DICTIONARY OF THE NORTH-WEST SEMITIC INSCRIPTIONS

PART ONE

HANDBUCH DER ORIENTALISTIK
HANDBOOK OF ORIENTAL STUDIES

ERSTE ABTEILUNG

DER NAHE UND MITTLERE OSTEN
THE NEAR AND MIDDLE EAST

HERAUSGEGEBEN VON

H. ALTENMÜLLER · B. HROUDA · B.A. LEVINE
K.R. VEENHOF

EINUNDZWANZIGSTER BAND

DICTIONARY OF THE NORTH-WEST SEMITIC INSCRIPTIONS

PART ONE

DICTIONARY OF THE NORTH-WEST SEMITIC INSCRIPTIONS

BY

J. HOFTIJZER AND K. JONGELING

WITH APPENDICES BY

R.C. STEINER, A. MOSAK MOSHAVI AND B. PORTEN

PART ONE

ʾ – L

E.J. BRILL
LEIDEN · NEW YORK · KÖLN
1995

The paper in this book meets the guidelines for permanence and durability of the Committee on Production Guidelines for Book Longevity of the Council on Library Resources.

Library of Congress Cataloging-in-Publication Data

Hoftijzer, J. (Jacob)
Dictionary of the North-West Semitic inscriptions /J. Hoftijzer & K. Jongeling : with appendices by R.C. Steiner, A. Mosak Moshavi and B. Porten.
p. cm.— (Handbuch der Orientalistik. Erste Abteilung, Der Nahe und Mittlere Osten ; 21. Bd., T. 1-2
Based on: Dicxtionnaire des inscriptions sémitiques de l'ouest / C.F. Jean and J. Hoftijzer.
Includes bibliographical references.
ISBN 9004098178 (v. 1). — ISBN 9004098208 (v. 2)
1. Inscriptions, Semitic—Dictionaries—English. 2. Semitic languages, Northwest—Dictionaries—English. I. Jongeling, K. II. Steiner, Richard C. III. Moshavi, A. Mosak. IV. Porten, Bezalel. V. Jean, Charles-F.
(Charles-François), b. 1874. Dictionnaire des inscriptions sémitiques de l'ouest. V. Title. VI. Series.
PJ3085.H63 1995
492—dc20 94-39945
CIP

ISSN 0169-9423
ISBN 90 04 09817 8 (*Vol. 1*)
ISBN 90 04 09820 8 (*Vol. 2*)
ISBN 90 04 09821 6 (*Set*)

PRINTED IN THE NETHERLANDS

THIS BOOK IS DEDICATED
TO THE MEMORY OF

JOHANNES HENDRIK HOSPERS

1921 - 1993

Contents

Part one

Part two

Introduction

This dictionary of the Northwestsemitic epigraphic material is based on the *Dictionnaire des inscriptions sémitiques de l'ouest* by C.F.Jean and J.Hoftijzer (DISO), published in five fascicles (I/II in 1960, III in 1962 and IV/V in 1965). Lexemes from texts first published after the completion of fascicles I and II were not included in the later fascicles, but new comments on texts already known were. Since 1960 not only quite a number of previously unknown texts have been published, but also many texts previously known have been commented upon anew. Consequently the authors have made many additions to the original text, and in many instances they have proposed other solutions than the ones favoured in DISO. What remains, however, is the structure of the book and the presentation of the material.

As in DISO the discussion of a lexeme is normally divided into two: - a) the enumeration of the various grammatical forms (wherever appropriate in their various orthographical representations) attested in the texts, grouped by language - b) the translation of the lexeme, with special attention to contextual data (see also below). In an optional third part, references are given to other lexemes where the lexeme under discussion is mentioned.

As in the previous edition no etymological information is given, except in the case of loan words, or in those instances where the context makes a reference unavoidable. This does not mean we are not interested in etymological questions, but we are of the opinion that Semitic etymology has to be dealt with by specialists. Etymology cannot be treated as a mere complement in a dictionary mainly devoted to one language or language group.

The first part of the discussion of a lexeme is subdivided according to the languages in which it is attested. The order of the subdivision is the following: Old Can(aanite), Ph(oenician), Pun(ic), Mo(abite), Amm(onite), Edom(ite), Hebr(ew), Samal(ian) (Yaudic), D(eir) A(lla dialect), Old Ar(amaic), Off(icial) Ar(amaic), Nab(atean), Palm(yrenean), Hatra, Waw, J(ewish) A(ramaic).

This subdivision is necessary because the Northwestsemitic epigraphic texts are very heterogeneous from a linguistic point of view, but it would be incorrect to see it as absolute.

As in DISO, Ugaritic is not treated in this dictionary. This does not mean that the authors do not consider it highly desirable to have a new and complete dictionary of this language which includes also extensive references to the various readings and interpretational proposals. Our decision not to include Ugaritic was a purely practical one, based on the difference in approach between the study of Ugaritic and that of Northwestsemitic epigraphics. On the absence of Syriac, see below.

Old Canaanite. Under this *siglum* are gathered the Canaanite glosses which are found in the Tell El-Amarna correspondence if they are indicated as such by a *Keil.* We are aware that there are many words in these letters which are of Canaanite origin or show a (strong) influence of the Canaanite language/dialect of the scribe. However, by not putting a *Keil* before such a word, the scribe did not indicate that he meant to write a non-Akkadian word. For that reason such words and forms should be (and are) included in Akkadian dictionaries. The Old Canaanite words and forms in the Tell El-Amarna correspondence do not, of course, belong to one language or dialect. They were written by scribes from different regions who were probably speaking different languages or dialects. It would be a grave mistake to consider this material to represent only one language. Under this head the lexemic material from a few Canaanite texts written in syllabic script is also included.

Phoenician. Under this head are gathered all those lexemic forms that are attested in Phoenician texts. These texts are not all written in the same type of Phoenician. Some are in Official Phoenician, some in the Phoenician of Byblos and some in other dialects (cf. the magical texts from Arslan Tash and the text published in Epigraphica Anatolica ix). Under this head the texts from Cyprus and Egypt are also treated. In addition, the texts in Official Phoenician and in the Phoenician of Byblos show clear signs of diachronic development. In this edition, as in the French one, we have nevertheless abstained from further subdividing this material because, had we done so, we would have had to subdivide material found under other *sigla* as well, and as a result the presentation of the morphological material would have become confusingly complex. Moreover, it is a nearly impossible task to give a satisfactory subdivision of the Official Phoenician material according to diachronic rules.

Punic. Under this *siglum* are gathered all those lexemic forms that are attested in Punic texts, including those texts written in non-Semitic script. In nearly all instances we have maintained the geographical distinction between Phoenician and Punic texts commonly used, although we are aware that this distinction has only a relative value. There are many Punic texts which show none or only slight linguistic differences from texts written in Official Phoenician. Moreover, the material gathered under the *siglum* Punic is neither linguistically nor orthographically uniform. There are clear signs of diachronic linguistic development and in some instances also indications of dialectal differences. But in this case too it is impossible to give a satisfactory subdivision of the material that can be used in a dictionary. Often in one and the same text forms are attested which, according to their orthography, belong to different linguistic levels. This means that an "old-fashioned" orthography cannot prove that a text in which it is used represents an older linguistic level. So, a subdivision based on orthography is less useful. A subdivision between Punic and Neopunic texts, which is sometimes made, is based on non-linguistic palaeographical grounds. There is no reason to believe that this subdivision coincides with a diachronic linguistic subdivision. Therefore and for the general reason mentioned under the heading "Phoenician" we have preferred not to introduce any subdivisions into the Punic material. Mainly for practical reasons we have however maintained the division between Phoenician and Punic material.

Under the headings "Phoenician" and "Punic" we have also included forms of Phoenician and Punic lexemes attested in Greek and Latin texts, e.g. the plays of Plautus and the works of Dioscurides and Augustine. We are aware that we don't have to do here with Northwestsemitic epigraphical material in the strict sense. Nevertheless we have included this material in the dictionary to supplement the scanty material known from Phoenician and Punic epigraphical texts.

Moabite. Under this head are gathered those lexemic forms that are attested in the texts from the kingdom of Moab: the Mesha-inscription, some inscriptional fragments and a number of seal inscriptions which can be identified as Moabite in origin. Moabite has its own linguistic character, which is different from that of other Northwestsemitic languages or dialects of the relevant period (see below), and also from Classical Hebrew.

Ammonite. Under this *siglum* are gathered those lexemic forms that are attested in the texts from the Ammonite kingdom: some inscriptional fragments, an inscription on a bottle, a number of ostraca and quite a number of seal inscriptions which can be identified as being of Ammonite origin. This *siglum* is introduced because these texts have their own orthographical and linguistic character, which differs from that of other Northwestsemitic languages or dialects of the relevant period (see below).

Hebrew. Under this *siglum* are gathered those lexemic forms that are attested in Hebrew epigraphic texts. The Hebrew texts of the relevant period (see below) are, of course, neither orthographically nor linguistically uniform. A number of subdivisions might be made in the material in question, e.g. a subdivision based on diachronic arguments or a division between Northern Israelite Hebrew (e.g. found in the Samaria ostraca) and Southern Israelite (Judean) Hebrew. The older Southern Israelite epigraphical texts are not orthographically and linguistically uniform either. However, we have decided to collect this heterogeneous material under one head in order to avoid unnecessary complications.

Deir Alla. Under this *siglum* are collected those lexemic forms that are found in the Deir Alla plaster texts. The language or dialect reflected in these texts stands completely on its own and is neither strictly Canaanite nor strictly Aramaic in type. This necessitates its special treatment.

Samalian. Under this *siglum* are gathered those lexemic forms that are attested in the three texts written in the local language or dialect of Sam'al. Although this language is considered to be Aramaic by many authors and although it undoubtedly possesses many linguistic characteristics which can be considered as Aramaic, it also possesses a number of characteristics absent from other Aramaic languages or dialects. Therefore it seems undesirable to include the relevant material under the heading "Old Aramaic".

Old Aramaic. Under this *siglum* are gathered those lexemic forms that are attested in Aramaic epigraphical texts from the period before 700 B.C. These texts are not linguistically homogeneous. The Tell-Fekheriye inscription especially has its own characteristics, but the other texts also differ from each other. However, in order to avoid making the presentation of this material too complicated we have decided to present it under one *siglum* and to refrain from further subdividing it. The *terminus ad quem* is chosen, because around 700 B.C. Aramaic begins to be used as *a lingua franca.* However, we are aware of the fact that not all Aramaic material from before that date can be clearly distinguished from some of the Aramaic material which has to be dated after 700 B.C.

Official Aramaic. Under this *siglum* are gathered those lexemic forms that are attested in Aramaic epigraphical texts from the period after 700 B.C., in as far as they are not written in Nabatean or Palmyrenean script, are not written in Jewish Aramaic, and are not written in Hatrean (or the related Assur) Aramaic; included is the text from Warka in syllabic cuneiform script. Although all these texts are to a certain extent linguistically uniform (Aramaic having been used for quite a period as *a lingua franca* in the Near East), there are also many internal differences. These differences are caused by the decreasing influence of the *lingua franca* (especially after the fall of the Achaemenid empire), by the influence of the Aramaic dialects of the scribes (or their non-Aramaic languages), sometimes already at an early date (cf. the Hermopolis-papyri), and by linguistic development. However, in order to avoid making the presentation of this material too complicated, we have decided to present it under one *siglum*. This decision was also taken because many of the texts are written in an official language influenced to a greater or lesser degree by the dialect or language of the scribe. This makes a further subdivision very difficult, if not impossible. Under the heading "Official Aramaic" we have also included references to the Aramaic ideograms found in Parthian, Pehlevic, Sogdian and Chwarezmian texts. Although we are not concerned here with Northwestsemitic epigraphic material in the strict sense, it is clearly material related to the Official Aramaic material and for that reason is best presented in this dictionary.

Nabatean. Under this head are gathered all those lexemic forms that are attested in Aramaic texts written in some form of Nabatean script. For practical reasons we have followed here the generally accepted way of dividing the Aramaic material, although this division is not based on linguistic grounds and the texts in question are often greatly influenced by the *lingua franca* mentioned above and quite a number of them do not show any differences from texts belonging to the Offical Aramaic material. On the other hand one should be aware that the Nabatean material is not absolutely homogeneous, texts with different geographical backgrounds, for example, sometimes differing from each other.

Palmyrenean. Under this *siglum* are gathered all those lexemic forms that are attested in Aramaic texts written in some form of Palmyrenean script. Here also we have, for practical reasons, followed the generally accepted division of the Aramaic material, although this division is not based on linguistic grounds and these texts are still influenced by the *lingua franca* mentioned above. Nevertheless, they display more differences from texts belonging to the Official Aramaic material than the texts written in Nabatean script. Material which differs from that found in Official Aramaic texts and material which does not is often found in one and the same text. This makes a subdivision of the Palmyrenean material less advisable.

Hatra. Under this *siglum* are gathered all those lexemic forms that are attested in the Aramaic epigraphic texts found in Hatra and in some other epigraphic texts written in the same script, but found elsewhere. These texts show a (sometimes much) greater linguistic difference from the Official Aramaic material, than the Nabatean and Palmyrenean texts. This fact alone justifies their being gathered under one heading. Under the same heading we have also gathered the lexemic forms which are attested in Aramaic texts from the first centuries A.D. from Assur, which are palaeographically, orthographically and linguistically similar to the Hatrean texts (although there are some differences).

Waw. Under this *siglum* are gathered those lexemic forms that are attested in the amulet AMB 6. Although this text is written in Syriac (see below), we have decided to include it in the dictionary because the other amulets of the collection published in AMB are also included.

Jewish Aramaic. Under this *siglum* are gathered those lexemic forms that are attested in Jewish Aramaic epigraphic texts. This material is not subdivided, in order to avoid making the presentation too complicated, although it is clearly not linguistically homogeneous.

As in the first edition we have not included divine names, personal names, geographical names and names of months.

We have used the terms "inscription" and "epigraphic" in their widest sense. We have not only included lexemes from inscriptions on stone, but also those attested in texts on ostraca, coins, seals, on papyrus or leather, in stamps and graffiti. Only forms of lexemes which are attested in texts published with transcription and commentary have been included.

From a strictly linguistic point of view objections may be raised against a dictionary containing only lexemes from epigraphical material, if not only epigraphical but also non-epigraphical texts of the language in question have been preserved. According to this, in itself linguistically correct, point of view the epigraphic southern-Israelite material ought to be treated in the same dictionary as the biblical Hebrew texts, the Hebrew texts from Qumran and the Hebrew fragments of Sirach, and the epigraphic Jewish Aramaic texts ought to be treated in the same dictionaries as the Rabbinic Jewish Aramaic texts. However, in the past dictionaries have been mainly based upon certain collections of texts, resulting in dictionaries of the Old Testament, of Rabbinic literature, etc. Although there is change for the better at this moment, not all the relevant material is dealt with in this way yet. For this reason it is still fully justified, and even advisable, to publish a dictionary of only the epigraphic material of languages of which non-epigraphic texts have also been preserved. We have also included in this dictionary (as was done in DISO) comprehensive references to the scholarly literature on the relevant texts, which is not done in, e.g., the more recent dictionaries of, e.g., Classical Hebrew, Jewish Aramaic, etc.

Because, from the Hebrew and Jewish Aramaic texts, only words from epigraphical material are included, we have maintained the decision already taken in DISO not to include the literary, non-epigraphic texts from Qumran, Massada, etc.

As a rule we have included in this dictionary only the forms of the lexemes which are attested in epigraphic texts which with reasonable certainty can be dated to the period before 300 A.D. The decision not to include material from a later date is of course a subjective one, but any decision on this point is subjective in one way or another. However, the decision not to draw a line somewhere would mean that all published Hebrew and Jewish Aramaic epigraphic material of later periods would have to be included. This would mean that texts from the Middle Ages and from modern times (as far as they have been published) would have had to be included. The line we have drawn includes the epigraphic material of all other languages in the dictionary (also the Palmyrenean material). In those instances where texts from a period after 300 A.D. have been published in the same text edition as a large number of texts from a period before that date, we have included them in the dictionary (e.g. texts published in Frey or in MPAT).

The line drawn here has as a consequence that the material from Syriac epigraphical texts is not included. Only a minority of them could have been included, and it seems wrong to divide them from the majority which are to be dated after 300 A.D.

In the second part of an *entry* the translation of the lexemes in question is given. However, because the semantic field of a lexeme belonging to a certain language is often not identical with that of a single lexeme in another language, not only translations are given. It is impossible to define the semantic value of a lexeme without insight into the various context types in which it occurs. For that reason these various context types are also described.

The forms of the lexemes attested for the relevant Northwestsemitic languages are transcribed in italics. We have decided not to use the well-known Hebrew square script at all, because its use would convey a pretence of originality, whereas for a huge majority of the texts it would only be a different transcription, since they are being written in other script types themselves.

In case of verbs, the root radicals are used as *headwords.* In a number of instances the root does not consist of three (or more) radicals, but of two. However, for practical reasons, we have conformed ourselves to the practice still common in dictionaries in our field of constructing a root with at least three radicals.

In case of nouns, the singular absolute form is used as the *headword*, and for adjectives the singular masculine absolute form is used. The feminine ending in nouns is always indicated by *-h* (according to the Hebrew and Aramaic way), unless it is also indicated by *-t* in these languages. Parallel lexemes from different languages which are etymologically related, but which (e.g. because of different developments in the phoneme structure) are differently spelled for different languages, are normally collected under the same heading (cf. *zhb* - *dhb* "gold", *šwb* - *twb* "return"). If such a lexeme is attested in both Canaanite and Aramaic texts, the Canaanite spelling (*zhb*, *šwb*) is used to indicate the lexeme. In these instances cross-references are given referring the reader to the Canaanite form of the lexeme (e.g. *dhb* v. *zhb*). If, for some reason, etymologically related words are not gathered under the same heading, there are cross-references with both *entries*. In case a lexeme is only attested for (an) Aramaic language(s), an Aramaic form is used as indication of the *headword*.

Possible lapsus and orthographical variants of any form listed in the first part of an entry are also included there. For these lapsus and orthographical variants usually no special *entries* with cross-references are introduced.

A list of text references like Cowl 1^1, 2^1, 3^1, Krael 1^1, 2^1, 3^1, Driv 1^1, 2^1, 3^1, etc., etc. does not exclude the possibility that there are other attestations of the relevant form from Cowley and Kraeling than those listed.

Although the general interpretation of epigraphic texts is mostly reasonably certain (even though there are quite a number of exceptions to this rule), the interpretation of details often offers many difficulties. Therefore we do not want to present the solutions preferred by us as certain. This is the reason why we not only present the solutions we prefer (with references to the relevant scholarly literature), but also references to other solutions (again with references to the relevant literature). We want to underline that in those instances where we indicate a certain solution as preferable, only our personal preference is concerned. Unfortunately a dictionary does not give the opportunity to present arguments for one's preferences.

Although in the first part of an entry forms gathered under the same heading can occur in texts from very different times, we have, for practical reasons, decided to abstain from giving the (approximate) date of a text with every quotation.

In 1977 we started the provisional collecting of new material for this dictionary. In 1981 we started writing the provisional text. This work was finished at the beginning of 1991. Material published since that date is not included. Since then we have added text references and references to additional scholarly literature.

To the text of the dictionary a list of words from the Amherst Papyri is added (namely those words the interpretation of which is reasonably certain). We wish to thank Prof. R.C. Steiner and Mrs. A. Mosak Moshavi for their willingness to prepare this list. Prof. B. Porten was so kind as to compile a list of those words for which a new reading and/or interpretation was proposed in the recent Achiqar edition prepared by him and Dr. Yardeni. This list is also added to the dictionary.

We wish to thank all those who have helped us in any way with our work on this dictionary, with their advice, or by sending books and offprints. We want to mention especially the names of Prof. M.G. Amadasi Guzzo, Prof. J.C. Greenfield and Prof. B. Porten. We owe much to the staff of the Library of Leiden University and that of the Library of the "Nederlands Instituut voor het Nabije Oosten" in Leiden. The help they gave us was invaluable. We want to thank Drs. P. Goedegebuure, Drs. S.B. ter Haar Romeny and Drs. M. Oldenhof, and Dr. H.Neudecker for the help they gave us in checking and computerizing the text. The book was typeset with the use of the typesetting program TeX(LaTeX) by Dr. K. Jongeling. During the preparation of the text we had useful contacts with the publishing house of Brill. We particularly want to mention the names of the late Drs. F.H. Pruyt and of Dr. F. Dijkema and to express our gratitude for their help.

The work on this book, which has taken a long time, could not have been realized without the financial aid of the Dutch Organization for Scientific Research (NWO) and of the Faculty of Arts of Leiden University. We are glad to be able to express our great thanks and indebtedness to them.

We dedicate this book to the memory of Prof. J.H. Hospers of Groningen University, who died in 1993, whom we remember with warm respect as a colleague, friend and teacher.

Leiden, November 1994. J. Hoftijzer, K. Jongeling.

List of abbreviations.

AA Acta Archaeologica.
AAALT Arameans, Aramaic and the Aramaic Literary Tradition, ed. M.Sokoloff, Ramat-Gan, 1983.
AAG see a) Degen - b) Segert.
AAS Les Annales Archéologiques de Syrie. Revue d'archéologie et d'histoire syriennes (since vol. xvi: (Les) Annales Archéologiques Arabes Syriennes. Revue d'archéologie et d'histoire).
AASOR The Annual of the American Schools of Oriental Research.
AAW see Altheim & Stiehl.
Abbadi PIH S.Abbadi, Die Personennamen der Inschriften aus Hatra (= Texten und Studien zur Orientalistik, Band 1), Hildesheim/Zürich/New York, 1983.
ABC see Stevenson.
abbrev. abbreviation/abbreviated.
Abessinier see Glaser.
abs. absolute.
Abydos see Kornfeld.
acc. accusative.
ACF Annuaire du Collège de France. Résumé des cours et travaux.
act. active.
ActAntHung Acta Antiqua Academiae Scientiarum Hungaricae.
ActHyp Acta Hyperborea.
ActIr Acta Iranica.
ActOr Acta Orientalia.
ActOrHung Acta Orientalia Academiae Scientiarum Hungaricae.
ADAJ Annual of the Department of Antiquities of Jordan.
ADD C.H.W.Johns, Assyrian Deeds and Documents recording the transfer of property ..., Vol. 1 (sec. edition), Cambridge 1924, Vol. 2, Cambridge, 1901, Vol. 3, Cambridge, 1901, Vol. 4, Cambridge, 1901.
adj. adjective.
Adonis und Esmun see Baudissin.
adv. adverb.
AE Ancient Egypt.
a.e. and elsewhere.
Aeg Aegyptus. Rivista italiana di egittologia et di papyrologia.
AEPHE Annuaire de l'École Pratique des Hautes-Études (Ve section, sciences religieuses).
AfO Archiv für Orientforschung. Internationale Zeitschrift für die Wissenschaft vom Vorderen Orient.
AfrIt Africa Italiana.
AG N.Aimé-Giron, Textes araméens d'Égypte, Le Caire, 1931.
AGG Göttingische Gelehrte Anzeigen.
AGPPS see Hölbi.
AGWG Abhandlungen der königlichen Gesellschaft der Wissenschaften zu Göttingen; philologische-historische Klasse. Neue Folge.
AH An Aramaic Handbook (ed. F.Rosenthal), Wiesbaden, 1967.
Aḥiq The story and wisdom of Aḥiqar quoted after the edition in Cowl pp. 204-248.
Ahlström RANR G.W.Ahlström, Royal Administration and National Religion in ancient Palestine (= Studies in the history of the ancient Near East, I, ed. M.H.E.Weippert), Leiden, 1982.
AHW see v.Soden.
AI see Clay.
AIA see Kaufman.
AIAI see Borowski.
AION Istituto (universitario) Orientale di Napoli; Annali nuova

serie.
AION-SL Istituto orientale di Napoli; Annali, sezione linguistica.
AIPHOS Annuaire de l'Institut de Philologie et d'Histoire Orientales et Slaves.
AIS see Fitzmyer.
AISN see Hinz.
Aistl J.Aistleitner, Wörterbuch der ugaritischen Sprache, ed. O.Eissfeldt (= Berichte Über die Verhandlungen der sächsischen Akademie der Wissenschaften zu Leipzig; philologisch-historische Klasse, Band 106, Heft 3), Berlin, 1963.
AIT see Humbach.
AJ The Antiquaries Journal.
AJBI Annual of the Japanese Biblical Institute.
AJC see Reifenberg.
AJSL The American Journal of Semitic Languages and Literatures.
AJT American Journal of Theology. The divinity faculty of the university of Chicago.
Akkad. Akkadian.
a.l. ad locum.
Albright Archeology W.F.Albright, Archeology and the religion of Israel (sec. edition), Baltimore, 1946.
Albright PSI W.F.Albright, The Proto-Sinaitic Inscriptions and their decipherment, Cambridge (Mass.), 1966.
Albright Religion W.F.Albright, Die Religion Israels im Lichte der archäologischen Ausgrabungen, München/Basel, 1956.
ALIA see Jackson.
Altheim LuG F.Altheim, Literatur und Gesellschaft im ausgehenden Altertum, Band I, Halle (Saale), 1948, Band II, Halle (Saale), 1950.
Altheim & Stiehl AAW F.Altheim & R.Stiehl, Die Araber in der Alten Welt, Band I, Berlin, 1964, Band II, Berlin, 1965, Band III, Berlin, 1966, Band IV, Berlin, 1967, Band V/1, Berlin, 1968, Band V/2, Berlin, 1969.
Altheim & Stiehl ASA Die aramäische Sprache unter den Achaimeniden, Band I, Geschichtliche Untersuchungen, Frankfurt am Main, 1963.
Altheim & Stiehl CRM F.Altheim & R.Stiehl, Christentum am Roten Meer, Band I, Berlin/New York, 1971, Band II, Berlin/New York, 1973.
Altheim & Stiehl, Das erste Auftreten der Hunnen; supplement to Altheim & Stiehl Suppl.
Altheim & Stiehl GH F.Altheim & R.Stiehl, Geschichte der Hunnen, Band I, Berlin, 1959, Band II, Berlin, 1960, Band III, Berlin, 1961, Band IV, Berlin, 1962.
Altheim & Stiehl GMA F.Altheim & R.Stiehl, Geschichte Mittelasiens im Altertum, Berlin, 1970.
Altheim & Stiehl Phil F.Altheim & R.Stiehl, Philologia sacra (= Aparchai, Untersuchungen zur klassischen Philologie und Geschichte des Altertums, Band 2), Tübingen, 1958.
Altheim & Stiehl Suppl F.Altheim & R.Stiehl, Supplementum aramaicum. Aramäisches aus Iran, Baden-Baden, 1957.
AltorForsch see Winckler.
Alvarez Delgado ILC J.Alvarez Delgado, Inscripciones líbicas de Canarias. Ensayo di interpretación líbica, La Laguna, 1964.
AM a) Asia Maior (NS) - b) see Cardascia.

AMB J.Naveh & Sh.Shaked, Amulets and Magic Bowls, aramaic incantations of late antiquity, Jerusalem/Leiden, 1985.
AMCS The Age of the Monarchies: Culture and Society, edd. A.Malamat & I.Eph ʿal (= The world history of the Jewish people, First series, ancient times, Vol. IV/2), Jerusalem, 1979.
Amm Ammonite.
AMSMG Atti e Memorie della Società Magna Grecia, NS.
AN Abr-Nahrain.
anc. ancient.
ANET Ancient Near Eastern Texts relating to the Old Testament (third edition, with Supplement), ed. J.B.Pritchard, Princeton, 1969.
AnOr Analecta Orientalia.
ANR Aufstieg und Niedergang der römischen Welt. Geschichte und Kultur Roms im Spiegel der neueren Forschung, II Principat, Band 8, edd. H.Temporini & W.Haase, Berlin/New York, 1977.
AnSt Anatolian Studies. Journal of the British Institute of Arachaeology at Ankara.
Ant Antonianum. Periodicum philosophico-theologicum.
Antas Ricerche puniche ad Antas. Rapporto preliminare della missione archeologica dell'università di Roma e della soprintendenza alle antichità di Cagliari di E.Acquaro, F.Barreca, S.M.Cecchini, D.Fantar, M.Fantar, M.G.Guzzo Amadasi, S.Moscati (= Studi Semitici 30), Roma, 1969.
AnthGraec Anthologia Graeca quoted after the second edition by H.Beckby (4 volumes), München, 1957, 1957, 1958, 1958.
AO Aula Orientalis. Revista de estudios del próximo oriente antiguo.
AOAT xvi J.C.de Moor, The seasonal pattern in the Ugaritic myth of Ba ʿlu according to the version of Ilimilku (= Alter Orient und Altes Testament Band 16), Neukirchen/Vluyn, 1971.
AOAW Anzeiger der Österreichische Akademie der Wissenschaften. Philosophisch-historische Klasse.
AoF Altorientalische Forschungen.
AOTS Archaeology and Old Testament Study. Jubilee Volume of the Society for Old Testament Study, 1917-1967 (ed. D.W.Thomas), Oxford, 1967.
AP see Löw.
APA see Lindenberger.
APCI Actes du Premier Congrès International de linguistique sémitique et chamito-sémitique, Paris 16-19 Juillet 1969, edd. A.Caquot & D.Cohen, The Hague/Paris, 1974.
Aph Aphel.
API see Herzfeld.
app. apposition.
Apul Pseudo Apulei Platonici Herbarius, quoted after the edition in Corpus Medicorum Latinorum, Vol. IV (edd. E.Howard & H.E.Sigerist), Lipsiae/Berolini, 1927, pp. 15-225.
Ar a) Aramaic - b) see Dupont-Sommer.
Arab Arabic.
AramaicScript see Naveh.
AramOT see Rowley.
Arch see Porten.
ArchClass Archeologia Classica. Rivista dell'istituto di archeologia della università di Roma.
ArchOr Archív Orientální.
ARNA F.V.Winnett & W.L.Reed, Ancient Records from North Arabia, with contributions by J.T.Milik &

J.Starcky (= Near and Middle East Series 3), Toronto & Buffalo, 1970.
ArPap see Ungnad.
AS i Ausgrabungen in Sendschirli ausgeführt und herausgegeben im Auftrage des Orient-Comités zu Berlin, I, Einleitung und Inschriften (= Mittheilungen aus den orientalischen Sammlungen, Heft xi), Berlin, 1893.
ASA see Altheim & Stiehl.
ASAE Annales du Service des Antiquités de l'Égypte.
AsAfS Asian and African Studies. Annual of the Israelite Oriental Society.
ASB Ancient Seals and the Bible (edd. L.Gorelick & E.Williams-Forte; = Occasional Papers on the Near East 2.1), Malibu, 1983.
ASGM Atti del Sodalizio Glottologico Milanese.
Ashera see Maier, Olyan.
ASI see Hüttenmeister.
ASPG see Sukenik.
ASR Ancient Synagogues Revealed (ed. L.I.Levine), Jerusalem, 1981.
Ass see LidzbAss,
ASS see Dietrich.
ASSL see Steiner.
Assur The Aramaic inscriptions and graffiti from Assur quoted after the edition by B.Aggoula, Inscriptions et graffites araméens d'Assour (=Supplemento n.43 agli Annali-vol. 45 (1985), fasc. 2), Napoli, 1985.
At ʿAtiqot, Journal of the Israel Department of Antiquities.
ATAT see Gressmann.
ATNS J.B.Segal, Aramaic Texts from North Saqqâra with some Fragments in Phoenician, London, 1983.
AttiTor Atti della R. Accademia delle Scienze di Torino, Classe di scienze morali, storiche e filologiche.
ATTM see Beyer.
AUA M.Lidzbarski, Altaramäische Urkunden aus Assur (= 38. wissenschaftliche Veröffentlichung der deutschen Orient-Gesellschaft), Leipzig, 1921.
Aug Augustinianum. Periodicum quadrimestre Collegii Internationalis Augustiniani de Urbe.
August de Serm Dom Augustinus, De Sermone Domini in monte libri duo quoted after the edition in Corpus Christianorum, Series Latina, Volume XXXV, Turnholti, 1967.
August Enarr in Ps Augustinus, Enarrationes in Psalmos quoted after the edition in Corpus Christianorum, Series Latina, volumes xxxviii-xl, Turnholti, 1956.
August Ep ad Rom Augustinus, Expositio quarundam propositionum ex Epistola ad Romanos quoted after the edition in Sancti Aureli Augustini Opera, Sect IV, Pars I, Vindobonae, 1971.
August Epist the letters of Augustinus quoted after the edition in S.Aureli Augustini Hipponiensis episcopi epistulae, ed. A.Goldbacher, Pars I, Pragae, Vindobonae, Lipsiae, 1895, Pars II, Pragae, Vindobonae, Lipsiae, 1898, Pars III, Vindobonae, Lipsiae, 1904, Pars IV, Vindobonae, Lipsiae, 1911, Pars V, Vindobonae, Lipsiae, 1923.
August In Ioan Ev Augustinus, In Ioannis Evangelium Tractatus CXXIV quoted after the edition in Corpus Christianorum, Series Latina, Volume XXXVI, Turnholti, 1954.
August Quaest in Hept Augustinus, Quaestionum in

Heptateuchum libri VII quoted after the edition in Corpus Christianorum, Series Latina, Volume XXXIII, Turnholti, 1958.
August Sermones Augustinus, Sermones, quoted after the edition in Patrologiae cursus completus ..., series latina, tomus 38, ed. J.P.Migne, Parisiis 1845 (cf. also Sancti Aurelii Augustini Sermones de Vetere Testamento id est sermones I - L secundum ordinem vulgatum insertis etiam novem sermonibus post Maurinos repertis, ed. C.Lambot, Turnholti, 1961 (= Corpus Christianorum, Series Latina, Vol. XLI)).
AUSS Andrews University Seminary Studies. The journal of the Seventh-day Adventist Theological Seminary of Andrews University.
Avishur PIB Y.Avishur, Phoenician Inscriptions and the Bible, studies in stylistic and literary devices and selected inscriptions, 2 volumes, Jerusalem, 1979 (Hebrew).
Avishur SSWP Y.Avishur, Stylistic Studies of Word-Pairs in Biblical and ancient semitic literatures (= AOAT Band 210, edd. K.Bergerhof, M.Dietrich & O.Loretz), Neukirchen/Vluyn, 1984.
AVTA see Watanabe.
Ayad JACA B.Ayad Ayad, The Jewish-Aramaean Communities in Ancient Egypt, Cairo, 1975.
BAAI see Spronk.
Bab. Babylonian.
Babelon E.Babelon, Les rois de Syrie, de l'Arménie et de Commagène (Catalogue des monnaies grecques de la Bibliothèque Nationale), Paris, 1890.
BAG Beiträge zur Achämenidengeschichte (ed. G.Walser; = Historia, Zeitschrift für Alte Geschichte ..., Einzelschriften, Heft 18), Wiesbaden, 1972.
BAGN Beiträge zur Alten Geschichte und deren Nachleben, Festschrift für Franz Altheim zum 6.10.1968, Band I, Berlin, 1969, Band II, Berlin, 1970.
BAIBL Bulletin de l'Académie des Inscriptions et Belles Lettres.
BAO see v.Soden.
BAr Bulletin Archéologique du comité des travaux historiques et scientifiques.
BAR Biblical Arachaeology Review.
Barrois A.G.Barrois, Manuel d'archéologie Biblique, Tome I, Paris, 1939, tome II, Paris, 1953.
BASOR Bulletin of the American Schools of Oriental Research.
BAT Biblical Archaeology Today. Proceedings of the international congress on Biblical archaeology, Jerusalem, April 1984, Jerusalem, 1985.
Baudissin Adonis und Esmun W.W.v.Baudissin, Adonis und Esmun. Eine Untersuchung zur Geschichte des Glaubens an Auferstehungsgötter und an Heilgötter, Leipzig, 1911.
BCH Bulletin de Correspondance Hellénique. École française d'Athènes.
BDB Hebrew and English lexicon of the Old Testament with an appendix containing the Biblical Aramaic based on the lexicon of William Gesenius ... by F.Brown, S.R.Driver & Ch.A.Briggs, Boston/New York, 1907.
Beamtennamen see Eilers
Beh The aramaic text of the Behistun inscription quoted after the edition in Cowl pp. 248ff. (For

the text, cf. also Greenfield & Porten BIDG).
BeihAfO Archiv für Orientforschung. Beiheft.
Ben-Chayim LOT ii Z.Ben-Chayim, The Literary and Oral Traditions of Hebrew and Aramaic amongst the Samaritans, Vol. II, Jerusalem, 1957 (Hebrew).
Benveniste Titres E.Benveniste, Titres et noms propres en Iranien ancien (= Travaux de l'Institut d'Études Iraniennes de l'Université de Paris, 1), Paris, 1966.
Benz F.L.Benz, Personal names in the Phoenician and Punic inscriptions (= Studia Pohl 8), Rome, 1972.
Ber Berytus. Archaeological Studies.
BethSh iii N.Avigad, Beth She'arim, Vol. III, The archeological excavations during 1953-1958, The catacombs 12-23, Jerusalem, 1971 (Hebrew).
Betlyon CMP J.W.Betlyon, The Coinage and Mints of Phoenicia, the pre- Alexandrine period (= Harvard Semitic Monographs no 26), Chico, 1982.
Beyer ATTM K.Beyer, Die aramäischen Texte vom Toten Meer samt den Inschriften aus Palästina, dem Testament Levis aus der Kairoer Genisa, der Fastenrolle und den alten talmudischen Zitaten. Aramaistische Einleitung, Text, Übersetzung, Deutung, Grammatik/Wörterbuch, deutsch-aramäische Wortliste, Register, Göttingen, 1984.
BG see Dunand.
BHL see Ullendorff.
BIA Bulletin of the Institute of Archaeology. University of London.
BiAr (The) Biblical Archaeologist.
Bibl Biblica. Commentarii periodici Pontificii Instituti Biblici.
BIDG see Greenfield & Porten.
BIES Bulletin of the Israel Exploration Society.
BIFAO Bulletin de l'Institut Français d'Archéologie Orientale.
Bikerman IS E.Bikerman, Institutions des Séleucides, Paris, 1938.
BiOr Bibliotheca Orientalis.
Birnbaum MarDeed S.A.Birnbaum, The Bar Menasseh Marriage Deed. Its relation with other Jewish marriage deeds (= Uitgaven van het Nederlands Historisch en Archaeologisch Instituut te Istanbul, XIII), Istanbul, 1962.
BJ Bonner Jahrbücher des rheinischen Landesmuseums in Bonn (im Landschaftsverband Rheinland) und des Vereins von Altertumsfreunden im Rheinlande.
BJPES Bulletin of the Jewish Palestine Exploration Society.
BK see Yadin.
BKA see Schäfer.
BL H.Bauer & P.Leander, Grammatik des Biblisch-Aramäischen, Halle (Saale), 1927.
Blau PC J.Blau, On Pseudo-Corrections in some Semitic languages, Jerusalem, 1970.
BLKA i Beiträge zur Lexikographie des klassischen Arabisch Nr 1 (= M.Ullmann, Wa-ḫairu l-ḥadīṯi mā kāna laḥnan, mit einem Anhang von R.Degen (= Bayerische Akademie der Wissenschaften, philosophisch-historische Klasse, Sitzungsberichte, Jahrgang, 1979), München, 1979.
BLRF Louis M.Rabinowitz Fund for the exploration of ancient synagogues. Bulletin.

BMB Bulletin du Musée de Beyrouth.
BMQ The British Museum Quarterly.
BMS see Stol.
BN Biblische Notizzen. Beiträge zur exegetischen Diskussion.
BO Bibbia e Oriente. Rivista bimestrale per la conoscenza della Bibbia.
Böhl F.M.Th.Böhl, Die Sprache der Amarnabriefe mit besonderer Berücksichtigung des Kanaanismen (= Leipziger Semitistische Studien, V. Band, Heft 2), Leipzig, 1909.
Boisacq E.Boisacq, Dictionnaire étymologique de la langue Grecque étudiée dans ses rapports avec les autres langues indo-européennes (second edition), Heidelberg/Paris, 1923.
boll see Dir and Mosc.
Bonnet Melqart C.Bonnet, Melqart: cultes et mythes de l'Héracles Tyrien en Méditerranée (= Studia Phoenicia viii), Leuven, 1988.
Borowski AIAI O.Borowski, Agriculture in Iron Age Israel, Winona Lake, 1987.
bot. botanical.
BR6 M.San-Nicolò & H.Petschow, Babylonische Rechtsurkunden aus dem 6. Jahrhundert v. Chr. (= Bayerische Akademie der Wissenschaften, Philosophisch-historische Klasse, Abhandlungen, Neu Folge, Heft 51), München, 1960.
v.d.Branden GP A.v.d.Branden, Grammaire Phénicienne (= Bibliothèque de l'Université Saint-Esprit, Kaslik-Liban 11), Beyrouth, 1969.
Brekelmans Ḥerem C.H.W.Brekelmans, De Ḥerem in het Oude Testament, Nijmegen, 1959.
BRL Biblisches Reallexikon (second edition; ed. K.Galling; = Handbuch zum Alten Testament 1, Reihe 1), Tübingen, 1977.
Brockelmann Grundriss C.Brockelmann, Grundriss der vergleichenden Grammatik der semitischen Sprachen, Band I (Laut- und Formenlehre), Berlin, 1908, Band II (Syntax), Berlin, 1913.
Bron RIPK F.Bron, Recherches sur les inscriptions phéniciennes de Karatepe (= Hautes Études Orientales 11), Paris, 1979.
Brown LP J.P.Brown, The Lebanon and Phoenicia. Ancient texts illustrating the physical geography and native industries, Vol. I, The physical setting and the forest, Beirut, 1969.
Brugnatelli QMS V.Brugnatelli, Questioni di Morfologia e Sintassi dei numerali cardinali semitici (= Pubblicazioni della Facoltà di Lettere e Filosofia dell'Università di Milano XCIII), Firenze, 1982.
Brünnow ProvArab R.E.Brünnow & A.v.Domaszewski, Die Provincia Arabia auf Grund zweier in den Jahren 1897 und 1898 unternommenen Reisen beschrieben, 3 Bände, Strassburg, 1904-1909.
Bruston EtPhén C.Bruston, Études Phéniciennes, Paris, 1903.
BSAE British School of Archaeology in Egypt and Egyptian Research Account.
BSh The Aramaic Ostraca of Beer Sheva quoted after: a) BSh i (= Excavations at Tell Beer Sheba 1969-1971 seasons (ed. Y.Aharoni), Tel Aviv, 1973, pp. 79-82 (ostraca 1-26)) and b) TeAv vi 182-195 (ostraca 27-67).

BSOAS Bulletin of the School of Oriental and African Studies, University of London.
BTDA see Hackett.
Buber KG M.Buber, Königtum Gottes (third edition; = Das Kommende, Untersuchungen zur Entstehungsgeschichte des messianischen Glaubens 1), Heidelberg, 1956.
Bull de la Soc Arch de Sousse Bulletin de la Société Archéologique de Sousse.
Bunnens EPM G.Bunnens, L'expansion phénicienne en méditerranée. Essai d'interprétation fondé sur une analyse des traditions littéraires (= Études de Philologie, d'Archéologie et d'Histoire anciennes publiées par l'Institut historique Belge de Rome, Tome XVII), Bruxelles/Rome, 1979.
BySt Byzantine Studies.
BZAW Beiheft zur Zeitschrift für die alttestamentliche Wissenschaft.
CAD The Assyrian Dictionary of the Oriental Institute of the University of Chicago.
Caecus see Plautus.
CAI W.E.Aufrecht, A Corpus of Ammonite Inscriptions (= Ancient Near Eastern Texts & Studies 4), Lewiston/Queenston/Lampeter, 1989.
CAL Cuneiform Archives and Libraries. Papers read at the 30e Recontre Assyriologique internationale, Leiden 4-8 Juli 1983 (ed. K.R.Veenhof; = Uitgaven van het Nederlands Historisch-Archeologisch Instituut te Istanbul, 57), Istanbul, 1986.
Can Canaanite.
CanMyths see Driver.
Cantineau Gramm J.Cantineau, Grammaire du Palmyrénien épigraphique (= Publications de l'Institut d'Études Orientales de la Faculté des Lettres d'Alger IV), Le Caire, 1935.
Cantineau Nab J.Cantineau, Le Nabatéen, Tome I (Notions générales - Écriture, Grammaire), Paris, 1930, Tome II (Choix de textes - Lexique), Paris, 1932.
Capp. Cappadocia.
card. cardinal.
Cardascia AM G.Cardascia, Les Archives de Murašû. Une famille d'hommes d'affaires Babyloniennes à l'époque Perse (455-403 av.J.-C.), Paris, 1951.
Carth. Carthaginian.
cas. casus/case.
cas.obl. casus obliquus.
caus. causative.
CB Cahiers de Byrsa.
CBE see Drijvers.
CBQ The Catholic Biblical Quarterly.
CC Commémoration Cyrus. Actes du congrès de Shiraz 1971 et autres Études rédigées à l'occasion du 2500e anniversaire de la fondation de l'empire Perse. Hommage universel II (= Acta Iranica première série, 2), Leiden/Téhéran/Liège, 1974.
CDPA see Spijkerman.
Ceresko JLNS A.R.Ceresko, Job 29-31 in the Light of Northwest Semitic, a translation and philological commentary (= Biblica et Orientalia 36), Rome, 1980.
cert. certain.
CF F.M.Cross & D.N.Freedman, Early Hebrew orthography, a study of the epigraphic evidence (= American Oriental Series, Vol. 36), New Haven, 1952.
cf. confer.
CGSL see Moscati.
Chabot Choix Choix d'inscriptions

de Palmyre, trad. et commentées par J.B.Chabot, Paris, 1922.
Chal The Nabatean inscription from Chalasa, quoted after the edition by A.Cowley, Palestine Exploration Fund Annual '14/15, pp. 145ff.
Charrier L.Charrier, Description des monnaies de la Numidie et de la Mauretanie, 1912.
CHC see McDonald.
Chemistry see Thompson.
Choix see Chabot.
chron a) chronology - b) chronological.
Chrond'Eg Chronique d'Égypte. Bulletin périodique de la fondation égyptologique Reine Élisabeth.
ChwIr The Aramaic ideograms occurring in the chwarezmic texts, quoted after Ir.
CIFE M.J.Fuentes Estañol, "Corpus de las inscripciones fenicias de España", FPI pp. 5-30.
CIL Corpus Inscriptionum Latinarum.
Cil. Cilicia.
circumst. circumstantial.
CIS Corpus Inscriptionum Semiticarum.
CISFP i Atti del I Congresso Internazionale di Studi Fenici e Punici, Roma, 5-10 Novembre 1979 (= Collezione di Studi Fenici 16), 3 volumes, Roma, 1983.
Clay AI A.T.Clay, "Aramaic Indorsements on the documents of the Murašu sons", Old Testament and Semitic studies in memory of William Rainey Harper (edd. R.F.Harper, F.Brown, G.F.Moore, Vol. I, Chicago, 1908, pp. 287-321.
Clermont-Ganneau Et Ch.Clermont-Ganneau, Études d'archéologie orientale (= Bibliothèque de l'École des Hautes Études, Sciences philologiques et historiques, fasc. 44 & 113), Tome I, Paris, 1880, Tome II, Paris, 1897.
ClRh Clara Rhodos. Studi e materiali pubblicati a cara dell'Istituto Storico-archeologico di Rodi.
CM see Heider.
CMHE see Cross.
CMP see Betlyon.
COAI see Stefanovic.
coh. cohortative.
Cohen SVS M.Cohen, Le système Verbal Sémitique et l'expression du temps (= Publications de l'École Nationale des Langues Orientales Vivantes, Sér. V, Tome XI), Paris, 1924.
coll collective.
comb combination.
comm. commodi.
comp. a) comparative - b) comparable.
conc. concave.
cond. conditional.
conj. conjunction.
Conn. Transactions of the Connecticut Academy of Arts and Sciences
(**later** Transactions published by ...).
Conn. xix Essays on the Ancient Near East in memory of Jacob Joel Finkelstein (ed. M.de Jong Ellis; = Memoirs of the Connecticut Academy of Arts & Sciences, Vol. XIX), Hamden (Conn.), 1977.
conv. convex.
Cooke NSI G.A.Cooke, A text-book of the North-Semitic Inscriptions, Moabite, Hebrew, Phoenician, Aramaic, Nabataean, Palmyrene, Jewish, Oxford, 1903.
Cowl A.Cowley, Aramaic papyri of the fifth century B.C., Oxford, 1923.

cp. compare.
CPTJ see Grabbe.
CRAI Académie des Inscriptions et Belles Lettres. Comptes Rendus.
CRM see Altheim & Stiehl.
Cross CMHE F.M.Cross, Canaanite Myth and Hebrew Epic. Essays in the history of the religion of Israel, Cambridge (Mass.), 1973.
CSBA see Loewenstamm.
CSI see Reviv.
CSL see Tomback.
CSOI P.Bordreuil, Catalogue des Sceaux Ouest-sémitiques Inscrits de la Bibliothèque nationale, du Louvre et du Musée Biblique et Terre Sainte, Paris 1986.
cstr construct.
CT Les Cahiers de Tunisie. Revue de sciences humaines.
DA a) Aramaic texts from Deir ʿAlla (edd. J.Hoftijzer & G.v.d.Kooij with contributions by H.J.Franken, V.R.Mehra, J.Voskuil, J.A.Mosk; = Documenta et Monumenta Orientis Antiqui XIX), Leiden, 1976 - b) the plaster texts published in this volume.
DAE see Grelot.
Dahood PNSP M.Dahood, Proverbs and Northwest Semitic Philology (= Scripta Pontificii Instituti Biblici 113), Roma, 1963.
Dahood Ps M.Dahood, Psalms, introduction, translation and notes, Vol. I 1-50, Garden City/New York, 1966, Vol. II 51-100, Garden City/New York, 1968, Vol. III 101-150 with an appendix "The grammar of the Psalter", Garden City, New York, 1970.
Dahood UHP M.Dahood, Ugaritic-Hebrew Philology (= Biblica et Orientalia 17), Rome, 1965.
Dalman G.Dalman, Arbeit und Sitte in Palästina, Band I/1 (Jahreslauf und Tageslauf, Herbst und Winter), Gütersloh, 1928, Band I/2 (Jahreslauf und Tageslauf, Frühling und Sommer), Gütersloh, 1928, Band II (Der Ackerbau), Gütersloh, 1932, Band III (Von der Ernte zum Mehl, Ernten, Dreschen, Worfeln, Sieben, Verwahren, Malen), Gütersloh, 1933, Band IV (Brot, Öl und Wein), Gütersloh, 1935, Band V (Webstoff, Spinnen, Weben, Kleidung), Gütersloh, 1937, Band VI (Zeltleben, Vieh- und Milchwirtschaft, Jagd, Fischfang), Gütersloh, 1939, Band VII (Das Haus, Hühnerzucht, Taubenzucht, Bienenzucht), Gütersloh, 1942.
Dalman Grammatik G.Dalman, Grammatik des jüdisch-palästinischen Aramäisch nach den Idiomen des Palästinischen Talmud des Onkelostargum und Prophetentargum und der Jerusalemischen Targume (second edition), Leipzig, 1905.
dam damaged.
Day MGHS J.Day, Molech, a God of Human Sacrifice in the Old Testament (= University of Cambridge Oriental Publications no 41), Cambridge/New York/New Rochelle/Melbourne/Sydney, 1989.
DBKP The Documents from the Bar Kokhba Period in the cave of letters, Greek papyri (ed. N.Lewis), Aramaic and Nabatean signatures and subscriptions (edd. Y.Yadin & J.C.Greenfield), Jerusalem, 1989.
DCC see Mullen.
DCD see Harris.
DD a) The Phoenician texts published in M.Dunand & R.Duru, Oumm El-ʿAmed, une ville del'époque Hellénistique aux échelles de Tyre (= République Libanaise,

Ministère de l'Éducation Nationale, Direction Générale des Antiquités, Études et Documents d'Archéologie, Tome IV), Paris, 1962, pp. 181-196 - b) see Glueck.

DDA Dialoghi di Archeologia, rivista quadrimestrale.

DDS see Weinfeld.

Degen AAG R.Degen, Altaramäische Grammatik der Inschriften des 10.- 8. JH v. Chr. (= Abhandlungen für die Kunde des Morgenlandes, Band XXXVIII, 3), Wiesbaden, 1969.

Del L.Delaporte, Épigraphes araméens, étude des textes gravés ou écrits sur des tablettes cunéiformes, d'après les leçons professées au Collège de France pendant le semestre d'hiver 1910-11, Paris, 1912.

dem. demonstrative.

DemDenkm see Spiegelberg.

DEP C.Bradford Welles, R.O.Fink, J.Frank Gilliam, The Parchemnts and papyri (= The Excavations at Dura-Europos conducted by Yale University and the French Academy of Inscriptions and Letters, Final Report V, Part I), New Haven, 1959.

der. derivated.

design. designation.

Dessau Inscriptiones latinae selectae, ed. H.Dessau, Vol. I, Berolini 1892, Vol. II Pars I, Berolini, 1902, Vol. II Pars II, Berolini, 1906, Vol. III Pars I, Berolini, 1914, Vol. III Pars II, Berolini, 1916.

DF J.T.Milik, "Le iscrizioni degli ossuari", in P.B.Bogatti & J.T.Milik, Gli scavi del "Dominus Flevit" (Monte Oliveto-Gerusalemme), Parte I La necropoli del periodo Romano (= Pubblicazioni dello Studium Biblicum Franciscanum n. 13), Gerusalemme, 1958, pp. 70-109.

DGSP see Garr.

DHC see Dupont-Sommer.

Dietrich ASS M.Dietrich, Die Aramäer Südbabyloniens in der Sargonidenzeit (700-648) (= Alter Orient und Altes Testament, Veröffentlichungen zur Kultur und Geschichte des Alten Orients und des Alten Testaments, Band 7; edd. K.Bergerhof, M.Dietrich & O.Loretz), Neukirchen/Vluyn, 1970.

diff. a) difficult - b) different.

Dion P.-E.Dion, La langue de Ya'udie, description et classement de l'ancien parler de Zencirli dans le cadre des langues sémitiques du nord-ouest, 1974.

Diosc Dioscurides, De materia medica, quoted after Pedanii Dioscuridis Anazarbei de materia medica libri quinque, ed. M.Wellmann, Vol. I, Berolini, 1907, Vol. II, Berolini, 1906, Vol. III, Berolini, 1914.

Dir D.Diringer, Le iscrizioni antico-ebraiche palestinesi (= Pubblicazioni dell R. Università degli Studi di Firenze, Facoltà di Lettere e Filosofia III Serie, Vol. 2), Firenze, 1934.

dir. of direction.

Dir boll the Hebrew stamps published in Dir pp. 111ff.

Dir misc the Hebrew miscellanea published in Dir pp. 291ff.

Dir ostr the Hebrew ostraca published in Dir pp. 21ff.

Dir pes the Hebrew inscriptions on weights and measures published in Dir pp. 263ff.

Dir sig the Hebrew seals published in Dir pp. 159ff.

distr. distributive.

div. a) division - b) dividing.
DJD ii Discoveries in the Judaean Desert, Vol. II (Les grottes de Muraba ʿât par P.Benoit, J.T.Milik, R.de Vaux avec des contributions de G.M.Crowfoot, E.Crowfoot & A.Grohmann), Texte, Oxford, 1961.
DJD iii Discoveries in the Judaean Desert of Jordan, Vol. III (Les "petites grottes" de Qumrân, exploration de la falaise, le grottes 2Q, 3Q, 5Q, 6Q, 7Q à 10Q, le Rouleau de Cuivre par M.Baillet, J.T.Milik & R.de Vaux avec unde contribution de H.W.Baker), Textes, Oxford, 1062.
DJPA see Sokoloff.
DLPS see Peckham.
DM a) Damaszener Mitteilungen - b) see Fantar.
DO see Timm.
Dothan HT M.Dothan, Hammath Tiberias, early synagogues and the Hellenistic and Roman remains, Jerusalem, 1983.
DOTT Documents from Old Testament Times translated with introductions and notes by members of the Society for Old Testament Study (ed. D.W.Thomas), London, 1958.
DRBE The Defence of the Roman and Byzantine East. Proceedings of a colloquium held at the University of Sheffield in April 1986, Part II (= British Institute of Archaeology at Ankara, Monograph no 8 = BAR International Series 297 (ii); ed. Ph.Freeman & D.Kennedy), Oxford, 1986.
Dréd The Latino-libyc texts published in R.Goodchild, "La necropoli Romano-libica di Bir ed-Dréder", Quaderni di Archeologia della Libia iii, pp. 91-107.
Drijvers CBE H.J.W.Drijvers, Cults and Beliefs at Edessa (= Études préliminaires aux Religions orientales dans l'Empire Romain, Tome 82), Leiden, 1980.
Driv G.R.Driver, Aramaic documents of the fifth century B.C. with help from a typescript by E.Mittwoch, W.B.Henning, H.J.Polotsky and F.Rosenthal (second edition), Oxford, 1957.
Driv1 G.R.Driver, Aramaic documents of the fifth century B.C. transcribed and edited with translation and notes (with help from a typescript by E.Mittwoch, W.B.Henning, H.J.Polotsky and F.Rosenthal), Oxford 1954.
Driver CanMyths G.R.Driver, Canaanite Myths and legends (= Old Testament Studies published under the auspices of the Society for Old Testament Study no 3), Edinburgh, 1956.
Driv F Fragments of Aramaic documents published in Driv1, pp. 37-43.
Driver HTBS S.R.Driver, Notes on the Hebrew Text and the topography of the Books of Samuel (second edition), Oxford, 1913.
Dronkert MOT K.Dronkert, De Molochdienst in het Oude Testament, Leiden, 1953.
DRS see Dussaud.
DSK see Malamat.
Dunand BG M.Dunand, Byblia Grammata. Documents et recherches sur le développement de l'écriture en Phénicie (= République Libanaise, Ministère de l'Éducation Nationale et des Beaux-Arts, Direction des Antiquités, Études et Documents d'Archéologie, Tome II), Beyrouth, 1945.
Dupont-Sommer Ar A.Dupont-Sommer, Les Araméens

(= L'Orient ancien illustré 2), Paris, 1949.
Dupont-Sommer DHC A.Dupont-Sommer, "Une inscription Araméenne et la déesse Kubaba", in A.Dupont-Sommer & L.Robert, La Déesse de Hiérapolis Castabala (Cilicie) (= Bibliothèque archéologique et historique de l'Institut Français d'archéologie d'Istanbul XVI), Paris, 1964, pp. 7-15.
Dupont-Sommer Sf A.Dupont-Sommer, Les inscriptions araméennes de Sfiré (Stèles I et II), avec la collaboration de M. l'Abbé J.Starcky (= Extrait des Mémoires présentés par divers savants à l'Académie des Inscriptions et Belles-Lettres, Tome XV), Paris, 1958.
Duprez JDG A.Duprez, Jésus et les Dieux Guérisseurs, à propos de Jean, V (= Cahiers de la Revue Biblique 12), Paris, 1970.
Dussaud DRS R.Dussaud, Les découvertes de Ras Shamra (Ugarit) et l'Ancien Testament (second edition), Paris, 1941.
Dussaud MPJ R.Dussaud, Les Monuments Palestiniens et Judaïques (Moab, Judée, Philistie, Samarie, Galilée), Paris, 1912.
Dussaud Orig R.Dussaud, Les Origines Cananéennes du sacrifice israélite (second edition), Paris, 1941.
Dussaud THSA R.Dussaud, Topographie Historique de la Syrie Antique et médiévale (= Haut-Commissariat de la République Française en Syrie et au Liban, Service des Antiquités et des Beaux-Arts. Bibliothèque Archéologique et Historique, tome IV), Paris, 1927.
DWJ see Koffmahn.
EA a) The Akkadian texts from Amarna quoted after Die El-Amarna Tafeln mit Einleitung und Erläuterungen (ed. J.A.Knudtzon), Teil 1, Die Texte, Leipzig, 1915 - b) see Rainey.
EAS see Sader.
EB Estudios Bíblicos (Organo de la Asociación para el Fomento de los Estudios Bíblicos en España (A.F.E.B.E.)).
Ebeling Frah E.Ebeling, Das aramäisch-mittelpersische Glossar Frahang-i-Pahlavik im Lichte der assyriologischen Forschung (= Mitteilungen der altorientalischen Gesellschaft, Band XIV, Heft 1), Leipzig, 1941.
EDE vii/viii The excavations at Dura-Europos conducted by Yale University and the French Academy of Inscriptions and Letters. Preliminary Reprot of the seventh and eighth seasons of Work 1933-1934 and 1934-1935 (edd. M.I.Rostovtzeff, F.E.Brown & C.B.Welles), London/Leipzig/Prague, 1939.
Editto Un Editto bilingue Greco-aramaico di Asoka. La prima iscizione Greca scoperta in Afghanistan, testo, traduzione e note a cura di G.Pugliesi Caratelli e di G.Levi Della Vida (= Istituto Italiano per il Medio ed Estremo Oriente. Serie Orientale Roma, Vol. XXI; ed. G.Tucci), Roma, 1958.
Edom Edomite.
EFM L'Espansione Fenicia nel Mediterraneo, relazione del colloquio in Roma, 4-5 Maggio 11970 di F.Barreca, M.Bekkari, a.o. (= Studi Semitici 38), Roma, 1971.
e.g. exempli gratia.
Egypt. Egyptian.

EHA see Naveh.
EI Eretz-Israel. Archaeological, historical and geographical studies.
Eilers Beamtennamen W.Eilers, Iranische Beamtennamen in der keilschriftlichen Überlieferung (= Abhandlungen für die Kunde des Morgenlandes XXV/5), Leipzig, 1940.
Eissfeldt Molk O.Eissfeldt, Molk als Opferbegriff im Punischen und Hebräischen und das Ende des Gottes Moloch (= Beiträge zur Religionsgeschichte des Altertums, Heft 3), Halle (Saale), 1935.
Eissfeldt Ras Schamra und Sanch O.Eissfeldt, Ras Schamra und Sanchunjaton (= Beiträge zur Religionsgeschichte des Altertums, Heft 4), Halle (Saale), 1939.
Elam. Elamite.
Elayi RCP J.Elayi, Recherches sur les Cités Phéniciennes à l'époque Perse (= Supplemento n. 51 agli Annali, Vol. 47 (1987), fasc. 2), Napoli, 1987.
Elayi SCA J.Elayi, Sidon, Cité Autonome de l'empire Perse (second edition), Paris, 1990.
Ellenbogen M.Ellenbogen, Foreign words in the Old Testament, their origin and etymology, London, 1962.

EM Études Mithriaques, Actes du 2e congrès international Téhéran, du 1er au 8 Septembre 1975 (= Acta Iranica, première série, Volume IV; = Acta Iranica Vol. XVII), Leiden/Téhéran-Liège, 1978.
emph. emphatic.
Ench Enchoria, Zeitschrift für Demotistik und Koptologie.
enclit. enclitic.
energ. energic.
enumer. enumeration.
EpAn Epigraphica Anatolica. Zeitschrift für Epigraphik und historische Geographie Anatoliens.
Eph M.Lidzbarski, Ephemeris für semitische Epigraphik, Band I, Giessen, 1902, Band II, Giessen, 1908, Band III, Giessen, 1915.
Epigr Epigraphica. Rivista Italiana di epigrafia.
Epigraphische Miscellen see Euting.
EPM see Bunnens.
EpVos Epigrafika Vostoka.
Eranos Acta philologica suecana.
Erman Religion A.Erman, Die Religion der Ägypter. Ihr Werden und Vergehen in vier Jahrtausenden, Berlin/Leipzig, 1934.
ERS see Lagrange.
ESBNT see Fitzmyer.
Et see Clermont-Ganneau.
etc. et cetera.
EtPhén see Bruston.
etym. a) etymology - b) etymological.
Euting Epigraphische Miscellen J.Euting, "Epigraphische Miscellen" (erste Reihe), Sitzungsberichte der königlich preussischen Akademie der Wissenschaften zu Berlin 1885, 16 Juli, Sitzung der philosophisch-historischen Classe, pp. 669-688; (zweite Reihe), ibid. 1887, 12 Mai, Sitzung der philosophisch-historischen Classe, pp. 407-422.
Euting Nab Inschriften J.Euting, Nabatäische Inschriften aus Arabien, Berlin, 1885.
Euting Sin Inschrift Sinaitische Inschriften (ed. J.Euting), Berlin, 1891.
EVO Egitto e Vicino Oriente.
EW East and West. Quarterly published by the Istituto Italiano per il Medio ed Estremo Oriente.
explic. explication.

f. a) feminine - b) following.
Fantar DM M.Fantar, Le Dieu de la Mer chez les Phéniciens et les Puniques (= Studi Semitici 48), Roma, 1977.
FB M.Dunand Fouilles de Byblos, Tome Ier 1926-1932, (= Haut-Commissariat de la République Française en Syrie et au Liban. Service des Antiquités, Bibliothèque Archéologique et Historique Tome XXIV), Paris, 1939.
FDE F.Cumont, Fouilles de Doura Europos (1922-1923) avec un appendice sur la céramique de Doura par M. et Mme Massoul, Texte (= Haut- Commissariat de la République Française en Syrie et au Liban. Service des Antiquités et des Beaux-Arts, Bibliothèque Archéologique et Historique, Tome IX), Paris, 1926.
Festus Sexti Pompei Festi De verborum significatu quae supersunt cum Pauli epitome, quoted after the edition of W.M.Lindsay, Lipsiae, 1913.
Février Essai J.G.Février, Essai sur l'histoire politique et économique de Palmyre, Paris, 1931.
Février Rel J.G.Février, La Religion des Palmyréniens, Paris, 1931.
ff. and following pages.
FG see Winter.
fin. final.
Fitzmyer AIS J.A.Fitzmyer, The Aramaic Inscriptions of Sefîre (= Biblica et Orientalia 19), Rome, 1967.
Fitzmyer ESBNT J.A.Fitzmyer, Essays on the Semitic Background of the New Testament (second edition; = Sources for Biblical Studies 5), Missoula, 1974.
Fitzmyer GenAp J.A.Fitzmyer, The Genesis Apocryphon of the Qumran Cave I, a commentary (second edition; = Biblica et Orientalia 18A), Rome, 1971.
Fitzmyer TAG J.A.Fitzmyer, To Advance the Gospel, New Testament studies, New York, 1981.
Fitzmyer WA J.A.Fitzmyer, A Wandering Aramean, collected Aramaic essays (= Society of Biblical Literature Monograph Series 25, edd. L.E.Keck & J.L.Crenshaw), Missoula Montana, 1979.
FLEM see Marrassini.
FO Folia Orientalia.
foll. following.
Forschung see Rosenthal.
FP Frahang i Pahlavık edited with transliteration, transcription and commentary from the posthumous papers of Henrik Samuel Nyberg by Bo Utas with the collaboration of Christopher Toll, Wiesbaden, 1988.
FP (followed by date, e.g. FP '60) Palmyre, Fouilles Polonaises (ed. K. Michałowski).
FPI Los Fenicios en la Peninsula Iberica, Vol. II, Epigrafía y lengua, glíptica y numismática, expansión e interacción cultural, appendice: El elemento púnico en la cultura talayótica (edd. G.Del Olmo Lete & M.E.Aubet Semmler), Sadabell (Barcelona), 1986.
FR J.Friedrich & W.Röllig, Phönizich-Punische Grammatik (= Analecta Orientalia 46), Roma, 1970.
fr fragment.
Frah a) the Frahang-i-Pahlavik quoted after FP - b) see Ebeling.
Frah-app the appendix to Frahang-i-Pahlavik quoted after FP pp. 53-54 and 98-100.
Frah-S1 addition to

Frahang-i-Pahlavik quoted after FP pp. 59 and 111-112.
Frah-S2 addition to Frahang-i-Pahlavik quoted after FP pp. 113-124.
Fremdw see Zimmern.
Frey J.B.Frey, Corpus inscriptionum iudaicarum, Vol. I, Roma, 1936, Vol. II, Roma, 1952. For the first volume the reedition is quoted: Corpus of Jewish inscriptions, Jewish Inscriptions from the third century B.C. to the seventh century A.D. (Prolegomenon by B.Lifshitz), New York, 1975.
Frey Prol. B.Lifshitz, Prolegomenon, in: J.B.Frey, Corpus of Jewish Inscriptions, Vol. I, Europe, New York, 1975, pp. 21-97.
Friedr J.Friedrich, Phönizisch-Punische Grammatik (= Analecta Orientalia 32), Roma, 1951.
Fritz TZ V.Fritz, Tempel und Zelt. Studien zum Tempelbau in Israel und zu dem Zeltheiligtum der Priesterschrift (= Wissenschaftliche Monographien zum Alten und Neuen Testament 47), Neukirchen/Vluyn, 1977.
Frye Heritage R.N.Frye, The Heritage of Persia, London, 1962.
FS Albright i The Bible and the Ancient Near East. Essays in honor of William Foxwell Albright (ed. G.E.Wright), London, 1961.
FS Albright ii Near Eastern Studies in honor of W.F.Albright (ed. H.Goedicke), Baltimore, 1971.
FS Andersen Perspectives on language and text. Essays and poems in honor of Francis I.Andersen's sixtieth birthday Juli 28, 1985 (edd. E.W.Conrad & E.G.Newing), Winona Lake, 1987.
FS Asmussen A green leaf. Papers in honour of Professor Jes P.Asmussen (= Acta Iranica 28, 2e série, Hommages et opera minora, Vol. 12), Leiden, 1988.
FS Beek Travels in the world of the Old Testament. Studies presented to Professor M.A.Beek on the 0ccasion of his 65th birthday (edd. M.S.H.G.Heerma v.Voss, Ph.H.J.Houwink ten Cate & N.A.v.Uchelen), Assen, 1974.
FS Bertholet Festschrift Alfred Bertholet zum 80. Geburtstag gewidmet von Kollegen und Freunden (edd. W.Baumgartner, O.Eissfeldt, K.Elliger, L.Rost), Tübingen, 1950.
FS Brunner Fontes atque Pontes, eine Festgabe für Hellmut Brunner (ed. M.Görg; = Ägypten und Altes Testament, Studien zu Geschichte, Kultur und Religion Ägyptens und des Alten Testaments, Band 5), Wiesbaden, 1983.
FS Cazelles Mélanges Bibliques et orientaux en l'honneur de M. Henri Cazelles (edd. A.Caquot & M.Delcor; = Alter Orient und Altes Testament, Veröffentlichungen zur Kultur und Geschichte des Alten Orients und des Alten Testaments, Band 212), Neukirchen/Vluyn, 1981.
FS Christian Festschrift für Prof. Dr. Viktor Christian, gewidmet von Kollegen und Schülern zum 70. Geburtstag (ed. K.Schubert in Verbindung mit J.Botterweck & J.Knobloch), Wien, 1956.
FS Collart Mélanges d'histoire ancienne et d'archéologie offerts à Paul Collart (= Cahiers d'Archéologie romande de la Bibliothèque historique vaudoise no 5; edd. H.Bögli & C.Martin), Lausanne, 1976.

FS Cross Ancient Israelite religion. Essays in honor of Frank Moore Cross (edd. P.D.Miller, P.D.Hanson & S.D.McBride), Philadelphia, 1987.

FS Daube Daube noster. Essays in legal history for David Daube (ed. A.Watson), Edinburgh/London, 1974.

FS Delcor Mélanges Bibliques et orientaux en l'honneur de M. Mathias Delcor (edd. A.Caquot, S.Légasse & M.Tardieu; = Alter Orient und Altes Testament, Veröffentlichungen zur Kultur und Geschichte des Alten Orients und des Alten Testaments, Band 215), Neukirchen/Vluyn, 1985.

FS Driver Hebrew and Semitic studies presented to Godfrey Rolles Driver ... in celebration of his seventieth birthday 20 August 1962 (edd. D.W.Thomas & W.D.McHardy), Oxford, 1963.

FS Duchesne-Guillemin Orientalia J.Duchesne-Guillemin emerito oblata (= Acta Iranica Vol. 23, deuxième série, Hommages et Opera minora, vol. 9), Leiden, 1984.

FS Dussaud Mélanges Syriens offerts à Monsieur René Dussaud, secrétaire perpétuel de l'Académie des Inscriptions et Belles-Lettres par ses amis et élèves, Tome I, Paris, 1939, Tome II, Paris, 1939.

FS Eissfeldt Festschrift Otto Eissfeldt zum 60. Geburtstag 1 September 1947 dargebracht von Freunden und Verehrern (ed. J.Fück), Halle (Saale), 1947.

FS Elliger Wort und Geschichte. Festschrift für Karl Elliger zum 70. Geburtstag (edd. H.Gese & H.P.Rüger; = Alter Orient und Altes Testament, Veröffentlichungen zur Kultur und Geschichte des Alten Orients und des Alten Testaments, Band 18), Neukirchen/Vluyn, 1973.

FS Fensham Text and context, Old Testament and Semitic Studies for F.C.Fensham (ed. W.Claassen; = Journal for the Study of the Old Testament, Supplement Series 48), Sheffield, 1988.

FS Fitzmyer To touch the text, Biblical and related studies in honor of Joseph A.Fitzmyer S.J. (edd. M.P.Horgan & P.J.Kobelski), New York, 1989.

FS Fleischer Morgenländische Forschungen. Festschrift Herrn Prof. Dr. H.L.Fleischer zu seinem fünfzigjährigen Doctorjubiläum am 4. März 1874 gewidmet von seinen Schülern H.Derenbourg, H.Ethé, O.Loth, A.Müller, F.Philippi, B.Stade, H.Thorbecke, Leipzig, 1875.

FS Freedman The Word of the Lord shall go forth. Essays in honor of David Noel Freedman in celebration of his sixtieth birthday (edd. C.L.Meyers & M.O'Connor; = American Schools of Oriental Research, Special Volume Series no 1), Winona Lake, 1983.

FS Friedrich Festschrift Johannes Friedrich zum 65. Geburtstag am 27. August 1958 gewidmet (edd. R.v.Kienle, A.Moortgat, H.Otten, E.v.Schuler & W.Zaumseil), Heidelberg, 1959.

FS Gaster = JANES V.

FS Glueck Near Eastern archaeology in the twentieth century. Essays in honor of Nelson Glueck (ed. J.A.Sanders), Garden City/New York, 1970.

FS Gonin Pro munere grates studies opgedra van H.L.Gonin deur oud-studente en kollegas (ed. D.M.Kriel), Pretoria, 1971.

FS Gordon i Orient and Occident. Essays presented to Cyrus H.Gordon on the occasion of his sixty-fifth birthday (ed. H.A.Hofner; = Alter Orient und Altes Testament, Veröffentlichungen zur Kultur und Geschichte des Alten Orients und des Alten Testaments, Band 22), Neukirchen/Vluyn, 1973.
FS Gordon ii The Bible World. Essays in honor of Cyrus H.Gordon (edd. G.Rendsburg a.o.), New York, 1980.
FS Grelot La vie de la Parole, de l'Ancien au Nouveau Testament, études d'exégèse et d'herméneutique Bibliques offertes à Pierre Grelot Professeur à l'Institut Catholique de Paris, Paris, 1987.
FS Haupt Oriental studies published in commemoration of the fortieth anniversary (1883-1923) of Paul Haupt as Director of the Oriental Seminary of the John Hopkins University Baltimore, MD (edd. C.Adler & A.Ember), Baltimore/Leipzig, 1926.
FS Horn The archaeology of Jordan and other studies presented to Siegfried H.Horn ... (edd. L.T.Geraty & L.J.Herr), Berrien Springs (Michigan), 1986.
FS Hospers Scripta signa vocis. Studies about scripts, scriptures, scribes and languages in the Near East presented to J.H.Hospers by his pupils, colleagues and friends (edd. H.L.J.Vanstiphout, K.Jongeling, F.Leemhuis & G.J.Reinink), Groningen, 1986.
FS Isserlin Oriental studies presented to Benedikt S.J.Isserlin by friends and colleagues on the occasion of his sixtieth birthday 25 Februari 1976 (edd. R.Y.Ebied & M.J.L.Young; = Leeds University Oriental Society Near Eastern Researches II), Leiden, 1980.
FS Iwry Biblical and related studies presented to Samuel Iwry (edd. A.Kort & S.Morschauser), Winona Lake, 1985.
FS Lambdin "Working with no data". Semitic and Egyptian studies presented to Thomas O.Lambdin (ed. D.M.Golomb), Winona Lake, 1987.
FS Lebram Tradition and re-interpretation in Jewish and early Christian literature. Essays in honour of Jürgen C.H.Lebram (edd. J.W.v.Henten, H.J.de Jonge, P.T.v.Rooden & J.W.Wesselius; = Studia Post-Biblica 36), Leiden, 1986.
FS Loewenstamm i Studies in Bible and the Ancient Near East presented to Samuel E.Loewenstamm on his seventieth birthday (edd. Y.Avishur & J.Blau), Jerusalem, 1978.
FS Loewenstamm ii Meḥqarim bamiqra uvemizraḥ haqadmon mugashim liShmuel E.Loewenstamm bemil'at lo shiv ʿim shana (edd. Y.Avishur & J.Blau), Jerusalem, 1978.
FS Martini Studi in onore del cardinale Martini (= Atti del xxvi Settimana Bithia), Brescia, 1982.
FS Miles Near Eastern numismatics, iconography, epigraphy and history. Studies in honor of George C.Miles (ed. D.K.Kouymjian), Beirut, 1974.
FS Molin Meqor ḥajjim. Festschrift für Georg Molin zu seinem 75. Geburtstag (ed. I.Seybold), Graz, 1983.
FS Moran Lingering over words. Studies in ancient Near Eastern literature in honor of William

L.Moran (edd. T.Abusch, J.Huehnergard & P.Steinkeller), Atlanta, Georgia, 1990.

FS Morton Smith Christianity, Judaism and other Greco-Roman cults. Studies for Morton Smith at sixty, Part III, Judaism before 70 (ed. J.Neusner; = Studies in Judaism in late Antiquity, Vol. 12), Leiden, 1975.

FS Nyberg Monumentum H.S.Nyberg I (= Acta Iranica, deuxième, Vol. 1, Hommages et Opera minora), Leiden/Téhéran-Liège, 1975.

FS Oppenheim Studies presented to A.Leo Oppenheim, June 7, 1964, Chicago, 1964.

FS Pagliaro Studia Classica et Orientalia Antonino Pagliaro oblata (3 vols.), Roma, 1969.

FS Pedersen Studia orientalia Ioanni Pedersen septuagenario A.D. VII Id. Nov. Anno MCMLIII a collegis, discipulis, amicis dicata, Hauniae, 1953.

FS v.d.Ploeg Von Kanaan bis Kerala. Festschrift für Prof. Mag. Dr. Dr. J.P.M.v.d.Ploeg O.P. zur Vollendung des siebzigsten Lebensjahres am 4 Juli 1979 ... (edd. W.C.Delsman a.o.; = Alter Orient und Altes Testament, Veröffentlichungen zur Kultur und Geschichte des Alten Orients und des Alten Testaments, Band 211), Neukirchen/Vluyn, 1982.

FS Rendtorff Die hebräische Bibel und ihre zweifache Nachgeschichte. Festschrift für Rolf Rendtorff zum 65. Geburtstag (edd. E.Blum, Chr. Macholz & E.W.Stegemann), Neukirchen/Vluyn, 1990.

FS Rinaldi Studi sull'Oriente e la Bibbia offerti a Giovanni Rinaldi nel 60o compleanno da allieve, colleghi, amici (edd. H.Cazelles a.o.), Genova, 1967.

FS Seidl Festschrift für Erwin Seidl zum 70 Geburtstag (edd. H.Hübner, E.Klingmüller & A Wacke), Köln, 1975.

FS Rundgren = OrSu xxxiii-xxxv.

FS v.Selms De fructu oris sui. Essays in honour of Adrianus van Selms (edd. I.H.Eybers a.o.; = Pretoria Oriental Series Vol IX), Leiden, 1971.

FS Stinespring The use of the Old Testament in the New and other essays. Studies in honor of William Franklin Stinespring (ed. J.M.Efird), Durham, N.C., 1972.

FS Thomas Words and Meanings. Essays presented to David Winton Thomas on his retirement from the Regius Professorship of Hebrew in the University of Cambridge, 1968 (edd. P.R.Ackroyd & B.Lindars), Cambridge, 1068.

FS Tisserant i Mélanges Eugène Tisserant, Vol. I, Écriture Sainte - Ancient Orient (= Studi e Testi 231), Città del Vaticano, 1964.

FS Tufnell Palestine in the bronze and iron ages. Papers in honour of Olga Tufnell (ed. J.N.Tubb; = Institute of Archaeology occasional Publication no 11), London, 1985.

FS Ubach Miscellanea Biblica B.Ubach (ed. R.M.Díaz; = Scripta et Documenta 1), Montisserati, 1953.

FS de Vogüé Florilegium ou recueil de travaux d'érudition dédiés à Monsieur le Marquis Melchior de Vogüé à l'occasion du quatre-vingtième anniversaire de sa naissance, 18 Octobre 1909, Paris, 1909.

FS Volterra vi Studi in onore di

Edoardo Volterra, VI (= Pubblicazioni della Facoltà di Giurisprudenza dell'Università di Roma 45), Milano, 1971.
FS Vööbus A tribute to Arthur Vööbus. Studies in early Christian literature and its environment, primarily in the Syrian East (ed. R.H.Fischer), Chicago, 1977.
FS Ziegler Wort, Lied und Gottesspruch, Festschrift für Jsoeph Ziegler (ed. J.Schreiner; = Forschung zur Bibel 1, 2), Vol. I, II, Würzburg, 1972.
FS Zucker Festschrift für Friedrich Zucker zum 70. Geburtstag, Berlin, 1954.
FSR see Garbini.
FuB Forschungen und Berichte. Staatliche Museen zu Berlin.
FUCUS FUCUS, a Semitic/Afrasian grathering in remembrance of Albert Ehrman (ed. Y.L.Arbeitman; = Amsterdam Studies in the Theory and History of Linguistic Science, Series IV, Current Issues in Linguistic Theory, Vol. 58), Amsterdam, 1988.
FuF Forschungen und Fortschritte. Nachrichtenblatt der deutschen Wissenschaft und Technik.
Fuhs HZH H.F.Fuhs, Sehen und Schauen. Die Wurzel ḥzh im Alten Oreint und im Alten Testament. Ein Beitrag zur prophetischen Offenbarungsempfang (= Forschung zur Bibel, Band 32), Würzburg, 1978.
Fussbekleidung see Salonen.
FX Fouilles de Xanthos, Tome VI, La stèle trilingue de Letôon, Paris, 1979.
GAG a) see Sivan - b) see v.Soden.
Gall K.Galling, "Beschriftete Bildsiegel des ersten Jahrtausends v. Chr. vornehmlich aus Syrien und Palästina. Ein Beitrag zur Geschichte der phönikischen Kunst", ZDPV lxiv pp. 121-202.
Galling TGI see TGI.
Garb G.Garbini, L'Aramaico antico (= Atti della Accademia nazionale dei Lincei. Memorie, Classe di Scienze morali, storiche e filologiche, Serie 8, Vol. 7, fasc. 5), Roma, 1956.
Garbini FSR G.Garbini, I Fenici, Storia e Religione (= Istituto Universitario Orientale, Seminario di Studi Asiatici, Series Minor xi), Napoli, 1980.
Garbini ISN G.Garbini, Il Semitico Nordoccidentale, studi di storia linguistica (= Studi Semitici - Nuova Serie 5), Roma, 1988.
Garbini ISNO G.Garbini, Il Semitico di Nord-Ovest (= Quaderni della Sezione Linguistica degli Annali, I), Napoli, 1960.
Garbini Kand G.Garbini, The Aramaic section of the Kandahar inscription (= Serie Orientale Roma (ed. G.Tucci) Vol. XXIX estratto), Roma, 1964.
Garbini LS-Amm G.Garbini, "La lingua degli Ammoniti", Lel Lingue Semitiche, Studi di storia linguistica (= Pubblicazioni del Seminario di Semitistica, Ricerche ix), Napoli, 1972, pp. 97-108.
Garr DGSP W.R.Garr, Dialect Geography of Syria-Palestine, 1000-586 BCE, Philadelphia, 1985.
Gawlikowski MFP M.Gawlikowski, Monuments funéraires de Palmyre (= Travaux du Centre d'Archéologie méditerranéenne de l'Académie Polonaise des Sciences sous la direction de K.Michałowski, Tome 9), Warszawa, 1970.
Gawlikowski TP M.Gawlikowski, Le Temple Palmyrénien. Étude

d'épigraphie et de topographie historique (= Palmyre VI), Warszawa, 1973.
GCAV Gratz College Anniversary Volume on the occasion of the seventy-fifth anniversary of the founding of the College, 1895-1970 (edd. I.D.Passow & S.T.Lachs), Philadelphia, 1971.
GCPA see Schulthess.
GD see Schmökel.
gen. genitive.
GenAp see Fitzmyer.
Georg. Georgia.
Gezer ii see Macalister.
GGA Göttingische Gelehrte Anzeigen.
GH see Altheim & Stiehl.
GHPO Géographique Historique au Proche-Orient (Syrie, Phénicie, Arabie, Grecques, Romaines, Byzantines). Actes de la Table Ronde de Valbonne, 16-18 Septembre 1985 (edd. P.L.Gatier, B.Helly & J.P.Rey-Coquais; = Centre National de la Recherche Scientifique, Centre de Recherches Archéologiques, Notes et Monographies techniques no 23), Paris, 1990.
Gibeon see Pritchard.
Gifts see Yaron.
Gildemeister the transcription by J.Gildemeister of Punic parts of the Poenulus of Plaute in T.Macci Plauti Poenulus (= T.Macci Plauti Comoediae recensuit instrumento critico et prolegomenis auxit F.Ritschelius sociis operae adsumptis G.Loewe, G.Goetz, F.Schoell, Tomi II Fasciculus V; edd. G.Götz & G.Loewe), Lipsiae, 1884, pp. 114-116 (cf. also pp. xv-xix).
Ginzberg Volume Louis Ginsberg Jubilee Volume on the occasion of his seventieth birthday, English section, New York, 1945.
GIPP Ph.Gignoux, Glossaire des Inscriptions Péhlévies et Parthes (= Corpus Inscriptionum Iranicarum, Supplementary Series, Vol. I), London, 1972.
Glaser die Abessinier E.Glaser, Die Abessinier in Arabien und Afrika aud Grund neuentdeckter Inschriften, München, 1895.
GLECS Comptes Rendus du Groupe Linguistique d'Études Chamito- Sémitiques.
Glueck DD N.Glueck, Deities and Dolphins, the story of the Nabataeans, New York, 1965.
GLL see Krauss.
Gloss see Gordon.
GMA see Altheim & Stiehl.
Good SHP R.M.Good, The Sheep of His Pasture. A study of the Hebrew noun ʿAm(m) and its Semitic cognates (= Harvard Semitic Monographs 29), Chico, 1983.
Gordon Gloss the "Glossary" in C.H.Gordon, Ugaritic textbook, grammar, texts in transliteration, cuneiform selctions, glossary, indices (= Analecta Orientalia 38), Rome, 1965, pp. 347-507.
Gordon Introduction C.H.Gordon, Introduction to Old Testament times, Ventnor, N.J., 1953.
Gottheil R.J.H.Gottheil, "Vocabula Punica" in G.Lodge, Lexicon Plautinum I, Lipsiae, 1924, pp. 915-917.
GP see v.d.Branden.
GPP see Segert.
gr gramme.
GR i Grotta Regina I. Rapporto preliminare della missione congiunta con la Soprintendenza alle Antichità della Sicilia Occidentale (edd.

A.M.Bisi, M.G.Guzzo Amadasi, V.Tusa; = Studi Semitici 33), Roma, 1969.

GR ii Grotta Regina II. Le iscizioni Puniche. Rapporto della missione congiunta con la Soprintendenza alle Antichità della Sicilia Occidentale (edd. G.C.Polselli, M.G.Guzzo Amadasi, V.Tusa; = Studi Semitici 52), Roma, 1979.

Grabbe CPTJ L.L.Grabbe, Comparative philology and the text of Job, a study in methodology (= Society of Biblical Literature, Dissertation Series no 34), Missoula, 1977.

Gramm a) see Cantineau - b) see Nöldeke.

Grammatik see Dalman.

Greek a) the Greek language - b) see Lieberman.

Green RHS A.R.W.Green, The Role of human Sacrifice in the ancient Near East (= American Schools of Oriental Research, Dissertation Series 1), Missoula, 1975.

Greenfield & Porten BIDG J.C.Greenfield & B.Porten, The Bisitun Inscription of Darius the Great, Aramaic Version, text, translation and commentary (= Corpus Inscriptionum Iranicarum, Part I, Inscriptions of Ancient Iran, Vol. V, The Aramaic Versions of the Achaemenian Inscriptions, etc, Texts I), London, 1982.

Grelot DAE P.Grelot, Documents araméens d'Égypte, introduction, traduction, présentation, Paris, 1972.

Gressmann ATAT Altorientalische Texte zum Alten Testament in Verbindung mit E.Ebeling, H.Ranke, N.Rhodokanakis herausgegeben von H. Gressmann (2d edition), Berlin/Leipzig, 1926.

Gröndahl PTU F.Gröndahl, Die Personennamen der Texte aus Ugarit (= Studia Pohl 1), Rom, 1967.

Grundriss see Brockelmann.

Gsell HAAN S.Gsell, Histoire Ancienne de l'Afrique du Nord, Tome I (second edition), Paris, 1920, Tome II, Paris, 1920, Tome III, Paris, 1920, Tome IV, Paris, 1920, Tome V, Paris, 1927, Tome VI, Paris, 1927, Tome VII, Paris, 1928, Tome VIII, Paris, 1928.

GTT Gereformeerd Theologisch Tijdschrift.

Hackett BTDA J.A.Hackett, The Balaam Text from Deir ʿAllā (= Harvard Semitic Monographs no 31, ed. F.M.Cross), Chico, 1984.

HAHL see Pardee.

HAL Hebräisches und aramäisches Lexikon zum Alten Testament von L.Koehler & W.Baumgartner (third edition), Vol. I neu bearbeitet von W.Baumgartner unter Mitarbeit von B.Hartmann & E.Y.Kutscher, Leiden, 1967; Vol. II neu bearbeitet von W.Baumgartner unter Mitarbeit von B.Hartmann & E.Y.Kutscher (edd. B.Hartmann, Ph.Reymond & J.J.Stamm), Leiden, 1974; Vol. III neu bearbeitet von W.Baumgartner & J.J.Stamm unter Mitarbeit von Z.Ben-Ḥayyim, B.Hartmann & Ph.H.Reymond, Leiden, 1983; Vol. IV neu bearbeitet von J.J.Stamm unter Mitarbeit von Z.Ben-Ḥayyim, B.Hartmann & Ph.H.Reymond, Leiden/New York/København/Köln, 1990.

HAlSe see Tursinai.

Hama see Ingholt.

Handb see Lidzbarski.

Haph Haphel.

Haran TTS M.Haran, Temples and Temple Service in ancient Israel. An inquiry into the character of cult phenomena and the historical setting of the Priestly School, Oxford, 1978.
Harr Z.S.Harris, A grammar of the Phoenician language (= American Oriental Series, Vol. 8), New Haven, 1936.
Harris DCD Z.S.Harris, Development of the Canaanite Dialects. An investigation in linguistic history (= American Oriental Series, Vol. 16), New Haven, 1939.
hasm. hasmonean.
Hatra the Hatrean texts quoted after a) the edition in F.Vattioni, Le iscrizioni di Ḥatra (= Supplement no 28 agli Annali, vol. 41, fasc. 3), Napoli 1981 (no 1 - 341) - b) Syr lxiv p. 91ff. (no 342-344) - c) Syr lxiii pp. 353ff. (no. 345-387) - d) Syr lxvii pp. 397ff. (no. 388-416) - e) Syr lxiv pp. 223ff. (Ibr 9, 14, 20, 21).
Hazor ii the Hebrew inscriptions found at Hazor published in Hazor II, an account of the second season of excavations, 1956, by Y.Yadin, Y.Aharoni, R.Amiran, T.Dothan, I.Dunayevsky, J.Perrot with a contribution by S.Angress, Jerusalem, 1960, pp. 70-75.
Hazor-SL see Yadin.
HBTJ N.Avigad, Hebrew Bullae from the Time of Jeremiah, remnants of a burnt archive, Jerusalem, 1986.
HDAI see Smelik.
HDS Hommages à André Dupont-Sommer, Paris, 1971.
Hebr Hebrew.
Hehn KH V.Hehn, Kuturpflanzen und Hausthiere in ihrem Übergang aus Asien nach Griechenland und Italien sowie in das übrige Europa. Historisch linguistische Skizzen (neu ausgegeben von O.Schrader mit botanischen Beiträgen von A.Engler; seventh edition), Berlin, 1902.
Heider CM G.C.Heider, The Cult of Molek, a reassessment (= Journal for the Study of the Old Testament Supplement Series 43), Sheffield, 1985.
Hen Henoch, studi storicofilologici sull'ebraismo redatti presso la Biblioteca PAUL KAHLE dell'Istituto di Orientalistica dell'Università di Torino.
Henning Zoroaster W.B.Henning, Zoroaster, politician or witchdoctor?, London, 1951.
Heritage see Frye.
Herm E.Bresciani & M.Kamil, Le lettere Aramaiche di Hermopoli (= Atti della Accademia Nazionale dei Lincei, Memorie, Classe di Scienze morali, storiche e filologiche, Serie VIII, Vol. XII, fasc. 5), Roma, 1966.
Herzfeld API Altpersische Inschriften (ed. E.Herzfeld; = Erster Ergänzungsband zu den Archaeologischen Mitteilungen aus Iran), Berlin, 1938.
Herzfeld PE E.Herzfeld, The Persian Empire. Studies in geography and ethnography of the Ancient Near East edited from the posthumous papers by G.Walser, Wiesbaden, 1968.
Hesychius EtymMagna Hesychius Etymologia Magna published in Hesychii Alexandrini Lexicon post Ioannem Albertum (ed. M.Schmidt), Vol. I Ienae, 1858, Vol. II, Ienae, 1860, Vol. III, Ienae, 1861, Vol. IV Pars 1, Ienae, 1862, Vol. IV Pars 2, Ienae, 1864.
Heth Hethitica.
Hill (Phoen) Catalogue of Greek

coins in the British Museum (ed. G.F.Hill), Phoenicia, London, 1910.
Hillers TC D.R.Hillers, Treaty-Curses and the Old Testament prophets (= Biblica et Orientalia 16), Rome, 1964.
Hinz AISN W.Hinz, Altiranisches Sprachgut der Nebenüberlieferungen unter Mitarbeit von P.M.Berger, G.Korbel & A.Nippa (= Göttinger Orientforschungen, Veröffentlichungen des Sonderforschungsbereiches Orientalistik an der Georg-August-Universität Göttingen, III. Reihe Iranica, Band 3), Wiesbaden, 1975.
Hinz NW W.Hinz, Neue Wege im Altpersischen (= Göttinger Orientforschungen, Veröffentlichungen des Sonderforschungsbereiches Orientalistik an der Georg-August Universität Göttingen, III. Reihe Iranica, Band 1), Wiesbaden, 1973.
Hiph Hiphil.
Hipht Hiphta ʿal.
HISG see Pritchard.
Hitnaph Hitnaph ʿal.
Hitp Hitpa ʿel.
Hitt Hittite.
Hittanaph Hittanaph ʿal.
HJB see Neusner.
HO iii Handbuch der Orientalistik (ed. B.Spuler), erste Abteilung, dritter Band, Semitistik; Erster Abschnitt, Leiden-Köln, 1953, Zweiter und dritter Abschnitt, Leiden, 1954.
Hölbi AGPPS G.Hölbi, Ägyptisches Kulturgut im phönikischen und punischen Sardinien, Vol. I, Leiden, 1986, Vol. II, Leiden, 1986 (= Études préliminaires aux Religions Orientales dans l'Empire Romain, ed. M.J.Vermaseren, Vol. 102, 1 and 2).
Hoffmann Ueber einige phön Inschr G.Hoffmann, Ueber einige phönikische Inschriften, AGWG 1889, Band XXXVI 1.
Hofra A.Berthier & R.Charlier, Le sanctuaire Punique d'El-Hofra à Constantine, Paris, 1955.
Hofra Gr The Greek texts (or transcriptions of Punic texts in Greek script) published in Hofra pp. 167-176.
Hoftijzer RelAr J.Hoftijzer, Religio Aramaica, godsdienstige verschijnselen in Aramese teksten (= Mededelingen en Verhandelingen van het Vooraziatisch-Egyptisch Genootschap Ex Oriente Lux, Vol. XVI), Leiden, 1968.
Hoph Hophal.
HP see Nyberg.
HR see Niehr.
HT see Dothan.
HTBS see Driver.
HTSO Humour, Travail et Science en Orient (edd. A.Théodoridès, P.Naster & J.Ries), Leuven, 1988.
Hübschmann Studien H.Hübschmann, Persische Studien, Strassburg, 1895.
HUCA Hebrew Union College Annual.
Humbach AIT H.Humbach, Die aramäische Inschrift von Taxila (= Akademie der Wissenschaften und der Literatur, Mainz, Abhandlungen der geistes- und sozialwissenschaftlichen Klasse, Jahrgang 1969, nr 1.), Mainz, 1969.
Hurr. Hurrian.
Huss W.Huss, Geschichte der Karthager (= Handbuch der Altertumswissenschaft 3.Abt T. 8), München, 1985.
Hüttenmeister ASI

F.Hüttenmeister, Die antiken Synagogen in Israel I, Die jüdischen Synagogen, Lehrhaüser und Gerichtshöfe (= Beihefte zum Tübinger Atlas des Vorderen Orients, Reihe B, Geisteswissenschaften, nr 12/1; ed. W.Röllig), Wiesbaden, 1977.
Hvidberg-Hansen TNT F.O.Hvidberg-Hansen, La déesse TNT, une étude sur la religion Canaanéo-Punique, Vol. I, II, Copenhague, 1979.
HZH see Fuhs.
IAM Inscriptions Antiques du Maroc, Inscriptions Libyques par L.Galand, Inscriptions Puniques et Néopuniques par J.Février, Inscriptions Hébraïques par G.Vajda, Paris, 1966.
IAS see Lemaire & Durand.
IAT see de Vaux.
ibid. ibidem.
Ibr see Hatra.
ICO M.G.Guzzo Amadasi, Le Iscrizione Fenicie e Puniche delle Colonie in Occidente (= Studi Semitici 28), Roma, 1967.
ICO-App. the texts published in the appendix of ICO pp. 157ff.
ICO-Malta the (Neo)punic texts from Malta published in ICO pp. 15ff.
ICO-Sard the (Neo)punic texts from Sardinia published in ICO pp. 83ff.
ICO-Sic the (Neo)punic texts from Sicily published in ICO pp. 53ff.
ICO-Spa the (Neo)punic texts from Spain published in ICO pp. 137ff.
id. idem.
i.e. id est.
IEJ Israel Exploration Journal.
IGLS L.Jalabert & R.Mouterde, Inscriptions Grecques et Latines de la Syrie, Tome I Commagène et Cyrrhestique, Paris, 1929, Tome II Chalcidique et Antiochène, Paris, 1939, Tome III/1 Région de l'Amanus, Antioche, Paris, 1950, Tome III/2 Antioche (suite), Antiochène, Paris, 1953, Tome IV Laodicée, Apamène, Paris, 1955, Tome V Emesène, Paris, 1959.
IGRR Inscriptiones Graecae ad Res Romanas pertinentes auctoritate et impensis Academiae Inscriptionum et Litterarum Humaniorum collectae et editae, Vol. I, Paris, 1911 (ed. R.Cagnat, auxiliantibus J.Toutain & P.Jouguet), Vol. III, Paris, 1906 (ed. R.Cagnat, auxiliante G.Lafaye), Vol. IV, Paris, 1927 (ed. G.Lafaye).
IH see a) Lemaire - b) Vattioni.
IIJ Indo-Iranian Journal.
IKM see Smend & Socin.
ILC see Alvarez Delgado.
Imper. Imperative.
Impf. Imperfect.
imposs. impossible.
improb. improbable.
IN see Justi.
indef. indefinite.
Indologen Tagung '71 Indologen Tagung 1971. Verhandlungen der indologischen Arbeitstagung im Museum für indische Kunst, Berlin, 7.-9.Okt. 1971 (= Glasenapp-Stiftung, Band VIII; edd. H.Härtel & V.Moeller), Wiesbaden, 1973.
inexplic. inexplicable.
Inf. Infinitive.
Ingholt Hama H.Ingholt, Rapport préliminaire sur sept campagnes de fouilles à Hama en Syrie (1932-1938) (= Det Kgl. Danske Videnskabernes Selskab. Archaeologisk-kunsthistoriske Meddelelser III,1), København, 1940.
Ingholt PaS H.Ingholt, Studier over Palmyrensk Skulptur,

Kbenhavn, 1928.
Ingholt PSH H.Ingholt, Parthian Sculptures from Hatra, Orient and Hellas in art and religion (= Memoirs of the Connecticut Academy of Arts & Sciences, VOL. XII, July 1954), New Haven.
Inschrift see Nöldeke.
InscrP J.Cantineau, Inscriptions Palmyréniennes, Damas, 1930.
InscrSem see Pedersen.
instrum. instrumental.
interj. interjection.
interpret. interpretation(s).
interrog. interrogative.
intrans. intransitive.
Introduction see Gordon.
Inv Inventaire des inscriptions de Palmyre, Fasc. I, II, III, IV (ed. J.Cantineau), Beyrouth, 1930, fasc. V, VI, VII (ed. J.Cantineau), Beyrouth, 1931, fasc. VIIIa (ed. J.Cantineau), Beyrouth, 1932, fasc. VIIIb (ed. J.Cantineau), Beyrouth, 1936, fasc. IX (ed. J.Cantineau), Beyrouth, 1933, fasc. X (ed. J.Starcky), Damas, 1949, fasc. XI (ed. J.Teixidor), Beyrouth, 1965, fasc. XII (edd. A.Bounni & J.Teixidor), Damas, 1975.
invar. invariable.
InvD Comte du Mesnil du Buisson, Inventaire des inscriptions Palmyréniennes de Doura-Europos (32 avant J.C. à 256 après J.C.) (second edition), Paris, 1939.
IP see Noth.
IPAA G.D.Davary & H.Humbach. Eine weitere aramäoiranische Inschrift der Periode des Aśoka aus Afghanistan (= Akademie der Wissenschaften und der Literatur, Mainz. Abhandlungen zur geistes- und sozialwissenschaftlichen Klasse, Jahrgang 1974, nr. 1), Mainz, 1974.
Ipht Iphtaʿal.
IPT G.Levi Della Vida & M.G.Amadasi Guzzo, Iscrizioni Puniche della Tripolitania (1927-1967), Roma 1987 (= Monografie di archeologia Libica - XXII)
Ipt Iptaʿal.
Ir Handbuch der Orientalistik. Erste Abteilung der nahe und der mittlere Osten (edd. B.Spuler & H.Kees), vierter Band: Iranistik; erster Abschnitt: Linguistik mit Beiträgen von K.Hoffmann, W.B.Henning, H.W.Bailey, G.Morgenstierne, W.Lentz, Leiden/Köln, 1958.
IR Inscriptions Reveal, documents from the time of the Bible, the Mishna and the Talmud, Jerusalem, 1972.
Iran Iran, Journal of the British Institute of Persian Studies.
Iran. Iranian.
Irâq Irâq. London, Brithish School of Archaeology in Iraq.
IrJu Irano-Judaica. Studies relating to Jewish contacts with Persian culture throughout the ages (ed. S.Shaked), Jerusalem, 1982.
IRT The Inscriptions of Roman Tripolitania (edd. J.M.Reynolds & J.B.Ward Perkins), Rome/London, 1952.
IRTS J.Reynolds, "Inscriptions of Roman Tripolitania: a Supplement", PBR xxiii (1955), pp. 124-127.
IS a)R.Hestrin & M.Dayagi-Mendels, Inscribed Seals, first Temple period, Hebrew, Ammonite, Moabite, Phoenician and Aramaic from the collections of the Israel Museum and the Israel Department of Antiquities and Museums, Jerusalem, 1979 - b) see Bikerman - c) see Solá-Solé.
ISC Inscriptions from fifty Safaitic Cairns (edd. F.V.Winnett &

G.L.Harding; = Near and Middle East Series 9), Toronto/Buffalo, etc., 1978.
ISN see Garbini.
ISNO see Garbini.
Isr. Israelite.
ISS see Tubach.
ISSM see Pognon.
Ithaph Ithaph ʿel.
Itp Itpaʿal/Itpeʿel.
Ittaph Ittaphʿal.
IUGP see Knauf.
J Jaussen et Savignac, Mission archéologique en Arabie (Mars-Mai 1907), Vol. I De Jérusalem au Hedjaz Médain-Saleh, Paris, 1909, Vol. II El-ʿEla, d'Hégra à Teima, Harrah de Tebouk, Paris, 1914.
JdesSav Journal des Savants.
JA a) Journal Asiatique, périodique trimestriel - b) Jewish Aramaic.
JACA see Ayad.
Jackson ALIA K.P.Jackson, The Ammonite Language of the Iron Age (= Harvard Semitic Monographs no 27), Chico, California, 1983.
JAOS Journal of the American Oriental Society.
JAOS Suppl Supplement to the Journal of the American Oriental Society.
JAP see Staerk.
J.Ar. Jewish Aramaic.
Jastrow M.Jastrow, A dictionary of the Targumim, the Talmud Babli and Yerushalmi and the midrashic literature, London/New York, Vol. I, 1903, Vol. II, 1903.
JBL Journal of Biblical Literature.
JC Y.Meshorer, Jewish Coins of the second Temple period, Tel Aviv, 1967.
JCS Journal of Cuneiform Studies.
JDG see Duprez.
JdesSav Journal des Savants.
JEA The Journal of Egyptian Archaeology.
JEAS B.Porten & J.C.Greenfield, Jews of Elephantine and Arameans of Syene. Aramaic texts with translation, Jerusalem, 1974.
JEOL Jaarbericht van het Vooraziatisch-Egyptisch Genootschap Ex Oriente Lux, gevestigd te Leiden, opgericht 22 Mei 1933.
Jenni Olam E.Jenni, Das Wort ʿōlām im Alten Testament, Berlin, 1953.
JGM see Scholem.
JHS The Journal of Hellenic Studies.
JJLG Jahrbuch der jüdisch-literarischen Gesellschaft (Sitz: Frankfurt am Main).
JJP The Journal of Juristic Papyrology.
JJS The Journal of Jewish Studies.
JKF Jahrbuch für kleinasiatische Forschung. Internationale orientalistische Zeitschrift.
JLNS see Ceresko.
JLTV Jewish Languages, Theme and Variations. Proceedings of the regional conferences of the Association for Jewish Studies held at the University of Michigan and New York University in March-April 1975 (ed. H.H.Paper), Cambridge Mass., 1978.
JNES Journal of Near Eastern Studies.
JNSL Journal of Northwest Semitic Languages.
Jongeling NINPI K.Jongeling, Names in Neo-Punic Inscriptions (thesis University of Groningen), 1984.
JournofPhil The Journal of Philology.
JPOS The Journal of the Palestine Oriental Society.

JQR The Jewish Quarterly Review.

JRAS The Journal of the Royal Asiatic Society of Great Britain and Ireland.
JRS The Journal of Roman Studies.

JS see Goodenough.
JSS Journal of Semitic Studies.
Jud. Judean.
JThSt The Journal of Theological Studies.
jur. juridical.
juss. jussive.
Justi IN F.Justi, Iranisches Namenbuch, Hildesheim, 1963.
KA texts from Kuntillet ʿAjrud, quoted according to the numbering in RSO lxiii, pp. 199ff.
Kadm Kadmos. Zeitschrift für vor- und frühgriechische Epigraphik.
KAI H.Donner & W.Röllig, Kanaanäische und aramäische Inschriften mit einem Beitrag von O.Rössler, Band I Texte (third edition), Wiesbaden, 1971, Band II Kommentar (third edition), Wiesbaden, 1973, Band III Glossare und Indizen, Tafeln (second edition), Wiesbaden, 1969.
Kand see Garbini.
Karge Rephaim P.Karge, Rephaim. Die vorgeschichtliche Kultur Palästinas und Phöniziens. Archäologische und religionsgeschichtliche Studien (second edition; = Collectanea Hierosolymitana, Veröffentlichungen der wissenschaftlichen Station der Görresgesellschaft in Jerusalem, Band 1), Paderborn, 1925.
Karth Karthago. Revue d'archéologie Africaine.
Kaufman AIA S.A.Kaufman, The Akkadian Influences on Aramaic (= The Oriental Institute of the University of Chicago, Assyriological Studies no 19), Chicago/London, 1974.
KB R.Cohen, Kades Barnea, a fortress from the time of the Judaean kingdom, Jerusalem, 1983.
Kent OPG R.G.Kent, Old Persian Grammar, Texts, Lexicon (= American Oriental Series Vol. 33), New Haven, 1950.
KG see Buber.
KGOT see Mulder.
KH see Hehn.
KI M.Lidzbarski, Kanaanäische Inschriften (Moabitisch, Althebräisch, Phönizisch, Punisch) (= Altsemitische Texte, erstes Heft), Giessen, 1907.
Kinnier Wilson NWL J.V.Kinnier Wilson, The Nimrud Wine Lists, a study of men and administration at the Assyrian capital in the eighth century B.C., London, 1972.
Kition M.G.Guzzo Amadasi & V.Karageorghis, Fouilles de Kition III, Inscriptions Phéniciennes, Nicosia, 1977.
KJK see Stähli.
KlF Kleinasiatische Forschungen.
Klio Klio, Beiträge zur Alten Geschichte.
Knauf IUGP E.A.Knauf, Ismael. Untersuchungen zur Geschichte Palästinas und Nordarabiens im 1. Jahrtausend v. Chr. (= Abhandlungen des deutschen Palästinavereins, edd. S.Mittmann & M.Weippert), Wiesbaden, 1985.
Knauf MUGP E.A.Knauf, Midian. Untersuchungen zur Geschichte Palästinas und Nordarabiens am Ende des 2. Jahrtausends v. Chr. (= Abhandlungen des deutschen Palästinavereins, edd. S.Mittmann & M.Weippert), Wiesbaden, 1988.

Koch TH M.Koch, Tarschisch und Hispanien, historisch-geographische und namenkundliche Untersuchungen zur phönikischen Kolonisation der iberischen Halbinsel (= Madrider Forschungen nr 14), Berlin, 1984.
Koffmahn DWJ E.Koffmahn, Fie Doppelurkunden aus der Wüste Juda, Recht und Praxis der jüdischen Papyri des 1. und 2. Jahrhunderts n. Chr. samt Übertragung der Texte und deutscher Übersetzung (= Studies on the Texts of the Desert of Judah, Vol. V, ed. J.v.d.Ploeg), Leiden, 1968.
Kokalos ΚΩΚΑΛΟΣ, studi pubblicati dall'Istituto di Storia Antica dell'Università di Palermo.
Koldewey WB R.Koldewey, Das wiedererstehende Babylon, die bisherigen Ergebnisse der deutschen Ausgrabungen (fourth edition), Leipzig, 1925.
Koopmans J.J.Koopmans, Aramäische Chrestomathie. Ausgewählte Texte (Inschriften, Ostraka und Papyri) bis zum 3. Jahrhundert n. Chr. für das Studium der aramäischen Sprache gesammelt, 1. Teil, Einleitungen, Literatur und Kommentare, Leiden, 1962.
Kornfeld Abydos W.Kornfeld, Neues über die phönikischen und aramäischen Graffiti in den Tempeln von Abydos (= Sonderdruck aus dem Anzeiger der philologisch-historischen Klasse der Österreichischen Akademie der Wissenschaften, 115. Jahrgang 1978, No 11 (pp. 193-204)), Wien, 1978.
Kornfeld OAA W.Kornfeld, Onomastica Aramaica aus Ägypten (= Österreichische Akademie der Wissenschaften, philosophisch-historische Klasse, Sitzungsberichte, 333. Band), Wien, 1978.
Koschaker Neue Rechtsurkunden P.Koschaker, Neue keilschriftliche Rechtsurkunden aus der El-Amarna-Zeit (= no 5 des 39sten Bandes der Abhandlungen der philologisch-historischen Klasse der sächsischen Akademie der Wissenschaften), Leipzig, 1928.
Kottsieper SAS I.Kottsieper, Die Sprache der Aḥiqarsprüche (= BZAW 194), Berlin/New York, 1990.
Krael E.G.Kraeling, The Brooklyn Museum Aramaic papyri. New documents of the fifth century B.C. from the Jewish colony at Elephantine, edited with an historical introduction, New Haven, 1953.
Krauss GLL S.Krauss, Griechische und lateinische Lehnwörter im Talmud, Midrasch und Targum mit Bemerkungen von I.Löw, Band I, Berlin, 1898, Band II, Berlin, 1899.
Krug M.Lidzbarski, Phönizische und aramäische Krugaufschriften aus Elephantine (aus dem Anhang der Abhandlungen der preussischen Akademie der Wissenschaften, 1912).
Kuhnigk NSH W.Kuhnigk, Nordwestsemitische Studien zum Hoseabuch (= Biblica et Orientalia 27), Rome, 1974.
KuK Kultur und Konflikt (edd. J.Assmann & D.Harth), Frankfurt am Main, 1990.
Kultische Kalender see Landsberger.
KZ Zeitschrift für vergleichende Sprachforschung auf dem Gebiete der Indogermanischen Sprachen. Begründet von A.Kuhn.

l. a) line - b) lege.
Lach i Lachish Vol. I, The Lachish Letter (edd. H.Torczyner a.o.; = The Welcome Archaeological Research Expedition to the Near East Publications, Vol. I), London/New York/Toronto, 1938.
Lach. iii Lachish Vol. III, The Iron Age (ed. O.Tufnell with contributions by M.A.Murray and D.Diringer), London/New York/Toronto, 1953.
Lagrange ERS M.J.Lagrange, Études sur les religions sémitiques (second edition), Paris, 1905.
Landsberger Kultische Kalender B.Landsberger, Der kultische Kalender der Babylonier und Assyrer, 1ste Hälfte (= Leipziger semitistische Studien VI 1/2), Leipzig, 1915.
Landsberger Sam'al B.Landsberger, Sam'al, Studien zur Entdeckung der Ruinenstätte Karatepe, Erste Lieferung (= Veröffentlichungen der türkischen historischen Gesellschaft VII. Serie, nr 16), Ankara, 1948.
Lat. Latin.
LatDict see Lewis & Short.
Law a) see Rabinowitz - b) see Yaron.
LC Literarisches Centralblatt für Deutschland (cf. LZ).
LDA Le Langage Dans l'Antiquité (= La Pensée linguistique, Vol. 3; edd. P.Swiggers & A.Wouters), Leuven/Paris, 1990.
Le Bas Wadd VoyArch Inscr Voyage Archéologique en Grèce et en Asie Mineure fait pendant les années 1843 et 1844 et publié par Phil. Le Bas et W.H.Waddington avec la coopération d'Eug.Landron, Paris, 1847-1877, IIe Partie, Inscriptions Grecques et Latines.
Leand P.Leander, Laut- und Formenlehre des Ägyptisch-aramäischen (= Göteborgs Högskolas Årsskrift xxxiv, 1928:4), Göteborg, 1928.
Lemaire IH A.Lemaire Inscriptions Hébraïques, Tome I, Les ostraca, introduction, traduction, commentaire, Paris, 1977.
Lemaire & Durand IAS A.Lemaire & J.M.Durand, Les Inscriptions Araméennes de Sfiré et l'Assyrie de Shamshi-Ilu (= École pratique des Hautes Études IVe Section, Sciences historiques et philologiques II, Hautes Études Orientales 20), Paris, 1984.
Lesh Lešonénu. A journal for the study of the Hebrew language and cognate subjects.
Lev(ant) Levant. Journal of the British School of Archaeology in Jerusalem (since Vol. XIII (1981) with subtitle: Journal of the British School of Archaeology in Jerusalem and the British Institute at Amman for Archaeology and History).
Levinson NAI J.H.Levinson, The Nabataean Aramaic Inscriptions, Diss. New York University, 1974.
Levy J.Levy, Neuhebräisches und chaldäisches Wörterbuch über die Talmudim und Midraschim nebst Beiträgen von H.L.Fleischer, Band I, Leipzig, 1876, Band II, Leipzig, 1879, Band III, Leipzig, 1883, Band IV, Leipzig, 1889.
Levy SG M.A.Levy, Siegel und Gemmen mit aramäischen, phönizischen, althebräischen, himjarischen, nabathäischen und altsyrischen Inschriften erklärt, Breslau, 1869.
Lewis & Short LatDict A Latin Dictionary founded on Andrew's edition of Freund's Latin dictionary,

revised, enlarged, and in great part rewritten by C.F.Lewis and C.Short (reprint), Oxford, 1980.
lex. lexical.
Lex see Vogt.
L'Heureux RACG C.E.L'Heureux, Rank Among the Canaanite Gods, El, Ba'al and the Repha'im (= Harvard Semitic Monographs no 21), Missoula, Montana, 1979.
Lib Libya.
Lib. Libian.
LibAnt Libya Antiqua.
LibStud Libyan Studies.
Liddell & Scott H.G.Liddell & R.Scott, A Greek-English Lexicon, a new edition revised and augmented throughout by Sir H.Stuart Jones ... with the assistence of R.McKenzie (2 volumes), Oxford.
Lidzbarski Handb M.Lidzbarski, Handbuch der nordsemitischen Epigraphik nebst ausgewählten Inschriften, Band I, Text, Weimar, 1898.
LidzbAss The Aramaic texts written on clay tablets published in AUA pp. 15-20.
Lieberman Greek S.Lieberman, Greek in Jewish Palestine. Studies in the life and manners of Jewish Palestine in the II-IV centuries C.E., New York, 1942.
Liḥy. Liḥyanite.
Lindenberger APA J.M.Lindenberger, The Aramaic Proverbs of Aḥiqar, Baltimore/London, 1983.
Lipiński Royauté E.Lipiński, La Royauté de Yahwé dans la poésie et le culte de l'ancien Israel (= Verhandelingen van de Koninklijke Vlaamse Academie ..., Klasse der Letteren, jrg. 27 nr 55), Brussel, 1965.
Lipiński Stud E.Lipiński, Studies in Aramaic inscriptions and onomastics I (= Orientalia Lovaniensia Analecta 1), Leuven, 1975.
LIS see Weippert.
litt. a) literal(ly) - b) literature.
Littmann Sardis E.Littmann, Sardis (= Publications by the American Society for the Excavation of Sardis, Vol. VI, Lydian Inscriptions, Part I), Leyden, 1916.
Liv Titi Livi, Ab urbe condita libri, quoted after the edition by G.Weissenborn & M.Mueller, Pars I, Libri I-X, Lipsiae, Pars II, Libri XXI- XXX, Lipsiae, Pars III, Libri XXXI-XL, Lipsiae, Pars IV, Libri XLI-CXLII, Fragmenta, Index, Lipsiae.
LJPM Le Livre de Jérémie, le prophète et son milieu, les oracles et leur transmission (edd. P.M.Bogaert, W.A.M.Beuken a.o.; = Bibliotheca Ephemeridum Theologicarum Lovaniensium 54), Leuven, 1981
ll. lines.
loc. local.
Löw I.Löw, Die Flora der Juden, Wien/Leipzig, Band Ia, 1926, Band Ib, 1928, Band II, 1924, Band III, 1924, Band IV (Wien), 1934.
Löw AP I.Löw, Aramäische Pflanzennamen, Leipzig, 1881.
Loewenstamm CSBA S.E.Loewenstamm, Comparative Studies in Biblical and Ancient oriental literatures (= Alter Orient und Altes Testament. Veröffentlichungen zur Kultur und Geschichte des Alten Orients und des Alten Testaments, Band 204), Neukirchen/Vluyn, 1980.
LOT ii see Ben-Chayim.
LP see Brown.
LS see Garbini.

LuG see Altheim.
LXX Septuagint.
Lyc. Lycia.
LZ Literarisches Zentralblatt für Deutschland (cf. LC).
m. masculine.
Macalister Gezer ii R.A.Stewart Macalister, The excavation of Gezer 1902-1905 and 1907-1909, Vol. II, London, 1912.
Macc. Maccabean.
MAI(BL) Mémoires présentés par divers savants à l'Académie des Inscriptions et Belles Lettres de l'Institut de France.
Maier Ashera W.A.Maier III, ›Ašerah: Extrabiblical Evidence (= Harvard Semitic Monographs 37), Atlanta, 1986.
Malamat DSK A.Malamat, Das davidische und salomonische Königreich und seine Beziehungen zu Ägypten und Syrien. Zur Entstehung eines Grossreichs (= Oesterreichische Akademie der Wissenschaften, Philosophisch-historische Klasse, Sitzungsberichte, 407.Band), Wien, 1983.
Malédictions see Parrot.
Malta '63 Missione archeologica italiana a Malta. Rapporto preliminare della campagna 1963 (= Serie archeologica 5), Roma, 1964.
Malta '64 Missione archeologica italiana a Malta. Rapporto preliminare della campagna 1964, Roma, 1965.
Malta '65 Missione archeologica italiana a Malta. Rapporto preliminare della campagna 1965, Roma, 1966.
MarDeed see Birnbaum.
Marrassini FLEM P.Marrassini, Formazione del Lessico dell'Edilizia militare nel Semitico di Siria (= Quaderni di Semitistica 1), Firenze, 1971.
Mas Masada I. The Yigael Yadin Excavations 1963-1965, Final Reports. The Aramaic and Hebrew ostraca and jar inscriptions (edd. Y.Yadin & J.Naveh), The coins of Masada (ed. Y.Meshorer), Jerusalem, 1989.
Mas + number the ostraca published in Mas.
Mas coin the coins published in Mas pp. 85ff.
Mašr Al-Machriq, revue catholique orientale.
Masson RPAE E.Masson, Recherches sur les plus anciens emprunts sémitiques en grec (= Études et Commentaires 67), Paris, 1967.
Masson & Sznycer RPC O.Masson & M.Sznycer, Recherches sur les Phéniciens à Chypre (= Centre des Recherches d'Histoire et de Philologie II, Hautes Études Orientales 3), Genève/Paris, 1972.
mat. of material.
Mazard J.Mazard, Corpus nummorum Numidiae Mauretaniaeque, Paris, 1955.
MC Mélanges de Carthage offerts à C.Saumagne, L.Poinssot, M.Pinard (edd. P.Amiet a.o.), Paris, 1966.
McCarthy TaC D.J.McCarthy, Treaty and Covenant, a study in form in the ancient oriental documents and in the Old Testament (second edition; = Analecta Orientalia no 21a), Rome, 1978.
McCarthy Treaty D.J.McCarthy, Treaty and Covenant (= Analecta Biblica no 21), Rome, 1963.
McDonald (CHC) G.MacDonald, Catalogue of Greek coins in the Hunterian Collection, University of

Glasgow, Glasgow, 3 volumes, 1899-1905.
MDAIA Mitteilungen des deutschen archäologischen Instituts, Athenische Abteilung.
MDJ see Vermes.
MDOG Mitteilungen der deutschen Orientgesellschaft zu Berlin.
Mel Gad Anth Meleager Gadarenus in Anthologia Graeca, quoted after the second edition by H.Beckby, München, Vol. I, 1957, Vol. II, 1957, Vol. III, 1958, Vol. IV, 1958.
MélDérenbourg Mélanges Hartwig Dérenbourg (1844-1908). Recueil de travaux d'érudition dédiés à la mémoire d'Hartwig Dérenbourg par ses amis et ses élèves, Paris, 1909.
Mélanges Glotz Mélanges Gustaves Glotz (2 volumes), Paris, 1932.
Melqart see Bonnet.
Meltô Meltô. Recherches orientales.

Mem Brockelmann Studia orientalia in memoriam Caroli Brockelmann (ed. M.Fleischhammer; = Wissenschaftliche Zeitschrift der Martin-Luther- Universität Halle-Wittenberg, Gesellschafts- und sprachwissenschaftliche Reihe, Heft 2/3, Jahrgang xvii, 1968), Halle (Saale), 1968.
Mem Craigie Ascribe to the Lord. Biblical and other studies in memory of Peter C.Craigie (edd. L.Eslinger & G.Taylor; = Journal for the Study of the Old Testament, Supplement Series 67), Sheffield, 1988.
Mem Henning W.B.Henning Memorial Volume, London, 1970.
Mem Herzfeld Archaeologica orientalia in Memoriam Ernst Herzfeld (ed. G.C.Miles), New York, 1952.
Mem Kutscher Studies in Hebrew and Semitic languages dedicated to the Memory of Prof. Eduard Yechezkel Kutscher (edd. G.B.Sarfatti, P.Artzi, J.C.Greenfield, M.Kaddari), Ramat-Gan, 1980.
Mem de Menasce Mémorial Jean de Menasce (edd. Ph.Gignoux & A.Tafazzoli), Louvain, 1974.
Mem Saidah Archéologie au Levant. Recueil à la Mémoire de Roger Saidah (= Collection de la Maison de l'Orient Méditerranéen no 12, Série archéologique, 9), Lyon/Paris, 1982.
Mem Seeligmann Isac Leo Seeligmann Volume. Essays on the Bible and the ancient world (edd. A.Rofé & Y.Zakovitch), Vol. III, non-Hebrew section, Jerusalem, 1983.
Mem Wright Magnalia Dei, the mighty acts of God. Essays on the Bible and archaeology in Memory of G.E.Wright (edd. F.M.Cross, W.E.Lemke & P.D.Miller), Garden City, N.Y., 1976.
Mem Yalon Henoch Yalon Memorial Volume (edd. E.Y.Kutscher, S.Lieberman & M.Z.Kaddari; = Bar-Ilan Departemental Researches 2), Jerusalem, 1974 (Hebrew).
Mess see Yadin.
metaphor. metaphorical(ly).
Mettinger SSO T.N.D.Mettinger, Solomonic State Officials, a study of the civil government officials of the Israelite monarchy (= Coniectanea Biblica. Old Testament Series 5), Lund, 1971.
MFP see Gawlikowski.
MGHS see Day.
MGWJ Monatsschrift für Geschichte und Wissenschaft des

Judenthums.
Michaud PA H.Michaud, Sur la Pierre et l'Argile (= Cahiers d'Archéologie Biblique no 10), Neuchatel/Paris, 1958.
mil. military (term).
MINF Mémoires de l'Institut (national) de France. Académie des Inscriptions et Belles Lettres.
MiOr Mitteilungen des Instituts für Orientforschung.
MLAHE see Zevit.
MLE Materiali Lessicali ed Epigrafici - I (= Collezione di Studi Fenici, 13), Roma, 1982.
MM Madrider Mitteilungen. Deutsches Archäologisches Institut, Abteilung Madrid.
MME Midian, Moab and Edom, the history and archaeology of late Bronze and Iron Age Jordan and North-West Arabia (edd. J.F.A.Sawyer & D.J.A.Clines; = Journal for the Study of the Old Testament Supplement Series 24), Sheffield, 1983.
MO Le Monde Oriental. Revue des études orientales.
Mo Moabite.
Molk see Eissfeldt.
MonAnt Monumenti antichi pubblicati per la cura della reale Accademia dei Lincei.
MontSir Monte Sirai II. Rapporto preliminare della missione archeologica dell'Università di Roma e della Soprintendenza alle Antichità di Cagliari (edd. M.Guzzo Amadasi, F.Barreca a.o.; = Studi Semitici 14), Roma, 1965.
de Moor NYC J.C.de Moor, New Year with Canaanites and Israelites (= Kamper Cahiers 21/22), Vol. I, Description, Kampen, 1972, Vol. II, The Canaanite sources, Kampen, 1972.
Mosc S.Moscati, L'epigrafia ebraica antica 1935-1950 (= Biblica et Orientalia 15), Roma, 1951.
Moscati CGSL An introduction to the Comparative Grammar of the Semitic Languages, phonology and morphology by S.Moscati, A.Spitaler, E.Ullendorff, W.v.Soden (ed. S.Moscati; = Porta Linguarum Orientalium, Neue Serie VI), Wiesbaden, 1964.
Mosc boll the Hebrew stamps published in Mosc pp. 73ff.
Mosc pes the Hebrew inscriptions on weights published in Mosc pp. 101ff.
Mosc sig the Hebrew seals published in Mosc pp. 52ff.
Mosc var the Hebrew miscellanea published in Mosc pp. 111ff.
MOT see Dronkert.
Moz(ia) Mozia. Rapporto preliminare della missione archeologica della Soprintendenza alle Antichità della Sicilia occidentale e dell'Università di Roma, Vol. I (edd. A.Ciasca, M.Forte a.o.; = Studi Semitici 12), Roma, 1964, Vol. II (edd. A.Ciasca, M.Forte a.o.; = Studi Semitici 19), Roma, 1966, Vol. III (edd. I.Brancoli, A.Ciasca a.o.; = Studi Semitici 24), Roma, 1967, Vol. IV (edd. A.Ciasca, G.Garbini a.o.; = Studi Semitici 29), Roma, 1968, Vol. V (edd. A.Ciasca, M.G.Guzzo Amadasi a.o.; = Studi Semitici 31), Roma, 1969, Vol VI (edd. A.Ciasca, M.G.Guzzo Amadasi a.o.; = Studi Semitici 37), Roma, 1970, Vol. VII (edd. F.Bevilacqua, A.Ciasca a.o.; = Studi Semitici 40), Roma, 1972, Vol. VIII (edd. A.Ciasca, V.Tersa, M.L.Uberti; = Studi Semitici 45), Roma, 1973, Vol. IX (edd. A.Ciasca, G.C.Polselli a.o.; = Studi Semitici

50), Roma, 1978.
MP H.S.Nyberg, A Manual of Pahlavi, Part II, Ideograms, glossary, abbreviations, index, grammatical survey, corrigenda to Part I, Wiesbaden, 1974.
MPAT J.A.Fitzmyer & D.J.Harrington, A Manual of Palestinian Aramaic Texts (= Biblica et Orientalia 34), Rome, 1978.
MPAT-A the Appendix (Palestinian Aramaic inscriptions of later date, synagogal, funerary and other) in MPAT pp. 251ff.
MPJ see Dussaud.
MS manuscript.
MSN = RAI xxv.
MSS manuscripts.
MStSW Münchener Studien zur Sprachwissenschaft.
Müll(er) L.Müller, Numismatique de l'ancienne Afrique (3 volumes), Copenhague, 1860-1862.
Müll-Suppl Supplement to Müll(er) published Copenhague, 1874.
Muffs Y.Muffs, Studies in the Aramaic legal papyri from Elephantine (= Studia et Documenta ad Iura Orientis Antiqui pertinentia, edd. M.David & B.Landsberger, Vol. VIII; second edition), New York, 1973.
MUGP see Knauf.
Mulder KGOT M.J.Mulder, Kanaänitische Goden in het Oude Testament (= Exegetica, vierde reeks, vierde en vijfde deel), Den Haag, 1965.
Mullen DCC E.Th.Mullen, The Divine Council in Canaanite and early Hebrew literature (= Harvard Semitic Monographs 24, ed. F.M.Cross), Chico, 1980.
Mus Le Muséon. Revue d'études orientales.
MUSJ Mélanges de l'Université Saint-Joseph, Beyrouth (Liban).
n. note.
Nab a) Nabatean - b) see Cantineau.
NabInschrift see Euting.
NAI see Levinson.
Naveh AramaicScript J.Naveh, The development of the Aramaic Script, thesis submitted for the degree "Doctor of Philosophy" to the Senate of the Hebrew University, November, 1966.
Naveh EHA J.Naveh, Early History of the Alphabet, an introduction to West Semitic epigraphy and palaeography, Leiden, 1982.
NC Y.Meshorer, Nabataean Coins (= Qedem Monographs of the Institute of Archaeology, 3), Jerusalem, 1975.
n.d. divine name.
NdS Atti della R.Accademia dei Lincei, Notizie degli Scavi di antichità.
Neo-Babyl Neo-Babylonian.
NESE Neue Ephemeris für semitische Epigraphik (edd. R.Degen, W.W.Müller & W.Röllig), Band 1, Wiesbaden, 1972, Band 2, Wiesbaden, 1974, Band 3, Wiesbaden, 1978.
Neusner HJB v J.Neusner, A History of the Jews in Babylonia, Vol. V (= Studia Postbiblica 15), Leiden, 1970.
n.g. geographical name.
NGWG Nachrichten von der königlichen Gesellschaft der Wissenschaften zu Göttingen (philologisch-historische Klasse).
Niehr HR H.Niehr, Herrschen und Richten. Die Wurzel špṭ im Alten Orient und im Alten Testament (=

Forschung zur Bibel, Band 54), Würzburg, 1986.
NINPI see Jongeling.
Niph Niphal.
Nisa The Aramaic ideograms found in documents from Nisa quoted after: Corpus Inscriptionum Iranicarum, Part II, Inscriptions of the Seleucid and Parthian period and of eastern Iran and central Asia, Vol. II, Parthian, Parthian economic documents from Nisa, Texts I, pp. 1-80, by I.M.Diakonoff & V.A.Lifshits (ed. D.N.MacKenzie), London.
Nisa-b И.М.Дьяконов, В.А.Лившиц, Новые Находки Документов в Старой Нисе, Переднеазиатский Сборник II, pp. 134ff.
Nisa-c И.М.Дьяконов, В.А.Лившиц, Документы Из Нисы I в. до и.э., Москва, 1960.
Nitp Nitpael
n.l. place name.
nn. notes.
NOG see Tigay.
Nöldeke Gramm Th.Nöldeke, Kurzgefasste syrische Grammatik, second edition, Leipzig, 1898.
Nöldeke Inschrift Th.Nöldeke, Die Inschrift des Königs Mesa von Moab (9. Jahrh. vor Chr.), Kiel, 1870.
nom. a) nominal - b) nominative.
nom.gent. name of people.
Noth IP M.Noth, Die israelitischen Personennamen im Rahmen der gemeinsemitischen Namengebung (= Beiträge zur Wissenschaft vom Alten und Neuen Testament, III,10), Stuttgart, 1928.
NouvClio La Nouvelle Clio. Revue mensuelle de la découverte historique.
NP List of texts in Neopunic script published in Schroed 63ff. and Harr 160f.
n.p. personal name.
NSH see Kuhnigk.
NSI see Cooke.
NSPBS see Penar.
Num see Roschinski.
NumChr The Numismatic Chronicle and journal of the Royal Numismatic Society.
NW see Hinz.
NWL see Kinnier Wilson.
NWSem Northwest Semitic.
Nyberg HP H.S.Nyberg, Hilfsbuch des Pehlevi II, Glossar, Uppsala, 1931.
NYC see de Moor.
OA Oriens Antiquus. Rivista del Centro per le Antichità e la Storia dell'Arte del Vicino Oriente.
OAA see Kornfeld.
OAC xiii Orientis Antiqui Collectio XIII = Atti del 1o convegno italiano sul vicino oriente antico (Roma, 22-24 Aprile 1976), Roma, 1978.
OAG see Pincher.
obj. (of) object.
obl. see cas.obl.
OBS see Speiser.
obsc. obscure.
obv. obverse.
o.c. opus citatum.
Odeberg H.Odeberg, The Aramaic portions of Bereshit Rabba with grammar of Galilaean Aramaic, Vol. II, Short grammar of Galilaean Aramaic (= Lunds Universitets Årsskrift, NF Avd. 1. Bd 36. nr 4), Lund/Leipzig, 1939.
OffAr Official Aramaic.
OIC Oriental Institute Communications (University of Chicago).
Olam see Jenni.
OldAr Old Aramaic.
OldCan Old Canaanite.

OLP Orientalia Lovaniensia Periodica.
Olyan Asherah S.M.Olyan, Asherah and the Cult of Yahweh in Israel (= Monograph Series, Society of Biblical Literature, no. 34), Atlanta, Georgia, 1988.
OLZ Orientalistische Literaturzeitung.
OMRO Oudheidkundige Mededelingen uit het Rijksmuseum van Oudheden te Leiden.
OPG see Kent.
Oph Ophal.
Or Orientalia.
ord. ordinal.
Oriens Oriens. Journal of the International Society for Oriental Research.
Orient Orient. Report of the Society for Near Eastern Studies in Japan.
Orig see Dussaud.
orig original(ly).
OrSu Orientalia Suecana.
orthogr a) orthography - b) orthographical.
OTOS see Soggin.
p. page
PA see Michaud.
PAAES iv Publications of an American Archeological Expedition to Syria, Part IV, Semitic inscriptions, New York/London, 1905.
PAAJR Proceedings of the American Academy for Jewish Research.
PAES Publications of the Princeton University Archaeological Expeditions to Syria in 1904-1905 and 1909, Division IV, Semitic inscriptions by E.Littmann, Leyden, 1914.
Paik E.Herzfeld, Paikuli, monument and inscription of the early history of the Sassanian empire, Berlin, 1924.
Palm Palmyrenean.
Palmyra see Wiegand.
par. parallel(s).
Pardee HAHL D.Pardee, Handbook of Ancent Hebrew Letters, with a chapter on Tannaitic letter fragments by S.David Sperling, with collaboration of J.David Whitehead and Paul E.Dion (= Society of Biblical Literature, Sources for Biblical Study, no 15), Chico, 1982.
Parrot Malédictions A.Parrot, Malédictions et violations de tombes, Paris, 1939.
Part. a) participle - b) particle.
part. partitive.
partic particle.
PaSb Palestinskiy Sbornik.
pass. passive.
Paul ex Fest Pauli Excerpta ex libris Pompei Festi de significatione verborum, quoted after the edition by W.M.Lindsay, Lipsiae 1913 (in the same edition also Festus is published).
PBP Palmyre, Bilan et Perspectives, colloque de Strasbourg (18-20 Octobre 1973) organisé par le C.R.P.O.G.A. à la mémoire de Daniel Schlumberger et de Henri Seyrig (= Université des Sciences Humaines de Strasbourg, Travaux du Centre de Recherche sur le Proche Orient et la Grèce Antiques), Strasbourg, 1976.
PBR Papers of the British School at Rome.
PC see Blau.
PE see Herzfeld.
Peckham DLPS J.B.Peckham, The Development of the Late Phoenician Scripts (= Harvard Semitic Series XX), Cambridge

(Mass.), 1968.
Pedersen InscrSem Inscriptiones semiticae collectionis Ustanowianae (ed. J.Pedersen; = Symbolae Osloensis Pasc. Supplet. II), Osloae, 1928.
Penar NSPBS T.Penar, Northwest Semitic Philology and the Hebrew fragments of Ben Sira (= Biblica et Orientalia 28), Rome, 1975.
PEQ Palestine Exploration Quarterly.
Pers R.A.Bowman, Aramaic ritual texts from Persepolis (= The University of Chicago Oriental Institute Publications, Vol. XCI), Chicago, 1970.
Persepolis ii see Schmidt.
PF R.T.Hallock, Persepolis Fortification tablets (= The University of Chicago Oriental Institute Publications, Vol. XCII), Chicago, 1969.
Pf. Perfect.
PFP ii K.Michałowski, Palmyre, Fouilles Polonaises, Vol. II, Paris, 1962.
Ph Phoenician.
Phoenix Phoenix, Bulletin uitgegeven door het Vooraziatisch-Egyptisch Genootschap Ex Oriente Lux.
PI see Vriezen & Hospers.
PIB see Avishur.
PICS Proceedings of the International Conference on Semitic studies held in Jerusalem, 19-23 July 1965, Jerusalem, 1969.
PIH see Abbadi.
Pinches OAG Th.G.Pinches, An Outline of Assyrian Grammar, London, 1910.
PJB Palästinajahrbuch des deutschen evangelischen Instituts für Altertumswissenschaft des heiligen Landes zu Jerusalem.
pl. a) plural - b) plate.
Plautus Caecus The fragments of the Caecus of Plautus quoted after the edition by W.M.Lindsay, T.Macci Plauti Comoediae, Tomus II, Oxonii, 1974 (under Fragmenta).
Pléiade A.Dupont-Sommer, "Littérature araméenne", Histoire des Littératures, I (ed. R.Quenau), Éditions des Pléiades, Paris, 1955, pp. 631- 646.
Plin C.Plinii Secundi Naturalis Historiae Libri XXXVII quoted after the edition of L.Ian & C.Mayhof (5 volumes), Leipzig, 1906, 1909, 1892, 1897, 1897 (Vol. VI Indices composuit L.Ian, Stutgardiae, 1920).

Plur. Plural.
Plusquampf. Plusquamperfectum.
Plut Sulla The life of Sulla after Plutarch quoted after the edition in Plutarchi Vitae Parallelae recognoverunt Cl.Lindsberg & K.Ziegler, Vol. III Fasc 2, iterum recensuit K.Ziegler, Leipzig, 1973, pp. 131-193.
PNO D.Schlumberger, La Palmyrène du Nord-Ouest, villages et lieux de culte de l'époque impériale, recherches archéologiques sur la mise en valeur d'une région du désert par les Palmyréniens, suivie du recueil des inscriptions sémitiques de cette région par H.Ingholt et J.Starcky avec une contribution de G.Ryckmans, Paris, 1951.
PNPI see Stark.
PNSP see Dahood.
PO Parole de l'Orient.
Poeb A.Poebel, Das appositionell bestimmte Pronomen des 1. Pers. sing. in den westsemitischen Inschriften und im Alten Testament, Chicago, 1932.

Poen the texts of the Punic parts of the Poenulus of Plautus quoted after the edition in Sznycer PPP.
Pognon ISSM H.Pognon, Inscriptions Sémitiques de la Syrie, de la Mésopotamie et de la région de Mossoul, Paris, 1907.
Pol Polel.
Porten Arch B.Porten, Archives from Elephantine, the life of an ancient Jewish military colony, Berkeley/Los Angeles, 1968.
poss. possible.
PP a) La Parola del Passato. Rivista di studi antichi - b) see Teixidor.
pp. pages.
PPP see Sznycer.
PPT see Schiffmann.
prec. preceded.
prep. preposition.
pret. pretii/of price.
princ. principal.
Pritchard Gibeon J.B.Pritchard, Gibeon where the sun stood still, the discovery of the Biblical city, Princeton, New Yersey, 1962.
Pritchard HISG J.B.Pritchard Hebrew Inscriptions and Stamps from Gibeon, Philadelphia, 1959.
prob. probable/probably.
Proc v CJS Proceedings of the 5th World Congress of Jewish Studies, the Hebrew University, Jerusalem, 3-11 Aug 1969 (ed. P.Peli), Vol. I, Jerusalem, 1971.
Prol Prolegomena.
pron. pronoun.
prop. proposed.
Prophet see Thomas.
prosth. prosthetic.
ProvArab see Brünnow.
PRU Le Palais Royal d'Ugarit.
PS R.Payne Smith, Thesaurus Syriacus, Vol. I, Oxonii, 1879, Vol. II, Oxonii, 1901.
Ps see Dahood.
Ps. Psalm.
PSBA Proceedings of the Society of Biblical Archeology.
PSH see Ingholt.
PSI see Albright.
PTT G.G.Cameron, Persepolis Treasury Tablets (= The University of Chicago Oriental Institute Publications, Vol. LXV), Chicago, 1948.
PTU see Gröndahl.
publ. published.
Pun Punic.
Punica J.B.Chabot, Punica; Appendice Glanures Palmyréniennes, remarques sur le tarif de Palmyre, Paris, 1918.
PW a) Paulys Realencyclopädie der classischen Altertumswissenschaft. Neue Bearbeitung, begonnen von G.Wissowa, fortgeführt von W.Kroll und K.Mittelhaus, unter Mitwirkung zahlreicher Fachgenossen herausgegeben von K.Ziegler, Stuttgart - b) Phönizier im Westen, die Beiträge des internationalen Symposiums über "Die phönizische Expansion im westlichen Mittelmeerraum" in Köln vom 24. bis 27. April 1979 (ed. H.G.Niemeyer; = Madrider Beiträge, Band 8), Mainz am Rhein, 1982.
Qadm Qadmoniot. Quarterly of the Department of Antiquities of Eretz-Israel and Bible Lands.
QDAP The Quarterly of the Department of Antiquities in Palestine.
Qedem vi A.Negev, The inscriptions of Wadi Haggag, Sinai (= Qedem Monographs of the Institute of Archaeology, the Hebrew University of Jerusalem, 6), Jerusalem, 1977.

QMS see Brugnatelli.
Quintilianus M.Fabi Quintiliani Institutionis oratoriae libri xii quoted after the edition by M.Winterbottom (2 volumes), Oxonii, 1970.
RA Revue d'Assyriologie et d'archéologie orientale.
RAA Revue des Arts Asiatiques. Annales du Musée Guimet.
Rabinowitz Law J.J.Rabinowitz, Jewish Law, its influence on the development of legal institutions, New York, 1956.
rabb. rabbinical.
EACG see L'Heureux.
RAI Rencontre Assyriologique Internationale.
Rainey EA A.F.Rainey, El-Amarna tablets 359-379, Supplement to J.A.Knudtzon, Die Al-Amarna Tafeln, second edition (= Alter Orient und Altes Testament. Veröffentlichungen zur Kultur und Geschichte des Alten Orients und des Alten Testaments, Band 8), Neukirchen/Vluyn, 1978.
RANR see Ahlström.
RAO Ch.Clermont-Ganneau, Recueil d'Archéologie Orientale, Vol. I, Paris, 1888, Vol. II, Paris, 1898, Vol. III, Paris, 1900, Vol. IV, Paris, 1901, Vol. V, Paris, 1903, Vol. VI, Paris, 1905, Vol. VII, Paris, 1906, Vol. VIII, Paris, 1924.
RB Revue Biblique.
RCL Atti della Accademia Nazionale dei Lincei, Rendiconti, Classe di scienze morali, storiche e filologiche.
RCP see Elayi.
RDAC Reports of the Department of Antiquities, Cyprus.
REA Revue des Études arméniennes, nouvelle série.
Rec Dhorme Recueil Édouard Dhorme. Études Bibliques et orientales, Paris, 1951.
rect recto.
REHR Religions en Égypte Hellénistique et Romaine. Colloque de Strasbourg 16-18 Mai 1967, Paris, 1969.
Reifenberg AJC A.Reifenberg, Ancient Jewish Coins (second edition), Jerusalem, 1947.
REJ Revue des Études Juives.
Rel a) see Février - b) see Vincent.
rel. relative.
RelAr see Hoftijzer.
relig. religious.
Religion a) see Albright - b) see Erman.
Renan MP E.Renan, Mission de Phénicie, Paris, 1864.
Rephaim see Karge.
RES a) Répertoire de l'Épigraphie Sémitique, publié par la Commission du Corpus Inscriptionum Semiticarum (always quoted with a number: e.g. RES 1205) - b) Revue des Études Sémitiques. Organe de l'Institut d'Études Sémitiques (since 1937 with sub-title: Organe de l'Institut d'Études Sémitiques de Paris; since 1941 with title: Revue des Études sémitiques et Babyloniaca; always quoted with year indication, e.g. RES '45).
RESL G.Conti, Rapporto tra egiziano e semitico nel Lessico egiziano dell'agricultura (= Quaderni di Semitistica 6), Firenze, 1978.
resp. respectively.
rev. reverse.
RevAfr Revue Africaine publiée par la Société Historique Algérienne (with different sub-titles).
RevArch Revue archéologique ou recueil de documents et de mémoires relatifs à l'étude des monuments et à

la philologie de l'Antiquité et du Moyen Age.
RevEg Revue d'Égyptologie.
RevEtAnc Revue des Études Anciennes.
Reviv CSI H.Reviv, A Commentary on Selected Inscriptions from the period of the monarchy in Israel, Jerusalem, 1975 (Hebrew).
RGP see Verger.
RHA Revue Hittite et Asianique.
RHR Revue de l'Histoire des Religions.
RHS see Green.
RIDA Revue Internationale des Droits de l'Antiquité (3e série).
RIL J.B.Chabot, Recueil des Inscriptions Libyques, Paris, 1940.
RIN Rivista Italiana di Numismatica.
RIP M.Gawlikowski, Recueil d'inscriptions Palmyréniennes provenant de fouliies Syriennes et Polonaises récentes à Palmyre (= MAIBL xvi), PAris, 1974.
RIPK see Bron.
RivBib Rivista Biblica Italiana.
RN Revue Numismatique.
RoAr see Shahîd.
Rob Mélanges Bibliques rédigés en l'honneur de André Robert (= Travaux de l'Institut Catholique de Paris, 4), Paris, 1955.
Rofé SB A.Rofé, Sefer Bil ʿam (= "The Book of Balaam", (Numbers 22:2-24:25). A study in methods of criticism and the history of Biblical literature and religion, with an appendix: Balaam in the Deir ʿAlla inscription), Jerudalem, 1979.
Roschinski Num H.P.Roschinski, "Die Mikiwsan-Inschrift aus Cherchell", Die Numider, Reiter und Könige nördlich der Sahara (edd. H.G.Horn & Chr.D.Rüger; = Kunst und Altertum am Rhein, Führer des Rheinischen Landesmuseums Bonn herausgegeben im Auftrag des Landschaftsverbandes Rheinland nr. 96), Köln/Bonn, 1979, pp. 111-116.
Rosenthal Forschung F.Rosenthal, Die aramaistische Forschung seit Th.Nöldeke's Veröffentlichungen, Leiden, 1939.
Rosenthal Sprache F.Rosenthal, Die Sprache der palmyrenischen Inschriften und ihre Stellung innerhalb des Aramäischen (= Mitteilungen der vorderasiatisch-aegyptischen Gesellschaft, 41. Band, 1. Heft), Leipzig, 1936.
Rowley AramOT H.H.Rowley, The Aramaic of the Old Testament, a grammatical and lexical study of its relations with other early Aramaic dialects, London, 1929.
Royauté see Lipiński.
RPAE see Masson.
RPC see Masson & Sznycer.
RPIM The Role of the Phoenicians in the Interaction of Mediterranean civilizations. Papers presented to the Archaeological Symposium at the American University of Beirut; March 1967 (ed. W.A.Ward), Beirut, 1968.
RQ Revue de Qumran.
RS Revue sémitique d'épigraphie et d'historie ancienne.
rs/Rs reverse.
RSF Rivista di Studi Fenici.
RSO Rivista degli Studi Orientali.
RTAT Religionsgeschichtliches Textbuch zum Alten Testament (ed. W.Beyerlin; = Grundrisse zum Alten Testament, Das Alte Testament Deutsch, Ergänzungsreihe, Band 1), Göttingen, 1975.
RTP Recueil des Tessères de

Palmyre par H.Ingholt, H.Seyrig, J.Starcky, suivi de remarques linguistiques par A.Caquot (= Institut français d'Archéologie de Beyrouth, Bibliothèque archéologique et historique, tome LVIII), Paris, 1955.
Ryckmans RelArabPréisl G.Ryckmans, Les Religions Arabes Préislamiques, second edition (= Bibliothèque du Muséon, Vol. 26), Louvain, 1951.
s. singular.
SAB Atti della Settimana Sangue e Antropologia Biblica (Roma, 10-15 Marzo 1980), ed. F.Vattioni, Vol. I, Roma, 1981, Vol. II, Roma, 1981.
Sach E.Sachau, Aramäische Papyrus und Ostraka aus einer jüdischen Militärkolonie in Elephantine, altorientalische Sprachdenkmäler des 5. Jahrhunderts vor Chr., Leipzig, 1911.
Sader EAS H.S.Sader, les États Araméens de Syrie depuis leur fondation jusqu'à leur transformation en provinces Assyriennes (= Beiruter Texte und Studien, Band 36), Beirut, 1987.
Saf. Safaitic.
Salonen Fussbekleidung A.Salonen, Die Fussbekleidung der alten Mesopotamier nach sumerisch-akkadischen Quellen. Eine lexikalische und kulturgeschichtliche Untersuchung (= Annales Academiae Scientiarum Fennicae, Ser. B, tom. 157), Helsinki, 1969.
Salonen Hausgeräte A.Salonen, Die Hausgeräte der alten Mesopotamier nach sumerisch-akkadischen Quellen. Eine lexikalische und kulturgeschichtliche Untersuchung (= Annales Academiae Scientiarum Fennicae, Ser. B, tom. 139 and 144), Teil I, Helsinki 1965, Teil II (Gefässe), Helsinki, 1966.
Salonen Möbel A.Salonen, Die Möbel des alten Mesopotamien nach sumerisch-akkadischen Quellen. Eine lexikalische und kulturgeschichtliche Untersuchung (= Annales Academiae Scientiarum Fennicae, Ser. B, tom. 127), Helsinki, 1963.
Salonen Türen A.Salonen, Die Türen des alten Mesopotamien. Eine lexikalische und kulturgeschichtliche Untersuchung (= Annales Academiae Scientiarum Fennicae, Ser. B, tom. 124). Helsinki, 1961.
Salonen Wasserfahrzeugen A.Salonen, Die Wasserfahrzeugen in Babylonien nach sumerisch-akkadischen Quellen (mit besonderer Berücksichtigung der 4.Tafel der Serie ḪAR-ru = ḫubullu). Eine lexikalische und kulturgeschichtliche Untersuchung (= Studia Orientalia edidit Societa Orientalis Fennica, VIII.4), Helsingforsiae, 1939.
Sam Samaria-Sebaste. Reports of the work of the joint expedition in 1931-1933 and the British expedition in 1935, no 3, The objects from Samaria by J.W.Crowfoot, G.M.Crowfoot & K.M.Kenyon with contributions by S.A.Birnbaum, J.H.Iliffe, J.S.Kirkman, S.Lake, E.L.Sukenik, London, 1957.
Samal Samalian.
Sam'al see Landsberger.
Samar the Samaria papyri quoted after D.M.Gropp, The Samaria papyri from Wâdi ed-Dâliyeh, the slave sales, Ph.Diss. Harvard University, 1986.
Sanch the references to the lost work of Sanchuniaton in Eusebii Caesariensis Praeparatio Evangelica,

liber I, cap. 9, 10 quoted after the edition in Eusèbe de Césarée, La préparation évangélique Livre I, introduction, texte Grec, traduction et commentaire ... par J.Sirinelli & E. des Places (= Sources Chrétiennes no 206), Paris, 1974.
SANSS L.G.Herr, The Scripts of Ancient Northwest Semitic Seals (= Harvard Semitic Museum, Harvard Semitic Monograph Series, ed. F.M.Cross, no 18), Missoula, 1978.
SANSS-Amm The Ammonite seals quoted in SANSS pp. 55ff.
SANSS-App The seals listed in Appendix A, SANSS pp. 197-201.
SANSS-Ar The Aramaic seals quoted in SANSS pp. 7ff.
SANSS-Edom The Edomite seals quoted in SANSS pp. 161ff.
SANSS-Hebr The Hebrew seals quoted in SANSS pp. 79ff.
SANSS-Moab The Moabite seals quoted in SANSS pp. 153ff.
SANSS-Ph the Phoenician seals quoted in SANSS pp. 171ff.
Sar the Phoenician inscriptions from Sarepta published in J.B.Pritchard, Sarepta IV, The objects from area II, X (= Publications de l'Université Libanaise, Section des Études archéologiques II), Beyrouth, 1988, pp. 7-17.
Sardis see Littmann.
SAS see Kottsieper.
SaSt M.Back, Die sassanidischen Staatsinschriften. Studien zur Orthographie und Phonologie des Mittelpersischen der Inschriften zusammen mit einem etymologischen Index des mittelpersichen Wortgutes und einem Textcorpus der behandelten Inschriften (= Acta Iranica 18, troisième série, textes et mémoires, Vol. VIII), Leiden/Téhéran-Liège, 1978.
SAT see de Vaux.
SbPAW Sitzungsberichte der preussischen Akademie der Wissenschaften zu Berlin, philosophisch-historische Klasse.
SBS Chr.Dunant, Le Sanctuaire de Baalshamin à Palmyre, Vol. III, Les inscriptions (= Bibliotheca Helvetica Romana X/III), Rome, 1971.
SBS-Tess The tesserae published in R.Fellmann & Chr. Dunant, Le Sanctuaire de Baalshamin à Palmyre, Vol. VI, Kleinfunde, objets divers (- Bibliotheca Helvetica Romana XVI), Rome, 1975, pp. 113-116.
SC Aramaic papyri discovered at Assuan, ed. A.H.Sayce with the assistance of A.E.Cowley and with appendices by W.Spiegelberg and S.de Ricci, London, 1906.
sc scilicet.
SCA see Elayi.
Schaed H.H.Schaeder, Iranische Beiträge (= Schriften der königsberger Gelehrten Gesellschaft, geisteswissenschaftliche Klasse 6.Jahr, Heft 5), Halle (Saale), 1930.
Schäfer BKA P.Schäfer, Der Bar Kokhba Aufstand. Studien zum zweiten jüdischen Krieg gegen Rom (= Texte und Studien zum antiken Judentum, 1), Tübingen, 1981.
Schiffmann PPT Пальмирцкий Пошлинный Тариф, Введение, перевод и комментарий И.Ш.Шифмана, Москва, 1980.
Schmidt Persepolis ii E.F.Schmidt, Persepolis II. Contents of the treasury and other discoveries (= The University of Chicago Oriental Institute Publications, Vol. 69), Chicago, 1957.

Schmökel GD H.Schmökel, Der Gott Dagan, Thesis Heidelberg, 1928.
Scholem JGM G.Scholem, Jewish Gnosticism, Merkabah Mysticism and Talmudic Tradition, New York, 1962.
Schroed P.Schroeder, Die phönizische Sprache. Entwurf einer Grammatik nebst Sprach- und Schriftproben mit einem Anhang enthaltend eine Erklärung der punischen Stellen im Pönulus des Plautus, Halle, 1869.
Schulthess GCPA F.Schulthess, Grammatik des christlich-palästinischen Aramäisch, Tübingen, 1924.
SCO Studi Classici e Orientali.
SDB Supplément au Dictionnaire de la Bible.
SE Studi Etruschi.
SEA Svensk Exegetisk Årsbok.
sec secundary.
Sef Sefarad. Revista de la Escuela de Estudios Hebraicos (since 1945 with sub-title: Revista del Instituto Arias Montano de Estudios Hebraicos y Orient Proximo; since 1973 with sub-title: Revista del Instituto Arias Montano de Estudios Hebraicos, Sefardies y de Oriente Proximo).
SEG Supplementum Epigraphicum Graecum.
Segert AAG S.Segert, Altaramäische Grammatik mit Bibliographie, Chrestomathie und Glossar, Leipzig, 1975.
Segert GPP S.Segert, A Grammar of Phoenician and Punic, München, 1976.
SEL Studi Epigrafici e Linguistici sul Vicino Oriente antico.
Sem Semitica. Cahiers publiés par l'Institut d'Études sémitiques de l'Université de Paris (since 1974 with sub-title: Cahiers publiés par l'Institut d'Études sémitiques; since 1990 with sub-title: Cahiers publiés par l'Institut d'Études sémitiques du Collège de France).
Seneca de tr an Seneca, De Tranquillitate Animi, quoted after the edition in L.Annaei Senecae Dialogorum Libri Duodecum (ed. L.D.Reynolds), Oxonii, 1976, pp. 207-238.
SeYi Sefer Hayishuv I, Hayishuv limqomotav mime ḥorban bet sheni ʿad kibush 'ereṣ Yisra'el ʿal yede ha ʿaravim (ed. S.Klein), Jerusalem, 1939.
Sf see Dupont-Sommer.
SFAV The Seventh-Fifth Anniversary Volume of the Jewish Quarterly Review (edd. A.A.Neuman & S.Zeitlin), Philadelphia, 1967.
SG see Levy.
SGC see Testa.
SH Scripta Hierosolymitana. Publications of the Hebrew University, Jerusalem.
Shaph Shaphel.
Shahîd RoAr I.Shahîd, Rome and the Arabs, a prolegomenon to the study of Byzantium and the Arabs, Washington, D.C., 1984.
Shn Shnaton, an annual for Biblical and ancient Near Eastern studies (Hebrew).
SHP see Good.
SicArch Sicilia Archaeologica. Rassegna periodica di studi, notizie e documentazione a cura dell'Ente Provinciale per il Turismo di Trapani.
sign signification.
Sing. Singular.
SinInschrift see Euting.
Sivan GAG D.Sivan, Grammatical

Analysis and Glossary of the Northwest Semitic vocables in Akkadian texts in the 15th-13th C.B.C. from Canaan and Syria (= Alter Orient und Altes Testament. Veröffentlichungen zur Kultur und Geschichte des Alten Orients und des Alten Testaments, 214), Neukirchen/Vluyn, 1984.

SL Studia Linguistica. Revue de linguistique générale et comparée.

SM J.Naveh, On Stone and Mosaic. The Aramaic and Hebrew Inscriptions from ancient synagogues, Jerusalem, 1978 (Hebrew).

SMEA Studi micenei ed egeo-anatolici.

Smelik HDAI K.A.D.Smelik, Historische Dokumente aus dem alten Israel, Göttingen, 1987.

Smend & Socin IKM Die Inschrift des Königs Mesa von Moab (edd. R.Smend & A.Socin), Freiburg i.B., 1886.

SMI M.G.Amadasi Guzzo, Scavi a Mozia - Le Iscrizioni (= Collezione di Studi Fenici 22), Roma, 1986.

SMIM Studies in the Mesha Inscription and Moab (ed. A.Dearman; = American Schools of Oriental Research, the Society of Biblical Literature, Archaeology and Biblical Studies, Number 02), Atlanta, 1989.

SMSR Studi e Materiali di Storia delle Religioni pubblicati dalla Scuola di Studi Storico-religiosi della R.Unversità di Roma.

v.Soden AHW W.v.Soden, Akkadisches Handwörterbuch unter Benutzung des lexikalischen Nachlasses von B.Meissner (1868-1947), Band I, Wiesbaden, 1965, Band II, Wiesbaden, 1972, Band III, Wiesbaden, 1981.

v.Soden BAO Bibel und Alter Orient, altorientalische Beiträge zum Alten Testament von Wolfram von Soden (ed. H.P.Müller; = BZAW 162), Berlin/New York, 1985.

v.Soden GAG W.v.Soden, Grundriss der akkadischen Grammatik (= Analecta Orientalia 33), Roma, 1952.

Sogd The Aramaic ideograms attested in Sogdian texts.

Sogd ii The Aramaic ideograms mentioned in E.Benveniste, Essai de grammaire Sogdienne, deuxième partie, Morphologie, syntaxe et glossaire (= Mission Pelliot en Asie Centrale, Série Petit In-Octavo, tome III), Paris, 1929.

Sogd B The Aramaic ideograms mentioned in Textes Sogdiens éd., trad. et comm. par E.Benveniste, Paris, 1940.

Sogd Bb The Aramaic ideograms mentioned in W.Henning, Ein manichäisches Bet- und Beichtbuch (= Abhandlungen der preussischen Akademie der Wissenschaften 1936, Philosophisch-historische Klasse, no 10), Berlin, 1937.

Sogd Gi The Aramaic ideograms mentioned in Berliner Soghdische Texte. 1. Bruchstücke einer soghdischen Version der Georgpassion (C 1) (ed. O.Hansen; = Abhandlungen der preussischen Akademie der Wissenschaften 1941, Philosophisch-historische Klasse, no 10), Berlin, 1941.

Sogd Ka The Aramaic ideograms mentioned in O.Hansen, Zur soghdischen Inschrift auf dem dreisprachigen Denkmal von Karabalgasun, Journal de la Société finno-ougréenne xiv.

Sogd ML The Aramaic ideograms mentioned in F.W.K.Müller &

W.Lentz, Soghdische Texte II, SbPAW '34, pp. 504-607.
Sogd R The Aramaic ideograms mentioned in H.Reichelt, Die Soghidischen Handschriftenreste des britischen Museums, Band I, Heidelberg, 1928, Band II, Heidelberg, 1931.
Sogd Ta The Aramaic ideograms mentioned in W.B.Henning, Sogdian Tales, BSOAS xi 465-487.
Sogd Ve The Aramaic ideograms mentioned in Vessantara Jātaka, texte Sogdien, édité, traduit et commenté par E.Benveniste (= Mission Pelliot en Asie Centrale, Série In-Quarto IV), Paris, 1946.
Soggin OTOS J.A.Soggin, Old Testament and Oriental Studies (= Biblica et Orientalia 29), Rome, 1975.
Sokoloff DJPA M.Sokoloff, A Dictionary of Jewish Palestinian Aramaic of the Byzantine period, Ramat-Gan, 1990.
Solá-Solé IS J.M.Solá-Solé, L'Infinitif Sémitique. Contribution a l'étude des formes et des fonctions des noms d'action et des infinitifs sémitiques (= Bibliothèque de l'École Pratique des Hautes Études, Section des Sciences Historiques et Philologiques, fascicule 315), Paris, 1961.
SOLDV Studi Orientalistici in onore di Giorgio Levi Della Vida (= Pubblicazioni dell'Istituto per l'Oriente 52), Vol. I, Roma, 1956, Vol. II, Roma, 1956.
Souéïda M.Dunand, Mission archéologique au Djebel Druze I, Le Musée de Souéïda, inscriptions et monuments figurés (= Haut Commissariat de la République Française en Syrie et au Liban. Service des Antiquités, Bibliothèque archéologique et historique, Vol. XX), Paris, 1934.
SPC F.Bertrandy & M.Sznycer, Les Stèles Puniques de Constantine, Paris, 1987.
SPDS Studies in the Period of David and Solomon and other essays. Papers read at the international symposium for Biblical studies, Tokyo, 5-7 December 1979 (ed. T.Ishida), Tokyo, 1982.
spec. a) (of) specification - b) special(ly).
Speiser OBS Oriental and Biblical Studies. Collected writings of E.A.Speiser (edd. J.Finkelstein & M.Greenberg), Philadelphia. 1967.
SPGA see Stadelmann.
Spiegelberg DemDenkm W.Spiegelberg, Die demotischen Denkmäler 30601-31166 i (= Die demotischen Inschriften), Leipzig, 1904.
Spijkerman CDPA A.Spijkerman, The Coins of the Decapolis and Provincia Arabia edited with historical and geographical introduction (= Studii Biblici Franciscani Collectio maior 25; ed. M.Piccirillo), Jerusalem, 1978.
Sprache see Rosenthal.
Spronk BAAI K.Spronk, Beatific Afterlife in Ancient Israel and in the ancient Near East (= Alter Oreint und Altes Testament. Veröffentlichungen zur Kultur und Geschichte des Alten Orients und des Alten Testaments, 219), Neukirchen/Vluyn, 1982.
SSI J.C.L.Gibson, Textbook of Syrian Semitic Inscriptions, Vol. I, Hebrew and Moabite inscriptions, Oxford, 1971, Vol. II, Aramaic inscriptions including inscriptions in the dialect of Zenjirli, Oxford, 1975, Vol. III, Phoenician inscriptions

including inscriptions in the mixed dialect of Arslan Tash, Oxford, 1982.
SSMA Sacrificio e società nel mondo antico (edd. C.Grottanelli & N.F.Parise), Roma/Bari, 1988.
SSO see Mettinger.
SSWP see Avishur.
Stähli KJK H.P.Stähli, Knabe, Jüngling, Knecht, Untersuchungen zum Begriff n‘r im Alten Testament (= Beiträge zur biblischen Exegese und Theologie, Band 7, edd. J.Becker & H. Graf Reventlow), Frankfurt am Main/Bern/Las Vegas, 1978.
Stadelmann SPGA R.Stadelmann, Syrisch-Palästinensische Gottheiten in Ägypten (= Probleme der Ägyptologie, Band 5), Leiden, 1967.
Staerk JAP W.Staerk, Die jüdisch-aramäischen Papyri von Assuan sprachlich und sachlich erklärt (= Kleine Texte für theologische Vorlesungen und Übungen, ed. H.Lietzmann 22/23), Bonn, 1907.
Stark PNPI J.K.Stark, Personal Names in Palmyrene Inscriptions, Oxford, 1971.
stat. status.
Stefanovic COAI Z.Stefanovic, Correlations between Old Aramaic Inscriptions and the Aramaic section of Daniel, Ann Arbor, 1987.
Steiner ASSL R.C.Steiner, Affricated Ṣade in the Semitic Languages (= The American Academy for Jewish Research Monograph Series no 3), New York, 1982.
Stevenson ABC J.H.Stevenson, Assyrian and Babylonian Contracts with Aramaic reference notes transcribed from the originals in the British Museum, with transliteration, translation and commentary, New York/Cincinnati/Chicago, 1902.
Stol BMS Een Babyloniër Maakt Schulden, Leiden, 1983.
Strabo Strabo, Geographica, quoted after the edition of A.Meineke, Vol. I, Lipsiae, 1899, Vol. II, Lipsiae, 1907, Vol. III, Lipsiae, 1913 (for Libri I-VI see also the edition in 2 volumes of A.Alföldi in Antiquitas Reihe 1, Abhandlungen zur alten Geschichte unter Mitwirkung von V.Burr & J.Straub, Band 9, Bonn, 1968, Band 19, Bonn 1972).
STU Spätbabylonische Texte aus Uruk, Teil I (bearbeitet von H.Hunger; = Ausgrabungen der deutschen Forschungsgemeinschaft in Uruk-Warka, Band 9), Berlin, 1976, Teil II (bearbeitet von E.v.Weiher; = same series, Band 10), Berlin, 1983, Teil III (bearbeitet von E.v.Weiher; same series, Band 12), Berlin, 1988.
Stud see Lipiński.
Studien see Hübschmann.
StudIr Studia Iranica.
StudMagr Studi Magribini.
StudSard Studi Sardi.
SUBH Scripta Universitatis atque Bibliothecae Hierosolymitanarum Orientalia et Judaica.
subj. subject.
subst. a) substantive - b) substantivated.
suff. suffix.
Sukenik ASPG E.L.Sukenik, Ancient Synagogues in Palestine and Greece (= The Schweich Lectures of the British Academy 1930), London, 1934.
Sum Sumer. A journal of archaeology in Iraq (since 1958 with

subtitle A journal of archaeology and history in Iraq; since 1973 with sub-title A journal of archaeology & history in Arab world).

Sum. Sumerian.

Sumer Sumer, a journal of archaeology in Iraq (since 1958 with subtitle: A journal of archaeology and history in Iraq; since 1973 with subtitle: A journal of archaeology & history in Arab world).

Suppl see Altheim & Stiehl.

SV Schrijvend Verleden, documenten uit het oude Nabije Oosten vertaald en toegelicht (ed. K.R.Veenhof), Leiden/Zutphen, 1983.

s.v. sub voce.

SVM L.Jakob-Rost, Die Stempelsiegel im vorderasiatischen Museum, Berlin, 1975.

SVS see Cohen.

SVT Supplements to Vetus Testamentum.

SY Sefer Yerushalayim (The book of Jerusalem. Jerusalem, its natural conditions, history and development from its origins to the present day), ed. M.Avi-Yonah, Vol. I, Jerusalem/Tel Aviv, 1956 (Hebrew).

Syn C.H.Kraeling, The Synagogue (= The Excavations at Dura-Europos conducted by Yale University and the French Academy of Inscriptions and Letters, Final Report VIII, Part 1), New York, 1979 (augmented edition).

Syn D The great great inscriptions of the synagogue of Dura-Europos quoted after the edition of J.Obermann, Ber. vii 89ff.

Syr Syria. Revue d'art orientale et d'archéologie.

Sznycer PPP M.Sznycer, Les Passages Puniques en transcription Latine dans le "Poenulus" de Plaute (= Études et Commentaires 65), Paris, 1967.

TA La Toponomie Antique (Actes du Colloque de Strasbourg 12-14 Juin 1975) (= Université des Sciences Humaines de Strasbourg. Travaux du Centre de Recherche sur le Proche-Orient et la Grèce antiques, 4), Leiden [1977].

TA-Ar the Aramaic texts from Tell Arad, published in Y.Aharoni, Arad Inscriptions, in cooperation with J.Naveh, with contributions by A.F.Rainey, M.Aharoni, B.Lifshitz, M.Sharon & Z.Gofer, Jerusalem, 1981, pp. 153ff.

TaC see McCarthy.

TADAE B.Porten & A.Yardeni, Textbook of Aramaic documents from ancient Egypt, Vol. 1, Letters, Jerusalem, 1986, Vol. 2, Contracts, Jerusalem, 1989, Vol. 3, Lietrature, Accounts, Lists, Jerusalem, 1993.

taf table.

TAG see Fitzmyer.

TA-H The Hebrew texts from Tell-Arad, published in Y.Aharoni, Arad Inscriptions, in cooperation with J.Naveh, with contributions by A.F.Rainey, M.Aharoni, B.Lifshitz, M.Sharon & Z.Gofer, Jerusalem, 1981, pp. 11ff.

Tarbiz Tarbiz. A quarterly review of the humanities (since Vol. XXIV with sub-title: A quarterly for Jewish studies).

TC a) Textes cunéiformes. Musée du Louvre. Département des Antiquités orientales - b) see Hillers.

TeAv Tel Aviv. Journal of the Institute of Archaeology of Tel Aviv University.

Teb M.Fantar, Stèles anépigraphes

et stèles à inscriptions Néopuniques (= MAIBL XVI, pp. 379-431), Paris, 1974.

Teixidor PP J.Teixidor, The Pantheon of Palmyre (= Études préliminaires aux Religions Orientales dans l'Empire Ropmain, Vol. 79), Leiden, 1979.

Tell F the Aramaic inscription of Tell Fekheriye quoted after the edition in A.Abou-Assaf, P.Bordreuil, A.R.Millard, La statue de Tell Fekheriye et son inscription bilingue Assyro-Araméenne, Paris, 1982.

Tell Halaf M.v.Oppenheim, Tell Halaf, une civilisation retrouvée en Mésopotamie, Paris, 1939.

temp. temporal.

Testa SGC E.Testa, Il Simbolismo dei Giudeo-Cristiani (= Pubblicazioni dello Studium Biblicum Franciscanum, 14), Jerusalem, 1962.

TGI Textbuch zur Geschichte Israels (second edition) in Verbinding mit E.Edel und R.Borger herausgegeben von K.Galling, Tübingen, 1968.

TH a) The Aramaic texts published in Die Inschriften von Tell Halaf. Keilschrifttexte und aramäische Urkunden aus einer assyrischen Provinzhauptstadt, herausgegeben und bearbeitet von J.Friedrich, G.R.Meyer, A.Ungnad, E.F.Weidner (= Beiheft AfO 6), Berlin, 1940, pp. 70-78 - b) see Koch.

ThLZ Theologische Literaturzeitung.

Thomas The Prophet D.W.Thomas, "The Prophet" in the Lachish ostraca, London, 1946.

Thompson Chemistry R.C.Thompson, The Chemistry of the ancient Assyrians, London, 1925.

THP Temples and High Places in Biblical times. Proceedings of the colloquium in honor of the centennial of Hebrew Union College - Jewish Institute of Religion, Jerusalem 14-16 March 1977 (ed. A.Biran), Jerusalem, 1981.

THSA see Dussaud.

ThWAT Theologisches Wörterbuch zum Alten Testament.

Tigay NOG J.H.Tigay, You shall have No Other Gods: Israelite Religion in the light of Hebrew inscriptions (= Harvard Semitic Series no. 31), Atlanta, Georgia, 1986.

Timm DO S.Timm, Die Dynastie Omri: Quellen und Untersuchungen zur Geschichte Israels im 9.Jahrhundert vor Christtus (= Forschungen zur Religion und Literatur des Alten und Neuen Testaments, H.124), Göttingen, 1982.

Titres see Benveniste.

TK Tell Keisan (1971-1976). Une cité phénicienne en Galilée sous la direction de J.Briend et J.B.Humbert, assistés de E.Puech ... (= Orbis Biblicus et Orientalis, Series archaeologica 1), Paris, 1980.

TMP Comte du Mesnil du Buisson, Les Tessères et les Monnaies de Palmyre. Un art, une culture et une philosophie grecs dans les moules d'une cité et d'une religion sémitiques, Paris, 1962.

TNT see Hvidberg-Hansen.

Tomback CSL R.S.Tomback, A Comparative Semitic Lexicon of the Phoenician and Punic Languages (= Society of Biblical Literature Dissertation Series no 32), Missoula (Montana), 1978.

tot. totally.

TP see Gawlikowski.
TPC H.Bénichou-Safar, Les Tombes Puniques de Carthage, topographie, structures, inscriptions et rites funéraires, Paris, 1982.
TPI N.Slouschz, Thesaurus of Phoenician Inscriptions edited with commentary, Tel-Aviv, 1942 (Hebrew).
TPOA J.Briend & M.J.Seux, Textes du Proche-Orient Ancien et histoire d'Israël, Paris, 1977.
Traditio Traditio, studies in ancient and medieval history, thought and religion.
Trans Transeuphratène. Études sur la Syrie-Palestine et Chypre à l'époque Perse.
trans. transitive.
transl. a) translated - b) translation.
Trip Tripolitanian Inscriptions, cf. a) Lib iii pp. 92-116 (no. 1-26) - b) AfrIt vi pp. 1-27 (no. 27-29) - c) AfrIt vi pp. 104-109 (no 30) - d) RANL '49, pp. 399-412 (no. 31-35) - e) RevEtAnc lv pp. 358-60 (no 30) - f) RANL '55 pp. 550-561 (no. 37) - g) LibAnt i pp. 57-63 (no 38-40) - h) RANL '63 pp. 463-482 (no. 41-50) - i) Or xxxiii pp. 1-14 (no. 51) - j) Mem Brockelmann pp. 127-132 (no. 52) (for these texts, see now IPT).
TTS see Haran.
TUAT Texte aus der Umwelt des Alten Testaments (ed. O.Kaiser), Band I, Rechts- und Wirtschaftsurkunden, historisch-chronologische Texte, Gütersloh, 1982-1985 (6 facicles), Band II, Orakel, Rituale, Bau- und Votivinschriften, Lieder und Gebete, Gütersloh, 1986-1991 (6 facicles), Band III, Weisheitstexte, Mythen und Epen, Gütersloh, 1990- .
Tubach ISS J.Tubach, Im Schatten des Sonnengottes. Der Sonnenkult in Edessa, Ḥarrān und Ḥaṭrā am Vorabend der christlichen Mission, Wiesbaden, 1986.
Tur-Sinai HalSe N.H.Tur-Sinai, HaLashon wehaSefer (three volumes), Jerusalem 1954-1956.
TZ see Fritz.
Ug. Ugaritic.
UHP see Dahood.
Ullendorff BHL Is Biblical Hebrew a Language? Studies in Semitic languages and civilizations, Wiesbaden, 1977.
UMS xx University of Michigan Studies. Humanistic Series, Vol. XX (= Royal orrespondence of the Assyrian empire (ed. L.Waterman), Part IV with an interpretation of the Assur ostracon by R.A.Bowman, Ann Arbor, 1936).
uncert. uncertain.
Ungnad ArPap A.Ungnad, Aramäische Papyrus aus Elephantine. Kleine Ausgabe unter Zugrundlegung von Eduard Sachau's Erstausgabe, Leipzig, 1911.
UP M.Graas, P.Rouillard & J.Teixidor, l'Univers Phénicien, Paris, 1989.
v. vide.
var. variant.
Vattioni IH F.Vattioni, Le Iscrizioni di ḥatra (= Supplemento n. 28 agli Annali - vol. 41 (1981) fasc. 3), Napoli, 1981.
Vatt sig ar Aramaic seals published by F.Vattioni in "I sigilli, le monete egli avori aramaici", Aug xi pp. 47-87.
Vatt sig eb the Hebrew seals published by F.Vattioni in "I sigilli ebraici", Bibl l pp. 357-388, "I sigilli ebraici II", Aug. xi pp. 447-454 and "I sigilli ebraici III", AION xxviii pp. 227-254.

de Vaux IAT R.de Vaux, Les Institutions de l'Ancien Testament, Vol. I, Paris, 1958, Vol. II, Paris, 1960.
de Vaux SAT R.de Vaux, Les Sacrifices de l'Ancien Testament (= Cahiers de la Revue Biblique 1), Paris, 1964.
VD Verbum Domini.
VDI Vestnik Drevnej Istorii.
verb. verbal.
Verger RGP A.Verger, Ricerche Giuridiche sui Papyri Aramaici di Elefantina (= Studi Semitici 16), Roma, 1965.
Vermes MDJ G.Vermès, Les manuscrits du Désert de Juda, Tournai, 1953.
VF M.J.Fuentes Estañol, Vocabulario Fenicio (= Biblioteca Fenicia Volumen 1.), Barcelona, 1980.
Vincent Rel A.Vincent, La Religion des Judéo-Araméens d'Éléphantine, Paris, 1937.
VO Vicino Oriente.
Vogt Lex E.Vogt, Lexicon linguae Aramaicae Veteris Testamenti, documentis antiquis illustratum, Roma, 1971.
Vogüé List of Palmyrenean texts quoted after the numbering in Syrie centrale, inscriptions Sémitiques, publiées avec traduction et commentaire par le Cte Melchior de Vogüé, Paris, 1868.
Vriezen & Hospers PI Th.C.Vriezen & J.H.Hospers, Palestine Inscriptions (= Textus Minores, Vol. XVII), Leiden, 1951.
vs/Vs obverse.
VT Vetus Testamentum. Quarterly published by the International Organization of Old Testament Scholars (since Vol. XVI with subtitle: Quarterly published by the International Organization for the Study of the Old Testament).
WA see Fitzmyer.
Wag C.G.Wagenaar, De Joodsche kolonie van Jeb-Syene in de 5de eeuw voor Christus, Groningen/den Haag, 1928.
Warka The Aramaic text from Warka in cuneiform script quoted after the edition by A.Dupont-Sommer, RA xxxix 35ff.
War Scroll see Yadin.
Watanabe AVTA K.Watanabe, Die *adê*-Vereidigung anlässlich der Thronfolgeregelung Asarhaddons (= Baghdader Mitteilungen, Beiheft 3), Berlin, 1987.
Waw a) A.Dupont-Sommer, La doctrine gnostique de la lettre "Wâw" d'après une lamelle Araméenne inédite (= Bibliothèque archéologique et historique, tome 41), Paris, 1946 - b) the text published in this book = AMB 6.
WB see Koldewey.
Weinfeld DDS M.Weinfeld, Deuteronomy and the Deuteronomic School, Oxford, 1972.
Weippert LIS M.Weippert, Die Landnahme der israelitischen Stämme in der neueren wissenschaftlichen Diskussion, ein kritischer Bericht (= Forschungen zur Religion und Literatur des Alten und Neuen Testaments, H. 92), Göttingen, 1967.
Welten P.Welten, Die Königs-Stempel, ein Beitrag zur Militärpolitik Judas unter Hiskia und Josia, Wiesbaden, 1969.
WGAV Wirtschaft und Gesellschaft im alten Vorderasien (edd. J.Harmatta & G.Komoróczy), Budapest, 1976.
Wiegand Palmyra Palmyra, Ergebnisse der Expeditionen in 1902

und 1917 (ed. Th.Wiegand), Berlin, 1932.
Winckler AltorForsch H.Winckler, Altorientalische Forschungen, Leipzig, 1893-1906.
Winter FG U.Winter, Frau und Göttin. Exegetische und ikonographische Studien zum weiblichen Gottesbild im alten Israel und in dessen Umwelt (= Orbis Biblicus et Orientalis 53), Göttingen, 1983.
WO Die Welt des Orients. Wissenschaftliche Beiträge zur Kunde des Morgenlandes.
WZKM Wiener Zeitschrift für die Kunde des Morgenlandes.
WZKMU Wissenschaftliche Zeitschrift der Karl-Marx-Universität Leipzig. Gesellschafts- und sprachwissenschaftliche Reihe.
WZUH Wissenschaftliche Zeitschrift der Martin-Luther-Universität Halle-Wittenberg.
Yadin BK Y.Yadin, Bar-Kokhba, the rediscovery of the legendary hero of the last Jewish revolt against imperial Rome, London, 1971.
Yadin Hazor-SL Y.Yadin, Hazor the head of all those kingdoms, Joshua 11:10, with chapter on Israelite Megiddo (= the Schweich Lectures of the British Academy 1970), London, 1972.
Yadin Mess Y.Yadin, The Message of the scrolls, London, 1957.
Yadin War Scroll Y.Yadin, The Scroll of the War of the sons of Light against the sons of Darkness edited with commentary and introduction, Oxford, 1962.
Yaron Gifts R.Yaron, Gifts in contemplation of death in Jewish and Roman law, Oxford, 1960.
Yaron Law R.Yaron, Introduction to the Law of the Aramaic papyri, Oxford, 1961.
YClSt Yale Classical Studies.
Yiph Yiphil.
Yitp Yitpa‘el.
Yoph Yophal.
YOS Yale Oriental Series.
ZA Zeitschrift für Assyriologie und verwandte Gebiete (since Vol. XLV: Zeitschrift für Assyriologie und vorderasiatische Archäologie).
ZAH Zeitschrift für Althebraistik.
ZÄS Zeitschrift für ägyptische Sprache und Altertumskunde.
ZAW Zeitschrift für die alttestamentliche Wissenschaft.
ZDMG Zeitschrift der deutschen morgenländischen Gesellschaft.
ZDMG-Suppl Zeitschrift der deutschen morgenländischen Gesellschaft. Supplement.
ZDPV Zeitschrift des deutschen Palästina-Vereins.
Zevit MLAHE Z.Zevit, Matres Lectionis in Ancient Hebrew Epigraphs (= American Schools of Oriental Research, Monograph Series, ed. D.N.Freedman, no 2), Cambridge MA, 1980.
Zimmern Fremdw H.Zimmern, Akkadische Fremdwörter als Beweis für babylonischen Kultureinfluss, second edition, Leipzig, 1917.
ZNW Zeitschrift für die neutestamentliche Wissenschaft und die Kunde des Urchristentums (since vol. xx (1921) with the title: Zeitschrift für die neutestamentliche Wissenschaft und die Kunde der älteren Kirche).
Zoroaster see Henning.
ZS Zeitschrift für Semitistik und verwandte Gebiete.
Zunz (L.)Zunz, Zur Geschichte und Literatur, Erster Band, Berlin, 1845.

v.Zijl A.H.v.Zijl, The Moabites (= Pretoria Oriental Series, Vol. III), Leiden, 1960.

ʾ

ʾ$_1$ v. *ʾdm*$_5$.

ʾ$_2$ v. *ʾdn*$_1$.

ʾ$_3$ v. *ʾmn*$_2$.

ʾ$_4$ v. *ʾmn*$_5$.

ʾ$_5$ v. *ʾmr*$_1$.

ʾ$_6$ v. *ʾsrtg*.

ʾ$_7$ v. *ʾrdb*, *kʾ*$_1$.

ʾ$_8$ v. *ʾšl*$_1$.

ʾ$_9$ v. *h*$_1$.

ʾ$_{10}$ v. *y*$_1$.

ʾ$_{11}$ v. *mšmn*.

ʾ$_{12}$ v. *qwm*$_1$.

ʾ$_{13}$ Milik Syr xliv 296f.: the α in Inv D. 51^2 (before βαρζαχιχη) = prep. (= on, for) :: Levi Della Vida FDE '22-23, 368: = (combined with prec. α) 2 :: du Mesnil du Buisson sub Inv D. 51: = part of n.p.; cf. also Teixidor Syr xlvii 376.

ʾb$_1$ **Ph** Sing. abs. *ʾb* KAI 24^{10}, 26A i 3, DD 16^2; + suff. 3 p.s.m. *ʾbh* KAI 1^1, *ʾby* CIS i 58^{3f} (= Kition B 3), KAI 34^1 (= Kition B 45), RDAC '84, 104^2; + suff. 1 p.s. *ʾb* (nom.) KAI 24^3 (cf. FR 234), *ʾby* (gen.) KAI $24^{5,9}$, 26A i 11 (or suff. 3 p.s.m. preferable?, cf. Lipiński RTAT 258, Amadasi Guzzo VO iii 94, Gibson SSI iii p. 47), *ʾby* CIS i 57^2 (= Kition B 2), KAI $43^{7,9}$; + suff. 3 p.pl.m. *ʾbnm* CIS i 60^{3f} (= Kition B 5), KAI 40^5 (cf. also Krahmalkov JSS xv 183); Plur. + suff. 2 p.s.m. *[ʾ]bytk* KAI 9A 2 (cf. Röllig NESE ii 11; ??, highly uncert., cf. also Schiffmann RSF iv 177: or = Sing. + suff. 2 p.s.m. of *byt*$_2$ (??)); + suff. 1 p.s. *ʾbyty* MUSJ xlv 262^6 (cf. Starcky ibid. 272, Röllig NESE ii 11, Schiffmann RSF iv 177; dam. context :: v.d.Branden BiOr xxxiii 12: poss. = Sing. + suff. 1 p.s. of *ʾbyt* (= desire)); cf. FR 240,1 - **Pun** Sing. abs. *ʾb* KAI 128^3; + suff. 3 p.s.m. *ʾbyʾ* Trip 38^2, *ʿbyʿ* Punica xi 12^4 (dam. context), xii 31^2, *ʿbwyʿ* (or *ʿbyʿ*?) Punica ix 3^4, cf. IRT $828^{1f.}$: *(l)obym* (prec. by prep. *l*$_5$, cf. Vattioni Aug xvi 538 :: idem AION xvi 48: l. *oby m...* :: Levi Della Vida OA ii 78: l. *loby[ni]m* = *l*$_5$ + Sing. + suff. 3 p.s.m. of *bn*$_1$); + suff. 3 p.pl.m. *ʿbnʾm* Trip 39^2, cf. IRTS 24^2: *abunom* (cf. Février with Levi Della Vida OA iv 60, cf. also Krahmalkov JSS xv 184 :: Levi Della Vida OA ii 75: = Sing. + suff. 3 p.pl.m. of *bn*$_1$, cf. however idem OA iv 60); Plur. + suff. 3 p.s.m. *ʾbty* KAI 126^8, cf. OA ii 83^2: *(l)ybythem* (prec. by prep. *l*$_5$; cf. FR p. 34 n. 1; :: Vattioni AION xvi 40, 49, Aug xvi 539: = *l*$_5$ + *b*$_2$ + *tm*$_1$); + suff. 3 p.pl.m. *ʾbʿthm* KAI 142^4 (:: reading *ʾbʿnhm*, cf. e.g. Cooke NSI p. 141 (: = Sing. +

suff. 3 p.pl.m., cf. also Röllig KAI a.l.)) - **Mo** Sing. + suff. 1 p.s. *ʾby* KAI 181^{2,3} - **Hebr** Sing. + suff. 3 p.s.m. *ʾbyw* Frey 630b 3; + suff. 2 p.s.m. *ʾbyk* DJD ii 45^{5}; diff. *ʾb* without context HUCA xl/xli 157 - **Samal** Sing. + suff. 3 p.s.m. *ʾbh* KAI 214^{29} (:: Donner KAI a.l.: or = Plur. + suff. 3 p.s.m.), 215^{1,2,3,7,9}, *ʾbwh* KAI 215^{3} (:: Schuster FS Landsberger 441 n. 44a: = Plur. + suff. 3 p.s.m.); + suff. 1 p.s. *ʾby* KAI 214^{8,9}, 215$^{1,5,6,8,10,14,15(?),16,18,19,20,21}$ (Lipiński BiOr xxxiii 232: l. poss. *ʾbty* (= *Plur.* + suff. 1 p.s.) in KAI 214^{12} (*ʾbt[y]*)^{,13} (*[ʾb]ty*); highly uncert. reading and interpret.) - **OldAr** Sing. + suff. 1 p.s. *ʾby* KAI 216^{4,7,12}, 217^{3}, 219^{4} (*ʾb[y]*), 223B 8, 224^{10,23,25}; Plur. + suff. 1 p.s. *ʾbhy* KAI 216^{16} - **OffAr** Sing. + suff. 3 p.s.m. *ʾbwhy* Cowl 71^{5,25}, Aḥiq 47, 85, 138, Krael 5^{11,14}, Driv 8^{4,6}, KAI 273^{5} (cf. Drijvers BiOr xxx 467), 279^{6} (cf. also Humbach MSSW xxvi 40f.), NESE i 11^{7} (*[ʾ]bwhy*, cf. Naveh & Shaked JAOS xci 381: poss. reconstr., cf. however Grelot DAE p. 505 (n. m): l. *[h]bwhy* = QAL Imper. pl.m. + suff. 3 p.s.m. of *yhb*, cf. also Porten Or lvii 78, 80, Porten & Yardeni sub TADAE A 3.10: l. *[yz]bnhy* = PAʿEL Impf. 3 p.s.m. + suff. 3 p.s.m. of *zbn$_1$* (less prob. reading) :: Shunnar CRM ii 286f.: l. *bnhy* (= Plur. + suff. 3 p.s.m. of *br$_1$*) :: Shunnar GMA 115: l. *bnhy* (= Sing. + suff. 3 p.s.m. of *br$_1$*)), Samar 8^{12}, *ʾbwh* Krael 5^{12} (cf. Milik RB lxi 250, Porten & Greenfield JEAS p. 48, Porten & Yardeni sub TADAE B 3.6 :: Krael a.l.: l. *ʾbwhy*); + suff. 3 p.s.f. *ʾbwh* Cowl 25^{7}, Aḥiq 55, Krael 7^{28}; + suff. 2 p.s.m. *ʾbwk* Cowl 44^{7}, Aḥiq 15, 27; + suff. 1 p.s. *ʾby* Aḥiq 33, Krael 4^{19}, Driv 8^{2,3}, Herm 1^{14}, 3^{14}, 4^{13}, ATNS 3^{7}, 52b 3 (*[ʾ]by*; ?, dam. context, cf. also Segal ATNS a.l.), 59^{1} (diff. reading, dam. context), 78^{3}, 144 (uncert. reading); + suff. 3 p.pl.m. *ʾbwhm* ATNS 28a 2; + suff. 2 p.pl.m. *ʾbwkm* Cowl 20^{6}; Plur. + suff. 3 p.pl.m. *ʾbyhm* Cowl 71^{2} (:: CIS ii sub 145: l. *ʾlhyhm* = Plur. + suff. 3 p.pl.m. of *ʾlh$_1$*), *ʾbhyhm* AE '23, 42 no. 12^{3}; + suff. 1 p.pl. *ʾbhyn* 30^{13}, 31^{12}; cf. Frah xi 8 (*ʾb*), 9 (*ʾby*), Paik 7 (*ʾby*), Sogd ii 205, R. 43, Ve 103 (cf. also Lemosín AO ii 110, GIPP 15, 45, SaSt 11, Toll ZDMG-Suppl viii 29, 31) - **Nab** Sing. cstr. *ʾb* CIS ii 224^{6}; + suff. 3 p.s.m. *ʾbwhy* CIS ii 196^{3}, 201^{2}, 207^{1}, 332^{3}; + suff. 3 p.s.f. *ʾbwh* CIS ii 224^{4}; + suff. 2 p.s.m. *ʾbwk* MPAT 64 i 12; + suff. 1 p.s. *ʾby* MPAT 64 i 6, 7, iii 1 - **Palm** Sing. cstr. *ʾb* Syr xlvii 314^{3} (?, l. poss. *ʾbʾ* ^{4} *ʾbwhy* :: Gawlikowski ibid.: l. *ʾbʾ* <*dy* *ʾb*> ^{4} *ʾbwhy*); emph. *ʾbʾ*?? Ber v 135B 3; + suff. 3 p.s.m. *ʾbwhy* CIS ii 3930^{3}, 4030^{6}, 4045^{4}, 4050^{5}, 4130^{2}, 4169, Inv iv 7^{2} (Greek par. τῷ πατρὶ αὐτοῦ), etc., *[ʾ]byhy* DM ii 39 iii 5, *ʾbwh* CIS ii 4044^{5}, 4061^{6}, 4067^{4}, Syr xii 127^{2}, *ʾbyh* CIS ii 3907^{8}, 4036B 3, RIP 114^{8}, *ʾbw* ?? CIS ii 4116^{6}; + suff. 3 p.s.f. *ʾbwh* Inscr P 78^{6}, *ʾblh* (lapsus) CIS ii 4401^{3}; + suff. 3 p.pl.m. *ʾbwhn* CIS ii 3978^{7}, Inv x 4^{3}, *ʾbhwn* Inv viii 58^{2}, *ʾbwhw[n]* CIS ii 4201^{2} (:: Cantineau sub Inv vii 4: l. *ʾbwh[n]* :: Vogüé 47: l. *ʾbwhy* :: Frey sub 820: l. *ʾbwtw*; Greek par. πατρὸς αὐτῶν); + suff. 1 p.pl. *ʾbwn* Ber ii 79b, SBS 60^{11} (= 61e 4 = RIP 143^{4} × Milik DFD 98, Teixidor PP 23: l. *ʾbwy* = Sing. + suff. 3 p.s.m.?); Plur. + suff. 3 p.pl.m. *ʾbhthwn* Inv viii 59^{3} (Greek par. τοῖς γονεῦσι αὐτῶν) - **Hatra** Sing. emph. *ʾbʾ* 28^{5}; + suff. 3 p.s.m. *ʾbwhy* 107^{7}, 416^{5}, *ʾbh* Syr xl 12^{9} (= app. 4); Plur. + suff. 3 p.pl.m. *ʾbhthwn* 214^{2} (cf. Degen WO v 224, Milik DFD 167 :: Teixidor Syr xlviii 484) - **JAr** Sing. emph. *ʾbʾ* MPAT 95A 1 (= Frey 1359), 116 (:: Lidzbarski Eph iii 52: = n.p.), DJD ii 87^{1} (or = n.p.?, cf. Milik a.l.), *ʾbh* MPAT 145C 2 (cf. Milik with Zayadine Syr xlvii 131, Fitzmyer & Harrington MPAT a.l. :: Lidzbarski Eph ii 197, Frey sub 1373: = n.p.), Syn D 273 no. 13^{2} (= SM 96b); + suff. 1 p.pl. *ʾbwnh* MPAT 95B 1 (= Frey 1359), 110^{1} (= Frey 1299); Plur. + suff. 1 p.pl. *ʾbhtnh* MPAT 67^{2} (= Frey 1300), 71^{1} (= Frey 1334; *ʾbntn[h]*, or *ʾbhtn[ʾ]* ?, cf. Fitzmyer & Harrington MPAT p. 224; or l. *ʾbhtn*?, cf. Sukenik ZDPV lv 127, Frey a.l.) - ¶ subst. m. 1) father: KAI 1^{1}, etc., passim; concerning problems of *ʾby* in Herm., cf. Porten & Greenfield IOS iv 27f., Hayes & Hoftijzer VT xx 104f.; *ʾb ʾbwhy* Sep. xlvii 314^{3}: his paternal grandfather (for the reading, v. supra); *ʾbʾ dbnyh* Hatra 28^{5}: the father of her sons (i.e. her husband) - **2)** Plur. a) ancestors: KAI 126^{8}, 216^{16}, Cowl 30^{13}, 31^{12}, Inv viii 59^{3}, Hatra 214^{2}, MPAT 67^{2} - b) parents: KAI 142^{4} (v. supra, cf. however Lat. par. *patri piissimo*; v. also *mṣbh*), OA ii 83^{2} - **3)** **byt ʾb*, CIS ii 3978^{7}: family - **4)** used metaphorically: a) of a king, who protects his subjects and contributes to their prosperity: KAI 24^{10}, 26A i 3 - b) of a counsellor, on whom the welfare of the nation is dependent; *ʾbwh zy ʾtwr klh* Aḥiq 55: the father of all Assyria (for a and b, cf. for parallels Weinfeld UF viii 405 n. 243) - c) *ʾbh lhwn* Syn D 273 no. 13^{2}: their superior (reading of *lhwn* however uncert., cf. Naveh sub SM 96b) - reading *ʾb* at the end of KAI 201^{2} prob., cf. Cross BASOR ccv 37f., but interpret. and division of context highly uncert. :: Lipiński Stud 16ff.: = Sing. cstr. of *ʾb$_1$* (cf. Millard JSS xxi 174f.). - on this word cf. also Masson RPAE 71f.

v. *ʾbšp*, *ʾbt*, *ʾm$_1$*, *byt$_2$*, *dʾb*, *pʿl$_1$*, *šḥt$_2$*.

ʾb$_2$ **JAr** Plur. abs. *ʾbyn* Mas 556^{4} (?, uncert. and dam. context) - ¶ subst. fruit, v. however supra.

v. *ʾdn$_1$*, *dʾb*.

ʾb$_3$ v. *b$_1$*.

ʾbb **Pun**, cf. Diosc iii 102: αβιβ (var. αβοιβ, αβαιβ), 122: αβιβ (var. αβοιβ, αββοιβ) = ear (bot.) - Driver PEQ '45, 6f.: l. in KAI 182 ii: *ʾby[b]* = spring-fruit (highly improb. interpret.; *ʾby* = n.p. or part of n.p.).

ʾbgdn v. *ʾbgrn*.

ʾbgrn (< Iran., cf. Schaed 264, Benveniste JA ccxxv 178ff., Eilers AfO xvii 332f., Hinz AISN 18 :: J.J.Rabinowitz Bibl xxxix 78f.: < Greek επίγραμμα) - **OffAr** Sing. abs. *ʾbygrn* Cowl 43^{6}, Krael 6^{17}, 8^{7},

9[20], 10[10,14], 12[30], ›*bgrn* Krael 5[8,14], 11[6] (for the reading cf. Porten & Greenfield JEAS p. 66, Porten & Yardeni sub TADAE B 3.13); emph. ›*bygrn*› Cowl 20[14], 25[15], 28[10], ›*bgrn*› Krael 11[7] (:: reading ›*b(y)gdn(*›*)* in Krael) - ¶ subst. fine, penalty (to be paid in case of breach of contract) :: Wag 69 n. 3, Porten & Greenfield JEAS a.l., Grelot e.g. DAE p. 90 a.e. = compensation, indemnity.

›**bd**$_1$ **OldCan** QAL Pf. 3 p.s.f. *a-ba-da-at* EA 288[52] (cf. Sivan GAG 138, 199) - **Ph** YIPH (or PI‹EL?, cf. Dupont-Sommer RA xli 205, H.P.Müller ZA lxv 110, Puech Sem xxix 22 :: Masson & Sznycer RCP 18: or = QAL?, cf. also Fuentes Estañol VF s.v. ›*bd* (cf. however Puech RB xcii 291)); Impf. 3 p.s.m. *y*›*bd* KAI 30[3] (dam. context; cf. also Puech Sem xxix 21f.: = Impf. 3 p.pl.) - **Mo** QAL Pf. 3 p.s.m. ›*bd* KAI 181[7] (v. ›*bd*$_2$) - **Hebr** QAL Pf. 3 p.pl. ›*bdw* DJD ii 45[7] - **Samal** ›*bd* KAI 215[5] (uncert. text) - **OldAr** PA‹EL Inf. ›*bdt* KAI 222B 36, 223B 7; HAPH Impf. 1 p.s. ›*h*›*bd* KAI 223C 4, ›*hbd* KAI 223C 5 (:: Degen Gramm 71f. n. 64: lapsus for ›*h*›*bd*, cf. also idem GGA '79, 24, Gibson SSI ii p. 45, Lemaire & Durand IAS 143, Garr DGSP 49 :: Lipiński Stud 47, BiOr xxxiii 234: = HAPH of *bdd*$_2$ (= to disperse, to eliminate)?) - **OffAr** QAL Pf. 3 p.s.m. ›*bd* Driv 8[2,4]; 3 p.pl.m. ›*bdw* Cowl 30[16]; Impf. 3 p.s.m. *y*›*bd* Cowl 15[27] (*[y]*›*bd*), Krael 7[25], Sem ii 31 conc. 3, xxi 85 conv. 5; 3 p.s.f. *t*›*bd* ? Cowl 71[28], KAI 226[10]; Part. act. s.m. abs. ›*bd* MAI xiv/2, 66[13] (cf. Dupont-Sommer ibid. 81, Porten & Yardeni sub TADAE B 1.1 :: Bauer & Meissner SbPAW '36, 415, 421: l. ›*dr* = Sing. abs. of ›*dr*$_2$); act. s.f. abs. ›*bdh* Aḥiq 94; HAPH Pf. 3 p.s.m. *hwbd* KAI 279[2] (cf. Garbini Kand 9 :: Nober VD xxxvii 370 (div. otherwise): l. *hwbdw* = HOPH Pf. 3 p.pl.m. :: Rosenthal EI xiv 97*f: or l. *hwbd/r* = pious? < Iran.?); Impf. 3 p.pl.m. *yh*›*bdw* KAI 225[11]; cf. GIPP 53 - **Nab** QAL (or PA‹EL?) Pf. 3 p.s.m. ›*bd* J 109[3] (= RES 1187, cf. RES 1291C; uncert. reading) - ¶ verb QAL - **1)** to perish, to go to ruin, to be devastated, to be lost - a) said of a country: EA 288[52] - b) said of a people or person: KAI 181[7], 226[10], Driv 8[2,4], DJD ii 45[7] (›*bdw bḥrb*) - c) said of someone's possessions: Cowl 30[16]; said of vegetables: Sem ii 31 conc. 3 (cf. Milik Bibl xlviii 554f., Porten Arch 126, Teixidor Syr xlviii 480 :: Dupont-Sommer Sem ii 33f.: to get lost (said of an animal; v. ›*lp*$_3$)); said of a hide: Sem xxi 85 conv. 5; said of a marriage price: Cowl 15[27], Krael 7[25] (to be lost, to go forfeit; :: Fitzmyer FS Albright ii 164, WA 265: or *mhrh y*›*bd* = he shall lose his (or her) bride-price; for parallels, cf. Muffs 181, 206) - d) said of wisdom: Aḥiq 94; of justice?: Cowl 71[28]; for MAI xiv/2, 66[13], v. *qwm*$_1$ - PA‹EL to cause to perish, to exterminate, to wipe out: KAI 222B 36, 223B 7 (+ obj., someone's name; cf. Greenfield FS Fitzmyer 48) - HAPH/YIPH to cause to perish, to destroy, to annihilate, to wipe out; + obj. - a) a country: KAI 223C

5 - b) persons: KAI 225[11] - c) an inscription: KAI 223C 4 - on this root, cf. Jenni SVT xvi 143ff.
v. *ʾbd₂*, *ʾdr₁*, *brr*.

ʾbd₂ **Mo** Sing. cstr. *ʾbd* KAI 181[7] - ¶ subst. destruction, downfall, ruin; *wyšrʾl ʾbd ʾbd ʿlm* KAI 181[7]: and Israel perished an everlasting perishing (i.e. perished utterly), cf. e.g. Segert Arch Or xxix 224 (cf. also Auffret UF xii 112f.) × he perished forever, the first *ʾbd* being QAL Inf. abs. of *ʾbd₁* and the second *ʾbd* being QAL Pf. 3 p.s.m. of *ʾbd₁*, cf. e.g. Solá-Solé IS 121, Gibson SSI i p 78, cf. also S.R.Driver HTBS p. lxxxix, Ceresko JLNS 140, Andersen Or xxxv 99, Jackson & Dearman SMIM 98 :: Dahood FS Horn 432, de Moor UF xx 152: *ʾbd* in both instances = QAL Pf. 3 p.s.m. of *ʾbd₁*; cf. also Held JANES iii 51 n.31.

ʾbhysyts (< Prakrit, cf. Henning BSOAS xiii 84, Kutscher, Naveh & Shaked Lesh xxxiv 128) - **OffAr** *ʾbhysyts* BSOAS xiii 82[6] - ¶ subst. (declensional form): of the anointed.

ʾbwl v. *ʾbl₃*.

ʾbzkr v. *ʾškr₁*.

ʾbṭyḥ **Hebr** Plur. abs. *ʾbṭyḥyn* SM 49[2] - ¶ subst. melon - on this word, cf. Borowski AIAI 137.

ʾby₁ v. *ʾbt*, *nʾb*, *yʾb*, *qwm₁*.

ʾby₂ **Hatra** Sing. emph. *ʾbyʾ* 345[3], 361[1], Ibr 9[1] - p subst. lord, patrician Hatra 345[3], 361[1], Ibr 9[1] (cf. also Segal JSS xxxi 60: prob. = cheikh) :: al-Najafi Sumer xxxix p. 176: = petty king.

ʾbyb v. *ʾbb*.

ʾbygdn v. *ʾbgrn*.

ʾbygrn v. *ʾbgrn*.

ʾbydh v. *ʿbdh*.

ʾbyt v. *ʾb₁*.

ʾbl₁ v. *ybl₁*.

ʾbl₂ v. *plʾ₁*.

ʾbl₃ (< Akkad., cf. Zimmern Fremdw 14, Kaufman AIA 32) - **Palm** Sing. emph. *ʾblʾ* RB xxxix 548[6] - **Hatra** Sing. emph. *ʾbwlʾ* 272[1], 297[2], 379, Ibr 14[3] - ¶ subst. m. - **1)** gateway: Hatra 272[1], 297[2], 379, Ibr 14[3] (for 297[2], v. *gd₁*) - **2)** (entrance-)hall: RB xxxix 548[6] (of tomb construction) - cf. Marrassini FLEM 126f.

ʾbl₄ = sad, mournful > Akkad. (*abbālu*), cf. v.Soden Or xlvi 183.

ʾbl₅ (< *ʾy₂* + *bl₃*, cf. FR 249,1) - **Ph** *ʾbl* KAI 10[13] - **Pun** *ʾbl* KAI 70[4], ICO-Spa 14 (??, no context preserved), *ʾybl* KAI 69[18,21], 74[11] (prob. also in CIS i 5510[4], cf. Février BAr '46/49, 171 :: Chabot BAr '41/42, 388, 393: l. *ʾyb* (= QAL Pf. 3 p.s.m. or QAL Part. act. s.m. abs. of

›*yb_1*?) + *l_5* = he was inimical towards) - ¶ negation, cf. FR 318,2c (:: Dunand BMB v 82: ›*bl* in KAI 10^{13} = affirmative particle) - poss. also in the comb. ›*ybl* ›*m*: KAI 119^7, cf. Février RA l 188, CB viii 39, Fuentes Estañol VF s.v. '*bl_1*: only (:: Segert JSS xvii 139: = derivative of root *ybl_1*? :: v.d.Branden BiOr xxxi 225 (cf. idem BiOr xxxvi 202; div. otherwise): l. ›*ybl*›*m* = YIPH Pf. 3 p.s.m. + suff. 3 p.pl.m. of *bly_1* (= to make use of (something/someone) completely)).

›**bl_6** v. *bn_1*.

›**bn_1** v. ‹*bn*.

›**bn_2** **Ph** Sing. abs. ›*bn* KAI 10^5; Sing./Plur. cstr. ›*bn* RES 1204^2 (diff. reading) - **Pun** Sing. abs. ›*bn* CIS i 3784^2, RES 165^1, 171^1, 779^1, KAI 78^5, $79^{7f.}$, IAM 123^1, etc., ‹*bn* RES 164^1, 167^1, 168^1, KAI 150^1, Punica xx 2^2 (rather than ‹*kn*, thus Chabot Punica a.l.), Sem xxxvi 33^1, etc., *hbn* Punica iv 7^1, xii 15^1, 25^1, KAI 151^1 (:: Röllig KAI a.l.: poss. = article + noun, cf. also Fuentes Estañol VF s.v. ›*bn_1*), *hb* Punica xii 17^1 (lapsus), *hbnt* Punica iv $7^{4f.}$ (prob. no lapsus); cf. also KAI 135^1 *ṭ*‹›*n* pro *ṭ*‹*n*› ›*bn* (lapsus?); cstr. ›*bn* IAM 2^1 (?, diff. and dam. context); Plur. abs. ›*bnm* KAI 100^2, 139^2 - **Samal** Sing. cstr. ›*bn* KAI 215^7 (:: Halévy RS i 219: l. *b*‹*l* (= Sing. cstr. of *b*‹*l_2*)); Plur. abs. (casus obliquus) ›*bny* KAI 214^{31} - **DA** Sing. cstr. ›*bn* DA p. 267 no. 2 - **OffAr** Sing. abs. ›*bn* Cowl 15^{16}, 30^{10}, 31^9, Krael 7^{19}; cstr. ›*bn* Krael 7^{18}; emph. ›*bn*› Cowl 30^9; Plur. cstr. ›*bny* Cowl 5^7, 6^{14}, 8^{14}, Krael 3^6, $4^{15,21}$, etc. - **Nab** Plur. cstr. ›*bny* DBKP 22^{33} (for this poss. reading, cf. Yardeni with Yadin & Greenfield DBKP a.l.) - **Palm** Sing. (or Plur.) emph. ›*bn*› MUSJ xxxviii 106^{10} (cf. Ingholt MUSJ xxxviii 117 n. 3) - **JAr** Plur. emph. ›*bny*› MPAT 50d 3 (›*bny[*›*]*; for this uncert. reading, cf. Beyer ATTM 316), 51^7 - ¶ subst. f. - **1)** stone (object): KAI 214^{31}, especially a) building stone: KAI 10^5, 100^2, MPAT 51^7 - b) tombstone, memorial stone: RES 168^1, 173^1, 779^1, Punica iv $6^{1,4}$, $7^{1,4f.}$, $8^{1,5}$, xiA 4^1 - c) votive stele: CIS i 3784^2, KAI 78^5, Hofra 106^1 - d) for KAI 139^2, cf. Sznycer Sem xxvii 56f. - **2)** stone (material); *mš* ›*bn* CIS i 3777^1: stele of stone (:: Dussaud BAr '22, 244f., CRAI '46, 383: divide *mš*› *bn* = sacrifice of a son; cf. however Dussaud Syr xvi 408); *mzbḥ* ›*bn* KAI 77^1: an altar of stone; cf. also Antas v 1 (for context, v *ḥrṣ*$_5$), Cowl 15^{16}, $30^{9,10}$, 31^9, Krael 7^{19} - **3)** weight; a) in *b*›*bny mlk*› = according to the royal weight: Cowl 5^7, 6^{14}, 8^{14}, Krael 3^6, etc. - b) in *[b*›*]bny ptḥ* Cowl 11^2: according to the weight of Ptah; cf. Wag 212f., Rainey BASOR clxxix 34f., Porten Arch 63f., 66, 68f., cf. also Trinquet SDB v 1240f.; Caquot & Lemaire Syr liv 190: ›*bn šr*‹› DA p. 267 no. 2: = weight of Sh. (less prob. interpret., cf. Franken DA p. 15); cf. poss. also *b*›*bny nbṭw* DBKP 22^{33} (uncert. reading, v. supra): according to the Nabatean weight (cf. Greek par. ζύγωι Μαωζ[ας]) and ›*bn ṣr* RES

1204^2 (v. supra): according to the weight of T. (cf. e.g. Cooke NSI p. 43, Chabot RES a.l., Teixidor Sem xxix 10f. :: Catastini RSF xiii 6f.: = stone of Tyre) - **4)** *ʾbn šḥt* KAI 215^7 designation of an usurpator (v. *šḥt*$_2$) :: Montgomery JAOS liv 423: *ʾbn* = *ʾbn*$_4$ (= *bn*$_1$ preceded by *alef* prosth.) - for *ʾbn ṣrp*, v. *ṣrp*$_2$; for *ʾbn šš*, v. *šš*$_1$ - Vattioni AION xvi 47: *aban* in IRT 886a 7f. = Sing. abs. (cf. however idem Aug xvi 545, *(yrir)aban* = n.p., cf. also IRT 886h 1 (cf. Aug xvi 548)).
v. *ʾdn*$_3$, *lbnh*$_1$, *pḥmt*.

ʾbn$_3$ v. *ʾdn*$_1$.

ʾbn$_4$ v. *ʾbn*$_2$, *bn*$_1$.

ʾbst **Pun** Sing. abs. *ʾbst* ICO-Malta 31^2 - ¶ subst. of uncert. meaning: receptacle, bowl?

ʾbr$_1$ cf. Frah x 37 (*ʾblh*): penis :: Schaeder with Ebeling Frah a.l.: l. *ʾyrh* = form of *ʾyr* (= penis) :: Ebeling Frah a.l.: *ʾyrh* = lapsus for *ysrh* (= form of *ysr*$_3$ (= penis)).
v. *ʾbr*$_3$.

ʾbr$_2$ **Hebr** Plur. + suff. 3 p.s.f. *ʾbryh* AMB 4^{17} - **Palm** Sing. (or Plur.?) emph. *ʾbr[ʾ]* SBS 51^3 - **JAr** Plur. abs. *ʾbryn* AMB 9^3 - ¶ subst. - **1)** limb: AMB 4^{17}, 9^3 - **2)** wing (mil.), cf. Caquot GLECS vii 77, Degen WO viii 132 - on nominal derivatives of the same root, cf. Masson RPAE 72.
v. *ʾmr*$_2$.

ʾbr$_3$ **Hatra** Sing. emph. *ʾbrʾ* 8 (for the reading, cf. Aggoula Ber xviii 88; v. infra) - ¶ subst. of uncert. meaning (diff. context); Aggoula Ber xviii 88: = plumber (cf. Vattioni IH a.l.) :: Altheim & Stiehl AAW ii 195: = Sing. emph. of *ʾbr*$_1$.

ʾbr$_4$ v. *ʾbrw*.

ʾbrh v. *ʾbrt*.

ʾbrw **Samal** Sing. abs. *ʾbrw* KAI 214^{15,21} - ¶ subst. force, power? (cf. e.g. Cooke NSI p. 168, Friedr 33*, Koopmans 36, Dion p. 134 (cf. also Lagrange ERS 493) :: Montgomery JAOS liv 422: = *brw* (= sonship) preceded by *alef* prosth. :: Nöldeke ZDMG xlvii 104: = Plur. m. + suff. 3 p.s.m. of *ʾbr*$_4$(= his members); diff. context - Kornfeld WZKM lxi 13f.: *ʾbrty* on sarcophage (no 2607) with J.Ar. inscription poss. = Sing. + suff. 1 p.s. of *ʾbrw* (imposs. interpret.; = n.p.).
v. *sʿd*.

ʾbrḥt v. *rḥ*$_1$.

ʾbrt **OffAr** Sing. abs. *ʾbrt* Krael 4^7, 9^7, 12^{8,16} (v. infra) - ¶ subst. only attested in the expression *lʾbrt*; uncert. meaning (cf. Grelot DAE p. 222 n. e), Cazelles Syr xxxii 79: = circumference?? (cf. also Porten & Greenfield JEAS p. 45; cf. Porten & Yardeni sub TADAE B 3.5 a.e.:

in area?) :: Krael p. 173: *ʾbrt* = Plur. cstr. of *ʾbrh*, *lʾbrt* = to an exterior (total) of, to the outside?, cf. the criticism of Kutscher JAOS lxxiv 235f.
v. *ʾdr_1*.

ʾbšwk (< Iran., cf. Driv p. 53, Hinz AISN 18) - **OffAr** Plur. abs. *ʾbšwkn* Driv 5^5 - ¶ subst. m., prob. meaning: deserter; Eilers AfO xvii 332: = mentioned above (< Iran.); Porten & Yardeni sub TADAE A 6.7: = presser?

ʾbšwn (< Iran., cf. R.A.Bowman Pers p. 47, 63, Hinz NWAP 45, AISN 19) - **OffAr** Sing. abs. *ʾbšwn* Pers 2^3, 3^4, 9^3, 12^2, 21^3, 26^4, 27^5, 28^3, 29^4, 37^4, etc.; emph. *ʾbšwnʾ* Pers 13^3 (*ʾb[š]wnʾ*; :: Naveh & Shaked Or xlii 455 n. 69: reading of last ʾ uncert.), 15^4 - ¶ subst. m. pestle; for survey of pestles in Persepolis, cf. R.A.Bowman Pers 48f.

ʾbšnp v. *ʾškp*.

ʾbšp **Hatra** Milik DFD 388: the *ʾbšpʾ* in Hatra 106A = Sing. emph. of *ʾbšp* (prob. indication of function); uncert. interpret.; Safar Sumer xviii 26, 27 n. 3, Caquot Syr xli 252: = n.p.; Aggoula MUSJ xlvii 38f.: = *ʾb_1* (Sing. cstr. = head) + *špʾ* (= Plur. emph. of *špy_2* (= sculptor)), less prob. interpret.; Tubach ISS 423 (n. 813): = *ʾb_1* (Sing. cstr.) + *špʾ* (= Sing. emph. of *šp_2* (= variant of *sp_3*)), less prob. interpret.

ʾbt **Ph** Sing. abs. *ʾbt* KAI 26A i 12 (v. however infra) - ¶ subst. of uncert. meaning: = a father's (legal) power, status of a father? (cf. Albright with O'Callaghan CBQ xi 240, O'Callaghan Or xviii 185, Alt WO i 281, Levi Della Vida RCL '49, 283f., Friedrich Or xx 203, Pedersen ActOr xxi 51, Rosenthal ANET 654, Donner OA viii 101, Röllig KAI a.l., FR 207, Paul Maarav ii 181, Puech RB lxxxviii 97) × Dupont-Sommer Oriens ii 124, Dunand BMB viii 30, Dahood PNSP 25 n. 2, Bibl xliv 70, 291, lx 429, Or xlvi 465, Ps iii 104, Ginsberg FS Gaster 138, Lipiński RSF ii 48, RTAT 258 n. 65, OLZ '82, 459, SV 48, Avishur PIB 228f., Bron RIPK 60ff., Swiggers BiOr xxxvii 339, Gibson SSI iii p. 58, Fuentes Estañol VF s.v. *ʾb_1*: = Plur. abs. of *ʾb_1* (cf. also Paul EI xiv 33 n. 23) :: v.d.Branden Meltô i 42: = honour :: Dupont-Sommer RA xlii 171, Obermann Conn xxxviii 22: = (good)will (< root *ʾby*) :: Marcus & Gelb JNES viii 119: = desire (< root *ʾby*) :: Gordon JNES viii 113, Zolli Sef x 168: = war (< root *ʾyb*). For the diff. context, v. *pʿl_1*.

ʾgbl v. *ʾlh_1*.

ʾgd_1 **Ph** QAL (?) Inf. cstr. (?, v. infra) *ʾgd* MUSJ xlv 262^5 - **Hebr** NIPH Part. s.m. abs. *nʾgd* SM 49^2; s.f. abs. *nʾgdt* SM 49^{2}- ¶ verb NIPH to be tied up; *pwl hmṣry hnʾgd bšyph* SM $49^{2f.}$: the Egyptian beans which are tied up with bark; *hmynth̠ hnʾgdt bpny ʿṣmh* SM 49^2: the mint which is tied up in its special way (for both instances, cf. Sussmann Tarb xliii 112) - the interpret. of MUSJ xlv 262[5] highly uncert. (verb?); Starcky MUSJ xlv 271, Röllig NESE ii 11: = to bind, to tie together (Starcky MUSJ xlv 262: > to collect; cf. also Cross IEJ xxix 44: to bind over (to)) :: v.d.Branden BiOr xxxiii 12: = Sing. abs. of *ʾgd_2* (= band > equipage) :: Schiffmann RSF iv 176f.: l. *lʾ gd* = *lʾ*$_1$ + derivative of root *gdd*$_1$ or *gwd*$_1$ (= to invade), highly improb. interpret.

ʾgd_2 v. *ʾgd_1*.

ʾgdd **Ph** Plur. abs. *ʾgddm* KAI 26A i 15 (cf. FR p. 37 n. 1) - ¶ subst. gang of bandits (cf. also Bron RIPK 67) - on this word, cf. also Garr DGSP 47.
v. *gdd*$_2$.

ʾgdyl v. *ʾryh*$_1$.

ʾgwz **Hebr** Plur. abs. *ʾgwzyn* SM 49[20] - ¶ subst. nut.

ʾgwr_1 (< Akkad. < Sum., cf. Zimmern Fremdw 68, Kaufman AIA 48, 139 (cf. also ibid. 161f., 164), Greenfield JNES xxxvii 95) - **OffAr** Sing. cstr. *ʾgwr* Krael 3[9]; emph. *ʾgwrʾ* Cowl 13[14], 25[6], 30[6,7], Krael 4[10], 12[18], etc., etc.; Plur. cstr. *ʾgwry* Cowl 30[14], 31[13] - ¶ subst. m. temple, sanctuary; mostly used of the temple of YHW in Elephantine; Cowl 30[14], 31[13]: temples of Egyptian gods.

ʾgwr_2 **Palm** Sing. emph. *ʾgwrʾ* CIS ii 3913 i 9, 11 - ¶ subst. m. tax farmer (cf. Greek par. i 10 μισθουμένῳ, i 13 μισθούμενον).

ʾgwr_3 v. *ʾgr*$_3$.

ʾgwr_4 (< Akkad., cf. Kaufman AIA 33 (n. 15), cf. also v. Soden AHW s.v. *agurru*) - **OffAr** Plur. abs. *ʾgwrn* FuB xiv 24[2] (diff. reading; Akkad. par. *a-gur-ru*) - ¶ subst. kiln-fired brick.

ʾgwry v. *ʾgr*$_3$.

ʾglh (< Akkad. < Sum., cf. Kaufman (& Lipiński) AIA 55 n. 115, Lipiński Stud 97ff. (cf. also id. WGAV 381f.), cf. however Millard JSS xxi 176) - **OffAr** Sing. abs. *ʾglh* KAI 236[2] (:: Lidzbarski AUA 17: l. *ʾplh* = n.p. :: Donner KAI a.l.: l. *ʾplʾ* = n.p.) - ¶ subst. palace (??, for litt., v. supra; highly uncert. interpret., cf. Fales OA xvi 66: prob. = n.l.).

ʾgm_1 **OffAr** Sing. emph. *ʾgmʾ* ATNS 68 i 7 (diff. and dam. context) - **JAr** (in Hebr. context) Sing. emph. *ʾgmh* SM 49[8] - ¶ subst. exact meaning unknown: reed (land) or uncleared ground?

ʾgm_2 v. *w*$_2$.

ʾgn_1 (for the origin, cf. Zimmern Fremdw 33, Ellenbogen 8, Kaufman AIA 33) - **Ph** Sing. abs. *ʾgn* MUSJ xlv 262[4] (v. infra :: v.d.Branden BiOr xxxiii 12: = Qal Impf. 1 p.s. of *gnn*$_1$), Kition D 35, EI xviii 117[1] (= IEJ xxxv 83) - **Hebr** Plur. abs. *ʾgnt* TA-H 1[10] - **OffAr** Sing. cstr.,

cf. Warka 5: *ag-gan-nu*, Warka 9: *ag-ga-nu*; Plur. abs. *ʾgnn* RES 1300[7] - **Nab** Sing. emph. *ʾgnʾ* CIS ii 423B 1 (for the reading, cf. Littmann PAES iv 88, Milik DFD 109) - **Palm** Sing. *ʾgnʾ* PNO 21a; cf. the fragment PNO 49: the same word?? - ¶ subst. m. crater, open bowl, basin (cf. Teixidor Syr lii 266); the *hʾgn hz* of Kition D 35 written on a fragment of a big jar or amphora; for the diff. text MUSJ xlv 262[4], cf. Starcky MUSJ xlv 270, Röllig NESE ii 10 - Greenstein JANES viii 50, 54: the *ʾagn* (= Sing. abs./cstr., cf. also Owen Sar p. 102) in Sar 6^1 = Ph. - on this word, cf. also Amadasi Guzzo Sem xxxviii 22f.
v. *ʾgn₂*, *yyn*.

ʾgn₂ **Palm** Sing. cstr. (?) *ʾgn* RTP 76, 77, 78, 79, etc. (v. infra) - ¶ subst. prob. kind of religious assembly (symposium?); cf. Milik DFD 108f.: = *ʾgn₁* (= crater, open bowl > symposium; cf. also Gawlikowski Syr xlviii 412) :: du Mesnil du Buisson TMP 456ff.: < Greek ἀγών :: Torrey JAOS xxvi 113 n. 2 (editorial note), Caquot RTP p. 143: = Aph Imper. s.m. of *gnn₁* :: Lidzbarski Handb 251: = Aph Pf. 3 p.s.m. of *gnn₁* :: Lidzbarski Eph ii 320: < *gnn₃* = to lie down (cf. also Caquot RTP p. 143) - occurring in the following formulae: a) *ʾgn bl* RTP 84, 85, 86, 87, 89, etc., etc. - b) *ʾgn bl wʾblʿly* RTP 93 (cf. Milik DFD 111) - c) *ʾgn bl wblʿstr* RTP 125 - d) *ʾgn bl bny bwlḥʾ* RTP 82 - e) *ʾgn bl bny bwlʿʾ* RTP 83, 107 - f) *ʾgn bl bny bḥr* RTP 106 (v. sub n) - g) *ʾgn bl bny gwgʾ* RTP 80, 100 - h) *ʾgn bl bny gwgw* RTP 81 - i) *ʾgn bl bny ḥnwr* RTP 97 (cf. Milik DFD 313) - j) *ʾgn bl bny ydyʿbl* RTP 124 (cf. also RTP 95) - k) *ʾgn bl bny nwrbl* RTP 123 - l) *ʾgn bl bny sknʾ* RTP 96 (Teixidor MUSJ xlii 178, Milik DFD 118: pro *sknʾ* l. *mknʾ*) - m) *ʾgn bl bny ʿgrwd* RTP 99 - n) *ʾgn bl bny qṣmyt* RTP 106 (v. sub f) - o) *ʾgn bl bny šmwn* RTP 79 - p) *ʾg[n bl] bny t–* RTP 102 (highly uncert. reading, cf. Milik DFD 118: l. *ʾr[ṣw] bny ḥ[lʾ]...*) - q) *ʾgn bl bʿltk* RTP 76, 77 (for *bʿltk*, v. *bʿl₂*; var. *ʾgn bltk*?, uncert. reading: RTP 437) - r) *ʾgn bl ḥrtʾ* RTP 133 - s) *ʾgn bl wḥrtʾ wnny* RTP 134 - t) *ʾgn bl yrḥy* RTP 88 - u) *ʾgn bl wnbw bny ʿlyy* RTP 137 - v) *ʾgn bl qšṭʾ* RTP 78 - w) *ʾgn bl šmš* RTP 138 - x) *ʾgn bl wšmš* RTP 140 - y) *ʾgn bl wšmš wbny zbdbwl* RTP 141 - z) *ʾgn grʿtʾ dy bl* RTP 680 (v. *grʿh*) - aa) *ʾgn šmš bny šʿdw* RTP 341 - bb) on Syr xxxvi 104 no. 3 *ʾgn* on itself? or to be combined with the *yrḥbwl* on the other side?

ʾgnn **Pun** Sing. abs. *ʾgnn* KAI 69[11], CIS i 3915[5] - ¶ subst. of uncert. meaning; only in the expression *ṣpr ʾgnn* = bird of enclosure > domesticated bird?? (*ʾgnn* derived from *gnn₁* = to protect, to enclose (cf. also Février CB viii 41)) × Dussaud Orig 141: = rooster (cf. Delcor Sem xxxviii 89f.) :: Tomback CSL s.v.: = bowl ?.

ʾgr₁ **OldAr** Qal Impf. 1 p.s. + suff. 2 p.s.m. *ʾgrk* KAI 223C 8 (reading *k* uncert., cf. Veenhof BiOr xx 144, Degen AAG p. 19, 71 (n. 63), cf.

also Rössler TUAT i 186 :: Fitzmyer AIS 82, 91: l. *ʾgr* (= QAL Impf. 1 p.s.) *w* (of same root; cf. also Lemaire & Durand IAS 118, 128) :: Gibson SSI ii p. 45f.: l. *ʾgr w*, *ʾgr* = QAL Part. pass. with meaning "hireling" :: Dupont-Sommer Sf p. 121, 142, Donner KAI a.l.: l. *ʾgr w*, *ʾgr* = QAL Impf. 1 p.s. of *gwr* (= to be exiled); cf. Segert ArchOr xxxii 126, AAG par. 5.7.6.9); Inf. *ʾgr* KAI 223C 8 (for problems concerning derivation, v supra (cf. also Ben-Chayyim Lesh xxxv 250) :: Gibson SSI ii p. 45: = QAL Part. act. s.m.) - **OffAr** QAL Pf. 2 p.s.m. *ʾgrt* ATNS 59[1] (?, dam. context; or = Sing. abs./cstr. of *ʾgrt*?); Impf. 1 p.s. *[ʾ]gr* MAI xiv/2, 66[14] (uncert. reading, cf. also Porten & Yardeni sub TADAE B 1.1: l. *lʾgr*? = *l*$_5$ + QAL Inf.; or preferably *ʾgr* = Sing. cstr. of *ʾgr*$_2$?, oral communication of Wesselius); Part. pass. m./pl.f. abs. *ʾgyrn* ATNS 73[4] (?, heavily dam. context) - **Nab** QAL Pf. 3 p.s.m. *ʾgr* MPAT 64 i 12 (dam. context); Impf. 3 p.s.m. *yʾgr* CIS ii 220[2], 224[9]; APH Impf. 3 p.s.m. *ywgr* CIS ii 197[7], 199[6], 206[4], 214[5], 217[6]; 3 p.pl.m. *ywgrwn* CIS ii 212[3] - **Palm** QAL Pf. 3 p.s.m. *ʾgr* CIS ii 3913 ii 77; ITP Pf. 3 p.s./pl.(?)m *ʾ[t]ʾgr* CIS ii 3913 ii 65 -
verb QAL - **1)** to hire, to engage; + *b*$_2$ obj. (or pret.?): CIS ii 3913 ii 77; in KAI 223C 8: to pay wages to, to reward (+ obj., v. however supra) - **2)** to hire, to take on lease; + obj.: CIS ii 220[2], 224[9] - APH to let, to rent (out); + obj.: CIS ii 197[7], 206[4], 214[5], etc. - ITP to be provided, to be laid down (sc. of contract of lease; dam. context) - a form of this root (*]ʾgr[*) in ATNS 60[6]?? - Segal ATNS a.l.: l. *ʾgyr* in ATNS 10 i a 7 and *ʾgr* in ATNS 10 i a 8, both forms of this root, reading however highly improb., cf. Porten & Yardeni sub TADAE B 8.2: l. *ʾyr* (= name of month) in both instances.

ʾgr$_2$ **OffAr** Sing. abs. *ʾgr* Cowl 69A 12, Aḥiq 164; cstr. *ʾgr* NESE i 11[3] - **Hatra** Sing. cstr. *ʾgr* 344[7] - **JAr** Sing. + suff. 3 p.pl.m. *ʾgrhwn* Syn D B 5 (= SM 88[20]; for this reading, cf. Torrey Syn 263) -
subst. - **1)** rent; *ʾgr ʾlpʾ* NESE i 11[3]: rent of the ship - **2)** wages, salary: Cowl 69A 12 (for the reading of the context, cf. Porten & Yardeni sub TADAE B 8.5); *bʿl ʾgr* Aḥiq 164: employer (cf. Lindenberger APA 165f., 268 nn. 502-503 :: Grelot RB lxviii 191, DAE p. 445: = (money) lender :: Ginsberg ANET 429: = neighbour, reading *ʾgr*$_4$ = wall (cf. Cowl p. 245: or = co-tenant, reading *ʾgr*$_4$ = wall > roof (for this meaning, cf. Zimmern Fremdw 31, Marrassini FLEM 90 n. 3)) - **3)** price: Hatra 344[7] - for *mr ʾgrʾ*, v. *mrʾ* - this word (Sing. abs./cstr.) poss. also in ATNS 44 ii 5 (heavily dam. context; Porten & Yardeni sub TADAE B 8.2: or = form of *ʾgr*$_4$?).
v. *ʾgr*$_{2,4}$, *mrʾ*.

ʾgr$_3$ **Palm** Plur. emph. *ʾgwryʾ* CIS ii 3913 i 5, *ʾgryʾ* CIS ii 3913 i 8 - subst. Plur. contract of lease (cf. Greek par. i ll. 6, 9: μισθώσει) ::

Cantineau Gramm 115: = Sing. emph. of subst. *ʾgwry* (with ending *-iy*), cf. Rosenthal Sprache 74.

ʾgr$_4$ (<Akkad., cf. Kaufman AIA 57) - **OffAr** Sing. abs. *ʾgr* Cowl 5^{4}, Krael 9^{9}, $10^{4,5,6}$, $12^{18,20}$; cstr. *ʾgr* Krael $9^{10,11}$, 10^{5}, cf. Warka 1: *ig-ga-ri* (also l. 28), cf. Landsberger AfO xii 251; emph. *ʾgrʾ* Cowl $5^{4,5,6,7}$, Krael 9^{8}, etc.; Plur. + suff. 3 p.s.m. *ʾgwrh* Krael 3^{4}; cf. Frah ii 16 (*ʿgl*; cf. Nyberg FP 62 :: Ebeling Frah a.l.: l. *ʾr* (= *ʾr$_3$* (= roof) < Akkad. *ûru*), cf. also Toll ZDMG-Suppl viii 29) - **JAr** Sing. emph. *ʾgrh* IEJ xxxii 8^{3} (?, heavily dam. context) -
subst. f. - **1)** wall: passim in **OffAr** texts, cf. Driver JRAS '32, 77, Krael p. 159 :: Wag 48 n. 1: vault :: Cowl p. 13: sort of archway, covered passage - *ʾgr bʾgr* Krael 9^{9}, $10^{4,5,6}$, $12^{18,26}$: wall to wall (said of two houses sharing a wall) - **2)** roof: IEJ xxxii 8^{3} (cf. Naveh EI xx 307 :: L.I.Levine IEJ a.l.: or = Sing. emph. of *ʾgr$_2$* (= wages)?); cf. also Frah ii 16 - this word also in Punic??: CIS i 5510^{10}, cf. Février BAr '46/49, 173 (v. also *gnh$_1$*).
v. *ʾgr$_2$*, *bny$_1$*, *gnh$_1$*.

ʾgr$_5$ v. *drg$_2$*.

ʾgrh v. *ʾgrt*.

ʾgrt (< Akkad., cf. Zimmern Fremdw 19, Ellenbogen 12, Kaufman AIA 48; cf. also Köbert Or xiv 278f., v.Soden Or xxxv 8, xlvi 185, Muffs 187 n. 4, Degen Or xliv 118) - **OffAr** Sing. abs. *ʾgrh* Cowl $30^{18,19,24,29}$, $31^{17,28}$, 40^{3}, NESE iii 48^{8}, *ʾgrt* Cowl 30^{7}, 31^{6}, 38^{10}, 41^{5}, Driv 10^{2}, 12^{1} (cf. Leand 58a; for the abs. form, cf. Wesselius AION xxx 267); cstr. *ʾgrt* CIS ii 30^{1} (= Del 19 = AECT 21), 37 (= Del 20 = AECT 35; prob. reading, heavily dam. context), KAI 233^{4}, Driv 12^{4}, AG 5^{4}, NESE iii 48^{9} (?), AECT F 2; emph. *ʾgrtʾ* Cowl 42^{7}, SSI ii 28 rev. 2, 6, RES 1808^{3} (= HDS 163 = Sem xxxiii 94^{6}), 1809^{3} (= HDS 165 = Semxxxiii 94^{4}); + suff. 1 p.s. *ʾgrty* Krael 13^{8}; Plur. emph. *ʾgrtʾ* Cowl 37^{15} - **Palm** Sing. emph. *ʾgrtʾ* CIS ii 3913 ii 104, 121, SBS 45^{7} (*ʾg[rtʾ]*) -
subst. f. (cf. however Cowl 30^{24}, Krael 13^{8}) - **1)** letter; *ʾgrt ʾršm* Driv 12^{4}: a letter from A., cf. Krael 233^{4}, AG 5^{4}, KAI 13^{8}, cf. also *ʾgrt mn ʾršm* Driv 12^{1}: idem; *ʾgrtʾ zylk ʿl ktwn* SSI 28 rev. 2: your letter about a tunic - **2)** contract; *ʾgrtʾ kspʾ* CIS ii 30^{1} (= Del 19 = AECT 21): contract concerning silver (cf. Paul Bibl lxv 107f.), cf. also AECT F 2.
v. *ʾgr$_1$*.

ʾd$_1$ v. *ʾdn$_1$*.

ʾd$_2$ v. *ʾḥd$_4$*.

ʾd$_3$ v. *ʾr$_2$*.

ʾd$_4$ v. *š$_{10}$*.

ʾdb v. *ʾrb*.

ʾdwn$_1$ (< Iran., cf. Driv p. 61, Hinz AISN 23) - **OffAr** Sing. emph. *ʾdwnʾ* Driv 6[5] -
subst. prob. meaning: stage of a journey (< way), cf. also Greenfield IrJu 10f.

ʾdwn$_2$ v. *ʾdn$_1$*.

ʾdwš (< Iran.?, cf. Altheim & Stiehl EW ix 193, x 244, GH ii 170, ASA 24f., GMA 347, cf. however Benveniste JA ccxlvi 38; v. also infra) - **OffAr** Plur. emph. (cf. Dupont-Sommer JA ccxlvi 24, Garbini Kand 9, Donner KAI a.l., cf. however Altheim & Stiehl EW ix 193, GH ii 170 n. 26, GMA 347 n. 20) *ʾdwšyʾ* KAI 279[2] -
subst. m. uncert. meaning; Altheim & Stiehl EW ix 193, ASA 265: who (/which) pleases not, is unfriendly, cf. also Nober VD xxxvii 372, Dupont-Sommer JA ccxlvi 25: = misfortune, adversity, trouble (cf. also Schwarzschild JAOS lxxx 156), cf. however Hinz AISN 34: l. *ʾrwšyʾ* = Plur. emph. of *ʾrwš* (= darkness) < Iran.

ʾdz v. *ʾrz$_3$*.

ʾdy$_1$ v. *ʾry$_1$*.

ʾdy$_2$ **Palm** obscure word in the expression *rḥymʾ ʾdyʾ* Inv viii 180[2], cf. Cantineau RB xlvi 307, Gramm 160, Syr xix 166.

ʾdyn **OffAr** Cowl 14[4], 20[1], Krael 6[1], 7[1], Driv 5[6], 7[1], ATNS 29 i 9 (cf. Porten & Yardeni B 8.1) etc., *ʾdn* Krael 5[1] (cf. Jansma BiOr xi 215); cf. Frah xxv 15, Paik 12-16, DEP 154 recto 3, GIPP 15, 45, SaSt 11 - **Hatra** Milik Syr xliv 297: l. *ʾdyn* in Hatra 49[3] (context highly uncert.; cf. also, with the same reading, Milik RN vi/iv 56 n. 2: *ʾdyn* = part of name of month); cf. Caquot Syr xxxii 54: poss. l. *ʾmyn* = amen) - **JAr** *dyn* (in *bdyn* < *bʾdyn*) MPAT 40[8,20,21] (*[b]dyn*) -
adv. then, on that day, at that moment, passim; after a specified date, *b 3 lkslw šnt 8 hw ywm 12 lthwt šnt 9 drywhwš mlkʾ ʾdyn byb byrtʾ ʾmr ydnyh* Cowl 25[1f.]: on the 3d of Kislev, year 8, that is the 12th of Thoth, the 9th year of king Darius, on that day Y. said in the fortress Yeb ..., cf. Cowl 20[1], 35[1], Krael 6[1], 8[1,9], 9[1,20], etc. (not a pecularity of a special scribe :: Joüon MUSJ xviii 63); *kzy* ... *ʾdyn* Driv 5[6], 7[1] (uncert. reading): when .... then - prec. by prep.: a) prec. by prep. *b$_2$*, *bdyn* (v. supra) MPAT 40[8,20,21]: now, at this moment - b) prec. by prep. *mn$_5$*, *mn ʾdyn* KAI 279[2]: since then (cf. Greek par. ἀπὸ τούτου) - on this word, cf. also Buth Maarav v/vi 33ff.

ʾdl v. *ʾry$_1$*.

ʾdm$_1$ **Ph** Sing. abs. *ʾdm* KAI 10[11,15], 13[3], 14[4,7,10,20], 26 A ii 4, iii 12f., iv 1, C iv 14, 30[4] (dam. context; cf. Honeyman Irâq vi 107, Albright BASOR lxxxiii 16, Röllig KAI a.l. (cf. also H.P.Müller ZA lxv 112f.), cf. however Dupont-Sommer RA xli 206ff., Masson & Sznycer RPC

18f., Puech Sem xxix 24: = n.d. :: Teixidor Syr l 423: or l. *ʾlm* (= Plur. abs. of *ʾl*$_1$)?; Puech Sem xxix 20 ff: l. this word also in KAI 30^{6} (heavily dam. context)), 37B 7 (for the reading, cf. e.g. Peckham Or xxxvii 305f., 322, Healy BASOR ccxvi 53, Masson & Sznycer RPC 26f., 62, Gibson SSI iii p. 126f., 131 :: e.g. Cooke NSI p. 68f., Röllig KAI a.l.: l. *ʾšm* = m. Plur. abs. of *ʾš*$_1$), 48^{4}, EpAn ix 5^{6}; cstr. *ʾdm* KAI 26A iii 13, C iv 14; Plur. abs. *ʾdmm* KAI 14^{6,22}, 37A 6, 60^{4,7} - **Pun** Sing. abs. *ʾdm* KAI 69^{14}, 75^{5}, 79^{9,11}, 89^{5}, 119^{5} (:: Levi Della Vida RSO xxxix 307: l. *ʾdn* = Sing. abs. of *ʾdn*$_1$), CIS i 169^{11}, 3783^{5}, 4937$^{2f.,6}$, 5510^{4} (*[ʾ]dm*), 5632^{4,7} (*[ʾ]dm*), RCL '66, 201^{7}, *ʿdm* KAI 165^{3} (cf. Levi Della Vida OA ii 83 n. 40, iv 65 :: Février BAr '51/'52, 41, 43, v.d.Branden RSF ii 145f. (div. otherwise): l. *ʿd* = *ʿd*$_7$ (cf. also Röllig KAI a.l.), v. also *kwn*$_1$); Plur. abs. *ʾdmm* KAI 69^{16,17}, CIS i 5510^{1,2,5} - **Hebr** Sing. abs. *ʾdm* KAI 194$^{5f.}$, DJD ii 43^{5} -

subst. m. man, person, someone: passim, in KAI 26A ii 4 coll.; *bn ʾdm* KAI 48^{4}: men, people (cf. KAI 165^{3}, v. supra); *kl ʾdm* KAI 10^{11}: everyone (KAI 13^{3}, 14^{4,7}, 75^{5}, 89^{5}, CIS i 169^{11}, 3783^{5}, 5632^{4}, DJD ii 43^{5}); + negation, no one - 1) *kl ʾdm ʾl ypth̟* KAI 14^{4}: let no one whoever open .... (cf. KAI 14^{20}) - **2)** *ʾyn šm ʾdm* KAI 194$^{5f.}$: there is no one there - **3)** *lbl gzly ʾdm* EpAn ix 5$^{5f.}$: so that no one might wrongfully seize it - Lipiński OLP viii 89: l. *ʾdm* (Sing. abs.) in KAI 193^{5} (highly uncert.) - Levi Della Vida OA ii 85: *adom* in IRT 879^{1} = Sing. abs. of *ʾdm*$_1$ (cf. FR 78a; cf. also Krahmalkov RSF iii 184, vi 29: = Sing. cstr.; uncert. interpret., cf. Vattioni AION xvi 41 (cf. idem Aug xvi 544): *adom* = part of n.p.) - Levi Della Vida OA ii 83 n. 40, 85: *adom* in Dreder 8^{2} = Sing. abs. of *ʾdm*$_1$, improb. interpret., cf. Vattioni Aug xvi 547: *adom* = part of n.p. - Milik DFD 298: l. *ʾdm* in Syr xvii 271^{8} (:: Cantineau Syr xvii 271: l. *ʾrn...*) = Ph. in text in palm script (diff. reading, cf. Gawlikowski Syr li 99) - Dupont-Sommer RA xli 207, Masson & Sznycer RPC 19: *ʾdm* in KAI 30^{4} = n.d. (improb. interpret., cf. Teixidor Syr l 423, cf. also H.P.Müller ZA lxv 112f.) - for the expression *mlk ʾdm* (instances not quoted supra), v. *mlk*$_5$.

v. *dm*$_1$, *šyr*$_1$, *šm*$_1$.

ʾdm$_2$ v. *dm*$_1$, *mlk*$_5$.

ʾdm$_3$ v. *mlk*$_5$.

ʾdm$_4$ v. *mlk*$_5$.

ʾdm$_5$ **Ph** Puech Sem xxix 36: ʾ in Kition D 14^{2} poss. = abbrev. of *ʾdm*$_5$ (= red); highly uncert. interpret. - Puech Sem xxix 29f.: ʾ (above name) in RPC 112b poss. = abbrev. of *ʾdm*$_5$ (= red wine); highly uncert. interpret.

ʾdmh **Pun** Sing. (:: Krahmalkov RSF iii 191: Plur.) abs. *ʾdmt* KAI 145^{3} -

subst. land (:: Krahmalkov RSF iii 191: = landed property, estate), cf. Sznycer Sem xxii 38. The reading *›dm[h]* in KAI 222A 10 prob., cf. also Degen AAG p. 9, ZDMG cxix 173, OLZ '71, 264 (uncert. whether noun Sing. abs. or n.l., cf. Fitzmyer AIS 36, Donner KAI a.l., Gibson SSI ii p. 36f., Degen AAG p. 48; or l. *›dm* (= n.g.)?, cf. Zadok AION xliv 530f., Sader EAS 128 (n. 43)).
v. *mlk$_5$*.

›dn$_1$ m. **Ph** Sing. abs. *›dn* CIS i 9[1] (*[›]dn*; for the reading, cf. DD 3[1]), RES 504a 1, b 1, KAI 43[9,14]; cstr. *›dn* KAI 14[18], 18[5], 19[5], 40[1], 43[4,5,6,8], MUSJ xlv 262[3], *›d* (assimilation of the *n* to the first consonant of the following word: *›dmlkm*; cf. FR 99b) KAI 42[2]; + suff. 3 p.s.m. *›dny* KAI 31[2], 32[4] (= Kition A 2), 41[3], RES 234[1], 930[2], 1213[4], Kition A 3[7] (= CIS i 14), A 5B (= CIS i 16), A 10 (= CIS i 23), A 25 (= CIS i 39), A 30[3], F 1[3] (= CIS i 88), DD 13[1] (:: Milik DFD 425: = Sing. + suff. 1 p.s.), 14[1], BMB xviii 106 iii; + suff. 1 p.s. *›dny* KAI 18[7], 26A i 10 (:: Lipiński RTAT 258: = Plur. + suff. 1 p.s.), Mus li 286[2,4,5] (cf. however Lane BASOR cxciv 44: = Plur.), cf. AnthGraeca vii 419,8: Αὐδονίς (= *ḥw* (Imper. s.m. of *ḥwy$_2$*) + *›dny*); + suff. 3 p.pl.m. *›dnnm* KAI 40[5] (cf. also Krahmalkov JSS xv 182), RES 367 i 2 (cf. Delavault & Lemaire RB lxxxiii 569ff., cf. however Lidzbarski Eph i 285ff.); + suff. 1 p.pl. *›dnn* KAI 12[3], 29[2], Sar 2[2] - **Pun** Sing. abs. *›dn* KAI 61a 4f., 61b 4, 63[1], 64[1], 66[1], etc., *‹dn* KAI 94[1], 107[1], 167[1], CIS i 299[2], 4143[2], Hofra 34[1], 141[1], 166[1], etc., *hdn* NP 3[1] (cf. Levi Della Vida Lib iii 95), *ḥdn* RES 340[1], *›dm* (lapsus) CIS i 1296[1], 2271[2], *‹dm* CIS i 840[1], *›d* Hofra 163[1], 169[1], Punica xviii/ii 122[1], *dn* RES 792[1], CIS i 324[1], 3262[1], 4007[2], Hofra 41[1], 133[1], etc. (in *ldn*, cf. FR 29b), *[›]d‹n* CIS i 948[1f.] (uncert. reading), *dl* (lapsus for *dn*) CIS i 3722[2], *‹d›n* Punica xi 9b 1, *›bn* (lapsus) CIS i 3710[2], 3934[2], *bn* (lapsus) CIS i 3734[3] (in *lbn*), *›n* (lapsus?) CIS i 1919[2], 2087[2], 3561[2], 3942[3], 4765[2], *‹n* (lapsus?) CIS i 2347[2], *›* (lapsus) CIS i 4071[2] (in *l›*), *›‹n* (lapsus?) CIS i 4593[2], *rdn* (lapsus) CIS i 5127[2], *›šn* (lapsus) RES 1581[2], *›rn* (lapsus) CIS i 3749[2], 5740[1], *›rl* (lapsus) CIS i 2957[2], *bdn* (lapsus) CIS i 669[1], cf. KAI 175[1]: λαδουν (= *l›dn*; cf. Friedrich ZDMG cvii 284, FR 29b); cstr. *›dn* BAr-NS i/ii 228[1] (cf. Garbini AION xxv 258ff.; diff. interpret.); + suff. 3 p.s.m. *›dny* CIS i 4905[4], *›ny* (lapsus?) Hofra 43[3f.], *›dn›* BAr '55/56, 31 no. 3[1] (= IAM 3), *›dnm* CIS i 276[2], 293[2], 3781[4], 4901[3], 4902[4], 4903[3], 4904[2f.], *›dnw* CIS i 5939[2] (uncert. reading); + suff. 3 p.s.f. *›dny* CIS i 280[4]; + suff. 1 p.s., cf. Poen 998, 1001: *donni* (for 1001 :: Sznycer PP a.l.: l. *donnim* pro *donni*); + suff. 1 p.pl. *›dnn* KAI 47[1], CIS i 624[2f.], 634[1f.], 2763[2f.], Moz vi 107 i (= SMI 25), ix 158[1] (= SMI 39) - **Hebr** Sing. abs. *[›]dn* TA-H 71[3] (dam. context; uncert. interpret.); + suff. 1 p.s. *›dny* KAI 192[1,2,4], 200[1], TA-H 18[1], 21[3], 40[10] (:: Aharoni BASOR cxcvii 30: l.

ʾrb[ʿ]; cf. also Pardee UF x 325), etc., *ʾdwny* DJD ii 30^{27}; + suff. 1 p.pl. *ʾdwnnw* AMB 3^{18} - **Nab** Sing. + suff. 3 p.s.f. *ʾdwnh* DBKP 22^{34} (prob. reading) - **JAr** Sing. cstr. *ʾdwn* MPAT 61^{24} (= DBKP 15); + suff. 3 p.s.f. *ʾdwnh* DBKP 17^{40} (diff. reading) - f. **Ph** Sing. + suff. 3 p.s.m. *ʾdtw* KAI 6^{2}, 7^{4} (cf. e.g. Röllig KAI a.l., FR 112a, Huehnergard with Wallenfels JANES xv 107 n. 209 :: Albright JAOS lxvii 157 n. 41, CF 15, Wallenfels JANES xv 107 (n. 209): in both instances = Plur. + suff. 3 p.s.m.); + suff. 3 p.s.f. *ʾdty* KAI 29^{2} (for older literature, cf. Eissfeldt OLZ xli 489ff.; cf. also FR 57 :: Segert JSS xvii 138) - **Palm** Sing. + suff. 3 p.s.m. *ʾdth* Syr xvii 355^{1} -
subst. m. lord, f. lady - **1)** title of a god (/goddess): IAM 3^{1}, cf. a) of Amon: KAI 118^{1} - b) of Ashtarte: KAI 29^{2} - c) of Baʿa.l.: KAI 137^{1}, RES 1545^{1}, 1838^{2}, 1904^{2}, Hofra 40^{1}, 64^{1}, 76^{1}, ICO-Sic 16^{1}, etc. - d) of Baʿal-Addir: RES 330^{1}, Hofra 4^{1}, 5^{1}, 6^{1}, 8^{1}, etc. - e) of Baʿal Hamm: KAI 61a 3f., 63^{1}, CIS i 180^{2}, etc., etc. - f) of Baʿal-Lebanon: KAI 31^{1} - g) of Baʿal-Shamim: KAI 18^{7}, 64^{1} - h) of Baʿalat-Gebal: KAI 6^{2}, 7$^{3f.}$ - i) of El: RES 504a 1 - j) of Eshmun: KAI 66^{1}, BMB xviii 106 i, ii -k) of Melqart: KAI 43^{9}, 47^{1}, Mus li 286^{2,4}, CIS i 88^{3} (= Kition F 1) - l) of Milk-Ashtart: CIS i 9^{1} (= DD 3), DD 13^{1}, 14^{1} - m) of Osiris: Mus li 286^{5}, RES 504b (??) - n) of Reshef: RES 1214$^{2f.}$ - o) of Reshef-*ʾlhyts*: RES 1213$^{4f.}$ - p) of Reshef-*ḥeṣ*: KAI 32^{4} - q) of Reshef(/Arshaf)-Melqart: KAI 72a 1 - r) of Reshef-*mkl*: KAI 40^{5} - s) of Shadrapha: KAI 77^{1}, 119^{1}, 127 - t) of Shalman: RES 930^{2} - u) of Ṣid-Addir: Antas 51^{1}, 78a 1, 80^{1}, 81^{1} (Ṣid-Ha'addir), 82^{1}, 83^{1} (Ṣid-Ha['addir]) - v) of God, *ʾdwnnw* AMB 3^{18} - lapsus: a) *lʾdn ltnt*: CIS i 401^{1}, 402$^{1f.}$, 3048^{1}, 3913$^{1f.}$, 4328^{1}, Hofra 120^{1} - b) *lʾdn lrbt ltnt* CIS i 4796$^{1f.}$, 5468$^{1f.}$ - c) *lʾdn rbt ltnt*: CIS i 4994^{1} - pro *lʾd[n]n tnt* CIS i 5599$^{1f.}$ l. prob.: *lʾr[bt]n tnt* - **2)** title given to human superior: KAI 192^{1,2,4}, 200^{1}, TA-H 18^{1}, etc.; with the meaning guardian: MPAT 61^{24} (= DBKP 15; cf. Greek par. ἐπιτρόπου), DBKP 17^{40}, 22^{34}; *ʾdn mlkm* KAI 14^{18}, 18^{5}, 19$^{5f.}$, 40^{1}, 42^{2} (*ʾdmlkm*), 43^{4,5,6,8}, MUSJ xlv 262^{3}: lord of kings (cf. Fitzmyer Bibl xlvi 45ff., Gibson SSI ii p. 114, iii p. 113, Galling ZDPV lxxix 145ff., Peckham DLPS 80ff. :: e.g. Milik DFD 424: = lord of kingdoms), title used to indicate the king of an empire as distinguished from a local king (cf. also Gibson SSI iii p.113, Elayi SCA 238ff.); *ʾdny* in Poen 998, 1001 (*donni*; v. supra) used as a polite way of addressing someone (cf. also Αὐδονίς Anth. Graeca vii 419,8, v. supra); *ʾdwny* in DJD ii 30^{27} = my husband (cf. also CIS i 5939^{2}??, v. also supra) - **3)** Palm. *ʾdth* (v. supra) uncert. meaning: = his lady > his spouse?, cf. Noth OLZ xl 345f., Eissfeldt OLZ xli 489f. - for *byt ʾdn*, v. *byt$_2$* - the *ʾṣ* in Antas 91 abbrev. of *ʾdn ṣd*?, cf. Fantar a.l. - in KAI 192$^{5f.}$ poss. to restore *ʾ[dn]y* (= Sing. + suff. 1 p.s.), cf. e.g. Lemaire IH i 97, 100 :: Torczyner Lach i p. 43: poss. l. *ʾ[mr]y* = QAL Inf. cstr. of

ʾ*mr*$_1$ + suff. 1 p.s. (cf. also Röllig KAI a.l.) :: Hempel ZAW lvi 129f.: no restoration of signs between ʾ and *y* needed, ʾ*y* = ʾ*y*$_2$:: H.P.Müller UF ii 236f.: ʾ*y* = ʾ*y*$_4$ :: Lipiński OLP viii 89, BiOr xxxv 286: restore ʾ*[b]y* = Plur. cstr. of ʾ*b*$_2$ (= bud) - Burrows JRAS '27, 791: l. poss. ʾ*dnn* (= Sing. + suff. 1 p.pl.) in KAI 29[1] (for this poss. reading, cf. Amadasi Guzzo Or lix 60) - Garbini Mozia iv p. 98 l. poss. ʾ*dnn* (= Sing. + suff. 1 p.pl.) in SMI 7 (improb. reading, cf. Amadasi Guzzo SMI a.l. (div. otherwise): l. ʾ*dn* (= Sing. abs.)) - Amadasi Guzzo Mozia ix p. 157: l. ʾ*dnn* (= Sing. + suff. 1 p.pl.) in SMI 38 (less prob. reading, cf. Amadasi Guzzo SMI a.l.: l. ʾ*dn* (= Sing. abs.)).
v. ʾ*dm*$_1$, ʾ*dn*$_3$, ʾ*yn*$_1$, ʾ*l*$_1$, *byt*$_2$,*dm*$_1$, *ḥzn*$_1$, *mlk*$_5$, *pʾrt*, *pnh*$_1$.

ʾ**dn**$_2$ v. ʾ*wn*$_3$, ʾ*zn*$_2$, *dny*.

ʾ**dn**$_3$ **Ph** subst. of uncert. meaning (Sing. abs. ʾ*dn*) in KAI 37A 14 (= Kition C1 A; for the reading, cf. Peckham Or xxxvii 316, Healy BASOR ccxvi 56 :: e.g. CIS i sub 86A, Cooke NSI p. 65, Röllig KAI a.l., Masson & Sznycer RPC 26f., 51ff.: l. ʾ*bn* = Sing. abs. of ʾ*bn*$_2$ :: v.d.Branden BO viii 247, 256: pro ʾ*dn bbt* l. ʾ*š pn bt* :: Puech Sem xxix 32: l. ʾ*w* + *bn* (= Qal Pf. 3 p.pl. of *bny*$_1$). Cross with Peckham Or xxxvii 316 n. 2: poss. = base, foundation-platform (cf. also Healy BASOR ccxvi 56) × Peckham Or xxxvii 306, 316: = ʾ*dn*$_1$.
v. *znh*.

ʾ**dn**$_4$ v. ʾ*dyn*.

ʾ**dnwh** v. ʾ*rnwh*.

ʾ**dqwr** (< Akkad., cf. Abou-Assaf MDOG cxiii 16, Abou-Assaf, Bordreuil & Millard Tell F p. 29, Zadok TeAv ix 117, Kaufman JAOS civ 572, cf. also Leemhuis FS Hospers 141f n. 34) - **OldAr** Sing. abs. ʾ*dqwr* Tell F 3 - ¶ subst. ritual container for liquids; *wntn šlh wʾdqwr lʾlhyn klm* ʾ*ḥwh* Tell F 3f.: and giving rest and ritual containers to all the gods his brothers (i.e. who provides well-being (cf. also Geller BSOAS xlvi 546: = prosperity?) and sufficient sacrifices to ....; cf. Akkad. par. *na-din iš-qu u nin-da-bé-e*; cf. CAD *isqu* A 2 C2[1]; cf. Abou-Assaf, Bordreuil & Millard Tell F p. 29 (cf. also Vattioni AION xlvi 357, Delsman TUAT i 636, Stefanovic COAI 78, 234 (n. 1) :: Kaufman Maarav iii 161, 164: provider of ritual-sprinkling (= Sing. abs. of *šlh*$_2$) and libation vessel.... :: Muraoka AN xxii 82, 111 n. 20: provides a basket (= Sing. abs. of *šlh*$_3$), cf. also Gropp & Lewis BASOR cclix 45, 48 :: Zadok TeAv ix 117f.: *šlh* poss. = a term denoting solid offerings, related to Syriac *šalā* :: Wesselius SV 56: *šlh wʾdqwr* = income and meal-offering? :: Fales VO v 80ff.: *šlh* = goods, possessions :: Puech RB xc 596: pro *šlh* l. *šqh* (= Sing. abs.) = drink. - on this word, cf. also Greenfield FS Rundgren 149.

ʾ**dr**$_1$ **Ph** Qal Pf. 3 p.s.m. ʾ*dr* KAI 24[7] (:: Sanmartín UF ix 372 n. 2: =

Sing. m. abs. of ʾ*dr_7*, cf. also KAI iii s.v.); Impf. 3 p.s.m. *yʾdr* KAI 26A iii 10, C iv 10 (× Sanmartín UF ix 372 n. 2: = PUʿAL Impf. 3 p.s.m.); PIʿEL Pf. 3 p.s.m. *ʾdr* KAI 26A i 2; Part. pl.m. abs. *mʾdrm* KAI 14[16,17] (?, cf. e.g. CIS i sub 3 (cf. also Röllig KAI a.l.) :: the reading *šmm ʾdrm* pro *šm mʾdrm*, cf. e.g. Clermont-Ganneau RAO v 231f., Lidzbarski sub KI 7, Torrey JAOS xxiii 23f., lvii 400, 401, Eissfeldt Ras Schamra und Sanch 63, Rosenthal ANET 505, Lack CBQ xxiv 55, Milik Bibl xlviii 561 (n. 2), Avishur PIB 196, Mullen DCC 170, Olyan UF xix 167, Gibson SSI iii p. 109, 112, Hvidberg-Hansen TNT i 30, ii 28f. n. 246; cf. also Lidzbarski Eph ii 52f.) - ¶ verb QAL to be mighty, powerful: KAI 26A iii 10, C iv 10 (cf. however supra); + ʿ*l_7*, to have power over: *wʾdr ʿly mlk dnnym* KAI 24[7]: the king of the D. had power over me (cf. also Swiggers RSO lv 2 (n. 9) :: Garbini FSR 104ff.: I had power over the king of the D.) - PIʿEL 1) to make powerful, to elevate: KAI 26A i 2 (cf. Peckham DLPS 116f. n. 8 :: Swiggers BiOr xxxvii 337: = to exalt, to glorify) - **2)** to extol, to glorify: KAI 14[16,17] - poss. this verb also in NP 130[5] (*yʾdr*, = PIʿEL Inf. (cf. Février RHR cxli 21) or = Pf. 3 p.s.f.?) a form of this root (*ʾdrt*) poss. in ATNS viii (cf. Lemaire Syr lxi 341) :: Segal ATNS a.l.: l. *ʾbdt* or *ʾbrt*.
v. ʾ*dr_7*.

ʾdr_2 **OffAr** Sing. abs. *ʾdr* MAI xiv/2, 66[13], TH 5[2] (= AECT 57; highly uncert. reading: *[ʾ]dr*; cf. Lipiński Stud 140f.); emph. *ʾdrʾ* TH i vs. 5 (= AECT 53; for the reading of the context, cf. also Kaufman JAOS cix 100); Plur. abs. *ʾdrn* KAI 235 vs. 5 (= AECT 48; cf. also Fales OA xvi 66) - ¶ subst. Sing. and Plur. threshing floor; cf. Akkadian parallels, cf. v.Soden AHW s.v. *adru*, CAD s.v. *adru*, cf. also Goetze AJSL lii 159, Ungnad Beih AfO vi 49, Landsberger JNES viii 292, Koschaker Neue Rechtsurkunden 45, Marrassini FLEM 40f., Lipiński Stud 116f.
v. ʾ*bd_1*.

ʾdr_3 **Pun** Fantar Antas p. 72f.: l. Plur. cstr. *ʾdrʾ* (= coverings, sc. of roof, or = n.p.) in Antas 70[6] (dam. context; highly uncert. interpret.).

ʾdr_4 v. ʾ*dr_7*.

ʾdr_5 v. ʿ*rkh_1*.

ʾdr_6 v. ʾ*dr_7*.

ʾdr_7 **Ph** Sing. m. abs. *ʾdr* KAI 14[9], 19[6], 26A iii 4, 6, C iii 18, iv 1, 58, MUSJ xlv 262[2] (:: Garbini AION xxiv 412, FSR 58f. n. 4: = Sing. abs. of ʾ*dr_6* (= mantle)); Sing. f. abs. *ʾdrt* KAI 48[2], EpAn ix 5[5] (or = Plur. f. abs.?); Plur. m. abs. *ʾdrm* KAI 24[5f.]; f. abs. *ʾdrt* KAI 14[19], EI xviii 117[4] (= IEJ xxxv 83) - **Pun** Sing. m. abs. *ʾdr* KAI 161[5] (v. infra; :: Roschinski Num 112: = Sing. cstr. of ʾ*dr_4* (= splendour)), Antas 51[1], 78a 1, b 1, 80[1], 81[1], 82[1], 87[1], Punica ix 9[1], ʿ*dr* KAI 162[1] (?, reading of context uncert.); cstr. *ʾdr* KAI 62[4], 101[4] (*ʾd[r]*), 121[1], 126[2], CIS i

6000bis 7 (= TPC 84), Epigr xlii 196 (cf. also Uberti CISFP i 797); + suff. 3 p.pl.m. *ʾdrnm* KAI 65², 81⁵ (for both texts :: Schiffmann RSF iv 51f.: = Plur. abs. of *ʾdrn*$_1$ (= mighty one; for KAI 81⁵ :: v.d.Branden PO i 204, 210: = Plur. m. + suff. 3 p.pl.m.) :: Fuentes Estañol VF s.v. *ʾdr*$_2$: = lapsus for Plur. abs. *ʾdrm*); Sing. f. abs. *ʾdrt* CIS i 255⁴, 4842⁷, 4843⁴, Hofra 132¹ᶠ·, KAI 72B 3 (= ICO-Spa 10), *ʾdrʾ* KAI 161⁵ (?, v. infra :: Roschinski Num 112: = Sing. + suff. 3 p.s.m. of *ʾdr*$_4$); Plur. m. abs. *ʾdrm* CIS i 3920³, ICO-Spa 2 (??., uncert. reading; v. infra); cstr. *ʾdrʾ* KAI 119⁴, 126⁷; f. abs. *ʾdrt* KAI 145⁸ (??, or = art + Sing./Plur. abs. of *drh*$_2$?, cf. v.d.Branden RSF i 170 :: Krahmalkov RSF iii 194: l. *ʾdr t* = PIʿEL Pf. 3 p.s.m. (= he caused to grieve) of *ʾdr*$_1$ + nota obj.), *ʾdrʾt* KAI 145³ (v. however also *ʿṭrt*) - ¶ 1) adj. great, mighty, grand, illustrious, splendid; said of - a) a god/goddess, Ashtarte: CIS i 255⁴, 4842⁷, 4834⁴, Askan: KAI 58, Baʿal: Punica ix 9¹, KAI 162¹ (uncert., v. supra), Isis: KAI 48², Ṣid: Antas 51¹, 78a 1, 80¹, 81¹, 82¹, 87¹, Epigr xlii 196, Tinnit: Hofra 132¹ᶠ·, ICO-Spa 10B 3 (= KAI 72B) - b) a king: KAI 14⁹ (v. also *mmlkh*), 19⁶, 24⁵ᶠ· - c) a region, *ʾrṣt ... h ʾdrt* KAI 14¹⁹: the splendid regions ... - d) power, *ʿz ʾdr* KAI 26A iii 4: mighty power (cf. KAI 26A iii 6, C iii 18, iv 1) - e) curse: EpAn ix 5⁵ - f) building or part of it: KAI 145³ (v. *ʿṭrt*) - g) of an object: EI xviii 117⁴ (= IEJ xxxv 83) - for the context of ICO-Spa 2, v. *tr* - for the context of KAI 161⁵, v. *gm*$_1$, *tmh*$_2$ - **2)** subst. - a) chief; *ʾdrʾ ʾlpqy w(kl) ʿm ʾlpqy* KAI 119⁴, 126⁷: the notables of Lepcis and (all) the people of L. (cf. Levi Della Vida RCL '49, 406, Angeli Bertinelli CISFP i 256, Sznycer Sem xxv 66f.); for *ʾdr ʿrkt* KAI 62⁴, v. *ʿrkh*$_1$; for *ʾdr ʿzrm* KAI 121¹ᶠ·, 126², v. *ʿzr*$_3$; *[ʾ]dr ḥmšm hʾš* KAI 101⁴: chief (/commander) of fifty men (for Lib. par., cf. Février MC 88, Chaker AION xlvi 548ff.); *ʾdr špḥ* CIS i 6000bis 7: chief of a clan (v. also *špḥ*$_1$) - b) *ʾdrnm wʿd ṣʿrnm* KAI 81⁵ (cf. KAI 65²): (from) their large one to their small one (= (in) their totality)) - Lipiński Stud 146f.: l. *ʾdr* (Sing. m. abs. = oak or juniper) in the diff. *'drsw/pn* of KAI 258² (cf. also Millard JSS xxi 177; highly uncert. interpret., cf. Degen WO ix 169), cf. also Teixidor Syr xlvii 373f.: l. poss. *ʾdr skn* = n.d. preceded by epitheton *ʾdr* (less prob. interpret.), v. *ʾdrswn*, *spn* - Février AIPHOS xiii 169f.: l. poss. *ʾdrt* (= Sing. f. abs. of *ʾdr*$_7$) in KAI 162⁶ (uncert. reading and interpret., diff. context) - the interpretation of the context of *ʾdr* in MUSJ xlv 262² uncert. (v. *ʿg*, *bqš*); Starcky MUSJ xlv a.l.: = attribute to *ʿg* (cf. also Röllig NESE ii 2, 5); v.d.Branden RSF ii 143, Schiffmann RSF iv 172, 175: = indication of deity, the Mighty One (cf. also Cross IEJ xxix 41, 43: = shortening of *bʿl ʾdr*).

v. *ʾzr*$_4$, *gldgyml*, *ʿbn*.

ʾdrwn (< Greek ἀνδρών, cf. Starcky Syr xxvi 55ff., Rosenthal Sprache

90 n. 5, Milik DFD 142ff., 384, Gawlikowski TP 73f., cf. also PS s.v. *ʾdrwnʾ*; Telegdi JA ccxxvi 226: < Iran. :: Rosenthal Sprache 27, 90: < Akkad.) - **Palm** Sing. cstr. (?) *ʾdrwn* Syr xvii 280^4 (for this reading, cf. Milik DFD 310f.); emph. *ʾdrwnʾ* CIS ii 3917^4 - ¶ subst. refectory (in temple; to be used by religious communities) - du Mesnil du Buisson RES '42-45, 79, Milik DFD 270: l. Sing. emph. *[ʾd]rwnʾ* in Inscr P 31^5 (uncert. reading, cf. Gawlikowski Syr xlviii 414, 418f.: l. *bw[m]s*).
v. *ʾrn*$_1$.

ʾdrṭ (< Greek ἀνδριᾶς (-ντ-)) - **Palm** Plur. emph. *ʾdrṭyʾ* CIS ii 3913 ii 128 - ¶ subst. statue.

ʾdrn$_1$ v. *ʾdr*$_7$.

ʾdrn$_2$ v. *ʾrn*$_1$.

ʾdrng (< Iran., cf. Krael p. 243, Porten & Greenfield JAOS lxxxix 154, Hinz AISN 22f.) - **OffAr** Sing. abs. *ʾdrng* Krael 9^{18}, 10^{12}, 12^{27}; + suff. 1 p.s. *ʾdrngy* Krael 11^9 (or preferably Plur.?, cf. e.g. Grelot DAE p. 253, Porten & Greenfield JEAS p. 66, Porten & Yardeni sub TADAE B 3.13) - ¶ subst. m. of uncert. meaning; Porten & Greenfield ZAW lxxx 229, JAOS lxxxix 154: = guarantor (cf. also Porten Arch 216, Hinz AISN 22f., Porten & Greenfield JEAS p. 61 (a.e.), Porten & Yardeni sub TADAE B 3.10 (a.e.)), cf. however Yaron JSS xvi 243f.; de Menasce BiOr xi 161, Grelot DAE p. 245 (n. p): = creditor.

ʾdrswn **OffAr** Albright with Hanson BASOR cxcii 5: l. *ʾdrswn* in KAI 258^2 = subst. Sing. abs. (< Iran.) or l. *ʾdrswnh* = Sing. emph. of same word meaning fire-pillar (interpret. and reading highly uncert.); *ʾdrsw/pn* prob. = n.d., cf. Donner KAI a.l., Cross BASOR clxxxiv 10, Hanson BASOR cxcii 5, Gibson SSI ii p. 154, Delsman TUAT ii 578.
v. *ʾdr*$_7$, *spn*.

ʾdt v. *ʾdn*$_1$.

ʾh$_1$ **OffAr** The *ʾh* in Nisa b 22^5, c 355^{2,4} prob. abbrev. of measure of capacity (used here for wine).

ʾh$_2$ v. *z*$_1$.

ʾhb$_1$ **OffAr** Qal Pf. 2 (or 3?) p.s.f. + suff. 3 p.s.m. (or 2 p.s.m. + suff. 3 p.s.f.??) *ʾhbth* Cowl 75^3 (uncert. reading, the only time *ʾhb* is found in Ar.??) - ¶ verb Qal to love - prob. form of this root in Mo. text SSI i 83^2: *'h[b—]*, cf. already Reed & Winnett BASOR clxxii 9 - Dupont-Sommer MAI xliv 15, 25: l. *ʾhb* (= Qal Pf. 3 p.s.m.) in the Ph. text MAI xliv 15^5 (reading and interpret. highly uncert., cf. Teixidor Syr xlix 434: l. *ʾhd*), Puech RSF iv 13, 16f.: l. *šʾ hdr* (pro *š ʾhb-*) = "un mouton paré", *šʾ* = *š*$_1$ (Sing. abs.), *hdr* = Qal Part. pass. of *hdr*$_1$ (= to adorn, to festoon).
v. *mhr*$_2$.

ʾhb$_2$ v. *zhb*.

ʾhz v. *ʾš$_1$*.

ʾhzw **OffAr** diff. word (*[ʾ]hzw*) in PFT 2043[3]; lapsus or false transcription for *ʾḥzw* = QAL Pf. 3 p.pl.m. of *ʾḥz*?

ʾhl **Hebr** Sing. abs. *ʾhl* TA-H 15[5] (*[ʾ]hl*, ??, highly uncert. and dam. context) - **Nab** Plur. emph. *ʾhltʾ* (??; or = n.l.?, cf. Lidzbarski Eph ii 76, Littmann PAES ivA 46, Cantineau Nab ii 57) RES 2125[2f.] - ¶ subst. tent.

ʾhš v. *mlk$_5$*.

ʾw **Pun** KAI 159[8] (v. *ʿlh$_2$* :: Fuentes Estañol s.v. *w*: lapsus for *w$_2$*) - **Hebr** KAI 195[10] (for this reading, cf. Albright BASOR lxx 15 (cf. also e.g. Ginsberg BASOR lxxi 26, de Vaux RB xlviii 196, Elliger ZDPV lxii 75), reading however highly uncert.; cf. Michaud Syr xxxiv 47: l. *hw* (= part of n.p.), prob. reading, cf. also Torczyner Lach i a.l. (: = part of n.d.), Gibson SSI i p. 44f., Lemaire IH i 117), DJD ii 22,1-9[11], 30[14] -**Samal** KAI 214[16,25,26,27,30,32,33,34] - **DA** ii 9 - **OldAr** KAI 202B 21, 222B 26, 27, C 19, 224[1,4,5], etc. - **OffAr** Cowl 5[6,8,9], Krael 2[7,9,10], Driv 6[3], 7[8], 11[5], KAI 260B 4, 5, 6, 278[8], Samar 8[7], etc., etc.; cf. Nisa-b 780b 4, Sogd B 247, R 45, ML 578 - **Nab** CIS ii 197[6,7], 198[5,6], 199[5,6], etc., etc. - **Palm** CIS ii 3913 ii 3, 56, 111, 127, 4214, MUSJ xxxviii 106[10,11], etc. - **Hatra** 281[3,4] - **JAr** MPAT 41[9], MPAT-A 5[2] - ¶ connecting particle, or (connecting words/phrases or clauses); *mn zy yḥbl ʾw yprk* ... KAI 260B 6 whoever destroys or smashes ...; *ḥmr ʾw škr* Driv 6[3]: wine or beer; *dnr ʾw ytyr* CIS ii 3913 ii 127: a *denarius* or more; *wbnyk šlyṭn ... wlmn zy ... tntn ʾw zy tzbn lh* Krael 12[23f.]: and your children shall have power .... and(/or) to whomsoever you will give (it) ... (and/)or to whomsoever you will sell (it); *mn kndwṣ ʾlhʾ ʾw mn kmrʾ* FX 136[21f.]: from the god K or from the priest; *mdy yhwʾ mt[ʾʿ]l br mn tḥwmʾ ʾw mʾpq* CIS ii 3913 ii 111: whatever shall be imported from without the borders or be exported; *qm ʿyny ʾw dlḥ* KAI 216[30]: my eye is fixed or turbid; for DA ii 9, v. *h$_2$* - for DJD 30[14], v. *ʾm$_3$* - for the poss. reading *ʾw* in KAI 222B 35, v. *lqḥ*.
v. *ʾdn$_3$*, *ʾwmh*.

ʾwgrw **Nab** Sing. abs. *ʾwgrw* RES 1103[6], CIS ii 223[3] (cf. J 26, RES 1155) - ¶ subst. f. contract of lease.

ʾwdʾ v. *wdʾ*.

ʾwdys (< Iran., cf. Schaed 266, Hinz AISN 51) - **OffAr** Sing. abs. *ʾwdys* Cowl 33[12] - ¶ subst. information, inquiries (cf. Grelot Or xxxvi 176f., RB lxxxii 292 :: Porten & Greenfield JEAS p. 100, Porten & Yardeni sub TADAE A 4.10: = statement :: Cowl a.l.: = orders).

ʾwdn v. *ʾzn$_2$*, *ʾrnwh*.

ʾwzn v. *ʾwn₁*.

ʾwḥr v. *ʾḥr₅*.

ʾwṭqrṭwr (< Greek αὐτοκράτωρ) - **Palm** Sing. abs. *[ʾw]ṭqrṭwr* Inv ix 26[1] - ¶ subst. m. emperor.

ʾwy₁ v. *ʾwyn*.

ʾwy₂ **DA** derivative of this root (*tʾwh*) in viiib 2; uncert. whether noun or (complete?) verbal form. Meaning uncert.: to desire (?, or: to lament??), cf. Hoftijzer DA p. 260.

ʾwy₃ v. *nwh*.

ʾwy₄ **OffAr** *ʾwy* HDS 5[1] - ¶ interj.; *ʾwy ly* HDS 5[1f]: woe is me.

ʾwyn **OldAr** word of unknown meaning in KAI 222B 30 (dam. and diff. context). Donner KAI a.l.: poss. to be connected with Hebr. *'wn* = vanity, wickedness; Fitzmyer AIS 69: poss. = n.p.?; Lipiński Stud 38: = QAL Part. act. pl. abs. of *ʾwy₁* (= to seek refuge, to seek shelter; cf. also Sader EAS 131; improb. interpret.); for the interpret. of the context, cf. also Lemaire & Durand IAS 138.

ʾwyr v. *ʾḥz*.

ʾwl **OffAr** this subst. (Sing. emph.) perhaps in Warka 14: *mi-in-nu ul-la-ʾ* = from everlasting?? (uncert. reading and interpret.; for other interpret., cf. also Dupont-Sommer RA xxxix 47).

ʾwlm v. *ʿlm₄*.

ʾwlt **OffAr** word of uncert. reading in CIS ii 64[1] (cf. Kaufman AIA 34); normally explained as Sing. abs. of *ʾwlt* = female slave (< Akkad.; cf. e.g. CIS ii 64 a.l., Del sub 91, Vattioni Aug x 512) - cf. *ʾmlt* sub *ʾwmnt*.

ʾwmh **Waw** Dupont-Sommer Waw p. 11, 27f., 102: l. *ʾwmn* in AMB 6[14] = Plur. abs. of *ʾwmh* (= oath); less prob. interpret., cf. Naveh & Shaked AMB a.l.: l. *ʾw* + *mn* (= *mn₅*).

ʾwmn v. *ʾmn₂*.

ʾwmnt cf. Frah xiii 9 (*ʾwmntyʾ*; < Akkad.), cf. Nyberg FP 47, 82 = work-troops (:: Ebeling Frah a.l.: l. *ʾmlt* = female servant).

ʾwn₁ **Nab** Sing. emph. *ʾwnʾ* CIS 202[1] - **Palm** Sing. emph. *ʾwnʾ* Ber xix 77 (for the reading, cf. Gawlikowski Ber xxi 14 n. 68), SBS 87 (for the reading, cf. Gawlikowski Ber xxii 146, reading however highly uncert.; other proposals: a) Gawlikowski Ber xxii 146: l. *ʾwznʾ* = Sing. emph. of *ʾwzn* (= tub, sarcophage) - b) Dunant SBS a.l.: l. perhaps *ʾrwnʾ* = Sing. emph. of *ʾrn₁*) - ¶ subst. m. (habitation, abode >) sarcophage: Ber xix 77. The precise meaning in CIS ii 202[1] unknown (part of tomb) construction?, sarcophage?, cf. Gawlikowski Ber xix 78) - Telegdi JA ccxxvi 226: < Iran.; on this word, cf. also Rundgren OrSu xv 75ff., xxii

68f.
v. ʾ*wn*$_2$, ʾ*rz*$_3$.

ʾ**wn**$_2$ **OffAr** Sing. cstr. ʾ*wn* Aḥiq 160 - ¶ subst. force? (for context of Aḥiq 160, v. *gw*$_2$; cf. however Lindenberger APA 161, 266 n. 490, 288: = ʾ*wn*$_4$ (= wickedness) :: e.g. Baneth OLZ '14, 351: = ʾ*wn*$_1$ (= habitation)) - Lipiński Stud 40f.: l. Sing. cstr. ʾ*n* (with contracted diphtong) in KAI 222B 36 (less prob. explanation; perhaps other derivative of same root??) - Vattioni Aug xvi 547: *vn* in IRT 886f. 6 perhaps = Sing. cstr. with meaning "substance" (less prob. interpret.).
v. *nʿm*$_1$.

ʾ**wn**$_3$ cf. Frah x 3: ear (cf. Nyberg FP 75: < ʾ*dn*$_2$ (= ʾ*zn*$_2$); cf. also Toll ZDMG-Suppl viii 32).

ʾ**wn**$_4$ v. ʾ*wn*$_2$, *nʿm*$_1$.

ʾ**wsp** v. *ysp*.

ʾ**wp** v. ʾ*p*$_2$.

ʾ**wpkrt** (< Iran., cf. R.A.Bowman AJSL lviii 311, cf. however Schaed 263 n. 1) - **OffAr** Sing. emph. *[ʾ]wpkrtʾ* AJSL lviii 304B 12 (= AG 10B 4); + suff. 3 p.s.f. ʾ*wpkrth* Cowl 26^{5} - ¶ subst. of uncert. meaning; Bowman AJSL lviii 311: = part of a ship or a substructure upon which a boat will be set while being built or repaired, cf. however Hinz AISN 243f.: = estimate (sc. (in the context): estimate of the materials required for the reparation of a ship; cf. also Porten El xiv 177: = estimate, Porten & Yardeni sub TADAE A 6.2: = reckoning?) :: Cowl a.l. (cf. also Grelot Sem xx 27, DAE p. 287 n. i): = report.

ʾ**wpstʾ** (< Iran., cf. Segal ATNS a.l., cf. also Shaked Or lvi 410) - **OffAr** Sing. abs. ʾ*wpstʾ* ATNS 45b 3 - ¶ subst. help, support.

ʾ**wpšr** (< Iran., cf. Benveniste JA ccxlii 303, Hinz AISN 242f., cf. however Schaed 263 n. 1) - **OffAr** Sing. cstr. ʾ*wpšr* Cowl 26^{22}; + suff. 3 p.s.f. ʾ*wpšrh* Cowl 26^{3,6,9} (ʾ*wp[šrh]*, for the reading, cf. Porten & Yardeni sub TADAE A 6.2) - ¶ subst. of uncert. meaning; Grelot Sem xx 28, DAE p. 286 n. d (cf. Benveniste JA ccxlii 303): = support, prop. (used here to indicate a part of the structure of a wooden ship); Hinz AISN 242f.: what is required in a certain case (i.e. in the context, what is required for the reparation of a ship) :: Cowl a.l.: = repairs (cf. also Porten EI xiv 176, Porten & Yardeni sub TADAE A 6.2).

ʾ**wptštw** **OffAr** word of unknown meaning of non-Semitic origin in ATNS 1^{3,8}; = n.p. or title?, cf. Segal ATNS a.l.

ʾ**wṣbʿ** v. ʾ*ṣbʿ*.

ʾ**wṣlt** **OffAr** Ebeling Frah a.l.: l. ʾ*wṣlt* in Frah xv 11, prob. = some article of dress, v. ʾ*štl* (improb. reading and interpret., cf. Nyberg FP 48, 85: l. iranian word).

ʾwṣr **Hebr** Sing. abs. *ʾwṣr* DJD ii 24B 19; + suff. 3 p.s.m.? *ʾwṣrh* DJD ii 24C 17 - **Samal** Sing. cstr. (or abs.?) *ʾṣr* KAI 215[7] - **OffAr** Sing. cstr. *ʾwṣr* Krael 6[7], 10[4], 11[4]; emph. *ʾwṣrʾ* Cowl 2[12], 11[6], 50[6], Krael 3[9] - ¶ subst. treasure, treasury - a) treasury building: Krael 3[9], 6[7], 10[4] - b) treasury office; *spry ʾwṣrʾ* Cowl 2[12]: the clerks of the treasury - c) stores in the treasury building, from which one's salary is paid: Cowl 11[6], or one's monthly rations of grain: Krael 11[4] (here *ʾwṣr mlkʾ* // with *byt mlkʾ* in l. 6, cf. Cowl 2[12]) - cf. Porten Arch 60f., Galling SGI 103 - this word also in Hebr. text NESE ii 50 i 1??, l. *bʾṣr* ??, reading of *ṣ* uncert., cf. Millard with Mallowan Nimrud 598) :: Lemaire Sem xxvi 65f.: l. *bʾḥr* = *b*$_2$ + *ʾḥr*$_5$ (= behind).

ʾwṣtph v. *ʾṣbʿ*, *ṣbʿ*$_2$.

ʾwqynws (<Greek ὠκεανός) - **Waw** Sing. abs. *ʾwqynws* AMB 6[4f] - p subst. Ocean; cf. Dupont-Sommer Waw p. 16, 63, 66f.

ʾwr$_1$ v. *yrd*.

ʾwr$_2$ v. *yrd*.

ʾwrz **Hebr** Sing. abs. *ʾwrz* SM 49[3,20,23] - ¶ subst. rice.

ʾwrḥ v. *ʾrḥ*$_2$.

ʾwrḥwt v. *ʾrḥ*$_2$.

ʾwrḥtwt v. *ʾrḥ*$_2$.

ʾwryh$_1$ **JAr** e.g. Schwabe BIES xviii 162f.: poss. l. *[ʾ]wrytʾ* (= Sing. emph. (= law)) in SM 24[2] (uncert. reading and interpret., cf. Naveh SM a.l.: or *]wrytʾ* = part of n.p.?, Hüttenmeister ASI 439f. (div. otherwise): l. poss. *byth* (= Sing. emph. of *byt*$_2$)).

ʾwryh$_2$ v. *ʿryh*.

ʾwt$_1$ **Pun** Février AIPHOS xiii 163f.: the *ʾtʾ* in KAI 162[4] = Qal Pf. 3 p.s.f. of *ʾwt*$_1$ and the *ʾtʾ* in KAI 163[4] = Qal Pf. 3 p.s.m. + suff. 3 p.s.m. of *ʾwt*$_1$ (= to approve, to accept; cf. also v.d.Branden BO xiv 199: the *ʾtʾ* in KAI 162[4] = Qal Pf. 3 p.pl.), highly uncert. interpret. v. *ʾyt*$_3$.

ʾwt$_2$ v. *ʾt*$_1$.

ʾz$_1$ v. *z*$_1$, *mlk*$_5$, *š*$_{10}$.

ʾz$_2$ **Hebr** KAI 193[7] (*mʾz*), 196[13] (for this diff. reading, cf. e.g. de Vaux RB xlviii 197, 199, Albright BASOR lxxxii 23, Gibson SSI i p. 45 :: Albright BASOR lxx 15f.: pro *z* l. *y* (v. *qrʾ*$_1$) :: Torczyner Lach i p. 116f.: l. *ʾ[m]* = *ʾm*$_3$) - **Samal** KAI 214[7] (?, dam. context), 215[9] (cf. Dion 172 :: Koopmans 73: *wʾz* = *wʾ* (variant of *w*$_2$) + *z*$_2$ (= *zy*) :: Garb 259: *wʾz* = indef. pronoun, whatever :: Segert AAG p. 178: *ʾz* < *ʾy-zy* = that which, all sorts of things, medley) - ¶ adv. then, at that time: KAI 215[9]; *mʾz* (< *mn*$_5$ + *ʾz*) *šlḥk* KAI 193[7]: since your sending.

v. *ʾzy*, *ʿly₁*.

ʾz₃ v. *ʿnz*.

ʾzb Ebeling Frah a.l.: the *ʾzbʾ* in Frah ix 6 = fox; cf. Baumgartner BiOr xix 133: or misspelling for *zʾb*?; cf. however Nyberg FP 73: poss. = iranian word.

ʾzd (< Iran., cf. Schaed 266, Friedrich Or xxvi 41, Hinz AISN 52, Frah xv 10) - **OffAr** Sing. abs. *ʾzd* Cowl 27[8], ATNS 21[4] (for the reading, cf. Shaked Or lvi 409 :: Segal ATNS a.l.: l. *ʾzd/r* = n.p.) - ¶ subst. m. inquiry (:: Porten EI xiv 176, Porten & Greenfield JEAS p. 86: proclamation, Hinz AISN 52: announcement); *ʾzd ʿbdw* ATNS 21[4]: make an inquiry (:: Shaked Or lvi 409: make known); *ʾzd ytʿbd mn dynyʾ* Cowl 27[8f.]: an inquiry will be made by the judges.

ʾzdkr (< Iran., cf. Schaed 264, Eilers IIJ v 225f., Hinz AISN 52, Porten RB xc 413) - **OffAr** Sing. emph. *ʾzdkrʾ* Cowl 17[7]; Plur. emph. *ʾzdkryʾ* Cowl 17[5] - ¶ subst. m. inspector :: Porten Arch 52, RB xc 513, Porten & Yardeni sub TADAE A 6.1: = herald; cf. also Hinz AISN 52.

ʾzh v. *ʾlh₂*.

ʾzy **OffAr** KAI 233[6,14] - **Hebr** DJD ii 42[5] (cf. I.Rabinowitz BASOR cxxxi 21 (cf. Milik DJD ii a.l., Pardee HAHL 123) :: Yeivin At i 98f. (div. otherwise): l. *ʾz* (= *ʾz₂*) :: de Vaux RB lx 270, Sonne PAAJR xxiii 86, 91, Bardtke ThLZ lxxix 302: l. *ʾny₄*) - ¶ adv. then, afterwards; the reading *ʾzy* in KAI 279[4] (cf. Dupont-Sommer JA ccxlvi 28, Donner KAI a.l. (cf. also Rosenthal EI xiv 98*: l. poss. *ʾzy* < pers.)) prob. false, cf. Altheim & Stiehl EW ix 192, x 244, ASA 26, GMA 348, GH ii 171, Garbini Kand 11, Nober VD xxxvii 372, 375, Degen ZDMG cxxi 126: l. *wzy* - for the context of DJD ii 42[5], v. *ʾlly*.

ʾzl **OldAr** QAL Impf. 2 p.s.m. *tʾzl* KAI 222B 39 (cf. e.g. Degen AAG p. 71 :: Fitzmyer AIS 72, Lipiński Stud 43f.: = Impf. 3 p.s.f.) - **OffAr** QAL Pf. 3 p.s.m. *ʾzl* Cowl 27[3], 30[5], 31[4], 56[2], Beh 8 (Akkad. par. *it-ta-lak*), 12 (prob. lapsus for *ʾzlt* = Pf. 1 p.s., cf. e.g. Greenfield & Porten BIDG p. 33, and cf. Akkad. par. *at-ta-lak*; cf. however Sokoloff JAOS cix 686 = QAL Part. act. s.m. abs.), Cowl p. 267, 56 xiii 1 (for this prob. reading, cf. Greenfield & Porten BIDG p. 40f.; Akkad. par. *il-lik-ma*), ATNS 29 ii 5, etc.; 2 p.s.m. *ʾzlt* SSI ii 28 obv. 22; 1 p.s. *ʾzlt* Cowl 40[2], Aḥiq 22, 76, Sach 81 i 3 (?), ATNS 29 ii 2; 3 p.pl.m. *ʾzlw* Beh 4 (Akkad. par. *it-tal-ku*), 8 (*ʾzl[w]*; Akkad. par. *it-tal-ku-ʾ*), 10 (*ʾ[z]lw*), 24* (Akkad. par. *it-tal-ku-ʾ*), 26 (*ʾz[l]w*; for the reading, cf. also Greenfield and Porten BIDG p. 38; Akkad. par. *it-tal-ku-ʾ*), Sach 78 i B 1 (or = Imper. pl.m.?), ATNS 62[3] (dam. context); Imper. s.m. *ʾzl* Cowl 42[8], Beh 7 (Akkad. par. *a-lik-ma*), 18 (Akkad. par. id.), JRAS '29, 108[9] (*zwl* RES 1793[7], incorrect reading: l. *ʾl*, cf. Cowley PSBA '15,

222); s.f. *ʾzly* JRAS '29, 108^{5}; pl.m. *ʾzlw* Beh 39 (Akkad. par. *al-ka-ma*); Part. act. s.m. abs. *ʾzl* Driv 6^{2} (highly uncert. reading, cf. Porten & Yardeni sub TADAE A 6.9); pl.m. abs. *ʾzln* Driv 6^{4}, *ʾzlyn* AG 39^{4} (prob. reading); cf. Frah xx 9 (*ʾzlwn*), Paik 39 (*ʾzl*), 40-41 (*ʾzlwn*), Syn 313^{1,2} (cf. however Altheim & Stiehl EW ix 9f., Phil 61), GIPP 20, 48, cf. also SaSt 15 - **Hatra** QAL Impf. 3 p.s.f. *tʾzy[l]* 342^{7} - **JAr** QAL Pf. 1 p.s. *ʾzlt* IEJ xl 142^{1} - ¶ verb to go (to), to make (for); cf. *ʾzlt hškḥt lʾḥyq[r]* Aḥiq 76: I went (and) found Aḥiqar (cf. Aḥiq 110, Beh 18) - **1)** + acc. direct, *byty ʾzl mn ..* ATNS 67a 2: he went to my house from ..; *ʾzln ʿmh mṣryn* Driv 6^{4}: (those) who went with him to Egypt - 2) + *b$_2$*, *ʾzlt bʾrḥʾ zk* SSI ii 28 obv. 2: you went on that way - **3)** + *l$_5$*, *ʾzl lswn* Cowl 56^{2}: he went to Syene (cf. Aḥiq 22, cf. also *ʾzlw lʿrqh* Beh 4, 10: they went against him) - **4)** + *l$_5$* + Inf., *ʾzl lmnšʾ mʾkl* ATNS 29 ii 5: he went to carry food - 5) + *ʿl$_7$*, *ʾzl ʿl mlkʾ* Cowl 27^{3}: he went to the king (cf. Cowl 30^{5}, 42^{8}, Aḥiq 75, 120, Sach 81 i 3 - **6)** + *ʿm$_4$*, *ʾzlt ʿm šʾryt ..* ATNS 29 ii 2: I went with the rest of .. - Segal ATNS a.l.: the *ʾzt* (reading uncert.) in ATNS 82b 1 poss. = QAL Pf. 2 p.s.m. or 1 p.s. of *ʾzl* (less prob. interpret., cf. also Blau Lesh xlviii/xlix 217; = form of *ʾzt$_1$*?? (heavily dam. context)).

v. *ʾzt$_1$*, *zwl*, *mʾzl*.

ʾzn$_1$ v. *mʾzn$_2$*.

ʾzn$_2$ **Hebr** Sing. cstr. *ʾzn* KAI 193^{5} (for this reading, cf. Torczyner TL a.l., Briend TPOA 143, Lipiński OLP viii 89, Cross FS Iwry 45, for the reading of the second sign, cf. also Gibson SSI i p. 39 :: Torczyner Lach i a.l.: l. *rzm* = QAL Pf. 3 p.s.m. of root *rzm$_2$* (= to hint, to refer) :: Ginsberg BASOR lxxi 25 (especially n. 4), lxxx 11, Albright BASOR lxxiii 17f. n. 14: l. *ʿyn* (= Sing. cstr. of *ʿyn$_2$*), cf. also Diringer Lach iii 332) - **OffAr** Sing. + suff. 2 p.s.m. *[ʾ]dnk* Beh 53 (for the reading, cf. Greenfield & Porten BIDG p. 48f.); Dual abs. *ʾdnyn* Aḥiq 157, 216; + suff. 2 p.s.m. *ʾdnyk* Aḥiq 132; + suff. 3 p.pl.m. *ʾdnyhm* Aḥiq 97- ¶ subst. f. ear; for context of KAI 193^{5}, v. also *pqḥ*; for the context of Aḥiq 97, cf. Lindenberger APA 73 - Milik DFD 105, Vattioni IH a.l.: l. *ʾwdnyh* (= Dual + suff. 3 p.s.m.) in Hatra 173^{3} (improb. interpret., v. also *ʾrnwh*) - cf. *ʾwn$_3$*.

v. *ʾzn$_3$*, *dny*.

ʾzn$_3$ **Palm** subst. (Sing. abs. *ʾzn*) of unknown meaning in expression *ʾzn špyr* in Syr xiv 191^{3}; Milik DFD 104: = Sing. abs. of *ʾzn$_2$* (less prob. interpret.).

ʾzr$_1$ v. *ʾzr$_5$*, *mlk$_5$*.

ʾzr$_2$ **Ph** Plur. m. abs. *ʾzrm* KAI 14^{3,13} - ¶ adj. (?) of unknown meaning, short (??); *bn msk ymm ʾzrm* KAI 14$^{3,12f.}$: a son of a short number of days (litt. a number of short days)??, cf. Cooke NSI p. 33, cf. also

Torrey JAOS lvii 402 (Driver ZAW lxxx 178: *ʾzrm* = cut of prematurely < root *zrm*; cf. also Gibson SSI iii p. 110, cf. however Emerton ZAW lxxxix 70) :: Février JA ccxliii 62: *ʾzrm* = Sing. abs. of *ʾzrm*$_1$ (= young boy; cf. v.d.Branden BMB xiii 89, GP § 68; improb. interpret.; cf. also Röllig BiOr xxvii 377) :: Puech RB lxxxviii 99: = Plur. abs. of *ʾzr*$_3$ (= certain type of sacrifice; cf. Cazelles CISFP 674ff.) :: Siegel AJSL xlvi 58f.: = NIPH Impf. 1 p.s. of *zrm* (= to be cut off; cf. v.d.Branden BiOr xxxvi 202), cf. also Lipiński RSF ii 57: = QAL Impf. 1 p.s. of *zrm* (= to break off); improb. interpret.; cf. also Zorell s.v. *zrm*: = QAL pass. Impf. 1 p.s. of *zrm* (improb. interpret.) :: Cazelles SDB v 1342: *ʾzrm* = *ʾzr*$_6$ (= incubation rite) + adv. ending *-m* :: Dussaud Syr xi 202f.: = Plur. m. abs. of *ʾzr*$_4$ (= glorious).
v. *ʾzr*$_3$, *mlk*$_5$.

ʾzr$_3$ **Pun** for the diff. *ʾzrm* (= Plur. abs. of *ʾzr*$_2$ or Sing. abs. of *ʾzrm*$_2$) and its variants in the expression *mlk* (*bʿl*) *ʾzrm*, v. *mlk*$_5$.
v. *ʾzr*$_{2,5}$.

ʾzr$_4$ **Ph** this nominal form (f. Sing. abs. *ʾzrt*) poss. in Kition A 27^{3} (= CIS i 13^{3}), or = QAL Part. act. (/pass.) s.f. abs. of a root *ʾzr*?; meaning unknown (cf. E.Meyer ZAW xlix 11 n. 5) :: Kutscher JSS x 42: combine with root *ʾzr* in Ps xviii 33, xciii 1 (cf. Cooke NSI p. 59f.: she who girds on > protects) :: *ʾzrt* = QAL Part. act. s.f. abs. of *ʿzr*$_1$, cf. Cooke NSI p. 59, Röllig KAI ii p. 100, FR 16 (v. also *ʾzrh*$_1$) :: e.g. Cooke NSI p. 60: or *ʾzrt* = variant of *ʾdrt* (= variant form of *ʾdrt*, Sing. f. abs. of *ʾdr*$_7$; cf. also Dussaud Syr xi 202, Albright JAOS lxxi 263). The interpretation as Sing. abs. of *ʾzrh*$_2$ (meaning unknown) also poss.; for the problems involved, cf. also Amadasi sub Kition A 27, Hvidberg-Hansen TNT ii 17f. n. 28.
v. *ʾzr*$_2$, *ʾzrh*$_1$, *ʾm*$_1$.

ʾzr$_5$ **DA** Sing. abs. *ʾzr* i 14 (:: McCarter BASOR ccxxxix 51, 56, Levine JAOS ci 197: = Sing. cstr. (cf. Hackett BTDA 29, 52f., 94, Sasson UF xvii 288, 303)) - ¶ subst. loincloth (context however dam.; cf. Hoftijzer DA a.l., cf. also Rofé SB 67, Garbini Hen i 180f., 185 :: H.P.Müller ZAW xciv 218, 228f. (n. 91): = Sing. abs. of *ʾzr*$_3$ (= certain type of sacrifice/offering), cf. also Puech BAT 359, 362, FS Grelot 24, 28: = Sing. cstr. of *ʾzr*$_3$; for the context, cf. also Caquot & Lemaire Syr liv 201) - the interpret. of the *ʾzrn* in DA i 18 (reading uncert.) as Plur. abs. highly uncert., cf. Hoftijzer DA a.l. (cf. Puech FS Grelot 25, 28: = Plur. abs. of *ʾzr*$_3$ :: Lemaire CRAI '85, 281: = QAL Imper. s.m. of *ʾzr*$_1$ (= to gird))

ʾzrh$_1$ **Pun** Sing. abs. *ʾzrt* KAI 100^{5}; cstr. *ʾzrt* CIS i 3712^{4}, 4854^{4}, 4855$^{4f.}$, 4873^{4} (and CIS i 2758?, cf. Février BAr '46/49, 168), Syr xi 202 ii 1; + suff. 3 p.s.m. *ʾzrtm* Hofra 223^{3} (v. infra); + suff. 3 p.pl.m.

ʾzrtnm CIS i 5510², ʾzrtm CIS i 5510⁵ᶠ· - ¶ subst. prob. meaning *familia* (the clients and slaves included), cf. Février Sem vi 27, Karth x 54f., sub CIS i 5510 :: CIS i sub 3712: = *clientela* (cf. also Röllig sub KAI 100: 'Hilfmannschaft'?, Ferron Africa iii 86 :: Février BAr '46/49, 168ff., JA ccxxxix 9f.: = male issue (cf. Cazelles CISFP 673ff.: = offspring) :: CIS i sub 4854: = *vestiarium* :: Chabot sub RIL 1: = technical term connected with building (cf. also Alvarez Delgado ILC 179) :: Dussaud Syr xi 202, Albright JAOS lxxi 263: ʾzrt in Syr xi 202 ii 1 = excellence - interpret. of ʾzrtm in Hofra 223³ (isolated word) uncert., cf. Berthier & Charlier Hofra a.l.: = form of ʾzr₄ < root ʿzr₁.
v. mʿzrh.

ʾzrh₂   v. ʾzr₄.

ʾzrm₁   v. ʾzr₂.

ʾzrm₂   v. ʾzr₃.

ʾzt₁   (< Iran., cf. Benveniste JA ccxlii 299, Gershevitch JRAS '54, 126, de Menasce BiOr xi 161, Eilers AfO xvii 333, Hinz AISN 52, cf. also In Der Smitten BiOr xxviii 385 (cf. Benveniste Titres 26: < med)) - **OffAr** Sing. abs. ʾzt Krael 5⁴ - ¶ adj. free; ʾzt šbqtky Krael 5⁴: I have released you (cf. also Muffs 40 n. 1, Benveniste JA ccxlii 298f., Boyarin JANES iii 60: < Iran., cf. however Greenfield AAASH xxv 113) :: Krael p. 183: = QAL Pf. 1 p.s. of ʾzl?, cf. Milik RB lxi 249f.

ʾzt₂   v. mlk₅.

ʾztp   v. ʾštp.

ʾḥ₁   m **Ph** Sing. abs. ʾḥ KAI 24¹¹; cstr. ʾḥ EpAn ix 5⁹; + suff. 1 p.s. ʾḥ KAI 24³ (nom.; cf. e.g. FR 234, Gibson SSI iii p. 36 :: Röllig KAI a.l., Collins WO vi 184 (n. 9): or = Sing. + suff. 3 p.s.m.?); Dual abs. ʾ[ḥ]ym KAI 197ᶠ· - **Pun** Sing. + suff. 3 p.s.m. ʾḥy KAI 47², ʾḥyʾ NP 2² (= Trip 2²; or = Plur. + suff. 3 p.s.m.? :: Berger RA ii 38: lʾḥyʾ = lʾ (= l₁) + Plur. + suff. 3 p.s.m. of ḥy₁), ʿym Punica xii 30³ (?); + suff. 3 p.s.f., cf. IRT 826²,³: *via* (?, diff. context (for this interpret., cf. Vattioni Aug xvi 538) :: Krahmalkov JSS xvii 73f.: l. <a>via in l. 2 and *fel avia* pro *fela via* in l. 3, *avia* being Sing. + suff. 3 p.s.f. :: Levi Della Vida OA ii 84: *via* = part of n.p.); + suff. 1 p.s., cf. Poen 932: *ui* (cf. Gordon Or xxi 122, Friedrich OLZ '69, 47, FR 35c, cf. however Sznycer PPP 65); + suff. 3 p.pl.m., cf. IRT 24⁴: *unom* (highly uncert. interpret., cf. Krakmalkov RSF vii 177 :: Vattioni AION xvi 55, Aug xvi 549); Plur. + suff. 3 p.s.m. ḥym Punica xi 10⁶, 11² (or l. ḥymy ḥnbʿl pro ḥym yḥnbʿl?) - **Amm** Sing. + suff. 3 p.s.m. ʾḥh BASOR cclxiv 47¹ (= CAI 144) - **Hebr** Sing. cstr. ʾḥy Frey 630b³; + suff. 2 p.s.m. ʾḥk TA-H 15⁵ (ʾḥ[k], heavily dam. context), 16¹; + suff. 1 p.s. ʾḥy DJD ii 45⁸ (dam. context); Plur. + suff. 1 p.s. ʾḥy KAI 200¹⁰,¹¹ - **DA** Sing. abs. ʾḥ xd 3 (uncert. context) -**Samal** Sing. + suff. 2 p.pl.m. *ʾḥkm* KAI 214^{29} - **OldAr** Sing. + suff. 2 p.s.m. *ʾḥk* KAI 224^{18}; Plur. + suff. 3 p.s.m. *ʾḥwh* KAI 224^{17}, Tell F 4; + suff. 1 p.s. *ʾḥy* KAI 216^{14}, 224^{4,9,13} (or in KAI 224^{4,9,13} = Sing. + suff. 1 p.s.?) - **OffAr** Sing. abs. *ʾḥ* Cowl 1^{5}, 5^{8}, 6^{13}, Krael 4^{13,19}, etc., etc.; + suff. 3 p.s.m. *ʾḥwhy* Cowl 25^{21}, 28^{15}, Aḥiq 49, Krael 12^{19,20}, Driv 11^{5}, ATNS 28a 1 + 30b 1 (for the reading, cf. Porten & Yardeni sub TADAE B 8.4 :: Segal sub ATNS 28: l. *ʾḥn* (= Plur. abs.)), 111^{3} (dam. context), etc., *ʾḥwh* Cowl 25^{3} (:: e.g. Schulthess GGA '07, 191, Leand 12c: scribal error), Syr xli 285^{3} (× Naveh AION xvi 30: l. *ʾḥwh[y]*), ATNS 55a 5 (??, heavily dam. context; or = Paʿel Impf. 1 p.s. of *ḥwy*$_1$??); + suff. 3 p.s.f. *ʾḥwhʾ* RES 1300^{4}; + suff. 2 p.s.m. *ʾḥwk* KAI 233^{1}, Cowl 40^{1,5}, 42^{1,15} (for the reading, cf. Porten & Yardeni sub TADAE A 3.8), 68 i 2, RHR cxxviii 30^{1}, RES 1300^{2}, SSI ii 28 obv. 1, rev. 7, Sach 76 v 5 (or = suff. 2 p.s.f.?), ATNS 85^{5} (?, *]ʾḥwk[*; or = Paʿel Impf. 1 p.s. of *ḥwy*$_1$??), *ʾḥk* Herm 3^{5}; + suff. 2 p.s.f. *ʾḥwky* Cowl 68 viii 1, Herm 7^{1}, *ʾḥky* Herm 1^{1}, 2^{1}, 4^{2}; + suff. 1 p.s. *ʾḥy* Cowl 40^{1,5}, 41^{1}, 65 iv 1, 67 viii 2, RES 1300^{1,3}, RHR cxxviii 30^{1}, SSI ii 28 rev. 7, Herm 1^{8}, ATNS 77b 1, etc.; + suff. 2 p.pl.m. *ʾḥwkm* Cowl 21^{2,11}, 41^{9} (*[ʾ]ḥwkm*), NESE i 11^{1} (for the reading, cf. Porten Or lvii 78, Porten & Yardeni sub TADAE A 3.10), *ʾḥykwn* NESE iii 48^{3} (for the reading, cf. Ullendorf JSS xxv 246; lapsus for *ʾḥwkwn*?; :: Degen NESE iii a.l.: l. *ʾḥwkwn*); Plur. abs. *ʾḥyn* Cowl 20^{10}, ATNS 8^{1}, 50^{2} (dam. context, uncert. reading, cf. Porten & Yardeni sub TADAE B 5.6), *ʾḥn* ATNS 55a 3 (*ʾḥn[*), Samar 4^{6}; + suff. 3 p.s.m. *ʾḥwhy* IrAnt iv 122^{3}; + suff. 3 p.s.f. *ʾḥwh* CIS i 19^{4} (= Del 12; for this reading, cf. Fales sub AECT 17, cf. however Kaufman JAOS cix 99); + suff. 1 p.s. *ʾḥy* Cowl 21^{2,11}, NESE i 11^{1,9}, iii 48^{1,4} (in both instances Sing. poss.); + suff. 2 p.pl.m. *ʾḥykm* Cowl 20^{12}; cf. Frah xi 12 (*ʾḥ[y]*), Nisa-b 902 obv. 2, 6, 7, 8, rev. 4, 1760^{2} (*ʾḥy*), etc., Sogd B 242, GIPP 15, 45, cf. SaSt 12 (cf. also Toll ZDMG-Suppl viii 29) - **Nab** Sing. cstr. *ʾḥ* CIS ii 212^{5}, 231^{2}, 351^{1}, RES 675^{1}, J 34^{7}, on coins, cf. NC 37f.; + suff. 3 p.s.m. *ʾḥwhy* CIS ii 195^{4}, 814^{2}, 2611^{2}, *ʾḥwh* CIS ii 302^{2}, 1780, 2654^{2}, *ʾḥwhw* CIS ii 1627, *ʾḥwy* (?) RB xlvii 98^{2}, *ʾḥh* EI x 181,8^{2}; + suff. 3 p.s.f. *ʾḥwh* CIS ii 226^{2}; Plur. + suff. 3 p.s.m. *ʾḥwhy* CIS ii 209^{2,5}, ARNA-Nab 30, *ʾḥwyhw* RB xlii 420,13^{2}; + suff. 3 p.s.f. *ʾḥyh* CIS ii 213^{3} - **Palm** Sing. + suff. 3 p.s.m. *ʾḥwhy* CIS ii 3955^{4}, 4072^{4}, 4211 (*[ʾ]ḥwhy*; Greek par. ἀδελφὸν), 4328^{7}, 4329A 9, B 5, 4330^{4}, Inv xii 56^{4}, SBS 19^{4}, etc., *ʾḥwh* CIS ii 4072^{6} (or = Plur.?), 4518A 3, MUSJ xxviii 46^{5}, Ber v 137, Inv viii 200^{3}, xi 35^{5} (Milik DFD 294: l. *ʾḥyh* = Aph Pf. 3 p.s.m. + suff. 3 p.s.m. of *ḥyy*), xii 36^{1}, RIP 102a, *ʾḥyh* CIS ii 4305^{6}, RIP 108^{4}, 114^{8} (??), *ʾḥwhw* Ber v 137, SBS 67^{2} (?, dam. context :: Dunant SBS p. 79: = Plur. + suff. 3 p.s.m.; Starcky SBS p. 80 n. 1: l. *ʾḥwhn*), *ʾḥy* Inv xii 34^{4} (lapsus ?; :: Aggoula Sem xxix 115: = +

suff. 1 p.s.); + suff. 3 p.s.f. *ʾḥwh* CIS ii 4284^{6}, 4304, Ber ii 96^{3}; + suff. 3 p.pl.m. *ʾḥwhn* CIS ii 3995^{4} (cf. also sub *ʾḥwhw*); + suff. 1 p.pl. *ʾḥwnʾ* RIP 52^{4}; Plur. abs. *ʾḥyn* Ber v 106^{1}; emph. *ʾḥyʾ* CIS ii 4158^{2}; + suff. 3 p.s.m. *ʾḥwhy* CIS ii 3973^{6}, 3989^{3} (= RIP 131, SBS 13^{2}), 3998A 3 (= RIP 130^{8}), 4017^{5}, 4026^{4}, 4122^{3} (Greek par. ἀδελφοῖς), RB xxxix 530^{3} (Greek par. ἀδελφοῖς), RIP 106^{5}, 110^{5}, 112$^{4f.}$, 127^{10}, Inv xi 6^{7}, 12^{8}, SBS 1A 2, B 2 (cf. Cantineau Gramm 65), etc., *ʾḥwh* CIS ii 4018^{3}, RIP 115^{7}, 122^{5} (or = Sing.?), 143^{2}, SBS 14^{2}, Sem xxvii 117^{6} (cf. Cantineau Gramm 66), *ʾḥw* CIS ii 4024^{5}, *ʾḥyhy* PNO 39 (or = Sing.?), *ʾḥyh* PNO 14^{8}, Inv xi 7^{4} (or = Sing.?), *ʾḥywh* CIS ii 4029^{5}, *ʾḥwḥy* CIS ii 4021^{3} (or = Sing.?; lapsus); + suff. 3 p.s.f. *ʾḥyh* CIS ii 3988^{3} (= RIP 128), SBS 11^{7}, Syr xii 135^{1} (or = Sing.?), *ʾḥh* CIS ii 4067^{4} (or = Sing.?), 4532^{6}; + suff. 3 p.pl.m. *ʾḥyhwn* CIS ii 3986^{4}, Inv xii 46^{4}, 48^{3} (*ʾḥyhw[n]*), *ʾḥyhn* Syr xix 80^{5}; + suff. 3 p.pl.f. *'ḥyhn* SBS 10^{5} - **Hatra** Sing. emph. *ʾḥʾ*, cf. Assur 3 ii 5, 15a 4 (uncert. reading); + suff. 3 p.s.m. *ʾḥwhy* 34^{6}, 174^{2} (cf. also Assur 22^{6}), *ʾḥwh* 35^{6} (= KAI 249; cf. Degen ZDMG cxxi 125, Milik DFD 353, 366: l. *ʾḥwh w* pro *ʾḥwhy* (cf. also Vattioni IH a.l.), *ʾḥh*, cf. Assur 3 ii 2 (heavily dam. context), 27b 2, 44 (heavily dam. context), the reading *ʾḥw* in 288a 6 (Safar Sumer xxvii 9) uncert., cf. Degen NESE iii 80, 81, cf. also Vattioni IH a.l.); Plur. + suff. 3 p.s.m. *ʾḥyhy* 20^{3} (cf. Milik RN vi/iv 54, Teixidor Syr xliv 189 :: Safar Sumer vii 180, Caquot Syr xxix 99f., Altheim & Stiehl AAW ii 199, Aggoula Ber xviii 89: = Sing. + suff. 3 p.s.m. :: Vattioni IH a.l.: l. *ʾḥwhy* (= Plur. + suff. 3 p.s.m.)), 80^{4}, 192^{4}, 241^{2}, 272^{1}, 408^{5}, *ʾḥyh* Syr xl 12^{10} (= app. 4; reading *ʾḥwh* = Sing. + suff. 3 p.s.m. poss., cf. Teixidor Syr xli 275 n. 1) - **JAr** Sing. + suff. 3 p.s.m. *ʾḥh* MPAT 52^{5}, *ʾḥwh* SM 37^{2} (for the reading, cf. Naveh EI xx 307), *ʾḥwy* MPAT-A 42^{3} (= SM 20), EI xx 307 vii 1 (dam. context); + suff. 1 p.s. *ʾḥy* MPAT 89^{1} (:: Beyer ATTM 329: = derivative of root *ḥwy*$_2$*/ḥyy*) - f. **Ph** Sing. + suff. 2 p.s.f. *ʾḥtk* KAI 50^{2}; + suff. 1 p.s. *ʾḥty* KAI 50^{2} - **Pun** Sing. cstr. *ʾḥt* KAI 123^{2} - **OffAr** Sing. abs. *ʾḥh* Cowl 1^{5}, 5^{8}, 6^{13}, Krael 1^{8}, 4^{13,19}, etc., etc.; cstr. *ʾḥt* Cowl 22^{82}, 65 iv 3, Herm 2^{5}, ATNS 142^{4} (*]ʾḥt*; uncert. reading, heavily dam. context); + suff. 3 p.s.m. *ʾḥth* Cowl 82^{10}, Krael 7^{41} (*ʾḥ[t]h*; for the reading, cf. Porten & Yardeni sub TADAE B 3.8), KAI 264^{2}, *ʾḥthh* Herm 7^{4} (for this reading, cf. e.g. Kutscher IOS i 104, 106, Contini EVO ii 204, Kottsieper SAS 98; prob. lapsus for *ʾḥth*, cf. Degen Or xlvii 119; for interpret. as Sing. + suff. 3 p.s.m., cf. Grelot DAE p. 472, Gibson SSI ii p. 143 :: Kutscher IOS i 104, 106: = Sing. + suff. 3 p.s.f. (cf. also Porten & Greenfield JEAS p. 164, Porten & Yardeni sub TADAE A 2.7) :: Bresciani & Kamil Herm. a.l.: l. *ʾḥthy* = Sing. + suff. 3 p.s.m.); + suff. 3 p.s.f. *ʾḥth* Cowl 1^{2}, 34^{4}, 43^{2,13}; + suff. 2 p.s.m. *ʾḥtk* Krael 7^{3,4,5}; + suff. 1 p.s. *ʾḥty* Cowl 68 viii 3, KAI 264^{5}, Herm 1^{1}, 2^{1}, 4^{1}, 5^{1}, 6^{1}, 7^{2,5}; Plur. + suff. 3 p.s. (m. or f.?) *ʾḥwth*

Cowl 75[8]; cf. Frah xi 14, 15 (ʾ*ḥth*), cf. also Toll ZDMG-Suppl viii 31 - **Nab** Sing. cstr. ʾ*ḥt* CIS ii 224[6], 448[2]; + suff. 3 p.s.m. ʾ*ḥth* CIS ii 354[3] (*[ʾ]ḥth*), PEQ '81, 22[2], on coins, cf. NC 65 (cf. Meshorer Mas coin 3626; cf. also Spijkerman CDPA p. 32); Plur. + suff. 3 p.s.m. ʾ*ḥwth* CIS ii 199[3], 210[2], RES 1434[9] (prob. lapsus for Sing. + suff. 3 p.s.m. ʾ*ḥth*), RB xlii 408[4], ʾ*ḥth* CIS ii 207[4]; + suff. 3 p.pl.f. ʾ*ḥwthm* CIS ii 205[3] - **Palm** Sing. + suff. 3 p.s.m. ʾ*ḥth* CIS ii 4535B 3, Inv x 119b 2, Ber xix 71[7], RIP 193[3] (or + suff. 3 p.s.f.); + suff. 3 p.s.f. ʾ*ḥth* CIS ii 3907[5], 4568; + suff. 3 p.pl.m. ʾ*ḥthwn* CIS ii 4018[8] - **Hatra** Sing. cstr. ʾ*ḥt*, cf. Assur 11 i 2; + suff. 1 p.s. ʾ*ḥty*, cf. Assur 11 ii 1; + suff. 1 p.pl. *ḥtn* (in the comb. *wḥtn*, cf. Assur 11 i 1 (cf. Aggoula Assur a.l.) - ¶ subst. 1) m. brother, f. sister, passim (e.g. m.: KAI 24[3], 47[2], f.: Cowl 22[82], 82[10]; said of half-brothers: RB xxxix 530[3]; ʾ*ḥy* ʾ*byw* Frey 630b 3: his (paternal) uncle; ʾ*ḥt* ʾ*mm* KAI 123[2f.]: his (maternal) aunt; *bn*ʾ *ḥym* Punica xi 10[6]: his nephews, cf. Poen 932: *byn ui* = my nephew, cf. also IEJ xxxviii 164B i 3, Assur 3 ii 5; *b*ʿ*ly* ʾ*ḥyn* Ber v 106[1]: half-brothers; in the expression *lḥyy bnwhy w*ʾ*ḥwhy* (and parallels), ʾ*ḥwhy* (and variants) considered as Plur. - **2)** a) used in epistolary style among equals: my brother (the addressee or (other) people spoken of in the third person) and your brother (the sender), cf. KAI 50[1], 233[1], RES 1300[1f.], Cowl 21[2,11], 40[1,5], RHR cxxviii 30[1], etc.; for the problems of the Hermopolis papyri (meaning 1) or meaning 2)?), cf. Milik Bibl xlviii 549, Porten & Greenfield ZAW lxxx 227, 230f., IOS iv 15, 26ff., Porten Arch 264ff., cf. also Hayes & Hoftijzer VT xx 104 (especially on inconsistencies) - b) also used elsewhere indicating equals, ʾ*ḥy mlky*ʾ KAI 216[14f.]: my colleagues, the kings; ʾ*ḥy* KAI 200[10,11]: my fellow-workers (cf. Lemaire Sem xxi 73, Pardee Maarav i 49) - **3)** said of a king, who protects his subjects and contributes to their prosperity: KAI 24[11] - **4)** ʾ*ln* ʾ*[ḥ]ym* KAI 19[7f.]: the divine brothers, title of the ptolemaean king and his spouse (for Greek par., cf. Cooke NSI p. 51, Gibson SSI iii p. 121) - **5)** ʾ*ḥth* CIS ii 354[3], PEQ '81, 22[2], RES 1434[9] (cf. however supra) and on coins: his sister (sc. of the nabatean king); epitheton of nabatean queen; cf. also KAI 264[2] - **6)** ʾ*ḥ mlk*ʾ RES 675[1]: brother of the king, title of the nabatean prime minister, cf. ʾ*ḥ šqylt mlkt nbṭw* CIS ii 351[1f.]: prob. the prime minister of the nabatean queen-regent ShuqaiLat., cf. Strabo XVI iv 21, Clermont-Ganneau RAO ii 380f., vii 307ff. - Février CB viii 31: l. *ḥt*ʾ (= f. Sing. + suff. 3 p.s.m.) in NP 87 (uncert. reading and interpret.) × Février Sem vi 17 (cf. also Chabot sub Punica xviii/i 15 with also other poss. readings): l. *ḥn*ʾ = n.p. (for the context, v. ʿ*m*4) - Février sub IAM 123: l. ʾ*ḥt* (= f. Sing. cstr.) in IAM 123[2] (= RIL 881[2]), cf. already Sola Sole Sef xix 373, 375: l. ʾ*ḥt*ʾ (= f. Sing. + suff. 3 p.s.m.) :: Alvarez Delgado ILC 249, 260: l. ʾ*brt* (= article + Sing. cstr. of *brt* = covenant, treaty; cf. however Chabot sub RIL 881:

ʾ..t) - Amadasi Guzzo VO vi 187f.: l. poss. *]ʾḥy* (= Sing. + suff. 3 p.s.m./f.) in CIS i 124 - Puech RB xc 501: l. *ʾḥy* in Frey 1322[2] (= Sing. + suff. 1 p.s. or = n.p.) - Segal ATNS a.l.: l. prob. *ʾḥn* (= Plur. abs.) in ATNS 9[1] (improb. reading, cf. Porten & Yardeni sub TADAE B 8.6 (div. otherwise): l. poss. *wzy*) - Hüttenmeister ASI 338f.: l. *ʾḥwh* in SM 37[2], poss. = Sing. + suff. 3 p.s.m. (uncert. interpret. and reading, cf. e.g. Naveh SM a.l.).
v. *ʾḥrh, ʾḥrn, ʾyḥ, ʾnth$_2$, ʾsr$_3$, br$_1$,zy, ḥy$_2$, ḥwy$_2$, ḥn$_1$, mwt$_1$, šlḥ$_1$*.

ʾḥ$_2$ **Pun** Février Sem vi 18: *ʾḥt* in KAI 145[4] = Plur. cstr. of *'ḥ$_2$* (= brazier), *ʾḥt šmm* = the braziers (i.e. stars) of Heaven (highly uncert. interpret., cf. Röllig KAI a.l.) :: Krahmalkov RSF iii 191: = orthographical variant of *ʾyt$_3$* (improb. interpret.) :: v.d.Branden RSF i 168: = m. Sing. cstr. of *ʾḥd$_4$*; Ellenbogen 21: < Egypt.
v. *ḥrʾ$_1$*.

ʾḥ$_3$ v. *ʿṣ*.

ʾḥbr v. *ḥbr$_2$*.

ʾḥd$_1$ v. *ʾḥz*.

ʾḥd$_2$ v. *ʾḥd$_4$, tkd*.

ʾḥd$_3$ **OffAr** Plur. cstr. *ʾḥdy* (?) Aḥiq 99 - ¶ subst. of uncert. meaning; *ʾḥdy pmk* Aḥiq 99: the secrets(??) of your mouth (cf. Cowl a.l., cf. also Grelot RB lxviii 183 (reading *ʾḥydy* prob. misprint), DAE p. 437; cf. also H.P.Müller VT xx 479 n. 4: = ruse, trick, Lindenberger APA 77:= saying or riddle (less prob. interpret.), Kottsieper SAS 20, 186: = trap).

ʾḥd$_4$ **Ph** m. + suff. 1 p.s. *ḥdy* MUSJ xlv 262[1] (in combination *lḥdy*; Starcky MUSJ xlv 262, Röllig NESE ii 2f.: *ʾ* between *l* and *d* lost (uncert. interpret.); = prep. *l$_5$* + subst. *ḥd$_1$* (= oneness) + suff. 1 p.s.?; on *lḥd* in **Ph** cf. also (Greenfield with) Ginsberg FS Gaster 137) - **Pun** m. *ʾḥd* KAI 69[3,7,11,12,17], 74[7], RES 336[4], etc., *ḥd* KAI 143[4] (in *wḥd*, cf. FR 243,1), *hd* Punica xx 1[5] (in *whd*), *ʾd* KAI 158[3] (in *wʾd*, cf. FR 35c), *d* Punica xi A 4 (in *wd*, cf. FR 243,1); f *ʾḥt* KAI 120[1], 141[3], *ʾḥtt* (lapsus) KAI 110[3] - **Hebr** m. *ʾḥd* DJD ii 30[8], EI xii 146 ii 7, MPAT 40[1], 42[6] (*ʾḥ[d]*; all in dates in J.Ar. context), SM 106[9], AMB 1[19]; f. *ʾḥt* EI xx 256[7] and on coins of the second revolt, JC no. 165, 166, 168, 170-3, 176, DJD ii 22, 1-9[1], 46[6], 48[5] (dam. context) - **Samal** m. *ḥd* KAI 214[15(?),27], 215[5]; f. *ḥdh* KAI 214[28] (for the form *ḥd(h)*, cf. Dion p. 118) - **OldAr** m. *ḥd* KAI 216[13], 222B 26, 28, 30(?), 45 (?, cf. Fitzmyer AIS 73), 224[1,4,5,9,10,13,17,22]; + suff. 3 p.pl.m. *ḥdhm* KAI 222B 45 (?, cf. Fitzmyer AIS 73), 224[19]; f. *ḥdh* KAI 222B 8 - **DA** m. *ḥd* ii 10 - **OffAr** m. *ḥd* Cowl 10[6], 15[28], 26[11], Krael 7[40], 9[13], 10[2] (for the reading problems, cf. Porten & Szubin JAOS cvii 231, cf. also Porten & Yardeni sub TADAE B 3.11), Beh 38 (Akkad. par. *išten*), Driv $6^{3,4}$, Aḥiq 191 (for the reading problems, cf. Lindenberger APA 189), ATNS 10a 7, Samar 2^{4}, etc., etc.; emph. *ḥdʾ* NESE iii 28 (??, reading *ḥrʾ* (= Sing. emph. of *ḥr*$_1$) poss., cf. Degen NESE iii a.l.); f. *ḥdh* Cowl 15^{28}, 27^{6}, 30^{19}, 37^{12} (diff. and dam. context; cf. Cowl a.l., Grelot DAE p. 390, Porten & Greenfield JEAS p. 80, cf. however Porten & Yardeni sub TADAE A 4.2 = QAL Part. act. s.m. abs. of *ḥdy*$_1$), NESE i 11^{2} (for the reading, cf. Degen NESE i 14, Naveh & Shaked JAOS xci 380, Grelot DAE p. 504 (n. d), Golomb BASOR ccxvii 52, Porten Or lvii 78, Porten & Yardeni sub TADAE A 3.10 :: Shunar GMA 116ff., CRM ii 278, Macuch JAOS xciii 58f.: l. *ḥnh* = cabin (of a ship)), ATNS 26^{16}, etc.; cf. Frah xxv 18 (*ḥt*, cf. Nyberg FP 55, 102f.), xxix 1 (*ḥd*), Frah-S1 2 (*kḥdh*), cf. MP 3 (*ḥd*, *ḥt*, (cf. however SaSt 17), *kḥdh*), GIPP 23, 25, 52, SaSt 16 (*ḥd*), 18 - **Nab** m. *ḥd* RES 676^{5}, J 4^{7}, CIS ii $200^{7,8}$ (= J 30; for the reading, cf. Milik sub ARNA-Nab 79), 209^{6}, 224^{12}, ADAJ xx 121^{1}; f. *ḥdh* CIS ii 218^{4}, 221^{6}, 223^{5}, Syr xxxv 250b, on coins, cf. NC no. 46, 47, 47a, 48, *ʾḥdy* J 386^{5}, BAGN ii 88^{7} (arabism, cf. Cantineau Nab i 95f.) - **Palm** m. *ḥd* CIS ii 3913 ii 42, 45, 48, 69, 73, Ber ii $86^{11,13}$, 102 i 3, Sem xxxvi $89^{3,5}$, *ʾḥd* CIS ii 4158^{1}, SBS 45B 11, 12, Sem xxxvi 89^{1}; f. *ḥdʾ* CIS ii 3913 ii 60, 4199^{4}, Syr xii 138^{3}, *ʾḥdʾ* RB xxxix 548^{5} (for the forms *ʾḥd* and *ʾḥdʾ*, cf. Cantineau Gramm 124f., Rosenthal Sprache 31) - **Hatra** m. *ḥd* 281^{9}; f. *ḥdʾ* 245^{2} (for the reading, cf. Aggoula MUSJ xlvii 16, Vattioni IH a.l., cf. also Safar Sumer xxiv 18: l. *ḥd/rʾ* :: Degen JEOL xxiii 412: l. *hdʾ*) - **JAr** m. *ḥd* MPAT 52^{8}, MPAT-A 27^{1}, $28^{3,4}$, $29^{2,3}$, 56^{2} (= SM 74), 62^{12} (for the reading, cf. Yadin & Greenfield sub DBKP 27 :: e.g. Fitzmyer & Harrington MPAT a.l. (div. otherwise): l. *ḥdʾ* = m. emph.), SM 53^{2}, *hd* (lapsus, cf. Beyer ATTM 394) MPAT-A 41^{4} (:: Naveh sub SM 29: l. *ḥd* :: Fitzmyer & Harrington MPAT a.l.: l. *hdh*); emph. *ḥdʾ* Syr xlv 101^{2}; f. *ḥdh* MPAT 41^{1}, 43 i 3, MPAT-A 28^{2}, AMB $7^{17,18}$, Syn D A 9 (for the reading, cf. Naveh sub SM 88 :: Torrey Syn D p. 263: l. *šyt* = *šš*$_3$) - ¶ cardinal number, one: KAI 69^{17}, Punica ix 1^{4}, xi 13^{2}, etc., etc.; cf. also *ytyr mn zy kʿn ḥd ʾlp* Cowl 30^{3}: a thousand times more than now; indicating dates, *bšt ʿsrm wʾḥt* KAI 141^{3}: in the 21st year, cf. *šnt ʾḥt* on jewish coins (v. supra), *bʾḥtt ʾrbʿm št* KAI $110^{3f.}$, *šnt ḥdh* CIS ii 218^{4}, *šnt ḥdh lḥr[wt...]* MPAT 43^{1-3} (the first year of the liberation), *by(w)m ḥd* RES 676^{5}, J 4^{7}, *bʾsr wʾḥd lzyb* RES 336^{4} (on the 21st of (the month) Z.), *bḥd bʾyr* ADAJ xx 121^{1} (on the first of (the month) I.), *mḥd* (v. supra) *btmwz* MPAT 62^{12} (from the first of (the month) T.); cf. also *pʿmʾt ʿsr wʾḥt* KAI 120^{1}: for the 11th time - **1)** used as indefinite article, a(n): Cowl $27^{5,6}$, 30^{29}, 31^{28}, Aḥiq 38, Beh 38, Hatra 245^{2}; cf. *bywm ḥd bkp ḥdh* Cowl 15^{28}: on a certain day, at a certain moment; *ḥd zywk* Cowl 37^{3}: a certain Z.??, v. however *zywk* -

2) prec. by prep. - a) *bʾḥd* KAI 69[3,7,11]: apiece, each - b) *kḥdh* Cowl 28[3], MAI xiv/2, 66[6]: together; cf. *ḥd kḥd* Cowl 10[7]: alike - c) *lḥd* Cowl 24[28-30]: per head, each, Cowl 26[14-16,18-20]: apiece, each; cf. *lyrḥ ḥd* Cowl 10[6]: each month, monthly; *lʾrḥ ḥdʾ* CIS ii 3913 ii 60: for each journey; cf. also *lbʾḥd* KAI 69[12]: apiece, each; *ʾnk lḥdy* MUSJ xlv 262[1]: I only/alone - the *lḥdy* in KAI 26A ii 5f. prob. = *lḥd* + suff. 3 p.s.f., cf. Ginsberg with Obermann JAOS Suppl ix 24 n. 70, Levi Della Vida RCL '49, 277, 284, Röllig NESE ii 3, Avishur PIB 224, 231, Bron RIPK 84f., Gibson SSI iii p. 49, 59, Dahood Or xlvi 475, Lipiński SV 48 (cf. also Greenfield EI xiv 75ff., H.P.Müller TUAT i 642) :: Weippert GGA '64, 191f. (div. otherwise): l. *lḥd* (without pron. suff.) = alone + *yd* = with :: Honeyman Mus lxi 52 (div. otherwise): *lḥdy* = *l*$_5$ + PI ʿEL Inf. cstr. of *ḥdy*$_1$ (cf. O'Callaghan Or xviii 177, Marcus & Gelb JNES viii 119, cf. also Dunand BMB vii 94, viii 27, Leveen & Moss JJS i 191, Schiffmann RSF iv 172, Silverman JAOS xciv 268 :: Dupont-Sommer RA xlii 172 (cf. JKF i 303f.; div. otherwise): *lḥdy* = *l*$_5$ + QAL Inf. cstr. + suff. 1 p.s. of *ʾḥd*$_2$ (= to unite) :: Gordon JQR xxxix 46 n. 15, JNES viii 114 (div. otherwise): l. *(tk)l* (v. *tk*$_1$) + *ḥdy* (= QAL Inf. cstr. + suff. 3 p.s.m. of *ḥyd* (= to stray)) :: Rosenthal ANET 500 (div. otherwise): l. *(tk)l ḥdy* (translation *ad sensum*): was able to stroll, cf. also Röllig KAI a.l., Teixidor Syr xlix 430 :: Lipiński RSF ii 48, RTAT 259 (n. 66; div. otherwise): l. *(tk)l* (v. *tk*$_1$) + *ḥd* (= QAL Inf. cstr. of *ḥdy*$_1$) + *y(dl)* (v. *plk*$_1$) :: v.Selms JNSL i 53: l. *(tk)l* + *l*$_5$ + QAL Inf. of *ḥdy*$_2$ (= to see) :: Swiggers BiOr xxxvii 339: *ḥd* = Sing. abs. of *ḥd*$_3$(= joy) :: Swiggers UF xii 440: *ḥdy* = Sing. + suff. 3 p.s.f. of *ḥd*$_3$(= joy) :: v.d.Branden BMB xiii 92, Meltô i 44: = *l*$_5$ + *ḥdy* (= Sing. + suff. 1 p.s. of *ḥd*$_1$ (= sword)) :: Friedrich FuF xxiv 78: = *lḥ* (= Sing. abs. of *lḥ*$_1$ (= *lwḥ*)) + *dy* (= Sing. cstr. of *dy*$_1$ (= sufficiency)) :: Obermann JAOS Suppl ix 25: l. *lḥry* (= *l*$_5$ + QAL Inf. cstr. of *ḥry*$_2$ (= to strife)) :: Pedersen ActOr xxi 52 (div. otherwise): l. *(tk)l* (v. *tk*$_1$) *ḥr* (= Sing. abs. of *ḥr*$_1$) *y(dl)* (v. *plk*$_1$) :: Lemaire Sem xxvi 69: *ḥdy* = Sing. abs. of *ḥdy*$_2$ - d) *ʿl ʾḥd* KAI 74[7]: apiece, each - **3)** *ḥd(h) ... wḥd(h)* AMB 7[17f.]: the one ... the other; *ḥd mn ḥd* Samar 2[4]: mutually - *d* in EI xii 136[1] (jewish Greek inscription) = abbrev. of *ʾḥd*?? - Dupont-Sommer JKF i 203: l. *wḥd* = *w* + *ḥd* in AMB 7[4], improb. reading, cf. Naveh & Shaked AMB a.l.: l. *-yh* (= emph. ending) + *d* (= *d*$_3$ (= *zy*)) - the *ḥdʾ* in Mas 698 also form of *ʾḥd*$_4$?, cf. Yadin & Naveh Mas a.l. - Cowley a.l.: l. *ḥdʾ* (Sing. m. emph.) in BSAE xvii pl. xiiiA (cpl.f. xvi), less prob. reading, cf. Lemaire Sem xxxvii 54: l. 20 + 3 + 1 - for *kl ḥd*, v. *kl*$_1$, for *mn ḥd*, v. *mn*$_4$.

v. *ʾḥ*$_2$, *ʾḥr*$_4$, *znh*, *ḥwd*$_1$, *kḥd*, *pḥd*$_2$.

ʾḥd$_5$ v. *ʾḥr*$_4$.

ʾḥdh v. *ʾḥz*.

ʾḥdy$_1$ **Pun** *ʾḥdy* RCL '66, 201[6] - ¶ adverb (or subst. used as adverb): together (cf. Dupont-Sommer CRAI '68, 117).

ʾḥdy$_2$ v. *ʾḥd$_4$*.

ʾḥh v. *ʾḥ$_1$*.

ʾḥw **OldAr** Sing. + suff. 3 p.s.f. *ʾḥwh* KAI 222A 29, 32 (:: Segert ArchOr xxxii 123: = Sing. abs. of *ʾḥwh*) - ¶ subst. m. grass (or more generally: vegetation?), cf. Fitzmyer AIS a.l., Greenfield ActOr xxix 11 n. 34; cf. also Couroyer RB lxvi 588: reeds, rushes (as distinguished from *ḥṣr$_3$* and *yrq*).

ʾḥwh v. *ʾḥw*.

ʾḥwnyh **Hebr** Plur. abs. *ʾḥwnywt* SM 49[20] - ¶ subst. f. prune.

ʾḥwr v. *ʾḥr$_3$*.

ʾḥz **Mo** QAL Impf. 1 p.s. + suff. 3 p.s.f. *ʾḥzh* KAI 181[11,15f.,20]; Imper. s.m. *ʾḥz* KAI 181[14] - **Samal** QAL Pf. 3 p.s.m. *ʾḥz* KAI 215[11] (for the context, v. *p$_1$*); Impf. 3 p.s.m. *yʾḥz* KAI 214[15,20,25]; 1 p.s. *ʾḥz* KAI 214[3] - **OldAr** QAL Pf. 1 p.s. *ʾḥzt* KAI 216[11]; Impf. 3 p.s.m. *lʾḥz* Tell F 19 (:: Andersen & Freedman FS Fensham 35: = *l$_1$* + QAL Pf. 3 p.s.m.; cf. also Greenfield & Shaffer Shn v/vi 124) - **OffAr** QAL Pf. 3 p.s.m. ATNS 3[3], *ʾḥz* CIS ii 19[4] (= Del 12; for the reading, cf. Fales sub AECT 17), OA iii 56 conv. 1 (= CRAI '47, 181), *ʾḥd* Driv 5[7] (:: Segal JSS iv 70: l. *ʾḥr* = *ʾḥr$_4$*); 1 p.s. *ʾḥzt* ATNS 6[2] (dam. context; highly uncert. reading, cf. Porten & Yardeni sub TADAE B 8.12), *ʾḥdt* Beh 14 (Akkad. par. *uṣ-ṣab-bi-tú*), ATNS 97a 1 (?, or 2 p.s.m./3 p.s.f.?, heavily dam. context); 3 p.pl.m. *ʾḥzw* KAI 266[5], *ʾḥdw* Cowl 69A 3, Beh 1, 6 (*ʾḥd[w]*; Akkad. par. (*uṣ-ṣab-bi-tú*), 11 (Akkad. par. *uṣ-ṣab-bi-tú*), 34 (Akkad. par. *uṣ-ṣab-bi-tú*), BIDG l. 58 (= Cowl p. 266 ii 5), TADAE A 4.6[16] (*ʾḥ[d]w*); + suff. 3 p.s.m. *ʾḥdwhy* HDS 9[8] (for the reading, cf. Kaufman with Lipiński Stud 77 (cf. also Fales AION xxviii 277) :: Caquot HDS a.l.: l. *ʾḥrmhy* = APH Pf. 3 p.pl.m. + suff. 3 p.s.m. of *ḥrm$_1$*; 1 p.pl. *ʾḥzn* KAI 233[3,6] (heavily dam. context); Impf. 3 p.s.m. *yʾḥd* HDS 9[3f.] (for the reading, cf. Fales AION xxviii 277) :: Caquot HDS a.l., Lipiński Stud 79, ActOr Hung xxii 375, WGAV 375 (div. otherwise): l. *yʾḥrm* = APH Impf. 3 p.s.m. of *ḥrm$_1$*), *yʾḥdn* Aḥiq 171 (on this form, cf. Kottsieper SAS 136); 2 p.s.m. *tʾḥd* ATNS 26[5]; Inf. *mʾḥd* Cowl 2[17], *mḥd* Krael 11[10] (for this reading, cf. Yaron JNES xx 127, JSS xviii 277, Porten & Greenfield JEAS p. 66, Porten & Yardeni sub TADAE B 3.13 :: Krael a.l., Grelot DAE p. 253: l. *mḥr* = *mḥr$_1$*, cf. however Grelot RB lxxxii 290f.); Part. act. s.m. abs. *ʾḥd* Krael 3[5], 4[8], 6[4], 9[13], 10[2], 12[13] (Kutscher JAOS lxxiv 235: = Part. pass.); pl.m. abs. *ʾḥdn* KAI 279[4] (× Coxon JNES xxxvi 297:= QAL Pf. 3 p.pl.m.; cf. also Koopmans 176, Altheim

& Stiehl EW ix 194, GH 401, ASA 265, Stiehl AAW i 228; :: Rosenthal EI xiv 98*: = form with Iran. inf. ending *-n*); ITP Pf. 3 p.s.m. *ʾtʾḥz* KAI 226[4], ATNS 141[3] (*ʾtʾḥ[z]*; ?, heavily dam. context); 3 p.pl.m. *ʾtḥd[w]* Cowl 34[4]; cf. Frah xx 15 (*ʿḥdwn*), Paik 43 (*ʾḥd*), 44 (*ʿḥdwn*), cf. GIPP 19, 45, SaSt 13f. - **Nab** QAL Pf. 3 p.s.m. *ʾḥd* CIS ii 234[2], RES 1110C (= J 56, ARNA-Nab 92), 1111B (cf. however J 59: = PAʿEL), 1119A (= J 100), etc.; + suff. 3 p.s.m. (prob.) *ʾḥdh* RES 1292B; 1 p.s. *ʾḥdt* DBKP 22[32] (dam. context; for the reading, cf. Yadin & Greenfield DBKP a.l.) - **Palm** QAL Pf. 3 p.s.m. *ʾḥd* RIP 127[2,7], Inv xii 44[1]; Impf. 3 p.s.m. (or 3 p.pl.m.??, cf. Gawlikowski Sem xxiii 120, TP 43) + suff. 3 p.pl.m. *yḥdnh[n]* SBS 34[4] (:: Dunant SBS a.l.: l. *yḥdnh* = QAL Impf. 3 p.s.m. + suff. 3 p.s.m.); Part. pass. s.m. abs. *ʾḥyd* SBS 68[1], RIP 145[3] (:: Michałowski FP ii 250: l. *ʾwyr* = air, void); s.m. emph. *ʾḥydʾ* SBS 70; pl.m. abs. *ʾḥydyn* SBS 34[2]; pl.m. cstr. *ʾḥydy* RTP 40 (for the reading, cf. Milik DFD 286); pl.m. emph. *ʾḥydyʾ* RIP 199[4] (*ʾḥ[y]dyʾ*),[11] (:: Michałowski FP i 215 ad text 10a 9: l. *ʾḥyryʾ* = Plur. emph. of *ʾḥyr* (= *ʾḥr*$_3$)) - **Hatra** QAL Pf. 3 p.s.m. *ʾḥd* Assur 15d 2 (?, heavily dam. context); 3 p.pl.m. *ʾḥdw* 79[7] (cf. Aggoula MUSJ xlvii 31 :: Safar Sumer xvii 13, 17, Caquot Syr xl 2, 6, Teixidor Syr xli 280, Vattioni IH a.l.: l. *wʾḥrwhn w* (pro *wʾḥdw hnw*) = and their posterity and :: Aggoula Ber xviii 96: *wʾḥrwhn* = the others, cf. also Safar Sumer xvii 13 n. 11: poss. = others than them (cf. also Altheim & Stiehl AAW iv 243, 245: l. *ʾḥryhn* with same meaning)); Part. pass. s.m. cstr. *ʾḥd* 261, 263 (?, × Aggoula MUSJ xlvii 21: = QAL Pf. 3 p.s.m. (cf. also Vattioni IH a.l.) :: Degen JEOL xxiii 415: *ʾḥd* = part of n.p. (less prob.)) - **JAr** QAL Impf. 2 p.pl.m. *tḥdwn* MPAT 53[1] (for the reading, cf. Beyer ATTM 351); Inf. *mḥd* MPAT 53[3] - ¶ verb QAL to take, to seize, to take possession of; *wywnyʾ wkrkyʾ zy tʾḥd ṭr ʿmk* ATNS 26[5]: and the Ionians and Carians that you will seize, keep (them) with you - **1)** + acc. obj.: Cowl 2[17], CIS ii 234[2], RES 1110C, 1119A, 1121C, MPAT 53[1] (v. supra), etc.; to take (sc. a town): KAI 181[11,15f.,20], cf. *ʾḥz ʾt nbh ʿl yšrʾl* KAI 181[14]: take N. from Israel (*ʿl* prob. having a negative implication, against, cf. also Lipiński Or xl 334; on the subject, cf. also Dahood FS Horn 433f. (nn. 14-19), Sperling JAOS ci 449, Jackson & Dearman SMIM 114 :: Segert ArchOr xxix 228; Aartun BiOr xxviii 125: take N. in Israel (less prob.; cf. also Reviv CSI p. 23); to seize, to make prisoner/captive: Driv 5[7], Beh 14, 34, HDS 9[8] (v. supra; poss. also in HDS 9[4]); cf. *ḥyn ʾḥdw* Beh 1, 11: they took them alive (cf. Beh 6); *zy nwnyʾ ʾḥdn* KAI 279[4]: the fishermen (cf. Greek par. ἁλιεῖς); *yʾḥz ḥṭr wyšb ʿl mšby* KAI 214[20]: he will grasp the sceptre and sit on my throne (i.e. he will become king), cf. KAI 214[25], cf. also Greenfield FS Fitzmyer 48; *'ḥzt byt ʾby* KAI 216[11f.]: I have taken over my father's house (i.e. I assumed the headship of the dynasty, cf. Gibson SSI ii

p. 90f. :: Donner KAI a.l.: prob. architectural expression); *ʾḥd gšwrn kwn wdššn 2* Krael 12[13]: (said of a house) containing beams, windows and 2 doors, cf. Krael p. 160, Krael 4[8], 6[4], 10[2f.], cf. als Krael 9[13]: *ʾḥd gšwrn wkwn bh 3 dš ḥd* (cf. Krael 3[5]) - **2)** + obj. + *mn*$_5$, *wʾlp šʿryn lzrʿ wprys lʾḥz mnh* Tell F 19: may he sow a thousand measures of barley and may he get (only) a half-measure from it (cf. Akkad. par. *li-iṣ-bat*; cf. also Greenfield & Shaffer Irâq xlv 115) - **3)** + *b*$_2$ - a) *ʾḥz bknp m[r]ʾh* KAI 215[11]: he grasped the skirt of his lord (i.e. he submitted himself to his lord, he placed himself under the protection of his lord), cf. also Landsberger Samʾal 69 n. 178, cf. also Pardee UF ix 206, Younger JANES xviii 98 n. 31, Greenfield FS Fitzmyer 48, FS Moran 196ff.; *yʾḥdn ršyʿʾ bknpy lbšk* Aḥiq 171: a wicked man will grasp the fringe of your garment (in this case as a robber taking the garment, or a creditor confiscating it; cf. Lindenberger APA 174, 271 nn. 532, 533); - b) *wʾḥdw hnw ... bmrn* Hatra 79[7ff.] (v. supra): they are attached to our lord (i.e. they serve him piously) - c) *pmz ʾḥz byd[y]* KAI 214[3f.]: and whatever I will take in my hand (i.e. whatever I will undertake) - **4)** + *l*$_5$ in RES 1111B (diff. text): to take possession of (something) for?? (or PAʿEL?) - **5)** special semantic developments: - a) to choose, to select; *dy ʾḥd yrḥybwl ʾlhʾ* RIP 127[2]: whom Y. the god selected (cf. Greek text AAS vii 102 Gr 2ff.: ἐπιμελητὴς αἱρεθεὶς Ἔφκας πηγῆς ὑπὸ Ἰαριβόλου τοῦ θεοῦ), cf. Inv xii 44[1ff.]: *brbnwt ʿynʾ dy ʾḥd yrḥbwl ʾlhʾ tymw ....* (cf. also Aggoula Sem xxix 116, Teixidor Sem xxxiv 95 n. 238), cf. also *dy ʾḥd lh bwlḥʾ dnh rb ʿyn* RIP 127[7f.]: whom the said B. has selected as chief of the source (cf. SBS 34[4], dam. context); in RIP 149[4,11] *ʾḥydyʾ* prob. = functionaries, office-holders (cf. also RTP 40 (v. supra)), cf. Milik DFD 286f., Gawlikowski Sem xxiii 113ff. This word perhaps also in SBS 34[2] - b) pass. to be reserved; *ʾḥydʾ lbny* SBS 70: (place) reserved for B.; *ʾ[t]r ʾḥyd* SBS 68[1]: reserved p(la)ce; *ʾḥd wrwd* Hatra 261, 263: reserved (place) of W. (or: W has taken in possession; v. supra; cf. also J 56 (= ARNA-Nab 92): *ʿbdʿbdt ... ʾḥd ʾtrʾ dnh*)) - c) said of a door, *ʾḥd wptḥ* Krael 9[13]: closing and opening - **6)** Part. pass. with active function, *dkl ʾḥyd* RIP 145[3]: who is all-powerful (cf. also Gawlikowski TP 94) - ITP - 1) to be taken prisoner: Cowl 34[4] (?, cf. Cowl a.l.) - **2)** *pmy lʾtʾḥz mn mln* KAI 226[4]: my mouth was not closed to words (i.e. I was able to speak), cf. Cooke NSI p. 190, Lieberman Greek 168 n., Degen ZDMG cxxi 135, Tawil Or xliii 60ff., Greenfield FS Fitzmyer 48 - Porten & Yardeni sub TADAE B 3.8: l. form of this root *[ʾ]ḥdth* (= QAL Part. act. s.f. + suff. 3 p.s.m. or Pf. 3 p.s.f. + suff. 3 p.s.m.) in Krael 7[29] (uncert. interpret.; cf. Krael a.l.: l. *[ʾ]ḥdth* = Plur. + suff. 3 p.s.m. of *ʾḥdh* (= possession), Grelot DAE p. 236 n. c.: l. *[ʾ]ḥrth* = f. Sing. + suff. 3 p.s.m. of *ʾḥry*$_1$ (= trustee, executor)).

v. *ʾhzw*, *ʾḥry*$_1$, *ʾḥrn*, *mḥz*$_2$, *mḥzt*.

ʾḥzh v. *znh*

ʾḥyd v. *ʾḥz*.

ʾḥydw **Palm** Sing. abs. *ʾḥydw* Inv x 115^{3} - ¶ subst. office, function, cf. Milik DFD 286f. (cf. also Teixidor Sem xxxiv 95 n. 239; v. also *ʾḥz* sub 4); *bkl ʾḥydw klh* Inv x 115^{3}: in every function (cf. Greek par. πᾶσας λειτουργίας).

ʾḥyr v. *ʾḥz*.

ʾḥyryn v. *ʾtyṯk*.

ʾḥr$_1$ **Hebr** PIʿEL Impf. 2 p.s.m. *tʾḥr* TA-H 2^{6} - ¶ verb to loiter, to linger.
v. *ʾtḥr*.

ʾḥr$_2$ **Nab** Sing. cstr. *ʾḥr* CIS ii 200^{4} (= J 30; for the reading, cf. Milik sub ARNA-Nab 79)^{,6}; + suff. 3 p.s.m. *ʾḥrh* CIS ii 197^{2}, 201^{3}, 206^{8}, 208^{2}, ARNA-Nab 16^{2}, etc.; + suff. 3 p.s.f. *ʾḥrh* CIS ii 223^{2}, 224^{2}, 225^{2}; + suff. 3 p.pl.m. *ʾḥrhm* CIS ii 200^{2}, 209^{2,5}, 222^{5}, J 38^{3}, ADAJ xxi 144$^{2f.}$; + suff. 3 p.pl.f. *ʾḥrhm* CIS ii 198^{2,7}, J 14^{2} (= CIS ii 203; cf. also Ben-Chayyim EI i 137) - ¶ subst. posterity; mostly the children not included, cf. *lnpšh wyldh wʾḥrh* CIS ii 197^{2}: for himself, his children and his posterity (cf. also CIS ii 200^{2}, 201^{3}, 203^{2}, 206^{1}, etc.); cf. however *lh wlʾḥrh* J 22^{2}: for himself and his posterity (cf. also CIS ii 198^{2}, 222^{5}, ADAJ xxi 144$^{2f.}$, and *kmkm wbrth wʾḥrhm* CIS ii 198$^{6f.}$: K., her daughter and their posterity) - < Liḥy.?, cf. CIS ii sub 197, Cantineau Nab ii s.v., O'Connor JNES xlv 217ff., cf. however Milik ADAJ xxi 147.
v. *ʾḥr*$_4$, *ʾḥrh*, *ʾḥry*$_2$, *ʾšr*$_4$.

ʾḥr$_3$ **Hebr** Plur. m. abs. *ʾḥrym* DJD ii 22,1-9^{3,11,12} - **OffAr** Sing. m. emph. *ʾḥrʾ* KAI 278^{8} (for the reading, cf. Naveh AION xvi 32f., Hanson BASOR cxcii 11, Gibson SSI ii p. 156f. :: Dupont-Sommer DHC 11, 15, Donner KAI a.l.: l. *ʾḥrn* (= Sing. m. abs. of *ʾḥrn*)); f. abs. *ʾḥrh* Cowl 15^{32}, 64 xx 4?, 79^{3,4} (cf. Leand 43 v 1), Krael 7^{36} (*ʾḥr[h]*; for the reading, cf. Porten & Yardeni sub TADAE B 3.8); Plur. m. abs. *ʾḥrn* Cowl 15^{33} (:: Nöldeke ZA xx 136, Fitzmyer FS Albright ii 166: = lapsus for *ʾḥrnn* (= Plur. abs. of *ʾḥrn*)), *ʾḥwrn* FX 137^{25} (context however uncert.); emph. *ʾḥryʾ* Cowl 82^{7}; cf. Frah xxvii 8 (*ʾḥl*; cf. Nyberg FP 56, 106 :: Ebeling Frah a.l. (div. otherwise): l. *mʾḥr* = *mḥr*$_3$) - ¶ adj. other; *ʾyš ʾḥrʾ* KAI 278^{8} (v. supra): another man :: Gibson SSI ii p. 156f.: any person thereafter.
v. *ʾḥz*, *ʾḥr*$_5$, *ʾḥrh*, *ʾḥrn*, *ʾtyk*, *ḥrʾ*$_1$.

ʾḥr$_4$ **Pun** NP 2^{4} (cf. Levi Della Vida Lib iii 4)?? - **OffAr** Cowl 9^{8}, 13^{5}, 20^{8}, Krael 11^{3,6}, Driv 4^{3}, 5^{6,7} (:: Segal JSS iv 70: = *ʾḥr*$_5$; for this text, v. also sub *ʾḥz*), Samar 1^{9} (= EI xviii 8*), KAI 260B 3, 6,

262² (for the reading, cf. Hanson BASOR cxcii 6f., Lipiński Stud 163, Degen ZDMG cxxi 136 :: CIS ii sub 109: l. *ʾḥd₄*), 264⁴, RES 1785F 3, 4, 5, Beh 6 (Akkad. par. *ár-ki*), ATNS 6¹, 9^2,10, 16² (for the context, cf. Porten & Yardeni sub TADAE B 8.10), etc., etc.; cf. Frah xxv 48 (*ʾḥl*), Paik 52 (*ʾḥr*), Sogd ii 206, B 242, R 45, Ve 103, GIPP 15, 26 - ¶ adv. then, passim; cf. after imper Aḥiq 171: then; *hn* ... *ʾḥr* Cowl 28^9f., Krael 11^5f.,8,9f.: if ... then; also in the diff. text KAI 260B 3, cf. Kahle & Sommer KlF i 48ff., Hanson BASOR cxcii 8 (n. 13), Lipiński Stud 158 :: Lidzbarski ZA xxxi 128, Cowley CRAI '21, 11f.: l. *ʾḥd₅* = possession :: Torrey AJSL xxxiv 194: l. *ʾḥr₂*; the use of *ʾḥr* (picking up the train of thought: and, in sum, thus, then ...) in this text and also in ibid. l. 6 (bis) prob. under Iran. influence (for this influence, cf. also Cowl p. 206, Kutscher JAOS lxxiv 241, Driv p. 50, Whitehead JNES xxxvii 134 (n. 99)), cf. *mn zy ʿl* ... *ʾḥr mn zy yḥbl ʾḥr ʾrtmw zy klw wʾpšsy* ... *ybdrwnh* KAI 260B 4ff.: whoever is against (this stele) ... and whoever destroys (something) ... in his turn Artemis of C. and of E. will shatter him - Cowl p. 206: the *ʾḥr₄* in Aḥiq under Iran. influence (highly uncert., cf. also Lindenberger APA 31 n. 24).
v. *ʾḥz*.

ʾḥr₅ **Pun** NP 130² - **Hebr** DJD ii 44⁹ and diff. form in DJD ii 30²⁷; + suff. 2 p.s.m. *ʾḥryk* AMB 1² - **Mo** KAI 181³ - **OldAr** Tell F 10 (cf. Abou-Assaf, Bordreuil & Millard Tell F p. 24, 32, Zadok TeAv ix 125, Wesselius SV 56, Muraoka AN xxii 83, 111 n. 23, Gropp & Lewis BASOR cclix 46, 51, Vattioni AION xlvi 360, Delsman TUAT i 636 :: Kaufman Maarav iii 162: = Sing. m. abs. of *ʾḥr₃* (cf. also Greenfield & Shaffer Irâq xlv 113, Andersen & Freedman FS Fensham 23); for the context, cf. Pardee JNES xliii 254 n. 5) - **OffAr** Krael 4¹⁷, IPAA 11⁸; *ʾḥry* Cowl 44 (*scriptio anterior* l. 2; for the reading, cf. Porten & Yardeni sub TADAE B 7.3), Aḥiq 99, Krael 4²¹, 5¹⁴, Samar 4⁶ (*[ʾ]ḥry*), 6⁵; + suff. 3 p.s.m. *ʾḥrwhy* Cowl 9⁴, 13⁷, 38¹⁰, Aḥiq 210, Samar 1⁴ (= EI xviii 8*); + suff. 2 p.s.m. *ʾḥryk* Cowl 9¹³, 28^7,12, Krael 3^12,16,19, 12²³, Samar 1^6,11 (= EI xviii 8*); + suff. 2 p.s.f. *ʾḥryky* Cowl 8^9,15, 13⁸, Krael 4⁵, 9^19,21, 10⁹; + suff. 1 p.s. *ʾḥry* Cowl 67 xii (?), Beh 50 (Akkad. par. *ár-ki-iá*), Driv 3³ (cf. Milik RB lxi 593, Cazelles Syr xxxii 100, Degen GGA '79, 39), Samar 1⁶ (= EI xviii 8*); + suff. 2 p.pl.m. *ʾḥrykm* Cowl 9⁸, 25^9,16; + suff. 1 p.pl. Aḥiq 63 (*[ʾ]ḥryn*), BSOAS xiii 82⁸ (?, dam. context, cf. Henning BSOAS xiii 84 :: Birkeland ActOr xvi 232: l. *ʾḥnyn*); cf. Frah xxv 42 (*ʾwḥl*), 48 (*ʾḥl*), Paik 52 (*ʾḥr*), GIPP 15, SaSt 12, 21 - **Nab** CIS ii 158⁵? - ¶ prep. (< subst., cf. Frah xxv 42 (*lʾwḥl* = backwards), SaSt 21 - 1) after (temp.): KAI 181³, Cowl 9¹³, 28^7,12, Cowl 44 (*scriptio anterior* l. 2; v. supra), Krael 4²¹, 5¹⁴, etc.; for formulae like *bnyk ʾḥryk* (e.g. Cowl 28⁷, cf. Weinfeld JAOS xc 199

- **2)** after (loc.): Aḥiq 63; *[g]brn ʾḥrnn mlkʾ [yš]lḥ [ʾ]ḥryn* Aḥiq 62f.: the king will send other men after us; the *ʾḥr* of IPAA 11[8] prob. loc., but context very diff. - **3)** concerning: Cowl 9[4], 13[7], 38[10] (v. however *šym₂*) - 4) *ʾḥry kn* Tell F 10 (Akkad. par. *arkû*[ú]), Aḥiq 99: afterwards - **5)** *mn ʾḥry*, after (temp.) Cowl 13[8], Krael 3[12,16,19], 4[5], Samar 1[4,6,11], 6[5]; cf. also *zy [y]ʾth mn ʾḥrwhy* Aḥiq 210: what/who will come after it/him (dam. context) - **6)** *ʾḥr ʾš* NP 130[2]: after (conj.), cf. FR 258a - in Hebr. text NESE ii 45[2], l. perhaps *[ʾ]ḥry* (reading of *d* instead of *r* poss.) = + suff. 1 p.s.?, cf. Millard Irâq xxiv 45, 47, Röllig NESE a.l., Gibson SSI i p. 19f., for the context, cf. also Naveh Lesh xxx 67, Greenfield JAOS xciv 510; Lemaire Sem xxvi 69: l. *ḥdy₃*? = joy? (less prob. interpret.).
v. *ʾwṣr*, *ʾḥr₄*, *ʾḥrh*, *ʾḥry₁*, *ʾḥry₂*, *ʾḥrn*.

ʾḥrʾ v. *ḥrʾ₁*.

ʾḥrʾh v. *ḥrʾ₁*.

ʾḥrʾy v. *ʾḥry₁*.

ʾḥrh **OffAr** Sing. abs. *ʾḥrh* KAI 226[8]; + suff. 3 p.s.m. *ʾḥrth* KAI 226[10] - **Nab** Sing. + suff. 3 p.s.m. *ʾḥrth* Atlal vii 105[3] - ¶ subst. f. - **1)** future; *lʾḥrh* KAI 226[8]: in the future (cf. Dupont-Sommer Pléiade 637, Rosenthal ANET 505, Koopmans 94, Gibson SSI ii p. 97, Delsman TUAT ii 574 :: Garr DGSP 88: = *l₅* + *ʾḥr₅* + *ā*-ending :: Cooke NSI p. 190f.: = Sing. emph. of *ʾḥr₃*) - **2)** future (of a family), posterity: KAI 226[10] (:: Gevirtz VT xi 147f. n. 6: = future (cf. Cathcart CBQ xxxv 182; on the subject, cf. Hasel FS Horn 517f.: poss. = surviving remnant), Atlal vii 105[3] - **3)** *ʾḥrh* in KAI 225[13] diff., used adverbially: in the future, thereafter (??, cf. Dupont-Sommer AH i/2,1) × = *ʾḥr₅* + *ā*-ending (= in the future (cf. Garr DGSP 88)) :: = *ʾḥr₃* + emph. ending, cf. Cooke NSI p. 189, Koopmans 93 :: = *ʾḥr₂* or *ʾḥr₃* + suff. 3 p.s.m./f., cf. Donner KAI a.l. :: Stefanovic COAI 193, 289 n. 1: = subst. Sing. abs. (with abstract meaning: another (cf. however id. ibid. 289)) - also in NESE ii 87[6]??, Sing. + suff. 3 p.s.m./f. or 3 p.pl.m.: *ʾḥr[th(m)]*, cf. Degen NESE ii 86, Altheim & Stiehl CRM ii 243ff. :: Segal Irâq xxxi 172: l. poss. *ʾḥw[hy]* = Plur. + suff. 3 p.s.m. of *ʾḥ₁*.

ʾḥry₁ **Hebr** Sing. abs. *ʾḥry* DJD ii 22,1-9[2]; Plur. abs. *ʾḥrʾym* DJD ii 30[24] - **OffAr** Sing. cstr. *ʾḥry* ATNS 29[3] (uncert. interpret., dam. context; Segal ATNS a.l.: = Sing. abs.; Porten & Yardeni sub TADAE B 8.1: = *ʾḥr₅* + suff. 1 p.s.) - **JAr** Sing. abs. *ʾḥry* MPAT 47r 10, 51[11]; emph. *ʾḥryʾ* MPAT 45[4], 48[4]; + suff. 1 p.pl. *ʾḥryn* MPAT 46[3] (?, v. infra); Plur. abs. *ʾḥrʾyn* MPAT 41[12], 52[11], IEJ xxxvi 206[6] - ¶ subst. guarantee; *ʾḥry wʿrb lk* MPAT 47r 10: a guarantee and surety for you, cf. MPAT 41[12], 48[4] (for these contexts, cf. also Geller BSOAS li 315f.); cf. *ʾnh ʾḥry ʿrb l[k]* MPAT 51[11]: I am guarantee, surety for you (cf.

Milik Bibl xxxviii 264, RB lxii 253f., J.J.Rabinowitz BASOR cxxxvi 15 :: Abramson & Ginsberg BASOR cxxxvi 17, 19: l. *ʾḥwy ʿrb* (*ʾḥwy* = *ʾhwy* = QAL Impf. 1 p.s. of *hwy*$_{1}$) :: Birnbaum PEQ '57, 114, 127, 130: l. *ʾhwy ʿrb* (imposs. reading); *ʾḥryʾ wʿrbh [l]mrqʾ wlqymʾ* MPAT 45^{4}: the guarantee and surety to clear and confirm (cf. MPAT $52^{11f.}$, DJD ii 30^{24}, IEJ xxxvi 206^{6}; for the comb. of *ʾḥry*$_{1}$ and *ʿrb*$_{5}$, cf. also Greenfield RAI xxv 478); *nksy ʾḥryn* MPAT 46^{3}: our possessions, which (can) serve as guarantee (:: Milik DJD ii p. 139: l. *nksy<nh> ʾḥryn* = (we give) a guarantee (on) our possessions, cf. Fitzmyer & Harrington MPAT a.l.) - this word also in Inv xii 45^{3}??, cf. however Bounni & Teixidor Inv xii a.l., reading *ʾḥdy* (= QAL Part. pass. pl.m. cstr. of *ʾḥz*) = the functionaries/officials of poss. in context (cf. Aggoula Sem xxix 116: = the responsible ones), cf. also Bounni & Teixidor Inv xii a.l.: or = QAL Part. act. pl.m. cstr. of *ʾḥz* (= those who possess, are responsible; cf. also Naveh JAOS cii 184) - Segal ATNS a.l.: l. poss. *[ʾ]ḥrʾy* (= Sing. abs.) in ATNS 10a i 6 (context however heavily dam.) and *ʾḥr[yʾ]* (= Plur. emph.) in 29 ii 6 (Porten & Yardeni sub TADAE B 8.1: or = form of *ʾḥd*$_{1}$ (= *ʾḥz*)) and *ʾḥry* (= Sing. abs./cstr.) in ATNS 44 ii 5 (*scriptio anterior*; highly uncert. reading, cf. Porten & Yardeni sub TADAE B 8.2: l. numerical signs).
v. *ʾḥz*.

ʾḥry$_{2}$ **Ph** Sing. cstr. *ʾḥry* KAI 19^{9} (cf. FR 204a :: Ringgren Oriens ii 127: = Plur. of *ʾḥr*$_{5}$+ suff. 3 p.s.m. (= his rests)) - **Pun** Sing. cstr. *ʾḥry* KAI $69^{4,8,10}$ (:: Dahood RPIM 140: = Sing. + suff. 3 p.s.m. of *ʾḥr*$_{2}$ (= rest)) - ¶ subst. rest.

ʾḥry$_{3}$ v. *npš*, *ṣby*$_{1}$.

ʾḥry$_{4}$ v. *ʾḥr*$_{5}$.

ʾḥrn **OldCan** Sing. m. + suff. 3 p.s.m. *aḫ-ru-un-ú* EA 245^{10} (cf. Garr DGSP 31, Sivan GAG 133, 196) - **OldAr** Sing. m. abs. *ʾḥrn* KAI 224^{24} - **OffAr** Sing. m. abs. *ʾḥrn* Cowl 1^{4}, $5^{6,8}$, 8^{11}, Krael $2^{7,9}$, Driv 7^{9}, 8^{5}, 12^{7}, ATNS 13^{4} (??, or = Plur. m./f. abs. of *ʾḥr*$_{3}$ or l. *ʾḥdn* = QAL Part. act. pl.m. abs. or Pf. 1 p.pl. of *ʾḥd*$_{1}$ (= *ʾḥz*); heavily dam. context), ATNS 26^{12}, Samar 3^{5}, 9^{7}, etc., etc. (× Vogt Lex s.v. *ʾḥr*: in Cowl 38^{4}, Aḥiq 53, 64 *ʾḥrn* = Plur. abs. of subst. *ʾḥr* (> *ʾḥr*$_{5}$)); emph. *ʾḥrnʾ* Krael 4^{19}; Plur. m. abs. *ʾḥrnn* Cowl $8^{10,19}$, 9^{7}, RES 1793^{11} (= PSBA '15, 222^{5}), etc.; cf. Frah viii 6 (cf. Nyberg FP 44, 72 :: Ebeling Frah a.l.: l. *ḥḥwr* = raven), Frah S$_{2}$ 5, Paik 55, 56, Nisa 194^{4}, 459^{7}, 592^{7}, Syr xxxv 327^{61}, cf. GIPP 15, 45, SaSt 12 - **Nab** Sing. m. emph. *ʾḥrnʾ* CIS ii 215^{5} (obscure text), BASOR cclxiii 78^{2} - **Palm** Sing. m. abs. *ʾḥrn* Ber ii 85^{11}; emph. *ʾḥrnʾ* CIS ii 3914^{4} (cf. Cantineau Gramm 134 :: Rosenthal Sprache 53: = Plur. m. emph.), Ber ii 112^{4}; f. emph. *ʾḥrtʾ* CIS ii 4199^{5} (cf. Cantineau Gramm 134, Syr xix 170); Plur. m. abs.

ʾḥrnyn CIS ii 4173²; f. emph. *ʾḥrnytʾ* CIS ii 3913 ii 117 - **JAr** Sing. m. abs. *ʾḥrn* IEJ xl 132^3,5,7,11^, 144^12^ (on the contexts, cf. Yardeni ibid. 133f.); Plur. m. abs. *ʾḥrnyn* MPAT 52⁴, 60³ - ¶ adj. - **1)** other: Cowl 8^11,16^, 13⁹, Krael 3^19^, 4^16^, BASOR cclxiii 78², etc., cf. *ḥylʾ ʾḥrnn* Cowl 30⁸: other troops (cf. Joüon MUSJ xviii 41; prob. no lapsus, perhaps to be understood as a case of apposition or as a case of congruence *ad sensum*; for emph. followed by abs. attribute, cf. Syriac examples, Nöldeke Gramm 203); for the *ʾyš ʾḥrn* and *gbr ʾḥrn* in Elephantine contracts (cf. Cowl 8^11^, 13^8f.^, Krael 3^19^, 4^19,19f.^), cf. also Porten & Szubin Maarav iv 51ff.; cf. also *[š]mh ʾ[ḥ]rn* PIA 518-520²: his other name (cf. l. 1, and Akkad. par. *šumi-šú šá-nu-u*) - **2)** later, future; *ʿ[d] lywmn ʾḥrnn* Aḥiq 52: until other days, cf. Cowl 71⁴: *bywmn ʾḥrnn* (in afterdays) and Aḥiq 49: *ʿd zy lʿd[n ʾ]ḥrn wlywmn ʾḥrnn šgyʾn qrbtk* (until in aftertime and many days after I brought you ...); cf. also *mḥr (ʾw) ywm ʾḥrn* Cowl 1⁴ (for the reading *mḥr* pro *lmḥr*, cf. Porten & Greenfield JEAS p. 106, Porten & Yardeni sub TADAE B 5.1), 5^6,8^, Krael 2^7,9,10f.,12^, etc.: tomorrow or another day (= in the future; diff. to decide whether *ywm ʾḥrn* here orig. is some other day or the day after tomorrow, cf. J.J.Rabinowitz JNES xiv 59f., Law 159ff., Fitzmyer FS Albright ii 159, WA 261, Muffs 183f., 206f., Yaron RB lxxvii 415, Weinfeld JAOS xc 189 n. 43) - **3)** used as subst., another: KAI 224^24^, Cowl 8^19^, 9^7,9^, Driv 7⁴, 9² (uncert. reading), RES 1793^11^, Ber ii 112⁴ - **4)** used as subst., the rest: Cowl 26⁶ (:: Grelot Sem xx 28f., DAE p. 287: *ʾḥrn zy* = conj. after), 30^11^, cf. *wʾḥrn* Cowl 20^6,12^, 26⁵ (?): *et c etera* - **5)** prec. by prep. - a) *ʿd ʾḥrn* Krael 10^10^: until another time (in the context > for temporal use, temporally, cf. also Krael p. 254) - b) *ʿl ʾḥrn* Cowl 38⁴: afterwards (cf. ATNS 26^12^; cf. Greenfield BSOAS xl 371f.: *ʿd ʾḥrn* and *ʿl ʾḥrn* interchangeable (?)); prob. also in this meaning in Aḥiq 53 :: Grelot Sem xx 29, DAE p. 450: finally :: Driver JRAS '32, 87: more than another; also in Aḥiq 64, dam. context (v. also supra; cf. also Lidzbarski Eph iii 255, Leand 121o: in Cowl 38⁴, Aḥiq 53, 64 = finally) - **6)** used adverbially, *ʾḥrnʾ* CIS ii 3914⁴: moreover (?, v. supra); Krael p. 174: also in Krael 4^19^ (= later, afterwards), wrong interpret., cf. Driver PEQ '55, 92: *ḥlqy ʾḥrnʾ* = my other portion; cf. also the prepositional expression *aḫ-ru-un-ú* EA 245^10^: after him - Levi Della Vida OA ii 76: poss. l. *ʾḥrn* (Sing. m. + suff. 3 p.pl.m.) in IRTS 24^3f.^ (*yariunom* = *ʾḥrnm*)?? (improb. interpret.; poss. *(y)ari* = n.p., cf. Krahmalkov RSF vii 175ff., for *unom*, v. $ʾh_1$; :: Vattioni AION xvi 55: *ariunom* = either their grandson (= Sing. + suff. 3 p.pl.m. of $ʾry_4$) or their freedman (= Sing. + suff. 3 p.pl.m. of $ḥr_1$)) - a form (*ʾḥrn*) also in ATNS 17⁵ ??, or = form of $ʾḥd_1$ (= *ʾḥz*; Qal Pf. 1 p.pl. or Part. act. m.pl.f. abs.)??

v. $ʾḥr_3$, *ʾtyṭk*.

ʾḥrst v. *ḥrsh₁*.

ʾḥšyn (< Iran., cf. R.A.Bowman Pers p. 45, Naveh & Shaked Or xlii 456, cf. also Bernard StudIr i 173f. n. 8) - **OffAr** this word (prob. adj. = of dark colour, cf. however Hinz NW 34, AISN 25: = turquoise) occurring in the combination *ʾḥšynpyn* (Pers 11³, 75² (*ʾḥ[šy]np[y]n*), 76³ (*ʾḥšyn[pyn]*) and *'ḥšynpn* (Pers 101²) and possibly *[ʾḥš]nḥwyn* (Pers 74³)); meaning of elements *pyn* and *pn* uncert. (cf. R.A.Bowman Pers p. 84: = green, greyish-green?). The meaning of the element *ḥwyn* < Iran. = glowing or beautiful?? (cf. R.A.Bowman Pers p. 138, Hinz AISN 25).

ʾḥšn v. *ʾḥšyn*.

ʾṭbʿ v. *ʾṣbʿ*.

ʾṭh **OffAr** Segal ATNS a.l.: l. *ʾṭ[h]* (= Greek letter η?, used as mark of a slave) in ATNS 5⁸ (reading uncert., cf. Porten & Yardeni sub TADAE B 8.3: l. prob. *ʾḥ[* without interpret.).

ʾṭwmṭʾ **Pun** diff. phrase *bʿgl ʾš qrny lmbmḥsr bʾṭwmṭʾ* in KAI 69⁵, poss. meaning: with a calf the horns of which are still lacking by nature (cf. also v.d.Branden RSO xl 119) :: Garbini FS Pagliaro ii 155ff.: *ʾṭwmṭʾ* poss. < Greek ἔντομιδα = incision or perhaps < Greek ἐντόματα = which can be cut off > testicles :: CIS i sub 165: = non-castrated < Greek ἀτμητός? :: Dussaud Orig 320: *bʾṭwmṭʾ* = *bʾṭ* (= *bʿṭ*) *wmṭʾ* = which can stand on his legs and walk :: v.d.Branden RSO xl 119: *ʾṭwmṭʾ* = natural size; cf. also Rosenthal ANET 502: for a calf whose horns are *still lacking somewhat*. Perhaps < Greek αὐτόματον (cf. Hoffmann Ueber einige phon Inschr 16 n 2, Prätorius ZDMG lxii 407, Brockelmann HO iii 56), cf. however Friedrich VT xi 356 (n. 2), Röllig KAI a.l.; cf. also Lagrange ERS 470, 473, Lidzbarski sub KI 63, Capuzzi StudMagr ii 49f.

ʾṭm v. *yṭb*.

ʾṭr **OffAr** QAL Part. pass. s.m. abs. *ʾṭyr* Samar 3³, 7⁵ (heavily dam. context) - ¶ verb QAL to pay; Part. pass. paid, *ʾṭyr mkyr* Samar 3³: paid (and) received.

ʾṭrn **Hatra** the *ʾṭrn* in 332³, prob. = n.p., cf. Degen NESE iii 109.
v. *ṭrn*.

ʾy₁ **Pun** in the sense of peninsula only in connection with geographical names, cf. Harr 76, Berthier & Charlier sub Hofra 102, CRAI '41, 267, Bouchenaki EFM 50f., Sznycer TA 172f. For *y* pro *ʾy*, cf. Solá-Solé Sef xvi 326, cf. also Trip 41¹ -
v. *ʾy₃,₄*, *ḥzr₂*.

ʾy₂ **Ph** KAI 13⁴, 14⁵, RES 922⁴ (?, dam. context, cf. Masson & Sznycer RPC 105, 107) - ¶ negation, not - Dupont-Sommer CRAI '68, 117, 128:

l. *ʾy2* in RCL xxi 201[5] (uncert. reading).
v. *ʾbl5*, *ʾdn1*, *ʾy3,4*, *ʾyny*, *by2*, *mšmn*.

ʾy3 **Ph** Syr xlviii 396[5] - ¶ word of uncert. meaning. Poss interrogative pronoun, where?, cf. Lipiński RSF ii 51f., v.d.Branden BiOr xxxiii 13, Avishur PIB 267, 270, UF x 32, 34f., Gibson SSI iii p. 89, 91 × Caquot Syr xlviii 401, Röllig NESE ii 31: = *ʾy1*, *ʾy ʾlšyy* = the isle of the Alasians (= Cyprus; cf. also Gaster BASOR ccix 19) × Garbini OA xx 289, 292: = *ʾy2*:: Cross CBQ xxxvi 488f. (n. 25): = *ʾy6* (= exclamation: woe; cf. also de Moor JEOL xxvii 111) :: Liverani RSF ii 36f.: l. *ʾ<t>y* = *ʾt6* + suff. 3 p.s.m.
v. *hn3*.

ʾy4 **Ph** H.P.Müller ZA lxv 106f., UF ii 236f. (n. 78): the *ʾy* in KAI 30[1] = indef. pronoun = (whoever (prob. interpret.)) :: Albright BASOR lxxxiii 16, v.d.Branden OA iii 253: = *ʾy2* (cf. also Röllig KAI a.l., FR 249,1, Puech Sem xxix 21, Gibson SSI iii p. 29) :: Dupont-Sommer RA xli 203: = *ʾy1*.
v. *ʾdn1*, *ʾz2*.

ʾy5 **JAr** Syr xlv 101[16] (uncert. reading) - ¶ conj. if.

ʾy6 v. *ʾy3*.

ʾyb1 v. *ʾbl5*, *ʾyb2*.

ʾyb2 **Pun** Sing. abs. *ʾyb* StudMagr vii 12[2] (highly uncert. context, cf. also Rocco StudMagr vii 12f.) - ¶ subst. (or QAL Part. act. of *ʾyb1*) enemy.

ʾybl v. *ʾbl5*.

ʾyh1 **Nab** IEJ xxix 112[1] (uncert. reading, cf. Naveh IEJ xxix 113, cf. also Cross and Smith with Naveh ibid. 113 n. 7) - ¶ interjection oh!; cf. *y1*.

ʾyh2 v. *ʾyt3*.

ʾywmy **Nab** RES 1134B, uncert. reading, meaning unknown.

ʾyḥ **Samal** m. Plur. cstr. *ʾyḥy* KAI 215[3]; + suff. 3 p.s.m. *ʾyḥyh* KAI 214[27,28], *ʾyḥh* KAI 214[30], 215[17] (on both forms, cf. Garr DGSP 37); + suff. 1 p.s. *ʾy[ḥ]y* KAI 214[24] (?, cf. Dion p. 32; dam. context); f. Sing. + suff. 3 p.s.m. *ʾyḥt[h]* KAI 214[28] (cf. Dion p. 247 × Donner KAI a.l., Gibson SSI ii p. 69, 75: = Plur. + suff. 3 p.s.m.); Plur. + suff. 3 p.s.m. *ʾyḥth* KAI 214[31] (dam. context); on this word, cf. Dion p. 419 - ¶ subst.; in the context of KAI 214/215 prob. = m. kinsman, f. kinswoman (relation of *ʾyḥ* with *ʾḥ1* unclear, cf. on this point and related etymological problems: Cooke NSI p. 169, Poeb 44 n. 4, Ginsberg AJSL l. 2 (n. 10), Koopmans 38, Donner sub KAI 214[24], Dion p. 99, 419, Gibson SSI ii p. 74).

ʾyṭšry **OffAr** Sing. abs. *ʾyṭšry* ATNS 19[5], 20[4] - ¶ subst. of unknown meaning, prob. denoting some kind of agricultural produce; Segal sub ATNS 19: poss. < Egypt. = red barley?

ʾyyl v. *ʾyl$_2$*.

ʾyk **OldAr** *ʾyk* KAI 222A 35, 38, 39 - **OffAr** *ʾyk* Cowl 16^{7}, Aḥiq 37, Beh 52, ATNS 21^{4} (dam. context), SSI ii 28 obv. 6, PF 2043^{3}, KAI 279^{7}; cf. Frah xxv 4, Frah-S$_2$ 20, Paik 60-62, Nisa-c 287^{5}, ZDMG xcii 442A 14, Syn 311^{4}, 312^{1}, DEP 154 recto 3, verso 3, Sogd ii 211, B 247, R 46, 49, Ta 466, 467, 475, 478, Ka 22, Ve 106, JA cclix 12^{3}, ML 578, BSOAS xxxiii 148^{5,6}, cf. GIPP 15, 18, 28, 48, Lemosín AO ii 266 - ¶ particle - **1)** with interrogative function, how?; *ʾyk bytʾ ʿbyd wʾyk ...* SSI ii 28 obv. 6: how is the family faring and how ....? (cf. Bresciani RSO xxxv 19, 21, Naveh AION xvi 26, Gibson SSI ii a.l., Porten & Yardeni sub TADAE A 3.3, Grelot RB xcv 296 :: Fitzmyer JNES xxi 16, 20: = conj. (cf. below sub 2), as?, cf. also Grelot DAE p. 126 (n. d)) - **2)** with conj. function; *ʾyk ʾsrhy ḥlqwtʾ* KAI 279^{7}: as the dispositions of fate bound him (to do; v. *ʾsr$_1$*, *ḥlqw*), for this use of *ʾyk*, cf. Kutscher, Naveh & Shaked Lesh xxxiv 135 (cf. also Altheim & Stiehl GH i 405, ii 175, GMA 352) - **3)** with prep. function, according; *ʾyk zy* - a) just as (conjunctional function); *ʾyk zy tqd šʿwtʾ zʾ bʾš kn ...* KAI 222A 35: just as this piece of wax burns with fire, so ...., cf. KAI 222A 38, 39 (cf. also Hillers TC 18f.) - b) how (conjunctional function); *hwdʿ ʾyk zy ʿbyd* Beh 52: make known how it was done.
v. *ʾykh*, *ʾk$_2$*, *hyk*.

ʾykh **OldAr** KAI 222A 37 - ¶ particle, with prep. function; *ʾykh zy tqd šʿw[tʾ] zʾ bʾš kn ...* KAI 222A 37: just as this piece of wax burns with fire, so ...
v. *ʾyk*, *hyk*.

ʾykn **Hebr** SM 49^{25} - ¶ adv. where; *wʿd ʾykn sbyb lqysryn* SM 49^{25}: and until where in the region of Caesarea?

ʾyl$_1$ v. *ʾl$_7$*.

ʾyl$_2$ **Pun** Sing. cstr. *ʾyl* KAI 69^{5,9}, 74^{5}, CIS i 3915^{1} (dam. context) - **Hebr** Sing. abs. *ʾyyl*Frey 1164^{1} (= SM 44^{4}) - ¶ subst. ram: Frey 1164^{1}; meaning in Pun. texts uncert.: ram? × deer? (= *ʾyl$_3$*), for the problems involved, cf. Dussaud Orig 138ff., Röllig sub KAI 69^{5}, Capuzzi StudMagr ii 50f., Amadasi Guzzo SSMA 113f.; for the combination *ṣrb ʾyl* KAI
69^{9}, 74^{5}, v. *ṣrb$_1$*.
v. *ʾl$_1$*, *ybl$_2$*, *kly$_3$*.

ʾyl$_3$ **OffAr** m. Sing. emph. (:: Baumgartner ZAW xlv 92: = f. Sing. abs.) *ʾylʾ* Aḥiq 88; f. Sing. emph. *ʾyltʾ* Aḥiq 87 - ¶ subst. m. deer, stag, f. hind.

v. *ʾyl$_2$*.

ʾyl$_4$ in AMB 6^{2,11}, v. *ʾl$_1$*.

ʾylh v. *ʾyl$_3$*.

ʾylw v. *z$_1$*.

ʾyln **JAr** Plur. cstr. (?) *ʾyln[y]* Syr xlv 101^8 (dam. context) - ¶ subst. tree.

ʾym **OldAr** Lipiński Stud 43: l. *ʾym* (= Sing. abs.) = terror, frightful thing in KAI 222B 39 (uncert. interpret.); Lipiński Stud 46: l. *[ʾ]ym* = terror in KAI 223B 3f. (improb. interpret.); for the reading of the context of KAI 222B 39, cf. also *ʾnḥ$_2$*.

ʾymnš (< Iran., cf. Sims-Williams BSOAS xliv 6) - **OffAr** Sing. m. abs. *ʾymnš* Beh 55 - ¶ adj. weak, unsteady, insecure, careless.

ʾyms **OffAr** Kutscher, Naveh & Shaked Lesh xxxiv 127: l. *[ʾy]ms* (< Prakrit (= dem. pronoun + genitive ending)) in BSOAS xiii 82^4, cf. also Henning BSOAS xiii 85 (prob. restoration).

ʾymt v. *ʾmt*

ʾyn$_1$ **Pun** + suff. 3 p.s.m., cf. Poen 1006: *ynny* (var. *ennu*) - **Mo** *ʾn* KAI 181^{24} - **Hebr** *ʾyn* KAI 194^5, SSI i p. 24^1, DJD ii 30^6 (uncert. reading),^{28}, 45^4 (dam. context); + suff. 1 p.s. *ʾy[nn]y* KAI 194$^{7f.}$ (cf. e.g. Albright BASOR xcvii 26, Cross BASOR cxliv 24 n. 3 :: Torczyner Lach i p. 79: l. *ʾdny*), *ʾyny* DJD ii 46^2; + suff. 3 p.pl.m. *ʾynn* Mas 449^2, *ʾnn* Mas 451^2; + suff. 1 p.pl. *[ʾy]nnw* TA-H 40$^{13f.}$ - ¶ subst. - negation: (there is) not; *wbr ʾn bqrb hqr* KAI 181^{24}: there was no cistern inside the town; *rufe ynny cho* Poen 1006: there is no doctor here; *[ʾy]nnw yklm* TA-H 40$^{13f.}$: we are not able ...; *ʾyny ṣryk* DJD ii 46^2: I do not need; *ʾynn kšyr[yn]* Mas 449^2: they are not suited - the *ʾn* in DJD ii 51,2 the same word??, cf. also Milik DJD ii a.l. - for *bʾn ṣdn*, v. *ṣdn*.

ʾyn$_2$ v. *hn$_3$*.

ʾyny **Pun** RES 1543^5, uncert. reading and interpret.; Février BAr '51/52, 264: l. *ʾy$_2$+ n(ʾ)y* = it is not good??

ʾynyn v. *hʾ$_1$*.

ʾynth v. *ʾš$_1$*.

ʾyskwph (< Akkad., cf. Zimmern Fremw 31, Kaufman AIA 37 (n. 33)) - **JAr** Sing. emph. *ʾyskwpth* SM 22, *skwpth* MPAT-A 39^2 (= SM 42; for the form, cf. Sokoloff Maarav i 81) - ¶ subst. f. lintel - cf. *šqwp*.

ʾyph this subst. (Sing. abs.) poss. in Hebr. text: *ʾy[ph]*, cf. Wright with Yeivin Lesh xxxi 248f., cf. also Yeivin PEQ '69, 67f.; Ellenbogen 26: < Egypt.; cf. also Barrois ii 248ff., Trinquet SDB v 1222ff., de Vaux IAT i 303ff., and also EM iv 852ff. - Yassine & Teixidor BASOR cclxiv a.l.: l. in BASOR cclxiv 48 no. 6^1 poss. *ʾp* = abbrev. of *ʾPh./ʾyph*?? (reading and interpret. of context highly uncert.).

ʾyr v. *ʾbr*$_1$.

ʾyš$_1$ v. *ʾš*$_1$.

ʾyš$_2$ v. *ʾš*$_1$, *mlk*$_5$.

ʾyš$_3$ **OffAr** Sing. emph. *ʾyšʾ* JAOS liv 31[1] - ¶ subst. m. wall?, cf. Torrey JAOS liv 31.

ʾyšpr **OffAr** the reading *ʾyšpr* (= Sing. abs., v. *ʾšpr*, weaver) in Del 96 incorrect; l. *tʾšṭr* = n.p., cf. Kaufman AIA 60 n. 136.

ʾyštw **JAr** Plur. cstr. *ʾyštwt* Syr xlv 101[19] (:: Milik Syr xlv 102: Sing. cstr.) - ¶ subst. of unknown meaning; Milik Syr xlv a.l.: = sixth part.

ʾyt$_1$ **OffAr** Lipiński Stud 140ff.: l. *ʾyt* (= Sing. abs. of *ʾyt*$_1$ (= receipt)) in TH 5 vs. 4 (= AECT 57; highly uncert. interpret.; reading of context uncert., cf. also Degen NESE i 56).

ʾyt$_2$ v. *ʾyt*$_3$, *ʾyty*, *ʾt*$_3$.

ʾyt$_3$ **Ph** *ʾyt* KAI 10[8,15], 13[3], 14[4,5], 15, 19[9], 26A i 3, iii 3, 14f., 37A 4 (:: (Cross with) Healy: l. *mnt* = Sing. cstr. of *mnh*$_1$)[,10], 43[7], 50[4], CIS i 14[4], EpAn ix 5[7] (cf. Long & Pardee AO vii 209ff. :: Mosca & Russell EpAn ix 17f., Lemaire EI xx 125*: = *ʾyt* + suff. 3 p.s.m.), etc., *ʾt* KAI 10[3,7], 50[6] (for the instances from KAI 10, cf. Hoftijzer Mus lxxvi 195ff. :: Harr 63, Röllig BiOr xix 25, Gibson SSI iii p. 96, Krahmalkov RSF iii 195 n. 75, Izre'el Shn iii 206, Puech Sem xxxii 53ff. = *ʾt*$_6$; possibly also in KAI 48[3], Eph ii 170 (= KI 38; for the problems, cf. also Puech Sem xxxii 53)), cf. KAI 174[5]: θ (diff. context :: Sznycer, Sem viii 7f., 9, PPP 100: forms part of other word, v. *nšʾ*$_1$) - **Pun** *ʾyt* KAI 62[1,2,3], 72B 1 (= ICO-Spa 10), 80[1], 89[2,3,5], 115[2], CIS i 3604[6], 3916[6], RCL '66, 201[1,7], ICO-Sard 32[7], *ʾt* KAI 69[21], 119[5] (?), GR ii 38[1,3] (diff. reading :: Rocco AION xix 413, 416 (div. otherwise): l. *ʾ bn* (= Sing. cstr. of *bn*$_1$)), RES 303[1,2], 305[1], Punica xi 18[4], 19[4], 20[3], xii 10[4], Hofra 23[3], 43[5], Trip 43, 51[3,6], *t* KAI 79[7], 124[1,2], 129[2], 141[1], 160[1] (v. *lyh*), 161[3], 165[2,3], 172[3,4], CIS i 151[2], 3783[6], 3784[2], NP 130[1], Trip 41[1], etc., cf. Poen 930 (:: Izre'el Shn iii 207: = *ʾt*$_6$), 932, 935, 936, 937 (cf. Sznycer PPP 92ff., Glück & Maurach Semitics ii 111 :: Schroed 312, L.H.Gray AJSL xxxix 78: = Sing. cstr. of *ʾt*$_1$ :: Izre'el Shn iii 207: pro *yth em-* l. *ythem* = *ʾt*$_6$ + suff. 3 p.s.m.), 940: *yth*, Poen 939: *th*; + suff. 3 p.s.f. *ʾtʾ* CIS i 580[3] (:: FR 255: = + suff. 3 p.s.m.) - **Mo** (cf. Segert ArchOr xxix 236, Blau Maarav ii 150ff., Jackson & Dearman SMIM 106f., Khan BSOAS xlvii 471 n. 15, 488) *ʾt* KAI 181[5,6,7,9,10,11], etc. (prob. also in dam. text BASOR clxxii 7[3]: *ʾt[*, cf. also Weippert ZDPV lxxx 172) - **Edom** *ʾt* TeAv 97[3] - **Hebr** *ʾt* KAI 191B 3, 192[2,4,5] (dam. context :: Gibson SSI i p. 37f.: = Sing. abs. of *ʾt*$_1$ :: Galling TGI 75 (n. 5; div. otherwise): l. *ʾty* = QAL Part. act. pl.m. cstr. of *ʾwt*$_1$ (= to concern oneself with;

cf. already Elliger ZDPV lxii 66)), 193^{16}, 194^{12} (cf. Albright BASOR lxxxii 21, Cassuto RSO xvi 176, Gibson SSI i p. 42, Lemaire IH i p. 110 :: Gordon BASOR lxvii 32, Ginsberg BASOR lxxx 11: = Sing. cstr. of *ʾt*$_1$). 196$^{1f.,2}$ (diff. reading, for the context, v. *rʾy*), 197^{1}, 200^{2,6,8,9}, TA-H 16^{4,8,10}, 24^{16} (cf. Lemaire Sem xxiii 16), 40^{14}, DJD ii 17A 1 (uncert. reading, cf. Aharoni BASOR cxcvii 30 n. 44), 22,1-9^{2}, 24C 9, E 5, 30^{24}, SM 75^{3}, 80, *t* DJD ii 24C 16 (?, dam. context), E 8, 10, 43^{3,5}, 44^{7,8,9}, EI xx 256^{7}; + suff. 3 p.s.m. *ʾth* KAI 193^{12}, TA-H 17^{6}, *ʾwtw* SM 49^{26}; + suff. 3 p.s.f. *ʾth* DJD ii 22,1-9^{6}; + suff. 3 p.pl.m. *ʾtm* TA-H 24^{13} (interpret. *ʾtm* = pers. pron. 2 p.pl.m. less prob.) - **Edom** *ʾt* TeAv xii 97^{3} - **Samal** (cf. Dion 164f.) + suff. 3 p.s.m. *wth* KAI 214^{28} - **OldAr** *ʾyt* KAI 202B 5, 10, 11 (?, dam. context), 15, 16, 27, 222B 32, 223C 5, 14; + suff. 1 p.s. *ʾy[t]y* KAI 224^{11} (cf. Degen GGA '79, 45f. :: Segert AAG p. 363, 378: = *ʾyty*; for the reading, cf. Hopkins BSOAS xl 142); the *ʾyh*of KAI 224^{13} prob. lapsus for *ʾyth* (= + suff. 3 p.s.m.), cf. Dupont-Sommer BMB xiii 33, Vogt Bibl xxxix 272 (§ 4 n. g), Garbini RSO xxxiv 53, Fitzmyer AIS a.l., Donner KAI a.l., Puech RB lxxxix 584 - **OffAr** *wt* RES 1785F 1, 3, FuF xxxv 173^{10}; + suff. 3 p.s.m. *yth* Krael 3^{22} (cf. Milik RB lxi 249, cf. also Driver PEQ '55, 92, Grelot DAE p. 219 n. i :: Ginsberg JAOS lxxiv 157, Yaron BiOr xv 21: = QAL Impf. 3 p.s.m. of *ʾty*$_1$, cf. also Porten & Greenfield JEAS p. 42, Porten & Yardeni sub TADAE B 3.4); + suff. 3 p.pl.m. *ʾythm* KAI 233^{6} (?, dam. context; cf. Donner KAI a.l., Segert AAG p. 227, Coxon ZDMG cxxix 15 n. 24 :: Lidzbarski ZA xxxi 197: = *ʾyt*$_2$(= *ʾt*$_3$) + suff. 3 p.pl.m.; cf. also Dupont-Sommer Syr xxiv 37, Stiehl AAW i 222, Gibson SSI ii p. 106); cf. Frah xxv 36 (*lwth*), xxviii 31 (*lwth*), Paik 575 (*lwth*)< GIPP 27, 56, SaSt 22, cf. also Lemosín AO ii 267 - **Nab** + suff. 3 p.s.m. *yth* CIS ii 198^{5}, 200^{6} (= J 30; for the reading, cf. Milik sub ARNA-Nab 79), 211^{3}, 212^{6,7}, 217^{5,6}, 224^{10}; + suff. 3 p.s.f. *wth* MPAT 64 i 5; + suff. 2 p.s.m. *wtk* MPAT 64 i 5, 9; + suff. 3 p.pl.m. *ythm* RES 1102^{5} - **Palm** *yt* CIS ii 3932^{4}, *wt* CIS ii 4058^{7}, Inv x 127^{3}, Syr xii 139^{4,7}, SBS 48B 5, RIP 199^{2} (?, dam. context)^{,5}; + suff. 3 p.s.f. *wth* RIP 143^{4} - **JAr** *yt* MPAT 42^{19} (dam. context), 53^{3,4}, 54^{1} (dam. context), 56^{4}, 58^{2}, AMB 3^{14}, DBKP 18^{68}, *wt* MPAT 42^{8} (dam. context), 60^{2,3}, Frey 896^{3} (dam. context); + suff. 3 p.s.m. *yth* AMB 15^{17}, *ytyh* MPAT-A 22^{7}; + suff. 3 p.s.f. *yth* AMB 13^{4}; + suff. 2 p.s.m. *wtk* MPAT 60^{3}, *tk* MPAT 42^{19} (in combination *ltk*, prob. no lapsus for *lwtk*; cf. however Beyer ATTM 311: l. *lyk* = *l*$_5$ + suff. 2 p.s.f.); + suff. 3 p.pl.m. *ythwm* DBKP 17^{41}, *ythn* MPAT 53^{2}, 59^{2} (Beyer ATTM 352: l. *ythwn*), 60^{4}, *ythwn* MPAT-A 34^{3,5}; + suff. 2 p.pl.m. *ytkwn* AMB 10^{4} - ¶ prep. (not to be connected with *ʾt*$_3$ and *ʾyty*, cf. Kaufman BiOr xxxiv 94, Degen GGA '79, 20, 30 :: Segert ArchOr xxxii 126, AAG p. 227; cf. also Garbini ISNO 170f.; for Phoen./Pun., cf. also FR 256, Puech Sem xxxii 52) - **1)** used as *nota objecti*, passim - 2) followed by proleptic pron. suffix, used as demonstrative; *ʾth ršt* DJD ii 22,1-9^6: this right (of property); Milik DJD ii p. 120: *ʾt mqm* in DJD ii 22,1-9^2 = *oto-a-maqôm* (= *ʾtw hmqm*), diff. context, highly uncert. interpret. - **3)** used as introduction of grammatical subject with passive verbal form; *ytḥzh yt qmyʿh dn* AMB 3^{14} : this amulet will be seen, cf. Naveh & Shaked AMB p. 34 - **4)** + pron. suff., used to strengthen a preceding pron. suff.; *brh lh yth* Krael 3^{22}: (prob. interpret.) a daughter of his (v. also supra) - **5)** used temporarily; *yhw ʾṣlk tšbt hzw* (for the reading and interpret., cf. Pardee HAHL 132f.) DJD ii 44$^{5f.}$: they will be with you during this Sabbath; Milik DJD ii p. 125: temporal use of *ʾt* in DJD ii 24B 10 (improb. interpret. of dam. context) - **6)** in the combination *lwt* - a) with terminative meaning; *tšlḥ ... gbryn lwt yhwntn* MPAT 60$^{1f.}$: you must send ... men to Y., cf. also ibid. l. 3; *qrybn lwt yrḥ* RES 1785F 3: near to the Moon (cf. also ibid. l. 1f.); cf. poss. also FuF xxxv 173^{10} (diff. context) - b) with locative meaning; *ytbyn lwth* RIP 143^4: living with her - c) with meaning "belonging to"; *dy lwth* MPAT 64 i 5: what belongs to it (sc. the garden) - d) used as "*lwt* comm"; *ʾktb .... lwtk* MPAT 64 i 5: I will write .... on your behalf; cf. also Inv x 127^3; for MPAT 64 i 9, v. *bwʾ* - **6)** in the combination *mlwt* (= *mn*$_5$ + *l*$_5$ + *wt*); *wʾt šlḥ ʾḥrnyn mlwtk* MPAT 60^3: and you, send others from you - Chabot sub Punica ivA 2^2: l. *ʾt* in this text, cf. however Hoftijzer OMRO xliv 94: or (div. otherwise) l. *ʾtʾ* = *ʾt*$_5$ + suff. 3 p.s.m./f.?) - this word prob. also in KAI 194^8, cf. Albright BASOR cxliv 26: l. *ʾt hʿd[m]*, cf. also Gibson SSI i p. 41ff.: l. *ʾt hʿ[d]* :: Cross BASOR cxliv 24: l. *ʾth* (+ suff. 3 p.s.m.) *ʿw[d]*, cf. also Röllig KAI a.l., Lemaire IH i p. 110, 112: l. *ʾth ʿ/w[* :: May BASOR xcvii 23, 25: l. *ʾyh* + broken word :: Torczyner Lach i p. 81f.: l. *ʾyhw* = *ʾyh hw*, cf. Reviv CSI p. 82, cf. also de Vaux RB xlviii 195, Birnbaum PEQ '39, 100 - Milik DJD ii p. 120: l. this word (*t*) in DJD ii 22,1-9^2 (highly uncert., dam. context) - Vattioni Aug xvi 539: the *thy* in OA ii 83^1 = *ʾyt*$_3$, cf. also Polselli StudMagr xi 40, cf. however Levi Della Vida OA ii a.l.: = part of n.p. - the *wt* in *kwt* (v. *s.v.*) prob. etymologically related - Dupont-Sommer MAIBL xliv 281 l. *[ʾ]yt* (= as to) in Kition D 21^2 (cf. also Puech RSF iv 12, 14), reading and interpret. highly uncert., for other reading and/or interpret., cf. a) Teixidor Syr xlix 434: l. *[ ]yt*, text poss. in non-semitic language - b) Liverani RSF iii 37: l. *[ ]yt*, Ph. text, cf. also Amadasi Kition a.l. - c) Coote BASOR ccxx 47, 49: l. *wyt* = *w* + *yt* (= QAL Impf. 3 p.s.m. of *ʾty*$_1$) - Dupont-Sommer MAIBL xliv 281: l. prob. *ʾyt* (= as to) in Kition D 21^3 (Teixidor Syr xlix 434: l. *kyt*, text poss. non-Semitic), cf. also Puech RSF iv 12ff. (Liverani RSF iii 37, 40, Coote BASOR ccxx 47: *ʾyt* = *nota objecti*) - on this word, cf. also Garr DGSP 116, 191ff. - Cowl a.l. (cf. also Grelot DAE p. 282 n. m, Dion RB lxxxix

533 n. 39): l. *lwthm* = l_5 + *wt* + suff. 3 p.pl.m. in Cowl 17[7], less prob. reading, cf. Porten RB xc 406, 414f.: l. prob. *p/wtḥm* (= part of n.p.?; cf. also Porten & Yardeni sub TADAE A 6.1.).
v. *ʾḥ*$_2$, *ʾt*$_2$, *ʾt*$_6$, *dlt*$_2$, *lwh*, *mṭwtw*, *myl*, *ʿnš*$_1$, *šqlh*, *štʿ*$_1$.

ʾyth v. *ʾš*$_1$.

ʾyty **OffAr** *ʾyty* Cowl 8[23], 9[3], 15[19,32,33], Krael 7[31] (for the reading, cf. Porten & Greenfield JEAS p. 56, Porten & Yardeni sub TADAE B 3.8 :: Krael a.l.: l. *ʾyt*$_2$ (= *ʾt*$_3$)),[35], Driv 5[2], 8[1], 12[9], ATNS 4[5], 8[11], 21[6], SSI ii 28 obv. 7, NESE i 11[2], FX 136[10], KAI 279[7], etc., etc.; cf. Frah xxiv 8, Paik 71 (*ʾyty*), Nisa-b 211[3], SaSt 13, 21 - **Nab** *ʾyty* CIS ii 198[7], 199[7], 200[4], 205[9], etc. - **Palm** *ʾyty* Syr vii 129[6] (cf. Milik DFD 153 :: Ingholt Syr vii 135f., 141: = Aph Pf. 3 p.s.m. of *ʾty*$_1$) - **JAr** *ʾyty* MPAT 51[5] (cf. Milik RB lxii 254 :: Abramson & Ginsberg BASOR cxxxvi 17, Birnbaum PEQ '57, 110, 130: l. *yyty* = Qal Impf. 3 p.s.m. of *ʾty*$_1$),[10,12] (in *lʾyty*), 52[11], Mas 554[3,5], Syr xlv 101[17] (:: Milik Syr xlv 102: = Aph Pf. 3 p.s.m. of *ʾty*$_1$), IEJ xxxvi 206[6]; + suff. 1 p.s. *ʾytyny* MPAT 49,1[4] - ¶ subst. (prob. related etymologically to *ʾt*$_3$) only used in specific constructions: presence, existence (mostly to be translated, there is); *ʾyty spr mrḥq* Cowl 8[23]: there is a deed of renunciation; etc., etc.; on the use of *ʾyty* in letters, cf. Dion RB lxxxix 563f.; cf. *lʾ ʾyty*: there is not, cf. Aḥiq 105, 111, 112 (v. also *lyt*), cf. also MPAT 51[12]: *lʾyty*; cf. *ʾyty tbʾ šmh ... kzy [ʿ]dn yhwh nplg* Cowl 28[12f.]: there is T. by name (i.e. as to T. by name) ... when it is time we will divide ..., cf. also Driv 8[1f.] - *ʾyty* + subject clause, *ʾyty qṣt mn ywdnʾ* (v. *ywdn*) *zy mlkʾ ... ndšw* Cowl 27[4]: it is (a fact that) they demolished a part of the king's storehouse (cf. Hoftijzer VT ix 316f. :: Joüon MUSJ xviii 25: after *ʾyty* a *zy* lacking by mistake or presupposed :: Cowl a.l., Grelot DAE p. 402, Porten & Greenfield JEAS p. 87, Porten & Yardeni TADAE A 4.5: there is a part .... this they demolished - followed by prep.: - a) + l_5, *kl zy ʾyty lh* Cowl 15[19]: all that he has, cf. Cowl 15[32,33], NESE i 11[2], MPAT 52[11], IEJ xxxvi 206[16], etc.; with negation, *br dkr wnqbh lʾ ʾyty lh* Cowl 15[20f.]: she has no male or female child, cf. Cowl 15[17f.], Krael 7[34f.], MPAT 51[12], 64 i 8, Mas 554[5] - b) + l_5 + *byd*, *tqlʾ dy ʾyty ly bdkwn* Mas 554[3]: the shekel that you owe me - c) + l_5 + *ʿl*$_7$, *ʾyty lk ʿly ksp ...* Cowl 29[2f.]: there is to your credit against me the sum of ....., cf. Cowl 35[3] - d) + *ʿl*$_7$, *ʾyty ʿlwhy kpl dmy ʾtrʾ dnh klh* CIS ii 217[7f.]: he is indebted in (a sum which is) the double of the price of this place in its totality - e) + *ʿl*$_7$ + l_5, *ʾyty ʿlwhy ḥṭyʾh ldwšrʾ ..... ksp slʿyn ʾlp ḥd* CIS ii 224[11f.]: he owes D. ... a fine (viz.) a sum of one thousand *s.* - e) + *ʿm*$_4$ + l_5, *ʾyty ʿmh ldwšrʾ ... slʿyn ʾlp* CIS ii 199[7f.]: he owes D. ... (a sum of) thousand *s.*, cf. CIS ii 198[7f.], 200[6] (= J 30; for the reading, cf. Milik sub ARNA-Nab 79), 205[9f.], 206[7] (cf. also ATNS 8[11]: + l_5

+ *ʿm*$_4$ (dam. context)) - followed by subj. + pred, *ʾyty qbrʾ dnh ḥrm* CIS ii 206^{2}: this tomb must be considered as sacred, cf. CIS ii $210^{7f.}$, comparable also Aḥiq 159 (?) - *ʾyty zy*, a) + nom. clause, *lʾ ʾyty zy yqyr mn ...* Aḥiq 111: there is nothing which is heavier than ... - b) + verbal clause, cf. *ʾyty zy bpq[dwn] hpqdw* Cowl 20^{7}: it is a fact that they were placed on deposit (cf. Joüon MUSJ xviii 25, Grelot DAE p. 198 (n. d), cf. also Esr v 17 :: Cowl p. 60: poss. = they are things which are ...) - Altheim & Stiehl GH ii 175, ASA 29f., GMA 352 (cf. however id. GH i 406f.): the *lʾ ʾyty* in KAI 279^{7}: = the non-existence of ... (less prob. interpret., cf. Dupont-Sommer JA ccxlvi 31, Garbini Kand 17, Donner KAI a.l., Rosenthal EI xiv 97*) - cf. also *lyš*.
v. *ʾyt*$_3$, *ʾt*$_3$, *mll*$_1$, *ṣlqh*.

ʾk$_1$ v. *ʾnk*.

ʾk$_2$ v. cf. Paik 72: if; cf. also Paik 75; v. also *ʾyk*.
v. *kḥd*.

ʾkʾ v. *znh*.

ʾkb v. *ʿqb*$_2$.

ʾkd v. *tkd*.

ʾkdy = (certain type of) rooster > Akkad., cf. v.Soden Or xlvi 184.

ʾkḥd v. *kḥd*.

ʾkyn v. *kwn*$_2$.

ʾkl$_1$ **OldCan** Qal Inf. abs. *a-ku-lí* EA 148^{12}, cf. Böhl 13g - **Ph** *ʾklt* KAI $24^{6,7}$ (diff. form, FR 131, 156: = Qal Pf. 1 p.s., cf. also Torrey JAOS xxxv 366, Landsberger Samʾal 51, Dahood CBQ xxii 405, Röllig KAI a.l., Schuster FS Landsberger 443, Fales WO x 10ff., Sader EAS 157f. (n. 15) × Bauer ZDMG lxvii 686 (cf. Poeb 35, Dupont-Sommer Syr xxiv 46, Avishur PIB 208, 211, Gibson SSI iii p. 36f.): = Qal Part. act. s.f. abs. (cf. also Collins WO vi 184) :: Lidzbarski Eph iii 228: = Qal Part. pass. s.f. abs. or (less prob.) Pf. pass. 3 p.s.f.) - **Pun** v.d.Branden RSF ii 144: l. *[ʾ]k[l]* = Qal Inf. cstr. in KAI 161^{7} (highly uncert.) - **Samal** Qal Pf. 3 p.s.m. *ʾkl* KAI 214^{9}; 3 p.s.f. *ʾklt* KAI 215^{9}; Impf. 3 p.s.f. *tʾkl* KAI 214^{17} (*[tʾ]kl*)^{,21}; Inf. *ʾkl* KAI 214^{13} - **OldAr** Qal Impf. 3 p.s.m. *yʾkl* KAI 222A 27; 3 p.s.f. *tʾkl* KAI 222A 27; 3 p.pl.m. *lʾklw* Tell F 22 (cf. Abou-Assaf, Bordreuil & Millard Tell F p. 36, Zadok TeAv ix 122, Gropp & Lewis BASOR cclix 54, Huehnergard ZDMG cxxxvii 268 (n. 7), cf. however Kaufman Maarav iii 173, JAOS civ 572: or *lʾklw* = *l*$_5$ + Sing. abs. of *ʾklw* (= food)? :: Andersen & Freedman FS Fensham 40: *lʾklw* = *l*$_1$ + Pf. 3 p.pl.m. of *ʾkl*$_1$); Part. s.m. abs. *ʾkl* KAI 222A 30 - **DA** Qal Impf. 3 p.s.m. *yʾkl* ii 31, 37 (both in heavily dam. context); Imper. pl.m. *ʾklw* i 11 (cf. Hoftijzer DA p. 209, Levine JAOS ci 197, H.P.Müller ZAW xciv 218, 226f., Puech FS Grelot 23, 28 :: e.g. Caquot

& Lemaire Syr liv 199, Garbini Hen i 179, 185, Delcor SVT xxxii 57, McCarter BASOR ccxxxix 51, 55, H. & M. Weippert ZDPV xcviii 96, 103, Hackett BTDA 29, 97: = QAL Pf. 3 p.pl.m., cf. also Rofé SB 66 - **OffAr** QAL Pf. 3 p.s.f. + suff. 3 p.pl.m. *ʾklthm* KAI 233^{17} (:: Degen GGA '79, 50: l. *ʾklt hm<w>*, the *w* left out by haplography); Impf. 3 p.s.m. *yʾkl* Aḥiq 89; 2 p.s.m. *tʾkl* Aḥiq 127, 129; 3 p.pl.m. *yʾklw* KAI 270B 3; Imper. s.m. *ʾkl* Sach 76 i B 6 (?); Inf. *mʾkl* Cowl 61^{9}, Sach 80 iii A 2; cf. Paik 74 (*ʾklw*), MO xvii 187^{4} (cf. Nyberg ibid. 204), GIPP 45 - **JAr** Part. act s.f. abs. *ʾklh* AMB $7^{17,20}$ - ¶ verb QAL to eat: KAI 214^{9}, 215^{9}, Aḥiq 127, etc.; + obj. (own beard and hand, as symbol of extreme poverty): KAI $24^{6,7}$ (v. however supra); for DA i 11, v. *pḥd$_2$*; with animal subject (to devour): KAI 222A 27; with inanimate subject, viz fire (to devour): KAI 233^{17} - Part. act. used as subst., devourer: KAI 222A 30 (:: Tawil BASOR ccxxv 61: = crop-consuming devourer, i.e. special species of insect; cf. also Hillers TC 54ff.) - a form of this root poss. also in DA ii 3 (*ʾkl[*).
v. *ʾpl$_1$*, *ykl*.

ʾkl$_2$ **Amm** Sing. abs. *ʾkl* AUSS xiii $2^{1,4}$ (highly uncert. reading),^{8,9} - **Edom** Sing. abs. *ʾkl* TeAv xii $97^{3,6}$ - **JAr** Sing. (?) abs. (?) *ʾkl[* Syr xlv 101^{21} (uncert., dam. context) - ¶ subst. food (in Syr xlv 101^{21} imposs. to be specified in the context, v. also supra); in AUSS xiii $2^{1,4,8,9}$ prob. a cereal: grain, cf. also Cross AUSS xiii 3f., Jackson ALIA 52, 55, Aufrecht sub CAI 80 - Lemaire & Durand IAS 115, 125, 140: l. *ʾkl* (= Sing. abs.) in KAI 222B 40 (cf. also Lipiński Stud 43; highly uncert. reading).

ʾkldy v. *kldy*.

ʾklh **Nab** Sing. emph. *ʾkltʾ* BASOR cclxiii 78^{2} (cf. Jones BASOR cclxxv 43 :: Hammond, Johnson & Jones BASOR cclxiii ibid. (div. otherwise): l. *ʾklt* = APH Pf. 3 p.s.f. of *kly$_1$* (= to be completed)) - ¶ subst. food.

ʾklw v. *ʾkl$_1$*.

ʾkls **JAr** Beyer ATTM 352, 510: l. this subst. Sing. emph. (< Greek ὄχλος) *ʾklsh* (= crowd, throng) in MPAT 60^{5}.

ʾkm **OffAr** QAL Impf. 3 p.pl.m. (with f. subject, cf. also Ben-Chayyim EI i 136f.) *yʾkmw* Aḥiq 157 - ¶ verb QAL to become blind (said of eyes; cf. also Lindenberger APA 158, Kottsieper SAS 187).

ʾksdr (< Greek ἐξέδρα) - **Pun** Sing. abs. *ʿksndrʿ* KAI 129^{2} (cf. FR 109) - **Palm** Sing. emph. *ʾksdrʾ* CIS ii 4171^{2}, 4172^{1}, 4173^{1}, 4174^{4}, 4199^{8}, Inv xii 2^{3}, RIP 51^{2}, etc., *ʾkšdrʾ* CIS ii 4171^{2} (cf. also Blau PC 58 n. 17); Plur. abs. *ʾksdryn* RB xxxix 541^{3}, Ber ii 110^{1} (Greek par. ἐξεδρῶν) - ¶ subst. m. and f. exedra, room - in punic text prob. = part of sanctuary - in Palm. texts = room in tomb constructions - the *mksdrʾ* in Ber ii

107^2 = lapsus for *mn* ʾ*ksdr*ʾ?

ʾ**ksn** (or ʾ*ksny*?, cf. Cantineau Gramm 114; < Greek ξένος) - **Palm** Plur. emph. ʾ*ksny*ʾ CIS ii 3959^4 (= SBS 44B 4) - ¶ subst. m. stranger.

ʾ**kpl** v. ʾ*pkl*.

ʾ**kṣr** v. *kṣr*$_5$.

ʾ**kr** (< Akkad. (< Sum.), cf. Zimmern Fremdw 40, Ellenbogen 27, Kaufman AIA 58, cf. also Widengren HDS 224, Lipiński ZAH i 62f.) - **OffAr** Sing. emph. ʾ*kr*ʾ NESE iii 39^5 - ¶ subst. farmer.

ʾ**kryz** v. *krwz*$_1$, *krz*$_1$.

ʾ**kšdr** v. ʾ*ksdr*.

ʾ**l**$_1$ m. **Ph** Sing. (or Plur.?, cf. Röllig FS Friedrich 408, 410) cstr. ʾ*l* CIS i 8^1, 9^1, KAI 19^4 (cf. e.g. Röllig KAI a.l., Gibson SSI iii p. 119f.), DD 13^1 (cf. e.g. Gibson SSI iii p. 119f., 121 :: Dunand & Duru DD p. 192: = part of n.d.), etc.; + suff. 3 p.s.m. ʾ*ly* KAI 15^4, 38^1, CIS i 94^4, RES 289^3, 302^{10}, etc.; Plur. abs. ʾ*lm* KAI 26A i 8, ii 6, iii 11, 16, 19 (:: Driver FS Bakoš 102, Del Olmo Lete AO i 289: = n.d. + *m* enclit.), C iv 2, 12, 19, 27^{11}, 30^5 (v. also ʾ*r*ʾ*l*), 37B 4 (for the reading, cf. Peckham Or xxxvii 305, 319, Masson & Sznycer RPC 26, 59, Garbini AION xxiii 134, Healy BASOR ccxvi 53 :: CIS i sub 86, Cooke NSI p. 69, Lidzbarski Hand 376, KI sub 29, Röllig KAI a.l.: l. *šlm* = Sing. abs. of *šlm*$_3$), 44^2, 48^2, 59^2, 60^6 (:: Fuentes Estañol VF s.v. ʾ*l*$_4$ = lapsus for Sing. abs. of ʾ*l*$_1$), etc.; cstr. ʾ*l* KAI 4^{4,7}, 50^3, Mus li 286^9 (?) - **Pun** Sing. abs. ʾ*l* CIS i 4943^1 (Röllig FS Friedrich 415 n. 24: ʾ*l* lapsus for ʾ*lm*?; or ʾ*l* lapsus for ʾ*n* = ʾ*dn*$_1$?); Plur. abs. ʾ*lm* KAI 69^{13,16}, 74^8 (:: Fuentes Estañol VF s.v. *l*$_4$ = lapsus for Sing. abs. of ʾ*l*$_1$), 77^1, 90^3, 118^1, 120^1, Hofra 87^2, etc., ʾ*lym* NP 130^5 (??, thus Février RHR cxli 21); for Ph. and Pun., cf. also FR 240,4 - **Hebr** Sing. cstr. ʾ*l* AMB 12^{24} - **OffAr** Sing. abs. ʾ*l* Aḥiq 107, 154, 156, 161, 173 (?. v. infra) - **JAr** Sing. emph. ʾ*lh* AMB 7^{5,11,14,15} - f. **Ph** Sing. cstr. ʾ*lt* IEJ iv 224 - **Pun** Sing. abs. ʾ*lt* KAI 89^1 (the ʾ*lt* in Antas xix 1 more prob. = n.d., cf. Garbini AION xix 329; cf. also the ʾ*lt* in KAI 89^1, 172^3, etc., prob. = n.d. :: Röllig FS Friedrich 409f., KAI a.l.; for KAI 27^1, v. infra) - **Palm** v. infra - ¶ subst. m. god, f. goddess, cf. e.g. *bʿbr bʿl w*ʾ*lm* KAI 26A i 8: thanks to Baʿal and the gods (:: Röllig FS Friedrich 404: ʾ*lm* = deity); cf. also ʾ*lt ṣr* (= goddess of Tyre) on Ph. coin IEJ iv 224 (cf. Albright BASOR cxxxix 25, Dahood CBQ xxii 408); cf. ʾ*l ṣb*ʾ*wt* AMB 12^{24}: God of Hosts; Plur. ʾ*lm* used with Sing. meaning "god" (:: Dahood Bibl xliii 355 n. 3: = Sing. abs. + -*m* enclit., cf. also idem Bibl xlvii 412), *h* ʾ*lm z bʿl krntryš* KAI 26C iii 16 (cf. Gibson SSI iii p. 52): this god B.K., ʾ*lm nrgl* KAI 59^2: the god Nergal (:: Albright PSI 34: = Sing. + suff. 3 p.s.m.); ʾ*lm ʿwgsṭs* KAI 122^1: the divine August (*divus Augustus*), etc., cf. also *ʿwgsṭs bn ʾlm* KAI 120^{1}: *Augustus divi filius*; Plur. *ʾlm* used with Sing. meaning "goddess", *ʾlm ʾdrt ʾs ʾlm ʿštrt* KAI 48^{2}: the mighty goddess Isis (and) the goddess Ashtarte; etc.; cf. also *sml hʾlm* KAI 26C iv 19: the image of a/the god; *glb ʾlm* CIS i 257^{4}: barber in the service of a/the deity; *ksp ʾlm* KAI 60^{6}: treasure of the deity (> temple); *hʾlm z* Kar stat. iii 16 (cf. RA xlii 176): this god; etc.; for the use of the Plur. with Sing. meaning, cf. Hartmann MUSJ xlviii 67ff. :: Uffenheimer Lesh xxx 169: *ʾlm* = *ʾl* + *-m* enclit. (v.d.Branden Meltô i 65 (cf. also H.P.Müller TUAT i 641, 643): the *ʾlm* in KAI 26A i 8, ii 6 = Plur. with Sing. meaning (improb. interpret.)); - this word prob. also in **OffAr** (or = n.d.?, cf. Grelot RB lxviii 190), *yʾpk ʾl pm ʾpkʾ* Aḥiq 156: God will distort the mouth of the liar (v. *ʾpk*); *hqymny ʾl bṣdyq ʿmk* Aḥiq 173: o God, set me up as a righteous man with you; *zy ʾl ʿmh* Aḥiq 107, 154 (dam. context): with whom God is (cf. Seidel ZAW xxxii 296, Ginsberg ANET 429, Lindenberger APA 93, UF xiv 109ff. (*ʾl* = El) :: Grimme OLZ '11, 532, Koopmans 144: who is the like of him (*ʾl* = *ʾl$_6$*, *ʿmh* = Sing. + suff. 3 p.s.m. of *ʿm$_3$* (= juxtaposition)) cf. Cowl p. 238, cf. also Grelot RB lxviii 184: *ʾl* = *ʾl$_6$*, *ʿmh* = *ʿmh$_2$*, cf. however Grelot DAE p. 444 n. h: in Aḥiq 154 l. *zy ʾl ʿmhwn*), cf. also Aḥiq 161: *zy lh ʾl ʿmh* - this word prob. also in Waw, Sing. abs. *ʾyl*AMB 6^{17} (?, diff. and dam. context), emph. *ʾylʾ* AMB 6^{2,11}, + suff. 1 p.s. *ʾyly* AMB 6$^{15f.}$ (highly uncertain reading and interpret.), *ʾyl* here indication of God; < Hebr.??, thus Dupont-Sommer Waw p. 74 - this word (Plur. abs. *ʾlm*) prob. also in the Ph. text KAI 19^{2}, cf. Caquot Sem xv 31f., Milik DFD 424f., *hʾlm mlʾk mlkʿštrt* = the divine Mal'ak of Milkashtart (cf. also Cooke NSI p. 48: the *Elim* the envoys of M.-A. and Seyrig Syr xl 27: the *elim* the envoy of M.A.; v. also *mlʾk*) :: Meyer ZAW xlix 3: *ʾlm* = Plur. abs. of *ʾyl$_2$*(= rams > officials, notabilities; cf. Dahood Or xxxiv 86, Miller UF ii 182, Röllig FS Friedrich 407, KAI a.l., Dunand & Duru DD p. 186f., v.d.Branden BO vii 70f., Baldacci BiOr xl 131 (cf. also Healy UF x 89 n. 7: *ʾlm* indication of human beings)) - the *ʾlt* on KAI 27^{1} poss. = f. Sing. abs., cf. Albright BASOR lxxvi 7 n. 8, Dupont-Sommer RHR cxx 134f., Gaster Or xi 44, Röllig FS Friedrich 409, KAI a.l., Zevit IEJ xxvii 111, de Moor JEOL xxvii 108, Gibson SSI iii p. 83f. (:: Cross & Saley BASOR cxcvii 45: = f. Plur. abs. of *ʾl$_1$* (cf. also Röllig NESE ii 20) :: du Mesnil du Buisson FS Dussaud 424f.: prob. = f. Sing. cstr. of *ʾl$_1$*) × Torczyner JNES vi 20f., Rosenthal ANET 658, Caquot FS Gaster 46, Lipiński RTAT 265, Avishur PIB 248f., Garbini OA xx 281, 283, Sperling HUCA liii 3, 5: = Sing. cstr. of *ʾlh$_2$* - the *ʾlym* (= m. Plur. abs.) in the Palm. *gntʾ ʾlym* (SBS 45B 12) prob. canaanism, cf. Caquot GLECS vii 78, Dunant SBS p. 59, Milik DFD 5, Gawlikowski Ber xxii 146, Syr li 93f., TP 28, 50, cf. also Teixidor Syr li 333 :: Degen WO viii 131 (n. 12) - in the

fragmentary text of SicArch xii 6 (*lʾlk*), poss. form of *ʾl*$_1$ preserved??, or of *ʾl*$_6$??, or of *hlk*$_1$?? - the *ʿlm* in NP 1 (= Trip 1) prob. = *ʿl*$_7$ + *m[*, cf. Amadasi IPT p. 34 :: Berger RA ii 42, Levi Della Vida Lib iii 92f., Hoftijzer DA 224 n. 113: = Plur. abs. of *ʾl*$_1$ :: Vattioni RB lxxviii 243: = *ʿlm*$_4$ - for the combinations with *ʾlm*, v. *ʾmh*$_2$, *ʾrʾl*, *byt*$_2$, *bn*$_1$, *glb*$_2$, *ksp*$_2$, *mrzḥ*, *nšʾ*$_3$, *qwm*$_1$.
v. *ʾdm*$_1$, *ʾl*$_{3,7}$, *ʾlh*$_{1,2}$, *ʾlw*$_1$, *ʾlm*$_2$, *ʾlmh*, *ʾln*$_1$, *ʾnth*$_2$, *ʾšr*$_7$, *znh*, *ṭbwt*, *kkb*, *šlm*$_2$.

ʾl$_2$ (< prob. Arab., cf. Cantineau Nab ii 172, O'Connor JNES xlv 217ff.) - **Nab** Sing. cstr. *ʾl* CIS ii 164[1] (Greek par. δῆμος), 165, RES 2042, 2065, 2066[3], Syr xxxv 244[4], ARNA-Nab 130[2], ADAJ xxiv 42 - ¶ subst. m. family, clan, tribe - this word prob. also in RES 53[1] (Sing. cstr.).

ʾl$_3$ **Ph** KAI 13[3,4,5,6,7], 14[4,5,6,8,11,20,21], 24[14,15] - **Hebr** DJD ii 17A 2, TA-H 2[6] - **Samal** KAI 214[22,23,26] - **DA** i 8f., 9 - **OldAr** KAI 202A 13, 222A 21, 22, 23, 24, 28, 29, 33, 36, B 8, C 24, 223A 2, 224[7], Tell F 17, 18, 19, 20, 21, 22, 23 - **OffAr** Cowl 42[7,11,13], Aḥiq 52, 54, Driv 6[6], KAI 233[17], 266[7], PSBA '15, 222[4] (= RES 1793[9]), ASAE xxvi 25B 5, Herm 1[4,10], 2[3], ATNS 26[9], etc.; cf. Frah xxv 41, Paik 77, GIPP 15, SaSt 12 ¶ subst. absence - a) *ʾl ngh* DA i 8f.: absence of light = darkness (cf. Hoftijzer DA a.l., Dahood Bibl lxii 126; for comparable material, cf. also Dahood Bibl xli 176ff. :: e.g. Caquot & Lemaire Syr liv 196f., McCarter BASOR ccxxxix 51, H.P.Müller ZAW xciv 218, 224f., H. & M. Weippert ZDPV xcviii 92f., 103, Hackett BTDA 29, 43f.) - b) mostly used as adv. of negation (prohibitive), always with Impf. (cf. FR 249, 318,3, Degen AAG 47, 86b,c, Hoftijzer DA p. 294, 299f., Segert AAG p. 233, 426, cf. also Degen GGA '79, 36, 46, 49); sometimes doubled *ʾl ʾl* KAI 13[3,5] - Cross & Saley BASOR cxcvii 46 (nn. 29, 32): l. *ʾl* in KAI 27[24] and *ʾ.l* (lapsus for *ʾl*) in KAI 27[22] (cf. also Röllig NESE ii 19, 25; in both instances uncert. reading; for other readings, cf. e.g. v.d.Branden BiOr xxxiii 13, Avishur PIB 248, Caquot FS Gaster 50f.) - Liverani RSF ii 36f.: l. *ʾl šyy* = non equal in Syr xlviii 396[3,5f.], cf. however Cross CBQ xxxvi 488 (n. 20): = the god Spoiler (both interpretations less prob.; *ʾlšyy* prob. = Alasiote, cf. Caquot Syr xlviii 399, 403, Gaster BASOR ccix 19, Röllig NESE ii 31, Lipiński RSF ii 51f. × Garbini OA xx 288, 292, Sem xxxviii 134: l. *ʾl* (= *ʾl*$_1$) *šyy* (= n.d.), cf. also Avishur PIB 267f., UF x 30, 33; v. also *šyy*) - Hackett BTDA 60: the first *ʾl* in DA ii 6 poss. = *ʾl*$_3$ (less prob. interpret., prob. = n.d., cf. e.g. Hoftijzer DA a.l.) .
v. *hgy*$_2$, *kl*$_1$.

ʾl$_4$ v. *ʾnk*.

ʾl$_5$ v. *z*$_1$, *znh*.

ʾl$_6$ **Ph** KAI 50[1] (reading of *l* uncert. :: Cross Or xxxvii 446 n. 5: l.

ʾdt[ ], cf. also Röllig BiOr xxvii 379) - **Pun** Levi Della Vida OA ii 73: *yl* in IRT 906[3] prob. = *ʾl$_6$*, cf. also Vattioni Aug xvi 550 :: Vattioni AION xvi 51: = *ḥyl$_2$* - **Hebr** KAI 189[2,3,5], 192[1], 193[7,20,21], TA-H 1[1], 2[1], 3[1], etc.; + suff. 3 p.s.m. *ʾlw* KAI 200[13] (cf. e.g. Cross BASOR cxlv 44 nn. 38, 39 :: Talmon BASOR clxxvi 36: = *ʾlw$_2$*, interj., pray, behold); + suff. 2 p.s.m. *ʾlyk* DJD ii 17A 2, *ʾlk* DJD ii 30[19]; + suff. 1 p.s. *ʾly* KAI 193[11], TA-H 8[8] (heavily dam. context); + suff. 1 p.pl. *ʾlnw* DJD ii 42[5] - **DA** + suff. 3 p.s.m. *ʾlwh* i 1, 6 (for the reading, cf. McCarter BASOR ccxxxix 51, 53, Levine JAOS ci 196, 198, Hackett BTDA 25, 37, 100, Sasson UF xvii 287, 290, Wesselius BiOr xliv 593, 595f., Lemaire GLECS xxiv-xxviii 325, Weinfeld Shn v/vi 142, 146 :: e.g. Hoftijzer DA a.l., TUAT ii 140, H. & M. Weippert ZDPV xcviii 83, 86f. (n. 37), 103, Smelik HDAI 79: l. *ʾlqh* = n.p. :: Greenfield JSS xxv 251f.: l. poss. *ʾl* (= *ʾl$_6$*) + *qhl* (= Sing. abs. of *qhl$_2$*) :: Puech BAT 356, 361: l. *ṣlqh* = n.p.?) - **OldAr** KAI 202A 11, 224[1,19], Tell F 14, 15; + suff. 3 p.s.m. *ʾ[l]wh* KAI 224[8]; + suff. 1 p.s. *ʾly* KAI 202A 12, 224[20] - **OffAr** Cowl 30[1], 37[1,17], KAI 266[1], JRAS '29, 108[1], RHR cxxviii 30[1], cxxx 20[1], PSBA '15, 222[1f.], Herm 1[1,14], NESE iii 48[1], ATNS 26[9,16] (in both instances dam. context), etc. - ¶ prep. (on this prep., cf. also Pennachietti AION xxiv 182 (n. 42)), to, towards; *wyʾtw ʾlwh ʾlhn* DA i 1: the gods came to him; *ql ʾš qrʾ ʾl rʿw* KAI 189[2f.]: a man's voice calling to his mate; etc.; beginning of a letter (cf. Alexander JSS xxiii 159ff., Dion RB lxxxix 530, 536f., 541, Fitzmyer JBL xciii 211ff., WA 189ff., Pardee JBL xcvii 332f., Fales JAOS cvii 454), *ʾl ʾdny* KAI 192[1]: to my lord, cf. KAI 196[1], TA-H 1[1] (cf. also Pardee UF x 325f.), 2[1], 3[1], Cowl 30[1], 38[1], Herm 5[1], 6[1], 7[1], etc. (cf. *šlm byt nbw ʾl ʾḥty rʿyh mn ʾḥky mkbnt* Herm 1[1]: prosperity (be given to you from) the temple of N., to my sister R. from your brother M.; cf. also Herm 2[1], 4[1], compare Herm 3[1]: *ʿl$_7$* pro *ʾl$_6$*); beginning of the address of a letter (cf. also Fitzmyer JBL xciii 218f., WA 195, Dion RB lxxxix 533, 555, Porten EI xiv 167), *ʾl mrʾy yʾdnyh* Cowl 37[17]: to my lord Y., cf. KAI 50[1], Cowl 38[12], 39[5], Herm 1[14], 2[18], 3[14], etc. - in special contexts, *šʿrn lʾlmnny ʾl ndʿ[* TH iv vs. 1f.: (prob. meaning) barley which N. has to (re)pay to I. (for parallels, v. *ʿl$_7$*); *ʾl ʾlhn wʾl ʾnšn tyṭb* Tell F 14f.: may it be pleasant before gods and men (cf. Akkad. par. *eli ilāni u nišē ṭu-ub-bi*); for Tell F 15, v. *ytr$_1$*; *ʾl tšbq ʾl[* ATNS 26[9]: do not allow (?) to .... (context however dam.) - Greenfield JAOS xciv 511: l. *ʾly* (= *ʾl$_6$* + suff. 1 p.s.) in TA-H 17[5] (less prob. reading), Gibson SSI i p. 54: l. *l[y]* (uncert. reading), Aharoni TA a.l.: *lzp* (uncert. reading) = *l$_5$* + n.l. - Lemaire IH i 103: l. the first word of KAI 193[13] *ʾl* (poss. reading, cf. also Gibson JSS xxiv 11), for the context and other reading proposals, v. *ntn* - Hackett BTDA 59: the second *ʾl* in DA ii 6: prob. = *ʾl$_6$* (less prob. interpret.; prob. = n.d., cf. Hoftijzer DA a.l.) - Segal ATNS a.l.:

l. *ʾl* (= *ʾl$_6$*) in ATNS 6[1] (reading however uncert., cf. Porten & Yardeni sub TADAE B 8.12) - Bresciani RSO xlv a.l.: l. *ʾl* in RSO xlv 24a (reading of *ʾ* however highly uncert., cf. Porten FS Bresciani 435).
v. *ʾl$_{1,7}$*.

ʾl$_7$ **Ph** KAI 1[2] - ¶ conj., if (cf. par. text KAI 26A iii 12, cf. e.g. Avishur PIB 160f., Garbini ISN 55) :: Lidzbarski NGWG '24, 45: = *ʾl$_1$*(by God) :: Torrey JAOS xlv 272: = *ʾl$_6$*:: v.d.Branden Mašr liv 733ff.: poss. = QAL Pf. 3 p.s.m. of *ʾyl$_1$*(= to be powerful, mighty) or = QAL Pf. 3 p.s.m. of *ʾly$_1$* (= to swear); derivation uncert., cf. FR 258c; for the proposed solutions, cf. a) = *ʾillū*, cf. Dussaud Syr v 139, Vincent RB xxxiv 185, Segert GPP p. 164, Gibson SSI iii p. 15 - b) = *ʾūlay* > *ʾulē*, cf. Albright JPOS vi 80, JAOS lxvii 155 n. 23, CF 14 - c) // with Arab. *ʾin* with change of *n* to *l*, cf. Ronzevalle MUSJ xii 28, Vinnikov ActOrHung v 325, RA lii 245 - d) Moran CBQ xv 365f.: // with Amarna *allu*, particle with deictic force - cf. also Soggin Bibl xlvi 59 n. 3: = asseverative particle, certainly (improb. interpret.) - on this word, cf. also Garbini FSR 38 (n. 21), Healy CISFP i 664f.

ʾl$_8$ (< Arab.) - **Nab** RES 2052[6], J 17[7] (= RES 1175) - ¶ article; otherwise only in proper names (v. e.g. *rtb$_2$*), cf. Cantineau Nab ii 61f. - cf. also Diem Or lii 378.
v. *ṭbwt*.

ʾl$_9$ **Ph** inscr on jar, cf. RB lxxxiii 90, meaning unknown. Found together with jar with inscription *ʾlg*, cf. ibid., meaning also unknown.

ʾlʾ$_1$ (< Greek εἶλη; v. however infra) - **Palm** Sing. cstr. *ʾlʾ* Inv x 128[2] - ¶ subst. (army-)corps; Caquot GLECS vii 77, Dunant SBS p. 65: < Lat. *ala*, but less prob. (Greek par.: εἴλης; Greek εἶλη not < Lat. *ala*, but has par. meaning in later usage).

ʾlʾ$_2$ v. *z$_1$*.

ʾlʾ$_3$ **Hebr** *ʾlh* DJD ii 45[8], 46[6] - **Palm** *ʾlʾ* CIS ii 3913 ii 149 - ¶ conj. but, however; in CIS ii 3913 ii 149 perhaps to be translated: if it is not, cf. Cantineau Gramm 136; in the Hebr. texts prob. to be translated: except.
v. *znh*.

ʾlʾm v. *sgyl*.

ʾlb v. *ʾlp$_1$*.

ʾlg v. *ʾl$_9$*.

ʾlh$_1$ m. **Hebr** Plur. cstr. *ʾlhy* AMB 1[23], 4[24,34], SSI i p. 58A[1,2] (cf. Naveh IEJ xiii 84, 89f., Weippert ZDPV lxxx 162, Lemaire RB lxxxiii 558f., Lipiński OLP viii 94, Smelik HDAI 149 :: Cross FS Glueck 301, 305 nn. 6, 9 (cf. also Garr DGSP 106): l. in l. 1 for *ʾlhy kl* Plur. + suff. 2 p.s.m. *ʾlhykh* (cf. also Sarfatti Maarav iii 68, Miller SVT xxxii 321 (n.

23)), in l. 2 for *yhd lw lʾlhy* l. *yhdh wgʾlty*, *gʾlty* being QAL Pf. 1 p.s. of *gʾl* = to redeem (cf. also Miller SVT xxxii 321 (n. 27)), Frey 1398^{1}; + suff. 2 p.s.m. *ʾlhyk* KAI 196$^{12f.}$ - **Samal** Sing. abs. *ʾlh* KAI 215^{2} (?); cstr. *ʾlh* KAI 214^{29} (or = Plur. cstr.?); Plur. abs. (nom.) *ʾnhw* (lapsus; for the reading, cf. Gibson SSI ii p. 64, 70 :: e.g. Cooke NSI p. 159, 165, Röllig KAI a.l., Dion p. 129: l. *ʾlhw*) KAI 214^{2}; abs. (gen./acc.) *ʾlhy* KAI 214^{4,12} (for second instance :: Lipiński BiOr xxxiii 232: = Plur. cstr.; v. *mt₃*)^{,13,19}, 215^{23}; cstr. (nom./gen./acc.) *ʾlh* 215^{2}; cstr. (gen./acc.) *ʾlhy* KAI 215^{22} (cf. Friedr 30*, Friedrich FS Landsberger 425 :: Garb 260f.) - **DA** Plur. abs. *ʾlhn* i 1 - **OldAr** Sing. abs. *ʾlh* Tell F 5; Plur. abs. *ʾlhn* KAI 202B 9, 222A 30, B 6, 31, C 15, 21, 223B 2, 224^{2}, Tell F 14, *ʾlhyn* Tell F 4; cstr. *ʾlhy* KAI 202B 25, 217^{3}, 222A 10, B 5, 23, 33, 223B 9 (*ʾlh[y]*), C 13 (*ʾlh[y]*), 224^{4,14,17,23}; emph. *ʾlhyʾ* KAI 223C 3, 7, 10 (*[ʾ]lhyʾ*) - **OffAr** Sing. abs. *ʾlh* Cowl 13^{14}, IEJ xxv 118^{6} (on script and language, cf. Naveh ibid. 120ff.); cstr. *ʾlh* Cowl 30^{2,27}, 32^{2}, 38^{3,5}, ASAE xxxix 357^{3}; emph. *ʾlhʾ* Cowl 2^{16}, 3^{17}, 6^{4}, 13^{15} (for the reading, cf. Porten & Yardeni sub TADAE B 2.7, Lipiński Or lix 553 :: e.g. Cowl a.l.: l. *ʾ[l]hyʾ* = Plur. emph. (cf. also Grelot DAE p. 187, Porten & Greenfield JEAS p. 16), for the reading problems, cf. also Grelot RB xcvii 273), Krael 2^{2}, 3^{3,8}, ATNS 30a 7, RES 1817^{2}, KAI 229$^{3f.}$, 233^{19}, etc., etc.; + suff. 3 p.s.m. *ʾlhh* ATNS 23b 5; + suff. 1 p.pl. *ʾlhn* Cowl 7^{6} (:: Porten Arch 156: poss. = Plur. abs.); Plur. abs. *ʾlhn* Aḥiq 95, 115 (:: Kottsieper SAS 13, 21, 187: l. *ʾlh* = QAL Part. act. s.m. abs. of *ʾly₂* (= to lament)), 124, 128, 135, 160, KAI 228A 20, *ʾlhyn* RES 1785A 5; cstr. *ʾlhy* Cowl 30^{14}, 71^{8,26}, KAI 228A 3, 10, 13, 17, Atlal vii 109^{7}; emph. *ʾlhyʾ* Cowl 17^{1}, 21^{2}, Krael 13^{1}, Driv 13^{2}, etc.; cf. Frah i 10 (*ʿrḥyʾ*), Paik 78, 79 (*ʾlḥʾ*), 84, 86 (*ʾlḥyn*), 82, 83 (*ʿrḥyʾ*), 85, 87, 88 (*ʿrḥyʾn*), Syr xxxv 305^{1}, Syn 315 i 1, GIPP 45, SaSt 14 - **Nab** Sing. abs. *ʾlh* (??) RES 2092^{2} (or n.d.?); cstr. *ʾlh* CIS ii 174^{2}, 176^{4}, 208^{6}, 209^{8}, etc., etc.; emph. *ʾlhʾ* CIS ii 199^{7}, 200^{7}, 354^{1}, 572^{2}, J 72 (for the reading, cf. Milik sub ARNA-Nab 101), BASOR clxiii 23, etc.; + suff. 3 p.pl.m. *ʾlhhm* RES 2042; Plur. cstr. *ʾlhy* RB xlii 576$^{4f.}$; emph. *ʾlhyʾ* CIS ii 185^{6}, 211^{6,8}, 350^{3,4}, etc. - **Palm** Sing. cstr. *ʾlh* CIS ii 3978^{7}, 3991^{3}; emph. *ʾlhʾ* CIS ii 3911^{8}, 3919^{3}, 3959^{3} (= SBS 44B), 3972^{3}, 3973^{4}, Inv iii 22^{7}, etc., etc.; + suff. 3 p.s.m. *ʾlhh* SBS 58^{2}; Plur. abs. *ʾlhyn* Syr xii 130^{8}; cstr. *ʾlhy* CIS ii 3903^{1}, Syr xlvii 413^{1}; emph. *ʾlhyʾ* CIS ii 3914^{3}, 3955^{7}, 3974^{1}, Inv ix 1^{5}, xi 12^{6}, 73^{4} (for the reading, cf. Starcky RB lxxiii 66, cf. also Teixidor Syr xliv 186), xii 22^{5}, 55^{2} (reading *ʾlhy* mistaken, cf. Bounni FS Michałowski 318), SBS 14^{2}, etc., *ʾlhʾ* Syr xlvii 316^{2}, PNO 35c (prob. reading, cf. Milik DFD 343 :: Ingholt & Starcky PNO a.l.: l. *ʾlhyʾ*); + suff. 3 p.s.f. *ʾlhyh* Syr xvii 280^{8} (= SBS 48B); + suff. 3 p.pl.m. *ʾlhyhn* CIS ii 3903^{3}, 3923^{4}, SBS 40^{5}, *ʾlhyhwn* CIS ii 3929^{5}, 3930^{4}, Inv ix 12^{4}, SBS 39^{6}, RIP 160^{8} (the reading

-*hn* prob. misprint), *ʾlhwhwn* DFD 37[5] - **Hatra** Sing. abs. *ʾlh* 173[2]; emph. *ʾlhʾ* 23[1], 25[2] (× Aggoula Ber xviii 91: = Plur. emph.), 26[2] (× Aggoula Ber xviii 91: = Plur. emph., cf. also Degen WO v 236, Vattioni IH a.l.), 60 (?, dam. context, cf. also Aggoula Ber xviii 95), 67 (rather than Plur. emph., cf. Milik DFD 361), 82[3], 106b 4, 107[4], 228[3] (*[ʾ]lhʾ*), 232b 3, 272[1] (or = Plur. emph.?)[,2], 280[3], KAI 257[3] (cf. also Assur 7[2], 11 ii 5, 15d 1, 15f 2 (heavily dam. context), 17 i 4); Plur. emph. *ʾlhʾ* 17 (cf. Aggoula Ber xviii 89, Vattioni IH a.l. :: Caquot Syr xxix 98: = Sing. emph.), 21[2] (:: Caquot Syr xxix 101, Altheim & Stiehl AAW ii 200, Vattioni IH a.l., cf. also Milik RN vi/iv 52f.: = Sing. emph.), 23[1], 79[2] (:: Altheim & Stiehl AAW iv 244: = Sing. emph. (= the sun god)), 169 (or = Sing. emph.?), 173 (:: Caquot Syr xli 264: or = Sing. emph.), 184[2] (*ʾlh[ʾ]*), 200, 325[3] (for the context, cf. Degen NESE iii 107, Aggoula Sem xxvii 132), 346[5], 363[3], cf. also Assur 28a 3 - **JAr** Sing. abs. *ʾlh* MPAT 69[2], JKF i 203[5,11,14,15] (?, or in the JKF texts *ʾlh* = *ʾl₁* (Hebr. loanword) with emph. ending, thus Dupont-Sommer JKF i 214) - f. **OffAr** Sing. emph. *ʾlhtʾ* Cowl 72[16] (cf. Cowl a.l. :: CIS ii sub 146B 4: l. *rbty* = Sing. f. + suff. 1 p.s. of *rb₂*), JNES xviii 154, JKF i 46[1] (?), ATNS 6[7] (or Plur.??, dam. context), 181[3] (*ʾlht[ʾ]*), NESE ii 87[4] (dam. context, cf. Segal Irâq xxxi 171f., Degen NESE ii 86 :: Altheim & Stiehl AAW v/1, 75: = *ʾlh₃* + *tʾ[...])*, *ʾlhth* Cowl 14[5]; Plur. abs. *ʾlhn* KAI 264[6]; for *[ʾ]lhyt* in Sumer xx 19,10[5], v. infra - **Nab** Sing. cstr. *ʾlht* RES 2091, Atlal vii 105[2], BJ clxxx 265; emph. *ʾlhtʾ* CIS ii 336[3], RB xli 593[3], xlii 411[1], xliii 574[1] (for the reading, cf. Milik ADAJ xxi 144 n. 3), J 30[8] (= CIS ii 200; for the reading, cf. Milik sub ARNA-Nab 79), ADAJ xx 121 ii 1 (reading *ʾlht* mistake), 124, etc.; + suff. 3 p.pl.m. *ʾlhthm* CIS ii 182[1]; Plur. emph. *ʾlhtʾ* Atlal vii 105[2] - **JAr** Sing. cstr. *ʾlh* AMB 3[6]; emph. *ʾlhʾ* AMB 3[12], 5[3] (dam. context), cf. PEQ '38, 238[2]: ελαα (cf. Peters OLZ '40, 218f., Beyer ATTM 353; cf. also Milik LA x 154f.) - Plur. abs. in unknown West Semitic dialect (*ʾlhn*) in Sem xxxviii 52[1] (or = fraud?, cf. however Bordreuil & Pardee Sem xxxviii 65ff.) - ¶ subst. m. god, f. goddess, passim, cf. e.g. *wʾlhn wʾnš lʾ yhn[pq] ṣlmšzb ... mn bytʾ znh* KAI 228[20f.]: neither gods nor men shall eject S. ... from this temple (cf. also Tell F 14); *kwl ʾlh kwlyh* Hatra 173[2]: every god whomsoever; *wšpyrʾ ʾnt mn ʾlhn* KAI 264[6]: you are fairer than goddesses; in the Aramaic texts the emph. form often after the name of a god, *yhw ʾlhʾ* Cowl 22[1]: the god Y.; *ḥnwm ʾlhʾ* Krael 3[8]: the god Ch.; *nbw ʾlhʾ* ATNS 30a 7: the god N.; *yrḥbwl ʾlhʾ* Inv xii 44[2]: the god Y.; *bʿšmyn ʾlhʾ* Hatra 23[1]: the god B.; *bl ʾlhʾ* Assur 7[2]: the god B.; *ʾsy ʾlhtʾ* Cowl 72[16]: the goddess I. (cf. also ADAJ xx 121 ii 1f.); *tdh* (uncert. reading of *d*) *ʾlhtʾ* CIS ii 336[3]: the goddess T. (cf. ATNS 181[3]); cf. also *hdryn[ws] ʾlhʾ* CIS ii 3959[3]: the divine Hadrian (= *divus Hadrianus*) - for Plur. with Sing. meaning, see the Hebr. material, cf.

YHWH ʾlhy kl hʾrṣ SSI i p. 58A 1: Y. the God of the whole earth (cf. also Lemaire RB lxxxiii 566; v. also *ʾrṣ*$_1$); *ʾlhy yšrʾl* AMB 1[23], 4[34]: the God of Israel; *YHWH ʾlhyk* KAI 196[12f.]: Y. your God, etc. (cf. also *ʾlhy ṣbʾwt* Frey 1398[1], *ʾlhy mʿrkwt* AMB 4[24]); in Aramaic, cf. Aḥiq 126 (*ʾlhyʾ ysgh* = God will come to his help), cf. Joüon MUSJ xviii 27 (:: Perles OLZ '11, 502, Cowl p. 241, Grelot RB lxviii 187, DAE 440 n a: = lapsus for *ʾlhʾ* :: Lindenberger UF xiv 107f.: = gods, cf. also Segert AAG p. 334, 440); cf. however *ʾlhn* in Aḥiq 95, 115, 124, 128, 135 prob. with Plur. meaning :: Joüon MUSJ xviii 27ff.; the *ʾlhyʾ* in Cowl 21[2] Plur. meaning :: Porten Arch 160: poss. Sing. meaning, cf. also Ayad JACA 116f., Delsman TUAT i 253; cf. also *ʾlhyʾ* in Driv 13[2] designation of the Persian king (His Majesty), cf. Eilers AfO xvii 335 (cf. also Driv p. 85, Couroyer RB lxxviii 240f. Grelot DAE p. 326 (n. a); cf. however Porten & Yardeni sub TADAE A 6.16, Whitehead JNES xxxvii 134 (n. 103): = the gods) - *ʾlh ʾbh* KAI 214[29]: the god of his father (= his paternal god; Donner KAI a.l.: prob. the god of the dynasty); cf. *ʾlhy byt ʾby* KAI 217[3]: the gods of my father's house (sc. of the dynasty, cf. also Yadin FS Glueck 226 n. 34, H.P.Müller ZDPV xciv 66 n. 66); *šmš ʾlh byt ʾbwhn* CIS ii 3978[7]: Sh. the god of their father's house (of the clan or the family?) - *ʾlht ʾlhtʾ* Atlal vii 105[2]: the main goddess - *ʾlh mrʾnʾ* = the god of our lord (sc. of the king), title of the nabatean god Dushara: CIS ii 208[6], 211[6], 350[3], cf. *ʾlhy mrʾnʾ* RB xliii 576[4f.] and *ʾlhyʾ dy mrʾnʾ* CIS ii 185[6ff.], cf. also *ʾlh mnkw* PEQ '81, 22[1]: the god of M. (= the king of the Nabateans) - *ʾlhy ʿdyʾ* KAI 222B 23, 33, 224[4,14,17]: the gods of the treaty (sc. those who guarantee the treaty) - *ʾlh šmyʾ* Cowl 30[2,27f.], 32[3f.], 38[3,5]: the god of Heavens (cf. also AMB 3[6]), cf. KAI 202B 25: *ʾlhy šmy[n]* - *ʾlhy tymʾ* Atlal vii 109[7]: the gods of Taima - *ʾlhy tdmr* Syr xlvii 413[1f.]: the gods of Tadmor (= Palmyre) - Starcky MUSJ xlix 503ff.: the *ʾlhʾgbl* on Palm. stele = *ʾlh*$_1$ Sing. emph. + *gbl*$_3$ Sing. abs. (= the divine mountain; or rather *ʾlhʾgbl* = *ʾlh*$_1$ Sing. cstr. + *ʾgbl* < Arab. = pluralis fractus of *gbl*$_3$, the god of the mountains? or *ʾlh* here also < Arab.?) - Safar Sumer xx a.l.: l. poss. *[ʾ]lhyt* = f. Sing. form of *ʾlh*$_1$ in Sumer xx 19, 10[5] (however prob. = n.d.) - Naveh & Shaked AMB a.l.: l. poss. *ʾlwhh* (Sing. emph. or Sing. + suff. 3 p.s.f.) in AMB 14[3] (uncert. reading).
v. *ʾb*$_1$, *ʾlw*$_1$, *ʾnš*$_2$, *byt*$_2$, *brk*$_1$, *zḥl*, *znh*, *ṭb*$_2$, *mrlhʾ*, *plḥ*$_1$, *rb*$_2$, *rdwtʾlhʾ*, *škr*$_5$.

ʾlh$_2$ **Ph** Sing. cstr. *ʾlt* KAI 27[9,13,14,15] (*bʾl[t]*; Caquot FS Gaster 48: l. *bʾl[ty]* = *b*$_2$ + Sing. + suff. 3 p.s.m. of *ʾlh*$_2$ or *bʾl[m]* = *b*$_2$ + Plur. abs. of *ʾl*$_1$, cf. also Lipiński RTAT 265 :: Cross & Saley BASOR cxcvii 44f. (n. 12), Röllig NESE ii 18, 23, Zevit IEJ xxvii 111 (div. otherwise): l. in l. 15f. *ʾllt* = dittography for *ʾlt*; v. *ʾš*$_1$, v. also infra) - **Samal** Sing.

abs. ʾ*lh* KAI 215[2] (v. infra) - ¶ subst. f. - **1)** in KAI 27[9,13,14,15]: = (curse >) covenant, cf. Gaster Or xi 65f., Röllig FS Friedrich 416 n. 28, KAI a.l., NESE ii 18, Rosenthal ANET 658, Lipiński RTAT 265, Zevit IEJ xxvii 111, 114f., Caquot FS Gaster 46ff., Avishur PIB 248, 252f. × Sperling HUCA liii 3: ʾ*lt* in l. 9 = Plur. cstr. × Cross & Saley BASOR cxcvii 45: ʾ*lt* in ll. 13, 14, 15 = Plur. cstr. (= covenant oaths; cf. the authors also for the reading problems of ll. 15f.; cf. also Gibson SSI iii p. 83, 85) :: Garbini OA xx 283f.: the ʾ*lt* in l. 15 = Sing. abs. :: Cross & Saley BASOR cxcvii 45 (n. 16): ʾ*lt* in l. 9 = Plur. abs. :: du Mesnil du Buisson FS Dussaud 424: ʾ*lt* in ll. 14, 15 = f. Sing. abs. of ʾl_1, ʾ*lt* in ll. 9, 13 = f. Sing. cstr. of ʾl_1(cf. Dupont-Sommer RHR cxx 135) :: Albright BASOR lxxvi 8: ʾ*lt* in l. 9 = f. Sing. cstr. of ʾl_1, ʾ*lt* in l. 13 = f. Plur. cstr. of ʾl_1, ʾ*lt* in ll. 14, 15 = f. Plur. abs. of ʾl_1(cf. also v.d.Branden BO iii 43 the ʾ*lt* in ll. 9, 13 = f. Sing. cstr. of ʾl_1, the ʾ*lt* in ll. 14, 15 = f. Sing. abs. of ʾl_1, id. BiOr xxxiii 12: the ʾ*lt* of ll. 13, 14 = f. Sing. cstr. of ʾl_1(cf. also Vattioni Aug xiii 43 for l. 13), the ʾ*l[t]* of l. 15 = f. Sing. abs. of ʾl_1(cf. also Xella AION xxii 276), cf. also Cross HThR lv 237f.: the ʾ*lt* in l. 9 = f. Sing. cstr. of ʾl_1?(cf. also Jenni Olam 13f.)) - **2)** in KAI 215[2] poss. with the meaning conspiracy, cf. Cooke NSI p. 175 (for the reading, cf. Dupont-Sommer AH i/1, 7 n. 9, Hopkins BSOAS xl 143, ZDMG cxxi 133) :: Lidzbarski Handb 211, 442: l. ʾ*zh* rel. pronoun?, cf. also Schuster FS Landsberger 441, Stiehl AAW i 224, Dion p. 115, Segert AAG p. 491, 525, Sader EAS 165f., Faber ZDMG cxxxvii 279, Delsman TUAT i 628.
v. ʾl_1, ʾlw_1.

ʾ**lh**$_3$ v. ʾlh_1, ʾlw_1, *z*, *znh*.

ʾ**lh**$_4$ v. ʾlʾ$_3$.

ʾ**lw**$_1$ **Ph** the diff. ʾ*lw* in KAI 27[3] poss. = ʾl_1 (Sing. abs.) + dittographical. *w*, cf. Cross & Saley BASOR cxcvii 44 n. 7, Röllig NESE ii 21 (ʾl_5 + dittographical. *w*), Gibson SSI iii p. 82ff. (cf. however Teixidor AO i 106: l. ʾ*lw.* as against ʾ*lw*) :: Dupont-Sommer RHR cxx 136, Garbini OA xx 281, 283: = Sing. + suff. 3 p.s.m. of ʾl_1:: Caquot FS Gaster 47: = ʾlw_3 (= these; cf. also Lipiński RTAT 265, Baldacci BiOr xl 127) :: Sperling HUCA liii 3, 5: l. ʾ*lt* = Sing. abs. of ʾlh_2:: Albright BASOR lxxvi 8 (n. 11), Gaster Or xi 42 n. 5, 44, Röllig FS Friedrich 411 n. 3, KAI a.l., de Moor JEOL xxvii 108: l. ʾ*lh* = Sing. abs. of ʾlh_1:: du Mesnil du Buisson FS Dussaud 424, 426: l. ’*lh* = Sing. + suff. 3 p.s.m. of ʾl_1 :: v.d.Branden BO iii 43f.: l. ʾ*lh* = exorcist (= QAL Part. s.m. abs. of ʾly_1 (= to utter imprecations)) :: Rosenthal ANET 658 n. 1: l. ʾ*lh* = ʾlh_3(= these) :: Torczyner JNES vi 21, 28: l. ʾ*lh* = Sing. abs. of ʾlh_2.

ʾ**lw**$_2$ v. ʾl_6, ʾlp_4.

ʾlw$_3$ v. *ʾlw$_1$,z$_1$*.

ʾlw$_4$ v. *ʾlp$_3$, znh*.

ʾlwh v. *ʾlh$_1$*.

ʾlwk **OffAr** Sing. abs. *ʾlwk* Beh 23 - ¶ subst. of unknown origin and meaning (Akkad. par. *al-lu-ka-ʾ*, cf. CAD s.v. *alluka*). Cowl p. 258: = neighbourhood? (cf. ibid. p. 262 for Akkad. par.: = barracks?); Altheim & Stiehl ASA 92: = palace :: v.Soden Or xlvi 184: *alluka* poss. < Ar. *hlkh$_2$* = hither (used with temp. sense).

ʾlwš v. *ʾnš$_3$*.

ʾly$_1$ v. *ʾl$_7$, ʾlw$_1$*.

ʾly$_2$ v. *ʾlh$_1$*.

ʾlk$_1$ v. *hlk$_1$*.

ʾlk$_2$ v. *ʾnk*.

ʾlk$_3$ v. *zk$_2$*.

ʾlky v. *zk$_2$*.

ʾll **Pun** CIS i 360[4]; subst. (?) of uncert. meaning, title or function? poss. subst. *ll$_1$* of unknown meaning preceded by article?

ʾlly **Hebr** DJD ii 42[5] - ¶ conj. if it is not; *ʾlly šhgyym qrbym ʾlnw ʾzy ʿlty* ... DJD ii 42[5]: if it were not that the heathens are approaching us, (then) I would come up ... (cf. I.Rabinowitz BASOR cxxxi 23, Ginsberg ibid. 26, Lehmann & Stern VT iii 393, Sonne PAAJR xxiii 87, 90, Yeivin At i 98, Milik DJD ii a.l.).
v. *ʾzy*.

ʾlm$_1$ **DA** in ii 30 prob. derivative of root *ʾlm* (uncert. meaning: to be wrathful or to make mute??), an imperfect form 3 p.s.m. *yʾlm*?? (reading *y* and *l* uncert.), cf. Hoftijzer DA p. 250.

ʾlm$_2$ **Amm** Sing. abs. (?, dam. context) *ʾlm* BASOR cxciii 8[6] - ¶ subst. portico (for this prob. interpret., cf. Horn BASOR cxciii 13, Cross ibid. 19 (with other interpret. of context), Garbini AION xx 254, LS 104f., v.Selms BiOr xxxii 6, 8 (with other interpret. of context), Fulco BASOR ccxxx 42, Aufrecht sub CAI 59 × Albright BASOR cxcviii 38: = Plur. abs. of *ʾl$_1$*(cf. also Cross AUSS xiii 12 n. 34, R.Kutscher Qadm v 27f., Puech & Rofé RB lxxx 541, Dion RB lxxxii 31, 33, Shea PEQ '79, 18, 20, '81, 105, 108, Sasson PEQ '79, 118, 123, Jackson ALIA 10, 23f., 25, Baldacci AION xlv 519); for the context, v. also *byn$_2$*.
v. *ʾlmh, šlm$_2$*.

ʾlm$_3$ v. *sgyl*.

ʾlm$_4$ v. *ʿlm$_4$*.

ʾlm$_5$ **Pun** Février AIPHOS xiii 166, 170: the *ʾlm* in KAI 163[2] = Sing. m. abs. of *ʾlm$_5$* (= mute); highly uncert. interpret., diff. context.

ʾlmh **Pun** a Sing. abs. of this word poss. in KAI 145[2] (*ʾlʿmt*), cf. Sznycer Sem xxii 41, or = Plur. abs. of *ʾlm$_2$*or *ʾlmh*?, cf. Clermont-Ganneau RAO iii 327 :: Février Sem vi 17: = -ʾ + *l$_5$* + *ʿmt* (= Sing. cstr. of *ʿmh$_2$* (= juxtaposition; *lʿmt* used as prep. "as", cf. also Good SHP 156 n. 69; cf. also Krahmalkov RSF iii 187f., 190, 202 *lʿmt* used adverbially, side by side) :: Cooke NSI p. 153f.: = *ʾl* (= *ʾl$_5$*) + Sing. cstr. of *ʿmh$_2$* (used as prep.: beside), cp Röllig KAI a.l. :: Lidzbarski Eph i 48: = Sing. cstr. of *ʾl$_1$* + Sing. abs. of *ʿmh$_1$* (= people, congregation), cf. also ibid. 176) :: Halévy RS ix 271: = Sing. cstr. of *ʾl$_1$* + Sing. abs. of *ʾmh$_3$* (= clan), with deviating orthography :: Berger (cf. MAIBL xxxvi/2, 150): l. *ʾlʿmn* = Sing. abs. of *ʾl$_1$* + n.d. (Ammon).

ʾlmt **Ph** Sing. abs. KAI 14[3,13] - ¶ subst. widow, cf. FR 214. A Sing. cstr. also in KAI 28[1]?? (*ʾl[mt]*).

ʾln$_1$ m. **Ph** Plur. abs. *ʾlnm* KAI 10[10], 14[9,16,22], 48[2,4], DD 13[3] (for the context, cf. Pardee Mem Craigie 56 (n. 5)), RES 1512[1]; cstr. *ʾln* KAI 10[16], 14[18], 19[7], 26A iii 5, 37A 3, B 3 (= Kition C1 = CIS i 86, v. infra) - **Pun** Sing. abs. *ʾln* RES 328[1] (:: Röllig FS Friedrich 405: *ʾln* = variant for *'lm* (= Plur. abs. of *ʾl$_1$*)); cstr. *ʾln* KAI 104[1] (or abs.?, v. infra; :: Röllig FS Friedrich 405: = variant for *ʾlm* (= Plur. abs. of *ʾl$_1$*) :: Röllig ibid. 414 n. 11: certainly = abs.); Plur. abs. *ʾlnm* KAI 137[4], CIS i 6000bis 5 (= TPC 84), *ʿlnm* KAI 117[1] (*ʿl[nm]* :: Friedrich AfO x 83, Röllig FS Friedrich 406, 414 n. 15: or l. *ʿl[n]ʾ* = Plur. cstr.?), Karth xii 53 iii 1 (cf. Février & Fantar Karth xii a.l. :: Krahmalkov RSF iii 178, 184, 203: = *ʿl$_7$* + suff. 3 p.pl.m.), cf. Poen 930, 933, 940, 942: *alonim* (cf. Sznycer PPP 50), IRT 892[4f.]: *allonim* (cf. Vattioni Aug xvi 551; ?, highly uncert. context) - f. **Pun** Plur. abs., cf. Poen 930: *alonuth*, cf. Poen 940: *aloniuth* - ¶ subst. - **1)** m. god, f. goddess: KAI 10[16], 14[18], 26A iii 5, 48[2], 137[4], DD 13[3], CIS i 6000bis 5, Poen 930, 933, 940, 942; cf. also - a) *h ʾlnm hqdšm* KAI 14[9]: the holy gods, cf. also KAI 14[22]; *lʾln ʾqdš* KAI 104[1] (for the reading, cf. RES 327): to the god of the sanctuary (or: to the holy god?, v. supra) - b) *lʿl[nm] ʾrʾpʾm* KAI 117[1]: to the divine shades of the dead (cf. Lat. par. *D(is) M(anibus) Sac(rum)*, cf. also Ferron MC 69ff.) - c) for *ʾln ʾ[ḥ]ym*, v. *ʾḥ$_1$* - d) for *šd ʾlnm*, v. *šd$_1$* - e) *lʿn ʾlnm wlʿn ʿm ʾrṣ* KAI 10[10]: for the eyes of the gods and the people of the land; cf. also *lʿn ʾlnm wbn ʾdm* KAI 48[4] - **2)** dignitary, notable man; *ʾln ḥdš* KAI 37A 3, B 3: the dignitaries of the new moon feast (prob. those to whom the organization of this feast was entrusted), cf. v.d.Branden BO viii 247f., Masson & Sznycer RPC 33ff., cf. also Teixidor AJA lxxviii 189, Amadasi Kition p. 107f., Gibson SSI iii p. 125f., Delcor UF xi 151 :: e.g. Cooke NSI p. 66, Röllig KAI a.l.: the gods of the new moon :: Healy BASOR ccxvi 53: the god of the new moon (for the interpret. with god(s), cf. also Peckham JNES xxxv 286); prob. the same meaning in Karth xii 53 iii 1 (diff. context), cf. v.d.Branden RSF v 61 :: Février & Fantar Karth xii 53: = divine statues (v. also supra).

ʾln$_2$ v. *hykylyn*, *znh*.

ʾlp$_1$ **Samal** Paᶜel Impf. 2 p.s.m. *tʾlb* KAI 214^{34} (cf. e.g. Cooke NSI p. 171, Dion p. 210 :: Donner KAI a.l.: = Qal; for the *b*, cf. Garb 258, Garbini Ant xxxi 310f., xxxii 427f., RSO xxxiv 43, ISNO 25f., Dion p. 88f.; cf. however Rosenthal JBL xcv 154) - **OffAr** Itp Impf. 3 p.s.m. *ytʾlp* Aḥiq 80; cf. Frah xviii 6 (*ʾlpwn*), cf. Toll ZDMG-Suppl viii 38 - **Nab** Itp Impf. 3 p.s.m. *ytʾlp* CIS ii 197^{7}, 217^{10}, 224^{10} (Cantineau Nab ii 172: Nab. *ʾlp$_1$* < Arab., less prob. interpret., cf. O'Connor JNES xlv 218 (n. 27)) - **Hatra** Paᶜel Pf. 3 p.s.m. *ʾlp* 106b 5 (for *ʾlp hnw*, v. *hʾ$_1$*) - ¶ verb Paᶜel to instruct - a) + obj.: Hatra 106b 5 - b) + obj. + *l$_5$* + Inf. (to instruct someone to, to instigate, to incite): KAI 214^{34} (cf. Tawil JNES xxxii 479ff.); :: O.Connor JNES xlv 218: = to write - Itp 1) to be instructed, to be disciplined: Aḥiq 80 - **2)** to compose, to draw up (an inscription) for oneself, on one's behalf - a) + *b$_2$* (loc.): CIS ii 217^{10} - b) + *b$_2$* + obj.: CIS ii 224^{10} - c) + *ᶜl$_7$* + obj.: CIS ii 197^{7}; :: Levinson NAI 128: Itp in Nab. = to be added.
v. *ʾlp$_4$*, *mlh*.

ʾlp$_2$ **Ph** Sing. abs. *ʾlp* KAI 24^{11}, 26A iii 1 (:: Gordon JNES viii 111, 115: = *ʾlp$_5$*); Plur. abs. *ʾlpm* KAI 26A iii 8, C iv 8 (*[ʾ]lpm*) - **Pun** Sing. cstr. *ʾlp* KAI 69^{3}; cf. Diosc iv 127: (λασουν)αφ, varr: -αλφ, -ααφ, and PsApul xli note 13: *(lasim)saph*, varr: *-safh*, *-saf* (cf. also Sznycer PPP 51; v. also *lšn*) - ¶ subst. ox (:: Dussaud Orig 138: in KAI 69^{3} = bull) - this word Sing. emph. *ʾlpʾ* also in Irâq xxxi 174^{3}??, or = *ʾlp$_3$* or *ʾlp$_5$*?
v. *ʾlp$_3$*, *ʾpl$_2$*.

ʾlp$_3$ (< Akkad., cf. Zimmern Fremdw 45, v.Soden AHW s.v. *eleppu(m)*, cf. however Kaufman AIA 48) - **OffAr** Sing. abs. *ʾlp* Herm 6^{9} (cf. Milik Bibl xlviii 548, 554f., Grelot RB lxxiv 436, DAE p. 166, Vogt Lex s.v. *bᶜh*, Porten & Greenfield IOS iv 23f., JEAS p. 162, Porten & Yardeni sub TADAE A 2.6 :: Bresciani & Kamil a.l.: or = *ʾlp$_2$*), NESE i 11^{2} (cf. Naveh & Shaked JAOS xci 379f., Degen NESE i 14; for the context, v. *'ḥd$_4$*), KAI 271B 9 (for the reading, cf. RES sub 495A 9, Degen NESE i 28, 30 :: CIS ii sub 138B, Donner KAI a.l. (cf. also Brown Bibl lxx 208): l. *yglp* = Qal Impf. 3 p.s.m. of *glp*; or = cstr.?); cstr. *ʾlp* RES 1792A 2 (:: Grelot DAE p. 93 (n. d): = Sing. abs.), KAI 271A 2, 5 (for the reading, cf. Lidzbarski Eph ii 242, RES sub 495B 2, 5, Degen NESE i 28, 30 :: CIS ii sub 138A, Donner KAI a.l.: l. *ʾlw* = pron. pers. 3 p.pl.; in A 5 heavily dam. context, could be Sing. abs.), B 3 (for the reading, cf. RES sub 495A 3, Degen NESE i 27, 29 :: CIS ii sub 138B, Donner KAI a.l.: l. *gṭp* = part of n.p.); emph. *ʾlpʾ* RES 1795A 3 (?,

dam. context, cf. Lidzbarski Eph ii 236, Milik Bibl xlviii 555), Sem ii 31 conc. 2 (cf. Milik Bibl xlviii 554f., Porten JNES xxviii 116, Arch 126, Grelot DAE p. 370 (n. d), Teixidor Syr xlviii 480 :: Dupont-Sommer Sem ii 32f.: = *ʾlp*$_2$), NESE i 11[3,8] (*ʾlp[ʾ]* :: Shunnar GMA 114f.: l. *q[ym]* (= Qal Part. act. s.m. abs. of *qwm*$_1$) *lb[ytk]* (= *l*$_5$ + Sing. + suff. 2 p.s.m. of *byt*$_2$) :: Shunnar CRM ii 286f.: l. *pqd* (= Pa ʿel Imper. s.m. of *pqd*$_1$) *l[pṭmḥw]* (= *l*$_5$ + n.p.)); Plur. cstr. *ʾlpy* RES '41-45, 67[4] (cf. Milik Bibl xlviii 555, Degen NESE i 17 n. 11, BiOr xxix 212, Grelot DAE p. 136 (n. b) :: Dupont-Sommer RES '41-45, 73: = n.p.) - ¶ subst. f. boat (Milik Bibl xlviii 555: smaller boat for private use; cf. *spynh*) - Shunnar GMA 114ff., Macuch JAOS xciii 59: l. a second *ʾlp* in NESE i 11[2], l. however *zyly*, cf. Degen NESE i 15.
v. *ʾlp*$_{2,5}$, *ḥlq*$_3$.

ʾlp₄ **OffAr** Sing. abs. *ʾlp* Pers 52[3], 118[3] (:: Bowman Pers a.l., and p. 34, 67: = Sing. cstr., cf. however idem ibid. p. 66, 192 s.v. *plg* = myriarch; cf. also Teixidor Syr li 331f. :: Hinz FS Nyberg 379: = *ʾlp*$_6$ (as usually, according to custom) :: Delaunay cc 203f.: = Qal Part. pass. s.m. abs. of *ʾlp*$_1$ (instructed, accustomed) :: Naveh & Shaked Or xlii 454f.: poss. l. *ʾlw* = *ʾlw*$_2$(= behold)) - ¶ subst. prob. title, exact meaning unknown (:: Bowman Pers p. 34: = chiliarch, cf. also Bowman Or xxxix 459, Grelot RB lxxx 595, Millard JRAS '73, 63): = chief, commander?
v. *ʾlp*$_5$, *plg*$_6$.

ʾlp₅ **Ph** Sing. *ʾlp* Mus li 286[8] (reading uncert.) - **Pun** Sing. *ʾlp* RCL '66, 201[7] - **Mo** Plur. abs. *ʾlpn* KAI 181[16] (reading of *n* less cert.) - **Hebr** Sing. *ʾlp* KAI 189[5], Mosc var. 10[1] (*ʾl[p]*; for this reading, cf. e.g. Maisler JNES x 266, Gibson SSI i p. 17, Lemaire IH i p. 252, cf. however Catastini Hen vi 137 (div. otherwise): l. *mlkʾl* (= n.p.)); Plur. abs. *ʾlpm* FS Brunner 303 iii 12, 306 vi 10, *ʾlpy[n]* SM 76[4] - **OldAr** Sing. *ʾlp* Tell F 19 - **OffAr** Sing. *ʾlp* Cowl 24[40], 31[27], ATNS 97b 2 (*]ʾlp*; heavily dam. context), *lp* Cowl 30[28], 50[9], 73[3], Beh 3, 9 (Akkad. par. *limi*), 11 (akad. par. *limi*), ATNS 24[7], 48a 4, 5, etc.; Plur. cstr. *ʾlpy* Cowl 71[16] (v. infra); cf. Nisa-c 100+91[3], 164[9] (*lp*) Sogd B 260, R 50, Ve 115, cf. MP 4 (*p*, cf. also MP 99), GIPP 45 - **Nab** Sing. *ʾlp* CIS ii 198[9], 199[8], 200[7,8] (= J 30), etc.; Plur. abs. *ʾlpyn* CIS ii 206[7], 212[8] - **Palm** Plur. abs. *ʾlpyn* Sem xxxvi 89[2,3,4,6] - **JAr** *lp* Mas 577[3] (dam. context), 589 - ¶ cardinal number, thousand: passim; cf. also *ʾrbʿt ʾlpy[n]* = 4000 in SM 76[4] - **1)** followed by a noun - a) in Plur., *ʾlp šʿrn* Tell F 19: thousand (measures of) barley; *šbʿt ʾlpn g[b]rn wgrn* ... KAI 181[16]: seven thousand men and clients ... (for the context, cf. also Segert ArchOr xxix 263, Andersen Or xxxv 91f.) - b) in Sing., *mʾtyn wʾlp ʾmh* KAI 189[5]: twelve hundred yards; *ʾl[p] šmn wmʾh* Mosc var. 10[1f.]: eleven hundred (measures) of oil - **2)** preceded by a noun in

Plur., *knkrn ʾlp* Cowl 31^{27} (cf. Cowl 30^{28}): a thousand talents; *slʿyn ʾlp* CIS ii 198^{9}, 199^{8}: a thousand drachmes; *slʿyn ʾlp ḥd* CIS ii $200^{7,8}$: one thousand drachmes (for the reading, cf. Milik sub ARNA-Nab 79; cf. also CIS ii 224^{12}) - the significance of *ʾlpy mlkʾ* Cowl 71^{16} uncert.: the thousands of the king? × CIS ii sub 145B 7: *ʾlpy* = Plur. cstr. of *ʾlp$_4$*× Milik Bibl xlviii 555: = Plur. cstr. of *ʾlp$_3$*?(context heavily dam.) - this word also in Pun. text RES 1847: *lp*?, cf. Clermont-Ganneau RAO vi 149 n. 6, Lidzbarski Handb 303 (v. *mslh$_2$*); cf. also the Pun. text RCL '66, 201^{7}: *ksp ʾlp 1 lp* (= thousand silver ("pieces", i.e.) 1000), for the reading, cf. Dupont-Sommer CRAI '68, 132 :: Mahjoubi & Fantar RCL '66, a.l.: l. *ksp ʾlp ylp* (*ylp* without interpret.) - cf. also Galling SGI 87f.
v. *ʾlp$_2$*,*hʾ$_1$*.

ʾlp$_6$ v. *ʾlp$_4$*.

ʾlṣ$_1$ v. *ʿlṣ$_1$*.

ʾlṣ$_2$ v. *mlṣh*.

ʾm$_1$ **Ph** Sing. abs. *ʾm* KAI 24^{10}, 26A i 3, CIS i 13^{3} (= Kition A 27); cstr. *ʾm* KAI 11 and on coins (v. infra); + suff. 3 p.s.m. *ʾm* KAI 24^{13} (or = Sing. abs.?, cf. e.g. Röllig KAI a.l., Avishur PIB 213), *ʾmy* KAI 34^{3} (= Kition B 45), RDAC '84, 104^{3}; + suff. 1 p.s. *ʾmy* KAI 14^{14}; + suff. 3 p.pl.m. *ʾmnm* KAI 48^{3} (cf. also Krahmalkov JSS xv 183), cf. also Hesychius EtymMagn s.v. >Ἀμμάς: = ao the Mother - **Pun** Sing. abs. *ʾm* CIS i 195, 380^{3}, cf. Poen 1141: *amma*; cstr. *ʾm* NP 4 (= Trip 4 = IRT 655 = CIL viii 16; cf. Lat. par.: *mater*, Greek par. μήτηρ); + suff. 3 p.s.m. *ʾmm* KAI 123^{3}, Trip 38^{3}, NP 130^{2} (for the reading, cf. Février RHR cxli 120), CIS i 151^{4} (= ICO-Sard NPu 2; cf. Février JA ccxlvi 444); for *ʾmʾ* in CIS i 177, v. infra - **Hebr** Sing. + suff. 1 p.pl. *ʾmnw* RB lxiii 77,14 (= DF 39) - **OffAr** Sing. + suff. 3 p.s.m. *ʾmh* Cowl $28^{4,5}$, Aḥiq 138, Krael 2^{14}, ATNS 8^{1}, JA xi/xviii $57^{1,2,3,4}$, KAI 267A 2, *ʾmwhy* KAI 279^{6} (Greek par. μητρὶ ; for this form, cf. Dupont-Sommer JA ccxlvi 30, Altheim & Stiehl EW ix 197, GH 405, Garbini Kand 15f., 21, Humbach MSSW xxvi 40f., Kutscher, Naveh & Shaked Lesh xxxiv 134f., Drijvers BiOr xxx 467); + suff. 3 p.s.f. *ʾmh* Krael 6^{3}; + suff. 2 p.s.m. *ʾmk* Cowl 29^{4} (for this reading, cf. Porten JNES xlviii 163, Porten & Yardeni sub TADAE B 4.5 :: e.g. Cowl a.l.: Grelot DAE p. 86: l. *ʾmr* = QAL Part. act. s.m. abs. of *ʾmr$_1$*), SSI ii 28 obv. 2, rev. 3, 5; + suff. 1 p.s. *ʾmy* Krael 4^{19}, JRAS '29, 108^{1}, KAI 261^{3}, RSO xxxv 22^{1} (*ʾm[y]*)^{,5}, 23^{1}, Herm 3^{2}, 4^{13}, 6^{11}, 7^{1}; + suff. 3 p.pl.m. *ʾmhm* Cowl 25^{3}, 28^{13}, RES 1793^{3} (= PSBA '15, 222^{8}); + suff. 1 p.pl. *ʾmn* Cowl 28^{3}; cf. Frah xi 10 (*ʾm*), 11 (*ʾmy*), GIPP 16, 45, SaSt 12 (cf. also Toll ZDMG-Suppl viii 29, 31) - **Nab** Sing. cstr. *ʾm* CIS ii 161 ii 1, 185^{5}, 221^{3}, 224^{6}, J 18A 2; + suff. 3 p.s.m. *ʾmh* CIS ii 199^{2}, 443^{2} (= RES 1462), J 17^{3}, on coins, cf. Meshorer NC p. 72 no. 142-146, cf. also Milik & Starcky ADAJ xx 113; + suff. 3 p.pl.m. *ʾmhm* CIS ii 222^2 - **Palm** Sing. cstr. *ʾm* CIS ii $4287^{5,7}$; emph. *ʾmʾ* Ber v 106^2; + suff. 3 p.s.m. *ʾmh* CIS ii 3971^6, 4017^4, 4190^3, 4502^3, 4573^2, RIP 37^6, 103b 3, Inv iv 4b (*[ʾ]mh*, cf. Milik DFD 86, Gawlikowski Syr xlviii 424 :: Cantineau Inv iv a.l.: l. *[š]mh* = Sing. + suff. 3 p.s. of *šm_1*), 7^2 (Greek par. τῇ μητρί), xi 14^6 (or + suff. 3 p.s.f.?, dam. context), xii 3, DM ii 39 iii 5, etc.; + suff. 3 p.s.f. *ʾmh* Inscr P 78^5; + suff. 3 p.pl.m. *ʾmhn* CIS ii 3911^{11}, 4231E 4, *ʾmhwn* CIS ii 4018^6, 4056^6, 4615^5, RB xxxix 542 ii 7, RIP 71A 2, Syr xlviii 422b 2; + suff. 1 p.pl. *ʾmn* Ber ii 81f. (*ʾmwn* false reading, cf. Ingholt Ber iii 126) - **Hatra** Sing. emph. *ʾmʾ* 28^1 (prob. l. $28^{1f.}$ *ʾmʾ* *<dy>* *ʿbdsmyʾ*, cf. also Degen Or xxxvi 79 × Altheim & Stiehl GH iv 81f., GMA 580: Sing. emph. used as *regens*), 36^4 - **JAr** Sing. emph. *ʾmʾ* MPAT 114 (or rather n.p.?, cf. also Oelsner OLZ '86, 475); + suff. 3 p.s.m. *ʾmh* LA xxxii 358 (cf. Puech RB xc 517f. :: Puech LA xxxii a.l. = n.p.), AMB 12^7 (or = + suff. 3 p.s.f.?, heavily dam. context), BASOR ccxxxv 34 no. 11b (or = Sing. emph.? (cf. also (Naveh with) Hachlili BASOR ccxxxv 55); cf. Greek par. μητρὸς); + suff. 1 p.pl. *ʾmnh* MPAT 96a (= Frey 1363), *ʾmn* MPAT 96b (= Frey 1363; for the reading, cf. Savignac RB xxxviii 233f., Beyer ATTM 342, Puech RB xc 504f. :: Sukenik JPOS viii 117, Fitzmyer & Harrington MPAT a.l.: l. *ʾm(ʾ)*, see also Fitzmyer & Harrington MPAT p. 231; reading of last sign uncert., other poss. reading *ʾmw* = hebraism?) - ¶ subst. f. - **1)** mother, passim; for the *ʾmy* in Herm. and RSO xxxv 22^1, 23^1 (cf. 22^5), cf. Greenfield & Porten IOS iv 15, 27f., Porten Arch 265ff., Hayes & Hoftijzer VT xx 104f.; *bnʾ ʾmʾ* Ber v. 106^2: uterine brothers; for *ʾḥt ʾmm*, v. *ʾ$ḥ_1$*; for the order mother-father in KAI 279^6, cf. Benveniste JA ccxlvi 42, Teixidor Syr xlvi 349 - **2)** used metaphorically of a king who protects his subjects and contributes to their prosperity; *wʾnk lmy kt ʾb wlmy kt ʾm ...* KAI 24^{10}: as to me, for some I was (like) a father, for others I was (like) a mother ...; *pʿln bʿl ldnnym lʾb wlʾm* KAI 26A i 3: Baʿal made me a father and a mother for the Danunites - **3)** used as a title - a) of the goddess Tinnith, *lʾm lrbt pn bʿl* CIS i $380^{4f.}$: to the mother, to the lady, face of Baʿal (cf. CIS i $195^{1f.}$; cf. Teixidor Syr xlvi 332); the *ʾmʾ* in CIS i 177 prob. = n.d. (cf. E.Meyer ZAW xlix 11: = Mother (i.e. divine mother), cf. also Hvidberg-Hansen TNT i 20) and not Sing. + suff. 3 p.s.m. - b) of the goddess Allath, *ʾm ʾlhyʾ dy mrʾnʾ rbʾl* CIS ii $185^{5ff.}$: mother of the gods of our lord R. - c) of goddess in difficult context, *lrbty lʾm hʾzrt* CIS i 13^3 (= Kition A 27), v. also *ʾzr_4* - **4)** used to indicate the function of metropolis, on Ph. coins, *lṣr ʾm ṣdnm* = of Tyre the mother of the Sidonians, cf. Hill Phoen cxxxiii, cf. also Hill Phoen 155 (cf. Lewy HUCA xviii 439f.), cf. however Malamat UF xi 535 (n. 43) - for KAI 46^5 and context, v. *ṣ$bʾ_3$* - Puech LA xxxii a.l.:

the ʾ*mkh* in LA xxxii 358 = Sing. + suff. 2 p.s.m. (improb. interpret., cf. Puech RB xc 517f.: = n.p.).
v. ʾm_2, ʾmh_2, mʾ$š_1$, $š_{10}$.

ʾ$\mathbf{m_2}$ **OffAr** Sing. abs. ʾ*m* Sem xxiii 95 recto 5 (:: Lipiński WGAV 377 (div. otherwise): l. *l*ʾ*m* = Sing. abs. of *l*ʾm_1(= eponym) :: Kaufman Conn xix 121: (div. otherwise): l. *l*ʾ*m* = abbrev. of l_5 + QAL Inf. of ʾmr_1 (stage between *l*ʾ*mr* and *lm*), v. also infra :: Wesselius AION xlv 507f. (div. otherwise): l. ʾ*mh* (= Sing. + suff. 3 p.s.m. of ʾm_1)); + suff. 3 p.pl.m. ʾ*mhm* Sem xxiii 95 recto 2 (:: Lipiński ActAntHung xxii 378 (= WGAV 378): = Plur. + suff. 3 p.pl.m. of ʾmh_1 :: Wesselius AION xlv 507f.: = Sing. + suff. 3 p.pl.m. of ʾm_1) - ¶ subst. meaning unknown. Bordreuil Sem xxiii 98: = matter, affair (cf. Teixidor Syr li 330, lvi 391; cf. also Kaufman Conn xix 121f.: in l. 2 = word, statement < QAL Inf. of ʾmr_1 (less prob. derivation), in l. 5 preceded by l_5 (< *l*ʾ*mr*) = as follows (related to *lm*)), v. supra); Weinfeld Maarav iii 46 (n. 90) = word, settlement; Fales AION xxvi 544: < Akkad. *ummu* = demarcation point of landed property (*ummu* normally = mother, v. also ʾm_1), cf. also Fales sub AECT 58: = boundary-stone, boundary-marker, cf. also id. ibid. p. 96, Kaufman JAOS cix 100.

ʾ$\mathbf{m_3}$ **Ph** KAI 3^{3}, 10^{13}, 13^{6}, $14^{6,7,10,11}$, 26A iii 12, 14, 17, C iv 13 (ʾ*[m]*), 14 (*[*ʾ*]m*), 16, RES 922^{2} (cf. Masson & Sznycer RPC 105f.) - **Pun** KAI $69^{3,5,7,9,11,12,15}$, 74^{5}, CIS i $3915^{2,3,5}$, etc. - **Hebr** KAI $193^{9,11}$, 194^{9}, $200^{11,12}$ (for both uncert. instances in KAI 200 however, v. infra), TA-H 2^{7}, 21^{8}, 28^{6} (dam. context), DJD ii 22,1-9^{10} (dam. context), $30^{3,14}$, 44^{6}, SM 49^{26} - **Samal** KAI 214^{29} (v. infra) - **JAr** MPAT $41^{6,8}$, 53^{2}, 59^{2} - ¶ A) conj. - **1)** introducing a conditional clause: if - a) + Impf. (with future meaning), *w*ʾ*m ptḥ tptḥ* KAI $13^{6f.}$: if you do open ..., cf. also KAI 3^{3} (or used with ellips of the main clause and to be translated as negation?, cf. McCarter & Coote BASOR ccxii 19); *w*ʾ*m* ʾ*bl tšt šm* ʾ*tk* KAI 10^{13}: and if you do not place my name with you (i.e. with yours) ...; *w*ʾ*m l*ʾ *tšdrwn ythn* MPAT 59^{2}: and if you do not send them ... (cf. also MPAT 53^{2}); cf. also ʾ*m* ... ʾ*m* introducing alternative conditional clauses (cf. FR 258b, 320,1), ʾ*m bḥmdt ys*ʿ ʾ*m bšn*ʾ*t wbr*ʿ *ys*ʿ *hš*ʿ*r z* KAI 26A iii 17f.: if he either removes this gate with good intentions or out of Hatr.ed and evil (v. also *ḥmdh*); for ʾ*m* ʾ*p* (KAI 26A iii 14, C iv 16) and ʾ*p* ʾ*m* (KAI 146), v. ʾp_2 - b) + Pf. (with past meaning), ʾ*m šmt* ʾ*mrt* ʾ*l bpm* ... KAI 214^{29}: if I have put these words in the mouth of ... (cf. also Driver AnOr xii 47; diff. and dam. context; or to be understood as a case of ellips like KAI $193^{9,11}$ quoted infra?, thus Dion p 34, 316); used with ellips of the main clause and to be translated as negation, ʾ*m nsh* ʾ*yš* KAI $193^{9f.}$: if a man has tried (i.e. no one has tried) ..., cf. also KAI $193^{11f.}$, for the interpretational problems, cf. e.g.

H.P.Müller UF ii 238f., WO viii 66, Teixidor Syr l. 416, liii 326, or *ʾm* in l. 11 to be understood as conj. introducing a conditional clause?, cf. Gibson SSI i p. 39f., Lemaire IH i 101f. - c) + nom. clause, *wʾm ʿwd ḥmṣ* TA-H 2[7]: and if there is still vinegar; cf. also *wʾm mlk bmlkm wrzn brznm ʾm ʾdm ʾš ʾdm šm ʾš ymḥ* KAI 26A iii 12f.: if there is a king among kings, a prince among princes (or) if (there is) a man who is a man of renown, who will wipe out .... (for the translation, v. *šm*$_1$; on this text, cf. also Amadasi Guzzo VO iii 91); cf. also SM 49[26]; cf. also CIS i 3917[2] (cf. idem l. 3 = KAI 74[2,3]): *[wtb]rt lbʿl hzbḥ ʾm ltt lkhn ʾyt [...*, the rest is for the sacrificer provided he gives the priest the ... (cf. also Février CB viii 38f.) - **2)** introducing an object clause, *ḥzw ʾm yḥpṣw ...* DJD ii 44[6]: see that they are satisfied ... - B) used as copula: or - **1)** used before all parts of an enumeration, except the first one, *kl ʾdm ʾš yptḥ ... ʾm ʾš yšʾ ... ʾm ʾš yʿmsn* KAI 14[7]: every person who will open ... or who will lift up ... or who will remove ... (cf. also KAI 14[10,11]); *dl mqnʾ ʾm dl ṣpr* KAI 69[15]; who is poor in cattle or poor in fowl (cf. also KAI 69[3,5,7,9,11], etc.) - **2)** used in the combination *ʾm ... ʾw*, *ʾm ytyr ʾw ḥ[sr]* DJD ii 30[14]: either more or less (cf. ibid. l. 3; for the context, v. also Milik DJD ii a.l.) - C) cf. also the following diff. instances: - **1)** for *ky ʾm* in KAI 194[9], SBS 47B 2, v. *ky* - **2)** poss. *ʾm* also in the Palm. text Syr xvii 271[4] (dam. context, exact meaning unknown), cf. also Milik DFD 296: used as a copula (either), v. supra sub B - **3)** for KAI 200[11], v. *ʾmn*$_5$ - **4)** for KAI 200[12], v. *mlʾ*$_1$ - Altheim & Stiehl FuF xxxv a.l.: l. *ʾm*$_3$ in FuF xxxv 173[4] (cf. also idem ASA 244; diff. and uncert. context).
v. *ʾz*$_2$, *ʾm*$_4$, *kn*$_4$, *mlk*$_3$, *msʿ*.

ʾm$_4$ (prob. etymologically identical with *ʾm*$_3$ :: Milik RB lxi 249: < exclamative particle *ʾay/ʾê/ʾî* + *m* :: Cowl sub 13[11]: = lapsus for *ʾpm*,cf. however ibid. sub 34[6] :: Segert AAG p. 233: < *ʾpm*) - **OffAr** Cowl 13[11], 34[6], Krael 3[16,19], 9[21], 10[11,14] - ¶ adv. of emphasis, underlining the following word (not only underlining the attribute in a nominal clause :: Milik RB lxi 249, cf. Cowl 34[6]): also, furthermore; often used to confirm a disputed right, *byt ʾm dylky* Cowl 13[11]: the house will be assuredly (/still) be yours - for SBS 45B 7, v. *dyṭgm*.
v. *hn*$_3$.

ʾm$_5$ v. *š*$_{10}$.

ʾm$_6$ v. *ʾpy*.

ʾmh$_1$ **Hebr** Sing. abs. *ʾmh* KAI 189[5,6]; Plur. abs. *ʾmt* KAI 189[2], *ʾmwt* Mas 585[1, 3] - **OffAr** Sing. abs. *ʾmh* Cowl 79[2,3], ATNS 52b i 10 (dam. context); Plur. abs. *ʾmyn* Krael 12[8,15], *ʾmn* Cowl 8[4,5], 9[4], Krael 4[6,7,8], ATNS 49[3], etc., etc. - **Nab** Plur. abs. *ʾmyn* J 14[3,4] (= CIS ii 203) - **Palm** Plur. emph. *ʾmmʾ* (??) RB xxxix 548[7] (cf. Cantineau RB xxxix

549, Rosenthal Sprache 75 n. 3, 78) - **JAr** Plur. abs. *ʾmyn* MPAT 67^{3} - ¶ subst. f. (cf. KAI 189^{2}, Krael 6^{4}, MPAT 67^{3}, cf. however Cowl 26^{12} (*ʾmn tryn*) and Cowl 26^{14} (*ʾmn ḥmšh*), cf. also Segert AAG p. 332) cubit, passim; cf. *lbš 1 ... bʾmn 6* Krael 7^{9}: one garment ... of 6 cubits, cf. also Cowl 26^{12}, Krael 7^{6} - for a discussion of the specific length of the *ʾmh* in Hebr. texts, cf. e.g. Trinquet SDB v 1213ff., Yeivin Lesh xxxi 244ff., D.Sperber JJS xx 81ff., Puech RB lxxxi 208ff., Ben-David PEQ '78, 27f. - cf. also Cohen Shn v 25*ff. - Porten & Yardeni sub TADAE B 8.2: l. prob. *ʾmn* (= Plur. abs. of *ʾmh$_1$*) in ATNS 10a ii 1 (prob. reading and interpret.) :: Segal ATNS a.l.: l. *ʾ* (= abbrev. of *ʾrdb*) + number.
v. *ʾm$_2$*.

ʾmh$_2$ **Ph** Sing. cstr. *ʾmt* KAI 29^{1} - **Pun** Sing. abs. *ʿmt* CIS i 3776^{4}; cstr. *ʾmt* CIS i 378^{3}; + suff. 3 p.pl.m. *ʾmtnm* CIS i 2632$^{3f.}$; Plur. abs. *ʿmt* CIS i 263^{3} (v. infra; :: CIS i a.l., Slouschz TPI p. 235, Harr 133: = Sing. abs. of *ʿmh$_1$* = community (cf. also Hvidberg-Hansen TNT i 28, ii 27f. n. 234, Good SHP 24, 156 n. 69, v.d.Branden BiOr xxxvi 158)) - **Hebr** Sing. + suff. 3 p.s.m. *ʾmth* KAI 191B 2 (for the reading, cf. Röllig KAI al) - **Amm** Sing. cstr. *ʾmt* Vatt sig. eb. 116 (= Herr SANSS-Amm 13, Garbini LS-Amm vii = IS 29 = Jackson ALIA 81 no. 57 = CAI 44), 157 (= Mosc sig. 39 = Herr SANSS-Amm 12, Garbini LS-Amm v = IS 28 = Jackson ALIA 80 no. 52 = CAI 36; cf. Puech RB lxxxiii 61 n. 13) - **OffAr** Sing. abs. *ʾmh* Cowl 10^{10}, Aḥiq 84, ATNS 9^{8} (dam. context; or = Sing. + suff. 3 p.s.m./f. of *ʾm$_1$*?; cstr. *ʾmt* ATNS 54^{6}, 55a 4 (heavily dam. context), Vatt sig. eb. 315 (= Herr SANSS-Ar 45 = Avigad Qedem iv no. 14); emph. *ʾmtʾ* CIS ii 19a 1 (= Del 12 = AECT 17), ATNS 8^{3} (for this reading, cf. Shaked Or lvi 409, cf. also Porten & Yardeni sub TADAE B 5.6); + suff. 3 p.s.m. *ʾmth* Krael 5^{3}, ATNS 54 i 4 (or = + suff. 3 p.s.f.??, dam. context); + suff. 3 p.s.m./f. *ʾmth* ATNS 10 i 3 (*[ʾ]mth*; cf. Porten & Yardeni sub TADAE B 8.2 (prob. restoration) :: Segal ATNS a.l. (div. otherwise): l. *mth* (= Sing. + suff. 3 p.s.m. of *mt$_1$*)); + suff. 2 p.s.m. *ʾmtk* Krael 2^{3} (reading uncert.); + suff. 2 p.s.f. *ʾmtky* ATNS 30b 4; Plur. abs. *ʾmhn* Samar 7^{7} - ¶ subst. f. slave-girl, servant. passim; in KAI 191B 2 indication of a second wife?, cf. Avigad IEJ iii 145f. (cf. however Galling TGI 66 (n. 4)) - cf. the following constructions: 1) *ʾmt ʾlm* CIS i 378^{3}: servant of the gods, exact meaning uncert., cf. *ʿmt šʿštrt ʾrk* CIS i 3776^{4}, *ʾš bʿmt ʾš ʿštrt* CIS i 263^{3} (who belongs to the servants of A.); cf. also CIS i 2632$^{3f.}$ and proper names composed with *ʾmt*, cf. Benz PNP 270 - **2)** for the *ʾmh* in Vatt sig. eb. 116, 157, 315 (prob. indicating female official), cf. Avigad PEQ '46, 126ff., Qedem iv pp 11ff., 31f., FS Cross 206, Albright FS Ubach 134, Zayadine Syr li 136, Cross AUSS xiii 12 n. 33, cf. also

Lipiński BiOr xliii 450: *ʾmt* in Amm. seals = wife (cf. also Aufrecht sub CAI 36) - this word (Sing. abs. *ʾmh*) also in Aeg xxxix 4 recto 2? (cf. Hoftijzer VT xii 341 (: or = *ʾm*$_1$+ suff. 3 p.s.?) :: Milik Aeg xl 79f.: l. *ymhw* (= Sing. emph. of *ywm* + *hw* (= *hʾ*$_1$)) :: Swiggers Aeg lx 94: l. *ʾmh* = Sing. abs. of *ʾmh*$_3$ (= people, men)) - Fales sub AECT 17: l. *ʾmt<ʾ>* (= Sing. emph.) in CIS ii 19^4 (= Del 12), highly uncert. reading.
v. *ʾmt*, *mtnh*.

ʾmh$_3$ v. *ʾlmh*, *ʾmh*$_2$.

ʾmwnh v. *ʾmn*$_5$.

ʾmyn for poss. adverbial use in Hatra, v. *ʾdyn*.
v. *ʾmr*$_1$, *mym*.

ʾmkyl v. *mkyl*.

ʾml Pun QAL (??) Impf. 3 p.s.m. *yʾml* CIS i 5510^3 - ¶ verb QAL (??) to wither; *yʾml yd[...* CIS i 5510^3: may he wither as to (his) hand (i.e. may (his) hand wither), cf. Dahood Bibl liii 394, UF i 17 (:: v.d.Branden BiOr xxxvi 202: *yʾml* = form with causative meaning: they make to wither).

ʾmlgyʾ (< Greek ὁμολογία) - **Palm** Sing. abs. *ʾmlgyʾ* Syr xiv 184^2 (reading of first ʾ uncert., cf. Rosenthal Sprache 36) - ¶ subst. exact meaning uncert., *bʾmlgyʾ* Syr xiv 184^2: by consent/agree-ment (or as payment/redemption??).

ʾmlt v. *ʾwmnt*; cf. also *ʾwlt*.

ʾmm v. *ʾpy*, *tmʾ*$_2$.

ʾmn$_1$ Palm Gawlikowski Ber xxii 146: l. *ʾmyn* (= verbal form, he has instituted; PAʿEL Pf. 3 p.s.m.?) in Syr xvii 280^4 (= SBS 48B 3), highly uncert. reading, especially of *m* - for *ʾmn* in Syr xiv 177^3 (heavily dam. context), cf. Milik DFD 313f.: -ʾ + *mn*$_5$.
v. *ʾmn*$_1$, *hymn*, *mn*$_4$.

ʾmn$_2$ (< Akkad., cf. Zimmern Fremdw 25, Ellenbogen 30, Kaufman AIA 109, cf. also Lipiński ZAH i 63) - **Pun** Sing. abs., cf. KAI 178$^{2f.}$: *ymman(nai)*, cf. Cassuto with Levi Della Vida Lib iii 109, Levi Della Vida OA ii 92, Friedrich ZDMG cvii 296, Röllig KAI a.l., FR 205, Vattioni AION xvi 41, Aug xvi 537 - **OffAr** Sing. abs. *ʾmn* Driv 6^4; + suff. 2 p.s.m.? *ʾmnk* JRAS '29, 111^3 (or n.p.?); Plur. abs. *ʾmnn* Driv 7^{3,6} - **Nab** Sing. emph. *ʾmnʾ* CIS ii 164^4, 166, RES 53^3, 807^3, 1093^2, 2117^7, Souëïda 196^2, Syr xxxv 236b; Plur. emph. *ʾmnyʾ* RB xlii 413^2 - **Palm** Sing. emph. *ʾmnʾ* CIS ii 4258^5, 4261^4, 4261bis 5, AAS iii 19 i 3, ii 7 - **JAr** Sing. emph. *ʾwmnh* MPAT-A 9 (= SM 3^2), 14 (= SM 47) - ¶ subst. m. craftsman, architect, sculptor, passim; making - a) a tomb: RES 1093^2 - b) a stele: RB xlii 413^2 - c) a statue, of a man: CIS ii

164^4, of an eagle: Souéïda 196^2, Syr xxxv 236b; cf. Driv $7^{3,6}$: the *ʾmnn* slaves belonging to the household of Arsham (cf. l. 7) - abbrev. ʾ??, cf. RB xlvi 408, cf. however Milik Syr xxxv 237.

ʾmn$_3$ **Samal** Sing. abs. *ʾmn* KAI 214^{11} - ¶ subst. firmness, steadfastness, faithfulness - used in KAI 214^{11}, prob. to indicate a sure covenant, cf. Halévy RS i 149f., D.H.Müller WZKM vii 52, Lagrange ERS 493, Driver AnOr xii 46 (: l. *ʾmn[h]*), cf. also Koopmans 35, Marrassini FLEM 81, Gibson SSI ii p. 67, 71, Dion p. 28, 381 n. 7 :: Lidzbarski Handb 220, Cooke NSI p. 162: = surety? :: Donner KAI a.l.: context untranslatable - this word also in - a) KAI 215^{21}??, cf. Lidzbarski Handb 220, Cooke NSI p. 180, Koopmans 76, Lipiński Stud 33, or = *ʾmn$_5$* used as adjective?, cf. Halévy RS i 238f., Lagrange ERS 497, Gibson SSI ii p. 85, or used adverbially?, cf. Marrassini FLEM 81, Dion p. 171 (cf. however D.H.Müller WZKM vii 40, Donner KAI a.l.: context untranslatable) - b) KAI 222B 7?? (*[ʾ]mn*), cf. Lipiński Stud 33 (highly uncert.; for other text restoration, cf. e.g. Fitzmyer AIS 16f., Donner KAI a.l.: l. *[lʿl]mn* = *l$_5$* + Plur. abs. of *ʿlm$_4$*).

ʾmn$_4$ **Hatra** Plur. abs. *ʾmnyn* 292^5 (:: Safar Sumer xxvii 13f.: l. *ʾd/rnyn* = pocket?) - ¶ subst. of uncert. meaning, prob. designation of certain object; Degen NESE iii 91: = vessel, poss. metathesis of *mʾn*, or lapsus for the same, cf. also Aggoula Syr lii 195.

ʾmn$_5$ **Hebr** KAI 200^{11} (for this division of words, cf. Naveh IEJ x 131, 133, 135, Lesh xxx 69, Vogt Bibl xli 183, Cross BASOR clxv 43, 45 n. 49, Amusin & Heltzer IEJ xiv 153 n. 20, Talmon BASOR clxxvi 34f., Lemaire Sem xxi 74, Strugnell HThR lxvii 178f., Sasson BASOR ccxxxii 60, 61, 62 n. 9, Pardee Maarav i 51, HAHL 21f., cf. also Gibson SSI i p. 28, 30, Suzuki AJBI viii 5, 15ff., Conrad TUAT i 250, Smelik HDAI 90 :: Yeivin BiOr xix 5: l. *ʾm$_3$*+ *n-* (cf. also Delekat Bibl li 468f.) :: Albright ANET 568 n. 10: l. *ʾm$_3$*+ *ntn* (cf. also Albright with Cross BASOR clxv 45 n. 49); cf. also Röllig KAI a.l., Weippert FS Rendtorff 461 (n. 32)), Frey 599^5 (for the reading, cf. Leon JQR xliv 268 n. 4), 630b 5, 650, 651^5, 661^5, 1398^6, SM 75^6, 111^2 - **JAr** MPAT-A 3^2 (= SM 60), 5^8 (= SM 64), 9 (= SM 3^2; *[ʾ]mn*), 13^3 (= SM 46), 22^8 (= SM 70^{16}), 26^{10} (= SM 32), $27^{3,4}$ (= SM 33), $28^{2,4}$ (= SM 34), 29^5 (= SM 35; *ʾm[n]*), 30^3 (= SM 26), 33^2 (= SM 50), 35 (= SM 16), 36^5 (= SM 30), 39^4 (= SM 42^5), Frey 845^4 (= SM 104), SM 24^2, 73^1, $105^{3,4}$, AMB 1^{12}, etc. - ¶ (adj. used as) adv.: surely, truly (for the context of KAI 200^{11}, v. *nqy$_1$*) - **1)** *ʾmn* used as affirmative exclamation in synagogue inscriptions: a) at the end of an inscription: MPAT-A 3^2, 5^8, 13^3, 36^5, Frey 630b 5, 661^5, SM 24^2, 75^6, 111^2; doubled and combined with *slh$_2$* (*ʾmn ʾmn slh*): MPAT-A 26^{10}, 27^4, $33^{2f.}$, 39^4 (cf. also Frey $1398^{6f.}$, MPAT-A 22^8: *ʾmn wʾmn slh*); combined with *slh šlwm* (*ʾm[n sl]h šlwm*): MPAT-A

29^5 (cf. also MPAT-A 35), cf. also *ʾmn ʾmn šlwm* SM 105$^{3f.}$ (:: Naveh sub SM 105: l. *ʾmn šlwm ʾmn*) and the combination *ʾmn ʾmn slh wly ʾmn* MPAT-A 30^3 (cf. Sokoloff Maarav i 81, v. also *wly*$_3$) - b) at the beginning of an inscription combined with *slh* (*[ʾ]mn slh*): MPAT-A 9 (cf. Frey 650^1: *ʾmn ʾmn*) - c) in the midst of an inscription combined with *slh šlwm* (*ʾmn ʾmn slh šlwm*): MPAT-A 27^3, 28^{2,4} (*[slh]*) - d) in the expression *wymrwn kl ʿmh ʾmn wʾmn slh* MPAT 22^8: let all the people say: Amen and Amen Selah - 2) in the midst of an amulet in the comb. *ʾmn ʾmn slh*, AMB 1^{12,18} (uncert. restoration)^{,19} (uncert. restoration), 2^{11} and *ʾmn ʾmn slh hllwyh* AMB 4^{23} - this exclamation also used in Greek transcription: e.g. ἀμέν (EI x 186), ἀμήν (ZDPV lxxviii 182f. and Frey 867), ἀμνν (Frey 732), in Lat. transcription *amen* (Frey 661 ii 7) - Lipiński Stud 44f.: l. *ʾm[n]*$_5$ in KAI 222B 42 (highly uncert. interpret.) - prob. this word used as adj. (Sing. f. abs.) *ʾmnh* (= faithful) in Hebr. text Frey 634^4 (or = *ʾmnh* (= faith, Torah)?; cf. Lifshitz Frey^2 p. 49) :: Frey a.l.: l. *ʾmw[nh]* (= *ʾmnh*) - for abbrev. *ʾ*, cf. Frey 904.

ʾmnh **Pun** Sing. + suff. 1 p.s., cf. Poen 937: *emanethi* (cf. variant reading *emanehti*, cf. Sznycer PPP 46 (or div. otherwise: l. *manethi* = QAL Pf. 1 p.s. of *mny* (= to count > to remit) :: Izreel Shn iii 207: pro *yth emanethi* l. *ythem* (= *ʾt*$_6$ + suff. 3 p.s.m.) *anechi* (= *ʾnk*)) :: Krahmalkov Or lvii 63 ff (div. otherwise): l. *ythem* (= *ʾt*$_6$ + suff. 3 p.s.m.) *aneth* (= lapsus for *ʾnk*) - ¶ subst. prob. meaning: proof, in the context: written proof of identity (credentials), cf. Sznycer PPP 92ff. (also for older literature), J.J.Glück & Maurach Semitics ii 111. v. *ʾmn*$_{3,5}$.

ʾms$_1$ v. *mss*$_1$.

ʾms$_2$ **OffAr** Ebeling Frah a.l.: l. *ʿwztwn* in Frah xxi 4 = form of *ʾms*$_2$ (= to beat), improb. interpret., cf. Nyberg FP 52, 95: l. iranian word.

ʾmprʿṭr (< Lat. *imperator*) - **Pun** Sing. abs. *[ʾmp]rʿṭr* KAI 173^2 (= ICO-Sard-Npu 8) - ¶ subst. imperator.

ʾmṣ$_1$ **Hebr** PIʿEL Imper. s.m. *ʾmṣ* TA-H 88^2 (dam. context; v. however infra) - ¶ verb PIʿEL to make strong, to strengthen + obj. (*zrʿ*$_3$), or = adj. *ʾmṣ*$_2$ (or QAL Part. act.?) Sing. m. cstr. (= strong)?, cf. also Yadin IEJ xxvi 9ff., Millard PEQ '78, 26, Green ZAW c 277ff.

ʾmṣ$_2$ v. *ʾmṣ*$_1$.

ʾmr$_1$ **Ph** QAL Pf. 3 p.s.f. *ʾmr* KAI 50^2; Impf. 3 p.s.m. *yʾmr* KAI 26C iv 14f. (*yʾm[r]*), 17; Inf. cstr. *ʾmr* KAI 14^2; Imper. s.m. *ʾmr* KAI 50^2 (cf. also v.d.Branden BO xxii 216) - **Pun** obscure form of this root: *imur* in Poen 948??, cf. L.H.Gray AJSL xxxix 78, cf. however Schroed 292, Sznycer PPP 128 - **Hebr** QAL Pf. 3 p.s.m. *ʾmr* KAI 193^8 (less prob.

kyʾmr = haplography for *ky yʾmr* (= QAL Impf. 3 p.s.m.), on this point, cf. e.g. Seeligmann VT xi 209 n. 3, Röllig KAI a.l., H.P.Müller UF ii 238f., WO viii 65f., Reviv CSI 77, Lehman JNES xxvi 93ff., Millard JSS xv 7), DJD ii 17A 1 (diff. and uncert. reading, cf. also Aharoni BASOR cxcvii 30 n. 44; for this text, cf. Pardee JBL xcvii 334f., HAHL 121), 24B 5, C 5, D 5 (*ʾm[r]*), E 4, I 5 (*ʾm[r]*; dam. context); 2 p.s.m. *ʾm[rt]* TA-H 40^{5}; Inf. cstr. *ʾmr* KAI 193$^{14,20f.}$; Part. act. pl.m. abs. *ʾwmryn* SM 49^{20}; Part. pass. s.m. abs. *ʾmwr* DJD ii 42^{6} (:: Lehmann & Stern VT iii 391, 394: l. *ʾmyr* = QAL Part. act. s.m. abs., cf. however Birnbaum PEQ '55, 27) - **Amm** QAL Imper. s.m. *ʾmr* BASOR cclxiv 47^{1} (= CAI 144) - **Edom** QAL Pf. 3 p.s.m. *ʾmr* TeAv xii 97^{1}; Imper. s.m. *ʾmr* TeAv xii 97^{1} - **Mo** QAL Pf. 3 p.s.m. *ʾmr* KAI 181^{6}; Impf. 3 p.s.m. *yʾmr* KAI 181^{6,14,32} (*[y]ʾmr*); 1 p.s. *ʾmr* KAI 181^{24} - **Samal** QAL Pf. 3 p.s.m. *ʾmr* KAI 215^{21} (?, highly uncert. context, cf. Donner KAI a.l., cf. also Cooke NSI p. 180: or = QAL Impf. 1 p.s.? and Gibson SSI ii p. 85, Dion p. 42: or = Sing. abs. of *ʾmr$_3$*?); Impf. 3 p.s.m. *yʾmr* KAI 214^{17,21,29}; Imper. s.m. *ʾmr* KAI 214^{30} (?, cf. Donner KAI a.l., Gibson SSI ii p. 69 :: Dion p. 304: prob. = QAL Part. act. s.m. abs. :: Cooke NSI p. 170: or = QAL Pf. 3 p.s.m.? :: D.H.Müller WZKM vii 68: or = QAL Impf. 1 p.s.?); ITP Impf. 3 p.s.m. *ytmr* KAI 214^{10} (?, cf. D.H.Müller WZKM vii 57f., Koopmans 34, Dion p. 108f., Gibson SSI ii p. 71, Garr DGSP 119, Stefanovic COAI 171 :: Lidzbarski Hand 386: < root *tmr$_1$* = to avail :: Donner KAI a.l. (div. otherwise): l. *ytmrb* = HITP Impf. of root *mrb*??) - **DA** QAL Pf. 3 p.pl.m. *ʾmrw* i 8; Impf. 3 p.s.m. *yʾmr* i 6f.; 3 p.pl.m. *yʾmrw* i 4; a form of this root prob. also in DA ii 17 (*ʾmr[*) - **OldAr** QAL Pf. 1 p.pl. *ʾmrn* KAI 222C 1 (:: Vriezen JEOL xvii 209f.: instead of *kh ʾmrn* divide *k$_4$* + *hʾmrn* = HAPH Pf. 1 p.pl.); Impf. 3 p.s.m. *yʾmr* KAI 202A 15, 222C 18, 223C 1f. (*[y]ʾmr*), 4 (*[y]ʾmr*), 7, 8f. (*[y]ʾmr*); 2 p.s.m. *tʾmr* KAI 222B 24, 26, 223B 5, 224^{5,7,18,21}; Impf. pass. 3 p.s.f. *tʾmr* KAI 222A 33, 36 (:: Lipiński Stud 32, 50: = QAL Impf. 2 p.s.m.) - **OffAr** QAL Pf. 3 p.s.m. *ʾmr* KAI 233^{8}, 264^{3} (with f. subject)^{,4}, 267A 3, 271B 4, Cowl 2^{1}, 5^{1}, 6^{2}, Aḥiq 139 (cf. Grelot RB lxviii 188, DAE p. 442 n. m, Watson OA ii 257 :: Cowl a.l.: = QAL Impf. 1 p.s., cf. however idem p. 243; cf. also Ginsberg ANET 429, Lindenberger APA 137f.), Krael 1^{2}, 2^{1}, 3^{1}, ATNS 1^{2}, Beh 27 (*ʾm[r]*; Akkad. par. *iq-bu-u*), 37 (Akkad. par. *i-qab-bi*), Aeg xxxix 4 recto 4 (cf. Hoftijzer VT xii 342, Swiggers Aeg lx 94 × Porten & Yardeni sub TADAE A 3.11: = QAL Imper. s.m. :: Bresciani Aeg xxxix 7, Milik Aeg xl 79: = QAL Impf. 1 p.s.), etc., etc.; 3 p.s.f. *ʾmrt* KAI 269^{2}, Cowl 1^{1}, 10^{2}, 68 iv obv., Aḥiq 119, Krael 5^{11}, ATNS 3^{6}, RES 1801^{3}; 2 p.s.m. *ʾmrt* Cowl 55^{5} (for the reading of the heavily dam. context and interpret., cf. e.g. Porten & Yardeni sub TADAE A 3.2 verso 13 :: Cowl a.l.: = QAL Pf. 1 p.s.); 1 p.s. *ʾmrt* Cowl 9^{5}, 16^{3,5}, 43^{6}, Aḥiq 24, 45, 49, Beh

7 (Akkad. par. *al-ta-par um-ma*), 18 (Akkad. par. *al-ta-par um-ma*), ATNS 12[3] (dam. context), RES 1295[1], Sem xxi 85 conv. 4, Sach 76 ii A 4 (cf. the peculiar *ʾmr* in Krael 6[2], where one should expect *ʾmrt*, cf. also Szubin & Porten BASOR cclxix 36); 3 p.pl.m. *ʾmrw* Cowl 26[3,9], 32[1], 41[4], 80[2] (for the reading, cf. also Porten & Yardeni sub TADAE A 5.5), Aḥiq 58, 121, ATNS 28a 2, 52b 7 (dam. context), KAI 271B 2 (= NESE i 27A 2), AJSL lviii 302A 2; 1 p.pl. *ʾmrn* Cowl 40[2], Krael 6[5]?, ATNS 2[3], 6[5] (:: Porten & Yardeni sub TADAE B 8.12: or = QAL Part. act. pl.m. abs.), 101[3] (heavily dam. context); Impf. 3 p.s.m. *yʾmr* KAI 233[10], Cowl 15[27], 37[9], Aḥiq 194, 207, Beh 53 (for the context, cf. Greenfield & Porten BIDG p. 48f.), Krael 2[7], 7[41,42], ATNS 1[3] (*yʾm[r]*; dam. context), Samar 3[7], NESE i 11[2]; + suff. 3 p.s.m.? *yʾmrnh* Aḥiq 158 (on this form, cf. also Lindenberger APA 284, 299 n. 19); 3 p.s.f. *tʾmr* Cowl 15[23], 18[3], Krael 2[9], 7[25]; 2 p.s.m. *tʾmr* RES 1298B 5; 2 p.s.f. *tʾmrn* Sem ii 31 conv. 4; 1 p.s. *ʾmr* Cowl 5[12], 8[20], 9[14], 10[11], 15[31,33], 47[8], 49[2] (cf. Degen NESE iii 19f.), Aḥiq 57, 139, Krael 6[15], 10[9,10]; 3 p.pl.m. *yʾmrwn* Cowl 71[32], ATNS 26[2]; 1 p.pl. *nʾmr* Samar 5[9], 7[11] (*nʾm[r]*, diff. reading); Inf. *mʾmr* Aḥiq 115, *mmr* Cowl 32[2], *ʾmr* KAI 233[17], Cowl 1[5] (for this prob. reading, cf. Porten & Yardeni sub TADAE B 5.1, cf. also Porten & Greenfield JEAS p. 106 :: Cowl a.l.: poss. l. *nm[r]* = QAL Impf. 1 p.pl.), 2[3], 5[3,12], Krael 1[3], 2[3], 3[3], ATNS 8[2], etc. etc.; Imper. s.m. *ʾmr* NESE iii 29B 1, Sach 76 ii A 1, cf. Warka 18, 43: *a-ma-ar*; s.f. *ʾmry* ASAE xxvi 27[3]; pl.m. *ʾmrw* Cowl 80[8], RES 1797B 2; Part. act. pl.m. abs. *ʾmrn* Cowl 26[23], 27[10], 30[4], 31[22], 33[7], 37[6], *ʾmryn* Cowl 30[22]; QAL pass. Pf. 3 p.s.m. (or Part. pass. s.m. abs.?) *ʾmyr* Cowl 76[1] (for this reading, cf. Porten & Yardeni sub TADAE A 5.4); Part. pass. s.m. abs. *ʾmyr* SSI ii 28 obv. 4, Aḥiq 210 (for this diff. reading, cf. Puech RB xcv 591; cf. also Kottsieper SAS 14, 23, 188: = QAL. pass. Pf. 3 p.s.m.), ATNS 1[2] (for this poss. reading, cf. Porten & Yardeni sub TADAE B 8.8 :: Segal ATNS a.l.: l. *ʾmyn* = Sing. m. abs. of *ʾmyn* (adj. used adverbially = verily)), 96[1] (dam. context) - **Nab** QAL diff. form *ʾmr* CIS ii 235B, prob. = Pf. 3 p.s.m., cf. Cantineau Nab i 78 :: Guidi RB xix 424: = QAL Imper. s.m. or Impf. 1 p.s. - **Palm** QAL Impf. 3 p.s.m. *yʾmr* Syr xvii 353[7]; 3 p.pl.m. *yʾmrwn* RIP 199[13]; Part. act. s.m. abs. *ʾmr* CIS ii 3973[10]; *ʾmry* in RIP 134[4] = n.p. :: Michałowski FP '60, 248: = form of root *ʾmr$_1$* - **Hatra** QAL Pf. 3 p.s.f. *ʾmrt* 35[4]; Impf. 3 p.s.m. *lmr* 24[2] (for the reading, cf. Degen ZDMG cxxi 125, Donner KAI ii p. 343, Vattioni IH a.l. :: reading *lm? dy* (cf. Safar Sumer vii 182; cf. also Safar Sumer ix 14*: l. *lmn* (?) *dy* without interpret. and Pennacchietti FO xvi 62: l. *lm.dy* = Impf. form) :: Milik RN vi/iv 55: l. *lqry* = QAL Impf. 3 p.s.m. of *qrʾ$_1$* :: reading *lmdy* (cf. Donner KAI sub 245, cf. also Silverman JAOS xciv 271: *lmdy* = rather, rather much)), 53[3] (cf. Aggoula Ber xviii 95, Degen NESE ii 100, Vattioni IH a.l. (for

the reading, cf. Safar Sumer ix 247) :: Caquot Syr xxxii 56: l. *lmn* = *l*$_5$ + *mn*$_4$; cf. after Pennacchiotti FO xvi 62 n. 4), 101^{2} - **JAr** QAL Pf. 3 p.s.m. *ʾmr* MPAT 47,1-2 recto 1, 49 i 5, 9, 51^{2}, IEJ xxxvi 206^{1}, AMB 15^{17}, EI xx 161*; 1 p.s. *ʾmrt* AMB 7^{19} (cf. Beyer ATTM 373, Naveh & Shaked AMB a.l. :: Dupont-Sommer JKF i 203, 210: or: = QAL Pf. 2 p.s.m.?, cf. Scholem JGM 86 :: Levine with Neusner HJB v 361: = QAL Part. act. s.m. abs. + pronoun 2 p.s.m.), IEJ xl 142^{2}; Impf. 2 p.s.m. *tʾmr* MPAT 45^{7} (:: Beyer ATTM 314: = lapsus for *tʾmrn* (= QAL Impf. 2 p.pl.m.)), 46^{5}; 2 p.s.f. *tmryn* MPAT 40^{10,24} (*[t]mryn*); 3 p.pl.m. *ymrwn* MPAT-A 22^{8} (= SM 70^{16}); 2 p.pl.m. *tmrwn* IEJ xxxvi 206^{7}; Part. act. s.m. abs. *ʾmr* MPAT 49 i 4, 55^{3}, MPAT-A 22^{2} (= SM 70^{10}, cf. also Sokoloff Maarav i 82); pl.f. abs. *ʾmrn* AMB 7^{22} (or = Pf. 3 p.pl.f.?, cf. Naveh & Shaked AMB a.l. :: Dupont-Sommer JKF i 203, 210 (div, otherwise): l. *ʾmr* = QAL Imper. s.m.) - QAL Pf. 3 p.pl.m. (*ʾmrw*) in unknown West-Sem. dialect: Sem xxxviii 52^{1} (or = fraud?, cf. however Bordreuil & Pardee Sem xxxviii 65ff.) - ¶ verb QAL to speak, to say, passim; for *ʾmr* of KAI 181^{6}, cf. Lipiński Or xl 329f. - **1)** + direct speech - a) without introduction: KAI 26C iv 17, 50^{2}, 181^{6,14,32}, 193^{8}, 214^{17,21,29,30}, 222B 24, C 18, 264^{3}, Cowl 1$^{1f.}$, 13$^{1ff.}$, 20^{7}, Krael 5^{11}, Driv 4^{1}, ATNS 2^{5}, 3^{6}, 4^{9}, 9^{4}, 21^{4}, CIS ii 3973^{10}, Hatra 101^{2}, MPAT-A 22^{8} (= SM 70^{16}), etc. - b) introduced by *lʾmr*, v. sub 10 - c) introduced by *zy/dy*, *ʾmr zy šmʿ hwyt* MPAT 49 i 5: he said: I have heard, cf. EI xx 161* - d) introduced by *kzy*, *yʾmr kzy ʾn[h]* Samar 3^{7}: he will say as follows: I ... - **2)** + indirect speech - a) without introduction, *šlʾ thy ʾmr ... lʾ ʿlty* DJD ii 42^{6}: in order that it is not said (or: you will not say) ... (that) I did not come - b) introduced by *dy*, *mn dy lmr dy dkryn lṭb* Hatra 24^{2} (= KAI 245; for the reading, v. supra): whoever will say that they may be remembered for good (cf. also Hatra 53^{3} (for the reading, v. supra)) - **3)** + obj. - a) words: Cowl 37^{9}, 71^{12}, ATNS 1^{2} - b) counsel: Aḥiq 57 - c) truth?: Aḥiq 158 - d) calumny: KAI 269^{2} (v. also *krṣ*; cf. also Greenfield FS Fitzmyer 48) - **4)** + obj. + *ʿl*$_7$ + *l*$_5$, *ʾmr lšn byš ʿl ḥbryh lʿmmyh* MPAT-A 22$^{2f.}$ (= SM 70$^{10f.}$): speaking slander against his fellow to the gentiles - **5)** + *bnbš-*, *tʾmr bnbšk* KAI 223B 5: you will say in your soul (cf. Greenfield FS Fitzmyer 48, Zevit Maarav v/vi 340) - **6)** - a) + *l*$_5$ (to): KAI 50^{2} (on this text, cf. Pardee JBL xcvii 334f.), 181^{14}, 202A 15, 222B 26, 223C 8f., Cowl 1$^{1f.}$, 2$^{1f.}$, Krael 2$^{1f.}$, 3$^{1ff.}$, ATNS 90^{1}, MAI xiv/2,66$^{1f.}$, Syr xvii 353^{7}, AMB 7^{19}, Sem xxi 85 conv. 4, NESE i 11^{2}, Hatra 35^{4} (v. also *btlh*), MPAT 55^{3}, IEJ xxxvi 206^{1,7} - b) + *l*$_5$ (to) + direct speech: KAI 181^{24}, 223C 7f., 224^{5,7,18,21}, 264$^{4f.}$, DA i 8, Sem xxxviii 52^{1} (v. however supra), DJD ii 24E 4 (cf. also C 5), MPAT 40^{10,24}, 45^{7}, 46^{5}, 51$^{2f.}$, BASOR cclxiv 47^{1}, TeAv xii 97^{1}, AMB 15^{17}, etc. - c) + *l*$_5$ (to) + *lʾmr* + direct speech, v. sub 10 - d) + *l*$_5$

(to) + ʿl_7 (concerning): RES 1295[1f.], MPAT 49 i 4 (*lʾ ʾytyny ydʿ lmn hwh ʾmr ʿl[*: I do not know to whom he was speaking about ...) - **7)** + l_5 (concerning) + direct speech: Krael 7[41] (cf. Krael a.l. :: Yaron JSS iii 28, Porten & Greenfield JEAS p. 56f., Grelot DAE p 48, Porten & Yardeni sub TADAE B 3.8: l_5 here = to); cf. Samar 5[9] (+ l_5 + *kzy* introducing direct speech (dam. context)) - 8) + l_5 + Inf., *[y]ʾmr lhldt* KAI 223C 1: he will purpose to efface (cf. e.g. Donner KAI a.l., Gibson SSI ii p. 45, Swiggers BiOr xxxvii 341 :: Fitzmyer AIS 83, 89: he (will) give orders (cf. also Lipiński Stud 54, Gibson SSI iii p. 55, 64)); cf. also KAI 26C iv 14f. - **9)** +qdm_3 (before, sc. an authority), Cowl 16[5], 37[9]; cf. also Cowl 32[2f.] (+ qdm_3 + ʿl_7 (concerning), for the *scriptio anterior* of this text, cf. Porten EI xiv 173f.) - **10)** *lʾmr* + direct speech preceded by - a) a form of ʾmr_1: KAI 233[10], Krael 1[2f.], cf. also KAI 233[8], Cowl 5[1ff.,12], 20[1ff.], Krael 2[1ff.] (form of ʾmr_1 + l_5 (to) + lʾ*mr*) and Cowl 25[2ff.], Krael 8[1ff.] (form of ʾmr_1 + qdm_3 + l_5 (to) + *lʾmr*; for last mentioned text, v. also qdm_3); cf. also *kn ʾmyr ln lʾmr* SSI ii 28 obv. 4: we were told as follows - b) a form of dbr_1: KAI 14[2] - c) a form of *mll* (v. mll_1): Herm 1[6] (combined with l_5 (to)) - d) a form of ngd_2: KAI 193[13f.] (combined with l_5 (to)) - e) a form of qwm_1: Krael 5[13] (*hn qmn lʾmr lʾ nsblnk*: if we rise up saying: we will not provide for you) - f) a form of $ršy_1$: Cowl 20[4f.,6] - g) of form of $šlḥ_1$: Cowl 16[8], 30[7] - h) for KAI 193[19], v. *bwʾ*; cf. Kutscher JAOS lxxiv 234 for the relation between *lʾmr* and *lm(ʾ)mr*, cf. also Fitzmyer FS Albright ii 148 on *lʾmr* - QAL pass. to be said, to be mentioned: KAI 222A 33, 36, ATNS 96[1] (+ ʾl_7), etc. - ITP (?, v. supra) diff. and dam. context, meaning uncert.: KAI 214[10], cf. Gibson SSI ii p. 67: *ytmr* = command was given × Dion p. 28: *ytmr* = it was said :: D.H.Müller WZKM vii 52: *ytmr* = he was appointed (for the context, v. also $nṣb_5$) - Lemaire & Durand IAS 117, 127: l. poss. *tʾmr* (= QAL Impf. 2 p.s.m.) in KAI 223B 15 (highly uncert. reading) - Dupont-Sommer FX p. 142: the ʾ at the end of FX 136[5] = ʾ<*mr*> (= QAL Pf. 3 p.s.m. (less prob.; last letter of n.l.?)) - Segal ATNS a.l.: l. in ATNS 35[1] ʾ*mrt* (= QAL. Pf. 1 p.s.), reading however less prob., cf. Porten & Yardeni sub TADAE B 4.7: l. *zy swn* (= *zy* + n.l.).

v. ʾdn_1, ʾm_1, ʾm_2, ʾ$mr_{2,3}$, ʾsr_1, ʾ$šm_1$, *zkm*, kh_1, lm_2, mlk_5 (ad *mlk ʾmr*), qwm_1.

ʾ**mr**$_2$ **Pun** Sing. abs., cf. Poen 1017: *umer* (var. *umir*; cf. Sznycer PPP 143f., J.J.Glück & Maurach Semitics ii 122, cf. also L.H.Gray AJSL xxxix 82: divide *palu mer* = *plwʾ ʾmr*) - **Amm** Sing. cstr. *ʾmr* BASOR cclxiv 47[1] (= CAI 144; or = QAL Pf. 3 p.s.m. of ʾmr_1?) - **Edom** Sing. cstr. *ʾmr* TeAv xii 97[1] (× Beit Arieh & Cresson TeAv xii a.l.:, Israel RivBib xxxv 339f.: = QAL Pf. 3 p.s.m. of ʾmr_1) - ¶ subst. - **1)** speech:

Poen 1017 - **2)** message: BASOR cclxiv 47^{1}, TeAv xii 97^{1} (for both instances, v. however supra) - Milik DFD 365f.: l. this subst. Sing. + suff. 3 p.s.f. (*ʾmrh*) in Hatra 31^{3} (*rbt ʾmrh* = the lady of the promise), poss. interpret. :: Safar Sumer viii 188, Caquot Syr xxx 238, Degen WO v 229, Vattioni IH a.l.: divide *rbtʾ* (= n.p.) + *mrh* (= Sing. + suff. 3 p.s.f. of *mrʾ*) - Cowl a.l.: l. poss. *ʾ[m]ryk* = Plur. + suff. 2 p.s.m. in Aḥiq 102 (uncert. reading and interpret., heavily dam. context, cf. also Kottsieper SAS 12, 20, 185: l. *ʾ[b]ryk* (= Plur. + suff. 2 p.s.m. of *ʾbr*$_2$ (= limb)).
v. *spr*$_3$.

ʾmr$_3$ Ph Sing. abs. *ʾmr* KAI $27^{4f.}$ (cf. du Mesnil du Buisson FS Dussaud 424, 426, Albright BASOR lxxvi 8, Gaster Or xi 44, 51f., Röllig KAI a.l., NESE ii 18, Cross & Saley BASOR cxcvii 45, Zevit IEJ xxvii 111, 114, Avishur PIB 248, 251, de Moor JEOL xxvii 108, Gibson SSI iii p. 83ff., Butterweck TUAT ii 436 (cf. also Healy CISFP i 666) × Torczyner JNES vi 21, 28: = QAL Imper. s.m. of *ʾmr*$_1$,cf. also Rosenthal ANET 658, Caquot FS Gaster 47, Lipiński RTAT 265, Garbini OA xx 281, 283, Sperling HUCA liii 3, 5f. :: Dupont-Sommer RHR cxx 134, 137: = QAL Pf. 3 p.s.m. of *ʾmr*$_1$ :: v.d.Branden BO iii 43f.: = QAL Impf. 1 p.s. of *ʾmr*$_1$) - **Pun** Sing. abs. *ʾmr* KAI 61B 2, 69^{9}, 109^{2}, 110^{1} (diff. reading *ʾmr* or *ʾtr*, cf. Hofra p. 51), CIS i 307^{5} (*[ʾ]mr* :: Slouschz TPI p. 247: l. *[b]šr*), 3915^{3}, Punica xviii/i $58^{3f.}$, Hofra 54^{3} - **OldAr** Sing. abs. *ʾmr* KAI 222A 23, Tell F 20 - **OffAr** Sing. abs. *[ʾ]mr* Driv 6^{3} (highly uncert. reading, cf. Porten & Yardeni sub TADAE A 6.9); emph. *ʾmrʾ* RES 496^{1} (cf. Driver AnOr xii 58 :: Sach 77 i 1 (= RES 496^{1}): l. *ʾmrh*); Plur. abs. *ʾmrn* PF 695; emph. *ʾmry[ʾ]* Aḥiq 121 - **Palm** Plur. emph. *ʾmryʾ* CIS ii 3913 ii 42 - ¶ subst. m. lamb, sheep; for *ḥnqt ʾmr*, cf. *ḥnq*; for *mlk ʾmr*, v. *mlk*$_5$.
v. *ʾmr*$_1$.

ʾmrh Samal Plur. abs. *ʾmrt* KAI 214^{29}; + suff. 3 p.s.m. *ʾmrth* KAI $214^{26,32}$ (or = Sing.?) - **OldAr** Sing. cstr. *ʾmrt* Tell F 10, 14 (cf. Abou-Assaf, Bordreuil & Millard Tell F p. 46 :: Abou-Assaf MDOG cxiii 17: in l. 10 = Plur. cstr.) - ¶ subst. word, utterance; *ʾmrt pmh* Tell F 10, 14: the utterance of his mouth (Akkad. par. *qí-bit pi-ia/qí-bit pî-šú*); in KAI 214 prob. meaning: command; *ʿl ʾmrth* KAI $214^{26,32}$: on his order(s).

ʾmš Hebr KAI 193^{6} - ¶ adv. yesterday (evening).
v. *mšmn*.

ʾmt (< Akkad., cf. Kaufman AIA 58, cf. also Zimmern Fremdw 70) - **OffAr** RES 1793^{4} (= PSBA '15, 222^{9}); cf. Frah xxv 7, 8 (*ʾymt*, *ʾmt*), Frah-S$_2$ 20 (*ʾmt*), Paik 96, Syn 300^{2}, 301^{3}, 304^{2}, etc., cf. GIPP 16, 45, SaSt 12 - **Hatra** 342^{13} *ʾmty* - ¶ adv. when, cf. for RES 1793^{4}

Dupont-Sommer CRAI '45, 175, REJ cvii 47ff., Kutscher Kedem i 55f., Ben-Chayyim EI i 136, Grelot VT iv 378 n. 1, DAE p. 376, Degen GGA '79, 29 :: interpret. as a form of *ʾmh$_2$*,cf. e.g. RES sub 1793, Driver AnOr xii 56, Segert AAG p. 208 (v. also *ʿbd$_1$*); *ʾmt tʿbdn psḥʾ*, when will you celebrate the Passover?

ʾn$_1$ v. *ʾwn$_2$*.

ʾn$_2$ v. *ʾyn$_1$*, *ṣdn*.

ʾn$_3$ **OldAr** KAI 223C 3 - **OffAr** Cowl 15^{25,29}, Krael 7^{24} (dam. context); cf. MP 2, GIPP 46 - ¶ adv. where(ever); *thk lh ʾn dy ṣbyt* Cowl 15$^{28f.}$: she can go wherever she wants to (cf. also Cowl 15^{25}); *bty ʾlhyʾ ʾn zy y[r]šmn* KAI 223C 2f.: the *Bethels* where they are written (on).

ʾn$_4$ v. *hn$_3$*, *ndd*, *nṣb$_3$*.

ʾn$_5$ v. *ʾny$_4$*, *ʾnk*.

ʾn$_6$ v. *ʾnh$_3$*.

ʾn$_7$ v. *hn$_3$*.

ʾnʾ$_1$ **Nab** QAL (or PAʿEL?) Impf. 3 p.s.m. *yʾnʾ* CIS ii 199^6 (= J 1) - ¶ verb of uncert. meaning; Greenfield Mem Yalon 82f. : < Akkad. *enû* = to change; Cantineau Nab ii 65: = PAʿEL (= to detain, to retard); Jaussen a.l.: = caus. with the same meaning; CIS ii a.l.: = to profit by :: Euting Nab Inschr 35: = to rent for a certain time.

ʾnʾ$_2$ v. *hnh*.

ʾnʾ$_3$ v. *ʾnh$_3$*.

ʾnʾ$_4$ v. *znh*.

ʾnb v. *ʿnb*.

ʾngyn Ebeling Frah a.l.: l. *ʾngyn* (= assembly) in Frah xii 9 (improb. reading and interpret., cf. Nyberg FP p. 46, 81: l. Iran. word).

ʾndwm v. *ʾndm*.

ʾndwt Ebeling Frah a.l.: l. *ʾndwt* in Frah vii 10 (= chamois, word related to Hebr. *ʿtd*, Arab. *catūd* and Akkad. *atūdu*; less prob. reading and interpret., cf. Nyberg FP 43, 70: l. *hangūt* (= Iran. word)).

ʾndm **OffAr** Cowl 22^{133} - ¶ reading uncert. (*ʾndm* or *ʾnrm*), meaning uncert., possibly n.p., cf. Grelot DAE p. 89, Porten & Greenfield JEAS p. 147 - the same word or a related one perhaps in Cowl 72^{20} (dam. context, reading *ʾndwmʾ* highly uncert., cf. Cowl a.l.).

ʾnh$_1$ Kottsieper SAS 34, 189: the *]ʾnhy* in Aḥiq 161 = Sing. + suff. 1 p.s. of *ʾnh$_1$* (= sighing); uncert. interpret., cf. Grelot DAE p. 444 n. c: = end of verbal form, v. also *hwn$_2$*.

ʾnh$_2$ v. *ʾnḥ$_2$*.

ʾnh$_3$ **OldAr** *ʾnh* KAI 202A 2, 13, 14, B 3f. (*ʾn[h]*), 216^{1,20}, 217^{1,5}, 218, 223C 8, 224^6 - **OffAr** *ʾnh* KAI 226^5, 233^{2,4}, 261^{1,5,6}, 264^{3,7}, 270A

3 (:: Dupont-Sommer ASAE xlviii 120: l. *ʾph* = QAL Part. pass. s.m. abs. of *ʾpy*; for the reading, cf. CIS ii 137 a.l., Donner KAI a.l., Levine JAOS lxxxiv 19 (n. 2)), 276^{1}, Cowl 5^{3,11}, 6^{5}, 43^{2} (for the reading, cf. Porten JNES xlviii 176, Porten & Yardeni sub TADAE B 5.5 :: Cowl a.l. (div. otherwise): l. *mbtḥyh* (= n.p.)), 47^{8} (for the reading, cf. Porten & Yardeni sub TADAE B 5.4 l. 2 :: Cowl a.l.: l. *ʾnt*), Krael 1^{9}, 2^{3}, 3^{10}, 6^{12} (for the reading, cf. Porten & Greenfield JEAS p. 50, Porten & Yardeni sub TADAE B 3.7), Driv 3^{6}, 8^{5}, Herm 1^{4,7}, ATNS 2^{5}, 4^{5b}, Beh 21* (Akkad. par. *a-na-ku*), 24 (Akkad. par. *ana-ku*), AE '23, 40 no. 2^{3}, FuF xxxv 173^{1} (= ASA 244), Samar 1^{5,8} (= EI xviii 8*), 2^{3} (dam. context)^{,7,8}, etc., etc., cf. Warka 10, 26: *a-na-ʾ*; cf. Frah-S$_1$ 3 (*ʾnh*), S$_2$ 27 (*ʾnh*), Paik 102, 103 (*ʾnh*), Syr xxxv 305^{1}, cf. GIPP 16, 46, SaSt 12 - **Nab** *ʾnh* MPAT 64 i 7, 8, 9, iii 1, CIS ii 340 (doubtful, cf. Cantineau Nab i 51) - **Palm** *ʾnʾ* Syr xlvii 413^{2}, *ʾnh*, cf. Cantineau Gramm 61 - **Hatra** *ʾnʾ* 24^{1,3}, 72 (for the reading, cf. Milik DFD 166, Vattioni IH a.l. :: Safar Sumer xi 12 (n. 41; div. otherwise): l. *-ʾ ?ʾ* (cf. also Aggoula Ber xviii 96, v. also *klb*$_1$)), 272^{3}, 288a 3 (cf. Assur 11 i 4, 21 ii 3, 27h) - **JAr** *ʾnh* MPAT 39^{3,5}, 40^{2,13} (*ʾ[n]h*), 41^{9}, 42^{14,17,18}, 44 i 5, 6, 47,1-2 recto 6, 9, 50e 2, 51^{3,11,12}, 52^{8,10}, 68$^{1,2f.}$, MPAT-A 9^{2} (= SM 3), 23, Syn 273 no 13^{1} (= SM 96b), 16^{1} (= SM 97), IEJ xxxvi 206^{3,5,6}, AMB 1^{12}, 8^{3}, DBKP 17^{40} (written as one word together with preceding *mwdy*), 18^{70}, 19^{28}, ZDPV xcvi 59^{1}, etc., *ʾnʾ* Syn 269 no. 2^{1} (uncert. reading, cf. du Mesnil du Buisson Syr xl 309f., Naveh sub SM 90), 273 no. 15 (= SM 96d), 274 no. 17^{1} (= SM 98) - ¶ pers. pronoun, I, me; *byty ʾnh drgmn* Cowl 6^{8}: my house (i.e.) of me D. (cf. Muraoka JSS xi 166 n. 7), cf. Cowl 28^{5}; *wʾpqny ʾnh wbry* Herm 6^{4}: he has brought me out (i.e.) me and my son (cf. also Porten & Greenfield IOS iv 20); *wʾnh nktny ḥwyh* Herm 5^{8}: as to me, a serpent has bitten me - the *ʾn* in AMB 8^{8} prob. = lapsus for *ʾnh*$_3$.

v. *ʾnḥ*$_1$, *ʾny*$_4$, *ʾnk*, *ʾnth*$_2$.

ʾnhnh v. *ʾnḥn*$_2$, *hwy*$_1$.

ʾnw v. *znh*.

ʾnwky v. *ʾnk*.

ʾnwn v. *hʾ*$_1$.

ʾnwpṭyptyʾ (< Prakrit, cf. Benveniste JA ccliv 447, 450, Kutscher, Naveh & Shaked Lesh xxxiv 129) - **OffAr** JA ccliv 440^{6} (cf. also p. 462b) - ¶ subst. (declensional form) with esteem (for), in obedience (to).

ʾnwpṭyptmnh (< Prakrit, cf. Benveniste JA ccliv 449, Shaked JRAS '69, 119ff., Kutscher, Naveh & Shaked Lesh xxxiv 128) - **OffAr** JA ccliv 440^{3} (cf. also p. 462b; for the reading, cf. Dupont-Sommer JA ccliv 457) - ¶ verbal form: has conformed itself.

ʾnwš v. *ʾnš$_3$*.

ʾnḥ$_1$ **DA** NIPH Part. s.m. abs. *nʾnḥ* ii 12 (cf. Hoftijzer DA p. 236 :: Lemaire CRAI '85, 277: = NIPH Impf. 1 p.pl. :: H.P.Müller ZAW xciv 219, 235: the first *nʾnḥ* = nomen actionis; for the context, cf. also Caquot & Lemaire Syr liv 205) - ¶ verb NIPH to sigh, to moan; a form of this root also in DA viic 2?? (*ʾnḥ*, or l. *ʾnh* = *ʾnh$_3$*??, cf. Hoftijzer DA a.l.).

ʾnḥ$_2$ **OldAr** prob. form of this root (non-verbal form) in KAI 222B 39 (*ʾnḥ*), meaning unknown; Lipiński Stud 43: l. *ʾnh* (= *ʾnh$_2$*(= distress), *lḥm ʾnh* = bread of distress (uncert. reading and interpret.)), cf. also Lemaire & Durand IAS 115, 124, 139f. (div. otherwise): l. poss. *lklkly* (= *l$_5$* + Palp Inf. + suff. 1 p.s. of *kwl$_1$* (= to maintain, to support)).

ʾnḥn$_1$ **Ph** *ʾnḥn* KAI 14^{16,17}, IEJ xxxii 120 (cf. Avigad & Greenfield IEJ a.l., Guzzo Amadasi SEL iv 121f., Lemaire SEL vi 100 :: Catastini FS Bresciani 111f.: l. *ʾnsk* = Sing. abs. of *ʾnsk* (= libation)) - **Hebr** *nḥnw* KAI 194$^{10f.}$ - ¶ personal pronoun, we - cf. also *ʾnḥnw* in Syr xvii 271^{8} (= phoen (?) form in text in Palm. script), cf. also Gawlikowski Syr li 99f. :: Milik DFD 298: = YIPH Impf. 1 p.s. + suff. 3 p.s.m. of *nwḥ$_1$*.
v. *ʾnḥn$_2$*, *hwy$_1$*, *ḥnn$_1$*.

ʾnḥn$_2$ **OffAr** *ʾnḥn* Cowl 1^{2,5}, Krael 3^{3,5,7}, Herm 4^{8}, 6^{9}, B-Sh 35^{4} (heavily dam. context), AE '23, 42 no. 11^{2}, etc., etc., *ʾnḥnh* Cowl 2^{9,11,15}, ATNS 2^{3}, 3^{5}, Samar 4^{8}, 7^{16}, etc., etc. > Akkad. *anī/ēnu*, cf. v.Soden GAG § 41j sub 15, AHW sv. - **JAr** *ʾnḥnh* MPAT 58^{2}, DJD ii 26,2^{2} (no. context), *[ʾ]nhnh* (lapsus?, cf. Milik DJD ii p. 139) MPAT 46^{2} - ¶ personal pronoun, we - Lemaire Syr lxi 341: l. poss. *ʾnḥnh* in ATNS 143^{2} (poss. reading; Segal ATNS a.l.: l. *ṣḥnh* (without interpret.)) - on the form of this word, cf. also Cook Maarav v/vi 61f. (n. 35).
v. *ʾnḥn$_1$*, *ntn*.

ʾnḥnh v. *ʾnḥn$_2$*.

ʾnḥnw v. *ʾnḥn$_1$*.

ʾny$_1$ v. *ʿny$_1$*.

ʾny$_2$ v. *ʾnyʾ*.

ʾny$_3$ **OldCan** Sing. abs. *a-na-ji* EA 245^{28} (cf. Sivan GAG 18, 197) - ¶ subst. boat - Puech RB xc 496: l. poss. *ʾnywt*, Plur. abs. in IEJ xvii 110 l. 2 (highly uncert. reading and interpret.).
v. *ʾnyh*.

ʾny$_4$ **Hebr** *ʾny* TA-H 88^{1}, DJD ii 22,1-9^{4,5}, 24B 6, C 5 (*ʾn[y]*), E 5, H 3, L 6 (heavily dam., no context), 30^{5,6,22,25}, 36,1-2^{1} (dam. context), 43^{3,5}, 48^{3} (*ʾn[y]*), Frey 843, AMB 4^{28,32}, EI xx 256^{5}, *ʾn* EI xx 256^{7} (on the orthography, cf. Broshi & Qimron EI xx 258) - ¶ personal pronoun,

I, me; the *ʾn* in the Ph. texts RES 1308 (= KAI 49[38] :: Kornfeld sub Abydos 11: = n.l.), 1335[1] (= KAI 49[45]; cf. also Kornfeld sub Abydos 14) the same word?? (doubtful, cf. Greenfield Lesh xxxii 360f. n. 8); *ʿmy ʾny* EI xx 256[5] with *me* - Vattioni Aug xvi 543: *ana* in IRT 877[2f.] = personal pronoun 1 p.s. (uncert. interpret., cf. also Levi Della Vida OA ii 87, Röllig KAI ii p. 166) - Vattioni Aug xvi 550: *ana* in IRT 906[5] = personal pronoun 1 p.s. (uncert. interpret., cf. Vattioni AION xvi 51f.: = part of n.p. (cf. also Levi Della Vida OA ii 74: without interpret.)) - Cross FS Glueck 301, 305 nn. 4, 5, 10: l. *[ʾ]ny* before *YHWH* in SSI i p. 58A 1 (uncert. reading, cf. Lipiński OLP viii 93: no traces of signs visible).
v. *ʾzy*, *ʾnh*$_3$, *ʾnk*.

ʾny$_5$ v. *hʾ*$_1$

ʾnyʾ **Nab** word of highly uncert. meaning in IEJ xxix 112[2]; Naveh IEJ xxix 116: perhaps = interjection, Naveh IEJ xxix 114: or = QAL Part. act. s.m. emph. of *ʾny*$_2$(= to ripen)??

ʾnyh this word = boat > Egypt. *ʾi-na-ja(t)*, cf. also Stadelmann SPGA 36.
v. *ʾny*$_2$.

ʾnk **Ph** *ʾnk* KAI 10[1,2], 11, 12[2], 13[1], 14[3], 17[2], 24[1,8], 26A i 1, 6, 43[2], Mus li 286[4,5,6,8], MUSJ xlv 262[1], Kition B 1[1] (= KAI 35), 2[1], 38 (= CIS i 56), etc., etc., *ʾnky* KAI 49[6,7,13], *'lk* KAI 49[15,18,21] (cf. FR 56b), *ʾl* (lapsus?) KAI 49[29], *ʾk*(lapsus?; or l. *ʾn*??, cf. RES 1361) KAI 49[39] - **Pun** *ʾnk* KAI 79[8], CIS i 6000bis 3 (= TPC 84), Punica xviii/i 31[4], *ʾnky* KAI 89[2], cf. Poen 995: *anech* (var. *annech*), Poen 947: *anec* (var. *anehc*), Poen 949: *anec* (var. *enehc*), Poen 1142: *annac* (??, only in Ambrosian s.m., diff. reading and interpret., cf. Sznycer PPP 138, 145; in Palatine mss: *ammac*); for the forms in Poen, cf. FR 111,1, Aartun UF iii 5 - **Mo** *ʾnk* KAI 181[1,2,21-23,25-29] (on this form, cf. Blau Maarav ii 146ff., Garr DGSP 31, Jackson & Dearman SMIM 100) - **Samal** *ʾnk* KAI 214[1], *ʾnky* KAI 215[19] - ¶ personal pronoun, I, me; *bymty ʾnk* KAI 26A ii 5: in my days; *qbry ʾnk ʿbdy* NESE i 3[1]: my tomb, (namely) of me A.; *šm ʾnk yḥwmlk* KAI 10[12]: my name (namely) of me Y., cf. also KAI 43[2] (cf. Röllig KAI a.l., Lane BASOR cxciv 44, cf. however v.d.Branden OA iii 248ff.); for the construction *qṭl ʾnk* (and related ones) in Ph. texts (prob. = Pf. 3 p.s.m. + personal pronoun 1 p.s.), cf. Driver JBL lxxiii 128f., PICS 61ff., Hammershaimb FS Driver 85ff., Hoftijzer BiOr xxiv 29 - cf. also *ʾnwky* in Syr xvii 271[3,4] (= Ph.(?) form in text in Palm. script), cf. Milik DFD 291, Teixidor Syr l. 412, Gawlikowski Syr li 98, Lipiński BiOr xxxiii 233f., AAALT 19 - for the diff. *ʾnk* in the Pun. text BAr-NS i-ii 228 ii 2, v. *ḥnk*$_1$.
v. *ʾmnh*, *ʾnh*$_3$, *ʾny*$_4$, *nʾlk*, *šnh*$_2$.

ʾnky v. *ʾnk,nʾlk.*

ʾns v. *hns.*

ʾnsk v. *ʾnḥn$_1$*

ʾnp$_1$ **Mo** QAL Impf. 3 p.s.m. *yʾnp* KAI 181^{5} - ¶ verb QAL to be angry; *ky yʾn.p. kmš bʾrṣh* KAI 181$^{5f.}$: for Chemosh was angry with his land.

ʾnp$_2$ **OldAr** Sing. cstr. *ʾp* NESE ii 40 ii; Dual cstr. *ʾpy* KAI 222A 28; + suff. 3 p.s.m. *ʾpwh* KAI 224^{2}; + suff. 3 p.s.f. *ʾpyh* KAI 222A 42 (:: Lipiński Stud 50: + suff. 3 p.s.m.) - **OffAr** Sing. + suff. 2 p.pl.m. *ʾnpkm* Sem xxxiii 94^{4} (= RES 1801^{3} = TADAE A 5.1; or = Dual?); Dual abs. *ʾnpyn* Aḥiq 134; cstr. *ʾnpy* KAI 228A 14, Cowl 15^{19}, Aḥiq 14, 101 (*[ʾ]npy*), ATNS 40^{4}; + suff. 3 p.s.m. *ʾnpwhy* Aḥiq 133, 201, 202; + suff. 2 p.s.m. *ʾnpyk* Krael 13^{4}, SSI ii 28 obv. 3, *ʾpyk* Herm 3^{2}; + suff. 2 p.s.f. *ʾpyky* Sem ii 31 conv. 5, Herm 2^{2}, 6^{2}, *ʾpyk* Herm 1^{2}, 4^{2}; + suff. 1 p.s. *ʾnpy* Sem ii 31 conv. 4; + suff. 2 p.pl.f. *ʾpykn* Herm 5^{2}; + suff. 1 p.pl. *ʾnpyn* Cowl 37^{8,9}; cf. Frah x 16 (*ʾnph*), Syn 300^{5}, 301^{6}, 311^{3} - **Palm** Sing. cstr. *ʾp* Inv D 39^{3}; Dual cstr. *ʾpy* CIS ii 3913 ii 102, 105, 135, *ʾpʾ* RB xxxix 526^{3}, 548^{6} - **JAr** Dual cstr. *ʾnpy* MPAT 49,1^{6}; + suff. 3 p.s.m. *ʾpwh* MPAT-A 22^{6} (= SM 70^{14}); + suff. 1 p.s. *npy* (in *bnpy*) MPAT 39^{3} (for another reading of the context, cf. Beyer ATTM 306; on reading and interpret., cf. also Bennett Maarav iv 254f.) - ¶ subst. Sing. - **1)** front, front side; *ʾp krsʾ* NESE ii 40 ii: the front side of the throne; cf. also *ʾp bbʾ* Inv D 39^{3}: the front of the gate (less prob.: in front of the gate, cf. du Mesnil du Buisson a.l., cf. also Röllig NESE ii 41) - **2)** face: Sem xxxiii 94^{4} (for this interpret., cf. Porten Sem xxxiii 97, Porten & Yardeni sub TADAE A 5.1 :: Sznycer HDS 172f.: prob. = anger) - Dual - **1)** nostrils: KAI 224^{2} (v. *bʿy*) - **2)** face: KAI 222A 42, Aḥiq 14, 134 (for a discussion of the context, cf. Lindenberger APA 130f., 257f. nn. 404-406), Sem ii 31 conv. 4f., Herm 1^{2}, 2^{2}, 3^{2}, 4^{2}, 5^{2}, 6^{2}, SSI ii 28 obv. 3, MPAT-A 22^{6} (= SM 70^{14}); *ʾpy dnr* CIS ii 3913 ii 102: (calculate) to a *denarius* (cf. Greek par. l. 181: εἰς δηνάριον), cf. CIS ii 3913 ii 106 (Greek par. l. 183: πρὸς ἀσσάριον ...), 135; *bʾnpy yhwḥnn* MPAT 49,1^{6}: in the presence of Y., cf. Aḥiq 201, MPAT 39^{3}; *lʾpʾ* RB xxxix 526^{3}, 548^{6}: towards; *ʿqhy ʾšh lʾnpy kršn 10* ATNS 40^{4}: pieces of fire-wood at the cost of 10 *k.* (for this prob. interpret., cf. Segal ATNS a.l.); *ʿl ʾnpy ʾrʿʾ* Cowl 15^{19}: on the face of the earth, cf. KAI 222A 28; *mn ʾpy tymʾ* KAI 228A 14f.: (remove) from T. - **3)** anger: Cowl 37^{9}, cf. prob. also Cowl 37^{8} (cf. Sznycer HDS 173, Grelot DAE p. 97 (n. k), Porten & Greenfield JEAS p. 81 × Cowl a.l.: = face, *glyn ʾnpyn* = we had appeared (cf. Porten & Yardeni sub TADAE A 4.2, cf. also Porten & Greenfield JEAS p. 81: or = presence?)) - Altheim & Stiehl Suppl 94f.: in AM ii 174^{3}: l. *mn* (= *mn$_5$*) *b* (= *b$_2$*)-*ʾnpy* (= Dual cstr.) *zy* = in front of, before (uncert. reading & interpret., cf. also Henning AM ii

174).

v. *ʾpn*.

ʾnph **DA** Sing. abs. *ʾnph* i 10 - ¶ subst. type of bird, cormorant? (cf. Hoftijzer DA a.l.), or heron? (cf. Caquot & Lemaire Syr liv 198, McCarter BASOR ccxxxix 51, 55, H.P.Müller ZAW xciv 218).

ʾnš$_1$ v. *ʾnš$_3$*.

ʾnš$_2$ v. *ʾnš$_3$*.

ʾnš$_3$ **Samal** Sing. abs. *ʾnš* KAI 215[23] - **DA** Sing. abs. *ʾnš* ii 10 (cf. Hoftijzer DA p. 232, TUAT ii 146, Rofé SB 68, Dahood Bibl lxii 126, Dijkstra GTT xc 173 :: e.g. Caquot & Lemaire Syr liv 294f. (div. otherwise): l. *yʾnš* = PAʿEL (?) Impf. 3 p.s.m. of *ʾnš$_1$* (= to make kind, to restore friendship), cf. Ringgren Mem Seeligmann 94 :: Garbini Hen i 186: l. *yʾnš* = QAL Impf. 3 p.s.m. of *ʾnš$_1$*(= to be favorable) :: Levine JAOS ci 200f.: l. *yʾnš* = QAL Impf. 3 p.s.m. of *ʾnš$_2$* (= to be mortally ill, wounded; cf. Hackett BTDA 30, 66, 97, 127: = to be weak, to falter); on this subject, cf. also H.P.Müller ZAW xciv 234) - **OldAr** Sing. abs. *ʾnš* KAI 224[16] - **OffAr** Sing. abs. *ʾnš* Cowl 28[8,10], Krael 8[5,8], KAI 228A 20, BSOAS xiii 82[2] (*ʾnš[*, dam. context), *ʾynš* KAI 276[10], *nš* FuF xxxv 173[4] (= ASA 244; diff. context); Sing. emph. *ʾnšʾ* Aḥiq 116 (or Plur. emph.??), 122 (*ʾn[š]ʾ*; or Plur. emph.??), 124 (*ʾn[šʾ]*), 151 (*[ʾn]šʾ*), 162 (or Plur. emph.?), 167 (:: Halévy RS xx 72, Seidel ZAW xxxii 297: l. *ʾlhyʾ* = Plur. emph. of *ʾlh$_1$*), 190 (dam. context); cf. GIPP 49 - **Nab** Sing. abs. *ʾnwš*CIS ii 197[7], 206[3,5,6], 209[5], etc., (cf. Cantineau Nab i 47f.), *ʾlwš*(lapsus?) J 9[4] (= CIS ii 212, cf. Jaussen a.l.) - **Palm** Sing. abs. *ʾnš* CIS ii 3913 i 11, Inv ix 11[6], RIP 105[5] (= Inv xii 17), 199[3] (dam. context), Sem xxvii 117[7]; cstr. *ʾnwš* Inv ix 12a 3 (cf. Cantineau Gramm 51f., Rosenthal Sprache 27) - **Hatra** Sing. abs. *ʾnš* 74[7], 79[12], 293[3]; Plur. emph. *ʾnšʾ* 346[5], 363[3] - **JAr** Sing. abs. *ʾnš* MPAT 59[2], 69[1], Syr xlv 101[18] (dam. context), At xiv 55[1] (diff. context), EI xx 161*; emph. *ʾnšʾ* Mas 556[2] - ¶ subst. m. - **1)** man, person: Krael 8[5], Inv ix 28[2], MPAT 69[1]; + negation, *wlʾ yptḥh ʾnš* RIP 105[4f.]: may no one open it, cf. Hatra 79[12], 293[3]; repeated *ʾnš ʾnš* Sem xxvii 117[7]: every person whosoever - a) *ʾnš zyly* Cowl 28[8]: someone who represents me, cf. Cowl 28[10] (on this and related expressions in Elephantine contracts, cf. Porten & Szubin Maarav iv 58ff.) - b) *kl ʾnwš* CIS ii 206[3,5,6], J 38[7]: everyone, cf. *kl ʾnš mtqwʿ* MPAT 59[2]: everyone from T.; *kwl ʾnšʾ* Mas 556[2]: every person; + negation, no one (whosoever): CIS ii 212[4], cf. EI xx 161* - c) *ʾnwš klh* CIS ii 217[4]: everyone, cf. also *ʾnš kwlh* Hatra 74[6f.]: (prob. translation) everyone (i.e.) every man (cf. also CIS ii 3913 i 13: *kl mʾ gns klh*, any kind of goods whatsoever); + negation, no one (whosoever): CIS ii 209[5], 350[5], J 12[8] - d) someone: CIS ii 197[7], 210[3,5], 3913 i 11; + negation: Krael 8[8], Inv ix 11[6], CIS ii 212[7], 214[5], 219[3],

etc. - e) *br ʾnš*, KAI 224^{16}: someone (cf. e.g. Fitzmyer WA 147), cf. KAI 276$^{9f.}$ - **2)** coll., people, mankind: DA ii 10, Aḥiq 116, 122, 124, 151, 162, 167 (v. however supra: in some instances Plur. form poss.) - a) *qdm ʾlhy wqdm ʾnš* KAI 215^{23}: before gods and men (cf. KAI 228A 20: *ʾlhn wʾnš*, Hatra 346^5: *ʾlhʾ wʾnšʾ*, cf. also Hatra 363^3) - b) *ʾnwš ʿnwštʾ* Inv ix 12^3: the people of the financial administration, i.e. the treasurers (cf. Greek par. οἱ ἀργυροτομίαι) - for the Plur. forms, v. *ʾš$_1$*.
v. *ʾš$_1$*.

ʾnšwt cf. Frah xi 1 (*ʾnšwtʾ*), cf. SaSt 12: mankind, men (cf. also GIPP 16).
v. *ʾš$_1$*.

ʾnt v. *ʾnth$_2$*.

ʾntʾ v. *ʾnth$_2$*.

ʾnth$_1$ v. *ʾš$_1$*.

ʾnth$_2$ s.m. **Ph** *ʾt* KAI 13^3, 14^{4,20} - **Pun** cf. Poen 1017: *etha* (with haplography of *e*: *gadetha* pro *gade etha*, cf. variant *gadectha*, cf. however L.H.Gray AJSL xxxix 82 :: Schroed 296: *gadetha* = Qal Pf. 2 p.s.m. of *gdʿ*(= to garble, to disfigure)), Poen 1142: *ete* (cf. L.H.Gray AJSL xxxix 83; ??, highly uncert. context, cf. Sznycer PPP 145 :: Schroed 298: = *ʾt$_5$* + suff. 3 p.s.m. :: J.J.Glück & Maurach Semitics ii 124 (div. otherwise): l. *eten* = Qal Impf. 1 p.s. of *ntn*) - **Amm** *ʾt* BASOR cclxiv 47^2 (= CAI 144) - **Edom** *ʾt* TeAv xii 97^2 - **Hebr** *ʾth* AMB 3^{18}, 15^{23} - **Samal** *ʾt* KAI 214^{33} (?, diff. and dam. context) - **OldAr** *ʾt* KAI 224^{11,20} - **OffAr** *ʾnt* Cowl 2^{16,17}, 5^{11,14}, Krael 2^{14},3^{11}, 11^{10}, Driv 1^3, 3^7, Beh 52, Samar 1^{7,9} (= EI lxviii 8*), ATNS 26^7, etc., etc., *ʾt* KAI 225^5, 226^8, 233^{2,19}, 259^2 (:: Cross with Hanson BASOR cxcii 11: = *ʾt$_1$*; for poss. haplography involved, v. *šwb$_1$*); cf. Paik 108 (*ʾnt*), GIPP 46 - **Nab** *ʾntʾ* MPAT 64 i 5, 9 (cf. Levinson NAI 27), *ʾnt* DBKP 22^{31} - **Palm** *ʾnt* CIS ii 4199^{4,7} - **JAr** *ʾnth* MPAT 51^{10} (× Fitzmyer & Harrington a.l., Beyer ATTM 320: = lapsus for *ʾnh$_3$*), *ʾnt* MPAT 49 i 9, *ʾth* Syr xlv 101^{22}, *ʾtʾ* Frey 845^5 (cf. Milik DFD 410f.: l. *wʾtʾ* = *w$_1$* + *ʾtʾ* (= *ʾnth$_2$*) × Naveh sub SM 104: l. *wʾtʾ* = *w$_1$* + Qal Pf. 3 p.s.m. of *ʾty$_1$*? :: du Mesnil du Buisson Bibl xviii 170f., Frey a.l.: l. *zʾtʾ* = demonstrative pronoun f.), Mas 556^3 (poss. interpret. :: Yadin & Naveh Mas a.l.: = f. form of *ʾš$_1$* (= woman)), *ʾt* MPAT 60^3 - s.f. **Ph** *ʾt* KAI 50^2 - **OffAr** *ʾnty* Cowl 8^{9,11,12}, Krael 5^{8,10}, 6^{10} (*ʾnt[y]*, for the reading, cf. Porten & Yardeni sub TADAE B 3.7)^{,13} (for the reading, cf. Porten & Yardeni ibid.), 9^{11}, RES 496^1, Sem ii 31 conv. 4, etc., *ʾnt* Krael 9^{14}, KAI 264^{5,6} - **JAr** *ʾnty* MPAT 40^{3,10} (cf. Milik DJD ii p. 108 :: Fitzmyer & Harrington MPAT a.l.: = f. Sing. + suff. 1 p.s. of *ʾš$_1$*), MPAT 40^5 (? × Milik DJD ii p. 108: = f. Sing. + suff. 1 p.s. of *ʾš$_1$* or lapsus for *ʾntty*, cf. also Fitzmyer & Harrington MPAT a.l.), *'nt* MPAT

42^{12} (heavily dam. context), DBKP 20^{41}, *ʾty* MPAT 40^{17}, *ʾt* MPAT 40^{5} - pl.m. **OffAr** *ʾntm* Cowl 21^{4}, 38^{5,6}, Driv 7^{5}, 8^{5}, 10^{4}, ATNS 202 (heavily dam. context), TADAE A 5.5 (dam. context), etc. - **JAr** *ʾtwn* AMB 7^{4} (cf. Naveh & Shaked AMB a.l. :: Dupont-Sommer JKF i 203, 205: l. *ʾtt* = f. Sing. cstr. of *ʾš*$_1$, cf. also Beyer ATTM 372: l. *ʾtt* = lapsus for *ʾḥt* = f. Sing. cstr. of *ʾḥ*$_1$ :: Scholem JGM 86, 88: l. *ʾtt* = QAL Pf. 3 p.s.f. of *ʾty*$_1$), 10^{3} - ¶ personal pronoun, you (s. and pl., m. and f.), *ʾnt šm ṭʿm* Driv 3^{7}: you, issue an order (cf. also Driv 8^{5}, 10^{4}); *bytk ʾnt ʿnny* Krael 12^{17}: your house, sc. (of) you A. (cf. Cowl 25^{8}, 28^{3}); *lky ʾnty mrym* MPAT 40$^{3f.,14}$ (v. supra): you (*l*$_5$ objecti), sc. you M. (cf. also Samar 1^{7,9} MPAT 64 i 5, 9, DBKP 20^{41}); *ʿmk ʾnt* Samar 1^{7}: with *you* (cf. Samar 1^{9}) - Glück & Maurach Semitics ii 124f.: *este* in Poen 1142 = lapsus for *ette* (= personal pronoun 2 p.s.m. (improb. interpret.)) - the reading *ʾth* in the Hebr. text SSI i p. 58B (cf. also Naveh IEJ xiii 85f.) uncert. (cf. Cross FS Glueck 302, 306 n. 13: l. *ʾl* = Sing. abs. of *ʾl*$_1$, Lemaire RB lxxxiii 560f. : pro *hmwryh ʾth* l *pqd*? (= QAL Imper. s.m. of *pqd*$_1$ (= to intervene)) *YHWH*?) - for the constructions *my ʾt, mn ʾt, mn (zy) ʾt, qnmy ʾt*, v. resp. *my*$_1$, *mn*$_4$, *nšṭ*, *qnmy*. v. *mh*$_2$, *nšʾ*$_1$.

ʾntw **OffAr** Sing. abs. *ʾntw* Cowl 14^{4}, 15^{3}, 48^{3}, Krael 2^{3}, 7^{3,37}, 12^{25}; + suff. 3 p.s.f. *ʾntwth* Krael 12^{9a} (original text, half erased, cf. Krael p. 277, Ginsberg JAOS lxxiv 162, Porten & Greenfield JEAS p. 68, Porten & Yardeni sub TADAE B 3.12)^{,18}; + suff. 2 p.s.f. *ʾntwtky* Cowl 35^{5}, Krael 10^{10}, *ʾnttky* Krael 10^{7} (for a *scriptio anterior* *ʾnttky* in the same line, cf. Porten & Szubin JAOS cvii 231) - ¶ subst. f. marriage (< status of married woman, wifehood); for the expression *lʾntw* (Cowl 15^{3}, 48^{3}, Krael 2^{3}, 7^{3}), cf. Fitzmyer FS Albright ii 149, Muffs 6; cf. *spr ʾntwtky* Cowl 35^{5}: your marriage contract, cf. also Krael 10$^{7,9f.}$, 12^{18}, the interpret. of *spr ʾntw* in Cowl 14^{4} depends partly on the interpret. of *nprt* in l. 3, v. *npr*$_2$ (cf. also Porten Arch 222, 247 (n. 21)).

ʾnty v. *ʾnth*$_2$.

ʾntm v. *ʾyt*$_3$, *ʾnth*$_2$.

ʾs$_1$ (< Lat. *as*?) - **Hatra** Sing. abs. *ʾs* 47^{1}, 225^{1} (for the reading, cf. Aggoula MUSJ xlvii 45, Degen JEOL xxiii 412 n. 35, Vattioni IH a.l. :: Degen WO v 229f.: l. *ʾs(kpy)* = Plur. emph. of *ʾskp* (= threshold) or l. *ʾsppy* (cf. also Safar Sumer xxi 39) related to *ʾsp*$_3$ (= portico) :: Milik DFD 167: l. *ʾspky* (epithet derived from n.l.) or *ʾsppy* (epithet either derived from n.l. or < pers. = subst. rider, horseman), 245^{2}, 246^{3}, 292^{7} - ¶ subst. certain weight (14 grammes, cf. Hatra 47)/ certain amount of money; *yhb gd[ʾ] ... ʾs 5 lsgyl* Hatra 246^{1,3}: G. gave ... 5 *as* for the *Segil* - Aggoula MUSJ xlvii 41 (cf. also Vattioni IH a.l.): l. *ʾs* in Hatra 191^{2} (instead of *ʾlm 3 wʾl?* (cf. Caquot Syr xli 267) l. *[s]gyl mn[y]n*

1 (vel: *2*) *wʾs 5* (uncert. reading)) - Aggoula MUSJ xlvii 42: l. *ʾs* in Hatra 192[2] (instead of *d/r lʾm 13* (cf. Caquot Syr xli 268) l. *dy [sgy]l ʾs 8* (poss. reading)) - for Hatra 191, 192, v. also *sgyl*.
v. *ʾsr$_4$*, *ʾstr*.

ʾs$_2$ Ebeling Frah a.l.: in Frah iv 13 l. *ʾsʾ* = myrtle (highly uncertain reading and interpret., cf. also Nyberg FP 66: l. *ʿnytʾ* = lapsus for *ʿnydʾ* (= dead; uncert. interpret.)).

ʾs$_3$ v. *ʿs*.

ʾsgd cf. Frah xix 13 (*ʾsgdh*) = adoration, cf. SaSt 23 s.v.
v. *sgd$_3$*.

ʾsd v. *ʾsr$_1$*.

ʾsw v. *ʾsy$_1$*, *mqlw*.

ʾsḥr v. *ʾtḥr*.

ʾsṭw (< Greek στοά) - **Palm** Sing. emph. *ʾsṭwʾ* CIS ii 3955[4] (*ʾsṭ[wʾ]*), 4168[3], Inv xii 48[1,2], 49[5], RIP 153[2] (*ʾsṭ[w]ʾ*; heavily dam. context); Plur. + suff. 3 p.s.m. *ʾsṭwwhy* Inv xii 48[2], 49[7] (cf. Gawlikowski TP 83, Aggoula Sem xxix 118 :: for both texts du Mesnil du Buisson CRAI '66, 170, 172, Bounni & Teixidor Inv xii a.l.: = Sing. + suff. 3 p.s.m.) - **Hatra** Sing. emph. *ʾsṭwʾ* 290[1] (for the context, cf. Teixidor Sem xxx 64; cf. also Aggoula Syr lxv 204) - ¶ subst. portico, cf. Rosenthal Sprache 73 n. 5 - cf. *sṭwh*.

ʾsṭplyn (< Greek σταφυλῖνος) - **Hebr** Plur. abs. *ʾsṭplyny* SM 49[2] - ¶ subst. Plur. kind of carrot, parsnip, cf. Sussmann Tarb xliii 112.

ʾsṭrbyl (< Greek στρόβιλος) - **Palm** Plur. emph. *ʾsṭrbylyʾ* CIS ii 3913 ii 114 - ¶ subst. pine apple; Greek par. κώνου, cf. Rosenthal Sprache 36 n. 4 - the same word poss. also in EI xv 67*[3] (*ʾstrbls[*; for the reading problems, cf. Cross EI xv a.l.).

ʾsṭrṭg (< Greek στρατηγός, cf. also Rosenthal Sprache 31 n. 5) - **Palm** Sing. abs. *ʾsṭrṭg* CIS ii 3932[2], Syr xiv 179[1]; emph. *ʾsṭrṭgʾ* Inv D 19[1], DFD 37[2], *ʾsṭrgʾ* (lapsus) CIS ii 3939[4] - ¶ subst. m. commander/high official (denoting function not necessarily military, cf. CIS ii sub 3934[4]; *ʾsṭrṭg lqlnyʾ* CIS ii 3932[2] (Greek par. στρατηγήσαντα) and *ʾsṭr<ṭ>gʾ dy qlnyʾ* CIS ii 3939[4] (Greek par. στρατηγὸς τῆς λαμπροτάτης κολωνείας): commander of the Colony = Palmyre; cf. *ʾsṭrṭg ʿl ʿnʾ wgmlʾ* Syr xiv 179[1]: commander of A. and G. - for the function of *strategos* in Palmyre, cf. also Ingholt PBP 124ff.
v. *ʾsrṭg*.

ʾsṭrṭgw (< Greek στρατηγός + suffixed element -*ū*) - **OffAr** Sing. + suff. 3 p.s.m. *ʾsṭrṭg[wth]* Sumer xx 13[3] (cf. Milik DFD 258 :: Safar Sumer xx a.l.: l. *ʾsṭrṭg[wt]* = Sing. cstr., reading *ʾsṭrṭy[* mistake) - **Palm** Sing. cstr. *ʾsṭrṭgwt* Syr xl 47[4f.]; + suff. 3 p.s.m. *ʾsṭrṭgwth* CIS ii

3934[4]; Plur. abs. *ʾsṭrṭgwn* Inv x 44[4] - ¶ subst. f. office of *ʾsṭrṭg*.

ʾsṭrṭwm (< Greek στράτευμα) - **Palm** Sing. emph. *ʾsṭrṭw[mʾ]* CIS ii 3959[4] (= SBS 44B 4, in SBS mistake in transliteration) - ¶ subst. army.

ʾsy$_1$ **JAr** PA‘EL Impf. 3 p.s.m. *[y]ʾsy* AMB 1[13]; Imper. s.m. *ʾsy* AMB 3[20] (:: Naveh & Shaked AMB a.l.: or l. *ʾsw* = Sing. abs. of *ʾsw*(= healing, cure); pl.m. *ʾswn* AMB 3[22] (for the form, cf. Naveh & Shaked AMB a.l.); Inf. *mʾsyh* AMB 2[1] (on the form, cf. Naveh & Shaked AAALT 85); ITP Imper. s.m. *ʾtʾs[y]* AMB 1[10] - ¶ verb PA‘EL to heal: AMB 1[13]; + obj.: AMB 3[22]; + obj. + *mn$_5$* (= from): AMB 2[1f.]; + *l$_5$* (obj.): AMB 3[20] - ITP to be cured + *mn$_5$* (= from): AMB 1[10f.] - L.H.Gray AJSL xxxix 79: l. QAL Imper. pl.m. of the same root (= to console) in Poen 943: *esu* (highly uncert. interpret., cf. Sznycer PPP 126 :: Schroed 291f. (div. otherwise): l. *es* (= Sing. abs. *ʾš$_1$*) + *u(lic)* (= QAL Part. act. s.m. abs. of *hlk$_1$*)) - Février CB viii 32f.: l. *ʾsy* = QAL Pf. 3 p.s.m. + suff. 3 p.s.m. of the same root in Hofra 107[3] (uncert. reading and interpret., cf. Berthier & Charlier Hofra a.l.: l. *wsy*??).

ʾsy$_2$ (< Akkad., cf. Kaufman AIA 37, 158) - **OffAr** Sing. m. emph. *'syʾ* AG 67[1]? - **Nab** Sing. m. emph. *ʾsyʾ* CIS ii 206[1] - **Palm** Sing. m. emph. *ʾsyʾ* CIS ii 4513[2], Ber ii 90[2], 97[1], 98[1], 99 ii 1, v 120[2] (Greek par. ἰατρός), Inv xii 45[4] - ¶ subst. m. physician - the *ʾšyʾ* in Hatra 92 = Sing. m. emph. of *ʾšy* (= *ʾsy$_2$*)??, cf. e.g. Caquot Syr xl 9, Vattioni IH a.l.

ʾsyw **JAr** Sing. + suff. 3 p.s.m. *ʾsywth* AMB 1[15] (or = Sing. emph.?),[18] (or = Sing. emph.?) - ¶ subst. cure, recovery.
v. *mqlw*.

ʾskp v. *ʾs$_1$*.

ʾsm$_1$ **Hebr** QAL (?, or PI‘EL?, cf. e.g. Weippert FS Rendtorff 465) Pf. 3 p.s.m. *ʾsm* KAI 200[5] (cf. Delekat Bibl li 462, Lemaire Sem xxi 68, Pardee Maarav i 42f., HAHL 21, 237, Garr DGSP 183f. × Cross BASOR clxv 44f. n. 43, Naveh Lesh xxx 70, Röllig KAI a.l., Gibson SSI i p. 29, Solá-Solé IS 90: = QAL (?) Inf. abs. (cf. also Amusin & Heltzer IEJ xiv 151f. n. 7, Booij BiOr xliii 643, Weippert FS Rendtorff 464 n. 40) :: Naveh IEJ x 134: = QAL Impf. 1 p.s. :: Yeivin BiOr xix 4 (div. otherwise): l. *ʾsmk* = QAL Part. act. s.m. + suff. 2 p.s.m. :: Albright ANET 568 (n. 5): = Sing. abs. of *ʾsm$_2$* (= storage of grain) :: Garbini AION xxii 99ff.: = Sing. abs. of *'sm$_2$* (= certain quota of grain)), KAI 200[6f.] (× Booij BiOr xliii 643: = QAL Inf. abs. :: Yeivin and Garbini interpreting the form as in l. 5) - ¶ verb QAL (?) to gather, to store (grain) - on this word, cf. also Borowski AIAI 71ff.
v. *ʾsm$_2$*.

ʾsm$_2$ v. *ʾsm$_1$*; Garbini AION xxii 99ff. interprets *ʾsm* in KAI 200[4] also as *ʾsm*$_2$, improb. interpret., prob. part of n.l. *ḥṣr-ʾsm* (v. also *ḥm*$_2$).

ʾsn (< Akkad., cf. Zimmern Fremdw 54) - **OffAr** Plur. abs. *ʾsnyn* Del 92 (= Eph ii 201D; cf. also Akkad. par.) - ¶ subst. date from Telmun, date palm.

ʾsnb v. *snb*.

ʾsnl Ebeling Frah a.l.: the *ʾsnl* in Frah xxvii 5 = day before yesterday, cf. Akkad. *am/nšala-a/i* (less prob. interpret., cf. Nyberg FP 56, 106: l. Iran. word).

ʾsp$_1$ **Ph** QAL Part. pass. s.m. abs. *ʾsp* MUSJ xlv 262[1] (or: *znʾsp* = haplography for *zn nʾsp* (= NIPH Part. s.m. abs.)?) - **Pun** NIPH Pf. 3 p.pl. *nʿspʾ* Punica xiv 3[4] - ¶ verb QAL to gather; Part. pass. (v. however supra) gathered (said of dead body in a coffin.); *ʾnk škb bʾrn zn ʾsp bmr* ... MUSJ xlv 262[1]: I am lying in this coffin gathered in myrrh ... (cf. however also Cross IEJ xxix 41: prepared for burial in myrrh) - NIPH to be gathered + *b*$_2$ (said of bones in a grave): Punica xiv 3[4f.] - a form of the NIPH of this root prob. also in KAI 161[6]: *nʿsp* (for this reading, cf. Février RA xlv 143f. :: v.d.Branden RSF ii 144: = NIPH Pf. 3 p.s.m. of *ysp* :: Berger RA ii 36 (div. otherwise): l. *nʿzk*?); for an interpret., cf. Février RA xlv 144, Roschinski Num 112, 115. v. *ʾsp*$_2$, *ysp*, *nʾsph*.

ʾsp$_2$ **Hebr** Sing. abs. *ʾsp* KAI 182[1] (:: Segal JSS vii 219: = QAL Imper. s.m. of *ʾsp*$_1$?) - ¶ subst. ingathering (sc. of agricultural produce); in the context of KAI 182[1] prob. of grapes and olives (cf. Gibson SSI i p. 3, cf. also Cassuto SMSR xii 109, Talmon JAOS lxxxiii 183 n. 46, Conrad TUAT i 247, Smelik HDAI 27; less prob. Albright BASOR xcii 22 n. 30: ingathering of olives (cf. also Borowski AIAI 32, 34; cf. also Dalman i/2, 552ff., iii 77, 197).

ʾsp$_3$ v. *ʾs*$_1$.

ʾsp$_4$ **Hatra** Aggoula Syr lxii 368: l. *ʾsp* (= Sing. cstr. of *ʾsp*$_4$ = group (cf. *sp*$_3$)) + *pṭʾ* (= Sing. of *pṭʾ* < Iran. (= chef, master)) in Hatra 382, *ʾsp pṭʾ* = prefect :: Al-Nagafi Sumer xxxix 197, 198 n. 31: = epithet: rider, horseman.

ʾsph v. *ysp*, *nʾsph*, *ʿbr*$_1$.

ʾspk(y) v. *ʾs*$_1$.

ʾsply (< Greek ἀσφάλεια) - **JAr** Sing. emph. *ʾsplyʾ* MPAT 53[2] - ¶ subst. assurance, bond, pledge; exact meaning of *bʾsplyʾ* in MPAT 53[2] diff. to establish because of dam. context (Beyer ATTM 351, 519: = under strict care (cf. van Bekkum SV 122)); cf. also Kutscher Lesh xxv 119, Fitzmyer CBQ xxxii 523.

ʾsppy v. *ʾs*$_1$, *ʾsp*$_4$.

ʾsprn (< Iran., cf. Driv p. 76, Benveniste JA ccxlii 304, Cazelles Syr xxxii 100, Nober EB xvi 393ff., xix 111f., Bibl xxxix 195* no. 3269, Ellenbogen 33f., Altheim & Stiehl ASA 141, Cameron JNES xvii 173f., Hinz AISN 246, Cook Maarav v/vi 66; on this word, cf. also Rosenthal Forschung 25) - **OffAr** *ʾsprn* KAI 263 (= CIS ii 108), Driv 10^{4}, *ʾsprnʾ* RA i 67 - ¶ adv. exact, completely, in full amount; *ʾsprn lqbl zy stryʾ zy kspʾ* KAI 263: (a weight) exactly corresponding to the (weight of) silver staters (v. also *str$_3$*); *ʾsprn whdʾbgw* Driv $10^{4f.}$: completely and with interest.

ʾsprng **OffAr** Word of unknown meaning (Plur. emph. *ʾsprngyʾ*) in ATNS 43b ii 4 (Segal ATNS a.l.: = quince, cf. also Zadok WO xvi 175).

ʾsr$_1$ **Ph** QAL Pf. 3 p.s.m. *ʾsr* Syr xlviii 396^{2} (:: Cross CBQ xxxvi 488 (n. 19): = QAL Part. s.m. abs./cstr.) - **Mo** QAL Part. pass.m. pl. cstr. *ʾsry* KAI $181^{25f.}$ (uncert. reading; :: Andersen Or xxxv 107f.: = PI ʿEL Inf. cstr. + suff. 1 p.s., cf. also Dahood FS Horn 436f. :: Lipiński Or xl 337f.: = QAL Inf. cstr. + ending *-y*, cf. also de Geus SV 28) - **Hebr** QAL Part. act. pl.m. abs. *ʾwsryn* SM 49^{24}; pass. s.m. abs. *ʾswr* SM 49^{9}; pl.m. abs. *ʾswryn* SM $49^{1,19}$; pl.f. abs. *ʾswrwt* SM $49^{9,11}$; NIPH Part. m. s. abs. *nʾsr* SM 49^{13} - **OldAr** QAL Impf. 3 p.s.m. *yʾsr* KAI 224^{18} (× Dupont-Sommer Sf p. 34, Rosenthal BASOR clviii 30: poss. = QAL Impf. pass., cf. also Degen AAG p. 71 n. 62); Imper. s.m. + suff. 3 p.s.m. *ʾsrh* KAI 224^{18} - **OffAr** QAL Pf. 3 p.s.m. + suff. 1 p.s. *ʾsrny* Cowl 38^{3}; 3 p.pl.m. *ʾsrw* TADAE A 4.6^{16}; + suff. 3 p.s.m. *ʾsrwhy* Cowl 69A 3, *ʾsrhy* KAI 279^{7} (cf. Altheim & Stiehl EW x 246, GH ii 174f., ASA 29, 266, GMA 351f., Koopmans 177, Kutscher, Naveh & Shaked Lesh xxxiv 135, Levine JAOS lxxxvii 186f. :: Dupont-Sommer JA ccxlvi 30f., Donner KAI a.l., Garbini Kand 16, Teixidor Syr xlvi 349, Segert AAG p. 308 (on Segert, cf. Degen GGA '79, 39f.): = QAL Pf. 3 p.s.m. + suff. 3 p.s.m. :: Altheim & Stiehl EW ix 197, GH 405: l. *ysrhy* = PA ʿEL Pf. 3 p.pl.m. + suff. 3 p.s.m. of *ysr$_1$* = (to warn) :: Levine JAOS lxxxvii 186f.: or = Sing. + suff. 3 p.s.m./pl. of *ʾsr$_3$* (= prohibition), cf. also Levi Della Vida Editto 27 :: Rosenthal EI xiv 98*: l. perhaps *ʾsdhy* = subst. *ʾsd*(= foundation) + suff. 3 p.s. (ideogrammatic)); Part. act. s.m. abs., cf. Warka 5, 8: *a-si-ir* (cf. Gordon AfO xii 106 n. 9 × Garbini HDS 33: = Part. act. s.m. cstr.); QAL pass. Pf. 3 p.pl.m. *ʾsyrw* Cowl 56^{3} (for the reading, cf. Porten & Greenfield JEAS p. 84, Porten & Yardeni sub TADAE A 4.4 :: Cowl a.l.: l. poss. *ʾzybw* = n.p.); Part. pass.m. pl. abs. *ʾsyrn* Cowl 64 xxix 1, *ʾsrn* ATNS 50^{9}; pl.m. emph. *ʾsyryʾ* AM ii 171 i 3, ii 2 (cf. Henning AM ii a.l.; uncert. interpret. × Shaked BSOAS xxvii 287: = n.p.; cf. also Altheim & Stiehl Suppl 92, ASA 266, AAW i 653f.: = QAL part pass. (= servant, retainer)); pl.f. abs. *[ʾ]syrn* Cowl 34^{3}; ITP Impf. 3 p.s.m. *ytsr* Aḥiq 80 (cf. Cowl a.l., Leand 3f. (cf. also Kottsieper SAS 42, 50, 145) :: Barth OLZ '12, 11: l. *ytsd* = ITP Impf.

3 p.s.m. of *sdd* (= to be put in the stocks) :: Sach p. 160, Grelot RB lxviii 180: preferably ITP from *ysr*$_1$ = to be corrected, to be punished; on this form, cf. also Lindenberger APA 46f., 222f. nn. 17-25); cf. Frah xx 17 (*ʾslwn*), Paik 116 (*ʾsr*), 117 (*ʿslwn*), GIPP 19, 47 - **Palm** QAL Pf. 3 p.pl.m. *ʾsrw* Syr xvii 351^{12} (dam. and diff. context, cf. Cantineau Syr xvii 352, Milik DFD 304 :: Gawlikowski TP 57: l. *ʾmrw* = QAL Pf. 3 p.pl.m. of *ʾmr*$_1$); Part. pass.m. pl. emph. *ʾsyrʾ* CIS ii 3913 i 10 (cf. transcription (Ῥαβ)ασείρη in Greek par.) - ¶ verb QAL to bind; used with the following shades of meaning - a) to harness; *ʾsr mrkbty* Syr xlviii 396^2: he harnessed his chariot (:: Garbini OA xx 288, 292: *ʾsr* = he closed, v. also *mrkbh*) - b) to bind, sc. magically; *pa-tu-ú-ri a-si-ir li-iš-ša-an* Warka 5, 8: the tablet that binds the tongue (cf. Landsberger AfO xii 254f. :: Dupont-Sommer RA xxxix 39: the tablet of the one who binds the tongue) - c) to imprison + obj.: KAI 224^{18}, Cowl 38^3, 69A 3 - d) to bind someone (sc. to do something): KAI 279^7, v. *ʾyk* (cf. also Dupont-Sommer JA ccxlvi 30f., Kutscher, Naveh & Shaked Lesh xxxiv 135 (cf. also Altheim & Stiehl GH ii 176) :: Teixidor Syr xlvi 349: = to forbid) - e) to forbid + obj.: SM 49^{24} - f) exact meaning diff. to establish in Syr xvii 351^{12}, poss. = to determine, to oblige, cf. Cantineau a.l., Milik DFD 304 - QAL pass. to be imprisoned: Cowl 56^3 (v. supra); Part. pass. - a) prisoner: KAI $181^{25f.}$ (cf. however supra; cf. also Andersen Or xxxv 107), Cowl 34^3 (v. supra), 64 xxix 1; cf. *byt ʾsrn* ATNS 50^9: prison; cf. also *rb ʾsyrʾ* CIS ii 3913 i 10, *hyklʾ dy rb ʾsyrʾ* prob.: = the temple of R. (cf. Greek par. [ἱ]ερ[οῦ] λεγομένου Ῥαβασείρη, prob. = the temple of (the god) called R.), *rb ʾsyrʾ* prob. = the lord of the enchained ones (cf. e.g. Pognon ISMM 84 n. 2, du Mesnil du Buisson CRAI '66, 176f., Milik Syr xliv 300, Teixidor Syr xlv 359f., xlvii 377); this meaning also in *ʾsrtʾ* (= QAL. Part. pass. s.f. emph.?) in the Nab. text ADAJ xxvi 366^2 (dam. context)?? (Zayadine ADAJ xxvi 366f.: = concubine) - b) forbidden: SM $49^{9,11,19}$; cf. *hpyrwt hllw ʾswryn b...* SM 49^1: these fruits are forbidden in ... - NIPH to be forbidden: SM 49^{13} - ITP prob. meaning to be subjected to binding obligations :: Cowl p. 222, Ginsberg ANET 428: to be taught - a form of this root (*ʾsrn* = QAL Part. pass. m. pl. abs.) in ATNS 3^1 (uncert. interpret., heavily dam. context) .

v. ʾsr_3

ʾsr_2 v. ʿsr_1.

ʾsr_3 **OffAr** Sing. emph. *ʾsrʾ* Samar 1^{11} (= EI xviii 8*), $2^{4,6,10}$, 3^9, 7^{11}; + suff. 3 p.s.f. *ʾsrh* ATNS 8^{10} (for this poss. reading, cf. Porten & Yardeni sub TADAE B 5.6 :: Segal ATNS a.l.: l. *ʾḥw[h]y* (= Sing. + suff. 3 p.s.m. of *ʾḥ*$_1$); Plur. abs. *ʾsrn* ATNS 3^1 (cf. Porten & Yardeni sub TADAE B 8.10 :: Segal ATNS a.l.: = QAL Part. pass. pl.m. abs.

of *ʾsr*$_1$), 30a 5 (cf. Porten & Yardeni sub TADAE B 8.4 :: Segal ATNS a.l.: or = QAL Part. pass.m. pl. abs. of *ʾsr*$_1$); emph. *ʾsryʾ* ATNS 8^{10} (cf. Porten & Yardeni sub TADAE B 5.6 :: Segal ATNS a.l.: = QAL Part. pass. pl.m. emph. of *ʾsr*$_1$)- ¶ subst. bond, covenant. v. *ʾsr*$_1$.

ʾsr$_4$ (< Greek ἀσσάριον) - **Palm** Sing. abs. *ʾsr* CIS ii 3913 ii 105, 133, 135; emph. *ʾsrʾ* CIS ii 3913 ii 42, 69, 73: Plur. abs. *ʾsyrn* CIS ii 3913 ii 12, 47, 49, 50, 52. etc. - ¶ subst. certain coin (cf. Greek ἀσσάριον, Lat. *as*); cf. *ʾsr ʾtlq[ʾ]* CIS ii 3913 ii 105, 133: the Italian *as* (as distinguished from the Greek ἀσσάριον, cf. Cooke NSI p. 336, cf. Greek par. ἀσσάριον ἰτα[λικὸν]; cf. also Ben-David PEQ '71, 112ff., Teixidor Sem xxxiv 81
v. *ʾs*$_1$.

ʾsr$_5$ v. *ʿšr*$_5$.

ʾsrṭ (prob. < Greek στρατός) - **Hebr/JAr** Plur. abs. *ʾsrṭyn* Mas 611^1 (*ʾsrṭy[n]*)^{,2} - ¶ subst. soldier or band, cf. Yadin & Naveh Mas a.l.

ʾsrm v. *ʿšrm*.

ʾsrtg (< Greek στρατηγός) - **Nab** Sing. emph. *ʾstrgʾ* CIS ii 160^2, $161^{3,6}$, $195^{2,4}$, 196^2, etc., *ʾsrtygʾ* CIS ii 238^1 (cf. however J 61: l. *ʾstrgʾ*), *ʾsrtwgʾ* CIS ii 287 (cf. however J 84: l. *ʾsrtgʾ*), *ʾstrtgʾ* CIS ii 319a (uncert. reading); Plur. emph. *ʾsrtgyʾ* CIS ii 235A 2 (on the Nab. material, cf. also Levinson NAI 131) - ¶ subst. commander/high official, cf. Starcky RB lxiv 201ff., Negev RB lxxxiii 223ff., Peters JAOS xcvii 267 - the *ʾ*. in J 216 poss. = abbrev. of *ʾsrtg*.
v. *ʾsṭrṭg*.

ʾst v. *z*$_1$.

ʾstwdn (< Iran., cf. Shaked with Hanson BASOR cxcii 7 n. 9, Hinz AISN 47) - **OffAr** Sing. emph. *[ʾ]stwdnh* KAI 262 - ¶ subst. m. grave (the Iran. original = bone-container, the word in KAI 262 refers to rock tomb; Greek par. τάφον; cf. also Lipiński Stud 163f.).

ʾstr$_1$ (< Greek στάτηρ?, cf. Degen JEOL xxiii 410) - **Hatra** Sing. abs. (?) *ʾstr[*- ¶ subst. *stater* (cf. for this text also Aggoula MUSJ xlvii 14); *ʾs*$_1$perhaps abbrev. of this word??
v. *str*$_3$, *sttr*, *sttry*.

ʾstr$_2$ v. *ʾštr*.

ʾstrbls v. *ʾsṭrbyl*.

ʾstrtg v. *ʾsrtg*.

ʾʿ v. *ʿṣ*.

ʾʿšr v. *ʿšr*$_5$.

ʾp$_1$ v. *ʾnp*$_2$.

ʾp$_2$ **Ph** KAI 14^6, 26A i 12, iii 14, C iv 16, 50^2, EpAn ix $5^{3,\ 5}$, C 1 - **Pun** CIS i 169^2, KAI 162^4 (?, uncert. context), Hofra 277^4 (??), StudMagr vii 12[4] (?, dam. context) - **Hebr** DJD ii 42[5], *’wp* SM 49[20] - **OffAr** Cowl 4[2,3], 6[7], 7[10], Krael 4[13,18], 7[36,39], Driv 5[2], 7[2,4,5], Herm 2[11,12], 5[3], RES 1792B 8, JRAS ’29, 108[13], AG 90, KAI 273[11], 279[3], Sem xxxiii 94[4,6] (= RES 1808 = TADAE A 5.1), FX 136[19], NESE i 11[3], Beh 54 (for the context, cf. Porten & Greenfield BIDG p. 49), Samar 6[8] (dam. context), ATNS 7[2], 26[12], 36[1] (*scriptio anterior*, uncert. reading), etc., etc.; cf. Paik 120-123, ZDMG xcii 442A 14, Sogd ii 208, R ii 44, Ve 105, ML 576, GIPP 16, SaSt 12 (cf. also Lemosín AO ii 265, 267; Ebeling Frah a.l.: l. this word in Frah xxiv 6, 14 (less prob. interpret., cf. Nyberg FP 54f., 101: l. Iran. word)) - **Palm** CIS ii 3913 ii 46, 47, 53, 68, 93, 113, 3917[3,4], SBS 48B 7, Inv xii 48[2], etc. - ¶ conj. also, moreover, even, passim, cf. also v.d.Branden GP § 312b, 322,5 - for special usage, cf. - **1)** introducing a repetition, *zn’ byt’ .... ’nh ‘nny yhbth lyhwyšm‘ ... ’p yhbt lh* Krael 9[16ff.]: this house ... I, A., gave it to Y. ... surely I have given it to her ... - **2)** having a meaning almost identical with the copula *w_2*: and, e.g. Cowl 31[7] - **3)** *’p ... ’p, hlw mnyn hmw ’p lḥm ’p qmḥ* JRAS ’29, 108[12f.]: behold, they count and bread and wheat - **4)** *’p ’m* and *’m ’p*, even if/moreover if; *’p ’m ’dmm ydbrnk ’l tšm‘* KAI 14[6]: even if people speak to you (sc. press the point with you), you must not listen; *w’m mlk bmlkm .... ’š ymḥ šm ’ztwd ... wšt šm ’m ’p yḥmd ’yt hqrt z* KAI 26A iii 12ff.: and if there is a king among the kings ... who wipes out the name of A. ... and puts his (own) name (in place), moreover if he covets this town ... (cf. KAI 26C iv 16) - **5)** *’p ... w, ’p yhkwn bdyn wl’ yṣdqwn* Cowl 10[19]: even, should they go to law, they shall not win their case - **6)** *’p zy* in KAI 279[3], JA ccliv 440[2] (*[’]p zy*), prob. = ’p_2 perhaps with some added emphasis, cf. Dupont-Sommer JA ccxlvi 25f., Shaked JRAS ’69, 120, Kutscher, Naveh & Shaked Lesh xxxiv 133, Rosenthal EI xiv 97* (cf. also Dupont-Sommer JA ccliv 455), for other less prob. interpret., cf. Altheim & Stiehl EW x 244f., GH i 400, ii 171f., ASA 26f., GMA 348f., Nober VD xxxvii 375, Levi Della Vida Editto 23, 34; also *’p zy* in ATNS 43a i 5, context however heavily damaged (cf. also Segal ATNS a.l.: or = n.p.?) - Lidzbarski Eph i 48: *p* in KAI 145[2] (*pḥnt*) = ’p_2 (cf. Cooke NSI p. 152f., Röllig KAI a.l., FR 29e; uncert. interpret.), for other interpret., cf. Halévy RS ix 270 (*pḥnt* = orthographical variant of *pnt*, cf. also v d.Branden RSF i 166f., Krahmalkov RSF iii 190), Février Sem vi 17 (:= p_1) - this word also in KAI 43[14]?, cf. Lipiński RTAT 251 (n. 33) :: v.d.Branden OA iii 259 (div. otherwise): l. *’pdt* = Plur. abs. of *’pdh* = (sheathing) - for a poss. reading *w’p* (*w’p šty* instead of *r’m šty*) in KAI 279[3], v. *šty*$_3$ - Rocco StudMagr vii a.l.: l. *’p* in StudMagr vii 12[4] (highly uncert. reading and interpret.).

v. *’pl*$_2$, *’pm*, *pḥnt*, *rwm*$_1$.

ʾp3 v. *ʾyph.*

ʾpgnzbr (< Iran., cf. R.A.Bowman Pers p. 30, 63, Hinz AISN 243) - **OffAr** Sing. emph. *ʾpgnzbrʾ* Pers 13[4], 14[4], 26[5], 28[5], 31[5], 32[5], 33[5], 36[2], etc. - ¶ subst. sub-treasurer; for this function, cf. R.A.Bowman Pers p. 30ff., Naveh & Shaked Or xlii 448ff., Bernard StudIr i 167f., Hinz FS Nyberg 374, cf. also Harnack with Altheim & Stiehl GMA 547.
v. *gnz*, *gnzbr*.

ʾpdh v. *ʾp2*.

ʾpdyʿ v. *ʾpryʿ*.

ʾpdt v. *ʾp2*.

ʾph v. *ʾyph.*

ʾpw **OffAr** Aḥiq 52, 140 - ¶ adv. used to underline the clause (:: Cowl a.l., p. 221, 232, Beyer ATTM 106 n. 1, 520: = also); *lqbl zy ʾnh ʿbdt lk kn ʾpw ʿbd ly* Aḥiq 52: according as I did to you, treat me in just the same way; *wmn ʾpw ṣdqny* Aḥiq 140: who then has justified me?; cf. Joüon MUSJ xviii 12: < Hebr.?, cf. however Lindenberger APA 138, 261 n. 435.

ʾpwḥs **OffAr** Krael 13[2] - ¶ prob. subst., meaning unknown (dam. context), cf. also Grelot DAE p. 421 n. b.

ʾpwn **Hebr** Plur. abs. *ʾpwnyn* SM 49[4] - ¶ subst. m. bean; *hʾpwnyn hgmlwnyn* SM 49[4]: the large-sized beans, cf. Sussmann Tarb xliii 113.

ʾpwnzh **OffAr** word(?) of unknown meaning in ATNS 145.

ʾpwtyqy (< Greek ἀποθήκη, cf. Torrey Syn 276) - **JAr** Sing. abs. *ʾpwtyqy* Syn D 275 no. 22[2] (= SM 103; reading uncert.) - ¶ subst. prob. indicating function; Torrey Syn 275f.: = commissary (of army), or person in charge of some important repository, cf. also Ellis & Ingholt Syn 457; Naveh sub SM 103: = pawn-broker.

ʾpṭrp (< Greek ἐπίτροπος) - **Palm** Sing. emph. *ʾpṭrpʾ* CIS ii 3938[2], 3939[1], 3940[1], 3943[2] - **JAr** Sing. emph. *ʾp[ṭrpʾ]* MPAT 62[12] (= DBKP 27; cf. ἐπίτροπος in Greek part of the text l. 16, cf. EI viii 50), *ʾpṭpʾ* (prob. lapsus) DBKP 20[41] - ¶ subst. m. - **1)** guardian: MPAT 62[12], DBKP 20[41] - **2)** *procurator*, high administrator of Roman Empire, in the Palm. texts in the combination *ʾpṭrpʾ d(w)qnrʾ*, *procurator ducenarius* i.e. *procurator* receiving a salary of 200.000 sesterces (an imperial revenue officer), cf. *ʾpṭrpʾ dqnrʾ* CIS ii 3940[1f.] with Greek par. ἐπίτροπον Σεβαστοῦ δουκηνάριον (cf. CIS ii 3943; cf. also *ʾpṭrpʾ dwqnrʾ dy qsr mrn* CIS ii 3938[2f.], Greek par. ἐπί[τρ]οπον [Σεβ]αστο[ῦ τοῦ κυριοῦ] δουκη[νάριον].
v. *ʾpyṭrpy.*

ʾpy **Ph** Qal Pf. 3 p.pl. *ʾp* KAI 37A 10; Part. act. pl.m. abs. *ʾpm* KAI 37A 10 (for the reading in both instances, cf. Peckham Or xxxvii 313f.,

cf. also Masson & Sznycer RPC 48, Healy BASOR ccxvi 55, Amadasi sub Kition C1 A 9, Delcor UF xi 155f., Gibson SSI iii p. 124, 128 :: CIS i sub 86A 9: l. resp. *ʾšm* (= Plur. abs. of *ʾš*$_1$) and *ʾm*$_6$(meaning unknown), cf. Cooke NSI p. 67, Lidzbarski sub KI 29, Röllig KAI a.l., cf. also v.d.Branden RSF ii 141f.: l. *ʾšm* and *ʾm* (= QAL Pf. 3 p.pl. of *ʾmm*(= to hit)) - **OldAr** QAL Impf. 3 p.pl.f. *lʾpn* Tell F 22 (for the form, cf. Kaufman Maarav iii 150, Huehnergard BASOR cclxi 94, ZDMG cxxxvii 275 (n. 31) :: Andersen & Freedman FS Fensham 38: prob. = *l*$_1$ + Pf. 3 p.pl.f.) - **OffAr** Ebeling Frah a.l.: l. *ʾppwn* in Frah xix 9 < root *ʾpy*, cf. however Nyberg FP 50, 91: l. *ḥppwn* < *ḥpp*$_2$ (= to cover) - ¶ verb QAL to cook, to bake; *lʾpn btnwr lḥm* Tell F 22: may they bake bread in an oven (cf. Kaufman Maarav iii 170) - Zauzich & Röllig Or lix 327ff.: the *ʾph* in Or lix 325[3] poss. = QAL Part. act. s.m. abs. of *ʾpy* (highly uncert. interpret.).
v. *ʾnh*$_3$, *br*$_1$, *hlk*$_1$.

ʾpyṭrpy (< Greek ἐπιτροπεία) - **Nab** Sing. emph. *ʾpyṭrpyʾ* J 302 - p subst. function of ἐπίτροπος (v. *ʾpṭrp*), in this text military function, cf. Negev RB lxxxiii 227, cf. also Clermont-Ganneau RAO vii 305ff.

ʾpylw **Hebr** SM 49[21] - ¶ conj. however.

ʾpyty (derivation from Akkad. less prob., cf. Kaufman AIA 35, cf. also Grelot DAE p. 287 n. m :: Cowl p. 94) - **OffAr** Cowl 26[9] - ¶ adv. or adj.?, meaning unknown; poss. interpret.: immediately, cf. Cowl a.l., cf. also Torczyner OLZ '12, 399, Leand 61m (cf. however Grelot DAE p. 287 (n. m), 288 (n. r): = necessary, cf. also Porten & Yardeni sub TADAE A 6.2; cf. also Whitehead JNES xxxvii 133 n. 90: = required).

ʾpk **OffAr** QAL Impf. 3 p.s.m. *yʾpk* Aḥiq 156; Part. act. s.m. emph. (or = noun of *qattāl*-type? (cf. also Kottsieper SAS 190)) *ʾpkʾ* Aḥiq 156 - ¶ verb QAL to twist, to distort; + obj., *yʾpk ʾl pm ʾpkʾ* Aḥiq 156: God will distort the mouth of the liar, cf. Greenfield HDS 51f., 56ff., cf. also Driver AnOr xii 56, Grelot RB lxviii 190, DAE p. 444; Part. act. liar, treacherous one, perverse one Aḥiq 156; // of *hpk*? (cf. e.g. Lindenberger APA 156f., 264 n. 468, 265 n. 472, cf. also Tropper UF xxi 423 n. 18).

ʾpkl (prob. < Sum., via Akkad.? (cf. Zimmern Fremdw 29, Rosenthal Sprache 90) or via Arab.? (cf. Cantineau Gramm 150, cf. also Kaufman AIA 34)) - **Nab** Sing. abs. *ʾpkl* RB xlii 411[3]; cstr. *ʾpkl* BIA x 58[1] (?, dam. context; for the reading, cf. Teixidor Syr xlvii 378, Milik BIA a.l. :: Altheim & Stiehl AAW v/2, 25 (div. otherwise): l. –ʾ *wkl*); emph. *ʾpklʾ* CIS ii 198[8] (:: Levinson NAI 74, 174: l. *ʾkplʾ*(= twice)), 2674[1] (reading *ʾkplʾ* mistaken, cf. Negev IEJ xxvii 224), RHR lxxx 4[8], *ʾkplʾ* CIS ii 2188[1], 2660[2], 2667[1], 2672[2], 2673[2], 2677[1], 2678[1f.], 2714[1] (*ʾkpl[ʾ]*), EI x 184 no. 33[2], IEJ xxvii 227 no. 24[2], xxix 220 (cf. Cantineau Nab i 41) - **Palm** Sing. emph. *ʾpklʾ* CIS ii 3974[2], 4064[5] (*ʾpkl[ʾ]*), 4065[4] (*ʾ[pk]lʾ*), RTP 116 (poss. reading *ʾp[k]lʾ*, cf. Milik DFD 157) - **Hatra** Sing. emph. *ʾpk[l]ʾ* 67[3], 345[4], 352[2], 361[1] (poss. also in Hatra 33, cf. Teixidor Syr xliii 92) - ¶ subst. m. title of religious functionary, priest (cf. Jaussen RB xx 554, cf. Lidzbarski Eph i 203: = celibate priest? :: Savignac RB xlii 412: the foremost religious authority of the nation (cf. Hatra 67: *ʾpk[l]ʾ rbʾ dʾlhʾ* (cf. also Hatra 361[1f]), Hatra 345[4f]: *ʾpklʾ rbʾ dšmš ʾlhʾ*); cf. also Gawlikowski TP 112; *ʾpkl ʾlhʾ* BIA x 58[1f.]: the priest of I.; *ʾpkl[ʾ dy] mṣb ʿynʾ* CIS ii 4064[5f.]: the priest of the stele of the source, sc. the source Ephka (cf. also CIS ii 4065[4]; cf. Gawlikowski Sem xxiii 119); for Arabic par., cf. G.Ryckmans Les rel. Arab. préisl 20, 30, Borger Or xxvi 8ff.; cf. also for Hatra, Teixidor Syr xliii 91ff.; cf. however also Aggoula Syr lxiii 354: judge (interpretation as priest impossible) - Milik DFD 158: l. poss. in RTP 610: *ʾp[k]ly[ʾ]* (Plur. emph.; highly uncert. reading) - Milik ADAJ xxi 144 n. 3: l. *[ʾ]pkl[ʾ]* in Nab. text RB xlii 574[3] (uncert. reading).

ʾpl₁ **OffAr** QAL (?) Pf. 1 p.s. *ʾplt* Cowl 13[4] (for the reading, cf. Sayce & Cowley APA sub text E, Cowl p. 39 :: Grelot DAE p. 185 n. d, Porten & Greenfield JEAS p. 14, Porten & Yardeni sub TADAE B 2.7: l. *ʾklt* = QAL Pf. 1 p.s. of *ʾkl₁*:: Wag 64 n. 2: *ʾplt* lapsus for *ʾplty* = PAʿEL Pf. 2 p.s.f. + suff. 1 p.s.) - ¶ verb of uncert. meaning; Sayce & Cowley APA sub text E: = to take in exchange, Cowl p. 39: = to acknowledge.
v. *šʾplt*.

ʾpl₂ **OldAr** *ʾplʾ* in KAI 222B 43 prob. = subst. Sing. emph. of unknown meaning. Fitzmyer AIS 72: = metathesis for *ʾlpʾ* (= Sing. emph. of *ʾlp₂*)?; Lipiński Stud 45: = late born lamb; Silverman JAOS xciv 270: = not even (*ʾp₂*+ *lʾ₁*); Lemaire & Durand IAS 115, 125: l. poss. *ʾply* = *ʾp₂* + *l₅* + suff. 1 p.s. (poss. reading).

ʾpm (< *ʾp₂*+ *-m*?, cf. Joüon MUSJ xviii 29f., cf. however Leand 61q, Rundgren ZAW lxx 212 n. 12 (: poss. < Iran.; cf. also Hinz AISN 30f.)) - **OffAr** Cowl 5[8,11], 6[15], Krael 4[16,22], etc. - ¶ adv. used in contrastive contexts: still, as well, moreover (cf. also Krael p. 229, Porten & Greenfield JEAS p. 4, 5 a.e., Rundgren ZAW lxx 212 (n. 12), Porten & Yardeni sub TADAE B 2.1 a.e.); *ʾgrʾ zylk ʾpm* Cowl 5[10f.]: the wall will still be yours (i.e. notwithstanding an eventual process against you; cf. Skaist AAALT 31ff., cf. also Porten & Szubin JAOS cvii 236); *hn hškḥt ksp [ḥ]t lʿbq whn lʾ hškḥt ʾpm ḥt [lʿ]bq* Cowl 42[7f.]: if you have found silver, come down at once, and if you have not found (it), still come down at once - less exact translations: - a) in addition, cf. Joüon MUSJ xviii 30, J.J.Rabinowitz Law 50f., Krael p. 162, cf. also Grelot DAE p. 131 a.e. - b) again, cf. Yaron Bibl xli 270f., Law 84ff., 88,

T(ournay) RB lxix 626 - c) assuredly, cf. Cowl p. 11, Segert AAG p. 412 - Grelot DAE p. 90 n. 9, Porten JNES xlviii 176, Porten & Yardeni sub TADAE B 5.5: l. *[ʾ]pm* in Cowl 43^6 (poss. reading, dam. context) :: Cowl p. 146: l. *[k]pm* = k_1 + pm_1 :: Seidel ZAW xxxii 294: l. pm_2 = variant of *ʾpm* - Porten & Yardeni sub TADAE B 3.13: l. *ʾpm* in Krael 11^2 (prob. reading, cf. also Porten & Greenfield JEAS p. 66 :: e.g. Krael a.l., Grelot DAE p. 253 (n. a): l. *[k]nm*).
v. $ʾm_4$, $ʾps_3$.

ʾpmlṭ (< Greek ἐπιμελητής) - **Palm** Sing. *ʾpmlṭʾ* CIS ii 4157^3 - ¶ subst. m. one who has the charge of something, *curator*; *ʾpmlṭʾ dy nmšʾ* (i.e. *npšʾ*) *dh* CIS ii 4157^3: the *curator* of this grave; cf. Starcky RB lxiv 216.

ʾpmlṭw (< *ʾpmlṭ* + suff. *-ū*) - **Palm** Sing. cstr. *ʾpmlṭwt* CIS ii 3968^2 (= RIP 157^4); Plur. abs. *ʾpmlwṭn* CIS ii 3976^2 (lapsus for *ʾpmlṭwn*?, cf. Cantineau Gramm 155, Rosenthal Sprache 13) - ¶ subst. f. function of *curator*, *curator*-ship.

ʾpn **OffAr** Sing. emph. *ʾpnʾ* Cowl $81^{15,60}$ (for this interpret., cf. Grelot DAE p. 108 (n. o), 112 (n. z) :: Leand 12w: *ʾpnʾ* = Dual + suff. 1 p.pl. of $ʾnp_2$)- ¶ subst. fixed time; *slq lʾpnʾ* Cowl 81^{15}: he has acquitted (his debts) falling due :: Harmatta ActAntHung vii 348f.: poss. = he has reached a conditional agreement (cf. also ibid. 402); cf. Cowl 81^{60} *bʾpnʾ* (diff. context, uncert. interpret., cf. also Harmatta ActAntHung vii 364).

ʾpnrtṭ (< Greek ἐπανορθωτής) - **Palm** Sing. emph. *ʾpnrtṭʾ* CIS ii 3971^3 - ¶ subst. m.; *ʾpnrtṭʾ dy mdnḥʾ klh*, restorer (/corrector) of the whole Orient (title of the Palm. king), cf. Greek par. ἐπανορθωτοῦ πάσης ἐπαρχίας; for par. title, cf. *mtqnn*.

$ʾps_1$ v. $ʾps_3$.

$ʾps_2$ **OldCan** Sing. + suff. 3 p.s.f., cf. EA 366^{34}: *up-sí-ḫi* (cf. Rainey EA p. 98) - ¶ subst. extremity - on this word, cf. Lipiński ZAH i 63.

$ʾps_3$ **Ph** KAI 26A iv 1 - ¶ adv. only (cf. e.g. FR 248c, Röllig KAI a.l., Avishur PIB 236, Gibson SSI iii p. 53, 63, cf. also Joüon MUSJ v 408f. :: Marcus & Gelb JNES viii 120: = totally :: Dupont-Sommer RA xlii 175: = provided that :: O'Callaghan Or xviii 181, 188: *ʾdm šm ʾps* = a notable (or) a nobody :: Obermann Conn xxxviii 37: = QAL Pf. 3 p.s.m. of $ʾps_1$(= to destroy) :: v.d.Branden GP p. 123: l. *ʾpm* = assuredly or only.

ʾpsy **OffAr** Sing. abs. (?) *ʾpsy* Cowl 26^{12} (:: e.g. Cowl a.l.: = Plur. cstr.) - ¶ subst. m. (?) certain type of cross-beam in shipbuilding, cf. Grelot DAE p. 291 n. f (: < Egypt.; cf. also Porten & Yardeni sub TADAE A 6.2: = stanchions), cf. also Holma Öfversigt af Finska

Vetenskaps-Societetens Förhandlingar '15 B 5, p. 12.

ʾpṣ v. *npṣ*.

ʾpq **OldAr** Lipiński Stud 36: l. *mʾpq[y]k* in KAI 222B 29 = PAʿEL Part. act. pl.m. + suff. 2 p.s.m. of *ʾpq* (= to break through): the brave ones (highly uncert. reading and interpret.).

ʾpr v. *ʿpr*$_1$.

ʾprḥ **DA** Plur. cstr. *ʾprḥy* i 10 - ¶ subst. young bird - on this word, cf. Garr DGSP 48.

ʾpryʿ **OffAr** Driv 9^3 (reading of *r* uncert.) - ¶ adv. prob. meaning immediately, cf. Black JSS i 66, Grelot DAE p. 319 (n. e), cf. also Driv p. 74: reading *ʾpdyʿ*less prob.; the reading *[ʾ]pryʿ* in Driv 9^{5*} (cf. Driv a.l.) highly uncert., cf. Porten & Yardeni sub TADAE A 6.12.

ʾprytr (< Iran., cf. Segal sub ATNS 26, Shaked Or lvi 411 :: Teixidor JAOS cv 733: < Greek) - **OffAr** Plur. abs. *ʾprytrn* ATNS 26^{15} - ¶ subst. (?) of uncert. meaning; Shaked Or lvi 411: hero, heroic man :: Segal sub ATNS 26: = adj. more praised, most worthy.

ʾṣbʿ **OffAr** Plur. abs. *ʾṣbʿn* Pers 43^4 (for the reading, cf. Degen BiOr xxxi 126, Naveh & Shaked Or xlii 455f., Delaunay CC 217 (cf. also Hinz FS Nyberg 385) :: Bowman sub Pers 43, Or xxxix 459: l. *ʾṭbʿn* = Plur. abs. of *ʾṭbʿ*(= certain coin = 1 shekel)); cf. Frah x 31 (*ʾwṣbʿth*), cf. Nyberg FP 45, 77 :: Ebeling Frah a.l. : l. *ʾwṣtph*. ¶ subst. finger; in the context of Pers 43^4 = certain measure.
v. *ṣbʿ*$_2$.

ʾṣdq (< Arab., cf. Cantineau Nab i 88, cf. also O'Connor JNES xlv 216f., 219) - **Nab** Sing. abs. *ʾṣdq* CIS ii 201^3, 206^2, 207^6, 208^2, etc.; + suff. 3 p.s.m. *ʾṣdqh* CIS ii 220^2, 223^4, 224^8, J 5^8; + suff. 3 p.pl.m. *ʾṣdqhm* CIS ii 215^2, J 38^4; Plur. + suff. 3 p.pl.m. *ʾṣ[d]qyhm* CIS ii 219^6 (= J 4, uncert. reading) - ¶ subst. - **1)** legitimate heir; *kl ʾnwš ʾṣdq wyrt* CIS ii 206^3: every heir (both words *ʾṣdq* and *yrt* indicating the same person) :: J i p. 147: *ʾṣdq* = testamentary heir, *yrt* = natural heir (the two words indicating different persons; cf. however MPAT 64 i 7) :: RES sub 1289C (following Guidi): *ʾṣdq* = legitimate heir, *yrt* = testamentary heir; *ʾṣdq bʾṣdq* CIS ii 201^3, 206^2, 207^6, 208^{2,3}, 209^3, etc.: heir after heir (> on legal right, *iure haereditatis*, cf. also Cooke NSI p. 226) - **2)** coll. (always with pron. suff.) the heirs: CIS ii 215^2, 220^2, 223^4, 224^8, J 5^8, 38^4.

ʾṣyl **OffAr** Sing. abs. *ʾṣy[l]* Aḥiq 143 (prob. reading, cf. Lindenberger APA 143, cf. however Perles OLZ '11, 502: l. *kṣy[r]*$_3$ = little, Sach p. 172: l. *[ḥ]ṣy[p]* = impudent, Kottsieper SAS 9, 16, 204: l. *[ḥ]ṣyp* = strong, inflexible) - ¶ adj. noble (?, v. supra; v. Ex xxiv 11, cf. Grelot RB lxviii 189, cf. however Nöldeke AGWG xiv/4, 17).

ʾṣl₁ **Nab** Sing. emph. *ʾṣlʾ* CIS ii 350[3] - ¶ subst. prob. meaning: property (cf. Clermont-Ganneau RAO ii 130, Nöldeke ZA xii 4, Cooke NSI p. 243; < Arab.?) :: Milik RB lxvi 560: = Sing. emph. of *ʾṣl₂* = (side >) certain architectonic element :: Barth AJSL xiii 275: *ʾṣlʾ* = adv. completely :: de Vogüé JA ix/viii 313 (improb. reading); cf. also Cantineau Nab i 64.

ʾṣl₂ **Ph** Sing. cstr. *ʾṣl* KAI 9B 2 - **Pun** Sing. cstr. *ʿṣʾl* KAI 165[4] (v. however *mṣʾ₁*) - **Hebr** Sing. + suff. 2 p.s.m. *ʾṣlk* DJD ii 42[7], 44[4,5]; + suff. 1 p.s. *ʾṣly* DJD ii 46[4]; + suff. 2 p.pl.m. *hṣlkm* DJD ii 43[4] (cf. Birnbaum PEQ '54, 29, Milik DJD ii a.l., Pardee HAHL 130 :: Yeivin At i 106: l. *ʾṣlkm* = *ʾṣl₂* + suff. 2 p.pl.m. :: Milik RB lx 277, 285: l. *hṣlt* = Hiph Pf. 2 p.s.m. of *nṣl* (= to deliver; cf. Vogt Bibl xxxiv 421, Teicher JJS iv 133f., J.J.Rabinowitz RB lxi 192, Delcor SDB v 1390, Vermès MDJ 203; cf. also Cross RB lxiii 47f. n. 6: l. *hṣlt* or possibly *hṣlth* or *hṣltm*) :: Ginsberg BASOR cxxxi 25 n. 5: l. *hṣlty* (= Hiph Pf. 1 p.s. of *nṣl*; cf. also Bardtke ThLZ lxxix 297) :: Sonne PAAJR xxiii 98: l. *ḥṣltm* = Qal Pf. 2 p.pl.m. of *ḥṣl₂* (= variant of *ḥsl₁* = to devour)) - ¶ subst. - **1)** side; *bʾṣl hmšk[b]* KAI 9B 2: at the side of the tomb - **2)** used as prep., next, with; *lʾ ʿlty ʾṣlk* DJD ii 42[7]: I did not ascend to you; *kn ʾṣly bʿyn gd[y]* DJD ii 46[4]: here with me at E.-G. (cf. DJD ii 44[5]); diff. *hgllʾym šhṣlkm* DJD ii 43[4] prob.: the Galileans who are with you; for DJD ii 44[4], v. *ydʿ₁*; the diff. *ʿṣʾl* in KAI 165[4] = prep.??, cf. Février BAr '51/52, 42f., Röllig KAI a.l., v.d.Branden RSF ii 146 (less prob. interpret.; for an other division of words, v. *mṣʾ₁*) - Milik sub ARNA-Nab 111, DFD 212: l. *ʾṣl* (Sing. cstr.) in RES 1434[5] (poss. reading; subst. exact meaning uncert.). v. *ʾṣl₁*.

ʾṣlʾ v. *ʾṣl₁*.

ʾṣph = matting > Akkad. *a-ṣu-pa(-a)-tu4/ta*, cf. v.Soden Or xlvi 185.

ʾṣr v. *ʾwṣr*.

ʾqbr v. *qbr₃*.

ʾqlwt₁ v. *mqlw*.

ʾqlwt₂ (< Greek ἀκόλουθος) - **Hatra** Sing. emph. *ʾqlwtʾ* 112[7] - ¶ subst. follower (cf. Caquot Syr xli 254, cf. also Safar Sumer xviii 33: commissioner, representative).
v. *ʾqlt*.

ʾqlt **Hatra** in *bny ʾqltʾ dy brmryn* Hatra 280[1f.], *ʾqltʾ* prob. = Sing. emph., exact meaning unknown: poss. < Greek ἀκόλουθος = following, attending on (?), *bny ʾqltʾ* = the followers?, cf. Drijvers EM 161, cf. also Tubach ISS 258f. (n. 23): = a certain group of cultic staff :: Aggoula MUSJ xlvii 27: = the sons of the acolyte (= Sing. emph. of *ʾqlwt₂*, cf. Vattioni IH a.l.) :: Safar Sumer xxiv 31: *ʾqltʾ* = name of tribe (cf. also

Degen JEOL xxiii 421).
v. *mqlw* (for CIS ii 3927).

᾽qn᾽ Ph meaning of the *᾽qn᾽* in MUSJ xlv 262[4] unknown; Röllig NESE ii 9f., Cross IEJ xxix 44: = subst. Sing. abs. (= lapis lazuli/purple), cf. also (Mazar with) Cross IEJ xxix 44: = 'Phoenician' blue/purple; less prob. interpretations: - **1)** Starcky MUSJ xlv 270: = QAL Impf. 1 p.s. of *qny* - **2)** v d Branden BiOr xxxiii 12: = Sing. abs. of qnh_1 prec. by prosthetic *alef*

᾽qns v. qns_1.

$᾽r_1$ v. *mwddw*, *p᾽r*, rzm_1.

$᾽r_2$ OffAr Sing. abs. *᾽r* Cowl 26[10] (reading *᾽d* poss.) - ¶ subst. certain kind of wood (for the discussion, cf. Cowl p. 91, Ungnad ArPap sub no. 8, Grelot DAE p. 288f. n. s) - this word (Plur. emph. *᾽ry᾽*) also in BSh 50[1], meaning "beams of *᾽r*-wood"?, cf. Naveh BSh a.l.

$᾽r_3$ v. $᾽gr_4$.

᾽r᾽l **Mo** the diff. *᾽r᾽l* in KAI 181[12] word of unknown meaning (cf. e.g. Andersen Or xxxv 90 n. 2, Reviv CSI p. 21f.). Poss interpret.: - **1)** military term denoting more than one person, cf. Reviv o.c.; prob. subst. Sing. cstr. - **2)** altar hearth, cf. Lidzbarski Handb 225, Cooke NSI p. 11, v.Zijl 190 (n. 7), Röllig KAI a.l., Segert ArchOr xxix 219, 240, Galling TGI 52 (n. 8), Smelik HDAI 35 (cf. also de Moor UF xx 153); prob. subst. Sing. cstr. - **3)** n.p., cf. Praetorius ZDMG lix 34f., Albright Archaeology[2] 218 n. 86, Lipiński Or xl 332ff., de Geus SV 26, 28 n. k (cf. also McDonald AN xvii 67) - less prob. interpret. - 1) champion, cf. Albright with Andersen Or xxxv 90 n. 2; subst. Sing. cstr. - **2)** lion figure, cf. Gibson SSI i p. 80; subst. Sing. cstr. - **3)** certain type of priest, cf. Halévy RS viii 289f., Grimme OLZ '01, 43ff., cf. also Lidzbarski Eph i 278, Beeston JRAS '85, 144f., 147 - **4)** cherub?, cf. Mazar VT xiii 316 n. 2; for litterature on the subject, cf. also Tur-Sinai HalSe i 34, Bernhardt ZDPV lxxvi 145 n. 32, Miller UF ii 185f., Teixidor Syr xlviii 467f., Jackson & Dearman SMIM 112f., Mattingly SMIM 235ff. and EM i 558f. - the reconstruction *᾽[r᾽]ly* = Plur. cstr. in KAI 181[17f.] less prob., cf. e.g. Röllig KAI a.l., v. also kly_3 - Albright BASOR lxxxiii 16 n. 12: l. Plur. abs. *᾽r᾽lm* also in KAI 30[5] (= shades), cf. also idem Archaeology[2] 218 n. 86 (cf. also Mazar VT xiii 316 n. 2: l. *᾽r᾽lm* = champions); heavily dam. context, less prob. reading, cf. Honeyman Irâq vi 106ff.: l. *[ḥ]br.᾽lm* = resp. Sing. cstr. of $ḥbr_3$ and Plur. abs. of $᾽l_1$(cf. also H.P.Müller ZA lxv 106, 112, Baldacci BiOr xl 126, Gibson SSI iii p. 29f.) × Dupont-Sommer RA xli 209: l. *[š]᾽r.᾽lm* = Sing. cstr. of $š᾽r_2$ + Plur. abs. of $᾽l_1$ (cf. also Masson & Sznycer RCP 19); cf. also Puech Sem xxix 21, 23 (div. otherwise): poss. l. *br* (= Sing. abs. of br_4 (= grain, corn)) + *᾽l* (= $᾽l_6$) + *mḥ* (= Sing. abs. of $mḥ_1$ (=

fat)).
v. *kly*$_3$.

ʾrb OffAr Sing. cstr. *ʾrb* Aḥiq 99 (:: Ginsberg ANET 428 n. 6: l. *ʾdb* = instruction?) - ¶ subst. m. ambush; *ʿzyz ʾrb pm mn ʾrb mlḥm* Aḥiq 99: the ambush of the mouth is stronger than the ambush of the war (Grelot RB lxviii 183, DAE p. 437: transl. trick, device (cf. Kottsieper SAS 20, 190), cf. also Lindenberger APA 77f., 237 n. 186: = treachery).

ʾrbh OldAr Sing. abs. *ʾrbh* KAI 222A 27 (cf. Fitzmyer AIS 46, Degen AAG p. 39 :: Garb 247, 266: = Sing. emph.) - ¶ subst. m. locust (in the context of KAI 222 coll.; cf. also Cathcart CBQ xxxv 186) - on this word, cf. also Borowski AIAI 153f.

ʾrbwʿ v. *rbʿ*$_3$.

ʾrbl = seave > Akkad. *arballu*, cf. v.Soden Or xlvi 184.

ʾrbn = (papyrus) reeds/rushes > Akkad. *urbānu*, cf. v. Soden Or xxxvii 269, xlvi 196.

ʾrbʿ Ph m. abs. *ʾrbʿ* KAI 14[1], 39[1] - **Pun** m. abs. *ʾrbʿ* KAI 120[1], 130[5], 137[6]; the *ʿrbʾ* in RES 779[6] false reading, cf. Chabot sub Punica xi 10; f. + suff. 3 p.pl.m. *ʾrbtnm* Trip 38[5] - **Hebr** m. abs. *ʾrbʿ* IEJ xii 30[2] (with masc noun), SM 13[1], Mas 585[1], 586 (heavily dam. context), on coins of the first revolt, cf. Meshorer JC no. 161-163 (cf. Meshorer Mas coin 3492, 3493), DJD ii 30[8] (for the reading, cf. Milik DJD ii a.l., cf. however Hartman CBQ xxiii 519), AMB 4[17]; s.f. abs. *ʾrbʿh* DJD ii 22,1-9[13], 29[9], SM 106[13], EI xx 256[6]; f. cstr. *ʾrbʿt* TA-H 2[3], DJD ii 24B 17 (diff. reading), SM 76[4] - **OffAr** m. abs. *ʾrbʿ* Cowl 26[16], Samar 9[2]; f. abs. *ʾrbʿh* Cowl 10[4], 29[5]; cf. Frah xxix 4 (*ʾlbʾ*), GIPP 15 - **Nab** m. abs. *ʾrbʿ* CIS ii 202[4], 212[9], 225[3], J 38[9], MPAT 64 iii 2, 3, PEQ '81, 22[6], on coins, cf. Meshorer NC no. 55; s.f. abs. BASOR cclxiii 78[4] - **Palm** m. abs. *ʾrbʿ* CIS ii 3913 ii 23, 4199[15], Inv x 44[3], 54[5], Sem xxxvi 89[5], Syr lxii 277 ii 4 (heavily dam. context); f. abs. *ʾrbʿʾ* CIS ii 3913 i 13, ii 138, 4158[2], 4171[1,3], 4172[2], 4174[3], SBS 19[1], 48B 5, Sem xxvii 117[9], FS Miles 50 ii 6, etc.; f. emph. *ʾrbʿtʾ* CIS ii 3962[2] (v. infra); f. + suff. 3 p.pl.m. *ʾrbʿtyhwn* Inv x 44[2] (the *yod* analogous to the *yod* in forms like *tryhwn*?) - **JAr** m. abs. *ʾrbʿ* MPAT-A 52[6], *rbʿ* MPAT-A 50[7]; f. abs. *ʾrbʿh* MPAT 50e 1 - ¶ card. number, four: KAI 137[6], IEJ xii 30[2], CIS ii 4171[1,3], 4172[3], 4174[3], SBS 19[1], 48B 5, Sem xxvii 117[9], FS Miles 50 ii 6, SM 106[13] (*ʾrbʿh ʿšr*); cf. the following constructions - **1)** used in dating, *bšnt ʾrbʿ 4 l...* KAI 39[1]: in the fourth (4) year of ...; *bʾrbʿh ʿšr lʾlwl* DJD ii 29[9]: on the fourteenth (day) of (the month) Elul (cf. KAI 14[1], Meshorer JC no. 161-163, CIS ii 202[3f.], 4199[15], MPAT 50e 1, Meshorer NC no. 55, BASOR cclxiii 78[4], etc.); cf. also *šnt ʾrbʿ mʾh wtltyn wḥmš šnyn l ....* MPAT-A 52[5ff.]: the four hundred and thirty-fifth year of ...; cf. also *mynkd pʿmʾt ʿsr wʾrbʿ* KAI 120[1]: *imperator* for the fourteenth

time (cf. Lat. par. *imp(erator) xiiii*) - **2)** *lʾrbʿt hymm* TA-H $2^{2f.}$: for four days (cf. also Pardee UF x 297f.), cf. DJD ii 24B 17 (diff. reading), cf. also *ʾrbʿt ʾlpy[n]* SM 76^{4}: 4000 - **3)** *ṣlmyʾ ʾln ʾrbʿtyhwn* Inv x 44^{2}: these four statues - **4)** *lʾrbtnm* Trip 38^{5}: for the four of them - 5) *lgywnʾ dy ʾrbʿtʾ* CIS ii 3962^{2}: the legion which is no. 4 (i.e. the fourth legion), cf. Cantineau Gramm 125, Starcky sub Inv x 17 (cf. also Lat. par. *iiii Scy(thicae)*, cf. Inv x 17) :: Rosenthal Sprache 81f.: the legion of the "fourness" (*Vierheit*), i.e. the fourth legion :: Lidzbarski Eph ii 291: *ʾrbʿtʾ* = n.l.? (cf. also CIS ii sub 3962) - Lipiński Stud 108f.: restore *[ʾr]bʿt* (*b* uncert.) in Lidzb Ass 6^{1} (highly uncert. reading).
v. *ʾdn₁*, *ʾrbʿm*, *rbʿ₃*.

ʾrbʿy **Pun** Sing. m. abs. *ʾrbʿy* KAI 76B 1 (cf. FR 244) - ¶ ord. number, fourth; *ym hʾrbʿy* KAI 76B 1: the fourth day.
v. *rbʿy*.

ʾrbʿym v. *ʾrbʿm*.

ʾrbʿyn v. *ʾrbʿm*.

ʾrbʿm **Pun** abs. *ʾrbʿm* KAI $110^{3f.}$, $111^{3f.}$, 141^{5}, RES 336^{5}, 1543^{4}, Punica ix 1^{4}, xiv 1^{2}, 8^{3}, NP 65^{3} (= Punica xii/i 33), etc., *ʿrbm* KAI 143^{4}, NP 23^{3} (= Punica xi 2), 60^{3} (= Punica xii/i 28), Sem xxxvi 33^{3} - **Hebr** abs. *ʾrbʿym*Frey 630b 4, AMB 4^{17} - **Mo** abs. *ʾrbʿn* KAI 181^{8} - **OffAr** emph. *ʾrbʿyʾ* Cowl 81^{60} (dam. context, cf. Harmatta ActAntHung vii 365, Degen GGA '79, 30) - **Nab** abs. *ʾrbʿyn* CIS ii 196^{8}, 209^{9}, 210^{8}, 212^{9}, DBKP 22^{33}, etc. - **Palm** abs. *ʾrbʿyn* Sem xxxvi 89^{3} - **JAr** abs. *ʾrbʿyn* AMB 9^{3}, DBKP 21 back - ¶ card. number, forty: RES 1543^{4}, NP 65^{3} (= Punica xii/i 33), etc. - used in dating, *[ʾ]rbʿt ʾrbʿm št mlky* RES 336^{5}: the forty-fourth year of his reign, cf. Hofra $57^{3ff.}$, $59^{4f.}$, KAI $110^{3f.}$, $111^{3f.}$; *šnt ʾrbʿyn* CIS ii 209^{9}: in the fortieth year, cf. CIS ii 196^{8}, 210^{8}, 212^{9}, etc. - for *ʾrbʿn št* in KAI 181^{8}, cf. Röllig KAI a.l., Wallis ZDPV lxxxi 180ff., Lipiński Or xl 330ff., Miller PEQ '74, 16 n. 35, Smelik HDAI 47: forty years (meant as an approximate number of years), cf. also CF 39 n. 13 :: Reviv CSI p. 18f.: indication of one generation (cf. also Liver PEQ '67, 19, Bonder JANES iii 87f., Gibson SSI i p. 79, Teixidor Syr lii 277); on the subject, cf. also Timm DO 162ff., Graham SMIM 80f., Dearman SMIM 164ff., Smelik HDAI 47).
v. *ʾrbʿ*.

ʾrbʿn₁ **Nab** Sing. emph. *ʾrbʿnʾ* RES 2036^{1} - ¶ subst. prob. meaning *cella*, tetragonal niche, chapel - cf. *rbʿh₂*.

ʾrbʿn₂ v. *ʾrbʿm*.

ʾrg₁ v. *ʾrg₂*.

ʾrg₂ **Pun** Sing. abs. *ʾrg* Hofra 50^{2} (for the reading, cf. Février Hofra a.l. :: Berthier & Charlier Hofra a.l.: l. *bʾrg* prob. = b_2 + n.l.); cstr. *ʾrg* CIS i 344[3] - ¶ subst. m. (or = Qal Part. act. of *ʾrg*$_1$ (= to weave?)), prob. meaning weaver; for the diff. expression *ʾrg ʾmlqḥ*, v. *mlqḥ*.

ʾrgbṭ (< Iran., cf. Telegdi JA ccxxvi 228, Frye Or xv 352f. (cf. however Altheim & Stiehl AAW i 636f.), Chaumont JA ccl 11ff., Greenfield Mem Henning 183 n. 18, Harnack with Altheim & Stiehl GMA 540ff.) - **Palm** Sing. emph. *ʾrgbṭʾ* CIS ii 3940[2] (Greek par. ἀργαπέτην), 3943[2] (Greek par. ἀργαπέτην), 4105ter, Ber iii 94 - ¶ subst. m. governor of a city.
v. *hdrpṭ*.

ʾrgwn (< Akkad., cf. Zimmern Fremdw 37, Kaufman AIA 35f., cf. also Lipiński ZAH i 63f., cf. however Ellenbogen 38f.) - **Palm** Sing. emph. *ʾrgwnʾ* CIS ii 3913 ii 137 (cf. l. 11: *ʾ[rg]wnʾ*), Inv x 102b 3 - ¶ subst. red purple.

ʾrgl v. *drg*$_2$.

ʾrgmyt **Hatra** 281[12] (cf. Aggoula Syr lii 183, Sem xxvii 143 :: Safar Sumer xxvii 5 n. 10, Degen AION xxvii 488ff., NESE ii 68, 72, Vattioni IH a.l.: = Aph Pf. 1 p.s. of *rgm* = (to let be stoned)) - ¶ adv. accursedly (for this interpret. of the root, cf. also Safar Sumer xxvii 5 (n. 10) :: Aggoula Syr lii 182, Sem xxvii 143: = by stoning (cf. also Tubach ISS 275 (n. 114).

ʾrgr v. *drg*$_2$.

ʾrdb (< Iran., cf. Hallock JNES xix 92 n. 5, Hinz ZDMG cx 238, NWAP 101, AISN 204f.) - **OffAr** Sing. abs. *ʾrdb* Cowl 2[4], 3[8], ASAE lv 277 recto; Plur. abs. *ʾrdbn* Cowl 2[4,5,7,8], 3[5], 33[14] - ¶ subst. measure of capacity, cf. Malinine Kêmi xi 17: 1 χοῖνιξ = 1/40 *ardab* = 1.14 l. (cf. also Porten Arch 70f., EI xiv 177); abbrev. *ʾ*: Cowl 24[1], 81[4,5], 83[4], ATNS 41[1,4], 45a 6, b 2, etc., etc. (cf. Cazelles Syr xxxii 94 (n. 3), Driv p. 68).
v. *ʾmh*$_1$, *ʾšl*$_1$, *kʾ*$_1$, *prs*$_2$.

ʾrdh **JAr** word of unknown meaning in MPAT-A 27[3] (subst. Sing. emph. ??); for the problems involved, cf. Sukenik JPOS xv 142f.; Fitzmyer & Harrington MPAT a.l.: = the builder?, cf. also Naveh sub SM 33: = lapsus for *ʾrdklh* (= Sing. emph. of *ʾrdkl*), cf. however Beyer ATTM 385, 730: = np.

ʾrdykl v. *ʾrdkl*.

ʾrdkl (< Akkad., cf. Kaufman AIA 35, 150f., cf. also Oppenheim ArchOr xvii[2] 227ff.) - **OffAr** Sing. abs. *ʾrdkl* Cowl 15[2], *ʾrdykl*Cowl 14[2] - **Hatra** Sing. emph. *ʾrdklʾ* 1[2] (= KAI 237), 16[2] (= KAI 241), 106b 2, 3, 207[1], 208 (*ʾrd[klʾ]*, for the reading, cf. Milik DFD 391), 211 (*ʾrd[klʾ]*, uncert. reading, cf. also Milik DFD 391), 216, 217, 225[1]

(*ʾr[dkl]ʾ*), 232b 2, c 2, 305, 334^2 (Aggoula Sem xxvii 134: l. *ʾrkdlʾ*), 335^5, 403^1; cf. also Assur 41 (heavily dam. context) - ¶ subst. m. architect, cf. also Fitzmyer FS Albright ii 147, WA 250; *ʾrdkl zy mlkʾ* Cowl 15^2: architect of the king (i.e. in royal service); *ʾrdklʾ dbrmryn ʾlhʾ* Hatra 232b 3f.: architect (in the service) of the god Barmarayn; for the texts from Hatra, cf. also Aggoula Syr lxv 210ff.
v. *ʾrdh.*

ʾrh$_1$ **Pun** Sing. abs./cstr. *ʾrt* CIS i 3918^3 (complete word?, heavily dam. context) - ¶ subst. hearth (v. however supra).
v. *ʾrw$_1$*, *ʾrwh.*

ʾrh$_2$ **OffAr** Herm $1^{5,8}$ - ¶ interj. behold! (on this word, cf. M.L.Brown Maarav iv 211 ff); this word poss. also in KAI 233^{19} (cf. e.g. Lidzbarski ZA xxxi 202, Bowman UMS xx 278, 282, Bresciani & Kamil Herm a.l., Kutscher IOS i 112, Donner KAI a.l.; context however dam.).
v. *ʾrw$_1$*.

ʾrw$_1$ **Ph** Plur. abs. *ʾrwm* KAI 32^3 (= Kition A 2; :: e.g. CIS i sub 10, Lidzbarski sub KI 18, Röllig KAI a.l.: or = Dual abs.?) - ¶ subst. m. of uncert. meaning; poss. interpret. - **1)** lion (placed at the side of an altar) - **2)** altar hearth; for the interpret., cf. CIS i sub 10, Cooke NSI p. 56, Praetorius ZS ii 12, Röllig KAI a.l., Dahood Bibl xlix 356f., lx 430, UF xi 144, Amadasi Kition a.l. (on the interpret. of *ʾrw*, cf. also Teixidor Syr lvi 385) - Bivar & Shaked BSOAS xxvii 276f.: the diff. *blʾrw* in BSOAS xxvii 272 iii 2 = *bl* (=nd) + either *ʾrw$_1$* (Sing. abs.) or *ʾrw$_2$* (= behold; v. *ʾrh$_2$*), improb. interpret., prob. = *b$_1$* + *lʾrw* (= n.l.), cf. Sznycer JA ccliii 6f.
v. *ʾrh$_1$*, *ʾrwh*, *blʾrw.*

ʾrw$_2$ **JAr** Beyer ATTM 329, 521: l. *ʾrw$_2$* (= behold) in MPAT 89^1 (*[ʾ]rw*), highly uncert. reading, cf. also Avigad IEJ xvii 102f., Fitzmyer & Harrington MPAT a.l.: l. *dy* (= *dy$_2$*); on reading and interpret., cf. also Bennett Maarav iv 253.
v. *ʾrw$_1$*.

ʾrwd **Pun** Sing. abs. (?) *ʾrwd* CIS i 5343 - ¶ subst.? name of profession?? (dam. context; word division uncert.); CIS i a.l.: the man from Arwad? (??; cf. *ʾrwdy*, Greek par. Ἀράδιος, NESE i 3^2 and KI 38).

ʾrwh **Pun** Sing. abs. *ʾrwt* Punica xviii/ii 129^3 - ¶ subst. f. female profession: cook??, cf. Praetorius ZS ii 12.
v. *ʾrh$_1$*, *ʾrw$_1$*.

ʾrwn v. *ʾrn$_1$*.

ʾrwndkn v. *rwndkn.*

ʾrwst (< Iran., cf. Bailey JRAS '43, 2f., Nyberg Eranos xliv 238, Kent OPG 170, Henning Ir 39, Metzger JNES xv 24, Grelot Sem viii 14f.,

Donner sub KAI 276[4], Kutscher & Naveh Lesh xxxiv 312) - **OffAr** Sing. abs. *ʾrwst* KAI 276[4] (:: Grelot Sem viii 13 (n. 2): = orthographical variant for *ʾrwstʾ*), FuF xxxv 173[7,12,14] (= ASA 244; diff. and uncert. context) - ¶ subst. of uncert. meaning, poss. = capability > accomplishment. On the subject, cf. Bailey JRAS '43, 2f., Nyberg Eranos xliv 235ff., Metzger JNES xv 24, Grelot Sem viii 14ff., Altheim & Stiehl ASA 45, 260, Donner KAI a.l., Kutscher & Naveh Lesh xxxiv 312. For *wnṣyḥ wkbyr ʾrwst ʿbydʾ* KAI 276[3f.] (Greek par. τοῦ πολλὰς νείκας ποιήσαντος), v. *nṣyḥ*; for the poss. par. text FuF xxxv 173[14], v. *ʿbd₁*.

ʾrwš v. *ʾdwš*.

ʾrz₁ Zauzich & Röllig Or lix 327: a form of this root (QAL Part. pass. s.m. abs.) = to fasten poss. in Or lix 325[2] (uncert. interpret.).

ʾrz₂ **OffAr** Sing. abs. *ʾrz* Cowl 26[10,13,14,17], 30[11], 31[10]- ¶ subst. cedar (?, cf. Grelot DAE p. 288 n. s: or = certain type of pine?, cf. also Donner sub KAI 252); *ʿqy ʾrz* Cowl 26[10]: cedar (?) wooden boards (cf. Cowl 26[13,14,17]).
v. *ʾrz₃*.

ʾrz₃ (< Iran., cf. Telegdi JA ccxxvi 254f., Hinz AISN 203) - **OffAr** Sing. emph. *ʾrzʾ* Aḥiq 175 (v. infra) - **Hatra** Sing. emph. *ʾrzʾ* 60 (cf. Caquot Syr xxxii 263f., Aggoula MUSJ xlvii 65, Milik DFD 167, Teixidor Syr li 335, Vattioni IH a.l. :: Safar Sumer xxi 33 n. 3: l. *ʾdzʾ* = Sing. emph. of *ʾdz* < Lat. *aedes* = sanctuary, temple, cf. Degen WO v 223f.; v. also infra), 214[1] (cf. Aggoula MUSJ xlvii 43, Milik DFD 167, Teixidor Syr li 335 :: Safar Sumer xxi 33 (n. 3): l. *ʾdzʾ* = Sing. emph. of *ʾdz*, v. supra, cf. Degen WO v 223f. :: Teixidor Syr xlviii 484: l. *ʾwnʾ* = Sing. emph. of *ʾwn₁*), 403[2] (*ʾ[r]zʾ*, cf. Aggoula Syr lxii 281, lxv 207, Vattioni AION xliv p. 678f. :: as-Salihi Irâq xlv 140f.: l. *ʾdzʾ* = Sing. emph. of *ʾdz*, v. supra) - ¶ subst. - **1)** secret: Aḥiq 175 (cf. Driver JRAS '32, 89 :: Cowl p. 225, Grelot RB lxviii 192, DAE p. 446, Lindenberger APA 179, Kottsieper SAS 18, 190: = Sing. emph. of *ʾrz₂*)- **2)** mystery temple: Hatra 60, 214[1] (cf. Aggoula MUSJ xlvii 43, 65ff., Milik DFD 167, Teixidor Syr li 335, Drijvers EM 173 (cf. however (Shaked with) Greenfield FS Asmussen 138 (n. 22):= Sing. emph. of *ʾrz₄* (< Iran.; = building)) :: Safar Sumer xi 5: = Sing. emph. of *ʾrz₂*, cf. also Donner KAI sub 252 (: mystery temple also possible) - cf. *rz*.

ʾrz₄ v. *ʾrz₃*.

ʾrzwš **OffAr** diff. word in KAI 273[4]. Humbach AIT 10: < Iran., poss. meaning: endowed with reason (cf. also Drijvers BiOr xxx 467f., Kutscher, Naveh & Shaked Lesh xxxiv 126, Hinz AISN 219); Altheim LuG ii 181, Altheim & Stiehl Suppl 13, ASA 266: = n.p., cf. also Donner KAI a.l., In der Smitten BiOr xxviii 310 :: Andreas NGWG '32, 9,

11f.: l. *ʾszwš* = friend of a town (cf. Greek φιλόπολις).

ʾ**rḥ**$_1$ **Pun** PIʿEL Part. (v. infra) s.m. abs. *mʾrḥ* KAI 66^{1} (= CIS i 143; Lat. par. *merre*, Greek par. μηρρη; cf. FR 143, Segert GPP p. 140, v.d.Branden GP p. 87) - ¶ verb PIʿEL (interpret. as verb form not absolutely certain, cf. Amadasi ICO p. 92: or = n.l. or = n.d.); Part. epitheton of the god Eshmun (Lat. par. *Aesculapio*, Greek par. Ἀσκληπίῳ), uncert. meaning: guide?; for the proposed interpret., cf. CIS i sub 143, Nöldeke ZDMG xlii 472, Lidzbarski Handb 305, Hoffmann ZA xi 238, Cooke NSI p. 109f., Baudissin Adonis und Esmun 43, Röllig KAI a.l. :: Dahood Or xlvi 472: pro *ʾšmn mʾrḥ* l *ʾšmnm* (= n.d. + enclit. *-m*) *ʾrḥ* (= Sing. abs. of *ʾrḥ*$_2$): Eshmun of the Way.
v. *mtrḥ*.

ʾ**rḥ**$_2$ **Samal** Sing. abs. *ʾrḥ* KAI 215^{18} - **OldAr** Sing. emph. *ʾrḥʾ* KAI 224^{9} - **OffAr** Sing. cstr. *ʾrḥ* Cowl 25^{6}; emph. *ʾrḥʾ* SSI ii 28 obv. 2, 37^{3}, IPAA 11^{7}, CRAI '70, 163^{3}; + suff. 3 p.s.f. *ʾrḥh* Aḥiq 187 (cf. however Lindenberger APA 185, Kottsieper SAS 11, 190: l. poss. *ʾrḥʾ* = Sing. emph.) - **Palm** Sing. abs. *ʾrḥ* CIS ii 3913 ii 60 - **JAr** Sing. emph. *ʾwrḥʾ* MPAT 52^{5}, EI xx 305 iii 3 (heavily dam. context); Plur. + suff. 3 p.s.m. *ʾwrḥwtyh* MPAT-A 48^{1} (cf. however Naveh sub SM 15: unreadable :: Klein MGWJ lxxvi 554 (n. 2), Frey sub 979: l. *ʾwrḥwth* :: Beyer ATTM 393: l. *ʾwrḥth* :: Fitzmyer & Harrington MPAT a.l.: l. *ʾwrḥtwh*) - ¶ subst. f. (cf. CIS ii 3913 ii 60, cf. however SSI ii 37^{3}: *ʾrḥʾ znh*) - **1)** road, way: KAI 215^{18} (:: Driver JThSt-NS xii 62: = *ʾrḥ*$_7$ (= food), cf. Degen OLZ '71, 265), 224^{9} (v. *ptḥ*$_1$), IPAA 11^{7}, CRAI '70, 163^{3} (in both these instances diff. context), MPAT 52^{5}; *ʾrḥ mlkʾ* Cowl 25$^{6f.}$: the highway of the king; figuratively used, *npšy lʾ tdʿ ʾrḥh* Aḥiq 187: my soul (i.e. I) does not know its path - **2)** travel, journey: SSI ii 28 obv. 2 (cf. Bresciani RSO xxxv 211, Naveh AION xvi 26, Gibson SSI ii a.l.: way :: Bresciani RSO xxxv 20, Fitzmyer JNES xxi 18, WA 222, Dupont-Sommer CRAI '66, 54: = caravan), CIS ii 3913 ii 60; for *byt dh dʾwrḥwtyh*, v. *byt*$_2$ - in the diff. text SSI ii 37^{3} *ʾrḥʾ* prob. = way, cf. Cross BASOR clxxxiv 9 n. 21, Altheim & Stiehl AAW v/1, 73f., Gibson SSI ii a.l., Lipiński Stud 151, Degen Or xliv 120, Porten FS Bresciani 432, Porten & Yardeni sub TADAE A 3.3 :: Delcor Mus lxxx 310f.: = Sing. emph. of *ʾrḥ*$_3$ (= traveller) :: Dupont-Sommer CRAI '66, 47, 54f.: = caravan (cf. also Grelot DAE p. 125).
v. *ʾrḥ*$_{1,4}$.

ʾ**rḥ**$_3$ v. *ʾrḥ*$_2$.

ʾ**rḥ**$_4$ **OffAr** Sing. abs. *ʾrḥ* Aḥiq 196 (dam. context); emph. *ʾrḥʾ* Aḥiq 80 - ¶ subst. m. of uncert. meaning; poss. meaning: fetter, cf. Cowl p. 234, Ginsberg ANET 428 (n. 2; cf. also Kaufman AIA 158 n. 83), Grelot RB lxviii 180, DAE p. 435, Lindenberger APA 46ff., 224 nn. 28-34,

Kottsieper SAS 190 :: Lipiński BiOr xxxi 120: = *ʾrḥ$_2$*:: Montgomery OLZ '12, 535: = Sing. emph. of *ʾrḥ$_6$* (= millstone)?? (cf. also Muraoka JSS xxxii 187: poss. = grinding slab, hand mill).

ʾrḥ$_5$ **Amm** (?) Sing. abs. *ʾrḥ* AUSS xiii 2[5,11] - ¶ subst. young cow, heifer, cf. Cross AUSS xiii 5f.; *ʾrḥ bt 2* AUSS xiii 2[5]: a two year old young cow, cf. *ʾrḥ bt 3* in l. 11.

ʾrḥ$_6$ v. *ʾrḥ$_4$*.

ʾrḥ$_7$ v. *ʾrḥ$_2$*.

ʾry$_1$ **Ph** QAL Pf. 3 p.pl. *ʾr* KAI 13[4] (cf. e.g. FR 156, 174, 254a, 318,2b, v.d.Branden GP p. 9, 86, cf. also Röllig BiOr xix 24 (n. 9), KAI a.l., Lipiński RSF ii 55f., Puech RB lxxxviii 99, Gibson SSI iii p. 103f. :: Praetorius ZDMG lxii 154: l. *ʾd* = PIʿEL Pf. 3 p.pl. of *ʾdy$_1$* = (to provide; cf. also Gibson SSI iii p. 104) :: Brockelmann FS Eissfeldt 67: l. *ʾd* = QAL Pf. 3 p.pl. of *ʾdy$_1$* = (to give) :: Siegel AJSL xlvi 59 (div. otherwise): l. *ʾdln* = QAL Pf. 3 p.pl. + suff. 1 p.s. of *ʾdl* (= to place) :: Halévy JA ix/xx 350 (div. otherwise): l. *ʾdln* = prosth. *alef* + *dl$_4$* + suff. 1 p.s., cf. Masson & Sznycer RCP 107 (n. 3), cf. also Cooke NSI p. 27, 29, Ginsberg FS Gaster 144 n. 58, Avishur PIB 174 :: v.Selms JNSL i 56: l. *ʾdln* = Sing. cstr. of *dl$_2$* (= finished work) prec. by prosth. *alef* and + mimation) - ¶ verb QAL to amass; *ʾy ʾr ln ksp ʾy ʾr ln ḥrṣ* KAI 13[4f.]: they have not amassed with me (?) neither silver nor gold.

ʾry$_2$ v. *ʾryh$_2$*.

ʾry$_3$ **Hebr** Sing. abs. *ʾry* SM 70[3] - **OffAr** Sing. emph. *ʾryʾ* Aḥiq 110, *ʾryh* Aḥiq 89, 117 (cf. however Kottsieper SAS 191: = Sing. abs. of *ʾryh*) - **Palm** Sing. emph. *ʾryʾ* PNO 61[1] - ¶ subst. m. lion; in SM 70[3] indicating sign of Zodiac.

ʾry$_4$ v. *ʾḥrn*.

ʾry$_5$ **Nab** Starcky ADAJ x 44f., RB lxxii 95, Levinson NAI 132, 168: l. *ʾry$_5$* (= because) in ADAJ x 44 ii 2, less prob. reading, cf. Degen with Weippert ZDPV lxxxii 297 (n. 140b), Milik ADAJ xxi 150 n. 15: pro *wyqr ʾry* l. *wyqrʾ dy*, v. also *qry$_1$*.

ʾryh$_1$ **Hebr** Sing. abs. *ʾryh* SM 27[5], Frey 1206[5] (= SM 67), *ʾryyh* Frey 1162[5] (= SM 45) - **OldAr** Sing. abs. *ʾryh* KAI 223A 9 - **OffAr**, cf. Frah ix 4 (cf. Nyberg FP 44, 73 :: Ebeling Frah a.l.: l. *ʾgdyl* = lion) - ¶ subst. lion; in SM 27[5], Frey 1162[5], 1206[5] indicating sign of Zodiac; for KAI 223A 9, cf. Hillers TC 55f.
v. *ʾry$_3$*.

ʾryh$_2$ **Pun** Sing. (or Plur.?) cstr. *ʾryt* Mus lxxxiii 253[1] - ¶ subst. prob. meaning: ashes; Ferron Mus lxxxiii 252f.: = QAL Part. pass.f. s./pl. cstr. of *ʾry$_2$*(= to burn).

ʾryk v. *ʾrk$_4$*.

ʾrk$_1$ **Ph** YIPH Impf. 3 p.s.m. *yʾrk* KAI 4^{3} (cf. FR 156, v.d.Branden GP p. 88 × FR 146, Röllig KAI a.l.: = 3 p.pl., cf. also Segert GPP p. 143); 3 p.s.f. *tʾrk* KAI 6^{2}, 7^{4}, 10^{9} - **OldAr** QAL Inf. *mʾrk* Tell F 7, 14 (cf. Abou-Assaf, Bordreuil & Millard Tell F p. 50, Zadok TeAv ix 122, Kaufman Maarav iii 150, Gropp & Lewis BASOR cclix 49, Andersen & Freedman FS Fensham 20 :: Abou-Assaf MDOG cxiii 17: = Sing. cstr. of *mʾrk* (= length; cf. also Vattioni AION xlvi 359) - **OffAr** QAL Impf. 3 p.pl.m. *yʾrkwn* Beh 58 (Akkad. par. *[lu-ur]-rik*); HAPH Pf. 3 p.s.m. *hʾrk* KAI 226^{3} - ¶ verb QAL to be numerous; *wywmyk yʾrkwn* Beh 58: and may your days be numerous; *lmʾrk ywmh* Tell F 7: for the prolongation of his days (cf. Tell F 14) - YIPH/HAPH, to make numerous; *tʾrk bʿlt gbl ymt šptbʿl wšntw ...* KAI $7^{4f.}$: may the lady of G. make numerous the days and years of Sh., cf. KAI $4^{3ff.}$, $6^{2f.}$, 10^{9}, cf. also KAI 226^{3} (for these expressions, cf. Tawil Or xliii 49, Degen ZDMG cxxi 127, Avishur PIB 68, 78f., Pardee UF ix 207, Barré Maarav iii 181).
v. *ʾrk$_4$*.

ʾrk$_2$ **Ph** Sing. cstr. *ʾrk* KAI 26A iii 5, C iii 20 - **Pun** Sing. cstr. *ʾrk* CIS i 135^{1} (cf. however Herrmann MiOr xv 28 n. 62, 32 (nn. 85, 86), 35 (n. 108): = n.l.) - **Samal** Sing. cstr. *ʾrk* KAI 25^{7} - **OffAr** Sing. abs. *ʾrk* Cowl 8^{0} (for the reading, cf. Porten & Yardeni sub TADAE B 2.3), $15^{8,9}$, Krael $7^{11,12}$, etc.; emph. *ʾrkʾ* Cowl $26^{18,19,20}$; + suff. 3 p.s.m. *ʾrkh* Cowl 8^{4} - **JAr** Sing. abs. *ʾrk* MPAT 67^{3} - ¶ subst. length, said of - **1)** articles of dress: Cowl $15^{8,9,11}$, Krael 7^{11} - **2)** a house: Cowl 8^{4}, Krael $12^{7,15}$ - **3)** a sepulchral chamber: MPAT 67^{3} - **4)** days, *ʾrk ymm* KAI 26A iii 5, C iii 20: length of days, i.e. longevity (for this expression, cf. Avishur PIB 68, 78, cf. also Barré Maarav iii 180f.), cf. also KAI 25^{7}: *ʾrk ḥy*, CIS i 135^{1}: *ʾrk ḥym* with same meaning - Segal ATNS a.l.: l. poss. *ʾrk* (Sing. abs.) in ATNS 64a 9 (uncert. reading and interpret.).

ʾrk$_3$ v. *rqrq*.

ʾrk$_4$ **Ph** Sing. m. abs. *ʾrk* CIS i $67^{3f.}$ (= Kition B 12; v. infra) - **Pun** Sing. f. abs. *ʾrkt* KAI 78^{5} - **OffAr** Plur. m. abs. *ʾryknC*owl 30^{3}, 31^{3} (= QAL Part. pass. of *ʾrk$_1$*?), *ʾrykyn* FuF xxxv 173^{3} (diff. and uncert. context; v. infra); cf. Frah xxv 20 (*ʾlyk*), cf. also GIPP 15, SaSt 13 - **Hatra** Sing. m. emph. *ʾrykʾ* 48^{2} (or = QAL Part. pass. of *ʾrk$_1$*?) - ¶ adj. long, said of - **1)** a stone: KAI 78^{5} - **2)** a life: Cowl 30^{3}, 31^{3} - prob. used as cognomen, *ḥyrw ʾrykʾ* Hatra 48^{2}: Ch. the long one; a comparable cognomen also in CIS i $67^{3f.}$?? (dam. context; cf. also Amadasi sub Kition B 12) - a *ʾrk* (= cognomen) also to be restored in CIS i $67^{1f.}$ (*ʾr[k]*; = Kition B 12)?? - the expression *mn ʾrykyn* (FuF xxxv 173^{3}) of uncert. interpret. :: Altheim & Stiehl FuF xxxv 173, 175,

ASA 266: = since a long time.

ʾrkʾ (< Greek ἀρχή, cf. Rosenthal Sprache 91, Gawlikowski TP 43f., Sem xxiii 121 :: Cantineau Gramm 155: < Greek ἀρχεῖον) - **Palm** Sing. abs. *ʾrkʾ* Syr xiv 183[3], 184[2] - ¶ subst. magistracy, civil authority, only in the expression *bt ʾrkʾ* = the office of the civil authorities (cf. Gawlikowski TP 43f., Sem xxiii 121 (cf. also Teixidor Sem xxxiv 61f.) :: Cantineau Syr xiv 184: compare Syriac *byt ʾrkʾ* = archives, cf. also Gawlikowski MFP 203, Milik DFD 227.

ʾrkdl v. *ʾrdkl.*

ʾrkh (< Lat. *arca*?) - **Nab** Sing. emph. *ʾrktʾ* RES 471[1] - ¶ subst. meaning unknown: portico??, cf. Cantineau Nab ii 67 :: Clermont-Ganneau sub RES 86: = sarcophagus (cf. also Levinson NAI 132).

ʾrkwn (< Greek ἄρχων) - **Palm** Sing. abs. *ʾrkwn* SBS 34[5] (for the context, cf. also Gawlikowski Sem xxiii 120, TP 43); Plur. emph. *ʾrkwnyʾ* CIS ii 3913 i 2, 7, 10 - **JAr** Sing. abs. *ʾrkwn* Syn D A 5 (cf. Torrey Syn 263, Naveh sub SM 88 :: Obermann Ber vii 97: l. *ʾrknʾ*), C_1 6 (= SM 89a; *ʾrk[wn]* :: Frey sub 828a: l. *ʾrkny* = archon), C_2 4 (poss. reading, cf. Torrey Syn 268, cf. also Naveh sub SM 89b :: Obermann Ber vii 94f.: l. *ʾrkwn[ʾ]*) - ¶ subst. m. archon, chief civil magistrate; for a discussion of this function in Doura, cf. Obermann Ber vii 103f., Naveh sub SM 88.

ʾrkn v. *ʾrkwn.*

ʾrkny v. *ʾrkwn.*

ʾrm v. *mwddw.*

ʾrmlh **OffAr** Sing. abs. *ʾrmlh* Cowl 30[20] (cf. Segert AAG p. 110; cf. also Fraenkel HUCA xxxi 81f.) - ¶ subst. f. widow.

ʾrmlw **JAr** Sing. abs. *ʾrmlw* MPAT 41[11], 42[15] (*ʾrm[lw]*) - ¶ subst. widowhood.

ʾrn$_1$ **Ph** Sing. abs. *ʾrn* KAI 1[1,2], 9A 2, B 4, 11[1], 13[2,3,5], 29[1], MUSJ xlv 262[1,2] - **Pun** Sing. cstr. *ʾrn* CIS i 6043 (= TPC 72); Plur. abs. *ʾrnt* CIS i 326[3] (reading certain :: CIS i a.l.), 3333 - **Hebr** Sing. abs. *ʾrwn*IEJ vii 244[1]; Plur. abs. *ʾrwnwt* IEJ vii 241[1], *ʾrwnn* (with Aramaic Plur. ending) IEJ vii 245 - **OffAr** Sing. abs. *ʾrwn* Herm 5[4] (cf. Kutscher IOS i 116: prob. < Ph. or Hebr. (uncert.)); Plur. abs. *ʾrnn* CIS ii 111[5] - **Nab** Sing. emph. *ʾrnʾ* CIS ii 173[1] - **Palm** v. infra - **Hatra** v. *ʾrnwh* - **JAr** Sing. cstr. *ʾrwn* Syn 269 no. 2[2] (for this reading, cf. du Mesnil du Buisson Syr xl 308f.; uncert. reading, cf. Torrey Syn a.l., Naveh sub SM 90); emph. *ʾrnh* EI xx 161*, *ʾrwnh* Syn 269 no. 2[1] (for this reading, cf. Torrey Syn 269, Naveh sub SM 90; cf. however du Mesnil du Buisson Syr xl 308: l. *ʾrwn* = Sing. abs.), Frey 853[3] (= SM 37; for this reading, cf. Naveh EI xx 307) - ¶ subst. m. (in IEJ vii 241[1], 245: f.) - **1)**

small chest, box: KAI 29^{1}, Herm 5^{4} (cf. Milik Bibl xlviii 584: coll.); cf. *ḥrš ʾrnt* CIS i 326^{3}, 3333: trunk-maker - **2)** ossuary: CIS i 6043 - 3) sarcophagus: KAI $1^{1,2}$, 9A 2, B 4, 11^{1}, $13^{2,3,5}$, MUSJ xlv $262^{1,2}$, CIS ii 111^{5}, 173^{1}, IEJ vii 241^{1}, 244^{1}, 245, EI xx 161* (cf. also Marcus JANES vii 89f.) - for *byt ʾrwnh* in Syn 269 no. 2^{1}, Frey 853^{3} (v. supra), v. *byt*$_2$; for the eventual. *ʾrwn hqdš* in Syn 269 no. 2^{2}, v. *qdš*$_2$ - Cantineau Syr xvii 269: l. poss. Sing. emph. *[ʾ]rnʾ* in Palm. text Syr xvii 268^{6} (prob. restoration :: Milik DFD 220, Gawlikowski TP 61f.: l. *[ʾd]rnʾ* = Sing. emph. of *ʾdrn*$_2$ (= *ʾdrwn*) - on this word, cf. also Bénichou-Safar TPC p. 189ff. - Ellenbogen 40: < Akkad.
v. *ʾwn*$_1$, *ʾrnwh*, *znh*.

ʾrn$_2$ Nyberg FP 43, 70: l. *ʿlln* in Frah vii 10 = form of *ʾrn*$_2$ (= ram), uncert. interpret. :: Ebeling Frah a.l.: l. *gdlln*, the first element, *gd*, being a form of *gdy*$_2$.

ʾrnb **OldAr** Sing. abs. *ʾrnb* KAI 222A 33 - **DA** Plur. abs. *ʾrnbn* i 11 (or = Plur. abs. of *ʾrnbh/t*?) - ¶ subst. hare; for KAI 222A 33, cf. Hillers TC 44ff.

ʾrnbh/t v. *ʾrnb*.

ʾrnwh **Hatra** this word in 173^{3}, reading uncert., meaning unknown; cf. Caquot Syr xli 264f.: l. poss. *ʾrnwh* or *ʾdnwh* :: Milik DFD 105, Vattioni IH a.l.: l. *ʾwdnyh* = Dual + suff. 3 p.s.m. of *ʾwdn* (= *ʾzn*$_2$) - prob. not to be connected with *ʾrn*.

ʾrs **JAr** the *ʾrs* in MPAT 47 recto 4 poss. = verbal form of this root (= to join, to engage, to betroth; = QAL Impf. 1 p.s.??).

ʾrʿ v. *ʾrṣ*$_1$.

ʾrʿʾ (= *ʾrʿy*; being found on earth) > Akkad. (*arrāʾu*), cf. v.Soden Or xxxv 6f., xlvi 184 - this word (Sing. f. emph.: *ʾrʿyyth*) also in SM 49^{12} in n.l. *ḥnwth ʾrʿyyth* (= Löwer Ch.), cf. Sussmann Tarbiz xliii 126.

ʾrʿy v. *ʾrʿʾ*.

ʾrṣ$_1$ **Ph** Sing. abs. *ʾrṣ* KAI 10^{10}, $14^{16,18}$(v. infra)^{,20}, 19^{10}, 26A i 9, iii 18, 27^{13} (:: Cross & Saley BASOR cxcvii 44f.: = Sing. cstr.)^{,15}, $43^{2,6}$; cstr. *ʾrṣ* KAI 15 (= RES 287^{3}, 288^{2}), 26A i 4, ii 15, etc.; Plur. abs. *ʾrṣt* KAI 14^{19}, 26A i 18 - **Pun** Sing. abs. *ʾrṣ* KAI 121^{1}, $126^{4,5}$, 129^{1}; Plur. abs. *ʾrṣt* KAI 161^{2}, *[ʾ]rṣʾt* KAI $161^{9f.}$ (?, or cstr.?); cstr. *ʾrṣt* KAI 141^{1} - **Mo** Sing. abs. *ʾrṣ* KAI $181^{29,31}$; cstr. *ʾrṣ* KAI 181^{10}; + suff. 3 p.s.m. *ʾrṣh* KAI $181^{5f.}$ - **Hebr** Sing. abs. *ʾrṣ* RB lxxx 579 (?, dam. and diff. context), SSI i p. 58A 1 (cf. Naveh IEJ xiii 84, 89f., Weippert ZDPV lxxx 162, Lemaire RB lxxxiii 558f., 566, Smelik HDAI 149 :: Lipiński OLP viii 93f. (div. otherwise): pro *ʾrṣ h* l *ʾrṣh* = Sing. + suff. 3 p.s.m. :: Cross FS Glueck 301f. (div. otherwise): pro *ʾrṣ h* l. *ʾrṣh* = QAL Impf. 1 p.s. of *rṣy* (= to accept), cf. also Miller SVT xxxii 321ff. (n.

24)), AMB 3[19]; cstr. *ʾrṣ* SM 49[13] - **Samal** Sing. abs. *ʾrq* KAI 214[7], 215[14]; cstr. *ʾrq* KAI 214[5,6], 215[5,7]; Plur. abs. (nom.) *ʾrqw* KAI 214[13] (??, dam. context :: Lipiński OLP viii 101: = Aph Pf. 3 p.pl.m. of *rqy*₁ (= to favour), cf. also Lidzbarski Handb 227, Cooke NSI p. 167, Lagrange ERS 494 :: Montgomery JAOS liv 421: = Qal form with prosth. *alef* (cf. however the remarks of Dion p. 116, 417) :: Gibson SSI ii p. 72: = Sing. abs. of *ʾrqw* (= favour) or (div. otherwise) l. *wʾ* (= *w*) + Sing. abs. of *rqw* (= favour)?) - **OldAr** Sing. abs. *ʾrq* KAI 202B 26, 222A 26, Tell F 2; emph. *ʾrqʾ* KAI 216[4], 217[2] (*ʾr[qʾ]*); + suff. 3 p.s.f. *ʾrqh* KAI 222A 28, 223A 8 (dam. context, cf. also Lemaire & Durand IAS 117, 126: l. poss. *ṣrʾh*, without interpret.); + suff. 2 p.s.m. *ʾrqk* KAI 224[6]; + suff. 1 p.s. *ʾrqy* KAI 222B 27 - **OffAr** Sing. abs. *ʾrq* Cowl 6[7], 8[3,8], 9[3] (or = Sing. cstr.?, cf. e.g. Cowl a.l., Porten & Yardeni sub TADAE B 2.4), JA ccliv 440[3] (cf. Kutscher, Naveh & Shaked Lesh xxxiv 128, Shaked JRAS '69, 119f. :: Dupont-Sommer JA ccliv 456: = Sing. cstr.), WO vi 44C 4 (cf. also Périkhanian REA-NS viii 174), *ʾrʿ*Krael 3[5], ATNS 3[5]; cstr. *'rq* CIS ii 28 (= Del 11 = AECT 23), 35[1] (dam. context), Eph ii 209x 2 (= Del 70); emph. *ʾrqʾ* KAI 266[2], 279[3], CIS ii 1[1], 2[2], 3[2] (for the CIS ii texts, cf. Vattioni Aug xi 175f.), RES 1785B 3, 5, Cowl 6[5,6,7,12,13], REA-NS viii 170A 5, B 5, etc., etc., *ʾrʿʾ* Cowl 5[5], 6[16], 15[19], 30[9], 31[8], 68 xi obv. 3; Plur. cstr. *ʾrqt* Eph ii 206n 1 (= Del 77); emph. *ʾrqtʾ* Driv 12[6] (v. infra); cf. Frah ii 1, viii 3 (*ʾlkʾ*, cf. Nyberg FP 72 :: Ebeling Frah a.l. (div. otherwise): l. *dyrkʾ*, lapsus for *dykrʾ* = form of *zkr*₃), xvi 1 (*ʿrkʾ*, cf. Nyberg FP 48, 86 :: Ebeling Frah a.l.: l. *nrqʾ* = form of *nrq* (= possessions, riches) < Akkad., cf. also Baumgartner BiOr xxvii 14), SaSt 14f. - **Nab** Sing. emph. *ʾrʿʾ* CIS ii 964[3] - **Palm** Sing. abs. *ʾrʿ* Syr xvii 271[7] (??, cf. Cantineau Syr xvii 271, 273, Gawlikowski Syr li 99 × Milik DFD 298: = Qal Impf. 1 p.s. of *rʿʿ* or l. *ʾdʿ* = Qal Impf. 1 p.s. of *ydʿ*₁); for the variant *rʿ* in the divine epithet *q(w)nrʿ*, v. *qny*₁; cstr. *ʾrʾ* Ber i 38[10] - **Hatra** for the Sing. emph. form *rʿh/rʿʾ* in the divine epithet *qnh dy rʿh/rʿʾ*, v. *qny*₁ - **JAr** Sing. emph. *ʾrʿh* MPAT-A 22[5] (= SM 70[13]), AMB 9[6] - ¶ subst. f. - **1)** earth: KAI 27[15], SSI i p. 58A 1 (v. supra and v. *ʾlh*₁), Aḥiq 108, Cowl 15[19], RES 1785B 3, 5, MPAT-A 22[5] (= SM 70[13]), AMB 9[6], (for JA ccliv 440[3], v. *lkdnʾ*); *ʾl qn ʾrṣ* KAI 26A iii 18: El the creator of the earth, cf. KAI 129[1] (v. also *qny*₁); *rbʿy ʾrqʾ* KAI 216[4]: the four quarters of the earth (cf. KAI 215[14], 217[2]); *ʾlhy šmy[n wʾlh]y ʾrq* KAI 202B 25f.: the gods of heaven and earth; *bʾrq wbšmyn* KAI 222A 26: on earth and in heaven (i.e. everywhere), cf. also KAI 27[13], 266[2] (on this text, cf. e.g. Porten BiAr xliv 36ff.); *ʾdwnnw hrwpʾ kl hʾrṣ* AMB 3[19]: our Lord, the healer of all the earth, i.e. of all the people on earth; for Tell F 2, v. *gwgl* - 2) ground, soil; *yʿbdw ʾrq wkrm* KAI 214[7]: they till the soil and the vineyard(s); *mn ʾrʿʾ* Cowl 5[5]: from the ground upwards;

ndšwhy ʿd ʾrʿʾ Cowl 30[9]: they destroyed it to the ground (cf. Cowl 31[8]); *bʾrʿ gwmḥʾ* Ber i 38[10]: in the lower part of the niche - **3)** land, region, territory: KAI 10[10] (cf. also Dahood Bibl l 349f.), 14[20] (on this text, cf. Elayi RCP 12), 26A i 9, 18, 181[29,31], 222A 28, B 27, 223A 8, 224[6], CIS ii 2a 2; *ʾrṣh* KAI 181[5f.]: his land, sc. of the god Kemosh (i.e. Moab); *bʾrṣ ʾṭrt* KAI 181[10]: in the land/region of Atarot (:: Dahood FS Horn 432f.: in the city of A.); *ʾrq yʾdy* KAI 215[5,7]: the land of Y. (cf. KAI 26A i 4, 181[10], CIS ii 28, SM 49[13]); *ʾrṣt dgn* KAI 14[19]: regions producing grain, corn-lands (cf. e.g. Cooke NSI p. 32, Röllig KAI a.l., FR 299, Elayi SCA 53 :: Praetorius ZDMG lxii 407, Schmökel GD 45, Dussaud DRS 105, Dhorme RHR cxxxviii 133, Montalbano CBQ xiii 391, Rosenthal ANET 505, Hvidberg-Hansen ActOr xxxv 73f. n. 80, Butterweck TUAT ii 592: the lands of (the god) Dagan (cf. also Delcor VT xiv 145f., Avishur PIB 198; on the subject, cf. also Gibson SSI iii p. 109, 113), cf. also KAI 214[5,6]; for the *ʾrṣt* in KAI 141[1], cf. Picard FS Piganiol 1257ff., Karth xv 6f., Huss 470: *ʾrṣt tškʿt* = *pagus Tuscae* (cf. also Teixidor Syr li 301)); v. also *ḥbb*1, *myšr*, *ʿm*1, *rb*2, *šql*1 - **4)** field, plot, land: Cowl 6[5,6,7,12,13,14,15], 8[3,8], etc., etc.; *ḥlq ʾrq byn qryʾ* REA-NS viii 170A, B 4f. : he divided the field between the villages (for the reading, v. also *byn*2), cf. also WO vi 44A 4ff., B 3ff., C 3ff.; *ʿbwr ʾrqtʾ* Driv 12[6]: the crop from the field (:: Driv p. 82f.: *ʾrqtʾ* = Sing. emph. of *ʾrqh* // Akkad. *irṣitu* :: Milik RB lxi 595: *ʾrqtʾ* = Sing. emph. of *ʾrqh* = *nomen unitatis* ("terre > terrain") of *ʾrq*)); with the meaning 'unbuilt land' poss. in ATNS 3[5]; for Cowl 8, 9, Krael 3, v. *byt*2, *trbṣ* - **5)** diff. texts: a) *bṣdn ʾrṣ ym* KAI 14[16,18] - b) *bṣdn ym šmm rmm ʾrṣ ršpm ṣdn mšl ʾš bn wṣdn šr* KAI 15 (= RES 287[2ff.], 288[2], 289[2f.], 290[2ff.], 294[2ff.], RES 296A 3f., B 3f.); here *ʾrṣ* (*ršpm*), *ym*, *šmm rmm*, *ṣdn mšl* and *ṣdn šr* prob. the names of five wards of Sidon, for *ṣdn mšl*, v. *mšl*1, for *ṣdn šr*, v. *šr*2, for *šmm rmm*, v. *šmym*; for this interpret. of *ʾrṣ* (*ršpm*), *ym*, cf. Eissfeldt Ras Schamra und Sanch 109ff. (for KAI 15, but erroneously connecting *ṣdn ym*, cf. also Milik Bibl xlviii 575 n. 6; in KAI 14 erroneously taking *ṣdn ʾrṣ ym* for one ward), Röllig sub KAI 15, Teixidor Syr xlvi 332 (for KAI 15), for *ʾrṣ ršpm*, cf. also Xella WO xix 54 :: e.g. CIS i sub 3, Cooke NSI p. 32, Lidzbarski sub KI 7 (with reserve), Torrey JAOS xxiii 162, lvii 400, 406, Eissfeldt Ras Schamra und Sanch 110, Rosenthal ANET 662, Röllig sub KAI 14, Teixidor Syr xlvi 332f., Avishur PIB 189: *ʾrṣ ym* in KAI 14 = the land of the sea, the land on the seaside (cf. also Elayi SCA 82f., RCP 12ff., Gibson SSI iii p. 112) :: Lewy HUCA xviii 472 (n. 225): *ʾrṣ* in *ʾrṣ ym* in KAI 14 = quarter :: Torrey JAOS xxiii 164f. (div. otherwise): pro *ʾrṣ ršpm ṣdn ...*, l. in KAI 15 *ʾrṣ ršp mṣdn* = the Resheph district belonging to Sidon :: Hoffmann ThLZ '02, 633f.: *ʾrṣ ršpm* in KAI 15 designation of two distinct wards :: Lidzbarski Eph ii 53f.: *ʾrṣ ršpm* = name of

temple :: v.d.Branden GP p. 33: *ʾrṣ ršpm ṣdn* in KAI 15 = name of one ward :: Lewy HUCA xviii 472 (n. 228): *ʾrṣ* in *ʾrṣ ršpm* in KAI 15 = quarter, cf. also Ceresko JLNS 57: *ʾrṣ ym* = the city by the sea (cf. also Dahood Bibl xlvii 280, lx 432); cf. also Elayi SCA 83); *ʾrṣ* and *ʾrṣ ršpm* prob. designation of "netherworld", v. also *ršp*; on this subject, cf. also Meyer ZAW xlix 1ff., Albright FS Haupt 148 (cf. Torrey JAOS lvii 406: l. *ʾr[ṣ y]m* also in CIS i $4^{4f.}$ (highly uncert. reading)) - the *ʾrq ršp* in KAI 214^{11} prob. = n.d. (< *ʾrq* + *ršp*), cf. e.g. Vattioni AION xv 57 (n. 117), Silverman JAOS xciv 270, Lipiński AAALT 15ff. (cf. also Albright FS Haupt 147f. (n. 4)) - the *bʾrṣt* on Pun. coins (cf. Müll ii 91) prob. = b_2 + Plur. abs. of *ʾrṣ* (= in the districts/regions?, cf. also e.g. Huss 491) × = Sing. abs. of *ʾrṣh* (= land, country), cf. Harr 81 (cf. also Müll ii 125 n. 6) :: Müll ii 125: *bʾrṣt* = n.l. (Byrsa), cf. also Müll ii 86: restore coin legend *ʾrṣt* to *[b]ʾrṣt* (less prob.) - > Akkad. (*ārā*), cf. v.Soden Or xlvi 184, v. also *ʾrʿʾ*.
v. *šʿbṣ*.

ʾrṣ2 v. *mwddw*.

ʾrṣh **OffAr** Sing. *ʾrṣth* KAI $225^{7,12}$; + suff. 3 p.s.m. *ʾrṣth* KAI 225^{4}; + suff. 1 p.s. *ʾrṣty* KAI 226^{8} - ¶ subst. f. sarcophagus (prob. < underworld, cf. Akkad. *irṣitu*), cf. Driver AnOr xii 49 (transl. however: grave; cf. also Driver PEQ '45, 11, Driv p. 82f.), Kutscher JSS x 42, Gibson SSI ii p. 96 (transl. ibid. p. 95ff. however: grave), Delcor Mus lxxx 305 :: Kaufman AIA 49f. (n. 89): or = skeleton corpse?, cf. Akkad. *eṣittu* :: Clermont-Ganneau Et ii 196, Lidzbarski Handb 227, Garbini ISNO 55 (cf. also Garb 271), Koopmans 92, Rosenthal ANET 505, Segert AAG p. 527 (cf. however Kaufman BiOr xxxiv 97): = couch (> sarcophagus), etymologically related to root *ʿrš* (cf. also Moscati CG p. 42) - on this word, cf. also Marcus JANES vii 91.
v. *ʾrṣ1*, *ḥrsh1*.

ʾrq v. *ʾrṣ1*.

ʾrqh v. *ʾrṣ1*.

ʾrqw v. *ʾrṣ1*.

ʾrr1 **Hebr** QAL Part. pass. s.m. abs. *ʾrr* IEJ xiii 79^{1} (for the context, v. *ʾšr7*, *mḥy1*), xxv 229^{1} (cf. Bar-Adon ibid. 228ff., Conrad TUAT ii 561), *ʾrwr* KAI 191B 2, JPOS xxi 135^{1} (cf. Puech RB lxxxi 208 n. 46); POL Part. pass. s.m. abs. *mʾrr* HUCA xl/xli 159^{3} (for the reading, cf. Garbini AION xxviii 192, cf. also Teixidor Syr xlix 428, Garr DGSP 108 :: Lemaire RB lxxxiv 599, 601f., Miller SVT xxxii 317f., Zevit BASOR cclv 41ff., Hadley VT xxxvii 51, 54ff., O'Connor VT xxxvii 225, 228f. (div. otherwise): l. *mṣryh* = m_{12} (= mn_5) + Plur. + suff. 3 p.s.m. of *ṣr2*, cf. also Tigay FS Cross 174f., Margalit VT xxxix 372f., 377 n. 12, Smelik HDAI 139 :: Mittmann ZDPV xcvii 144, 146ff. (div.

otherwise): l. *mmṣr* = m_{12} (= mn_5) + Sing. abs. of $mṣr_1$ (= distress, oppression) :: Naveh BASOR ccxxxv 28, Angerstorfer BN xvii (n. 14; div. otherwise): l. *nṣry* = Qal Part. act. s.m. abs. of $nṣr_1$ :: Spronk BAAI 308 (n. 2; div. otherwise): l. *mmṣr* = m_{12} (= mn_5) + Sing. abs. of $mṣr_1$ (= distress) :: Shea VT xl 110, 112 (div. otherwise): l. *mṣryh* = Sing. m. + suff. 3 p.s.m. of *mṣry* (= Egyptian) = his Egyptian (sc. servant)) - ¶ verb Qal to curse; Part. pass. cursed - Pol to be cursed; Part. cursed - other forms of this root in 3 small Hebr. inscriptions, cf. Naveh IEJ xiii 80f., Lemaire RB lxxxiii 562f. (cf. also Miller SVT xxxii 323f.), v. also $ḥrp_1$.
v. $ʾrr_3$, *yṭb*.

ʾrr₂ v. *zḥl*.

ʾrr₃ **Pun** Plur. abs. *ʾrrm* Trip 51[7] - ¶ subst. or adj.?, in the combination *ṣyprm ʾrrm* Trip 51[7]: (birds who are) birds of decoy (cf. Levi Della Vida Or xxxiii 13, IPT 135; uncert. interpret.; dam. context), relation with $ʾrr_1$ less prob.

ʾrš₁ **Pun** Qal Pf. 3 p.s.f. *ʾrš* KAI 277[6] (cf. e.g. Fitzmyer JAOS lxxxvi 292, Gibson SSI iii p. 157, Friedrich BAGN i 208 :: Kutscher with Naveh Lesh xxx 236 (n. 5), Altheim & Stiehl AAW iv 225f., v.d.Branden Meltô iv 103: = Piʿel Pf. 3 p.s.f. :: Nober VD xliii 204: = Qal 3 p.s.f. + suff. 3 p.s.m. :: Ferron OA iv 190, 193: = Qal Pf. 3 p.s.m. :: Vattioni (with Milik) AION xv 295, 297: = Qal Part. pass. s.m. abs. (= promised, devoted) :: Garbini FSR 216ff.: = Piʿel Pf. 3 p.s.f. (= to give in possession, to concede) :: Pfiffig OA v 212, 220f., AOAW cii 327f.: = Qal Pf. 3 p.s.f. of $ʾrš_2$ (= to be mighty, merciful, helpful) :: Février OA iv 175ff., CRAI '65, 13, JA ccliii 11, BAr-NS i-ii 187, Delcor Mus lxxxi 246f., RSF ii 64: = Puʿal Pf. 3 p.s.f. (= to be married; cf. also Lipiński RTAT 261 (n. 78)) :: Ferron Mus lxxxi 523, 529ff.: = $'rš_4$ (= mighty) // with Akkad. *urša(nat ili)* = the mighty one among the gods) - ¶ verb Qal to desire, to wish; *ʿštrt ʾrš bdy* KAI 277[6]: A. requested (it) from him (cf. Röllig KAI a.l., Dahood UHP 52, Nober VD xliii 204, Fitzmyer JAOS lxxxvi 287, 292f., Fischer & Rix GAA '68, 68ff., Pardee UF ix 207 (cf. also Moscati RSO xxxix 258ff., Naveh Lesh xxx 236, Höfner AfO xxi 254, Friedrich BAGN i 208: A. requested (it) through him; for the problems involved, cf. also Amadasi ICO p. 165f.) :: Garbini RSF xvii 181ff.: *ʾrš* = Iph Pf. 3 p.s.f. of *ʾrš* = to possess :: Nober VD xliii 204: A. requested it (v. supra) from my hand (cf. Gibson SSI iii p. 154, 157, cf. also Amadasi ICO p. 161, 165f., Dahood Bibl lx 431, Fuentes Estañol VF s.v. *ʾrš*: A. requested it through me) :: Levi Della Vida with Garbini OA iv 42: A. has chosen (it) through him :: Dupont-Sommer CRAI '65, 16f., JA cclii 292: A. has favoured her client (*bdy* = Sing. + suff. 3 p.s.f. of bd_1; cf. also Heltzer PEQ '78,

8 n. 49: A. elected her dependent) :: Ferron OA iv 190, 193: he has chosen A. of his own accord :: v.d.Branden Meltô iv 101, 103 (v. also supra): A. has manifested her desire (to get) her chapel (*bdy* = Sing. + suff. 3 p.s.f. of *bd*$_2$ (= orthographical variant of *bt*$_1$ = *byt*$_2$)) :: Lipiński RAI xvii 53: *ʾrš* = to marry (a virgin); for a discussion of the problems involved, cf. Garbini ArchClass xvi 71f., OA iv 44ff., Pfiffig OA v 212ff., AOAW cii 313ff., Heurgon JRS lvi 10ff., Kharsekin & Heltzer VDI xciii 111f., Bonnet Melqart 280ff., Hvidberg-Hansen ActHyp i 58ff. (v. also *yd*).
v. *myṭb*.

ʾrš$_2$ v. *ʾrš$_1$*,*myṭb*.

ʾrš$_3$ v. *ʿrš*.

ʾrš$_4$ v. *ʾrš$_1$*.

ʾršh **Pun** Sing. cstr. *ʾršt* JA ccxliii 56 - ¶ subst. of uncert. meaning; Février JA ccxliii 56: *ʾršt šry* = the price of his flesh (sc. of his child = sacrifice of substitution??).

ʾrths **OffAr** Kutscher, Naveh & Shaked Lesh xxxiv 127: this word = subst. + gen. ending (< Prakrit) = intention (cf. also Henning BSOAS xiii 85) in BSOAS xiii 82^{4}.

ʾš$_1$ s.m. **Ph** Sing. abs. *ʾš* KAI 26A i 15, 30^{1} (cf. Masson & Sznycer RPC 15, 16f., Gibson SSI iii p. 29, Puech Sem xxix 20f.: pro *rʾš* l. *hʾš* :: Honeyman Irâq vi 107, Albright BASOR lxxxiii 16, Dupont-Sommer RA xli 204, v.d.Branden OA iii 253, Meltô i 33 n. 40, H.P.Müller UF ii 236 (n. 78), ZA lxv 106f., 113: l. *rʾš* = Sing. abs. of *rʾš$_1$*) :: v.Selms FS Gonin 194: l. *rʾš*, poss. = Sing. abs. of *rʾš$_2$* (= kerchief)), 51 Rs 2, 60^{5}; cstr. *ʾš* KAI 55^{2}, 57, RES 388, Mem Saidah 187^{2} - **Pun** Sing. abs. *ʾš* KAI 101^{4}, CIS i 3917^{1}, 5997 (= TPC 82), NP 130^{3}, Punica xiv 1^{3}, *ʾyš*KAI 143^{3}, 160^{2} (diff. context, cf. Février Sem iv 21, Röllig KAI a.l. :: Krahmalkov RSF iii 184: = variant form of *z*$_1$), cf. Poen 935: *ys* (cf. Sznycer PPP 81 :: J.J.Glück & Maurach Semitics ii 108f.: = *yš*), Poen 1006: *is* (cf. Sznycer PPP 142, J.J.Glück & Maurach Semitics ii 120), Poen 944: *es* (cf. Sznycer PPP 126f.; cf. however L.H.Gray AJSL xxxix 78 (div. otherwise): l. *esse* = *h*$_1$ + *z*$_1$ :: Schroed 291f. (div. otherwise): l. *esse* = m. Sing. abs. of *ʾš$_1$*) - **Mo** Sing. abs. *ʾš* KAI 181^{20,25}; cstr. *ʾš* KAI 181^{10,13} - **Hebr** Sing. abs. *ʾš* KAI 189^{2,4}, *ʾyš* KAI 193$^{9f.}$, TA-H 40^{7} (dam. context)^{,8} (dam. context) - **DA** Sing. abs. *ʾš* i 1 (cf. e.g. Hoftijzer DA a.l., Caquot & Lemaire Syr liv 194, H. & M. Weippert ZDPV xcviii 84, Puech RB xciii 286 :: Garbini Hen i 173, Hackett BTDA 31, 101, Or liii 60, Cross with Hackett BTDA 31 n. 4: = *ʾš$_4$* (= *š$_{10}$*)), ii 8 (:: McCarter with Hackett BTDA 83: = *ʾš$_2$*) - **Samal** Sing. abs. *ʾš* KAI 214^{34} - **OldAr** Sing. abs. *ʾš* KAI 202A 2 (v. *ʿnh$_2$*), 223B 16; emph. *ʾš[ʾ]* KAI 222C 21f. - **OffAr** Sing. abs. *ʾš* Herm 2^{13}, 3^{11}, 4^{9},

8[5] (*[ʾ]š*??, heavily dam. context), *ʾyš* Cowl 8[11,12,16], 20[10,12], Krael 4[19], 8[4], Driv 5[8], KAI 269[2], 278[5,8], SSI ii 37[4], HDS 9[1], Aḥiq 49, 104, Beh 38 (Akkad. par. *amelu*), 50 (Akkad. par. *amelu*), Samar 9[8], etc., etc.; cf. Frah xi 3 (*ʾyš*), Paik 69 (*ʾyš*), cf. GIPP 18, 48, SaSt 13 - **Palm** Sing. abs. *ʾyš* CIS ii 4214, Inv viii 86[2] - pl.m. **Ph** Plur. abs. *ʾšm* KAI 26A i 15; cstr. *ʾš* KAI 40[2] (v. infra), RES 367 i 2 (v. *ʿrkh*$_1$) - **Pun** Plur. abs. *ʾšm* KAI 80[1], CIS i 3919[3] - **Hebr** Plur. (from other root) abs. *ʾnšm* TA-H 24[19]; cstr. *ʾnšy* DJD ii 43[2]; + suff. 3 p.s.m. *ʾnšw* KAI 193[18] (:: Zevit MLAHE 29f.: or = Sing. + suff. 3 p.s.m. of *ʾnš*$_3$ with coll. meaning) - **Samal** Plur. (from same root as Hebr.) abs. (gen./acc.) *ʾnšy* KAI 214[30] (:: Donner KAI a.l.: = Plur. cstr.; cf. also Hoftijzer DA p. 184 n. 3) - **OldAr** Plur. (from same root as Hebr.) abs. *ʾnšn* Tell F 14; + suff. 3 p.s.m. *ʾnšwh* Tell F 9, 22 - **OffAr** Plur. (from same root as Hebr.) abs. *ʾnšn* CIS ii 149BC 12, KAI 279[2,4,5,6,8]; emph. *ʾnšyʾ* KAI 279[7]; + suff. 3 p.s.m. *ʾnšwh* CIS ii 17[2] (= Del 14 = AECT 5; for the reading instead of *ʾnš* (= Sing. abs. of *ʾnš*$_3$), cf. Kaufman JAOS cix 98 (n. 8)) - **Nab** Plur. (from same root as Hebr.) + suff. 3 p.pl.m. *ʾnwšyhm* RB xliv 266,3 (reading *ʾnwšhm* false) - **Palm** Plur. (from same root as Hebr.) emph. *ʾnšyʾ* Inv D 25[2], Inv ix 28[2], *ʾnšʾ* Inscr P 31[2] (cf. Cantineau Gramm 103, Rosenthal Sprache 76); + suff. 3 p.s.m. *ʾnšwhy* DM ii 38 i 4, Inv vi 5b 3 (*ʾnšwh[y]*?, or l. *ʾnšwh*?, cf. Gawlikowski ad RIP 130, cf. also idem TP 94) - **JAr** Plur. (from same root as Hebr.) cstr. *ʾnšy* MPAT-A 34[4] (cf. also Naveh sub SM 69 :: Sokoloff Maarav i 82: = f. Plur. cstr.) - s.f. **Ph** (from same root as s.m.??) Sing. cstr. *ʾšt* KAI 33[2], 36[2], CIS i 64[1] (= Kition B 9), DD 15[2] (*[ʾ]št*), Gall 144; + suff. 1 p.s. *ʾšty* KAI 35[2f.]; + suff. 3 p.s.m. (or 1 p.s.) *ʾšty* CIS i 40[2] (= Kition E 2) - **Pun** (from the same root as s.m.??) Sing. abs. *ʾšt* NP 130[1], ICO-Sard 35 (for this interpret., cf. Guidi MonAnt xxi 165f., Lidzbarski Eph iii 285, Amadasi ICO-Sard a.l. (uncert. interpret.) :: Garbini RSO xl 210ff.: = Sing. + suff. 3 p.s.m. :: Hoftijzer VT xiii 338 (div. otherwise): l. *št* (= Qal Pf. 3 p.s.m. of *šyt*$_1$ (cf. also Lidzbarski Eph iii 285: l. poss. *št* = Qal Pf. 3 p.pl. of *šyt*$_1$)); cstr. *ʾšt* KAI 67[2f.], 70[2], 88[3], 91[2], 93[2] (= TPC 12), 95[2] (= TPC 50), CIS i 3822[3], 4650[4], 4808[3], 5844[5], RES 501[2] (= CIS i 5961 = TPC 23), 502 (= CIS i 5941 = TPC 3), 539 (= CIS i 5959 = TPC 20), etc., *ʿšt* KAI 149[3], CIS i 232[4], 3185[4], NP 12[4], Punica xii 28[2]; + suff. 3 p.s.m. *ʾštʾ* RES 1226[2] (= CIS i 5945 = TPC 7), KAI 117[4] (*ʾšt[ʾ]*), 142[3] (*ʾš[t]ʾ*), *ʾšty* Trip 38[4], *ʾštm* KAI 169[4f.], 171[2], Punica xiA 1[2], cf. IRT 828[2]: *ystim* (diff. context, cf. Levi Della Vida OA ii 78f. :: Vattioni AION xvi 48: divide *(lil)y stim* = *l*$_5$ + Plur. cstr. of *ʿl*$_5$ (= child) + f. of *šnym* :: Vattioni Aug xvi 538: divide *(lil)y stim* = *l*$_5$ + *ʾl*$_5$ + f. of *šnym*), OA ii 83[3]: *ysthim* (cf. Levi Della Vida OA ii 84, Vattioni Aug xvi 539) - **Hebr** (from other root than s.m. and pl.m.) Sing. abs. *ʾšh* Frey 634[2] (:: Frey a.l.: l. *ʾšt*); cstr. *ʾšt* Dir sig. 62-64 (= Vatt sig. eb. 62-64), Mosc sig. 33 (= Vatt sig. eb. 152 = IS 32), 39 (= Vatt sig. eb. 157), Mas 400, DJD ii 30^{6}, Frey 621^{1}, 1294, 1295, 1313, 1314; + suff. 3 p.s.m. *ʾštw* RES 499 (= Frey 1247), Frey 1399^{2}, DJD ii 30^{25} - **OffAr** (a. from the same root as Hebr. s.f.) Sing. abs. *ʾnth*Cowl 8^{10}, 15^{32,33}, Krael 7^{36}, OA iii 56 conc. 5 (= CRAI '47, 181; dam. context), ATNS 8^{9}, etc.; cstr. *ʾšt* CIS ii 15 (= Del 4; or < Akkad.??, or belonging sub b.??; cf. also Stiehl AAW i 222 n. 11, Kaufman JAOS cix 99 :: Fales sub AECT 30: = Sing. cstr. of *ʾšw* (= marriage; < Akkad., cf. also Fales AECT p. 56)), *ʾntt* KAI 264^{8} (v. *lb*), Cowl 63^{2}, RES 1305, *ʾtt* Cowl 34^{3}, NESE ii 75 recto 6 (dam. context), BIFAO xxxviii 38^{2} (cf. Segal Maarav iv 72: = Palm.), ATNS 98^{3} (dam. context), Aug x 517 no. 128^{1} (the *ʾntt* in Krael 7^{22,25}, prob. = Sing. abs. acc., cf. Wesselius AION xxx 267, cf. also Kutscher JAOS lxxiv 236; the *ʾntt* in KAI 264^{3}, 276^{3} cstr. form with relative clause as *rectum*?, cf. Donner KAI a.l., Kutscher & Naveh Lesh xxxiv 312, Degen GGA '79, 43 × Silverman JAOS xciv 271: = Sing. abs. :: Segert AAG p. 336: in KAI 264^{3} = lapsus :: Grelot Sem viii 13: = orthographical variant for *ʾnttʾ*; cf. also Altheim & Stiehl EW x 251, GH i 428f., ASA 43f.); emph. *ʾnttʾ* Cowl 7^{9}, RES 493^{3}, ATNS 134^{3}; + suff. 3 p.s.m. *ʾntth* Cowl 15^{18}, 46^{9,11}, Krael 4^{2,25}, 7^{29}, KAI 264^{2}, ATNS 7^{2}, 29 ii 8, 30b 4, etc.; + suff. 2 p.s.m. *ʾnttk* Cowl 6^{4}, 9^{4,6}; + suff. 1 p.s.*ʾntty* Cowl 7^{5}, 15^{4}, Krael 2^{3,7}, 7^{4,21}, 12^{24}; (b. from other root than s.m. and Hebr. s.f., but identical with pl.m. in Hebr., Samal. and Ar. :: Coxon ZDMG cxxix 15f.: of same root as a.) Sing. + suff. 3 p.s.m. *ʾnšth* Herm 3^{3}, 4^{14} (cf. Porten & Greenfield ZAW lxxx 221, Kutscher IOS i 115f., Greenfield Lesh xxxii 367 (n. 45), Swiggers AION xlii 136f. :: Rosenthal with Porten & Greenfield IOS iv 22 n. 12: = Sing. + suff. 3 p.s.m. of *ʾnšwt*= (wo)men-folk), cf. also Porten & Yardeni sub TADAE A 2.1/4: = household); cf. GIPP 46 - **Nab** (from same root as Hebr. s.f.) Sing. abs. *ʾnth* IEJ xxix 112^{8} (diff. context); cstr. *ʾntt* ADAJ xxvi 366^{1} (dam. context), RES 2103^{2} (*[ʾ]ntt*); + suff. 3 p.s.m. *ʾntth* CIS ii 169^{5}, 173$^{3f.}$, 204^{3}, 207^{2}, 209^{6}, etc., *ʾtth* CIS ii 158^{4} (prob.), 161F, 194^{3}, RB xlvi 405^{4}, BAGN ii 87^{3} - **Palm** (from root as Hebr. s.f.) Sing. cstr. *ʾtt* CIS ii 3969^{2} (= Inv xi 84), 3988^{2} (= RIP 128), 4146^{2}, 4149^{2}, 4151^{2}, 4153^{4}, 4155^{4}, 4247^{4}, 4249^{4}, RIP 39B 1, 40A 4, RIP 147^{1} (cf. Michałowski FP '59, 117, 211f., du Mesnil du Buisson BiOr xx 172: l. *ʾtt* ‘- :: Gawlikowski a.l.: l. *ʾtth*; cf. also Milik DFD 168f.), Inv xi 69^{2} (:: Milik DFD 262: l. *ʾtth* = Sing. + suff. 3 p.s.m.), xii 5, 6^{2}, DM ii 41 ii 4, AAS xxxvi/xxxvii 168 no. 9^{2}, etc., etc.; emph. *ʾttʾ* CIS ii 3913 ii 48; + suff. 3 p.s.m. *ʾntth* RB xxxix 539^{3}, Inv xii 17^{8} (= RIP 105), *ʾtth* CIS ii 4115bis 4, 4237B 2, 4353B 1, 4410, 4458bis, 4501^{4}, RIP 21^{2}, 22^{2}, 24^{5}, 63^{4}, Inv xii 25^{2}, etc., *ʾtḥh* MUSJ xxviii 52^{5} (lapsus) - **Hatra** (from same root as Hebr. s.f.) Sing. cstr. *ʾntt* 35^{3}, 63^{1}

- **JAr** (from same root as Hebr. s.f.) Sing. abs. *ʾnth* MPAT 41^{3}, *ʾth* MPAT-A 28^{2}; cstr. *ʾntt* MPAT 45^{3} (?, dam. context: *ʾntt[)*, 98 (= Frey 1356), 122, *ʾyntt* MPAT 147 (= Frey 1384; cf. however Beyer ATTM 342: l. poss. *ʾntt*), *ʾtt* MPAT 51^{12} (*ʾt[t]*), 84, 97a (= Frey 1362), 103 (= Frey 1341), 104 (= Frey 1338), Mas 399, 402, *ʾytt* MPAT 94b 1 (= Frey 1353); emph. *ʾntʾ* MPAT 40^{18}, *ʾnt* MPAT 40^{6} (prob. lapsus for *ʾntʾ*, cf. l. 18 :: Milik DJD ii p. 108: lapsus for *ʾnth* = Sing. abs.); + suff. 3 p.s.m. *ʾtth* MPAT-A 2^{6} (= Frey 1198, SM 59), EI xii 146 ii 3, *ʾtt* At iii 107^{1} (lapsus, cf. Beyer ATTM 346: l. *ʾtt<h>* :: Rahmani At iii a.l.: l. *ʾtt<w>*); + suff. 1 p.s. *ʾntty* MPAT 40^{16}, DBKP 18^{71} - pl.f. **Ph** (from same root as Ph. s.f.) Plur. cstr. *ʾšt* KAI 27^{18} (cf. Gibson SSI iii p. 87 :: v.d.Branden BO iii 43: = Sing. cstr.); Plur. + suff. 3 p.s.m. *ʾštw* KAI 43^{11} (?, uncert. reading, cf. Honeyman JEA xxvi 64, JRAS '41, 33, cf. also Röllig KAI a.l., Lane BASOR cxciv 43 :: v.d.Branden OA iii 258, Gibson SSI iii p. 137, 140: = Sing. + suff. 3 p.s.m., cf. Teixidor Syr xliv 171) - **Samal** (from a root related etymologically to that of the Hebr. pl.m.) Plur. cstr. (or abs.?) *nšy* KAI 214^{16} (??, dam. context, uncert. reading), 215^{8} - **OldAr** (from same root as Samal. pl.f.) Plur. abs. *nšwn* Tell F 21, 22 (for the form, cf. Abou-Assaf, Bordreuil & Millard Tell F p. 35f., Zadok TeAv iv 122, Kaufman Maarav iii 169, Wesselius BiOr xl 182, Pardee JNES xliii 256, Greenfield & Shaffer RB xcii 50f., Gropp & Lewis BASOR cclix 53, Huehnergard BASOR cclxi 93, Israel ASGM xxiv 79f., Andersen & Freedman FS Fensham 37, Garr DGSP 96); cstr. *nšy* KAI 222A 41 - **OffAr** (from same root as Samal. pl.f.) Plur. abs. *nšn* Cowl 8^{2}, 10^{2}, Krael 3^{2,3}, 4^{2}, 5^{2}, 7^{3}, 9^{2}, Or lvii 34^{3}, 35^{3,6,8}, *nšyn* Krael 12^{1} (for the form *nš(y)n*, cf. Grelot RB lxxix 616: poss. no Plur.); cstr. *nšy* Krael 7^{38}, Driv 8^{2,4}, 9^{2} (in these three Driv texts < Akkad. *niše*, cf. Ginsberg ANET 633 n. 4, cf. also Kaufman AIA 78, Muffs 203, v. infra), Driv F iii 2^{2}, 13^{2,3}; emph. *nšyʾ* Cowl 30^{20}, 34^{2}, cf. Warka 12, 37: *ni-še-e*; + suff. 1 p.pl. *nšyn* Cowl 30^{15,26}, 31^{14}; cf. Frah xi 5 (*nyšh*, diff. reading), cf. MP 5, GIPP 30, SaSt 21 - **Hatra** (from same root as Samal. f. pl.) Plur. emph. *nšʾ* 30^{10} (cf. Aggoula MUSJ xlvii 28f., Vattioni IH a.l. × Milik DFD 381, Silverman JAOS xciv 271: = pl.m. emph. :: Aggoula Ber xviii 91: = Sing. m. emph., l. *[ʾ]nšʾ* :: Caquot Syr xxx 237: = n.p. :: Safar Sumer viii 187 n. 16: = subst. derivated from root *nšʾ*$_2$ (= to forget)) - **JAr** (from same root as Samal. pl.f.) Plur. emph. *nšyʾ* Syn D B 2 (for the reading, cf. Naveh sub SM 88 :: Torrey Syn D p. 266: l. *kšym* = *k*$_1$ + Sing. cstr. of *šym* (= *šm*$_1$) :: Obermann Ber vii 114: l. *tšyt* = **Hebr** Qal Impf. 2 p.s.m. of *šyt*$_1$); + suff. 3 p.pl.m. *[n]šyhwn* Syn D A 14 (= SM 88) - ¶ subst. - **1)** m. man, f. woman; *ʾšm rʿm* KAI 26A i 15: bad men; *ʿšrt hʾšm* KAI 80^{1}: the *decemviri*; *ʾš[ʾ h]ʾ* KAI 222C 21: that man; *ʾn ʾškḥt ʾš mhymn* Herm 4^{9}: if I find a trustworthy man; *ʾyš ḥd* Beh 38: a certain man; *lʾšt* *nʿmt* NP 130[1]: for an agreeable woman; *lʾ ʾyty ly br wbrh ... wʾnth wʾyš ʾḥrn* Cowl 8[10f.]: I have no son or daughter .... or other woman or man ....; etc.; cf. also *ḥdh ʾth ʾnṭwlyh* MPAT-A 28[2f.]: a certain lady A.; *wkl ʾš lsr* KAI 79[6f.]: and every man (sc. everyone) who will remove; *kl ʾnth* OA iii 56 conc. 4f.: every woman; for the *ʾyš zy ...* in HDS 9[1], cf. Lipiński Stud 77ff., ActAntHung xxii 376f., Fales AION xxviii 273ff., 280; for *ʾnth sʿnh*, v. *sʿn*; etc. - special uses and meanings: - a) m. husband; *hʾš šlʾ* Punica xiv 1[3]: her husband (cf. KAI 143[3], for this text, cf. also Röllig KAI a.l., FR 99a, Sznycer Sem xxxiii 54, 56 and NP 130[3]) - f. wife, spouse; *šblt ʾšt gwmzʿl* Punica xiv 1[1f.]: Sh. the wife of G.; *tdmr brt hnʾy ... ʾntth* Inv xii 17[6ff.]: T. the daughter of H. ... his wife; cf. also KAI 33[2], 36[2], CIS i 5844[5], Trip 38[4], CIS ii 11[2], 47[2], Dir sig. 62-64 (= Vatt sig. eb. 62-64), Cowl 15[18], 46[9], Herm 3[3], 4[14], ATNS 7[2], 30b 4, CIS ii 169[5], 173[3f.], 3969[2] (= Inv xi 84), 4146[2], RIP 39B 1, 40A 4, Inv xii 5, 6[2], AAS xxxvi/xxxvii 168 no. 9[2], Hatra 35[3], 63[1], DJD ii 30[6], MPAT 41[3], 51[12], 84, 97a, etc., etc. - b) everyone (with distributive function after pl.); *hkw hḥṣbym ʾš lqrt rʿw* KAI 189[4]: the stone-masons struck, everyone towards his colleague; cf. KAI 181[25], 189[1f.] - c) + negation, no one; *bl ʾš ʿbd* KAI 26A i 15: no one served ...; *wlh ʾškḥt ʾš* Herm 3[11]: I found no one (cf. KAI 223B 16, Cowl 30[14], Aḥiq 116, Driv 5[8], Herm 2[13], SSI ii 37[4]); cf. also *ʾm nsh ʾyš* KAI 193[9f.]: no one has tried - d) a person, someone: *wlʾ yhwn [šl]ṭyn ... lʾḥbwrʾ bh ʾyš* CIS ii 4214: they won't have the right ... to have someone participating in it (sc. as joint-owner); cf. Aḥiq 49, KAI 278[5], FX 136[20], Inv viii 86[2]; cf. *ʾyš ... ʾyš* CIS ii 145A 6, 7: the one ... the other; cf. also *ʾyš zylky* Cowl 8[12]: someone who represents you (cf. Cowl 20[10,14], Samar 9[8], v. also *ʾnš₃*); *ʾyš lkm* Cowl 20[12] (cf. Krael 8[4f.,5,6]); *ʾnth wʾyš ly* Cowl 25[10] (cf. Cowl 25[11,12,14]); on these expressions in Elephantine contracts, cf. also Porten & Szubin Maarav iv 58ff.; cf. also *klhm ʾnšn* KAI 279[2]: all people (cf. Greek par. τοὺς ἀνθρώπους; cf. ibid. ll. 4, 5, 6, 7, 8); *ʾnšy btyhwn* MPAT-A 34[4f.]: the people of their household (cf. also DJD ii 43[2]); *nšy bytn* Driv 8[2]: the women of our house (× Ginsberg ANET 633 n. 4, Kaufman AIA 78, Muffs 203: < Akkad. *nišē biti* = household personnel); cf. also *lšlm byth wlšlm zrʿh wlšlm ʾnšwh* Tell F 8f.: for the wellfare of his house, his descendants and his people (i.e. prob. the people belonging to his (sc. the royal) household; cf. ibid. l. 22); cf. also DM ii 18 i 4; cf. *ʾnšwh zy ʾdrʾ[š]* CIS ii 17[2] (for the reading, v. supra; = Del 14 = AECT 5): the men of U. (prob. slaves, cf. Akkad. par.); *ʿbdny ʾš ʿzbʿl* Mem Saidah 187[1f.]: A. the man of A. (indicating A. being in military service of A.??, cf. Bordreuil ibid. 190) - e) preceding another noun in apposition; *ʾyš gnb* Aḥiq 125: a thief; *ʾnšy ṣry* KAI 214[30]: enemies (or: my enemies?); *ʾš ḥzh ʾlhn* DA i 1: a seer of the gods; *ʾyš zr* KAI 214[34]: a stranger - f) *ʾš ʾlm* Lévy SG-Ph 18: a man of god (or: the gods), i.e. a prophet?? (cf. Lipiński RSF ii 54f. :: Cooke NSI p. 361: *ʾlm* here poss. = Plur. abs. of *ʾyl*$_1$ (cf. also Miller UF ii 182) :: Herr SANSS-Ph 5 (prob. same text; div. otherwise): l. *ʾšʾl* = n.p.) - g) *ʾš kty* KAI 55[2]: a man from Kition (cf. Greek par. Κιτιεύ[ς]), cf. KAI 57 (cf. Greek par. Κιτιεύς), RES 388, 1225 (= CIS i 5997 = TPC 82), cf. also *ʾš knʿn* KAI 116[3], *ʾš knbm* Hofra 103[3] (??) and *ʾš kty* KAI 40[2]: the men of Kition (cf. Cooke NSI p. 78, Röllig KAI a.l., FR 240,7 :: Lidzbarski Handb 222: = Sing. cstr.); for *ʾš ṣdn*, v. *ṣdn* - **2)** coll.: mankind, men; *ʿn ʾš* KAI 60[5]: before mankind (:: Fuentes Estañol VF s.v. *ʾš*$_1$: = lapsus for Plur. abs. *ʾšm*); *ʾš gd* KAI 181[10]: the men of Gad; cf. KAI 51 Rs 2, 181[13]; cf. also *bny ʾš* DA ii 8: the sons of men (i.e. mankind); *mʾtn ʾš* KAI 181[20]: two hundred men; *ʾdr ḥmšm hʾš* KAI 101[4]: commander of fifty men, cf. CIS i 3917[1] - **3)** Plur. f. with sing meaning: woman, *nš(y)n*: Cowl 8[2], 10[2], Krael 3[2,9], 4[2], 5[2], 7[2], 9[2], 12[1] (cf. Joüon MUSJ xviii 51f., Krael p. 274 :: Cowl p. 23, 24 (cf. also Wag 41 n. 1): spinster), used in the contracts from Elephantine to indicate women possessing contractual capacity; on the interpret. of *nšn rbh* Or lvii 35[3,6,8], cf. Porten Or lvii 34f. (exact meaning uncert.) - **4)** exact interpret. of *ʾnšwh* or *ʾnšwhy* in Inv vi 5b 3 (= RIP 130) diff. :: Cantineau Inv vi a.l., Aggoula Syr liv 283: = his parents (cf. Gawlikowski sub RIP 130) - Krahmalkov JSS xvii 72f.: the diff. *ysa* in IRT 827[2] = Sing. + suff. 3 p.s.f. of *ʾš*$_1$ (uncert. interpret.) :: Vattioni Aug xvi 539: = Sing. + suff. 3 p.s.m. of *ʾš*$_1$ (cf. also idem AION xvi 48, Levi Della Vida OA ii 85) - Vattioni Aug xvi 544: the diff. *ysy* in IRT 877a 1 = Sing. + suff. of *ʾš*$_1$ (highly uncert. interpret.) - Vattioni AION xvi 41, Aug xvi 544: divide the diff. *ysysy* in IRT 879[1] in *ysy* (= Sing. + suff. 3 p.s.m. of *ʾš*$_1$??) and *sy* (= *š*$_{10}$) :: Krahmalkov RSF iii 184f., vi 28f. (div. otherwise): = *ys* (= Sing. abs. of *ʾš*$_1$) + *ysy* (= *z*$_1$); cf. also Levi Della Vida OA ii 85 - Vattioni Aug xvi 546: the *ysy* in IRT 886e 16 (dam. context) = Sing. + suff. off *ʾš*$_1$ (highly uncert. interpret.) - for the diff. expression *mlk (bʿl) ʾzrm ʾš* and related ones, v. *mlk*$_5$ - Dupont-Sommer FX p. 156: the diff. *ʾš* or *[ʾ]š* at the end of FX 137[25] = m. Sing. abs. of *ʾš*$_1$ (cf. also Teixidor JNES xxxvii 184 (n. 22), Contini OA xx 233; highly uncert. interpret.) - cf. also *ʾyš* (Sing. abs.) in Syr xvii 271[7] (text in Palm. script with Ph. (?) influence), cf. also Milik DFD 297f. - this word (f. Sing. abs.) *ʾšt* also in KAI 26A ii 5, cf. Gordon JNES viii 114, Alt WO i 281, Levi Della Vida RCL '49, 277, 284, Ginsberg with Obermann JAOS Suppl ix 24 n. 70, JANES v 136, Rosenthal ANET 500, Röllig KAI a.l., NESE ii 3, Starcky MUSJ xlv 262, Teixidor Syr xlix 430, Schub Lesh xxxviii 148, Lipiński RSF ii 48, ii 259, SV 48, Avishur PIB 224, 231, Swiggers BiOr xxxvii 339, Greenfield EI xiv 75ff. (cf. also Bron RIPK 78ff., Gibson SSI iii p. 49) :: Honeyman Mus lxi 55, PEQ '49, 32f.: = Qal Impf. 1 p.s. of *šyt*$_1$ (cf.

also O'Callaghan Or xviii 186f., Leveen & Moss Irâq x 65, Friedrich FuF xxiv 78, Pedersen ActOr xxi 40, 52f., Dunand BMB viii 31, Zolli Sef x 169, v.d.Branden BMB xiii 93, Meltô i 44) :: Marcus & Gelb JNES viii 119: = QAL Pf. 1 p.s. of *ʾyš$_1$* (= to weaken) :: Dupont-Sommer RA xlii 172: = Sing. cstr. of *ʾšt$_1$* - du Mensil du Buisson FS Dussaud 422, 424, 428, Gaster Or xi 61f., Gibson SSI iii p. 82f., 86, Sperling HUCA liii 4,8: l. prob. *[ʾ]št* (= f. Sing. cstr.) in KAI 27[16] (poss. reading) :: Albright BASOR lxxvi 9, Röllig KAI a.l.: l. *[ʾ]št* = f. Plur. cstr. :: Cross & Saley BASOR cxcvii 44 (n. 12; div. otherwise): l. *ʾl[l]t* = lapsus for *ʾlt* (= Plur. cstr. of *ʾlh$_2$*), cf. also Röllig NESE ii 18, 23, Zevit IEJ xxvii 111f.: l. *ʾl[l]t* = lapsus for *ʾlt* (= Sing. cstr. of *ʾlh$_2$* (cf. also Baldacci BiOr xl 128: l. *ʾlt*)) :: Caquot JANES v 49: l. *[lḥ]št* = Sing. cstr. of *lḥšh* :: Torczyner JNES vi 24f. (div. otherwise): l. *št* = QAL Imper. s.m. of *šyt$_1$* - l. *ʾ[š]t* in RES 126[2] (= RES 931 = CIS i 6066)? = f. Sing. cstr. (cf. Ferron Mus lxxix 446, Garbini StudMagr xi 23f.; uncert. reading) - Garbini Hen i 172, 183, 186: l. *ʾšt[k]* = f. Sing. + suff. 2 p.s.m. of *ʾš*, in DA ii 11 (cf. also Delcor SVT xxxii 61; for the reading, cf. also Caquot & Lemaire Syr liv 205); reading of *t* less certain, cf. v.d.Kooij DA p. 124: l. prob. *m* (highly uncert. interpret., diff. context; cf. also Hackett BTDA 30, 67, 98, 134: l. *ʾšm* (= QAL Impf. 1 p.s. of *šym$_1$*)) - Ferjaoui Sem xxxviii 115f.: l. prob. *št* (= f. Sing. cstr.) in Sem xxxviii 114[2] (uncert. reading and interpret.).

v. *ʾdm$_1$*, *ʾnth$_2$*, *ʾsy$_1$*, *ʾsr$_{1,4}$*, *ʾpy*, *ʾš$_{1,2}$*, *ʾšh$_2$*, *ʾšr$_4$*, *ʾškmst*, *ʾšm$_4$*, *byt$_2$*, *kbl$_4$*, *krṣ*, *lb*, *mlk$_5$*, *mṣbh*, *nš$_1$*, *nšʾ$_4$*, *ʿnh$_2$*, *ʿrkh$_1$*, *ʿšy*, *ṣbʾ$_3$*, *qrt$_1$*, *š$_{10}$*, *šm$_1$*, *šmm$_1$*, *šnym*.

ʾš$_2$ **OldAr** Sing. abs. *ʾš* KAI 222A 35, 37, 37f. (*[ʾ]š*) - **OffAr**, cf. Frah xiii 5 (*šyʾ* in *mršyʾ*) - ¶ subst. fire; this word (Sing. abs.) prob. also in DA i 2 (cf. Hoftijzer DA p. 187, Rofé SB 65, Lemaire BAT 318, CRAI '85, 279f. × e.g. Caquot & Lemaire Syr liv 194, H. & M.Weippert ZDPV xcviii 86, 103, Sasson UF xvii 287, 293 n. 19, Puech FS Grelot 27: = Sing. abs. of *ʾš$_1$*:: Garbini Hen i 174f.: = *ʾš$_4$* (= *š$_{10}$*, cf. also Hackett BTDA 35)), diff. and dam. context - this word (Sing. abs.?) poss. also in KAI 222A 25, cf. Gibson SSI ii p. 30f., 39 (cf. already Rosenthal ANET 659 :: e.g. Dupont-Sommer Sf p. 17, 20, 42, Donner KAI a.l., Fitzmyer AIS 14f., 45, Rössler TUAT i 180 (div. otherwise): l. *ʾšr* = n.g.), *zy ymlk ʾš* KAI 222A 25: where fire will reign ... (for the context, v. also *ḥl$_2$*, *mlk$_1$*).

v. *ʾš$_1$*, *ʾšh$_2$*, *mlk$_5$*, *mrʾ*, *š$_{10}$*.

ʾš$_3$ **Hatra** Milik RN vi/iv 55: l. *lʾš* in Hatra 24[3] = *l$_5$* + Sing. abs. of *ʾš$_3$* (= abundance; *lʾš* = much), highly uncert. reading and interpret. - Milik RN vi/iv 55: l. *lʾš* (v. supra) in 100[2], highly uncert. reading and interpret. (for the reading, cf. also Safar Sumer xvii 33) :: Caquot Syr xl 10: l. poss. *ʾlhʾ* or *byš* (= Sing. abs. of *bʾš$_2$*).

ʾš$_4$ v. *mʾš$_1$*,*mlk$_5$*, *nšl$_2$*, *ʿnh$_2$*, *ʿrkh*, *š$_{10}$*.

ʾš$_5$ v. *hš*.

ʾš$_6$ v. *yš*, *š$_{10}$*.

ʾšd **OffAr** QAL (or PAʿEL?) Impf. 3 p.s.m. *yʾšd* Aḥiq 89; ITTAPH Pf. 3 p.s.f., cf. Warka 9: *it-ta-ši-da-at* (cf. Driver AfO iii 50 × Dupont-Sommer RA xxxix 45: = same form but of the root *šdy$_1$* :: Gordon AfO xii 115f.: = ITPEʿEL Pf. 3 p.s.f. :: Koopmans 184: = ITPAʿAL Pf. 3 p.s.f.; on this form, cf. also Kaufman JAOS civ 89); ITP Impf. 2 p.s.m. *ttʾšd* SSI ii 28 obv. 7 - ¶ verb QAL to pour (out), to spill, to shed; *wdmh yʾšd* Aḥiq 89: and he will shed his blood - ITTAPH (v. however supra) to be spilled, to be poured out (cf. Driver AfO iii 50, Dupont-Sommer RA xxxix 39, 45 (v. however supra), Gordon AfO xii 115f. (v. however supra) - ITP diff. interpret., Fitzmyer JNES xxi 16, 20, WA 220, 225: = to dissipate oneself, cf. however Naveh AION xvi 27, Kutscher with Naveh ibid. n. 23, Gibson SSI ii a.l.: = to be troubled, Bresciani RSO xxxv 19, 21: = to let oneself go, Porten FS Bresciani 432, Porten & Yardeni sub TADAE A 3.3: = to weep? - for the root, cf. also Bongini AION xix 182ff.

ʾšh$_1$ v. *ʾš$_1$*.

ʾšh$_2$ **OffAr** Sing. abs. *ʾšh* KAI 233^{17}, Cowl 30^{12}, Aḥiq 103, 104, 222, ATNS 40^{4}; emph. *ʾštʾ* Cowl 31^{11}, RES 1785A 3 - **JAr** Sing. abs. *ʾšʾ* AMB 14^{2} (or = Sing. emph. of *ʾš$_1$*?); emph. *ʾšth* AMB 2^{2,8,12}, 3^{22}, 9^{1} - ¶ subst. f. - **1)** fire; *ʿqhy ʾšh* ATNS 40^{4}: pieces of fire-wood; for Cowl 30^{12}, cf. Joüon MUSJ xviii 8: cf. also Warka 21, 32: *iš-ša-ʾ* = Sing. abs. (or = Sing. emph. of *ʾš$_2$*?)- **2)** fever: AMB 14^{2} (v. however supra); *ʾšth wʿryth* AMB 2^{2}: the fever and the shiver (cf. AMB 2^{8,12}, 3^{22}, cf. also AMB 9^{1}), cf. also Naveh AAALT 85ff., Naveh & Shaked sub AMB 2^{2} - this word also in Frey 1407 (= MPAT 107): Sing. emph. *ʾštʾ*?? (cf. also Beyer ATTM 343, 524).

ʾšh$_3$ **Ph** Puech Sem xxix 20f., 24f.: l. *ʾšm* (= Plur. abs. of *ʾšh* (= fire-offering)) in KAI 30^{7}, reading of *ʾ* uncert., diff. and uncert. context. v. *mlk$_5$*, *š$_{10}$*.

ʾšw v. *ʾš$_1$*.

ʾšwḥ **Mo** Sing. abs. *ʾšwḥ* KAI 181^{9,23} (*ʾšw[ḥ]*) - ¶ subst. prob. water reservoir, for a discussion on the precise meaning of this technical term, v. *klʾ$_2$* and cf. e.g. Galling BiOr xxii 244, Yadin IEJ xix 18 (and context), BiAr xxxii 70 (n. 18), Lipiński Or xl 335f., Meshel TeAv i 140 n. 12, H.P.Müller TUAT i 648, Jackson & Dearman SMIM 110 :: Torczyner JPOS xvi 5f.: = grave-sanctuary (> sacred building) - this word poss. also in Mo. fragment BASOR cxxv 21^{1}: *[ʾ]šwḥ*, cf. Albright

with Murphy BASOR cxxv 22, Dearman SMIM 173 - on this word, cf. also Brock & Diringer FS Thomas 43f.
v. *ʾšḥh.*

ʾšḥ v. *ʾšḥh.*

ʾšḥh **Amm** Plur. abs. *ʾšḥt* Ber xxii 120[5] (× Zayadine & Thompson Ber xxii 136: = Plur. abs. of *ʾšḥ* (for the interpret. as Plur., cf. also Thompson & Zayadine BASOR ccxii 9f., Teixidor Syr li 318, Coote BASOR ccxl 93, Briend TPOA 141) × Dion RB lxxxii 25: = Sing. abs. (cf. also Baldacci VT xxxi 364ff., Garr DGSP 59, Aufrecht sub CAI 78 :: Baldacci AION xlv 519: = Sing. abs. of *šḥt*$_4$ (= pit) with *alef prostheticum* :: Krahmalkov BASOR ccxxiii 56f., Loretz UF ix 171, Emerton FS v.d.Ploeg 372, 376: = NIPH Impf. 1 p.s. of *šḥt*$_1$, cf. also Shea PEQ '78, 109 (cf. however Garr DGSP 121) :: Becking BiOr xxxviii 275: = QAL Impf. 1 p.s. of *šḥt*$_1$ (= to destroy); for reading problems of the *t*, cf. Thompson BASOR ccxlix 88) - ¶ subst. prob. water reservoir, cistern, cf. e.g. Ahlström PEQ '84, 13, cf. however Coote BASOR ccxl 93: rather = pool/pond - on this word, cf. also Garr DGSP 48.
v. *ʾšwḥ.*

ʾšy v. *ʾsy*$_2$.

ʾšybh **OffAr** Henning with Bivar & Shaked BSOAS xxvii 273f.: l. this subst. (= oath) in BSOAS xxvii 272 i 1, ii 1, v 1, *bʾšybh* = under oath (:: Bivar & Shaked ibid. 272, Altheim & Stiehl AAW iii 69f., 72f., GMA 558: *bʾšybh* = title < Iran., cf. also Teixidor Syr xliv 182), improb. interpret., *ʾšybh* prob. = n.l., cf. Sznycer JA ccliii 4f.

ʾšyt **Hatra** Sing. emph. *ʾšytʾ* 408[7,8]; Plur. + suff. 3 p.s.m. *ʾšyth* 408[3] - ¶ subst. wall, Hatra 408[3]; *ʾšytʾ mʿrbytʾ* Hatra 408[8]: the western wall, cf. Hatra 408[7].

ʾškmst **Pun** word or words (division uncert.) of unknown meaning in KAI 153[5]. Poss division *ʾškm st* (= dem. pron.), cf. Chabot sub RIL 31 :: Alvarez Delgado sub ILC 240: divide *ʾš* (= Sing. cstr. of *ʾš*$_1$)+ *kmst* (= Plur. abs. of *kms/š* (= land of Moab)) = the Moabite men.

ʾškp (< Akkad., cf. Zimmern Fremdw 28, Kaufman AIA 39) - **Hatra** Sing. emph. *ʾškpʾ* 212[2] (reading highly uncert., for first *ʾ*, cf. Teixidor Sumer xx 79f.: or l. *bw*?, for *k*, cf. Milik DFD 388f.: l. *n* (prob.) :: Milik DFD 389: l. poss. *ʾbšnpʾ* = variant of *'bšpʾ*, v. *ʾbšp*) - ¶ subst. leatherworker (v. however supra), Teixidor Sumer xx 79f., Syr xliv 189: = saddler (cf. Vattioni IH a.l.); Aggoula Ber xviii 100: = shoe-maker.

ʾškr$_1$ (< Akkad., cf. Zimmern Fremdw 10, Ellenbogen 42, Kaufman AIA 59 (n. 135), cf. also Lipiński ZAH i 64) - **Hebr** Sing. cstr. *ʾškr* KB xix (cf. Lipiński ZAH i 64 :: Cohen KB a.l.: = Sing. abs.) - **OffAr** Sing.

cstr. *ʾškr* Pers 1^4, 2^5, 3^5, 4^4, 5^4, 8^4, 9^5, 10^6, etc., etc. (:: R.A.Bowman Pers a.l.: in Pers 62^3 = Sing. abs. :: Altheim & Stiehl GH i 430, ASA 18, 20f.: l. *ʾbzkr* = title, function) - ¶ subst. tax, tribute, cf. Naveh & Shaked Or xlii 452, Levine JAOS xcii 72 n. 14, 78 (nn. 66, 68), Degen BiOr xxxi 125 (n. 6), Grelot RB lxxx 597f., Millard JRAS '73, 64, de Menasce with Bernard StudIr i 176, Gignoux RHR clxxxi 87, Hinz FS Nyberg 376f., Oelsner OLZ '75, 475 (cf. also Kaufman AIA 59) :: Cameron with Schmidt Persepolis ii 55: = gift :: Delaunay with Teixidor Syr l 432, Delaunay CC 212f.: = *ʾškr*$_2$ (= series; < Akkad.) :: R.A.Bowman Pers p. 53ff.: = *ʾškr*$_3$ (= intoxicating drink, intoxicant).

ʾškr$_2$ v. *ʾškr*$_1$.

ʾškr$_3$ v. *ʾškr*$_1$.

ʾšl$_1$ (< Akkad., cf. Zimmern Fremdw 35, Kaufman AIA 39) - **OffAr** Sing. abs. *ʾšl* Sach 75 ii 6, 11, 12, 16 (v. infra), ATNS 48^5; Plur. abs. *ʾšln* Cowl 75^5 (and prob. l. 7), MAI xiv/2, 66^3, Sach 75 ii 6, 8 (v. infra), ATNS 48^{4,6}, 57^{2,3,4,5}, etc. - ¶ subst. surface measure (cf. Driver AnOr xii 57; cf. Akkad. *ašlu* = linear measure and surface measure, cf. CAD s.v. × Sach p. 232, Grelot DAE p. 104 (n. f): in Sach 75 *ʾšl*/*ʾšln* forms of *ʾšl*$_2$ = tamarisk) - the abbrev. ʾ - a) in Cowl 81^{11} as linear measure?? - b) in Driv 8^{2,4} as surface measure? × Driv p. 68: = abbrev. of *ʾrdb*.

ʾšl$_2$ v. *ʾšl*$_1$.

ʾšlb v. *šlb*$_2$.

ʾšm$_1$ **Pun** the *assam* (var. *issam*) in Poen 1016 poss. = QAL Pf. 3 p.s.m. of *ʾšm*$_1$ (= to be guilty), cf. L.H.Gray AJSL xxxix 81 (or PIʿEL?); J.J.Glück & Maurach Semitics ii 121f.: = Sing. abs. of *ʾšm*$_2$ (= sinner); Schroed p. 296 (div. otherwise): l. *assamar* = *ʾš*$_4$ + QAL Pf. 3 p.s.m. of *ʾmr*$_1$; or l. *assamar* = Sing. abs. of *ʾš*$_1$ + QAL Pf. 3 p.s.m. of *ʾmr*$_1$; cf. also Sznycer PPP 143.

ʾšm$_2$ v. *ʾšm*$_1$.

ʾšm$_3$ v. *šm*$_1$.

ʾšm$_4$ **DA** word (?) of unknown meaning (*]ʾšm[*) in i 11 (diff. reading; cf. Rofé SB 68: = QAL Impf. 1 p.s. of *šym*$_1$ :: Caquot & Lemaire Syr liv 205: l. *ʾšt* = f. Sing. cstr. of *ʾš*$_1$).

ʾšn v. *ʾdn*$_1$.

ʾšnm v. *šnym*.

ʾšph **Hebr** the *ʾšpt* in Lach xiii 3 prob. = Plur. (abs. or cstr.) of *ʾšph* (= quiver); heavily dam. context; cf. Torczyner Lach i p. 159f., Baumgartner BiOr xix 134, Pardee HAHL 109; Ellenbogen 45f.: < Akkad.

ʾšpzkn (< Iran., cf. Telegdi JA ccxxvi 233) - **Hatra** a Sing. + suff. 3 p.s.m./f. poss. to be found in 287^2 (*[ʾ]špzknh*) = his/her majordomus;

reading and interpret. uncert. Safar Sumer xxvii 7: l. *špy?knh*; Degen NESE iii 78: *n* doubtful (cf. also Vattioni IH a.l.: l. *[ʾ]špzkh* (cf. also Aggoula Sumer lxiii 362)), for this and other reading/interpret. proposals, cf. Degen ibid.; cf. also 364[5] (*ʾšpzknh*), cf. e.g. Aggoula Sumer lxiii 362: = his majordomus

ʾšpr **Hatra** Sing. emph. *ʾšprʾ* prob. in 283[2]; meaning uncert.: weaver? (< Akkad., cf. Zimmern Fremdw 27, Kaufman AIA 59); other proposals: a) cleaner of clothes, cf. Safar Sumer xxvii 6 n. 14 - b) majordomus, for this interpret., cf. Degen NESE iii 74.
v. *ʾyšpr*.

ʾšr$_1$ v. *ʾšr$_7$*, *yšb$_1$*, *yšr$_1$*.

ʾšr$_2$ **Ph** v.d.Branden BiOr xxxiii 12: the *ʾšr* in KAI 27[10] = QAL Imper. s.f. of *ʾšr$_2$* (= to leave, to go); less prob. interpret. Prob. = n.d. (Ashur), cf. the discussion (also for reading problems) with Röllig KAI a.l., Avishur PIB 252, Sperling HUCA liii 6f., Gibson SSI iii p. 83, 85 :: Cross & Saley BASOR cxcvii 45 (n. 17): = n.d. (Ashera), cf. also Baldacci BiOr xl 128: = n.d. f. :: Lipiński RTAT 265: = Sing. abs. of *ʾšr$_5$* (= charter) :: v.d.Branden BO iii 43f.: = Sing. abs. of *ʾšr$_3$* :: du Mesnil du Buisson FS Dussaud 424, Torczyner JNES vi 22, Garbini OA xx 282ff.: = *ʾšr$_7$*.

ʾšr$_3$ **Pun** Sing. cstr. *ʾšr* KAI 145[11] - ¶ subst. joy; in the expression *bʾšr lbn* KAI 145[11]: with joy of heart, cf. Février Sem vi 26, Röllig KAI a.l., Krahmalkov RSF iii 197.
v. *ʾšr$_2$*.

ʾšr$_4$ **Pun** Sing. cstr. *ʾšr* KAI 277[1] (or = Sing. abs., v. *qdš$_2$*), CIS i 3779[6] (cf. Garbini OA iv 37 (cf. also Levi Della Vida ibid.), Fitzmyer JAOS lxxxvi 288f., Ferron Mus lxxxi 527 × = Sing. abs., cf. CIS i a.l.; cf. also Dupont-Sommer JA cclii 292, Naveh Lesh xxx 235, Vattioni AION xv 292) - **DA** Sing. cstr. *ʾšr* i 11 - **Samal** Sing. cstr. *ʾšr* KAI 214[27]; + suff. 3 p.s.m. *ʾšrh* KAI 214[32] (for both instances, v. infra; the *ʾšr* in KAI 215[18] most prob. = n.l. (Assur), cf. e.g. Dupont-Sommer Ar 66, AH i/2, 2, Donner KAI a.l., Dion p. 72, 400 :: e.g. Cooke NSI p. 179, Landsberger Samʾal 70, Koopmans 75, Sader EAS 168 (n. 47): = Sing. abs. or cstr. of *ʾšr$_4$*) - **OldAr** Sing. + suff. 3 p.s.m. *ʾšrh* KAI 222A 5 (*ʾšr[h]*), B 3, 224[7]; + suff. 2 p.pl.m. *ʾšrkm* KAI 224[5] - **OffAr** Sing. abs. *ʾtr* ATNS 5[5], Aḥiq 34 (× Kutscher Or xxxix 182, Degen WO viii 130 (n. 7), GGA '79, 43: = Sing. cstr.), Sem xxvii 72 conc. 4?), 97, Driv 6[6], 7[2,4,6,9], FuF xxxv 173[8] (= ASA 244; or cstr.?, diff. and uncert. context), also in Cowl 17[2] (cf. for this interpret. also Porten RB xc 411) cstr. *ʾtr* Cowl 71[20], NESE iii 48 conc. 6; emph. *ʾtrʾ* Cowl 13[19], KAI 261[6]; + suff. 3 p.s.m. *ʾšrh* KAI 225[8] (or + suff. 3 p.s.f.??, cf. Stiehl AAW i 221), *ʾtrh* Cowl 6[2], 32[8], OMRO lxviii 45[3] (*[ʾ]trh*; for the reading, cf. Hoftijzer OMRO lxviii 46), IPAA 11[8] (for the use of the suffix, cf. Davary & Humbach IPAA a.l.); + suff. 2 p.s.m. *ʾšrk* KAI 225[10]; cf. Frah xxv 48 (*bʾtr*), Paik 177 (*ʾtrh*), 191, 192 (*bʾtr*), GIPP 20, 47, 49 - **Nab** Sing. abs. *ʾtr* RES 1181[1] (= J 83; on this form, cf. Diem Or l 354f.), 2052[6]; cstr. *ʾtr* MPAT 64 i 2, J 30[3,5] (= CIS ii 200; for the reading in both instances, cf. Milik sub ARNA-Nab 79 :: Jaussen & Savignac sub J 30: l. *bʾḥr* = b_2 + Sing. cstr. of *ʾḥr*₂, cf. CIS ii sub 200); emph. *ʾtrʾ* CIS ii 217[7], 235A 2, RES 1110A (= J 54), C (= J 56, ARNA-Nab 92), 1119A (= J 100), 1174[1] (= CIS ii 270, J 43), Chal 1; Plur. emph. *ʾtryʾ* CIS ii 350[3] - **Palm** Sing. abs. *ʾtr* CIS ii 3913 ii 131, 132, 3949[4], 4011[5], SBS 24[4], 68[1] (*ʾ[t]r*), RIP 143[5]; emph. *ʾtrʾ* PNO 2ter 7, Ber v 110[4], Syr xix 159[1,2]; + suff. 3 p.s.m. *ʾtrh* CIS ii 3917[4] - **JAr** Sing. abs. *ʾtr* MPAT-A 26[7], AMB 3[14]; emph. *ʾtrʾ* MPAT 47 recto 2, 52[3,5,9], *ʾtrh* MPAT-A 3[2] (= SM 60), 5[3,7] (= SM 64), 7[3,4] (*ʾtr[h]*; = SM 65), 13[2], 30[2], 35[1]; Plur. emph. *ʾtryʾ* IEJ xxxvi 206[4] - ¶ subst. m. place, passim; for KAI 224[5], cf. Greenfield ActOr xxix 4; the Plur. in CIS ii 350[3] has no Sing. meaning :: Lipiński OLP viii 115 n. 88; cf. - a) *mn ʾtr ʾḥrn* Driv 7[2,4,6,9]: from elsewhere - b) *bkl ʾtr* Aḥiq 97, CIS ii 4011[5], MPAT-A 26[7], AMB 3[13f.]: everywhere (cf. *bkl ʾtr* <*k*>*lh* CIS ii 3949[5]: everywhere, cf. also RIP 143[5] *bkl ʾtr klh*, cf. Aggoula Syr liv 284 :: Gawlikowski Syr xlvii 314, RIP a.l., TP 97 (no. 21): in the whole place (i.e. sanctuary)) - c) *ʾtr dy dms* CIS ii 3913 ii 131: public place, cf. CIS ii 3913 ii 132: *ʾtr dy mtknšyn* = the place where they assemble - d) *tbʿh ʾtr zy ʾnt thškḥ* Aḥiq 34: search (for him) where you may find him - e) *ʾtr ym[ʾ]* Cowl 71[20]: a place situated near the sea/on the seaside? (dam. context) - f) *ʾšr rḥln* DA i 11: a place fit for breeding ewes (for other interpret., v. *ybl*₁); cf. prob. also *ʾtr ʿbwrʾ* NESE iii 48 conc. 6f.: a place where corn is extant - specialized meanings: - **1)** site; *tḥwmy ʾtrʾ dk* MPAT 52[3]: the boundaries of that site, cf. also MPAT 47 recto 2 (?, heavily dam. context), 52[5,9], IEJ xxxvi 206[4]; cf. also Syr xix 159 i 2: *ʾtrʾ* = a site to build upon, cf. Milik DFD 177 (:: Ingholt Ber v 99 n. 1: = base or floor, cf. also Teixidor sub Inv xi 81) - **2)** base upon which an object is placed, sockle; *ḥmnʾ klh hw wʾtrh* CIS ii 3917[3f.]: the whole incense altar, (i.e.) itself and its sockle (cf. Ingholt Ber v 99 n. 1 :: Lipiński OLP iii 116: *ʾtrh* = its sanctuary (for this meaning, v. infra) :: Milik DFD 143: *hw wʾtrh* = he (i.e. the donor) and his substitute; for the text, cf. also Clermont-Ganneau RAO vii 10f., Starcky Syr xxvi 52, Teixidor Syr liii 307) - **3)** locality, region; *yhb lʾbgl šlṭnʾ bʾtrʾ klh* PNO 2ter 6ff.: he has given to A. authority over the whole region; this meaning prob. also in KAI 224[7] (v. *pny*) and Cowl 13[19] - **4)** station, situation; *drgmn ... zy ʾtrh byb byrtʾ ʿbyd* Cowl 6[2f.]: D. .... whose office is in the fortress of Yeb (cf. OMRO lxviii 45[3]), cf. Nöldeke ZA xx 146, for the context, v. *ʿbd*₁; cf. poss. also Cowl

13¹⁹ - **5)** vestiges of someone's existence; *yṣhw šmk wʾšrk mn ḥyn* KAI
225⁹ᶠ·: may they pluck out your name and the traces of your existence
from among the living (cf. also Gevirtz VT xi 148 (n. 3) :: Cathcart
CBQ xxxv 182: *ʾšrk* = your house; for the context, v. *ḥy₂*) - **6)** seat
(or: stand?): RES 1110A (= J 54), C (= J 56, ARNA-Nab 92), 1119A
(= J 100), 1174 (= J 43, CIS ii 270), SBS 68¹ - **7)** building; in CIS ii
217⁷ used to indicate a tomb construction, in CIS ii 235A 2 to indicate
a chapel/sanctuary (cf. Clermont-Ganneau RAO iv 110ff. :: Milik Bibl
xlviii 554: in both texts = place); in SBS 24⁴ prob. indicating part
of temple (gate), cf. also Garbini OA xiv 179 :: Degen WO viii 130:
ʾtr dy = the place where ...; *ʾšr qdš* KAI 277¹ (v. supra): holy place,
sanctuary (cf. also Margalit VT xl 292 n. 42; v. also *qdš₂*), cf. also CIS
i 3779⁶: *ʾšr hqdš* (:: Milik Bibl xlviii 573 (n. 3): = train, suite, retinue,
cf. also idem in Bibl xxxviii 253 n. 3); *hdn ʾtrh qdyšh* MPAT-A 5⁷: this
holy place (i.e. synagogue), cf. MPAT-A 3² (= SM 60), 5³ᶠ· (= SM 64),
13²ᶠ·, 30², 35¹, cf. also *ʾtrh* MPAT-A 7³: synagogue (dam. context, cf.
also Naveh sub SM 65); cf. also Vattioni Aug ix 461f. - **8)** preceded by
prep. *b₂* and in this combination used prepositionally - a) in the place
of; *bnwh zy ysqn bʾšr[h]* KAI 222A 5: his sons who will come in his place
(prob. with temporal feature: after (cf. Fitzmyer AIS 31, Lemaire &
Durand IAS 131)); *mlk zy [ysq wymlk] bʾšrh* KAI 222B 2f.: a king who
(will come up and rule) in his place - b) after; *wdy hn yhwʾ bʾtr mnʿt
dnh* CIS ii 200²ᶠ· (= J 30; for the reading, cf. Milik sub ARNA-Nab 79):
and if there will be (someone) after (the death of) M. mentioned above
..., cf. also CIS ii 200⁵ (= J 30, for the reading, cf. Milik sub ARNA-Nab
79) - c) meaning of *bʾšr* in KAI 214²⁷,³² uncert., cf. e.g. Dion 33: in
the region of, Cooke NSI p. 162f., 170, Donner KAI a.l.: after (cf. also
Gibson SSI ii p. 75) - **9)** preceded by prep. *mn₅ + b₂* - a) in the place
of; *ʾṣdqh mn bʾtrh* RES 1103⁸ (= J 5): his heir in his place (probably
with temporal feature: after) - b) *mn bʾtr d* = conj. after: MPAT 64²ᶠ·
:: Fitzmyer & Harrington MPAT a.l.: = prep., in accordance with (cf.
also Starcky RB lxi 165, 168) - Gibson SSI ii p. 66, 71: pro *yqḥ* (= QAL
Impf. 3 p.s.m. of *lqḥ*) *ʾš* (= Sing. abs. of *ʾš₁*) *rʿyh* (= Sing./Plur. m.
+ suff. 3 p.s.m. of *rʿ₁* (= neighbour) or = f. Sing. abs. *rʿ₁* (= female
companion)) *wytr* (= QAL/PA ʿEL Pf. 3 p.s.m. of *ytr₁*) in KAI 214¹⁰ᶠ·
l. *yqḥ[w]* (= QAL Impf. 3 p.pl.m. of *lqḥ*) *ʾšrw* (= Plur. abs. (nom.) of
ʾšr₄) *yh[b]yt* (= Sing. cstr.) *hdd* = the districts received the bounty of
Hadad (uncert. reading and interpret., preferable however to the older
one, for which, cf. e.g. Donner KAI a.l., Dion 28) - Cooke NSI p. 174,
179: the *ʾšr* in KAI 215¹⁸ = Sing. abs. of *ʾšr₄* (improb. interpret.) =
n.l. cf. e.g. Donner KAI a.l., Gibson SSI ii p. 81, 85 - the *ʾšr* in Hatra
40², meaning unknown, heavily dam. context (Milik DFD 340: = part
of n.p.?) - Beyer ATTM 352, 526: l. *ʾtryn* = Plur. abs. in MPAT 59².

v. *ʾšr₅*, *btr*, *ʿšrm*, *qṣr₆*, *šʾr₃*, *tqʾ*.

ʾšr₅ **OldAr** Sing. cstr. *ʾšr* KAI 202B 15, 16 (*ʾš[r]*) - ¶ subst. of uncert. meaning (dam. contexts); Lidzbarski Eph iii 10 (cf. also Donner KAI a.l.): = inscription; Rosenthal ANET 656, Dupont-Sommer AH i/2, 2 s.v., Lipiński Stud 23, Tawil Or xliii 52, Gibson SSI ii p. 11, 16, Sader EAS 209: = achievements, accomplishments :: Dussaud RevArch '08, 233f.: = *ʾšr₄*(= temple; cf. also Degen AAG p. 45) :: Torrey JAOS xxxv 363: = *ʾšr₇*.
v. *ʾšr₂*.

ʾšr₆ v. *ʾšrn*, *ʾtr₄*.

ʾšr₇ **Mo** KAI 181[29] - **Hebr** KAI 191B 1, 2, 192[6], 193[5,11], 194[2,4,11], 200[6,8], SSI i p. 48 xviii 2, TA-H 5[10] (dam. context), 8[9] (?, heavily dam. context), 18[7], 21[7] (*ʾš[r]*, dam. context), 29[7] (dam. context), 40[5,15] (*ʾš[r]*, dam. context; cf. also Aharoni BASOR cxcvii 29f.), 71[2], IEJ xxv 229[1], xxx 171[2], DJD ii 17A 2, Mosc sig. 30 (= Vatt sig. eb. 149; *[ʾ]šr*), Mosc var. B 1 (?, heavily dam. context; cf. Sam p. 32), 2[2] (heavily dam. context; for context, cf. Ussishkin BiAr xxxiii 44), JPOS xxi 135[2] (cf. Puech RB lxxxi 208 n. 46), HBTJ 1, 2, 3 - **Edom** TeAv xii 97[4] - ¶ nota relationis - **1)** used to introduce - a) relative clause, *qrn ʾšr yspty ʿl hʾrṣ* KAI 181[29]: the towns which I annexed to the land (cf. KAI 191B 2, 192[6], 193[5,11], 194[11], SSI i p. 48 xviii 2, TA-H 18[7]); cf. also *kkl ʾšr šlḥ ʾdny kn* ... KAI 194[2f.]: in accordance with all (the instructions) which my lord has sent me, so .... (cf. also KAI 194[3f.]) - b) subject clause, *ʾrr ʾšr ymḥh* IEJ xxv 229[1]: cursed be he who will efface - c) relative phrase, ... *ʾšr lʾdn gdy* ... TA-H 71[2f.] (dam. context): .. which belongs to (my) lord G.; *lplʾyhw ʾšr ʿl hms* IEJ xxx 171: belonging to P. who is over the corvée; for *ʾšr ʿl hbyt*, v. *byt₁* - **2)** preceded by prep. *k₁* (with temporal function), *kʾšr klt ʾt qṣry* ... *lqḥ ʾt bgd ʿbdk* KAI 200[8f.]: after I had finished my grain, he took the garment of your servant (cf. also KAI 200[6f.]) - poss. also *ʾšr₇* in Hebr. text HUCA xl/xli 159[3] (for context, v. also *yd*) :: Garbini AION xxviii 193 (div. otherwise): l. *ʾšrt* prob. = PIʿEL (?) Pf. 3 p.s.f. of *ʾšr₁*(= to bless > to curse; for this reading, cf. Teixidor Syr xlix 428; cf. also Catastini Hen vi 133ff.) :: Lemaire RB lxxxiv 599, 601ff., Naveh BASOR ccxxxv 28, Miller SVT xxxii 317f., Hadley VT xxxvii 51, 55ff. (div. otherwise): l. *ʾšrth* = Sing. + suff. 3 p.s.m. of *ʾšrh₂* (cf. also Zevit MLAHE 17, Winter FG 488f., Tigay FS Cross 174f., Margalit VT xxxix 372ff., Shea VT xl 110, 112, Smelik HDAI 139 :: Mittmann ZDPV xcvii 144, 147 (div. otherwise): l. *ʾl* (= Sing. cstr. of *ʾl₁*) *šrth* (= Sing. + suff. 3 p.s.m. of *šrt₃* (= service)) :: Zevit BASOR cclv 42ff.: l. *ʾšrth* = n.d. *ʾšrt* with double fem. ending (cf. also Angerstorfer BN xvii 11ff., O'Connor VT xxxvii 225, 228f., Conrad TUAT ii 557) :: Spronk BAAI 308 (n. 7; div. otherwise): l.

šrth = PIʿEL Inf. cstr. + suff. 3 p.s.m. of *šrt*$_1$ - Bar-Adon IEJ xxv 231: in the diff. text IEJ xiii 79$^{1f.}$ (ʾʾ*rr yšr*) *yšr* prob. mistake for ʾ*šr*$_7$, cf. however Lemaire RB lxxxiii 561f.: ʾʾ*rr yšr ...* mistake for ʾ*rr* ʾ*šr y...* (highly uncert. interpret., v. also *mḥy*$_1$) - on this word, cf. also Garr DGSP 85f.
v. ʾ*šr*$_{2,5}$, ʿ*šr*$_4$.

ʾ**šrh**$_1$ **Hebr** Sing. + suff. 3 p.s.m. ʾ*šrth* KA 7^2, 9^1, ʾ*šrt* KA 8^6 - **Ph** Sing. cstr. ʾ*šrt* KAI 19^4, EI xviii 117^2 (= IEJ xxxv 85) - **OldAr** Sing. + suff. 3 p.pl.m. ʾ*šrthm* KAI 222B 11 (cf. Fitzmyer AIS 17, 65 × Lipiński Stud 34: = Plur. + suff. 3 p.pl.m., cf. also Kaufman AIA 153, Lemaire & Durand IAS 123; cf. also Dupont-Sommer Sf p. 74, Donner KAI a.l.) - **OffAr** Sing. emph. ʾ*trt*ʾ KAI 260^3 - ¶ subst. prob. meaning: sanctuary; for KAI 19^4, cf. Halévy REJ xii 109f., Cooke NSI p. 50f., Lidzbarski sub KI 16, Chabot sub RES 1215, Röllig KAI a.l., FS Friedrich 415 n. 23, DD p. 187, v.d.Branden BO vii 70, 73f., Lipiński OLP iii 114, Gibson SSI iii p. 119f. :: e.g. E.Meyer ZAW xlix 9f.: = ʾ*šrh*$_2$ (= sacred pole (of wood)), cf. Milik DFD 424: = ʾ*šrh*$_2$ > divine female consort, cf. also idem Bibl xlviii 573 n. 3; for EI xviii 117^2, cf. Dothan EI a.l., IEJ xxxv 86; for KAI 222B 11, cf. Dupont-Sommer Sf p. 74, Fitzmyer AIS 65, Donner KAI a.l. :: Kaufman AIA 153: = ʾ*šrh*$_2$?, v. also supra; for KAI 260^3, cf. Driver AnOr xii 53, Lipiński OLP iii 115 :: Cowley CRAI '21, 9f.: = ʾ*šrh*$_2$, cf. also Hanson BASOR cxcii 8 n. 13 :: Kahle & Sommer KlF i 33f.: = ʾ*šrh*$_3$ (= site (cf. also Donner KAI a.l.)); for ʾ*šrh* in KA 7^2, 8^6, 9^1 = divine female consort, cf. e.g. Angerstorfer BN xvii 7ff., North FS Fitzmyer 118ff. or = cultic symbol or sacred tree, cf. Lemaire BAR x/6 47ff., RB lxxxiv 603ff., Emerton ZAW xciv 14, Hadley VT xxxvii 204, Olyan Ashera, Maier Ashera 169ff.; for this word, cf. also Tigay NOG 26ff., Scagliarini RSO lxiii 207 (with literature). - the same word also in KA 12^1 (ʾ*šrt*, heavily dam. context).
v. ʾ*šr*$_7$.

ʾ**šrh**$_2$ v. ʾ*šr*$_7$, ʾ*šrh*$_1$.

ʾ**šrh**$_3$ v. ʾ*šrh*$_1$.

ʾ**šrn** (< Iran., cf. Benveniste JA ccxlii 303, Degen Or xliv 120, Hinz AISN 21) - **OffAr** Sing. abs. ʾ*šrn* Krael 3^{23} (cf. Milik RB lxi 249, Ginsberg JAOS lxxiv 157, Kutscher JAOS lxxiv 235, Torrey JNES xiii 152 :: Krael p. 101 n. 6, 163: = Plur. abs. of ʾ*šr*$_6$(= pole, log)), ATNS 26^{8,10}; emph. ʾ*šrn*ʾ Cowl 26^{5,9,21}, 27^{18}, 30^{11} - ¶ subst. m. prob. meaning, timber, panelling, woodwork (cf. Joüon Bibl xxii 38ff., Torrey JNES xiii 151f., cf. also Barth ZA xxi 192, Galling TGI 86, Grelot Sem xx 25, DAE p. 287 n. k, 404 n. p), the working materials of a carpenter like nails included, cf. Cowl 26$^{15f.}$ (cf. also Tuland JNES xvii 271ff., Hinz AISN 21; cf. Porten & Greenfield JEAS p. 42: = fittings?) ::

Nyberg MO xxiv 138f.: = equipment, outfit < Iran., cf. Hinz NWAP 41: 'Ausstattungsgegenstände', 'Möbel', cf. also Koopmans 129: or = beams, rooftimbers? (cf. also Nober VD xxxvi 103) :: Torczyner OLZ xv 399f.: = construction materials :: Wag 20 n. 3: = tools :: Lagrange RB xvii 326, 334, Vincent Rel 314: = decoration :: Galling OLZ xl 473ff.: = specification; cf. also Cowl p. 93, 102, Milik RB lxi 249, Segal sub ATNS 26.

'šš v. mn_4.

'št_1 (or *'šth*?; < Akkad., cf. Masson & Sznycer RPC 52, Kaufman AIA 37 (n. 32)) - **Ph** Sing. (or Plur.?) cstr. *'štt* KAI 37A 14 (= Kition C 1 A 13), B 5 (= Kition C 1 B 5) - ¶ subst. of uncert. meaning, pillar, pillar hall?, cf. e.g. Cooke NSI p. 67, Harr p. 83 (or: = stylobate?), Dahood Ps i 69, Peckham Or xxxvii 306, 316, Teixidor Syr l. 424, Healy BASOR ccxvi 56, Masson & Sznycer RPC 52f., Amadasi & Karageorghis sub Kition C 1 (cf. also Delcor UF xi 158ff., Gibson SSI iii p. 99, 125); Röllig KAI a.l.: = fundament, foundation (cf. also Lidzbarski sub KI 29, Dahood UF xi 143); Vincent RB xxxvii 539: = sacred stone (bethel) with emblem(s); v.d.Branden BO iv 48f., viii 258, 260: = incense burner (cf. also idem PO ii 404) - for KAI 26A ii 5, v. also *'š*$_1$ - Dupont-Sommer Sem iii 43: l. *'št* (Sing. abs.) also in KAI 10[14]??
v. *'š*$_1$, *tḥt*.

'št_2 v. mlk_5.

'šth v. *'š*t_1.

'štl **OffAr** Sing. emph. (?) *'štl'* RES 1300[9] - ¶ subst. of unknown meaning, probably movable object. Lidzbarski Eph iii 24: < Greek στολή? = article of dress, cloak, cf. also Grelot DAE p. 144 (n. f): prob. < Greek στολή = (military) equipment - cf. *'wṣlt*.

'štp **Pun** word (?) of unknown meaning and reading (l. *'ztp*?) in Antas 18[2], cf. Garbini AION xix 328.

'štr (< Akkad., cf. also Kaufman AIA 60) - **OffAr** Sing. emph. *'štr'* CSOI-Ar 140 (diff. reading) - **Palm** Sing. emph. *'štr'* Syr xii 133[4], 134[3], Inv xi 87[4], *'s[t]r'*RIP 152[1] (= CIS ii 3985 = Inv vi 1; heavily dam. context) - **Hatra** Sing. emph. *'štr'*, cf. Assur 17 i 5, 19[5], 23c 3 (*'štr['])*, 27d 2, 29c (*[']štr'*), j 3, k 2 - ¶ subst. (< n.d.) goddess; *sr 'štr'* Assur 17 i 4f.: the goddess S. (cf. Assur 23c 3, 27d 2, 29c, j 3, k 2); *l'štr[t'] 'štr' ṭbt'* Syr xii 134[2f.]: to Ashtarte the good goddess.

't_1 **Hebr** Plur. abs. *'tt* KAI 194[11] - ¶ subst. signal, code-signal (cf. e.g. Thomas Prophet 22, Gibson SSI i p. 43, Reviv CSI p. 84, Lemaire IH i p. 113 :: Torczyner JQR xxxix 365ff.: = miracle) - Dupont-Sommer Waw a.l.: *b'wt* in AMB 6[8,13] = b_2 + *'wt* (= Sing. abs. of *'wt*$_2$ (= orthogr. variant of *'t*$_1$)), *b'wt* = litterally, to the letter?? (highly uncert. reading

and interpret., cf. Gordon Or xviii 339ff., Naveh & Shaked AMB p. 62f., 67: l. *zbʾwt* = variant of *ṣbʾwt* used as part of n.d.).
v. *ʾyt*$_3$, *ʾnth*$_2$, *ʾt*$_6$, *hlkt*, *lʾy*.

ʾt$_2$ (< Akkad.?) - **OffAr** Sing. cstr. *ʾt* CIS ii 65^{2} (= Del 101)- ¶ subst. prob. rent, cf. Del a.l. :: Lidzbarski Handb 230: = *ʾt*$_5$ (= *ʾyt*$_3$).

ʾt$_3$ **OffAr** *ʾyt*MAI xiv/2, 66^{15}, Cowl 46^{3}, 54^{4}, *ʾt* Herm 1^{9}; cf. Nisa-b 447^{2}, 526^{2} (*[ʾ]yt*), 556^{2}, 661^{2}, 676^{2} (*ʾyt*); cf. also GIPP 18, 48, MP 2 - **Palm** *ʾyt* CIS ii 3913 ii 124, 4175^{7}, RB xxxix 541^{2} - **JAr** *ʾyt* MPAT 42^{16} (dam. context) - ¶ noun (prob. related etymologically to *ʾyty*), only used in specific constructions: presence, existence (mostly to be translated: there is) - a) + prep. *b*$_2$, for CIS ii 3913 ii 124, v. *tgrh* - b) + prep. *l*$_5$, *ʾyt lk ḥmrn 10* Cowl 54$^{4f.}$: you have 10 donkeys, cf. MAI xiv/2, 66^{15}, RB xxxix 541^{2} - c) for *ʾt* + *ʿl*$_7$ in Herm 1^{9}, v. *ʿrb*$_4$ - cf. also *lyš*$_2$ - Segal ATNS a.l.: a form *ʾyt* in ATNS 29 i 6 (context however heavily dam.: *]ʾyt*, reading highly uncert., cf. Porten & Yardeni sub TADAE B 8.1).
v. *ʾyt*$_3$, *ʾyty*,*ṣly*.

ʾt$_4$ v. *ʾnth*$_2$.

ʾt$_5$ v. *ʾyt*$_3$, *ʾt*$_{2,6}$.

ʾt$_6$ **Ph** KAI 10^{16}, 13^{8}, 14^{8,9}, 26A i 11, 37A 11 (= Kition C 1 A 10), 60^{8}, Mus li 286^{2}; + suff. 3 p.s.m. *ʾty* Syr xlviii 396^{3} (cf. Caquot Syr xlviii 400, Liverani RSF ii 36f., Lipiński RSF ii 51, Gaster BASOR ccix 19, Cross CBQ xxxvi 488 :: Gibson SSI iii p. 89f. (cf. also Garbini OA xx 288, 292): = + suff. 1 p.s. :: Röllig NESE ii 30f., v.d.Branden BiOr xxxiii 13, xxxvi 202, Avishur PIB 268, UF x 33, de Moor JEOL xxvii 111: = Qal Pf. 3 p.s.m. of *ʾty*$_1$); + suff. 2 p.s.m. *ʾtk* KAI 10^{13} - **Pun** KAI 124^{3}, 141^{4} (v. infra), RES 942^{7}; + suff. 1 p.s.; cf. Poen 947: *itte* (var. *ette*; :: Krahmalkov Or lvii 63ff.: l. *itt/ett* (without pron. suffix)); for Poen 937, v. *z*$_1$, for Poen 936, v. *tny*$_1$ - **Hebr** KAI 193^{20}, 196$^{1f.,2}$ (:: Gordon BASOR lxx 17: = Sing. cstr. of *ʾt*$_1$:: Torczyner Lach i p. 117 (div. otherwise): l. *ʾth* = *ʾth*$_2$ (v. *rʾy*)), TA-H 24^{19}; + suff. 3 p.s.m. *ʾtw* DJD ii 24A 10 (heavily dam. context), *ʾth* KAI 191B 2; + suff. 2 p.s.m. *ʾtk* TA-H 5^{2}, 6^{2}, 9^{2} (*ʾt[k]*; dam. context), 16^{7} (dam. context); + suff. 1 p.s. *ʾty* KAI 200^{10}; + suff. 3 p.pl.m. *ʾtm* TA-H 3^{6} (cf. Aharoni TA a.l. :: Pardee UF x 300f., HAHL 238 (cf. also Hospers SV 103): = *ʾt*$_5$ (= *ʾyt*$_3$) + suff. 3 p.pl.m.); + suff. 2 p.pl.m. *ʾtkm* TA-H 24^{17}, BiAr xxxix 10 (dam. context) - ¶ prep. with, near, beside; *mškb ʾt rpʾm* KAI 13^{8}: a resting-place with (i.e. among) the shades (cf. KAI 14^{8}); *hqṣrm ʾty* KAI 200^{10}: (those) who were reaping together with me; *wʾm ʾbl tšt šm ʾtk* KAI 10^{13}: and if you do not put my name with (i.e. next to) yours; cf. also KAI 191B 2; in special contexts: - a) *wysgrnm hʾlnm hqdšm ʾt mmlk<t> ʾdr* KAI 14^{9}: the holy gods will deliver them to a mighty prince (v. *mmlkh*; cf. Dahood Bibl l 341f.: may they imprison them with ...) - b) *wšt ʾnk šlm ʾt kl mlk* KAI 26A i 11f.: and I made peace with every king; cf. *brkt ʾtkm* BiAr xxxix 10: blessings (be) with you (dam. context) - c) *wdbr hmlk ʾtkm bnbškm* TA-H $24^{17f.}$: the word of the king (i.e. his command) is incumbent upon you for your very life (cf. Pardee HAHL 60, cf. also Dion JAOS ciii 472) - d) *hʾnšm ʾt ʾlyšʿ* TA-H $24^{19f.}$: the men have to be with (i.e. under the commandment of) E. (cf. Aharoni TA-H a.l., Pardee UF x 322, HAHL 61, JNES xliv 70 (cf. also Hospers SV 104) :: Aharoni BASOR cxcvii 7f.: (get) the men to E. :: Lemaire Sem xxiii 17, IH i p. 188, 190: the men under the commandment of E. (apposition to preceding *-km*) :: Dahood Or xlvi 331 (comb. otherwise): *šlḥty lhʿyd ... hʾnšm ʾt ʾlyšʿ* = I have sent men from E. to testify); cf. also *wnntn ʾt hkhnm ʾt ʾrš wʾt bdʿštrt* RES $942^{6f.}$: and they are placed under the supervision of the priests, of A. and B. (prob. interpret.) - e) *ʾt pn kl ʾln g[bl]* KAI 10^{16}: in the presence of all the gods of G.; *[yt]t sml ... z ... ʾt pn ʾdny ʾt pn mlqrt* Mus li 286^{2}: I have placed this statue ... in the presence of (i.e. before) my lord, before M.; cf. also *ʾdmm ʾš pʿl mšrt ʾt pn gw* KAI $60^{7f.}$: the men who have held office in the presence of (i.e. at the service of) the community - f) preceded by other prep. - **1)** mn_5, *šlḥ mʾtk ... hqmḥ* TA-H $5^{2f.}$: send on your part ... meal, cf. also TA-H $6^{2ff.}$ (cf. Levine Shn iii 292); *mʾt hnbʾ* KAI 193^{20}: by the prophet (prob. interpret. (cf. Hoftijzer FS Hospers 87f., cf. also Smelik PEQ '90, 134f.), for the context, v. also $nbʾ_2$); for KAI 124^{3}, v. $ʿly_1$ - **2)** $ʿd_6$, *lmbʾbn ʾš ʿl ... wʿd ʾt ʾbn z* KAI $141^{4f.}$: from the stone which is at ... unto this stone (:: Chabot BAr '43/45, 66: *ʾt* = $ʾt_5$ (= $ʾyt_3$) :: Février BAr '51/52, 118, Röllig KAI a.l.: *ʾt* = Sing. cstr. of $ʾt_1$:: Février CB vii 121: pro *ʾt*l *ṣt* = prep. meaning towards, near < $ṣdt_2$) - Guidi MonAnt xxi 165f.: *ʾt* in ICO-Sard 35 = $ʾt_6$ (cf. also Garbini RSO xl 212, FR 250a, Amadasi ICO a.l.), uncert. interpret. :: Hoftijzer VT xiii 337ff. (div. otherwise): l. *ʾtʾ* = $ʾt_5$ + suff. 3 p.s. (v. also $ʾš_1$).

v. $ʾy_3$, $ʾyt_3$, *ʾmnh*, hn_3, mwt_1, *mṭwtw*, $nšʾ_1$, *ṣlqh*, *qnmy*, *tkk*.

ʾtʾ v. $ʾnth_2$, $nšʾ_1$.

ʾth₁ v. $ʾš_1$.

ʾth₂ v. $ʾnth_2$, $ʾt_6$, *nšṭ*.

ʾtwn v. $ʾnth_2$.

ʾtḥn v. *ʾtḥr*.

ʾtḥq v. *ʾtḥr*.

ʾtḥr **Amm** Sing. abs. *ʾtḥr* Ber xxii 120^{4} (:: Cross with Zayadine & Thompson Ber xxii 131: or l. *ʾsḥr*?= enclosure wall (cf. also BASOR ccxii 10; Coote BASOR ccxl 93: = enclosure, park) :: Krahmalkov

BASOR ccxxiii 56: = HIPHT (Dt) of ʾ*ḥr*$_1$ (= to be delayed, to be left behind), cf. also Loretz UF ix 170: = Gt or Dt of ʾ*ḥr*$_1$, cf. also Becking BiOr xxxviii 274f.: = verbal adjective with infixed *t* (with pass. meaning): that what is retained (i.e. store) :: Shea PEQ '78, 109: = HITP Impf. 1 p.s. of *ḥry*$_1$ (= to enflame oneself), cf. also Emerton FS v.d.Ploeg 372ff., 376: = to vex oneself; reading ʾ*tḥn*poss. but less prob., cf. Zayadine & Thompson Ber xxii 131: = throne, platform, cf. also BASOR ccxii 10, BiAr xxxvii 17), v. also infra - ¶ subst. of unknown meaning; Zayadine & Thompson Ber xxii 131: = hiding-place?, hole?, cf. also BASOR ccxii 10 (cf. Aufrecht sub CAI 78: = hollow); Dion RB lxxxii 25: = tunnel? (cf. also Briend TPOA 141, Baldacci VT xxxi 365f.); Jackson ALIA 38: poss. = surface pond of some sort; Ahlström PEQ '84, 13f.: = pool or shaft :: Ahlström ibid.: or = object made of leather (wine/waterskin), barrel (?) of leather :: Ahlström ibid. 14: or l. ʾ*tḥq* (< root *ḥqq*) - on this word, cf. also Garr DGSP 48.

ʾ**ty**$_1$ **Pun** QAL Pf. 3 p.s.m. ʾ*t*ʾ Trip 51^{2} (bis, cf. Levi Della Vida Or xxxiii 9, cf. also Röllig BiOr xxvii 379, FR 174, cf. however Amadasi IPT 131, 133: = ʾ*t*$_5$ + suff. 3 p.s.m., for the first occurrence: or l. *mn*ʾ (= QAL Pf. 3 p.s.m. of *mny*); uncert. and diff. context) - **DA** QAL Impf. 3 p.pl.m. *y*ʾ*tw* i 1; Part. act. s.m. abs. (or Pf. 3 p.s.m.) ʾ*th* ii 14 (dam. and uncert. context) - **OldAr** QAL Impf. 3 p.s.m. *y*ʾ*th* KAI 222B 28 (bis × Lipiński Stud 36, Lemaire & Durand IAS 115, 124, 138 (div. second form otherwise): l. -*y* ʾ*th* = QAL Imper. s.m.), 32, 223B 13, 224^{11,12,20}; 2 p.s.m. *t*ʾ*th* KAI 222B 31, 224^{11}; 2 p.pl.m. *[t*ʾ*]twn* KAI 222B 32 (for the ending, cf. Degen AAG p. 77 n. 78, GGA '79, 32) - **OffAr** QAL Pf. 3 p.s.m. ʾ*th* Cowl 37^{11}, Herm 5^{6} (or = Part. act. s.m. abs.?, cf. Grelot RB lxxiv 435f.), Beh 31 (for this prob. reading, cf. also Greenfield & Porten BIDG p. 41; Akkad. par. *it-[ta]-lak*), ATNS 14^{3}, 80^{3}, RES 1298B 5, 1372A 1 (for the reading of the context, cf. AG p. 79), AJSL lviii 303B 4, JRAS '29, 108^{4}, NESE iii 48 conv. 5, Sach 80 vi B 3 (?, diff. context), Syr xli 285^{3}; 1 p.s. ʾ*tyt* Cowl 5^{3}, Krael 2^{3}, 7^{3}, 11$^{2f.}$, 14^{3}, ATNS 80^{5} (dam. context, or = 2 p.s.m.?), KAI 233^{7}; 3 p.pl.m. ʾ*tw* KAI 266^{4}, CIS ii 149BC 8, Cowl 30^{8}, 80^{2} (for the reading, cf. Porten & Yardeni sub TADAE A 5.5), ATNS 30a 4, 112^{2} (ʾ*hw* printers error), TADAE A 4.6^{11} (heavily dam. context), RES 1367^{4}, 1372B 3; Impf. 3 p.s.m. *y*ʾ*th* KAI 233^{11}, Cowl 41^{3} (*y[*ʾ*]th*; for this prob. reading, cf. Porten & Yardeni sub TADAE A 3.5), 82^{11}, Aḥiq 210 (*[y]*ʾ*th*; dam. context), 214 (heavily dam. context), Driv 9^{5*} (highly uncert. reading, cf. Porten & Yardeni sub TADAE A 6.12), 10^{5}, 11^{5}, ATNS 8^{6} (for this poss. reading, cf. Porten & Yardeni sub TADAE sub B 5.6), OA iii 56 conv. 1 (= CRAI '47, 181), *y*ʾ*ty* Driv 10^{3*} (highly uncert. reading, cf. Porten & Yardeni sub TADAE A 6.13); 3 p.s.f. *t*ʾ*th* Aḥiq 97, PSBA '15,

222$^{3f.,8}$ (= RES 1793$^{3,9f.}$); 2 p.s.m. *tʾth* Driv 12^{7}, SSI ii 28 obv. 7, rev. 5; 3 p.pl.m. *yʾtw* Driv 1^{3}, *yʾtwn* ATNS 26^{4}; 2 p.pl.m. *tʾtwn* SSI ii 28 obv. 5, Driv F vi 10^{2} (reading uncert.); Imper. s.m. *ʾth* Sach 76 i A 6; s.f. *ʾty* Aḥiq 118, ATNS 58^{4}; Inf. *mʾth* NESE iii 48^{6,8}; Part. act. pl.m. abs. *ʾtyn* Cowl 38^{5}, ATNS 65b 4 (dam. context, or = Pf. 1 p.pl.?); HAPH/APH Pf. 3 p.s.m. *hyty* Cowl 24^{36,48}, Driv 9^{1}, 13^{3}, ATNS 29^{3}, 31^{5}, etc.; 2 p.s.f. *htty* Herm 4^{6}; 1 p.s. *hytt* RES 492A 5 (?, diff. context, cf. also RES sub 1800), *ʾytyt* SSI ii 28 rev. 3; 3 p.pl.m. *hytw* Driv F iv 1^{4}, *hytyw* Driv 12^{4}; Impf. 3 p.s.m. *yhyth* Cowl 26^{13} (or = HOPH Impf. 3 p.s.m.?, cf. Grelot DAE p. 291 n. i), Driv 10^{3,5}, AG 49, NESE i 11^{6} (*[yh]yth*); 1 p.s. *ʾth* Herm 4^{10}; 3 p.pl.m. *yhytw* Driv 9^{3}, ATNS 46^{2}, *[y]hytwn* Krael 13^{3} (for this prob. reading, cf. Porten & Yardeni sub TADAE A 3.9), *yhtw* Herm 5^{4}, *ytw* Herm 3^{12}, 4^{7}, 5^{5}, 8^{6} (dam. context); + suff. 3 p.s.m. *yhytwn[h]* Driv 1^{1*} (diff. reading), *ytwnh* Herm 6^{10} (for the problem of the suffix, cf. Porten & Greenfield IOS iv 23f.); 2 p.pl.f. *thytn* Herm 5^{5}; 1 p.pl. + suff. 3 p.s.m. *nhytyh* ATNS 24^{4} (diff. reading, uncert. interpret., cf. also Bennett Or lvi 88); Imper. s.f. + suff. 3 p.s.m. (?) *ʾtyh* Herm 1^{10}; Inf. *hytyh* Cowl 27^{14}, 76^{3} (for the reading, cf. Porten & Yardeni sub TADAE A 5.4 :: Porten & Yardeni ibid.: = Inf. + suff. 3 p.s.m./f. :: Cowl a.l.: l. *y[d]nyh* = n.p.), Driv 10^{5}, Eph ii 211C 4, *mtyh* Herm 3^{11}, *mytyt* Herm 3^{11} (cf. Wesselius AION xxx 266 (n. 9); :: Greenfield Lesh xxxii 365 n. 38, JNES xxxvii 96 n. 25, Kaufman BiOr xxxiv 93: l. *mytyt<hm>* = Inf. + suff. 3 p.pl.m.); Part. s.m. abs. *mhyth* Driv 10^{4}, 11^{2}, Krael 17^{2} (?), *myty* Aeg xxxix 4 verso 1 (cf. Bresciani Aeg xxxix 7, Hoftijzer VT xii 342, Swiggers Aeg lx 94, Porten & Yardeni sub TADAE A 3.11 :: Milik Aeg xl 79: = HOPH Part. s.m. cstr.); pl.m. abs. *mhytyn* Driv 10^{2}, 11^{2}; cf. Frah xx 7, 18 (*yḥytywn*), Paik 169 (*ʾty*), 171, 172 (*ʾtyh*), 170, 173, 174 (*yʾtwn*), 175 (*yʾt[)*, 390 (*hytt*), 391 (*hytywt*), Nisa 14^{3}, 18^{5}, 19^{4}, 20^{4}, 22^{4}, 26^{5}, 27^{4}, 29^{4}, 30^{6}, etc. (*hyty*), 345^{7}, Nisa-b 1673a 5 (*hytyw*), Syn 301^{4}, 304^{3}, 306^{4}, 307^{2}, 308^{2}, 309^{2}, 310^{2}, 311^{2}, 313^{1}, cf. also MP 6, 7, GIPP 24, 37, 48, 54, SaSt 18, 24 and Sprengling AJSL liii 138, Lemosín AO ii 108, 110f., Toll ZDMG-Suppl viii 37, 39 - **Nab** QAL Impf. 3 p.s.m. *yʾtʾ* CIS ii 217^{2} (for CIS ii 219^{4} = J 4, v. *bʿy₁*), BASOR cclxiii 77^{1} - **Palm** QAL Pf. 3 p.s.m. *ʾtʾ* CIS ii 3959^{3} (*ʾt[ʾ]*)^{,4} (= SBS 44B), Syr xl 47^{3}; APH Pf. 3 p.s.m. *ʾty* CIS ii 3932^{4} (cf. Cantineau Gramm 87 (cf. also Kutscher IOS i 107 n. 22) :: Rosenthal Sprache 18: = PAʿEL) - **Hatra** APH Pf. 3 p.s.m. *ʾyty* 243^{1}, 244^{1}, 245^{1} - **JAr** QAL Pf. 3 p.s.m. *ʾth* Syr xlv 101^{17} (dam. and diff. context); 1 p.s. *ʾtt* IEJ xl 142^{3}, 144^{5}; Impf. 3 p.s.m. *yth* MPAT 58^{2}; Part. act. s.m. abs. *ʾty* Syn D. B 6 (× Naveh sub SM 88^{21}: l. *ʾtw* = Pf. 3 p.pl.m.); APH/HAPH Pf. 3 p.s.m. *ʾyty* LA xxxii 358; 1 p.s. *htyt* MPAT 70^{1} (cf. Sokoloff Maarav i 80 :: Sukenik PEQ '31, 218, Tarb ii 290, J.N.Epstein Tarb ii 293, Albright BASOR xliv 8, Kutscher SY 349, AH i/1, 52 n. 6, i/2, 55,

Fitzmyer & Harrington MPAT a.l., Beyer ATTM 343, 525, Delsman TUAT ii 576: = Hoph Pf. 3 p.s.f.; against the authenticity of this text, cf. however Garbini OA xxiv 67ff.); Impf. 3 p.s.m. *yʾ[y]tʾ* Mas 556[2] (?, uncert. interpret.) - ¶ verb Qal to come, to go; cf. *ʿlmh dʾty* Syn D. B 5f.: the coming world (cf. however Naveh sub SM 88[20f.]: l. *ʿlmh wʾtw*) - 1) + acc. direct; *tʾtwn mṣryn* SSI ii 28 obv. 5: you will come to Egypt (cf. RES 1367[4]; cf. also RES 1372B 3: *zy ʾtw ʿd lpnh*); *ʾtw pnh* Cowl 80[2] (= TADAE A 5.5[6]): they came to P.; *ʾnh [ʾ]tyt bytk* Cowl 15[3]: I come to your house (:: Fitzmyer FS Albright ii 149: scribal error?), cf. KAI 233[11], JRAS '29, 108[4] (cf. Joüon MUSJ xviii 4) - **2)** + *ʾl₆*; *wyʾth ʾly* KAI 224[20]: he will come to me; *wyʾtw ʾlwh ʾlhn blylh* DA i 1: the gods came to him (i.e. appeared to him, cf. Hoftijzer DA al) in the night (cf. also Weinfeld Shn v/vi 141) - **3)** + *b₂* - a) in; *kzy tʾth bznh* Driv 12[7]: when you come here; *lmʾth bʾtr ...* NESE iii 48[6]: to come in a place of ... (cf. AJSL lviii 303B 4, Syr xl 47[3]) - b) with; *ltʾth bḥylk* KAI 222B 31: you will not come with your army - **4)** + *l₅* - a) to; *ʾtw lbyrt yb* Cowl 30[8]: they came to the fortress of Yeb; *yʾth lky* OA iii 56 conv. 1: he will come to you; *mh dy yʾtʾ lh mn ksp wdhb* BASOR cclxiii 77[1]: whatever comes to him of silver and gold (cf. also Jones BASOR cclxxv 42); cf. Cowl 37[11], ATNS 58[4], 65b 4, TADAE A 4.6[11], RES 1372A 1 (v. supra), OA iii 56 conv. 1 - b) + *l₅* + Inf. (+ *l₅* + obj.); *ʾth lmḥth lbmrsry ʾtryh* Herm 5[6]: he came to bring the *ʾtryh* (v. *ʾtr₄*) to B. - **5)** + *mn₅* (from): ATNS 112[2] - **6)** + *ʿl₇*; *ʾnh ʾtyt ʿlyk* Cowl 5[3]: I came to you (cf. Cowl 41[3] (v. supra), Driv 1[3], 11[5], ATNS 14[3], 30a 4; cf. *ʾtyn tmh ʿlykm* Cowl 38[5]: coming there to you); cf. also a) + *ʿl₇* + *b₂*; *ʾnh ʾtyt ʿlyk bbytk* Krael 11[2f.]: I came to you in your house (cf. Krael 7[3], (for the reading of the context, cf. Porten & Greenfield JEAS p. 52, Porten GCAV 247, Porten & Yardeni sub TADAE B 3.8), Krael 14[3]) - b) *[kl m]lh [zy] tʾth ʿl blk* Aḥiq 97: (every w)ord (which) comes into your mind (cf. Greenfield FS Fitzmyer 49) - **7)** + *ʿm₄*; *ʾth ʿm ʾḥwh ... lʾbwd ... qdm ʾwsy[ry]* Syr xli 285[3f.]: he came with his brother ... to A. ... before O.; *yʾth ʿm gnzʾ* Driv 10[5]: he must come with the treasure; cf. also MPAT 58[2] - Haph/Aph to bring, to forward - **1)** + obj.: ATNS 24[10], 52b 3, Aeg xxxix 4 verso 1; cf. also *ʾyty ʾšlm ... mnyn 3* Hatra 243[1f.]: A. brought (i.e. donated) three *m.* (cf. also Hatra 244[1f.], 245[1f.]) - cf. also - a) + obj. + acc. dir.; *lʾ ʾytyt hmw mnpy* SSI ii 28 rev. 3: I did not bring them to M.; cf. *nhytyh gbrn 200* ATNS 24[4]: we will bring him 200 men (v. however supra) - b) + obj. + *l₅*; *mndʿm lʾ mhyth ly* Driv 11[2]: bringing me nothing (cf. LA xxxii 358, Herm 1[10], 6[10], for the context, cf. also Milik Bibl xlviii 554) - c) + obj. + *ʿl₇*; *klʾ yhyth ... ʿl gnzʾ* Cowl 26[13]: everything he will bring .... to the treasury (cf. Driv 10[2]) - **2)** + acc. dir.; *bgsrw hyty šwšn* Driv 9[1]: B. brought (them) to S. - **3)** + *l₅*, *lmtyh lkn ... lmytyt lkn* Herm 3[11]:

(bis) to bring to you (v. also supra), cf. ATNS 46[2] (dam. context); cf. also - a) + l_5 + obj.; *ʾth lkn mdʿm* Herm 4[10]: I will forward something to you; *whn tkln thytn ln tqm ytw byd ḥrwṣ* Herm 5[5]: and if you are able to forward to us castor oil, let them do (it) through Ch.; *ʾty lkʾ yt lgynyʾ* CIS ii 3932[4]: he has brought the legions hither; *lkh htyt ṭmy ʿwzyh* MPAT 70[1f.]: hither I brought the bones of U. (v. also supra); cf. Herm 3[12], 4[7], 5[4] - b) + l_5 + acc. dir.; *htty ly swn* Herm 4[6]: you have forwarded (it) to me to S. - **4)** + *ʿl_7*; *yhytw ʿly* Driv 9[3]: they will bring (them) to me, cf. Driv 12[4], 13[3], ATNS 31[5], NESE i 11[6]; cf. also - a) *wyhyth ʿly ʿm mndtʾ* Driv 10[3]: let he bring it to me together with the rent - **5)** for the diff. forms *ʾyṭy* and *ʾṭyy* in Waw 14bis (= AMB 6), cf. Dupont-Sommer Waw p. 28f.: = APH Imper. s.m. and s.f. (highly uncert. reading and interpret.) - **6)** for *dyṭwl* in Hatra 173[3] (read by Milik DFD 105: *dyṭy* = d_2 + QAL (or APH) Impf. 3 p.s.m. of *ʾty_1*), v. *nṭl* - a HAPH form of this root in ATNS 24[10]: *]ytyh* - Porten & Yardeni sub TADAE A 3.8: l. prob. *lʾyty* (= l_5 + APH Inf.) in Cowl 42[14] (highly uncert. reading and interpret.).

v. *ʾyt_3*, *ʾyty*, *ʾnth_2*, *ʾt_6*, *bʿy_1*, *mṭ*, *ndr_1*, *nšʾ$_1$*, *sgy_1*.

ʾty₂ v. *ʾnth_2*.

ʾtyṭk **OffAr** the *ʾtyṭkʾ* in AM ii 171 i 3 (// with *ʾtykʾ* in ibid. ii 2) = noun (Sing. emph.) of unknown meaning??, cf. Henning a.l.; cf. however Bivar & Shaked BSOAS xxvii 287: *ʾtyṭkʾ* misspelling for *ʾtykʾ* (= n.p.); less prob. Altheim & Stiehl Suppl 90, 92, ASA 265: l. *ʾḥyrynʾ* = Sing. m. emph. of *ʾḥyryn* = other (cf. also idem AAW i 654).

ʾtyk **OffAr** the *ʾtykʾ* in AM ii 171 ii 2 (// with *ʾtyṭkʾ*in ibid. i 3) = noun (Sing. emph.) of unknown meaning??, cf. Henning a.l.; cf. however Bivar & Shaked BSOAS xxvii 287: = n.p.; less prob. Altheim & Stiehl Suppl 92f., ASA 265: l. *ʾḥrʾ* = Sing. m. emph. of *ʾ$ḥr_3$*.

ʾtml **OffAr** *ʾtml* Sem xxxix 32[4] (dam. context, *ʾtml[*); cf. Frah xxvii 6 (*ytmʾl*; cf. Nyberg FP 56, 106 :: Ebeling Frah a.l.: l. *swmsʾl* < Akkad. *šamšala* = the day before yesterday) - ¶ adv. yesterday.

ʾtn **OffAr** Sing. emph. *ʾtnʾ* Cowl 44[4], Aḥiq 91 - ¶ subst. she-ass.

ʾtnʿmh v. *ršʾt*.

ʾtph **OffAr**, cf. Nisa 593[2], 594[1], 598[1], 599[2], etc.: irrigation canal (prob. interpret.); cf. also GIPP 47.

ʾtr₁ v. *ytr_1*.

ʾtr₂ v. *ʾ$šr_4$*, *mlk_5*, *$qṣr_6$*, *tqʾ*.

ʾtr₃ v. *ʾmr_3*.

ʾtr₄ **OffAr** Plur. emph. *ʾtryh* Herm 5[6] - ¶ subst. of unknown meaning; Bresciani & Kamil Herm a.l.: prob. = *ʾ$šr_6$*(cf. however Grelot RB lxxiv 435, DAE p. 163 n. e, Lipiński OLP iii 115 n. 88, cf. also Porten &

Greenfield JEAS p. 161).

ᵓtrg **JAr** Plur. abs. *ᵓtrgyn* MPAT 60^3 - ¶ subst. *ethrog.*

ᵓtrh v. *ᵓšrh*$_1$.

ᵓtrwdn (< Iran., cf. Benveniste JA ccxlii 304) - **OffAr** Sing. abs. *ᵓtrwdn* Cowl 27^{17} - ¶ subst. f. brazier? (cf. Benveniste JA ccxlii 304, Porten & Greenfield JEAS p. 89, Porten EI xiv 173, Porten & Yardeni sub TADAE A 4.5, Hinz AISN 49 (: = 'Feuerwedel'); cf. however Grelot DAE p. 404: = burnt-offering?; Cowl a.l.: = fire?

ᵓtrmsyn **Palm** word of unknown meaning in CIS ii 4036A 3, B 2.

B

b_1 v. *bn*$_1$, *mrᵓ*, *ᶜmq*$_2$

b_2 *b* passim, other spellings: *ᵓb* KAI $43^{3,7}$, 163^2(?), 277^5, RES 1200^3 (cf. FR 95b); transcriptions: - **1)** *by*: Poen 933, IRT 906^3 - **2)** *bi*: IRT 828^3 - **3)** *b*: IRT 828^3 (in *baiaem* = *bḥym*) - **4)** *ba-ᵓ*: Warka 21, 24; > Akkad. *ba*, cf. v.Soden Or xlvi 185, 186; cf. Paik 186, Nisa 20^1, 22^1, 24^1, 26^3, 30^3, 31^3, 48^3, 61^2, 77^2, etc. - ¶ prep. (on this prep., cf. also Pennachietti AION xxiv 181ff.) - **1)** local a) in - α) in, inside (enclosed space); *bᵓrn z* KAI $13^{2f.}$: in this sarcophagus; *ᶜšw lkm ᵓš br bbyth* KAI $181^{24f.}$: make, each of you, a cistern for yourselves in his house; *bzqyn* CIS ii 3913 ii 29: in wine-skins; *bqbrᵓ dnh* CIS ii 350^5: in this tomb; *wqbrth bmᶜrth* MPAT $68^{6f.}$: I buried him in the cave; *mn dbgwh* MPAT 69^2: the one who is within it (sc. in the ossuary); *btnwr* Tell F 22: in an oven (for the context, v. *ᵓpy*) - β) in a certain place, region; *bhr* KAI 14^{17}: on the mountain; *bmqmm bᵓš* KAI 26A i 14: in the places in which ..; *krmm bšd zbl* EpAn ix 5^4: vineyards in the field of the Prince; *ltnt blbnn* KAI 81^1: for Tinnit-on-the-Lebanon (i.e. whose dwelling is on the L.); *lmlqrt bṣr* Syr lxv 438: belonging to (the god) M. in Tyre; also in Antas 51^1: *lṣd ᵓdr bᵓby* = to Ṣid the Mighty in A.?? (cf. Fantar Antas p. 54f.), cf. Antas 78b1, 82 (*bᵓ[by]*), 84a (*[b]ᵓby*) and Antas 80^1 (*bby* pro *bᵓby*), cf. however Garbini AION xix 318ff.: *bᵓby* = father (epithet of the deity) < indigeneous language, Mazza RSF xvi 47ff.: *bᵓby* = n.d. < Egypt *bᵓby* :: Ferron StudSard xxii 281f. *bᵓby* < reduplicated Semitic root *ᵓb* = progenitor; *špṭm bᵓlpqy* KAI 119^3: suffetes in Lepcis; *bšd lwbym* KAI 118^2: in the territory of the Libyans (v. *šd*$_1$); *llᵓdkᵓ ᵓš bknᶜn* CHC 49 no. 53, 96 no. 54: (coin) from Laodicea in Canaan (cf. Hill 1, 52); *bᵓrq yᵓdy* KAI 215^5: in the land of Y.; *kl mlkyᵓ zy ymlkn bᵓrpd* KAI 222B 22: all kings who will reign in A.; *btnwr* TellF 22: in an oven (for the context, v. *ᵓpy*); *bswn byrtᵓ* Krael 11^1: in the fortress S.; *bmnpy* ATNS 29^1: in Memphis; *bḥthrbᵓ mdyntᵓ* ATNS 103^2: in the province Ch. (for this interpret., cf. Zauzich

Ench xiii 117f.); *byt bnt bswn* Herm 2^{1}: the temple of B. in S.; *bʾtr ḥd* Driv 6^{6}: in a single place; *bznh* Driv 3^{2}: here; *rb mšrytʾ dy blḥytw* CIS ii 196^{4}: the commander of the army camp in L.; *dwšrʾ ʾlhʾ dy bdpnʾ* BASOR cclxix 48^{3}: the god D. who is in D.; *bgntʾ ʾlym* SBS 45B 12: in the holy garden (cf. Greek parallel: [ἐ]ν ἱερῷ ἄλσει); *bkl ʾtr klh* RIP 143^{5}: everywhere; *dkyrn lʿlm bḥṭrʾ...* Hatra 79^{14}: may they be remembered in Hatra ...; *ytb bmṣdʾ* MPAT 40^{9}: living in M.; *bšwq mḥwz ʿgltyn* MPAT 64 iii 5: in the market of M.-E.; *drth wbyth dy bh* DBKP 19^{28}: the courtyard and the house therein - γ) on the surface of, on; *mly sprʾ zy bnṣbʾ znh* KAI 222C 17: the words of the inscription which is on this stele; *wktšwny bkp yd 10 bkp rgl* it 6 ATNS 30a 5 + 28b 4: and they struck me on the palm of the hand ten (times and) on the sole of the foot six (times; on this reading and interpret., cf. Porten & Yardeni sub TADAE B 8.4); *ktb .... bgllʾ ...* CIS ii 3913 i 9: they have written (it) ... on the stele (cf. Greek parallel ἐνγραφῆναι ... στήλῃ λιθίνῃ); *wkl mn dy ytʾlp bkprʾ dnh...* CIS ii 217^{10}: and everyone who composes (an inscription) for himself (and writes it) on this tomb; *wḥtmw bgwh* MPAT 51^{14}: and they set a seal on it - b) among, in the midst of; *mlk bmlkm* KAI 1^{2}: a king among the kings (i.e. a certain king); *my bbny ...* KAI $24^{13f.}$: who from among my sons ... ; *bḥym* KAI 13^{7}: among the living; *ʾš bʿm ʾlpqy* Trip 35: who belongs to the people of L. (v. *ʿm*$_1$); *qtlw bhm* it 504[6] Beh 3: they killed 5064 (men) among them (i.e. of them); *ytqbr bhm* CIS ii 219^{4}: he will be buried among (i.e. with) them; *wdy hw yhwʾ bʾḥr mnʿt dnh* CIS ii $200^{2f.}$: and who belongs to the posterity of the said M.; *pršyʾ bʾbr[ʾ] dy gml wʿnʾ* SBS $51^{3f.}$: the cavalarists belonging to the wing of G. and A. - c) besides, with; *bʾrn zn ʾnk ... škbt bswt* KAI 11: in the sarcophagus I ... repose with a garment; *wʾnk ʿšty hmslt bʾrnn* KAI 181^{26}: and I made the highway alongside (the river) A. (cf. however Segert ArchOr xxix 229 (n. 168), Andersen Or xxxv 95, Röllig KAI a.l., Gibson SSI i 82, Dahood FS Horn 437, de Geus SV 26; cf. also HP Müll TUAT i 650, Dearman SMIM 191ff.); *bʾrḥ* KAI 215^{18}: next to the road, by the way; *rṣt bglgl mrʾy* KAI $216^{8f.}$: I ran at the wheel (i.e. beside the chariot) of my lord; *ltʾth bḥylk* KAI 222B 31: you will not come with your army; *dy yhʾ qyr bh* CIS ii 3972^{4}: that he may be a client with him (sc. the god; i.e. that he (the god) may be his patron); *bymnh* ATNS 90^{3}: at its right; *bʾnpy yhwḥnn* MPAT 49^{6}: in the presence of Y.; cf. also *yrḥ byrḥ* Cowl 11^{5}: month by month; for *ʾgr bʾgr*, v. *ʾgr*$_4$ - d) from within, from; *wʾl yʿmsn bmškb z* KAI $14^{5f.}$: don't let him remove me from this resting-place (cf. Albright JAOS lxvii 158 n. 42, Gordon Or xxi 121, H.P.Müller ZA lxv 112 (cf. also Swiggers AO v 153f.) :: FR 54b, 251 I: *b* dissimilation of original. *m* (= *mn*$_5$)); *lʿptʾ bḥdr ḥšk ʿbr* KAI $27^{19f.}$: o flier-goddess, from the dark room pass. away (cf. Cross & Saley BASOR cxcvii 46 ::

e.g. Röllig KAI a.l., Avishur PIB 248, 255: o flier-goddess in the dark room, pass. away; cf. prob. also *bmṣrm* KAI 5[2]: from Egypt); *ymḥ šm ›ztwd bš‹r z* KAI 26A iii 13f.: he will expunge the name of A. from this gate (cf. also Swiggers AO v 153), cf. Tell F 11; for these transl., cf. also Zevit JANES vii 103ff. - e) fig. uses connected with the meanings sub a), b), c); *hn t›mr bnbšk* KAI 223B 5: if you say in your soul (i.e. to yourself); *ksph zy hwh bydy* Herm. 2[4f.]: the silver which was in my possession; *ntn nḥm šmn byd hkty* TA-H 17[8f.]: N. has delivered the oil in the hand of (i.e. to) the K.; *dy qrw lh b‹q›* RIP 119[7]: because they have invoked him in (their) distress; *yḥzny ›pyk bšlm* Herm 1[2]: that he may show me your face in peace; *ytn brkth b‹mlhwn* MPAT-A 26[9f.]: may He set His blessing on their undertakings; *[dy]hb bhdn ›trh [q]dyšh* MPAT-A 5[3f.]: who has contributed in (i.e. for) this holy place (sc. the synagogue); *›lh hwt bbyt ›bwh* KAI 215[2]: there was a conspiracy (?; v. *›lh₂*) in the house of his father; *bspr› znh* Krael 9[12]: in this document; *bnmws›* CIS ii 3913 ii 4: in the law; *grmnqws qysr b›grt› dy ktb ... pšq* CIS ii 3913 103f.: G.C. has explained in a letter he wrote ...; *›š bmmlht* KAI 66[1]: who is in charge of the salt-mines; *ḥštrpn› zy bkrk* FX 136[4f.]: the satrap of K.; cf. also MPAT 51[10]; *l› mštm‹n ly bṣbwt mr›y* Driv 4[1f.]: they do not obey me in the matters of my lord; *ktb ... bkpr› hw* CIS ii 198[9f.]: a document ... concerning this tomb; *nbš ytm b›m* KAI 24[13]: the attachment of the fatherless to (his) mother; *wyhw› bh ḥlp mwt* CIS ii 212[6]: the fate of death will befall him; *ḥlqy b›gr ›lp›* NESE i 11[3]: my share of the rent of the ship; cf. also *wbšbw‹h dkl* MPAT-A 46[3]: with an oath that everyone ... (i.e. on this grave there is the curse that everyone ...) - **2)** temporal, in, on, during; *bymy* KAI 24[12]: in my days; *byrḥ bl bšnt ‹sr w›rb‹* KAI 14[1]: in the month B., in the 14th year; *bymm 6 lyrḥ bl bšnt 21* KAI 32[1]: on the sixth day of the month B. in the 21st year; *bḥy ›by* KAI 43[8f.]: during the lifetime of my father; *byrḥ mp‹ lpn› b›ḥtt ›rb‹m št* KAI 110[3f.]: in the first month M. in the 41st year; *bllh* KAI 181[15]: during the night (cf. also Dahood FS Horn 434f.: throughout the night); *ygl wyšmḥ bywmt rbm wbšnt rḥqt* Ber xxii 120[6ff.]: may he rejoice and be glad for many days and long years; *bṭrm y‹br hḥdš* TA-H 5[12f.]: before the month is over; *bšlšt* TA-H 20[1f.]: on the third (day) (or: in the third (year)?); *bywmyh* KAI 215[9]: in his time; *bkl ‹dn* Krael 13[1]: always; *bz› šnt›* ATNS 3[3]: in this year; *bywmt kbwzy* ATNS 34a 3: in the days of Cambyses; *b* it 20 *l›dr* Samar 1[1] (= EI xviii 8*; cf. Samar 3[11], 6[1]); *bmwty* Krael 9[17]: at my death; *bḥywhy* ADAJ xxi 144[3]: during his life (cf. CIS ii 197[4]); *bzbny› qdmy›* CIS ii 3913 i 4: in former times; *bšt› dh* SBS 34[2]: in that year; *bh bšt›* RIP 199[10]: in that year; *b›pmlṭwt yrḥbwl›* RIP 157[4]: during the *curator*-ship of Y.; *brbnwth* AAS xxxvi/xxxvii 169 no. 10[5]: during his presidency; *bywm 9. ... btšry* Hatra 49[1f.]: on the 9th day ... in (the month) T.; *bywm 11* *bnysn bšnt 517* Assur 20[1]: on the 11th day in (the month) N. in the year 517; *b>ḥd bmrḥšwn* MPAT 40[1]: on the first of (the month) M.; *b 14 ltmwz* BSh 1[1] (cf. also ibid. 2[1], 3[1], Mas 564[1], etc.); *b 10 lšbṭ* MPAT 43 i 3: on the tenth of (the month) Sh. (cf. also IEJ xvii 109a and b); *b 22* Mas 560[1]: on the 22nd (day); *mḥd* (v. *>ḥd₄*) *1 btmwz* DBKP 27[12]: from the first (day) in (the month) T. - **3)** instrumental, by, by means of, with, through; *b>sry yšr>l* KAI 181[25f.]: by means of (with) Israelite prisoners; *wḥtm >th bḥtmk* TA-H 17[5]: and seal it with your seal; *plktšh b>bny* KAI 214[31]: and let them stone him to death (with stones); *>yk zy tqd š‹wt> z> b>š ...* KAI 222A 35: just as this wax will be burned by fire; *zy yḥyh bh >yš* Cowl 49[3]: by which a man lives; *wsṭrw bšnt> zyly* Driv 7[7]: mark them with my mark; *shdt lh bdgm bwl> wdms* SBS 48B 4: she (i.e. the Senat) has testified about him by decree of Senat and People; *w>ḥydyn bh* SBS 34[2]: and chosen by him; *>lh> bḥlm> >lphnw* Hatra 106b 4f.: the god has instructed them by a dream - a) (fig) uses connected with the instrumental use; *wbrk b‹l ... bḥym wbšlm wb‹z* KAI 26C iii 16ff.: and may Ba‹al bless (him) ... with life, well-being and power; *‹l> bbn m>t m‹qr ... bktbt ...* KAI 124[3]: he became (v. *‹ly₁*) the adoptive son of M. ... by the document of ... (v. *dbr₃*); *blḥṣ ‹lb y[mt]* KAI 223C 10: and may he die by oppressive torment; *wṭyb lbbn bdmy> zy yhbt ln* Krael 3[6f.]: our heart is contented with the price you have given us; *byty zy zbnt bksp* Krael 9[3]: my house that I bought with silver (cf. e.g. CIS ii 19[2]); *wyhb bgšrn* Herm 3[9]: and he will give (it) (in exchange) for beams, cf. Herm 4[5] (cf. Grelot DAE p. 160 :: Milik Bibl xlviii 553, 583: as); *ym>t ly bYHW* Cowl 6[11]: you have sworn to me by Y. (cf. also Cowl 14[5], etc.); *bm‹rth dzbnt bgṭh* MPAT 68[6f.]: in the cave I had acquired by the writ; *ymwt bswp byš* MPAT-A 45[4]: he will die of an evil end; *ršy >l‹zr bzbn bth dk ...* MPAT 51[6f.]: E. has authority by the purchase of that house ...; *>tr> dk bthwmh wbmṣrh .. dk zbnt ...* MPAT 52[5ff.]: *this site* confined by its boundary and border ... that I have sold ... - **4)** causal, because of; *bṣdqy wbḥkmty* KAI 26A i 12f.: because of my loyalty and wisdom, cf. KAI 215[19], 226[2]; *bzy z‹yrn >nḥnh* Cowl 37[7]: because we are few; *p>yty ‹mh ldwšr> >lh> bḥrm> dy ‹l>* CIS ii 199[7]: and he shall be charged (to pay) to the god D. on account of the consecration formula (v. *ḥrm₃*) mentioned above; *ytqbr bqbr> dnh ... btqp> dy bydh* CIS ii 207[5f.]: he may be buried in this grave ... in virtue of the warrant which is in his hand (i.e. which he possesses); *ḥrm ... dwšr> ... bšṭry ḥrmyn* CIS ii 350[3f.]: the inviolable possession ... of D. ... on account of the deeds containing the consecration formulae (v. *ḥrm₃*) - a) (fig.) uses connected with the causal use; *>m bḥmdt ys‹ >m bšn>t wbr‹ ...* KAI 26A iii 17: if he tears (it) down in greed or in hate and malice ...; *>l ytn lh l>kl brgz* KAI 214[23]: let he not suffer him to eat in anger; *byt> zy >nh yhbt lyhwyšm‹ brty brḥmn* Krael 9[5]: the

house I gave to my daughter Y. in affection - **5)** circumstantial (*beth essentiae* included); *bbn* ... KAI 124[3]: as son of ... (for the context, v. *ʿly*$_1$); *ʿṭrt ḥrṣ bdrknm 20* KAI 60[3]: a golden crown worth 20 drachmes (cf. also Brown JBL c 177); *brʾšt nḥšt* KAI 31[1]: of first rate bronze; *zy lʾ bʾgr yhbt lh* Cowl 69A 12: which I did not give to him as payment; *zy yhyb bmkl* Cowl 24[35]: which is delivered as food; *znh ḥlqʾ zy mṭʾk bḥlq* Cowl 28[3]: this is the share which comes to you as a share (cf. Krael 1[5]); *hqymny ʾl bṣdyq* Aḥiq 173: set me up, o God, as a righteous man (v. *qwm*$_1$; cf. also Lindenberger APA 176); *ʾl tzbny bkst* Herm 1[10]: do not buy anything as clothing (cf. Porten & Greenfield ZAW lxxx 226, 228, Grelot DAE p. 152 n. 1 :: Milik Bibl xlviii 550: in exchange of); *bʾbny mlkʾ* Cowl 5[7]: according to royal (i.e. official) weight; *dy ʾt ršyʾ bnpšky lmhk* ... MPAT 40[5f.]: that you on your part are free to go ... - **6)** hostile, against; *wyzq bspr z* KAI 24[14]: and he will damage this inscription; *wʾltḥm bqr* KAI 181[11]: and I fought against the town; *wʾšʾh byhṣ* KAI 181[20]: I led it up against Y. (:: Segert ArchOr xxix 229, xxxi 335: I conveyed it to Y.); *wdbr hmlk ʾtkm bnbškm hnh šlḥty lhʿyd bkm hym* TA-H 24[17ff.]: the word of the king is incumbent upon you for your very life, see I have sent you (sc. this message) to warn you now; *šqrt bʿdyʾ ʾln* KAI 222B 38: you have been false to these treaty-conditions; *ytn ʾpwh bgbrh hhw* MPAT-A 22[6f.]: may he set his face against that man - for *by* in KAI 79[8,9], 5522[4], v. *by*$_2$ - for *bn* in KAI 30[4], v. *byn*$_2$, for *bn* in KAI 43[13], v. *mn*$_5$ - for *bn* in KAI 60[1], v. *nʾsph* - for constructions with *b*, cf. also under the different verbs.
v. *bwʾ*, *by*$_2$, *bn*$_6$, *bny*$_1$, *mn*$_5$, *pwn*.

b$_3$ = abbrev. of *byt*$_2$, v. *bb*$_1$, *šyt*$_1$.

b$_4$ v. *bb*$_1$.

b$_5$ v. *bqʿ*$_2$.

b$_6$ v. *bt*$_3$.

b$_6$ The *b* in CIS ii 1[1], 2[1], 3[1], 4[1] poss. indication of duplication; *mnn 3 b* CIS ii 3[1f.]: 3 double *mines*?; cf. also *b* in Lidzb Ass 5[7] after n.p.: = the second one??

b$_7$ Inscription *b* on tags, meaning unknown, cf. Yadin IEJ xv 112, Yadin & Naveh Mas p. 12f.

b$_8$ v. *w*$_2$.

bʾby v. *b*$_2$.

bʾh v. *tbʾh*.

bʾyš v. *bʾš*$_2$

bʾr **Pun** Sing. abs. *bʾr* Trip 38[1] (cf. Vattioni AION xvi 39 :: Levi Della Vida LibAnt i 57f.: l. *[q]bʾr* = *qbr*$_3$), *bʿʾr* KAI 173[5] (??, dam. context); Plur. abs. *bhrm* KAI 173[3] (??; cf. FR 108,2) - **OffAr** Sing. abs. *bʾr* Cowl 27[6] - **Nab** Plur. cstr. *bʾrwt* CIS ii 350[2] (cf. Cantineau Nab i 47, 92, 93) - ¶ subst. f. well, cistern; cf. *bʾrwt myʾ* CIS ii 350[2]: wells of

water; in Trip 38^{1} indication of grave (cf. Vattioni AION xvi 39 (nn. 20-22)) - Vattioni AION xvi 40, Aug xvi 539 (sub 6): *bur* in OA ii 84^{1} = Sing. abs. of *bʾr*, cf. also Polselli StudMagr xi 40, cf. however Levi Della Vida OA ii 83: = part of n.p. - Segal ATNS a.l.: l. *bʾrn* in ATNS 62^{3}, poss. = Plur. abs. (uncert. reading and interpret.).
v. *byr*$_1$.

b ʾrh Vattioni Or xlviii 141: l. *bʾrk* (without interpret.) in FuB xiv 20^{2} (uncert. reading).

b ʾš$_1$ **OffAr** Haph Impf. 3 p.pl.m. *yhbʾšw* KAI 226^{9} - **JAr** Aph Part. s.f. abs. *mbʾšh* AMB 3^{4} - ¶ verb Haph to make miserable; *yhbʾšw mmtth* KAI 226$^{9f.}$: may they make his death miserable; *rwḥ byšh wnbʾšh* AMB 3^{4}: an evil and evil-doing spirit.

b ʾš$_2$ **OffAr** Sing. m. abs. *bʾyš* Cowl 31^{16}, Driv 5^{8}, KAI 269^{2}, *byš* KAI 258^{3}; Sing. f. abs. *bʾyšh* Cowl 38^{6}; emph. *bʾyštʾ* Cowl 30^{17} - **Palm** Sing. m. emph. *byšʾ* Inv viii 172; f. cstr. *byšt* CIS ii 4486ab^{3}, Inscr P 3ab 3 (= CIS ii 4486^{3}?) - **Hatra** Sing. abs. *bš* 74^{8} (for the context, v. *mdʿm*) - **JAr** Sing. m. abs. *byš* MPAT-A 22^{3}, 45^{4}, 46^{6}; m. emph. *[b]ʾšh* Syr xlv 101^{17}; Plur. m. abs. *byšyn* AMB 13^{5} (*[by]šyn*), 9 (*byš[yn]*); Sing. abs. *byšh* AMB 3^{4} (or = Hebr.?), 13^{6}, *byšʾ* AMB 14^{2}; f. emph. *byšth* AMB 2^{3}, 7^{6,12} - ¶ adj. bad, evil; *mlh bʾyšh* Cowl 38^{6}: a bad thing (i.e. a fault; cf. Dion RB lxxxix 567f.); *mndʿm bʾyš* KAI 269^{2}: something evil (cf. Driv 5^{8}, Hatra 74^{8} (v. supra)); *lšn byš* MPAT-A 22^{3}: evil tongue (i.e. calumny); *swp byš* MPAT-A 45^{4}, 46$^{5f.}$: an evil end; *ʿynh byšth* AMB 2φ.: the evil eye (cf. AMB 13^{6}, 14^{2}; cf. also Naveh AAALT 86); *rwḥh byšth* AMB 7^{6} (cf. AMB 7^{12}): an evil spirit/demon; *mzqyn byš[yn]* AMB 13^{9}: evil tormentors (kind of evil demons; cf. also AMB 13^{5}); *byšt gdʾ* CIS ii 4486$^{3f.}$: the unfortunate one, cf. Inscr. P 3ab 3f. - subst. adj. something bad/evil: Cowl 30^{17}, 31^{16}, KAI 258^{3}, Inv viii 172 - cf. also Plur. (or Sing.?, cf. Kaufman JAOS civ 90) f. + suff. 1 p.s. (< Akkad.) *bi-ʾi-šá-ti-ia* Warka 35: what is evil to me (i.e. what affects me badly), on this form, cf. also Kaufman AAALT 48, 50 - Segal ATNS a.l.: l. *byšh* (= f. Sing. abs.) in ATNS 1^{10} (dam. context, reading highly uncert.; cf. Porten & Yardeni sub TADAE B 8.8: prob. l. *xʿšh*).
v. *ʾš*$_3$.

b ʾšybh v. *ʾšybh*.

b ʾt v. *gll*.

b ʾtr v. *ʾšr*$_4$; v. also *btr*.

bb$_1$ (< Akkad., cf. Zimmern Fremdw 30, Kaufman AIA 40f.) - **OffAr** Sing. cstr. *bb* Cowl 66 vii 2 (?), Aḥiq 9 (*[b]b*), 17, 23; emph. *bbʾ* Krael 10^{4}; + suff. 3 p.s.m. *bbh* Cowl 34^{4}, Krael 10^{3} (for the reading, cf. Milik RB lxi 251, Grelot DAE p. 248 (n. b), Porten & Greenfield JEAS p. 62, Porten & Yardeni sub TADAE B 3.11 :: Krael a.l.: l. *wbh*); Plur. cstr. *bby* ATNS 26^{13}; emph. *bbyʾ* ATNS 26^{7}; cf. Frah ii 17 (*bbʾ*), Paik 193 (*bb*ʾ), GIPP 20, SaSt 15 - **Palm** Sing. emph. *bb*ʾ CIS ii 3917[3], 4172[2], 4197[2], 4199[9], 4204[1], RIP 163b 3, SBS 24[3], Ber ii 78[2] (for the reading, cf. Cantineau with Ingholt Ber iii 126 :: Ingholt Ber ii a.l.: l. *bn*ʾ = Sing. emph. of *bn*$_3$ (= intermediate part), Syr xix 156[2] (Greek par. θύρωμα) etc.; Plur. emph. *bby*ʾ Inv D 32 (?) - ¶ subst. m. gate, passim; *bb*ʾ *rb*ʾ SBS 24[3f.]: the great gate (:: Garbini OA xiv 178f.: designation of other part of the temple: niche?); *bb*ʾ *wtrʿwhy* CIS ii 3917[3]: the gate and its door leaves; *bbh lmnpq* Krael 10[3]: its gate (through which) to go forth, cf. *bb*ʾ *zylk lmnpq* Krael 10[4] (for the context, cf. also Porten & Szubin JAOS cvii 233f.); *bbb hykl*ʾ Aḥiq 17: in the gate of the palace (i.e. in the chancellary, cf. Teixidor Syr liii 309, cf. also Kaufman AIA 40f.), cf. Aḥiq 9, 23 - cf. Warka 2: *di-a-ba-ba-*ʾ (= *dy* ʿ*l bb*ʾ, cf. Gordon AfO xii 106 n. 8): which is at the gate - this word also in Cowl 81[5,16,17], etc., etc. with the meaning "account, bank (< gate)"?, cf. Driver JRAS '32, 83 :: Grelot DAE p. 106 n. h: *bb* = *b*$_2$ + *b*$_3$ (= abbrev. of *byt*$_2$) :: Harmatta ActAntHung vii 342ff.: *b*$_2$ + *b*$_3$ (= abbrev. of *byt spry*ʾ) - Harmatta ActAntHung vii 369: the *b* in Cowl 81[106] prob. = *bb* (in Cowl 81[5,16,17]; etc.), uncert. interpret.

bb$_2$ v. *dbb*.

bby$_1$ **Hatra** Sing. emph. *bby*ʾ - ¶ substantivated adj. banker (for this uncert. interpret., cf. Aggoula Syr lxvii 417; cf. also id. ibid.: or = ethnicon ? :: as-Salihi Sumer xliv 106 n. 54: = adj. right).

bby$_2$ v. *b*$_2$.

bbn v. *byn*$_2$.

bg (< Iran., cf. Telegdi JA ccxxvi 233, Driv p. 39f., Friedrich Or xxvi 41, Eilers AfO xvii 333, Hinz AISN 53) - **OffAr** Sing. cstr. *bg* ATNS 47[4,5,6,7,8]; emph. *bg*ʾ Driv 10[1], ATNS 41[6] (diff. and dam. context); + suff. 3 p.s.m. *bgh* Driv 8[2,3,5]; + suff. 1 p.s. *bgy* Driv 11[4] (cf. however Porten & Yardeni sub TADAE A 6.14: l. preferably *bg*ʾ = Sing. emph.); Plur. emph. *bgy*ʾ Driv 1[2],2[2,3], 5[5], etc. - ¶ subst. m. domain, fief - Segal ATNS a.l.: l. *bgy* (= Plur. cstr.) in ATNS 46[5] (uncert. interpret., dam. context).

v. *bz*$_1$

bgd **Hebr** Sing. cstr. *bgd* KAI 200[8,9]; + suff. 1 p.s. *bgdy* KAI 200[12] - ¶ subst. garment (for the context, cf. Amusin & Heltzer IEJ xiv 154f.).

bgmwt v. *gmwt*.

bgn$_1$ v. *bgn*$_2$.

bgn$_2$ **Hatra** Sing. cstr. *bgn* 23[4] (= KAI 244; for the reading, cf. Caquot Syr xl 16f., Milik RN vi/iv 54, Degen ZDMG cxxi 125, NESE ii 100, Vattioni IH a.l. :: Caquot Syr xxix 102: pro *wbgn šḥrw* l. *whnšḥd/rw* (without interpret.)), 29[1] (= KAI 247), 30[5], 53[1], 74[6], 75, 101[2], 247[1], 281[1] - ¶ subst. invocation, appeal (cf. Caquot Syr xxx 235, Hillers BASOR ccvii (ccvi *sic*!) 55, Ingholt AH i/2, 43, Pennachietti FO xvi

63f.), subst. always construed with prep. *ʿl*$_7$ (= against); *wbgn mrn ʿl kwl mn ʾnš kwlh* Hatra 74[6f.]: invocation of our lord against everyone ... (i.e. may everyone ... be cursed by our lord), cf. also Degen NESE ii 99ff. :: Safar Sumer viii 185 n. 7: = *bgn*$_3$ (= woe to) :: Aggoula Ber xviii 91: = PA ʿEL Imper. s.m. of *bgn*$_1$ (= to cast a spell on, to charm) - > Akkad. (cf. Brockelmann OLZ xlii 666ff., CAD s.v. *bagani* :: Schaeder OLZ xli 593ff., v.Soden AHW s.v. *bagani*, Or xxxv 8, xlvi 186: < Ar. *bgn* = *b*$_2$ + *gn*$_4$ (= protection)): *ba-ga-ni-ʾ*.
v. *gnh*$_1$.

bgn$_3$ v. *bgn*$_2$.

bgr **OffAr** Segal ATNS a.l.: l. *bgrw* (= QAL Pf. 3 p.pl.m. of *bgr* (= to reach maturity)) in ATNS 73[3] (reading *waw* uncert., dam. context, uncert. interpret.).

bgrh **OffAr** Segal ATNS a.l.: l. *bgrtʾ* (= Sing. emph. of *bgrh* (= mature age)) in ATNS 44 i 4 (less prob. reading and interpret., cf. Porten & Yardeni sub TADAE B 8.2 (div. otherwise): l. *bgdt* = n.p. (prob. reading and interpret.))

bd$_1$ v. *ʾrš*$_1$, *bd*$_5$.

bd$_2$ v. *ʾrš*$_1$.

bd$_3$ **Ph** Plur. + suff. 3 p.pl.m. *bdnm* KAI 14[6] (cf. Dérenbourg JA vi/xi 102, Torrey ZA xxvi 85, Gibson SSI iii p. 110f. :: Ginsberg FS Gaster 143: = *bd*$_4$ + suff. 3 p.pl.m. :: Barth ZDMG xli 643 n. 2: = lapsus for *dbrnm* (= Plur. + suff. 3 p.pl.m. of *dbr*$_3$) :: Cooke NSI p. 35: lapsus for *bdbrnm* = *b*$_2$ + Plur. + suff. 3 p.pl.m. of *dbr*$_3$, cf. also Röllig KAI a.l., Segert GPP p. 268, Bron RIPK 115f., Puech RB lxxxviii 100; for older litt. on the subject, cf. also CIS i 3 a.l.)- ¶ subst. Plur. idle talk.

bd$_4$ v. *yd* (v. also *bd*$_{3,5}$).

bd$_5$ **OffAr** diff. word *bu-di* in Warka 12 (for the reading, cf. Landsberger AfO xii 257 n. 49). Interpret. highly uncertain; Landsberger AfO xii 257 n. 49, Dupont-Sommer RA xxxix 46: = Sing. abs. of *bd*$_1$ (= community; less probable interpret.; v. also sub *yd*); Garbini HDS 33: = *bd*$_4$ (highly improb. interpret.

bd$_6$ v. *zy*.

bdʾ **OffAr** QAL Pf. 3 p.s.m. *bdʾ* Aḥiq 30 (uncert. reading, cf. Cowl p. 229) - ¶ verb, poss. meaning: to devise falsehood (dam. context).

bdʾq **OffAr** diff. word in AM ii 174[3]; poss. n.p., cf. Altheim & Stiehl Suppl 95, ASA 267 :: Henning AM ii 174 n. 1: *br bdʾq* = outside the fissure (*br* = *br*$_3$).

bdd$_1$ **Ph** diff. word in Syria xlviii 403[3], reading uncert. (cf. Caquot Syr xlviii 404), reading *brd* also possible, cf. Gaster BASOR ccix 25 n. 35, Röllig NESE ii 32, v.d.Branden BiOr xxxiii 13, xxxvi 202 (cf. also Teixidor AO i 108: l. *bdr*). For the interpret., cf. Gaster BASOR ccix 19, 25: = QAL Imper. s.m. of *bdd*$_2$ = to keep distance (cf. de Moor JEOL xxvii 111, cf. also Baldacci BiOr xl 129: = to fly, Garbini OA xx 290, 29[2]: = to retreat, Gibson SSI iii p. 90f.: = to separate oneself); Röllig NESE ii 29: = QAL (?) Imper. s.m. of *bdd$_2$* (= to remove); Caquot Syria xlviii 404, 406: = QAL Part. s.m. abs. of *bdd$_2$* (= to disperse, to destroy) :: Avishur PIB 267, UF x 32, 35f.: = QAL Part. s.m. abs. of *bdd$_2$* (= to be isolated) :: Lipiński RSF ii 53: = *b$_2$* + *dd$_2$* (= breast) :: vd Branden BiOr xxxiii 13, xxxvi 202: l. *brd* = *b$_2$* + *rd$_1$* (= reason, intelligence).

bdd$_2$ v. *ʾbd$_1$*, *bdd$_1$*, *bdr$_1$*.

bdd$_3$ v. *pwd*.

bdykr (< Iran., cf. Driv p. 72 × de Menasce BiOr xi 162: reading *brykr* preferable < Iran., v. also infra) - **OffAr** Plur. abs. *bdykrn* (× *brykrn*) Driv 9[2] - ¶ subst. artist (cf. also Eilers AfO xvii 333, Porten & Yardeni sub TADAE A 6.12; cf. also Hinz NWAP 41f., AIS 64: l. *brykr* = artist) × de Menasce BiOr xi 162, Grelot DAE p. 318 n.c: l. *brykr* = polisher of stones?

bdyl v. *zy*.

bdyn v. *ʾdyn*.

bdl v. *pwd*.

bdlḥ **Ph** Sing. abs. (dam. context) *bdl[ḥ]* MUSJ xlv 262[1] (for the reading, cf. Starcky MUSJ xlv 264, Röllig NESE ii 4) - ¶ subst. bdellium (v. also *mr$_1$*) - on the use of bdellium, cf. Nielsen SVT xxxviii 30.

bdm v. *brm$_1$*.

bdmrk **Hatra** Sing. emph. *bdmrkʾ* 23[2] (reading uncert.: *bd/rmd/rkʾ*, cf. Caquot Syria xl 15, Degen ZDMG cxxi 125 :: Safar Sumer vii 182, Milik RN vi/iv 54, Donner sub KAI 244: pro *bdmrkʾ dy* l. *br mrkʾdy* :: Aggoula Ber xviii 90 (div. otherwise): l. *br mdkʾ* (= Sing. emph. of *mdk* (= apothecary)) *dy* (cf. also Vattioni IH a.l.: *mdkʾ* = n.p.) :: Caquot Syria xxix 102: or l. *mrnʾdy* = n.p.?) - ¶ subst. designation of (religious) function, exact meaning unknown.

bdṣ v. *dṣ*.

bdr$_1$ **OffAr** PAʿEL (?) Impf. 3 p.pl.m. (with fem. subject) + suff. 3 p.s.m. *ybdrwnh* KAI 260[8] (:: Driver AnOr xii 54: l. *ybddwnh* = PAʿEL Impf. 3 p.pl.m. + suff. 3 p.s.m. of *bdd$_2$* (= to scatter) :: Lipiński Stud 155, 159f.: l. *ybdrw* = PAʿEL (?) Impf. 3 p.pl.m. + *nh* = (precative interjection; = *nʾ*); cf. Degen WO ix 170) - ¶ verb PAʿEL (?) to disperse, to scatter + acc. obj. (person).

bdr$_2$ **Hatra** Segal Irâq xxix 9 n. 28: l. this noun (Sing. abs.) *bdr* in app. 4[5] (= function of religious character), improb. interpret. (cf. Safar Sumer xvii 38 (div. otherwise): l. *br* (= Sing. cstr. of *br$_1$*) + *d* (= first letter of n.p., cf. also Caquot Syria xl 13, Teixidor Syria xli 273, Vattioni IH a.l.); for the context, v. also *ḥny*).

bdš v. *brš$_2$*.

bhwwrd v. *hwwrd.*

bhl Garbini StudMagr xii 90f.: the *bel* in Poen 1027 = Sing. cstr. of *bhl* (= splendour), highly uncert. interpret., cf. Gray AJSL xxxix 82: = Bel (cf. also Sznycer PPP 144).

bhlh v. *kbh.*

bhmd› **OffAr** diff. word *bhmd/r›* in PF 2043[2] (cf. Or xlviii 144 no. 264), function indication (Sing. emph.)? or = b_2 + n.l.?

bhmh v. *‹td*$_1$.

bhmyth **OffAr** for this diff. word (?) in Cowl 9[5], v. *‹td*$_1$.

bhr$_1$ **Pun** the *bhr* in CISFP i 913 (for the reading problems, cf. Johnstone CISFP i a.l.) prob. = noun indicating some part of ship. Exact meaning unknown. Johnstone CISFP i 914ff.: = keel (highly uncert. etymology).

bhr$_2$ v. *b›r.*

bw v. *bz*$_1$.

bw› **Ph** QAL Impf. 1 p.s. *›b›* KAI 27[5]; 2 p.pl.f. *tb›n* KAI 27[6] (cf. e.g. Albright BASOR lxxvi 8 (n. 13), Röllig KAI a.l., Avishur PIB 248, Cross & Saley BASOR cxcvii 45, Caquot FS Gaster 47 × Gibson SSI iii p. 83, 85: prob. = impf 2 p.pl.m. :: v.d.Branden BiOr xxxiii 12: = Impf. 2 p.s.f. + *nun* parag. :: du Mesnil du Buisson FS Dussaud 422: l. *tb›* = QAL impf 3 p.s.f. (for this reading, cf. also Teixidor AO i 106)) - **Pun** QAL Pf. 3 p.pl. *b›* KAI 137[4]; Impf. 3 p.pl.m. *yb›* (or 3 p.s.m.?; FR 166: YIPH?, cf. also vd Branden PO i 209) KAI 81[4] (cf. also Röllig KAI a.l.); YIPH Pf. 3 p.s.m. (?) *›yb›* Trip 41[1] - **Hebr** QAL Impf. 3 p.s.m. *yb›* KAI 193[11], 200[7]; *ybw* DJD ii 46[7]; 3 p.s.f. *tb›* TA-H 24[20], Frey 974 (= SM 1); Imper. s.m. *b›* TA-H 17[1f.]; Inf. cstr. *b›* KAI 193[15], NESE ii 45[3] (??, heavily dam. context :: Millard Irâq xxiv 47: poss. QAL Inf. abs.), *bw* DJD ii 44[6] (cf. Pardee HAHL 132 :: Milik DJD ii a.l. (div. otherwise): l. *lbw* = Sing. + suff. 3 p.s.m. of *lb*); Part. act. s.m. abs. *b›* KAI 193[19] (cf. e.g. Albright BASOR lxi 13, Cassuto RSO xvi 173, Ginsberg BASOR lxxi 26, Hoftijzer FS Hospers 87ff., Smelik PEQ '90, 133 :: Torczyner Lach i p. 59: *hb›* = HIPH Pf. 3 p.s.m.), Frey 661[4]; pl.m. abs. *b›yn* SM 49[24]; HIPH impf 2 p.s.m. *tby* DJD ii 44[6] (cf. Pardee HAHL 132: :: Milik DJD a.l.: l. *tbw* = QAL impf 2 p.s.m.) - ¶ verb to come, to go, to enter: KAI 200[7] - a) + subst./name/adv. followed by *-h* loc., *pn tb› ›dm šmh* TA-H 24[20]: lest Edom should go there, cf. KAI 193[15f.], TA-H 17[1f.] (on this text, cf. Pardee JNES xliv 70) - b) + subst. (without ending), *bt ›b› bl tb›n* KAI 27[5f.]: the house I enter, you may not enter - c) + *›l*$_7$, KAI 193[11]; cf. also *spr ṭbyhw ... hb› ›l šlm ... m›t hnb› l›mr hšmr* KAI 193[19ff.]: the letter of T. ... which has reached Sh. from the side of the prophet (v. *›t*$_6$, *nb›*$_2$) with the accompanying message: "Be on your guard" (cf. Hoftijzer FS Hospers 88f. :: e.g. Albright BASOR lxi 13, Dussaud Syr

xix 267, Hempel ZAW lviii 132, de Vaux RB xlviii 193, Michaud PA 98f., Röllig KAI a.l., Gibson SSI i p. 41, Lemaire IH i 105f., Smelik PEQ '90, 135f.: a letter ..... saying: "Be on your guard" (or beginning with this word; cf. also KAI 196[3ff.]) - d) + *b*$_2$, *tbʾ brkh bmʿ<š>yw* Frey 974 (= SM 1): may a blessing come upon his works - e) + *l*$_5$: DJD ii 46[7] (dam. context) - f) + *mn*$_5$, *hbʾyn mhr hmlk* SM 49[24]: coming from the king's mountain - g) + *ʿlt*, *bʾ hʾlnm ʾl ʿlt hmqdšm ʾl* KAI 137[4f.]: these gods came to these sanctuaries, cf. also KAI 81[4] - YIPH/HIPH to bring, + obj.: DJD ii 44[2f.] (v. supra); in the context of Trip 41[1] > to add (sc. something to a building; ?), cf. Levi Della Vida RCL '63, 465f., 468, cf. however Amadasi IPT 83: = to offer - Lipiński RTAT 260, Gibson SSI iii p. 55, 64: the *bbʾ* KAI 26C iv 20 = *b*$_2$ + QAL Inf. cstr. (= at the coming/entrance of ... ; uncert. context and interpret.; cf. however Lipiński SV 50 (n.j.) (div. otherwise): l. *šbr* (= QAL Impf. 1 p.s. of *šbr*$_1$)?? - Albright JAOS lxvii 157 (n. 38), Röllig KAI a.l.: l. *[y]bʾ* = YIPH Pf. 3 p.s.m. (= to bring) in KAI 5[1] (reading and restoration however uncert., cf. Gibson SSI iii p. 21; cf. also Swiggers AO v 153) - Fitzmyer & Harrington ad MPAT 64[9]: the *by* in this line poss. = form of the root *bwʾ* (imposs. interpret.), prob. = *b*$_2$ + suff. 1 p.s., cf. also Starcky RB lxi 165, *by ʾnh ʾlʿzr dnh lwtk ʾntʾ ymlyk dnh* prob. = on me said Eleazar there rests an obligation to you said Yamlik - cf. also the expression *hʿwlm hbʾ* Frey 661[4]: the coming world - Röllig NESE ii a.l.: l. poss. form of this root (*bʾ*) in NESE ii 45[3] (reading of *b* uncert., cf. also Millard Irâq xxiv 47) - l. a form of this root in Frey 626[2]: *bwʾ[* (= QAL Imper. s.m.? :: Frey a.l.: l. *ybwʾ* = QAL Impf. 3 p.s.m.) - Gibson SSI iii p. 55, 64: the *bʾ* in KAI 26C iv 20 = derivative of this root (= entrance), interpret. of context however highly uncert., cf. also Bron RIPK 127f. -
v. *byk*, *bʿy*$_1$, *ḥk*, *ybl*$_1$, *yṭb*, *tbʾh*.

bwz **Pun** Rocco AION xxiv 476, 479 l. *bz* = QAL Imper. s.m. of *bwz* (/ *bzy*$_1$/*bzz*$_1$) = to despise in GR ii 36 no. 20[5] (highly uncert. interpret., cf. Polselli GR a.l.).

bwl v. *ybl*$_1$.

bwlʾ (< Greek βουλή) - **Palm** Sing. abs. *bwlʾ* CIS ii 3913 i 1, 7, 3914[1], 3919[2], 3927[2], 3959[1] (= SBS 44B 1), etc. - ¶ subst. f. Senate; cf. *bwlʾ wdm(w)s* CIS ii 3913 i 2, 3914[1], 3930[1], 3931[1], 3932[8], 3934[1], 3936[3], 3959[1], Inv x 44[1], 115[1], 129[3], Inscr P 32[3], SBS 48B 4, 7, DFD 13[17], 37[1]: the Senate and the People (cf. also Février Essai 21f., Gawlikowski TP 42); in many instances Greek par.: βουλή.

bwlbs **Hebr** Plur. abs. *bwlbsyn* SM 49[4,24] - ¶ subst. bulbous root; v. also *bylbwš*.

bwms v. *bms*.

bws **Pun** Rocco AION xxiv 471: l. 8 times *bs* = QAL Imper. s.m.

(?) of *bws* (= to crush, to trample down); highly uncert. interpret. and reading, cf. Polselli sub GR ii 18 - Rocco AION xxiv 475f.: l. *bs* in GR ii 36 no. 20^5 = QAL Imper. s.m., and *lbs* in GR ii 36 no. 20^1 = l_1 + QAL Imper. s.m. of *bws* (uncert. interpret.; cf. also Polselli sub GR ii 20) - Rocco StudMagr vii 12: l. *bs* in l. 3 = QAL Imper. pl.m. of *bws* (uncert. interpret.).

bw' v. *b'y*$_1$.

bwp **Pun** *hbwp* (reading *b* uncert.) in Hofra 95^3 = h_1 + *bwp* (Sing. abs.), meaning unknown, = title or indication of function? Or = lapsus for *hrwp*?? = h_1+ QAL Part. act. s.m. abs. of *rp'*$_1$.

bwṣ v. *bṣ*.

bwṣyn cf. Frah iv 24: gourd, cucumber.

bwt$_1$ **JAr** Naveh & Shaked AMB a.l.: the diff. *b't'* in AMB 12^{11} (dam. context) prob. = QAL Part. act. s.f. abs. of *bwt*$_1$/*byt*$_1$ (= to lodge); uncert. interpret.

bwt$_2$ **OffAr** Sing. abs. *bwt* Aḥiq 90 - ¶ subst. of unknown meaning; Baneth OLZ '14, 297, Ginsberg ANET 428, Grelot RB lxviii 181, DAE p. 426: = burden, cf. however Seidel ZAW xxxii 295, Epstein ZAW xxxiii 228: = shame, Kottsieper SAS 192: = trouble, distress, cf. also Cowl a.l., Lindenberger APA 62f., 231 n. 102, 288 :: Joüon MUSJ xviii 86: = thrashing.

bwt$_3$ v. *byt*$_3$.

bwt$_4$ **Waw** Sing. + suff. 2 p.s.m. *bwtk* AMB 6^{10} (cf. Naveh & Shaked AMB a.l. :: Dupont-Sommer Waw p. 11, 23f.: l. *kwtk* (= Sing. + suff. 2 p.s.m. of *kwh*) :: Gordon Or xviii 339: l. *kwtk* = *kwt* (used as prep., as) + suff. 2 p.s.m.) - ¶ subst. desire.

bz$_1$ **OffAr** this word and *bzy*$_3$ in Pers texts: 5^3 (*bz*, for the reading, cf. Naveh & Shaked Or xlii 456 :: Bowman Pers a.l.: pro *bz kp* ... l. *bprk* = b_2 + *prk*$_4$ (= (ceremony of) crushing) :: Gershevitz Mem de Menasce 70: = b_2 + *prk*$_5$ (= pestle) :: Levine JAOS xcii 75f.: l. *bprk* = b_2 + *prk*$_6$ (= chamber, sanctuary); for the reading, cf. also Degen BiOr xxxi 127), 48^5 (*bzy*, for the reading, cf. Degen BiOr xxxi 127 :: Naveh & Shaked Or xlii 456: l. *bz* :: Bowman Pers a.l.: l. *bw*.), 52^4 (*bzy*, for the reading, cf. Degen BiOr xxxi 127 :: Naveh & Shaked Or xlii 455: l. *bz* :: Bowman Pers a.l.: l. *bg* = good fortune, cf. Bowman ibid. p. 50: < Iran.), 91^3 (*bz*), 92^5 (*bzy*), 112^5 (*bzy*), 116^3 (*bz*), 163^3 (*bzy*). In Pers 47^3 l. poss. also *bzy*, cf. Naveh & Shaked Or xlii 456 n. 74, Degen BiOr xxxi 127 :: Bowman Pers a.l.: l. [*bg*]. Poss. subst. or adj. of unknown meaning; occurring in the following expressions: a) *bz* in *hwn zy gll zy bz* Pers 116$^{2f.}$ (cf. also *[hwn] zy gll bz* Pers 91$^{2f.}$, *hwn znh [zy gll] bz* Pers 5$^{2f.}$) - b) *bzy* in *sḥr znh z'yr bzy* Pers 52$^{3f.}$ and in comparable expressions with *sḥr*$_3$: Pers 48$^{4f.}$, 52$^{3f.}$, 92$^{4f.}$, 112$^{4f.}$, 163$^{2f.}$; > doubtful whether *bz* and *bzy* are the same word. Naveh & Shaked

Or xlii 456: *bz/bzy* < Iran. = tribute, cf. also Degen BiOr xxxi 127 n. 15, Levine JAOS xcii 79 n. 71. Bowman Pers p. 63: *bz/bzy* < Iran., designation of kind or quality of stone?

bz$_2$ Ebeling Frah a.l.: the *btyʾ* in Frah xxx 20 = lapsus for *bzyʾ* (= form of *bz$_2$* (= breast)), cf. however Nyberg FP 110: = form of *bṭ* (= breast).

bzʾ **JAr** Puech RB xc 496: l. poss. *ybzʾ* = QAL Impf. 3 p.s.m. of *bzʾ* (= to destroy) in IEJ xvii 110 (highly uncert. reading).

bzh v. *zbnwt*.

bzz$_1$ **Ph** *mbzt* KAI 27^{21} (for this uncert. reading, cf. du Mesnil du Buisson FS Dussaud 424, Albright BASOR lxxvi 9, Gaster Or xi 44, JNES vi 187, Röllig KAI a.l. (= YIPH Part. s.m. abs. of *bzz* (= to spoil, to kidnap), cf. FR 164; cf. also Gaster Or xi 49); for the problems of this reading, cf. Caquot FS Gaster 50) × Dupont-Sommer RHR cxx 144: l. *mbt*? = *mn$_5$* + Sing. abs. of *byt$_2$*, cf. Avishur PIB 248, 256: *mbt* = *mn$_5$* + Sing. + suff. 1 p.s. of *byt$_2$*?, cf. also Lipiński RTAT 266, transl.: from the h[ou]se :: Cross & Saley BASOR cxcvii 46, Gibson SSI iii p. 83, 87: l. *bbt* = *b$_2$* + Sing. abs. of *byt$_2$* :: Torczyner JNES vi 26, 29: l. *šmn zt* = Sing. cstr. of *šmn$_2$* + Sing. abs. of *zyt$_1$* - in FuF xxxv 173^{10} poss. form of this root (*bz* = QAL Pf. 3 p.s.m.).
v. *bwz*.

bzz$_2$ **OffAr** Sing. abs. *bzz* (uncert. reading :: Porten & Greenfield JEAS p. 80, Porten & Yardeni sub TADAE A 4.2 : l. *b 2*) Cowl 37^7 - ¶ subst. plunder?; *ndḥl bzy zʿyrn ʾnḥnh bzz* Cowl 37^7: because we are few, we fear plunder/robbery (uncert. transl.; dam. context).

bzy$_1$ this root in KAI 233^8??: *bzyt* = QAL Pf. 1/2 p.s.(m.) of *bzy$_1$* (= to despise), cf. Dupont-Sommer Syr xxiv 40, Donner KAI a.l.: or = PIʿEL Pf. 1/2 p.s.(m.) of *bzy$_2$* (= to divide?) :: Lidzbarski ZA xxxi 199, Kaufman Conn xix 122 n. 31: *bzyt* = *b$_2$* + Sing. abs. of *zyt* (cf. Bowman UMS xx 277, cf. also Lidzbarski AUA 11: or l. *ḥzyt* ? = QAL Pf. 1/2 p.s.(m.) of *ḥzy$_1$* and Gibson SSI ii p. 103, 107: l. prob. *ḥzyt* = QAL Pf. 2 p.s.m. of *ḥzy$_1$*).
v. *bwz*.

bzy$_2$ v. *bzy$_1$*.

bzy$_3$ v. *bz$_1$*.

bzyzh **OffAr** Sing. cstr. *bzyzt* Aḥiq 168 - ¶ subst. booty, loot (prob. meaning, for the uncert. context, cf. also Grelot RB lxviii 192, DAE p. 445 n. g, Lindenberger APA 172).

bzʿ **OffAr** QAL Pf. 3 p.s.m. *bzʿ* Aḥiq 41 - **JAr** QAL Pf. 3 p.s.m. *bzʿ* Frey 834^4 (= SM 91a), 835^1 (= SM 91c; *b[z]ʿ*) - ¶ verb - **1)** to tear, to rend + obj. (a garment): Aḥiq 41 - **2)** to cleave + obj. (the sea; said of Moses): Frey 834^4, $835^{1f.}$.

bzq$_1$ cf. Frah viii 7 (*bzkwn*), xviii 21 (*pzkwn*) to scatter, cf. Nyberg FP

49, 90 :: Ebeling Frah a.l.: l. *pshwn* = form of *psy* (= to extend).

bzq₂ **OffAr** Sing. abs. *bzq* Aḥiq 206 - ¶ subst. pebble (cf. Lindenberger APA 205).

bzr cf. Frah iv 5: corn, seed.

bḥh **Hebr** The *]bḥh[* on bowl rim (BiAr xxxiv 118, cf. also Dever RB lxxvii 395) without interpret.

bḥl v. *pḥl*.

bḥn **OffAr** QAL Imper. s.m. *bḥn* RES 1792A 7; Part. pass. s.m. abs. *bḥyn* Aḥiq 203 (?, diff. and dam. context; or = QAL pass. Pf. 3 p.s.m.?) - ¶ verb QAL to examine + obj. (vessels): RES 1792A 7, cf. Dupont-Sommer REJ '46/47, 46 - Aḥiq 203: dam. context (cf. also Kottsieper SAS 22, 192).
v. *šnʾ₁*.

bḥr = to select, to levy (troops) > Akkad., cf. v.Soden Or xxxv 7, xlvi 185, cf. also v.Soden AHW s.v. *beḫēru* and CAD s.v. *beḫēru* - a form of this root prob. in Irâq xxxii 74[4] (*bḥr*), cf. Segal a.l. - cf. poss. Frah xviii 18 (*mbḥlwn*), Nyberg FP 89: = form of *bḥr* :: Ebeling Frah a.l.: l. *mšlwn* to be related to Akkad. *šullû* (= to bring in, to gather in).

bḥš = to examine > Akkad.?. cf. v.Soden Or xlvi 185.

bṭ v. *bz₂*.

bṭwṭ **Nab** Naveh IEJ xxix 113, 119: the *bṭwṭʾ* in IEJ xxix 112[9] prob. = Sing. emph. of *bṭwṭ* (= spark; highly uncertain context and interpret.).

bṭḥ **OldCan** QAL Pf. 1 p.s. *ba-ti-i-ti* EA 147[56] (cf. also Sivan GAG 141, 212) - ¶ verb QAL to trust: EA 147[56] - a form of this root also in KAI 50[5]? (diff. and dam. context).

bṭḥš (< Iran., cf. Nyberg Eranos xliv 237, Metzger JNES xv 21f., Eilers IIJ v 209, Altheim & Stiehl LuG ii 41ff., Suppl 77ff., 88f., ASA 83f., 267, Harnack with Altheim & Stiehl GMA 528ff., Henning Ir 62 (n. 2), cf. also Rundgren OrSu xxx 179f.) - **OffAr** Sing. abs. *bṭḥš* KAI 276[2] (Greek par. πιτιάξου; :: Grelot Sem viii 13:= orthogr. var. of Sing. emph. *bṭḥšʾ*) - **Hatra** Sing. emph. *bṭḥšʾ* 143 - ¶ subst. m. designation of high official; cf. Frye SOLDV i 316ff., BAG 89, Altheim & Stiehl Suppl 77ff., GH i 248 n. 41, 428, iv 23ff., Toumanoff Traditio xvii 8ff., Chaumont JA ccliv 492 n. 15, cclvi 27 n. 42 (cf. also Benveniste Titres 65 n. 2, Amiranachvili RSO xxxiv 156f.); cf. also *pdḥš*, *pyṭḥš*, and cf. also *bytyʾḥš*: Altheim LuG ii 47.
v. *brš₂*.

bṭṭ₁ v. *lwṭ*.

bṭṭ₂ **JAr** Yadin & Naveh Mas a.l.: the diff. *ʾytbṭ* in Mas 556[5] poss. = ITP Pf. 3 p.s.m. of *bṭṭ₂* (= to bloom), uncert. interpret.

bṭyt = pitcher, jar, CAD s.v. *baṭû*: > Akkad.? (less prob. interpret., cf. v.Soden Or xlvi 185).

bṭl₁ **JAr** PAʿEL Imper. pl.m. *bṭlwn* AMB 5[4] - ¶ verb PAʿEL to eliminate, to annul + obj.: AMB 5⁴.

bṭl₂ **Palm** PA ʿEL Part. pass. s.m. abs. *mbṭl* CIS ii 3913 i 10 - ¶ verb PA ʿEL to occupy oneself with; *yhwʾ mbṭl lʾrkwnyʾ ... dy ...* CIS ii 3913 i 10f.: it will be made the concern of the archonts ... that (cf. Greek par.: ἐ[πι]μελεῖσθαι δὲ τοὺς ... ἄρχοντας ...).

bṭln **JAr** Sing. abs. *bṭln* DJD ii 25 i 7, 26 i 5 - ¶ adj. idle, without legel effect.

bṭn₁ **OldCan** Sing. abs. *ba-aṭ-nu-ma* EA 232[10] (cf. Rainey EA p. 85 s.v. *pandu*, Kossmann JEOL xxx 56, Sivan GAG 131, 210) - **OffAr** Sing. abs. *bṭn* Aḥiq 161 (?; for the dam. context, cf. Lindenberger APA 163), 217 (diff. and dam. context); emph. *bṭnʾ* Cowl 26[11]; + suff. 1 p.s. *bṭny* Aḥiq 139; + suff. 3 p.pl.m. *b[ṭn]hm* Cowl 71[1] (??) - ¶ subst. - **1)** belly, cf. *br bṭny* Aḥiq 139: my own son (cf. also Lindenberger APA 137, Greenfield FS Fitzmyer 49) - **2)** hold (of a ship): Cowl 26[11] (cf. Cowl a.l., Grelot DAE p. 290 n. z).
v. *bṭn₂*.

bṭn₂ **Pun** Sing. + suff. 3 p.s.m./f. *bʾṭnʾ* KAI 119[2] - **Amm** Sing. abs. (or cstr.?, cf. Cross BASOR cxciii 19) *bṭn* BASOR cxciii 8[5] - ¶ subst. (same word as *bṭn₁*?), prob. designation of architectural element: KAI 119[2] (cf. Dussaud Syr xxxiv 199, Röllig KAI a.l., Amadasi IPT 76), BASOR cxciii 8[5] (cf. Garbini AION xx 253, Teixidor Syr xlvii 367, Fulco BASOR ccxxx 41f. :: Horn BASOR cxciii 12 (also proposing other solutions), Puech RB lxxx 534, 538f.: *dlt bṭn* prob. = the inner door (litt. the door of the interior, *bṭn* = *bṭn₁*), cf. Sasson PEQ '79, 118, 122f., Aufrecht sub CAI 59: *dlt bdlt bṭn* = the innermost door, cf. also Shea PEQ '79, 18ff., '81, 105, 107: = interior, inner part (obj. of verb), transl. adverb.: inward :: v. Selms BiOr xxxii 6: *bṭn* = *bṭn₁* used adverb.: inside :: Cross BASOR cxciii 19 (n. 15): *bṭn* = *bṭn₁* (= bowl, bottom of basin (of a laver; v. *kbh*)) :: Rofé RB lxxx 534, 538: = n.l. :: Albright BASOR cxcviii 38f.: = *bṭn₃* (= terebinth), cf. also Dion RB lxxxii 33; cf. also R.Kutscher Qadm v 28, Jackson ALIA 22.

bṭn₃ v. *bṭn₂*.

bṭq (< Akkad.?, cf. Cowl p. 95, cf. also v.Soden AHW s.v. *baṭqu*, cf. however CAD treating this word s.v. *batqu*) - **OffAr** Sing. abs. *bṭq* Cowl 26[10] - ¶ subst. (?), damage, damaged part > repair (?), for the context, cf. also Grelot DAE p. 289 n. u; cf. also Whitehead JNES xxxvii 133 n. 90: = part of boat.

by₁ v. *byt₁*.

by₂ (< *b₂* + *ʾy₂*, cf. Février Sem iv 15f., RA xlvi 224, cf. also Röllig sub KAI 79, FR 320,3, v.d.Branden GP 304 :: FR 258d, 283,11 (v. infra) :: Chabot Mus xxxvii 155f. (v. infra) :: v.d.Branden BiOr xxiii 144f.: = orthogr. var. of *b₂* (cf. also Levi Della Vida RSO xxxix 304, Segert GPP 56.212) :: Lidzbarski ThLZ xlix 296: = *b₂* + suff. 1 p.s. used as exclamation) - **Pun** KAI 79$^{8, 9}$, CIS i 5522^4 - ¶ prep. prob. meaning: without; *ḥnm by ksp* CIS i 5522^4: free of expense, without money (i.e. without paying); *by py ʾnk wby py ʾdm bšmy* KAI 79$^{8ff.}$: without my personal order or without the order of anyone (acting) in my name (cf. also Gevirtz VT xi 152 (n. 3), Röllig KAI a.l.) :: FR 258d, 283,11: *by py* ... *by py* = or .... or ... (cf. Roschinski TUAT ii 612) :: Chabot Mus xxxvii 155f.: *by py* .... *by py* .... = except ... except ... :: Segert GPP 56.212: *by py* = according to my instruction (twice).

by$_3$ v. *bn$_1$*.

byk **Pun** Février CB vii 123, CIS i a.l.: l. *byk ršm* in CIS i 5523^2 (= KAI 96; = Sing. abs. of *byk* (= curtain) + *ršm* (= QAL Part. pass. s.m. abs. of *ršm* (= painted, embroidered)), uncert. interpret., diff. context; cf. also Lidzbarski Eph ii 58f. (div. otherwise): l. *tby* (highky uncert. interpret.) + *kršm* (= Plur. abs. of subst. *krš$_2$*)? (cf. also Clermont-Ganneau RAO viii 99f.: *tby* = verbal noun of root *bwʾ* (= production, product)??).

bylbwš cf. Frah iv 17 (*bylbwšyʾ*): aegle marmelos (a citracé), cf. Ebeling Frah a.l., Nyberg FP 66; cf. also *bwlbs*.

bylwṭ (< Greek βουλευτής, cf. Rosenthal Sprache 20, cf. also Littmann with Cantineau Syria xix 170 :: Cantineau Gramm 49f.: *bylwṭʾ* lapsus for *bwlwṭʾ*?) - **Palm** Sing. abs. *blwṭ* Inv x 29^2; emph. *bylwṭʾ* CIS ii 3937^2 (Greek par. βουλευτὴν) - ¶ subst. m. senator; cf. also Teixidor Sem xxxiv 63f.

bylwp **OffAr** Cowl 61^{5,7} (for the reading, cf. Cowl a.l.) - ¶ word of unknown meaning.

byn$_1$ **Hebr** NIPH Part. s.f. abs. *nbwnh* Frey 634^2 - **Palm** APH Impf. 3 p.pl.m. *ybn[w]n* CIS ii 3913 i 8 (cf. Greek par. διακρείνοντας) - ¶ verb APH to cause to understand > to lay down in rules; *dy ybn[w]n mdʿm dy msq bnmwsʾ*: that they should lay down in rules whatever was not specified in the law - NIPH Part. sensible: Frey 634^2 - a derivative of this root poss. also in the diff. *bynny* Poen 938, cf. Schroed p. 290, 313, Sznycer PPP 100ff. :: L.H.Gray AJSL xxxix 78: *bynny* = *b$_2$* + suff. 1 p.pl. :: J.J.Glück & Maurach Semitics ii 112: *bynny* = *b$_2$* + Sing. + suff. 1 p.s. of *ʿyn$_2$* or rather *bynn* = *b$_2$* + Sing. abs. *ʿnn$_2$* (= cloud).

byn$_2$ **Ph** *bn* KAI 30^4 (v. however infra) - **Hebr** *byn* AMB 4^{29,30,31} - **OldAr** *bny* KAI 224^{21} (for this prob. interpret., cf. e.g. Dupont-Sommer BMB xiii 29, Donner KAI a.l., Degen AAG p. 62 n. 39a :: Fitzmyer AIS 118, Grelot RB lxxv 285: = Plur. cstr. of *br$_1$*; cf. also Gibson SSI ii p. 55); + suff. 3 p.pl.m. *bnyhm* KAI 224^{18,19} (for OldAr.. material, cf. Fitzmyer AIS 116, Degen AAG p. 62 n. 39a) - **OffAr** *byn* Cowl 5^{13}, 7^{8,10}, Krael 2^{11,12} (for the dittography in the *scriptio anterior*, cf. Yaron JSS xiii 207 (n. 1), cf. also Porten & Yardeni sub TADAE B 3.3), 6^{11} (for this reading, cf. Szubin & Porten BASOR cclxix

39f., Porten & Yardeni sub TADAE B 3.7), Driv 1^{2}, Aḥiq 113, 206, Irâq xxxiv 133a (= AECT 45), WO vi 44B 4 (= KAI 275 :: Dupont-Sommer Syr xxv 61: l. *byn[yt›]* = Sing. emph. of *bynyt* (= carp or barbel), cf. also Donner KAI a.l., Silverman JAOS xciv 272), C 4, etc., *bny* REA-NS viii 170A 5, B 5; + suff. 1 p.s. *byny* NESE i 11^{2}; + suff. 1 p.pl. *bynyn* Cowl $5^{13,14}$, 28^{14}; + suff. 3 p.pl.m. *bynyhm* Krael $3^{8,10}$, 6^{6}, Samar $1^{5,11}$ (= EI xviii 8*), Sem xxiii 95 verso 3 (= AECT 58), *bnyhm* Cowl 13^{14}, 25^{7}, Krael $4^{10,11}$, *bynyhn* Krael $12^{19,21}$, *bynym* Krael 10^{5} (lapsus (cf. Porten & Szubin JAOS cvii 232)?, cf. however Kutscher JAOS lxxiv 237); cf. Frah xxv 38 (*byn*), Frah-S$_2$ 127 (*bbynyḥwn*), Paik 207 (*byn*), Syn 306^{4}, GIPP 21, SaSt 16 - **Nab** + suff. 2 p.s.m. *bynyk* MPAT 64 recto i 13, ii 2; + suff. 1 p.s. *byny* MPAT 64 recto i 13 - **Palm** *byny* CIS ii 3913 i 7, Syr xvii 351^{12} (*byny[*; dam. context), *bny*? CIS ii 3913 ii 75; + suff. 3 p.pl.m. *bynyhwn* CIS ii 3915^{3}, *bnyhwn* Ber v 125^{9} - **JAr** *bn* MPAT-A $5^{4,5}$ (= Frey 1203, SM 64), 22^{2} (= SM 70^{10}) - ¶ prep. - **1)** loc. - a) between; *by[n] ṭwry› [›l]h tryn* Aḥiq 62: between these two mountains; *wšq› bnyhm* Cowl 13^{14}: the street (which is) between them, cf. Cowl 25^{7}, Krael $3^{8,10}$, $4^{10,11}$, $10^{4f.}$, $12^{19,21}$; *bšwq› zy bynyn wbyn byt ppṭ‹wnyt* Cowl $5^{12f.}$: in the street which is between us and the house of P.; *›rq› bny qry›* REA-NS viii 170A 5, B 5: the land between the villages (cf. also WO vi 44C 4); *byn yd z› wlbb›* Irâq xxxiv 133: between this side and the centre (cf. Akkad. par.: *bir-ti idi lìb-bi*; reading and interpret. of Ar. text however uncert., cf. Fales sub AECT 45, v. also *yd*) - b) among, in the midst of; *byn krmy›* Aḥiq 40: among the vineyards, cf. KAI 269^{4} - c) in (this meaning influenced by Persian usage, cf. Rosenthal Forschung 81, Eilers AfO xvii 335, Whitehead JNES xxxvii 134 (n. 100)); *byn bgy› zyly* Driv 1^{2}: in my domains, cf. Driv 2^{2}, 5^{5} and Frah xxv 7 - d) fig. uses related to the loc. meaning; *ḥrb tdlḥ myn špyn byn r‹yn ṭbn* Aḥiq 113: a sword (i.e. war?) will trouble calm waters between good friends (for this translation, cf. Driver JRAS '32, 88, Ginsberg ANET 429, Grelot DAE p. 439 :: Cowl a.l.: a sword will trouble calm waters whether they be bad (or) good; v. also *r‹*$_1$); *‹bd šlm› bynyhwn* CIS ii 3915^{3}: he made peace between them (cf. also Sem xxiii 95 verso 3, Samar 1^{5}); *kl mn dyhyb plgw bn gbr lḥbryh* MPAT-A 22^{2}: everyone who will set discord between a man and his fellow; *kl› nḥšb byny lbynyk* MPAT 64 recto i 13: we will calculate everything between me and you (i.e. between us; v. *ḥšb*$_1$); *sbrnyn hww byny tgr› lbyny mksy›* CIS ii 3913 i 7: disputes arose between the merchants and the tax-collectors (cf. also KAI $224^{17f.}$); *nksn zy yhwwn byn tmt wbyn ‹nny* Krael $2^{12f.}$: the possessions that are between T. and A. (i.e. their joint possessions; cf. e.g. Krael p. 148, Kutscher JAOS lxxiv 241f., Hoftijzer & Pestman BiOr xix 217 n. 7, Porten Arch 211 n. 39, Muffs 33f. n. 3), cf. with same meaning Krael 2^{11}: *nksn zy yhwwn byn ‹nny*

wtmt, cf. also NESE i 11[2] (cf. Degen NESE i 12, Grelot DAE 504 (n. d), Naveh & Shaked JAOS xci 380); *wspr plgnn nktb bynyn* Cowl 28[14]: and we will write between us our deed of partition - **2)** temp. - a) during; *byn ywmy[ʾ]* Cowl 21[9]: during (these) days, cf. Grelot VT iv 366 - b) within (cf. Kutscher JAOS lxxiv 242); *byn ywmn 30* Krael 3[20]: within 30 days, cf. Krael 11[7] and poss. also Cowl 29[6] (heavily dam. text, cf. Cowl a.l.; on the restoration, cf. also Porten FS Freedman 535, Porten & Yardeni sub TADAE B 4.5) and Cowl 45[7] (cf. Porten RB xc 571, 573f., cf. also Grelot DAE p. 97), cf. also Yaron JSS xvi 243 - **3)** *b(y)n ... b(y)n* = either ... or; *[dy]hb ... bn dhb bn [k]sp bn kl mqmh* MPAT-A 5[3ff.]: who has contributed ... either gold or silver or any object; *mšbyʿ ʾny ʿlykm ... byn mywm ly[wm] byn mšbt lšbt byn mšnh lšnh byn mḥdš lḥdš* AMB 4[28ff.]: I adjure you ... whether it is from day to day, or from week to week, or from year to year, or from month to month .... ; this expression also in KAI 30[4]?? (*]bn yd bʿl wbn yd ʾdm wb[n])*, cf. Honeyman Irâq vi 107, Albright BASOR lxxxiii 16, FR 258d, 320.2, Röllig KAI a.l., cf. however - a) Dupont-Sommer RA xli 206, Masson & Sznycer RPC 15, 18f., Puech Sem xxix 20f.: *bn* = between - b) H.P.Müller ZA lxv 111f., Gibson SSI iii p. 30: *bn* = bn_6 (= allomorph of b_2) - for the diff. *byn* in Cowl 7[8,10], v. nqm_2 - the diff. *bbn* in the Amm. text BASOR cxciii 8[6] poss. = b_2 + bn_5 (= byn_2), *bbn ʾlm* ... poss. = in the midst of the porch (cf. Cross BASOR cxciii 19, Fulco BASOR ccxxx 41f.; *byn* having its original nom. function?) × Horn BASOR cxciii 8, 13, Puech & Rofé RB lxxx 534, 541, Dion RB lxxxii 31ff.: *bbn* = b_2 + Plur. cstr. of bn_1 (cf. also Cross AUSS xiii 12 n. 34, Shea PEQ '79, 18, 20, '81, 105, 108) :: Albright BASOR cxcviii 38, 40: *bbn* = b_2 + Sing. cstr. of bn_1 (cf. also R.Kutscher Qadm v 27f., Sasson PEQ '79, 118) :: v.Selms BiOr xxxii 6, 8: *bbn* = Sing. cstr. of *bbn* (= outside; comp. Akkad. *babânu*) :: Palmaitis VDI cxviii 120, 125: l. *zbl* = Sing. cstr. of zbl_4 (= residence), cf. however Teixidor Syr li 318 - for this prep., cf. also Barr JSS xxiii 1ff. - this prep. poss. also in FuF xxxv 173[8] (cf. also Altheim & Stiehl FuF a.l.).
v. *bynh*, mn_5, *nbnh*, $nṣr_1$.

bynbn **OffAr** Sing. abs. *bynbn* Herm 5[5] - ¶ subst. of unknown meaning; Bresciani & Kamil Herm a.l.: < Egypt. = beam? of cedar wood (cf. also Porten Arch 267; Porten & Greenfield ZAW lxxx 222: < Egypt.?; cf. however Grelot RB lxxiv 435, DAE p. 163 n. c).

bynh **OffAr** word of unknown meaning in ATNS 43b i 2 (= byn_2 + suff. 3 p.s.m./f.?); for the reading *bynh* in ATNS 44 ii 6, v. bny_1.

bynwt **Palm** *bynwt* Ber ii 104[4] (cf. Ingholt Ber ii 105) - ¶ prep. between; *bynwt trtn kpyʾ* Ber ii 104[4]: between the two rooms.

byny v. byn_2.

bynyt v. byn_2.

bys **OffAr** Sing. emph. (?) *bys›* AJSL lviii 304C 11- ¶ subst. baker's trough??, cf. Bowman AJSL lviii 313.

by‘t v. *ytn*$_2$.

byr$_1$ **Mo** Sing. abs. *br* KAI 181^{24,25} (for the relation to *b›r*, cf. Segert ArchOr xxix 218f., xxxi 335) - **OldAr** Sing. emph. *byr›* KAI 222B 34, 34f. (*by[r›]*; for the relation to *b›r*, cf. Segert ArchOr xxxii 126, Degen AAG p. 28 :: Fitzmyer AIS 70; cf. also Garr DGSP 49) - **OffAr**, cf. Frah iii 5 (*byr›*), GIPP 21 - ¶ subst. well (cf. Frah iii 5), cistern.
v. *b›r*.

byr$_2$ v. *kbyr*.

byrby **Hebr** Sing. abs. *byrby* SM 75^{2,5}, Frey 892^{2}, 893^{2}, 951 - **JAr** Sing. abs. *byrby* SM 43^{5} (cf. Naveh SM a.l.; Fitzmyer & Harrington sub MPAT-A 11: l. *]rby*; Beyer ATTM 377: l. *ydy rby*), *brryby* Frey 1042 - ¶ subst. (< Sing. cstr. of *bn*$_1$ + Plur. abs. of *rb*$_2$; cf. Naveh sub SM 75) title of jewish scholars.
v. *rbrb*.

byrh (< Akkad., cf. Zimmern Fremdw 14, Kaufman AIA 44, AAALT 53, Lipiński ZAH i 64f. :: Lemaire & Lozachneur Syr lxiv 261f.: poss. from NorthWest-Semitic > Akkad.) - **OffAr** Sing. cstr. *byrt* Cowl 6^{3}, 27^{5}, 30^{8}, ATNS 73^{1}, FuF xxxv 173^{7} (the *byrt* in FuF xxxv 173^{11} poss. Sing. abs.?); emph. *byrt›* Cowl 6^{3,4,17}, Krael 2^{2}, 4^{2,4}, Driv 5^{7}, Pers 1^{1}, 5^{1} FX 136^{3}, etc. etc., *brt›* Cowl 35^{2}, Beh 2 (Akkad. par. *al*), 46 (*[b]rt›*; for the prob. reading, cf. Greenfield & Porten BIDG 44f.; Akkad. par. *al*), Krael 3^{4}, 5^{2}, etc., cf. poss. also *byrt* in Cowl 13^{4} (diff. form, haplography?: *byrt ›klt* pro *byrt› ›klt*?) and in Pers 4^{1}, 46^{1} (in both instances at the end of the line, shortened form of *byrt›*?, cf. also R.A.Bowman Pers p. 20, 66) and *byrtn* in Pers 77^{2} (poss. lapsus for *byrt›*?, reading of last sign however uncert. :: R.A.Bowman Pers a.l.: = *byrt* + pers. ending *-na*, cf. however Bowman Pers p. 20, 66 n. 33); cf. Paik 211 (*br*, *brt›*, *byrt›*), Nisa-b 1693 (*byrt›*), GIPP 50; for *byrh* as a loanword in ancient Iran. texts, cf. PTT 36^{2}, 44^{2}, 44a^{2}, cf. also Cameron PTT p. 86 - **Nab** Sing. emph. *byrt›* CIS ii 164^{3} (cf. Greek par. τὸ ἱερὸν), RES 2023^{3} - **Hatra** Sing. emph. Ibr 20^{2}, 21^{3} - **Palm** Sing. emph. *byrt›* Syr xxxvi 106 no. 14 (for the reading, cf. Dunant Syr xxxvi 108 and with du Mesnil du Buisson BiOr xvii 238; × Milik Syr xxxvii 94: = n.l.) - ¶ subst. f. - **1)** fortress: passim; *yb byrt›* Cowl 6^{3,4}, Krael 2^{2}, etc.: the fortress of Yeb; cf. *swn byrt›* Cowl 6^{17}, 8^{28}, Krael 8^{1}, etc., *ṭbh byrt›* Cowl 82^{3}, *tgr šmh brt›* Beh 2, *b›wrn byrt›* FX 136^{3} (for *hst byrt›*, *srk byrt›* and *prkn byrt›*, v. resp. *hst*, *srk*$_2$ and *prkn*$_2$); *byrt yb* Cowl 6^{3}, 27^{5}, 30^{8}: the fortress of Yeb; *byrt mnpy* ATNS 73^{1}: the fortress of Memphis; cf. also Altheim & Stiehl GMA 566, 568, cf. however Herzfeld Paik p. 68 and sub 211; cf. also Hatra Ibr 20^{2}, 21^{3} (cf. Aggoula Syr lxiv 226, 227f., cf. however Segal JSS xxxi 57ff.??: = temple) - **2)** temple, sanctuary:

CIS ii 164[3], RES 2023[3] (cf. 1 Chr. xxix 1, 19); du Mesnil du Buisson BiOr xvii 238: this meaning also in Syr xxxvi 106 no. 14 (less. prob.) - Cowl a.l.: l. poss. *b[r]t[ʾ]* (= Sing. emph.) in Beh 23, less prob. reading, cf. Greenfield & Porten BIDG 36f., l. *b[ʾ]nz* = *b*$_2$ + *ʾnz* (= n.g.) - the Akkad. (neo-Bab.) Plur. *birānātu* < Ar.?, cf. Albright BASOR cxliii 33, cf. also v.Soden AHW s.v. *birtu(m)* - for this word, cf. also Marrassini FLEM 105f., Cameron PTT p. 141, Lemaire & Lozachmeur Syr lxiv 262ff.

v. *gnh*$_1$, *lbyn*.

byš v. *bʾš*$_2$.

byt$_1$ v. *bwt*$_1$.

byt$_2$ **Ph** Sing. abs. *bt* KAI 4[1], 14[17,18], 15, 16, 24[16], 37B 5 (= Kition C 1 B 5), CIS i 45 (= Kition B 36), etc.; cstr. *bt* KAI 24[5], 26A i 10 (:: Dupont-Sommer Oriens ii 123: = Plur. cstr., cf. id. ArchOr xviii/3, 44), 16, ii 15, iii 11, C iv 12, 27[5] (cf. e.g. FR 292, Röllig KAI a.l.), 37A 5 (= Kition C 1 A 4), 14 (= Kition C i A 13), 60[2,3,4,5], Mus li 286[6]; + suff. 3 p.s.m. *bty* Mus li 286[5]; Plur. abs. *btm* KAI 4[2] (:: Dahood Ps iii 142: = Plur. cstr. + *-m* enclit., cf. also Baldacci BiOr xl 125), 14[17]; cstr. *bt* KAI 14[15] - **Pun** Sing. abs. *bt* KAI 124[4], 277[5], Trip 41[1], Hofra 25[2]; cstr. *bt* KAI 62[2,3], 69[1], 86[4], 115[2], CIS i 124[1], 247[5], 248[3], 3779[5], 4834[5], 4835[3], 6000 bis 8, etc.; + suff. 3 p.s.m. *btm* CIS i 5522[5] (:: v.d.Branden BiOr xxiii 145: + suff. 3 p.pl.m.); + suff. 3 p.s.f. *bty* KAI 277[10]; Plur. + suff. 3 p.s.m. *btʾy* KAI 118[1] (cf. e.g. FR 235, Röllig KAI a.l., Amadasi IPT 110 :: Levi Della Vida PBR xix 67: = Plur. + suff. 1 p.s. :: Clermont-Ganneau RAO vii 88, 95, Lidzbarski Eph iii 60: l. *btʾ* = Sing. + suff. 3 p.s.m.) - **Mo** Sing. cstr. *bt* KAI 181[23]; + suff. 3 p.s.m. *byth* KAI 181[25], *bth* KAI 181[7] - **Hebr** Sing. abs. *byt* KAI 191B 1, Mosc sig. 30 (reading of *t* uncert.; = Vatt. sig. eb. 149 = SANSS-Heb 18), HBTJ 1, 2, 3, DJD ii 30[18] (diff. reading), SM 13[2], Frey 1398[2]; cstr. *byt* KAI 194[5], TA-H 18[9], RB lxxxviii 236 (*by[t]*), DJD ii 30[2], 42[7], SM 6[2] (= Frey 977); cstr. + *h* loc. *byth* TA-H 17[2] (:: Cross FS Glueck 305 n. 3: = Sing. + suff. 3 p.s.m.); + suff. 3 p.s.m. *bytw* DJD ii 30[28] (dam. context, reading of *y* uncert., cf. also Milik DJD ii a.l.); + suff. 2 p.s.m. *bytk* TA-H 16[2,4], 21[2], DJD ii 17A 1, 30[27]; + suff. 1 p.s. DJD ii 44[3], 45[2] (dam. context), EI xx 256[11] (prob. reading) - **DA** Sing. abs. *byt* ii 7; cstr. *byt* ii 6 - **Samal** Sing. abs. *byt* KAI 215[22]; cstr. *byt* KAI 214[9], 215[2,3,7,9]; + suff. 3 p.s.m. *byth* KAI 215[19]; + suff. 1 p.s. *byty* KAI 215[5] - **OldAr** Sing. *by* KAI 216[16] (in the comb. *by ṭb* < *byt ṭb*, cf. FR p. 39 n. 2, Garb 274, Degen AAG p. 43 (n. 46), Donner KAI a.l. :: Gordon Or xxi 122, Fitzmyer Or xxxix 583, Segert AAG p. 209: *by* = shortened form of *byt*); cstr. *byt* KAI 203 (*[b]yt*), 216[7,12,13,17,18,19], 217[3], 222A 6, C 7, 224[9f.], *bt* Tell F 17; emph. *bytʾ* KAI 216[10]; + suff. 3 p.s.m. *byth* KAI 222C 16, 22, Tell F 8; + suff. 2 p.s.m. *bytk* KAI 222B 40; + suff.

1 p.s.. *byty* KAI 216[15], 222B 32 (*b[y]ty*), 40, 44, 224[21]; + suff. 2 p.pl.m. *bytkm* KAI 222B 21; Plur. cstr. *bty* KAI 202B 9, 223C 2f., 7, 9f.; + suff. 3 p.pl.m. *btyhm* KAI 223C 16 - **OffAr** Sing. abs. *byt* Cowl 13[11] (cf. however Degen GGA '79, 29: *byt ʾm* haplography for *bytʾ ʾm* (?), cf. also Beyer ZDMG cxx 200), Krael 3[21], *by* Cowl 3[18], 8[3] (for the reading, cf. e.g. Porten & Yardeni sub TADAE B 2.3. :: Cowl a.l.: l. prob. *byt* (= Sing. abs.)), 9[3], 10[9], 13[21] (for the reading, cf. Porten FS Freedman 529, Porten & Yardeni sub TADAE B 2.7), Krael 4[8,25], 6[3] (for this prob. reading, cf. Porten & Yardeni sub TADAE B 3.7), ATNS 8[4] (for the reading, cf. Porten & Yardeni sub TADAE B 5.6 :: Segal ATNS a.l.: l. *br* (= Sing. cstr. of *br*$_1$)), CIS ii 20 (= Del 7; for the interpret., cf. Fales sub AECT 28 :: Delaporte Del a.l.: = Sing. cstr.), etc. (cf. also Degen GGA '79, 22), cf. Warka 4, 7: *ba-a-a* (on this form, cf. also Garbini HDS 31f.); cstr. *byt* CIS ii 54, KAI 228A 12, Cowl 5[5,13], 6[8], 13[15] (for the reading, cf. Porten & Yardeni sub TADAE B 2.7), Krael 3[8], 6[6,7] (*scriptio anterior*, cf. Szubin & Porten BASOR cclxix 33, cf. also Porten & Yardeni sub TADAE B 3.7)[,8], Driv 7[5], 8[2,4], Herm. 1[1], 2[1], 3[1], NESE iii 39[2], TA-Ar 38[3], TeAv vi 192 no. 50[1] (cf. however Naveh a.l.), ATNS 29[1], Atlal vii 109[3] (*by[t]*, cf. Beyer & Livingstone ZDMG cxxxvii 286, 293 :: Livingstone Atlal vii a.l.: = Sing. abs.), etc., etc., *bt* Herm 2[12]; emph. *bytʾ* KAI 228A 22, Cowl 5[3,4], 8[8], Krael 3[7,12,13], Driv 4[2], 6[2], 7[2], HDS 9[5], ATNS 30a 4, 44 i 3 (*]bytʾ*, cf. Segal ATNS a.l. :: Porten & Yardeni sub TADAE B 8.2: l. *]mstʾ* without interpret.), etc., etc., *btʾ* Del 93, *byth* Krael 4[20], 12[9]; + suff. 3 p.s.m. *byth* KAI 260[7], Cowl 15[18, 30], Aḥiq 197 (heavily dam. context, diff. reading, cf. Kottsieper SAS 13), Krael 3[4], 4[11], Driv 9[2], HDS 9[2f.,5f.], *bth* Herm 2[15]; + suff. 3 p.s.f. *byth* Cowl 81[24]; + suff. 2 p.s.m. *bytk* Cowl 7[8,9], 15[3], Aḥiq 52, Krael 3[21], etc., + suff. 2 p.s.f. *bytky* Cowl 8[15,22]; + suff. 1 p.s. *byty* Cowl 5[5], 6[8], Aḥiq 22, 139, Krael 4[21,22], 6[10] (*[b]yty*; on this text, cf. Szubin & Porten BASOR cclxix 37f.), Herm 1[12] (for the reading, cf. Bresciani & Kamil Herm a.l., Porten & Greenfield ZAW lxxx 219 n. 11, Kutscher IOS i 114), NESE i 11[4], ATNS 67a 2, etc.; + suff. 1 p.pl. *bytnʾ* Cowl 81[110], *btnʾ* Cowl 81[115] (?; :: Harmatta ActAntHung vii 372: poss. = Plur. + suff. 1 p.pl.), *bytn* Krael 12[3,5,12], Driv 8[2], F vi 2; Plur. cstr. *bty* JA xi/xviii 60[11]; emph. *btyʾ* Cowl 34[6], Beh 23 (on the dam. context, cf. Porten & Greenfield BIDG 36f.), Krael 6[14] (for the reading and the *sc riptio anterior btʾ* (lapsus), cf. Szubin and Porten BASOR cclxix 33)[,16]; + suff. 3 p.pl.m. *btyhm* Cowl p. 265[2] (for the reading, cf. Greenfield & Porten BIDG 54 :: Cowl a.l.: l. *btyhwm*); + suff. 1 p.pl. *btyn* Cowl 38[8], NESE i 11[6] (cf. Degen a.l. :: Shunnar with Altheim & Stiehl GMA 115: = Sing. + suff. 1pl); cf. Frah ii 15, 16 (*bytʾ*), viii 5, ix 9, xii 7 (in comb. *br/lbytʾ*), Paik 212, 213 (*bytʾ*), 224, 225 (in comb. *br/blbytʾ*), ZDMG xcii 442A 10, Syr xxxv 321[49,50], 327[60,61], Syn 300[5],

301^{5}, GIPP 20, 21, 49, SaSt 15f. - **Nab** Sing. cstr. *byt* CIS ii 196^{5}, 209^{9}, IEJ xxi 50^{1}, *bt* RES 2053^{2}; emph. *byt›* CIS ii 182^{1}, 184^{1} (cf. Milik Syr xxxv 227 :: CIS ii sub 184: l. *qbr›* = Sing. emph. of *qbr*$_3$), 235A 2, J 59, RB xlii 413^{1}, BIA x 58^{1} (:: Altheim & Stiehl AAW v/2, 25: l. *šqy* = Sing. abs. of *šqy*$_3$ (= irrigation)); + suff. 1 p.s. *bty* MPAT 64 recto i 10, 11; Plur. cstr. *bty* CIS ii 350^{1}; emph. *bty›* CIS 350^{2} - **Palm** Sing. cstr. *byt* CIS ii 3978^{7}, RTP 525, RIP 199^{5}, *bt* CIS ii 3914^{5}, 3915^{4}, 3923^{4} (cf. Inv xii 35), 4116^{1}, 4121^{2}, RIP 21^{2}, 24^{3}, Inv xii 26, SBS 45^{11}, etc., etc.; emph. *byt›* CIS ii 3977^{3}, 4176B 3, C 2, RIP 143^{3}, Inv xi 6^{8} (uncert. reading), 78$^{3f.}$ (for the reading, cf. Gawlikowski TP 75 (rather than *byyt›*, cf. Milik DFD 176) :: Teixidor Inv xi a.l.: l. *(mr)byyn›*? = Sing. emph. of *mrbyn*), *bt›* Inv xii 49^{8} (??, highly uncert., dam. context; or l. *bt ›[lh›/y›]*?, cf. also Gawlikowski TP 83); + suff. 3 p.s.m. *byth* CIS ii 3972^{4}, 3997^{2}, 4009^{6}, 4026^{5}, 4033^{6}, 4036A 4, 4051^{3}, 4054^{3}, 4235^{3}, PNO 2ter 4, RIP 108^{4}, 119^{6}, 134^{5}, Inv xi 8^{6}, 16^{4}, 17^{5}, 20^{6}, 25^{3}; + suff. 3 p.pl.m. *bythwn* CIS ii 3981^{5}; Plur. abs. *btyn* Syr xii 130^{8} (dam. context; cf. Milik DFD 48) - **Hatra** Sing. cstr. *byt* 49^{3}, 66, 107^{5} (for the context, v. *ḥdy*$_3$), 272^{1,2}, cf. also Assur 7^{2}, *bt* 3^{2} (cf. Caquot Syr xxix 91), cf. also Assur 27g (dam. context), 33f. 3, *by* (in *byldh*) 79^{3} (v. *yld*$_3$); emph. *byt›* in *rbyt›*, v. *rbyt*, *bt›* 232c 4 (× Degen JEOL xxiii 404: or = Plur. emph.?); + suff. 3 p.s.m. *byth* 200^{6}, 290^{7}; + suff. 3 p.s.f. *byth* 290^{3}; + suff. 2 p.s.m. *bytk* 232e 3 - **JAr** Sing. abs. *byt* Frey 979^{1} (= MPAT-A 48), AMB 15^{4} (?, diff. context), *bt* MPAT 42^{14}(:: Beyer ATTM 310, 530: l. *bty* = Sing. + suff. 1 p.s.)^{,15}; cstr. *byt* Frey 853^{3} (= SM 37; uncert. reading, cf. Naveh SM a.l.), 1415^{1}, MPAT 41^{7}, 44 i 4, 50b 1 (heavily dam. context), c 1, 52^{2}, MPAT-A 50^{8} (= Frey 1208), 51^{8}, 52^{8}, Syn D 269 no. 2^{1} (= SM 90), Syr xlv 101^{16}, IEJ xxxvi 206^{4}, *bt* Frey 1077^{1}, MPAT 41^{9} (?, dam. context), *by* Frey 1418^{1}; emph. *byth* Syn D A 1 (= SM 88), C$_1$ 1 (= SM 89a), C$_2$ 1 (= SM 89b; *byt[h]*), AMB 1^{17} (diff. context), IEJ xxxvi 206^{2,3}, DBKP 19^{28}, *bth* MPAT 51^{3,7,8,11,13}; + suff. 3 p.s.m. *bth* ZDPV xcvi 59^{2}; + suff. 2 p.s.m. *btk* MPAT 51^{4}; + suff. 1 p.s. *byty* MPAT 42^{11}; + suff. 3 p.pl.m. *bythwn* MPAT 42^{15}; Plur. + suff. 3 p.pl.m. *btyhwn* MPAT-A 34^{5} (= SM 69) - Sing. abs. (*byt*) in unknown west Sem dialect: Sem xxxviii 52^{2} (or = fraud?, cf. however Bordreuil & Pardee Sem xxxviii 65ff.) - ¶ subst. m. - **1)** house, building; *b› byth ›lyšb* TA-H 17$^{1f.}$: go to the house of E.; *‹šw lkm ›š br bbyth* KAI 181$^{24f.}$: each (of you) make for yourselves a cistern in his house; *wyhbt ly tr‹ byt› zylk* Cowl 5^{3}: you have given me the gateway of your house; cf. DA ii 7, Cowl 5^{5,13}, 6^{8}, Herm 1^{12}, 2^{15}, NESE i 11^{4}, KAI 260^{7}, CIS ii 350^{2}, Hatra 200^{6}, DJD ii 30^{27}, MPAT 44 i 4, 51^{3,7}, etc. etc.; for HDS 9$^{2f.}$, v. *qryh*; with specialised meaning: - a) palace; *›nh bnyt byt› znh* KAI 216^{20}: I have built this palace; *byt štw› ... byt kyṣ›* KAI 216$^{18f.}$: a winter palace ... a summer palace; cf. also KAI

216^{13,15,16,17} - b) temple; *bt z bny yḥmlk* KAI 4^1: the temple which Y. built; *bnn bt l›šmn* KAI 14^{17}: we have built a temple for Eshmun; *w›nš l› yhn[pq] ṣlmšzb ...mn byt› znh* KAI 228A 20ff.: and no. man shall eject S. ... from this temple; cf. also KAI 4^2, 37B 5, 277^{5,10} (:: Dahood Ps ii 87: = grave), Frey 1398^2, CIS ii 182^1, Inv xii 49^8, Hatra 232e 3, etc.; cf. *ḥrbn hbyt* SM 13$^{1f.}$: the destruction of the Temple (i.e. the second temple in Jerusalem); cf. also *b(y)t* + n.d., *bt hdd* Tell F 17: the temple of H.; *byt nbw* Herm. 1^1: the temple of N.; *‹bd bt ‹štr[t]* CIS i 3779$^{5f.}$: the servant of the temple of A. (cf. TA-H 18^9, CIS i 251 (cf. also Lipiński UF xx 140), KAI 69^1, 86^4, 115^2, 228A 12, Herm 2^{12}, CIS ii 3914^5, SBS 48^6 (cf. Greek par. τῷ τοῦ βήλου ἱερῷ), Hatra 49^3, 272^4, etc. - cf. also *byt byt YHH* ASAE xxvi 27^3 poss. = building belonging to the temple of Y., Dupont-Sommer JA ccxxxv 80f., 83, Grelot DAE p. 369 (× Aimé-Giron ASAE xxvi a.l.: = lapsus for *byt YHH* :: Couroyer RB lxviii 534f.: the grounds of the temple of Y. :: Krael p. 96: the *adyton* of the temple of Y.); cf. poss. also *bt ›šmn* CIS i 2362^6: the temple of Eshmun (cf. Xella RSF xvi 21ff.) - c) synagogue, cf. Syn D A 1, C$_1$ 1, C$_2$ 1 (= resp. SM 88, 89a, 89b) - d) tomb: CIS i 45 (= Kition B 36; *bt z*, cf. Greek par. text ἐνθάδε κεῖμαι); prob. also in LA ix 331 (*b[y]t[›]*; for the context, v. *wgr* :: Milik LA ix 337: prob. = temple) - e) room, Krael 6^{14,16}, cf. Szubin & Porten BASOR cclxix 37 - cf. also the following combinations: - a) *byt dh d›wrḥwtyh* Frey 979^1 (= MPAT-A 48; for the reading, v. *›rḥ$_2$*): this hostel of his (cf. Billig with Klein MGWJ lxxvi 554 n. 2) - b) *bt ›lm* Mus li 286^6, KAI 60$^{2,3,4f.,5}$: temple; cf. *bt ›lhyhn* CIS ii 3923^4: their temple, cf. also CIS i 6000bis 8, KAI 202B 9, IEJ xxv 118^6, SBS 48^8, Syr xvii 280^9, DFD 37^5, 217^1, Hatra 272^1, MPAT 149^6 - the *bty ›lhy›* in KAI 223C 2f., 7, 9f. (*bty [›]lhy›*) = designation of a bethel, sacred stone, cf. e.g. Dupont-Sommer Sf p. 117, 119, Donner ZAW lxxiv 68ff., KAI a.l., Fitzmyer AIS 90 McCarthy CBQ xxvi 187 (n. 21), Milik Bibl xlviii 609 (cf. also ibid. 565ff., Rössler TUAT i 186) :: Greenfield JBL lxxxvii 241, Lemaire & Durand IAS 142: = temples (cf. also Lemaire & Durand IAS 128) - c) *byt ›srn* ATNS 50^9: prison - d) *byt ›rwnh* Syn D 269 no. 2^1 (= SM 90; for the reading, v. *›rn$_1$*): Torah shrine, cf. also Frey 853^3 (= SM 37; v. *›rn$_1$*) - e) *bt dy ›rm[lw dy lk]* MPAT 42^{15}: the house where you will live as a widow - f) *byt bky›* NESE iii 39^2, v. *bky$_2$* - g) for *bt gb›*, v. *gb$_2$* - h) *byt ḥdy›* Hatra 107^5, v. *ḥdy$_3$* - i) *by zy lbnn*, v. *lbnh$_1$* - j) *byt mdbḥ›* Cowl 32^3: (house of sacrifice, i.e.) temple - k) *byt mdršw* SM 6$^{2f.}$: his house of learning, school - l) *bt mlk* KAI 181^{23}: palace, cf. KAI 222A 6; *byt mlk›* Cowl 2^{12,14,16}, 43^8, Krael 11^6, ATNS 31^3 (:: Wesselius BiOr xli 706: in this text = royal domain): (the house of the king, i.e.) the (local) centre of government and administration, cf. also Porten Arch 60 - m) *bt mqbrt›* CIS ii 4170: tomb, cf. *bty mqbryn* CIS ii 350^1 (for the construction, cf.

Milik RB lxvi 558) - n) *byt mqdšh* MPAT-A 50[8], 51[8], 52[8]: the Temple (i.e. the second Temple in Jerusalem); cf. also *mqdš bt ʿštrt* KAI 62[3]: the sanctuary of A. (:: e.g. Cooke NSI p. 105, Röllig KAI a.l.: the inner sanctuary of the temple of A. (cf. also v.d.Branden OA iii 251f.); cf. also CIS i 132 comm. a.l.), cf. KAI 62[2] and poss. KAI 118[1] (diff. context, v. also supra) - o) *byt mšḥʾ* RIP 199[5], v. *mšḥ$_3$* - p) *byt mšry* ATNS 43a 4, v. *mšry* - q) *bt nṭrʾ* Inscr. P 31[9], v. *nṣr$_1$* - r) *bt npšʾ* Frey 1077[1]: sepulchral monument; cf. also *bnpšʾ* (= *b(y)t npšʾ*) Frey 1024[1] - s) *byt spyntʾ* AJSL lviii 303B 4 (heavily dam. context), AG 5[11] (*byh* is a misprint, cf. Daniels Or l. 193; heavily dam. context): house of boats (i.e. dockyard, shipyard?), cf. also Verger RGP 42 - t) *byt sprʾ* AG 71[2]: archives? - u) *bt ʿlm* CIS i 124[1]: grave/tomb (cf. Gawlikowski Ber xxi 13, H.P.Müller WO ix 88 n. 48); cf. IEJ xxi 50[1], CIS ii 4119[2,6f.,8], 4121[2], 4123[1], 4159[1], 4168[3], 4192[1], 4193[4], 4199[1], 4216, 4473, 4490, RIP 21[2], 24[3] (Greek par. τὸ σπήλαιον), 25[7] (Greek par. τὸν ταφ[εῶ]να), 164[2], 167[1], Inv xii 26, Ber xix 74[1], cf. also Ber xix 69[2], Frey 1418[1], etc.; *lbyt ʿlmʾ thk* MPAT 41[7]: you will go to the grave (i.e. you will die); cf. also *byt ʿlmn* DA ii 6: graves (?, cf. Hoftijzer DA a.l., H.P.Müller ZDPV xciv 63 (n. 42) × Levine JAOS ci 200f.: = grave, eternal home (cf. also H.P.Müller ZAW xciv 219, 231f.) :: Hackett BTDA 30, 59: = grave > underworld (cf. Levine BAT 333) :: Caquot & Lemaire Syr liv 203: *ʿlmn* = Plur. abs. of *ʿlm$_5$* = (youth); cf. also Rofé SB 68)) - v) *byt prsʾ* Krael 9[4,7f.], v. *prs$_3$* - w) *bt qbwrʾ* CIS ii 4160[1], 4163[1f.], 4165[1], 4166[1f.] (= Inv xii 16), Inv viii 62[1], Syr xix 153[2], 160[1f.]: tomb, grave - x) *byt qwrh*, v. *qwrh* - y) *byt škn* ATNS 44 ii 2, v. *škn$_2$* - z) *byt šltwnhm* CIS ii 196[5]: their government house - aa) *byt šʿt* Sem iv 21[2] (= KAI 160), v. *šʿt* - bb) *by tḥty* Krael 9[12f.], 10[2,12,13], v. *tḥty* - cc) *byt tnbh* TA-Ar 38[3], v. *tnb* - **2)** - a) designation of plot intended for building upon - α) a plot which is walled in, cf. the *byt* in Krael 3 - β) a plot which is not walled in, cf. the *byt* (// *ʾrq* = plot) in Cowl 8, 9; cf. the appositional phrases *by 1 'rq* Cowl 8[3]: a *byt*, namely a plot; *'rq by 1* Cowl 9[3]: a plot, namely a *byt*, cf. Hoftijzer VT ix 312f., for partly different interpret. of Krael 3, Cowl 8 and 9, cf. also Joüon MUSJ xviii 32f., Kutscher JAOS lxxiv 234f., Porten Arch 214, 240, Muffs 34 n. 2, Ayad JACA 279 n. 30 - b) designation of a field (not intended for building upon; cf. Kaufman AIA 44, Whitehead JNES xxxvii 135): in the following comb.: *byt zrʿ* Driv 8[2,4], DJD ii 30[2], MPAT 52[2]: sowing land/corn land (cf. Koffmahn DWJ 173; *byt zrʿ ʾ[rdb] 30* Driv 8[2,4]: a corn field measuring a seed requirement of 30 ardab (cf. Ginsberg ANET 633 (n. 3)); *byt zrʿ ḥṭym 5* DJD ii 30[2]: a corn field measuring a seed requirement of 5 (measures) of wheat; *byt zrʿ ḥntyn sʾyn tlt wqbyn tlth* MPAT 52[2]: a field measuring a seed requirement of 3 *s.* and 3 *q.* of wheat, cf. Milik Bibl xxxviii 260, Beyer ATTM 322 :: Fitzmyer & Harrington MPAT a.l.: (yielding) wheat etc.); for *byt sygly* Syr xlv 101^{16}, v. *sygl* - **3)** family, house(hold); *byth dnpš[h]* Hatra 290^{3}: his own house/family, cf. KAI 181^{7}, 215^{5,19}, 222B 32, 40, C 16, 22, 224^{21}, Tell F 8, TA-H 16^{2}, 21^{2}, DJD ii 17A 1, CIS ii 3997^{2}, 4009^{6}, Inv xi 8^{6}, Hatra 290^{7}; for Driv 8^{2}, v. *ʾš$_1$*; exact meaning of *br bth* in ZDPV xcvi 59^{2} uncert., cf. Meehan ZDPV xcvi 63f.; *bny byth* CIS ii 3972^{4}: the members of his household (cf. also CIS ii 4033^{6}, 4054^{3}, RIP 134^{5}, Inv xi 16^{4}, 25^{3} (the *bnytʾ* in CIS ii 4048^{5} prob. lapsus for *bny bytʾ*, cf. CIS ii a.l.)); cf. also Frah viii 5 *sws br bytʾ* = swallow belonging to the house (= martin (cf. Ebeling Frah a.l.)); in some texts the (members of the) household mentioned apart from (certain) members of the family, cf. - a) *ʾbwhy wbny byth* Inv xi 20$^{5f.}$: his father and the members of his household - b) *ʾḥwhy wbny byth* PNO 2ter 3: his brothers and the members of his household, cf. also RIP 108^{4} - c) *bnwhy wbny byth klhn* CIS ii 4036A 4: his sons and all the members of his household, cf. CIS ii 4051$^{2f.}$, 4235^{3} (Greek par. τ[οῖς] ἰδ[ίοι]ς, Lat. par. *suis*), RIP 199$^{5f.}$ - d) *bytk wbnyk* Cowl 34^{7}: your household and your sons - e) *šmhtwn wdbnyhwn wdʾnšy btyhwn* MPAT-A 34$^{4f.}$: their names and those of their children and of the people of their households; in some texts (Driv 4^{2}, 6^{2}, 7^{2,3,5,6,7,9}, 8^{6}, 12^{7}) designation of the fief of Arsham in Egypt, including its complete household (slaves, etc.) - f) cf. also the following combinations: - α) *bt ʾby* KAI 24^{5}: my paternal family (i.e. the family to which I belong (of a royal family = dynasty, cf. also Ishida BZAW cxlii 100f., 113)), cf. KAI 214^{9}, 215^{2,3,7,9}, 216^{7,18}, 217^{3}, 224$^{9f.}$, CIS ii 3978^{7} - β) *bt ʾdny* KAI 26A i 10: the house of my lord (i.e. in the context: the dynasty of my overlord), cf. Weippert ZDMG-Suppl i^{1} 193 n. 8 :: Dupont-Sommer RA xlii 170f.: = the house of my lord = the house of (the king) my father = my (royal) house (cf. also v.d.Branden, Meltô i 41) :: Alt WO i 281: = the house of my sovereignty = my lordly house, cf. Pedersen ActOr xxi 51, Röllig KAI a.l. :: O'Callaghan Or xviii 177: = the house of AdaniSamal. (for this text, v. also *ʾdn$_1$* and supra) - γ) for *[b]yt mlkh* in KAI 203, v. *mlk$_3$* - δ) *rkbʾl bʿl byt* KAI 215^{22}: R., the lord of the house, i.e. the special dynastic god (cf. KAI 24^{16}) - ε) *br bytʾ* Driv 2^{1*}: royal prince, cf. Driv 5^{1*}, 10^{1}, Cowl 30^{3}, Frah xii 7, Paik 224, 225 (cf. also Eilers AfO xvii 335, Benveniste Titres 23ff., 35f., 41f., Harnack with Altheim & Stiehl GMA 519ff., Whitehead JNES xxxvii 133f.; cf. Frah ix 9: *bḥl br bytʾ* = princely elephant = strong elephant bull (cf. Ebeling Frah a.l.)), cf. however Nyberg FP 44, 74: l. *ʿbd brbytʾ* = servant member of the house; in *br bytʾ* in Krael 10^{19}, 11^{14}, 12^{34} *bytʾ* prob. is n.p., cf. also Grelot DAE p. 468, RB lxxxii 291, Kornfeld OAA 43 :: Porten Arch 230 (n. 89): *br bytʾ* in these instances = title of some official :: Krael ad 10^{19}: poss. = the houseborne slave (cf. Segal BSOAS xxxiv 142, cf. also Porten & Greenfield JEAS p. 64, 66, 73, Porten &

Yardeni sub TADAE B 3.13 a.e.: the houseborn; the same interpret. for *br byt*ʾ in ATNS 53^{12,16,17}, 74^3 :: Segal sub ATNS 53: = person born of a union between a female slave and her master (cf. however Naveh IEJ xxxv 211), cf. also Grelot RB xcvii 274) - ζ) *bktbt dbr*ʾ *hbt šg*ʿ*y* KAI 124$^{3f.}$: by document of the affairs of the house of Gaius, i.e. by testamentary disposition of G. (cf. Lat. par. *testamento*) - η) *mr*ʾ *byt*ʾ*/mrt byt*ʾ, v. *mr*ʾ - θ) ʾ*šr* ʿ*l hbyt* KAI 191B 1, Mosc sig. 30, HBTJ 1, 2, 3 : who is over the (royal) household, i.e. the majordomus; for this function, cf. Katzenstein EI v 108ff., IEJ x 149ff., Yeivin Lesh xxxv 173, Greenfield Mem Henning 84, Welten Stempel 138ff., Mettinger SSO 70ff., Good RB lxxxvi 580ff., ZAW xcv 110f., Loretz ZAW xciv 124ff., Layton JBL cix 633ff. (:: Brand Tarbiz xxxvi 221ff.: head of Temple administration) - ι) extended meaning, family > people, cf. *byt yšr*ʾ*l* DJD ii 47^7 - Dupont-Sommer MAIBL xliv 281: l. *bt* (= Sing. cstr.) in Kition D 21^3 (cf. also Puech RSF iv 13f.), reading of *t* uncert., for other readings and/or interpretations, cf. - a) Liverani RSF iii 37, Amadasi & Karageorghis Kition a.l.: l. *b[*ʾ*]* - b) Teixidor Syr xlix 434: l. *bl*, text poss. in non-semitic language - c) Coote BASOR ccxx 47: l. *bl* = decrepit one (= QAL Part. s.m. abs. of *bly*$_1$?) - Dupont-Sommer CRAI '48, 15: for the diff. *btršš* in KAI 46^1: l. *bt* (Sing. cstr.) + *rš* (= Sing. abs. of *r*ʾ*š*$_1$ (= cape)) + *š*$_{10}$, cf. Röllig KAI a.l., Delcor Syr xlv 332f., 351 (cf. also - a) Dhorme with Février RA xliv 124: *btršš* = *bt* (Sing. cstr.) + *rš* (= Sing. abs. of *r*ʾ*š*$_1$ (= head); *bt rš* = main temple, cf. also v.d.Branden Mašr lvi 286f.) + *š*$_{10}$ - b) Ferron RSO xli 285f., 288: *btršš* = *bt* (Sing. abs.) + *rš* (= Sing. abs. of *r*ʾ*š*$_1$ (= first)) + *š*$_{10}$ - c) v.d.Branden Mašr lvi 287: *btršš* = *bt* (Sing. abs.) + *rš* (= Sing. abs. of *r*ʾ*š*$_1$ (= head)) + *š*$_{10}$); less prob. interpretations, preferably *btršš* (= *b*$_2$) + *tršš* (= n.l.), cf. Albright BASOR lxxxiii 19, Mazar with Silverman JAOS xciv 268f., Lipiński BiOr xlv 63 :: CIS i sub 144, Lidzbarski Handb 370, 427, sub KI 60, Cooke NSI p. 110f.: l. *[mṣ]bt* (= Sing. cstr. of *mṣbh*) + *rš* (= n.p.) + *š*$_6$ (on *btršš*, cf. also Bunnens EPM 31f., 37ff., Gibson SSI iii p. 27) - Lipiński RTAT 251: l. *bt* (Sing. abs.) in KAI 43^{14} (??, highly uncert. context) - Février Sem ii 21ff.: l. *byt* (Sing. cstr.) *kblt* (Sing. abs. = doubleness) in KAI 9A 2 = double house/grave (improb. interpret., cf. Röllig KAI a.l.) - the diff. ʾ*btm* in KAI 119^7 = article + Plur. abs.??, cf. Levi Della Vida RCL '55, 560; uncert. interpret. × Février RA l 189: = Plur. + suff. 3 p.s.m. of ʾ*b*$_1$ (cf. also Röllig, KAI a.l.: = Plur. + suff. 3 p.pl.m.? of ʾ*b*$_1$) - the diff. *bt*ʾ in Trip 51^5 poss. = Sing. + suff. 3 p.s.m. (reading however uncert., or l. *bn*ʾ = Sing. + suff. 3 p.s.m. of *bn*$_1$?, or = form of *bny*$_1$, cf. Levi Della Vida Or xxxiii 12, 14, cf. however Amadasi IPT 134f.: without interpret.) - the *byt* in IEJ xviii 168^{10} prob. = part of geogr. or family name (cf. also Yadin IEJ xxvi 10 n. 4) - Sayce PSBA

'06, 174f., '08, 41: the 3 inscriptions *by* in a quarry at Assuan: = Sing. abs., uncert. interpret. - the *byt* in Cowl 81[24, 109] (Sing. cstr.), *bytn›* in Cowl 81[110] of uncert. meaning (Grelot DAE p. 106 n. h, 108, 116: = account, uncert. interpret.) - the *bt* in RCL '66, 201[6], prob. = Plur. cstr. (cf. Dupont-Sommer CRAI '68, 120, Ferron Mus xcviii 59, 61 :: Mahyoubi & Fantar RCL '66, 208: = Sing. cstr. (= group)) - Ahlström RANR 15: the *bt* (twice) in KAI 181[30] = not part of n.g., but Sing. cstr. (= temple); cf. already Andersen Or xxxv 94, Miller PEQ '74, 14 (n. 26), poss. interpret.
v. *›b$_1$*, *›wryh$_1$*, *›lp$_3$*, *›rš$_1$*, *bb$_1$*, *bzz$_1$*, *byt$_4$*, *bn$_1$*, *bny$_1$*, *btlh*, *ywm*, *ytn$_2$*, *lb*, *mqr›$_2$*, *mrbyn*, *mrkbh*, *ṣbyt*, *qqbtn*, *rbyt*, *rzn*, *šyt$_1$*.
byt$_3$ **OffAr** word of uncert. reading and interpret. in RES 1300[8] (Sing. abs.); Lidzbarski Eph iii 24: l. *byt* = receptacle ('Behälter') :: Chabot sub RES 1300: l. *bwt*? = Sing. abs. of *bwt$_3$* (= dish, charger)?
byt$_4$ **OffAr** diff. word *ba-a-a-ti* in Warka 28 in the construction *mi-in ba-a-a-ti ig-g[a-ri]*; Dupont-Sommer RA xxxix 51: = prep. between (from between the wall), cf. however Landsberger AfO xii 251: = Sing. cstr. of *byt$_2$* (from a walled house; cf. also Garbini HDS 32).
byty **Nab** Sing. emph. *byty›* CIS ii 1814, 1969[1], 2068[2], 2514[2], 2648[1], 2845[1f.] - ¶ subst. m. prob. meaning administrator, comptroller (par. with Greek διοιxητής or όιxονόμος?), prob. hereditary function, cf. Díez Merino LA xix 274f. - l. this word in CIS ii 1612, 1985, 2086, 2226, 2501? (cf. also Negev IEJ xxvii 229).
bk$_1$ v. *bky$_1$*.
bk$_2$ v. *bky$_2$* (for f. *bkh/bkth*, v. *br$_1$*).
bkw v. *kwh*.
bky$_1$ **Samal** QAL (cf. Friedr 28*, Donner KAI a.l. × Cooke NSI p. 179, Dion p. 200, 219, 465 n. 3, Segert AAG p. 305: = PI‹EL) Pf. 3 p.pl.m. (× 3 p.s.m., cf. Cooke NSI a.l., Friedr 28*, Dion p. 219, 277, Donner KAI a.l. Segert AAG p. 305) + suff. 3 p.s.m. *bkyh* KAI 215[17]; 3 p.s.f. + suff. 3 p.s.m. *bkyth* KAI 215[17] - **DA** QAL Impf. 3 p.s.m. *ybkh* i 6; 2 p.s.m. *tbkh* i 6 - **OffAr** QAL (cf. Donner KAI a.l., Degen GGA '79, 38, 39 :: Cooke NSI p. 190f., Segert AAG p. 301, 305) Pf. 3 p.pl.m. + suff. 1 p.s. *bkwny* KAI 226[5f.]; cf. Frah xxi 2 (*bkywn*), cf. Toll ZDMG-Suppl viii 37 - ¶ verb to lament, to weep; + obj.: KAI 215[17], 226[5f.] - Caquot & Lemaire Syr liv 194f.: l. *bkh* = QAL Inf. abs. in DA i 3, 6 (combining both lines; prob. reading and interpret., cf. also Rofé SB 61, Garbini Hen i 175 (v. also *škm$_1$*), H.P.Müller ZAW xciv 216, 221, Puech FS Grelot 17, 19f., 27) - L.H.Gray AJSL xxxix 79: *bic* in Poen 943 = nom. derivative of this root: weeping (highly uncert. interpret., cf. on this line Sznycer PPP 126). - Segal ATNS a.l.: the *]bky* in ATNS 58[3] perhaps = form of this root (highly uncert. interpret., heavily dam. context; for other interpret., cf. Segal a.l.).

v. *br$_1$*.

bky$_2$ **OffAr** diff. word *bky*ʾ in NESE iii 39[2] (*byt bky*ʾ); Degen NESE iii 40f.: *bky*ʾ poss. = a) Sing. emph. of *bky$_2$* = weeping, mourning (*byt bky*ʾ = house of mourning) or b) Plur. emph. of *bky$_3$* = mourner (*byt bky*ʾ = house of mourners); less prob. interpret. *bky*ʾ = Plur. emph. of *bk$_2$* = rooster, cf. Degen NESE iii a.l. :: v.d.Branden BiOr xxxvi 341: pro *bky*ʾ l. *bsy*ʾ (< root *bss*, Plur. emph. of *bs*?), *byt bsy*ʾ = silo, warehouse.

bky$_3$ v. *bky$_2$*.

bky$_4$ v. *kp$_1$*.

bkyr **Hebr** Plur. f. abs. *bkyrwt* SM 49[20] - ¶ adj. first-ripening, early; ʾ*ḥwnywt hbkyrwt* SM 49[20]: early prunes.
v. *bkr$_2$*.

bkr$_1$ **Hebr** the *ybkr* in KAI 192[5] (for the reading, cf. Birnbaum PEQ '39, 92f., Diringer Lach iii 332 n., cf. also infra) diff. to explain, for the proposals, cf. - a) Torczyner Lach i p. 43: = PIʿEL Impf. 3 p.s.m. of *bkr* (= *bqr$_1$*) = to examine (less prob. interpret.) - b) Vincent J des Sav '39, 64, Michaud Syr xxxiv 43f.: = PIʿEL Impf. 3 p.s.m. of *bkr$_1$* (= to privilege, to favour; cf. Torczyner Lach i p. 41, Röllig KAI a.l., cf. also H.P.Müller UF ii 235 (nn. 64, 65): to privilege, to favour used as euphemism for to punish (less prob. interpret.)) - c) Dussaud Syr xix 261 n. 2: = PIʿEL Impf. 3 p.s.m. of *bkr$_1$* (= (to give as firstling/first fruit >) to reveal), cf. Lemaire IH i p. 97, 99, Briend TPOA 143, Lipiński OLP viii 89, BiOr xxxv 286, cf. also Pardee HAHL 79f., 242: = to give first knowledge?, cf. further v. Raalte Kerygma ii 73 - d) Gibson SSI i p. 37f.: = PIʿEL or Hiphil of *bkr$_1$* (= to make early) :: e.g. Albright BASOR lxiii 36 (following alternative reading proposed by Ginsberg BJPES iii 80), lxx 13, Ginsberg BASOR lxxi 25: l. *yʿkr* = QAL Impf. 3 p.s.m. of *ʿkr* (= to afflict, to punish; cf. also Galling TGI 75 (n. 4), Albright ANET 322) :: Ginsberg BJPES iii 80: l. *yzkr* = HIPH Impf. 3 p.s.m. of *zkr$_1$*, cf. also Cassuto RSO xvi 167f., 393: = QAL Impf. 3 p.s.m. of *zkr$_1$* :: Reider JQR xxix 231f.: l. *ynkr* = PIʿEL Impf. 3 p.s.m. of *nkr$_1$* (= to reject, to disavow), cf. also Albright BASOR lxxiii 17 (cf. however Albright BASOR lxxxii 19).

bkr$_2$ **Ph** Sing. abs. EpAn ix 5[2] (v. infra) - ¶ subst. first-born; *šd bkr* EpAn ix 5[2]: the field of the first-born (or = n.l.?, cf. Mosca & Russell EpAn ix 9) - Garbini StudMagr x 10: l. *bkr* (Sing. abs.) = first-born in MAI xvi 38 no. 29 (improb. reading).
v. *bkyr*.

bkr$_3$ **DA** Garbini Hen i 182, 185: l. *bkrn* (= Plur. abs. of *bkr$_3$* (= young camel)) in DA i 17 + ii 2 (highly uncert. interpret., reading of *k* less prob., cf. v.d.Kooij DA p. 118).

bkt v. *br$_1$*.

bkth v. *br*$_1$.

bl$_1$ **OffAr** Sing. + suff. 2 p.s.m. *blk* Aḥiq 97 (:: Kselman JBL cv 115 pro *blk* l. *lbk* (= Sing. + suff. 2 p.s.m. of *lb*)) - ¶ subst. mind, cf. Lieberman Greek 172ff.

bl$_2$ v. *bn*$_1$.

bl$_3$ **Ph** KAI 14^{3,12}, 24^{2,3,4,5,11,12}, 26A i 15, 19, ii 16, 27^{6,8}, EpAn ix 5^{6} - **Pun** KAI 69^{15}, 74^{6}, CIS i 170^{2,3} - **Hebr** AMB 4^{18} - ¶ negation, not: KAI 24^{2,3,4}, 26A i 19, CIS i 170^{2,3}; with prohibitive sense: KAI 27^{6,8}, 69^{15}, 74^{6}, AMB 4^{18}; + subst. *bl ʿty* KAI 14^{3,12}: before my time (for this expression, cf. Degen ZDMG cxxi 127 :: v.d.Branden BMB xiii 88f.: *bl* = variant form of *mn*$_5$, cf. however idem GP p. 114 :: Joüon RES iii 89f. (cf. also Gibson SSI iii p. 109): *bl* here = *b*$_2$ + *l*$_2$ (= *l*ʾ$_1$; cf. Garbini ISNO 169 n. 7)); prec. by *l*$_5$, *qb ... qbt ʾdrt lbl gzly ʾdm* EpAn ix 5$^{5f.}$: he cursed a mighty curse so that no one might wrongfully seize it; v. also *ʾbl*$_5$.
v. *ʾbl*$_5$, *ybl*$_1$.

bl$_4$ **Nab** J 213, RES 1431 (reading uncert.) - **Palm** CIS ii 4207 - **Hatra** 24^{1,3,4}, 48^{1}, 51, 53^{5}, 99, 100, 104, 122, 123, 125, 127, 129, etc., etc. - ¶ interjection underlining the contents of the following words (cf. also Joüon MUSJ xviii 98ff.: = optative particle: *utinam*) :: Aggoula Ber xviii 90: = also :: Caquot (following Safar) Syr xxix 103: = n.d. used in exclamation, cf. also Pognon ISMM 84, Altheim & Stiehl AAW iv 258, v. also infra (rejection notwithstanding formulae like *bl brmryn dkyr* Hatra 128 and *mrh dkyr* Hatra 121) :: Aggoula MUSJ xlix 477: *bl*$_4$, *bl*ʾ$_3$, *bly*$_3$ derivatives of *bly*$_1$, meaning: is decayed, is dead (cf. however idem ibid. n. 5: or *bl* = n.d.?); mostly in formula *bl dkyr PN*, cf. CIS ii 4207, Hatra 24^{1,3,4}, 48^{1}, 51, 53^{5}, 99, etc., etc.; cf. also the formulae *bl dkrt ʾlt* J 213 (v. *zkr*$_1$) and *bl NP dkyr* Hatra 136 and *lṭb bl dkyr NP* Hatra 321; v. also *bl*ʾ$_3$, *bly*$_3$.

blʾ$_1$ **OffAr** Qal Pf. 3 p.s.f. *blʾ[h]* Cowl 26^{1} (heavily dam. context) - ¶ verb Qal to deteriorate (prob. said of a boat) - the *blʾ* (reading uncert.) in RSO xxxv 22^{3} prob. = n.p. (cf. Bresciani RSO xxxv 23, Naveh AION xvi 30 :: Bresciani RSO xxxv 23: or = verbal form of *bl*ʾ$_1$) - the diff. *blʾ* in DA i 2 (reading highly uncert., cf. v.d.Kooij DA p. 102f., cf. also Caquot & Lemaire Syr liv 194ff.) = Qal Part. act. s.m. abs. of *bl*ʾ$_1$?? (cf. Hoftijzer DA p. 188, cf. also Koenig Sem xxxiii 82ff.: = Sing. cstr. of *bl*ʾ$_2$ (= annulment, discontinuance; cf. also Puech FS Grelot 18, 27), cf. however H. & M. Weippert ZDPV xcviii 85, 103: = *b*$_2$ + *l*ʾ$_1$ (cf. also Puech BAT 356, 360, Wesselius BiOr xliv 593, 595) :: Rofé SB 61, 65: pro *blʾ* l. *ʿdʾ* = n.l. :: Garbini Hen i 174: l. *zdʾ* = Sing. abs. of *zdʾ* (= pride) :: Lemaire BAT 317f. (div. otherwise): l. poss. *nhrʾ* = Sing. emph. of *nhr*$_3$ (= light)).

blʾ$_2$ v. *bl*ʾ$_1$.

bl$ʾ_3$ **Nab** CIS ii 246, 285[1] (or l. *bly$_3$*?, cf. Milik sub ARNA-Nab 75), 757[2] (or l. *klʾ*?) - ¶ interjection underlining the contents of the following words (v. *bl$_5$*; :: Levinson NAI 56f.: = *b$_2$* + *lʾ$_2$*), occurring in the following formulae: *blʾ šlm PN* (CIS ii 266, 285), *blʾ dkyr [PN] bṭb* (CIS ii 246), *šlm PNN bṭb wšlm blʾ* (CIS ii 757, v. however supra).
v. *bl$_4$*, *bly$_3$*, *kl$_1$*.

blʾrw **OffAr** Bivar & Shaked BSOAS xxvii 276f.: the diff. *blʾrw* in BSOAS xxvii 272 iii 2 = title (= (keeper of) the altar (*ʾrw*) of Bel (*bl*) ?), cf. also Altheim & Stiehl AAW iii 69ff., 73, GMA 558: = title < Akkad. *bel uru* (= lord of the stable, equerry) cf. Teixidor Syr xliv 183. Interpretation as title less prob., cf. Sznycer JA ccliii 6f. = *b$_2$* + *lʾrw* (= n.l.).

blh$_1$ v. *bly$_1$*.

blh$_2$ v. *blt$_1$*, *bnḥ*.

blw (< Akkad.?, cf. Rosenthal Forschung 51 n. 3, Baumgartner KB s.v., Altheim & Stiehl ASA 149, Kaufman AIA 44) - **OffAr** Sing. + suff. 3 p.s.m. (?) *blwh* RES 492B 3 (= RES 1800 :: Driver AnOr xii 56f.: = Sing. + suff. 3 p.s.f.) - ¶ subst. of uncert. meaning: *blwh* = his payment, reward (?), cf. Lidzbarski Eph ii 239f. :: Driver AnOr xii 57: = her task or earnings - Segal ATNS a.l.: l. this word (Sing. abs.) in the Ph. text ATNS xxiv (highly uncert. interpret., cf. the *bly* in the Ph. text ATNS v (Segal ATNS a.l.: prob. = n.p., not a variant of *blw*).

blwṭ v. *bylwṭ*.

blḥwd v. *ḥwd*.

blzm **Hebr** Sing. abs. *blzm* MPAT 66 - **JAr** Sing. emph. *blzmh* MPAT 66 - ¶ subst. balsam (the Hebrew and Aramaic word both occurring on the same storage jar); cf. *blsn*.

bly$_1$ **OffAr** QAL Part. act. s.m. abs. *blh* Krael 7[10] (for the reading, cf. Porten & Yardeni sub TADAE B 3.8); s.f. abs. (v. infra; :: Vogt Lex s.v. *blh*: = QAL Part. pass.) *blyh* Krael 7[12] - ¶ verb QAL Part. act. (or adject. of same root?) worn (said of a gown) - Lipiński Stud 44f.: *blh* in KAI 222B 42 = QAL Pf. 3 p.s.m. of *bly$_1$* (= to decay; interpret. of context highly uncert.).
v. *ʾbl$_5$*, *byt$_2$*, *bl$_4$*, *bly$_2$*, *ybl$_1$*.

bly$_2$ **Hatra** Sing. (?) emph. *blyʾ* 416[2], app. 5[2] (diff. reading; Altheim & Stiehl AAW iv 252: l. *bnyʾ* = QAL Part. pass. pl.m. emph. of *bny$_1$* (= buildings) :: Caquot Syr xl 14: = Plur. emph. of *bly* = rags (< *bly$_1$*) > remnants) - ¶ subst. designation of (certain type of) tomb, cf. Aggoula MUSJ xlix 476, Syr lxvii 419, Vattioni sub IH app. 5.

bly$_3$ **Nab** CIS ii 243, 272, 293, 303, ARNA-Nab 17[3], 65[1], etc., etc. - ¶ interjection underlining the contents of the following words (v. *bl$_4$*), occurring in the following formulae: a) *bly dkyr PN* (cf. CIS ii 243, 272, 293, J 157[1], 255, 281, ARNA-Nab 17[3], 65[1] (dam. text)) - b) *bly šlm*

PN (cf. CIS ii 303, J 44, 95, 103, 115, 189, 192, 194, RES 1431A 2 (? dam. context)) - c) *bly NP šlm* (cf. J 185) - d) *bly PN* (cf. CIS ii 347, cf. also Starcky RB lxxv 207) - e) also in the combination *bly wly* (= wly_3) J 373 underlining the following words (cf. Cantineau Nab i 105). v. bl_4, bl'_3.

bll **Pun** Sing. abs. *bll* KAI 69[14], 75[1], 76A 7 - ¶ subst. certain type of offering, oblation, prob. farinaceous food mixed with oil; cf. also Dussaud Orig 153, Rosenthal ANET 503 n. 2, Amadasi ICO p. 180f. - a derivative of the same root (Sing. cstr. *bll*) also in BASOR cclxiv 46[2] (diff. context).

blm to tie, to muzzle > Akkad.?, cf. v.Soden Or xxxvii 269f., xlvi 185, Dietrich ASS 121 n. 1.

blsn **JAr** Sing. emph. *blsnh* Mas 544 - ¶ subst. balsam; cf. *blzm*.

blʿ **Nab** Qal (?) Pf. 3 p.s.m. *blʿ* MPAT 64 ii 5 - ¶ verb to swallow, to receive blows, exact meaning in the dam. context uncert., Fitzmyer & Harrington MPAT a.l.: = to suffer loss - on this root, cf. also Rundgren OrSu xv 86ff.

blʿd **OffAr** *blʿdy* MAI xiv/2, 66[12], Aḥiq 122 (*blʿ[dy]*) - **Nab** *blʿd* CIS ii 198[9], 209[6] - ¶ prep. except(ed): CIS ii 198[9], cf. also *blʿd hn* CIS ii 209[6]: excepted if - preceded by prep. mn_5, *mn blʿdy* MAI xiv/2, 66[12]: without (for the context, v. mlk_3)

blʿdy v. *blʿd*.

blr Ebeling Frah a.l.: l. *blrwn* in Frah app. 8 = derivative of root *blr* (< Akkad. < Sumer; = to traverse, to cross); improb. reading and interpret., cf. Nyberg FP 99: l. *bllwn* prob. = variant for *ʿblwn* (< root $ʿbr_1$).

blt_1 (or *blh*?) **OffAr** Sing. cstr. *blt* Del 95 - ¶ subst. word of unknown meaning (cf. Altheim & Stiehl ASA 149; for the reading and interpret. problems, cf. Lindenberger APA 222 n. 14 :: Henning Or iv 292: = Sing. cstr. of blh_2 indicating some kind of taxation).

blt_2 **Ph** KAI 13[5] - ¶ adv. used as conj. (cf. also FR 249.3): except that.

bm_1 v. bn_1.

bm_2 v. $ʿm_1$.

bmh **Mo** Sing. abs. *bmt* KAI 181[3] - ¶ subst. f. high place, cf. Landsberger JNES viii 276 n. 91; for discussion on the exact meaning, cf. e.g. Yadin EI xiv 78ff. (cf. idem BASOR ccxxii 5ff.), G.R.H.Wright VT xxi 588ff., Welten ZDPV lxxxviii 19ff., P.H.Vaughan, The meaning of 'Bāmā' in the OT, Cambridge, 1974, Boyd Barrick VT xxv 565ff., SEA xlv 50ff., Fenton BSOAS xxxix 434, Grintz VT xxvii 112, Fowler ZAW xciv 203ff., Brown JSS xxv 1ff., Mattingly SMIM 227ff., Dothan THP 77ff., Biran THP 142f., 148ff., H.Weippert ZDPV c 182f., M. KuK 154f., Fritz TZ 71ff., Haran TTS 18ff., Heider CM 384ff. - Garbini AION xxv

442: the βουμα in ibid. 441^2 = transcription of Sing. abs. of *bmh* (uncert. interpret., cf. also La Lomia StudMagr vi 47, 49f.: = Greek word in transcribed Punic text, βουμα = punicized form of βῆμα, βᾶμα = platform, *podium*) - Andersen Or xxxv 94: *bt bmt* in KAI 181^{27} poss. = cultic building and not a n.l. (uncert. interpret.) - on this word, cf. also H.Lewy KZ lv 32: > Greek βωμός (uncert. interpret.) - Ferron MC 76f.: the φαεμα in KAI 174^8 = Sing. abs. of *bmh* (improb. interpret., cf. Sznycer Sem viii 9: = n.d. (prob. interpret.) :: Milik MUSJ xxxi 11 = n.p.).
v. *bny*₁, *tw*.

bmys v. *bms*.

bms (< Greek βωμός) - **Nab** Sing. cstr. *bwms* RES 2117^5; emph. *bms*ʾ Lev vii 16^1 - ¶ subst. m. altar: Lev vii 16^1; in the expression *bwms ṣlm* RES 2117^5 prob. altar with statue of ... (text on pedestal in form of altar, cf. also Levinson NAI 136: *bwms* = pedestal), cf. Starcky SDB vii 1010 - Dussaud RevArch '97 ii 322f.: l. *hbmys* in RES 56^1 (= RES 1594) = *h*₁ + Sing. abs. of *bmys* (= altar) < Greek βωμίς, however pro *hbmys* l. *hrmys* = n.p., cf. Clermont-Ganneau sub RES 56, RAO iv 196ff., Lidzbarski OLZ '98, 9f., Handb 504, Eph i 283, Teixidor Syr lvi 146, 148, cf. also Benz PNP 194.
v. ʾ*drwn*.

bn₁ m. **Ph** Sing. abs. *bn* KAI 14^8; cstr. *bn* KAI 1^1, 7^2, 10^1, 11^1, 12^3, 13^1, 14^2, 27^2 (v.d.Branden BO iii 43: = *bn*₄ (= *mn*₅)), etc., etc., *bm* CIS i 112b 1, c 1, 2 (cf. FR 53), *bl* KAI 49,15, 18 (cf. FR 56b; cf. also the *bl* Irâq xix 140 ii 5 (v. infra), cf. Segert AsAfS i 149f. (against reading *bl* pro *bn*, cf. however Puech RB xcii 292)), ʾ*bl* KAI 49,30, *b* (with assimilation of *n* to the first consonant of the following word, cf. FR 99b) KAI 6^1, 7^3, 8, RSF i 5B (= SSI iii 3 (cf. Gibson SSI iii a.l.)); + suff. 3 p.s.m. *bny* CIS i 8^2 (= DD 2; × = Plur. + suff. 3 p.s.m.; cf. also FR 240,9), KAI 40^4 (× = Sing. + suff. 3 p.s.f. (cf. FR 240,9, Röllig KAI a.l. :: FR 240,9: or = Plur. + suff. 3 p.s.f. ?)), Kition A 30^3; Plur. cstr. *bn* KAI 26A iii 19, 27^{11} (:: Torczyner JNES vi 22, 28, Sperling HUCA liii 3, 7: = Sing. cstr.), 40^4, 47^3, CIS i 88^6 (= Kition F 1), EI xviii 117^1 (= IEJ xxxv 83); + suff. 1 p.s. *bny* KAI $24^{13f.}$; + suff. 3 p.pl.m. *bnm* DD 9^3 - **Pun** Sing. cstr. *bn* KAI $62^{5,6,7}$, $63^{1,2}$, 64^2, $65^{5,6,7,8,9,10}$, ICO-Spa 16^3 (cf. Gibson SSI iii p. 65f. :: Solá-Solé RSO xli 102f., Amadasi ICO a.l., Heltzer OA vi 266ff. (div. otherwise): l. *bny* = Plur. cstr. (cf. also Ross HThR lxiii 13 n. 38) :: Krahmalkov OA xi 211 (div. otherwise): l. *bny* = Plur. + suff. 3 p.s.m. :: v.d.Branden RSO xliv 104, 106 (div. otherwise): l. *bny* = Qal Pf. 3 p.pl.m. + suff. 3 p.s.m. of *bny*₁; cf. however Amadasi ICO a.l.: or l. *bn yš*ʾ*l* (= n.p.)?), etc., etc., ʾ*bn* KAI 133^3 (?, diff. text, cf. also Röllig KAI a.l.), *bm* CIS i 840^2, 2960^4, Hofra 169^2 (cf. FR 53), *b* CIS i 3247^3, 4058^6, 4825^4, 4853^3, Punica xviii/i 31^4, *bt* (lapsus) CIS i 1118[4], 1538[4], 1543[4], 2397[5], 3347[1], 4644[4], 5129[4], *nb* (lapsus) CIS i 4748[2], *dn* (lapsus) CIS i 2637[4], *n* (lapsus) CIS i 1239[2,3], *rr* (lapsus) CIS i 2954[3], cf. Poen 932, 995 (par. text), Dred. 2[3] (= IRT 886b; cf. Vattioni Aug xvi 545), 4[2] (= IRT 886d; cf. Vattioni ibid. 546), 5[21] (= IRT 886e, cf. Vattioni ibid. 546), 9[2] (= IRT 886h, cf. Levi Della Vida OA ii 82), 14[3] (cf. Vattioni Aug xvi 548), 16 (dam. context, cf. Vattioni ibid. 549), IRT 906[2] (cf. Levi Della Vida OA ii 74): *byn*, KAI 175[3] (= Hofra Gr 1), 177[3] (= Hofra Gr 8): βυν (cf. Friedrich ZDMG cvii 287, FR 240,9); Dred 1[2] (= IRT 886a; cf. Levi Della Vida OA ii 81, Polselli StudMagr xi 42): *bn*; Dred 17[2] (cf. Vattioni Aug xvi 549): *bun* (dam. context), IRT 877[4] (cf. Levi Della Vida OA ii 87): *by* (uncert. interpret.; Vattioni Aug xvi 543: *by* = b_2; Röllig sub KAI 179: pro *by* l. *bu* = part of n.p.), IRT 865: *bean* (uncert. interpret., cf. Vattioni AION xvi 42, Aug xvi 541); + suff. 3 p.s.m. *ʾbny* Trip 38[4] (in *lʾbny*; cf. FR 95b), *bnʾ* KAI 163[2] (diff. and uncert. context), 172[4], *bnm* KAI 84 (or = Plur. + suff. 3 p.s.m.?), CIS i 2805[5] (or = Plur. + suff. 3 p.s.m.?), 3135[2], 3180[6], cf. Poen 936 (:: L.H.Gray AJSL xxxix 77, 79: = *bn* (Sing. cstr.) + *ʿmy* (= Sing. + suff. 1 p.s. of $ʿm_1$) :: J.J.Glück & Maurach Semitics ii 110: = Plur. abs.), KAI 179[1] (= IRT 889, cf. Février JA ccxli 467), IRT 873[4] (cf. Levi Della Vida OA ii 79, Polselli OAC xiii 237): *binim*, Aug xvi 553 no. 65[5]: *bun[im]* (cf. Levi Della Vida OA ii 86; uncert. context, Levi Della Vida ibid.: or l. *bun[om]* = Sing. + suff. 3 p.pl.m.?); + suff. 3 p.s.f., cf. IRT 906[1] (?, cf. Levi Della Vida OA ii 72, 74): *byne* (Krahmalkov RSF vii 177: = Sing. + suff. 3 p.s.m. :: Krahmalkov JSS xvii 70: or = Plur. cstr.?); + suff. 1 p.s., cf. Poen 1141: *bane* (var. *bene* :: J.J.Glück & Maurach Semitics ii 124: = Sing. abs.); + suff. 3 p.pl.m., cf. Aug xvi 550, no. 55[9] (cf. Levi Della Vida OA ii 88): *bunom* (uncert. context), Aug xvi 550, no. 55[11]: *bannom* (uncert. interpret., cf. also Vattioni a.l.: or = form of root bny_1?, cf. also the poss. *banom* (uncert. reading or l. *banoni*) Aug xvi 552 no. 61[3]: = Sing. (or Plur.) + suff. 3 p.s.m./f. or 3 p.pl.m. (cf. Vattioni Aug xvi a.l.: or = form of root bny_1; or = part of n.p.?)); Plur. abs. *bnm* KAI 76B 9 (?, dam. context, cf. Röllig a.l.), cf. IRT 877[6f.] (uncert. interpret., cf. Levi Della Vida OA ii 87 :: Vattioni Aug xvi 543 (div. otherwise): l. *nbanem* = Niph form of bny_1): *banem*; cstr. *bn* KAI 68[2,3,4] (?, uncert. interpret., cf. Chabot Punica i :: e.g. Röllig KAI a.l.: = Sing. cstr.), 80[2] (?, dam. context, cf. e.g. Cooke NSI p. 130, Röllig KAI a.l.: = Sing. cstr.), 141[2] (?, cf. Garbini RSO xliii 15f. :: e.g. Röllig KAI a.l.: = Sing. cstr.?), Mozia vi p. 102[2] (= SMI 22; dam. context, cf. Amadasi Mozia and SMI a.l.), Trip 40[5] (diff. and dam. context), *bnʾ* KAI 118[3], 126[5,6], CIS i 4596[5], Trip 51[4], Sem xxxviii 114[2] (or rather = Qal Pf. 3 p.pl.m. + suff. 3 p.s.m. of bny_1?, cf. Ferjaoui Sem xxxviii 117); *bny* KAI 153[4] (diff. context, cf. Février JA ccxxxvii 88: or = Sing. + suff.

3 p.s.m.? × or = Plur. + suff. 3 p.s.m.? :: Delgado ILC 230: = Sing. + suff. 1 p.s.), cf. IRTS 24[4] (cf. Levi Della Vida OA ii 75f., 92): *b[y]ne*; + suff. 3 p.s.m. *bny* CIS i 134 (for the reading, cf. Amadasi sub ICO-Sic Npu 1; or = Sing. + suff. 3 p.s.m.?; dam. context), *bnyʾ* Trip 8[2] (prob. reading, or l. *btyʾ*?), *bnʾm* Trip 38[6], *bʿnm* Punica xvi 2[1]; + suff. 3 p.s.f. *bʿnyʿ* Punica xx 1[4] - **Mo** Sing. cstr. *bn* KAI 181[1], ZDPV ci 22[1] (Mo.?, cf. Taleb ZDPV ci 23ff.); + suff. 3 p.s.m. *bnh* KAI 181[6] (cf. e.g. Jackson & Dearman SMIM 97),[8] (:: e.g. Cooke NSI p. 9: prob. = Plur. + suff. 3 p.s.m., cf. also Röllig KAI a.l., Segert ArchOr xxix 222, 263, Galling TGI 52, Wallis ZDPV lxxxi 180ff., Bonder JANES iii 86ff.; cf. also Jackson & Dearman SMIM 97, 109f.: = Sing. or Plur., see further Dearman SMIM 164ff., 198, 200, 202, Smelik HDAI 47f.) - **Amm** Sing. cstr. *bn* SANSS-Amm 5 (= CAI 18), 6, 8 (= IS 104 = CAI 67), 10 (= IS 102 = CAI 70), 11 (= CAI 51), 15 (= IS 108 = CAI 30), 16 (= CAI 49), AUSS xiii 2[3] (= CAI 80), etc.; Plur. cstr. *bn* Ber xxii 120[1,2,3] (= CAI 78; :: Block AUSS xxii 208ff.: or = Sing. cstr.?), ADAJ xii/xiii 65[2] (= CAI 58; ?, dam. context; cf. Oded RSO xliv 188f.: = Sing. cstr., cf. also Dayani ADAJ xii/xiii 66: = Sing. cstr. as part of n.p.) - **Edom** Sing. cstr. *bn* RB lxxiii 399[3] (heavily dam. context) - **Hebr** Sing. cstr. *bn* Lach 1[1,2,3,4,5] (= Gibson SSI i p. 36), Vatt. sig. eb. 19, 20, 22 (= resp. SANSS-Hebr 151, 150, 90), etc., etc.; + suff. 3 p.s.m. *bnw* IEJ vii 239[5], 245, SM 75[6]; + suff. 3 p.s.f. *bnh* DF 8, 14 (?, dam. context); + suff. 2 p.s.m. *bnk* TA-H 21[1]; + suff. 2 p.pl.m. *bnkm* TA-H 40[1] (or = Plur. + suff. 2 p.pl.m.??, cf. Aharoni BASOR cxcvii 29f.); Plur. cstr. *bny* TA-H 16[5] (:: Pardee UF x 311 (div. otherwise): or l. *bn* = Sing. cstr.?), 49[1,2,4,16], MPAT 91A 1, 2 (= Frey 1352a), Frey 1360, SM 49[4], etc. (for poss. *bny* in TA-H 55, cf. Heltzer Shn ii 58), *bnʾ* DF 22[2]; + suff. 3 p.s.m. *bnyw* IEJ vii 241[3], 245; + suff. 1 p.s. *bny* DJD ii 22,1-9[6]; + suff. 1 p.pl. *bnynw* SM 111[2] - **Nab** Sing. cstr. *bn* J 240, 261, 262, 387 - f. **Ph** Sing. cstr. *bt* KAI 14[15], 29[1], 34[4] (= Kition B 45), 35[3] (= Kition B 1), 36[1] (= Kition B 31), 40[2,3], 50[1], 59[1], ASAE xl 436, DD 11[2], Kition B 14[2] (= CIS i 69), B 20[2] (= CIS i 75, dam. context), D 42, RDAC '84, 104[3] (for the context, cf. Puech Sem xxxix 100ff. :: Heltzer AO vii 195: = Sing. cstr. of *byt₂*), 108 no. 5a 2, b 2 (for the context, cf. Puech Sem xxxix 104f.); + suff. 3 p.s.m. *bt* EpAn ix 5C 1 (for this interpret., cf. Mosca & Russell EpAn ix 22f.) - **Pun** Sing. cstr. *bt* KAI 70[1] (uncert. reading), 87[4], 91[1], 93[1], 95[1], 109[3], 123[3], NP 130[6], Punica xii 5[2], xvii 6[2], Sem xxxvi 35[2], etc., etc., *bʿt* KAI 162[2] (diff. context), Punica xii 3[3], *bn* (lapsus) CIS i 712[3], 2069[4], 3640[3], 4614[3], etc., *rt* (lapsus) CIS i 1518[2], cf. IRT 901[3]: *byth* (uncert. reading, cf. Krahmalkov JSS xxiv 26, Polselli StudMagr xi 40 (cf. also CIL iii 744), cf. however CIL viii 10991, Vattioni AION xvi 49f., Aug xvi 552: l. *buth*; CIL viii ad 10971, IRT a.l.: l. *buch*), Aug xvi 552 no. 61[3]: *buth* (diff. and uncert. context,

cf. Vattioni a.l.: or = *byt*$_2$?), IRTS 20[2]: *ryth* or *ruth* (prob. lapsus for *byth* or *buth*; cf. however Levi Della Vida OA ii 77: = lapsus for *byn* :: Vattioni AION xvi 50 (n. 75), Aug xvi 553: = *rt* (= subst. denoting a certain grade of parentage, daughter-in-law?)); + suff. 3 p.s.m. *btʾ* CIS i 5702[5], Punica xi 38[2] (diff. context, cf. Chabot a.l., Jongeling NINPI 149f.), xviii/i 15[4] (?, for this interpret., cf. Février CB viii 30f.); + suff. 3 p.s.f., cf. IRT 901[5]: *ruthi(a)* (prob. lapsus for *buthi(a)* :: Milik with Vattioni AION xvi 50 (div. otherwise): l. *ruthi* = variant of *buthi* (= Sing. + suff. 3 p.s.f.) :: Krahmalkov JSS xxiv 26: *ruthia* is part of n.p. *uruthi(a)* :: Vattioni AION xvi 50: or *ruthi* = Sing. + suff. 3 p.s.f. of *rt* (v. supra)? :: Polselli StudMagr xi 40: l. *byth* = Sing. cstr. of *byt*$_2$); Plur. + suff. 1 p.s., cf. Poen 932: *bynuthi* - **Amm** Sing. cstr. *bt* SANSS-Amm 4 (= Vatt sig. eb. 103 = Jackson ALIA 75 no. 40 = CAI 23; cf. also Bordreuil Syr l. 186, Garbini LS-Amm iv), 7 (= Vat sig. eb. 59 = CSOI-Amm 78 = Jackson ALIA 80 no. 51 = CAI 9), CAI 117, 121, 126, AUSS xiii 2[5,11] (= CAI 80?) - **Hebr** Sing. cstr. *bt* SANSS-Hebr 98 (Vatt sig. eb. 226 = CSOI-Hebr. 54), 117 (= Vatt sig. eb. 60), 143 (= Vatt sig. eb. 61), Vatt sig. eb. 324, Syr lxiii 309, IS 34, Frey 1253, 1265[2], 1296, 1311, 1317a, etc.; + suff. 3 p.s.m. *btw* IEJ vii 239[1,4], 244[2] - ¶ subst. m. son, f. daughter, passim; for the context of KAI 181[8], v. *ʾrbʿm*, *ḥṣy*$_2$; *bn bn* KAI 10[1]: grandson, cf. KAI 14[14], 40[4], Hofra 143[3], 263[1], etc.; *ytm bn ʾlmt* KAI 14[3]: a fatherless child, the son of a widow - special usages: - a) designation of someone belonging to a family, a tribe or another community; *NP ʾš bbnʾ mʿsnkʿw* KAI 118[3]: NP who is a member of the M. tribe, cf. KAI 68[2,3,4] (for litt. v. supra), 141[2] (v. supra), Frey 1352a 2 (= MPAT 91a), 1394[3]; *bnʾ ʿm* KAI 126[5,6]: (the sons of the people, Lat. par. resp. *civium*, *patriae*, v. also *ʿm*$_1$; i.e.:) the citizens/compatriots; *bn ḥrš* EI xviii 117[1]: the handicraftsmen; *bn nsk* ES xlv 60: someone belonging to the corporation of the casters; *bn ʾdm* KAI 48[4]: men, people, mankind, cf. KAI 165[3] (v. *ʾdm*$_1$); *bn ʾlm* Trip 11: the son of god, i.e. the divine, epithet of Roman emperor (cf. Amadasi IPT 41f. :: Levi Della Vida Lib iii 99: l. *bt* (= Sing. cstr. of *bt*$_1$) + *ʾlm*); *bn ʾlm* KAI 26A iii 19: the gods, cf. KAI 27[11] (:: Cross & Saley BASOR cxcvii 44f. (n. 9): *ʾlm* = *ʾl* (= n.d.) + encl *m*; for BASOR cxciii 8[6], v. *byn*$_2$); this meaning also in KAI 190[1,2,3?], cf. Gibson SSI i p. 25; cf. also *bṣlyn bny mdynh* SM 49[4]: onions grown in the district - b) designation in epistolary style of a person of lower standing; *bnk yhwkl šlḥ* TA-H 21[1]: your son Y. sends ..., cf. TA-H 40[1] (:: Pardee UF x 310: or = real son?) - c) used in formulae indicating the age of a person; *bt šmnm št* NP 130[6]: (a woman) eighty years old, cf. KAI 133[3], 136[2f.], 148[2f.], Punica xvii 8[3f.], IEJ vii 239[3f.,6f.]; cf. *ʾrḥ bt 2* AUSS xiii 2[5]: a two year old cow, cf. also ibid. l. 11 - for *bn ʾḥ*, v. *ʾḥ*$_1$, for *bn/t hmlk*, v. *mlk*$_3$, for *bn msk ymm*, v. *msk*$_3$, for *bn ṣdq*, v. *ṣdq*$_2$, for *bny rkš*, v.

rkš - Dupont-Sommer RDAC a.l.: the *bty* in RDAC '84, 104^3 = f. Sing. + suff. 3 p.s.m. (cf. also Heltzer AO vii 195), less prob. interpret., cf. Puech Sem xxxix 100ff. = part of n.p. - L.H.Gray AJSL xxxix 76ff.: the *bin* in Poen 943 = m. Sing. abs. (highly uncert. interpret., cf. Sznycer PPP 126) - L.H.Gray AJSL xxxix 76ff.: the *bat* in Poen 943 = f. Sing. abs. (highly uncert. interpret., cf. Sznycer PPP 126) - *bn* in KAI 166^4 (= Sing. cstr., cf. e.g. Röllig KAI a.l. or Plur. cstr., cf. Segert JSS xvii 139) probably misread, cf. Chabot Punica xi 7 - Rainey BASOR ccii 26: l. *bny* in TA-H 25^2 (improb. reading, cf. Aharoni TA a.l.: l. *ʿnym* = n.l.) - *bn* (Sing. cstr.) poss. in Syr xvii 271^7 (Ph. (?) text in Palm. script), cf. Milik DFD 297f. - the *bnm* in BAr-NS i-ii p. 228^2 prob. = Sing. (or Plur.) + suff. 3 p.s.m., cf. Garbini StudMagr vi 30 :: Février BAr a.l.: = QAL Part. pl.m. abs. of *bny*$_1$ - Naveh Maarav ii 164 n. 5: the *bl* in the Nimrud ostracon l. 15 = Sing. cstr., with dissimilation, cf. however Segal Irâq xix 140, 143 (div. otherwise): l. *blmtn* or *blntn* = n.p., cf. also Albright BASOR cxlix 34 n. 15: l. *blntn* (= n.p.) - CIS i sub 144, Cooke NSI p. 111: in KAI 46^7 l. *bn* = Sing. cstr. (uncert. interpret.), cf. Peckham Or xli 459, 464f., Cross BASOR ccviii 15ff., Gibson SSI iii p. 27 (div. otherwise): l. *šbn* = n.p. (poss. interpret.) :: Dupont-Sommer CRAI '48, 15, 18, JA cclii 30, Février RA xliv 124, 126, Delcor Syr xlv 331, 349, 351, Ferron RSO xli 285, 287f.: l. *bn* = QAL Pf. 3 p.s.m. of *bny*$_1$ (cf. also Röllig KAI a.l.) :: Albright BASOR lxxxiii 19 (dividing otherwise): l. *[y]šb* (= QAL Impf. 3 p.s.m. of *šwb*) + *w* - v.d.Branden BO xiv 196, 200: the *bnm* in KAI 162^5 = Sing. + suff. 3 p.s.f..

v. *ʾb*$_1$, *ʾbn*$_2$, *ʾyt*$_3$, *byn*$_2$, *byrby*, *byt*$_2$, *bny*$_1$, *br*$_1$, *zrʿ*$_2$, *ḥly*$_2$, *kwn*$_1$, *ktʾ*, *mnḥh*$_1$, *nʾsph*, *nbnh*, *ʿly*$_1$, *ʿmq*$_2$, *ṣd*$_1$, *qrdm*, *qšt*$_2$, *šbʿh*$_1$, *tʾr*, *tm*$_{1,3}$, *tṣʾh*.

bn$_2$ v. *pnh*$_1$.

bn$_3$ v. *bb*$_1$.

bn$_4$ v. *mn*$_5$.

bn$_5$ v. *byn*$_2$, *mn*$_5$, *nbnh*.

bn$_6$ (= allomorph of *b*$_2$) v. *byn*$_2$, *bny*$_1$, *mn*$_5$, *nʾsph*.

bnʾ$_1$ v. *bny*$_1$.

bnʾ$_2$ v. *btʾ*.

bnʾy **OffAr** Segal ATNS a.l.: l. *bnʾy* (Sing. abs.) = builder in ATNS 44 i 8 (uncert. interpret. and reading, cf. also Porten & Yardeni sub TADAE B 8.2).

bnh$_1$ **Ph** Sing. abs. *bnt* Syr xlviii 403^4 (= or Plur. abs.??, cf. Is. xxvii 11; diff. context, cf. Röllig NESE ii 33 :: Teixidor AO i 108: l. pref. *bmt* (without interpret.) :: Garbini OA xx 290, 292: l. *ʿnt* = QAL Pf. 1 p.s. of *ʿny*$_1$ :: Cross CBQ xxxvi 487ff.: l. *ʿnt* = Plur. abs. of *ʿyn*$_2$ (= eyes) :: Avishur PIB 267, 271: l. *ʿnt* = Sing. abs., variant of *ʿyn*$_2$, cf. also idem UF x 32, 36) - ¶ subst. intelligence.

v. *zbnwt*.
bnh$_2$ v. *bny$_1$*.
bnw v. *bnwy*.
bnwy **OffAr** Sing. emph. *bnwy*ʾ (cf. Leand 439"', or Plur. emph. of a noun *bnw*?) Cowl 9[12] - ¶ Subst. construction, building (translation 'improvement' (cf. Cowl a.l., Porten & Greenfield JEAS p. 15) too narrow).
bnḥ **OffAr** Sing. abs. *bnḥ* Del 78[1], 79[1] (= AM 110), 80[1] (:: Henning Or iv 292: l. *blh* (= Sing. abs. of *blh$_2$*, indicating some kind of tax); less prob. reading, cf. Lindenberger APA 222 n. 14) - ¶ subst. gift (??, cf. Akkad. par. *ni-din-tum* with Del 79 and cf. Clay AI sub 26, Lidzbarski Eph iii 16, Del a.l., Driver AnOr xii 54f., Altheim & Stiehl ASA 149, cf. also Vattioni Aug x 510 (n. 152)); in the context of Del 78-80 prob. = payment for dues connected with feudal rights.
bnwt v. *zbnwt*.
bny$_1$ **Ph** QAL Pf. 3 p.s.m. *bny* KAI 4[1], 7[1], *bn* KAI 15 (twice :: Milik Bibl xlviii 575f. n. 6: the first *bn* = *bn$_6$* used adverbially: there), 16, 19[2,9] (for KAI 19, cf. Milik DFD 424f. × e.g. Cooke NSI p. 48, Röllig KAI a.l., FR 174, Gibson SSI iii p. 119: = QAL Pf. 3 p.pl.; for the context of l. 2, v. *ʾl$_1$*, *mlʾk$_1$*), 26A i 13, 17, ii 9, 17 (for KAI 26, cf. FR 174, 267b, also for litt.; interpret. as Inf. (abs.), cf. also Gai Or li 254ff., less prob.), 46[7] (poss. interpret., context prob. dam., cf. Albright BASOR lxxxiii 17ff., FS Albright i 346; Dupont-Sommer CRAI '48, 15, 18, JA cclii 301, Février RA xliv 126, v.d.Branden Mašr lvi 286, 291, Ferron RSO xli 288, Amadasi ICO p. 86, Delcor Syr xlv 349, 351, cf. also Röllig KAI a.l. (cf. also Bunnens EPM 37: l. *bn* (= QAL Pf. 3 p.s.m.) + *ngr* (= Sing. abs. of *ngr$_3$* (= commander)) and Lipiński BiOr xlv 63: *ngr* = herald) :: CIS i sub 144, Cooke NSI p. 111: = Sing. cstr. of *bn$_1$* :: Cross CMHE 220 n. 5 (div. otherwise): l. *šbn* (= n.p.) *ngd* (= Sing. abs. of *ngd$_3$* (= commander)), cf. also Peckham Or xli 459, 464f. :: Albright BASOR lxxxiii 19 (div. otherwise): l. *[y]šb* (= QAL Impf. 3 p.s.m. of *šwb*) *w ngr[š]* (= NIPH Pf. 3 p.s.m. of *grš$_1$*)), 60[3], CIS i 4[3]; + suff. 3 p.s.f. *bny* KAI 26A ii 11 (v. supra sub *bn* in KAI 26; cf. also Chiera Hen x 134f.); 1 p.s. *bnt* KAI 14[4]; + suff. 3 p.s.m. (?) *bnty* KAI 18[4]; 3 p.pl. *bn* KAI 37A 5 (= Kition C 1 A 4); 1 p.pl. *bnn* KAI 14[15,17]; Inf. cstr. *bnt* KAI 26A ii 11 (cf. Gibson SSI iii p. 60: or = + suff. 3 p.s.f.?? (cf. also Bron RIPK 89)); Part. act. s.m. abs. *bnh* KAI 12[2] (diff. form., cf. FR 102 n. 1, 178b); pl.m. abs. *bnm* KAI 37A 5 (= Kition C 1 A 4) - **Pun** QAL Pf. 3 p.s.m. *bn* KAI 77[1] (dam. context: *bn[ ]*), 277[5] (for the context, v. *tw$_1$*), *bn*ʾ KAI 129[1], 145[1] (cf. e.g. FR 174 :: Röllig KAI a.l.: = Pf. 3 p.pl.), *b*ʾ*n*ʾ KAI 118[1] (uncert. reading), *b*ʿ*n*ʾ CIS i 151[4] (= ICO-Sard Npu 2; cf. Février JA ccxlvi 444, interpret. however uncert.; or = Pf. 3 p.s.m. +

suff. 3 p.s.m./f.?; Amadasi ICO a.l.: or = subst. Sing. cstr., *bʿnʾ kʿbd* = building of honour; or *ʾmm bʿnʾ* = haplography for *ʾmm mbʿnʾ*?; :: FR 234, 240,9: = Sing. + suff. 3 p.s.m. of *bn*$_1$); + suff. 3 p.s.m. *bny* Trip 38^{5} (or + suff. 3 p.s.f.? :: Levi Della Vida LibAnt i 59f.: or = QAL Part. pass. s.m. abs.?), *bʿnʾ* Punica xxi 3 (dam. context, or = Pf. 3 p.s.m. or = Pf. 3 p.pl.?), BAr '21 cclx 1f. (for this prob. reading, cf. also Jongeling NINPI 11f.), cf. IRT 865: *baneo* (or + suff. 3 p.s.f.?; cf. Vattioni AION xvi 42, Aug xvi 541; uncert. interpret.); 3 p.s.f. *bnʾ* KAI 140^{1}, *bʿnʿ* KAI 117^{3}; 3 p.pl. *bnʾ* KAI 101^{1}, Punica xx 1^{4}; + suff. 3 p.s.m. *bnyʾ* KAI 146^{2}; Inf. cstr. *bnʾt* KAI 172^{3}, *bnʾ* KAI 137^{2} (diff. form, cf. FR 174: = *Verbalsubstantiv*; or = subst.?); Part. act. s.m. abs. *bnʾ* KAI 65^{11}, 123^{4}, Trip 41^{1} (dam. context; FR 119: = Part. act. pl.m. cstr.?), 52^{2}, ICO-Sard 32^{8}, cf. IRT 906^{4}: *buny* (cf. Levi Della Vida OA ii 74, Polselli OAC xiii 239 :: Vattioni AION xvi 50: l. *byny* = Sing. + suff. 3 p.s.f. of *bn*$_1$ :: Vattioni Aug xvi 550: l. *buny* = Sing. + suff. 1 p.s. of *bn*$_1$); pl.m. abs. *bnm* KAI 100^{2}, Trip 40^{5}, *bnʾm* KAI 65^{1} (for the reading, cf. Chabot sub Punica xiii (cf. also Lidzbarski Eph iii 284, Amadasi sub ICO-Sard 36), diff. and dam. context; for interpret., cf. Schiffmann RSF iv 51; for other poss. interpret., cf. - a) Chabot ibid.: or = QAL Pf. 3 p.s.m./pl. + suff. 3 p.pl.m. (cf. Amadasi sub ICO-Sard 36) - b) or = QAL Pf. 3 p.s.m./pl. + suff. 3 p.s.m. :: Lidzbarski Eph iii 284 (div. otherwise): l. *bnʾ* (= QAL Pf. 3 p.pl.) *mbn*; cf. also Röllig KAI a.l.), 101^{6}, *bʿnym* KAI 140^{6}, cf. IRTS 24^{3}: *bunem* (cf. Levi Della Vida OA ii 75f., Polselli OAC xiii 239, Krahmalkov RSF vii 177 :: Vattioni Aug xvi 549: l. *bynem* = Sing. + suff. 3 p.pl.m. of *bn*$_1$); Part. pass. s.m. abs. *bnʾ* Sem xxxviii 114^{1} (cf. Ferjaoui Sem xxxviii a.l.; or = QAL Pf. 3 p.pl.?); PIʿEL Pf. 3 p.s.m. + suff. 3 p.s.m., cf. StudMagr vi 46^{2}: βινιω (cf. La Lomia StudMagr vi 48 × Garbini AION xxv 441: = PIʿEL Pf. 3 p.pl. + suff. 3 p.s.m.); NIPH Pf. 3 p.s.m. *nbnʾ* KAI 146^{1}; 3 p.s.f. *nbnʿ* KAI 149^{1} - **Mo** QAL Pf. 3 p.s.m. *bnh* KAI 181^{18}; 1 p.s. *bnty* KAI 181$^{21,22,23,26,27,29f.}$; Impf. 3 p.s.m. *ybn* KAI 181^{10}; 1 p.s. *ʾbn* KAI 181^{9} - **Amm** QAL Impf. 1 p.s. *ʾbnh* ADAJ xii/xiii 65^{1} (cf. (Sauer with) Fulco JNES xxxviii 38, Cross AUSS xiii 11, Sivan UF xiv 223, 231, Jackson ALIA 45, Aufrecht sub CAI 58; heavily dam. context (cf. also Puech RB xcii 290: uncert. reading), poss. interpret.; Dayani ADAJ xii/xiii 66f.: = part of n.l.); Imper. s.m. *bnh* BASOR cxciii 8^{1} (cf. Albright BASOR cxcviii 38, R.Kutscher Qadm v 28, Dion RB lxxxii 29, Sasson PEQ '79, 118ff., Shea PEQ '81, 105, Jackson ALIA 10, 14, 25, 28, Aufrecht sub CAI 59, Smelik HDAI 84; or + suff. 3 p.s.m./f.?, cf. also Garbini LS p. 105f., AION xx 253, 255: or = verbal/nominal form of root *bny*$_1$ + suff.; cf. however Horn BASOR cxciii 9, v.Selms BiOr xxxii 8, Puech & Rofé RB lxxx 534 (Rofé ibid.: or + suff. 3 p.s.m.?), Fulco BASOR ccxxx 41, Shea PEQ '79, 18: = QAL Pf. 3 p.s.m. :: Cross BASOR cxciii 18 n. 8: = QAL Inf. abs. :: Palmaitis VDI cxviii 119: l. *bmh* (cf. however Teixidor Syr li 318); on the form, cf. also Sivan UF xiv 222f., 230f.) - **Hebr** QAL Impf. 2 p.s.m. *tbnh* Frey 1398^{2}; NIPH Pf. 3 p.s.m. *nybnh* SM 13^{2} - **Samal** QAL Pf. 1 p.s. *bnyt* KAI 214^{14} (for the context, v. *mt$_6$*); Inf. *bn›* KAI 214^{13,14} (uncert. reading) - **OldAr** QAL Pf. 1 p.s. *bnyt* KAI 202B 9 (*[b]nyt*), 10, 216^{20} - **OffAr** QAL Pf. 3 p.s.m. *bnh* Cowl 5^{20}, IEJ xxv 118^{6} (for script and language, cf. Naveh ibid. 120ff.), *bn›* JAOS liv 31^{1}; 2 p.s.m. *bnyt* Cowl 9^{12}; 3 p.pl.m. *bnw* Cowl 30^{13}, 31^{12}, Krael 10^{4} (for the *scriptio anterior*, cf. Porten & Szubin JAOS cvii 231); + suff. 3 p.s.m. *bnhw* Krael 9^{9} (diff. form; lapsus for *bnwh(y)*?, cf. Krael a.l.; Rosenthal with Krael a.l.: lapsus *bnh* corrected to *bnw* without deletion of *h*? :: Segert AAG p. 131); Impf. 2 p.s.m. *tbnh* Cowl 9^{8}, Krael 3^{22}; 3 p.pl.m. *ybnwn* Cowl 71^{3}; Imper. s.m. *bny* Cowl 9^{5}; s.f. *bny* Cowl 8^{19}; Inf. *mbnh* Cowl 5^{3,6,9,11}, etc.; + suff. 3 p.s.m. *mbnyh* Cowl 30^{23,25}, 32^{8}, etc.; Part. pass. s.m. abs. *bnh* Cowl 27^{6}, 30^{14,25}, 31^{13}, 32^{4}, 33^{9} (*[b]nh*, for this prob. reading, cf. also Porten & Yardeni sub TADAE A 4.10), Krael 4^{8} (:: Grelot DAE p. 222, RB lxxxii 290: = Sing. abs. of subst. *bnh$_2$* (= construction, building)); s.f. abs. *bnyh* Cowl 27^{6}, Krael 3^{5}; ITP Pf. 3 p.s.m. *›tbn›* ATNS 67b 6 (diff. reading, dam. context); Impf. 3 p.s.m. *ytbnh* Cowl 30^{27}, 33^{8} (for this prob. reading, cf. Porten & Yardeni sub TADAE A 4.10); cf. Frah xviii 7 (*bnywn* // *‹bd$_1$* = to make), Paik 215 (*bny*), AM ii 176^{3} (*bnyt*), GIPP 49 - **Nab** QAL Pf. 3 p.s.m. *bnh* CIS ii 162, 163^{3}, 164^{3} (Greek par. ὑπεροικοδομήσαντα), 182^{1}, 191^{3}, HDS 151^{1}, ARNA-Nab 16^{1}, ADAJ xxi 143^{1} (*bn[h]*, Greek par. [ἐπ]οίησ[ε]), BIA 58^{1}, etc., *bn›* J 386^{1}, CIS ii 333^{2}; 3 p.pl.m. *bnw* J 18A 2 (= ARNA-Nab 89, for the reading, cf. Milik ARNA a.l., cf. however Jaussen & Savignac sub J 18: l. *bny* = QAL Part. act. pl.m. cstr.); Part. act. s.m. abs. *bn›* RB xlii 416,6; s.m. emph. *bny›* J 171, Syr xxxv 231^{3}, RB xlii 417,7^{2}, 8^{2}, etc.; pl.m. emph. *bny›* J 18A 1 (= ARNA-Nab 89 :: Milik ARNA a.l.: = s.m. emph.), RB xlii 418,9^{1} (cf. Milik ADAJ xxi 145 n. 5 :: Savignac RB a.l.: = n.p.); ITP Pf. 3 p.s.m. *›tbny* IEJ xiii 118^{1}, *›bny* CIS ii 158^{5} (??, highly uncert., cf. Cantineau Nab i 71) - **Palm** QAL Pf. 3 p.s.m. *bn›* CIS ii 3959^{5} (= SBS 44), 3966^{5} (= RIP 156^{14}; cf. Greek par. κτίσμασιν), 4116^{4}, 4123^{2} (Greek par. ᾠκοδόμησεν), 4134^{1} (Greek par. ἔκτισαν), 4164^{1}, 4192 (Greek par. ἔκτισεν), 4202 (Greek par. ἔκτισεν), Inv vii 5^{1} (Greek par. ἔκτισεν), viii 59 (Greek par. ἀνῳκοδόμησαν), xi 81^{2}, xii 35^{4}, RIP 127^{3}, etc., *bnh* Inv viii 57^{1} (Lat. par. *fec it*, Greek par. ἐποίησεν); + suff. 3 p.s.m. *bnhy* Syr xiv 191B 3; 3 p.pl.m. *bnw* CIS ii 4109A 3, B 2, 4124^{1} (Greek par. ᾠκοδόμησ[αν]), 4158^{2}, 4168^{3} (Greek par. ἔκτισαν), 4171^{1}, Inv viii 58^{1} (Greek par. [ᾠ]κοδόμησα[ν]); Part. act. s.m. abs. *bnh* Inv xii 26a 4, b 3, c 4, d 3, e 3 (uncert. interpret., or = n.p. (cf. *b(w)n›*)??); pl.m. abs. *bnn* Ber v 95^{9}, RTP 522 - **Hatra** QAL Pf. 3 p.s.m. *bn›* 60^{1}, 62^{1}, 107^{6},

199, 232c 3 (cf. Degen JEOL xxiii 404, Aggoula MUSJ xlvii 9, Vattioni IH a.l. :: Safar Sumer xxiv 9 n. 7: or = QAL Part. act.?), 272^{1,2} (cf. Degen JEOL xxiii 417, Vattioni IH a.l. :: Safar Sumer xxiv 25 n. 51 (cf. also Aggoula MUSJ xlvii 23f.): = QAL Part. act.), 294^2 (*b[n]ʾ*), 333, 334^1; 1 p.s. *bnyt* 272^3 (cf. Degen JEOL xxiii 418 :: Safar Sumer xxiv 26 n. 58 = PAʿEL); 3 p.pl.m. *bnw* 293^2; Part. act. s.f. cstr. *bnyt* 34^3 (for the uncert. reading, cf. Milik DFD 373, Vattioni IH a.l. :: e.g. Safar Sumer viii 189f., ix 18, Caquot Syr xxx 239: pro *bnyt kwl* l. *bt* (= f. Sing. cstr. of *br*$_1$) *tkdm* (= n.p.)) - **JAr** QAL Pf. 3 p.s.f. *bnt* AMB 15^4; 2 p.s.m. *bnt* MPAT 89^1 (cf. Avigad At iv 34, 35, IEJ xvii 103, 105 :: Fitzmyer & Harrington MPAT a.l. = QAL Pf. 3 p.s.f. :: Beyer ATTM 329, 533: = QAL Pf. 1 p.s. :: Puech RB xc 485f., 489: l. prob. *byt* (Sing. abs. of *byt*$_2$)); 3 p.pl.m. *bnwn* MPAT-A 48^1 (cf. Beyer ATTM 393 :: Fitzmyer & Harrington MPAT a.l.: l. *bnyn* = QAL Part. act. pl.m. abs. (= Frey 979, SM 15)); Part. act. s.m. cstr. *bnh* MPAT 85A (cf. Naveh IEJ xx 34, cf. also Beyer ATTM 344, 533; or rather Hebr.? :: Tzaferis Proc v CJS i 4: certainly Aramaic :: Yadin with Naveh IEJ xx 35 n. 17 (div. otherwise): l. *bn* (= Sing. cstr. of *bn*$_1$) + *h*?), *bnʾ* MPAT 85B 2 (:: Yadin with Naveh IEJ xx 35 n. 17 (div. otherwise): l. *bn* (Sing. cstr. of *bn*$_1$) + *ʾ*?); m. emph. *bnyʾ* Mas 561^2 (diff. reading); Part. pass. s.m. abs. *bny* SM 89a 1 (= Syn D C$_1$ 1); s.m. emph. *bnyh* MPAT 51^8 (for this reading, cf. Milik Bibl xxxviii 264, 267, Puech RQ ix 217, cf. also Beyer ATTM 320, 533 :: Fitzmyer & Harrington MPAT p. 310: = Sing. abs. of *bnh*$_2$ (= building) :: Birnbaum PEQ '57, 112, 123: l. *ʿprh* = Sing. emph. of *ʿpr*$_1$ :: Milik RB lxi 186: l. poss. *mndh*$_2$ = *mndʿ*$_2$ (= something) :: J.J.Rabinowitz BASOR cxxxvi 15: l. poss. *mrqʿʾ* = *mn*$_5$ + Sing. emph. of *rqʿ*$_2$ (= sky) :: Abramson & Ginsberg BASOR cxxxvi 17: l. poss. *[mn* (= *mn*$_5$) *ʾ]grh* = Sing. emph. of *ʾgr*$_4$ (= roof)); ITP Pf. 3 p.s.m. *ʾtbny* SM 88^1 (= Syn D A), 89b 1 (= Syn D C$_2$) - ¶ verb QAL - **1)** to build, to construct (for texts from Hatra, cf. also Aggoula Syr lxv 198ff., 203) - a) (without gramm. object or prep. phrases) KAI 77^1 (said of stone altar), Punica xx 1^4 (tomb stone), Cowl 5^{20} (wall), 30^{23} (temple), Krael 10^4 (cert. building), CIS ii 184^1 (tomb; cf. also CIS ii 191^3, 332^2, 4116^4), 4193$^{1ff.}$ (statues), Inv xi 81$^{1f.}$ (statues with construction belonging to them), RES 2054^1 (building), HDS 151^1, BIA 58^1 (temple, cf. also Hatra 60, 272^3) - b) + obj., Krael 9^9 (cert. building), KAI 14^{15} (temples, cf. KAI 19^9, 37A 5, 145^1, 146^2, 181^{27}, Frey 1398^2, Cowl 30^{23}, CIS ii 164^3, 3959^5, Hatra 272^2, IEJ xxv 118^6, MPAT 149^6), KAI 60^3 (temple court), KAI 140^1 (tomb, cf. CIS ii 169^3, 4123, 4158^2, J 18A 2, ADAJ xxi 143^1, Ber v 95^9, Hatra 293^2), KAI 26A ii 9 (cf. however Sznycer RA lxxv 51ff.: = to rebuild), 11, 17 (town), KAI 181^{9,18,21,26} (fortifications of town), KAI 181^{22} (gates), Cowl 5$^{3f.}$ (wall, cf. poss. JAOS liv 31^1), KAI 181^{23}

(palace, cf. KAI 216[20]), RIP 127[3] (a building and a wall), Hatra 62[1] (stone table with stone pedestal), MPAT-A 48[1] (caravanserai), 49[1] - c) + obj. + acc. loci (?): Hatra 272[1] (wall and gateway) - d) + obj. + b_2 loci: KAI 18[4] (gateway with doors), KAI 26A i 13, 17 (wall of city), Cowl 30[25], 32[8] (temple), KAI 202B 9 (temples) - e) + obj. + l_5 comm.: KAI 14[17] (temple, cf. KAI 15, 16, 101[1], 172[3]), CIS ii 4124[1ff.] (tomb, cf. CIS 4168[1]), Syr xiv 191B 3 - f) + b_2 loci: Cowl 9[12] (building; cf. Krael 3[22]), Hatra 232C 3 (altar?) - g) + l_5 comm.: KAI 46[7], KAI 7[1ff.] (wall), RES 2025[1f.] (wall and other elements of construction), KAI 117[1ff.] (mausoleum), Punica xxi 3 (tombstone), Sem xxxviii 114[1] (temple, v. supra; cf. CIS ii 182[1], Hatra 107[6f.]), CIS ii 162 (tomb; cf. CIS ii 332[2], 4164, ARNA-Nab 16[1], Inv viii 58[1f.]) - h) + l_5 comm. + obj.: KAI 181[10f.] ((fortifications of) town; on this text, cf. H.P.Müller TUAT i 648), BASOR cxciii 8[1] (v. however supra, prob. gates), Inv xii 35[4] (building, cf. AMB 15[4]), MPAT 89[1] (tomb) - i) + l_5 comm. + b_2 loci: KAI 19[2ff.] (temple, cf. Cowl 30[13], 31[12]) - j) + ʿl_7 comm., CIS ii 163[3] (religious buildings), 4109A 3, B 2 (tomb, cf. J 386[1ff.]) - k) + *ʿlwy* loci: Cowl 5[6,9f.,11] (v. also *ʿlwy*) - Part. act. - a) architect, builder (often diff. to differentiate): KAI 12[2] (v. supra), 37A 5, 101[6], 140[6], Trip 40[5] (dam. context), 52[2], J 18A 1 (v. supra), 171, RB xlii 416,6, 417,7[2],8[2], 419[1], Syr xxxv 231[3], RTP 522, Hatra 211; cf. also *hbnm šʾbnm* KAI 100[2]: the builders of the stones (i.e. the stone-masons); *bnh hklh* MPAT 85A: the architect of the Temple, cf. MPAT 85B 2 - b) creator; *bnyt kwl* Hatra 34[3] the *creatrix* of everything (title of female deity; uncert. reading, v. supra) - Part. pass. built: Cowl 27[6] (wall, + b_2 loci)[,6f.] (well, + b_2 loci), 30[14] (temple, cf. 30[25], 31[13]), 32[4] (temple, + b_2 loci), Krael 4[8] (building), SM 89a 1 (synagogue) - in some texts with special meaning: to restore, to rebuild, to maintain, cf. e.g. KAI 4[1f.], 37A 5 (cf. however Delcor UF xi 150f.), 181[27], Cowl 30[23,25,27] (meaning often diff. to differentiate; cf. e.g. Sznycer RA lxxv 51ff.) - cf. also the foll. comb.: - a) forms of *bny_1* + *$qdš_1$*, v. *$qdš_1$* - b) forms of *bny_1* + *qrb_1*, v. *qrb_1* - c) forms of *$ḥpr_1$* + *bny_1*, v. *$ḥpr_1$* - **2)** to build upon, *ʾrqʾ zk tbnh* Cowl 9[8]: you will build upon that plot, cf. Cowl 8[19], 9[5] (for the context of 9[5], v. *ʿtd_1*; cf. also Milik Bibl xxxviii 267, Ginsberg ANET 222); Part. pass., built upon: Krael 3[5] (for the context, v. *trbṣ*), cf. also *bnyh wqrqʿʾ* MPAT 51[8]: which is built upon and which is not (:: Milik Bibl xxxviii 265, 267, Puech RB ix 215, Fitzmyer & Harrington MPAT a.l.: (the) building and terrain; v. also supra) - NIPH to be built: SM 13[2] (for the context, v. *srr*); + l_5 comm.: KAI 146[1] (temple), 149 (tomb) - ITP to be built: Cowl 30[27] (temple, cf. Cowl 33[8] (v. supra)), SM 88[1] (synagogue, cf. SM 89b 1), IEJ xiii 118[1] - Levi Della Vida LibAnt i 61f.: the *bnʾm* in Trip 39[3] prob. = QAL Part. act. pl.m. abs. of *bny_1* (uncert. interpret., diff. context) - the *bnʾ* in KAI 161[9] poss. =

QAL Pf. 3 p.s.m. (cf. Roschinski Num 112, 115, cf. however Février RA xlv 147: = QAL Part. s.m. abs.? and Röllig KAI a.l.: = QAL Part. act. pl.m. cstr.?; highly uncert. interpretations; cf. also Berger RA ii 43: = Sing. + suff. 3 p.s.m. of *bn$_1$*?, cf. Lidzbarski Handb 237) - Aggoula Ber xviii 97: l. *nbw* (= n.p.) + *bn*ʾ (= QAL Part. act. s.m. abs. of *bny$_1$* (= mason)) in Hatra 98 pro *nbwbn*ʾ (= n.p., cf. Safar Sumer xvii 32 (n. 76), Caquot Syr xl 10, Vattioni IH a.l.), less prob. interpret. - Aggoula Ber xviii 99: l. *nbw* (= n.p.) + *bn*ʾ (= QAL Part. act. s.m. abs. of *bny$_1$* (= mason)) in Hatra 211 pro *nbwbn*ʾ (= n.p., cf. e.g. Vattioni IH a.l.), less prob. interpret. (:: Teixidor Sumer xx 79: l. *b*ʾ?) - a derivative of *bny$_1$* poss. in the *bn*ʾ of Nisa 17[1], 19[1], 30[3], 67[1], 72[1], 73[1], 81[2], 94[2], etc. (cf. Diakonov & Livshitz Nisa-b p. 40: = fief, domain, cf. also Altheim & Stiehl AAW ii 224, GMA 471: = QAL Part. pass. with the meaning: building (i.e. main building of the fief); cf. also GIPP 49) - Ferron RSF ii 79f.: l. *b*ʿ*l* (= Sing. abs. of *b*ʿ*l$_2$*) *bn*ʾ (= QAL Part. act. s.m. abs. of *bny$_1$*) in WO v 119[4]: = architect (poss. reading, uncert. interpret. (cf. also Gibson SSI iii p. 144); cf. also Röllig WO v a.l. (div. otherwise): l. *r* ʿ*l b.*ʾ without interpret.) - for the diff. group of graphemes *bntw* in KAI 277[5f.], v. *tw$_1$* - Lipiński Or xl 327f.: l. form of *bny* (= QAL Pf. 1 p.s. + suff. 3 p.s.f.: *bn[th]*) in KAI 181[3] (for the reading of *n*, cf. Lidzbarski Eph i 4, Teixidor Syr xlix 428), for other interpretations and reading proposals (l. *bn[s]* = *b$_2$* + Sing. abs., of *ns* (= sign) or l. *bmt* = Sing. cstr. of *bmh*), cf. e.g. Röllig KAI a.l., Lipiński Or xl a.l., Auffret UF xii 110 (n. 6), cf. also H.P.Müller TUAT i 646: l. *bns[bt]*? = *b$_2$* + Sing. cstr. of *nsbh* (= turn), Smend & Socin IKM 12f., 17: l. *bmš*ʿ = *b$_2$* + Sing. abs. of *mš*ʿ$_1$ (= deliverance) - Porten & Yardeni sub TADAE B 8.2: l. prob. *bnh* in ATNS 44 ii 6 (= form of *bny$_1$*), diff. reading, cf. also Segal ATNS a.l.: l. *bynh* (less prob. reading), v. also *bynh*.

v. ʾ*dn$_3$*, *bly$_2$*, *bn$_1$*, *bnyn*, *br$_1$*, *dnb*, *zbn$_1$*, *mbny*, *mn$_5$*, *nbnh*, ʿ*bn*, *tw$_1$*, *tm$_1$*, *try$_3$*.

bny$_2$ v. *bny$_1$*.

bny$_3$ v. *byn$_2$*.

bnyh v. *bny$_1$*.

bnyn **OffAr** Sing. cstr. *bnyn* Cowl 30[10], 31[9] (for both texts, cf. Cowl a.l.: or = QAL Part. pass. pl.m. abs.?, cf. also Vogt Lex s.v. *bnh*, Grelot DAE p. 409); emph. *bnyn*ʾ Krael 3[22]; Plur. abs. *bnynyn* FuF xxxv 173[4] - **Nab** Sing. emph. *bnyn*ʾ RES 2054[1] - **Palm** Sing. cstr. *bnyn* RTP 114; emph. *bnyn*ʾ Inv ix 11[4], x 13[5], RIP 21[3], 127[3], Syr xii 130[10], xiv 177[6], RTP 115, 116, 117; Plur. cstr. *bnyny* Syr xiv 175[2] - **Hatra** Sing. emph. *bnyn*ʾ 191[1] (for the reading, cf. Aggoula MUSJ xlvii 41f. :: Safar Sumer xviii 54: l. *(l)b(?)*ʾ*n*ʾ or *(l)w*ʾ*n*ʾ?, cf. also Caquot Syr xli 267), 192[2] (for the reading, cf. Aggoula MUSJ xlvii 42, Vattioni IH a.l. :: Caquot Syr xli 268: l. *(l)byn*ʾ :: Safar Sumer xviii 55: l. *(l)b(?)*ʾ*(?)n*ʾ) - ¶ subst.

m. - **1)** building, construction: Krael 3[22], RES 2054[1], RIP 21[3] (for this text, cf. Gawlikowski TP 116), Syr xiv 175[2] (prob. interpret.; du Mesnil du Buisson Syr xl 313: = construction/building service (of the temple)); *bnyn ps(y)lh zy ʾbn* Cowl 30[10], 31[9] (said of a gateway): a construction made with hewn blocks of stone; *bnynʾ dnh dy ʿynʾ* RIP 127[3]: this construction of the well - **2)** the act of building/constructing: Syr xiv 177[6] (cf. Gawlikowksi TP 72), Inv ix 11[4f.] (cf. Gawlikowski TP 71), Hatra 191[1], 192[2] (v. supra, cf. also Aggoula Syr lxv 201f.) - **3)** fabric: RTP 114, 115, 116, 117 (for RTP cf. also Caquot RTP p. 141), Inv x 13[5] (cf. Gawlikowski TP 72), prob. also in Syr xii 130[10].

bnʿtm v. *tm₃*.

bnpqyr (< Greek βενεφικίαριος < Lat. *beneficiarius*) - **Palm** Sing. emph. *bnpqyrʾ* CIS ii 4292A 2- ¶ subst. m. *beneficiarius* (i.e. soldier who through the favour of his commander is exempt from menial duties (throwing up entrenchments, procuring wood and water, foraging, etc.); privileged soldier; cf. also Ingholt PBP 133 (n. 167)).

bnt₁ v. *pnt, tm₃*.

bnt₂ v. *tw*.

bntm v. *tm₃*.

bs v. *bky₂*.

bsʾmyn Ebeling Frah a.l.: l. *bsʾmyn* (= spring) in Frah xxvii 10 (prob. = derivative of the same root as in *bšm₁,₂*) = fragrance (improb. interpret., cf. Nyberg FP 56, 107: l. Iran. word); cf. also *bsym, bšm₃*.

bsy v. *ksy*.

bsym cf. Frah v 11: sweet, agreeable (cf. Lemosín AO ii 266, 268), cf. also *bsʾmyn, bšm₃*.

bslqʾ (< Greek βασιλικὴ) - **Palm** Sing. emph. *bslqʾ* CIS ii 3914[4] (= Inv ix 25; Greek par. βασιλικῇ), 3952[3] (= Inv v 3; :: Renan sub CIS i 88 (div. otherwise): l. *slmʾ* = Sing. emph. of *slm₃* = *slmh*), AAS xxxvi/xxxvii 167 no. 7[4] (*[b]slkʾ*; Greek par. βασιλικὴν) - ¶ subst. f. (CIS ii 3914[4], AAS xxxvi/xxxvii 167 no. 7[4]: *bslqʾ rbtʾ*), m. (CIS ii 3952[3]: *bslqʾ dnh*), portico (cf. Dunant SBS p. 13, Gawlikowski TP 74).

bss (< Greek βάσις) - **Nab** Sing. emph. *bssʾ* CIS ii 199[1] - ¶ subst. base (part of sepulchral construction, exact meaning uncert.) - cf. *bʿṣṣ*.

bsr₁ v. *zrd*.

bsr₂ cf. Frah v 6: unripe grape.

bsr₃ v. *bšr₂*.

bstr v. *šṭr₃*.

bʿbr v. *ʿbr₇*.

bʿd₁ **Palm** Qal (or Paʿel?) Pf. 3 p.s.f. *bʿdt* RB xxxix 548[4] (:: Cantineau Gramm 74: l. *bʿd/rt* = Qal Pf. 3 p.s.f. of *bʿd₁* of *bʿr₁* (= to dispose of)); Inf. *mbʿd* (or *mbʿdʾ*?) CIS ii 4214 (= Inv vii 2 :: Cantineau sub Inv vii 2, Gramm 78s.: l. *mbʿrʾ* = Qal Inf. of *bʿr₁* (= to dispose of)) - ¶ verb prob. meaning: to cede, to renounce (v. supra). v. *mb‘r₂*.

b‘d₂ v. *‘dh₁*, *‘wd₅*, *‘rbn*.

b‘dy v. *‘wd₅*.

b‘h (or **b‘t**) - **Pun** Sing. abs. *b‘t* KAI 119[8], CIS i 171[7], 3919[1f.] (*[b]‘t*), Trip 51[3]; cstr. KAI 69[1] (*b‘[t]*), 74[1] - ¶ subst. prob. meaning tariff, list (cf. however Delcor Sem xxxviii 88: = stipulation, fixing, notification or = what is asked, required); for the diff. context of Trip 51[3], cf. Levi Della Vida ibid. 10, Amadasi IPT 133.
v. *‘t₁*.

b‘w cf. Frah xxx 9: petition, rogation.

b‘y₁ **OldAr** Qal Impf. 3 p.s.m. *yb‘h* KAI 223B 8, 224[2,11]; 3 p.s.f. *tb‘h* KAI 222B 39; 2 p.s.m. *tb‘h* KAI 223B 17 - **OffAr** Qal Pf. 3 p.s.m. *b‘h* Cowl 31[16], 50[4], Driv 7[3]; 1 p.s. *b‘yt* ATNS 5[3] (or = Pf. 2 p.s.m.?, cf. Porten & Yardeni sub TADAE B 8.3, dam. context); 3 p.pl.m. *b‘w* Cowl 30[17]; 1 p.pl. *b‘n* Herm 6[9] (cf. Grelot RB lxxiv 436, DAE p. 166 n. m × Bresciani & Kamil Herm a.l.: pref. = Qal Part. act. pl.m. abs., cf. also Porten & Greenfield IOS iv 24 (n. 16)); Impf. 3 p.s.m. *yb‘h* Cowl 38[6], Aḥiq 53, KAI 258[5] (:: Torrey JAOS xxxv 372, 374: = Qal Impf. 3 p.pl. (or s.?) m. + suff. 3 p.s.); *yb‘y* Sach 80 iii A 1; 2 p.s.m. *tb‘h* Aḥiq 34; 2 p.s.f. *tb‘y* JRAS ’29, 108[15] (:: Degen GGA ’79, 36: = Impf. 2 p.s.m.); 3 p.pl.m. *yb‘wn* KAI 259[2f.] (for the reading, cf. Hanson (& Naveh) BASOR cxcii 9, 11, Teixidor Syr xlvii 374, Gibson SSI ii p. 154 :: Montgomery JAOS xxviii 166: l. *tṣbw..* (3) *pn*, Halévy RS xvi 435ff. (div. otherwise): l. *ṣbw y[s](3)pn* (cf. a) Lidzbarski Eph iii 64: = form of root *nṣb₂* (= *nsb*) - b) Driver AnOr xii 50ff.: = form of root *ṣby₂* (= to surround, to enclose) - c) Lidzbarski Eph iii 64, Chabot sub RES 956: l. *tṣbw..*(3) *sn*, meaning of *tṣbw..*: you will sm(ash it) (thus Chabot), *sn* = Qal Pf. 3 p.s.m. of *šn’₁* (cf. Segert AAG p. 296: = Qal Part. act. s.m. abs. of *šn’₁*)) :: Torrey ZA xxvi 91 (cf. also Koopmans 160, Donner KAI a.l., Dupont-Sommer FX 157): l. *ttb ytb* (3) *wn* (*ttb* = Haph Impf. 2 p.s.m. of *tbb* (= to destroy), *ytbwn* = Haph Impf. 3 p.pl.m. of *tbb*)), FX 137[27]; 2 p.pl.m. *tb‘wn* Driv 7[9]; Imper. s.m. *b‘y* Cowl 42[6], ATNS 22[2], 197[2] (heavily dam. context); s.f. *b‘y* Sem xxi 85 conv. 3; pl.m. *b‘w* Driv 7[7]; Part. act. s.m. abs. *b‘h* ATNS 29 ii 10 (dam. context); cf. Frah xxi 14 (*b‘yhwn*), Paik 456, 457 (*yb‘h*), 458, 459 (*b‘yḥwn*), GIPP 20, 37, 67 (cf. also Toll ZDMG-Suppl viii 37) - **Nab** Qal Pf. 1 p.s. *b‘yt* MPAT 64 recto 1[9]; Impf. 3 p.s.m. *yb‘’* J 4[4] (:: CIS ii sub 219: l. *y’t’* = Qal Impf. 3 p.s.m. of *’ty₁*); 2 p.s.m. *tb[‘y]* MPAT 64 recto 2[1]; 1 p.s. *’b‘y* MPAT 64 recto 2[1] - **Palm** Qal Impf. 3 p.s.m. *yb‘h* RIP 199[14]; Itp Impf. 3 p.s.m. *ytb‘’* CIS ii 3913 ii 70 - **Hatra** Qal Impf. 3 p.s.m. *lb‘’*, cf. Assur 11 ii 3 - ¶ verb Qal to search for, to look for, to want; for KAI 223B 39, v. *npš* - **1)** + obj.: Cowl

42^{6} (object: man), Aḥiq 53 (object: counsel), JRAS ’29, 108^{15} (*mh tb‘y*), Herm 6^{9} (object: boat), MPAT 64 recto 2^{1} (*kl dy ’b‘y*), Sem xxi 85 conv. 3 (object: hide); *yb‘’ dy yktb* J 4^{4} (v. supra): he wants to write; *yb‘h r’šy lhmtty* KAI 224^{11}: he seeks my head to kill me (cf. for parallels Greenfield Lesh xxvii/xxviii 306, ActOr xxix 7, cf. however also Kaufman AIA 154 n. 73); *yb‘h rwḥ ’pwh* KAI 224^{2}: he looks for the breath of his nostrils (i.e. he wants to save his life, he seeks asylum, cf. Dupont-Sommer BMB xiii 30f., Vogt Bibl xxxix 271, Lex s.v. *b‘h*, Donner KAI a.l., Gibson SSI ii 47, 52, Sader EAS 134, Rössler TUAT i 186 :: Rosenthal BASOR clviii 28 n. 1: *yb‘h* = Qal Impf. 3 p.s.m. of *b‘y*$_2$ (= to cause to boil), (transl.) he causes his breath to boil (i.e. he blows hot), cf. also Rosenthal ANET 660, Fitzmyer AIS 104, Grelot RB lxxv 284, Lipiński Stud 55 :: Fitzmyer CBQ xx 453: *yb‘h* = Qal Impf. 3 p.s.m. of *b‘y*$_1$ (transl.) he becomes enraged (cf. also Lemaire & Durand IAS 143) :: Vattioni AION xiii 279ff.: *yb‘h* < root *bw‘* (transl.) he causes the breath of his nostrils to boil :: Garbini RSO xxxiv 43f.: *yb‘h* < root *b‘y*$_3$ = **p‘y* (transl.) he blows through his nostrils (like a snake; i.e. he spits his venom., sc. against the king of KTK) :: Ben-Chayyim Lesh xxxv 246f.: *rwḥ ’pwh* is subject of *yb‘h*; v. also *rḥ*$_1$) - **2)** + obj. + *mn*$_5$, *wmlh zy ṣḥ’ ... yb‘h mnkm* Cowl 38^{6}: and the matter which S. asks of you - **3)** + obj. + *l*$_5$, *b‘w b’yš l’gwr’ zk* Cowl 30^{17}: they sought to do evil to that temple, cf. Cowl 31^{16} - **4)** + *l*$_5$, *wyb‘h lh šhr wšmš* KAI 258^{5} (v. supra): and may Sh. and Sh. search for him (i.e. punish him, cf. Lipiński Stud 150, cf. also Gevirtz VT xi 146 (n. 5), Cross BASOR clxxxiv 10, Hanson BASOR cxcii 11, Donner KAI a.l., Dupont-Sommer FX 157), cf. KAI 259$^{2ff.}$ (v. supra) - 5) + *mn*$_5$ - a) *wmn ’tr ’ḥrn l’ tb‘wn* Driv 7^{9}: you will not acquire (them) from elsewhere - b) *’lhy’ yb‘wn mnh* FX 137$^{26f.}$: may the gods require (it) from him (i.e. punish him) - **6)** + *mn*$_5$ + obj. - a) *mn ’tr ’ḥrn grd ... b‘w* Driv 7$^{6f.}$: acquire a staff of ... from elsewhere (cf. Driv 7$^{2f.}$) - b) *wb‘yt mnk dy ...* MPAT 64 recto i 9: and I required of you that ... - **7)** + *‘l*$_7$, prob. with special sense, to pray for: Assur 11 ii 3 - **8)** + *‘l*$_7$ + obj. - a) *]b‘h ‘lyk gbry’ d[* Cowl 50^{4}: he sought (i.e. incited) men against you (??, heavily dam. context) - b) *yb‘h ‘l gbr ḥṭ[* RIP 199^{14}: he will require from a man (his) ... (ie. poss. he will visit (his) ... on a man; ?? dam. and uncert. context; cf. however Milik DFD 287: *ḥṭ[* = attribute to *gbr*) - Itp be asked, required: CIS ii 3913 ii 70 - a form of this root poss. also in KAI 222B 35, cf. Silverman JAOS xciv 270, Lipiński Stud 40 - Schroed p. 308 (cf. also L.H.Gray AJSL xxxix 79): the *beat* in Poen 941 (l. however *beat[i]*) = Qal Pf. 1 p.s. (highly uncert. interpret., cf. also Sznycer PPP 122: *beat* or (div. otherwise) *mbeat* < root *bw’*?) - Segal Maarav iv 70f.: l. *b‘yt* = Qal Pf. 1 p.s. or 2 p.s.m. in ASAE xxvi 24^{5} (uncert. reading), Aimé-Giron AG a.l.:

l. *bʿkh* (without interpret.) - Segal ATNS a.l.: l. poss. *bʿʾt* (= Qal Pf. 1 p.s.) in ATNS 69b 3 (reading however highly uncert.).
v. *nbʿ*, *prʿ*$_2$, *rbʿ*$_3$.

bʿy$_2$ v. *bʿy*$_1$.

bʿy$_3$ v. *bʿy*$_1$.

bʿk v. *yrʿ*.

bʿl$_1$ **OffAr** Haph Inf. *hbʿlh* Krael 7[33] (?, prob. reading (cf. also Porten & Yardeni sub TADAE B 3.8) :: J.J Rabinowitz Law 58: = Niph Inf.) - ¶ verb Haph to marry (said of a woman); *lʾ šlyṭh yh[wyšmʿ l]hbʿh bʿl ʾḥrn* Krael 7[33]: Y. has no power [to] marry another husband (prob. interpret., cf. Yaron JSS iii 27, cf. also id. JSS v 68, Law 73, Verger OA iii 54f. :: Krael a.l.: Y. shall not have power to cohabit with (?) another man (cf. also Grelot DAE p. 237 (n. e): Y. shall not have conjugal relations with another husband)).

bʿl$_2$ m. **Ph** Sing. cstr. *bʿl* KAI 24[11,12,16], 47[1]; Plur. cstr. *bʿl* KAI 19[3] (:: Baldacci BiOr xl 131 = n.d or = Sing. cstr.; v. also *ʿbd*$_2$), 26A i 15, iii 8, 8f., 9, C iv 8, 9, 37B 4 (= Kition C 1; ?, v. *mym*), 60[6] (v. infra), DD 13[2] (for the reading of the context, cf. Milik DFD 425f. :: Caquot Sem xv 30: = Sing. cstr. :: Dunand & Duru DD a.l.: *bʿl ḥmn* = n.d.) - **Pun** Sing. abs. *bʿl* CIS i 4841[8] (v. however *qdš*$_3$); cstr. *bʿl* KAI 69[4,8,10,21], 72B 4, 74[2,3], 75[4], 81[9], 116[4], 120[2], 140[2], 145[5], 150[2], 152[1], Monte Sirai ii 80[3], CIS i 4911[5], Hofra 112[2], 113[1], 114[4], etc., cf. IRT 827[2], 889[2]: *bal*; + suff. 3 p.pl.m. *bʿlnm* ICO-Sard 35 (diff. context, cf. Guidi MonAnt xxi 165f. (or = + suff. 3 p.s.m.?), Garbini RSO xl 211f., Amadasi sub ICO-Sard 35 :: Hoftijzer VT xiii 337ff.: = + suff. 3 p.s.m.); Plur. abs. *bʿlm* NP 87[3] (= Punica xviii/1 15); cstr. *bʿl* KAI 137[1], on coins, cf. e.g. Sef ix 433, *bʿlʾ* KAI 101[1], 140[5], 155[2] (cf. Chabot sub Punica v 5 :: Röllig KAI a.l.: = part of n.p., cf. Lidzbarksi Eph ii 68), NP 7[2] (= Punica iv A 1), 45[2] (= Punica iv A 5), CRAI '16, 121 ii 2, 124[2] (*[b]ʿlʾ*), Karthago xii 48[2], Sem xxxvi 28[1], xxxviii 114[3] - **Samal** Sing. cstr. *bʿl* KAI 215[3,11,22]; Plur. cstr. *bʿly* KAI 215[10] - **OldAr** Plur. cstr. *bʿly* KAI 216[10,11], 222A 4, B 4; + suff. 3 p.s.f. *bʿlyh* KAI 224[23,26] - **OffAr** Sing. abs. *bʿl* Krael 7[33]; cstr. *bʿl* Cowl 5[9], 13[10], Aḥiq 42, 95, etc.; + suff. 3 p.s.m. *bʿlh* RN vi/xiii 17[5] (for the reading of the context, cf. also Naveh & Puech with Greenfield FS Grelot 10 (n. 30)); + suff. 3 p.s.f. *bʿlh* Cowl 15[4,21], Krael 2[4], 7[24,40], 14[4], AG 37[1] (?); + suff. 2 p.s.f. *bʿlky* Cowl 8[7]; + suff. 1 p.s. *bʿly* Cowl 15[23], Krael 2[9]; Plur. cstr. *bʿly* Cowl 30[22,23], 31[22,23], 83[21], FX 136[6,11], 171[3], 173[5] - **Nab** Sing. + suff. 3 p.s.f. *bʿlh* CIS ii 162; + suff. 1 p.s. *bʿly* DBKP 22[31] - **Palm** Sing. + suff. 3 p.s.f. *bʿlh* CIS ii 4010[5f.] (= Inv xi 23), 4027[4], 4518A 3, Inv xi 56[3], SBS 63[3], RIP 80[5], 104[4], 161[4] (?, or + suff. 3 p.s.m.?, cf. Gawlikowski RIP a.l.), RB xxxix 548[2], AAS xxxvi/xxxvii 168 no. 9[4]; Plur. cstr. *bʿly* Ber v 106[1] - **Hatra** Sing. + suff. 3 p.s.f. *bʿlh* 5[3], 30[4], 35[6] - f. **Ph** Sing. abs. *bʿlt* KAI 11 (or

= n.d.?); cstr. *b‘lt* KAI 5[2] (*b‘l[t]*), 6[2] (*[b]‘lt*), 7[3,4], 10[3,7,8,10] (*[b]‘lt*)[,15], 26A iii 7, C iv 6 (*b‘l[t]*), 56, Sem xxxv 10, *b‘l* (lapsus) KAI 4[3] (cf. e.g. Röllig KAI a.l., Oden CBQ xxxix 459 n. 9 :: Eissfeldt ZAW lvii 3: = m. Sing. cstr. :: Levi Della Vida RSO xxxix 301: poss. *t* (following *mpḥr*) in next line belongs here) - **Pun** Sing. cstr. *b‘lt* KAI 83, CIS i 4910[3] - **Palm** for *b‘ltk*, v. infra - ¶ subst. m. and f. - **1)** m. lord, chief, f. lady; *lb‘l ltnt b‘lm šl’* NP 87[2f.] (= Punica xviii/1 15): to Ba‘al (and) Tinnit, his lords; *hdd b‘lh* RN vi/xiii 17[4f.]: H. his lord (v. supra); *b‘l ṣr* KAI 47[1]: the lord of Tyre (epithet of Melqart; Greek par. Ἡρακλεῖ ἀρχηγέτει); *b‘lt gbl* KAI 7[3f.]: the lady of Byblos (epithet of the foremost goddess of Byblos (or = n.d.?; cf. Röllig KAI ii p. 7, cf. also KAI 4[3f.] (v. supra), 5[2], 6[2], 7[4], 10[3,3f.,7,8,10,15], Sem xxxv 10), cf. also Kition D 37: *b‘l kty* (heavily dam. context); for *b‘l byt/bt* = special god of the Yaudian dynasty, v. *byt*$_1$; for *b‘l ḥrdt*, v. *ḥrdh*; for *b‘lt hḥdrt*, v. *ḥdrh*; for *b‘l qdšn*, v. *qdš*$_3$; *b‘l ’gddm* KAI 26A i 15: chiefs of gangs of bandits, robberchiefs (cf. Avishur PIB 229); for *b‘l bn’*, v. *bny*$_1$; for *b‘l ḥrš*, v. *ḥrš*$_5$; for *b‘l pqt*, v. *pqt*$_1$; the *b‘ltk* in RTP 66, 76, 77, 200, 332, 437, 548, 714, 715, 716, 717, Syr xii 133[3], xxxvi 105 no. 12, 13 prob. = f. Sing. + suff. 2 p.s.m. > n.d., for this goddess, cf. also du Mesnil du Buisson TMP 364ff., Milik DFD 219, Gawlikowski TP 33f., Teixidor PP 87f.; for older interpret., cf. - a) = *b*$_2$ + Sing. + suff. 2 p.s.m. of *‘lh*$_1$) - b) = *b*$_2$ + Sing. + suff. 2 p.s.m. of *‘lh*$_3$ (= cause, interest)), cf. Caquot RTP p. 143 (cf. also Milik sub SDB vi 1101: = Sing. + suff. 2 p.s.m. of *b‘lh*$_3$ (= possession)) - **2)** owner, possessor, proprietor; *b‘l bqr* KAI 24[11f.]: an owner of cattle (cf. KAI 24[11], 26A iii 8, 8f., C iv 8, 9); *b‘l ksp wb‘l ḥrṣ* KAI 24[12]: an owner of silver and an owner of gold (cf. KAI 215[11], 216[10f.]); for *b‘ly rkb* KAI 215[10], v. *rkb*$_6$; for *b‘ly kpyry* KAI 215[10], v. *kpyr*; *b‘l šb‘ wtrš* KAI 26A iii 9: owner of abundance and wine (for the exact meaning, v. *trš*$_1$; cf. KAI 26A iii 7, C iv 6f., 9); for *b‘l ’gr* = employer, v. *’gr*$_2$; *b‘l ‘ṭt’ ṭbt’* Aḥiq 42: a good counsellor; for *b‘l ṭ[‘m]* Cowl 26[23], v. *ṭ‘m*$_2$; *b‘l (h)zbḥ* KAI 69[4,8,21], 74[2,3], 75[4], CIS i 3917[2,3]: person offering the sacrifice (cf. however the expression *b‘l šlm hršt* KAI 120[2], prob. title of religious functionary, v. *šlm*$_3$); *b‘ly ṭbtk wrḥmyk* Cowl 30[23f.], 31[23] : your wellwishers and friends (cf. JRAS '29, 108[3f.]; v. *ṭbh*$_1$); for *b‘ly ptwr’* Cowl 83[21]: money-lenders?, v. also *ptr*$_1$; cf. also *b‘ly ’ḥyn* Ber v 106[1]: half-brothers - **3)** m. husband: Cowl 8[7], 15[4], Krael 2[9], CIS ii 162, 4518A 3, Hatra 5[3], etc., etc.; cf. poss. *b‘l b‘l ‘nwt* Syr xxxiii 81[3]: Ba‘al the husband of ‘Anat (cf. also Porten Arch 170f., Grelot DAE p. 336 (n. d), cf. however Milik Bibl xlviii 566 n. 3: *b‘l ‘nwt* = citizen of *‘nwt*) - **4)** citizen, inhabitant; *b‘ly yb* Cowl 30[22], 31[22]: the inhabitants of Yeb; *b‘ly ’wrn* FX 136[6]: the citizens of O. (Greek par. ξανθίοις καὶ τοῖς περιοίκοις; cf. also Dupont-Sommer FX a.l. :: Teixidor JNES xxxvii 182: the landowners of O.); *b‘l tnsmt* KAI

137[1]: the citizens (or inhabitants?) of T.; *b‘l› hmkt‘rm* Karth xii 48[2]: the citizens (or inhabitants?) of Mactar (cf. CRAI ’16, 121 ii 2, 124[2], Sem xxxviii 114[3]); *b‘l mkd‘* NP 68[2] (= Punica iv A 8; cf. Chabot a.l.): the citizen (or inhabitant?) of M.; *b‘l› hmdm* Sem xxxvi 28[1f.]: the citizens (or inhabitants?) of Mididi (cf. also Fantar Sem xxxvi 38f.); *b‘l gwl* KAI 140[2]: the inhabitant of G. (cf. Lat. par. *[g]a[l]esis*); *b‘lt bznty* KAI 56: the female inhabitant of B. (cf. Greek par. βυζαντία), cf. also KAI 19[3] (v. also *‘bd₂*), 60[6] (:: e.g. Cooke NSI p. 94, 99: *b‘l ṣdn* = n.d. :: v.d.Branden BiOr xxxvi 160 = treasurer (< possessor; = Sing. or Plur. cstr.) of the *ṣdn* organisation, v. also *ṣdn*), 101[1], 116[4f.], 137[1], 150[2f.], 152[1], NP 10[2] (= Punica iv A 2, cf. also OMROL xliv 93f.), BAr ’89, 99[3] (dam. context; for the Pun. texts, cf. also Moscati RSO xliii 3f.), etc., etc.; in KAI 222A 4, B 4 *b‘ly ktk/b‘ly ›rpd* poss. indication of the local aristocracy of K. and A., cf. Sacchi RCL ’61, 186, Noth ZDPV lxxvii 130, Donner KAI a.l., Fitzmyer AIS 28, Gibson SSI ii p. 35 (also in KAI 224[23,26?]; cf. also Donner KAI a.l., BiOr xxvii 248, Fitzmyer AIS 119, Lipiński Stud 48, 57, cf. however Degen AAG p. 93: = inhabitants) - **5)** indication of membership of a certain group; *b‘l dgl wqryh* Cowl 5[9]: soldier and civilian (cf. J.J.Rabinowitz JJP xi/xii 173, Porten Arch 35 (n. 30)), cf. also Cowl 13[10], 20[10f.], 46[6]; cf. poss. also *bal ysrim* IRT 827[2]: a man of twenty years of age (?, cf. Levi Della Vida OA ii 85, Krahmalkov JSS xvii 72 (n. 1), cf. however Vattioni AION xvi 47: = commander of (a group of) twenty (men), cf. also idem Aug xvi 539) - a form of *b‘l₂* also in Herm 8[14]: *b‘l[* (heavily dam. context) - Sing. + suff. 1 p.s. (*b‘ly*) poss. also in one word Pun. text (OA iv 53), cf. Barréca a.l. (or = n.p.??) - Cross CBQ xxxvi 488 (n. 18): the *b‘l* in Syr xlviii 396[2] = Sing. abs. of *b‘l₂* (less prob. interpret., prob. = n.d.) - L.H.Gray AJSL xxxix 76f., Lipiński UF vi 171: the *balim* in Poen 943 = Plur. abs. of *b‘l₂* (highly uncert. interpret., cf. also Sznycer PPP 126) - v.d.Branden BiOr xxxiii 12: pro *b‘l* (= n.d.) in KAI 27[14] l. *b‘lt* (= f. Sing. cstr. of *b‘l₂*) = lady of ... (less prob. reading and interpret.), for the context v. also *›lh₂* - Garbini RSO xliii 16 (n. 1): the *b‘ly* in KAI 78[6f.,7] = Plur. + suff. 3 p.s.m. of *b‘l₂* (= citizen), less prob. interpret., cf. e.g. Röllig KAI a.l., Benz PNP 94, 242: = n.p. - Vanel BMB xx 65: the *b‘l* in BMB xx 62[6] poss. = Sing. abs. used as title (uncert. interpret.; prob. = (part of) n.p.) - for the expression *b‘l mym*, v. *mym* - Greenstein JANES viii 54, 56; the *b‘l* in Sar 6[2] (= part of n.d. or l. *b‘l[h]* = Sing. + suff. 3 p.s.m.) = Ph. (:: Owen Sar p. 104: *b‘l* = variant of *p‘l* (= Qal Pf. 3 p.s.m. of *p‘l₁*)).
v. *›bn₂, bl›rw, bny₁, b‘l₃, hbrk, lk, mb‘l, mlk₅, sbb₁, ‘ly₁, šyt₁*.

b‘l₃ **JAr** Plur. abs. *b‘lyn* MPAT 41[9], 42[12] (both instances in dam. context; cf. also Milik DJD ii p. 113 :: Birnbaum MarDeed 19f., Beyer ATTM 310, 534: = Plur. abs. of *b‘l₂*) - ¶ subst. Plur. marriage.

b ‘lh$_1$ v. *b ‘l$_2$*.

b ‘lh$_2$ **Pun** Sing. abs. *b ‘lt* on coins, cf. Mazard no. 594; cstr. *b ‘lt* on coins, cf. Sef ix 435, 436, Charrier 143, CHC 618 (no. 2-3), 664 (no. 19-21), Mazard no. 589-593, 610 - ¶ subst. community (of citizens); Alvarez Delgado ILC 237: l. *b ‘lt* = Sing. cstr. in KAI 153[5] (less prob. interpret.; for the reading, cf. also Chabot sub RIL 31).

b ‘lh$_3$ v. *b ‘l$_2$*.

b ‘lyn v. *b ‘l$_3$*.

b ‘ltk v. *b ‘l$_2$*.

b ‘nw **OffAr** the *b ‘nw* in RCL ’62, 259 iii 2, word of unknown meaning (or = *b$_2$* + *‘nw* = subst. of unknown meaning?), cf. also Bresciani RCL ’62, 262, Naveh AION xvi 36.

b ‘ ‘ v. *nb ‘*.

b ‘ṣṣ **Pun** Février JA ccxlvi 446: l. poss. *b ‘ṣṣ* (= Sing. abs. < Lat. *basis*) in CIS i 151[6] = pedestal (less prob. interpret., cf. Amadasi sub ICO-Sard Npu 2: pro *b ‘ṣṣ* l. *p/nd/‘ṣṣ* of uncert. interpret.) - cf. *bss*.

b ‘r$_1$ v. *b ‘d$_1$*, *mb ‘r$_1$*.

b ‘r$_2$ v. *‘r$_1$*.

b ‘r$_3$ **Amm** Plur. abs. *b ‘rm* AUSS xiv 145[3] (cf. also Cross AUSS xiv 147; heavily dam. context, cf. also Aufrecht sub CAI 94: or (div. otherwise) l. *b ‘r* (= Sing. abs./cstr.)?, cf. also Teixidor Syr lvi 378) - ¶ subst. ox (beast of burden?).

b ‘rr **Ph** plur abs. *b ‘rrm* KAI 24[14f.] - ¶ subst. prob. designation of the ruling class of Aramean conquerors in Sam ’al; cf. Lidzbarski Eph iii 235f., Alt ZÄS lxxv 18f., Röllig KAI a.l., Gibson SSI iii p. 38 (cf. also Dupont-Sommer Oriens ii 122, Sader EAS 158f. nn. 19, 23, 177f.) :: Joüon RES v 92: = cattle breeders (cf. also Segert GPP 46.3, cf. however Healy CISFP i 665) :: Poeb 38 n. 3: Plur. form *b ‘rrm* = cattle. For the problems involved, cf. also Landsberger Sam ’al 55f., v. *mškb$_2$*.

b ‘t$_1$ v. *bry$_2$*.

b ‘t$_2$ v. *b ‘h*.

bpywn cf. Frah ii 19: pavilion (< Greek < Lat. *papilio*, cf. Nyberg FP 63).

bṣ **Ph** Sing. abs. *bṣ* KAI 24[12f.] - **Pun** Sing. abs. *bwṣ* KAI 76A 6 - ¶ subst. byssus, fine white Egyptian linen - on this word, cf. Hurvitz HThR lx 117ff. - < Egypt.?, cf. Brown Bibl lxx 206; on Greek par. βύσσος (loan from semitic?), cf. Steiner ASSL 66 - on this word, cf. also Masson RPAE 20ff.

bṣy **OffAr** Itp Pf. 3 p.pl.m. *’tbṣyw* Cowl 50[5] - ¶ verb Itp prob. meaning to be sought, to be chosen.

bṣyr$_1$ **OffAr** Yassine & Teixidor BASOR cclxiv a.l.: l. poss. *b[ṣ]yr* (= Sing. cstr.) = vintage in BASOR cclxiv 48 no. 6[1] or l. *ḥmyr*? (= Qal

Part. pass. s.m. abs. of *ḥmr$_2$*)?? = fermented; reading and interpret. of context highly uncert.

bṣyr$_2$ **OffAr** Plur. abs. *bṣyrn* JA ccliv 440[7] (for reading problems, cf. Dupont-Sommer JA ccliv 460f., cf. also Shaked JRAS '69, 119, Kutscher Naveh & Shaked Lesh xxxiv 129) - ¶ adj. small, humble.

bṣl **Hebr** Plur. abs. *bṣlyn* SM 49[4] - ¶ subst. onion - Sing. cstr. *bṣl* poss. in the Ph. text BIFAO xxxviii 3[4] (?, reading and interpret. uncert., cf. Aimé-Giron BIFAO xxxviii 5f.) - on this word, cf. also Borowski AIAI 138.

bṣ'$_1$ **Nab** QAL (or PA'EL?) Pf. 3 p.s.m. *bṣ'* MPAT 64 recto i 5 - ¶ verb poss. meaning: to settle; + obj. (the price of something), cf. also Starcky RB lxi 170.
v. *bṣ'$_4$*.

bṣ'$_2$ v. *mbṣ'*.

bṣ'$_3$ **Pun** Plur. abs. *bṣ'm* KAI 119[6] - ¶ subst. m. uncert. meaning; Levi Della Vida RCL '55, 560: = gain × Février RA l 187: = levy, contribution (cf. also Röllig KAI a.l., vd Branden BO xxxi 226); *bṣ'm n'mm*: friendly contributions ? (cf. also Amadasi IPT 80f.).

bṣ'$_4$ **Pun** Sing. abs. *bṣ'* Karth x 61 (uncert. reading; or = QAL Part. act. s.m. abs. of *bṣ'$_1$*?) - ¶ subst. (v. however supra) prob. indicating function; cf. Février Karth x 63: = usurer, Berger Bull de la Soc. Arch de Sousse '03, 133: = carpenter.

bṣq **Hebr** Sing. abs. *bṣq* TA-H 3[6], Mas 548 (or **JAr**?) - ¶ subst. dough (for the context of TA-H 3[6], v. *'t$_6$*, *ṣrr$_1$*).

bṣr Ebeling Frah a.l.: l. *bṣr* in Frah x 37 = female genitals, vulva (Sem. word), improb. interpret., cf. Nyberg FP 45, 77f.: l. Iran. word.

bṣrh **Amm** Cross FS Horn 480: the *bṣrt* in FS Horn 476[14] poss. = Plur. abs. of *bṣrh* (= enclosure) or = n.l. (for this last interpret., cf. also Hamilton with Aufrecht sub CAI 137).

bq$_1$ v. *bql* - on *bq* = jar, cf. Masson RPAE 78ff.

bq$_2$ **OffAr** Sing. abs. *bq* PF 968[1] - ¶ subst. (?) of unknown meaning.

bq' **Palm** QAL Part. act. s.m. + suff. 3 p.s.m. *bq'h* RIP 107[2] (uncert. reading, cf. Gawlikowski RIP a.l., cf. Al-Hassani & Starcky AAS iii 148f.: l. *bm'h*, without interpret. :: Al-Hassani & Starcky AAS iii 148f.: or l. *nšm'h* (= form of *nšmh*)??) - ¶ verb QAL to search for, to seek (?) (v. however supra).

bqd v. *pqd$_1$*.

bqy v. *sbq*.

bql **OffAr** Sing. emph. *bql'* Sem ii 31 conc. 1 (cf. Milik Bibl xlviii 555, cf. also infra :: Dupont-Sommer Sem ii a.l. (div. otherwise): l. *bq* (= Sing. abs. of *bq$_1$* (= jar)) + *l'$_1$*, cf. also Lipiński UF ii 81); cf. Frah vi 1 (*bkl'*) - ¶ subst. vegetables (cf. Rosenthal AH i/2, 9, Porten JNES xxviii 116, Arch 84, Teixidor Syr xlviii 480 (cf. Arabic) × Milik Bibl xlviii 555: = malt (cf. Akkadian).

bq‘₁ **Mo** Sing. cstr. *bq‘* KAI 181[15] - ¶ subst. (or = verb QAL Inf. cstr.?, cf. e.g. Cooke NSI p. 12, Solá-Solé IS 122, Andersen Or xxxv 106, Degen OLZ ’71, 266, Gibson SSI i p. 80; HAL 143b: QAL Inf. cstr.); *mbq‘ hšḥrt* KAI 181[15]: from break of dawn.

bq‘₂ **Hebr** Sing. abs. *bq‘* Dir pes. 15-18, Mosc pes. 8, 9, BASOR clxxiii 57, HUCA xl/xli 180, Sem xxvi 35f. no. 7-10, 43f. no. 29, IEJ xxviii 212 - ¶ subst. weight, half a shekel, abbrev. *b* on Mosc pes. 10 (for this weight, cf. Barrois ii 253ff., and id. RB xli 69, Dir p. 280, Trinquet SDB v 1242ff., Wambacq VD xxix 342ff., 348, Scott BASOR clxxiii 57f., BiAr xxii 35, PEQ ’65, 136, 138f., I.T.Kaufman BASOR clxxxviii 41, Liver HThR lvi 182 n. 18, Shany PEQ ’67, 54f., EM iv 870ff., Dever HUCA xl/xli 180ff., Ben-David PEQ ’74, 79ff., Lemaire & Vernus Sem xxviii 56).
v. *bt₃*.

bq‘t **OldAr** the *bq‘t* in KAI 222B 10 (Sing. abs.) = valley prob. used as n.l. (cf. e.g. Sacchi RCL ’61, 183f., Noth ZDPV lxxvii 154, Fitzmyer AIS 64, Donner KAI a.l.).

bqr₁ **Nab** PA‘EL Part. act. s.m. emph. *mbqr’* CIS ii 2661[4], 2667[3], 2668[3], 2669[2], IEJ xxix 219[3] (cf. Cantineau Nab i 80, CIS ii sub 2661) - **JAr** PA‘EL Impf. 2 p.pl.m. *tbqrn* MPAT 53[1] (for the reading, cf. Beyer ATTM 351, 535) - ¶ verb PA‘EL to examine: MPAT 53[1]; Part. act. subst. one who examines the victims (i.e. a certain priest; cf. also Negev IEJ xxvii 229 :: Levinson NAI 140: = visitor (on this term, cf. also Teixidor Syr lvi 357f.)): CIS ii 2661[4], 2667[3], etc. - > Akkad. *buqquru*, cf. v.Soden Or xxxvii 270, Dietrich ASS 171 n. 1 - a form of this root prob. also in the Nab. text RB lxxiii 244[2] (cf. Starcky & Strugnell ibid. 246): *]tbqr* (= ITP?).
v. *bkr₁*, *bqr₁*.

bqr₂ **Ph** Sing. abs. *bqr* KAI 24[12] - ¶ subst. cattle.
v. *bqrlḥš*, *smr₁*, *qr₁*.

bqr₃ **Hebr** Sing. abs. *bqr* KAI 194[9] (cf. Cross BASOR cxliv 24 (cf. already Elliger PJB ’38, 49 n. 3, ZDPV lxii 71, Cassuto RSO xvi 175f., May BASOR xcvii 25, Albright BASOR xcvii 26), Röllig KAI a.l., Gibson SSI i p. 42f. :: Gordon BASOR lxvii 31: = PI‘EL Imper. s.m. of *bqr₁* :: Torczyner Lach i p. 82f.: = PI‘EL Pf. 3 p.s.m. of *bqr₁*, cf. however ibid. 82 n. 2; cf. also
Talmon BASOR clxxvi 31) - ¶ subst. morning; for the context, v. also *tsbh*.

bqrh v. *dqrh*.

bqrlḥš **DA** diff. combination in ii 37, cf. Hoftijzer DA p. 253f.; Puech FS Grelot 23 (div. otherwise): l. *bqr* (= Sing. abs. of *bqr₂*) *lḥšl* = *l₅* + *ḥšl* (= QAL Inf. of *ḥšl₂* (= to beat, to pound)).

bqš **Ph** PI‘EL (?, cf. FR 144) Impf. 3 p.s.m. *ybqš* KAI 14^{5} - **Hebr** PI‘EL Pf. 3 p.s.m. *bqš* TA-H 40^{12} (prob. interpret. dam. context; cf. however Dion with Pardee HAHL 65 (div. otherwise): l. *qš[r]* = Sing. abs. of *qšr*$_2$ (= treachery)) - ¶ verb PI‘EL (v. supra) to seek, to look for, to search; + obj.: TA-H 40^{12} (dam. context, v. supra; a document, letter); *ʾl ybqš bn mnm* KAI 14^{5}: may he not search for anything in it (sc. my grave; cf. e.g. Röllig KAI a.l., Ginsberg FS Gaster 144, Gibson SSI iii p. 107, 110 :: e.g. Cooke NSI p. 34: *bn* = *b*$_2$ + suff. 1 p.s./pl.) - a form of this root prob. in MUSJ xlv 262^{2}, cf. Cross IEJ xxix 41ff.: l. *bqšn* = PI‘EL Imper. s.m. + suff. 3 p.s.m. or + emph. ending *-n* (for this division of words, cf. also Garbini AION xxiv 412: l. *bqšn* of diff. interpret., cf. also id. FSR 58f. n. 4) :: Starcky MUSJ xlv 262, 264f. (div. otherwise): l. *ytbqšn* = HITP Impf. 3 p.s.m. + suff. 1 p.s. (= to look for; cf. Röllig NESE ii 4f. (= to revenge), cf. also Schiffmann RSF iv 175; reading of *y* highly uncert., *z* more prob., cf. Cross IEJ xxix 41f.) :: v.d.Branden RSF ii 142 (div. otherwise): l. *-yt bqšn* = PI‘EL Pf. 3 p.s.m. + suff. 1 p.s.; cf. also Teixidor Syr xlix 431.

br$_1$ m. **DA** Sing. cstr. *br* i 2, viiid 2; Plur. cstr. *bny* ii 8 (also xb 3 ??, heavily dam. context) - **Samal** Sing. cstr. *br* KAI 25^{3}, 214^{1,14}, 215^{1,15,19,20}; Plur. cstr. *bny* KAI 214^{10} (cf. e.g. Cooke NSI p. 167, Donner KAI a.l. :: Lagrange ERS 493f., Ronzevalle FS de Vogüé 523 n. 1, Rowley AramOT 48 n. 1, Landsberger Samʾal 64 n. 165, Dion 28, 392, Garr DGSP 140: = QAL Inf. of *bny*$_1$ :: Halévy RS vii 345: = PI‘EL Inf. of *bny*$_1$ (= to bring under cultivation) :: Lipiński BiOr xxxiii 233: = Plur. cstr. (casus obl.) of *lbnh*$_1$?); + suff. 1 p.s. *bny* KAI 214^{15,20}, 215^{5} (Samal. forms in Ph. context: Sing. cstr. *br* KAI 24^{1,4,9}) - **OldAr** Sing. cstr. *br* KAI 201^{2} (dam. context), 202A 4, 216^{2}, 217^{1}, 218, 221^{2} (dam. context), 222A 1, 3, 14, 223C 14, 224^{1,12,15,16,25}, 232 (*]br*; uncert. reading, cf. e.g. Röllig KAI a.l., Gibson SSI ii p. 5 :: Puech RB lxxxviii 546f., 561 (div. otherwise): l. *[q]rb* = PA‘EL Pf. 3 p.s.m. of *qrb*$_1$), BMQ xxxvi 145 n. 43, Tell F 6; + suff. 3 p.s.m. *brh* KAI 222A 25, C 8, 223C 11 (cf. Fitzmyer AIS 92, Donner KAI a.l., Degen AAG p. 19 :: Dupont-Sommer Sf p. 117, 123, 141, Segert ArchOr xxxii 126 n. 111: l. prob. *bnh* = Plur. + suff. 3 p.s.m.), 14, 224^{25}; + suff. 2 p.s.m. *brk* KAI 222B 25 (*br[k]*), 41, 45 (for the reading, cf. Fitzmyer AIS 73), 224$^{1,2f.,11,12,15}$; + suff. 1 p.s. *bry* KAI 222B 25, 27, C 3, 223B 8, 13, 224^{1,3,11,12,15,17} (*br[y]*)^{,26} (*[b]ry*); Plur. cstr. *bny* KAI 222A 2, B 1, 3, 223B 13; + suff. 3 p.s.m. *bnwh* KAI 222A 5, 223B 2bis, 6; + suff. 1 p.s. *bny* KAI 217^{6} (dam. context), 224^{10,21,22} - **OffAr** Sing. abs. *br* Cowl 1^{5}, 5^{8,9}, 6^{12}, Krael 3^{14,15,17}, NESE iii 16^{3} (add. to Cowl 49), WO vi 44A, B, C 2, etc., etc.; cstr. *br* Cowl 1^{9,10}, Krael 1^{2,10}, Driv 3^{1,3}, Herm 1^{14}, 2^{5,18}, Beh 61 (Akkad. par. *apil-šú*), ATNS 6^{6}, etc., etc., cf. Warka 22: *ba-ri*; emph. *brʾ* Aḥiq 2, 80, RES 954^{4} (heavily dam. context; for the prob. interpret., cf. Lipiński Stud 200), FuF xxxv 173^{1,2}, ATNS 11^{2}; + suff. 3 p.s.m. *brh* Cowl 30^{7}, 31^{6}, Aḥiq 1, Driv 2^{2}, Herm 6^{9}, NESE iii 48^{6}, ATNS 8^{5} (or + suff. 3 p.s.f.?, cf. Porten & Yardeni sub TADAE B 5.6), 21^{5} (for this prob. reading, cf. Porten & Yardeni sub TADAE B 8.11 :: Segal ATNS a.l.: l. prob. *byqn* = n.p.), etc.; + suff. 3 p.s.f. *brh* Cowl 28^{13}, Aḥiq 8, Herm 1^{12}; + suff. 2 p.s.m. *brk* Cowl 6^{5}, 68 x rev. 2, Aḥiq 81, Krael 5^{12,14}, ATNS 60^{2} (*brk[* ; heavily dam. context); + suff. 2 p.s.f. *brk* RSO xxxv 22^{1}; + suff. 1 p.s. *bry* Aḥiq 18, 30, 82, Krael 6^{2} (used for female person; *scriptio anterior brt* = lapsus for *brty* (= f. Sing. + suff. 1 p.s.), cf. Szubin & Porten BASOR cclxix 33)^{,3} (for the reading, cf. Porten & Yardeni sub TADAE B 3.7, v. also infra)^{,11} (for this reading, cf. Szubin & Porten BASOR cclxix 39, Porten & Yardeni sub TADAE B 3.7), 8^{5}, Herm 6^{4}, ATNS 166a 2 (heavily dam. context), etc.; the form *bry* (in *bry zy PN*, cf. also *brty zy PN* in l. 1) in KAI 276^{5} functioning as Sing. abs. or emph. (for emph., cf. Altheim & Stiehl FuF xxxv 174, Suppl 83; cf. the *br*ʾ in par. construction in FuF xxxv 173^{1}) differently explained: - a) = Sing. + suff. 1 p.s. (suff. having lost real meaning, but no ideographical use), cf. Altheim & Stiehl Suppl 71f., 83, EW x 249, GH i 265, iv 83ff., ASA 39, 247, 265, AAW ii 217ff., GMA 476f. - b) same explanation, but *bry* used ideographically, cf. Nyberg Eranos xliv 236 (cf. also Henning Ir 38, AM '52, 166, Segert ArchOr xxxviii 225) :: Grelot Sem viii 13f.: = Sing. + suff. 3 p.s.m. (cf. also Kutscher & Naveh Lesh xxxiv 311f. :: Dupont-Sommer Syr xxv 62 n.: = variant form of Sing. emph. (on the subject, cf. also Lipiński LDA 119); cf. also *bry NP* on coin in Hill plate xl 10-12, xli 2 (cf. Henning AM '52, 165f., cf. also ibid. 176^{2}); and *npšy zylh* in KAI 258^{3} (v. *npš*), *bry br[y z]y PN* Nisa-b 1760^{1} and *bry* ʾ*ḥy bry zy* (?) *PN* Nisa-b 1760^{2}); + suff. 2 p.pl.m. *brkm* ATNS 8^{2} (uncert. reading, diff. context, cf. Porten & Yardeni sub TADAE B 5.6); Plur. abs. *bnn* Cowl 15^{32}, 25^{12} (for this reading, cf. Porten & Yardeni sub TADAE B 2.10 :: e.g. Cowl a.l., Porten & Greenfield JEAS p. 26: l. *bny* = m. Pl. + suff. 1 p.s.)^{,17}, Aḥiq 3, 106, Samar 4^{6}; cstr. *bny* KAI 226^{5}, Cowl 20^{3,8,13}, Krael 12^{20}, ATNS 54^{12}, etc.; + suff. 3 p.s.m. *bnwhy* Cowl 40^{1}, Herm 3^{3}, KAI 273^{11} (dam. context; cf. also Drijvers BiOr xxx 467), Samar 1^{4} (= EI xviii 8*), 4^{5} (*bnwh[y]*)^{,7,11}, 6^{4}; + suff. 3 p.s.f. *bnyh* Cowl 15^{34}, 68 viii obv. 2, Herm 7^{3}, ATNS 4^{4} (for this reading, cf. Shaked Or lvi 408, Porten & Yardeni sub TADAE B 8.7 :: Segal ATNS a.l.: l. *bd/ryh* = n.p.), *bnwh* CIS ii 19^{4} (= Del 12; cf. Fales sub AECT 17 for this uncert. reading; on this point, cf. also Kaufman JAOS cix 99); + suff. 2 p.s.m. *bnyk* Cowl 9^{7,9,12}, 29^{4} (for this prob. reading, cf. Porten & Yardeni sub TADAE B 4.5, Porten JNES xlviii 163), Aḥiq 127, Krael 3^{12,16,19}, Samar 1^{6} (=

EI xviii 8*), JNES xlix 291[3], etc.; + suff. 2 p.s.f. *bnyky* Cowl 8[9,11], Krael 4[5], 9[19,20], etc.; + suff. 1 p.s. *bny* Cowl 10[15], 13[8], 14[9], Krael 4[17,18,20], Samar 1[6] (= EI xviii 8*), etc.; + suff. 3 p.pl.m. *bnyhwm* FX 171[4] (for the reading, cf. Dupont-Sommer Sem xxix 101f.), *bnyh[m]* ATNS 54[7] (heavily dam. context); + suff. 2 p.pl.m. *bnykm* Cowl 20[11,13,14], 25[16], *bnyk* (lapsus?) Cowl 25[9]; + suff. 1 p.pl. *bnyn* Cowl 20[10,13], 30[15,26], 31[14], Krael 3[21]; cf. Frah viii 5 (*bl*), ix 9 (*br*), xi 17 (*brh*), xii 7 (*bl*; v. also *nr*$_1$), Paik 224 (in the combination *brbyt*ʾ), 225 (*brbyt*ʾ/*blbyt*ʾ), 226 (*bry*), 227 (*brh*), 228 (in the comb. *bry lbry*), Sogd B 249, Syr xxxv 305[1,2], 321[49-51], 327[60], 329[65], ZDMG xcii 442A 6, B 6 (v. also supra), BSOAS xxiv 354, AM ii 176[2] (*bry*), cf. also Toll ZDMG-Suppl viii 29, GIPP 20, 49 - **Nab** Sing. cstr. *br* CIS ii 158[3,5], 160[2], 163[2], 164[2,4], IEJ xi 135[2] (for the reading, cf. Naveh IEJ xvii 188 :: Negev IEJ xi a.l. (div. otherwise): l. *bn*ʾ (= QAL Pf. 3 p.s.m. of *bny*$_1$)), etc., etc.; + suff. 3 p.s.m. *brh* CIS ii 161B, C, 209[1], 323[3], 476[2] (= ADAJ xxi 139), 509[2], ARNA-Nab 23, etc., etc.; + suff. 3 p.s.f. PEQ '81, 22[5]; + suff. 3 p.pl.m. *brhm* CIS ii 191[4]; Plur. cstr. *bny* CIS ii 157[3], 161 ii 3, 200[1], 212[2], 219[5] (for the reading, cf. J 4 :: CIS ii a.l. (div. otherwise): l. *br* (= *br*$_3$) + *g*..), 222[2], etc., etc.; + suff. 3 p.s.m. *bnwhy* CIS ii 202[3], 354[3], 1150[2], 1182[2] (?), HDS 151[6], ARNA-Nab 16[1], IEJ xxi 50[3], etc., *bnwhw*? RB xliv 269[3], *bnwh* CIS ii 192[3], *bnyhw* CIS ii 536[5], *bnyhy* CIS ii 536[4], *bnyh* CIS ii 545[3], 704[2] (?), 859[3], 969[3], 2674[3] (for the reading, cf. also Teixidor Syr lvi 397 :: Negev IEJ xxvii 224 sub 12[3]: l. *brth* = f. Sing. + suff. 3 p.s.m.), RB xlii 420, 12[2], etc., *bnyw* CIS ii 1185[2]; + suff. 3 p.s.f. *bnyh* CIS ii 212[3,4,5], 216[1]; + suff. 3 p.pl.m. *bnyhm* CIS ii 158[4], 209[2,5], 214[3], PEQ '81, 22[3] - **Palm** Sing. cstr. *br* CIS ii 4048[1,2], 4080[6], 4210[1,2], etc., etc.; + suff. 3 p.s.m. *brh* CIS ii 3931[3], 3957[4], 3990[4], 4000[6], 4023[3], 4259C 2, 4299[5], 4327[5], 4333B 1, 4372A 3, C 2, Inv xi 2[4], xii 26a 2, RIP 24[5], etc.; + suff. 3 p.s.f. *brh* CIS ii 4252B 2, 4268[9], 4373B 2, 4417[2], 4476B 4, 4594B 2, 4605[6], Inv viii 134[5], xi 63[6], RIP 40B 2, 64[4], 71C 2, 104[5], 123[5]; Plur. abs. *bnyn* CIS ii 4214, Ber v 94[6]; cstr. *bny* CIS ii 3922[2], 3923[2], 3924[3], 4112[6], Inv xi 6[7], 70[3], etc., etc., *bn*ʾ CIS ii 4018[3], 4054[3], 4159[5], 4209[3], Ber ii 60 i 2, 76[2], v 94[6], Syr xiv 185[5], xix 156[5], Inv xi 13[6], xii 36[1], RIP 119[5f.], etc., *bnw* (lapsus?) CIS ii 4125, *b*ʾ (lapsus?) CIS ii 4192; + suff. 3 p.s.m. *bnwhy* CIS ii 3902[2], 3922[3], 3993[4], 4028[6], 4119[8], 4122[3] (Greek par. υἱοῖς αὐτοῦ), Inv xi 12[7], 79[5] (prob. reading, cf. Starcky RB lxxiii 616 :: Teixidor Inv xi a.l.: l. *bnwh*), xii 45[6], RIP 24[3,6], Inscr P 36[2] (*b[n]why*, cf. however Milik DFD 233: l. ʾ*ḥwhy* = Plur. + suff. 3 p.s.m. of ʾ*ḥ*$_1$), etc., etc., *bnwhw* CIS ii 4175[8], *bnwh* CIS ii 4012[4], 4035[4] (cf. also Milik DFD 106 :: Teixidor sub Inv xi 15 (div. otherwise): l. *bnwhw*), 4171[3], 4175[9], 4202, 4209[3], Syr xiv 185[6], xix 156[5], Ber ii 95, v 110[7], xix 71[7], Inv xi 4[4] (diff. context), 33[6], xii 36[1], 45[6] (:: Naveh JAOS cii 184 (div. otherwise): l. *bnwhw*), RIP 115[6], 119[5], Sem xxvii

117[6], *bnw* CIS ii 4015[5], 4043[2] (reading *bnw[h]*, cf. Inv xi 18[3], less prob.), *bnyhy* Ber ii 99 i 2, 100 i 2, Inv xi 32[7] (dam. context), 34A 4 (?, l. *bnyh* or *bnyh[y]*?), *bnyh* CIS ii 4051[2], RB xxxix 532[3], Ber ii 99 i 2, 100 i 2 (cf. Ber iii 127), *bnh* CIS ii 4081[4] (cf. Rosenthal Sprache 13), Syr lxii 275 i 3 (Greek par. υἱῶν), *bnwhn* SBS 14[2] (lapsus for *bnwhy*?, cf. also Garbini OA xiv 177, Degen WO viii 132f., cf. however FS Collart 161[7] where the same form is attested); + suff.3 p.s.f. *bnh* CIS ii 4053[3], Ber ii 88[7,8], 103[7], 110[2], 112[9], v 135A 2, *bnyh* CIS ii 3988[3] (= RIP 128), Inv xi 24[3], SBS 11[6], *byh* (lapsus?) Ber ii 103[8], *bnyhw* (lapsus?) Ber ii 112[10]; + suff. 3 p.pl.m. *bnyhwn* CIS ii 3978[9], 3981[5], 3986[4], Ber ii 77[2], v 95[10], Syr xix 160[4], lxii 273[2] (Greek par. υἱωνοὺς), Inv xi 70[3], xii 1[2], 34[5], SBS 19[6], RIP 113[2], 116[6], 153[3], FS Miles 50 i 2, etc., *bnyhn* CIS ii 3911[10], 3996[7], 4163[3], 4206[2], Syr xix 166[3f.], *bnhw[n]* CIS ii 4002[5], *bnwhwn* CIS ii 4056[7]; + suff. 3 p.pl.f. *bnyhn* SBS 10[5] - **Hatra** Sing. cstr. *br* 1[1], 4[4], 5[2,4], etc., etc. (cf. also Assur 4[3], 7[2], 15a 1, etc.); + suff. 3 p.s.m. *brh* 4[6] (for the reading, cf. Caquot Syr xxix 92 :: Safar Sumer vii 174: l. *bdh* (?) = *b*$_2$ + *dh*), 62[2], 101[1], 192[3] (*br[h]*), 195[3], 287[5], app. 5[4] (cf. also Assur 4[7]), *bry* 191[3] (??; cf. Caquot Syr xl 267f., Vattioni IH a.l. :: Safar Sumer xviii 55: l. *brh*); + suff. 3 p.s.f. *brh* 34[4]; Plur. cstr. *bny* 242[2], 280[1], 293[2] (cf. also Assur 3 ii 5), *bn*ʾ 79[5,12], 207[2] (cf. Aggoula Sem xxii 53, Syr lii 195, Vattioni IH a.l. :: Teixidor Sumer xx 78, Syr xliv 188f., Milik DFD 391: = Qal Part. act. m. emph. of *bny*$_1$), 334[1], 409 iii 4 (:: as-Salihi Sumer xlv 103: = Qal part act. s.m. abs. of *bny*$_1$); + suff. 3 p.s.m. *bnyhy* 68[3], 79[11], 80[6,10], 206[2], 223[8], 225[2] (for the reading, cf. Safar Sumer xxi 39, Degen WO v 229, Vattioni IH a.l. :: Milik DFD 167: l. *bnwhy*), 241[2], 245[3], 272[1], 287[7], 335[2] (*bn[y]hy*; for the reading, cf. Degen NESE iii 110), 408[4,6], cf. also Assur 15d 2, *bnyh* 1[2] (cf. Milik DFD 391, Altheim & Stiehl AAW iv 255, Aggoula Ber xviii 86 (cf. however p. 89), Degen ZDMG cxix 174, Vattioni IH a.l. :: Teixidor Sumer xx 78, Syr xliv 189, xlviii 485: l. *bnyh[y]* :: Safar Sumer ix 8*, Caquot Syr xxix 90: l. *bnyh* = Qal Part. act. s.m. emph. of *bny*$_1$, cf. also Donner sub KAI 237, Altheim & Stiehl AAW ii 191f.), app. 4[10]; + suff. 3 p.s.f. *bnyh* 28[5]; + suff. 1 p.s. *bny* 288c 7 (cf. Degen NESE iii 83, Vattioni IH a.l. :: Safar Sumer xxvii 10: l. *bnyhy*); + suff. 3 p.pl.m. *bnyhwn* 34[7], 79[8], *bnyhn* 62[2] - **JAr** Sing. cstr. *br* MPAT 36[1], 38[4], 39[2,3,9,11], Frey 824[2], 1301, 1308b, etc., etc., cf. also SEG xvi 837 (= xx 438), IEJ xxii 231: βαρ (cf. also Vattioni RB lxxx 261ff.); + suff. 3 p.s.m. *brh* MPAT 61[26] (= DBKP 15), 110[3] (= Frey 1299), MPAT-A 7[3] (= Frey 1204 = SM 65), 26[4,6] (= Frey 856 = SM 32), Frey 892[1], Syn 269 no. 2[2] (= SM 90; highly uncert. context, v. *qdš*$_2$; du Mesnil du Buisson Syr xl 309f.: *brh* = Sing. abs. of *brh*$_3$ (= construction), less prob. interpret. :: Torrey sub Syn 269: l. ʿ*bd* = Qal Pf. 3 p.s.m. of ʿ*bd*$_1$), Mas 426[2], *bryh* MPAT 145C 2 (= Frey 1373, cf. however Milik with Zayadine Syr xlvii 131, Beyer ATTM 342: l. *bdnh* = b_2 + *dnh*$_3$), MPAT-A 44^{3} (= Frey 1196 = SM 87), Mas 461, 504; + suff. 3 p.s.f. *brh* MPAT 97A (= Frey 1362), B (= id.), AMB $3^{5,16}$, $15^{11,23}$ (prob. reading); + suff. 1 p.s. *bry* MPAT 62^{12} (= DBKP 27); Plur. abs. *bnyn* AMB 15^{1}; cstr. *bny* MPAT $41^{2,17}$, 91A 1, 2 (= Frey 1352), B 2 (= id.), MPAT-A 11^{4} (= Frey 1165 = SM 43), 13^{1} (= SM 46), Frey 1357a, b, 1360, SM 83, *bnh* Frey 845^{2} (= SM 104), *bry* MPAT 91B 3 (= Frey 1352b :: Beyer ATTM 341: = lapsus for *bny*); + suff. 3 p.s.m. *bnwh* MPAT-A 22^{1} (= SM 70^{9}), *bnwy* MPAT-A 36^{2} (= Frey 987 = SM 30), 48^{1} (= SM 15; cf. e.g. Klein MGWJ lxxvi 554 :: Frey sub 979: l. *bnyw*), SM 85^{1}, Frey 975 (= SM 2; diff. reading :: Fitzmyer & Harrington sub MPAT-A 49: l. *bn[h]w* = Qal Pf. 3 p.s.m. + suff. 3 p.s.m. of *bny*$_1$), *bwny* MPAT-A 56^{2} (lapsus?, or l. with Naveh sub SM 74: *bnwy*?), *bnwyy* SM 81; + suff. 3 p.s.f. *bnyh* AMB 5^{7} (dam. context); + suff. 2 p.s.f. *bnyk* MPAT 42^{13}; + suff. 3 p.pl.m. *bnyhwn* MPAT-A 26^{6} (= Frey 856 = SM 32), 34^{4} (= SM 69), Syn A 14 (= SM 88) - f. **Samal** Plur. cstr. *bnt* KAI 215^{14} - **OldAr** Plur. + suff. 3 p.s.m. *bnth* KAI 222A 24 (for this uncert. reading, cf. Bauer AfO viii 7, Hillers TC 71ff., Kutscher with Greenfield AcOr xxix 12 n. 39, Garbini AION xvii 89f., Degen AAG p. 10 n. 47, Weinfeld DDS 125 n. 5, Gibson SSI ii p. 30, 38, Lemaire Hen iii 165ff., Syr lxii 33, 35 (cf. also Lemaire & Durand IAS 113, 121, 133), Kaufman Maarav iii 170 × Ronzevalle MUSJ xv fasc. 7 pl. 2 l. 5, Epstein Kedem i 38, Driver AfO viii 203f., Dupont-Sommer Sf p. 40, AH i/1, 4, i/2, 3, Donner KAI a.l., Fitzmyer JAOS lxxxi 195, AIS 43, Lipiński Stud 28, Swiggers HTSO 319: l. *bkth* of diff. interpret.: - a) Dupont-Sommer: = Sing. abs. with double f. ending < *bkh* = hen, followed by Donner, Segert ArchOr xxxii 123, cf. also Fitzmyer, Swiggers HTSO 320 - b) Lipiński Stud 28: = Plur. + suff. 3 p.s.m. of *bkh*, cf. also Galling ZDPV lxxxiii 134f. (n. 2) :: Puech RB lxxxix 579ff.: l. *ʾpth* (= Qal Part. act. f. pl. + suff. 3 p.s.m. of *ʾpy*) :: Driver AfO viii 203f.: l. *bkth* = Qal Part. act. pl.f. emph. of *bky*$_1$ (= weeping women)? :: Epstein Kedem i 39: l. *bkth* = Sing. emph. of *bkt* (= weaveress); for the context, v. also *šwṭ*); for the text, cf. also Puech RB lxxxii 615 - **OffAr** Sing. abs. *brh* Cowl 1^{5}, 5^{8}, $6^{12,13}$, Krael $3^{14,15,17}$, etc., etc., *brʾ* Cowl 14^{9}; cstr. *brt* Cowl $1^{1,2}$, 8^{36}, 10^{2}, Krael 3^{2}, $4^{13,17}$, ATNS 54^{8}, etc., etc., *bt* (?, text Aramaic ??) SEL vii 108, cf. CIL iii 14392: *barath* (cf. Milik DFD 417f.: = part of n.p. (?)); emph. *brtʾ* ATNS 88^{1}; + suff. 3 p.s.m. *brth* Cowl 8^{3}, $13^{2,21}$, Krael $9^{2,27}$, $10^{2,21}$, Or lvii 34^{4} (*br[t]h*; heavily dam. context; or + suff. 3 p.s.f.?), 38^{5} (heavily dam. context; or + suff. 3 p.s.f.?), ATNS 5^{2} (dam. context), 28a 3, 4, 30b 3 (dam. context), $54^{13,14}$ (*[b]rth*; dam. context), 61b 1, 2 (dam. context), 109^{1} (dam. context), 180^{1} (*[b]rth*)^{,2} (heavily dam. context); + suff. 3 p.s.f. *brth* Cowl 18^{2} (or + suff. 3 p.s.m.?, cf. Cowl a.l.), 39^{2}

(or + suff. 3 p.s.m.?, dam. context), Krael 5^{11}, Del 15^{2} (*brt[h]*;, for the reading, cf. Fales sub AECT 14; or + suff. 3 p.s.m.?), CIS ii 19a 2 (= Del 12; for the highly uncert. reading, cf. Fales sub AECT 17); + suff. 2 p.s.m. *brtk* Cowl $15^{3,5}$, 48^{3}; + suff. 2 p.s.f. *brtky* Krael $5^{4,6,9,10}$, Herm 8^{13}, *brtk* Krael 5^{7}; + suff. 1 p.s. *brty* Cowl $9^{4,7}$, Krael $6^{8,11}$ (for the reading, cf. Szubin & Porten BASOR cclxix 39, Porten & Yardeni sub TADAE B 3.7)^{,17,19}, etc.; + suff. 1 p.pl. *brtn* Krael 12^{18} (for the *brty* in *brty zy NP* KAI 276^{1}, v. supra); Plur. + suff. 3 p.s.m. *bnth* Herm 8^{9}; + suff. 2 p.s.m. *bntk* Krael 12^{26}; + suff. 2 p.pl.m. *bntkm* Cowl 20^{13}; + suff. 1 p.pl. *bntn* Cowl $20^{10,13}$; cf. Frah xi 18 (*brth*), Syr xxxv $321^{50\text{-}52}$ (cf. also Benveniste Titres 35), GIPP 20, 49, SaSt 15f. - **Nab** Sing. cstr. *brt* CIS ii 161 i 2, 173^{4}, 175^{1}, 198^{1}, 200^{5}, etc., etc.; + suff. 3 p.s.m. *brth* CIS ii 212^{2}, 1076, RES 2045 (?), 2063^{2}, RB xlii 419^{11}, PEQ '81, 22^{5}; + suff. 3 p.s.f. *brth* CIS ii $198^{2,6,10}$; Plur. cstr. *bnt* CIS ii 205^{3}, 207^{4}, 209^{4}, 210^{2}; + suff. 3 p.s.m. *bnth* CIS ii 202^{3}, 209^{7}, J 5^{2}; + suff. 3 p.s.f. *bnth* CIS ii $205^{2,6}$, 211^{2}, $212^{2,5}$, 216^{1}; + suff. 3 p.pl.m. *bnthm* CIS ii 207^{2} - **Palm** Sing. cstr. *brt* CIS ii $4048^{3,4}$, 4080^{3}, 4115bis 3, 4153^{1}, 4247^{2}, RIP 21^{2}, 48, 105^{6} (= Inv xii 17), Inv xi 5^{2}, 23^{3}, xii 5, 6^{1}, SBS 10^{3}, etc., etc., *bt* CIS ii 3901, $3907^{2,3,4}$, 3917^{7}, 4053^{2}, 4080^{7}, SBS 63^{1}, etc., etc., *br* (lapsus) Inv viii 118^{3}; + suff. 3 p.s.m. *brth* CIS ii 4058^{4}, 4259B 2, D 2, 4405B 2, 4537B 2, RIP 1^{4}, 124^{4}, 175, Inv x 119B 1, xii 8, 10, 11, MUSJ xlvi 184, 186A, B, 190, 191, DM ii 39 ii 5, DFD 163^{6}, cf. EDE vii/viii 124 no. 437: βαρτε (for the reading, cf. Milik DFD 139); + suff. 3 p.s.f. *brth* CIS ii 4014^{6}, 4594A 5, Inscr P 2^{3}, RIP 71B 2, Inv xii 12b 2, 13b 1 (*brt[h]*); Plur. cstr. *bnt* SBS 10^{2}, 11^{3}, FS Miles 50 ii 3; Plur. + suff. 3 p.s.m. *bnth* AA iii 1 n. 3, Syr xvii 355^{2}; + suff. 3 p.s.f. *bnth* Inv viii 118^{2} - **Hatra** Sing. cstr. *brt* 5^{1}, $30^{1,4}$, 35^{2}, 36^{2}, 37^{2}, 228^{1} (cf. also Assur 15b 2); emph. *brt*ʾ 341^{3} - **JAr** Sing. cstr. *brt* MPAT 40^{4}, 42^{2} (dam. context), $51^{12,16}$ (*b[r]t*), 62^{11} (= DBKP 27), 63^{1}, 74^{1}, 88^{1}, 94a 1, b 2 (= Frey 1353), 111^{1}, 119^{1}, 134a 1 (= Frey 1245), MPAT-A 3^{1} (= Frey 1199 = SM 60), DJD ii 10A i 1, 3, ii 1, 2, 30^{33}, Frey 1297, BASOR cxxxv 34 no. 7a, c, IEJ xxxvi 39^{2}, etc.; + suff. 3 p.s.m. *brth* MPAT 141^{4} (= Frey 1222, in **Palm** script), MPAT-A 51^{2}, 52^{2}, Frey 896^{2} (?), AMB 2^{1} (diff. reading), etc.; + suff. 3 p.s.f. *brth* MPAT 88^{2} (diff. context, cf. also Naveh IEJ xx 37, Fitzmyer & Harrington MPAT p. 228f.), AMB 4^{16}, $11^{4,9}$, 13^{3} (*[b]rth*); + suff. 1 p.s. *brty* DBKP 18^{68}; Plur. abs. *bnn* MPAT 41^{8} (cf. Milik DJD ii p. 111, Birnbaum MarDeed 20, 24 :: Fitzmyer & Harrington MPAT a.l.: = m. Plur. abs.) - ¶ subst. m. son, f. daughter, passim; *br brh* KAI 223C 14: grandson, cf. KAI $224^{1,12,15,25}$, CIS ii 1256^{2}, $3957^{3f.}$, $4334^{1f.}$, J $157^{1f.}$, IEJ xi 131, RES 955^{2}, Inv xii 23^{1}, Inv D 35 (for ideogram *(l)brylbry*, cf. Bivar Iran xix 81); *br brt*ʾ ATNS 88^{1}: the grandson by a daughter; *bt brth* MUSJ xlvi 190: his granddaughter by his daughter; *bny bnwh* CIS ii 4171^{3}:

his grandchildren, his descendants, cf. KAI 222A 2, 223B 13, CIS ii
4172[3], 4173[2f.], 4174[6], 4175[8f.], 4199[11f.], 4209, Inv xi 70[3] (dam. context),
RB xxxix 532[3] (Greek par. ἐγγόνοις), Inv xii 1[2], 16[4] (= CIS ii 4166),
45[6], RIP 24[3,6], 163B 5, Ber xix 71[7]; *bry yhwh* Krael 8[5]: he will be my
son (adoption formula, cf. Krael a.l., Paul EI xiv 33, Maarav ii 179f.,
Greenfield SVT xxxii 123, cf. also Verger RCL '64, 297; cf. poss. also
Aḥiq 2, cf. prob. also *thwh lh br*ʾ ATNS 11[2]: you will be a son to him
(cf. Segal ATNS a.l., context however dam.); *bry zy l*ʾ *bry* Aḥiq 30:
my son who was (in reality) not my son, i.e. my adoptive son?) - with
more general meaning: child, *bry* Krael 6[3] : my child (said of a woman;
scriptio anterior brt = lapsus for *brty*, cf. Szubin & Porten BASOR
cclxix 33), cf. RB xlii 408[3], PEQ '81, 22[3]; *br dkr wnqbh* Cowl 15[20]: a
male or female child, cf. Krael 7[28f.], CIS ii 4214[1], 4256A, RES 369[6],
Ber ii 60[2], 109[3]; cf. also *mrym ywʿzr šmʿwn bny yḥzq* MPAT 91a 1 (=
Frey 1352): M., Y., S. children of Y.; *bny rbʿ* KAI 226[5]: descendants of
the fourth generation; for ʾ*b*ʾ *dbnyh*, v. ʾ*b₁*, for *bn*ʾ ʾ*m*ʾ, v. ʾ*m₁*, for *br*
bṭny, v. *bṭn₁*, for *br mlk*ʾ, v. *mlk₃*, for *brmryn*, v. *mr*ʾ - special usages:
- a) designation of someone belonging to a family, tribe or another
community; *bny* ʾ*š* DA ii 8: the sons of men (= mankind), cf. KAI
224[16], 276[9f.]; *bny khnbw* Inv xi 83[2]: the members of the K. tribe (cf.
CIS ii 3922[2], 3923[2], Inv xi 84[4] (v. *kmr₂*), 85[1], AAS xxxvi/xxxvii 165
no. 4[3] (cf. also - α) ʾ*mtlt b[r]t .. dy mn bnt myt*ʾ SBS 11[2f.]: A. daughter
of .. who belongs to the women of the M. tribe; cf. also MPAT 91b 3)
- β) *pḥd bny mʿzyn* SBS 11[5]: the tribe of the Maʿzianites, cf. CIS ii
4119[5], SBS 38[3], cf. poss. also RES 53[1]); for *br byt*ʾ and *bny byt*ʾ, v.
byt₂; *bny gš* KAI 222B 3: inhabitants of G.; *br tdmryh* MPAT 53[3]: the
Tadmorean; *bny qrth* SM 83: the inhabitants of the town, cf. also PNO
78[1f.]; *bnt mwq*ʾ *šmš ... wbnt mʿrb* KAI 215[14]: women living in the east
... and women living in the west; *bny mzrḥ* RTP 301: the members of
the *thiase*; *bn*ʾ *plḥt*ʾ Hatra 409 iii 4f.: the servants; *bny šyrt*ʾ CIS ii
3916[2]: the members of a caravan, cf. CIS ii 3928[2], 3933[3], 3948[2], 3963[2],
Inv x 81[4], 124[2], SBS 45[10]; *kl bny ḥbwrth qdyšth* MPAT-A 13[1] (= SM
46): all the members of the holy community; for *br ḥrn*, v. *ḥr₁*; for *br*
nr, v. *nr₁*; for *bn*ʾ ʿ*šrt*ʾ, v. ʿ*šr₅* - b) designation in epistolary style of
a person of lower status: SSI ii 28 obv. 1 (cf. rev. 7), cf. also Hayes &
Hoftijzer VT xx 104 n. 2 (for *br* in Herm., cf. Porten & Greenfield IOS
iv 26ff.) - c) used in formulae indicating the age of a person; *brt šnt*
18 Hatra 30[4f.]: (a woman) 18 years of age, cf. Krael 4[17,18], BAGN ii
88[7], CIS ii 3908[5], Inv viii 168[4] - for *br smy*ʾ, v. *sm*ʾ - the form *bnyt*ʾ
CIS ii 4048[5] prob. = lapsus for *bny byt*ʾ - the *bnyhwn bnyhwn* in FS
Miles 50 ii 8f. prob. lapsus for *lbnyhwn wlbny bnyhwn* - in RTP 211 l.
prob. *bny* (= Plur. cstr.), cf. also Milik DFD 47 :: Caquot RTP a.l. (cf.
also RTP p. 143): l. *gny* = QAL Part. pass. s.m. cstr. of *gn*ʾ = *gny₁*

(= to lie down) - Kaplan EI xix 285: l. *brt* (= f. Sing. cstr.) in Frey 896^{2} (uncert. interpret., cf. also Frey a.l. (div. otherwise): l. *brth* = f. Sing. + suff. 3 p.s.m.) - CIS ii sub 94, Galling ZDPV lxiv 179, Herr sub SANSS-Ar 10: l. *br* (Sing. cstr.) in CIS ii 94 (uncert. reading, cf. Bordreuil & Lemaire Sem xxvi 57 (div. otherwise): l. *[ʿ]bdmlkm* = n.p. × Cross AUSS xi 128 n. 6, Garbini JSS xix 161f. (div. otherwise): l. *[ʿ]bd* (= Sing. cstr. of *ʿbd*$_2$) *mlkm* (= n.d.)) - Puech RB xc 507f.: l. *brh* in MPAT 141^{3} (= Sing. + suff. 3 p.s.m.) - Garbini Hen i 183f., 186: the *bt* in DA ii 13 = f. Sing. cstr. of *br*$_1$ - Lemaire & Durand IAS 117, 127: l. poss. *brk* (= Sing. + suff. 2 p.s.m.) in KAI 223B 13 (less prob. reading) - Segal ATNS a.l.: l. *br*ʾ (= Sing. emph.) in ATNS 9^{7} (improb. interpret.; prob. = part of n.p., cf. Porten & Yardeni sub TADAE 8.6) - on the relation between *br*$_1$ and *bn*$_1$, cf. Testen JNES xliv 143ff.
v. *ʾb*$_1$, *bdr*$_2$, *byn*$_2$, *byt*$_2$, *bny*$_1$, *br*$_3$, *brk*$_1$, *gbr*$_2$, *gdh*$_2$, *dbr*$_3$, *hwy*$_1$, *znh*, *ḥbr*$_2$, *ḥlh*$_1$, *ḥny*, *yrʿ*, *kbr*$_2$, *lbb*$_2$, *lbnh*$_{1,3}$, *lqḥ*, *mrʾ*, *mšlḥ*, *mšb*$_1$, *nyḥ*, *npš*, *smʾ*, *ʿbd*$_2$, *ʿrbn*, *qlbh*.

br$_2$ v. *byr*$_1$.

br$_3$ **OffAr** Sing. cstr. *br* Krael 2^{14}, 3^{21}, 7^{33}; emph. *br*ʾ (cf. Kottsieper SAS 81; :: orig. acc. ending? cf. Leand 47b), Aḥiq 109, Krael 6^{14}, ATNS 50a; cf. Frah xxv 32 (*br*ʾ), Paik 221 (*br*), 222 (*br*ʾ, *bl*ʾ), 574 (in comb. *lbr*ʾ), 767 (id.), BSOAS xxxiii 152, GIPP 20, 49, 56, SaSt 15, cf. also Lemosín AO ii 267 - **Palm** Sing. cstr. *br* CIS ii 3913 ii 111, 119, 4172^{2}; emph. *br*ʾ RIP 127^{4} (for the reading, cf. Milik DFD 257, Gawlikowski RIP a.l. :: Al-Hassani & Starcky AAS vii 111f.: l. *bry*ʾ = Sing. m. emph. of *bry*$_2$) - **Hatra** Sing. abs. *br* 79^{8} - **JAr** Sing. abs. *br* Frey 894^{4} (for this interpret., cf. Kaplan EI xix 285 :: Frey a.l.: = Sing. cstr. of *br*$_1$; heavily dam. context); emph. *br*ʾ AMB 1^{17} (diff. context), DBKP 17^{42} (diff. context; comb. *br*ʾ *mn*) - ¶ subst. what is outside; *]tbyr hnpqh br*ʾ Aḥiq 109: a broken one (i.e vessel) lets it (sc. the contents) go forth outside (cf. Krael 6^{14}); *ktl*ʾ *dy br*ʾ RIP 127^{4}: the outer wall (cf. Gawlikowski RIP a.l. :: Milik DFD 256f.: the wall of the open space (sc. before the well)) - cf. also the following comb. - a) preceded by *l*$_5$, *wnk[s]yhwn dlbr wlgw* Hatra 79$^{8f.}$: their possessions which are outside and inside (i.e. all their possessions); cf. also *dy lbr mn kpt*ʾ CIS ii 4172^{2}: which are outside the vaulted room - b) followed by *mn*$_5$ - α) loc. outside; *mdy yhw*ʾ *mt[*ʾʿ*]l br mn tḥwm*ʾ CIS ii 3913 ii 111: whenever it shall be imported (sc. in Palmyre) from outside (cf. Greek par. ὅταν ἔξωθεν τῶν ὅρων εἰσά[γηται]), cf. also CIS ii 3913 ii 119 (with Greek par. l. 194) - β) with spec. meaning beside, except; *l*ʾ *šlyṭh ... [l]hbʿlh bʿl ʾḥrn br [mn] ʿnny* Krael 7^{33}: she does not have the power ... to marry another man other than A.; *l*ʾ *ʾkl ʾnṣl lplṭy mn tḥt lbbk br mn zy ʾnt ttrk l*ʾ*mh* Krael 2$^{13f.}$: I will not be able to take away P. from under your heart except if you drive out his mother; cf.

Krael 3^{21}, ATNS 52a 9 (*br› mn* in dam. context; uncert. interpret.) - γ) cf. also CIS ii 3915^{3f}, *wprns br mnhwn bkl [ṣ]bw* he supported them in everything, when he was far from them (??), cf. Rosenthal Sprache 85 (or: = instead of them he attented to everything?? or *brmnhwn* = subst. + suff. 3 p.pl.m. or = b_2 + subst. + suff. 3 p.pl.m.??, cf. also Clermont-Ganneau RAO ii 84 (n. 4), Cooke NSI p. 294, Chabot sub CIS ii 3915) - > Akkad. *barru* (= non-cultivated land), cf. v.Soden Or xxxv 7, xlvi 185.
v. *bd›q*, br_1.

br_4 **Hebr** Michaud PA 62 (n. 3): the *brk* in KAI 188^2 = Sing. of br_4 (= corn) + suff. 2 p.s.m., cf. Yeivin with Mosc p. 38 n. 2: or + suff. 2 p.s.f., cf. also Galling ZDPV lxxvii 181f.: = Sing. abs. of br_4 + *k* (abbrev. of ksp_2, $krš_1$ or kp_1), less prob. interpret., cf. e.g. Albright PEQ '36, 212, ANET 321, Lipiński OLP viii 86: = n.p., cf. also Röllig KAI a.l., Gibson SSI i p. 15, Lemaire IH i 246f. :: Birnbaum Sam p. 12f.: = QAL Part. pass. s.m. abs. of brk_1.
v. *›r›l*.

br› **Pun** QAL Part. act. (?) s.m. abs. *br›* CIS i 347^4, CB viii 31^4 - **Hebr** NIPH Pf. 3 p.s.m. *nbrh* SM 76^5 - ¶ verb QAL Part. act. (?) indication of profession: engraver??: CIS i 347^4, CB viii 31^4 (cf. Février CB viii 32), cf. however Tomback p. 55: = diviner? '(cf. Ribichini UF xxi 307f.); on this word, cf. also Bonnet SEL vii 118 - this word also in NP 87^4 (= Punica xiii/1 15)?? (cf. Février CB viii 31f.), Chabot Punica a.l.: l. *ḥd›* or *ḥb›*, poss. lapsus for *ḥn›* (= n.p.), Février Sem vi 17: l. *ḥn›* (= n.p.) - Lipiński Stud 200, 202: the *br›h* in RES 954^3 = QAL Pf. 3 p.s.m. + suff. 3 p.s.m. (= he built it; cf. however Degen WO ix 171), heavily dam. context - NIPH to be created (said of the world): SM 76^5.

brby v. *rbrb*.

brd_1 **OldAr** Sing. abs. *[b]rd* KAI 222A 26f. - ¶ subst. hail.

brd_2 L.H.Gray AJSL xxxix 77, 79: the *barde* in Poen 942 = Sing. + suff. 1 p.s. of brd_2 (= case, right; highly uncert. interpret.).

brh_1 v. br_1.

brh_2 v. *byrh*.

brh_3 v. br_1.

brw v. *›brw*.

brwqh **JAr** Sing. abs. *brwqh* AMB 1^{16} - ¶ subst. prob. meaning: cataract (eye illness; cf. also Naveh & Shaked AMB a.l.).

brzl (derivation unknown; cf. also Ellenbogen 52, Weippert LIS 78 n. 4 (with litt.), HAL s.v., Artzi JNES xxviii 268f.) - **Ph** Sing. abs. *brzl* CIS i 67^{4f} (= Kition B 12) - Sing. abs. *brzl* CIS i 3014^3, 5943^2 (= TPC 5), KAI 100^7 - on this word, cf. also Sawyer MME 129ff. - ¶ subst. iron; *nsk brzl* CIS i 67^{4f}: iron-founder, cf. CIS i 3014^3, 5943^{1f}, KAI 100^7; cf. also *pzrl*.

brzmdn (< Iran., cf. Schaed 260, 264) - **OffAr** Sing. emph. *brzmdn*ʾ RES 1806[1] - ¶ subst. indication of object, receptacle for sacred twigs? (cf. Andreas with Lidzbarski Eph ii 222 n. 1, Grelot DAE p. 334 n. g) or (more generally) building with ritual function, temple?, cf. Andreas (v. supra), Bogoljubov PaSb xv 41ff. (cf. also Hinz AISN 67) :: Schaed 264: priest holding the sacred twig.

brḥ$_1$ **Ph** QAL Impf. 3 p.s.f. *tbrḥ* KAI 1[2]; Imper. s.m. *brḥ* Syr xlviii 403[2] (cf. Caquot Syr xlviii 404, 406, Gasser BASOR ccix 19, 24f., Röllig NESE ii 29, 32, v.d.Branden BiOr xxxiii 13, Garbini OA xx 290, 292, de Moor JEOL xxvii 111 :: Baldacci BiOr xl 129: = Sing. (abs./cstr.?) of *brḥ$_4$* (= evil) :: Lipiński RSF ii 53: = QAL Pf. 3 p.s.m. :: Cross CBQ xxxvi 488f.: = QAL Inf. abs. :: Avishur PIB 267, UF x 32, 35: = QAL Imper. s.f.) - ¶ verb QAL to flee: Syr xlviii 403[2]; *nḥt tbrḥ ʿl gbl* KAI 1[2]: the well-being will flee from G. (cf. e.g. Semkowski Bibl vii 95, Lidzbarski OLZ xxx 455f., Ronzevalle MUSJ xii 26, 36, Vinnikov RA lii 245, Röllig KAI a.l., Avishur PIB 159, Gibson SSI iii p. 16 (cf. also Metzger UF ii 157f.) :: v.d.Branden Mašr liv 732, 734f.: the peace will abandon the heights (*ʿl* = Plur. cstr. of *ʿl$_1$*) of G. :: Bauer OLZ xxviii 132: peace will come on G. :: Vincent RB xxxiv 187: peace will hover over G. :: Lane BASOR cxciv 42: may his resting-place (v. *nḥt$_2$*) flee from Byblos :: Dussaud Syr xi 184 (n. 4; cf. already Syr v 136): the destruction/terror (*tbrḥ* = subst. Sing. abs.) will descend on/fall upon G. (*nḥt* = QAL Pf. 3 p.s.f. of *nwḥ$_1$*)).
v. *rḥ$_1$*.

brḥ$_2$ v. *rḥ$_1$*.

brḥ$_3$ **Palm** Sing. (or QAL Part.?) cstr. *brḥ* (v. however infra) Inv D 39[1] - ¶ subst. m. one who bolts; *brḥ bb[ʾ]* Inv D 39 [1f]: the gate-keeper (litt. the one who bolts the gate); or l. *brḥ[ʾ dy] bb[ʾ]*??

brḥ$_4$ v. *brḥ$_1$*.

brḥ$_5$ cf. Frah vii 8 (*blḥ(n)*): chamois, mountain goat.

bry$_1$ v. *brr*.

bry$_2$ **Palm** Sing. m. emph. *bry*ʾ Ber xii 86[12]; Plur. m. abs. *bryyn* Ber v 124[2] - **Nab** Sing. f. emph. *bryt*ʾ RES 2023[3] - **Hatra** Sing. m. emph. *bry*ʾ 336[9], 343[8]; f. emph. *bryt*ʾ 35[7] (for the reading, cf. Aggoula Ber xviii 92f., MUSJ xlvii 44, Milik DFD 353, 366, Starcky Sem xxii 64f. (n. 2), Vattioni IH a.l. :: Safar Sumer ix 19* (n. 61), Caquot Syr xxx 240f.: l. *bʿyt*ʾ = QAL Part. pass. s.m. emph. of *bʿt$_1$* (= to send; i.e. collector (Safar), delegated (Caquot, cf. also Donner sub KAI 249))) - ¶ adj. 1) exterior; *gwmḥʾ ḥd bry*ʾ Ber ii 86[11f]: one outer niche (i.e. the niche in a tomb which is nearest to the entrance, cf. Ingholt Ber ii 88), cf. Ber v 124[2]; *byrtʾ gwytʾ wbyrtʾ bryt*ʾ RES 2023[2f]: the inner and the outer temple (cf. however Teixidor Syr xlviii 485); *šwrʾ bry*ʾ Hatra 336[10]: the exterior wall: for Hatra 35[7], v. also *dyr* - **2)** foreign: Hatra

343^{8}.
v. *br$_3$*.

bry$_3$ **Hatra** diff. word in 202 no. 10, 12; prob. function indication: exorcizer, diviner? (cf. also Kaufman AIA 41).

bry$_4$ v. *srbyl*.

bry’h **Pun** Sing. abs. *bry’t* NP 2^{4} (= Trip 2)? - ¶ subst. tranquillity, security (??, cf. Levi Della Vida Lib iii 4).

bryh$_1$ **OffAr** Plur. abs. *bryw[t]* IPAA 11^{4}; cstr. *brywt* CRAI ’70, 63^{2bis} - ¶ subst. creature (for the context of both texts, cf. Dupont-Sommer CRAI ’70, 165).

bryh$_2$ **JAr** Sing. cstr. *bryt* BASOR ccxxxv 34 no. 16 - ¶ subst. diminutive form of *br$_1$* f.: little daughter, cf. Hachlili BASOR ccxxxv 53 (highly uncert. interpret.).

brykr v. *bdykr*.

brk$_1$ He QAL Part. pass. sing. m. abs. *brk* KA 4; PI‘EL Pf. 1 p.s. *brkt* KA 7^{1}; + suff. 2 p.s.m. *brktk* KA 8^{4} - **Ph** PI‘EL (or QAL??, cf. Friedrich ZDMG cvii 288, FR p. 67 n. 1, cf. also Rosenthal Or vii 171) Pf. 3 p.s.m. *brk* KAI 26A iii 2, C iii 16; 1 p.s. + suff. 2 p.s.f. *brktk* KAI 50^{2}; Impf. 3 p.s.m. *ybrk* KAI 12^{4} (or = 3 p.pl.m.?, cf. Lidzbarski OLZ ’27, 458, Röllig KAI a.l.), 32^{4} (= Kition A 2), 38^{2} (cf. however Gibson SSI iii p. 132f.: = Impf. 3 p.s.m. + suff. 3 p.s.m.), 39^{3}, 41^{6}, 58, CIS i 25 (= Kition A 12), 94^{5}, RES 930^{2}, 1213^{6}, DD 7$^{4f.}$ (*[y]brk*; = RES 504A), 8^{6} (= RES 504B), 13^{3} (cf. however Gibson SSI iii p. 122: = Impf. 3 p.s.m. + suff. 3 p.s.m. :: Milik DFD 425f. (div. otherwise): l. *-y brk* (= PI‘EL Pf. 3 p.s.m.) or l. *-y <y>brk*), 14^{3}, 15^{4} (*[y]brk*; uncert. reading, cf. Dunand & Duru DD a.l.: or l. *[d]br[y]* = Plur. + suff. 3 p.s.m. of *dbr$_3$*), Kition D 10^{2} (= RES 1517B), F 1^{7} (cf. Amadasi Kition a.l. :: e.g. CIS i sub 88, Cooke NSI p. 73: l. *ybrk[m]* = Impf. 3 p.s.m. + suff. 3 p.pl.m.), Mus li 286^{3}, BMB xviii 106 (cf. however O’Connor RSF v 6, Gibson SSI iii p. 115f.: = Impf. 3 p.s.m. + suff. 3 p.s.m. :: Mullen BASOR ccxvi 25: = PU‘AL Impf. 3 p.s.m.); + suff. 1 p.s. *ybrkn* KAI 18^{8} (cf. Amadasi sub Kition A 30: or + suff. 1 p.pl.?), RES 826A 2 (*[yb]rkn*; heavily dam. context; or + suff. 1 p.pl.?), Kition A 30^{30} (or + suff. 1 p.pl.?); + suff. 3 p.pl.m. *ybrkm* KAI 40^{5} (cf. BMB xii 45^{3}); 3 p.s.f. *tbrk* KAI 10^{8}, RSF vii 18^{2} (heavily dam. context); + suff. 3 p.s.m. *tbrky* KAI 29^{2} (:: Gibson SSI iii p. 72: = PI‘EL Impf. 2 p.s.f. + suff. 3 p.s.f.); 3 p.pl.m. *ybr[k]* Mus lxi 48 leo 8 - **Pun** QAL Pf. 3 p.s.m. + suff. 3 p.s.m. *b‘rk’* CIS i 3135^{3}, Punica xii 10^{4}, xvii 1, RES 303^{2}, Sem xxxvi 30^{4}, *bḥrk’* RES 340^{2}, cf. KAI 175$^{4f.}$: βαραχω (cf. Friedrich ZDMG cvii 288, FR p. 67 n. 1); Part. pass. s.m. abs.? *brk* CIS i 150 (= ICO-Sard Npu 1), RES 304^{1}, 331^{4}, Punica xix 1, CRAI ’16, 128a 1, b 1, Teb. 16^{1}, 18^{1}, 19^{1}, 20^{1}, 24^{1}, 25^{1}, GR i 48^{1,2}, 58^{1}, ii 32 (or = PI‘EL Imper. s.m.?, cf. Rocco AION xxiv 470), ICO-Malta pu 9^{2} (cf. Levi Della Vida RSO xxxix 318

:: Garbini Malta '63, 84: = *brk*$_2$ (= knee > small pillar)), BAr-NS i-ii 228 i 1, *bʿrk* RES 303^{1} (for the reading, cf. RES 305; v. also *ʿpṣ*), Teb. 17^{1}, 21^{1}, 22^{1}, 23^{1}, 26^{1} (*bʿr[k]*), BAr-NS i-ii 226^{1} - PIʿEL (?, or QAL?, v. supra) Pf. 3 p.s.m. + suff. 3 p.s.m. *brkʾ* KAI 106^{4}, 107^{5}, Hofra 15^{2}, 29^{4}, NP 8^{2}, Sem xxxvi 26^{4}, etc., etc., *brkm* Punica iv 5^{2}, KAI 68^{5} (for the reading, cf. Guidi with Chabot sub Punica i :: Lidzbarski Eph iii 281f., Röllig KAI a.l., Dahood Ps iii 75, Silverman JAOS xciv 269, Baldacci VT xxxi 367: l. *brbm* = *b*$_2$ + Plur. m. abs. of *rb*$_2$ :: Lidzbarski Eph iii 283: or = *b*$_2$ + Plur. abs. of *rb*$_3$ (= quarrel, dispute); for the reading *brbm*, cf. also Amadasi sub ICO-Sard 34), *brʾ* (lapsus) Hofra 84^{4}, 179^{3}, *bkʾ* (lapsus?) Hofra 78^{3}, *ʿrkm* (lapsus) Hofra 160^{4}; + suff. 3 p.s.f. *brkʾ* Punica xvii 2^{4}; + suff. 3 p.pl.m. *brkm* KAI 159^{7}, Punica iv 1^{2} (:: FR 187: + suff. 3 p.s.m.), Eph i 44 iii 4 (cf. Sznycer Sem xxxii 60, 65 :: v.d.Branden RSF ix 12, 16: + suff. 3 p.s.m.), Sem xxxvi 28^{3}; 3 p.pl. *brk* CIS i 511^{4}, 580^{3}, 678^{4}, 2787^{4}; + suff. 3 p.s.m. *brkʾ* CIS i 182^{3}, 242^{4}, 4044^{5}, 4051^{5}, etc., etc., *brky* CIS i 4575^{4}, RevAfr. xci 43^{4}, *brkyʾ* KAI 105^{4}, 119^{8} (= Trip 37), Hofra 177^{3}; + suff. 3 p.s.f. *brkʾ* CIS i 3599$^{4f.}$, 4740^{7}, 4746^{6}, *brkm* (or + suff. 3 p.s.m./pl.?), KAI 164^{3}; Impf. 3 p.s.m. *ybrk* GR i 49^{1} (= ii 55; :: Rocco AION xix 413f. (div. otherwise): l. *mqdš* (= Sing. abs. of *mqdš*)), 61a 1 (heavily dam. context); + suff. 3 p.s.m. *ybrkʾ* KAI 63^{3}, 98$^{4f.}$ (or div. otherwise l. *brkʾ* = Pf. 3 p.pl. + suff. 3 p.s.m.), RevAfr. xci 41^{4}, 44^{5}, Antas p. 61^{2} (dam. context), 85a (heavily dam. context), ICO-Sic 10^{3}; + suff. 1 p.s. *ybrkn* GR i 47 (= GR ii 46); + suff. 3 p.pl.m. *ybrkm* KAI 47^{4}; 3 p.s.f. (:: Alt ZAW lx 156ff.: all the *t*-forms in punic votive texts dedicated to Tinnit and Baʿal-Hamm are 3 p.pl.m.) *tbrk* CIS i 2521^{6}, 3797^{3}, 4872^{5}, 5597^{6}, 5688^{7}, 5714$^{5f.}$; + suff. 3 p.s.m. *tbrkʾ* KAI 79^{6}, CIS i 180^{5}, 327$^{5f.}$, 3712^{6}, 3777^{2}, 5507^{4}, 5518^{5}, 5657^{7}, 5709^{4f}, Antas 78b 3, etc., *tprrʾ* (lapsus for *tbrkʾ*?) CIS i 4469^{4} (:: CIS i a.l.: = derivative of *prr*$_2$ (= to let (s.o.) prosper)), *tbrkʾy* CIS i 5194^{5}; + suff. 3 p.s.f. *tbrkʾ* CIS i 4717^{4}, 4771$^{4f.}$; + suff. 1 p.pl. *tbrkn* CIS i 418^{6} (uncert. interpret.; or + suff. 1 p.s., for the context, v. also *ql*$_1$); 2 p.pl.m. + suff. 3 p.s.m. *tbrkʾ* Hofra 172^{3}, *tbrkyʾ* Hofra 21^{3}; 3 p.pl. *ybrk* CIS i 2642^{4}, 2723$^{4f.}$, 3822^{6}, cf. Poen 931: *ibarui* (lapsus for *ibarcu*, cf. Sznycer PPP 59 :: J.J.Glück & Maurach Semitics ii 104 (div. otherwise): l. *thibarui* = PIʿEL Impf. 2 p.pl.m. of *brk*$_1$); + suff. 3 p.s.m. *ybrkʾ* CIS i 181^{5}, 195^{5}, 271^{5}, 3937^{5}, 3941^{4}, 5917^{5}, etc., etc., *ybrky* KAI 78^{1}, CIS i 3737^{8}, 4945^{4}, 4949^{6}, 5226^{3}, *ybrkyʾ* CIS i 3604^{6}, 3709^{7}, 4503^{5}, *ybrkʿʾ* CIS i 277^{4} (dam. context), *ybrkm* (or + suff. 3 p.pl.m.?) CIS i 197^{6}, *yrk[ʾ]* (lapsus?) CIS i 3522^{4}; + suff. 3 p.s.f. *ybrkʾ* KAI 88^{6}, CIS i 1885^{6}, 4628^{4}, RSF iii 51 ii 4, *ybrky* CIS i 4620^{4}, *ybrkyʾ* CIS i 4665^{8}, 4742^{5}; + suff. 3 p.pl.m. *ybrkm* CIS i 5702^{6}; Imper. s.m. + suff. 3 p.s.m. *brkʾ* Hofra 2^{3}, 3^{3}, 4^{4}, 5^{2}, etc., *bʿrkʾ* Hofra 161$^{3f.}$; + suff. 3 p.s.f. *brkʾ* Hofra 67^{4}, 162^{4}; s.f. *brk* CIS i 3962^{4}; pl.m. *brk* CIS i 3962[4]; + suff. 3 p.s.m. *brk›* Hofra 80[3], 231[3], *brky* CIS i 5716[6f.]; Inf. abs. *brk* (for the reading, cf. Berthier & Charlier Hofra a.l.) Hofra 172[3] (for the interpret., cf. Février Hofra a.l.) - **Amm** QAL Part. pass. s.m. abs. *brk* SANSS-Amm 9 (= Vat sig.eb. 225 = CSOI-Amm 76 = ALIA no. 36 = CAI 55 :: Bordreuil sub CSOI-Amm 76: = QAL Part. act., cf. however Puech RB xcvi 591), 45 (= Vat sig.eb. 229 = CAI 57), 46 (= CAI 61; 45 & 46 prob. forgeries, cf. Naveh & Tadmor AION xviii 448ff., Herr SANSS a.l., cf. however Garbini AION xviii 453f., xx 252 (= LS 101), cf. also Bordreuil Syr l. 183); PI‹EL (?, or QAL; v. supra) Impf. 3 p.s.f. (or 2 p.s.f.?) + suff. 3 p.s.m. *tbrkh* SANSS-Amm 36 (= CSOI-Amm 80 = ALIA no. 49 = CAI 56; cf. also Bordreuil & Lemaire Sem xxix 80f.) - **Edom** HIPH Pf. 1 p.s. + suff. 2 p.s.m. *hbrktk* TeAv xii 97[2] (cf. Beit-Arieh & Cresson TeAv xii 98, Misgav IEJ xl 215) - **Hebr** QAL Part. pass. s.m. abs. *brk* IEJ xxv 229[4,6,7], HUCA xl/xli 159[2] (cf. e.g. Dever HUCA a.l., Lemaire RB lxxxiv 599, 601, Hadley VT xxxvii 54, 61 :: Zevit BASOR cclv 41, 43f.: l. *brkt* (= PI‹EL Pf. 1 p.s.) :: O'Connor VT xxxvii 224f., 228f.: l. *brkt* (= PI‹EL Pf. 2 p.s.m.); *brkt* less prob. reading, cf. also Conrad TUAT ii 557), J ii 642 no. 2 (or = PI‹EL Imper. s.m.?), *brwk* AMB 3[18], 15[23]; PI‹EL (or QAL?; v. supra) Pf. 1 p.s. + suff. 2 p.s.m. *brktk* TA-H 16[2f.] (for the reading, cf. Pardee UF x 311, HAHL 49), 21[2], 40[3] (for the reading, cf. Pardee UF x 324) - **OffAr** QAL Part. pass. s.m. abs. *bryk* KAI 267[1], RES 1367[1], 1368, 1372B 1, 2, 1376, ASAE xxxix 352[2], 353[2], 356[1], *brk* RES 608, 960, 961, 962, SSI ii 28 obv. 2, etc.; pl.m. abs. *brykyn* Sumer xx 18,8[4]; s.f. abs. *brykh* KAI 269[1,3], *brkh* RES 1788, *brk›* CIS ii 135; PA‹EL (:: Swiggers AION xli 145: in the Herm. instances = QAL) Pf. 1 p.s. + suff. 2 p.s.m. *brktk* RHR cxxx 20[3], Herm 3[1]; + suff. 2 p.s.f. *brktky* Herm 1[2], 2[2], 4[2], 6[1], 8[1]; 1 p.pl. + suff. 2 p.pl.f. *brknkn* Herm 5[1f.] - **Nab** QAL Part. pass. s.m. abs. *bryk* CIS ii 491[2], 590, 861, 868[1], 875[1], 878, etc., etc., *brk* (prob. reading) BSOAS xv 13 no. 31c; s.f. abs. *brykh* CIS ii 874, 877; ITP Part. s.f. abs. *mtbrkh* (reading cert.?), RES 529[2] - **Palm** QAL Part. pass. s.m. abs. *bryk* CIS ii 3999[1], 4000[1], 4001[1], 4002[1], 4007[1], 4008[1], etc., etc., *brk* CIS ii 4024[1], 4046[1], *bryl* (lapsus) CIS ii 4040[1], 4083[1] (cf. Rosenthal Sprache 13), *brlky* (lapsus for *lbryk*) Inv xi 22[1]; pl.m. abs. *brykyn* InscrP 31[2], Inv xi 77[1], SBS 61B 2, Syr vii 129[6], xl 33[1], PNO 18c, Inv D 25[1], RTP 244 (or l. *bryky›* = Plur. emph.?; identical text in SBS-Tess 4); s.f. emph. *brykt›* CIS ii 3976[1]; PA‹EL Impf. 3 p.s.m. *ybrk* RTP 92, 108, 109, 110, 134, 304, 305; 3 p.s.f. *tbrk* RTP 722 (after *k* a sign; du Mesnil du Buisson TMP 216: l. *tbrk›* = Plur. cstr. of *tbrk* (= blessing)); 2 p.pl.f. *tbrkn* RTP 242; Inf. *mbrkw* RIP 136[2] (cf. Gawlikowski RIP a.l. :: Milik DFD 230: l. *mbrkw[t]* :: Strelcyn FP iii p. 244: = PA‹EL Part. s.m. + suff. 3 p.s.m.?; for the context, cf. also Aggoula Syr liv 283) - **Hatra** QAL Part. pass. s.m. abs. *bryk* 23[1], 25[1],

77[1], 81[1], 146[1,2], 225[2], 296 (cf. also Assur 12[2], 14[2], 27d 1, i 2); cstr. *bryk* 21[2]; pl.m. abs. *brykyn*, cf. Assur 28a 2 - **JAr** QAL Part. pass. pl.m. abs. *brykyn* MPAT-A 32[1] (for the reading, cf. Naveh sub SM 39, Beyer ATTM 386 :: Avi-Yonah QDAP iii 129: l. *brwkh* (= Hebr. QAL Part. pass. s.f. abs., cf. also Frey sub 885, Fitzmyer & Harrington MPAT a.l., Hüttenmeister ASI 183f.) - ¶ verb QAL, PI‹EL, PA‹EL to bless - **1)** + obj. (men), *ybrk šdrp› ›t ḥnb‹l* GR i 49[1f.] (= GR ii 55): may Sh. bless Ḥ; cf. passim - **2)** + obj. + acc. instrum., *wbrk b‹l ... ›yt ›ztwd ḥym wšlm ...* KAI 26A iii 2f.: and Ba‹al ... blessed A. with life and well-being ... (:: Dahood Bibl xlix 364 n. 2, Driver PICS 52 (n. 10): may Ba‹al bless ...; on this text, cf. Greenfield FS Albright ii 265, Amadasi Guzzo VO iii 93) - **3)** + obj. + b_2, *wbrk b‹l .. ›yt ›ztwd bḥym wbšlm ...* KAI 26C iii 16ff.: and Ba‹al ... blessed A. with life and well-being ... - **4)** + obj. + l_5 (+ n.d.), *brkt ›tkm lYHWH* KA 7[1f.]: I mention you in blessing formulae in (the name of) the Lord (cf. KA 8[4f.]); *brktk lb‹lṣpn ...* KAI 50[2f.]: I mention you in blessing formulae in (the name of) B.-S.; *brktk lYHWH* TA-H 16[2f.]: I mention you in blessing formulae in (the name of) the Lord (cf. also RHR cxxx 20[3], TA-H 21[3f.]; cf. S.Smith PEQ '49, 57, Fitzmyer JBL xciii 215, Pardee JBL xcvii 338, HAHL 49, Dion RB lxxxvi 558ff.); *brktky lptḥ zy yḥzny ›pyk bšlm* Herm 1[2]: I mention you in blessing formulae in (the name of) Ptah, that he may show me your face in peace (cf. also Herm 2[3], 3[1f.], 4[2], 5[1f.], 6[1f.]; cf. Alexander JSS xxiii 159, Fitzmyer JBL xciii 215, WA 192f., Weippert VT xxv 208ff., Dion RB lxxxvi 562ff., Fales JAOS cvii 459f.); v. also infra sub Part. pass. (cf. also Kutscher IOS i 111f.) - **5)** + l_5 (obj.): RTP 92, 108, 134, 242, 722 - **6)** Part. pass. QAL: blessed, passim; cf. e.g. *bryk hw ›b› wbnyhy* Hatra 225[2]: blessed be he, A. and his sons; *qynw bryk* CIS ii 1696: may Q. be blessed; etc.; *bryk NP ... bṭb* Qedem vi 13 no. 12: blessed be NP ... in good memory; *bryk NP ... bṭb wšlm* CIS ii 1150: blessed be NP ... in good memory and peace (v. also sub *zkr*$_1$); *bym n‹m wbrk* RES 304[1]: on a propitious and blessed (i.e. favorable) day, cf. Punica xix 1, Teb. 16[1], 17[1], 18[1], etc. (v. also *ywm*); *bryk ›lh›* Hatra 21[2]: blessed by the gods (v. also *›lh*$_1$); *bryk šmh l‹lm›* CIS ii 3999[1]: the one whose name is blessed in eternity (epithet of the so-called anonymous god in Palmyra); for a survey, cf. Díez Merino LA xxi 103f., Vattioni Aug xii 503ff., cf. also Teixidor PP 115ff.), cf. CIS ii 4000[1f.], 4001[1], etc., etc. (in RIP 114[2] this epithet without *l‹lm›*, lapsus?); *brwk ›th ›dwnnw* AMB 3[18]: blessed are You, our Lord - a) + l_5 (+ n.d.; cf. Lipiński Chron d'Egypt. l. 96ff.), *brk lmlkm* SANSS-Amm 9: blessed in the name of Milkom, i.e. blessed by Milkom, cf. also KA 4, CIS ii 135, 4091[2], RES 960, 961, 962, 1366, 1788, GR i 58[1] (dam. context), ii 49[2] (= GR i 48), cf. also Meshel IEJ xxvii 53 (*brk h› l ..*); cf. HUCA xl/xli 159[2]) - b) + *qdm*$_3$, *bryk ›bh ... qdm ›wsry ›lh›* KAI 267[1f.]: blessed be A. before (i.e.

by) the god Osiris (for this text, cf. also Lévy JA ccxi 285, 291ff.), cf. also RES 1364, 1368, Hatra 23^1, 25^1, etc.- HIPH to bless: + obj. + *l*$_5$, *hbrktk lqws* TA xii 97^{2f}: I Bless you by Q. - a form of this root in Nisa-b 54^6 *]wybrk[* (??, heavily dam. context) - Dupont-Sommer JKF i 203, 206: l. *brk* (= PA ʿEL Imper. s.m.) in AMB 7a 8 and *br[k]* (= idem) in AMB 7b 4 (cf. Scholem JGM 86: l. *brk* = QAL Part. pass. s.m. abs. of *brk*$_1$; improb. reading, cf. Naveh & Shaked AMB a.l. (div. otherwise): l. in both instances *br* (= Sing. cstr. of *br*$_1$)) - forms of this root also in KA 11^1, 12^3 (dam. context).
v. *br*$_4$, *brkh*, *hbrk*, *pgr*$_2$.

brk$_2$ Ebeling Frah a.l.: the *bzʾnrk* in Frah x 40: poss. = contamination of Iran. word and *brk*$_2$ (= knee); improb. interpret., cf. Nyberg FP 45, 78: l. *bzʾnwk* = *b*$_2$ + Iran. word.
v. *brk*$_1$.

brkh$_1$ **Pun** Sing. (or Plur.) abs. (?) *brkt* KAI 147^3 - **Hebr** Sing. abs. *brkh* Frey 625, 629^2, 635, 661^4, 892^3, IEJ vii 244^3, SM 1 (= Frey 974) - **OffAr** Sing. abs. *brk[h]* JRAS '29, 108 conc. 1 - **JAr** Sing. abs. *brkh* EI xii 146a 1 (or = Hebr.?); emph. *brktʾ* AMB 12^5 (heavily dam. context), *brkth* MPAT-A 13^3 (= SM 46), 15^3 (= Frey 982 = SM 18), 19^2 (*brkt[h]*, heavily dam. context; = SM 9), 20^3 (= SM 10), 25^4 (= Frey 976 = SM 12), 29^5 (= Frey 859 = SM 35), 30^3 (= SM 26), 36^4 (= Frey 987A = SM 30), 37^3 (*brkt[h]*; = Frey 987B = SM 31; heavily dam. context), Syn D A 12 (= Frey 828b = SM 88), IEJ xxxii 8^4 (*[b]rkth*, heavily dam. context); + suff. 3 p.s.m. (or emph.??) *brkth* MPAT-A 26^9 (= Frey 856 = SM 32), $27^{3,4}$ (= Frey 857 = SM 33), $28^{2,3}$ (= Frey 858 = SM 34) - ¶ subst. blessing; *zkr ṣdyq lbrkh* Frey 635: the memory of the just is a blessing (cf. Frey 625, 629^2, $661^{3f.}$, $892^{2f.}$, IEJ vii $244^{2f.}$); *thy lh brkth* MPAT-A $20^{2f.}$: may a blessing be upon him (cf. MPAT-A 13^3, 15^3, $25^{3f.}$, $29^{4f.}$, 30^3, 36^4); *mlk ʿlmh ytn brkth bʿmlhwn* MPAT-A $26^{9f.}$: may the King of the Universe give His blessing on their undertakings (cf. MPAT-A $27^{2f.,4}$, $28^{2,3}$); *brk[h] šlḥt lky* JRAS '29, 108 conc. 1f.: a blessing I send to you - poss. Sing. abs. also in TA-H 28^1 (*b[r]kh*)^{,7} (or = form of *brk*$_1$ + suff. 3 p.s.m./f., cf. v.Dyke Parunak BASOR ccxxx 26; heavily dam. contexts).
v. *ʿpṣ*.

brkh$_2$ **Hebr** Sing. abs. *brkh* KAI 189^5 - ¶ subst. pool.

brm$_1$ **Hatra** QAL Pf. 3 p.s.m. *brm* 408^7 (:: as-Salihi Sumer xlv 102 (n. 31): l. *bdm* = QAL Pf. 3 p.s.m. of *bdm* (= to repair)) - ¶ Verb QAL to redress: Hatra 408^7.

brm$_2$ **OffAr** cf. Paik 223: but, however (*brʾm*).

brn cf. Frah vii 8 (*blln*): wild (cf. Nyberg FP 70).

brprwn JA Dupont-Sommer JKF i 207: the *brprwn* in AMB 7^{10} poss. = Sing. abs. of *brprwn* (< Greek πόρφυρον), improb. interpret., cf.

Scholem JGM 86, Naveh & Shaked AMB a.l.: = part of magical name.

brq **OffAr** Sing. abs. *brq* Aḥiq 101 - ¶ subst. lightning.
v. *plg*$_8$.

brr **Nab** PAʿEL Imper. s.m. *brr* IEJ xxix $112^{3,9}$ (cf. Naveh IEJ xxix 113, 117; interpret. of context in both instances however highly uncert.) - **Palm** APH Pf. 3 p.s.m. + suff. 3 p.s.m. *ʾbrh* SBS 60^5 (cf. Garbini OA xiv 177f. :: Gawlikowski TP 18: = APH Pf. 3 p.s.m. + suff. 3 p.s.m. of *brʾ/bry*$_1$ (= to remove, to purify; cf. also Dunant SBS a.l.) :: Drijvers JAOS cii 538f.: l. *ʾbd* = PAʿEL Pf. 3 p.s.m. of *ʾbd*$_1$ (= to do away with)); OPH Pf. 3 p.s.m. *ʾbr* SBS 60^3 (cf. Garbini OA xiv 177f., cf. also Teixidor Syr liii 336 :: Gawlikowski TP 18 (div. otherwise): l. *ʾbrw* = lapsus for *ʾbry* (= APH Pf. 3 p.s.m. of *brʾ/bry*$_1$; cf. also Dunant SBS a.l.) :: Drijvers JAOS cii 538f.: l. *ʾbdh* = PAʿEL Pf. 3 p.s.m. + suff. 3 p.s.m. of *ʾbd*$_1$ (= to do away with)); cf. for both texts, Degen WO viii 132 - ¶ verb PAʿEL to make clear, to explain: IEJ xxix $112^{3,9}$ (v. however supra) - APH to purify + obj. (grave, tomb); *ptḥh wʾbrh* SBS 60^5: he opened it and purified it - OPH to be purified (subj. grave, tomb): SBS 60^3 - on this root, cf. also Collini SEL iv 21, 35.

brš$_1$ **Pun** Sing. abs. *brš* CIS i 348^3 - ¶ subst. of unknown meaning, title or function indication: stone-cutter, stone-mason?? (cf. e.g. CIS i a.l., Huss 481 (cf. however Heltzer UF xix 434)), cf. however Tomback CSL 57: = candlestick maker?, cf. also Slouschz TPI p. 312 (on this word, cf. also Bonnet SEL vii 117f.) - related to *brš*$_2$?

brš$_2$ **Hatra** the diff. *334ʾ* (or l. *bdšʾ*?) in 188^1 prob. = Sing. emph. of adj./subst. denoting prob. either surname or title/function; Aggoula MUSJ xlvii 41: *brš*$_2$ = many-coloured; Safar Sumer xviii 53 (n. 49): l. *bdšʾ* *bdš* poss. = variant of *bṯḥš*; Caquot Syr xli 267: *bdšʾ* poss. = shortened form of *rb dḥšʾ* (= Plur. emph. of *dḥš*) :: Vattioni IH a.l.: l. *[w]ʿbsʾ* = *w* + n.p.
v. *brš*$_1$.

brt v. *ʾḥ*$_1$.

bš v. *bʾš*$_2$.

bšym v. *bšm*$_3$.

bšl **OffAr** QAL Impf. 1 p.s. *ʾbšl* Sach 80 vi b 2 (heavily dam. context); cf. Frah xix 10 - ¶ verb to cook.

bšm$_1$ **Pun** Sing. abs. *bšm* KAI 138^4 (cf. Dussaud BAr ’14, 620, Février Sem ii 27, Röllig KAI a.l. (cf. also Sznycer Sem xxx 39, 41) × Lidzbarski Eph iii 289: = *b*$_2$ + Sing. cstr. of *šm*$_1$) - ¶ subst. perfume, spices (in KAI 138 for cultic use) - on this word, cf. also Masson RPAE 77f., Nielsen SVT xxxviii 67.

v. *bšm$_3$*, *mšḥ$_3$*.

bšm$_2$ **JAr** Yadin & Naveh Mas a.l.: the *bšm[ʾ]* in Mas 471 = Sing. emph. of *bšm$_2$* (= druggist?; uncert. interpret.).

bšm$_3$ **OffAr** Sing. m. abs. *bšm* Krael 2^5, Herm 2^{12}, 3^{11} (in all these instances poss. = Sing. abs. of *bšm$_1$*, v. also *mšḥ$_3$*) - **Palm** Sing. m. emph. *bšymʾ* CIS ii 3913 ii 13, 17, 47 - ¶ adj. perfumed (said of oil, v. *mšḥ$_3$*) - a derivative of the same root also in Krael 7^{20}, cf. Krael p. 214: l. *m[b]šym*?? (for this reading, cf. also Porten & Yardeni sub TADAE B 3.8) or *bšym*?? - cf. *bsʾmyn*, *bsym*.

bšr$_1$ v. *bšr$_2$*.

bšr$_2$ **Pun** Sing. abs. *bšr* CIS i 302^5, 304^6, 305^5, 306^5, 2678^6, etc., *bšʾr* CIS i 301^6, 4894^2, *bšʿr* CIS i 299^5, 300^5; + suff. 3 p.s.m. *bšry* KAI 79$^{5f.}$, CIS i 4929^3, 5111^5, *bšʾry* CIS i 296^2 (or + suff. 3 p.s.f.?), *bšrm* KAI 104^2, 106^2, 107^4, CIS i 297^5, 2441$^{4f.}$, 3737^8, 3745^4, 3746^6, Punica xviii/ii 37 (for the reading, cf. Bertrandy & Sznycer sub SPC 104), etc., etc., *bšʾrm* KAI 162^2, CIS i 3731$^{8f.}$, 4872^4, *bšʿrm* KAI 105^3, CIS i 294^4, Hofra 29$^{1f.}$, 33^1, etc., *bšrʾm* KAI 108^3, Hofra 50^2 (?, poss. reading), *bšrʿm* RES 335^3 (:: RES a.l.: l. *bšʿrm*; cf. CIS i/1 p. 365, Chabot sub Punica xviii/ii 100), *bšrn* Hofra 37^3; + suff. 3 p.s.f. *bšryʾ* CIS i 3822^5; diff. form *[b]šʿrʾt* CIS i 3886^2, reading *[b]šʿrʾm* preferable? (+ suff. 3 p.s.m.), cf. Hoftijzer VT viii 292 n. - **Hebr** (or **JAr**?) Sing. abs. *bšr* Mas 547 - **OffAr** Sing. abs. *bšr* Aḥiq 104; + suff. 3 p.s.m. *bšrh* Aḥiq 89; cf. Frah x 2 (*bsl(y)ʾ*, cf. Lemosín AO ii 266), GIPP 20, SaSt 16 - **Palm** Sing. abs. *[b]šr* Syr xvii 353^1 - ¶ subst. flesh, meat; in the punic texts: child, offspring, cf. Hoftijzer VT viii 291f., Röllig sub KAI 79, de Vaux SAT 71 :: Février RHR cxliii 15, JA ccxliii 54, 56: *bšrm* (and variants) = *b$_2$* + Sing. + suff. 3 p.s.m./f. of *šr* (= *šʾr$_3$*) = in exchange of his/her child (cf. also Garbini GLECS xi 144, v.d.Branden BO xv 202f., xxiii 47 (n. 75), RSF ix 14) :: CIS i sub 3822: *bšrm* (and variants) = derivative of root *bšr$_1$* (= to be glad, to rejoice)) // Lat. *libens animo*, *laetus merito* (cf. also Lipiński RTAT 252 (n. 38): *bšrm* = QAL Part. (or adj.) pl.m. abs. of *bšr$_1$*, id. RAI xvii 32 (n. 7): *mqm ʾlm bšʾrm* CIS i 4872^4: the reviver of the blessed god (improb. interpret., v. *qwm$_1$*)) :: CIS i sub 294: = *b$_2$* + n.l., cf. Kornfeld WZKM li 292f., Charlier Karthago iv 25ff., 30ff., 45f., v. also *mlk$_5$*, *tm$_{1,2}$* (on the subject, cf. also Eissfeldt Molk 19ff., Sznycer GLECS xi 146) - this word (Sing. abs./cstr.) poss. also in ATNS 52a 11 (= meat; interpret. of context diff.), also to be restored in ATNS 52a 10 (*bš[r]*)? Segal ATNS a.l.: or (div. otherwise) restore in l. 10 *lbš[n]* (= Plur. abs. of *lbš$_2$*)?? v. *swr$_3$*.

bšr$_3$ v. *bšrwn*.

bšrwn **Hebr** Sing. abs. *bšrwn* DJD ii 42^6 (for the reading, cf. I.Rabinowitz BASOR cxxxi 23, Birnbaum PEQ '55, 32 :: de Vaux RB lx 270,

272: l. *bšryn* = Plur. abs. of *bšr$_3$* (= good tiding) :: Feuchtwanger with Lehmann & Stern VT iii 394: l. *kšryn* = n.l. (< Lat. *castra*)) - ¶ subst. disdain, contempt.

bt$_1$ v. *byt$_2$*, v. also *›rš$_1$*.

bt$_2$ v. *bn$_1$*, *br$_1$*, *zbnwt*, *kt›*, *šb‹h$_1$*, *tm$_{1,3}$*.

bt$_3$ **Ph** Sing. abs. *bt* EI ix 86 (= RSF vii 7 no. 10) - **Hebr** Sing. abs. *bt* Dir pes. 25, Mosc var. 2 - ¶ subst. *bat*, liquid measure; for the discussion on its volume, cf. e.g. Dir p. 290, Inge PEQ '41, 106ff., Albright AASOR xxi/xxii 58f. n. 7, Barrois ii 248ff., Trinquet SDB v 1223ff., Milik Bibl xl 988ff., de Vaux IAT i 304, Scott BiAr xxii 29ff., Yeivin Lesh xxxi 243ff., PEQ '69, 63ff. (cf. also id. EI ix 86f.), EM iv 853, Schmitt BRL 205, Welten Stempel 131ff., Pardee UF x 302 n. 57; abbrev. *b* in TA-H 1^3, 2^2, 3^2, 4^3 (cf. Aharoni a.l., cf. also Pardee UF x 303, HAHL 31), 5^{12} (dam. context), 7^5, 8^5, 9^3 (dam. context), 10^2 (cf. Aharoni a.l., cf. also Pardee UF x 308), 11^3 (dam. context), 61^2 (heavily dam. context), 79 (heavily dam. context), BS i 71^2, BASOR cclxiv 46^2; on the abbrev. stroke following *b*, cf. Pardee UF x 293f. - Lipiński OLP viii 91: abbrev. *b* also in TA-H 20^1 (highly uncert. interpret., cf. on this text also Aharoni a.l., Lemaire VT xxiii 243f.) - Lemaire & Vernus FS Brunner 308: the *b* in FS Brunner 303 i 2 prob. = abbrev. of *bt$_3$*, or = abbrev. of *bq‹$_2$* (interpret. of context highly uncert.), the same abbrev. in FS Brunner 323 iii 9.

v. *‹b$_2$*, *tš‹y*.

bt› **Palm** *bt›* Ber ii 98^1, 100 i 2 (reading *bn›* in both texts incorrect, cf. Cantineau with Ingholt Ber iii 127) - ¶ prep. prob. meaning between (loc.) - l. this word also in Ber ii 97^1 instead of *bn›*?

btk **Samal** PA‹EL (?) Impf. 3 p.s.m. + suff. 3 p.s.m. *lbtkh* KAI 214^{23} (for this reading and interpret., cf. Gibson SSI ii p. 68, 74 :: e.g. Cooke NSI p. 169, Friedr 41*, Koopmans p. 38, Donner KAI a.l., v.Dijk VT xviii 26, Stefanovic COAI 176: l. *lytkh* (for this reading, cf. also D.H.Müller WZKM vii 50bis, Lidzbarski Handb 441) = *l$_1$* + APH Impf. 3 p.s.m. + suff. 3 p.s.m./f. of *ntk$_1$* (= to pour forth), cf. also Dahood UF i 36, Or xlv 383) - ¶ verb PA‹EL (?) uncert. meaning; Gibson SSI ii p. 69, 74: to confound, to confuse.

btwlh v. *btlh*.

btlh **Hebr** Sing. abs. *btwlh* Frey 1162^6 (= SM 45), 1206^6 (= SM 67), SM 27^6, 70^3, IEJ vii 239^3 - **OffAr** Sing. abs. *btwlh* Aḥiq 134 - **Hatra** Sing. abs. *btlh* 35^4 (cf. Milik DFD 344, 353, 365, 374, Vattioni IH a.l. :: Safar Sumer viii ix 18*f., Caquot Syr xxx 240, Gawlikowski TP 78 (n. 70) (div. otherwise): l. *bt* (= Sing. abs. of *byt$_2$*) + *lh* (= *l$_5$* + suff. 3 p.s.m./f.), cf. also Donner sub KAI 249) - **JAr** Sing. abs. *btwlh* DBKP 18^{68} - ¶ subst. f. virgin, maiden, young woman; in Hatra 35^4 used as epithet of a goddess (v. supra); in Frey 1162^2, 1206^6, SM 27^6,

70^3 indicating sign of zodiac - Naveh IEJ xxix 113, 117: l. Sing./Plur. emph. of this word (*btlt›*) in IEJ xxix 112^4: = virgin(s) > closed (virgin) flower(s) (highly uncert. context) - for this word, cf. also Winham VT xxii 326ff.

btm v. *tm*$_1$.

btn$_1$ v. *tm*$_1$.

btn$_2$ v. *qqbtn*, *tm*$_1$.

btr **OffAr**, cf. Frah xxv 48 (*b›tl*), SaSt 15 - **Palm** CIS ii 3913 ii 95, 3920^3, 3927^5 (:: Gawlikowski TP 51: pro *btr dy myt* l. *]lt dmysyt* (= at the expense of the state < Greek δημοσίοις); diff. reading), 4171^2, 4175^6, RIP 24^1, 25^9, 103c 4, Inv x 4^4, 53^3, 119a 4, RB xxxix 539^3, Ber ii 78^2, 84^1, 85^7, 98^1, MUSJ xxxviii 106^7; + suff. 3 p.s.m.

btrh Ber ii 86^{12}, v 106^4, CIS ii 4194^6 (or + suff. 3 p.s.f.?) - **JAr** + suff. 3 p.s.m. *btrh* AMB 15^{15}; + suff. 1 p.s. *btry* MPAT 41^{11} (*bt[ry]*), 42^{12} (*btr[y]*), AMB 10^6 (on this uncert. reading, cf. Naveh & Shaked AMB a.l.) - ¶ prep. (< *b*$_2$ + *›tr*$_2$, v. also *›šr*$_4$) - **1)** loc. behind, beyond; *rdpw btrh* AMB 15^{15}: they chased him; *›ksdr› dy btr bb›* (v. *bb*$_1$) Ber ii 78^2: the exedra which is beyond the porch (cf. CIS ii 4171^2, 4175^6, Ber ii 84^1, 98^1, v 106^4, MUSJ xxxviii 106^7, etc.) - **2)** temp. after; *btr mwth* RIP 103c 4: after his death (for the context, cf. Aggoula Syr liv 282f.; cf. Inv x 53^3, 119a 4 (Greek par. μετὰ τὴν τε[λε]υτὴν)); *btr dy*, *btr dy myt* Inv x 4^4: after they had died (cf. CIS ii 3920^3 (Greek par. μετὰ τὴν τελευτὴν), 3927^5) - **3)** preceded by *mn*$_5$ - a) loc. behind; *mn btr gwmḥ› qdmy›* Ber ii $104^{3f.}$: beyond the first niche - b) temp. after; *m]n btr[y]* MPAT 42^{12}: after me (i.e. after my death), cf. MPAT 41^{11}; *mn btr dy*, *mn btr dy myt šlmlt* RIP 24^4: after Sh. had died (cf. RIP 25^9 (?): *]btr dy*) - **4)** for *btr kwt*, v. *kwt* - > Akkad.??, cf. v.Soden Or xxxv 7, xlvi 185 - this word poss. also in FuF xxxv 173^{13} - Beyer ATTM 307: l. prob. *btr* in MPAT 39^6 (on the reading problems, cf. Bennett Maarav iv 255f.).

v. *kwt*, *pny*.

btt **Pun** the diff. *›bt* in CIS i 6000bis 8 (= TPC 84) poss. = Qal Impf. 1 p.s. of *btt* (= to cut, to engrave), cf. Février BAr '51/52, 80, CB viii 30f., sub CIS i a.l., HDS 193, v.d.Branden BO xxiii 156, Ferron StudMagr i 77, Bonnet SEL vii 113f. - Février CB viii 30f., HDS 193f.: l. *bt* (= Qal Pf. 3 p.s.m. of *btt*) in NP 7^5 (= Punica iv A 1), uncert. interpret. - Février IAM a.l: l. poss. *bt* (= Qal Pf. 3 p.s.m.) in IAM 13? (highly uncert. interpret., diff. context).

v. *ptytw*.

G

g_1 v. *grb_1*.
g_2 v. *gryw*.
g_3 **JAr** MPAT-A 51[5] indication of number 3.
g'wlh v. *g'lh*.
g'l v. *'lh_1*, *gly*.
g'lh **Hebr** Sing. cstr. *g'lt* DJD ii 24B 2, D 2, E 1, EI xx 256[2] and on coins of the first and second revolt: JC no. 162, 163, 165, 166, 168, 170-173, 176 (cf. Meshorer Mas coin 3492, 3493), *g'wlt* DJD ii 22,1-9[1], 30[8] - ¶ subst. liberation; on coins of the first revolt, *lg'lt ṣywn* JC no. 162, 163: of the liberation of Sion; on coins of the second revolt, *lg'lt yšr'l* JC no. 165, 166, 168, 170-173, 176: of the liberation of Israel; cf. also on documents of the same period: DJD ii 22,1-9[1], 24B 2, D 2, E 1f., 30[8], EI xx 256[2]; for the coins of the second revolt, cf. Kanael IEJ xxi 39ff., Schäfer BKA 62f., 85ff.
g'n **Pun** Plur. cstr., cf. Poen 1027: *gune* - ¶ subst. exaltation, majesty; *gune bel balsamen* (var. *guneb balsamen*) Poen 1027: exaltations of Bel, the lord of heavens (cf. e.g. Schroed 318, Sznycer PPP 144 (cf. also Garbini StudMagr xii 89) :: J.J.Glück & Maurach Semitics ii 123: *gune* = QAL Imper. s.m. + suff. 1 p.s. of *gnn_1* (= to protect, to rescue)).
gb_1 **Palm** Sing. emph. *gb'* RB xxxix 532[2] - ¶ subst. side; *bsṭr' gb' dy sml'* RB xxxix 532[2]: at the north side (sc. of a part of a tomb construction; Greek par. ἀρκτικοῦ πλευροῦ; for the diff. context, cf. Cantineau a.l.) - cf. also GAB-DI in Ass text, cf. Fales DDA iii 72.
v. *gbl_1*, *šrgb*.
gb_2 (not < Arab., cf. Rosenthal Forschung 90 (cf. also O'Connor JNES xlv 216f.) :: Cantineau Nab ii 76) - **Nab** Sing. emph. *gb'* RES 1432[1] - **Palm** Sing. emph. *gb'* RIP 127[4] (for the reading, cf. Gawlikowski a.l., Milik DFD 256) - ¶ subst. well, cistern; *bt gb'* RIP 127[4]: water reservoir (cf. Gawlikowski RIP a.l., TP 116, cf. however Aggoula Syr liv 283) - for this word (and related ones), cf. de Geus PEQ '75, 72ff., Gottlieb PEQ '77, 53f. - > Akkad., cf. v.Soden Or xxxv 8, xlvi 186.
v. *gb't*, *šrgb*.
gb_3 cf. Frah x 33: back (*gnb(m)h*, *gb(m)h*, *gph*).
gb_4 **OffAr** word of unknown meaning in FuB xiv 17[2].
gb_5 v. *qb_2*.
gb_6 **Hatra** Sing. emph. *gb'* 342[9] - ¶ subst. stealing > seduction (for this interpret., cf. Aggoula Syr lxiv 96f.).
gb' v. *gby_1*.
gb't **Palm** Sing. emph. *gb't'* Inv xii 39; Plur. abs. *gb'tn* PNO 22 (for the reading, cf. Gawlikowski sub RIP 127, TP 84 n. 104 :: Ingholt & Starcky PNO a.l. (div. otherwise): l. *gb'* (= Sing. emph. of *gb_2*)+ *t-*, cf.

Gawlikowski Syr xlviii 410 n. 3) - ¶ subst. crater (:: Bounni & Teixidor sub Inv xii 39: < Akkad. *gubbû*).
v. *ml'h*₂.

gbgb Ebeling Frah a.l.: l. *gbgb'/gbgp'* and *gbyb'/gbyp'* in Frah vi 6 (= grass, hay), cf. however Nyberg FP 69: l. *giyā(h)* = Iran. word.

gbh₁ cf. Frah app. 3 (*ygbḥwn*): to be high (cf. Nyberg FP 53, 98 :: Ebeling Frah a.l.: l. *zgbhwn* = contamination of *zqp* (= to erect) and *gbh*₁).
v. *gbh*₄.

gbh₂ **Hebr** Sing. cstr. *gbh* KAI 189⁶ - ¶ subst. height; *gbh hṣr* KAI 189⁶: the height of the rock.

gbh₃ v. *gbh*₄.

gbh₄ **OffAr** Sing. m. abs. *gbh* Aḥiq 107 (:: Kottsieper SAS 144f., 194 (div. otherwise): l. *gbhh* = PA‘EL Pf. 3 p.s.m. + suff. 3 p.s.m. of *gbh*₁) - ¶ adj. haughty (said of voice): Aḥiq 107, cf. Grelot RB lxviii 184, DAE p. 438 (cf. also Ginsberg ANET 429: = loud) :: Cowl a.l.: = high (on the subject, cf. also Lindenberger APA 93, 244 nn. 263, 264) - Joüon MUSJ xviii 12: < Hebr. (less prob.) - the same word (Sing. abs. preceded by article: *hgbh*) poss. also in Vatt sig. eb. 228 (= SANSS-Hebr 127): = epithet or title?? (cf. however Avigad IEJ xvi 51f.: = *gbh*₃(= locust; used as family name), cf. also Naveh Qadm i 105, Borowski AIAI 155f.).

gbwl v. *gbl*₁.

gbwrh v. *gbrh*₂.

gby₁ **OffAr** QAL Pf. 2 p.s.m. *gbyt* ATNS 35⁴ (or = 1 p.s.?, cf. Segal ATNS a.l.; highly uncert. reading, cf. Porten & Yardeni sub TADAE B 4.7: l. prob. *hnbg* (= Sing. cstr. of *hnbg*)); Impf. 2 p.pl.m. *tgbwn* ATNS 43⁶ (heavily dam. context); ITP Impf. 3 p.s.m. *ytgbh* ATNS 22⁴ (heavily dam. context) - **Palm** QAL Pf. 3 p.s.m. *gb['*]* CIS ii 3913 ii 62; Impf. 3 p.s.m. *ygb'* CIS ii 3913 ii 38, 47, 50, 52, etc.; Part. act. s.m. abs. *gb'* CIS ii 3913 i 6, 11, ii 107; pl.m. abs. *gbn* CIS ii 3913 ii 123 (Rosenthal Sprache 69: = Part. pass.??; for the context, v. also *kpr*₁); Part. pass. s.m. abs. *gby* CIS ii 3913 i 14; pl.m. abs. *gbn* CIS ii 3913 ii 106; ITP Impf. 3 p.s.m. *[ytg]b'* CIS ii 3913 ii 70; 3 p.pl.m. *ytgb[wn]* CIS ii 3913 ii 129 (thus CIS ii sub 3913, Cantineau Gramm 91, Rosenthal Sprache 69, l. however rather: *ytgb['*]*, cf. Reckendorff ZDMG xlii 382, Lidzbarski Handb 468, Cooke NSI p. 330); Part. s.m. abs. *mtgb'* CIS ii 3913 ii 141, 143, 149; pl.f. abs. *mtgbyn* CIS ii 3913 i 5 (uncert. interpret., diff. context: *hww*!, cf. Rosenthal Sprache 17 n. 5; v. infra and cf. also Ben Chayyim EI i 137 (n. 3a)) - ¶ verb QAL to levy, to collect - **1)** + obj. - a) said of tax: CIS ii 3913 ii 38, 107, cf. 122f. - b) said of the collection of debts: ATNS 35⁴ (v. however supra) - 2) + obj. + *l*₅, *lgml' kdy yt'y‘l sryq ygb' d 1* CIS ii 3913 ii 61: for (each) camel, when it is brought in without load, he (sc. the publican) shall levy one *d.* (cf. CIS ii 3913 i 13f., ii 59) - **3)** + obj. + *mn*$_5$, to levy something (as tax) of someone: CIS ii 3913 i 11, ii 47f., 49f., 51f. - **4)** + *mn*$_5$, *ʾp ygbʾ [mks]ʾ mn gnsyʾ klhwn hyk ktyb* ... CIS ii 3913 ii 68: the publican will also levy (sc. tax) from goods of all kinds as it is written .... - Part. pass. being levied (said of tax); *ṭʿwn qrs ... lʾrbʿʾ ṭʿwnyn dy gmlyn mksʾ gby* CIS ii 3913 i 13f.: for a wagon-load ... the tax shall be levied as for four camel-loads (cf. Greek par. γόμος καρρικὸς παντὸς γένους τεσσάρων γόμων καμηλικῶν τέλος. ἐπράχθη; cf. also CIS ii 3913 ii 105f.) - ITP 1) to be levied (said of tax): CIS ii 3913 ii 110, 129 (if reading *ytgb[wn]* is right (v. supra), meaning as sub 2)), 141, 149 - **2)** to be liable to taxation?: CIS ii 3913 i 5 (uncert. interpret. based on the presupposition that *mtgbyn* = f.) - Greek par. derived from the root πράττω/πράσσω - a form of this root (*gbyʾ*) also in ATNS 38[6]: = QAL Part. act./pass. s./pl.m. emph.? (collector/what is collected, receipt?) or = subst. Plur./Sing. emph.? (heavily dam. context).

gby$_2$ v. *gnby.*

gbyb v. *gbgb.*

gbyḥy **JAr** Yadin & Greenfield sub DBKP 27: l. poss. *g[by]ḥyh* = Sing. emph. of *gbyḥy* (= hunchback) in MPAT 62[11] (cf. however Fitzmyer & Harrington MPAT a.l.: l. *b[r yhw]ḥnn*), cf. Greek par. κυρτῷ.

gbyn **OffAr**, cf. Frah x 12 (*gbyntʾ*, *gbynh*): forehead.

gbl$_1$ **Ph** Sing. cstr. *gbl* KAI 14[20], 26A ii 2 (× e.g. Röllig KAI a.l., Gibson SSI iii p. 49: = Plur. cstr.), 43[9]; + suff. 1 p.s. *gbly* KAI 26A i 21 (:: v.d. Branden Meltô i 46, 74: = Sing. m. abs. of *gbly*$_2$ (= adj. at the border)); Plur. abs. *gblm* KAI 26A i 14 - **Pun** Plur. abs., cf. Poen 938: *gubulim* - **Samal** Sing. cstr. *gbl* KAI 215[15] (for the reading, cf. e.g. Cooke NSI p. 172, Gibson SSI ii p. 80 :: Donner KAI a.l.: l. *gbwl* (prob. misprint)); + suff. 3 p.s.m. *gblh* KAI 215[15] - **OldAr** Sing. + suff. 3 p.s.f. *gblh* KAI 224[23]; + suff. 1 p.s. *gb[ly]* KAI 202B 8f. (for the reading, cf. Dupont-Sommer AH i/1, 2, Gibson SSI ii sub 5B, cf. Greenfield Lesh xxxii 363 n. 21a, JNES xxxvii 95 n. 15: l. *gb[l]*, cf. also Lipiński Stud 23 :: e.g. Pognon ISMM 174, 176, Donner KAI a.l., Vogt Lex s.v. *gb*, Degen AAG p. 7 (n. 33): l. *gb* (= Sing. abs. of *gb*$_1$)) - ¶ subst. border, boundary, territory within boundary (often diff. to distinguish); *yšbm ʾnk bqṣt gbly* KAI 26A i 20f.: I made them live in the outskirts of my territory; *wbn ʾnk ḥmyt ʿzt bkl qṣyt ʿl gblm* ... KAI 26A i 14: and I built strongwalls at all ends at the frontiers; *wkn ... bkl gbl ʿmq ʾdn* KAI 26A ii 1f.: they were (settled) ... in the whole territory of the valley of A.; *wyspnnm ʿlt gbl ʾrṣ* KAI 14[19f.]: and we annexed them to the territory of the country; *[wtlʾy]m wkpryh wbʿlyh wgblh* KAI 224[23]: T, its villages, its inhabitants (or local aristocracy?, v. *bʿl*$_2$) and its territory (cf. also Cazelles HDS 18); cf. also KAI 43[9],

215[15], 202B 8f., Poen 938 (cf. Lat. par.: *regionibus*).
v. *gbl*$_2$.

gbl$_2$ (< Arab.?, cf. Rosenthal Sprache 89, 94f.; or = *gbl*$_1$?) - **Palm** Sing. cstr. *gbl* CIS ii 3923[3], Inv ix 12a 3 - ¶ subst. collectivity, people; *gbl tdmry›* CIS ii 3923[3]: the collectivity of the Palmyreneans, cf. also Inv ix 12a 3 (Greek par. Παλμυρηνῶν ὁ δῆμος; cf. also Gawlikowski TP 42, Teixidor Sem xxxiv 9).

gbl$_3$ v. *›lh*$_1$.

gbl$_4$ v. *gzt*.

gbly$_1$ **Hatra** Sing. (or Plur.?, cf. Degen NESE iii 70) emph. *gblyt›* 281[6] - ¶ subst. certain object/tool, exact meaning unknown: = tile-mould?, cf. Degen NESE iii 68, 70, cf. however Safar Sumer xxvii 4f. (n. 6): = plasterer's hob (cf. also Aggoula Syr lii 282, lxv 208, Vattioni IH a.l.).

gbly$_2$ v. *gbl*$_1$.

gbn$_1$ = cheese > Akkad., cf. v.Soden Or xxxv 8, xlvi 186, cf. also CAD s.v. *gubnatu*.
v. *gbn*$_2$.

gbn$_2$ the diff. γοβνιν in Inv D 51[1] (Plur. abs.) in comb. γοβνιν δααβ (v. *zhb*), prob. indication of object (used as votive offering); exact meaning unknown; Levi Della Vida FDE '22-23, 367f.: = ingot; du Mesnil du Buisson ad Inv D 51: = globe; Milik Syr xliv 289ff., Aggoula Sem xxxii 110: = *gbn*$_1$; Teixidor Syr xlvii 375f.: = cheese-mould (= *gbn*$_1$?), cf. also Beyer ZDMG Suppl iii/1, 651.

gbnh **OffAr** Sing. abs. *gbnh* CRAI '47, 180[2]; cf. Frah vii 20: (*gwbyn›*, *gwbyt›* (cf. Nyberg FP 44 71, :: Ebeling Frah a.l.: l. *gwpt›* = cheese)) - ¶ subst. cheese (as object): CRAI '47, 180[2], cf. Porten Arch 87, cf. also Dupont-Sommer CRAI '47 al.

gbr$_1$ **OldAr** Qal (?) Impf. 3 p.s.m. *ygbr* KAI 223B 19 (v. however infra) - ¶ verb Qal (?) to be mighty/strong: KAI 223B 19 (heavily dam. context; cf. e.g. Dupont-Sommer Sf p. 105, 115, Donner KAI a.l., Fitzmyer AIS 82, 89, Degen AAG p. 18, 68, cf. however Lemaire & Durand IAS 117, 128, 142 (div. otherwise): l. *gbr* (= Sing. cstr. of *gbr*$_2$; poss. reading and interpret.), cf. already Lipiński Stud 54) - the diff. *mgbr* RTP 722 poss. form of this root (Qal Inf.?, Pa‘el/Aph Part. pass. s.m. abs.? or nominal form *mgbr* Sing. m. abs.?, cf. Caquot RTP p. 142, cf. also Gawlikowski TP 117).

gbr$_2$ m. **Ph** Sing. abs. *gbr* KAI 24[8], 30[2] (dam. context) - **Mo** Plur. abs. *g[b]rn* KAI 181[16] - **OldAr** Sing. abs. *gbr* KAI 224[1f.]; cstr. *gbr* KAI 222A 39, B 24 - **OffAr** Sing. abs. *gbr* KAI 228A 12, Cowl 13[8,11], 25[11], Aḥiq 42, 98, 130, Krael 3[3,19], SSI ii 28 obv. 7 (*gb[r]*), Samar 6[6], 7[9], 8[7], etc., etc.; emph. *gbr›* Beh 45 (Akkad. par. *a-me-lu*), Krael 4[20], AG 6[1], ATNS 1[7]; Plur. abs. *gbrn* Cowl 2[7,8], 3[7], Aḥiq 37, Driv 3[5], 5[2,5], TA-Ar 7[2], RES 1809[1] (for this prob. reading, cf. Sznycer HDS 165),

ATNS 24^4, $26^{7,14}$, etc.; emph. *gbry›* Cowl 2^{13}, 34^4, Aḥiq 56, NESE iii 48^{10}, ATNS 19^6, etc., cf. Warka 12: *ga-ab-ri-e*, Warka 37: *ga-ba-ri-e* (cf. Degen GGA '79, 24 :: Segert AAG p. 134; cf. also Gordon AfO xii 111, Kaufman JAOS civ 89); cf. Frah xi 4 (*gbr›*), Paik 234, 235 (*gbr›*), BSOAS xxxiii 152^{10}, GIPP 22, 51, 57, SaSt 16 - **Nab** Sing. abs. *gbr* J 295, IEJ xxix 112^8 - **Hatra** Sing. emph. *gbr›* 343^6, 342^{11} (*[g]br›*, cf. Aggoula Syr lxiv 96, cf. however Aggoula Syr lx 101: l. *dbr›* = QAL Part. act. m. Sing. emph. of *dbr*$_2$) - **Palm** Sing. abs. *gbr* PNO 2ter 9, RIP 199^{14}; emph. *gbr›* RTP 507 (?, cf. Caquot RTP p. 142) - **JAr** Sing. abs. *gbr* MPAT $40^{6,19}$, 53^3, MPAT-A 22^2 (= SM 70^{10}); emph. *gbrh* MPAT-A 22^6 (= SM 70^{14}); Plur. abs. *gbryn* MPAT 60^2 - f. **Mo** Plur. abs. *gbrt* KAI 181^{16} - ¶ subst. - **1)** m man, f. woman, passim; *gbr ‹dn* KAI 222B 24: a man (with whom one has concluded) a treaty, i.e. an ally (cf. also Fitzmyer AIS 66, Parnas Shn i 243); *gbr š‹wt›* KAI 222A 39: the man of wax (i.e. the wax figurine, cf. Weinfeld UF viii 400f., cf. also Hartman CBQ xxx 259); *bn gbr lḥbryh* MPAT-A 22^2: between a man and his fellow; *gbrn ḥlkyn tryn* Driv $6^{4f.}$: two Cilician men (i.e. two Cilicians); *gbr yhwdy* MPAT $40^{1f.,19}$: a Jewish man (cf. MPAT 53^2); *gb[r] hwy* SSI ii 28 obv. 7: be a man; *lgbr lgbr* Cowl 2^7, 22^1, Driv $6^{4f.}$: pro person - **2)** functioning as indefinite pronoun - a) everyone; *wgbr ḥlqh nhḥsn* Cowl 28^{14}: we will take possession each of his share - b) + negation, no one: Aḥiq 98 - **3)** - a) *gbr zy*, everyone who, whosoever; *gbr zy tzbnwn lh byt› zk* Cowl 25^{11}: whomsoever you will sell this house to ... (cf. also KAI 228A 12f., Cowl 30^{28}, 31^{27}, Krael 4^{20} and Krael 5^9: *gbr ›ḥrn*, somebody else) - b) *kl gbr zy/dy*, everyone who, whosoever: KAI $224^{1f.}$, J 295, PNO 2ter 9f. - for the context of *gbry›* in NESE iii $48^{10f.}$, v. *ntyrh* - Sperling UF xx 326f.: the *br* in KAI 24^4 = lapsus for *gbr* (Sing. abs.), less prob. interpret. - Puech RB xc 496: l. Plur. cstr. *gbry* in IEJ xvii 110 l. 2 (highly uncert. reading and interpret.).

v. *gbr*$_1$,*gnb*$_2$, *m‹brh*.

gbr$_3$ **Hebr** Sing. abs. (?, dam. context) *[g]ybwr* AMB 12^{31} (heavily dam. context) - **OldAr** Sing. abs. *gbr* TellF 12 - **JAr** Sing. emph. *gybr›* AMB 1^8 - ¶ subst. hero (in TellF 12 used as epithet for Hadad; Akkad. par. *qar-du* (cf. Kaufman Maarav iii 167)).

gbrh$_1$ v. *gbr*$_2$.

gbrh$_2$ **Samal** Sing. (cf. e.g. Cooke NSI p. 163, 171, Donner KAI a.l. × Dion p. 439 n. 2: or = Plur.?) + suff. 3 p.s.m. *gbrth* KAI 214^{32} - **Palm** Sing. (cf. Gawlikowski RIP a.l. × Milik DFD 294: = Plur.) emph. *gbwrt›* RIP 142^2 - ¶ subst. force, might(y deed); in RIP 142^2 mighty deed, miracle worked by a god.

v. *gybrh*, *m‹brh*.

gg$_1$ **Pun** Sing. abs. *gg* ICO-Sard $32^{2,3}$, Antas p. 70^6 (dam. context; ::

Fantar Antas a.l.: or = *gg₂* (= roofer or navvy)) - **Hebr** Sing. cstr. *gg* DJD ii 24C 17 - ¶ subst. roof; *mwdd ʿl gg ʾwṣrh* DJD ii 24C 17: paying (v. *mdd₁*; sc. the tithes) on the roof of the Treasury, cf. Milik DJD ii a.l., cf. also DJD ii 24F 15.

gg₂ v. *gg₁*.

ggg the peculiar comb. *ggg* in FuF xxxv 173[13], unknown abbrev.??, cf. Altheim & Stiehl FuF xxxv 177.

ggl **Hebr** peculiar *ggl* in JC no. 27: *hkhn hgdggl* (lapsus for *hgd(w)l wggl* (prob. lapsus for repeated *gd(w)l*).

ggʿ **Pun** Sing. abs. *ggʿ* Hofra 42[2] - ¶ subst. of unknown meaning; indication of function or occupation: roofer, shingler??

ggp **Pun** Plur. abs. *ggpm* CIS i 339[4] - ¶ subst. of uncert. meaning, indicating certain object; *pʿl ggpm* CIS i 339[4]: maker of ...; Tomback JNSL v 68: *gg* in *hggpm* indicating lengthening of *g* after article, *gpm* = Plur. abs. of *gp₃* (= fence).

gd₁ **Pun** Sing. abs. *gd* KAI 72B 4; cstr. *gd* KAI 147[2] - **OffAr**, cf. Frah i 8 (*gdh*), Paik 236 (*gdh*), BSOAS xxxiii 152[7], GIPP 16, 22, 51 (cf. Toll ZDMG-Suppl viii 29) - **Nab** Sing. emph. *gdʾ* RES 53[1] - **Palm** Sing. cstr. *gd* CIS ii 3991[4] (cf. Milik sub ARNA-Nab 111, DFD 211 × Chabot CIS ii a.l.: l. *gdʾ* = Sing. emph.), PNO 51, 63, RTP 130-132, 135, 213, 224, 273, 274, Syr xvii 271[2], etc.; emph. *gdʾ* CIS ii 3976[1], 4486[4], Inscr P 3ab 4, PNO 42[4], SBS 23[3], Inv D 13, 28, 31, RTP 718, MUSJ xxxviii 125[2], 133[6]; + suff. 3 p.s.f. *gdh* PNO 42[3] - **Hatra** Sing. emph. *gdʾ* 288a 8, 297[2], 406, 407, 408[3], 409 iii 6, *gndʾ* 58[2], 79[4,9] (:: Altheim & Stiehl AAW iv 244, 249: = Sing. emph. of *gd₃* (= army)), 235[1] (:: Aggoula MUSJ xlvii 12: = Plur. emph.), 288b 3, 296, 413 i 3, iii 3; + suff. 3 p.s.m. *gdh* 74[4] (:: Milik DFD 402, Vattioni IH a.l.: l. *nšrh* = Sing. emph. of *nšr₂*), *gndh* 79[1] (:: Altheim & Stiehl AAW iv 244f., 250f.: = Sing. + suff. 3 p.s.m. of *gd₃* (= army)), 125[2]; + suff. 3 p.pl.m. *gndhwn* 79[10] (:: Altheim & Stiehl AAW iv 244, 249: = Sing. + suff. 3 p.pl.m. of *gd₃* (= army)) - ¶ subst. fortune, fate; *gdʾ ṭbʾ lbny bwlḥʾ* RTP 718: good fortune to the Banu B.; for CIS ii 4486[3f.], Inscr P 3ab 3f., v. *bʾš₂*; *gdʾ rbʾ* Hatra 407: the great "Fortune" (cf. Hatra 408[3], 413 iii 3) - in most texts indication of a deity, (semi-)divine being, abstract divine quality, cf. *Fortuna*, Τύχη - a) used without other qualifications, *hgd* KAI 72B 4 (cf. Garbini RSO xl 212f., Amadasi ICO p. 145, Delcor Sem xxviii 47f.: = epithet of Tinnit, less prob. interpret.), *gdʾ* RES 53[1], Inv D 13, Hatra 288a 8, *gndʾ* Hatra 296 (cf. also *gdy* IrAnt iv 122[2], cf. Dupont-Sommer ibid. 124f.) - b) specified - **1)** with non-proleptic pron. suff., *mrn wgdh* Hatra 74[4]: our lord and his "Fortune" (cf. also Hatra 125[2], for the context, cf. also Degen NESE ii 101 n. 10); *zkyʾ dgndh ʿm ʾlhʾ* Hatra 79[1f.]: (epithet) the victorious one, whose "Fortune" is with the gods (cf. also Teixidor Syr xlvi 329; v. also supra) - **2)** specified by

name of people or tribe, *bgnd› d‹rb* Hatra 79[9f.]: by the "Fortune" of the Arabs (cf. Hatra 288b 3); *gd› dr/dmgw* Hatra 406, 409 iii 6f., 413 i 3f.; *gd blm›* RTP 130, *gd› dy ydy‹[b]l* SBS 23[3f.], *gd ‹grwd* RTP 213, 224, *gd tymy* RTP 135, 273, 274, etc., etc. - **3)** specified by noun/name indicating part of the universe/territory/locality, etc., *gd hšmm* KAI 147[2]: "Fortune" (i.e. god) of the heavens; *gd› dy dwr›* Inv D 28: the "Fortune" of D.; *gd tdmr* Syr xvii 271[2]: the "Fortune" of T. (cf. also Inv D 31); *gd qryt›* PNO 51: the "Fortune" of the village (cf. PNO 42[3f.], MUSJ xxxviii 133[6]); *gnd› dy kṣry›* Hatra 58[2f.]: the "Fortune" of K. (?, v. *kṣry›*); *gd› dy gny›* MUSJ xxxviii 125[2f.]: the "Fortune" of the gardens (cf. PNO 42[4f.]); *gd› dy ‹yn› brykt›* CIS ii 3976[1]: the "Fortune" of the blessed well; *gd› dy ›bwl›* Hatra 297[2]: the "Fortune" of the gateway - **4)** specified by noun indicating certain substance, *gd mšḥ›* RTP 131, 132: the "Fortune" of the oil (v. also *mšḥ*$_3$) - **5)** specified by n.p., etc., *wbgndhwn dsnṭrwq mlk› wzr‹h wbnyhy klhwn dl‹lm* Hatra 79[10f.]: and by the "Fortune" of king S., his posterity and all his descendants forever - **6)** specified by diff. or unexplained element, *gd n›wm/q* PNO 63 (*n›wm/q* prob. name; cf. Ingholt & Starcky PNO a.l.); *gnd› d‹mh* Hatra 235[1] (: the "Fortune" of his people, cf. Aggoula MUSJ xlvii 12 (v. supra and *‹m*$_1$) × Degen JEOL xxiii a.l.: the "Fortune" which is with him, cf. also Safar Sumer xxiv 11 (n. 12)); *gd› [›]nbṭ/gd ›nbṭ* (v. supra) CIS ii 3991: the "Fortune" of the Nabateans (cf. Milik DFD 211) × Chabot CIS ii a.l.: = G. the Nabatean; *bbyldh dgnd›* Hatra 79[3f.]: on the birthday of (his) "Fortune", cf. Teixidor Syr xli 280 (n. 2), Aggoula Ber xviii 96, MUSJ xlvii 31 :: Caquot Syr xl 3: on his fortunate birthday (cf. also Milik DFD 379: on his birthday, (day) of the "Fortune" (v. also *yld*$_3$)) - for the divine being, cf. also Février Rel 64f., Solá-Solé Sef xvi 341ff., N.Glück DD 288, 396ff., 409ff., 428, Hoftijzer RelAr 59f., Milik DFD 290, As-Salihi Sumer xxix 99f. (Engl.), 151ff. (Arab.), Teixidor PP 92ff., Tigay FS Cross 163, 167.
v. *gdh*$_2$, *gr*$_1$, *grh*$_2$.

gd$_2$ v. *gr*$_1$.

gd$_3$ v. *gd*$_1$.

gd›$_1$ **Pun** Sing. abs. *gd›* KAI 69[9], CIS i 3915[3], cf. Poen 1017: *gade* (v. *›nth*$_2$; cf. Sznycer PPP 143f.: diff. context) - **OldAr** Sing. abs. *gdh* KAI 223A 2 - ¶ subst. m. goat.
v. *gdy*$_2$.

gd›$_2$ v. *gwd*$_1$.

gdd$_1$ v. *›gd*$_1$.

gdd$_2$ = marauding band > Akkad., cf. v.Soden Or xxxv 9, xlvi 186 (cf. however CAD s.v. *gudūdu*).
v. *›gdd*.

gdh$_1$ v. *gd›*$_1$.

gdh$_2$ **Hatra** Sing. cstr. *gdt* (v. however infra) 37[2] - ¶ subst. of uncert. reading and meaning; poss. indication of female function, cf. Milik DFD 372: = lady of honour (sc. of princess), reading *grt* poss.; Maricq Syr xxxii 282: l. *gdt* = child (cf. also Aggoula MUSJ xlvii 29: l. *grt* = Sing. cstr. of *grt* (= whelp); cf. also Weippert ZAW lxxxiv 485 n. 116, Vattioni IH a.l.) :: Safar Sumer viii 193 (n. 42): l. *gdt* = poss. lapsus for *brt* (= f. Sing. cstr. of *br*$_1$or = f. of *gd*$_1$?:: Caquot Syr xxx 242f.: l. *brt* = f. Sing. cstr. of *br*$_1$);for the context, cf. also Degen Or xxxvi 79f.; reading *grt* = Sing. cstr. of *grh*$_2$ (= female servant) preferable.

gdwl v. *gdl*$_2$.

gdy$_1$ = to cut off > Akkad., cf. v.Soden Or xxxv 9, xlvi 187 (cf. however CAD-ḫ p. 27b s.v. *ḫadû*, v. sub (5)) - a form of this root prob. also in Nisa-b 2067[3] (*gdyt*), cf. also GIPP 51.

gdy$_2$ **Hebr** Sing. abs. *gdy* SM 27[10], 70[4] - ¶ subst. goat; in SM 27[10], 70[4] indication of one of the signs of the zodiac; > Akkad., cf. v.Soden Or xxxv 8, xlvi 186 (cf. CAD s.v. *gadû*).
v. *gd*’$_1$.

gdy$_3$ Zadok WO xii 198: this word (= fortunate, lucky) > Akkad. *gaddā*’*a* (indication of an official), highly uncert. interpret. (cf. also CAD s.v.: poss. < Iran.); cf. also AHW s.v. *gaddāja*.
v. *tgr*$_1$.

gdy$_4$ **Hatra** the reading and interpret. of the *gdy* in *[g]dynšr*’ in 229b 2 highly uncert., cf. Degen WO v 232, v. also *nšr*$_2$.

gdyl Ebeling Frah a.l.: l. *gdyln* (= form of *gdyl* (= string of garlic)) in Frah vi 2, cf. however Nyberg FP 69: l. *šōn* (= Iran. word).

gdl$_1$ **JAr** PA‘EL Part. pass. s.m. emph. *mgdlh* AMB 7[16] - ¶ verb PA‘EL to extol; Part. pass. extolled (epithet of God).

gdl$_2$ **Hebr** Sing. m. abs. *gdl* NESE ii 45[2], IEJ xxxvi 39[3], Vatt sig. eb. 348, RB lxxvii 51, on coins, cf. JC no. 12, 14, 17, 18, 18a, 19, 20, 20a, 21, 22, 23, 26, 29, *gdwl*on coins, cf. JC no. 13, 28, *gdggl* (lapsus) on coin, cf. JC 27 (v. *ggl*); f. abs. *gdwlh* SM 49[18] - ¶ adj. great; *drk hgdwlh hhwlkt lmydbr* SM 49[18]: the highway leading to the desert; *hkhn hgdl* JC no. 18: the highpriest (cf. IEJ xxxvi 39[3], Vatt sig. eb. 348, JC no. 12, etc., cf. also Meshorer Mas coin 96, 101, 103); *mmlk gdl* NESE ii 45[2]: from the great king (prob. the king of Assyria, cf. Millard Irâq xxiv 47, Malamat DSK 20, Gibson SSI i p. 20, Röllig NESE ii a.l., Naveh Lesh xxx 67 (:: Lemaire Sem xxvi 69: or = epithet of God?; for restoration of the context, cf. also Greenfield JAOS xciv 510)); for the diff. *nqm gdl* RB lxxvii 51, v. *nqm*$_3$.

gdm = bunch of dates > Akkad., cf. v.Soden Or xxxv 8, xlvi 186, cf. also CAD s.v. *gidmu*.

gd‘ v. ’*nth*$_2$.

gd‘h v. *gr‘h*.

gdr **Pun** Sing. + suff. 1 p.s. *gydry* Trip 51^7 (uncert. interpret., dam. context, cf. also Amadasi IPT 135); Plur. cstr. *gdr*ʾ Trip 11 (??, cf. however IRT p. 11) - **DA** Sing. abs. *gdr* ii 15 (uncert. reading, cf. v.d. Kooij DA p. 131f., cf. also Caquot & Lemaire Syr liv 207; Levine JAOS ci 200, 202 (div. otherwise): l. poss. *mgdr* = Sing. abs. of *mgdr* (= fence, hedge)) - **Nab** Sing. emph. *gdr*ʾ RES 90^1 (= RES 2025) - ¶ subst. m. wall (cf. also Marrassini FLEM 50ff.) - Pritchard HISG p. 9f.: for the diff. *gdd/r* in HISG no 1, 3, 7, 8, 10, 14, 15, etc. l. *gdr* (= Sing. cstr. (in no. 51 Sing. abs.)) = wall > walled plot, walled enclosure (said of vineyard), cf. Pritchard BASOR clx 4, Eissfeldt OLZ '60, 148, cf. also Kutscher Lesh xxvii/xxviii 185f., Stern AMCS 257, Teixidor Syr xlix 425f. :: Demsky BASOR ccii 20ff.: l. *gdr* = name of clan :: de Vaux RB lxvii 636: l. *gdd/r* = n.p. (cf. Galling BiOr xxii 244f.; cf. also Avigad IEJ ix 130ff., Yadin IEJ ix 187: l. *gdd* = n.p.) :: Pritchard BiAr xxiii 25: or = n.g.; for the reading problems, cf. also Michaud VT x 104ff., Cross BASOR clxviii 20 - on this word, cf. Borowksi AIAI 105f.

gdš$_1$ **DA** Sing. abs. *gdš* ii 8 (cf. Hoftijzer DA a.l., Levine JAOS ci 200f., Hackett BTDA 30, 62, 128, Knauf ZDPV ci 188 :: Kaufman BASOR ccxxxix 73f. (div. otherwise): l. *ngrš* = Niph-form (Pf. 3 p.s.m.?) of *grš*$_1$ (= to be driven)) - ¶ subst. grave (cf. e.g. Hoftijzer DA p. 226 n. 120 :: Caquot & Lemaire Syr liv 204, H.P.Müller ZAW xciv 219, 233 (n. 130): = *gdš*$_2$ (= misfortune) :: Lemaire CRAI '85, 276: = *gdš*$_3$ (= mill-stone)).

gdš$_2$ v. *gdš*$_1$.

gdš$_3$ v. *gdš*$_1$.

gh v. *gw*$_2$.

ghn **OffAr** QAL Pf. 1 p.s. *ghnt* Aḥiq 13 - ¶ verb QAL to bow down, to prostrate oneself.

gw$_1$ **Ph** Sing. abs. *gw* KAI 60^{2,5,7,8} - **Pun** Sing. abs. KAI 164^3 (uncert. reading) - ¶ subst. community, corporation, cf. Greek par. τὸ κοινὸν (for KAI 60, cf. Dombrowski HThR lix 294, Kutler JANES xiv 76).
v. *gw*$_2$.

gw$_2$ **Ph** Sing. cstr. *gw* KAI 17^1 (cf. e.g. Lidzbarski Eph iii 53, Röllig KAI a.l., Healy CISFP i 666, Delcor CISFP i 780ff. :: Milik Bibl xlviii 572f., Teixidor Syr liii 315: = Sing. cstr. of *gw*$_1$:: Gibson SSI iii p. 117: = Sing. abs. of *gw*$_1$(cf. also Puech with Delcor CISFP i 782)) - **OldAr** Sing. + suff. 3 p.s.f. *gwh* KAI 202B 3 - **OffAr** Sing. abs. *gw* Cowl 2^9, 5^{15}, 8^{28}, Krael 1^{4,5,7,10}, Driv 8^2, ATNS 3^5, etc., etc.; cstr. *gw* FuF xxxv 173^8; + suff. 3 p.s.m. *gwh* Aḥiq 160 (??; for the reading, cf. Lindenberger APA 161f. (cf. also Kottsieper SAS 10, 194), cf. also Cowl p. 244: or l. *gwp[h]*? = Sing. + suff. 3 p.s.m. of *gwp* :: Epstein ZAW xxxiii 231: l. *gwh[m]* = Sing. + suff. 3 p.pl.m. :: Baneth OLZ '14, 351: l. *gphm* = Sing. + suff. 3 p.pl.m. of *gp*$_4$ (= wing)) - **Nab** Sing. cstr. *gw*

CIS ii 158[6], 211[2] (= J 11); emph. *gw*ʾ CIS ii 350[1], MPAT 64 recto iii 5 - **Palm** Sing. abs. *gw* CIS ii 3913 ii 106, 146, RIP 21[3], Ber ii 82[1], 85[9], RB xxxix 539[2], Syr xiv 185[2], FS Miles 38[2]; cstr. *gw* Ber ii 60[1]; emph. *gw*ʾ Ber ii 102 i 3, FS Miles 38[1]; + suff. 3 p.s.m. *gwh* CIS ii 4206[2], Ber ii 82[1], Inscr P 77[2]; + suff. 3 p.pl.m. *gwhwn* FS Miles 38[3] - **Hatra** Sing. abs. *gw* 79[9], 336[9], 343[5,6] - **JAr** Sing. cstr. *gw* MPAT 51[5,10], MPAT-A 29[4] (= Frey 859 = SM 35), IEJ xxxvi 206[2], *gh*MPAT 51[4]; + suff. 3 p.s.m. *gwh* MPAT 51[14]; + suff. 3 p.s.f. *gwh* MPAT 69[2], MPAT-A 45[3] - ¶ subst. interior; cf. *gwmḥʾ ḥd dy hw gwʾ ʿl ymynʾ* Ber ii 102 i 3: the one niche which is inside (immediately) to the right; *mʿrtʾ dnh dy gwʾ* FS Miles 38[1]: this hypogeum which is inside (i.e. behind the door on the lintel of which the inscription is written) - combined with prep. - a) *gw(ʾ) mn* - **1)** behind; *wṣryḥʾ zʿyrʾ dy gwʾ mnh* CIS ii 350[1]: the small room which lies behind it (cf. Milik RB lxvi 556 :: CIS ii sub 350: within it) - **2)** within; *trty ḥnwtʾ wtwnyʾ dy gwʾ mnhm* MPAT 64 recto iii 5: the two shops and the rooms which are within them (or: which are behind them??) - **3)** less than; *gw mn dnr* CIS ii 3913 ii 106: less than a denarius - b) *bgw* (st abs.; cf. Whitehead JNES xxxvii 135 (n. 112)) - **1)** thereon, within; *tb bgw ʿm ʾnttk* Cowl 9[6]: dwell thereon (sc. on the plot in question) with your wife; *lʾ ʾrʿ bgw* ATNS 3[5]: there is no unbuilt land within (for this poss. interpret., cf. Porten & Yardeni sub TADAE B 8.10 :: Segal ATNS a.l.: *bgw* = inclusive) - **2)** including (in several types of lists); *ksp kršn 31 šqln 8 bgw lYHW k 12 š 6* Cowl 22[122f.]: 31 *k.* and 8 *sh.* silver of which 12 *k.* and 6 *sh.* are for YHW (cf. Cowl 26[10], 72[5], 78[2], 79[2,3]; cf. also *ksp kršn 2 ḥlrn 3 bgw kspʾ zy ʾtwsp ʿl mks pṭʾsy*, ATNS 19[3f.]: silver 2 *karaš*, 3 *ḥallur* including the silver which was added to the tax of P. (uncert. interpret., cf. Segal ATNS a.l.: *bgw* = inclusive, *kspʾ* begins a new clause), cf. also ATNS 41[1], 43b 2, 48[5], 52a 4, 95b 4?? (in all these instances diff. and dam. context) - **3)** as to that; *ṭyb lbbn bgw* Cowl 2[9]: as to that our heart is content (cf. Cowl 15[5f.,15], 20[9], Krael 12[6,26]); *qblt ʿly bgw* Krael 1[4]: you complained against me about this; in contracts, *šhdyʾ bgw* Cowl 5[15], 8[28], 9[16f.], Krael 1[10], 2[14f.], 3[22a], etc., etc.: witnesses concerning this (i.e. thereto; :: J.J.Rabinowitz BASOR cxxxvi 16, Law 156f., Yaron JSS ii 45f., Law 16f.: = the witnesses within (i.e. mentioned at the inside of the document); cf. also Krael p. 137, Fitzmyer FS Albright ii 167) - 4) in consequence; *zk ʾbd wbgh ... ʾštbq bgw ...* Driv 8[2]: this (man) perished ... and in consequence his fief was abandoned (:: Driv a.l.: *bgw* here = thereupon) - c) *bgw* (st cstr.) inside, within; *lrbty lʿštrt ʾš bgw hqdš* KAI 17[1]: to my lady A. who is inside the sanctuary (cf. KAI 202B 3, CIS ii 158[6], 4206[2], Ber ii 82[1]); *dbgwh* MPAT 69[2]: who is within it (sc. in the ossuary), cf. also MPAT-A 45[3]; *wršh lʾ ʾyty lk ... bgw drth dk* MPAT 51[4]: there is no authority for you ... inside that courtyard (i.e. over that courtyard), cf. also MPAT 51[10]; *wḥtmw bgwh* MPAT 51[14]: they set a seal inside it (i.e. on the inside of the document) - d) *lgw* (st abs.) - **1)** inside; *nk[s]yhwn dlbr wlgw* Hatra 79[8f.]: their possessions which are outside and inside (i.e. all their possessions) - **2)** to the inside; *mn qrqs› wlgw* Ber ii 82[1]: from the *kerkis* (v. *qrqs*) and further; *m‹lyk lgw* FS Miles 38[2]: when you enter (further) to the inside; also instance in RB xxxix 541[3]? (*lgw dy[*) - e) *lgw/h* (st cstr.) - **1)** into; *dy ptyḥ ṣpn lgh drty* MPAT 51[4]: which opens at the north side into my courtyard (cf. also end of same line); cf. IEJ xxxvi 206[2] - **2)** for, on behalf of; *dyhb ḥd plgwt dynr lgw hdn [psyp]sh* MPAT-A 29[3f.] (for the reading, cf. SM 35): who gave half a denarius for this mosaic - f) *lgw mn* - **1)** within; *lgw mn m‹rt›* Syr xiv 185[2]: within the hypogeum; cf. also Hatra 336[9], 343[5,6] - **2)** further within, behind; *lgw mn ṣlmy› ›ln* RIP 21[3f.]: behind these images; *lgw mn qrqs›* Ber ii 85[9f.]: further inside than the *kerkis* (v. *qrqs*) - g) *mn lgw* (st abs.), inside: RB xxxix 539[2] - h) in the diff. text Aḥiq 160: *›wn gwh* = the force of his interior (= his own force)? (cf. also Grelot RB lxviii 190, DAE p. 444; v. also supra) - Segal ATNS a.l.: l. *gw* (= inclusive) in ATNS 45a 2, 3, 4, b 2 (uncert. interpret., l. poss. *g* (= abbrev. of *gryw*) *1*?) - Segal ATNS a.l.: l. poss. *gw* (= included) in ATNS 52a 8 (highly uncert. reading and interpret.) - Segal ATNS a.l.: l. *gw* (= including) in ATNS 23a 4, b 4 (uncert. interpret.).

v. *gw$_3$*.

gw$_3$ **OffAr** Sing. emph. *gw›* Krael 12[24] - ¶ subst. of uncert. meaning: female slave? (cf. e.g. Porten & Greenfield JEAS p. 71, Grelot DAE p. 259f. n. o; for a poss. Iran. background, cf. Benveniste JA ccxlii 308f. :: J.J.Rabinowitz Bibl xxxix 77f., Law 36, Meyer UF xi 605: = graecism, *gw›* = body > slave // σῶμα = body > slave :: Milik RB lxi 251: *gw›* = Sing. emph. of *gw$_2$* > slave, who stays at the house (cf. Porten & Yardeni sub TADAE B 3.12: = (the one belonging to) the inner (chamber)) :: Krael p. 278f.: poss. coarse expression for slave girl, cf. JAr *gw›* = belly, cf. also Grelot DAE p. 260 n. o) - Teixidor Sumer xxi 88: in *lṭb gw ngr›* in Hatra 202 no. 4, *gw* = servant, *gw ngr›* = servant carpenter (uncert. reading and interpret., cf. also Safar Sumer xviii 62: l. *ṭw‹z* (= n.p.) *ngr›*, Caquot Syr xli 271: l. *ṭw‹y* (= n.p.) *ngr›* (cf. also Vattioni IH a.l.).

gwby Ebeling Frah a.l.: l. *gwby›* in Frah x 5 (= Semitic word for tongue); improb. interpret., cf. Nyberg FP 76: = Iran. word.

gwbyn v. *gbnh*.

gwgl (< Akkad. < Sum., cf. Abou-Assaf MDOG cxiii 16, Abou-Assaf, Bordreuil & Millard Tell F p. 28, Kaufman Maarav iii 164, Zadok TeAv ix 118, Andersen & Freedman FS Fensham 16) - **OldAr** Sing. cstr. *gwgl* Tell F 2, 4 - ¶ subst. inspector of canals; *gwgl šmyn w›rq* Tell F 2: canal inspector in heaven and earth (cf. Akkad. par. *gú-gal šamê-e u erṣeti-ti*; cf. also CAD s.v. *gugallu* Ad); *gwgl nhr klm* Tell F 4: inspector of all the water courses (Akkad. par. *gú-gal nārāti*); in both instances epithet of Hadad.

gwgn v. *gḥgn*.

gwd₁ **OldAr** Lipiński Stud 40f.: the diff. *gdʾ* in KAI 222B 36 = Sing. emph. of noun (= attacker) derived from root *gwd₁* (= to raid, to attack), uncert. interpret., v. also *ʾwn₂*.
v. *ʾgd₁*.

gwd₂ = leather bottle > Akkad., cf. v.Soden Or xlvi 186, cf. also CAD s.v. *gūdu*.

gwd₃ **Pun** Sing. abs. *gwd* BAr '55/56, 31 no. 3[2] (= IAM 3) - ¶ subst. of uncert. meaning; Février sub IAM 3: = war.

gwz v. *ḥzy₁*.

gwḥ (< Akkad., cf. Kutscher EI viii 273ff., Kaufman AIA 64 (n. 160), 139, 142f., Lipiński Stud 201f. n. 6, cf. also Zimmern Fremdw 68, O'Connor JNES xlv 218; v. *gmḥ*) - **Nab** Sing. emph. *gwḥʾ* CIS ii 211[1,4,7], 215[5], 226[1]; Plur. abs. *gwḥyn* CIS ii 350[1]; emph. *gwḥyʾ* CIS ii 213[5,6,7], J 2[1] - ¶ subst. niche, *loculus*, passim; in J 2[1]: small galery with several tombs, cf. Guidi RB xix 424, Chabot sub RES 1285; cf. also Milik RB lxvi 558, Kutscher EI viii 273ff.

gwy₁ v. *gy*.

gwy₂ **Nab** Sing. f. emph. *gwytʾ* RES 803[3] (= 2023) - **Palm** Sing. m. emph. *gwyʾ* CIS ii 4227[3], 4239, Inv xii 45[4], RB xxxix 532[2] (Greek par. ἐσωτέρας), 539[3]; Plur. m. abs. *gwyyn* CIS ii 4174[3], Ber ii 88[5], *gwyn* Ber ii 102 ii 4; m. emph. *gwyʾ* SBS 19[3], Ber ii 107[3] - **Hatra** Sing. m. emph. 336[10], 343[7]; Sing. f. emph. *gwytʾ* 35[7] (for the reading, cf. Aggoula Ber xviii 92f., Milik DFD 353, 366, Starcky Sem xxii 64 (n. 2), Degen ZDMG cxxi 125 (cf. also Teixidor Syr xlviii 485) :: Safar Sumer ix 19*, Caquot Syr xxx 240f., Donner sub KAI 249: l. *gzztʾ* = Sing. emph. of *gzzh* (= storekeeper, treasurer)) - ¶ adj. interior: RB xxxix 532[2], 539[3], RES 803[3], SBS 19[3], Hatra 35[7]; innermost: CIS ii 4174[3], 4227[3], Ber ii 88[5], 102 ii 4, 107[3] - substantivated adj. in Hatra 336[10], 343[7]: who belongs inside, i.e. a citizen (cf. Aggoula Syr lxiv 92); in CIS ii 4239, indication of function: eunuch?, cf. Chabot CIS ii a.l., Cantineau sub Inv viii 193 × Milik RB lxi 251: = domestic servant - the meaning of *gwyʾ* in the function indication *ʾsyʾ gwyʾ* Inv xii 45[4] uncert. (Teixidor Inv xii a.l.: = the domestic physician?; cf. also Aggoula Sem xxix 116: = house physician (i.e. physician belonging to a household)).

gwyh **Nab** Sing. + suff. 3 p.s.f. *gwyth* (?, uncert. reading, cf. Lidzbarski Eph ii 252) RES 2126[3] - ¶ subst. interior.

gwmḥ v. *gmḥ*.

gw‘ v. *ng‘*$_1$.

gw‘r **Pun** Levi Della Vida Or xxxiii 11: l. poss. this subst. (Sing. abs.; meaning unknown) in Trip 51[4], cf. however Amadasi IPT 134 n. 1: or (div. otherwise) l. *gw* (= *gw*$_1$ or *gw*$_2$) + *‘r* (without interpret.); uncert. context and interpret.

gwp v. ,*gw*$_2$,*gp*$_1$.

gwpt v. *gbnh*.

gwr v. *’gr*$_1$.

gwrn v. *ywdn*.

gwšk (< Iran., cf. Schaed 264, Eilers Beamtennamen 22f., Hinz AISN 105) - **OffAr** Plur. emph. *gwšky’* Cowl 27[9] - ¶ subst. hearer (function indication), prob. member of intelligence system, cf. Euting MAI I/xi/2 ('04), 307f., Cowl a.l., Porten Arch 50f., Frye BAG 89, Grelot DAE p. 403 n. j, Hinz AISN 105f., cf. also Wag 208, Couroyer BiOr xxvii 249 n. 4, Hinz NWAP 98ff.

gzby (< Lib., cf. Chabot sub Punica xxv 2) - **Pun** Sing. abs. *gzby* KAI 101[3] - ¶ subst. indication of function, meaning unknown; cf. Chaker AION xlvi 547: poss. = supervisor, guardian or inspector.

gzbr v. *gnzbr*.

gzh **OffAr** Sing. + suff. 3 p.s.f. (or m.) *gzth* Herm 2[8] (cf. e.g. Milik Bibl xlviii 551, Porten & Greenfield ZAW lxxx 224 n. 29, Porten Arch 268 n. 8, Hayes & Hoftijzer VT xx 99 n. 3, Donner FS Albright ii 84 (n. 47) :: Bresciani & Kamil Herm a.l.: = QAL Pf. 2 p.s.f. + suff. 3 p.s.m. of *gzz*) - ¶ subst. fleece.

gzz **OffAr** QAL Impf. 2 p.s.m. + suff. 3 p.s.f. *tgznh* Sach 76 i A 8; Imper. + suff. 3 p.s.f. *gzh* Sach 76 i A 6; Inf. *mgz* Sach 76 i A 3 - **Palm** QAL Inf. *mgz* CIS ii 3913 ii 147 - ¶ verb QAL to shear, to clip (of sheep); + obj. (sheep): Sach 76 i A 6, 8 (for the interpret. of the context, cf. Perles OLZ xiv 503, Lidzbarski Eph iii 256, Greenfield Or xxix 98ff.). v. *gzh*,*gzy*, *gzr*$_1$.

gzzh v. *gwy*$_2$.

gzy **Pun** QAL Part. act. s.m. abs. *g‘z* (??) Trip 18[1] - ¶ verb QAL Part. act. carver?? (or < *gzz*?,cf. Levi Della Vida Lib iii/ii 20f.; cf. also Bonnet SEL vii 120).

gzl$_1$ **Ph** QAL Inf. cstr. + suff. 3 p.s.m. *gzly* EpAn ix 5[6] (cf. also Long & Pardee AO vii 213 n. 31); NIPH Pf. 1 p.s. *ngzlt* KAI 14[2,12] - ¶ verb QAL to seize by force, acquire illegitimately: *lbl gzly ’dm bd špḥ klš* EpAn ix 5[6]: so that no one might wrongfully seize it from the possession of the family of K. - NIPH to be snatched (sc. from life); *ngzlt bl ‘ty* KAI 14[2f.,12]: I was snatched before my time - QAL = to rob, to plunder > Akkad., cf. v.Soden Or xlvi 186.

gzl$_2$ **Pun** Sing. abs. *gzl* CIS i 2643[2], 3415 - ¶ subst. indicating function or title, meaning unknown (cf. Bonnet SEL vii 120).

gzr$_1$ **OldAr** QAL Pf. 3 p.s.m. *gzr* KAI 222A 7; Impf. 2 p.s.m. *tgzr* KAI 222B 43 (diff. context, v. *ʾpl*$_2$); Impf. pass. 3 p.s.m. *ygzr* KAI 222A 40; 3 p.pl.m. *ygzrn* KAI 222A 40; IPHT Impf. 3 p.s.m. *ygtzr* Tell F 23 (cf. Kaufman Maarav iii 150, 173, Segert AfO xxxi 93, Muraoka AN xxii 95, Greenfield & Shaffer RB xcii 50, Gropp & Lewis BASOR cclix 54 :: Abou-Assaf, Bordreuil & Millard Tell F p. 37, 50: = ITP; cf. on the problem, cf. also Leemhuis FS Hospers 138f., Greenfield & Shaffer Shn v/vi 128) - **OffAr** QAL Pf. 3 p.s.m. *gzr* JRAS '29, 108[9] (uncert. reading); Part. pass. s.m. abs. *gzyr* Aḥiq 134; s.f. abs. (or s.m. emph.?) *gzyrh* RSO xxxii 404[5] (dam. context) - ¶ verb QAL - **1)** to cut; *mkdb gzyr qdlh* Aḥiq 134: a liar whose throat is cut (cf. Vogt Lex s.v. *gzr* :: e.g. Cowl a.l., Grelot DAE p. 441: a liar has his throat cut :: Lindenberger APA 130: a liar should have his throat cut (on the context, cf. also id. ibid. 256 n. 396) :: Grelot RB lxviii 188: a liar, throat to be cut :: Ginsberg ANET 429: a liar's neck is cut (i.e. he speaks very softly?)) - **2)** to conclude (sc. a treaty, a covenant); *ʿdyʾ ʾln zy gzr brgʾ[yh]* KAI 222A 7: this treaty, which B has concluded (cf. Fitzmyer AIS 32f., McCarthy TaC 92ff., Polzin HThR lxii 235ff., Weinfeld Shn i 72f.; cf. also Tadmor Shn v/vi 160) - **3)** to order?; *gzr ly lm ...* JRAS '29, 108[9]: he has ordered me saying ... (:: Cowley JRAS '29, 110: he has promised me ...) - QAL pass. to be cut in pieces: KAI 222A 40 (:: Bauer AfO viii 10: to be castrated), for the covenantal background of the context, cf. e.g. Fitzmyer AIS 56f., Hillers TC 20 n. 27, Weinfeld UF viii 400 n. 195 - IPHT to be destroyed, to be cut off; *mwtn ... ʾl ygtzr mn mth* Tell F 23: let the plague not be cut off from his country (for the context, cf. Greenfield & Shaffer RB xcii 58f.) - Fitzmyer AIS 72, Lipiński Stud 43, 52: l. *ygz[rn]* (= QAL Impf. 3 p.pl.m.) in KAI 222B 41 (poss. restoration (cf. also Lemaire & Durand IAS 115, 125, 140) :: Silverman JAOS xciv 270 (div. otherwise): l. *ygz* = QAL Impf. 3 p.s.m. of *gzz*) - Lipiński Stud 43, 52: l. *t[g]zr* (= QAL Impf. 2 p.s.m.) in KAI 222B 40 (poss. interpret., cf. also Lemaire & Durand IAS 115, 125, 140) - a form of this root poss. in EA 244[14] (*ka-[z]i-ra*), cf. Rainey EA p. 77: or < root *qṣr*$_1$?
v. *gzr*$_2$.

gzr$_2$ **OffAr** diff. word in IrAnt iv 113; Dupont-Sommer ibid. 113ff.: prob. = n.p. (or l. *ʿzr*? = n.p., cf. also Naveh AION xvi 21); Teixidor Syr xliv 184: = Sing. abs. of *gzr*$_2$ (= exorcist, cf. also Dupont-Sommer IrAnt iv 114) or = QAL Pf. 3 p.s.m. of *gzr*$_1$(= to cut > to inscribe).

gzr$_3$ **OffAr** word of unknown meaning in ATNS 43b 3 (Sing. abs.), Segal ATNS a.l.: prob. = carrot (dam. and diff. context).

gzrh v. *gzt*.

gzt **Pun** Solá-Solé Sem iv 30, Sef xv 50: l. poss. *gzt* (= Sing. abs.) in KAI 72B 1 (= wall of hewn stones; cf. also Röllig KAI a.l., Amadasi sub ICO-Spa 10), reading of *zt* improb. Delcor Sem xxviii 39ff.: l. *gbl* (= Sing. abs. of gbl_4(= small statue made of clay)), reading poss., highly uncert. interpret. :: v.d.Branden BiOr xxxvi 202: pro *gzt* l. *gt* = Sing. abs. of gt_2 (= wine press) + *st* (v. z_1) :: Litmann FuF '32, 179: *gz[rt]* = figure?

gḥgn **Hatra** Sing. abs. (?) *gḥgn* 106a (for the reading, cf. Safar Sumer xviii 26, Caquot Syr xli 252, Aggoula MUSJ xlvii 38f. :: Vattioni IH a.l.: l. *grgn* (= Gorgon) :: Teixidor Ber xvii 8 (n. 46), Syr xliv 189f.: l. *gw/ygn* (= Sing. cstr.) = (inner room of) temple) - ¶ subst. Gorgon, demon (cf. Safar Sumer xviii 26f. n. 2, Aggoula MUSJ xlvii 38f. :: Caquot Syr xli 252: = n.p.), v. also *ʾbšp*.

gḥn **OffAr** a form of this root (= to bow down) prob. in AM ii 174^5. Altheim & Stiehl Suppl 97, ASA 267, Vinnikov PaSb iv 226: poss. = QAL Part. act. s.m. abs. (cf. also Shaked BSOAS xxvii 288 (n. 80)); Henning AM a.l.: = subst. of this root.

gḥrʿ **Nab** Sing. emph. *gḥrʿʾ* J 22^1 (prob. reading) - ¶ subst. of unknown meaning indicating function or title?, cf. also Negev RB lxxxiii 226.

$gṭ_1$ (< Akkad. *giṭṭu* = parchment, document, cf. Zimmern Fremdw 19, Kaufman AIA 52) - **OffAr** Sing. emph. *gṭʾ* Samar 3^{12}; cf. Paik 247 (*gṭy*), 248 (*gṭky*) - **JAr** Sing. cstr. *gṭ* MPAT $40^{8,21}$; emph. *gṭh* MPAT 68^7 - ¶ subst. writ, document, deed: MPAT 68^7, Samar 3^{12}; *gṭ šbqyn* MPAT 40^8: a writ of divorce, cf. also MPAT 40^{21}.

$gṭ_2$ inscription *gṭ* on tags, meaning unknown, cf. Yadin IEJ xv 112, Yadin & Naveh Mas p. 12f.

gṭyp = what is picked, what is loose (said of garlic) > Akkad. (*giṭīpu*), cf. v.Soden Or xxxvii 270, xlvi 186 (× :: v.Soden AHW, CAD: l. *gidipū*).

gy **Hebr** Plur. abs. *gyym* DJD ii 42^5 (for this reading, cf. Birnbaum PEQ '55, 25, Milik DJD ii a.l. :: Lehmann & Stern VT iii 391: l. *gwym*) - ¶ subst. Plur. the heathens.

gybwr v. gbr_3.

gybr v. gbr_3.

gybrh **Pun** Sing. (v. however infra) + suff. 3 p.s.m. *gybrtm* KAI 145^6 (for the reading, cf. Février Sem vi 16, Krahmalkov RSF iii 187 × e.g. Lidzbarski Eph i 49, Cooke NSI p. 154, Röllig KAI a.l.: l. *gbrtm* (with erasure between *g* and *b*), cf. also Halévy RS ix 277: l. *gbrtm* = Sing. + suff. 3 p.pl.m.; for the reading, cf. also Clermont-Ganneau RAO iii 334f., CRAI '99, 528) - ¶ subst. might, power (or = Plur. (= mighty deeds?), cf. Röllig KAI a.l.).
v. $gbrh_2$.

gygn v. *gḥgn*.

gyd **OffAr**, cf. Frah x 6 (*gydyʾ*), cf. Nyberg FP 45, 75 :: Ebeling Frah a.l.: l. *šʾr<n>*, cf. Akkad. *šerʾânu*, Syriac *šeryānā* (and Arab., Mand.) :: Schaeder with Ebeling Frah a.l.: = lapsus for *šbʾ* (cf. Syriac *šbʾ*) ::

Ebeling Frah a.l.: or l. *šy*ʾ? - **JAr** Plur. + suff. 3 p.s.m. *gydwhy* AMB 1[22], *gydw[y]* AMB 5[5] - ¶ subst. tendon.

gywr **JAr** Sing. emph. *gywrh* Syn D A 8 (= Frey 828b (line 8 left out), SM 88) - ¶ subst. proselyte.

gyzbr v. *gnzbr*.

gyl **Amm** Qal Impf. 3 p.s.m. *ygl* Ber xxii 120[6] (cf. Sivan UF xiv 230, Jackson ALIA 41 :: Shea PEQ '78, 110f., Becking BiOr xxxviii 275, Coote BASOR ccxl 93: = Hiph (for the causative interpret., cf. also Aufrecht sub CAI 78: = Qal or Hiph (= to cause rejoicing)) :: Baldacci VT xxxi 367: = Hoph Impf. 3 p.s.m. (= to be gratified)) - ¶ verb Qal to rejoice.

gyml v. *gldgyml*.

gynh v. *gnh$_1$*.

gyr v. *gr$_1$*.

gl$_1$ v. *gly*.

gl$_2$ v. *gly*.

glʾ v. *ngl*.

glb$_1$ v. *plb*.

glb$_2$ **Ph** Plur. abs. *glbm* KAI 37A 13 (= Kition C 1 A 12, cf. e.g. Röllig KAI a.l., Masson & Sznycer RPC 50f., Delcor UF xi 156ff., Gibson SSI iii p. 125, 129 :: (Cross with) Healey BASOR ccxvi 56: = Plur. abs. of *glb$_3$* (= someone shaved, tonsured)) - **Pun** Sing. cstr. *glb* CIS i 257[4], 258[4], 259[3], 588[4], RES 125 (cf. 931, 1598, diff. reading, cf. Lidzbarski Eph i 171) - **Nab** Sing. emph. *glbʾ* RES 1416[1] - ¶ subst. barber; cf. *glb ʾlm* CIS i 257[4], 258[4f.], 259[3], 588[4f.]: barber with function in temple, cf. also *glbm pʿlm ʿl mlʾkt* KAI 37A 13: the barbers performing their duties for cultic purposes - for this word, cf. Kaufman AIA 51 (cf. however also Zimmern Fremdw 28) - Février BAr '55/56, 157: l. *glb* (Sing. cstr.) in Hofra 48[2]? (diff. reading and interpret., cf. however Berthier & Charlier Hofra a.l.: l. Sing. cstr. of *glgl$_2$*, poss. = craftsman working on the turning lathe).
v. *mglb*.

glb$_3$ v. *glb$_2$*.

glgl$_1$ **Pun** Sing. abs. (or cstr.?) *glgl* RES 907A - **Samal** Sing. cstr. *glgl* KAI 215[13] - **OldAr** Sing. cstr. *glgl* KAI 216[8] - ¶ subst. wheel (the exact meaning of the word in RES 907A uncert., dam. context; Dahood Bibl xlv 399: = pitcher, jar); v. *rwṣ* - for this word, cf. also Kutscher Lesh xxvii/xxviii 186ff., Lesh xxx 23.

glgl$_2$ v. *glb$_2$*.

glgn Ebeling Frah a.l.: l. *(g)lgny/k* in Frah iv 4 poss. to be related to *glgn* (= a species of lentils); improb. reading, cf. Nyberg FP 42, 65: l. Iran. word.

gld$_1$ **OffAr** Sing. emph. *gldʾ* Sem xxi 85 conv. 3; + suff. 1 p.s. *gldy*

Aḥiq 119, 211; Plur. cstr. *gldy* Driv 13^3; cf. Frah vii 21 (*glt*ʾ) - **Palm** Plur. emph. *gldy*ʾ CIS ii 3913 ii 122 (v. however infra) - ¶ subst. hide, skin (cf. also Lozachmeur Sem xxi 92 n. 3, 4); *gldy*ʾ *dy gmly[*ʾ*]* CIS ii 3913 ii 122: camel-hides (:: Ingholt MUSJ xlvi 194ff., PBP 104f.: = the camel leaders (*gldy*ʾ = Plur. emph. of *gld₂*)); *gldy twl*ʿ Driv 13^3: skins coloured purple (cf. Driv p. 85f.); *gldy* ʾ*l tlqḥn* Aḥiq 119: don't take my skin away (i.e. don't kill me) - > Akkad., cf. v.Soden Or xxxv 8, xlvi 186, cf. also CAD s.v. *gildu* - cf. *glyd.*

gld₂ v. *gld₁,gldgyml.*

gldgyml **Pun** Sing. abs. *gldgyml* KAI 101^4 (cf. Lib. par.: *gldgmyl*) - ¶ subst. of uncert. meaning, prob. indicating title or function, consisting of two elements: *gld, gyml, gld* prob. = *gld₂*(= leader, master: < Lib.?, cf. e.g. Rössler sub KAI 101 num), *gyml*poss. = *gml* (cf. Ingholt MUSJ xlvi 193ff., PBP 104 n. 9, *gldgyml* = camel leader, cf. also Delgado ILC 172ff.), cf. also Lib. *gldmṣk* KAI 101 num 5 // with Pun. ʾ*d[r] ḥmšm h*ʾ*š* in KAI 101^4; Février MC 89 = high priest?? (on this word, cf. also Chaker AION xlvi 550f.).

glh v. *mglh.*

glwp (*nomen agentis* of the root *glp*, prob. < Greek γλύφω :: Starcky sub Inv x 110: < Greek γλυφεύς) - **Palm** Sing. emph. *glwp*ʾ CIS ii 3974^4, Inv x 110^2 (*glwp[*ʾ*]*), RIP 159^6 (*[g]lwp*ʾ) - ¶ subst. sculptor (cf. also QAL Part. act. of *glp*).

gly **Ph** QAL Impf. 3 p.s.m. *ygl* KAI 1^2; YIPH Pf. 3 p.s.m. *ygl* EpAn ix 5^7 (:: Lemaire EI xx 125*: = QAL Impf. 3 p.s.m. of *g*ʾ*l*) - **OffAr** QAL Pf. 1 p.pl. *glyn* Cowl 37^8; Impf. 2 p.s.m. *tgly* Aḥiq 141; cf. Frah viii 1 (*gly*ʾ :: Ebeling Frah a.l.: l. *ṭyr*ʾ = form of *ṭyr* (= bird)) - **JAr** QAL Pf. 3 p.s.m. *gl*ʾ MPAT 68^5; Part. act. s.m. abs. (?) *gly* MPAT-A 22^4 (= SM 70^{12}) - ¶ verb QAL - **1)** to reveal, to uncover; + obj., *wygl* ʾ*rn zn* KAI 1^2: and he will uncover this sarcophagus; *glyn* ʾ*npyn* ʿ*l* ʾ*ršm* Cowl 37^8: we had revealed our face before Arsham (i.e. we had shown ourselves in A.'s presence, cf. Cowl a.l., Vogt Lex s.v. *glh*, Porten & Yardeni sub TADAE A 4.2 × Grelot DAE p. 389 n. k: we had shown our anger to A., cf. also Porten & Greenfield JEAS p. 81); *mn dgly rzh dqrth* MPAT-A 22^4: one who reveals the secret of the town, cf. Aḥiq 141 (+ *qdm*) - **2)** to go into exile; *ylyd byrwšlm wgl*ʾ *lbbl* MPAT $68^{4f.}$: he was born in Y. and went into exile to B.; YIPH to drive into exile; + obj.: EpAn ix 5^7 (for the context, cf. Mosca & Russell EpAn ix 17f., Long & Pardee AO vii 209ff.) - > Akkad., cf. v.Soden Or xxxv 8, xlvi 186 - Dupont-Sommer Sem iii 44: l. poss. QAL Impf. 2 p.s.m. *tgl* in KAI 10^{14} (cf. e.g. also Röllig KAI a.l., Gibson SSI iii p. 94f., 99) - a derivative of this root poss. in Syr xlviii 396^4 (*gl(*ʿ*n)*), cf. Caquot Syr xlviii 399f.: = QAL Part. pass. s.m. cstr. (cf. also Gaster BASOR ccix 19, Röllig NESE ii 29, cf. also Cross CBQ xxxvi 487ff. (n. 24), de Moor

JEOL xxvii 111 (n. 20) × Dupont-Sommer with Caquot Syr xlviii 399, Avishur PIB 267, 270, UF x 30f. 34, Garbini OA xx 292: = Sing. m. cstr. of gl_2(= round) :: Lipiński RSF ii 51, v.d.Branden BiOr xxxiii 13, xxxvi 202: = Plur. cstr. of gl_1(= wave)).
v. *mglh*, $qr{}^{\text{ʾ}}{}_1$.

glyd **Palm** Sing. + suff. 3 p.s.m. *glydh* MUSJ xlvi 183 - ¶ subst. of unknown meaning, poss. indicating function or social status, cf. Ingholt MUSJ xlvi 193ff. = master of the camels (highly uncert. interpret., cf. Teixidor Syr xlix 441); cf. also gld_1.
v. *ʿlym*.

gll **OffAr** Sing. abs. *gll* Pers 4^{4}, 8^{3} (for this prob. reading, cf. Naveh & Shaked Or xlii 455 :: R.A. Bowman Pers p. 40, 65, 80: pro *zy gll* l. *lḥšl* (= l_5 + QAL Inf. of $ḥšl_2$ (= to pound)); cf. also Levine JAOS xcii 79 n. 71, Degen BiOr xxxi 125 n. 2), 10^{4}, 13^{2}, 20^{4}, 22^{3}, 31^{3}, 32^{3}, 103^{3}, 108^{4}, 113^{3}, 116^{3}, 118^{4}, 143^{3} (in direct comb. with words denoting colour or quality in Pers 1^{2}, 11^{3}, 75^{2}, 91^{3}, 101^{2}, 105^{3}, 122^{2}, uncert. whether abs. or cstr.), PF 1587^{2}; cf. Frah xvi 10 (*gʾl(l)ʾ*), cf. Nyberg FP 48, 87 :: Ebeling Frah a.l.: l. *šllʾ* (var. *šlʾ*) = stone, cf. Hebr. *slʿ* and Syriac *šlʿ* - **Palm** Sing. emph. *gllʾ* CIS ii 3913 i 9 - ¶ subst. - **1)** stone (object): CIS ii 3913 i 9 (cf. Greek par. στήλη λιθίνη (on this text, cf. also Williamson BASOR cclxxx 86)) - **2)** stone (material): Pers 1^{2}, 4^{4}, 10^{4}, PF 1587^{2}, etc., etc. (cf. also Schmidt Persepolis ii 55 n. 68; on these texts, cf. also Williamson BASOR cclxxx 83ff., 86, on the Pers instances, cf. also Greenfield FS Rundgren 154 :: Delaunay CC 205: *zy gll* = reference to the manner the object is wrought, sc. by turning, cf. already Herzfeld with Schmidt Persepolis ii 55 n. 68) - > Akkad., cf. v.Soden Or xxxv 8, xlvi 186 (cf. also CAD s.v. *galālu*) - Naveh & Shaked Or xlii 455: *ʾbšwn zy zy* (dittography) *g[ll]* in Pers 29^{4} (prob. reading; for reading, cf. also Degen BiOr xxxi 127) :: R.A.Bowman Pers p. 100: l. *ʾbšwn zy bʾ[t]*, *bʾt* < Iran. = wine, cf. idem ibid. p. 63.

$\textbf{glm}_1$ **JAr** Plur. emph. *glmth* AMB 9^{8} - ¶ subst. hill.

$\textbf{glm}_2$ v. $ʿgl_1$.

glmt **Pun** word of unknown meaning in CIS i 204^{3} (CIS i a.l., Slouschz TPI p. 314: = n.l.?).

gln **Ph** Plur. abs. *glnm* EI xviii 117^{2} (= IEJ xxxv 83) - ¶ subst. poss. meaning cup (cf. also Dothan EI xviii 118, IEJ xxxv 86f.).

glp (< Greek γλύφω?, cf. also Brown Bibl lxx 208) - **Palm** QAL Pf. 3 p.s.m. *glp* PNO 52b 2; Part. act. s.m. abs. emph. *glpʾ* Inv D 47^{2} (for the reading, cf. Ingholt YClSt xiv 138) - **Hatra** QAL Pf. 3 p.s.m. *glp* 4^{1}, 46 (or Pf. 3 p.pl., cf. however 45, cf. also Degen WO v 227), 221^{3} (or Pf. 3 p.pl., cf. Degen WO v 227), 237^{2} (cf. Degen JEOL xxiii 407 n. 22, Aggoula MUSJ xlvii 13 :: Safar Sumer xxiv 12: = subst. or QAL Part. act. s.m. abs., cf. Vattioni IH a.l.), 258^{4} (cf. also Assur 9^{1}), 398,

413 i 1; 3 p.s.f. *glpt* 31[1], 32[1]; 3 p.pl. *glpw* 383; Part. act. s.m. emph. *glp›* 34[8], 289b; pl.m. emph. *glp›* 1[3] (cf. Teixidor Sumer xx 78, Syr xliv 189, Altheim & Stiehl AAW iv 255, Aggoula Ber xviii 86, Milik DFD 391, Degen ZDMG cxix 174, Vattioni IH a.l. :: Caquot Syr xxix 90: = s.m. emph., cf. also Donner KAI sub 237, Altheim & Stiehl AAW ii 191f.), 399 - ¶ verb QAL to sculpture, to make to be sculptured (a statue: Hatra 4[1], 34[8], a bas-relief: Hatra 31[1], a marble tablet with inscription: Hatra 221[3], 237[2], 258[4] (or object to which the tablet belonged?; :: Degen JEOL xxiii 415: = to write); + obj. (an altar): PNO 52b 2, Assur 9; QAL Part. act.: sculptor (or = noun?; v. *glwp*) - the diff. *glp* in Hatra 5[4] poss. = QAL Pf. 3 p.s.m. (cf. Caquot Syr xxix 93, Vattioni IH a.l. :: Safar Sumer vii 175 (n. 20): = part of n.p.), cf. also the *glp* in Hatra 5[2] (for the reading, cf. Aggoula Ber xviii 87); for this root in Hatra, cf. also Aggoula Syr lxv 213ff.
v. *›lp*$_3$, *glwp*.

glph **Palm** Sing. emph. *glpt›* PNO 57 - ¶ subst. f. sculpture (bas-relief) - Vattioni IH a.l.: l. *[gl]pt›* (= Sing. emph.) in Hatra 80[3] (uncert. interpret.).

glt Brown JSS xxv 5f.: prob. > Greek γαυλός (= bowl), γαῦλος (round Phoenician ship), cf. Hebr. *gullā*.

gm$_1$ **Pun** Sing. abs. *gm* KAI 161[5] - ¶ subst. of unknown meaning in expression *gm ›dr tm› ›dr›* (cf. Février RA xlv 143f., 148: = the illustrious Majesty, the illustrious Perfection, cf. also Röllig KAI a.l., Bron RIPK 102 :: Roschinski Num 114f.: *gm* = *gm*$_2$).

gm$_2$ **Mo** KAI 181[6] - **Hebr** KAI 193[10] - **Samal** KAI 214[8,9], 215[5] (v. also *w*$_2$)[,16] - ¶ adv. also, moreover - this word prob. also in TA-H 17[4], cf. Lipiński OLP viii 92.
v. *gm*$_1$,*lqḥ*.

gm› (< Egypt.?, cf. W.M.Müller OLZ iii 51 (n. 2), Grelot RB lxxviii 517 (n. 8), cf. however Lambdin JAOS lxxiii 149 (n. 35)) - **OffAr** Sing. abs. *gm›* Cowl 15[15], Krael 7[17] - ¶ subst. reed.

gmd **OffAr** Segal ATNS a.l: restore this subst. (Sing. abs. *gm[d]* = cloth) poss. in ATNS 9[9] (less prob. reading, cf. Porten & Yardeni sub TADAE B 8.6: l. *mn* (= *mn*$_5$)).

gmh v. *ym*$_1$.

gmwt **Palm** this word poss. in Inv xii 43[4] in the comb. *bgmwt*.Gawlikowski Syr xlviii 408f., TP 84: < Greek γάμος = hierogamy, *gmwt* = lapsus for *gmwthwn* (cf. however Starcky, Bounni & Teixidor sub Inv xii 43); cf. however Aggoula Sem xxix 116f.: or *bgmwt* = n.p. (poss. interpret.) or *gmwt* = n.l.

gmḥ (< Akkad., cf. Kutscher EI viii 273ff., Kaufman AIA 64 (n. 160), 139, 142f. (?), Lipiński Stud 201f. n. 6, cf. also Zimmern Fremdw 68; v. *gwḥ*) - **Palm** Sing. abs. *gwmḥ*Ber ii 85[11]; emph. *gwmḥ›*CIS ii 4175[7],

4218[3], 4227[2], 4292[8], RIP 105[1], etc.; Plur. abs. *gwmḥyn*CIS ii 4172[2], 4174[3,5], 4175[5], 4212[1], MUSJ xxxviii 106[7], FS Miles 50 ii 6, etc., etc., *gmḥyn* CIS ii 4171[1,2,3], 4173[2], 4195[7], etc.; emph. *gwmḥy*ʾ CIS ii 4194[6], RB xxxix 532[3] (Greek par. νεκροθή(κ)ων), Ber ii 82[1], 84[1], DM ii 43 ii 1, etc.; + suff. 3 p.s.m. *gwmḥwhy* Ber v 106[4], *gmḥwhy*MUSJ xxxviii 106[8] - ¶ subst. m. niche, *loculus*, passim; sometimes containing more than *one* burial site, cf. CIS ii 4175[7f.].

gmydh **OffAr** Sing. abs. *gmydh* Krael 7[7] (for the reading, cf. e.g. Kutscher JAOS lxxiv 236, Driver PEQ '55, 93, Porten & Yardeni sub TADAE B 3.8 :: Krael a.l.: l. *gmyrh* = garment) - ¶ subst. certain type of garment; on this word, cf. also Porten Arch 88 (n. 132), Kaufman AIA 51, Grelot RB lxxviii 518f., Zadok WO xii 198f.

gmyr v. *yqyr*.

gmyrh v. *gmydh*.

gml **OffAr** Sing. abs. *gml* TA-Ar 24[1]; emph. *gml*ʾ Aḥiq 91; Plur. abs. *gmln* AG 90; cf. Frah vii 1 (*gmr*ʾ), cf. also Lemosín AO ii 266 - **Nab** Sing. abs. *gml* J 109[3] (= RES 1187; uncert. reading); Plur. emph. *gmly*ʾ CIS ii 157[1] - **Palm** Sing. abs. *gml* CIS ii 3913 ii 16, 30, 32, 60, 66, 120; emph. *gml*ʾ CIS ii 3913 ii 7, 8, 17, 27, 36, 43, 61 (Greek par. καμήλου); Plur. abs. *gmlyn* CIS ii 3913 i 13; emph. *gmly*ʾ CIS ii 3913 ii 118 (Greek καμήλων), 122 (*gmly[*ʾ*]*) - ¶ subst. m. camel (on the camel in CIS ii 3913, cf. also Klíma FS Bakoš 147ff. (v. however *ṭ*ʿ*n*₁ and *srq*)); in *ḥṭ gml* TA-Ar 24[1], *ḥṭ* prob. = n.p.; for the comb. with *ṭ*ʿ*n*₂, v. *ṭ*ʿ*n*₂ - on this word, cf. also Masson RPAE 66f.

v. *gldgyml*.

gmlwn **Hebr** Plur. m. abs. *gmlwnyn* SM 49[4] - ¶ adj. large-sized, v. ʾ*pwn*.

gmnsyrks (< Greek γυμνασίαρχος) - **Palm** Sing. abs. (?) *gmnsyrks* Inv x 102b 1 - ¶ subst. m. gymnasiarch, master of a gymnasium.

gmr₁ **Pun** QAL Pf. 3 p.s.m. + suff. 3 p.s.m.? *gmr*ʾ CIS i 3918[2] - **Samal** ITP (or HITP, cf. Dion 206f., cf. also Huehnergard JAOS ciii 590 n. 179, ZDMG cxxxvii 268 n. 11) Impf. 3 p.pl.m. (preceded by *l*₁, cf. Dion 166f.) *ltgmrw* KAI 214[30] (cf. also Poeb 44 :: e.g. Cooke NSI 171, Friedr 16*e, Garb 262, Donner KAI a.l., Sader EAS 164: = QAL Impf. 2 p.pl.m.) - ¶ verb QAL to complete; + obj. (an altar): CIS i 3918[2] - ITP (v. supra) to assemble - the form *gmyr* KAI 276[8] prob. = QAL Part. pass. s.m. abs. (:: Grelot Sem viii 13: orthographical var. of *gmyrh* = QAL Part. pass. s.f. abs.; for form and context, v. *prnwš*) - a derivative of this root poss. also in FuF xxxv 173[11] (cf. Altheim & Stiehl ASA 267: = QAL Part. act. s.m. abs.?)

v. *gnb*₁, *yqyr*, *mgmr*₁.

gmr₂ **Ph** subst. of uncert. meaning in the comb. *gmr lmlk* in CISFP i 752; Bordreuil ibid.: = tax ? (< Akkad.?), cf. however Mantovani Hen vii 341.

gmr$_3$ = charcoal > Akkad., cf. v.Soden Or xxxv 9, xlvi 186, cf. however CAD s.v. *gumāru*: poss. Akkad. > Ar.

gmr$_4$ **OffAr** Plur. m. abs. *gmyrn* Samar 1^3 (= EI xviii 8*), Samar 2^2 (*[g]myrn*, dam. context); cf. GIPP 51 - **JAr** Plur. m. abs. *gmryn* MPAT 51^6, IEJ xxxvi 206^5 - ¶ adj. complete; *dmyn gmryn* MPAT 51^6: the total price (cf. Samar 1^3, IEJ xxxvi 206^5; cf. also Muffs 181 n. 7), cf. *mgmr$_2$*.

gn$_1$ **OffAr** Sing. abs. *gn* Cowl 81^{41} (on the context, cf. also Harmatta ActAntHung vii 355f.); Plur. emph. *gny*ʾ ATNS 107^1 - **Nab** Plur. cstr. *gny* DBKP 22^{31}; emph. *gny*ʾ CIS ii 350^2 (v. however infra) - **Palm** Plur. emph. *gny*ʾ PNO 42^5, MUSJ xxxviii 125$^{2f.}$ - ¶ subst. garden; *gny tmyry*ʾ DBKP 22^{31}: the Palm. orchards; context of CIS ii 350^2 diff., cf. e.g. Cooke NSI p. 242 × Milik RB lxvi 558f.: *gny*ʾ = Plur. emph. of *gn$_2$* (= seat, couch) - > Akkad., cf. v.Soden Or xxxv 8, xlvi 186 (cf. also Aro ZDMG cxiii 479, Zadok WO xii 199), cf. however CAD s.v. *gannatu* - on this word, cf. also Masson RPAE 74.

gn$_2$ v. *gn$_1$*.

gn$_3$ v. *bgn$_2$*.

gn$_4$ **Pun** for the diff. *gn* in CIS i 4981, Mozia ii p. 115b, cf. Garbini Moz ii p. 115ff.

gnʾ **Hatra** Qal Part. s.m. abs. *gn*ʾ 408^6 - ¶ verb to stretch oneself out; + *b$_2$*: Hatra 408^6 (cf. Aggoula Syr lxvii 409).
v. *br$_1$*.

gnb$_1$ **Pun** Qal Inf. cstr. *gnb* CIS i 3784$^{1f.}$; Part. act. s.m. abs. (?, cf. Gevirtz VT xi 151 n. 5 :: FR 131: = Pf. 3 p.s.m.) *gnb* CIS i 3783^5 - **Samal** Qal Impf. 3 p.s.m. *ygnb* KAI 214^{28} (for the reading, cf. e.g. Lidzbarski Handb 251, 442, Cooke NSI p. 161, 170, Donner KAI a.l., Dion p. 33, 192, Sader EAS 162, 164 × D.H.Müller WZKM vii 66, Gibson SSI ii p. 68, 75: l. *ygmr* (Müller: = Qal Impf. 3 p.s.m. of *gmr$_1$*, Gibson: = Paʿel Impf. 3 p.s.m. of *gmr$_1$*;dam. context; cf. also Poeb 44)) - **OffAr** Qal Pf. 3 p.pl.m. *gnbw* ATNS 10a 7; Qal pass. Pf. 3 p.s.m. *gnyb* ATNS 5^2 (cf. Porten & Yardeni sub TADAE B 8.3 :: Segal ATNS a.l.: = Qal Part. pass. s.m. abs.); Part. s.m. abs. *gnyb* Cowl 38^4 - Hatra Qal Impf. 3 p.s.m. *lgnwb* 336^8, 343^5 - **Palm** Qal Impf. 3 p.s.m. *ygnb* Inv viii 86^2, Syr xvii 353^2 - **JAr** Qal Part. act. s.m. abs. *gnyb* MPAT-A 22^3 (= SM 70^{11}) - ¶ verb Qal to steal, to rob: Hatra 336^8, 343^5 - **1)** + obj.: CIS i 3783$^{5f.}$, 3784$^{1f.}$ (on this text, cf. Krahmalkov RSO lxi 74ff.), MPAT-A 22$^{4f.}$ - **2)** + *l$_5$* (obj.): ATNS 10a 7 - Qal pass. to be stolen: ATNS 5^2 (probably said of a slave) - a form of this root in ATNS 10b 2 (*gnb[*).
v. *gnb$_2$*.

gnb$_2$ **OldAr** Sing. emph. *gnb*ʾ KAI 222A 36 - **OffAr** Sing. m. abs.

gnb Aḥiq 125, 221 (??, heavily dam. context); cf. Frah xiii 13 (*gnb*ᵓ; cf. Nyberg FP 47, 83 :: Ebeling Frah a.l.: l. *zlb*ᵓ (related to Akkad. *ṣalpu*??)); f. abs. *gnbh* Aḥiq 84 - ¶ subst. thief (or in Aḥiq 84, 125: = QAL Part. act. of gnb_1??);KAI 222A 36 diff. context, Dupont-Sommer Sf p. 53f.: = thief > bandit (cf. Gibson SSI ii p. 31, 42), or = gnb_3 (= tail??, cf. also Donner KAI a.l.), Lipiński Stud 31: = thief, for the problems involved, cf. also Fitzmyer AIS 54, Grelot RB lxxv 282f., Degen AAG p. 46, OLZ '71, 268; Lemaire & Durand IAS 114, 122, 135: l. poss. *gbr*ᵓ (= Sing. emph. of gbr_2).
v. *gnby*.

gnb₃ v. gb_3,gnb_2.

gnby **JAr** Sing. abs. *gnby* MPAT 127 (= Frey 1190) - ¶ subst. of uncert. meaning; Fitzmyer & Harrington MPAT a.l.: = thief?, l. perhaps *gnb*ᵓ = Sing. emph. of gnb_2? (or interpret. as variant of gby_2(= collector of charities, manager) preferable?).

gnbyt **OffAr** *gnbyt* Cowl 37[5] - ¶ adv. as a thief.

gnd₁ v. gd_1.

gnd₂ cf. Frah-S_2 104 (*gnd*ᵓ): band, troupe.

gndn **Hatra** Sing. emph. *gnd[n*ᵓ*]* 380 - ¶ adj. fortunate, *snṭrwq mlk*ᵓ *gnd[n*ᵓ*]* Hatra 380: S. the fortunate king.

gngn **OffAr** Plur. emph. *gngny*ᵓ ATNS 40[1] - ¶ subst. prob. meaning gardener (Segal sub ATNS 40: *gngn-* = Plur. form of gnn_4).

gnh₁ **Pun** Sing. abs. *gnt* CIS i 5510[10] (?, cf. Février BAr '46/49, 173: div. ᵓ*gr gnt* = the wall (Sing. cstr. of ᵓgr_4) of the garden :: Garbini RSO xlii 12f.: ᵓ*grgnt* = ᵓ$_8$ + *grgnt* (= Pun. f. form < Greek Γοργών = head (sculptured) of Gorgon, cf. also idem JSS xii 112, FSR 165 n. 13) :: Krahmalkov RSF ii 174, v.d.Branden BiOr xxxvi 202: ᵓ*grgnt* = n.l., *Agrigentum*) - **Amm** Plur. (?, cf. Zayadine & Thompson Ber xxii 136, BASOR ccxii 10, Smelik HDAI 85 (cf. also Baldacci VT xxxi 364f.) × Krahmalkov BASOR ccxxiii 56, Emerton FS v.d.Ploeg 372, 376, Jackson ALIA 36, 38, 40, Garr DGSP 59: = Sing.; cf. also Becking BiOr xxxviii 275 (n. 20)) abs. *gnt* Ber xxii 120[4] (:: Loretz UF ix 170: = Sing. or Plur. abs. of gnh_2 (= wine press); on this word, cf. also Aufrecht sub CAI 78) - **OffAr** Sing. emph. *gnt*ᵓ CRAI '70, 163[3bis] (diff. context), IPAA 11[8] (diff. context) - Nab. Sing. cstr. *gnt* CIS ii 350[2]; emph. *gnt*ᵓ MPAT 64 recto i 2, 3, 4 - **Palm** Sing. cstr. *gnt* Inv xi 80[6] (?, dam. context: *gnt[*; for the reading, cf. Degen NESE ii 104 n. 22, cf. also Milik DFD 2, 4, Gawlikowski Syr xlvii 324 (: l. *gnt[*ᵓ*]* = Sing. emph.) :: Teixidor Inv xi a.l.: l. *(b)gnw[*, perhaps = Sing. abs. of bgn_2(= prayer) + *w*); emph. *gnt*ᵓ RIP 162[4], SBS 45[12] (v. infra) - **JAr** Sing. emph. (?) *gynth* Syr xlv 101[18] (dam. context) - ¶ subst. f. garden; *gnt smk*ᵓ CIS ii 350[2]: (walled) garden used for funeral banquet, cf. Nöldeke ZA xii 4, Starcky Syr xxvi 64, Milik RB lxvi 559, cf. also Cooke NSI p. 242,

Gawlikowski TP 93 (n. 31) :: Clermont-Ganneau RAO ii 372 n. 1: *gnt* = baldachin, canopy; *gnt› ›lym* SBS 45[12] (Greek par. for *bgnt› ›lym* = [ἐ]ν ἱερῷ ἄλσει): the sacred garden/forest (for the construction, cf. Caquot GLECS vii 78, Dunant SBS a.l., Gawlikowski Syr li 93f.), indication of (part of) one of the tribal sanctuaries in Palmyre (cf. Gawlikowski Syr xlvii 322f., li 93f., TP 49ff., Dunant SBS a.l., Milik DFD 7ff.), cf. *gnt› mtq[dšt›]* RIP 162[4]? - in RES 954[1] prob. l. *gnt›* (= Sing. emph.), cf. Lidzbarski Eph iii 65 (for the context, cf. Lipiński Stud 200f., cf. however Degen WO ix 171 :: Chabot sub RES 954: l. *byrt›* = Sing. emph. of *byrh*, cf. also Sprengling AJSL xlv 280 :: Vattioni Aug xi 185f.: l. *pgrt›* (= Sing. emph. of *pgrh* (= tomb), cf. however Teixidor Syr li 329f.)).

gnh$_2$ v. *gnh$_1$*.

gnz (< Iran., cf. Telegdi JA ccxxvi 237, Schaed 245 n. 3, 264, Driv p. 77, Diakonov & Livshitz Nisa-b p. 40, Sznycer Sem xiii 34ff., Hinz AISN 102) - **OffAr** Sing. emph. *gnz›* Cowl 26[4,13], 69B 2 (*gnz[›]*, for this prob. reading, cf. Porten & Yardeni sub TADAE B 8.5), 3, Driv 10[5] - ¶ subst. - **1)** treasure: Driv 10[5] - **2)** treasury: Cowl 26[4,13].
v. *›pgnzbr*, *gnzbr*.

gnzbr (< Iran., cf. Telegdi JA ccxxvi 237, Diakonov & Livshitz Nisa-b p. 40, R.A.Bowman Pers p. 63, Harnack with Altheim & Stiehl GMA 547ff., Sznycer Sem xiii 35, Hinz AISN 102; cf. also Hinz NWAP 31) - **OffAr** Sing. emph. *gnzbr›* Pers 1[4], 12[3], 14[3], 15[5], 18[3], 19[4], 20[5], 21[5], etc., etc. (for this form in pers., cf. also R.A.Bowman Pers p. 67) - **Hatra** Sing. emph. *gzbr›*,cf. Assur 15c, 22[8] - **JAr** Sing. emph. *gyzbrh*Syn D A 6f. (= SM 88) - ¶ subst. m. treasurer (for Pers, cf. R.A.Bowman Pers p. 28ff., Naveh & Shaked Or xlii 448ff.; cf. also Altheim & Stiehl GMA 558).
v. *›pgnzbr*,*gnz*.

gny$_1$ v. *br$_1$*.

gny$_2$ **OffAr** Grelot DAE p. 404 n. t: l. *[y]gnwn* (= Pa‹el/Aph Impf. 3 p.pl.m. of *gny$_2$* (= to protect; cf. also Porten & Greenfield JEAS p. 88, Porten & Yardeni sub TADAE A 4.5: l. *[yh]gnwn* = Haph Impf. 3 p.pl.m. of *gny$_2$*) :: Cowl a.l.: l. *[yn]gnwn* = Pa‹el Impf. 3 p.pl.m. of *ngn* (= to injure)).

gny$_3$ cf. Frah-S$_2$ 70 (*gny›*), prob. = Qal Part. pass. (= ugly, disgusting) of *gny$_3$* (= to blame), cf. Nyberg FP 118.

gny$_4$ (< Arab.?, cf. Starcky Syr xxvi 254ff.) - **Palm** Sing. abs. *gny* PNO 41; emph. *gny›* PNO 5, 6bc, 17[4] (*g[n]y›*), 23, 43[3] (cf. Starcky PNO a.l., Schlumberger MUSJ xlvi 214f.), 68 (*gn[y]›*), Inv xi 66[2], Sem xxii 59[2]; Plur. emph. *gny›* RTP 248 (cf. Schlumberger MUSJ xlvi 217f.), Sem iii 47, PNO 14[4] (:: Milik DFD 343: = Sing. emph.), 16[5], 39, 48[2], Inv D 20, MUSJ xlii 178 ii (dam. context), Syr xii 135[1], FS Collart 327[4];

Sing. or Plur. emph. *gnyʾ* PNO 78^{6} (cf. Schlumberger MUSJ xlvi 215), RTP 225, 226 (cf. Schlumberger MUSJ xlvi 217f.) - ¶ subst. m. *genius* (i.e. divine being); for these divine beings and the problem of *gny* as n.d., cf. Seyrig & Starcky Syr xxvi 230ff., Schlumberger PNO pp 135-137, MUSJ xlvi 209ff., Starcky MUSJ xlix 506 n. 1, FS Collart 329f. (nn. 16-18), Milik Bibl xlviii 602f., Teixidor Syr xlvi 326, Milik with Teixidor Syr xlviii 464, Teixidor Syr xlix 421f., PP 77ff., 95ff.; cf. also *gnyt*.

gny$_5$ **JAr** Sing. emph. *gnyh* Syr xlv 101^{15} (diff. reading) - ¶ subst. m. gardener.

gnyt **Hatra** Sing. emph. 410^{1} - ¶ subst. female divine being, cf. *gny*$_4$; cf. Aggoula Syr lxvii 413.

gnn$_1$ v. *ʾgn*$_{1,2}$, *ʾgnn*, *gʾn*, *gnn*$_2$, *nwh*.

gnn$_2$ **Pun** YIPH Pf. 3 p.s.m.? *ygn* KAI 124^{2} - ¶ verb YIPH of uncert. meaning + obj.; Levi Della Vida RCL '49, 402: = to repair?, Röllig KAI a.l.: = to cover (= *gnn*$_1$;cf. also v.d.Branden PO i 436, Amadasi IPT 64).

gnn$_3$ v. *ʾgn*$_2$.

gnn$_4$ **OffAr** Sing. abs. *gnn* Krael 9^{10}, 10^{6} - ¶ subst. m. gardener; *gnn zy ḥnwm ʾlhʾ* Krael 9^{10}, 10^{6}: the gardener of the god Chnum.
v. *gngn*.

gnn$_5$ v.d.Branden BO xxii 220, 224: l. *gnn* = Sing. abs. (= protection) in RSF vii 18 no. 38.

gns (< Greek γένος) - **Palm** Sing. abs. *gns* CIS ii 3913 i 13, 3966^{6} (= RIP 156^{15}), Inv ix 11^{4}; Plur. emph. *gnsyʾ* CIS ii 3913 ii 68 - **JAr** Plur. + suff. 3 p.pl.m. *gnsyh[wn]* Syr xlv 101^{13} (dam. context) - ¶ subst. m. kind, species, passim; *bkl gns klh* CIS ii 3966^{6}, Inv ix 11^{4}: in every way; *dy klmʾ gns klh* CIS ii 3913 i 13: of any kind (sc. of goods) whatsoever.

gnsṭs (< Greek γνώστης, cf. Littmann with Wiegand Palmyra p. 11, Rosenthal Sprache 20 n. 4, 92) - **Palm** Sing. abs. *gnsṭs* RB xxxix 548^{3} - ¶ subst. prob. meaning: witness :: Cantineau RB xxxix 548f.: = posterity? (cf. however idem Syr xix 171).

gntl **Hebr** the *gntl* IEJ ix 191 (uncert. reading, cf. Tsori IEJ ix a.l.: or l. *gwtl*, *pntl*, *pwtl*) on spindle whirl = n.p.?

gsʾsṭr **JAr** Dupont-Sommer JKF i 207: the *gsʾstr* in AMB 7^{10} (< Greek γῆς ἀστήρ) prob. = talc (improb. interpret., cf. Naveh & Shaked AMB a.l.: *gs* = part of magical name, *ʾsṭr* = magical name (cf. also Scholem JGM 86)).

gst$_1$ (< Iran., cf. Driv p. 50, Eilers AfO xvii 333, Hinz AISN 103) - **OffAr** Sing. cstr. (or abs.?) *gst* Driv 4^{3}, 7^{9} - ¶ subst. m. in the expression *gst ptgm* Driv 4^{3}, 7^{9}: = bad thing > punishment, cf. Greenfield IrJu 9f. :: bad (/adverse) word > rebuke (cf. Driv p. 50f., Porten EI xiv 176, Hinz AISN 103, Porten & Yardeni sub TADAE A 6.8/10) :: >

sanction (cf. Grelot DAE p. 305f. n. d) :: J.J.Rabinowitz Bibl xli 74: > crime :: Segert ArchOr xxiv 390: = the presenting of (= Sing. cstr. of *gst*$_2$) the bill (i.e. the calling to account).

gst$_2$ v. *gst*$_1$.

gʿz v. *gzy*.

gʿr **JAr** QAL Imper. pl.m. *gʿwrw* AMB 2^8; Inf. *mgʿwr* AMB 2^{11}; ITP Imper. s.m. *ʾgʿr* AMB $9^{2,4}$ (cf. Naveh & Shaked AMB a.l. :: Greenfield Mem Kutscher xxxviiif.: = QAL Impf. 1 p.s.) - ¶ verb QAL to turn back, to drive out (cf. Greenfield Mem Kutscher xxxviii, Naveh AAALT 88); + obj. + *mn*$_5$, *gʿwrw ʾšth ... mn pgrh* AMB $2^{8f.}$: drive out the fever ... from her body (cf. AMB $2^{11f.}$) - ITP to be driven out (v. supra); + *mn*$_5$, *ʾgʿr mn gwph* AMB 9^2: be driven out from her body (cf. AMB 9^4).

gp$_1$ **OffAr** Sing. abs. *gp* CIS ii 146^5; emph. *gpʾ* Cowl 73^1 (= CIS ii 147A 1; ?, heavily dam. context); + suff. 3 p.s.m.? *gph* NESE iii 39^9 (dam. context); + suff. 3 p.s.f. *gph* NESE iii 39^7; Plur. emph. *gpyʾ* Cowl $73^{1,8}$ (= CIS ii 147A 1, D 1; heavily dam. context) - **Hatra** Sing. + suff. 3 p.s.m. *gwph*74^7 (for the uncert. reading, cf. Caquot Syr xxxii 270, Donner sub KAI 256, Degen NESE ii 100 (n. 6), Ingholt AH i/1, 44, i/2, 44 :: Milik DFD 401ff., Vattioni IH a.l.: pro *bgwph* l. *bh zpʾ* (= Sing. emph. of *zp*$_1$ (= lie, falsification))) - **JAr** Sing. + suff. 3 p.s.f. *gwph*AMB 9^2 - ¶ subst. person, in Hatra 74^7 (v. supra): = corpse, dead body (cf. Degen NESE ii 102 (n. 15)); *bgp* CIS ii 146^5: in person, personally (cf. also NESE iii $39^{7,9}$); Cowl $73^{1,8}$, CIS ii 149BC 9 (*gwpn* (= Sing. + suff. 1 p.pl.?)) obscure contexts - Segal ATNS a.l.: l. *bgpn* (= *b*$_2$ + Plur. abs. of *gp*$_1$) = individually in ATNS 28b 1 (improb. interpret., cf. Shaked Or lvi 410: *bgpn* = n.p., cf. also Porten & Yardeni sub TADAE B 8.4).
v. *gw*$_2$.

gp$_2$ v. *gb*$_3$.

gp$_3$ v. *ggp*.

gp$_4$ **Nab** Naveh IEJ xxix 113, 117: the *gpyn* in IEJ xxix 112^3 = Plur./Dual abs. of *gp*$_4$ (= wing); interpret. of context highly uncert.
v. *gw*$_2$.

gṣ **Hatra** Sing. emph. *gṣʾ* $344^{5,10,11}$ - ¶ subst. mortar: Hatra $344^{5,10,11}$, cf. also Aggoula Syr lxv 210.

gqwl **Hebr** diff. word poss. occurring in ossuary inscription IEJ xx 35: *ḥ/hgqwl*. Naveh IEJ xx a.l.: l. *ḥgqwl* = n.p. (cf. also Yadin with Naveh IEJ xx a.l.); Yadin IEJ xxiii 18ff.: l. *hgqwl* = *h*$_1$ + *gqwl* (= var. of *ʿqwl* (= QAL Part. pass. s.m. abs. of *ʿql*$_1$ (= to distort)), i.e. the distorted one = one crucified in a special way (on this point, cf. Møller-Christensen IEJ xxvi 35ff.; less prob. interpret.)). For the problems involved, cf. also Fitzmyer CBQ xl 495ff., TAG 126ff.

gr_1 m. **Ph** Plur. abs. *grm* KAI 37A 16, B 10 (= Kition C 1 A 15, B 10; v. infra) - **Nab** Sing. + suff. 3 p.pl.f. *grhm* (or Plur.??) J 12[5,6]; Plur. + suff. 3 p.pl.f. *gryhm* J 12[4] - **Palm** Sing. abs. *gr* CIS ii 4218[5] (for the reading, cf. Chabot sub RES 1071, sub CIS ii a.l. :: Ledrain RA iii 27, Clermont-Ganneau Et i 121, Lidzbarski Handb 248, 480, Cooke NSI p. 311: l. *gd* (= Sing. abs. of gd_1;Clermont-Ganneau Et i 121: or = Sing. abs. of gd_2(= descendant)?), *gyr*CIS ii 3972[4]; + suff. 3 p.s.m. *grh* CIS ii 4035[4] (for the reading, cf. Chabot sub CIS ii a.l., Milik DFD 106 :: Teixidor sub Inv xi 15: l. *gdh* (= Sing. + suff. 3 p.s.f. of gd_1)),*gyrh* CIS ii 3973[8] - **JAr** Sing. emph. *gyr>* Mas 420[7] - f. **Hebr** Sing. abs. *gyrt* RB lxiii 77,23 (= DF 31) - ¶ subst. - **1)** *cliens*, client, follower - a) of a man: CIS ii 4035[4], 4218[5], J 12[4,5,6] - b) of a god: CIS ii 3972[4]; cf. KAI 37A 16, B 10? (cf. e.g. Lidzbarski Handb 251f., Cooke NSI p. 67f., Harr 92, Thomas VT x 425, Segert ArchOr xxix 240, Röllig KAI a.l., cf. also Puech RB xcii 292) × interpret. as forms of gr_2 (v.d.Branden BO viii 259, BMB xiii 92, Masson & Sznycer RPC 66ff., Delcor UF xi 163, Lemaire Syr lxiv 208: = young animal > young boy > young male prostitute (cf. also Amadasi sub Kition C 1); Peckham Or xxxvii 306, 317 (n. 4): = lion (i.e. in the context man with lion-mask), cf. also Healey BASOR ccxvi 53, 54, 56: = lion-man, Gibson SSI iii p. 125, 130: "lion's whelps", indication of cultic profession (prob. related to sacred prostitution)) - **2)** proselyte: RB lxiii 77,23 (= DF 31), Mas 420[7] (cf. Yadin & Naveh Mas a.l.) - **3)** giver of hospitality: CIS ii 3973[8] (cf. Cooke NSI p. 305, Teixidor FS Gaster 407) - on this word, cf. Teixidor GHPO 43 - cf. also O'Connor JNES xlv 218: not < Arab. (:: Cantineau Nab ii 172).
v. gr_2, grh_2, $ḥpr_2$.

gr_2 **Mo** Plur. abs. *grn* (prob. reading, cf. e.g. Lidzbarski Eph i 7) KAI 181[16] - ¶ subst. m. of uncert. interpret.: young boy (?; cf. e.g. Lidzbarski Eph i 7, Halévy RS viii 290, Albright ANET 320, v.Zijl 191, Andersen Or xxxv 88, Liver PEQ '67, 25, Weippert ZAW lxxxiv 484f. (n. 116), Lemaire Syr lxiv 207f.) × = gr_1(= client > alien resident, cf. e.g. Segert ArchOr xxix 240, xxxi 335, Röllig KAI a.l., Galling TGI 52, Gibson SSI i 76, 80f., Reviv CSI p. 24, de Geus SV 26, 28 n. n, de Moor UF xx 153, Briend TPOA 91, Jackson & Dearman SMIM 98) - in KAI 181[16f.] f. Plur. abs. prob. to be restored: *[gr]t*.
v. gr_1,grh_2, *gry*.

gr_3 v.Soden Or xxxv 8, xlvi 186, AHW s.v. *girû*: Ar. gr_3 (= carob seed) > Akkad. (= 1/24 shekel; ?, cf. also CAD s.v.).
v. *zz*.

grb_1 **OffAr** Sing. abs. *grb* Cowl 81[8,9,83]; Plur. abs. *grbn* Cowl 81[8,9,42], *grbyn* Cowl 81[10,40,43] - ¶ subst. large bottle, flagon - abbrev. *g* prob. in At ix-x 201[2] - *g* in Mas 591, 592 = abbrev. of grb_1? (cf. Yadin & Naveh

Mas a.l.) - Harmatta ActAntHung vii 345f.: < Iran. :: Hinz AISN 108: = *grb$_6$* (< Iran. = bushel).
v. *gryw*, *pg*.
grb$_2$ v. *ʿrb$_5$*.
grb$_3$ **Hatra** Plur. emph. *grbʾ* 281^9 - ¶ subst. of unknown meaning; v.d.Branden BiOr xxxvi 341: cf. Arab. *girāb* (bag in which utensils are collected); Degen AION xxvii 488, NESE iii 71, Aggoula Syr lxiv 101f., lxv 208: = water-skin, jar? (= *grb$_4$*), cf. also Vattioni IH a.l., Tubach ISS 274 (n. 111).
grb$_4$ = bag, reinforcement around an earthenware jar > Akkad., cf. v.Soden Or xxxv 9, xlvi 186, AHW s.v. *gurābu*, CAD sv.
v. *grb$_3$*.
grb$_5$ Aggoula Ber xviii 96: l. *grbʾ* (= Sing. m. emph. of *grb$_5$* (= leprous)) in Hatra 71. Prob = n.p.
grb$_6$ v. *grb$_1$*.
grbdr Ebeling Frah a.l.: l. *grb(d)rʾ* (< Akkad./Sum.) = sword in Frah xiv 5 (improb. reading and interpret., cf. Nyberg FP 47, 84: l. Iran. word).
grbyy **Palm** Sing. m. emph. *grbyyʾ* Ber ii 91^2, 98^1, 99 ii 1, v 95^7, 106^3 - ¶ adj. northern.
grgn v. *gḥgn*.
grgnt v. *gnh$_1$*.
grgr **Hebr** Sing. abs. *grgr* Mas 537 (*gr[gr]*), 540 (*gr[gr]*), 541, 542 - ¶ subst. berry (cf. also Yadin & Naveh sub Mas 537: in Mas 537, 540 = dried fig(s) (uncert. interpret.)).
grd (< Iran., cf. Driv p. 63, Benveniste JA ccxlii 306, de Menasce BiOr xi 162, Eilers AfO xvii 333, Altheim & Stiehl ASA 171, Hinz AISN 107, cf. also Hinz NWAP 53f.) - **OffAr** Sing. cstr. *grd* Driv 7^{2,6}, 9^2; emph. *grdʾ* Driv 7^{1,4,5,8}, 12^{8,9,10} - ¶ subst. domestic staff, passim; *grd ʾmnn* Driv 7$^{2f.,6}$: a staff of craftsmen (cf. also *grd bdykrn* (or *brykrn*?, v. *bdykr*): Driv 9^2) - cf. also Frye BAG 86 (n. 5), Ingholt PBP 104.
grh$_1$ **Hebr** Sing. abs. *grh* Or xlix 342 no. 3 i 9 (uncert. reading), 11 (uncert. reading), iii 2 (*gr[h]*, uncert. reading), 3 (*gr[h]*, uncert. reading), 6 (reading of *h* uncert.), 7 (reading of *h* uncert.), 8, 9 (reading of *h* uncert.) - ¶ subst. indicating certain small weight (cf. e.g. Barrois ii 253ff., Trinquet SDB v 1242, EM iv 863ff., Wambacq VD xxix 343, Lemaire & Vernus Or xlix 344 n. 10).
grh$_2$ **OffAr** Sing. abs. *grh* Aḥiq 219 (heavily dam. context) - ¶ subst. of uncert. meaning, f. of *gr$_1$*or *gr$_2$*?(Cowl a.l.: = f. of *gr$_2$*,cf. also Kottsieper SAS 23, 195: = Sing. + suff. 3 p.s.m. of *gr$_1$*;Sach p. 180: l. *gdh* (= Sing. + suff. 3 p.s.m. of *gd$_1$*));cf. also Lindenberger APA 218, 274f. nn. 573-575.
v. *gdh$_2$*.

grwb Ebeling Frah p. 38: the *grwb* in Frah xvii 2 = lapsus for *ʿrbn*, cf. however Nyberg FP 48, 87: l. Iran. word here.
grzn **Hebr** Sing. abs. *grzn* KAI $189^{2,4}$ - ¶ subst. pick(axe).
grṭyʾ v. *grmṭyʾ*.
gry (not < Akkad., cf. Kutscher JAOS lxxiv 238 :: Krael p. 135, Sperling JANES i/1 39f.; cf. also Muffs 31 n. 2, 196f., Kaufman AIA 88) - **OffAr** QAL Pf. 3 p.s.m. + suff. 2 p.s.m. *grk* Krael 1^{8}; + suff. 2 p.s.f. *grky* Cowl 14^{9} (cf. Leand p. 64 :: BL p. 126h', Altheim & Stiehl GH ii 175, GMA 352: = 3 p.pl.m. + suff. 2 p.s.f.); 1 p.s. + suff. 2 p.s.m. *grytk* Cowl 67 iii 2; + suff. 2 p.s.f. *grytky* Cowl 14^{8}, Krael 4^{14}; 3 p.pl.m. *grw* Krael 3^{18}; + suff. 2 p.s.m. *grwk* Krael 3^{18}; 1 p.pl. *gryn* Krael 3^{14}, ATNS 187^{2} (?, heavily dam. context); + suff. 3 p.s.m. *grnh* ATNS 13^{2} (cf. also Bennett Or lvi 88; dam. context, uncert. interpret.); + suff. 2 p.s.m. *grynk* Krael 3^{14}; Impf. 3 p.s.m. *ygrh* Krael 3^{19}; + suff. 2 p.s.m. *ygrnk* Cowl 6^{14}, 67 v 3, Krael $3^{17,19}$; + suff. 2 p.s.f. *ygrnky* Cowl 1^{6}, 3^{10}, Krael 4^{14}, *ygrnk* Krael 4^{16}; 1 p.s. + suff. 2 p.s.m. *ʾgrnk* Cowl 6^{12}, Krael 1^{4}; + suff. 2 p.s.f. *ʾgrnky* Cowl 14^{7}; + suff. 2 p.pl.m. *ʾgrnkm* Cowl 25^{10}; 3 p.pl.m. + suff. 3 p.s.m. *ygrwhy* RSO xxxv 22^{4}; + suff. 2 p.s.f. *ygrwnky* Cowl 1^{6}; 1 p.pl. *ngrh* Krael 3^{14}; + suff. 2 p.s.m. *ngrnk* Krael 3^{12}; + suff. 2 p.s.f. *ngrky* Cowl 1^{4} - ¶ verb QAL to sue, to institute suit against - **1)** + obj. (cf. however Muffs 31 n. 2, 196f.: indirect object), *hn grwk* Krael 3^{18}: if they start action against you, cf. Cowl 1^{6}, Krael 3^{19}, RSO xxxv 22^{4} - **2)** + obj. + instrum. (cf. however Muffs 31 n. 2, 196f.: = object, cf. also idem ibid. 182), *hn gbr ʾḥrn ygrnk dyn* Krael 4^{16}: if another man starts legal action against you; cf. *hn grytky dyn wdbb* Cowl $14^{8f.}$ (cf. Cowl 13^{10}, 25^{10}, Krael 3^{14}; cf. also Muffs 182, 196f.) - **3)** + obj. + b_2 instrum., *grytk bdyn* Cowl 67 iii 2: I start legal action against you (for the context, cf. Porten & Yardeni sub TADAE B 5.2 :: Joüon MUSJ xviii 38) - **4)** + obj. + b_2 caus., *ngrky bmntʾ zky* Cowl 1^{4}: we will sue you in the matter of this your share (cf. Cowl 1^{6}); cf. also + *bšm*, *wgrky ... bšm mwmʾh dky* Cowl 14^{9}: he sues you in the matter of this your oath (cf. Krael 1^{8}, 4^{14}) - **5)** + obj. + *bšm* + $ʿl_7$ (in the matter of), *ygrnk bšmy ʿl ʾrqʾ zk* Cowl 6^{14}: he will sue you in the matter of this land - **6)** + obj. + instrum. + *bšm*: Cowl $14^{7f.}$, Krael $1^{4f.}$, $3^{12f.,17}$, 4^{14} - **7)** + obj. + instrum. + $ʿl_7$ (in the matter of): Cowl $6^{12f.}$ - **8)** + l_5 (obj.): Krael $3^{14,14f.,18,19f.}$ - for the use of the root in the Elephantine papyri, cf. also Joüon MUSJ xviii 36ff. - the *gry* in DA i 12 prob. = QAL Part. act. pl.m. cstr. (or nominal form of this root?), cf. Hoftijzer DA a.l. and p. 272, Levine JAOS ci 197, 199, H.P.Müller ZAW xciv 218, 228 (n. 85), H. & M.Weippert ZDPV xcviii 98, 103, Puech BAT 359, 362, Smelik HDAI 79 :: Caquot & Lemaire Syr liv 200, Garbini Hen i 180, 185, Delcor SVT xxxii 58, McCarter BASOR ccxxxix 51, Hackett BTDA 29, 51, 128, Sasson UF xvii 288,

301 (n. 40), Puech FS Grelot 23, 28: = Plur. cstr. of *gr*$_2$(= young of animal); for the context, cf. also H.P.Müller ZDPV xciv 62 n. 39.

gryw **OffAr** the *g* in Cowl 2^{7}, $24^{38,41}$, Eph iii 300A 3, 4, prob. = abbrev. of *gryw* (= certain dry measure), cf. Epstein ZAW xxxiii 148, Maricq Syr xxxv 319 n. 7, Porten Arch 70f. (n. 48), Grelot DAE p. 268, 274 :: Lidzbarski Eph iii 300: = abbrev. of *grb*$_1$ - Segal ATNS a.l.: the *g* in ATNS 24^{8}, 42b 1, 69a, 95b 4 prob. = abbrev. of *gryw* - for *gryw* and *g* used as ideograms, cf. Maricq Syr xxxv 319 n. 7 (for the relevant texts, cf. AJSL lvii 387, 390, 391, 416).
v. *gw*$_2$,*ḥpn*.

grl **Ph** Sing. abs. *grl* EpAn ix 5^{1} - ¶ subst. allotment (of land), cf. Mosca & Russell EpAn ix 8, cf. also Greenfield Sem xxxviii 157.

grm$_1$ **OffAr** Plur. + suff. 2 p.s.m. *grmyk* Cowl 71^{15} - **J.Ar.** Plur. cstr. *grmy* MPAT 67^{2} (= Frey 1300); emph. *grmy*› LA xxxii 358, *grmyh* AMB $1^{20,21}$; + suff. 3 p.s.m. *grmwhy* AMB 1^{22} - ¶ subst. Plur. bones; v.Soden Or xxxv 10, xlvi 187, AHW s.v. *ḫarmil*: > Akkad. = cartilage, cartilaginous meat (cf. however CAD s.v. *ḫarmel*) - for *rwḥ grmyh* AMB $1^{20,21}$, v. *rḥ*$_1$.
v. *dm*$_1$.

grm$_2$ (< Greek γράμμα) - **JAr** Plur. abs. *grmyn* MPAT-A 27^{2} (= Frey 857 = SM 33) - ¶ subst. gram(me); cf. Frey a.l.: = third part of silver *denarius* (?; cf. Naveh SM p. 11 n. 41).

grmṭws (< Greek γραμματεύς) - **Palm** Sing. abs. *grmṭws* CIS ii 3913 i 2, 3959^{2} (= SBS 44B), Inscr P 6^{2} (cf. Inv x 39) - ¶ subst. m. scribe; *grmṭws dy trty*› CIS ii 3959^{2}: scribe for the second time (cf. Greek par. γραμμ[α]τέα γενόμενον τὸ δεύτερον), cf. Nöldeke ZDMG xxiv 102 and also Syr xiv 177^{5} *bgrmṭy*› *qdmt*›: during the first secretaryship.

grmṭy› (< Greek γραμματεία) - **Palm** Sing. abs. *grmṭy*› CIS ii 3913 i 2, Inv x 13^{4}, Syr xiv 177^{5}, Inscr P 6^{3} (the reading *grṭy*›mistake in transcription, cf. Starcky sub Inv x 39) - ¶ subst. f. secretaryship, secretariat(e), function of a scribe.

grs **OffAr** PA‘EL (or QAL?) Pf. 3 p.pl.m. *grsw* RES 1793^{1} (= PSBA xxxvii 222^{6}; uncert. reading, cf. Cowley PSBA a.l.; Kutscher Kedem i 55: l. *grst* = QAL Pf. 2 p.s.m.); Impf. 1 p.s. ›*grs* (›*grs[*) FS Driver 54 conv. 2 - ¶ verb PA‘EL (v. supra) to grind; in FS Driver 54 conv. 2 dam. context; in RES 1793^{1} uncert. context + obj. (*lḥm*$_4$; v. also supra), cf. Cowley PSBA xxxvii 222, Grelot DAE p. 376 (n. f): = to consume, to devour (interpret. based on other div. of context, v. *lḥm*$_4$) - Zadok JAOS cii 115f. (cf. also id. WO xii 199): a derivative of this root (= grits, groats) > the first element of Akkad. *girisuakarrānu* (highly uncert. interpret.; cf. also Eilers Beamtennamen 54 n. 5, CAD s.v. *girisu-akarrānu*, AHW s.v.).

gr‘h **Palm** Sing. emph. *gr‘t*› RTP 680 (for the reading, cf. Milik DFD

150f. :: Caquot RTP a.l.: l. *gd‘t’*) - ¶ subst. the hairdressers (coll.); *gr‘t’ dy bl* RTP 680: the hairdressers (functioning in the temple) of Bel.

grṣh = loaf of bread > Akkad., cf. v.Soden Or xxxv 8, xlvi 186, AHW s.v. *ga/irīṣ(t)u* (cf. also CAD s.v. *gariṣtu*).

grr **Pun** Sing. abs. *grr* CIS i 4873[3] - ¶ subst. m. title of unknown function; *curator*??, cf. CIS i sub 4873 in the combination *hgrr š’zrt b‘lysp* (v. *’zrh*$_1$).

grš$_1$ **Mo** PI‘EL (cf. Segert ArchOr xxix 226) Impf. 3 p.s.m. + suff. 3 p.s.m. *ygršh* KAI 181[19] - ¶ verb QAL to drive away; *wygršh kmš mpny* KAI 181[19]: and Kemosh drove him away before me - a form of this root postulated in KAI 46[2] by Albright BASOR lxxxiii 17ff. (l. *ngrš* (= NIPH Pf. 3 p.s.m.) + *h’*$_1$, cf. also Sarna JBL lxxviii 310), Cross BASOR ccviii 15f. (l. *w* + *grš* (= PI‘EL Inf. abs.) + *h’*$_1$), Peckham Or xli 457 (l. *w* + *grš* (= QAL pass. Inf. abs.) + *h’*$_1$), Mazar with Silverman JAOS xciv 269, Lipiński BiOr xlv 63 (l. *w* + *grš* (= PU‘AL Pf. 3 p.s.m.) + *h’*$_1$; for this reading, cf. also Gibson SSI iii p. 27), cf. however Février RA xliv 124, v.d.Branden Mašr lvi 283: l. *ngr* (= n.p.) + *š*$_{10}$ + *h’*$_1$ × Dupont-Sommer CRAI ’48, 15f., JA cclii 301, Delcor Syr xlv 331, 334ff., 351, Röllig KAI a.l.: l. *ngr* (= n.l.) + *š*$_{10}$ + *h’*$_1$ :: CIS i sub 144, Cooke NSI p. 110f.: l. *ngd* (= n.p.) + *š*$_{10}$ + *h’*$_1$ :: Ferron RSO xli 285, 288: l. *nqdš* (= NIPH Pf. 3 p.s.m. of *qdš*$_1$) + *h’*$_1$ (on these problems, cf. also Bunnens EPM 33f., 37f.) - a derivative of this root prob. in Sach 79 i 3: *grš’*.
v. *bny*$_1$,*gdš*$_1$,*ngd*$_3$.

grš$_2$ v. *krs*.

grt v. *gdh*$_2$.

gšwr v. *gšr*.

gšwt Ebeling Frah a.l.: l. *gšw/‘t’* in Frah xv 6 = writing material (cf. Hebr. *qst*), highly uncert. reading and interpret., cf. Nyberg FP 47, 85, l. *qšrt’* (form of *qšrh* = girdle).

gšy **Hatra** Aggoula Ber xviii 100: l. *gšy’* (= Sing. emph.) = blind in 212[3]? (highly uncert. reading and interpret.; cf. Teixidor Sumer xx 79: l. *‘šy’* = n.p. (cf. also Vattioni IH a.l.)).

gšyš **OffAr** Sing. emph. *gšyš’* BSOAS xxvii 272 i 1 - ¶ subst. (?) of uncert. meaning, prob. title or function; Bivar & Shaked BSOAS xxvii 274ff.: prob. = var. of *qšyš’* (= Sing. emph. of *qšyš* (= elder), cf. also Segal Irâq xxix 10: indicating priestly status, Sznycer JA ccliii 3f.: > chief, senator?); Altheim & Stiehl AAW iii 67ff.: < root *gšš* (cf. Bivar & Shaked BSOAS xxvii a.l., Sznycer JA ccliii a.l.: poss. (< *gšš* = to spy) = observer, supervisor, inspector.

gšr (> Akkad., cf. Zimmern Fremdw 31, Kaufman AIA 53) - **OffAr** Sing. abs. *gšr* Herm 2[15], 3[10]; Plur. abs. *gšrn* Krael 3[5], Herm 2[14], 3[9], *gšrn* Krael 3^{5}, Herm 2^{14}, 3^{9}, *gšwrn*Krael 4^{8}, 6^{4}, 9^{13}, 10^{2}, 12^{13} - ¶ subst. beam.

gšš **OffAr** HAPH Pf. 3 p.s.m. *hgšš* Aḥiq 139 (on the form, Lindenberger APA 137, 216 n. 430, cf. Kottsieper SAS 158) - ¶ verb HAPH prob. meaning to spy out (:: Kottsieper SAS 16, 195: = to discredit); *br bṭny hgšš byty* Aḥiq 139: my own son spied out my house.
v. *gšyš*.

gt$_1$ (< Arab., cf. Cooke NSI p. 223, Cantineau Nab ii 172, O'Connor JNES xlv 217ff.) - Nab. Sing. abs. *gt* CIS ii 198^{6}; + suff. 1 p.s. *gty* ADAJ xxvi 366^{4} (heavily dam. context) - ¶ subst. corpse.

gt$_2$ v. *gzt*.

D

d$_1$ v. *ʾḥd*$_4$.

d$_2$ v. *dy*$_1$.

d$_3$ v. *zy*.

d$_4$ v. *dnr*.

dʾ v. *znh*.

dʾb cf. Frah ix 5 (*dybʾ*): wolf - Baneth OLZ '14, 352: l. prob. *[d]ʾbʾ* (= Sing. emph.) in Aḥiq 199 (heavily dam. and uncert. context, cf. Lindenberger APA 197: or l. *ʾbʾ* = Sing. emph. of *ʾb*$_1$? and Kottsieper SAS 22, 185: = Sing. emph. of *ʾb*$_2$).
v. *db*.

dʾt (< Arab.) - **Nab** Sing. cstr. *dʾt* RES 2052$^{5f.}$ (for the reading, cf. Milik Syr xxxv 229 :: RES a.l.: l. *rbt* = Sing. f. cstr. of *rb*$_2$) - ¶ dem. pronoun f. she of; *lʾlt dʾt ʾl ʾtr* RES 2052$^{5f.}$: for Allāt the one of Al-Atar.

db **OffAr** Sing. emph. *dbʾ* Aḥiq 120 (for this reading, cf. Sach p. 167, Nöldeke AGWG xiv/4, 15, Ginsberg ANET 429, Grelot RB lxviii 186, DAE p. 440 (n. f), Lindenberger APA 110, 250 n. 323, Kottsieper SAS 13, 196 :: Cowl a.l., Gressmann ATAT 459: l. *rbʾ* (= Sing. m. emph. of *rb*$_2$ (= the master)) :: Nöldeke AGWG xiv/4, 15: or l. *dbʾ* (= Sing. emph. of *dʾb*??)); cf. Frah ix 7 (*dwb*) - ¶ subst. bear.
v. *dbhh*, *rb*$_2$.

dbb (< Akkad., cf. Zimmern Fremdw 24, Kaufman AIA 42f.) - **OffAr** Sing. abs. *dbb* Cowl 6^{12}, 8^{14,20}, Krael 1^{5}, 3^{13,14}, etc., etc., *zbb* Krael 3^{17} (for the orthography, cf. Driver PEQ '55, 92, Blau PC 47, Coxon ZDMG cxxix 13), *bb* (lapsus) Cowl 13^{10} - ¶ subst. process.
v. *dn*$_1$.

dbbh v. *dbhh*.

dbh v. *dbhh*.

dbhh **OldAr** diff. noun (Sing. abs.) in KAI 222A 31; Gibson SSI ii p. 40: dittography for *dbh* (= f. Sing. abs. of *db* (= bear); prob. interpret. :: Fitzmyer AIS 48f.: = variant form of *dbh* (= bear; cf. also Hillers TC 55 n. 34, Donner KAI a.l., Delcor BiOr xxv 380, Millard JSS xxi 175, cf. also Wittstruck JBL xcvii 100) × Dupont-Sommer Sf p. 46: = lapsus for *dbrh*$_2$ (= bee, wasp; cf. also Segert ArchOr xxxii 121, Koopmans 52 (or = Sing. abs. of *dbrh*$_3$ (= plague demon)?), Degen AAG p. 11 n. 53, 48, Rosenthal ANET 660 (n. 6), Rimbach JBL xcvii 565, Lemaire & Durand IAS 134 (cf. however Degen OLZ '71, 268)) :: Lipiński Stud 29 (div. otherwise): = *db* (= Sing. cstr. of *db* (= bear)) + *hh* (= subst. Sing. abs. (= woe)), against this interpret., cf. also Fitzmyer CBQ xxxix 263 :: Thomas JSS v 283: or l. *dbbh* (Sing. abs.) = flies?).

dbḥ$_1$ v. *zbḥ*$_2$.

dbḥ$_2$ v. *zbḥ*$_3$.

dbyḥh **Palm** the diff. word *dbyḥtʾ* in CIS ii 4029^4 (reading of *d* uncert., cf. also Lidzbarski Handb 248, 475: l. *gbyḥtʾ* = surname?) poss. = Sing. emph. of *dbyḥh* (= offering, gift??), cf. Chabot CIS ii a.l., cf. however Milik DFD 152: = *d*$_2$ + *byḥtʾ* (= n.l.).

dblh **Hebr** Sing. abs. *dblh* Mas 516, 521, 522, 523, 524, etc. - **JAr** Sing. abs. *dblʾ* IEJ xl 132^{4,6,9}; Plur. abs. *dblyn* IEJ xl 132^{12} - ¶ subst. fig-cake - for this word, cf. Borowski AIAI 115.

dbq **OffAr** QAL Impf. 3 p.s.f. *tdbq* Cowl 5^5; Part. act. s.m. abs. *dbq* Cowl 8^6, 25^5, Krael 3^9, 4^{9,11}, 9^{9,10}, Herm 4^5, etc.; s.f. abs. *dbqh* Cowl 5^4 (:: Segert AAG p. 371: = QAL Part. pass. s.f. abs., cf. however Degen GGA '79, 46) - **Palm** Part. act. pl.m. abs. *dbqyn* Ber ii 102 ii 4 - ¶ verb QAL to cling, to cleave, to be contiguous - **1)** + obj., *mnhwn trn ... gwyn dbqyn ʿrsʾ* Ber ii 102 ii 3f.: of the two (niches) ... the innermost ones next to the couch - **2)** + *l*$_5$, *byt hwšʿ ... dbq lh* Cowl 25^5: the house of H. ... adjoins it (sc. another house), cf. Cowl 5^{4,5}, 25^8, Krael 3^9, 4^{9,11}, 9^{9,10}, etc. - **3)** used figuratively + *l*$_5$, *lbby lh dbq lh* Herm 4^5: my heart is not attached to it (i.e. I do not like it).

dbr$_1$ **Ph** PIʿEL Pf. 3 p.s.m. *dbr* KAI 14^2; Impf. 3 p.pl.m. + suff. 2 p.s.m. *ydbrnk* KAI 14^6 - **Pun** QAL Part. act. s.m. abs., cf. Poen 944: *duber* (cf. Sznycer PPP 127, APCI 211, or = PIʿEL (?) Pf. 3 p.s.m. (?) :: L.H.Gray AJSL xxxix 86: = PUʿAL Pf. 3 p.s.m.); pl.m. abs., cf. Poen 935: *dobrim* (cf. L.H.Gray AJSL xxxix 77, FR 139, Sznycer PPP 81, APCI 211, J.J.Glück & Maurach Semitics ii 109); PIʿEL Pf. 1 p.s., cf. Poen 936: *dyburth* (cf. Sznycer PPP 87ff., 127, 128 :: L.H.Gray AJSL xxxix 77, FR 214, J.J.Glück & Maurach Semitics ii 110: = Sing. abs. of *dbrh*$_1$ (= rumour)), cf. Poen 946: *duberit*, Poen 948: *dubert* (in both instances same references) - **Hebr** PIʿEL Impf. 3 p.s.m. *ydbr* DJD ii 17A 2 - ¶ verb to speak, to say - **1)** + pron. suff., *ʾm ʾdmm ydbrnk* KAI 14^6: if men speak to you (i.e. if they try to persuade you) - **2)** +

ʾl$_6$ (to): DJD ii 17A 2 - **3)** + *lʾmr*: KAI 14[2].
v. *ʾmr$_1$*, *dbr$_{2,3}$*.

dbr$_2$ **OffAr** QAL Pf. 3 p.s.m. *dbr* Cowl 30[8], 31[7]; cf. Frah xx 20 (*dblwn*; cf. Nyberg FP 51, 94 :: Ebeling Frah a.l.: l. *yzlwn* = form of *nzl* (= to lead)), GIPP 37, SaSt 16 - **Palm** QAL Pf. 3 p.s.m. *dbr* CIS ii 3932[6] - **Hatra** QAL Impf. 3 p.s.m. + suff. 3 p.pl.m. *ldbrhn* 79[12] - **Waw** PAʿEL Part. act. pl.m. abs. *mdbryn* AMB 6[5] - ¶ verb QAL to lead; + obj., *npyn dbr mṣryʾ ʿm ḥylʾ ʾḥrnn* Cowl 30[8]: N. led out the Egyptians with the other forces (cf. Cowl 31[7]); for the context of Hatra 79[12], v. *qṭyr$_1$*; used figuratively, *dbr ʿmrh škytyt* CIS ii 3932[6]: he led his life in an honourable way - PAʿEL to lead, to direct; *mdbryn myʾ ... bmʿbrtʾ* AMB 6[5f.] directing the water in the ford (cf. already Gordon Or xviii 339 :: Dupont-Sommer Waw p. 11, 16: *mdbryn* = the leaders, chiefs, archonts) - in RES 1295[7] prob. QAL Imper. s.m. (*dbr*) = to go, to proceed to (*ʿl$_7$*), cf. Grelot DAE p. 372 n. e :: Lidzbarski Eph iii 119ff., Joüon MUSJ xviii 13: = PAʿEL Imper. s.m. of *dbr$_1$*.
v. *zkr$_1$*, *ybl$_1$*, *mdwbr*.

dbr$_3$ **Ph** Sing. abs. *dbr* KAI 13[6] - **Pun** Plur. cstr. *dbrʾ* KAI 124[3] (:: v.d.Branden PO i 437: = Plur. + suff. 3 p.s.m.); + suff. 3 p.s.m. *dbry* KAI 61A 6 (:: Honeyman JRAS '41, 35: = Sing. + suff. 3 p.s.m.), Moz vi 104[3f.] (= SMI 23), 105[4] (= SMI 24), 109[4] (= SMI 29), Mont Sir ii 80[3], SMI 2[2], Malta '65, 54[4], *dbrw* CIS i 3784[7] (prob. lapsus for *dbry*); + suff. 3 p.pl.m. *db[r]nm* ICO-Spa 16[5] (cf. e.g. Solá-Solé RSO xli 98, Gibson SSI iii p. 65f. :: Krahmalkov OrAnt xi 214: = Sing. + suff. 3 p.pl.m., cf. also Puech RSF v 86 :: Heltzer OrAnt vi 268: = Dual abs. of *dbrn* (= speech)) - **Hebr** Sing. abs. *dbr* KAI 192[6] (cf. e.g. Lemaire IH i 97 :: Michaud Syr xxxiv 45: = PIʿEL Imper. s.m. of *dbr$_1$* :: Hempel ZAW lvi 129, 130 n. g, H.P.Müller UF ii 237: = QAL Part. act. s.m. abs. of *dbr$_1$*; cf. also Röllig KAI a.l.), TA-H 24[17], DJD ii 17A 2, 46[7,8]; cstr. *dbr* KAI 189[1], 194[5], 200[2], TA-H 18[6f.] (or abs.?; :: Albright ANET 569 (n. 21): = Sing. abs. of *dbr$_4$* (= sanctuary)), 24[17]; Plur. abs. *dbrym* DJD ii 30[6]; Plur. cstr. *dbry* KAI 196[5] - **DA** Sing. cstr. *dbr* ii 17 (cf. Hoftijzer DA a.l. :: Caquot & Lemaire Syr liv 207, Garbini Hen i 186: = Sing. abs. :: Hackett BTDA 30, 73, 95, 128: = PAʿEL Pf. 3 p.s.m. of *dbr$_1$*) - **OffAr** Sing. abs. *dbr* ATNS 14[1]; cstr. *dbr* Cowl 6[6,16], 28[8,10,11], 40[3] (v. however infra), 62[5] (dam. context), 71[30], Krael 13[2,6] (dam. context), Aḥiq 202, ATNS 4[7b] (dam. context), 28b 6, 81[5] (*db[r]*; dam. context), Sem ii 31 conv. 1, Irâq xxxi 174[1] (heavily dam. context, diff. reading); + suff. 3 p.s.m. *dbrh* Krael 4[13]; + suff. 3 p.s.f. *dbrh* Cowl 6[5,8]; + suff. 3 p.pl.m. *dbrhm* ATNS 8[6] - ¶ subst. m. - **1)** word; *šmʿ ql dbry* KAI 61A 5f.: he has heard the sound of his words (cf. CIS i 3784[7], Moz vi 104[3f.] (= SMI 23), 105[4] (= SMI 24), Mont Sir ii 80[3], SMI 2[2], Malta '65, 54[4], ICO-Spa 16[5]); *yšmʿ ʾdny ... ʾt dbr ʿbdh* KAI 200[1f.]: may my

lord ... hear (/listen to) the word (i.e. the complaint) of his servant (cf. DJD ii 17A 2); for TA-H 24^{17}, v *ʾt*$_6$, *npš* - **2)** story; *dbr hnqbh* KAI 189^{1}: the story of the breach - **3)** affair, matter; *tʿbt ʿštrt hdbr hʾ* KAI 13^{6}: such a matter (i.e. act) is an abomination to A.; *wldbr ʾšr ṣwtny* TA-H $18^{6ff.}$: and as to the matter (in) which I ordered you (cf. KAI 192^{6}, DJD ii $46^{7,8}$); *ktbt dbrʾ hbt* KAI $124^{3f.}$: document concerning the affairs of the family, i.e. testament (cf. Lat. par. *testamento*); *pn yqrh ʾt hʿyr dbr* TA-H $24^{16f.}$: lest something befalls to the city; *ʿl dbr* KAI 194^{5}: concerning, with regard to (cf. Cowl $6^{5,6,8,16}$, ATNS 8^{6}, etc.); cf. also Cowl 45^{3}: *ʿdbr* (lapsus?, cf. however Greenfield BSOAS xl 371f.: = *ʿd*$_7$ + *dbr*); *ʿl dbr kn* Cowl 40^{3}: about/on this matter (cf. e.g. Cowl a.l., Porten & Yardeni sub TADAE A 3.6 × Grelot DAE p. 129: *dbrkn* = Sing. + suff. 2 p.pl.m., with regard to you); on *ʿl dbr*, cf. Zuckerman JANES xv 123f. - in TA-H 111^{4} a form of this noun in dam. context: *dbr* x[- Gawlikowski sub SBS 34^{1}: l. *bdbry* (= *b*$_2$ + Plur. cstr.) *k[* or *bdbr* (= *b*$_2$ + Sing. cstr.) *yk[* pro *br* (= Sing. cstr. of *br*$_1$) + *bryky* (= n.p.), cf. Dunant SBS a.l. (cf. also Gawlikowski Sem xxiii 120, TP 43) - a form of *dbr*$_3$ poss. also in IRT 892^{4}: *dubren*?, cf. Vattioni Aug xvi 551 sub no. 58 (highly uncert. context and interpret.).
v. *bd*$_3$, *brk*$_1$, *rʾš*$_1$.

dbr₄ **Pun** diff. word in KAI 173^{5}; Levi Della Vida Atti Tor lxx 196: = adj. Sing. m. abs. (= situated in the rear; cf. also Röllig KAI a.l., Amadasi sub ICO-Sard NPu 8); or poss. = subst. Sing. abs. (= hindmost chamber, i.e. the holy of holiest in a temple)?
v. *dbr*$_3$.

dbrh₁ v. *dbr*$_1$.

dbrh₂ v. *dbhh*.

dbrh₃ v. *dbhh*.

dbrn v. *dbr*$_3$.

dbš **OffAr** Sing. abs. *dbš* Cowl 37^{10} (cf. Driver JRAS '32, 80, Grelot DAE p. 389, Porten & Greenfield JEAS p. 80, Porten & Yardeni sub TADAE A 4.2); cf. Frah v 10 (*dwbšʾ*) - ¶ subst. honey.
v. *rbʿ*$_3$.

dg **Hebr** Plur. abs. *dgym* Frey 1162^{12} (= SM 45), 1206^{12} (= SM 67), SM 27^{12}, 70^{4} - **JAr** Sing. emph. *dgʾ* Mas 552, *dwgh* Mas 553 (or l. *dygh* = Sing. emph. of *dyg* (= fisherman, used as nickname)?) ¶ subst. fish; in all Hebr. instances sign of the Zodiac (*Pisces* (cf. also Mirsky Tarbiz xl 376ff.)) - used coll.: Mas 552, 553 (v. however supra).

dgl (Garbini Hen iv 166f.: < Akkad., less prob.) - **OffAr** Sing. abs. *dgl* Cowl 5^{9}, 13^{10}; cstr. *dgl* Cowl $5^{2,3}$, 6^{3}, Krael 2^{3}, 3^{2}, 5^{2}, ATNS 9^{7} (for the reading, cf. Naveh IEJ xxxv 211, Porten & Yardeni sub TADAE B 8.6 :: Segal ATNS a.l.: l. poss. *lbyl* = *l*$_5$ + n.d.)^{,8} (cf. Porten & Yardeni sub TADAE B 8.6 :: Segal ATNS a.l.: l. *lbyl* = *l*$_5$ + n.d.), 63^{3},

AG 5^{7}, TA-Ar 12^{2}, etc., etc.; emph. *dglʾ* Cowl 9^{2}, 20^{4}, 65 iii 2, 69^{8} (for the reading, cf. Porten & Yardeni sub TADAE B 8.5), Krael 7^{2}, 11^{2}, ATNS 3^{6} (*dgl[ʾ]*; for this prob. reading, cf. Porten & Yardeni sub TADAE B 8.10 :: Segal ATNS a.l.: l. *dgl* (= Sing. abs.)), 15^{2}; + suff. 3 p.s.f. *dglh* Cowl 43^{2}; + suff. 3 p.pl.m. *dglhm* Cowl 80^{3} (for the prob. reading, cf. Porten & Yardeni sub TADAE A 5.5); Plur. abs. *dg[l]n* Cowl 27^{1} (for this reading, cf. also Porten & Yardeni sub TADAE A 4.5) - ¶ subst. military term denoting a subdivision of a military colony (detachment < standard, banner), consisting of foreign reserve-troops (κληροῦχοι). Thus it can be explained that certain texts speak of females as belonging to the *dgl*: Cowl 43^{2}, Krael 3^{2}; for the *dgl* in Elephantine papyri, cf. Clermont-Ganneau RAO viii 135f., Wag 171ff., Widengren OrSuec v 161, Volterra RCL '63, 131ff., Bresciani SCO vii 148, Verger RCL '64, 78ff. (nn. 14, 15, 16, 17), 83 n. 30, RGP 67ff., Porten Arch 28ff., 200ff., 300, cf. also Yadin War Scroll 49ff., Temerev FS Freedman 523f. - for *bʿl dgl*, v. *bʿl*$_2$; for *rb dglʾ*, v. *rb*$_2$ - a form of this noun poss. also in Cowl 69^{5} (*dgln* = Plur. abs.? or Sing. + suff. 1 p.pl.?, for the reading, cf. Porten & Yardeni sub TADAE B 8.5 (id. ibid.: or l. *rgln* = Dual abs. or Sing. + suff. 1 p.pl. of *rgl*$_2$, less prob. reading)).
v. *rgl*$_2$.

dgm (< Greek δόγμα) - **Palm** Sing. abs. *dgm* SBS 48B 4 (cf. Greek par. ψηφισμάτων); emph. *dgmʾ* CIS i 3913 i 1; Plur. abs. *dgmyn* DFD 13^{10} (cf. Greek par. ψηφίσμασι) - ¶ subst. decree, enactment; *dgmʾ dy bwlʾ* CIS ii 3913 i 1: decree of the Senat (cf. Greek par. δόγμα βουλῆς).

dgn **Ph** Sing. abs. *dgn* KAI 14^{19} - **Hebr** Sing. abs. *dgn* DJD ii 45^{3} (dam. context) - **OffAr** Sing. emph. *dgnʾ* Aḥiq 129 - ¶ subst. grain; for *ʾrṣt dgn* in KAI 14^{19}, v. *ʾrṣ*$_1$ - for this word, cf. Borowski AIAI 87f.

dgr v. *drg*$_2$.

dd$_1$ **OffAr** Plur. + suff. 3 p.s.m. *dwdhy* IrAnt iv 122^{3} (cf. Dupont-Sommer CRAI '64, 286, cf. however Kutscher with Naveh AION xvi 34 n. 52: prob. = lapsus for *ddwhy*) - **Nab** Sing. + suff. 1 p.s. *ddy* MPAT 64 i 7, 8, ii 3 - **Palm** Sing. + suff. 3 p.s.m. *ddh* RIP 117^{5}, RB xxxix 536^{4}, 539^{2}, 547^{3}, Ber xix 69^{3}, Syr lxii 271^{5}, 277 ii 2, FS Collart 161^{10}; + suff. 1 p.s. *ddy* RB xxxix 539^{4}; + suff. 3 p.pl.m. *ddhwn* RB xxxix 536^{2} - **Hatra** Sing. + suff. 3 p.s.m. *ddh* 408^{6} (:: As-Salihi Sumer xlv 102 (n. 29): l. *drh* = Sing. + suff. 3 p.s.m. of *dr*$_1$), Ibr 21^{4} - ¶ subst. m. paternal uncle: passim; cf. *bny ddh* RB xxxix 536^{4}: his paternal cousins (cf. RB xxxix 536^{2}, $539^{2,4}$, 547^{3}, Syr lxii 271^{5}, 277 ii 2, Hatra 408^{6}).
v. *dwr*$_2$, *zy*.

dd$_2$ v. *bdd*$_1$, *kdd*$_2$.

dd$_3$ **DA** Plur. abs. *ddn* ii 4 - ¶ subst. Plur. (joys of) love (cf. e.g. Hoftijzer DA p. 221, H.P.Müller ZAW xciv 219, 232 :: Garbini Hen i 185: = lovers).

dd_4 v. *dr_1*.
dd_5 v. *zy*.
dd_6 v. *dwd_2*.
ddq v. *kdd_2*.
dh v. *br_1*, *znh*.
dhb v. *zhb*.
dhm **Hebr** NIPH (?) Impf. 2 p.s.m. *tdhm* KAI 200[14] (cf. Naveh IEJ x 134, xiv 158f., cf. also idem Lesh xxx 71, 80, Lemaire Sem xxi 76, Gibson SSI i p. 28, 30, Weippert FS Rendtorff 462 n. 33 (cf. also Pardee Maarav i 36, 54, HAHL 21f.: l. *tdhm[)* × Yeivin BiOr xix 5f., 8 (div. otherwise): l. *tdhmn* = HIPH Impf. 2 p.s.m. + suff. 1 p.s. of *dhm* (= to stun; cf. also Margalit UF xv 117: l. *tdhmw* or *tdhmn[w]* = HIPH Impf. 2 p.s.m. + suff. 3 p.s.m.: let him come to grief) :: Cross BASOR clxv 44f. n. 40, Suzuki AJBJ viii 5, 24ff. (div. otherwise): l. *tdḥnw* = QAL Impf. 2 p.s.m. + suff. 3 p.s.m. of *dḥy* (= to drive away; cf. Talmon BASOR clxxvi 36, Röllig KAI a.l.) :: Vinnikov ArchOr xxxiii 551f. (div. otherwise): l. *trhnn[y]* = HIPH Impf. 2 p.s.m. + suff. 1 p.s. of *rhn* (= to deposit as pledge)) - ¶ verb NIPH (?) to remain silent (cf. Naveh IEJ x 134f.: to be helpless; Amusin & Heltzer IEJ xiv 150, 154: to be speechless; Weippert FS Rendtorff 462 n. 33: > to remain inactive): KAI 200[14] (v. however supra).
dhmpṭypṭyš **OffAr** this word (< Prakrit) prob. to be restored in JA ccliv 440[1] (*[dhmpṭyp]ṭyš* = accordance to the law, cf. (Naveh with) Shaked JRAS '69, 119, Kutscher, Naveh & Shaked Lesh xxxiv 128 :: Dupont-Sommer JA ccliv 440, 454: l. *].šyš*.
dhn **Palm** Sing. cstr. *dhn* Sem xxxix 150[2] (diff. and dam. context); emph. *dhn*ʾ CIS ii 3913 ii 29, 31 - ¶ subst. fat; cf. also Teixidor Sem xxxiv 75.
dwb v. *db*.
dwbš v. *dbš*.
dwg v. *dg*.
dwd_1 v. *dd_1*, *dwr_2*.
dwd_2 **Palm** Plur. (cf. Ingholt Syr vii 138f.) emph. *dwd*ʾ Syr vii 129[8] - ¶ subst. (big) cauldron; *dy hw* ʿ*l bt dwd*ʾ Syr vii 129[8]: the one who supervises the house of the cauldrons (i.e. the kitchen), cf. also Milik DFD 151 - Dupont-Sommer MAIBL xliv 281, Puech RSF iii 12f.: the *dd* in Kition D 21[3] = Sing. abs. of *dd_6* (= *dwd_2* (= receptacle)), highly uncert. interpret., cf. Amadasi sub Kition D 21 :: Coote BASOR ccxx 47, 49 (div. otherwise): l. ʿ*dd* (= QAL Imper. s.m. of ʿ*dd* (= to recite); cf. ʿ*dd_2*).
dwd_3 **Mo** Sing. + suff. 3 p.s.f. *dwdh* (v. however infra) KAI 181[12] - ¶ word (subst.?) of unknown meaning (cf. Andersen Or xxxv 90 n. 2) - poss. interpret. - **1)** = certain title (cf. Lipiński Or xl 332f.: =

commander? (cf. Prätorius ZDMG lix 34f., Albright Archaeology 218 n. 86, Dussaud Syr xxviii 348, Ap-Thomas VT xi 244f., de Geus SV 26, 28 n. k); comparison with supposed Akkad. *dawidum* mistaken, cf. (Landsberger with) Tadmor JNES xvii 130f., Stamm SVT vii 169ff., v.Zijl 174 (n. 5) :: McDonald AN xvii 52ff.) - **2)** = noun denoting deity or comparable divine being (cf. Röllig KAI a.l., Bernhardt ZDPV lxxvi 145 (n. 32), Beeston JRAS '85, 145, 147, v. Zijl 190 (n. 8), Segert ArchOr xxix 213, 241 (: = *dwd*$_4$ (= loved one), indicating a deity, cf. also Brock & Diringer FS Thomas 44, v.d.Branden BO iii 45, Galling TGI 52 (n. 8), de Moor UF xx 153; less prob. interpret.)) - **3)** *dwdh* = n.d., cf. Lidzbarski Handb 255, Cooke NSI p. 11 (cf. also Halévy RS viii 289, H.P.Müller TUAT i 648) - less prob. interpret.: - **1)** = n.p., cf. Reviv CSI p. 22, Gibson SSI i p. 80 - **2)** = defeat, cf. Albright with Andersen Or xxxv 90 n. 2 - **3)** Tur-Sinai HalSe 34: = name of cultic object - **4)** = champion, cf. McDonald AN xvii 52ff. - on this word, cf. also Soggin OTOS 155 n. 10, Jackson & Dearman SMIM 113.
v. *dr*$_1$.

dwd$_4$ **OffAr** Plur. cstr. (or Plur. emph.?) *dwdy* CRAI '70, 163^2, IPAA 11^4 - ¶ subst. friend (for the context of both texts, cf. Dupont-Sommer CRAI '70, 164f., Humbach IPAA 12f.).
v. *dwd*$_3$.

dwh **Hebr** Sing. m. abs. *dwh* KAI 193^7 (cf. however Gibson SSI i p. 40: or l. *dwy*?) - ¶ adj. ill, unhappy; *lb [ʿ]bd[k] dwh* KAI $193^{6f.}$: the heart of your servant is sick (cf. Pardee HAHL 85).

dwy v. *dwh*.

dwk **Pun** Rocco Stud Magr vii 13: l. *dkk* = Pol Imper. pl.m. of *dwk* (= to shatter) in Stud Magr vii 12^2 (uncert. reading and interpret.).

dwkh v. *dkh*$_1$.

dwl v. *plk*$_1$.

dwnprys (< Prakrit, cf. Henning BSOAS xiii 85f.) - **OffAr** Sing. BSOAS xiii 83^6 - ¶ subst., prob. meaning: beloved of the gods (cf. Henning BSOAS xiii 85f., Kutscher, Naveh & Shaked Lesh xxxiv 127f.).

dwṣ v. *dṣ*.

dwqnr v. *dqnr*.

dwr$_1$ v. *rd*$_3$.

dwr$_2$ **Palm** Sing. emph. *dwrʾ* Syr xvii 351^{11} (for the reading, cf. Milik DFD 304, Gawlikowski TP 57 :: Cantineau Syr xvii a.l.: l. *dwdʾ* = Sing. emph. of *dwd*$_1$ (= *dd*$_1$)) - ¶ subst. enclosed space (cf. also Marrassini FLEM 47 (n. 2)).
v. *dwrh*.

dwr$_3$ v. *dr*$_1$.

dwrh **OffAr** Sing. abs. *dwrh* Cowl $79^{2,3}$ (*dwr[h]*)^{,4} (v. infra) - ¶ subst. of uncert. meaning, thickness (sc. of a board)??, cf. Cowl a.l. :: Lidzbarski

Eph ii 218 (cf. also Chabot sub RES 1796): = Sing. + suff. 3 p.s.f. of dwr_2 (= circumference (cf. also Ungnad ArPap 112) :: Clermont-Ganneau RAO vi 247f.: = Sing. + suff. 3 p.s.f. of dwr_2 (= frame)).

dwš v. *dš*ʾ.

dwšwn (< Iran., cf. Shaked Or lvi 412) - **OffAr** Plur. m. abs. *dwšwnn* ATNS 30a 2 (for the reading, cf. Shaked Or lvi 410, Porten & Yardeni sub TADAE B 8.4 :: Segal ATNS a.l.: l. *bwšpnn* = b_2 + n.l.) - ¶ adj. of evil desire, ill-willed.

dwškrt (< Iran., cf. Schaed 264, Hinz AISN 90, cf. also Kent OPG p. 192) - **OffAr** Sing. emph. *dwškrt*ʾ Cowl 27[3] - ¶ subst. m. crime, evil act.

dḥ **Hatra** diff. word in 145[4]; Degen JEOL xxiii 420: = dittography of the first two signs of preceding *dḥšpṭ*ʾ (prob. interpret.).

dḥʾ v. *dḥy*.

dḥh v. *dḥy*.

dḥḥ v. *dḥy*.

dḥy **Pun** QAL Impf. 3 p.s.m. *ydḥ* KAI 75[6] - **OffAr** QAL Pf. 3 p.s.m. *dḥ*ʾ CRAI '70, 163[1], IPAA 11[3]; Part. pass.m. s. abs. *dḥh* Krael 9[14] (cf. Krael a.l., Driver PEQ '55, 93, Grelot DAE p. 245 n. k, cf. also Porten & Greenfield JEAS p. 58, Porten & Yardeni sub TADAE B 3.10 :: Milik RB lxi 251: *dḥh* = subst. indicating something overturned :: Wesselius AION xlv 503ff.: l. *rḥh* = Sing. abs. of *rḥh* (= millstone)) - ¶ verb QAL - **1)** to break; + obj.: KAI 75[6], cf. FR 174, cf. also Harr 195 (: or < root *dḥḥ*?; Levi Della Vida Mem Brockelmann 130: = to move, to give a new place to) :: Chabot JA xi/xvii 183 and CIS i sub 3916: < root *ndḥ* - **2)** to drive away: CRAI '70, 163[1], IPAA 11[3] (+ mn_5; diff. context) - Part. pass.: (what is) overturned, knocked over: Krael 9[14] - Levi Della Vida RCL '49, 411: the ʾ*dḥt* in Trip 35 prob. = YIPH/YOPH Pf. 3 p.s.f. of *dḥy* or *dḥḥ* - Levi Della Vida Mem Brockelmann 130: the diff. ʾ*ydḥ* in Trip 52[1] = YIPH Pf. 3 p.s.m. of *dḥy* (or *dḥḥ*; = to remove; on the problems of this text, cf. also Amadasi Guzzo FS Delcor 9ff., IPT 100f.) - a form of this root (*dḥh*) also in Hebr. text DJD ii 22,1-9[5], diff. and dam. context.

v. *dhm*.

dḥyl **JAr** Sing. m. emph. *dḥyl*ʾ AMB 1[8] (uncert. reading, cf. Naveh & Shaked AMB a.l.), *dḥylh* AMB 7[15] - ¶ adj. (or QAL Part. pass. of *dḥl*) terrifying, awe-inspiring: AMB 7[15] (epithet of God), AMB 1[8] (epithet of an angel; v. however supra).

dḥk v. *šṭyn*.

dḥl v. *dḥyl*, *zḥl*.

dḥn **OffAr** Sing. emph. *dḥn*ʾ Sach 75 ii 9, 10 - ¶ subst. of unknown meaning; Grelot DAE p. 104 (n. h): = millet (cf. also Sach p. 232: = Sing. emph. of *dḥn* = millet dealer).

dḥš (poss. < Iran., cf. Caquot Syr xli 259, Milik DFD 396, cf. also Brockelmann LS s.v. *daḥšā*, Greenfield FS Asmussen 140f.) - **Hatra** Plur. + suff. 3 p.s.m. *dḥšyhy* 140^4 - ¶ subst. Plur. guard, guardsmen; *rb dḥšyhy* Hatra 140^4: the commander of his guard(smen).
v. *brš*$_2$.

dḥšpṭ (< Iran., cf. Safar Sumer xviii 43 n. 38, Caquot Syr xli 259f., cf. also Degen JEOL xxiii 421 (n. 53); v. also *dḥš*) - **Hatra** Sing. emph. *dḥšpṭ*ʾ 145^3, 279a, app. 4^8 (for the reading, cf. Caquot Syr xli 260 n. 6 :: Safar Sumer xvii 39 (n. 98), Caquot Syr xl 12f.: l. *dḥšpš*ʾ = *d*$_2$ + n.l. (cf. also Teixidor Syr xli 273) :: Altheim & Stiehl AAW v/1, 83: l. *dḥšpš*ʾ = *d*$_2$ + form of root *ḥwš*/*ḥšš* (= to feel, to understand) + *pš*ʾ (= emph. form of *pš* (= variant of *ps*$_1$) = lot), *ḥš pš*ʾ = one who asks for an oracle by casting lots), *dšḥpṭ*ʾ (variant form with metathesis, cf. Milik DFD 397, Teixidor Syr li 335, Aggoula Sem xxvii 124 :: As-Saliḥi Irâq xxxv 67f. n. 14, Degen NESE iii 96: = lapsus) 81^4 (*[d]šḥpṭ*ʾ), 295^3 - ¶ subst. chief of the guards, used as epithet of Nergal/Nergol (cf. Milik DFD 396ff., Degen JEOL xxiii 420f.; Tubach ISS 402 (n. 701): = the lord of the servants; cf. also Altheim & Stiehl AAW iv 258, Harnack with Altheim & Stiehl GMA 546f., Drijvers EM 172, 179); Greenfield FS Asmussen 138ff.: in the relevant context > executioner.
v. *dḥ*.

dṭy v. *rṭy*.

dy$_1$ **Ph** Sing. cstr. *d* KAI $43^{11,12}$ - ¶ subst. sufficiency; only attested in the combination *md* (= *mn*$_5$ + *d*), *ym md ym* KAI 43^{11}: day by day; *yrḥ md yrḥ* KAI 43^{12}: month by month.
v. ʾ*ḥd*$_4$, *yd*, *mdy*$_2$.

dy$_2$ v. *zy*.

dyʾ**n** v. *znh*.

dyb$_1$ cf. Frah app. 14 (*ydybwn*) = form of *dyb*$_1$ (= to flow), cf. Nyberg FP 99, Toll ZDMG-Suppl viii 36 :: Ebeling Frah a.l.: l. *yq*ʾ*wn* < root *nq*ʾ$_1$ (= to pour out).

dyb$_2$ v. *d*ʾ*b*.

dyg v. *dg*.

dygmʿ **Pun** Sing. abs. *dygm*ʿ (or l. *dyg*ʾʿ?) Trip 51^6 - ¶ subst. (?) of unknown meaning; Levi Della Vida Or xxxiii 12f., Amadsi IPT 135: < Greek δεῖγμα? = sample?

dyd v. *zy*.

dydsk Ebeling Frah a.l.: l. *dydsk* in Frah v 8 (< Sum.: = sweet bar?); improb. reading and interpret., cf. Nyberg FP 43, 68: l. Iran. word.

dyw (< Iran., cf. Hinz AISN 81) - **Waw** Sing. emph. *dyw*ʾ AMB 6^{10} (for this reading, cf. Gordon Or xviii 339, 341, Naveh & Shaked AMB a.l.: :: Dupont-Sommer Waw p. 11, 22f. (div. otherwise): l. *dy* (= *dy*$_2$) *w*ʾ*w* (= Waw)) - ¶ subst. demon.

dyḥhytwy (< Prakrit, cf. Henning BSOAS xiii 86f.) - **OffAr** *dyḥhytwy* BSOAS xiii 82[5] - ¶ poss. meaning: to be seen (cf. also Kutscher, Naveh & Shaked Lesh xxxiv 127).

dyṭgm (< Greek διάταγμα) - **Palm** Sing. abs. *dy[ṭg]m* SBS 45[7] (for the reading, cf. Degen WO viii 132 :: Dunant SBS a.l.: l. *dy* (= dy_2) + *[ʾ]m* (= $ʾm_4$); cf. Greek par. διατάγματι) - ¶ subst. edict.

dykr v. zkr_1.

dyl_1 v.Soden Or xxxvii 270, xlvi 185, AHW s.v. *dajjālu*: Ar. dyl_1 = inspector > Akkad., cf. however CAD s.v. *dajālu*; cf. also Kaufman AIA 45.

dyl_2 v. *zy*.

dyn_1 **OffAr** the interpret. of form *ydnyh* in KAI 271A 3 as QAL Impf. 3 p.s.m. + suff. 3 p.s.m. (thus CIS ii sub 138, Donner KAI a.l.) mistaken; = n.p., cf. also Degen NESE i 31f. - Zimmern Fremdw 23f.: root *dyn* < Akkad. (cf. also Widengren HDS 224), cf. however Kaufman AIA 43 n. 56.
v. *ymʾ*, *ndd*.

dyn_2 v. dn_1.

dyn_3 **OffAr** Sing. abs. *dyn* Cowl 8[13], 10[13,19], Krael 1[6], 12[28]; cstr. *dyn* CIS ii 16 (= Del 1; cf. Vattioni Aug ix 368f.; or = n.p.?, cf. Vattioni Aug x 494 n. 14); emph. *dynʾ* Cowl 16[3,9], 42[2]?, CRAI '70, 163[4], IPAA 11[9]; Plur. abs. *dynn* (??, v. infra) Cowl 28[8]; cstr. *dyny* Cowl 1[3], 16[4] (for this prob. reading, cf. Porten & Yardeni sub TADAE A 5.2 :: Cowl a.l.: l. prob. *dyny[ʾ]* = Plur. emph.),[7]; emph. *dynyʾ* Cowl 6[6], 8[24], 17[6] (for this reading, cf. Porten RB xc 406, 413, Porten & Yardeni sub TADAE A 6.1), 27[9], 80[8], 82[1], ATNS 16[2], 27[2], 30a 2, 79[1] (*dyny[ʾ]*), 121[2] - **Nab** Sing. abs. *dyn* MPAT 64 recto ii 8 (:: Starcky RB lxi 166: = dn_1) - **JAr** Sing. abs. *dyn* MPAT-A 22[5] (= SM 70[13]; :: Naveh SM a.l.: = dyn_4 (= dem. pronoun)) - ¶ subst. m. judge, passim; for CRAI '70, 163[4] (and IPAA 11[9]), cf. Dupont-Sommer CRAI '70, 169f., de Menasce IOS ii 290; cf. *dyny mdntʾ* Cowl 16[7]: the judges of the district; *dyny mlkʾ* Cowl 1[3]: the royal (i.e. official) judges; the interpret. of Cowl 28[8] uncert., Cowl a.l.: = dyn_3, cf. however e.g. Grelot DAE p. 206, Porten & Yardeni sub TADAE B 2.11: = Plur. abs. of dn_1 - on the judge in Elephantine documents, cf. also Greenfield Trans iii 90.
v. dn_1, sgn_1.

dyn_4 v. dyn_3.

dynr v. *dnr*.

dyṣ v. *dṣ*.

dyqn v. zqn_2.

dyr **Nab** Sing. + suff. 3 p.s.m. *dyrh* CIS ii 209[3] (cf. J 36: reading doubtful) - **Palm** Sing. emph. *dyrʾ* CIS ii 4501[3], Sem xxii 59[4] - **Hatra** Sing. emph. *dyrʾ* 35[7] (for the reading, cf. Aggoula Ber xviii 92, MUSJ xlvii 44f., Degen ZDMG cxxi 125, Milik DFD 366, Vattioni IH a.l. :: Caquot Syr xxx 240f., Donner sub KAI 249: pro *dyr› klh* l. *dy$_2$* + *d›klh* (= n.p.?) :: Safar Sumer viii 191, ix 19*: l. *dyd›kh* = n.p.), 290[6], cf. also Assur 28a 6 - ¶ subst. (in every case the same noun?) - **1)** (part of) building/construction: CIS ii 209[3] (part of tomb-construction?, cf. also Gawlikowski Ber xxiv 36; v. also supra) - **2)** people pertaining to a certain building: Hatra 35[7], 290[6] (cf. Starcky Sem xxii 64, Milik DFD 353, 366 :: Aggoula Ber xviii 92f., MUSJ xlvii 44f.: = building with religious function (enclosure), cf. also Gawlikowski TP 78 n. 69, Degen NESE iii 88) - **3)** community (poss. religious): Sem xxii 59[4f.], CIS ii 4501[3] (cf. Starcky Sem xxii 63ff., Teixidor Syr l. 436 :: Aggoula Ber xviii 93 (for CIS ii 4501): = religious building, sanctuary (cf. also Segal Irâq xxix 9f., Milik DFD 367; cf. however Aggoula Assur p. 14 n. 27) :: Clermont-Ganneau RAO iii 108: = quarter, ward :: Lidzbarski Eph i 87: *dyr›* = n.l.? (cf. also Chabot sub CIS ii 4501)); on *dyr*, cf. also Teixidor Sem xxx 66; the meaning 'community' poss. also in Assur 28a 6? (cf. however Aggoula Assur p. 12, 14, 16: = building which is the meeting-place of those who administered the city or the sanctuary); for Hatra, cf. also Aggoula Syr lxv 207 - Milik DFD 301, 367: l. Plur. emph. *dyry›* in Syr xvii 353[5] (diff. reading, cf. also Gawlikowski TP 57) :: Cantineau Syr xvii a.l. : l. *kmry›* = Plur. emph. of *kmr$_2$*.

dyrn **OffAr** Segal ATNS a.l.: restore poss. *[d]yrn›* (= Sing. emph. of *dyrn* (= habitation)) in ATNS 56[2] (uncert. interpret., heavily dam. context).

dk v. *zk$_2$*.

dk› v. *zk$_2$*.

dkh$_1$ **Palm** Sing. emph. *dkt›* Syr xiv 185[1]; Plur. emph. *dkt›* Ber iii 88[2] (?, v. infra) - **Hatra** Sing. emph. *dkt›* 7[1] (:: Aggoula Ber xviii 87f.: l. *dnt›* = Sing. emph. of *dnh$_2$* (= basin, tub)), 254, 282, 284[1], *dwkt›* 259[1] - ¶ subst. f. place; in Syr xiv 185[1]: place without special connotation (indicating certain space in tomb structure), cf. Aggoula MUSJ xlvii 70 (:: Gawlikowski TP 79: = pure place); in Hatra 7[1], 254, 259[1], 282, 284[1] prob. indication of offertory-box, cf. Milik DFD 273f. (cf. also Downey Ber xvi 98ff.) :: Aggoula MUSJ xlvii 69ff., 76ff., Syr lxv 204: = shop (cf. also Vattioni sub IH 7) :: Ingholt with Downey Ber xvi 98 n. 11: = place with sacred connotation :: idem PSH 14f.: = place with funeral connotation :: Safar Sumer ix 10* n. 20: = basin (or place, platform?); in Ber iii 88[2] *br dkt›* prob. = member (of the association in charge) of the offertory-boxes, cf. Milik DFD 273f. :: Aggoula MUSJ xlvii 71 n. 1: = poss. - a) functionary (*dkt›* = Sing. emph. of *dkh$_2$* (= function)) - b) shopkeeper (v. supra) :: Gawlikowski TP 79: = the purified one (*dkt›* = Sing. emph. of *dkw*; cf. also Stark PNPI p. 78: = n.p. with same derivation), cf. also Ingholt Ber iii 89 :: Ingholt FS Miles 46f.: *dkt›* =

Sing. emph. of *dkt* (< Iran.; = daughter > lady of high rank, princess)?
dkh$_2$ v. *dkh$_1$*.
dkw v. *dkh$_1$*.
dky$_1$ v. *zky$_2$*.
dky$_2$ v. *zk$_2$*.
dky$_3$ **Ph** CIS i 102a 1; reading and interpret. uncert.; = n.l.??, cf. Lidzbarski Eph iii 109.
dkyw **Palm** Milik DFD 313f.: l. *dkyw* (Sing. abs. = purity, integrety) in Syr xiv 177[5] (poss. reading) :: Cantineau Syr xiv a.l.: l. *brkyw* (= n.p.) pro *bdkyw*. Milik ibid.: l. *[d]kyw* (Sing. abs.) in Inv x 39[10] (diff. reading) :: Cantineau sub Inv x 39: l. *špyr w* (= Sing. abs. of *špr$_4$* + *w*). In both instances Greek par. ἁγνῶς.
dkm v. *zkm*.
dkn v. *zky$_2$*.
dkr$_1$ v. *zkr$_1$*.
dkr$_2$ v. *zkr$_{1,2}$*.
dkr$_3$ v. *zkr$_3$*.
dkrh v. *zkr$_1$*.
dkrwn v. *zkrn*.
dkrn v. *zkrn*.
dl$_1$ **Ph** Sing. abs. *dl* KAI 37A 6 (= Kition C 1 A 5; cf. e.g. Cooke NSI p. 66f., Röllig KAI a.l. :: Masson & Sznycer RPC 40f., Delcor UF xi 153, Gibson SSI iii p. 125, 127f.: = Sing. cstr. :: Peckham Or xxxvii 306, 310: l. *sl* = Sing. abs./cstr. of *sl$_1$* (= route); on the problems concerned, cf. also Amadasi sub Kition C 1) - ¶ subst. door; also in CIS i 44[2]??, cf. v.d.Branden BMB xiii 90f. : *šrdl* = Sing. cstr. of *šr$_2$* + Sing. abs. of *dl$_1$*, cf. also Masson & Sznycer RPC 40 (uncert. interpret., poss. = cognomen?, cf. e.g. Amadasi Kition p. 89 (n. 2), cf. also Benz PNP 426, 436).
v. *dlt$_2$*.
dl$_2$ v. *dl$_4$*, *plk$_1$*.
dl$_3$ **Pun** Sing. m. cstr. *dl* KAI 69[15], 74[6], CIS i 3915[5] (dam. context) - ¶ adj. poor, deficient; *dl mqn*ʾ KAI 69[15], 74[6]: someone who is poor in cattle; *dl ṣpr* KAI 69[15]: someone who is poor in birds (:: Dussaud Orig 321 (for both instances): = *dl$_6$*, transl. possessor of :: Février CB viii 39f.: = *dl$_6$*, transl. at the same time as).
v. *dl$_6$*, *plk$_1$*.
dl$_4$ v. *plk$_1$*.
dl$_5$ v. *plk$_1$*.
dl$_6$ **Pun** KAI 80[1]. 81[2,3], 119[2], 161[3] (for the context, cf. Roschinski Num 112, 114), 165[6], CIS i 5510[11], 6000bis 4 (= TPC 84), Punica xii 29[3] (= NP 61), NP 130[4] (highly uncert.; for the reading, cf. Février RHR cxli 21) - ¶ prep. with, provided with (cf. FR 250); *tsdt bn mtʿt*

bn gwṭʿl ... dl ʿṭrt wdl šm tʿṣmt KAI 165[5ff.]: T. son of M. son of G. ... (who is) provided with a crown and with a glorious name (v. also *tʿṣmh*), cf. *dl šm nʿm* Punica xii 29[3]: with a good name/reputation (cf. Polselli CISFP i 774); for CIS i 5510[11], v. *šlm*$_2$; *hmṭbḥ z dl pʿmm* KAI 80[1]: this slaughtering-table provided with legs (cf. Röllig KAI a.l., FR 250 :: Friedr 308,2: = *dl*$_3$ (= ruinous; cf. also Lidzbarski Eph i 22 n. 1 (with reserve), Cooke NSI p. 130, Lidzbarski sub KI 68, Harr 95 (: faulty in)) :: Lidzbarski Handb 256: = *dl*$_3$ (= without, lacking), cf. also CIS i sub 175); *wdl mlkt hḥrṣ wdl kl mnm* KAI 81[2]: with gold work and with everything whatever (cf. also KAI 81[3]), cf. e.g. CIS i sub 3914, Röllig KAI a.l., FR 250 :: Lidzbarski Eph i 21f., sub KI 69: = *dl*$_3$ (= ruinous; cf. also Cooke NSI p. 128), cf. also KAI 119[2], 161[3] (v. also *qbr*$_3$); *dl ṭhrt* NP 130[4]: provided with purity (?; cf. Février RHR cxli 21; diff. reading and interpret.); in all forementioned texts v.Selms JNSL i 54f.: = Sing. cstr. of *dl*$_2$ (= work); for CIS i 6000bis 4, v. *rḥ*$_1$ - poss. also in KAI 10[14] (cf. Röllig KAI a.l., FR 250) - Février Sem vi 20, 25: this word with meaning "on" in KAI 145[9] (highly uncert. context; Krahmalkov RSF iii 195f. (div. otherwise): l. *dlʿ*$_2$ = orthogr. variant of *dl*$_6$ meaning "also").
v. *ʾry*$_1$, *dl*$_3$, *plk*$_1$.

dlʾ v. *mdl.*

dlh v. *ktb*$_1$.

dlḥ$_1$ **Samal** QAL Pf. 3 p.s.m. *dlḥ* KAI 214[30] (cf. Dion p. 34, 181, 276f., cf. however Gibson SSI ii p. 76: prob. = QAL Part. pass. s.m. abs. :: Cook Maarav v/vi 65 = Pf. 3 p. dual) - **OffAr** QAL Impf. 3 p.s.f. *tdlḥ* Aḥiq 113 - ¶ verb QAL - **1)** to stir up, to trouble; + obj., *ḥrb tdlḥ myn špyn* Aḥiq 113: a sword will trouble calm waters - **2)** to be troubled (said of eyes): KAI 214[30] (v. however supra).

dlḥ$_2$ **Samal** Sing. abs. *dlḥ* KAI 214[24] - ¶ subst. m. prob. meaning: confusion (cf. Dion p. 32, 130), terror (cf. e.g. Cooke NSI p. 169, Donner KAI a.l.).

dlḥh **Pun** Sing. (or Plur.?) abs. *dlḥt* CIS i 3104[3] - ¶ subst. of unknown meaning in the expression *spr hdlḥt*: scribe of the ... (cf. Slouschz TPI p. 333: = Plur. abs. of *dlḥh* (= drain)), cf. also CIS i a.l.

dly$_1$ v.Soden Or xlvi 185: = to lift up > Akkad. *dalû* D (cf. also idem AHW s.v.; uncert. interpret.).
v. *dlt*$_2$, *mdl.*

dly$_2$ **Hebr** Sing. abs. *dly* SM 27[11] (in mirror writing), 70[4], Frey 1162[11] (= SM 45) - ¶ subst. bucket; in all instances indication of sign of Zodiac (*Aquarius*); cf. also Mirsky Tarbiz xl 376ff., Brand Tarbiz xl 510f.

dlyt v. *lyš*$_2$.

dll v. *plk*$_1$.

dlmn **Hatra** Ingholt AH i/1, 45 (sub no. 7): l. *dlmn* (meaning?) in 25[2] (less prob. reading); Caquot Syr xxix 104: l. *dy*$_2$ + *mn*$_4$? (cf. Donner sub KAI 246); Degen ZDMG cxix 174: pro *wdlmn/wdy mn* l. *h[w]* + *w* + *mn*$_4$? (uncert. reading); Vattioni IH a.l.: l. *hw* + *mn*$_4$, v. also *h*’$_1$.

dl‘$_1$ **OffAr** Plur. abs. *dl‘n* RES 1801^{6} (= RES 493; for the reading, cf. also Lidzbarski Eph ii 402, Cowley PSBA xxxvii 221) - ¶ subst. gourd (cf. Porten Arch 86, 276).

dl‘$_2$ v. *dl*$_6$.

dlq **Hebr** QAL Part. act. s.f. abs. *dwlqt* Frey 1390 (v. however infra) - ¶ verb QAL to set ablaze; Part. act. = lamplighter? or the fervent/passionate one? (cf. Frey a.l.), cf. however Milik DF i p. 95: = the person from Doliche (= Sing. f. abs. of *dlqy*).

dlt$_1$ v. *dlt*$_2$.

dlt$_2$ **Ph** Sing. abs. *dlt* KAI 43^{12} (v. infra); Plur. abs. *dlht* KAI 18^{3} (cf. FR 241.12, Healy CISFP i 666) - **Pun** Sing. abs. *dlt* CIS i 5522^{5}; Plur. abs. KAI 122^{2} (cf. e.g. Amadasi IPT 56 :: Levi Della Vida AfrIt vi 23: = Sing.) - **Amm** v. infra - **Hebr** Sing. abs. *dlt* KAI 194^{3} - **JAr** Sing. cstr. *[d]lt* IEJ xxxvi 206^{3} - ¶ subst. - **1)** door: KAI 18^{3}, 122^{2}, IEJ xxxvi 206^{3} - **2)** poss. meaning: tablet, plaquette; *hdlt hnḥšt* KAI 43^{12}: the bronze plaquette (cf. Röllig KAI a.l., v. d Branden OA iii 248, 259, BiOr xxiii 145, Lipiński RTAT 251, Gibson SSI iii p. 137, 140 :: Clermont-Ganneau Et ii 175: < Greek δέλτος = tablet, cf. Honeyman JEA xxvi 64, cf. however Galling FS Albright ii 210f. (cf. also Albright BASOR cxcviii 39, Masson RPAE 61ff.: > Greek δέλτος) :: Lidzbarski sub KI 36: = door? (cf. also Cooke NSI p. 87) :: Berger RA iii 73f., 83: pro *hdlt* l. *ḥdlt* = Sing. cstr. of *ḥdlh* (= residue, rest), or l. *ḥršt*); for CIS i 5522^{5}, cf. Février CIS i a.l., Sem xi 6, v.d.Branden BiOr xxiii 143, 145 :: Février Sem iv 17: = door; for KAI 194^{3}, v. *ktb*$_1$ - this word prob. also in the diff. *tdltbdlt* in the Amm. text BASOR cxciii 8^{5}, prob. solutions: - a) *tdlt* = verbal form, cf. Albright BASOR cxcviii 38f.: *tdltbdlt* = *tdlt* (= PI‘EL Impf. 2 p.s.m. of *dlt*$_1$ (= to inscribe)) + *b*$_2$ + Sing. cstr. of *dlt* (= board; cf. also Dion RB lxxxii 33, Hicks VT xxxiii 53ff.); Puech & Rofé RB lxxx 534, 538f.: *tdltbdlt* = *tdlt* (= QAL (?) Impf. 2 p.s.m. of *dlt*$_1$ (= to pass.)) + *b*$_2$ + Sing. cstr. of *dlt* (= door, gate), cf. also Fulco BASOR ccxxx 41f.: *tdltbdlt* = *tdlt* (lapsus for *tdl* = QAL Impf. 3 p.s.f. of *dly*$_1$ (= to hang, to bungle)) + *b*$_2$ (= from) + Sing. abs. of *dlt* (= door), less prob. interpret. - b) first and second *dlt* = noun; Horn BASOR cxciii 8, 12: *tdltbdlt* = *t* (unexplained) + Sing. abs. of *dlt* (= door) + *b*$_2$ + Sing. cstr. of *dlt* (= door; cf. also Sasson PEQ ’79, 118, 123); Cross BASOR cxciii 17, 19: l. *]l.t* (lapsus pro *]lt* (unexplained)) + Sing. abs. of *dlt* + *b*$_2$ + Sing. abs. of *dlt* (door by door; cf. also Shea PEQ ’79, 18, ’81, 105, 107); v.Selms BiOr xxxii 6, 8: *tdltbdlt* = *t* (= *t*$_1$ (= ’*yt*$_3$); cf. also Sivan UF xiv 228) + Sing. abs. of *dlt* (= door) + *b*$_2$ + Sing. abs. of *dlt* (= the inner door), cf. also

R.Kutscher Qadm v 27f. - c) cf. also Garbini AION xx 253f., LS 104f.: *dlt* = either Sing. or Plur. (on the problems of *tdltbdlt*, cf. also Jackson ALIA 19ff., Puech RB xcii 289, Aufrecht sub CAI 59) - for this subst., cf. also Marrassini FLEM 27ff.
v. *dl*$_1$.
dm$_1$ **Ph** Sing. + suff. 3 p.s.m. *ʾdmy* (prec. by aleph prosth.) KAI 43^{11} (?, uncert. reading and interpret.; cf. Honeyman JEA xxvi 64, cf. also Röllig KAI a.l., Dahood RPIM 127f., Penna CISFP i 890 × + suff. 1 p.s., cf. also Lane BASOR cxciv 43f. × v.d.Branden OA iii 259, Gibson SSI iii p. 137, 140: = Sing. + suff. 1 p.s. of *ʾdm*$_1$ (my people) × Lipiński RTAT 251: = Sing. + suff. 3 p.s.m. of *ʾdm*$_1$ (his people) :: Clermont-Ganneau Et ii 168f., 181: = lapsus for *ʾdny* (= Sing. + suff. 1 p.s. of *ʾdn*$_1$)) - **OldAr** Sing. cstr. *dm* KAI 224^{12}; + suff. 1 p.s. *dmy* KAI 224^{11} - **OffAr** Sing. abs. *dm* Aḥiq 211 (uncert. reading and interpret., dam. context; cf. Cowl a.l.; Greenfield HDS 57 (n. 5), div. otherwise: *wdm* = Sing. abs. of subst. of unknown meaning :: Seidel ZAW xxxii 297 (div. otherwise): l. *ndm* = subst. Sing. abs. (= part < Iran.), for the reading *nd/rm*, cf. also Sach p. 179f., Lindenberger APA 212 (cf. id. APA 212, 279): lapsus for *grm*? (= Sing. abs. of *grm*$_1$)); cstr. *dm* Aḥiq 87; + suff. 3 p.s.f.? *dmh* Aḥiq 89, 120; cf. Frah x 3 (*dm(y)ʾ*), GIPP 50 - ¶ subst. blood; in KAI 43^{11} > kin? (v. however supra) - for *mlk ʾdm*, v. *mlk*$_5$ - the form *edom* (August Enarr in Ps 136, 18 with Ps cxxxvii 7) poss. = *dm*$_1$ prec. by article, cf. Hoftijzer VT viii 289 n. 2 :: Février RHR cxliii 11, Vattioni AION xv 63 n. 156: = *dm*$_1$ prec. by aleph prosth. (cf. also Penna CISFP i 890) - L.H.Gray AJSL xxxix 83: *dume* in Poen 1142: = Sing. + suff. 1 p.s. of *dm*$_1$ (highly uncert. interpret., cf. Sznycer PPP 145 :: J.J.Glück & Maurach Semitics ii 125 (div. otherwise): l. *dumet* (= Sing. of *dmw* (= form, shape, stature)) :: Schroed 298f. (div. otherwise): l. *asd* (= Sing. abs. of *ḥsd* (= grace)) + *u* (= *w*) + *me* (= *mh*).
dm$_2$ v. *rmy*$_1$.
dmʾ **OffAr** Qal Part. act. s.m. abs. *dmʿ* KAI 276^{10} (for the orthography, cf. e.g. Nyberg Eranos xliv 236, Altheim & Stiehl GH i 251 n. 53, Donner KAI a.l. ; prob. interpret.); cf. Frah xviii 1 (*mdmhn*), GIPP 50, SaSt 19, cf. Toll ZDMG-Suppl viii 39 - **Palm** Qal Part. act. m. s. abs. *dmʾ* CIS ii 3913 ii 60, 114; s.f. abs.? *dmyʾ* CIS ii 3913 ii 91 - ¶ verb Qal to be like, comparable - a) + *l*$_5$ (to), *wmdy dmʾ lhwn* CIS ii 3913 ii 114: and whatever is comparable to them - b) + *mn*$_5$, *br ʾynš lʾ dmʿ yhwh mn ṭbwt* KAI 276$^{9ff.}$: no one was (her) equal in goodness (cf. Greek par. ἥτις τὸ κάλλος. ἀμείμητον εἶχε) - *dmʾ* in Syr xlv 101^{19} also from this root?? (dam. context).
v. *dmr*$_2$, *rmy*$_1$.
dmw **OldAr** Sing. emph. *dmwtʾ* Tell F 1, 15 - **OffAr** Sing. cstr. *dmwt*

Krael 3^{21} - **Hatra** Sing. emph. *dmt*ʾ, cf. Assur 7^{2} - ¶ subst. - **1)** statue: Tell F 1 (on the context, cf. Dion FS Delcor 141, Israel SAB i 79ff.), 15 (Akkad. par. *ṣalmu*; cf. Gropp & Lewis BASOR cclix 47, Sasson ZAW xcvii 72, 97f., M.S.Smith ZAW c 426 n. 13), Assur 7^{2} - **2)** conformity, similarity; *byt ldmwt bytk* Krael 3^{21}: a house similar to yours - Dankwarth & Ch.Müller AfO xxxv 74, 76f.: l. *dmt* (= Sing. abs./cstr. (= statue)) in KAI 231 (uncert. reading and interpret.) - Lemaire Syr lxi 252ff.: l. poss. *[d]mw* (= Sing. cstr.) in IEJ i 220^{1} (less prob. reading, improb. interpret.), cf. also Zayadine Syr li 134: l. *]šw* (cf. also Yellin-Kallai IEJ iii 124f.: l. *š/ṣw*) :: Aharoni IEJ i 220f.: l. *šd* (= part of n.p.) :: O'Callaghan Or xxi 184: l. *št*?? :: Puech with Lemaire Syr lxi 254: l. *[s]ml* = Sing. cstr. of *sml*$_1$ - Kottsieper SAS 13, 22, 196: l. poss. *dmw[*ʾ*]* (= Sing. emph. of *dmw*) in Aḥiq 202 (highly uncert. interpret.).
v. *dm*$_1$.

dmws v. *dms*$_1$.

dmy$_1$ v. *dm*ʾ, *dmn*$_1$, *dmr*$_2$.

dmy$_2$ **OffAr** Plur. + suff. 3 p.s.m., cf. Warka 31: *di-ma-a-a-*ʾ*[i-i]* (for the reading, cf. Landsberger AfO xii 253 n. 21) - ¶ subst. Plur. poss. meaning rest, calmness, cf. Dupont-Sommer RA xxxix 52.

dmy$_3$ **OffAr** in the combination *dmy dty* in KAI 273^{2} (< Prakrit, cf. Humbach AIT 9, Degen Lesh xxxiv 317, Hinz AISN 81f.), meaning: the decreed (*dty*) Dharma (*dmy*), cf. Humbach AIT 7, 9, 12, Degen Lesh xxxiv 316f., Hinz AISN 81f. :: Altheim LuG ii 181, Altheim & Stiehl Suppl 13, ASA 268, GMA 341, Donner KAI a.l., Kutscher, Naveh & Shaked Lesh xxxiv 126, In Der Smitten BiOr xxviii 311: = n.p. (cf. also Cowley JRAS '15, 343).

dmy$_4$ **Hebr** Sing. abs. *dmy* SM 49^{1,5}, *dmyy* SM 49^{19} (or cstr.?)^{,22,24} - ¶ subst. suspicion > those fruits (etc.) which are doubtful as to tithing.

dmyn v. *dmn*$_1$.

dmysyt v. *btr*.

dmk **JAr** QAL Part. act. s.f. abs. *dmkh* AMB 7^{19,22} - ¶ verb QAL to sleep - instead of *dmyk* Frey 979^{2} (= MPAT-A 48) = QAL Part. pass. s.m. abs. (cf. e.g. Ben-Zevi JPOS xiii 95, Frey a.l., Fitzmyer & Harrington MPAT a.l.) l. *dmn* = *d*$_3$ + *mn*$_5$ (cf. Klein MGWJ lxxvi 554) :: Beyer ATTM 393, 707: l. *dsym* = *d*$_3$ + QAL Part. pass. s.m. abs. of *šym*$_1$.
v. *dmn*$_1$.

dmm **Ph** Teixidor Syr lvi 148, 150: the *dm* in RES 56^{3} = QAL Inf. cstr. of *dmm* (= to rest), highly uncert. interpret. (for the problems of the context, cf. also RES a.l.).

dmn$_1$ **OffAr** Plur. abs. *dmn* Cowl 30^{28}, *dmyn* Samar 1^{3} (= EI xviii 8*; cf. also Freedman & Andersen FS Fitzmyer 19f.); cstr. *dmy* Cowl 13^{6},

15^{14}, 29^4, Krael 1^3, 2^6, Samar 7^{15}, ATNS 4^1, etc., etc.; emph. *dmy*ʾ
Krael 3^7, 12^{6,14}, Samar 9^{10}; + suff. 3 p.s.m. *dmwhy* Cowl 13^3, 36b 1
(for the reading, cf. also Porten & Yardeni sub TADAE B 6.2, Porten
AN xxvii 90), Krael 1^7, 3^6, 9^3, 12^{13,25,32}, Samar 3^8; + suff. 3 p.pl.m.
dmyhm Cowl 45^6, ATNS 114^1 - **Nab** Plur. cstr. *dmy* CIS ii 199^8, 217^7,
MPAT 64 recto i 5 - **Palm** Plur. + suff. 3 p.s.m./f. *[d]mwh* DEP 27
(dam. context) - **Hatra** Plur. abs. *dmyn* 49^3 (for the reading, cf. Milik
RN vi/iv 36 n. 2, Syr xliv 297, Vattioni IH a.l. :: Caquot Syr xxxii
54: l. *dmyk* (for this reading, cf. also Safar Sumer ix 245) = QAL Part.
pass. s.m. abs. of *dmk* (= died; specialized meaning, cf. also Altheim &
Stiehl AAW iv 265) - **JAr** Plur. abs. *dmyn* MPAT 49 i 12 (for this poss.
reading, cf. Beyer ATTM 318), 50a 2 (dam. context), e 3 (dam. context
:: Beyer ATTM 316 (div. otherwise): l. *hyn* (= variant of *hn₃*)), 51^6,
52^8, IEJ xxxvi 206^5 - ¶ subst. m. Plur. price, value; *dmy bytn* Krael 12^5:
the price of our house (cf. Cowl 13^3, 29$^{3f.}$, Krael 1^{3,7}, 3^6, 9^3, 12^{13,25,32},
CIS ii 217^7 (for this text, cf. Greenfield Mem Yalon 70f.)); *dmy* ʿ*bdy* ʾ*lk*
ksp kršn 15 ATNS 6^1: the value of these slaves of mine is (in) silver 15
karaš (cf. Samar 3^8); *dmyn gmryn* MPAT 51^6: total price (cf. Samar 1^3,
IEJ xxxvi 206^5), cf. *ldmy mgmr* CIS ii 199^8: according to the full price,
cf. also Muffs 181 n. 7; *dmyn dnšr*ʾ Hatra 49^3 (v. supra): the price (to
be paid for the construction of the statue) of the eagle; *nksyky ... dmy*
ksp kršn 5 Cowl 13^6: your possessions valued in silver at 5 *karaš* (cf.
Cowl 36^{2,3,4}, Krael 7^{8,14,15,23}); *dmy mnn [2]* Samar 7^{15}: a sum of 2 *m.*;
*kl ksp*ʾ *wdmy nksy*ʾ *ksp ksp šqln 7* Krael 2^6: all the silver and the value
of the goods in silver is silver 7 *shekel*; *kl dmy lbš*ʾ *wnksy*ʾ ATNS 50^{10}:
the complete value of the clothing and possessions (context however
dam.); *nwnyk* ʾ*w dmyhm* Cowl 45^6: your fishes or an equivalent of
their value (cf. Cowl 44^9, 45^5); *dbḥn dmn kdmy ksp knkryn 1 lp* Cowl
30^{28}: offerings worth as much as 1000 talents of silver (cf. Cowl 31^{27}) -
Caquot RTP p. 144: Plur. cstr. of this subst. (*dmy*) in RTP 706, cf. also
du Mesnil du Buisson TMP 491 (uncert. interpret.; Milik DFD 189f.:
l. *dmy* or *rmy* (= *rmy₂*) nouns derived from root *dmy₁* (= to think, to
decide) or root *rmy₁* (= to decide)).
v. *rmn₂*.
dmn₂ v. *dn₁*.
dmndyn v. *dn₁*.
dms₁ (< Greek δῆμος) - **Palm** Sing. abs. *dms* CIS i 3913 i 2, 3914^1,
3921^2, 3930^1, 3931^1, 3936^3, SBS 48^{4,7}, DFD 13^{2,17}, 37^1, etc., *dmws* CIS
ii 3932^8, 3934^1, 3935^3, 3959^1 (= SBS 44B), Inscr P 32^3, Inv x 115^1 -
¶ subst. people, only in comb. *bwl*ʾ *wdm(w)s*, v. also *bwl*ʾ; in many
instances Greek par. δῆμος.
dms₂ **Nab** Plur. cstr. *dmsy* RES 2126^2 (uncert. reading) - ¶ subst. of
uncert. interpret., cf. Lidzbarski Eph ii 253: = wall?? (< Greek δόμος)

:: Clermont-Ganneau RAO vi 114: l. *drg* (*drg*$_2$) = stairs??; cf. also Cantineau Nab ii 83.

dms$_3$ v. *ms*$_2$.

dms$_4$ v. *rms*.

dm‘ v. *dm’*.

dmr$_1$ **Palm** Gawlikowski Syr xlviii 417 (cf. TP 77): l. *’dmr* (= APH Pf. 3 p.s.m.) for *’d/rmd/r* in Syr xlviii 413[3] (meaning: to be protector, to protect), cf. also idem Syr li 91f., Sem xxiii 122f. (highly uncert. reading and interpret.), v. also *mhdmr*.

dmr$_2$ **OffAr** PA‘EL Impf. 3 p.s.m. *ydmr* RN vi/xiii 17[3] (for the reading, cf. Naveh & Puech with Greenfield FS Grelot 10 (n. 30), cf. also Gawlikowski Ber xxx 123 :: Caquot RN vi/xiii 17: l. *ydmh* = QAL Impf. 3 p.s.m. of *dmy*$_1$ (= *dm’*)) - ¶ verb to praise the might of (+ *b*$_2$), cf. Greenfield FS Grelot 10ff.

dn$_1$ **OffAr** Sing. abs. *dyn* Cowl 6[12,16], 8[12,14,17,20], Krael 3[12,14], 4[13], ATNS 2[2] (for the reading, cf. Segal ATNS a.l.), 35[3] (for this prob. reading, cf. Porten & Yardeni sub TADAE B 4.7 :: Segal ATNS a.l.: l. *ntn* = QAL Pf. 3 p.s.m. of *ntn*), etc., etc., *dn* Krael 1[5], 10[15], 11[8,12], *zyn* Krael 3[17] (cf. Driver PEQ ’55, 92, Coxon ZDMG cxxix 13), *ydyn* (lapsus) Cowl 15[16]; cstr. *dyn* Cowl 15[31], 18[1], 20[4], Krael 7[32,39]; emph. *dyn’* Cowl 7[7], 14[3], 28[9], KAI 279[7], Samar 2[11]; + suff. 3 p.s.m. *dynh* Aḥiq 198 (dam. context, cf. Halévy RS xx 77: = Sing. + suff. 3 p.s.m. of *dyn*$_3$, cf. also Lindenberger APA 196); + suff. 3 p.pl.m. *dynhm* ATNS 8[8] (for this reading, cf. Shaked Or lvi 409, Porten & Yardeni sub TADAE B 5.6 :: Segal ATNS a.l.: l. *dynh* (= Sing. + suff. 3 p.s.m.)),[13]; Plur. abs. *dynn* Samar 1[10] (= EI xviii 8*), 3[5], *dynyn* Samar 2[5,9]; cf. Frah xiii 6 (*dyn’*) - **JAr** Sing. cstr. *dyn* MPAT 41[3] (dam. context) - ¶ subst. justice - **1)** process, judicial action, lawsuit: Cowl 6[16], 8[27], 14[3], 20[14], Aḥiq 198, Krael 4[13,14,16]; cf. the expression *dyn wdbb* Cowl 6[12], 8[20], 9[13], Krael 3[12f.,14], 9[18f.], etc., *dn wdbb* Krael 1[5], *zyn wzbb* Krael 3[17]: suit and process (i.e. judicial action; < Akkad., cf. Cowl p. xxix, Sperling JANES i/1 36f.), for par., cf. also Kutscher JAOS lxxiv 239f., J.J.Rabinowitz VT xi 64, Muffs 31f. nn. 2, 3, 196f.; *wl’ dyn* Cowl 25[17], 28[12,14], Krael 4[15,22], ATNS 35[3] (v. supra), *wl’ dn* Krael 11[8,12]: without (the possibility to contest the preceding stipulation(s) in) a lawsuit, cf. also *wl’ dyn wl’ dbb* Cowl 8[14,21f.], 9[15], 14[10], 15[29] (for the reading of the context, cf. Porten & Yardeni sub TADAE B 2.6), Krael 5[15] (cf. Fitzmyer FS Albright ii 163f.): without suit and process, *l’ dynyn* Samar 2[9]: without process and *l’ dynn wl’ lḥwbn* Samar 1[10]: without litigation or obligations; *’hk bdyn* Cowl 8[22]: I will start a lawsuit (cf. Driver PEQ ’55, 94; cf. also Muffs 185, cf. however Yaron RB lxxvii 415), cf. Cowl 10[19], Krael 10[15]; *wl’ ytlqḥ bdyn* Cowl 8[17]: it shall not be accepted in suit; v. *gry*, *np’*$_2$, *ršy*$_1$ - **2)** legal decision, legal stipulation; *y‘bd lh*

dyn šn ᵓh Krael 7³⁹: he will treat her according to the law of divorce
(cf. Cowl 18¹); *wy ᶜbd [lh] dyn spr ᵓ dnh* Krael 7³²: he will treat her
according to the stipulation of this contract (cf. Cowl 15³¹ (l. *y ᶜ[bd]* =
QAL Impf. 3 p.s.m. of *ᶜbd₁* pro *y ᶜ[dy]* = QAL Impf. 3 p.s.m. of *ᶜdy₁*),
cf. also J.J.Rabinowitz Law 48ff., Fitzmyer FS Albright ii 165, Grelot
DAE p. 196 (n. w), Porten & Greenfield JEAS p. 22, Porten & Yardeni
sub TADAE B 2.6); *wmqry ᵓ ᶜl ᵓlhn mṭ ᵓ ᶜly bdyn ᵓ* Cowl 7⁶ᶠ·: the appeal
to our god has been laid upon me by legal decision; *wl ᵓ t ᶜbd dyn ḥd
w[t]ryn l ᶜnnyh b ᶜlh* Krael 7⁴⁰: prob. meaning, she will refuse the sexual
connection with A., her husband (cf. Krael 7³⁸; cf. J.J.Rabinowitz Bibl
xxxviii 269ff., Law 54f., Vogt Lex s.v. *dīn*, Grelot DAE p. 237 (n. g),
cf. also Kutscher JAOS lxxiv 237, Porten & Greenfield JEAS p. 56f.,
Porten & Yardeni sub TADAE B 3.8 :: Krael a.l.: she shall not be able
to go to law in cooperation with (?) one or two (men) ... with respect
to A. her husband); *lk hmw ᶜm dynhm* ATNS 8⁸ (v. supra): they (i.e.
certain slaves) belong to you with the stipulations made about them
(diff. and dam. context), cf. also ATNS 8¹³ (for this text, cf. Porten &
Yardeni sub TADAE B 5.6); cf. also *kdyn m[wš h]* MPAT 41³: according
to the law of Moses (cf. also Koffmahn DWJ 116) - **3)** claim; *hwdt
dyn ᵓ* Samar 2¹¹: I acknowledge the claim (dam. context) - **4)** (divine)
judgment: KAI 279⁷ (cf. e.g. Dupont-Sommer JA ccxlvi 31, Koopmans
178, Altheim & Stiehl ASA 29f., GMA 352, Garbini Kand 17, Donner
KAI a.l. (cf. however Kutscher, Naveh & Shaked Lesh xxxiv 135: =
appeal) :: Rosenthal EI xiv 97*: = way of life) - J.J.Rabinowitz Bibl
xxxix 80f.: the *dmndyn* in Cowl 20⁴ = d_3 + mn_5 + Sing. abs. of *dyn₂*
(= the chief magistrate; less prob. interpret.); :: Ayad JACA 286 n.
5: = *dmn₂* (< Egypt. = city) + *dyn₂* (= the judge of the city); prob.
interpret.: l. *rmndyn* (= n.p.), cf. Schaed 258, Porten Arch 255, Grelot
DAE p. 198 n. b, Porten & Greenfield JEAS p. 24f., Hinz AISN 198 ::
Cowl a.l.: l. *dmndyn* (= n.p.) - this word (Sing. abs. *dyn*) prob. also in
SCO xxix 128 ii 3.

v. *dyn₃*, *sgn₁*, *prtrk*.

dn₂ = jar, amphora > Greek δάννα, δάνα, cf. Milik DFD 200f.; for this
word, cf. also Kaufman AIA 46 - this word poss. also in Assur 13 (Sing.
emph. *dn ᵓ*), context however heavily damaged.

dn₃ v. *znh*.

dn ᵓ₁ v. *dny*.

dn ᵓ₂ v. *znh*, *lkdn ᵓ*.

dnb Palm PA ᶜEL (or QAL?; cf. also Milik DFD 243) Pf. 3 p.s.m. *dnb*
Inv xii 23²; 1 p.s. *dnbt* CIS ii 4214 (cf. Rosenthal Sprache 82, Milik
DFD 243 :: Cantineau sub Inv vii 2: l. *rnbt* = *rb₂* + f. ending used
adverbially :: Joüon Syr xix 189f.: l. *rnbt* < *rbt* = variant form of *rbbt*
(= PA ᶜEL Pf. 1 p.s. of *rbb₁* (= to make great, to enlarge)) :: Nöldeke

ZDMG xxiv 103, Lidzbarski Handb 256: = lapsus for *dbnt* (= d_3 + QAL Pf. 1 p.s. of *bny_1*); v. also infra) - ¶ verb PA'EL (?, v. supra) of unknown meaning, poss. = to complete (cf. Rosenthal Sprache 82, Milik DFD 242f. (for the problems involved, cf. Bounni & Teixidor sub Inv xii 23)); cf. however Greenfield JNES xli 149: *dnb* = metathesis of *ndb_1* (= to donate)).

dng **Ph** Sing. abs. *dng* IEJ xxxvii 27 no. 4[2] (v. infra) - ¶ subst. wax (reading and interpret. highly uncert., cf. also Naveh IEJ xxxvii 28).

dngl v. *sgyl.*

dnh_1 v. *dnt.*

dnh_2 v. *dkh_1.*

dnh_3 v. *znh.*

dnwn v. *kdn.*

dnḥ **OffAr** QAL Impf. 3 p.s.m. *ydnḥ* Aḥiq 138 - ¶ verb QAL to rise, to shine, to be bright (said of the sun); for the interpret. of the context, cf. also Lindenberger APA 135, 260 nn. 423, 425.

dny **OffAr** APH Imper. s.m. *'dny* Aḥiq 171 (cf. Lindenberger APA 175, 271 n. 535 × Smend ThLZ xxxvii 392, Nöldeke AGWG xiv/4,18, Kottsieper SAS 40f., 135, 196: = ITP Imper. s.m.) - **Palm** APH Pf. 3 p.s.m. + suff. 3 p.s.m. *'dn'h* Inv xi 11[8] (cf. Teixidor Inv xi a.l. :: Milik DFD 104, Aggoula Sem xxix 110f. (div. otherwise): l. *'dn'* = Sing. emph. of *$'dn_2$*) - ¶ verb APH to approach; *w'dn'h* Inv xi 11[8]: he (sc. the god) has approached him (sc. to help him); *'dny lšmš* Aḥiq 171: approach Sh. (i.e. have recourse to Sh., cf. also Grelot RB lxviii 192; v. however supra).

dnyn v. *kdn.*

dnyt v. *dnt.*

dnr ((< Greek δηνάριον) < Lat. *denarius*) - **Pun** Sing. (or Plur.?; cf. FR 208c) abs. *dn'ry'* KAI 130[1,2,3], cf. IRT 906[3]: *denario* (cf. Levi Della Vida OA ii 73) - **Palm** Sing. abs. *dnr* CIS ii 3913 ii 102, 106, 110, 120, 126, 149, *dynr* CIS ii 3913 ii 48; emph. *dnr'* CIS ii 3913 ii 48, DEP 27; Plur. abs. *dnryn* CIS ii 3948[3], RB xxxix 548[4] - **Hatra** Plur. emph. *dnr'* app. 3[4] (= KAI 257; cf. Caquot Syr xxx 245) - **JAr** Sing. abs. *dynr* Frey 858[3] (= MPAT-A 28, SM 34), 859[4] (*[dy]nr*; = MPAT-A 29, SM 35); Plur. abs. *dnryn* DBKP 17[41], 18[70], MPAT-A 40[4] (for this reading, cf. Naveh sub SM 57, Beyer ATTM 366 :: Fitzmyer & Harrington MPAT a.l.: l. *dynryn*), *dynryn* Frey 856[8] (= MPAT-A 26, SM 32), MPAT 62[12] (= DBKP 27; *d[y]nryn*) - ¶ subst. m. *denarius* - for abbrev. *d*, cf. CIS ii 3913 ii 3, 8, 9, etc., etc. - cf. Meshorer Proc v CJS i 84; cf. also Ben-David PEQ '71, 109ff.
v. *'tq*, *rb'_3*.

dnt (< Akkad., cf. Lidzbarski Handb 256, Zimmern Fremdw 19, Kaufman AIA 46, Muffs 187ff., Lipiński Stud 141f.) - **OffAr** Sing. abs. *dnt*

KAI 236 vs. 4 (= AECT 49; cf. also Lipiński Stud 95, 100 :: Lidzbarski AUA 19, Donner KAI a.l.: = Sing. cstr.); cstr. *dnt* CIS ii 17[1] (= Del 14 = AECT 5), 18 (= Del 9 = AECT 24; *[d]nt*), 19a 1 (= Del 12 = AECT 17), 22 (= Del 8 = AECT 27), 23 (= Del 10 = AECT 31), 24 (= Del 17 = AECT 32), 27[1] (= Del 18 = AECT 10), 28 (= Del 11 = AECT 23), 29[1] (= Del 16 = AECT 19; dam. context), Del 13[5] (*[d]nt*; = AECT 4), 15[1] (= AECT 14), Irâq xxxiv 133,5 (*[d]nt*; = AECT 37), AECT F 1; cf. Frah xv 3 (*dnt›*, *tnt›*) - ¶ subst. document, contract; *dnt hwš‘* CIS ii 17[1]: document concerning H.; *dnt ḥql[›]* CIS ii 27[1]: document concerning a field; for this subst., cf. also Fales AECT p. 7f.; Cowl a.l.: l. *dnh* (= Sing. abs.) in Cowl 10[23], cf. also Grelot DAE p. 84 n. h, Muffs 189 (less prob. interpret., prob. = *dnh*$_3$, cf. Ungnad ArPap p. 48, Kaufman AIA 46 n. 72, 156, cf. also Zimmern Fremdw 19 n. 1 (cf. also Porten & Greenfield JEAS p. 112, Porten & Yardeni sub TADAE B 3.1: *dnh* = subst. of unknown meaning)) - Lipiński Stud 140, 141f.: l. *dnyt* = Sing. abs. in TH 5 obv. 4 (= AECT 57; highly uncert. reading, cf. Friedrich TH a.l.: l. *dwyt*, cf. however Degen NESE i 56).

ds v. *rsy*.

d‘k **OffAr** Qal (or Pa‘el?, cf. Grelot RB lxviii 189) Impf. 3 p.s.m. *yd‘k* Aḥiq 147 (reading of *d* uncert., cf. Cowl a.l.; dam. context; :: Perles OLZ '11, 503, Kottsieper SAS 16, 206: = Qal Impf. 3 p.s.m. + suff. 2 p.s.m. of *yd‘*$_1$) - ¶ verb Qal (v. however supra) to be extinguished, quenched (or to extinguish?, cf. Grelot DAE p. 443 (n. d); cf. also Lindenberger APA 147f.).

v. *yr‘*.

d‘pr› v. *‘pr*$_2$.

d‘t v. *yd‘*$_1$.

dp› v. *rp›h*.

dpny (< Iran. (orig. past Part.), cf. Shaked Or lvi 411f.) - **OffAr** Sing. m. abs. *dpny* ATNS 28b 3 (cf. Shaked Or lvi 410ff., Porten & Yardeni sub TADAE B 8.4 :: Segal ATNS a.l.: l. *rwn[..]* = n.p.) - ¶ adj. one who is to be mistreated, tortured, harmed, injured.

dpsr Ebeling Frah a.l.: l. *dpsr* in Frah xv 1 = scribe (cf. Ar./Hebr. *ṭpsr*), less prob. reading, cf. Nyberg FP 47, 84: l. Iran. word - on this word, cf. Kaufman AIA 138 n. 6.

v. *ṭpsrs*.

dṣ **Pun** Sing. abs. *dṣ* (or Qal Inf. cstr. of root *dwṣ/dyṣ*?, cf. Röllig KAI a.l. (cf. also e.g. Cooke NSI p. 122, Harr 95, Segert GPP p. 216, Dahood Bibl lx 431)) KAI 69[20] - ¶ subst. (v. supra), only in the comb. *bdṣ l* = contrary to; *kl khn ›š yqḥ mš›t bdṣ l›š št bps z* KAI 69[20]: every priest who takes a contribution against what is set down on this tablet.

dq **Pun** Sing. f. abs. *dqt* KAI 76B 6 - ¶ adj. pulverized, fine; *lbnt dqt*

KAI 76B 6: fine frankincense (in powder form) - cf. also *dqq*.

dqdq OffAr Plur. m./f. abs. *dqdqn* ATNS 73^3 - ¶ adj. small: ATNS 73^3 (or substantivated adj.: a small/little one); Segal ATNS a.l. *dqdqn* = little girls (uncert. interpret., heavily dam. context).

dqyqh JAr Sing. emph. *dqyqth* AMB 2^{12} - ¶ subst. hectic fever (cf. Naveh AAALT 86f., Naveh & Shaked AMB a.l.).

dql OffAr Plur. abs. *dqln* KAI 228A 18, 19; cf. Frah iv 12 (*dkr*ʾ) - ¶ subst. palm tree, date palm.

dqnr ((< Greek δουκηνάριος) < Lat. *ducenarius*) - **Palm** Sing. emph. *dqnr*ʾ CIS ii 3940^2, 3943^2, *dwqnr*ʾ CIS ii 3938^2, 3939^2 - ¶ subst. m. *ducenarius*; for the meaning, cf. *ʾpṭrp*.

dqq OffAr Sing. m. abs. *dqq* ASAE xlviii 112 conc. 3 - ¶ adj. fine (said of salt); cf. also *dq* - on the root *dqq*, cf. also Collini SEL iv 20; v. also *ṭrq*.

dqr$_1$ OffAr QAL Part. pass. s.m. abs. *dqyr* TA-Ar 7^2, 8^3, $9^{1,2}$, 10^2, 11^1; cf. Frah app. 16 (*dklwn*, *dkrwn*, *dkkwn*) - ¶ verb to beat: Frah app. 16; exact meaning in TA-Ar texts unknown, prob. indication of some type of grain/wheat having undergone special treatment (cf. Aharoni TA a.l.: *dqyr* prob. indication of pounded wheat) - Caquot Syr xli 260 n. 6: the *dqrqbš* in Hatra app. 4^4 prob. = QAL Part. act. s.m. abs./cstr. of *dqr* (= piercing) + *qbš* (= enigmatic word), improb. interpret., cf. Safar Sumer xvii 38 n. 90, 40: = *d*$_3$ + *qrqbš* (= name poss. < Iran.), cf. also Caquot Syr xl 13: *qrqbš* = n.l. (cf. Teixidor Syr xli 276f., Aggoula MUSJ xlvii 47, Sem xxvii 140f.; on the problems involved, cf. also Altheim & Stiehl AAW v/1, 82f.).

dqr$_2$ v. *dqrh*.

dqrh Ph Plur. abs. *dqrt* EI xviii 117^7 (= IEJ xxxv 83; for the reading of the *d*, cf. Dothan EI xviii 118 :: Dothan IEJ xxxv 88f.: l. poss. *bqrt* = young cattle; or = Plur. abs. of *dqr*$_2$?) - ¶ subst. indicating certain object, Dothan EI xviii 118, IEJ xxxv 88: = deep bowl.

dqrywn ((< Greek δεκουρίων) < Lat. *decurio*) - **Palm** Sing. emph. *dqrywn*ʾ Ber ii 93^1 - ¶ subst. m. *decurio*; exact meaning in context uncert., military title?, cf. Ingholt Ber ii 94.

dr$_1$ Ph Sing. cstr. *dr* KAI 26A iii 19, 27^{12} (:: v.d.Branden BO iii 43,45: l. *dd*$_4$ (= *dwd*$_3$)) - **Pun** Sing. + suff. 3 p.s.m. *drm* RES 164^2, KAI 150^2 (*[dr]m*; for the reading of both instances, cf. Levi Della Vida RCL '49, 410 :: RES a.l.: l. *wrdm* = Plur. abs. of *wrd*$_1$ (= descendant)), *dʿr*ʾ KAI 165^8 (uncert. reading, cf. Levi Della Vida RCL '49, 410 × Röllig KAI a.l., Levi Della Vida RSO xxxix 309: l. *dr*ʾ), *dr*ʾ Punica xvi 2^4 (poss. reading, cf. Levi Della Vida RCL '49, 410, cf. however Chabot Punica a.l.), KAI 128^2 (cf. prob. also RevArch ii/xxxi 176^3 (*]dr*ʾ; :: Dérenbourg ibid. 176f.: l. *[n]dr*ʾ = Sing. + suff. 3 p.s.m. of *ndr*$_2$)); + suff. 3 p.s.f. *dr*ʾ NP 130^1 - **Hebr** Sing. abs. *dr* AMB 4^{11}, *dwr* AMB 4^{11}

(diff. reading) - ¶ subst. - **1)** group of individuals belonging together, family: KAI 150^{2}, RES 164^{2}; *sk*ʿ*r d*ʿ*r*ʾ *l*ʾ*lm* KAI 165$^{7f.}$ (for the reading, v. supra): a memorial of (i.e. dedicated by) his family forever, cf. also KAI 128^{2}, Punica xvi 2$^{3f.}$; *skr dr*ʾ *l*ʾ*št n*ʿ*mt* NP 130^{1}: a memorial for a pleasant woman dedicated by her family (:: Krahmalkov JSS xxiv 27: remember (*skr* = QAL Imper. s./pl.m. of *zkr*$_1$) her lifetime as a good woman); *kl dr bn* ʾ*lm* KAI 26A iii 19: the whole assembly of the gods (cf. *dr kl qdšn* (v. *qdš*$_3$) KAI 27^{12}), for Ug. par., cf. Gaster Or xi 60, cf. also Neuberg JNES ix 215ff., Ackroyd JSS xiii 3ff., Gibson SSI iii p. 63 - **2)** period; *ldwr dr* AMB 4^{11}: forever (v. however supra) - a word *dr* also in DJD ii 17A 5 (heavily dam. context) - this subst. poss. also in Karth xii 54^{1} (*dr*ʾ = Sing. + suff. 3 p.s.m. (= family)), cf. Février & Fantar Karth xii a.l. :: Krahmalkov RSF iii 179, 186, 200: = Sing. + suff. 3 p.s.m. of *dr*$_1$ (= period, term (sc. of consul)) :: v.d. Branden RSF v 57, 62: = Sing. + suff. 3 p.s.m. of *dr*$_4$ (= domain) - this subst. (Sing. + suff. 3 p.pl.m. *dhrnm*) poss. in Hofra 21^{1} (cf. Février Rob 365), diff. reading (:: Berthier & Charlier Hofra a.l.: poss. = n.d.?) - for *dr*$_1$, *drh*$_{1,2}$, v. also Marrassini FLEM 47ff.
v. *bdd*, *dd*$_1$, *drh*$_2$, *rd*$_3$.

dr$_2$ **OffAr** Plur. cstr. *dry* Cowl 26^{20} - ¶ subst. of unknown meaning, prob. indicating an object: board, panel?, cf. also Grelot DAE p. 293 n. t (< Egypt.), Porten & Yardeni sub TADAE A 6.2.

dr$_3$ **Pun** Février RA xlv 146: l. poss. *dr* (subst. Sing. abs. = liquid) in KAI 161^{8}, in the combination *mr dr* (// Hebr. *mr drwr* Ex xxx 23) = liquid myrrh (cf. also Röllig KAI a.l.; highly uncert. interpret., cf. also Roschinski Num 112, 115 (div. otherwise): l. *wš*ʿ*wtm bd b*ʿ*l* without interpret.).

dr$_4$ v. *dr*$_1$.

dr$_5$ v. *ṣwr*$_1$.

drbr Ebeling Frah a.l.: l. poss. *drbr* in Frah vii 14 = sheep, improb. interpret., cf. Nyberg FP 71: l. *dō-brīt* = Iran. word.

drg$_1$ v. *drk*$_1$, *ngd*$_1$.

drg$_2$ **OffAr** Sing. emph. *drg*ʾ Krael 6^{10}, 9^{4,7,10,15}, *drgh* Krael 10^{3} (cf. Krael p. 249 × e.g. Grelot DAE p. 248, Porten & Greenfield JEAS p. 63, Porten & Yardeni sub TADAE B 3.11: = Sing. + suff. 3 p.s.m.) - **JAr** Plur. + suff. 3 p.s.m. *drgwh* Frey 981^{3} (= MPAT-A 16, SM 17; for this reading, cf. e.g. also Sukenik ASPG 60 n. 2; :: Marmorstein PEQ '27, 101, '30, 155, Koopmans 219: l. *drgwt* = (Hebr.) Plur. abs. :: Krauss REJ lxxxix 390f.: l. *drgwh* = Sing. abs. (f.) (= stairs; cf. also Klein SeYi i p. 98) :: Ory PEQ '27, 51f. (div. otherwise): l. *drg* (= Sing. abs.)) - ¶ subst. staircase, stairs - the *dgry*ʾ in MPAT 51^{7} lapsus for Plur. emph. *drgy*ʾ (cf. Milik Bibl xxxviii 264, cf. also Puech RQ ix 217 (n. 10), Beyer ATTM 320)?? or rather cf. Abramson &

Ginsberg BASOR cxxxvi 17f.: l. *ʾgryʾ* = Plur. emph. of *ʾgr*$_5$ (= brick) or l. *dgryʾ* = Plur. emph. of *dgr* (= pile (?) of building material), cf. also Birnbaum PEQ '57, 112, 123, 130: l. *hgryʾ* = Plur. emph. of *hgr* (= brick) :: Milik RB lxi 183, 186: l. *ʾrgryʾ* var. of *ʾrglyʾ* (< Greek ἐργαλεῖα) = tools, instruments - v.Soden Or xxxv 7, xlvi 185: > Akkad. (cf. also idem AHW s.v. *dargu*) -
v. *dms*$_2$, *šgʾ*$_3$.

drgwh v. *drg*.

drgš v.Soden Or xxxv 7, xlvi 185: Ar. *drgš* = couch > Akkad. (?, cf. idem AHW s.v. *dargiš*, CAD s.v.: = foreign word).

drdq **Hatra** Plur. emph. *drdqʾ* 336[5], 343[3] - ¶ adj. small; for Hatra 336[5], 343[3], v. *qšyš*.

drh$_1$ **JAr** Sing. cstr. *drt* IEJ xxxvi 206[2,4]; emph. *drtʾ* MPAT 44 vi 2 (heavily dam. context), *drth* MPAT 51[5,9,10], IEJ xxxvi 206[3] (*drt[h]*; on the diff. and uncert. context, cf. Broshi & Qimron IEJ xxxvi 209)[,4], DBKP 19[28]; + suff. 1 p.s. *drty* MPAT 51[4] - ¶ subst. f. courtyard - Obermann Ber vii 94f., 105: l. *drʾtyh*? (= Plur. + suff. 3 p.s.m.) in Syn D C$_2$ 4 (= SM 89B), highly uncert. reading, cf. Torrey Syn p. 268: l. *mlʾktyh*? = Sing. + suff. 3 p.s.m. of *mlʾkh*$_1$, Naveh sub SM 89B (div. otherwise): l. *ʿybydth* = Sing. emph. of *ʿbydh* (less prob. reading).
v. *dr*$_1$, *drh*$_2$, *mrzḥ*.

drh$_2$ **Pun** Sing. (or Plur.) abs. *drt* KAI 145[1] - ¶ subst. of unknown meaning (identical with *drh*$_1$??); Cooke NSI p. 153: poss. = Plur. abs. (= habitations); cf. also Février Sem vi 16, 21: = Sing. abs. = house > sanctuary (cf. also v.d.Branden Mašr lvi 290f., Good SHP 23); Berger MAI xxxvi 144, 149: poss. = Sing. abs. (= town)?, cf. Clermont-Ganneau RAO iii 325 n. 1, CRAI '98, 363ff.: = circle > administrative subdivision of the town (cf. Halévy RS ix 269), cf. also Sznycer Sem xxii 39: = district; :: Lidzbarski Eph i 48: = n.l. :: Krahmalkov RSF iii 188ff.: = n.d. :: Röllig KAI a.l.: = Plur. abs. of *dr*$_1$ (= generations).
v. *ʾdr*$_7$, *dr*$_1$, *mrzḥ*, *nbnh*.

drwm v. *drm*.

drwt (< Iran., cf. Andreas with Lidzbarski Eph ii 223 n. 2, Grelot DAE p. 334 n. j) - **OffAr** Sing. abs./cstr. *drwt* RES 438[5] (= RES 1806) - ¶ subst. peace, benediction (diff. and dam. context).

drḥt (< Iran., cf. Shaked with Hanson BASOR cxcii 8 n. 13, Lipiński Stud 156, Hinz AISN 88) - **OffAr** Sing. abs. *drḥt* KAI 260[2] (for the reading, cf. Lipiński Stud 155 n. 1); emph. *drḥtʾ* KAI 260[5] - ¶ subst. tree (cf. Shaked with Hanson BASOR cxcii 8 n. 13, Lipiński Stud 155ff., Hinz AISN 88 :: Kahle & Sommer KlF i 33: l. *rdḥtʾ* (= Sing. emph. of *rdḥh*) < Iran. = wall??; (cf. also Donner KAI a.l.); for other interpret., cf. Littmann Sardis 26, Cook JHS xxxvii 84, Lidzbarski ZA xxxi 126, Torrey AJSL xxxiv 193, Cowley CRAI '21, 9).

dry v. *ybl*$_1$.
dryk v. *drk*$_1$.
drykn ((< Greek δαρειχός) < Iran., cf. e.g. Brockelmann LS p. 167) - **Hatra** Plur. emph. *drykn*ʾ 292[5,6] - ¶ subst. Persian gold coin, exact type and value in Hatra unknown.
drymy **OffAr** Sing.(?) + suff. 1 p.s. *drymyy* Krael 9[3] (uncert. reading × Porten & Yardeni sub TADAE B 3.10: l. *drysy* (= Sing. abs.) = southern room) - ¶ subst. of unknown meaning (v. however also supra), certain type of present??; cf. also Grelot DAE p. 243 n. c; origin also unknown, Krael p. 240: < Iran.??, Yaron HUCA xxviii 49: < Greek δώρημα (cf. however Grelot DAE p. 243 n. c) - on this word, cf. also Hinz AISN 22, 25.
drysy v. *drymy*.
drk$_1$ **Ph** Qal Impf. 1p.s. *ʾdrk* KAI 27[7]; 2 p.pl.f. *tdrkn* KAI 27[8] (cf. e.g. Röllig KAI a.l., Avishur PIB 248, Cross & Saley BASOR cxcvii 45 :: v.d.Branden BO iii 44, BiOr xxxiii 12: = Impf. 2 p.s.f. + *nun* parag.) - **OffAr** Qal Pf. 3 p.s.m. *drk* Aḥiq 191 (:: Kottsieper SAS 41, 197: poss. = var. of *drg*$_1$ (= to proceed)); Part. act. pl.m. cstr. *drky* Aḥiq 108; cf. GIPP 67 - ¶ verb Qal to go (to), to enter; + obj., *ḥṣr ʾdrk bl tdrkn* KAI 27[7f.]: the courtyard I enter, do not enter (there); *drky ʾrqʾ* Aḥiq 108: those who walk on the earth (i.e. mankind (prob. interpret.), cf. however Grelot RB lxviii 184, DAE p. 438 n. m, cf. also Lindenberger APA 244 n. 267); with obj. *qšt*: to tread (i.e. to bend) the bow: Aḥiq 191 - Akkad. *darīku* prob. < Ar. Qal Part. pass. *dryk*, cf. Landsberger BeihAfO xvii 56, v.Soden Or xxxvii 270, xlvi 185, with meaning (container of) pressed dates (cf. also AHW, CAD s.v.) - Février Sem vi 20, 25: l. Qal Pf. 1 p.pl. *dʿrkn* in KAI 145[10] (highly uncert. interpret., cf. Röllig KAI a.l. :: Krahmalkov RSF iii 189, 196f.: *dʿrkn* = Sing./Plur. + suff. 1 p.pl. of *drk*$_2$) - Rocco AION xxiv 476, 479: l. *drkm* = Qal Imper. s.m. + suff. 3 p.pl.m. of *drk*$_1$ (= to trample) in GR ii 36 no. 20[7] (highly uncert. reading and interpret., cf. Polselli GR ii p. 36ff.).
v. *ndr*$_1$, *prk*$_3$.
drk$_2$ **Ph** Sing. abs. *drk* KAI 26A ii 5; Plur. abs. *drkm* MUSJ xlv 262[3] (cf. Röllig NESE ii 2, 7f., Schiffmann RSF iv 172, 176 :: Starcky MUSJ xlv 262 (div. otherwise): l. *drkmn* = Sing. abs. of *drkmn* :: Cross IEJ xxix 43f.: l. *drkm* = Plur. abs. of *drk*$_3$ (= dominion :: Starcky MUSJ xlv 267 n. 4: or = Plur. abs. of *drk*$_4$ (= governor) ??) - **Hebr** Sing. abs. *drk* SM 49[18] - ¶ subst. f. way, road; *wdrk hgdwlh hhwlkt lmydbr* SM 49[18]: the great road leading to the desert.
v. *drk*$_1$, *drkmn*.
drk$_3$ v. *drk*$_2$, *rḥq*$_3$.
drk$_4$ v. *drk*$_2$.

drkh **Ph** Teixidor Syr lvi 148f.: l. in RES 56^3 *drkt* (= Sing. abs. of *drkh* (= concubine)), highly uncert. interpret., for the interpret. problems, cf. RES a.l.

drkmn (prob. related to Greek δραχμή, cf. also BDB, HAL s.v.) - **Ph** Plur. abs. *drkmnm* KAI 60^6, *drknm* KAI 60^3 (lapsus?, cf. also Starcky MUSJ xlv 268ff. (v. however *drk*$_2$), cf. however Röllig KAI a.l., Guzzo Amadasi RAI xxv 388, 394 n. 28, Gibson SSI iii p. 150) - ¶ subst. drachm; in KAI 60^3 prob. weight, in KAI 60^6 coin (cf. Lidzbarski sub KI 52).
v. *drk*$_2$.

drm **Hebr** Sing. abs. *drwm* DJD ii 22,1-$9^{3,12}$ (*dr[wm]*), $30^{4,15,17}$, AMB 4^{12}, SM 49^6 - **JAr** Sing. abs. *drm* MPAT 51^9 (diff. reading; cf. Milik RB lxi 181 (× Beyer ATTM 320: l. *drm* = lapsus for *drm*ʾ (= Sing. emph.)) :: Milik Bibl xxxviii 264, 268, Koopmans sub no. 64, Fitzmyer & Harrington MPAT a.l. (div. otherwise): l. *drm*ʾ (= Sing. emph.)); emph. *drwm*ʾ MPAT 44,9-10^2 (heavily dam. context), 52^4, *drwmh* IEJ xxxvi 206^4 - ¶ subst. south; *drwm*ʾ MPAT 52^4: at the south side (cf. MPAT 51^9, DJD ii 22,1-$9^{3,12}$, $30^{4,17}$, IEJ xxxvi 206^4); *mhmʿrb whdrwm* DJD ii 30^{15}: at the west and south side.

drmdr ((< Greek δρομαδάριος) < Lat. *dromedarius*) - **Palm** Plur. emph. *drmdry*ʾ Inv x 128^2 - ¶ subst. m. soldier serving in a unit mounted on dromedaries (cf. Seyrig Syr xxii 235).

drʿ v. *zrʿ*$_3$.

drr **DA** Sing. abs. *drr* i 10 (for the reading, cf. Hoftijzer DA a.l.) - ¶ subst. indicating bird: swallow or dove?

drš **Pun** QAL Impf. 2 p.s.m. + suff. 3 p.s.m. *tdrš*ʾ BAr '55/56, 30 no. 3^1 (= IAM 3) - ¶ verb QAL prob. meaning to care for + obj. (cf. Février IAM a.l.).

dš (poss. < Akkad., cf. Zimmern Fremdw 30, Kaufman AIA 45, 141, Marrassini FLEM 28 (n. 4), cf. however v.Soden JSS xxii 82f.) - **OffAr** Sing. abs. *dš* Krael 9^{13}; Plur. (cf. Nöldeke ZA xxi 199) abs. *dššn* Krael 10^3, 12^{13}; emph. *dššy*ʾ Cowl 30^{11}; + suff. 3 p.pl.m. *dšyhm* Cowl 30^{10} - **JAr** Plur. emph. *dšyh* IEJ xxxvi 206^4 (for the diff. and dam. context, cf. Broshi & Qimron ibid. 209) - ¶ subst. m. door.

dšʾ **Amm** Sing. abs. *dš*ʾ AUSS xiii 2^9 (= CAI 80; :: Baldacci AION xlv 519: = derivative of root *dwš* (= "threshing")) - ¶ subst. grass, hay (on the context, cf. Cross AUSS xiii 7).
v. *r*ʾ*š*$_1$.

dšʾ**h** v. *rš*ʾ*t*.

dšḥpṭ v. *dḥšpṭ*.

dšy v. *ndš*.

dšn (< Iran., cf. Telegdi JA ccxxvi 241, Benveniste JA ccxlii 300f., Driv p. 43, Eilers AfO xvii 333, Hinz AISN 84) - **OffAr** Sing. emph.

dšn› Driv 2^{2*,3} (for the reading and location of the word, cf. Yardeni with Szubin and Porten JNES xlvi 42, cf. also Szubin & Porten BASOR cclxix 42, Porten & Yardeni sub TADAE A 6.4)^{,4}, IEJ xiv 186^{2}; Plur. emph. *dšny›* ATNS 41^{8} - ¶ subst. donation, gift; *dšny› lywm› yld› zy* .. ATNS 41^{8}: presents for the birthday of ... (cf. also Shaked Or lvi 410, v. also *plny*); in the Driv texts a revocable gift of land, cf. Szubin & Porten JNES xlvi 43ff., cf. also Greenfield IrJu 8.

dštw› v. *rštw›*.

dt$_1$ (< Iran., cf. e.g. Mayrhofer FX 184) - **Ph** Sing. cstr. *dt* KAI 37B 1 (for the reading, cf. Peckham Or xxxvii 318, Healey BASOR ccxvi 56 :: Amadasi sub Kition C 1 B 1: l. *dt* = Sing. cstr. of *dt$_2$* (= what is conform to) :: Masson & Sznycer RPC 55 (with older litt. and Röllig KAI al): vacat; cf. also Puech Sem xxix 33), EI xviii 117^{1} (= IEJ xxxv 83, for the reading problems, cf. Dothan IEJ xxxv 84, EI xviii a.l.) - **OffAr** Sing. emph. *dth* FX 136^{19} - ¶ subst. decree: FX 136^{19}; *bdt* EI xviii 117^{1}: by order of ... (cf. also Dothan EI a.l., IEJ xxxv 84); for KAI 37B 1, v. *‹qb$_4$* - As-Salihi xlv 103: l. this word in Hatra 410^{1}, cf. however Aggoula Syr lxvii 412 (div. otherwise): l. *hdyrt*, name of a female deity.

dt$_2$ v. *dt$_1$*.

dt$_3$ v. *zy*.

dtbr (< Iran., cf. e.g. Eilers Beamtennamen 94, Hinz AISN 85) - **OffAr** Plur. emph. *dtbry›* ATNS 13^{3}, 14^{5} (*[d]tbry›*) - ¶ subst. m. judge, law official.

dty v. *dmy$_3$*.

dtk v. *prtk*.

H

h$_1$ **Ph** *h* KAI 4^{2}, 9A 1, 10^{2,4}, 14^{9,15}, 24^{9,10} (:: Lipiński RSF ii 49f.: *h* functioning as rel.), 26A i 9, 19, 37B 6, CIS i 13^{1}, etc., etc. - **Pun** *h* KAI 65^{11}, 69^{1,2,3}, 70^{1}, 72B 3, 74^{2}, 76B 1, 80^{1}, CIS i 370^{3,4}, 373^{3}, 374^{2}, 376^{3}, etc., etc., *›* KAI 87^{5,6}, 89^{6}, 112^{6}, CIS i 239^{6}, 246^{4}, 322^{3}, 325^{5}, 328^{4}, 370^{5}, Hofra 118^{1}, 174^{2}, etc., etc., *‹* KAI 173^{5}, *ḥ* KAI 118^{1} (diff. reading, dam. context), 122^{2}, Hofra 65^{3} (for poss. *h‹*, v. *khn$_1$*), cf. Poen 937, 947: *a* (in resp. *aelychot*, *ahelicot*, v. also *hlkt*), August Enarr in Ps 136,18 with Ps cxxxvii 7: *e* (?, in *edom*; v. *dm$_1$*) - **Mo** *h* KAI 181^{1,3,9,11}, etc., etc. - **Amm** *h* Ber xxii 120^{4} (= CAI 78; :: Loretz UF ix 170: indicating vocative), SANSS-Amm 14 (cf. also Garbini LS-Amm no. 21, Vatt sig. eb. 261, Jackson ALIA 83 no. 59) - **Edom** *h* TeAv xii 97^{3,6} - **Hebr** *h* KAI 183^{1}, 184^{1}, 185^{1}, 186^{1}, 187^{1}, 189^{1,2,3}, 191A, B 1, 2, 193^{14,19,20}, 194^{3,7}, 195^{6}, 196^{1}, 200^{1,10}, TA-H 1^{4,5,6,10}, 2^{3,5}, 3^{2,7}, etc., etc. (in MPAT-A 22^{7} in J.Ar. context) - ¶ article; for orthography and usage of the Ph./Pun. article, cf. FR 33, 117-119, 296-301, Lambdin

FS Albright ii 326ff., Ullendorf BHL 170 (cf. also Pardee Mem Craigie 56 n. 5); for the usage of the Mo. article, cf. Segert ArchOr xxix 218, 231; for KAI 26A i 1, v. *hbrk*.

v. *hnkt*, *hš*, z_1, *znh*, *ḥṭl*, $ḥyh_1$, *n*ʾ*n*, $pqḥ_1$, tm_3.

$\mathbf{h}_2$ **Hebr** *h* KAI 196[8] - **Edom** *h* TeAv xii 97[2] - **DA** *h* ii 9 - ¶ interrogative particle; *hl*ʾ *tktb* KAI 196[8]: will you not write? (dam. context); *hšlm* ʾ*t* TeAv xii 97[2]: are you well?; the function of h_2 in DA ii 9 diff. to establish, Hoftijzer DA p. 229f.: asseverative function, Caquot & Lemaire Syr liv 204: interrogative function.

v. $ḥzy_1$, $pqḥ_1$, $ṣd$ʾ$_1$.

$\mathbf{h}_3$ = hw_1 (= *h*ʾ$_1$), v. $nš_1$.

$\mathbf{h}_4$ v. hn_1.

$\mathbf{h}_5$ v. *h*ʾ$_2$, $ṭ$ʿm_1, qwm_1.

$\mathbf{h}_6$ **Hebr** the *h* in TA-H 60[1] (in the comb. *kkl 4 h*, v. also kl_1, *nṭl*) prob. abbrev., meaning unknown - **OffAr** the *h* in PF 2059[3] prob. abbrev. of dry measure.

hʾ$_1$ **Ph** Sing. m. *h*ʾ KAI 1[2], 10[9,15], 13[6], 14[10], 26A iii 19, iv 1, EpAn ix 5[1], etc., *h*ʾ*t* KAI 4[2] (cf. Albright JAOS lxvii 156, Röllig KAI a.l., FR 111, Gibson SSI iii p. 18f., Puech RB xcii 292, Del Olmo Lete AO iv 40, FPI 40 :: e.g. Dunand RB xxxix 324: l. *z*ʾ*t* pron. dem. s.f. used adverbially: lo!); f. *h*ʾ KAI 10[13], 14[11,22], 26A iii 19, 40[2], CIS i 94[2]; Plur. *hmt* KAI 14[11] (:: Baldacci BiOr xl 131: = Hiph Pf. 3 p.s.m. of mwt_1)^{,22}, 24[13], 26A i 17, 43[5] (on this form, cf. also e.g. FR 111, Del Olmo Lete AO iv 40, FPI 40) - **Pun** Sing. m. *h*ʾ KAI 76B 4, 79[11], 81[4], 89[1] (uncert. context), 119[2,5], CIS i 171[7], 5632[7], ICO-Spa 10B 4, CRAI '68, 117[7], cf. Poen 946: *hu* (var. *hy*), 937: *hy*; f. *hy* KAI 130[3]; Plur. *hmt* KAI 69[17], CIS i 151[5] (cf. Février JA ccxlvi 445, cf. also Guzzo Amadasi sub ICO-Sard Np 2: reading uncert.), 5510[1,2,5,10] - **Mo** Sing. m. *h*ʾ KAI 181[6]; f. *h*ʾ KAI 181[27] - **Hebr** Sing. m. *h*ʾ TA-H 18[10], *hw*ʾ DJD ii 24E 6, 46[4,8], 50 ii 2 (heavily dam. context), SM 70[14] (in Ar. context), *hw* DJD ii 46[9] (in *mhw*, dam. context), SM 70[15] (in Ar. context); f. *hy* DJD ii 42[4], *hy*ʾ SM 49[6,7,8]; Plur. *hm* DJD ii 24E 9f., *hn* SM 49[10,19,21,24] - **DA** Sing. m. *h*ʾ i 1 (cf. e.g. Hoftijzer DA p. 185, Naveh IEJ xxix 134f. :: e.g. Caquot & Lemaire Syr liv 194, Garbini Hen i 173, McCarter BASOR ccxxxix 51f., Ringgren Mem Seeligmann 93, Lemaire BAT 318, GLECS xxiv-xxviii 325: = *h*ʾ$_2$ :: Wesselius BiOr xliv 594 (div. otherwise): l. perhaps *r*ʾ*w* = Qal Imper. pl.m. of *r*ʾ*y*??; v. also infra) - **Samal** Sing. m. *h*ʾ KAI 214[22] (?, dam. context × Ginsberg JAOS lxii 235 n. 31: = *h*ʾ$_2$, cf. also Dion p. 32, 177 (cf. however ibid. p. 150); cf. Gibson SSI ii p. 74)^{,30}, 215[11,22] (:: Dion p. 43: = *h*ʾ$_2$, cf. also ibid. p. 177; for Samal., cf. also Garbini AION xxvi 128) - **OldAr** Sing. m. *h*ʾ KAI 216[18,19], 222A 37 (cf. e.g. Degen AAG p. 55; cf. however Fitzmyer AIS 54: = Sing. f.), B 24, 42 (??, uncert. context, cf. Fitzmyer AIS 72), 223C 6, 224[8] (cf.

e.g. Fitzmyer AIS 96, 111, Donner KAI a.l., Degen AAG p. 20, 69 (n. 56), Gibson SSI ii p. 46 :: Dupont-Sommer BMB xiii 32, Sf p. 128, 130, AH i/1, 5, Garbini RSO xxxiv 46, Segert ArchOr xxxii 126 n. 111 (div. otherwise): pro *rḥm h*ʾ *ly* l. *rḥmh* ʾ*ly*)^{,13,22} (for the context, v. *mn*$_5$); f. *h*ʾ KAI 224^{12}; Plur. *hm* KAI 222B 6, *[h]mw* KAI 202A 9 - **OffAr** Sing. m. *hw* Cowl $5^{1,12}$, $6^{1,14}$, Krael 1^{1}, $2^{11,12}$ (for the dittography *hw hw*, cf. Yaron JSS xiii 207 (n. 1)), 3^{1}, 4^{4}, Herm 1^{8}, ATNS 5^{7} (cf. Segal ATNS a.l. :: Porten & Yardeni sub TADAE B 8.3: l. *hn* (= *hn*$_3$)), Samar 2^{6}, etc., etc., *hd* (lapsus for *hw*??, cf. Cowl p. 241 × Joüon MUSJ xviii 87: word of unknown meaning, cf. however Lindenberger APA 119, 252 n. 354: l. *hw* written less clearly :: Grelot RB lxviii 187, DAE p. 441 (n. c): l. *hk* = Sing. abs. of *hk* (= movement) :: Grimme OLZ '11, 537: l. *hd* pro *hdy(*ʾ*)* = resp. Sing. abs. and emph. of *hdy*$_2$ (= direction (aiming)), cf. Ginsberg ANET 429) Aḥiq 128; f. *hy* Cowl 5^{4}, 8^{25}, 9^{9}, Krael $2^{3,11}$, 3^{5}, Herm 4^{6}, 8^{3} (heavily dam. context), ATNS 29^{4}, etc., etc.; Plur. *hmw* KAI $233^{4,7,8,16}$, Cowl $9^{7,10,13}$, Krael $4^{17,18}$, JRAS '29, 108^{12}, NESE i 11^{5}, ATNS 4^{5} (for this poss. reading, cf. Shaked Or lvi 409, Porten & Yardeni sub TADAE B 8.7 :: Segal ATNS a.l.: l. *hnt[rt]* = HAPH Pf. 1 p.s. of *ntr*$_1$), $8^{5,7,8}$, Samar 4^{13}, etc., etc., *hm* Cowl 18^{3}, RES 492A 9 (cf. RES 1800; for the reading, cf. Grelot DAE p. 140 n. l), AE '23, 42 no. 11^{1}; f. *hny* KAI 233^{12} - **Nab** Sing. m. *hw* CIS ii 164^{3}, 198^{10}, 200^{4}, 207^{6}, MPAT 64 i 2, etc., etc., *hw*ʾ J 18^{3} (for the reading of the context, cf. Milik & Starcky sub ARNA-Nab 90), 38^{8} (transcription *hwh* false, cf. Cantineau Nab ii 84), RES 2025^{1}? (Kottsieper SAS 91: the two last mentioned instances = QAL Pf. 3 p.s.m. of *hwy*$_1$); f. *hy* CIS ii 161^{8}, J 17^{3}, RES 2026^{2}, RHR lxxx 4^{7} (= BSOAS xvi 227,81), MPAT 64 i 2, BASOR cclxix 48^{6}; Plur. *hm* J 18^{2} (= RES 1106, cf. Cantineau Nab i 52); *hm* in CIS ii 203^{3}, 210^{6} false reading, cf. resp. J 14 and 3 :: Levinson NAI 152 (for the Nab. material in general, cf. Levinson NAI 23ff.) - **Palm** Sing. m. *hw* CIS ii 3913 ii 7, 126, 3917^{4}, 3955^{4}, etc., etc.; f. *hy* CIS ii 3913 ii 128; Plur. *hnn* CIS ii 4171^{2}, 4173^{2}, Inv x 115^{2}, *hnwn* Ber ii 101^{5}, SBS 45^{10} (*[h]nwn*), FS Miles 50 ii 7 - **Hatra** Sing. m. *hw* 25^{2} (for the reading, cf. Milik RN vi/iv 55, 56 n. 1, Degen ZDMG cxix 174, cxxi 125: l. *h[w] wmn* (or: haplography *hwmn* pro *hw wmn*?, cf. also Vattioni IH a.l.: l. *hw mn*), cf. also Altheim & Stiehl AAW ii 201 :: Caquot Syr xxix 104: l. *dy mn*, cf. also Donner sub KAI 246; v. also *dlmn*), 52^{5} (prob. reading: *h[w] wmn*, cf. e.g. Caquot Syr xxxii 55 (cf. also Vattioni IH a.l.: l. *hw wmn*) :: Altheim & Stiehl AAW ii 203: l. *ḥw* = variant for *hw*), 116^{3} (for the reading, cf. Aggoula Ber xviii 98 :: Caquot Syr xli 255: l. *-hy*), 225^{2}, 235^{3}, 377; Plur. *hnw* 13^{4} (for the reading, cf. Milik Syr xliv 298, Aggoula Ber xviii 88, Vattioni IH a.l. :: Safar Sumer vii 178: l. *hny*? :: Caquot Syr xxix 96f.: l. *hny* = n.p. :: Donner sub KAI 240: l. *hny* = *hny*$_2$ (= see)), 79^{7} (cf. Aggoula MUSJ xlvii 30f.: l. *ʾḥdw hnw*, for other proposals, v. *ʾḥz*), 106B 5 (:: Caquot Syr xli 252: = pron. suff., cf. also Degen WO v 231 n. 1: poss. = lapsus for *-hwn*? :: Altheim & Stiehl AAW iv 255: l. *hny* = QAL Imper. s.m. of *hny*$_{1}$ (= to be useful) :: Safar Sumer xviii 27: l. *ʾlp* (= *ʾlp*$_{5}$)*hnw* (= benefactions, mercies)) - **JAr** Sing. m. *hw* MPAT-A 22^{7} (= SM 70^{15}; Hebr. form in Ar. context), *hwʾ* MPAT 48^{3} (for this uncert. reading, cf. Beyer ATTM 316), 52^{4}, MPAT-A 22^{6} (= SM 70^{14}), RB xc 522 no. 31 (cf. Greek par. αὐτοῦ), cf. PEQ '38, 238^{2}: ου (cf. Peters OLZ '40, 218, 220, Beyer ATTM 353; cf. also Milik LA x 154f.); f. *hyʾ* MPAT-A 5^{6} (= SM 64 = Frey 1203, cf. however Hüttenmeister ASI 327ff. (div. otherwise): l. *[y]hyʾ* = QAL Impf. 3 p.s.m. of *hwy*$_{1}$), 52^{5}, AMB 1^{21}; Plur. *hmwn* MPAT 50D 2, 51^{6}, 52^{7}, AMB 7^{16} (cf. Naveh & Shaked AMB a.l. :: Beyer ATTM 372f.: l. *ḥmyn* = QAL Part. pass. pl.f. abs. of *ḥmy* (= fit, worthy)), *hnwn* MPAT-A 7^{3} (= SM 65, Frey 1204), 13^{2} (= SM 46), *hnnwn* MPAT-A 26^{6} (= SM 32), *ʾnwn*MPAT-A 22^{10} (:: Naveh sub SM 70^{18}: l. *hnwn*, cf. also Hüttenmeister ASI 113f.), Syr xlv 101^{9} (*ʾnw[n]*; ??, uncert. reading, heavily dam. context); f. *ʾynyn*Syn D A 3 (= SM 88), Syn D C 1b 2 (= SM 89 :: Frey 828a: l. *ʾynwn<wn>*?) - ¶ 1) pron. pers. (subject) Sing. m. he, f. she, Plur. they; *bʿl ksp hʾ* KAI 215^{11}: he was an owner of silver; *wyʾmr gm hʾ* KAI 181^{6}: he too said ...; cf. also KAI 1^{2}, 10^{9}, 24^{13}, 40^{2}, 43^{5}, 181^{27}, DJD ii 24E 9, 46^{8}, KAI 216^{17,18,19}, 222A 37, B 42, 223C 6, 224^{12,13}, Cowl 5^{12}, 13^{7}, Krael 4^{4}, Herm 1^{8}, NESE i 11^{5}, Samar 1^{12}, CIS ii 163C, 164^{3}, 3917^{4}, 3955^{4}, Hatra 25^{2}, 52^{5} (for both texts, v. supra), MPAT 51^{6}, 52^{7}, MPAT-A 7^{3}, 13^{2}, 22^{6}, 26^{6}, 52^{5}, etc. - a) followed by noun/name in apposition, *hṣdʾ hny mlyʾ ʾlh* KAI 233^{12}: are these words true?; *ʾnh hw ʾḥyqr zy qdmn šzbk* Aḥiq 46: I am (the) Aḥiqar who formerly has saved you; *hw mksʾ yg[bʾ mk]sʾ* CIS ii 3913 ii 126: the said tax-collector shall levy the tax (cf. also SBS 45^{10}; *bryk hw ʾbʾ wbnyhy* Hatra 225^{2}: the said A. and his sons be blessed; cf. also *mʿrb šmš lh hw bbʾ zylk lmnpq* Krael 10^{4}: at the west side of it there is your gate to go forth, cf. Krael 9^{4,9}, 10^{3,6}; cf. also *sṭrʾ grbyyʾ dy hw ʾksdrʾ dy ʿl ymynʾ* Ber v 106^{3}: the northern wall of this exedra, which is on the right side - b) as apposition to a name, *ʾsḥwr hw yrtnh* Cowl 15^{21}: A. will inherit it, cf. Krael 2^{11,12} (for the double *hw* in this text, cf. Krael a.l., cf. also Yaron JSS xiii 207 (n. 1)); cf. also *ktnh zy htty ly swn hy ...* Herm 4^{6}: the garment you brought to me to Syene, that one ... (Kutscher IOS i 104, 106, Kaufman BiOr xxxiv 95: *hy* used here as object; or *ktnh ... hy* = casus pendens?); *ʾlnp br ʾšy hw ʿbd* SSI ii 37$^{1f.}$: A. the son of I. made (them), cf. however Lipiński Stud 151ff. (div. otherwise): l. *ʾšyhw* (= n.p.) - c) expressing identity, *b 18 lʾlwl hw ywm 28 lpḥns* Cowl 5^{1}: on the 18th of Elul that is the 28th day of P., cf. Cowl 6^{1}, 8^{1}, Krael 1^{1}, 3^{1}, Syr xli 285^{1}, etc.; *ksp kršn 20 hw ʿšrn* Cowl 6^{14}: a sum of 20 *k.* i.e. twenty, cf.

Cowl 8[14], Krael 4[15], 11[7], etc. (cf. also Cowl 15[25], Krael 6[4], 7[16]); *ksp š 2 hw [ks]p sttry 1* Cowl 35[4]: a sum of 2 shekels, i.e. a sum of 1 stater; *[b]rznrw .. hw ptw* OMRO lxviii 45[2]: B. ... who is also called P. (on the pers. pronoun expressing identity, cf. also Hoftijzer OMRO lxviii 45f.) - **2)** pron. pers. (object); *hm(w), hnw*: KAI 233[7,11,16], Cowl 15[35], 18[3], RES 492A 9 (v. supra), Krael 7[42], Driv 5[7], Hatra 106B 5, etc.; cf. KAI 181[18]: *w›sḥb.hm*, I dragged them, but prob. *hm* although separated from the prec. word = pron. suff., cf. Segert ArchOr xxix 217f., xxxi 335 :: idem ArchOr xxix 259: = independent pronoun (cf. also Dahood FS Horn 435f., Garr DGSP 112, Jackson & Dearman SMIM 116) - **3)** dem. pronoun; *h›dm h›* KAI 10[15], *›dm h›* KAI 14[10]: that man; *hmmlkt h›* KAI 26A iii 19: that king; *h›dmm hmt* KAI 14[22], *›dmm hmt* KAI 14[11]: these men; *bhšt hy* KAI 130[3]: in that year; *plg› hw* Cowl 9[12]: that part; *mn ‹dn› hw* KAI 270A 2f.: from that time; *kpr› hw* CIS ii 198[10]: that tomb; *gnt› hy* MPAT 64 i 2: that garden; *ddy hw* MPAT 64 i 8: that uncle of mine; *gbrh hhw* MPAT-A 22[7]: that man; etc., etc. - **4)** used as casus pendens; *h› wy›tw ›lwh ›lhn* DA i 1: as to him, the gods came to him (cf. Hoftijzer DA p. 185, H.P.Müller ZDPV xciv 57 n. 6, H. & M.Weippert ZDPV xcviii 84 :: Fitzmyer CBQ xl 94f., Naveh IEJ xxix 134f., Dahood Bibl lxii 125, Levine JAOS ci 196, Hackett BTDA 31f., Or liii 60 (n. 19): *h›* belongs to prec. clause; cf. also Hoftijzer TUAT ii 139f.; v. also supra) - **5)** the diff. *hw* in Cowl 22[6,26,27,28] prob. apposition to the prec. person; *symk br mšlm hw k š 2 lh* Cowl 22[27]: S. the son of M. from his side (litt. he) the sum of 2 shekels for Him (i.e. for YHW), cf. also Porten & Greenfield JEAS p. 135, 137, Grelot DAE p. 357 (for l. 6) :: Joüon MUSJ xviii 66f.: *hw* short for *br symk*; *mnḥm br ḥṣwl hw br šm‹[yh]* Cowl 22[26] poss. lapsus for ... *br šm‹[yh] hw* :: Grelot DAE p. 358 (n. o): = M. son of H., i.e. son of Sh. (explained as poss. case of levirate marriage with distinction of legal and natural father) - *hw ›ntth* RES 805[8] prob. haplography for *hw w›ntth* - Segal ATNS a.l.: l. *hw* (= Sing. m.) in ATNS 9[7] (improb. interpret., cf. Porten & Yardeni sub TADAE B 8.6: = part of n.p.) - Segal ATNS a.l.: the *›ny[*in ATNS 31[1] poss. = Plur. f. of *h›*$_1$ (highly uncert. interpret.).

v. *›mh*$_2$, *grš*$_1$,*h›*$_2$, *hwm*$_1$, *hwnny*, *ḥlp*$_1$, *khy*, *lpny*, *lqḥ*, *mh*$_2$, *š›l*$_1$.

h›$_2$ **OldAr** KAI 216[17] (cf. e.g. Ginsberg JAOS lxii 235 n. 12, Gibson SSI ii p. 91, Degen GGA '79, 41, cf. also Beyer ZDMG cxx 201 :: e.g. Cooke NSI p. 181, Garb 273, Segert AAG p. 320: = *h›*$_1$)- **OffAr** Cowl 6[7], 13[13], 25[4], Krael 3[7], 4[5], Driv 11[4] (for the reading, cf. Porten & Yardeni sub TADAE A 6.14), Irâq xxxi 173[4], ATNS 8[8], etc., etc. - **Palm** CIS ii 3913 ii 105 (cf. Rosenthal Sprache 83, Kottsieper SAS 92 :: Cantineau Gramm 61: = *h›*$_1$),Inv viii 6[3], 37b 1, xii 51[1], *h* Inv viii 8[3] - ¶ interjection - **1)** at the beginning of a letter, *‹bdkm [wš]ḥy h› šlḥt* *lnbwntn* Cowl $54^{1ff.}$: your servant W. (says): behold I have sent to N. ...; in the combination *kʿnt hʾ*, *šlm yslḥ kʿnt hʾ bqlʾ* (v. *bql*) *ʾwšr* Sem ii 31 conc. 1f.: greeting to Y., well now I will send the vegetables; cf. *bʾgrtʾ ... pšq dy hʾ kšr dy ...* CIS ii 3913 ii 104f.: in a letter ... he explained that it was indeed right that ... (litt. that behold it is right that ...); cf. also at the beginning of an inscription, *hʾ dkrn ṭb ldywn ...* Inv xii $51^{1f.}$: Yea, may there be a good memory of D. ... - **2)** introducing the second part of a comparison, *šgyʾn [k]wkb[y šmyʾ zy] šmhthm lʾ ydʿ ʾyš hʾ kn ʾnšʾ lʾ ydʿ ʾyš* Aḥiq 116: many are the stars of heaven whose names man knows not, so man knows not mankind; *ʾryʾ yhwh msmh lʾylʾ ... wdmh yʾšd wbšrh yʾkl hʾ kn pgʿhm zy [ʾnš]ʾ* Aḥiq 88f.: the lion chases (?, v. *smy*$_1$) the hart ... and sheds his blood and eats his flesh, so is the contact of men (cf. also Aḥiq 144f.) - **3)** introducing a new theme/topic, *hʾ tḥwmwhy* Cowl 25^{4}: behold his boundaries are ... (:: Segert AAG p. 325: *hʾ*$_2$ functioning here as *hʾ*$_1$?);*whʾ ʾlh tḥmy bytʾ* Krael 3^{7}: and behold these are the boundaries of the property/plot (cf. Krael $4^{5,8}$, 9^{8}, 12^{8}); *ʾp hʾ tḥwmy ʾrqʾ zk* Cowl 6^{7}: and behold the boundaries of this plot are (cf. Cowl 13^{13}); *kʿn hʾ ʾtyn tmh ʿlykm* Cowl 38^{5}: and now see they are coming to you over there (cf. Cowl 37^{7}); *wby ṭb lyšh lʾbhy mlky šmʾl hʾ byt klmw lhm phʾ ...* KAI $216^{15ff.}$: my fathers the kings of S. did not have a suitable palace, they had indeed the palace of K., but this ... (v. supra) - **4)** underlining the next word, *wyšmʿ mlh wlʾ yhḥwh hʾ znh yqyr [qdm] šmš* Aḥiq 93: he hears a word and does not reveal (it), *this* indeed is precious to Sh.; *lʾ hwt ʾrq ldrgmn zyly hʾ ʾnh* Cowl 6^{7}: the plot does not belong to D., i.e. to me (not to) me indeed; cf. *dkyryn [h]ʾ ʾln klhwn bṭb* CIS ii $3973^{10f.}$: may they all indeed be remembered with favour - **5)** *hʾ ... hʾ ...*, introducing to different enumerations, *whʾ znh ḥlqʾ zy mṭʾk ... whʾ znh ḥlqʾ zy mṭʾny ...* Cowl $28^{3,5}$: and note this is the share which comes to you ... and note this the share that comes to me ... (cf. Cowl $34^{2,4}$) - Albright BASOR lxxxiii 16 (n. 6): the *hʾ* in KAI 30^{1} = *hʾ*$_2$?, cf. also H.P.Müller UF ii 236f. n. 78, ZA lxv 106: = *hʾ*$_2$ used as conjunction (heavily dam. context, cf. FR 259,2; cf. however Honeyman Irâq vi 107, Dupont-Sommer RA xli 203, Röllig KAI a.l.: = *hʾ*$_1$)- Milik DFD 369: the *hw* in Inv D 1^{2} = variant of *hʾ*$_2$, less prob. interpret. (*hw* = *hʾ*$_1$)- Donner sub KAI 228 ad l. 15: *hʾ zʾ* = extended dem. pron. (cf. also e.g. Cooke NSI p. 198, Gibson SSI ii p. 151): this (less prob. interpret., cf. also Degen ZDMG cxxi 135: = *hʾ*$_2$ + *zʾ*$_1$) - Altheim & Stiehl FuF xxxv 175: the *h* in *hlzn* FuF xxxv 173^{3} = orthographical variant of *hʾ*$_2$ (diff. context).

v. *hʾ*$_1$,*hn*$_3$, *ṭʿm*$_1$, *qwm*$_1$.

hʾzʾ v. *hʾ*$_2$.

hʾyš v. *mlk*$_5$.

h'š v. *mlk$_5$*.
h't v. *h'$_1$*.
hb v. *'bn$_2$*.
hb'r Inscr with text of unknown meaning found in Cologne; Scheftelowitz OLZ xxxiv 509: = sound, noise??
hbn v. *'bn$_2$*.
hbrk (< Akkad., cf. e.g. Krebernik WO xv 89ff.) - **Ph** m. Sing. abs. *hbrk* Dir sig. 76 (= Vatt sig. eb. 76 = SANSS-Ph 9), 97 (= Vatt sig. eb. 97 = SVM 185), Vatt sig. eb. 399, Sem xxvii 33 i (fake?, cf. e.g. Bordreuil sub CSOI-Ph 38, Puech RB xcvi 590); cf. Lipiński OLZ '82, 457 :: e.g. Lemaire Sem xxvii 38, Puech RB xcvi 590: = QAL Part. pass. s.m. abs. of *brk$_1$*;Teixidor Syr lvi 370: all relevant texts fakes?; cstr. *hbrk* KAI 26A i 1 (v. infra); f. abs. *hbrkt* Vatt sig. eb. 398 (cf. Lipiński OLZ '82, 457 :: e.g. Lemaire Sem xxvii 38: = QAL Part. pass. s.f. abs. of *brk$_1$*)- ¶ subst. indicating high official, steward?; *hbrk b'l* KAI 26A i 1: the steward of Ba'al (cf. Lipiński RSF ii 45ff., RTAT 258 (n. 62); cf. already Rosenthal ANET 653 n. 1; cf. also e.g. Arbeitman JANES xii 9ff., Röllig WZKM lxxii 184f., Pardee JNES xlii 64f., xlvi 140, Lipiński ZAH i 61f. :: Lipiński OLZ '82, 457f.: or l. *hbrk* (= Sing. abs.) *b'l* (= Sing. abs. of *b'l$_2$*)= the chief steward? :: e.g. Alt WO i 274, 279, Barnett, Leveen & Moss Irâq x 63, 67, O'Callaghan Or xviii 175, 184, Gordon JNES viii 109, 112, Pedersen ActOr xxi 46, Dahood Bibl lii 396 n. 2, Lambdin FS Albright ii 329 n. 24, Lemaire Sem xxvii 38, Garbini FSR 115, Amadasi Guzzo & Archi VO iii 100f.: l. *h* (= *h$_1$*) *brk* (= QAL Part. s.m. cstr. of *brk$_1$*)*b'l* (= n. d.), the one blessed by Ba'al :: Bron RIPK 28ff.: l. *h* (= *h$_1$*) *brk* (= QAL Part. pass. s.m. abs. of *brk$_1$*)*b'l* (= n.d.), the one blessed by Ba'al :: Honeyman Mus li 49, PEQ '49, 30: l. *h* (= *h$_1$*) *brk* (= QAL Part. act. s.m. abs. of *brk$_1$*)*b'l* (= n.d.), the one who worships Ba'al :: Dupont-Sommer RA xlii 164: l. *h* (= *h$_1$* used as demonstrative) *brkb'l* (= n.d. or n.p.), the one of B.? (cf. also Steinherr WO vi 180f.); on this text, cf. also H.P.Müller TUAT i 641, O'Connor RSF vii 10).
hbrkt v. *hbrk*.
hbt v. *yhb*.
hgy$_1$ **DA** QAL (or PA'EL?) Impf. 2 p.s.f. *thgy* i 9 - ¶ verb QAL (or PA'EL?) diff. and dam. context: = to say? (cf. Hoftijzer DA p. 199, cf. H.P.Müller ZDPV xciv 65 n. 59 (cf. also Kaufman BASOR ccxxxix 73) :: e.g. Caquot & Lemaire Syr liv 198: = to make noise (cf. Levine JAOS ci 197, 198: = to raise (one's voice), and H.P.Müller ZAW xciv 218: = to grumble? (cf. also H. & M.Weippert ZDPV xcviii 93 (n. 78), 103) and Wesselius BiOr xliv 594, 597: = to moan); cf. also Sasson UF xvii 288 (n. 14), 298: l. *'l thgy* = keep thou silent, i.e. do not seek to rebel (cf. also id. AUSS xxiv 153f.), Puech FS Grelot 27: = do not plot)

:: Garbini Hen i 176f., 185: = form of *hgy$_2$* (= to remove, to disperse; cf. also McCarter BASOR ccxxxix 51, 54, Hackett BTDA 29, 46, 128) :: Rofé SB 66 (n. 29): *ʾlthgy* = compound noun (*ʾl$_3$*+ *thgy* = noun).
hgy$_2$ v. *hgy$_1$*.
hgm **OffAr** Aggoula Syr lxii 62f., 65, 69, 72ff.: the *hgm* in KAI 228A 10, 12 = Sing. abs. of *hgm* (= well, in the context indicating a sanctuary in Têma), the *hgmʾ* in KAI 228A 17 = Sing. emph. of *hgm*, less prob. interpret., cf. e.g. Cooke NSI p. 196f., Donner KAI a.l.: = n.g. and l. in KAI 228A 17 (div. otherwise) *hgm* (prob. interpret.).
hgmwn v. *hgmn*.
hgmn (< Greek ἡγεμών) - **Nab** Sing. emph. *hgmwnʾ* BIA x 55^5, 58^4 - **Palm** Sing. emph. *hgmwnʾ* CIS ii 3968^1 (= RIP 157^3), SBS 45^7, *hygmwnʾ* CIS ii 3913 ii 65, 74, 3932^4, SBS 48B 5; Plur. abs. *hgmnyn* DFD 13^9 - ¶ subst. prefect, governor of a province; for Greek par., cf. the following texts: CIS ii 3932^4 (*hygmwnʾ*// τοῦ ἡγησαμένου), DFD 13^9 (*hgmnyn*// τῶν ἑξῆς ὑπατικῶν), SBS 45^7 (*hgmwnʾ mrn*// [τοῦ διασ]ημοτάτου κυρίου ὑπατικ[οῦ]), 48B 5 (*hygmwnʾ*// τῷ διασημοτάτῳ ὑπά[ρχ]ῳ).
hgʿ v. *ngʿ$_1$*.
hgr v. *drg$_2$*.
hd$_1$ v. *ʾḥd$_4$*.
hd$_2$ v. *hʾ$_1$*.
hdʾ v. *znh*.
hdʾbgw (< Iran., cf. Driv p. 77, Benveniste JA ccxlii 304, Eilers AfO xviii 333, Hinz AISN 109) - **OffAr** *hdʾbgw* Driv 10^5 - ¶ adv. with interest; v. *ʾsprn*.
hdh v. *znh*.
hdy$_1$ **Palm** Sing. cstr. *hdy* Inv D 39^3 - ¶ subst. m. commander, chief.
hdy$_2$ v. *hʾ$_1$*.
hdy$_3$ v. *znh*.
hdy$_4$ **Palm** the diff. *hdy* in CIS ii 4199^{12} of uncert. meaning (cf. Cooke NSI p. 309) explained by Chabot sub CIS ii a.l. as lapsus for *hyk dy* :: Chabot sub RES 1604: l. *hky* = as.
hdyn v. *znh*.
hdyr **OffAr** Sing. m. abs. *hdyr* Aḥiq 207 - ¶ adj. magnificent, glorious.
hdn$_1$ v. *ʾdn$_1$*.
hdn$_2$ v. *znh*.
hds **JAr** Plur. abs. *hdsyn* MPAT 60^4 (*hdswn* printing error) - ¶ subst. myrtle branch.
hdr$_1$ v. *ʾhb$_1$*.
hdr$_2$ **Hebr** Sing. abs. *hdr* AMB 4^{27} - **OffAr** Sing. + suff. 3 p.s.m. *hdrh* Aḥiq 108 - ¶ subst. m. glory, splendour (in Aḥiq 108 said of a king).
hdrpṭ (< Iran., cf. Safar Sumer xvii 26 n. 60, Harnack with Altheim &

Stiehl GMA 497f., Altheim & Stiehl AAW iv 254) - **Hatra** Sing. emph. *hdrpṭʾ* 83^{2} - ¶ subst. function indication, prob. fire priest (cf. however Greenfield FS Asmussen 136 (n. 10)); or read with Teixidor Syr xliii 93: *hrkpṭʾ* = Sing. emph. of *hrkpṭ* < Iran. (= governor of city or fortress (v. also *ʾrgbṭ*)).

hh v. *dbhh.*

hw$_1$ v. *hʾ$_1$,ydʿ$_1$, mh$_2$, mḥr$_3$, mn$_4$, nš$_1$.*

hw$_2$ v. *hʾ$_2$.*

hwʾ$_1$ v. *hwy$_1$.*

hwʾ$_2$ v. *hʾ$_1$, lʾ$_1$.*

hwbd v. *ʾbd$_1$.*

hwbr v. *ʾbd$_1$.*

hwwyšt v. *hwwrd.*

hwwrd (< Iran., cf. e.g. Donner sub KAI 273, Kutscher, Naveh & Shaked Lesh xxxiv 126) - **OffAr** KAI 273^{7} in *bhwwrd*or *bhwwrdh* (= + suff. 3 p.s.m./f.?, cf. Altheim & Stiehl Suppl 15) - ¶ prob. subst. of uncert. meaning; Donner sub KAI 273, Kutscher, Naveh & Shaked Lesh xxxiv 126: = good breeding; cf. however - a) In der Smitten BiOr xxviii 310: < Iran. = many (things) - b) Humbach AIT 8, 11 (div. otherwise): *bhwwrd* = noun?< Iran., cf. Degen Lesh xxxiv 317 (cf. also Cowley JRAS '15, 344: *bhwwrdh*= poss. n.p. < Iran.) - c) Andreas NGWG '32, 13f.: = by his effort - d) Altheim LuG ii 182: = good protection, good support; Humbach AIT 8, 10, Degen Lesh xxxiv 315, 316: l. in KAI 273^{5}: *hww[rd]* = good breeding, increase (cf. however Humbach MStSW xxvi 39f.: l. *hww[yšt]* = the oldest, the seniors (< Iran.) and cf. Hinz AISN 129: or l. *hww[rz]*? (< Iran. = good activity)) :: e.g. Cowley JRAS '15, 343, Andreas NGWG '32, 13, Altheim & Stiehl ASA 268, Donner KAI a.l. (div. otherwise): *hww* = QAL Pf. 3 p.pl.m. of *hwy$_1$* (cf. also Altheim & Stiehl Suppl 14).

hwwrz v. *hwwrd.*

hwh v. *hwy$_1$.*

hwy$_1$ **Hebr** QAL Pf. 3 p.s.m. *hyh* KAI 189^{1,6}, 200^{3}, TA-H 111^{5}; 3 p.s.f. *hyt* KAI 189^{3} (on this form, cf. Garr DGSP 61); Impf. 3 p.s.m. *yhy* DJD ii 42^{3}, Frey 622^{4}, 630b 4, 973^{1} (= SM 3), 974^{1} (for the reading, cf. Naveh sub SM 1), SM 76^{6}, IEJ iv 98^{2}; 3 p.s.f. *thy* Frey 661^{3}; 2 p.s.f. *thy* DJD ii 42^{6}; 1 p.s. *ʾhy* DJD ii 45^{6} (dam. context), *ʾhʾ* DJD ii 24A 13 (heavily dam. context), B 15, C 13; 3 p.pl.m. *yhw* DJD ii 44^{5}; Imper. s.m. *hwy* DJD ii 46^{12}, *hwh* DJD ii 48^{6}, *hwʾ* DJD ii 44^{8}, *ʾhwh* DJD ii 42^{7} (:: I.Rabinowitz BASOR cxxxi 23, Bardtke ThLZ lxxix 302: = Impf. 1 p.s.) - **Samal** QAL Pf. 3 p.s.f. *hwt* KAI 215^{2}; 1 p.s. *hwyt* KAI 215^{5} (cf. Friedr 27*a, Garb 263, Dion p. 223, Sader EAS 167 :: Driver AnOr xii 48, Dion p. 77, 406 n. 39, Gibson SSI ii p. 83: = PAʿEL Impf. 1 p.s. of *hwy$_2$* (= to beat down (= to cause to fall)); cf. Cooke NSI p. 176:

= PA‘EL of either *hwy*$_1$ or *hwy*$_2$ (cf. also Koopmans 72, Segert ArchOr xxxviii 225)) - **OldAr** QAL Pf. 3 p.s.f. *[h]wt* KAI 224^{24}; Impf. 3 p.s.m. *yhwh* KAI 223A 4, *lhwy* Tell F 12; 3 p.s.f. *thwy* KAI 222A 25, 32, 223A 6; Imper. s.m. *hwy* KAI 224^{22} (v. *ḥlp*$_1$; :: Nober VD xxxvii 171: = QAL Pf. 3 p.s.m.) - **OffAr** QAL Pf. 3 p.s.m. *hwh* Cowl 26^{3,5} (for this prob. reading, cf. Porten & Yardeni sub TADAE A 6.2)^{,9}, 27^{4}, 30^{12} (cf. Cowl p. 283, Ben-Chayyim EI i 135, Degen GGA '79, 31 :: Segert AAG p. 248: = Pf. 3 p.pl.f.), 76^{2} (for this prob. reading, cf. Porten & Yardeni sub TADAE A 5.4 :: Cowl a.l.: l. poss. *brt* (= f. Sing. cstr. of *br*$_1$)), Driv 7^{6}, 8^{2,4}, Herm 2^{5} (:: Bresciani & Kamil Herm p. 422: = QAL Part. act. s.m. abs.), 6^{6} (Bresciani & Kamil Herm ibid.: idem), Beh 24 (*[h]wh*; for the reading, cf. Greenfield & Porten BIDG 36f., Akkad. par. *it-tur*), 59, ATNS 34b 2, 36^{2} (*hnh* prob. misprint), etc., etc., *hw*ʾ Sumer xx 16 v 2; 3 p.s.f. *hwt* Cowl 6^{7}, Krael 12^{24}, AG 34^{3}, Aḥiq 43, Beh 16 (Akkad. par. *ta-at-tur*), 21a* (Akkad. par. *ta-at-tur*), BSOAS xiii 82^{4} (reading uncert., heavily dam. context), ATNS 39^{1}, 72a 3; 1 p.s. *hwyt* Cowl 13^{4}, 41^{3,4}, Aḥiq 48, Krael 9^{17}, Driv 3^{2}, ATNS 29 ii 1 (*hwyt[*, or = 2 p.s.m./f.?), *hwt* Herm 5^{8}; 3 p.pl.m. *hww* Cowl 30^{9,10}, Driv 5^{5,6,8}, Beh 59 (Akkad. par. *it-tu-ru-*ʾ), ATNS 30a 2, Samar 5^{5}, FuF xxxv 173^{13}, etc.; 1 p.pl. *hwyn* Cowl 30^{15}, 31^{14}, Krael 5^{12}, SSI ii 28 rev. 5 (dam. context); Impf. 3 p.s.m. *yhwh* Cowl 8^{17}, 11^{5}, 40^{3} (for the reading, cf. Porten & Yardeni sub TADAE A 3.6 :: e.g. Cowl a.l.: l. *yhbh* = QAL Pf. 3 p.s.m. + suff. 3 p.s.m. of *yhb*), Aḥiq 2, 19, 97 (:: Kottsieper SAS 169f., 198: = PA‘EL Impf. 3 p.s.m. of *hwy*$_2$), Krael 8^{5}, Driv 2^{4}, 4^{3}, KAI 276^{9} (for this text, cf. Altheim & Stiehl EW x 251, GH i 266, ASA 45, Donner KAI a.l.)^{,10}, BSOAS xiii 82^{2} (*[y]hwh*; ?, heavily dam. context), ATNS 1^{6}, Samar 3^{4}, etc., *yhwy* Cowl 32^{2}, 34^{7}, Herm 2^{14}, Aḥiq 110, Driv 5^{2}, FuF xxxv 173^{11}, ATNS 1^{10} (for this reading, cf. Shaked Or lvi 408, Porten & Yardeni sub TADAE B 8.8 :: Segal ATNS a.l.: l. *yḥwb* (= QAL Impf. 3 p.s.m. of *ḥwb*$_1$)), 12^{2}, AE '23, 41 no. 3/4, etc., *yhw*ʾ RES 1785B 5 (for the reading, cf. Degen GGA '79, 31 (cf. also Lidzbarski Eph i 324, Chabot sub RES a.l., Catastini JSS xxxii 273f.) :: e.g. Koopmans 190, Segert AAG p. 233: l. *lhw*ʾ); 3 p.s.f. *thwh* Cowl 11^{3}, Krael 7^{22}, *thwy* Aḥiq 100, Sem xxxiii 94^{3} (for this poss. reading, cf. Porten Sem xxxiii 94, 97, Porten & Yardeni sub TADAE A 5.1); 2 p.s.m. *thwh* Aḥiq 149, Beh 50 (Akkad. par. *tel-la-a*), 55, ATNS 11^{2}, *thwy* Herm 8^{3} (?, heavily dam. context); 1 p.s. ʾ*hwh* Cowl 11^{7}, Krael 7^{25}, RES 497A 3; 3 p.pl.m. *yhwwn* Cowl 27^{7}, 71^{27}, Krael 2^{11,12}, ATNS 26^{4}, *yhww* ATNS 26^{6}; 1 p.pl. *nhwh* Samar 4^{12}; Imper. s.m. *hwy* Cowl 30^{3}, 31^{3}, RES 1299B 1, PSBA xxxvii 222^{10} (:: Sayce PSBA xxxiv 212, RES sub 1793^{5}: l. *ḥgy* = n.p.), SSI ii 28 obv. 7, Herm 3^{9}; s.f. *hwy* KAI 269^{3,4}, Herm 1^{11}, 2^{14}, 7^{2}; pl.m. *hww* Cowl 17^{3} (cf. Grelot DAE p. 281, Porten RB xc 407, 412, Porten & Yardeni sub TADAE A 6.1 ::

e.g. Cowl a.l.: = QAL Pf. 3 p.pl.m.), 21[6], 38[2] (for this reading, cf. e.g. Porten & Greenfield JEAS p. 82, Porten & Yardeni sub TADAE A 4.3 :: Cowl a.l.: l. *thww* = QAL Impf. 2 p.pl.m.); Part. act. s.m. abs. *hwh* Cowl 8[3], 10[5], 15[8,9,10] (for these texts, cf. Joüon MUSJ xviii 38ff., v. infra), Krael 4[6], 6[4], Herm 1[12] (cf. Bresciani & Kamil Herm p. 422 (cf. also Kutscher IOS i 114) :: Grelot DAE p. 153, Porten & Greenfield JEAS p. 152), *hw›* FUF xxxv 173[6,8,9]; m. pl. abs. *hwyn* KAI 279[5] (for Aḥiq 167, v. *nṭḥ*$_1$); cf. Frah xxii 2 (*yḥwwn*), xxviii 31 (*yḥwwn*), xxxi 37 (*ḥwh*), 40 (*ḥwh*), Frah-S$_2$ 28, 29 (*ḥwh*), Paik 359 (*ḥwy*), 360 (*ḥwh*), 475 (*yḥwh*), 476 (*yḥwwn*), Nisa-b 483[1], 525[2], 556[2], 621[2], 672[3], etc. (*hwh*), MP 6, DEP 153[2], 154 verso 3, GIPP 24, 37, 53, 54, 67, SaSt 17, 25, cf. also Lemosín AO ii 266 (on the use of *hwy*$_1$ in Off.Ar, cf. Kaddari AAALT 43ff.) - **Nab** QAL Pf. 3 p.s.m. *hwh* CIS ii 224[4], J 38[8], ADAJ x 44 ii 3 (= RB lxxii 95 :: Milik ADAJ xxi 150 n. 15: = QAL Part. act. s.m. abs.), MPAT 64 i 9, ii 2 (dam. context), DBKP 22[32], *hw›* RES 2025[1]; 3 p.pl.m. *hww* BASOR cclxiii 78[2] (for this prob. reading, cf. Jones BASOR cclxxv 43 :: Hammond, Johnson & Jones BASOR cclxiii a.l.: l. *‹wn* (= Sing. cstr. of *‹wn* (= delinquency or aid)); Impf. 3 p.s.m. *yhw›* CIS ii 200[3,5], 212[4,5,6], 219[6], 224[9] (× J 34: l. *yhwh*), *yhwh* RHR lxxx 4[4]; Inf. *mhw›* BIA x 55[4] - **Palm** QAL Pf. 3 p.s.m. *hw›* CIS ii 3913 i 5, 6 (:: Sachau ZDMG xxxvii 563 (n. 1): *whw›* = lapsus for *yhw›*), 3932[2], 3973[2], RIP 126[2], Syr vii 128[8], xxv 336[2], Inscr P 31[5,6,7], *hwh* Syr xiv 177[4] (cf. however Cantineau Syr xiv a.l.); 3 p.s.f. *hwt* CIS ii 3913 i 3; 3 p.pl.m. *hww* CIS ii 3913 i 5 (diff. context, cf. Cantineau Gramm 144, Syr xix 170; Rosenthal Sprache 17 n. 5: = lapsus??, v. *gby*$_1$), 7, ii 96, 113, 144, Inscr P 31[3], Syr xl 33[2], xlvii 413[4]; Impf. 3 p.s.m. *yhw›* CIS ii 3913 i 10, 11, ii 46, 72, 79, Inv xi 80[6] (cf. Teixidor Inv xi a.l., Gawlikowski Syr xlvii 324 × Milik DFD 1f. (div. otherwise): l. *dy hw›* (= QAL Pf. 3 p.s.m.; heavily dam. context), etc., etc., *yh›* CIS ii 3913 ii 107, 3972[3], MUSJ xxxviii 106[9], *yhwh* SBS 24[4], 34[5], 60[6]; 3 p.s.f. *thw›* CIS ii 3913 ii 94, 131, 149, *thwh* CIS ii 3913 ii 127, RIP 199[6] (*[t]hwh*; dam. context); 3 p.pl.m. *yhwn* CIS ii 3913 ii 123, 4214, RIP 199[10,11], Ber v 95[9], *yhn* CIS ii 3913 ii 57, 118, *yhw* MUSJ xxxviii 106[10] (or *yhw ›bn›* haplography for *yhw› ›bn›*?; v. also *›bn*$_2$); 3 p.pl.f. *thwyn* SBS 24[3] (cf. Caquot GLECS vii 77, Dunant SBS a.l., Degen GGA '79, 31, or rather = 3 p. dual f.?, cf. Garbini OA xiv 177); Inf. *mhw›* CIS ii 3913 ii 77; Part. act. s.m. abs. *hw›* CIS ii 3913 ii 116, SBS 44B 2 (?, cf. Greek par. γενόμενον; or = QAL Pf. 3 p.s.m.?); pl.m. abs. *hwn* CIS ii 3913 i 10, ii 148 (?); s.f. abs. *hwy›* CIS ii 3913 ii 134 - **Hatra** QAL Pf. 3 p.s.m. *hw›*, cf. Assur 27e 1; Impf. 3 p.s.m. *lhw›* 408[6] - **JAr** QAL Pf. 3 p.s.m. *hwh* MPAT 49 i 3, 4; 2 p.s.m. *hwyt* MPAT 89[3]; 2 p.s.f. *hwyt* MPAT 40[5]; 1 p.s. *hwyt* MPAT 49 i 5, 8, 14 (for this poss. reading, cf. Beyer ATTM 318; heavily dam. context), ii 2; Impf. 3 p.s.m. *yhwy* MPAT-A 34[1] (=

SM 69), *yhy* MPAT 40^{9}, MPAT-A 16^{3} (= Frey 981 = SM 17), 30^{1} (= SM 26), 46^{4}, *lhw›* MPAT 41^{6}, *lhwy* MPAT 40^{7}, *lhy* MPAT 40^{20}; 3 p.s.f. *thwy* MPAT-A 13^{3} (= SM 46), 29^{4} (= Frey 859 = SM 35), *thy* MPAT-A 20^{2} (= SM 10), 30^{3} (= SM 26), 32^{2} (= Frey 885 = SM 39), 36^{4} (= Frey 987 = SM 30), *ty* MPAT-A 15^{3} (for the reading, cf. Frey 982, Naveh sub SM 18, Beyer ATTM 390 :: Fitzmyer & Harrington MPAT a.l.: l. *t[h]y*), *t›h* MPAT-A 25^{3} (= Frey 976 = SM 12); 2 p.s.f. *thw›* MPAT 41^{3}; 3 p.pl.m. *[y]hyn* MPAT 42^{11} (for the reading, cf. Milik sub DJD ii 21 :: Beyer ATTM 310: l. *[l]hwyn* = Impf. 3 p.pl.m. :: Fitzmyer & Harrington MPAT a.l.: l. *yhwn*); 1 p.pl. *nhw›* Mas 556^{5} (dam. context); Inf. *mhy* MPAT 40^{6} (:: Beyer ATTM 308: l. *mhwy*)^{,18} (:: Beyer ATTM 308: l. *mhw* = lapsus for *mhwy*); Imper. s.m. *hw›* MPAT 55^{5}, 60^{5}, *hwh* MPAT 89^{1}; pl.m. *hww* MPAT 58^{3} - ¶ verb QAL - **1)** to be, to exist, to happen; *ky hyt zdh bṣr* KAI 189^{3}: for there was a fissure (?) in the rock; *yhw bw ›ṣlk* DJD ii 44^{5}: let them stay there with you; *yhy šlwm ‹l mnwḥtw* Frey $622^{4f.}$: let there be peace on his resting-place (cf. e.g. Frey 630b 4, 973^{1}); *zy hww b›gwr› zk* Cowl 30^{10}: which were in that temple; *kzy hwh lqdmn* Cowl 32^{8}: as it was before; *kzy [‹]dn yhwh* Cowl 28^{13}: when it will be time; *whn yhwh b›tr ḥd ytyr mn ywm ḥd* Driv 6^{6}: if he will stay in one place longer than one day; *kzy ywz› hwh bmṣryn* Driv 8^{4}: when there was revolt in Egypt; *mlk zy ›ḥry thwh* Beh 50: o thou king, who shalt be after me; *yhww tmh* ATNS 26^{6}: let them be there; *ksph zy hwh bydh* Herm $6^{6f.}$: the silver which was in his possession (cf. Herm $2^{4f.}$); *hn yhw› ḥwrw ... bḥgr›* CIS ii $212^{5f.}$: if Ch. ... will be in Ch.; *kdy hwh bktb› dnh* DBKP 28^{32}: according to what was (sc. written) in this document; *srbnyn hww* CIS ii 3913 i 7: disputes arose; *dy thwyn ‹lwt› ›ln ‹l bb› rb›* SBS $24^{3f.}$: that these altars may be situated at the great gate; *yhw ›bn›* MUSJ xxxviii 106^{10}: there must be stone(s) (v. *›bn$_2$*); *hw› nbr› dmṭr›* Assur 27e 1: there was a heavy rain (v. *nbr*) - a) + *l$_5$*, to belong to; *lk yhwh* Cowl 28^{12}: he will be yours (cf. ATNS 40^{2}); *ṣdqh yhwh lk qdm YHW* Cowl 30^{27}: it will be counted as your merit before YHW; *šlm yhwy lk* Aḥiq 110: peace be to thee; *dy yhw› kpr› hw lw›lt* CIS ii 212^{4}: that this tomb will belong to W.; *mn dy yhw› lh mlḥ* CIS ii 3913 ii 72: everyone who has salt in his possession; *lhwy lky mny spr ...* MPAT 40^{7}: you have from me a document of ...; *thwy lhwn brkth* MPAT-A 13^{3}: may blessing be their portion (cf. MPAT-A 29^{4f}, etc.); *yhy lh ḥwlq ‹m ṣdyqyh* (for the reading, v. *ṣdq$_3$*) MPAT-A $16^{3f.}$: may he have a portion with the righteous ones; etc., cf. also *thw› ly l›nth* MPAT 41^{3}: you shall be my wife (cf. also MPAT $40^{6f.,18f.}$); for Beh 16, cf. Greenfield FS Rundgren 152 - b) + *‹l$_7$*, to be dependent from, to be based on; *w‹l ‹ṭth wmlwhy ḥyl [›tw]r kl› hww* Aḥiq 60f.: by his counsel and his words the whole army of Assyria was guided - c) + *‹l$_7$*, to be in charge of; *‹gylw dy hw› ‹l ‹mwd›* (v. *‹md$_2$*) Inv ix 28^{6}

(= Inscr P 31): O. who is in charge of the .... - d) + *ʿm₄*; *zy qdmn ʿmy hww* Beh 59: who previously were with me - e) + verbal clause functioning as subject; *hwh trʿn zy ʾbn 5 ... ndšw* Cowl 30$^{9f.}$: it is a fact that they have wrecked 5 gates of stone (cf. also Hoftijzer VT ix 316f.) - **2)** to be + predicate; *wm[ʾ]t ʾmh hyh gbh hṣr* KAI 189$^{5f.}$: and the height of the rock was hundred cubits; *wzh hyh dbr hnqbh* KAI 189^{1}: and this is the story of how the breach was made; *wthwy ʾrpd tl* KAI 222A 32: let Arpad become a mound; *zy prtrk tnh hwh* Cowl 27^{4}: who was governor there; *knwth dynyʾ dwšwnn hww* ATNS 30a 2: his colleagues, the judges, were ill-willed (cf. also *dwšwn*); *hdd gbr lhwy qblh* Tell F 12: the hero H. will be his adversary (v. *qbl₁*); *gbr hwy* SSI ii 28 obv. 7: be a man; *hwyt ʾnty* MPAT 40^{5}: you have been my wife; *hwʾ šlm* MPAT 55^{5}: farewell (cf. DJD ii 46^{12}, MPAT 60^{5}, etc.; for this formula, cf. Pardee JBL xcvii 341); cf. *byt ... zyly hwh mšḥth ...* Cowl 8$^{3f.}$: my house ... being as to its measurements ...; *lbš 1 zy ʿmr ... hwh ʾrk ...* Cowl 15$^{7f.}$: one woollen robe being as to its length ... (cf. Krael 4^{8}, 6^{4}, Joüon MUSJ xviii 38ff.); *ksp ḥlrn 2 ltql lyrḥ hwh ksp ḥlrn 8 lyrḥ* Cowl 10$^{5f.}$: at the rate of 2 *ḥ.* per shekel per month, i.e. the sum of 8 *ḥ.* per month - a) predicate = Part. act.; *šʾhʾ šwql lk* DJD ii 24B 15: which I will pay to you (cf. DJD ii 24C 13); *hwt myt* Herm 5^{8}: I was dying (i.e. I was extremely ill), cf. MPAT 64 i 9, MPAT-A 46$^{4f.}$; *wyhwy zbn gšrn* Herm 2^{14}: and let him buy beams; *whwy lqḥ šʿrn ...* Herm 3^{9}: and do take barley ... (for other periphrastic imperatives, cf. Cowl 17^{3} (v. supra), Herm 1$^{11,11f.}$, 2^{14}, 7$^{2f.}$, KAI 269^{4}; cf. also Hammershaimb VT xviii 265f., Greenfield IEJ xix 199ff.); *šmʿ hwyt* MPAT 49 i 5: I have heard; *yhy qym wmšlm lrbʿyn* MPAT 40$^{9f.}$: let it be determined and paid fourfold (cf. MPAT 41^{6}) - b) predicate = Part. pass.; *šydʿ yhy lk* DJD ii 42$^{2f.}$: that it may be known to you; *šlʾ thy ʾmwr* DJD ii 42^{6}: that you will not say; *kd hwt bwlʾ knyšʾ* CIS ii 3913 i 3: when the Senate was assembled; *yhwh dkyr lʿlmʾ* SBS 60^{6}: let he be remembered for ever - c) + predicate + *l₅*; *brʾ lm yhwh ly* Aḥiq 2: he will be my son (cf. ATNS 11^{2}: + *l₅* + predicate); *zy hwt gwʾ lmšlm* Krael 12^{24}: who was a female slave (?, v. *gw₃*) of M.; *lʾ thwh ly ʾntt* Krael 7^{22}: she will not be my wife; *ʿbd yhwh lh l[ʿ]lmʾ* Samar 3^{4}: he will be his slave forever; etc.; cf. *thwʾ ly lʾnth* MPAT 41^{3}: you will be my wife (v. supra) - d) + predicate = prep. phrase; *zkrwnh thy lbrkh* Frey 661$^{3f.}$: let her memory be to a blessing; *yhwy dkrnhwn lṭb* MPAT-A 34^{1} (= SM 69): may their memory be for good - Gawlikowski Ber xxii 145: the *whyw* in SBS 39^{1} = *w* + QAL Pf. 3 p.pl.m. (improb. interpret., cf. Dunant SBS a.l. (div. otherwise): l. *[ʾqy]mwhy* (= HAPH Pf. 3 p.pl.m. + suff. 3 p.s.m. of *qwm₁*) *wq[rbw]* (= *w* + PA ʿEL Pf. 3 p.pl.m. of *qrb₁*) - Landsberger AfO xii 255 n. 39: the diff. *ma-a-a[-tu]* of Warka 10 prob. = QAL Pf. 1 p.s. (uncert. interpret., cf. also Gordon Or ix 31; Dupont-

Sommer RA xxxix 45: or l. perhaps *ma-a-a[-du]* = *m*ʾ*d*??) - the diff. *hwyn* in FuF xxxv 173^{5} explained by Altheim & Stiehl FuF xxxv 176 as Qal Part. act. s.m. + 1st person enclitic (diff. context) - Beyer ATTM 314: l. *nhwh* = Qal Impf. 1 p.pl. in MPAT 46^{2} :: Milik sub DJD ii 27: l. *[*ʾ*]nhnh* = variant of ʾ*nḥn*$_1$:: Fitzmyer & Harrington MPAT a.l.: l. *[*ʾ*]nḥnh* = ʾ*nḥn*$_1$- a form of this root (Qal Part. s.f. abs.) poss. in Aḥiq 199 (*hwyh*), cf. also Lindenberger 197, cf. however Kottsieper SAS 22, 198: poss. = Sing. + suff. 3 p.s.m. of *hwh* (= fall).

v. ʾ*ḥry*$_1$,*h*ʾ$_1$,*hwwrd*, *hwn*$_2$,*hndrz*, *yd*, *ym*ʾ, *mr*ʾ, *nhwyg*, *nṣyḥ*, ʿ*bd*$_1$, *qny*$_1$, *ryt*, *twy*$_2$.

hwy$_2$ v. *hwy*$_1$,*nṯḥ*$_1$.

hwk v. *hlk*$_1$, *tk*$_1$.

hwm$_1$ **OffAr** Qal Inf. abs. *hwm* KAI 226^{6} (cf. e.g. Lidzbarski Eph i 192f. (: abstract noun used as Inf. abs., cf. Cooke NSI p. 191, Gibson SSI ii p. 98), Donner KAI a.l., Dupont-Sommer AH i/2, 3, Segert AAG p. 390, Degen GGA '79, 26, 35, Garr DGSP 132 :: e.g. Kokowzoff JA ix/xiv 438ff., Degen ZDMG cxix 175: = *hwm*$_2$(= pron. pers. 3 p.pl.m.)); Itp Pf. 3 p.pl.m. ʾ*thmw* KAI 226^{6} - ¶ verb Qal to be distraught - Itp to be distracted, to be distraught (cf. Lidzbarski Eph i 192f., Gibson SSI ii p. 97f., cf. also Cooke NSI p. 190f.); > to lament (cf. Donner KAI a.l., Dupont-Sommer AH i/2, 3) :: Kokowzoff JA ix/xiv 438ff.: = Itp Pf. of *hmm* (= to make incisions), cf. also Segert AAG p. 390 (: > to mourn).

hwm$_2$ v. *hwm*$_1$.

hwmytk v. *ym*ʾ.

hwn$_1$ **OffAr** Qal Impf. 2 p.s.m. *thn* Aḥiq 103 (cf. Grelot VT xii 199f., RB lxviii 183, DAE p. 107 (n. h) :: Cowl p. 238: poss. = lapsus for *tntn* (= Qal Impf. 2 p.s.m. of *ntn*) :: Epstein ZAW xxxii 135, OLZ '16, 206, Nöldeke AGWG xiv/4, 13, Baneth OLZ '14, 298, Lindenberger APA 84f., 240 nn. 226, 229, Kottsieper SAS 12, 20, 220 (div. otherwise): l. *thnšq* (= Haph Impf. 2 p.s.m. of *nšq*$_1$ (= to kindle)) :: Ginsberg ANET 428 (div. otherwise): l. *thnšq* (= Hoph Impf. 3 p.s.f. of *nšq*$_1$ (= to be kindled, cf. also Fitzmyer Bibl lvi 256))) - ¶ verb Qal to place, to put; *[*ʾ*]l thn šq* ʿ*lyk* Aḥiq 103: do not put sackcloth on you.

hwn$_2$ **OffAr** Kottsieper SAS 10, 17, 198: l. *yhw[n]* in Aḥiq 161 (= Qal Impf. 3 p.s.m. of *hwn*$_2$ (= to be silent, to be quiet)), uncert. interpret., cf. Cowl a.l.: l. *yhw[h]* = Qal Impf. 3 p.s.m. of *hwy*$_1$ and cf. Grelot DAE p. 444 n. c (div. otherwise): l. *yhw[m]*ʾ*nhy* = Haph Impf. 3 p.s.m. + suff. 3 p.s.m. of *ym*ʾ (v. also ʾ*nh*$_1$).

hwn$_3$ **Ph** Sing. cstr. *hwn* MUSJ xlv 262^{5} (cf. Starcky MUSJ xlv 271, Röllig NESE ii 2, 11, Schiffmann RSF iv 171, Dahood Bibl lx 431, Butterweck TUAT ii 586 :: v. d Branden BiOr xxxiii 12 (div. otherwise): pro *hwn ym* l. *...]h wn*ʿ*m* (= Sing. abs. of *n*ʿ*m*$_1$ or *n*ʿ*m*$_2$)) - ¶ subst.

wealth (in *hwn ym* = the wealth of the sea?; uncert. interpret.). v. *znh*.

hwn$_4$ (< Iran., cf. R.A.Bowman Pers p. 45f., 63, Hinz NWAP 45, AISN 120) - **OffAr** Sing. abs. *hwn* Pers 1^2, 5^2, 8^2, 9^2, 13^2, etc., etc.) - ¶ subst. mortar (in most instances inscribed on mortar; in Pers 17^4, 24^4, 39^3 inscribed on pestle, Naveh & Shaked Or xlii 455 (n. 64): *hwn* describing both pestle and mortar (cf. also Bartholomae with Bowman Pers p. 45), this explanation poss. supported by Pers 24, 39, cf. however Pers $17^{4f.}$ (*[h]wn zy gll [ʿm ʾbš]wn*), cf. also Bowman Pers p. 45: or careless error involved?).

hwnny **Hatra** the reading *hwnny[ʾ]* in app. 4^{11} (cf. Safar Sumer xvii 40 (n. 103): = Sing. emph. of *hwnny* (= thinking, absorbed in thought; cf. also Caquot Syr xl 12f., Teixidor Syr xli 275 n. 3)) less prob., cf. Aggoula MUSJ xlvii 46, Sem xxvii 43, Milik DFD 395, Vattioni IH a.l. (div. otherwise): l. *hw* (= *hw*$_1$)+ *znʾ* (= n.p.), prob. reading and interpret. (cf. also Altheim & Stiehl AAW v/1, 80f.: l. poss. *hw* (= *hw*$_1$)+ *nny* (= n.p. of uncert. reading)).

hwnštwn (< Iran., cf. e.g. Andreas NGWG '32, 14f., Altheim LuG ii 182, Altheim & Stiehl Suppl 15, GMA 343, Humbach AIT 11f., Donner KAI a.l., Kutscher, Naveh & Shaked Lesh xxxiv 126, Hinz AISN 126) - **OffAr** Sing. abs. *hwnštwn* KAI 273^8 - ¶ subst. good order, cf. litt. mentioned above, Degen Lesh xxxiv 316 (:: In der Smitten BiOr xxviii 310: = good document) - cf. also *nštwn*.

hwptysty (< Iran., cf. Benveniste JA ccxlvi 42, ccliv 442, 449f., Altheim LuG ii 182, Altheim & Stiehl EW ix 197, x 246, Suppl 15, GH i 405, ii 174ff., GMA 342, 351 (n. 26), 352f., ASA 28, 30, Donner sub KAI 273, Kutscher, Naveh & Shaked Lesh xxxiv 134, Humbach AIT 10f., Hinz AISN 127, cf. also In der Smitten BiOr xxviii 310) - **OffAr** Sing. abs. *hwptysty* KAI 273^6, 279^6 (cf. Greek par. ἐνήκοοι) - ¶ subst. good obedience (cf. Benveniste JA ccxlvi 42, Schwarzschild JAOS lxxx 156, Kutscher, Naveh & Shaked Lesh xxxiv 134, Degen Lesh xxxiv 316, Humbach AIT 10ff., Hinz AISN 127, cf. also Andreas NGWG '32, 13, Rosenthal EI xiv 97*) :: interpret. as adj.: obedient (cf. Levi Della Vida Editto 26, Garbini Kand 14f., cf. also Nober VD xxxvii 373, Donner sub KAI 279) :: interpret. as subst.: good admonition, exhortation (cf. Altheim & Stiehl litt. mentioned above); cf. *ptystyknʾ*.

hwrʾh **JAr** Sing. abs. *hwrʾh* MPAT 41^8 (v. infra; dam. context) - ¶ subst. (prob. < Haph Inf. abs. of *yry*$_2$ (to teach), cf. Milik DJD ii p. 113) law.

hzpt v. *ntn*.

hy$_1$ v. *hʾ*$_1$, *mh*$_2$.

hy$_2$ (< Prakrit, cf. Benveniste JA ccliv 447f., Kutscher, Naveh & Shaked Lesh xxxiv 128) - **OffAr** JA ccliv 440^2 in *yʾnyhykʾnyš[* = tran-

scription of *yāni hi kānici* = everything which is made by.
hy3 **JAr** *hy* MPAT-A 22[2,3,4] (= SM 70[10,11,12]) - ¶ particle: or; in the combination *hy* ... *hy* ... *hy* = either ... or ... or. Sokoloff with Naveh sub SM 70: < Greek ἤ, cf. also Schulthess GCPA p. 57 (:: Fitzmyer & Harrington MPAT p. 350: < Greek εἰ).
hy4 v. *hyk*.
hy› v. *h›1*.
hygmwn v. *hgmn*.
hyd v. *hyr*.
hyy v. *hwy1,yd, ryt*.
hyk **OffAr** *hyk* KAI 276[9]; cf. GIPP 54 - **Palm** *hyk* CIS ii 3913 i 6, ii 54, 62, 64, 68, RIP 199[3] (for the reading, cf. Gawlikowski Sem xxiii 115 :: Milik DFD 286 (div. otherwise): l. *dy k...*), etc., etc., *hy* (lapsus) CIS ii 3913 ii 109 - ¶ prep. according to; *hyk ‹dt›* CIS ii 3913 ii 54: according to custom (cf. CIS ii 3913 ii 106f., 136); *ytgb[wn] hyk [nḥ]š›* CIS ii 3913 ii 129: they will be levied like bronze (v. however *gby1*); *hyk bnmws›* CIS ii 3913 ii 120: according to the law (litt. as in the law; cf. CIS ii 3913 i 6, ii 109, 134, 135 (??), 149); *lkl ... yhw› mks› hyk lybyš* CIS ii 3913 ii 115f.: for everything ... the tax shall be as for dry goods - cf. also the combination *hyk zy/dy*, as, like; *hyk dy ktyb* CIS ii 3913 ii 68: as it is written; *hyk dy ṣbyn* Ber v 95[9]: as they want; cf. CIS ii 3913 ii 103, 113, 120, 125 (for the context, v. *yḥ›*), 4214; for *hyk zy* in KAI 276[9], v. *hkyn*.
v. *›yk*, *›ykh,hdy,hykylyn, qdl*.
hykylyn **JAr** word of unknown meaning in MPAT 89[4] (cf. Avigad IEJ xvii 105: poss. = *hyk+ ylyn* (= orthographical variant for *›ln2*) :: Puech RB xc 488f.: l. *hyk*(= that, so that) + *ylyn* (= QAL Impf. 3 p.s.m. of *lyn1*) :: Beyer ATTM 329: l. *ḥy* (= Sing. m. abs. of *ḥy2*) + *kylwn* (= n.p.)).
hykl (< Akkad. < Sum., cf. Zimmern Fremdw 8; cf. however Lipiński Stud 26, ZAH i 65: < Sum.; cf. also Kaufman AIA 27: or < Sum.?) - **OffAr** Sing. emph. *hykl›* Aḥiq 9, 17, 23, 44, Irâq xxxiv 132 (= AECT 43) - **Palm** Sing. emph. *hykl›* CIS ii 3913 i 10, 3959[5] (= SBS 44B; Greek par. τὸν ναὸν), Inv ix 11[5], xii 45[3], 48[1,2], 49[6] (*[hy]kl›*), Inv D 1[6], SBS 32[1], Syr xiv 171[4], PNO 3, 7 - **Hatra** Sing. emph. *hykl›* 107[6] - **JAr** Sing. emph. *hklh* MPAT 85a 1, b 2 (for reading context, v. *bny1*) - ¶ subst. m. - **1)** palace: Aḥiq 9, 17, 23, 44 - **2)** temple: CIS ii 3913 i 10, 3959[5], Inv ix 11[5], xii 45[3], 48[1,2], 49[6], Inv D 1[6], SBS 32[4], Syr xiv 171[4], PNO 3, 7, Hatra 107[6], MPAT 85a 1, b 2 - cf. also prob. Greek transcription in IGRR iii 1093[5] (ναὸς) ἀειχάλας (cf. Schlumberger PNO p. 135, Aggoula MUSJ xlix 484).
v. *kl1*, *ksp2*.
hymn (in origin HAPH of *›mn1*) - **OffAr** Part. pass.m. s. abs. *mhymn*

Herm 4^{9}; pl.m. abs. *mhymnn* Samar 1^{12} (= EI xviii 8*), 4^{13}; cf. Frah xviii 3 (*ḥymnw*), cf. Toll ZDMG Suppl viii 39 - **Palm** Part. pass. s.m. emph. *mhymnʾ* CIS ii 4239 - **Hatra** Part. pass. s.m. abs. *[m]hymn* 232f. 4 (or = cstr.?, cf. Aggoula MUSJ xlvii 11); s.m. emph. *mhymnʾ* 100^{2} (dam. context; Caquot Syr xl 10 (div. otherwise): or l. *mhymn* = s.m. cstr.), 139^{3} (*[m]hymnʾ*), 290^{2} - ¶ verb to trust in; Part. pass. - **1)** trustworthy: Herm 4^{9}, CIS ii 4239, Samar 1^{12}, 4^{13}; in Hatra 100^{2}, 139^{3} prob. = title/indication of function (cf. Aggoula Syr lii 191, 205f.: = treasurer; Vattioni IH a.l.: = eunuch), also in Hatra 232f. 4f.? (l. *[m]hymn [m]lkʾ*?, cf. Aggoula MUSJ xlvii 11, Syr lii 206, Vattioni IH a.l.) - **2)** in Hatra 290^{2}: *ptwrʾ mhymnʾ*, Degen NESE iii 85f.: = permanent/regular table ... (cf. also Teixidor Sem xxx 64f.) :: Safar Sumer xxvii 12: = the big table (or rather *ptwrʾ mhymnʾ* = trustworthy *ptwr* (= title/function?, v. *ptr*$_1$), cf. Aggoula Syr lii 205).

hymnwt **OffAr** Sing. + suff. 3 p.s.m. *hymnwth* Aḥiq 132 - ¶ subst. trustworthiness - on this word, cf. also Kottsieper SAS 45, 146 n. 109: < Canaanite (uncert. interpret.).

hymnt v. *nḥt*$_4$.

hyn v. *dmn*$_1$,*hn*$_3$.

hyr **OffAr** Sing. emph. *hyrʾ* (or l. *hydʾ*?)Krael $1^{3,6,9}$, Cowl 68 vi obv. 1 (for the reading, cf. Krael p. 135 :: Cowl a.l. (div. otherwise): l. *yhybʾ* = QAL Part. pass. s.m. emph. of *yhb*) - ¶ subst. of uncert. meaning, cf. Milik RB lxi 248: object (either wooden tool or metal vase (for this interpret., cf. also Harmatta ActAntHung vii 360f.)), cf. also Grelot DAE p. 211 n. a :: Erichsen (with Krael p. 135): < Egypt.: = street, house (cf. also Ayad p. 288 n. 15) :: Rosenthal ibid.: < root *hrr*, cf. however Kutscher JAOS lxxiv 234 :: Cazelles Syr xxxii 77: l. *hydʾ*(cf. JA *hwdʾh*, *hwdyh* = confession, admission) :: Eilers AfO xvii 324 n. 6: l. *hydʾ*= Akkad. *idum* > Ar. (= rent??) :: Reider JQR xliv 339: = stony tract - Harmatta ActAntHung vii 360f.: for the diff. *hydḥ* in Cowl 81^{46}: l. poss. *hyrʾ* = Sing. emph. of *hyr* - Harmatta ActAntHung vii 360, 374: pro *hybʾ* l. poss. *hyrʾ* (= Sing. emph. of *hyr*) in Cowl 81^{118}.

hyš v. *mlk*$_5$.

hk$_1$ v. *hʾ*$_1$.

hk$_2$ v. *qdl*.

hkʾ **Hatra** *hkʾ* 29^{5} (the reading *hkh* in IH prob. misprint) - **JAr** *hkh* MPAT-A 26^{8} - ¶ adv. here (for the context of Hatra 29^{5}, v. *mšn*$_1$) - Ginsberg BJPES ii 47f., Naveh sub SM 21, Beyer ATTM 371: l. *hkh* in MPAT-A 1^{2} (poss. reading :: Klein BJPES ii 47f., Fitzmyer & Harrington MPAT a.l. (div. otherwise): l. *brkh* (= n.p.)).

hkh v. *hkʾ*.

hky v. *hdy*$_4$.

hkyn **OffAr** KAI 276^{9}, FuF xxxv $173^{3,4,8,10}$; cf. Frah xxv 9 (*ḥkyn*;

cf. Nyberg FP 55, 102 :: Ebeling Frah a.l.: l. Iran. word), GIPP 54 - **JAr** Syr xlv101[22] - ¶ adv. thus, how; *ḥzy hkyn ʿbdt* Syr xlv 101[22]: see how I have acted ...; in the combination *hkyn ... hyk zy*, *hkyn ṭb wšpyr yhwh hyk zy br ʾynš lʾ dmʿ yhwh* KAI 276[9f.]: she was so nice and pleasant that no one was (her) equal in beauty (for the context, v. *prnwš*) - Naveh & Shaked AMB a.l.: l. poss. *hkyn* in AMB 15[13] (reading however uncert.; dam. context).

hkl$_1$ v. *hykl.*

hkl$_2$ cf. Frah xxvii 8 (*mḥkl* = from here) :: Ebeling Frah a.l.: pro *mḥkl* l. *mʾkl/r* of diff. interpret. (Schaeder with Ebeling a.l.: lapsus for *mḥr$_3$*?).

hkn v.Soden Or xxxv 6, xlvi 184: > Akkad. *akanna* = here??

hknk v.Soden Or xxxv 6, xlvi 184: > Akkad. *akannaka* = there?? (CAD s.v. *akannaka*: the element *-kunu* in the variant *akannakunu* poss. < Ar. influence).

hlʾ v. *yd.*

hlh v. *hn$_3$*.

hlw **OffAr** KAI 233[9,11,13], 270A 1, B 4, Herm 1[7] (for the reading, cf. Milik Bibl xlviii 549, Grelot DAE p. 151 n. g, Kaufman AIA 69 (n. 190), Swiggers AION xli 145 :: Bresciani & Kamil Herm a.l.: l. *mlw* = QAL Imper. pl.m. of *mll$_1$* :: Hayes & Hoftijzer VT xx 99: l. *mlw* = QAL Pf. 3 p.pl.m. of *mll$_1$* :: Porten & Greenfield ZAW lxxx 222, 228, Porten & Yardeni sub TADAE A 2.3: l. *mlw* = particle, as much as (cf. also Porten Arch 270 (n. 13), Porten & Greenfield JEAS p. 152)),[8], 2[4], 6[6] (:: Wesselius FS Lebram 11, 13: *hlw* in Herm. 2[4], 6[6] = conjunction (= for, because)), JRAS '29, 108[2,9,12], etc. - ¶ interjection, behold (on this word, cf. M.L.Brown Maarav iv 211ff.) - **1)** introducing a letter - a) greeting formulae being absent, *kʿn hlw* KAI 270A 1: now, behold (i.e. well then); cf. *kʿnt hlw kn* RES 1792A 1 prob. = well then it is thus ... (:: Lidzbarski Eph ii 229f.: now isn't it thus? (*hlw* < *hlʾ hw*?) > now, surely ...) - b) used immediately after greeting formulae: Sach 76 i A 1f., JRAS '29, 108[2] (resp. *kʿn hlw* and *kʿnt hlw*) - **2)** introducing a new subject or a new aspect of the subject under discussion: KAI 233[9,13], 270B 4, RES 492B 5, 1792B 6, RES '41-'45, 67[5], Sem xxi 85 conc. 4, conv. 4, JRAS '29, 108[9,12]; *kʿn hlw*: Herm 6[6] (*[k]ʿn*; cf. however Porten & Greenfield IOS iv 16, 21, JEAS p. 162: l. *[s]wn* (= n.l.) *hlw*, cf. also Grelot DAE p. 166 (n. j), Porten & Yardeni sub TADAE A 2.6); *kʿt hlw*: Herm 1[8], 2[4]; *kʿnt hlw*: RES 1792A 3; cf. also the introductory formula *hlw kn* RES 492B 5: well, it is thus - for *kʿn lw*, v. *lw*.

hlyn v. *znh.*

hlk$_1$ **Ph** QAL Imper. s.f. *hlk* KAI 27[21] (cf. Albright BASOR lxxvi 9, Gaster Or xi 44, 67, FR 163 (cf. Röllig KAI a.l., NESE ii 19, Rosenthal ANET 658, v.d.Branden BiOr xxxiii 12f., de Moor JEOL xxvii 108; cf.

also Avishur PIB 248, 256, Gibson SSI iii p. 88: or = Inf. abs.?; cf. also Segert GPP p. 149: or = PI‘EL?) × Dupont-Sommer RHR cxx 144f., Baldacci BiOr xl 129: = QAL Inf. abs. (cf. also Cross & Saley BASOR cxcvii 46) :: Caquot FS Gaster 49f., Lipiński RTAT 266: = QAL Pf. 3 p.pl. :: Torczyner JNES vi 26, Garbini OA xx 285f.: = QAL Pf. 3 p.s.m. :: du Mesnil du Buisson FS Dussaud i 424: = QAL Part. act. s.m. abs. or = Sing. abs. of *hlk*$_2$); Inf. cstr. *lkt* KAI 26A ii 4; YIPH Pf. 1 p.s. *ylkt* MUSJ xlv 262[3] (dam. context; cf. Starcky MUSJ xlv al :: Schiffmann RSF iv 171, Röllig NESE ii 2, 7, Cross IEJ xxix 44: = QAL Pf. 1 p.s. of *ylk* = to go); Impf. 3 p.pl.m. *ylk* KAI 26A ii 19 (cf. e.g. Gibson SSI iii p. 60 :: Dupont-Sommer RA xlii 173: = Impf. 3 p.s.m. of YIPH or YOPH, or = Pf.? :: O'Callaghan Or xviii 187: = YIPH Inf. abs. :: Alt WO i 282, FR 158, Pardee UF ix 211: = YIPH Pf. 3 p.s.m. (cf. also Röllig KAI a.l., v. d Branden Meltô i 52f.: after *ylk* an *›nk* left out by lapsus, for this context type, cf. FR 267 (n. 1)) :: Del Olmo Lete AO i 289: poss. = QAL Impf. 3 p.s.m.) - **Pun** QAL Impf. 3 p.pl.m. *ylk* CIS i 5510[9] (cf. e.g. Segert GPP p. 149; diff. context, uncert. interpret.; poss. = YIPH Pf.?, cf. Garbini JSS xii 112, FSR 199, cf. also Krahmalkov RSF ii 177, v.d.Branden RSF v 140 (: < *ylk*)); Part. act. s.m. abs. *›lk* KAI 165[1] (or = *hlk*$_2$??); Imper. s.m., cf. Poen 1013: *lech* (var. *laech*, *lehc*); YIPH Impf. 3 p.s.m. *ylk* Trip 51[6] (??, highly uncert. context, cf. also Amadasi IPT 135: or = Pf.?) - **Mo** QAL Impf. 1 p.s. *›hlk* KAI 181[14f.] (cf. Rundgren ActOr xxi 316: or = PI‘EL?, cf. however Segert ArchOr xxix 226f.; on this form, cf. Blau Maarav ii 145f., Jackson & Dearman SMIM 114); Imper. s.m. *lk* KAI 181[14] - **Hebr** QAL Impf. 3 p.pl.m. *ylkw* KAI 189[4]; Part. act. s.f. abs. *hwlkt* SM 49[18] - **DA** QAL Pf. 3 p.pl.m. *hlkw* v d 3; Imper. pl.m. *lkw* i 7 - **OldAr** QAL Impf. 1 p.s. *›hk* KAI 224[6]; 3 p.pl.m. *yhkn* KAI 224[5]; 3 p.pl.f. *yhkn* KAI 222A 24 (:: Kaufman Maarav iii 170f.: l. *y›pn* = QAL Impf. 3 p.pl.f. of *›py*; the Impf. forms prob. < root *hwk*,cf. e.g. Nöldeke ZA xx 142, BL 46b, Fitzmyer AIS 108, Grelot RB lxix 282, lxxiv 586 :: e.g. Littmann OLZ '30, 450f., Rundgren ActOr xxi 304ff., Segert AAG 111f.: < root *hlk* (for litt., cf. Degen AAG p. 79 nn. 83, 84; on this problem, cf. also Garr DGSP 144ff.)) - **OffAr** QAL Impf. 3 p.s.m. *yhk* Krael 10[15], *yhkn* Krael 3[23a] (?, cf. however Ginsberg JAOS lxxiv 157: or = HAPH Impf. 3 p.s.m. of *kwn*$_2$?; Kutscher JAOS lxxiv 235: or = Impf. 3 p.pl.m.?); 3 p.s.f. *thk* Cowl 15[25,28], Krael 7[24] (dam. context)[,28]; 2 p.s.m. *thk* Cowl 71[13?,22], Aḥiq 102; 1 p.s. *›hk* Cowl 8[22], FS Driver 54 conv. 2; 3 p.pl.m. *yhkwn* Cowl 10[19]; Inf. *mhk* Cowl 54[14] (for this prob. reading, cf. Porten & Yardeni sub TADAE A 3.1 verso 3; for the context, v. also *qdm*$_3$), Sach 76 v 2 (diff. and dam. context) (Impf. and Inf. forms < root *hwk*,v. sub OldAr.); PA‘EL Part. act. s.m. abs. *mhlk* ATNS 5[4], Aḥiq 140 - **Nab** QAL Pf. 3 p.s.f. *hlkt* J 17[4] (<

Arab.?, cf. J p. 174, Cantineau Nab ii 172, Altheim & Stiehl AAW i 191, Diem Or l. 365 n. 83, O'Connor JNES xlv 217f.) - **Palm** QAL Pf. 3 p.s.m. *hlk* Inscr P 6^{3}, Inv x 53^{4}; PA ‘EL Part. act. pl.m. abs. *m[h]lkyn* CIS ii 3913 ii 139 (:: Cooke NSI p. 331: l. *mlkyn* = Plur. abs. of *mlk*$_3$) - **JAr** QAL Impf. 2 p.s.f. *thk* MPAT 41^{7}, 42^{12} (*[t]hk*); 1 p.s. *›hk* MPAT 42^{14}; Inf. *mhk* MPAT $40^{6,18}$ (*m[h]k*) (Impf. and Inf. forms < root *hwk*, v. sub OldAr.); PA ‘EL Part. s.f. abs. *mhlk[h]* AMB 1^{21} - ¶ verb QAL - **1)** to go: KAI 27^{21}, $181^{14,14f.}$, Cowl 71^{22}, MPAT $40^{6,18}$, cf. Poen 1013; *›hk ›grs* FS Driver 54 conv. 2: I shall go to grind; *lkw r›w p‘lt ›lhn* DA i 7: come to see the works of the gods; cf. also KAI 181^{14} - a) + name/noun without prec. prep. - α) *wyhkn ḥlb* KAI 224^{5}: they will go to A. - β) *llkt drk* KAI 26A ii 4f.: to walk on a road - b) + *b*$_2$, for KAI 222A 24, v. *šwt*$_1$; for Cowl 8^{22}, 10^{19}, Krael 10^{15}, v. *dyn*$_2$ - c) + *l*$_5$ comm., *wthk lh* Cowl $15^{28f.}$: she shall go away (cf. Cowl 15^{25}, Krael 7^{24}) - d) + *l*$_5$ loc., *wthk lbyt ›bwh* Krael 7^{28}: she will go to the house of her father (for the context, cf. Muffs 55 n. 5); *lbyt ‘lm› thk* MPAT 41^{7}: you will go to the house of eternity (i.e. you will die; cf. MPAT $42^{12,14}$); *wdrk hgdwlh hhwlkt lmydbr* SM 49^{18}: the great road leading to the desert - e) + *mn*$_5$ + *‘l*$_7$, *wylkw hmym mn hmwṣ› ‘l hbrkh* KAI $189^{4f.}$: the water flowed from the spring to the pool - f) + *‘l*$_7$, *kl ›šrn zy yhkn ‘l byt› zk* Krael 3^{23a}: all the timber which has gone into that house (?, v. supra) - g) + *‘m*$_4$, *hlk ‘mh špyr* Inv x 53^{4}: he behaved himself well towards him (cf. Pardee UF ix 211); cf. also Inscr P $6^{3f.}$ (= Inv x 39) - **2)** to die: J 17^{4} (v. supra), cf. also Aḥiq 102?, Cowl 71^{13}? (v. however *ḥyl*$_2$) - PA ‘EL to walk: ATNS 5^{4}; *w›nh mhlk byn krmy›* Aḥiq 40: I was walking among the vineyards, cf. also CIS ii 3913 ii 139 (?, heavily dam. context; v. also supra); *mhlk[h] bgydwhy wgrmwhy* AMB $1^{21f.}$: that walks within his tendons and bones (said of a spirit that causes illness) - YIPH + obj. + *l*$_5$, *wylk zbḥ lkl hmskt* KAI 26A ii 19f.: and let people bring sacrifices to all the cast images - Rocco AION xix 551^{1}: l. *tlk* = QAL Impf. 3/2 p.s.f., cf. however Amadasi GR i p. 45f.: completely uncert. reading and interpret. - L.H.Gray AJSL xxxix 81: *lachan* in Poen 1013 = QAL Imper. s. m. + *n›*??, cf. however Schroed 296, 318 (div. otherwise): l. *lachannan* (= *lknn* (= on the cross), cf. also Sznycer PPP 143: *lachannan* prob. = special oath formula of diff. explanation).

v. *›l*$_1$, *›sy*$_1$,*hlk*$_2$, *hlkw*, *hnh*, *kly*$_1$, *lyn*$_1$, *ml›kh*$_1$, *mlk*$_5$, *‘wp*$_1$, *tk*$_1$.

hlk$_2$ **Pun** Sing. abs., cf. Poen 934 (:: Schroed 310, Sznycer PPP 78 (div. otherwise): l. *thuulech* (= Sing. abs. of *thlk* (= *hospes*)) :: L.H.Gray AJSL xxxix 77f., 87: l. *thuulech* = Sing. + suff. 1 p.s. of *thlk* :: J.J.Glück & Maurach Semitics ii 105, 108 (div. otherwise): l. *noctothu* (v. *hnkt*) *ulech* (= *w* + *l*$_5$ + *k›*$_2$)), 1010: *uulech* (var. of *mi uulech* = *muialech*; or = QAL Part. act. s.m. of *hlk*$_1$?,cf. e.g. Segert GPP p. 149) - **DA** Sing.

abs. *hlk* ii 7 (cf. e.g. Hoftijzer DA a.l. :: H.P.Müller ZAW xliv 219, 232f. (nn. 124, 125): = Sing. abs. of *hlk*$_3$ (= one who is desirous, eager)) - ¶ subst. - **1)** traveller, guest: Poen 1010, DA ii 7 - **2)** *hospes*, one who receives a guest: Poen 934.
v. *hlk*$_1$.

hlk$_3$ v. *hlk*$_2$.

hlk$_4$ (< Akkad., cf. Kaufman AIA 58, cf. also Pognon JA xi/i 408; cf. however Driv p. 70, Altheim & Stiehl ASA 147f.) - **OffAr** Sing. emph. *hlk*ʾ Del 73^3 (= AM 112), 78^2, 79^1 (= AM 110), Driv 8^5 - ¶ subst. tax; in Driv 8^5 clearly ground tax. In Del 73^3, 79^1 Akkad. par. *ilku*.

hlk$_5$ v. *ḥrṣ*$_3$

hlkh$_1$ **OffAr** Sing. + suff. 2 p.s.m. *hlktk* Beh 52 - ¶ subst. behaviour (cf. Porten & Greenfield BIDG 47).

hlkh$_2$ v. *ʾlwk*.

hlkw **OffAr** Sing. cstr. *hlkwt* KAI 273^{10} (cf. Humbach AIT 8, 11, Davary & Humbach IPAA 12, Degen Lesh xxxiv 315 :: Andreas NGWG '32, 16, Altheim LuG ii 181, Altheim & Stiehl Suppl 11, 14, 16, Donner KAI a.l., Kutscher, Naveh & Shaked Lesh xxxiv 126 (div. otherwise): l. *hlkw* = Qal Pf. 3 p.pl.m. of *hlk*$_1$; heavily dam. context) - ¶ subst. conduct, way of living (for the context and parallels, cf. Humbach AIT 8, 11).

hlkt **Pun** Sing. abs., cf. Poen 937: *elichot* (variant *lychot*), Poen 947: *helicot* (variants: *helicos*, *elicos*) :: J.J.Glück & Maurach Semitics ii 111: *elichot* = *ʾl*$_6$ + suff. 3 p.s.m. + *k* + *ʾt*$_1$ (Sing. abs.). ¶ subst. hospitality (cf. e.g. Sznycer PPP 96f., Krahmalkov Or lvii 66).

hll v.d.Branden BO xiv 196, 200: the *thl* in KAI 162^5 = Qal Impf. 3 p.s.f. of *hll* (= to praise, to thank).
v. *myll*.

hllw v. *z*$_1$.

hlm$_1$ v. *kly*$_1$.

hlm$_2$ **Pun**, cf. Poen 944: *alem* (cf. e.g. Schroed 291f., L.H.Gray AJSL xxxix 76ff.; uncert. interpret., cf. also Sznycer PPP 126f.) - ¶ adv. here (v. however supra); Schroed 291, L.H.Gray AJSL xxxix 76ff.: *alum* in Poen 942 is same word (highly uncert. interpret., cf. Sznycer PPP 122ff.).
v. *ʿlm*$_5$.

hln v. *znh*.

hlss (< Greek ἄλσος, cf. Gawlikowski Syr xlvii 324, TP 49 and sub RIP 157, Milik DFD 8) - **Palm** Sing. abs. *hlss* RIP 157^4 (Greek par. ἄλσο[υς]) - ¶ subst. wood (cf. Gawlikowski Syr li 93f., TP 49ff., v. also *gntʾ ʾlym* sub *gnh*$_1$) :: CIS ii sub 3968: *hlss* = n.p. < Greek.

hm$_1$ v. *hʾ*$_1$.

hm$_2$ v. *mn*$_5$.

hmdkr v. *hmrkr*.
hmw v. *hʾ*$_1$.
hmwn$_1$ v. *hn*$_3$.
hmwn$_2$ v. *hʾ*$_1$.
hmwnyt (< Iran., cf. Schaed 255f., cf. also Koopmans 125) - **OffAr** Cowl 27^4, 30^5 - ¶ adv. in agreement, in league with; *hmwnyt ʿm wydrng* Cowl 27^4, 30^5: in agreement with W.
hmyh v. *hn*$_3$.
hmyt (< Iran., cf. Segal sub ATNS 26, Shaked Or lvi 412) - **OffAr** Sing. cstr. *hmyt* ATNS 26^{10,16} - ¶ subst. of uncert. meaning indicating something related to ships (in both instances ATNS 26^{10,16} in the combination *hmyt spyntʾ*); Shaked Or lvi 412: = (ship) appurtenances? or preferably = measured, alloted together (sc. with the ship?); Segal ATNS a.l.: = complement?
hmyth v. *ʿtd*$_1$.
hmkrygrb (< Iran., cf. Segal ATNS a.l., Shaked Or lvi 412) - **OffAr** Sing. abs. *hmkrygrb* ATNS 3^5 - ¶ subst. of unknown meaning; Shaked Or lvi 412: prob. =joint holding (cf. also Porten & Yardeni sub TADAE B 8.10); Segal ATNS a.l.: = pledge of collaboration ? (less prob. interpret.).
hml v. *hn*$_3$.
hmm v. *hwm*$_1$.
hmn$_1$ **OffAr** Cowl p. 144, 146: l. in Cowl 43^2: *hmnh*? (= Sing. + suff. 3 p.s.f. of *hmn* = compound < Iran. *ham-* + *n*? (= partner, twin??)), highly uncert. reading (especially of *nh*) :: Grelot DAE p. 89 n. e: l. *hmth* = Sing. + suff. 3 p.s.f. of *hmt*$_1$ (< Iran. = of the same mother; improb. reading), cf. also Porten JNES xlviii 176: l. rather *ywhdyh* (= f. Sing. abs. of *yhwdy* (= Judean)), cf. also Porten & Yardeni sub TADAE B 5.5.
hmn$_2$ v. *hn*$_3$, *pnh*.
hmr **OffAr** word of unknown meaning in ATNS 26^{13} (reading *hmd* also poss.); Shaked Or lvi 409: word < Iran., used as verb = to reckon, to calculate; Segal ATNS a.l.: < Iran. = reckoning, accounting.
hmrkr (< Iran., cf. Perles OLZ '11, 498f., Schaed 264, Eilers Beamtennamen 43ff., AfO xvii 333, Driv p. 75, Chaumont JA cclvi 23, Greenfield Mem Henning 180ff. (cf. also id. ActAntHung xxv 115f.), Hinz AISN 121, Brown Bibl lxx 201f.) - **OffAr** Sing. emph. *hmrkrʾ* PF 281; Plur. emph. *hmrkryʾ* Cowl 26^{4,23}, Driv 8^{1*} (for the diff. reading, cf. also Porten & Yardeni sub TADAE A 6.11), 10^{1*,3} (the reading *hmdkryʾ*in Cowl 26^{4,23} false, cf. Perles OLZ '11, 498f.) - ¶ subst. function indication: accountant; *hmrkryʾ zy gnzʾ* Cowl 26^4: the accountants of the treasury; for litt. on the subject, v. supra, cf. Porten Arch 58ff. (nn. 114-119), cf. also Chaumont JA cclvi 30 n. 88.

v. *hmrkrny*.

hmrkrygb (< Iran., cf. Segal sub ATNS 3, Shaked Or lvi 412) - **OffAr** Sing. abs. *hmrkrygb* ATNS 3[5] - ¶ subst. prob. meaning joint holding (cf. Shaked Or lvi 412 (cf. also Porten & Yardeni sub TADAE B 8.10) :: Segal ATNS a.l.: = pledge (of collaboration)); *hmrkrygb mhḥsnn ʾnḥnh* ATNS 3[5]: we possess a joint holding.

hmrkrny **OffAr** m.Sing. abs. (?) *hmrkrny* ATNS 49[4] - ¶ adj. of the accountant (?, uncert. interpret., cf. Segal sub ATNS 49; or preferably l. *hmrkr*(= Sing. abs./cstr. of *hmrkr*)+ *ny*?; *spr hmrkrny* ATNS 49[4] : an accountancy document (?, or a document (?) of the accountant (of ?)?).

hmš **OffAr** the diff. *hmš* (or *hmš[*?) in heavily dam. text Pers 105[4] unexplained. Poss. indication of type of stone; cf. however Hinz NWAP 88, AISN 112: < Iran. = the same, just as much.

hmt$_1$ v. *hmn*.

hmt$_2$ v. *hʾ$_1$*.

hn$_1$ (< Egypt., cf. e.g. Lambdin JAOS lxxiii 149; cf. also Ellenbogen 68, Trinquet SDB v 1225ff.) - **Hebr** Sing. abs. *hn* Dir pes. 23 - **OffAr** Sing. abs. *hn* RES 1791[2,3,4,5] - ¶ subst. *hin*, liquid measure (prob. = 1/6 *bat*, v. *bt$_3$*, cf. e.g. Barrois ii 248ff., EM iv 853ff.; cf. however Delavault & Lemaire RSF vii 7f.); abbrev. *h* prob. in EI ix 86 (= RSF vii 7 no. 10); poss. also in Nisa-b 2167[2-8], Nisa-c 355[1] (cf. Diakonov & Livshitz PaSb ii 144 n. 29, 171).

hn$_2$ v. *znh*, *pwd*.

hn$_3$ **Ph** *hn* KAI 2[2] (cf. e.g. Albright JAOS lxvii 156, Röllig KAI a.l., FR 259,1, Gibson SSI iii p. 17 :: Dussaud Syr v 143 (div. otherwise): l. *hny$_2$* = behold :: Vincent RB xxxiv 189 n. 1 (div. otherwise): l. *hnypd* (= HINPAʿAL Imper. s.m. of *ypd* (= to be on one's guard)); for the context, v. also *pwd*), MUSJ xlv 262[1] (:: Dahood Or xlv 337, Bibl lx 432, Teixidor Syr liv 267 (div. otherwise): pro *kn hn* l.: *k* (= *kʾ$_2$*) + *nhn* (= QAL Imper. s./pl.m. + suff. 1 p.s. of *nhy* (= to wail)); both instances may be orthographic rendering of *hnh*) - **Pun**, cf. Poen 931: *in* (for the reading *mlachthi in* for *mlachchun* (var. *mlahchun*), cf. Sznycer PPP 56f. :: Schroed 290, 305 (div. otherwise): *mlachchun* = Sing. + suff. 1 p.s. of *mlʾkn* (= business; cf. also L.H.Gray AJSL xxxix 77f.) :: J.J.Glück & Maurach Semitics ii 103: *mlachchun* = Sing. + suff. 1 p.pl. of *mlʾk$_2$* (= journey)?) - **Mo** *hn* SSI i 83[3] - **Hebr** *hn* TA-H 21[3], 40[9], IEJ vii 239[1] - **DA** *hn* ii 10 - **Samal** *hn* KAI 214[29] - **OldAr** *hn* KAI 222A 14, 15, 24, 29 (v. infra), B 28, 31, 36, 223B 4, 5, 224[4,6], etc. - **OffAr** *hn* KAI 225[11], 270B 1, 271B 2, Cowl 5[7,8,13], Krael 1[5,8], 3[14], Driv 3[5], 4[3], 5[8], 12[3] (cf. however Porten & Yardeni sub TADAE A 6.15: l. *hʾ* (= *hʾ$_2$*)),Herm 1[9], 2[8,9], Aḥiq 124 (for the reading, cf. Lindenberger APA 251 n. 336), ATNS 1[5], 2[1], Beh 58 (for the reading, cf. also Greenfield

& Porten BIDG 50; Akkad. par. *ki-i*), Samar 1^{5} (= EI xviii 8*), etc., etc., *hyn*NESE iii 48^{7}, *ʾn* RES 492A 2, B 3 (:: Segert AAG p. 233: = *ʾn*$_7$(= variant of *ʾm*$_4$)), Herm 4^{9}, *h* (in *hlh*< *hn*$_3$ + *lh*$_1$ = *lʾ*$_1$) Herm 2^{10} - **Hatra** *ʾyn* 343^{6,8} - **Nab** *hn* CIS ii 209^{6}, 212^{5}, J 5^{6}, 30^{2} (= CIS ii 200; for this reading, cf. Milik sub ARNA-Nab 79)^{,5} (the *hn* in CIS ii 224^{8} false reading, cf. J 34) - **Palm** *hn* CIS ii 3913 ii 6, 118, 127, 145, 146, *ʾn* CIS ii 3913 ii 149 (cf. Cantineau Gramm 44, Rosenthal Sprache 35), MUSJ xxxviii 106^{9} - **JAr** *hn* MPAT 39^{7}, 41^{9}, 42^{10} (heavily dam. context), Mas 556^{4,5}, *ʾn* AMB 3^{16}, 7a 7, 7b 3 - ¶ particle used with different functions - **1)** interjection, behold: KAI 2^{2} (cf. H.P.Müller ZAH ii 69 (n. 115)), 214^{29} (cf. Dion p. 172, 178f.; cf. also Driver AnOr xii 47), MUSJ xlv 262^{1}, Driv 12^{3} (v. however supra); for *hn lw*, v. *lw* - **2)** conj. introducing a conditional clause (cf. Kutscher JAOS lxxiv 234), if - a) + Impf. (future sense), *hn ʾmr* Cowl 15^{33}: if I say ...; *whn tkln thytn ln ...* Herm 5^{5}: if you are able to send us ...; cf. KAI 222A 14, 24, 225^{11}, Cowl 8^{20,26}, 9^{8}, Krael 3^{19}, 4^{16,18}, Driv 4^{3}, 6^{6}, ATNS 15^{3}, FX 136^{20}, CIS ii 212^{5}, J 30^{5}, CIS ii 3913 ii 6, 127, MPAT 39^{7}, AMB 3^{16}, etc., etc. - b) + Pf. (future sense), *hn lʾ šlmt lk kl kspk* Cowl 11^{7}: if I don't pay you all your silver; *kʿt hn mṭʾk ... šlḥ ly* Herm 3$^{5f.}$: now, if he reaches you ..., send me ...; cf. TA-H 21^{3} (for the problems of the context, cf. Pardee UF x 319, HAHL 58), 40^{9} (dam. context), TH 1^{4} (v. *lʾ*$_1$), Cowl 5^{7,8}, 7^{10}, 10^{7,14}, Krael 1^{5,8}, 3^{14}, Herm 4^{5,9}, RES 1793^{1} (for the context, v. *lḥm*$_3$), FS Driver 54 conv. 1, etc., etc.; cf. also *hlh*(v. supra) + Pf. (or Impf.??), *whlh yhb lky šlḥy ly* Herm 2^{10}: and if he does not give (it) to you, send me (sc. word); for a) and b), cf. Joüon MUSJ xviii 21 - c) + nom. clause, *hn ʾyt lk ḥmrn 10* Cowl 54$^{4f.}$: if you have 10 asses (cf. also Cowl 54$^{11f.}$?; cf. however Porten & Yardeni sub TADAE A 3.1.: pro *hn* l. *hw*?); *hn ṣbh ʾnt* Aḥiq 149: if you want; *whyn lʾ ṣbyn lmʾth* NESE iii 48$^{7f.}$: if they don't want to come; cf. Cowl 54^{11}, Herm 1^{9}, Aḥiq 103, 115, 124, NESE i 11$^{6f.}$, MUSJ xxxviii 106$^{9f.}$ - **3)** *hn lʾ* as elliptic subordinate clause, *ḥy lYHH hn lʾ npšk[y] ʾlqḥ* Sem ii 31 conc. 3f.: by the life of the Lord, if not, I will take your life (for reading and interpret., cf. Rosenthal AH i/1, 12, i/2, 11, Porten JNES xviii 116, Arch 126, Teixidor Syr xlviii 480 :: Dupont-Sommer Sem ii 31: l. *hn lʾ knšn ʾlqḥ*: yes, I will take barley??); cf. also the *hn lʾ* in Sem ii 31 conc. 7; cf. also the diff. *hn lhn* in KAI 222B 36, 224^{4,9,13,20} prob. = if not, then ..., *whn lhn šqrt lkl ʾlhy [ʿ]dyʾ* KAI 224^{14}: and if not, you will have been false to all the gods of the treaty, cf. KAI 222B 36, 224^{4,9,20} (for the interpret. of this formula as conditional clause, cf. - a) = *hn*$_3$ + *l*$_2$ + *hn*$_4$ (= pron. pers. 3 p.pl.f.), cf. Dupont-Sommer BMB xiii 31, Fitzmyer CBQ x 455, Donner sub KAI 224^{4}, Beyer ZDMG cxx 201 - b) = *hn*$_3$ + *l*$_2$ + *hn*$_3$ (= thus), cf. Ben-Chayyim Lesh xxxv 251, Lipiński Stud 37, cf. also Koopmans 57, BiOr xvii 52, Fitzmyer AIS

79f.; for the interpretation as compound conjunction, cf. Degen AAG p. 63 (n. 42), Gibson SSI ii p. 52; or to be interpreted as hn_3 + l_2 as elliptic conditional clause, the second *hn* (= hn_3, behold) introducing the principal clause?) - **4)** *hn d›* as elliptic subordinate clause: if so, ... : Mas 556[4] - **5)** *lmh hn, lmh hn y›bd* Sem ii 31 conc. 3: lest they should be spoiled (for the context, v. *›bd*$_1$, *bql*) - **6)** *hn ... (w)hn ...* - a) introducing single clause elements, *gmly› hn ṯ‹ynyn whn sryqyn* CIS ii 3913 ii 118: camels whether laden or empty; *wšydh w›n* (for the reading, cf. Dupont-Sommer JKF i 206) *dkr w›n nqbh* AMB 7a 6f.: and the demon be it male or female (cf. AMB 7b 3); *w›l ytšm‹ ql knr b›rpd wb‹mh hn lmrq whn [lṣ‹]qh wyllh* KAI 222A 29f.: the sound of the lyre will not be heard in Arpad nor among its people whether through sickness or through crying and lamentation (for the context, v. also *ṣ‹qh*; for the reading of both *hn*'s, cf. Rosenthal ANET 660 n. 5 (for the first one, cf. also Gibson SSI ii p. 30, 40) :: α) (for the first *hn*) e.g. Dupont-Sommer Sf p. 45, AH i/1, 4, i/2, 3, Brekelmans VT xiii 225ff., Fitzmyer AIS 47f., Donner KAI a.l. (div. otherwise), Lemaire & Durand IAS 114, 121: l. *hml* (= Sing. abs.; = noise, crash; cf. however Degen OLZ '71, 269); cf. also Hatra 343[6-8] - β) (for the second *hn*) e.g. Degen AAG 11 n. 52, Lipiński Stud 29 (n. 1), Lemaire & Durand IAS 114, 133 (div. otherwise): l. *hm[yt]* = Sing. cstr. of *hmyh* (= noise; cf. also Fitzmyer CBQ xxxix 263) :: Brekelmans VT xiii 227f.: l. *hm[yh]* :: Gibson SSI ii p. 30, 40 (div. otherwise): l. *hm[n]* = Sing. abs. of hmn_2 (= noise) :: e.g. Dupont-Sommer Sf p. 18, 45f., AH i/1, 4, i/2, 3, Fitzmyer AIS 48: l. *hm[wn]* = Sing. cstr. of *hmwn* (= noise, din; cf. also Donner KAI a.l.)) - b) introducing two mutually exclusive object clauses, *wlh šlḥtn hn ḥy ›nh whn mt ›nh* Herm 5[8f.]: and you did not send (a letter to ask) whether I were alive or dead - c) introducing complex conditional clauses, prob. in DA ii 10 (cf. Hoftijzer DA a.l., for the context, v. *›nš*$_3$) - Puech RB lxxxi 197, 199, 212 n. 56: in KAI 189[1] (first word) restore *hn* and not *z›t* (poss. interpret.) - Sznycer PPP 65ff.: the *edyn* (var. *aedin*) in Poen 932 poss. = *‹d*$_7$ + hn_3 (= until now, still) :: Schroed 308f.: = *›ydyn* (= *›y*$_3$+ deictic element *d* + pron. suff. 3 p.pl.f.. (= pers. pron. 3 p.pl.f.)) :: L.H.Gray AJSL xxxix 79 (div. otherwise): l. *iadedin* = PILPEL Impf. 1 p.s. prec. by *w* of *‹wd*$_3$ (= to take away; v. also *yḥd*$_2$) :: J.J.Glück & Maurach Semitics ii 105: *edyn* = *›t*$_6$ + suff. 3 p.pl.f. - L.H.Gray AJSL xxxix 77: *hem* in Poen 946 = hn_3 (= behold; cf. Schroed 291, 312 (div. otherwise): l. *em* = lapsus for *en* = hn_3 (= here)), cf. however Sznycer PPP 127.

v. *bl‹d*, dmn_1, *h›*$_1$, hn_3, *hnkt*, *ḥbr*$_2$, lhn_1, *ml›kh*$_1$, *nṣb*$_3$.

hn₄ v. *h›*$_1$, hn_3.

hn₅ **JAr** AMB 15[19] - ¶ adv. where; *kl hn d* AMB 15[19]: wherever.

hn› **OffAr**, cf. Frah xxv 25 (*hn›*), Paik 402, 403, 585, GIPP 23, 27,

SaSt 16f., 22 - **JAr** Frey 1415^{1}, 1418^{1} - ¶ dem. pron. m. this - Altheim & Stiehl AAW ii 195: l. in Hatra 8 *hnʾkʾ* = *hnʾ* + *kʾ*$_2$ (uncert. reading and interpret.), cf. also Vattioni IH a.l.: *hnʾkʾ* = adv. here (cp *hnkt*) - v.Soden Or xxxv 6, xlvi 184: Akkad. *ḫannû*, *ḫanniu* (= this) instead of *annû*, *anniu* influence of Ar. *hnʾ*.

hnbg (< Iran., cf. Schaed 264f., Eilers Beamtennamen 73, AfO xvii 333, de Menasce BiOr xi 161, Hinz AISN 115, cf. also Porten & Szubin Maarav iv 62) - **OffAr** Sing. abs. *hnbg* Krael 5^{5}, 9^{18}, 10^{12}, 12^{27}; emph. *hnbgʾ* Cowl 43^{9} - ¶ subst. m. associate (cf. Yaron JSS xvi 244, Porten & Yardeni sub TADAE B 3.6: = partner-in-land; cf. also Greenfield ActAntHung xxv 116ff.: = term referring to joint ownership of land (cf. also id. JLTV 33)).
v. *gby*$_1$,*hngyt*.

hngyt (< Iran., cf. Schaed 266, de Menasce BiOr xi 166, Eilers AfO xvii 333, xviii 126, Henning Zoroaster 44, Benveniste JA ccxlii 298 n. 3, Hinz AISN 116, cf. also Porten & Szubin Maarav iv 62) - **OffAr** Sing. abs. *hngyt* Cowl 43^{9}, Krael 5^{5}, 9^{18}, 10^{12}, 12^{27} - ¶ subst. m. partner (cf. Porten & Yardeni sub TADAE B 3.6: = partner-in-chattel), cf. the series *br ly wbrh wʾḥ ly wʾḥh wqryb wrḥyq hngyt whnbg* Krael 5^{5}: son of mine or daughter, brother of mine or sister, a relative or someone who is not a relative, partner or associate; for comparable enumerations, cf. Cowl 43^{9}, Krael 9^{18}, 10^{12}, 12^{27} - cf. also Greenfield ActAntHung xxv 116f.: = term referring to joint ownership of live stock (cf. also id. JLTV 33).

hndb v. *hndwp*.

hndwn (< Iran., cf. Schaed 266f., Hinz AISN 115f.) - **OffAr** Sing. + suff. 3 p.s.m. *hndwnh* Cowl $26^{5,17}$ - ¶ subst. paint (to paint wood), varnish, cf. however Grelot DAE p. 287 n. l: or = coating material? (cf. also Hinz AISN 115f., Porten & Yardeni sub TADAE A 6.2)

hndwp cf. Frah vi 4 (var. *ḥndwpʾ*) = endive, cf. Ar. *hndb*,cf. Ebeling Frah a.l., Nyberg FP 69.

hndz v. *hndyz*.

hndyz (< Iran., cf. Schaed 256ff., Driv p. 53f. (cf. however Widengren OrSuec v 153 n. 3), Benveniste JA ccxlii 301ff., de Menasce BiOr xi 162, Hinz AISN 116) - **OffAr** *hndyz* Cowl 27^{7}, Driv 5^{6}, *hndz*Cowl 13^{4}, AG 76a 3 - ¶ adj. (indecl.) prob. meaning: (said of soldiers) being held (sc. in the fortress), confined (sc. to the fortress), cf. Driv p. 53f., de Menasce BiOr xi 162, Grelot DAE p. 185, 309 (n. o), Hinz AISN 116, cf. also Porten & Greenfield JEAS p. 14, 86: on duty, Porten & Yardeni sub TADAE A 6.7: garrisoned? (cf. ibid. A 4.5, B 2.7) :: the transl. "being present at a review of arms", cf. Schaed 257f. (cf. also Eilers AfO xvii 333), "mobilized, called up" (cf. Benveniste JA ccxlii 302f. (cf. also Wag 16, 64, Milik RB lxi 593f.)).

hndrz (< Iran., cf. Driv p. 57, Eilers AfO xvii 333, Hinz AISN 115) - **OffAr** Sing. abs. *hndrz* Driv $10^{3,4}$; emph. *hndrzʾ* Driv 7^{1*} (for this prob. reading, cf. Porten & Yardeni sub TADAE A 6.10 :: Driv a.l.: l. *[z]y yh[w]h* (= QAL Impf. 3 p.s.m. of *hwy*$_1$)?,cf. Grelot DAE p. 313), 11^3; + suff. 1 p.s. *hndrzy* Driv 10^{1*} (cf. however Porten & Yardeni sub TADAE A 6.13: l. *hndrzʾ* = Sing. emph.) - ¶ subst. instruction, order; *ʾntm hndrz ʿbdw lḥtwbsty* Driv 10^4: you, do you instruct Ḥ.

hnh **Pun** + suff. 1 p.s., cf. Poen 939: *ynnynnu* (var. *ynnynu*), cf. e.g. Sznycer PPP 106f. (: poss. = lapsus for *ynnynny*; cf. J.J.Glück & Maurach Semitics ii 113f.) :: FR 33: = + suff. 1 p.pl. (cf. however ibid. 259,1; on this form, cf. also H.P.Müller ZAH ii 45 n. 5, 46 n. 10) - **Hebr** *hnh* KAI 196^5, TA-H 24^{18}, Frey 1164^1 (= SM 44^4) - **JAr** *hnh* Frey 841b - ¶ interj. behold; introducing a new subject: KAI 196^5, or a new aspect of a subject: TA-H 24^{18} (for the context, cf. Lemaire Sem xxiii 17f.) - the *ʾnʾ* in Karth xii 54^2 prob. = *hnh* (cf. Février & Fantar Karth a.l., v.d.Branden RSF v 57, 62) - Février BAr-NS a.l.: the *hnʿ* in BAr-NS i-ii 224^3 = *hnh* (uncert. interpret.) - Gray AJSL xxxix 77f.: the *hunc(c)* in Poen 935 = *hnh* :: Schroed 291, 311 (div. otherwise): l. *ulec* (= QAL Part. act. s.m. abs. of *hlk*$_1$) :: Krahmalkov Or lvii 59 (div. otherwise): l. *et* (= *ʾyt*$_3$); cf. also Sznycer PPP 127.
v. *hn*$_3$,*hnw*$_1$, *pwd*.

hnw$_1$ **Samal** KAI 214^{29} (*hn[w]*, cf. e.g. Dion p. 34, 172)^{,30,31} - ¶ (interj. >) conj. if; *phnw zkr hw* KAI 214^{30}: if he is a male (cf. Poeb 44, 48, Dion p. 34, 172f., 178f., 455 n. 3, JNES xxxvii 116) :: Friedr 41*, Garb 264 (cf. also Garbini AION xxvi 128), Donner KAI a.l.: = behold; for *hnw lw*, v. *lw*.
v. *hnh*.

hnw$_2$ v. *hʾ*$_1$.

hnwn v. *hʾ*$_1$.

hny$_1$ **Hebr** NIPH Impf. 3 p.pl. *yhnw* DJD ii 22^6 - **JAr** ITP Part. s.m. abs. *mthnh* MPAT 69^1 (for the reading, cf. Fitzmyer JBL lxxviii 61 (= ESBNT 95)) - ¶ verb NIPH to benefit; *wlʿlm bny yhnw ʾth ršt šlʿlm* DJD ii 22^6: forever my children will benefit of this eternal right of property - ITP to use at one's profit, to find to one's profit, + *b*$_2$ (something) - Milik DJD ii a.l.: l. poss. *yhnʾ* (= APH Impf. 3 p.s.m. (= to benefit)) in DJD ii 31 ii 1 (v. also sub **Hebr**).
v. *hʾ*$_1$.

hny$_2$ v. *hʾ*$_1$,*hn*$_3$, *pwd*.

hnyn v. *znh*.

hnk v. *hnkt*.

hnkt **Pun** *hnkt* KAI $136^{1f.}$ (for the reading, cf. Chabot BAr '36/37, 170, Hoftijzer VT xi 345, Röllig KAI a.l. :: Février Sem v 63, MC 93f.: l. *hknt* (= *h*$_1$ + *knt* (= Sing. abs. (var. form) of *khnh*), cf. also Garbini

FSR 182)), 152[2], 171[4], Punica iv A 6[4], 7[4], 8[4], vi 2[4] (cf. Hartmann & Hoftijzer Mus lxxxiv 534f., cf. also Teixidor Syr xlix 415 :: Hoftijzer VT xi 347f.: = h_1 + Sing. abs. of nkt_2 (= mortal remains??; cf. also Röllig sub KAI 136) :: Février CB viii 28f.: *nkt* = cave? or *hnkt* = orthographic variant of *ḥnkt* (= hidden room > cave)? :: Schedl VT xii 343f.: *hnkt* (= orthographic variant of *ḥnkt*) = memorial stone), cf. Poen 934: *ynnoctoth* (lapsus for *ynnochoth*), cf. e.g. Sznycer PPP 77f. :: Schroed 290f., 310, L.H.Gray AJSL xxxix 76ff., Gottheil 917 (div. otherwise): l. *ynnocho* (= *hnk(h)* (= here) :: Sznycer PPP 78, 89, H.P.Müller ZAH ii 45 n. 5: = hn_3+ suff. 3 p.s.m. + kh_2 (= here; cf. also FR 259,1) :: J.J.Glück & Maurach Semitics ii 105f. (div. otherwise): l. *-hyn* (= pron. suff. 3 p.pl.f.; cf. however p. 105) *noctothu* (= poss. lapsus for *noctophu*) = NIPH Pf. 3 p.pl. of $ḥṭp_2$ (= to be kidnapped)), Poen 936: *innochot* (variant *innochut*; cf. Gottheil 916 (div. otherwise): l. *hinnochot* (= also *hnkt*)) :: L.H.Gray AJSL xxxix 77f. (div. otherwise): l. *innocho* = *hnk(h)* (= here), cf. also Schroed 290f., 312 :: Sznycer PPP 89, H.P.Müller ZAH ii 45 n. 5: = hn_3+ suff. 3 p.s.m. + kh_2 (= here; cf. also FR 259,1, J.J.Glück & Maurach Semitics ii 110) - ¶ adv. here (v. also *ʿbn*); the diff. *ḥnʿkt* in Punica xvi 2[3] poss. = orthographical variant of *hnkt* (cf. Chabot Punica a.l., Hartmann & Hoftijzer Mus lxxxiv 535 n. 23).

v. *hnʾ*.

hnn v. $hʾ_1$.

hnnwn v. $hʾ_1$.

hns **OldAr** QAL (or PAʿEL? :: Cooke NSI p. 188: QAL or HAPH?) Impf. 3 p.s.m. + suff. 3 p.s.m. *yhnsnh* KAI 202B 20 - **OffAr** QAL (or PAʿEL?) Impf. 2 p.s.m. *thns* KAI 225[6], 226[8] (or Impf. pass. 3 p.s.f. in KAI 226[8]?, cf. Driver AnOr xii 49); + suff. 1 p.s. *thnsny* KAI 226[9] (for the root *hns*, cf. Barth OLZ '09, 11, Dupont-Sommer AH i/2, 3, Tawil JNES xxxii 481 n. 51, Gibson SSI ii p. 16, Segert AAG p. 532 :: Nöldeke ZA xxi 383, Donner sub KAI 202, Degen AAG p. 76: = HAPH of nws_1 :: Clermont-Ganneau Et ii 197f.: = HAPH of $nšʾ_1$, cf. also Cooke NSI p. 188 :: Hoffmann ZA xi 212: poss. = HAPH of *ʾns*(cf. also Koopmans 29)) - ¶ verb QAL (or PAʿEL?) to remove, to take away + obj.

hnpn (< Iran., cf. Krael 241, de Menasce BiOr xi 162, Hinz AISN 117) - **OffAr** Sing. emph. *hnpnʾ* Krael 9[9], 10[4] - ¶ subst. of uncert. meaning; Geiger with Krael 241: = shelter (cf. also de Menasce BiOr xi 162, Porten Arch 284f., Porten & Greenfield JEAS p. 58, 63, Porten & Yardeni sub TADAE B 3.10 a.e.); Grelot DAE p. 244 (n. g): = avenue; for this word, cf. also Couroyer RB lxi 558, lxxv 82ff., Eilers AfO xvii 333, Hinz AISN 117.

hsrm v. *ʿšrm*.

hst **OffAr** diff. word in Pers 36[1], 119[1], 120[1] (in all instances in the combination *bhst byrt›*); R.A.Bowman Pers p. 67: = subst. Sing. cstr.; for the interpret., cf. Emmerick with R.A.Bowman Pers p. 24 (n. 42): = a place where something is beaten (< Iran.), Harmatta ibid. p. 24: = *haoma* feast, Levine JAOS xcii 76: = a place or agency within the fortress or perhaps administrative term (non-semitic, cf. also Degen BiOr xxxi 125 n. 5), Segal BSOAS xxxv 354, Delauney CC 207, 209, 215: = treasury, part of temple (cf. Akkad. *e/isittu*; cf. Teixidor Syr l. 431, Delaunay with Teixidor ibid. (cf. also Gershevitz Mem de Menasce 53: prob. = place for sheep (indication of part of palace)), cf. also R.A.Bowman Pers p. 107 n. 171). Prob. interpret.: = n.l., cf. Cameron with R.A.Bowman Pers p. 21, Bernard StudIr i 171ff., Naveh & Shaked Or xlii 446f., Teixidor Syr li 331, Lipiński Stud 156 (n. 3), Hinz AISN 118, FS Nyberg 372ff. (cf. already Cameron with Schmidt Persepolis ii 55 n. 62).

hpwk **Nab** Sing. abs. *hpwk* BSOAS xv 16,46a 2 - ¶ subst. (??) return (?).

hpṭyn (< Greek ὀπτίων < Lat. *optio*, cf. Cantineau Gramm 157, Rosenthal Sprache 36, Starcky RB lxiv 201 n. 3) - **Palm** Sing. abs. *hpṭyn* CIS ii 3906 (Lat. par. *[op]tio*) - ¶ subst. m. adjudant, aide-de-camp, cf. also Clermont-Ganneau RAO viii 119f.

hpṭyq (< Greek ὑπατικός, cf. Cantineau Gramm 156, Rosenthal Sprache 91) - **Palm** Sing. emph. *hpṭyq›* CIS ii 3945[2] - ¶ subst. m. of consular rank, title borne by Palmyrenian ruler, cf. CIS ii sub 3945 (for this text, cf. Ingholt PBP 133ff.).

hpk **Ph** Iᴘʜᴛ Impf. 3 p.s.m. (?, cf. v.Dijk VT xix 441 n. 6, 444f., Dahood Or xlviii 97; v. *ks›*) *thtpk* KAI 1[2] (cf. FR 150) - **OldAr** Qᴀʟ Impf. 1 p.s. *›hpk* KAI 222C 19; 3 p.pl.m. *yhpkw* KAI 222C 21 - **Palm** Qᴀʟ Part. act. pl.m. abs. *hpkyn* CIS ii 3913 ii 57 (Greek par. μεταβόλοι) - ¶ verb Qᴀʟ - **1)** to overturn, to upset; + obj., *yhpkw ›lhn ›š[› h]› wbyth* KAI 222C 21: may the gods overturn that man and his house; for KAI 222C 19, v. *ṭbh* - **2)** to exchange, to barter: CIS ii 3913 ii 57 (cf. e.g. Cooke NSI p. 337 :: Chabot sub CIS ii a.l.: = intrans., to go about); *dy hpkyn bmdyt›* = (those) who barter in the city - Iᴘʜᴛ to be overturned, to be overthrown (said of a throne): KAI 1[2] (cf. e.g. also Hillers TC 39, Demsky Lesh xxxiv 185f.) - // of *›pk*? (for litt., v. also s.v. *›pk*).

v. *ypq*$_1$.

hpstywn (< Greek ʿΗφαιστίων, cf. Cantineau Nab i 38f., ii 88) - **Nab** Sing. abs. *hpstywn* CIS ii 201[2] - ¶ subst. (v. however infra) of diff. interpret., poss. to be combined with next word: *hpstywn klyrk›* = hephaestonian chiliarch, high military title (cf. Clermont-Ganneau RAO vii 247ff.), or = n.p.?, cf. e.g. CIS ii sub 201, Negev RB lxxxiii 225.

hpq (< Greek ἱππικός, cf. Cantineau Gramm 156, Rosenthal Sprache 91) - **Palm** Sing. emph. *hpq›* CIS ii 3937[1], 3943[4] (Greek par. ἱππεύς) - ¶ subst. m. someone of equestrian rank, knight, important person (cf. Chabot sub CIS ii 3937).
v. *pyq›*, *hpqws*, *ḥpqws*.

hpqws (< Greek ἱππικός, cf. Cantineau Gramm 156, Rosenthal Sprache 91) - **Palm** Sing. abs. *hpqws* CIS ii 3940[3] - ¶ subst. m. someone of equestrian rank, knight, important person.
v. *hpq*, *ḥpqws*, *pyq›*.

hprk$_1$ (< Greek ἐπαρχία or ἐπαρχεία) - **Nab** Sing. cstr. *hprk* Syr xxxv 244[5] (:: Milik Syr xxxv 246: = Sing. cstr. of *hprk$_2$*); emph. *hprk›* IEJ xiii 119[4] (:: Negev IEJ xiii 120: = lapsus for *hprky›*) - ¶ subst. eparchy, government by an eparch; cf. *bšnt tlt lhprk bṣr›* Syr xxxv 244[5]: in the third year of the eparchy of B.
v. *hprky›*.

hprk$_2$ (< Greek ἔπαρχος, cf. Cooke NSI p. 231, Starcky RB lxiv 201 n. 3, HDS 157f., Schottroff ZDPV lxxxii 198 × Cantineau Nab i 38, ii 88: < Greek ὕπαρχος × Negev RB lxxxiii 225 (n. 110): < Greek ἵππαρχος) - **Nab** Sing. emph. *hprk›* CIS ii 173[5], 207[2,4], 214[2], 221[1], 790[2], RES 1196, 2024[2], J 6[2], 38[1] - ¶ subst. m. governor, prefect (or = commander of cavalry?, cf. Chabot sub RES 2024, Starcky HDS 157, Negev RB lxxxiii 225).
v. *hprk$_1$*.

hprky› (< Greek ἐπαρχία or ἐπαρχεία) - **Nab** Sing. abs. *hprky›* J 159[2], IEJ xiii 118[2], *hprkyh* CIS ii 964[2] - ¶ subst. eparchy, government by an eparch; cf. *šnt 85 lhprkyh* CIS ii 964[2]: the year 85 of the eparchy; chronology starting in the year 106 AD, the occupation of Bosra by the Romans.
v. *hprk$_1$*.

hptḥ **OffAr** Segal ATNS a.l.: the *hptḥ* in ATNS 63[4] prob. = subst. Sing. abs. < Iran. indicating a title (diff. context, uncert. interpret., cf. Naveh Or lvi 412: prob. = n.p.).

hptḥpt (< Iran., cf. Krael p. 228, Eilers AfO xvii 333, Henning BZAW ciii 138ff., Bogolyubov PaSb lxxx 21f., 25, Hinz AISN 110, Lipiński LDA 103 :: J.J.Rabinowitz Bibl xli 73: = compound < Greek ἑπτά + ἱππευτής (= sevenfold knight)) - **OffAr** Sing. emph. *hptḥpt›* Krael 8[2,3] - ¶ subst. of uncert. meaning, prob. title or function indication; Henning BZAW ciii 138ff.: = guardian of a seventh part, i.e. of one of the districts of a province (cf. also Porten Arch 44, Grelot DAE p. 240 n. a, Hinz NWAP 29, 46, AISN 110, Porten & Yardeni sub TADAE B 3.9), cf. also Bogolyubov PaSb a.l.: the seventh is one of the seven climes of the earth (= the country, the land) and also Krael p. 228; Frye Heritage 282 n. 91: = combination of Semitic and Iran. (= one in

charge of supplies/the treasury).
hṣdʾ v. *ṣdʾ*.
hṣl v. *ʾṣl$_2$*.
hr **OldCan** Sing. abs. *ḫa-ar-ri* EA 74[20] - **Ph** Sing. abs. *hr* KAI 14[17] - **Pun** Sing. abs. (?) *hr* CIS i 3914[4] - **Hebr** Plur. cstr. *hry* SSI i p. 58A 1f. (for this reading, cf. Naveh IEJ xiii 84, Weippert ZDPV lxxx 162, Lemaire RB lxxxiii 559, 566, Smelik HDAI 149 :: Lipiński OLP viii 93f. (div. otherwise): l. *-h* (v. *ʾrṣ*) + zero (*ry* being absent) :: Cross FS Glueck 301f.: l. *-h* (v. *ʾrṣ$_1$*) *ʿry* (= Plur. cstr. of *ʿr$_1$*); cf. also Miller SVT xxxii 321f. (n. 25)) - ¶ subst. mountain.
hrbh v. *rby$_1$*.
hrg$_1$ **Mo** QAL Impf. 1 p.s. *ʾhrg* KAI 181[11,16] (:: Michaud PA 38 n. 7: l. *ʾhrs* = QAL Impf. 1 p.s. of *hrs$_1$*) - **Samal** QAL Pf. 3 p.s.m. *hrg* KAI 215[3,7]; Impf. 3 p.s.m. *yhrg* KAI 214[26]; 2 p.s.m. + suff. 3 p.s.m. *thrgh* KAI 214[33]; 2 p.pl.m. *thrgw* KAI 215[5]; Inf. + suff. 3 p.s.m. *hrgh* KAI 214[34] (cf. however Euting with v.Luschan AS i 51: pro *lhrgh* l. *yhrgh* = QAL Impf. 3 p.s.m. + suff. 3 p.s.m., cf. also Lidzbarski Handb 261, Dion 305, 384 n. 26, Dahood Or xlv 383) - **OldAr** QAL Impf. 3 p.pl.f. *yhrgn* KAI 222A 24 (on this form, cf. Beyer ZDMG cxx 201, Degen ZDMG-Suppl i 704 n. 4, Huehnergard ZDMG cxxxvii 270 n. 18) :: Puech RB lxxxix 582f.: QAL pass./PUʿAL Impf. 3 p.pl.f. (= to be killed), cf. also Lipiński Stud 28: = Impf. 3 p.pl.f. of pass. conjugation of *hrg$_1$* (cf. however Fitzmyer CBQ xxxix 263) :: Hillers TC 71ff.: = HAPH Impf. 3 p.pl.f. of *rgg* (= to seduce), cf. also Kutscher with Greenfield ActOr xxix 12f. n. 39, Weinfeld DDS 125f. n. 5 :: Lemaire Hen iii 167, Syr lxii 33, 35: = HOPH Impf. 3 p.pl.f. of *rgg* (= to de desired, to be coveted) :: Gibson SSI ii p. 38: = QAL Impf. 3 p.pl.f. of *hrg$_2$* (= to show concern; cf. however Garbini OA xv 353) :: Epstein Kedem i 39: = QAL Impf. 3 p.pl.f. of *hrg$_3$* (= to be able, in the context: to be able to do their work) :: Kaufman Maarav iii 171f.: l. *ymlʾn* (= PAʿEL Impf. 3 p.pl.f. of *mlʾ$_1$*) - ¶ verb QAL to kill: KAI 222A 24; + obj. (people): KAI 181[11,16], 214[33,34] (:: Tawil JNES xxxii 480ff.: = to destroy, cf. also Teixidor Syr li 328), 215[3,5,7].
hrg$_2$ v. *hrg$_1$*.
hrg$_3$ v. *hrg$_1$*.
hrh **Hebr** Mas 449[1], 451[1], 452[1] - ¶ interj. behold.
hry$_1$ **OldAr** QAL Impf. 3 p.s.f. *thry* KAI 222A 21 - ¶ verb QAL to conceive, to become pregnant.
hry$_2$ **Hebr** SM 49[21,23] - ¶ interj. behold.
hrkpṭ v. *hdrpṭ*.
hrs$_1$ **Mo** QAL Part. pass. s.m. abs. *hrs* KAI 181[27] (× Segert ArchOr xxix 224f., 226, 233, 241, xxxi 335: = *hrs$_2$* (= subst. ruins)) - ¶ verb QAL Part. pass. destroyed (said of a town).

v. *hrg*$_1$.
hrs$_2$ v. *hrs*$_1$.
hš **Pun** Plur. abs. (?, v. infra) *hšm* Hofra 101[3] - ¶ subst. (?) of unknown meaning in the combination *p'l hšm* = manufacturer of ... (or = *h* (= *h*$_1$) + *šm*$_3$ of unknown meaning??, or *hšm* = subst. Sing. abs.??). Perhaps related with the unexplained expression *p'l 'š* CIS i 337[4], 2806[4] (cf. also CIS i 336[3] (*p'l '[*)??).
hšm v. *hš*.
hšt v. *mlk*$_5$.

W

w$_1$ v. *ww*.
w$_2$ conjunction, in the relevant dialects and languages mostly written *w*; for **Pun**, cf. Poen 930, 940: *u*, IRT 906[1]: *u* (cf. Levi Della Vida OA ii 74, Vattioni AION xvi 50, Aug xvi 550, Krahmalkov JSS xvii 70f., FS Cameron 61), IRTS 24[1]: *u* (cf. Levi Della Vida OA ii 75f., Krahmalkov RSF vii 175 × Vattioni Aug xvi 549 (div. otherwise): l. *uy*), IRTS 24[3]: *u* (cf. Levi Della Vida OA ii 76 × Vattioni Aug xvi 549, Krahmalkov RSF vii 175 (div. otherwise): l. *uy*), Aug xvi 553,65[5]: *u* (cf. Levi Della Vida OA ii 86, Vattioni Aug xvi a.l.), Poen 931: *y* (cf. L.H.Gray AJSL xxxix 77f., Sznycer PPP 58f., J.J.Glück & Maurach Semitics ii 104 :: Schroed 289f., 305 (div. otherwise): pro *mycthib* l. *mythib* (= *myṯb* (= HIPH Part. s.m. abs. of *yṯb*), Poen 933: *uy* (var. *u*), OA ii 83[3]: *uy* (cf. Vattioni AION xvi 40, Aug xvi 539, Krahmalkov FS Cameron 58 × Levi Della Vida OA ii 83f.: l. *uu*), IRT 889[1] (= KAI 179): *uy* (cf. Vattioni AION xvi 45, Aug xvi 551, cf. also Garbini StudMagr vi 10 × Février JA ccxli 467, Friedrich ZDMG cvii 297, Levi Della Vida OA ii 86, Röllig KAI a.l., Polselli OAC xiii 237 (div. otherwise): l. *u* × Krahmalkov JAOS xciii 62f.: l. *uu*), Poen 944: *ue* (var. *ui*), KAI 175[1]: ου; for **Samal**, cf. the orthography *w'* KAI 215[5,6,12] (cf. Ginsberg JAOS lxii 235f., cf. also Koopmans 72 (for l. 5; Koopmans 72f. with hesitation for ll. 6, 12), Greenfield Lesh xxxii 361 n. 9 (for l. 5), Dion p. 61f., 116, 175, Dupont-Sommer AH i/2, 3 (for l. 5; for l. 6 however not, cf. AH i/2, 2), Gibson SSI ii p. 84 (for l. 12; for ll. 5, 6 however not, cf. ibid. p. 83; ibid. p. 72: poss. also in KAI 214[13], v. however *'rṣ*$_1$), Segert AAG p. 64f. (for l. 5 (cf. Hopkins BSOAS xl 140, Degen GGA '79, 20, Contini EVO ii 203f.); however not for l. 6, cf. ibid. p. 527) :: e.g. Cooke NSI p. 176, 178, Faber ZDMG cxxxvii 279 (div. otherwise): l. *w* + *'gm*$_2$ (= variant of *gm*$_2$) in l. 5 (v. also *ḥy*$_2$, *snb*), cf. also Friedr 43*, Friedrich FS Landsberger 427, Garb 264; on this problem, cf. also Andersen & Freedman FS Fitzmyer 10); for

OffAr, cf. Warka 10, 11, 12, etc.: *ú-ma-ʾ*, Warka 12, 36: *u* (for *umaʾ*, cf. Garbini HDS 29); cf. Paik 272, Nisa 604^{4}, GIPP 35, 66, SaSt 24; cf. also *b* as lapsus for *w* in Krael 3^{15} - ¶ - **1)** and, passim; for the use in the so-called consecutive imperfect in Hebr. and Mo., cf. (for Mo.) Segert ArchOr xxix 229, 262; for this use in OldAr., cf. Degen AAG p. 114f. n. 21; for this use in DA, cf. Hoftijzer DA p. 296 (n. 23); for this poss. use in Ph./Pun., cf. Février HDS 191ff.; for the use in the so-called consecutive Perfect in Ph./Pun., cf. FR 266,2, cf. also Février HDS 191ff. - **2)** or; *mlk bmlkm wskn bs<k>nm* KAI 1^{1}: a king among kings or a governor among governors; *br wbrh ly ʾḥ wʾḥh ly* Krael 8^{4}: a son or a daughter of mine, or a brother or a sister of mine; etc., etc.; *lh hwšr ly spr wmndʿm* Herm 5^{4}: he did not send me a letter or anything else; *hn ḥy ʾnh whn mt ʾnh* Herm 5^{9}: whether I was alive or dead; for the par. of *ʾw* and w_2, cf. *lkm ʾw lbnykm wlmn zy ...* Cowl 20^{14}: to you or your sons or whomsoever ... - **3)** but, however; *wʾdr ʿly mlk d[n]nym wškr ʾnk ʿly mlk ʾšr* KAI $24^{7f.}$: the king of the D. had power over me, but I hired the king of Assyria against him; *ʾm ʾmḥʾnk bry lʾ tmwt whn ʾšbqn ʿl lbbk ...* Aḥiq 82: if I chastise you, my son, you will not die, but if I leave (you) to your own heart ...; etc. - **4)** as so-called *waw explicativum*, namely, so; *ntnt ly ksp [šqln 4] ... wyrbh ʿly ksp ḥlrn 2 lksp š 1 lyrḥʾ ... wthwh mrbyt kspk ḥlrn 8 lyrḥ 1* Cowl $11^{1ff.}$: you have given me the sum (of 4 shekels) ... and interest shall be due from me at the rate of 2 *ḥ*. for the sum of one shekel per month, so that the interest on your money shall be 8 *ḥ*. each month - **5)** as so-called *waw apodosis* - a) between *casus pendens* and the rest of the clause, *wmy bl ḥz ktn lmnʿry wbymy ksy bṣ* KAI $24^{12f.}$: and as to him who had never seen linen from his youth, in my days byssus covered him (v. ksy_1); *ʾnt wgrdʾ zyly ʿbydh lʾ ʾyty lk* Driv 12^{9}: as for you, you have no business with my domestic staff; *hʾ wyʾtw ʾlwh ʾlhn* DA i 1: as to him, the gods came to him (v. also $hʾ_1$); *btḥtyh wmnʿlʾ kwyn ptyḥn tmh* Cowl 25^{6}: at the south side there are open windows above (sc. in the wall; cf. Hoftijzer VT ix 316, v. also $ʿl_1$, $ptḥ_1$, *tḥtyh*); cf. also *kṣʾty mbytk wšlḥty ...* TA-H $16^{3f.}$: as soon as I left your house, I sent ... - b) introducing a principal clause which follows on a subordinate one, *kmʾš qrʾt rbty bʿlt gbl wšmʿ ql* KAI $10^{7f.}$: when I invoked my lady the Mistress of Byblos, she heard (my) voice; *hn kn ʿbdw ʿd zy ʾgwrʾ zk ytbnh wṣdqh yhwh lk qdm YHW ʾlh šmyʾ* Cowl $30^{27f.}$: it they do thus so that this temple be rebuilt, (then) you will have a merit before YHW the God of Heavens; for comparable texts, cf. Grelot Sem xx 33ff., Or xxxvi 176, RB lxxxii 291f. - **6)** (in order) that (after imper or juss), *ptpʾ hb lh ... wyʿd ptkrn ...* Driv $9^{1f.}$: give a provision to him ... that he may execute sculptures ...; etc.; *mdʿm ʾl tzbny bkst wtšry lh* Herm 1^{10}: do not buy anything as clothing to send it to her (cf. Herm $2^{6f.,10,14}$,

4^7) - **7)** introducing a circumstantial clause, *wl› ›kl ›mr ... wspr› znh bydk* Cowl $10^{11f.}$: I shall have no power to say ... while this deed is in your hand - **8)** introducing direct speech, *›mr ›ḥtk bš› wšlm ›t* KAI 50^2: your sister B. says: are you in good health? (cf. Dupont-Sommer PEQ '49, 54, Röllig KAI a.l.), cf. also the beginning of the real letter after the introductory formula, *›l ›lyšb w‹t ntn lktym* TA-H $1^{1f.}$: To E., and now give to the K. (cf. also TA-H 2^1, 3^1, $5^{1f.}$, etc.) - **9)** *w ... w*, introducing two paratactic clauses of which the first one is of circumstantial or conditional nature, *w›nh ymyn sb l› khl hwyt bydy wsbltny* Krael 9^{17}: when I an old man was unable to use my hands, she supported me; *w›hk bdyn wl› ›ṣdq* Cowl 8^{22}: and if I go into court, I shall not win my case; etc. - Schroed 291, L.H.Gray AJSL xxxix 77f.: transcription *u* in Poen 945 (cf. however Sznycer PPP 127).
v. *›w*, *›z*$_2$, *ṣ›n*, for *›p ... w*, v. *›p*$_2$.

w› v. *w*$_2$.

w›z v. *›z*$_2$.

w›sh (prob. < Egypt., cf. Grelot DAE p. 131 n. d) - **OffAr** Sing. abs. *w›sh* Cowl 42^8 - ¶ subst. (?) of unknown meaning, used in description of garment.

wbl v. *ybl*$_1$.

wgr **OffAr** Sing. cstr. *wgr* LA ix 331^1 - **Nab** Sing. emph. *wgr›* J 11^2 (:: CIS ii sub 211: l *pgr›* = lapsus for *kpr›* (= Sing. emph. of *kpr*$_4$), cf. also Levinson NAI 202), 12^7 (cf. Cantineau Nab i 46); + suff. 3 p.s.f. *wgrh* CIS ii 183^2 (= Syr xxxv 227) - ¶ subst. m. - **1)** stela, betyle: CIS ii 183^2 (cf. Milik Syr xxxv 230, cf. however idem LA ix 22 (n. 14), cf. also O'Connor JNES xlv 216 n. 17, 219) - **2)** rock tomb: J 11^2, 12^7 (:: Levinson NAI 164: in both instances = stela) - **3)** uncert. meaning in LA ix 331^1, Milik LA ix 336f.: = monument (or "tomb construction" preferable??) - for the problems of etymology (< Arab.?), cf. Milik Syr xxxv 230, Gawlikowski Ber xxi 6 (n. 7), Segert AAG p. 107, 532, O'Connor JNES xlv 216f.

wd$_1$ v. *wd›*.

wd$_2$ v. *›ḥd*$_4$.

wd› **Palm** Sing. abs. *wd›* PNO 52ter a 3, b 3, Inv xii $45^{3,7}$ (:: Aggoula Sem xxix 116, Teixidor Sem xxx 62: = Plur. emph. of *wd*$_1$(= friend)) - ¶ subst. praise (:: Starcky sub PNO 52ter: *lwd›* = contraction of *l*$_5$ + *›wd›* (Sing. abs.) = in honour of, cf. also Bounni & Teixidor sub Inv xii 45); *dy glp ‹lt› lwd› dy yrḥbwl* PNO 52ter b 2ff.: who has sculpted the altar in honour of Y. (cf. PNO 52ter a 3, Inv xii 45^3). Context of Inv xii 45^7 unclear (*wd› l‹lm›* = praise/honour forever??).

wddh v. *mwddw*.

wdy v. *ydy*$_1$.

wdyy **Hebr** SM 49^{21} - ¶ adv. certainly.

wdm v. *dm*$_1$.

wdʿy **OffAr** diff. word (uncert. reading) in JAOS liv 31[3]. Torrey JAOS liv 32: = QAL Pf. 3 p.s.m. of *wdʿy* (= to lay out < Arab. *wdʿ*) + obj. (cemetery??, v. *nwyšh*); highly uncert. interpret.

ww **Pun** Sing. abs. *ww* CISFP i 909 - ¶ subst. nail (cf. Johnstone CISFP i 912); in some instances only *w* written, cf. Johnstone CISFP i 909, 912; on this word, cf. also Johnstone PEQ '77, 100f., Teixidor Syr lvi 376.

wzyk (< Iran., cf. Harmatta ActAntHung vii 351f., Grelot DAE p. 109 n. y, Hinz AISN 259) - **OffAr** Sing. emph. *wzykʾ* Cowl 81[31,32] - ¶ subst. draught-horse, cf. Harmatta ActAntHung vii 351f., Grelot DAE p. 109 n. y.

wḥd v. *yḥd*$_1$.

wḥy v. *twḥyt*.

wṭrn ((< Greek οὐετρανός) < Lat. *veteranus*, cf. Cantineau Gramm 157, Rosenthal Sprache 92) - **Palm** Sing. abs. *wṭrn* CIS ii 3913 ii 5 (prob. reading), 83, 86; emph. *wṭrnʾ* Ber v 104[2] - ¶ subst./adj. - **1)** veteran: Ber v 104[2] - **2)** in the expression *ʿlm wṭrn* CIS ii 3913 ii 5, 86: *mancipium veteranum*, slave who has served at least in the city (here: Palmyra).

wy **Hatra** 9[1] (for the reading, cf. Altheim & Stiehl AAW ii 195) - ¶ interjection, woe, alas (poss. interpret.).

wywmhlkʾn (< Prakrit, cf. Benveniste JA ccliv 450, Kutscher, Naveh & Shaked Lesh xxxiv 129) - **OffAr** *wywmhlkʾn* JA ccliv 440[6] (for the reading, cf. Shaked JRAS '69, 119, Kutscher, Naveh & Shaked Lesh xxxiv 129 (reading however *[wy]...*), Dupont-Sommer JA ccliv 440, 460 (reading however *wywmh[ʾ]lkʾn*)) - ¶ subst. (declensional form) of/for the old people.

wky v. *tk*$_1$.

wkl v. *kl*$_1$.

wld$_1$ v. *yld*$_2$.

wld$_2$ v. *yld*$_2$.

wly$_1$ v. *yly*.

wly$_2$ **Palm** Milik DFD 192f.: in RTP 705 pro *ply* = word of unknown meaning (cf. Caquot RTP p. 141) l. *wly* = Sing. abs. of *wly*$_2$ (= proximity > close relationship with a deity), highly uncert. interpret.; cf. also (Caquot with) du Mesnil du Buisson TMP 477: l. *wly* = *wly*$_4$ (= fittingly).

wly$_3$ **Nab** J 373 - **JAr** MPAT-A 30[3] (= SM 26), v. infra - ¶ interj.; in J 373 in the combination *bly wly*, v. *bly*$_3$; in MPAT-A 30[3] at the end of a synagogue inscription in the combination *ʾmn ʾmn slh wly ʾmn* (cf. also Dothan EI viii 185, Naveh sub SM 26, Sokoloff Maarav i 81: *wly* in this combination = fitting :: Fitzmyer & Harrington sub MPAT-A

26, Dothan HT 54, Hüttenmeister ASI 167: = *w* + *l*$_5$ + suff. 1 p.s.).
wly$_4$ v. *wly*$_2$.
wnqpr v. *nqpr*.
wspzn (< Iran., cf. Driv p. 64, Benveniste JA ccxlvi 62, Eilers AfO xvii 334, Nober VD xxxix 286) - **OffAr** Sing. m. abs. *wspzn* Driv 7^{3,7} - ¶ adj. of various kinds (said of craftsmen); Benveniste JA ccxlvi 63: or (less prob.) for various types of work (said of craftsmen: non-specialized).
wpdt v. *pdy*. *wpr* v. *pdy*.
wprt v. *pdy*.
wpt v. *pt*$_1$.
wqy$_1$ v. *qny*.
wqp **Nab** QAL (?) Pf. 3 p.s.m. *wqp* CIS ii 185^2 - ¶ verb QAL (?) to consecrate + obj. (a stela) + *l*$_5$ (comm., l. 4).
wrd$_1$ v. *dr*$_1$.
wrd$_2$ cf. Frah iv 14 (*wrtʾ*): rose (< Iran., cf. Telegdi JA ccxxvi 241; cf. also Nyberg FP 66, Hinz AISN 270).
wrdt v. *mwddw*.
wrš v. *yrš*.
wršbr (< Iran., cf. Driv p. 67, Benveniste JA ccxlii 300, de Menasce BiOr xi 162, Eilers AfO xvii 334) - **OffAr** Sing. abs. *wršbr* Driv 1^2, 8^1 - ¶ subst. m. of uncert. meaning; Driv p. 67: forester (less prob. interpret. in context, cf. Grelot DAE p. 302f. n. g); Hinz NWAP 42, AISN 140: table-steward, store-keeper, quarter-master; de Menasce BiOr xi 162: riding a stallion (cf. already Driv^1 p. 26: > mounted officer; cf. also Grelot DAE p. 302f. n. g: or = rearing stallions (cf. also already Driv^1 p. 26; cf. also other propositions ibid.)); Rosenthal AH i/2, 10: = farm expert?; Porten & Yardeni sub TADAE A 6.5/11: = plenipotentiary.
wršh **Palm** Sing. emph. *wrštʾ* CIS ii 4176B 3, C 2, 4184^3 - ¶ subst. f. heiress (:: Lidzbarski Eph i 205, ii 275: *w* + *rštʾ* (= Sing. emph. of *ršh*$_2$ = (female) owner, cf. also Rosenthal Sprache 24) :: Lidzbarski Eph ii 275 n. 1: or l. *yrštʾ* (= Sing. emph. of *yršh*$_1$ (= heiress) or QAL Part. act. s.f. emph. of *yrš* with same meaning)) - Cantineau Gramm 40f., 150: < Arab., cf. also Blau PC 46 n. 2, Diem ZDMG cxxiv 251, cf. however Diem Or xlix 71.
wrt$_1$ v. *wrd*.
wrt$_2$ v. *qrt*$_1$.
wt v. *ʾyt*$_3$, *knt*$_1$, *lwh*.
wtdr **Pun** word of unknown meaning in Hofra 82^3; subst. or tribal name?
wtḥ v. *mšḥ*$_5$.

Z

z_1 **Ph** Sing. m. *z* KAI 1[1], 4[1], 10[5], 13[3], 14[3], 15, 18[3], Sem xxvii 32 i 3 (= Dir sig. 97 = Vatt sig. eb. 97), etc., etc., *z*ʾ KAI 30[2] (twice), ʾ*z* KAI 38[1], CIS i 88[2], 91[1], etc.; f. *z* KAI 10[10,11], 14[3,11], 26A ii 9 , 17, iii 7, 15, 17, 60[4,6], RES 250[1] (= DD 5), DD 9[1], 10[1], 11[1], KI 11[1], *z*ʾ KAI 10[6,12,14] (or in these instances = f. form of zn_5??, cf. also Ockinga WO xii 71f.), PW 84[1], ʾ*z* KAI 34[1] (= Kition B 45), CIS i 44[1] (= Kition B 40), 57[1] (= Kition B 2); Plur. ʾ*l*KAI 4[3] (:: Dahood Ps iii 142: = n.d.), 12[1], 14[22], 30[3] (for this prob. reading, cf. Puech Sem xxix 20, 22, RB lxxxviii 98 :: e.g. Albright BASOR lxxxiii 16, Dupont-Sommer RA xli 202, 205, Masson & Sznycer RPC 15, 18, H.P.Müller ZA lxv 106, 110: l. *z*ʾ :: Honeyman Irâq vi 107: l.]*m*ʾ), 40[3], CIS i 14[5], RES 827, EpAn ix 5[8] - **Pun** Sing. m. *z* KAI 72A 2, 80[1], 89[6], 101[1], Punica ivA 4[1], xii 15[1], 18b[1], etc., etc., ʾ*z* KAI 277[2], NP 54[1], ICO-Spa 16[1], *s* KAI 146[1], *st* KAI 118[1] (diff. context), 172[3], Trip 41[1], 52[2] (or = f.?), ʾ*st*CIS i 151[2] (?, cf. Clermont-Ganneau RAO vii 91 n. 2, Février JA ccxlvi 443, Amadasi sub ICO-Sard Np 2; for the context, v. also mʾ$\check{s}_1$), cf. Poen 930, 940: *syth*, PBR xxviii 54,7[3]: *syt* (cf. Levi Della Vida OA ii 86), Poen 937: *sith* (cf. Sznycer PPP 97 (:: Schroed 290, 312f., L.H.Gray AJSL xxxix 78: = $\check{s}_{10}$ + ʾt_6 + suff. 1 p.s. :: J.J.Glück & Maurach Semitics ii 111: = *z*ʾ*t* meaning "here")); f. *z* KAI 69[3,6,10], 79[8], 133[1], 134[1], 149[1], CIS i 3731[3], 3783[6], RES 183[5], etc., *š*ʾ Trip 40[1] (?; cf. Levi Della Vida LibAnt i 62; or = $\check{s}_{10}$ + ʾ*[*??), *st* KAI 72B 2, 129[2], 165[3], Punica ivA 6[4], 7[5], 9[2], xii 29[1] (= KAI 152[2]; cf. Chabot sub Punica ivA no. 6, 7, 9), ʾ*st*KAI 151[1] (:: Röllig BiOr xxvii 378: = ʾ$_9$ (= h_1) + *st*), cf. IRTS 20[1] (cf. Levi Della Vida OA ii 77, Vattioni Aug xvi 553): *syth*; Plur. ʾ*l*KAI 81[2,3,4], 137[2,4,5,6], 145[2] (?, uncert. and diff. context), 277[11] (for context, v. *kkb*), ʾ*l*ʾKAI 130[1], 139[2], cf. Poen 938: *ily* (for the form, cf. also Garr DGSP 84; :: J.J.Glück & Maurach Semitics ii 112f. (div. otherwise): l. *chily* = kʾ$_2$ + l_5) - **Mo** Sing. f. *z*ʾ*t* KAI 181[3] (on this form, cf. Blau Maarav ii 148f.) - **Hebr** Sing. m. *zh* KAI 189[1], 193[18] (cf. Torczyner Lach i p. 51, 59, Michaud PA 98, H.P.Müller UF ii 240, Reviv CSI p. 79, Lemaire IH i p. 104, Briend TPOA 143, Hoftijzer FS Hospers 85ff., Conrad TUAT i 622, Smelik HDAI 113 :: e.g. Albright BASOR lxi 12f., Elliger ZDPV lxii 68, de Vaux RB xlviii 193, Galling TGI 76, Gibson SSI i p. 38f., 41 (div. otherwise): l. *mzh* = Sing. abs. of *mzh* (= food, provisions) :: Galling TGI 76 (n. 5): or *mzh* = storehouse :: Albright BASOR lxxxii 20 (div. otherwise): l. *myh* (for the reading, cf. also Diringer Lach iii p. 333, Röllig KAI a.l.) = lapsus for *mydh* (= m_{12} (= mn_5) + Sing. + suff. 3 p.s.m. of *yd*) :: Albright BASOR lxxiii 19, 23 (div. otherwise): or l. *myh* = Sing. abs. (= rations, allowance (of food))), 196[2], 200[9], TA-H 13[2], HUCA xl/xli 151[3], Frey 900[2], 974[1], 978,

994[1], SM 75[3], DJD ii 22,1-9[12] (uncert. reading), 30[4,7,26], etc., *z>* EI xx 256[9,12,13]; f. *z>t* KAI 191B 1, 3, 196[10], *zwt* Mas 449[1], *zw* DJD ii 44[6] (cf. Pardee HAHL 132 :: Milik DJD ii a.l. (div. otherwise): l. *ḥzw* = Qal Imper. pl.m. of *ḥzy*$_1$), IEJ iv 104, v 221, vii 245 (sub E), *zw>* IEJ vii 245, EI xx 256[7] (cf. also Broshi & Qimron EI xx 258f.); Plur. *>lh*DJD ii 24B 18 (heavily dam. context), C 16, E 13, AMB 1[3], *>lw*SM 49[21,23], IEJ vii 241[1], DJD ii 45[7], *>ylw*SM 49[5], *hllw*SM 49[1,19,22]; *>h* (lapsus for *>lh*) Mas 454[2] - **OldAr** Sing. f. *z>t* Tell F 15 (cf. Zadok TeAv ix 122, Kaufman Maarav iii 147, Muraoka AN xxii 93f., 114 n. 89) - ¶ group of words with deictic function (prob. belonging to the same paradigm) - **1)** used as dem. pronoun - a) used attributively, *mqm z* KAI 10[14]: this place (cf. *macom syth*: Poen 930, 940); *‹m z* KAI 26A iii 7f.: this people; *mṣbt >z* KAI 34[1]: this tombstone; *šdyt >l* EpAn ix 5[8]: these fields; *>bn st* Punica ivA 9[2] (= KAI 152[2]): this stone; *mqdšm >l* KAI 81[4]: these sanctuaries; *hbt z* KAI 15: this temple; *hsml z* KAI 43[2]: this statue; *hyšbm >l>* KAI 130[1]: these benches; *hbmt z>t* KAI 181[3]: this high place; *>lnm hqdšm >l* KAI 14[22]: these holy gods; *hsmlm h>l* KAI 40[3]: these statues; *h‹t hzh* KAI 196[2]: now, at this moment; *hpsypws hzh* SM 75[3]: this mosaic; *ptḥy z* KAI 10[5]: this door of mine (v. *ptḥ*$_3$); *dwsts zh* DJD ii 30[26]: the above-mentioned Dostes; cf. also *ily gubulim* Poen 938: this region, with noun as attribute (cf. Sznycer PPP 102f. and Lat. par. *hisce ... regionibus* × FR 316B: = nom. clause) - b) used independently, *>z ytn lb‹l ...* KAI 31[1]: he gave this to B. ...; *z mṣbt skr lb‹lytn* RES 250[1f.] (= DD 5): this is the memorial stela of B.; *ṯ[‹]n z ltw‹lb* KAI 148[1]: this has been erected for T.; *wzh hyh dbr hnqbh* KAI 189[1]: and this was the way the breach was made; *zw šl rby gmly>l* IEJ iv 104: this is (the grave) of Rabbi G.; *zh ‹šh šlwm* Frey 978: Sh. made this; *>lw >rwnwt* IEJ vii 241[1]: these are the sarcophagi; *...]m>lw >bdw* DJD ii 45[7]: ...] of these have perished; *lšlw zh* JKF i 203[2]: the one this belongs to; *kz>t* KAI 196[10]: thus; *h‹pr šhzh* DJD ii 24C 9: this above-mentioned plot (cf. prob. also DJD ii 24B 12 and Milik DJD ii a.l.); for KAI 200[9], v. *ywm* (cf. also KAI 193[18]: *mzh* = from here (v. supra)) - **2)** used as nota relationis (only in the Byblian dialect of Phoenician, cf. also Healy CISFP i 664); *bt z bny yḥmlk* KAI 4[1]: the temple which Y. built; cf. KAI 1[1], 6[1], 7[1]; cf. Friedrich FS Dussaud 39-47 (cf. however Rosén ArchOr xxvii 188 (n. 6), 190) - for the use in Ph./Pun., cf. FR 288, 289, 293, 300 (cf. also Loewenstamm CSBA 74f.); for Mo., cf. Segert Arch Or xxix 205, 218, 231, Andersen Or xxxv 90 - poss. transcription in KAI 174[7] εσαθ (cf. Milik MUSJ xxxi 10, Röllig KAI a.l. (cf. also Garbini ISN 61 n. 38); cf. however Sznycer Sem viii 8 (div. otherwise) l. ηδεσαθ = Sing. f. abs. of *ḥdš*$_3$, cf. also Ferron MC 76f.) - Vattioni AION xvi 42: *is* in IRT 865 = *z*$_1$ (highly uncert. interpret.) - Levi Della Vida OA ii 86: l. *syth* (= *z>t*) in PBR xxviii

54,7[3f] (*syt* at the end of l. 3 and *h* at the end of l. 4 to be combined); highly uncert. interpret. - Dupont-Sommer JKF i 211: l. *zh* (= Hebr. in J.Ar. context) in AMB 7b 4 (improb. reading, cf. Naveh & Shaked AMB a.l.: l. *nh* = part of n.p.) - for Hofra 43[5], v. *ndr*$_2$.
v. *ʾlw*$_1$, *ʾš*$_1$,*ʾškmst*, *gzt*, *hʾ*$_1$,*hn*$_3$, *zy*, *zky*$_2$, *mḥzt*, *mlk*$_5$, *qbr*$_3$, *š*$_{10}$, *št*$_6$.

z$_2$ v. *ʾz*$_2$, *zy*.

z$_3$ v. *zz*.

zʾ$_1$ v. *hʾ*$_2$,*z*$_1$.

zʾ$_2$ v. *znh*.

zʾb v. *ʾzb*.

zʾt v. *hʾ*$_1$,*hn*$_3$,*z*$_1$.

zʾtʾ v. *ʾnth*$_2$.

zb v. *zph*.

zbb v. *dbb*.

zbwn **Palm** Sing. emph. *zbwnʾ* CIS ii 3913 ii 6 - ¶ subst. m. buyer.

zbwqh **Palm** Sing. emph. *zbwqtʾ* Ber ii 78[2], 101[6f.] - ¶ subst. corner, recess.

zbzb cf. Frah i 11: sun (cf. Nyberg FP 61).

zbḥ$_1$ **Pun** QAL (or sometimes PIʿEL?) Pf. 3 p.s.m. *zbḥ* (or *šbḥ*?, cf. also Chabot sub Punica xi 20) Punica xi 20[1], *zbʾ* (or *šbʾ*?) Punica xi 32[3], *zʿbʾ* (or *šʿbʾ*?) Punica xi 19[1] (prob. QAL), *zwbʿ* Punica xi 18[1], *zʾb* Punica ii 1[1] (= Punica xi 25), *zb* Punica xi 34[1], *šbḥ* Punica xi 31[1], *šʿbʾḥ* (prob. QAL) Punica ix 9b 2, *šbʾ* Punica xi 21[1f], *šʿbʾ* (prob. QAL) Punica xi 26[1f], 27[2], (for these forms, cf. Chabot sub Punica xi 35); Impf. 3 p.s.m. *yzbḥ* KAI 69[15], CIS i 3915[4]; 3 p.pl.m. *yzbḥ* KAI 69[16]; Inf. cstr. *zbḥ* KAI 69[14] (on this text, cf. Krahmalkov RSO lxi 75f.) - **Samal** QAL (or PAʿEL?) Impf. 3 p.s.m. *yzbḥ* KAI 214[15,16,21] - **OffAr** QAL Part. act. s.m. abs. *zbḥ* FX 136[15]; cf. Frah xix 12 (*yzbḥwn*), GIPP 37, SaSt 24 - ¶ verb QAL (or sometimes PIʿEL/PAʿEL?) to offer as a sacrifice, to sacrifice, passim; + obj. + *l*$_5$: FX 136[15f.]; + indirect object, *wyzbḥ hdd* KAI 214[15f.]: and he will sacrifice to H.; + *l*$_5$ + *b*$_2$, *lʿdn bʿlmn zʾb bmlk* Punica ii 1[1]: he has sacrificed to the lord B. as a *molk* (v. *mlk*$_5$), cf. Punica xi 18[1f], 19[1f.], 20[1f.], 21[1f], etc. - in BAr-NS i-ii 228 ii 1 prob. QAL Pf. 3 p.s.m. (*zbḥ*), cf. Février BAr a.l. (or = Sing. cstr. of *zbḥ*$_2$?) :: Garbini AION xxv 261: = Sing. abs. of *zbḥ*$_2$ (diff. context) - Février BAr a.l.: the *šʿb* (uncert. reading) in BAr-NS i-ii 224[2] poss. = QAL Pf. 3 p.s.m. of *zbḥ*$_1$ (uncert. interpret.).
v. *nṣb*$_1$, *tbʾh*.

zbḥ$_2$ **Ph** Sing. abs. *zbḥ* KAI 26A ii 19, C iv 2, 37B 9 (or cstr.?, dam. context); cstr. *zbḥ* KAI 26A iii 1, C iv 4 (dam. context) - **Pun** Sing. abs. *zbḥ* KAI 69[4,8,14], 74[2,3], etc.; cstr. *zbḥ* KAI 69[12], 74[9] - **OffAr** Sing. abs. *dbḥ*ATNS 72b 3 (?, heavily dam. context); + suff. 1 p.s. (or Plur. cstr.?) *dbḥy*Krael 16G 3; Plur. abs. *dbḥn*Cowl 30[28], 31[27] - ¶ subst. m. sacrifice,

offering, passim (with collective meaning in KAI 26A ii 19); cf. - **1)** *zbḥ ymm* KAI 26A iii 1: annual sacrifice, cf. e.g. Dupont-Sommer RA xlii 173, FX 150, O'Callaghan Or xviii 179, Röllig KAI a.l., Teixidor Syr lii 288, Bron RIPK 99, Amadasi Guzzo VO iii 100, Gibson SSI iii p. 51, 61, cf. also de Moor NYC i 10, ii 29, AOAT xvi 58f., Lipiński SV 49, H.P.Müller TUAT i 643 :: Pedersen ActOr xxi 54: a regular sacrifice (cf. Dahood Bibl xliv 72: a seasonal sacrifice) :: Obermann Conn xxxviii 29, Leveen & Moss JJS i 192, Haran VT xix 372f., TTS 312f. (n. 40), Lipiński RTAT 259 (n. 71): a daily sacrifice :: Gordon JNES viii 111, 115: *zbḥ ymm ʾlp* = a sacrifice of the thousand days? (cf. Alt WO i 283, 287) - **2)** for *zbḥ ṣd*, v. *ṣd₁* - **3)** *zbḥ šmn* KAI 69[12], 74[9]: oil offering (cf. also Kaiser TUAT i 265, Delcor Sem xxxviii 92f.) - **4)** *zbḥ bmnḥt* KAI 74[10]: an offering in the form of a *minḥa* (v. *mnḥh₁*; cf. KAI 69[14]) - **5)** for *bʿl (h)zbḥ*, v. *bʿl₂* - cf. also *zbḥ šmš* KAI 277[4f.], CIS i 13[1] (= Kition A 27) and *zbḥ ššm* KAI 43[4] (cf. e.g. Röllig WO v 113, Avigad & Greenfield IEJ xxxii 126: *ššm* prob. lapsus for *šmš*), prob. names of months (cf. e.g. CIS i a.l., Cooke NSI p. 59, Röllig KAI 43 a.l., Garbini ArchClass xvi 69f., Amadasi sub Kition A 27, Lipiński RTAT 250 (n. 24)), or name of a festival in special month?, cf. v.d.Branden OA iii 252f., BiOr xxxvi 202, Koffmahn BZ x 203, Teixidor Syr xliv 171, li 317, cf. also Nober VD xliii 204, Vattioni Bibl xl 1013, Fischer & Rix GGA '68, 69, Gibson SSI iii p. 137f., Bonnet SEL vi 104 (cf. also Roschinski TUAT ii 604) - Dion p. 30, 130: the second *zbḥ* in KAI 214[16] = Sing. cstr. of *zbḥ₂*.
v. *zbḥ₁*, *zbḥh*, *špḥ₁*.

zbḥ₃ **Ph** Plur. abs. *zbḥm* KAI 37A 9 (= Kition C 1 A) - **Pun** Sing. abs. *zbḥ* KAI 62[6], 120[3] (Lat. par. *flamen*), 121[1] (Lat. par. *flamen*), 126[4] (Lat. par. *flamen*), 159[5], RES 332[3]; Plur. abs. *zbḥm* KAI 120[2] (Lat. par. *flaminib(us)*) - **Hatra** Sing. emph. *dbḥʾ*164[2] - ¶ subst. m. sacrificer (prob. high priestly function, cf. Lat. par. to Punic texts *flamen* (v. also *špṭ₂*) and Levi Della Vida FS Friedrich 313, Safar Sumer xviii 48 n. 44, Teixidor Syr lii 265f., Huss 544 n. 347 (cf. also Peckham Or xxxvii 313, Masson & Sznycer RPC 47f.) and cf. Février RA xlii 84f.: development from lower function to a higher one); cf. *zbḥ lk[l hʿ]t* KAI 126[4], Lat. par. *flamen perpetuus* (title of emperor Vespasian), cf. also Angeli Bertinelli CISFP i 256 - Milik DFD 26: l. Sing. abs./emph. *dbḥ(ʾ)* in MUSJ xlii 177[8] (less prob. interpret., cf. Teixidor MUSJ a.l.: l. *rbḥ* (= nomen familiae) - for *dbḥʾ dmlkʾ* Hatra 164[2]: the sacrificer of the king, v. also *mlk₃* - Aggoula MUSJ xlvii 17: the *dbḥʾ* in Hatra 47[2]: = Sing. emph. of *dbḥ₂* (= *zbḥ₃*; less prob. interpret., cf. Safar Sumer ix 244, Caquot Syr xxxii 53: = n.p.).

zbḥh **Samal** Sing. abs. *zbḥh* KAI 214[18,22] (cf. Hoffmann ZA xi 234, Donner KAI a.l. :: e.g. Cooke NSI p. 168: = Sing. + suff. 3 p.s.m. of *zbḥ$_2$*?(cf. also Dion p. 152)) - ¶ subst. f. sacrifice.

zbl$_1$ v.Soden Or xxxvii 269, xlvi 197, AHW s.v. *zabbīlu* (cf. also CAD s.v. *zabbilu*, Salonen Hausgeräte i 249): = basket > Akkad. (less prob., cf. Kaufman AIA 111: < Akkad., cf. also Zimmern Fremdw 34).

zbl$_2$ **Ph** Sing. abs. *zbl* EpAn ix 5^4 - ¶ subst. prince; *šd zbl* EpAn ix 5^4: the field of the prince.

zbl$_3$ **JAr** Plur. emph. *zblyyh* SM 70^8 - ¶ subst. dung heap.

zbl$_4$ v. *byn$_2$*.

zbn$_1$ **OffAr** QAL Pf. 3 p.s.m. + suff. 3 p.s.m. (or f.?) *zbnh* Krael 13^5 (or PA ʿEL?); 1 p.s. *zbnt* Krael 4^3, 9^3, Herm 2^{11}, 3^{10}, SSI ii 28 rev. 4; 3 p.pl.m. *zbnw* Cowl 42^5 (or PA ʿEL?); 2 p.pl.m. *zbntwn* NESE i 11^5; 1 p.pl. *zbn* Krael 12^{4,12}; Impf. 3 p.s.m. *yzbn* Cowl 42^6, Herm 2^{16}; 2 p.s.f. *tzbny* Herm 1^{10}; Imper. s.m. *zbn* Cowl 42^5 (or PA ʿEL?, cf. Porten & Yardeni sub TADAE A 3.8); s.f. *zbny* Herm 6^5; pl.m. *zbnw* RES '45, 67^4; Inf. + suff. 3 p.s.m. *mzbnh* NESE i 11^5 (for the reading and interpret., cf. Naveh & Shaked JAOS xci 379, 381, Degen NESE i 17, Golomb BASOR ccxvii 52f., Porten Or lvii 78, Porten & Yardeni sub TADAE A 3.10 :: Lindenberger APA 250 n. 328: = PA ʿEL Inf. :: Shunnar CRM ii 281f., 287: pro *lmzbnh* l. *ʿl mzbnh* :: Macuch JAOS xciii 59f.: pro *lmzbnh* l. *ʾl mzbnh* :: Shunnar GMA 115, 117: pro *lmzbnh* l. *ʿl mzbnwk* (= QAL Part. pass. s.m. + suff. 2 p.s.m.: what you have bought?)); Part. act. s.m. abs. *zbn* Herm 2^{14}; PA ʿEL Pf. 3 p.s.m. *zbn* Cowl 42^{11} (highly uncert. reading, cf. also Porten & Yardeni sub TADAE A 3.8, or QAL?), Krael 3^{25}, 12^{32,35}; 3 p.pl.m. + suff. 3 p.s.f.? *zbnwh* ATNS 67b 4 (or = QAL??, heavily dam. context; on the form, cf. Bennett Or lvi 88); 1 p.pl. *zbn* Krael 3^{3,7,10}, etc., etc.; *zbnʾ* Samar 4^9, 8^7 (*zbn[ʾ]*),^{9} (*[z]bnʾ*); + suff. 3 p.s.m. *zbnhy* Krael 3^5; Impf. 2 p.s.m. *tzbn* Krael 12^{24}; 2 p.s.f. + suff. 3 p.pl. *tzbnyhmw* KAI 270B 2 (:: Grelot DAE p. 138 (n. f): = QAL); 2 p.pl.m. *tzbnwn* Cowl 25^{11,14}; Inf. *zbnh* Cowl 9^6; + suff. 3 p.s.m. *zbnwth* NESE iii 48^{13} (cf. for form *mzbnw* PaSb ii 146 n. 36); cf. Frah xxi 16, 17 (*zbnwn, mzbnwn*), Paik 327 (*zbn*), 328 (*zbnw*), 613 (*mzbnw*), GIPP 59, 68, cf. Lemosín AO ii 108, Toll ZDMG-Suppl viii 38 - **Nab** QAL Pf. 3 p.s.m. *zbn*?? CIS ii 323^4 (or PA ʿEL?); Impf. 3 p.s.m. *yzbn* CIS ii 197^6, 198^5 (or PA ʿEL?), 199^5, 220^2, 224^9, J 38^7 (for the last three texts :: Cantineau Nab ii 91: PA ʿEL); PA ʿEL Pf. 1 p.s. *zbnt* DBKP 22^{31}; Impf. 3 p.s.m. *yzbn* CIS ii 197^6, 198^4 (or QAL?), 199^5, 200^3 (= J 30, for the reading *y[z]bn*, cf. Milik sub ARNA-Nab 79), 206^4, 209^5, 214^5; Part. act. s.m. abs. *mzbn* CIS ii 200^6 (= J 30; for the reading, cf. Milik sub ARNA-Nab 79); ITP Impf. 3 p.s.m. *ytzbn* CIS ii 208^4, *yztbn* J 5^5 - **Palm** QAL Pf. 3 p.pl.m. + suff. 3 p.s.m. *zbnwhy* Inv vi 11b (= RIP 132B 2; or PA ʿEL?, cf. Aggoula Syr liv 283 × Cantineau Inv vi a.l., Gawlikowski RIP a.l.: = Plur. + suff. 3 p.s.m. of *zbn$_2$* (= his purchases) :: Milik DFD 287: = his merchandise); Impf.

3 p.s.m. *yzbn* CIS ii 3913 ii 133; PA ʿEL Pf. 3 p.s.m. *zbn* RIP 51[1] (= Inv xii 14); Impf. 3 p.s.m. *yzbn* Ber v 133[3] (or QAL?); Part. act. s.m. abs. *mzbn* CIS ii 3913 ii 46; Part. pass. s.m. abs. *mzbn* CIS ii 3913 ii 136 (or ITP??, cf. Cantineau Gramm 86); ITP Impf. 3 p.s.m. *yzbn* CIS ii 3913 ii 5, 56 (cf. Cantineau Gramm 92, Rosenthal Sprache 56f.); Part. s.f. abs. *mtzbn*ʾ CIS ii 3913 ii 132 - **Hatra** PA ʿEL Impf. 3 p.s.m. *lzbyn* 344[4,9] (*lzby[n]*) - **JAr** QAL Pf. 3 p.s.m. *zbn* MPAT-A 12[5] (= SM 71 (for the reading, cf. Naveh Lesh xxxviii 298, SM a.l.) :: e.g. Sukenik ASPG 72, Frey sub 1195, Barag IEJ xxii 148, Hüttenmeister ASI 52: pro *dzbn* l. *dybn*? = *dy*$_2$ + *bn* (= QAL Pf. 3 p.s.m. of *bny*$_1$));1 p.s. *zbnt* MPAT 68[7], DBKP 21[28], IEJ xxxvi 206[3]; Part. act. m. s. emph. *zbnh* MPAT 51[8,9] (diff. reading, cf. Milik RB lxi 183, Beyer ATTM 320 :: Milik Bibl xxxviii 264, 268, Fitzmyer & Harrington MPAT a.l. (div. otherwise): pro *drm zbnh* l. *drm*ʾ (v. *drm*) *bnh* (= QAL Part. pass. s.m. abs. of *bny*$_1$);v. infra); pl.m. emph. *zbny*ʾ MPAT 52[9], *zbnyh* MPAT 45[8]; PA ʿEL Pf. 1 p.s. *zbnt* MPAT 43[5], 51[3,5], 52[7], IEJ xxxvi 206[5] (*zbn[t]*), *zbynt* MPAT 39[5]; Inf. *mzbnh* MPAT 52[9] (:: Fitzmyer & Harrington MPAT p. 317: QAL), *zbnh* MPAT 52[3] (or = Sing. abs. of *zbnh*??; dam. context); Part. s.m. emph. *mzbnh* MPAT 44 i 6, 52[11], IEJ xxxvi 206[6]; pl.m. abs. *mzbnyn* MPAT 46[2] - ¶ verb QAL to buy, passim (Part. act. = buyer: MPAT 45[8], 51[8,9] (:: Milik RB lxi 184: = the (plot) purchased), 52[9]) - **1)** + obj.: Krael 13[5], Herm 2[14,16], 3[10], 6[5], CIS ii 224[9], J 38[7], MPAT-A 12[5] - **2)** + obj. + *b*$_2$: Herm 1[10] (v. *b*$_2$ sub 5) - **3)** + obj. + *l*$_5$ (comm.): Herm 2[11], NESE i 11[5] (beginning of line; for the reading of the context, cf. Porten Or lvii 79f., Porten & Yardeni sub TADAE A 3.10) - **4)** + double obj., *zbntwn hmw* ʿ*bwr* NESE i 11[5]: you have bought corn for it (sc. the silver mentioned earlier in the context, cf. Degen NESE i 18) - **5)** + *b*$_2$ (instrum.), *zbnt bgṭh* MPAT 68[7]: I have acquired (it) by the writ - **6)** + *b*$_2$ (*pretii*): Krael 9[3] - **7)** + *b*$_2$ (*pretii*) + *mn*$_5$: Krael 12[4] - **8)** + *l*$_5$ (comm.) + obj.: SSI ii 28 rev. 4 - **9)** + *mn*$_5$, *zbnt mn* ʾ*wbyl* Krael 4[3]: I have bought from Ubil (cf. Krael 12[12], RES '45, 67[4], IEJ xxxvi 206[3], DBKP 21[28] - **10)** + *mn*$_5$ (part.) + obj. + *l*$_5$ (comm.): RIP 51[1f.] - PA ʿEL to sell, passim (Part. act. = seller: MPAT 44 i 6, 52[11], IEJ xxxvi 206[6]) - **1)** + obj.: NESE iii 48, KAI 270B 2, CIS ii 200[6] (for the reading, cf. ARNA-Nab 79), 206[4], 209[5], 3913 ii 46 - **2)** + obj. + *l*$_5$ (comm.): Krael 3[5], cf. Cowl 25[11] - **3)** + obj. + *l*$_5$ (comm.) + *b*$_2$ (*pretii*): MPAT 52[7] - **4)** + *l*$_5$ (comm.): Cowl 25[14], Krael 3[7,25], 12[32], IEJ xxxvi 206[5], Samar 4[9], 8[9], cf. also CIS ii 3913 ii 136 - **5)** + *l*$_5$ (obj.): Hatra 344[4] - **6)** + *l*$_5$ (comm.) + obj.: DBKP 22[31] - **7)** + *l*$_5$ (comm.) + *b*$_2$ (*pretii*): Krael 12[24], MPAT 43[5] (dam. context) - 8) + *l*$_5$ (comm.) + *l*$_5$ (obj.): MPAT 51[3] - **9)** + *mn*$_5$ (part.) + obj.: Hatra 344[9] - ITP to be sold - Sach p. 238: l. poss. a form of this root (*zbyn*) in Sach 77 iii 1 (uncert. reading, dam. and diff. context) - Vattioni Aug x

498: l. *zbn* in CIS ii 27^2 (= PA ʿEL Pf. 3 p.s.m.), highly uncert. reading, cf. CIS ii a.l., Del sub 18.
v. *ʾb$_1$*, *zbn$_2$*.

zbn$_2$ **JAr** Sing. cstr. *zbn* MPAT 51^{7,11} (*[z]bn*)^{,13}, SM 43^3 (= Frey 1165 = MPAT-A 11; for the reading, cf. Naveh SM a.l.), DJD ii 23^6 (for this uncert. reading, cf. Beyer ATTM 312); emph. *zbnʾ* MPAT 50c 1 (heavily dam. context, cf. Milik DJD ii p. 148), *zbnh* MPAT 52^{12} - ¶ subst. m. describing as well the act of purchasing as the act of selling (translation being dependent of context), or two different subst.? (one meaning purchase // QAL of *zbn$_1$*,one meaning sale // PA ʿEL of *zbn$_1$*);*ršy ʾlʿzr bzbn bth dk* ... MPAT 51$^{6f.}$: E. is given authority by the purchase of that house ... (cf. however Beyer ATTM 320: E. has authority over everything that comes within the sale ...); *mlyn lʾyty ly* ... *bzbn bth dk* MPAT 51$^{12f.}$: there are no claims for me ... on account of the sale of this house; *lqymʾ zbnh dk qdm[kn]* MPAT 52^{12}: to confirm that purchase for (you) - Segal ATNS a.l.: l. *zbnʾ* (Sing. emph. of *zbn$_2$*) in ATNS 44 ii 1 (improb. reading., cf. Porten & Yardeni sub TADAE B 8.2: l. *bnš* = part of n.p. (prob. reading and interpret.)) - Segal ATNS a.l.: l. poss. *zbnʾ* (Sing. emph.) in ATNS 54 i 8 (heavily dam. context, diff. reading; Segal ATNS a.l.: or l. *zrnʾ/zdnʾ* without interpret.??).
v. *zbn$_1$*, *zbnh*.

zbn$_3$ **Nab** Plur. abs. *zbnyn* CIS ii 186$^{3f.}$ - **Palm** Sing. abs. *zbn* CIS ii 3913 i 10; Plur. abs. *zbnyn* CIS ii 3913 i 6, 3932^5 (or l. *zbnn*?, cf. Cantineau Inv iii p. 31), 3949^3 (*[z]bnyn*), DFD 13^3 (*zb[nyn]*); emph. *zbnyʾ* CIS ii 3913 i 4 - ¶ subst. f. (once m.: CIS ii 3913 i 4, cf. Rosenthal Sprache 78f.) - **1)** time, moment in time; *zbnyn šgyn* CIS ii 3913 i 6: several times (Greek par. πλειστάκις), cf. CIS ii 186$^{3f.}$, 3932^5, DFD 13$^{3f.}$ (*bzb[nyn] šgyʾn wrbrbn*, Greek par. ἐν πολλοῖς καὶ μεγάλοις καιροῖς); *ʾrkwnyʾ dy hwn bzbn zbn* CIS ii 3913 i 10: the archonts who shall be (sc. in office) at any time (Greek par. τοὺς τυγχάνοντας κατὰ καιρὸν ἄρχοντας) - **2)** time, period of time; *bzbnyʾ qdmyʾ* CIS ii 3913 i 4: in former times (Greek par. ἐ[ν τ]οῖς πάλαι χρόνοις) -
v. also *zmn$_2$*.

zbn$_4$ **OffAr** word of unknown meaning in ATNS 43b ii 2, v. also *šbzbn*.

zbnh **OffAr** Sing. emph. *zbntʾ* Krael 12^{31} - ¶ subst. f. sale/purchase (cf. *zbn$_2$*); *sprʾ* ... *zy ktb ln bgzšt spr zbntʾ zy zbn ln* Krael 12$^{31f.}$: the document ... which B. wrote for us as document of sale (that is to say) that he sold us (:: Milik RB lxi 251: *zbntʾ* = the object which is sold, sc. the house).
v. *zbn$_1$*.

zbnwt **Hebr** Sing. abs. *zbnwt* DJD ii 42^4 (for the reading, v. infra) - ¶ subst. f. purchase; *bzbnwt* DJD ii 42^4: by purchase (for the reading, cf. I.Rabinowitz BASOR cxxxi 21f., Ginsberg ibid. 26, Bardtke ThLZ lxxix

300f. :: Milik DJD ii a.l.: l. *mzbnwt* = mn_5 + *zbnwt* (= by purchase) :: de Vaux RB lx 270, 272: l. *mn* (= mn_5) *bnwt* (= Plur. abs. of bnh_1)= as everybody knows (cf. Pardee HAHL 123f.: l. *mn bnwt* or *bn bnwt* without interpret.) :: Sonne PAAJR xxiii 86f., 89: l. *mn* (= mn_5) *bnwt* (= Plur. abs. of bt_2)= a group of villages surrounding a town (in the context: Bet-Mashko (cf. Birnbaum PEQ '55, 24, 33: = from daughters, cf. J.J.Rabinowitz with Yeivin At i 97 n. 12)) :: Lehmann & Stern VT iii 391, 393: l. *mn* (= mn_5) *bzwt* (= Plur. abs. of *bzh*)= from spoils :: Yeivin At i 97: l. *mn* (= mn_5) *knwt* (= Sing. abs. of *knwt*) = in very truth?).

zbr₁ **Pun** Plur. abs. *zbrm* KAI 137^6 - ¶ subst. m. vessel (prob. meaning).

zbr₂ v.Soden Or xxxvii 269, xlvi 159: = thyme > Akkad. *zambūru*, cf. however CAD s.v., Meissner ZA vi 294, Zimmern Fremdw 56.

zgp v. gbh_1.

zd v. *bl*$_1$.

zdh **Hebr** Sing. abs. *zdh* KAI 189^3 - ¶ subst. of uncert. meaning; for the diff. interpret., cf. e.g. Blake JAOS xxii 55ff., Röllig KAI a.l., Jepsen MiOr xv 3, Gibson SSI i p. 22f., del Olmo Lete UF x 44: = fissure, hole; Albright ANET 321: = overlap; Stoebe ZDPV lxxi 132ff.: = contact, meeting; Michaud VT viii 297ff., ix 205ff.: = ardour, excitement (cf. also Shea FUCUS 431, 433f.; cf. however Stoebe VT ix 99ff.); H.P.Müller UF ii 232ff. (with other etymology than Michaud): = excitement; Puech RB lxxxi 201ff.: = resonance (cf. also Briend TPOA 118, Conrad TUAT ii 556; cf. already Prätorius ZDMG lx 403: echo (cf. also Israel FS Martini 164)); for older interpret., cf. also Dir p. 86ff., Mosc p. 41f.

zdq v. $ḥdy_5$, $ṣdq_3$.

zh₁ v. z_1.

zh₂ v. *znh*.

zhb **Hebr** Sing. abs. *zhb* KAI 191B 1; cstr. *[z]hb* Mosc var. 11 (= SSI i p. 17B) - **Samal** Sing. abs. *zhb* KAI 215^{11} - **OldAr** Sing. abs. *zhb* KAI 216^{11} - **OffAr** Sing. abs. *zhb* Cowl 30^{28} (:: Joüon MUSJ xviii 78: = n.p.), 39^4, Aḥiq 193, *dhb*Cowl 10^9; emph. *zhb*ʾ Cowl 30^{12}, 31^{11}, ATNS 52b ii 3 (diff. reading); cf. Frah xvi 1 (*dḥb*), 4 (*dḥb*ʾ), Frah-S₂ 102 (*zḥb*), ZDMG xcii 442A 15, GIPP 38, SaSt 26 - **Nab** Sing. abs. *dhb*BASOR cclxiii 77^1; emph. *dhb*ʾRB lxxiii 244^1 (diff. and dam. context) - **Palm** Sing. abs. *dhb*CIS ii 3948^3, cf. Inv D 51^1: δααβ (for the context, v. gbn_2; for this interpret., cf. Milik Syr xliv 290, cf. also Beyer ZDMG-Suppl 3-1, 651 :: Levi Della Vida FDE '22-23, 376f., du Mesnil du Buisson sub Inv D 51 (div. otherwise): l. δααβα (= Sing. emph.) :: Aggoula Sem xxxii 110: = d_2 + QAL Pf. 3 p.s.m. of $ʾhb_2$ (= variant of *yhb*)); emph. *dhb*ʾCIS ii 3945^4 - **JAr** Sing. abs. *dhb*MPAT-A 5^4 (= Frey 1203 = SM

64), 26^9 (= Frey 856 = SM 32) - ¶ subst. m. gold; *[z]hb ʾpr* Mosc var. 11: gold of Ophir; *ḥmšh dynryn dhb* MPAT-A $26^{8f.}$: five golden dinars.
zhr **OffAr** ITP Imper. s.f. *ʾzdhry* Herm 2^{17}, 4^8; pl.m. *ʾzdhrw* Cowl 21^6 (this form poss. also in RES 492A 1 (for this poss. reading, cf. Lidzbarski Eph ii 401)) - ¶ verb ITP - **1)** abs., to take heed: Cowl 21^6 (cf. Grelot VT iv 360) - **2)** + b_2, to take care of: Herm 2^{17} - 3) + b_2 + mn_5, to protect (someone) against; *ʾzdhry bbytʾlntn mn ḥbb* Herm $4^{8f.}$: protect B. against Ch., cf. Hayes & Hoftijzer VT xx 105f., Porten & Greenfield JEAS p. 158f., Porten & Yardeni sub TADAE A 2.1 :: Bresciani & Kamil Herm a.l., Grelot DAE p. 161: pay attention to B. from the side of Ch. (cf. also Gibson SSI ii p. 138f.: on account of Ch.) :: Swiggers Aeg lxi 65ff.: pay attention to B. out of love (v. $ḥbb_2$) :: Milik Bibl xlviii 553: pay attention to B. (that he does not go to) the river (v. $ḥbb_2$) - the diff. *ʾzhr* in Beh 51 poss. = variant of or lapsus for *ʾzdhr* (= ITP Imper. s.m.), cf. also Greenfield and Porten BIDG 47 (Akkad. par. *ú-ṣur ra-man-ka*).
zw v. z_1.
zwʾ v. z_1.
zwg v. mzg_2.
zwd v. *nwr*.
zwz v. *zz*.
zwy **JAr** Beyer ATTM 329, 567: l. *zwy* in MPAT 89^4 (= corner), highly uncert. reading and interpret.
zwyh (cf. Marrassini FLEM 23ff., Kaufman AIA 90f.) - **OffAr** Sing. cstr. *zwyt* Cowl 5^5; + suff. 3 p.s.m. *zwyth* Cowl 5^4 - ¶ subst. corner; *mn zwyt byty* Cowl 5^5: from the corner of my house (cf. Cowl 5^4).
zwk **OffAr** Shaked Or lvi 410: l. poss. *zwk* in ATNS 52a 9, b i 10 (resp. Sing. cstr. and abs.) = group, heap (< Iran.), uncert. interpret., poss. reading (Segal ATNS a.l.: l. *zrk* poss. = certain type of solid measure).
zwl **OffAr** QAL (cf. e.g. Barth OLZ '12, 11, Seidel ZAW xxxii 293 :: Arnold JBL xxxi 26: = PAʿEL, cf. Leand 39g) Imper. pl.m. *zwlw* Cowl 38^8; Inf. + suff. 2 p.s.f. *mzlky* Krael 5^7 (for this interpret., cf. Krael p. 184 :: Milik RB lxi 249f.: = QAL Inf. of *ʾzl*) - ¶ verb QAL uncert. meaning, poss. = to sell + obj.: Cowl $38^{8f.}$ (in Krael 5^7 + obj. + acc. instrum.), cf. e.g. Cowl p. 137 (: or = to remove?, cf. Porten & Greenfield JEAS p. 46, 82: = to transfer; cf. Porten & Yardeni sub TADAE A 4.3: to lavish), cf. also Koopmans 114: = to sell at a bargain, Porten & Yardeni sub TADAE B 3.6: to traffic (with)?; cf. also Grelot DAE p. 226 (n. f), 393 (n. k): to estimate, to make a low estimate of.
zwlh **Hebr** Sing. + suff. 3 p.s.m. *zwltw* AMB 4^{19} - ¶ subst., poss. meaning removal, in the prepositional expression *mn zwltw* AMB 4^{19}: from someone else (?, diff. context).

zwmlyt **JAr** Naveh sub Mas 420[4]: *zwmlyt* poss. = nickname (= Sing. abs. of *zwmlyt* (= soup-ladle) < Greek ζωμάρυστρον? (highly uncert. interpret.)).

zwn$_1$ **OffAr** QAL Impf. 3 p.s.m. *yzwn* AM ii 174[5] (diff. context); PA ʿEL Pf. 3 p.s.m. *zyn* FuF xxxv 173[7,12] (diff. and uncert. context) - **JAr** ITP Part. s.f. abs. *mtznh* MPAT 41[10] (for the reading, cf. already Birnbaum MarDeed 19f. :: Birnbaum JAOS lxxviii 15ff. (div. otherwise): l. - a) *ymtynh* = APH Impf. 3 p.s.m. + suff. 3 p.s.m./f. of *mtn$_1$* (= to attend) - b) l. *wmtynh* = *w* + QAL Part. pass. s.f. abs./s.m. emph. of *mtn$_1$* - c) l. *wmtynh* = *w* + Sing. f. abs./m. emph. of *mtyn* (= adj. slow, careful)), 42[15]; pl.f. abs. *mtznn* MPAT 42[11] - ¶ verb QAL to feed (?, cf. Henning AM ii 174, Bivar & Shaked BSOAS xxvii 288f., cf. however Altheim & Stiehl Suppl 96, ASA 269: = to present, Vinnikov PaSb vii 206: = to adorn, to decorate) - PA ʿEL Altheim & Stiehl FuF xxxv 173, ASA 245, 269: = to feed, to strengthen; in both instances in the comb. *zyn zyn*ʾ ʾ*rwst* - ITP to be nourished: MPAT 41[10], 42[11,15].

zwn$_2$ **OffAr** Sing. abs. *zwn* Cowl 10[10,17] - **Nab** Sing. abs. *zwn* BASOR cclxiii 77[1] - ¶ subst. provisions - on the *zwn* in BASOR cclxiii 277[1], cf. also Jones BASOR cclxxv 42.

zwp v.Soden Or xxxvii 269, xlvi 197, AHW s.v. *zūpu*: = hyssop or majorana (origanum) > Akkad. (cf. however CAD s.v. *zūpu*: connect with Aramaic).

zwph v. *zph*.

zwt v. *z$_1$*.

zz (< Akkad., cf. Zimmern Fremdw 21, Kaufman AIA 114, Conn xix 123) - **Hebr** Sing. abs. *zwz*DJD ii 22,1-9[4], 30[21]; Plur. abs. *zwzyn* EI xx 256[6] - **OffAr** Sing. abs. *zwz*Cowl 2[15] (*zw[z]*, for the reading, cf. Porten & Yardeni sub TADAE B 4.4), 3[17] (for the reading, cf. Porten & Yardeni sub TADAE B 4.3; dam. context), 43[3] (for the reading, cf. Yaron Lesh xxxi 287, JSS xiii 203, xviii 277, Porten JNES xlviii 176, Porten & Yardeni sub TADAE B 5.5 :: Cowl a.l.: l. *r 1 1* (*r* being abbrev. of *rb*ʿ$_3$) :: Porten Arch 271 n. 15: = 2 zuz, cf. also Grelot DAE p. 90 (n. f): = 2 z(uz)), Krael 3[6,15,18], 7[17], 8[8] (for the reading in the Krael instances, cf. Yaron Lesh xxxi 288, JSS xiii 203, xviii 277, cf. also Porten & Greenfield JEAS p. 40, 42, 54, Grelot RB lxxxii 290, Porten & Yardeni sub TADAE B 3.4 a.e. :: Krael a.l.: l. *1 r 1* in Krael 3[6,15,18], 8[8] and *11 r* in Krael 7[17], *r* being abbrev. of *rb*ʿ$_3$, cf. Krael p. 39), Herm 2[6], 6[4], RES 957[8], Sem xxiii 95 verso 2 (= AECT 58); Plur. abs. *zwzn*Cowl 81[22,27,44,124], RES 957[1,4], REJ lxv 18[3], BASOR ccxx 55[3]; cf. Frah xvi 6 (*zwzn* :: Ebeling Frah a.l.: l. also *gryn* = Plur. abs. of *gr$_3$*), Frah-S$_2$ 105 (*zz*), BSOAS xxiv 353 (*zwzn*), IrAnt vii 148 (*zwzyn*, cf. also Bogoliubov PaSb lxxxvi 101f.), FS Nyberg 271 ii (*zwzyn*), iii (*zwzn*), 274 viii (*zwzn*), 275 xii (*zwzn*), xiii (*zwzn*), GIPP 68 - **Palm**

Sing. abs. *zwz*Sem xxxvi 89[5,7]; Plur. abs. *zwzyn*CIS ii 3934[5], Syr xiv 184[2], *zwzyyn* Sem xxxvi 89[1] (lapsus?) - **JAr** Plur. abs. *zzyn* MPAT 36[2], *zwzyn*MPAT 39[4], 41[5], 48[2] (*zw[z]yn*),[3,4], 51[6], 52[7], Mas 554[2] - ¶ subst. m. certain type of weight/coin; for Egypt in the fifth century BC prob. weight corresponding to a half shekel (v. *šql*$_3$), cf. Yaron Lesh xxxi 287, JSS xiii 203, Couroyer RB lxxvii 465 n. 2; *ksp zwz lkrš 1* Krael 3[6]: silver of a purity of 95 percent (cf. Yaron Lesh xxxi 287f., JSS xiii 202f.; cf. also Cowl 43[3], Krael 3[15f.,18], 7[17], 8[8], for the reading of these texts, v. supra); *ksp š 6 wzwz ksp zwz* Herm 2[6]: 6 1/2 shekel silver, of a purity of 95 percent (cf. Yaron JSS xiii 202f. :: Bresciani & Kamil Herm a.l.: 6 shekel and 1 zuz, a silver zuz (cf. also Grelot DAE p. 154) :: Milik Bibl xlviii 582: 6 shekel and 1 zuz (in coins?) of silver zuzes (cf. also Gibson SSI ii p. 133f.)) - in **Palm** and **JAr** (late Hebrew) a coin with the value of an Attic drachm = *denarius* = 1/4 shekel (for **JAr**, cf. also Ben-David PEQ '71, 109ff.); *bksp 40 zwz* DJD ii 22,1-9[4]: for the sum of 40 drachms (cf. DJD ii 30[21]); *ksp zwzyn m'h* MPAT 48[3]: a sum of 100 zuz (cf. MPAT 36[2], 39[4], 41[5], 48[2,4], 52[7], cf. also *bksp zwzyn dy hwn tmn[y]'* MPAT 51[5f.]); for the problems of Sem xxxvi 89, cf. Gawlikowski Sem xxxvi 93ff. - Lemaire Sem xxvi 37: l. *z*(= *zz*) on Mosc pes. 21 (= Lach iii 353f. no. 46), Sem xxvi 36 xi, 37 xii (uncert. interpret., cf. Diringer Lach iii 354f.: = *zayin* or mark, cf. also Scott BASOR clxxiii 62: l. *z* = poss. *z'r* (= Sing. m. abs. of *z'r*$_2$)) - Scott BASOR clxxiii 61: the sign on Mosc pes. 19, 20 (= Lach iii 353f. no. 49, 50) prob. no *zayin* but mark (cf. Diringer Lach iii 355: l. *z* or *š* (= *šlšt* (= 1/3)) or mark, cf. also idem PEQ '42, 96: prob. = no *zayin*, Kaufman BASOR clxxxviii 40: prob. = hieratic mark (8)) - Nyberg FP 120: *zz* in Frah-S$_2$ 105 = abbrev. for *zwzn* - Périkhanian REA-NS a.l.: the *z* in REA-NS viii 9 = abbrev. of *zz*, prob. interpret. - for the use of *zwz* as weight, cf. also Syr xlvii 375 (inscr. on silver bowl, around 500 AD) *mn zwzyn 105* IrAnt vii 148: from (silver weighing) 105 zuz (cf. also Azarpay & Henning IrAnt a.l.) - Lemaire & Vernus FS Brunner 309: the *z* in FS Brunner 303 i 3 prob. = abbrev. of *zz* (highly uncert. interpret.), the same abbrev. in FS Brunner 303 i 9 (?) and 323 iii 11.

zzr v. *zpr*.

zḥl (for the root, cf. Rabin IOS ii 362ff., cf. also Blau PC 54f.) - **OldAr** QAL Impf. 3 p.s.m. *yzḥl* KAI 223C 6; 2 p.s.m. *tzḥl* KAI 202A 13 - **OffAr** QAL Pf. 1 p.s. *dḥlt* Aḥiq 45; Impf. 2 p.s.m. *tdḥl*Aḥiq 54; 1 p.pl. *ndḥl*Cowl 37[7]; cf. Frah xxi 1 (*dḥllwn*:: Ebeling Frah a.l.: reading *y'rrwn* (= form of *'rr*$_2$)also poss.) - **Palm** QAL Impf. 3 p.s.m. *ydḥl*PNO 2ter 10; Part. act. m. s. cstr. *dḥl*Inv x 62[2], 74[2], Syr xix 77[2], SBS 47B 1, 90B 1 (heavily dam. context), DFD 13[3], pl.m. cstr. *dḥly*CIS ii 3930[3] (cf. Greek par. ἀρέσαντας), 3931[4], *dḥl'*CIS ii 3914[3] - **Hatra** QAL Pf. 3 p.s.m. + suff. 3 p.s.f. *dḥlh*31[4] (cf. Milik DFD 366, Vattioni IH a.l., v. also *'mr*$_2$ ::

Safar Sumer viii 188 (n. 21): l. *rḥlh* = QAL Pf. 3 p.s.m. + suff. 3 p.s.m. of *rḥl*$_1$ (= to fear, to venerate)); Part. act. m. s. cstr. *dḥl*200[8] - ¶ verb QAL - **1)** to be afraid, to fear: KAI 202A 13 (cf. also Greenfield Proc v CJS i 181ff., 185ff., Ross HThR lxiii 8f.), Aḥiq 45, 54 - a) + obj.: Cowl 37[7] (?, v. *bzz*$_2$) - b) + *mn*$_5$, to recoil from: KAI 223C 6 (for the interpret. of the context, cf. Veenhof BiOr xx 142f.) - **2)** to fear, to venerate (sc. god(s)); - a) + obj.: Hatra 31[4] - b) + *l*$_5$ (obj.): PNO 2ter 10 (for the context, cf. Gawlikowski TP 114f.); in the combination *dḥl* *ʾlhyʾ* Inv x 62[2], Syr xix 77[2] (Greek par. εὐσεβῆ): fearing the gods (i.e. pious, devout), cf. CIS ii 3914[3] (Greek par. εὐσε[βέσι]), 3930[3], 3931[4] (Greek par. εὐσεβεῖς), SBS 47B 1, DFD 13[3], Hatra 200[8].
v. *dḥyl*.

zy **Samal** *z*KAI 25[1] (cf. e.g. Dion p. 26, 157 (cf. also FR 293, Polselli RSF iv 139, Swiggers Or li 250) :: e.g. Röllig KAI a.l., Schuster FS Landsberger 440ff., Lipiński BiOr xxxiii 231: = *z*$_1$),214[3,4,22], *zy* KAI 214[1] - **OldAr** *zy* KAI 201[1,4], 202A 1, 16, 222A 5, 7, 25, 35, 37, 38, etc. - **DA** *zy* DA p. 267 no. 1 - **OffAr** *z*KAI 233[13] (cf. Degen GGA '79, 27), TH i 5, *zy* KAI 225[14], 228A 3, 5, 9, 10, 229[1], 231, 233[11,14,19], 234 vs. 1, Cowl 1[3,6], 3[12], Krael 1[3,5,6], Driv 2[2], 3[6], 4[1], ATNS 2[1], 3[6], 7[4], TA-Ar 41[1], Pers 4[4], 9[4], etc., etc., *dy* Cowl 13[7,11,16], Krael 3[12], 9[14], 12[30,31], Herm 1[4], 3[4]; cf. Frah xxiv 10, 15, 16 (*zy*), xxv 47 (*kzy*), xxviii 31 (*zy*), Paik 334, 337 (*zy*), Nisa 19[4], 20[1], 21[5], 22[1], 24[1], etc., Sogd B. 279, Ta passim, Ve 123, ML 602, Bb 141, ZDMG xcii 441[2], Syr xxxv 317[41], 319[46], GIPP 26, 39, 56, 68, SaSt 19, 27, etc., cf. also Warka 2, 29: *di*, 6: *di-ʾ* - **Nab** *zy* CIS ii 349[1,2,4], RES 1432[1] (on this form, cf. Levinson NAI 36f.), *dy* CIS ii 157[1,3], 158[2], etc., etc. - **Palm** *dy* CIS ii 3908[1], 3913 i 1, 2, Inv xi 100[4] (cf. Starcky SOLDV ii 514, RB lxxiii 616, Degen Or xxxviii 366 :: reading *dt*in Inv xi a.l.), etc., etc., *ry* (lapsus) CIS ii 4099[2], *d*CIS ii 3907[1], 3911[3], 3944[5], 4018[1], etc. - **Hatra** *dy* 3[1,2], 5[1], etc., etc. (cf. also Assur 3 ii 6, 4[2], 11 ii 1, etc.), *d*19[4], 25[1], 28[5], 29[5], etc., etc. (cf. also Assur 15a 3, 4, 17 ii, 21 ii 2, etc.) - **JAr** *zy* MPAT 48[3], 49 i 4, 5, 6, 7, 9, 89[3], *dy* MPAT 39[5,8], 40[5,7,10,16,19], 41[11], etc., etc., *d* MPAT 46[4], 53[3], 55[2], MPAT-A 1[3] (= SM 21), 2[1,3] (= Frey 1197 = SM 58), etc., etc., cf. PEQ '38, 238[2]: δα (cf. Peters OLZ '40, 218f., Beyer ATTM 353; cf. also Milik LA x 154f.) - ¶ **A)** introducing relative subordinate clause - **1)** verbal clause, *[n]ṣbʾ zy šm zkr* KAI 202A 1: the stele which Z. has erected (:: Rosén ArchOr xxvii 187f.: *zy* here = dem. pronoun; cf. Tell F 1); *ʿmwdyʾ ... zy hww tmh* Cowl 30[9]: the pillars ... which were there; *kspʾ zy ʾtwsp ʿl mks ptʾsy* ATNS 19[4]: the silver that was added to the tax of P.; *ywnyʾ wkrkyʾ zy tʾḥd* ATNS 26[5]: the Ionians and Carians that you will seize; *kl gšr zy yškḥ* Herm 2[15]: every beam which he can find; *ktnh zy ʾwšrty ly* Herm 4[4]: the tunic which you sent me; *ksph zy hwh bydy* Herm 2[4f.]: the silver which was in my possession; *[m]n ywm* *zy ʾzlt bʾrḥʾ zk* SSI ii 28 obv. 2: since the day you went on that way; *brbnwt ʿynʾ dy ʾḥd yrḥbwl ʾlhʾ* Inv xii 44[1f.]: during (his) supervision of the source for which function Y. the god had chosen (him); *bzmn dy tʾmr ly* MPAT 46[5]: on the time which you will say to me; *bmʿrth dzbnt bgṭh* MPAT 68[6f.]: in the cave which I had acquired by the writ; passim; cf. also relative clauses with deleted antecedent (the object the inscription is written upon being the "antecedent"), *zy šrʿʾ* DA p. 267 no. 1: (object) of Sh.; *dy bnh nṭyrʾl* RB xlvi 405[1]: (monument) which N. has built; *dy qrb nṭrʾl* ... CIS ii 174[1]: which N. has offered (cf. also CIS ii 4327[4f.], 4329B 4, 4330[5]); *dy bbly ... ktbyh* MPAT 62[13]: (document) which B. ... has written (cf. Greek par. Γερμαν[ὸς] ... ἔγραφα); etc.; for the comb. *ʾn zy/dy*, v. *ʾn*$_3$; for the comb. *ʾyk zy*, v. *ʾyk* - cf. also a) *mn zy/dy/d* + verbal clause, *wlmn zy ṣbyt tntn* Cowl 28[7]: and to whom you will, you may give (him); *kl mn dy yzbn* CIS ii 197[6]: whoever will sell; *mn dy yhwʾ mzbn* CIS ii 3913 ii 46: everyone who will sell ...; *mn dy yḥdnh* SBS 34[4]: whomsoever he will choose; *wmn dy lnsb ḥd mn grbʾ hlyn* Hatra 281[8ff.]: and whoever will take away one of these waterskins (?; v. *grb*$_3$); μαν δα ελαα σαβη PEQ '38, 238[1f.]: whom God wants (sc. to give it); *mn dy lbʿʾ* .... Assur 11 ii 2f.: whoever will pray ....; *kl mn dypth* MPAT-A 45[1]: and whoever will open ...; *mn dḥyh* AMB 9[5]: the One who lives (i.e. God), cf. AMB 15[18] - b) *m(h)/mʾ z(y)/dy*, + verbal clause, *wmz yšʾl* KAI 214[22f.]: and whatever he asks; *bkl mh zy ymwt br ʾnš* KAI 224[16]: in every case that a man dies; *mh zy lqḥt* Driv 12[9f.]: everything you have taken; *mh dy yʾtʾ lh mn ksp wdhb* BASOR cclxiii 77[1]: whatever comes to him of silver and gold (cf. also Jones BASOR cclxxv 42); *mh dy yštkḥ* BASOR cclxiii 78[3]: which was discovered (cf. Jones BASOR cclxxv 43); *wmdy ʾšr lʾgwrʾ* CIS ii 3913 i 9: and whatever is established with the tax farmer (cf. however Greek par. καὶ ἐπειδὰν κυρωθῇ τῷ μισθουμένῳ); *lṭʿwnʾ ʾqymt dy yhwʾ mtg[b]ʾ dnr mdy yhwʾ m[tʾʿl] ... ʾw mʾpq* CIS ii 3913 ii 109ff.: for a load I have ordained that a denarius should be levied (namely for) whatever is imported or exported (:: Reckendorff ZDMG xlii 388, 413, Cooke NSI p. 334, CIS ii a.l.: *mdy* = whenever), cf. also RIP 199[13] - **2)** + nominal clause, *ʾlh ... zy tṣlwth ṭbh* Tell F 5: the god ... to whom it is good to pray; *bytʾ zy tḥwmwhy ktybn mnʿl* Cowl 25[8]: the house whose boundaries are described above; *mdʿm dy lʾ msq bnmwsʾ* CIS ii 3913 i 8: everything which is not specified in the law; *lbth dyly dy ptyḥ ṣpn lgh drty* MPAT 51[3f.]: the house which belonged to me, which opens at the north side into my courtyard; *zwzyn dy hmwn tmn[y]ʾ* MPAT 51[6]: eight zuz; *dyn dʿynwh mšwṭṭn bkl ʾrʿʾ* MPAT-A 22[5] (= SM 70[13]): the Judge whose eyes range over all the earth; passim - cf. also - a) *mn zy/dy/d* + nom. clause, *mn dy šqlʾ ʾsryn tmnyʾ* CIS ii 3913 ii 112: one who takes eight *as*; *mn dy mpq* CIS ii 3913 ii 49: and whoever exports;

kl mn dyhyb plgw ... MPAT-A 22[2] (= SM 70[10]): whoever sets discord ...; *wmn drḥym lhwn* Hatra 35[7f.]: and whoever is beloved to them; etc. - b) *m(h)/m᾽ z(y)/d(y)* + nom. clause, *mh dy ‛l᾽ ktyb* CIS ii 199[6f.]: and what is written above; *mdy ktyb* CIS ii 3913 i 4: what is written (cf. also Syr xvii 351[10], 353[8]); for the context of KAI 276[7f.] (*m᾽ zy* ...), v. *prnwš* - **B)** introducing relative phrase (on this use, cf. also Kaddari PICS 104ff.; for Off.Ar., cf. Whitehead JNES xxxvii 128ff.) - **1)** *zy/dy/d* + noun (phrase) - a) indicating a possessive relation, *š‛rn zy br mlk᾽* CIS ii 39[1f.] (= Del 23 = AECT 9): wheat of the prince; *kl mlky᾽ zy sḥrty* KAI 224[7f.]: all the kings of my vicinity; *byt mdbḥ᾽ zy ᾽lh šmy᾽* Cowl 32[3f.]: the temple of the God of Heavens; *᾽wṣr᾽ zy mlk᾽* Krael 3[9]: the treasury of the king; *yqr᾽ dy bwl᾽ wdms* SBS 48B 7: the honour of (v. yqr_2) the Council and the People; *‛l ḥy᾽ dbnwh* Inv xi 33[6]: for the life of his sons; *šmy᾽ dmškn᾽* Hatra 79[11]: the standard (v. *sm᾽*) of the sanctuary; *rbyt᾽ dmrn* Hatra 195[2]: the majordomus of our lord; *šmhtwn wdbnyhwn* MPAT-A 34[4] (= SM 69): their names and (those) of their sons; etc. - with proleptic suffix, *᾽mhm zy ‛lymy᾽* Cowl 28[13]: the mother of the slaves; *‛bdh zy wrpby* (?) ATNS 9[3]: the slave of W. (for reading and interpret., cf. Porten & Yardeni sub TADAE B 8.6); *ṣyryhn zy dššy᾽* Cowl 30[10f.]: the hinges of the doors; *lyqrh dknyšth* MPAT-A 28[3] (= Frey 858): for the honour of the congregation; *lšmh drḥmnh* MPAT-A 22[10] (= SM 70[16]): in the name of the Merciful One - b) indicating non-possessive relations, *᾽bygrn᾽ zy ksp kršn ‛šrh* Cowl 20[14f.]: a fine of 10 k. silver; *‛mwdy᾽ zy ᾽bn᾽* Cowl 30[9]: the pillars of stone; *spr᾽ zy qymyhm* ATNS 27[3]: the document containing their covenants; *᾽bš[wn] zy gll* Pers 4[3f.]: a pestle of stone; *lbš 1 zy qmr* Krael 7[6]: a woollen garment; *qṣth zy ksp š 1* Herm 2[7]: her portion being 1 shekel silver; *[k]tn 1 zy ktn* SSI ii 28 rev. 4: one tunic of linen; *šṭr nbwkṣr ... zy tmrn* Irâq iv 18[1f.]: a document of N. ... concerning dates; *tmt šmh zy ᾽mtk* Krael 2[3]: Tamut by name who is your servant; *šṭr bnḥ ... zy šnt 3 dryhwš* Del 79: document concerning a gift (?, v. *bnḥ*) ... which is from the 3rd year of Darius; *‛ynt᾽ dy my᾽* CIS ii 3913 ii 63: wells of water; *ṣlm dy nḥš* SBS 48B 8: a statue of bronze; *ldkrnh dy ‛lm᾽* DFD 163[6]: for her eternal memory; *grmṭws dy trty᾽* CIS ii 3959[2]: scribe for the second time; *byrḥ nysn dy šnt 573* CIS ii 3938[5]: in the month N. of the year 573 (cf. Hatra app. 4[1f.]: *bnysn d 436* (or *456*?), etc., cf. Degen JEOL xxiii 410f. (n. 29)); *m‛rt᾽ dh dy bt ‛lm᾽* RIP 167[1]: this vault which (serves as) tomb; *yqrhwn dy bt ‛lm᾽* CIS ii 4121[2]: this magnificent tomb; *bywm 11 bnysn dšnt 421* Assur 17 ii 1f.: on the 11th day of (the month) N. in the year 421; etc. - **2)** *zy/dy/d* + name (phrase) - a) indicating possessive relation, *᾽rq᾽ zy nbw᾽tn* Del 83: the plot of N.; *8 šql ksp zy blšy* Lidzb Ass 5A 2: eight shekel silver of B.; *᾽gwr᾽ zy YHW* Cowl 30[6]: the temple of Y.; *kmry᾽ zy ḥnwb ᾽lh᾽*

Cowl 30[5]: the priests of the god Chn.; *kmry᾽ dy bl* Inv xi 100[2f.]: the priests of B.; *hykl᾽ dy mnwt* Inv xii 48[3]: the temple of M.; *mrbyn᾽ dy snṭrwq* Hatra 203[2]: the tutor of S.; *mwnyqh dswsyph* MPAT-A 27[1] (= SM 33): Monica (the wife) of S.; *br᾽ zy prsmn* FuF xxxv 173[1]: the son of P.; etc. - with proleptic suffix, *ʿbdyh zy mbtḥyh* Cowl 28[3]: the slaves of M.; *᾽bwhy zy ᾽srḥ᾽dn* Aḥiq 47: the father of A. (cf. also Samar 8[12]); *᾽bwh zy ᾽twr* Aḥiq 55: the father of Assur; *ḥtnh zy nbšh* Herm 6[3]: the son-in-law of N.; *᾽mh dy nbwzbd* RIP 37[6f.]: the mother of N.; *rbt᾽ dnny* Assur 15a 3: the majordomus of N.; *bnyhy dʿbdʿgylw* Hatra 80[10]: the sons of A.; *bbyth dnšryhb* Hatra 200[6f.]: in the house of N.; *bnwh dḥlpy* MPAT-A 22[1] (= SM 70[9]): the sons of Ch.; etc. - b) indicating a non-possessive relation, *dmwt᾽ zy hdysʿy* Tell F 1: the statue of H.; *᾽rmy zy yb brt᾽* Cowl 35[2]: an Aramean from the fortress Y.; *nbwšlm zy byt ʿdn* KAI 233[14]: N. from Bit-Adini; *kbbh zy pwšr* KAI 278[7]: K. (goddess) of P. (cf. Atlal vii 109[6]); *᾽bwd zy mṣryn* Syr xli 285[4]: Abydos in Egypt; *b᾽br[᾽] dy gml᾽ wʿn᾽* SBS 51[3f.]: of the wing of G. and A.; *hykl᾽ dy rb ᾽syr᾽* CIS ii 3913 i 10: the temple called R. (cf. Greek par. [ἱ]ερ[οῦ] λεγομένου ʽΡαβασείρη); *qlsṭ᾽ br šlm[n] dy mrql᾽* CIS ii 4565[1ff.]: Calistus son of Sh. also (called) Marcellus (cf. CIS ii 1365[2f.]); *ṣlm᾽ dy nny* Assur 15b 1: the image of N.; etc., cf. also *mlk gwzn wzy skn wzy ᾽zrn* Tell F 13: the king of G., S. and A. - **3)** *zy/dy/d* + prep. phrase, *ʿbdn hmw zly* KAI 233[13]: they are my servants; *khny᾽ zy byb byrt᾽* Cowl 30[1]: the priests in the fortress Y.; *ḥštrpn᾽ zy bkrk* FX 136[4f.]: the satrap in K.; *gnzbr᾽ zy bhrḥwty* Pers 43[5f.]: the treasurer in H.; *ʿl mn dbgwh* MPAT-A 45[3]: on the one who is within it; *šwq᾽ zy bynyn* Cowl 5[13]: the street between us; *ḥlq᾽ zyly* NESE i 11[2]: my portion; *᾽rq᾽ zyly* Cowl 6[5]: my plot; *byt᾽ zylk* Cowl 9[3]: your house; *plg᾽ dylk* Krael 9[14]: your half; *dgl[᾽] zy ln* ATNS 3[6]: our detachment (for the reading, cf. Porten & Yardeni sub TADAE B 8.10); *ʿbdy᾽ zylh* ATNS 4[4]: his slaves; *᾽lh᾽ zy lh* AE '23, 40 no. 2[5]: his god (for these and comparable Off.Ar. instances, cf. Swiggers FUCUS 458f.); *dnh kpr᾽ dy lhgrw* CIS ii 203[1]: this is the tomb of H.; *mh dy lk* MPAT 64 i 10: whatever is yours; *bth dyly* MPAT 51[3]: my house; *᾽rmlw dy lk* MPAT 41[11]: your widowhood; *bnyhy klhwn dlʿlm* Hatra 79[11f.]: all his sons for ever and ever; *w᾽sṭw᾽ dy lʿl mnh* Inv xii 48[2]: and the portico which is above it; *gys ... qṭrywn᾽ dy mn lgywn᾽* ... Inv xii 33[1]: Gaius ... the centurion from the legion ...; *zbyd᾽ ... dy mn bny mʿzyn* SBS 39[3f.]: Z. ... who belongs to the Benē M.; *ywsh ... dmn kpr nḥwm* MPAT-A 27[2]: Y. ... from Capernaum; *zbny᾽ dy mn ʿl᾽* MPAT 52[9]: the buyers who are (mentioned) above; *šhdy᾽ zy ʿl spr᾽ znh* Cowl 11[16]: the witnesses (mentioned) in this document; *ʿmrh zy ʿl mky* Herm 2[9]: the wool owed by M.; *ʿmwdyh dʿl mn kpth* MPAT-A 17[1f.]: the columns which are above the arches; *mṭll ... kl᾽ zy ʿm šyryt ᾽ šrn᾽* Cowl 30[11]: the whole ... roof with the rest of the woodwork;

w'sṭw' ... dy qdmwhy Inv xii 48[1f.]: the portico ... which is in front of it; etc. - **4)** + adverb, *wyhwdy' kl' zy tnh* Cowl 31[26]: and all the Judeans who are here (cf. also Cowl 30[24,26f.], 31[23]) - **5)** in the combination *dyd/dd* (prob. = dy_2 + d_3, cf. also Cantineau Gramm 131, Rosenthal Sprache 48), *bsṭr' dydh* MUSJ xxxviii 106[10]: on his side; *bn' ddhwn* Hatra 79[12]: their sons (cf. Teixidor Syr xli 280 n. 4 :: Safar Sumer xvii 15 n. 27, 17, Caquot Syria xl 6, GLECS ix 88: *ddhwn* = Sing. + suff. 3 p.pl.m. of dd_1);cf. also *šṭr' klh ... dydh dy 'kšdr'* CIS ii 4171[2]: the whole side of it ..., namely of the exedra - with proleptic suffix, *'l ḥyyhy ddh wd'ḥyhy* Hatra 20[2f.]: for his life and (that) of his brothers (cf. Milik RN vi/iv 54, Teixidor Syr xli 280 n. 4, Degen NESE iii 79 :: Safar Sumer vii 180 (n. 32): l. *ḥyy* (= Plur. cstr. of $ḥy_1$) *hyd*(?)*r*(?)*hwd* (= n.p.; cf. Caquot Syr xxix 99f.: l. poss. *hyrd hwr* = double n.p.) *'ḥyhy* = his brother :: Altheim & Stiehl AAW ii 198f.: l. *ḥyyhy* (= Plur. + suff. 3 p.s.m. of $ḥy_1$) + *d* + *rhwr* (= n.p.) + *'ḥyhy* (= his brother)) - **C)** introducing non-relative subordinate clause - **1)** verbal clause - a) subject/object/predicate in nominal clause, *wzy ygrnky ... yntn lky* Cowl 1[6]: whoever shall sue you ... shall pay to you; *zy t'bdwn lh l' ytkswn* Cowl 38[10f.]: what you do for him will not be hidden; *wzy ṣby y'bd lh* NESE i 11[3]: what he wants should be done for him; *wmhydh zy spr lh hwšrtn ly* Herm 5[7f.]: what is it that you did not send me a letter; *pqdwn dwšr' ... dy ... yt'bd* CIS ii 350[4]: it is the responsibility of D. ... that ... it should be done; *wb'yt mnk dy tnpq ly šṭr' ... hw* MPAT 64 i 9f.: and I requested of you that you produce for me that document of ...; *wyhw' mbṭl l'rkwny' ... dy l' yhw' gb'* CIS ii 3913 i 10f.: and it will be made the concern of the archonts ... that he will not levy; *mwd' hw ... dy lwt lh ...* MUSJ xxxviii 106[5f.]: he acknowledges ... that he has made him a partner; *kn 'mr zy šm' hwyt zy 'mr yhwḥnn* MPAT 49 i 5: he spoke thus: I have heard that Y. said ...; *ydy' yhw' lkn dy mnkn ''bd pr'nwt'* MPAT 59[3]: let it be known to you that I shall exact the punishment from you; etc.; cf. instances in clauses with deleted nominal predicate or verbal form, *wdy l' ytqbr bkpr' dnh lhn ...* CIS ii 208[3]: and (it is decided) that no one will be buried in this tomb, except ... (cf. CIS ii 208[4], 209[3], etc.; cf. also at the beginning of a letter after the address, *dy tšlḥwn ly yt 'l'zr* MPAT 56[4]: you are to send to me E. (cf. MPAT 36[1], 55[2], 57[2])) - b) functioning as "casus pendens", *wzy yld šmy mnh ... hdd ... lhwy qblh* Tell F 11f.: and whoever will efface my name from it ... may H. ... be his adversary; *wk't zy mlty lbty ... k't hlw kzy 'bd 'nh lḥrwṣ kwt t'bd bnt 'ly* Herm 1[6f.]: and now with respect to the fact that you are full of anger against me ... now as much as I am doing for Ch. thus may B. do for me - c) final/consecutive, *brktky lptḥ zy yḥzny 'pyk ...* Herm 1[2]: I bless you by Ptach that he may show me your face ...; *wyhb kpr' dnh l'mh ... dy t'bd kl dy tṣb'*

CIS ii 204[2f.]: and he gives this tomb to A. ... that she may do (with it) everything she wants; *dnh qbr› dy ‹bd ›rws ... dy ytqbr bqbr› dnh* CIS ii 207[1,5]: this is the tomb which A. made ... so that he may be buried in this tomb; *wl› ršyn ... dy yzbnwn* CIS ii 212[3]: they will not be allowed ... to sell; *wl› ykl ›nwš dy yzbn* CIS ii 220[2]: no one will be allowed to sell ...; *qrbw ... lb‹lšmn ›lh dy thwyn ‹lwt› ›ln ...* SBS 24[1ff.]: they have offered ... to the god B. with the intention that these altars may be ...; *mṣb› dnh nṣb ‹tntn ... lšdrp› ›lh› ... dy yh› gyr bh* CIS ii 3972[1ff.]: A. has erected this stele ... for the god Sh. ... that he may be client with him; *zbnt lk ... lbth dy ly ... dy tptḥnh lgh btk* MPAT 51[3f.]: I have sold you ... my house ... so that you may make an opening for it into your own house; etc. - d) causal, *šm br[h]dd ... lmlqrt zy nzr lh* KAI 201[1f.]: B. ... erected (it) for M., because he had made a vow to him ... (on this text, cf. also Greenfield IEJ xxviii 288f.; :: Donner KAI a.l., Gibson SSI ii p. 3, Lemaire Or liii 338f., 349: *zy* used relatively); *›qymw lh bny ... dy špr lhwn* SBS 39[4f.]: the sons of ... have erected for him ... because he was agreeable to them; *ṣlm› dnh dy ywlys ... dy ›qymt lh bwl› ... dy ›sq šyrt›* CIS ii 3936[1ff.]: this is the statue of J ... which the Council has erected for him ... because he has conducted the caravan; *mwd› n›ry ... w‹d› ... dy qrw lh b‹q› ...* RIP 119[3ff.]: N. ... and A. ... have expressed (their) gratitude because they called in distress to him (sc. the deity) ...; etc. - **2)** nominal clause - a) subject/object/predicate in a nominal clause, *td‹n zy md‹m lh mpqn ln ...* Herm 5[2f.]: you should know that nothing is brought to us; *l› ›yty zy yqyr mn ...* Aḥiq 111: there is nothing which is heavier than ...; *shd lh yrḥbwl ... dy rḥym mdyth* CIS ii 3932[6f.]: Y. has testified concerning him ... that he is patriotic; *pšq dy h› kšr* CIS ii 3913 ii 104f.: he has explained that it was indeed (v. *h›*$_2$) right; *dyd‹ šmhtwn wdbnyhwn ... yktwb ythwn bspr ḥyyh* MPAT-A 34[4f.] (= SM 69): He Who knows their names and those of their children ... will write them in the book of life; *dqbyr bhdyn šm‹wn* MPAT-A 46[1f.]: the one who is buried here is Sh.; etc. - b) final/consecutive, *šbq wmtrk ... ›nh ... lky ›nty dy ›t ršy› bnpšky lmhk ...* MPAT 40[2ff.]: I ... divorce and repudiate ... you my wife so that you are free on your part to go ...; etc. - c) causal, *wdy b[y]wm dy ktyb šṭr› dnh hwh m›t by ›nh ... lwtk ›nt›* MPAT 64 i 8f.: and because on the day that this document was written, he died, on *me* there rests an obligation to *you*; *wyth ‹mkwn dy ›nḥnh ṣrykyn lh* MPAT 58[2f.]: let him come with you because we are in need of him - **D)** introducing non-relative phrase, *hn hšb zy ly* KAI 224[20]: if he returns the one belonging to me; *ynṣr zy lk* KAI 225[13f.]: he will protect what is yours; *›gr› zk zylk hy* Cowl 5[4]: this wall is yours (for parallel of the formula *zylk hw/hy*, cf. Muffs 151 n. 3, cf. also ibid. 21 n. 1, 41 n. 2); *lk yhwh wzy bnyh ›ḥryk* Cowl 28[12]: it will be yours and of your children after you (on these Off.Ar. instances, cf. Swiggers

FUCUS 453ff.); *ḥdyn bh dylhwn* Hatra 79^4: the ones belonging to them rejoice in it (?, for the interpret., cf. Caquot Syr xl 3f., Teixidor Syr xli 280, Milik DFD 379f., cf. however Aggoula MUSJ xlvii 31; for the context, v. also *gd*$_1$, *ḥdy*$_1$); *wdy lwth [q]rb* MPAT 64 i 5: and what belongs to it he has offered (v. *qrb*$_1$); *dy ʿl* DBKP 20^{41}: what is (written) above; *tlh šwmyh dlh bšlšn* AMB $9^{5f.}$: He suspended the Heavens without chains (cf. AMB $9^{6f.}$); cf. *whn yhwh ... ytyr mn ywm ḥd ʾḥr zy ywmyʾ ʾlk ytyr ptp ʾl tntnw* Driv 6^6: if he wil be ... more than one day, then - as to these days - do not assign more provisions; cf. also instances with deleted antecedent, *zy kspʾ zy yhb bqṣ* Del 97^1: (document) concerning the silver B. gave; *ʾḥtr zy tmrn krn 100* Del 46: A., (document) concerning 100 k. of dates; *zy tʾšṭr* Del 96: (document) concerning T. (for the reading, cf. Kaufman AIA 60 n. 136) - **E)** *zy/dy/d* clauses preceded by prep. - a) preceded by prep. *ʾl*$_6$, *dmwtʾ zʾt ʿbd ʾl zy qdm hwtr* Tell F 15: he made this statue, made it better than before - b) prec. by prep. *b*$_2$ - α) because, *ʾtʿšt ʿl ʾgwrʾ zk lmbnh bzy lʾ šbqn ln lmbnyh* Cowl 30^{23}: take thought for that temple to (re)build (it) since they do not allow us to build it; *wbgh ... ʾštbq bgw bzy* (not l. *kzy*, cf. also Porten & Yardeni sub TADAE A 6.11) *nšy bytn klʾ ʾ[bdw]* Driv 8^2: and his fief in consequence was abandoned ... because all the women (or men?, v. *ʾš*$_1$) of our household perished; *ʾl tmly lbt bzy lʾ ʾytyt hmw ...* SSI ii 28 rev. 2: do not be angry, because I have not brought them - β) in the construction *bdlyt* Syr xvii $353^{5,6}$: in case there is not (v. *lyš*$_2$) - for SBS 45^7, v. *dyṭgm* - c) prec. by prep. *b*$_2$ in the combination *bdyldy*, *ṣlmʾ dnh dy nsʾ ... dy ʾqym lh bny šyrtʾ bdyldy špr lhwn* CIS ii $3916^{1ff.}$: this is the statue of N. ... which the members of the caravan erected for him, because he was agreeable to them; *ʾšʾlt ktb ydy lywlys ... bdyl dy lʾ ydʿ spr* MUSJ xxxviii $106^{3f.}$: I have lent the writing of my hand to J ... because he did not know writing; etc.; for *bdyl dy*, cf. also Ribera AO v 306ff.; for *bdylkwt*, v. *kwt* - d) preceded by the prep. *btr* (after), *btr dy myt* CIS ii 3920^3: after he died (cf. CIS ii 3927^5) - e) preceded by prep. *hyk*, *hyk dy ktyb* CIS ii 3913 ii 68: as it is written, v. *hyk* - f) preceded by prep. *k*$_1$ - **1)** temporal, when - α) + verbal clause, *kzy ḥbzw ʾlhn byt [ʾby]* KAI 224^{24}: when the gods struck the house (of my father); *kzy mrʾn ʾršm ʾzl ʿl mlkʾ* Cowl 27^2: when our lord A. went to the king; *kzy [ʿ]dn yhwh* Cowl 28^{13}: when it is time; *wkzy kznh ʿbyd* Cowl 30^{15}: and when this was done (v. *ʿbd*$_1$); *kzy mṣryn mrdt* Driv 5^6: when Egypt revolted; *kzy tʾth bznh* Driv 12^7: when you come here; *kd hwt bwlʾ knyšʾ* CIS ii 3913 i 3: when the Council assembled; *kdy ytʾyʿl* CIS ii 3913 ii 61: when it is brought in; *kdy ʾt[ʾ mr]n hdrynʾ ʾlhʾ* CIS ii 3959^3 (= SBS 44B): when our lord the divine H. came (Greek par. ἐπιδημία θεοῦ Ἁδρ[ι]ανοῦ) - β) + nom. clause, *kzy ʾnt ʿll* CIS ii $4199^{4f.}$: when you enter; *wdkyr qdm ʾln ʾnš ʾnš kd šwʾ*

... Sem xxvii 117$^{6f.}$: and may every individual be remembered before these when he accepts (??, v. *šwy*$_1$) - **2)** final, *kzy mnd‘m ksntw l’ hwh mn byt’ zyly* Driv 7^2: so that my estate suffered no loss whatever; *kzy m[n]d‘m ksntw l’ yhwh mn byt’ zyly* Driv 7^6: so that my estate may suffer no loss whatever; *kn ‘bd kzy ... l’ršm tḥd[y]* Driv 13^2: act so ... as to please A.; etc. - **3)** causal, *b[ry] ’l t[b]ṭ ytr’ ‘d tḥwh [kl m]lh [zy] t’th ‘l blk kzy bkl ’tr [‘yny]hm* Aḥiq 96f.: my son, do not chatter overmuch till you reveal every word which comes into your mind, for in every place are their eyes - **4)** explicative, *ṭ‘nwk ly mwm’h lmwm’ ... kzy l’ hwh ’rq ldrgmn* Cowl 6$^{6f.}$: they imposed upon you an oath to me ... that it was no (longer) the land of D.; *ytšm ṭ‘m kzy ’yš mnd‘m b’yš l’ y‘bd lpyrm’* Driv 5$^{8f.}$: let an order be issued that no one do any harm to P.; etc.; cf. also *kzy* introducing direct discourse: Samar 3^7, 5^9 - **5)** comparative, normative - α) + verbal clause, *kzy hwh lqdmn* Cowl 32^8: as it was before; *ḥzy ‘l ‘lymy’ wbyty kzy t‘bd lbytk* Cowl 41^6: look after the servants and my house as you would do for your own house; *l‘bq y‘bd kzy šym ṭ‘m* Cowl 26^{22}: let him do it at once according to the order issued; *w‘bdw ‘l byt’ zyly kn kzy pqydy’ [qd]my’ hww ‘bdn* Driv 7$^{7f.}$: attach them to my estate just as the former officers used to do (for *kn kzy*, cf. also Cowl 71^{19}, ATNS 26^{11}); *kzy qdmn ’mrt* ATNS 12^3: as I previously said (context however dam.); *kdy tkln t‘bdn lh ‘bd ’nh lh* Herm 1$^{4f.}$: just as you could do for him, I am doing for him; *kdy hwh bktb’ dnh* DBKP 22^{32}: according to what was (sc. written) in this document - β) + nominal clause, *kzy ‘bd ’nh lḥrwṣ kwt t‘bd bnt ‘ly* Herm 1^7: as much as I am doing for Ch. thus may B. do for me; *kdy mṭ’h ydy wk‘t ‘bd ’nh lh* Herm 3^4: as much as I am able, look, I am doing for him; *wmn‘lhm wmnpqhm kdy ’nw nqybyn bšmhn* MPAT 64 iii 5f.: their entrances and their exits as these are marked by their names; *ktybt* (v. *ktb*$_1$) *šhdt’ d’ kdy ‘l’ ktyb* MPAT 61^{25}: this testimony was written according to what is written above (cf. DBKP 17^{42}, 18^{69,71}); *kdy ḥzh* IEJ xxxvi 206^{5,7}: as is proper (v. *ḥzy*$_1$); etc. - γ) + noun/noun phrase, *kzy qdmn* Driv 5^9: as before; *kdy bktb’ hw* CIS ii 207^6: in accordance to the contents of this document; *mwdn ... zbdbwl wmqymw ... lrḥm<n>’ ... kdy l‘glbwl wmlkbl* CIS ii 3981$^{1f.,6}$: Z. and M. ... express their gratitude ... to the merciful one ... and likewise to A. and M.; *ksp r’š rbyn mn dmnh kdy bh* MPAT 64 iii 2: the interest is part of the principal sum, whatever there is from it (sc. from the interest) is as if it was part of it (sc. of the principal sum); *’ḥlp lky šṭr’ kdy ḥy’* MPAT 40$^{10f.}$: I shall replace for you the document as long as I am alive (cf. prob. also MPAT 40$^{24f.}$) - g) preceded by prep. *l*$_5$, *y’mr lzy lyd‘* KAI 224$^{7f.}$: he speaks to one who does not know; cf. preceded by *lmṭl*, *lwt lh ... lmṭl dy plg nsb* MUSJ xxxviii 106$^{6f.}$: he has made him a partner ... in such a way that he would take one half (cf. also *mṭwl d* in dam. context: Syr xlv 101[17]) - h) preceded by prep. mn_5 - **1)** temporal, since, *mn zy ḥnnyh bmṣryn ʿd kʿn* Cowl 38[7]: from the time that Ch. was in Egypt until now (cf. Herm 5[3], IEJ xl 142[3]) - **2)** causal, because, *mn dy špr lhn* CIS ii 3929[4]: because he was agreeable to them; etc. - **3)** separative, *lnsb ... mn dy brmryn* Hatra 281[9f.]: he will take away ... from what belongs to B.; cf. also *mn dylh* CIS ii 158[3]: on his costs (cf. poss. MPAT-A 39[2f.], v. *rḥmn*); *mn dlnh* MPAT 46[4]: from what is ours; cf. also *mn dydh* MPAT-A 2[3] (= Frey 1197 = SM 58): from his own resources (:: Fitzmyer & Harrington MPAT p. 351: *dydh* = d_3 + Sing. + suff. 3 p.s.m. of *yd*) - **4)** in the combination *br mn zy*, *lʾ ʾkl ʾnṣl lpltỵ mn tḥt lbbk br mn zy ʾnt ttrk lʾmh* Krael 2[13f.]: I will not be able to take P. from under your heart except if you will drive his out mother - **5)** in the combination *ytyr mn zy*, *ytyr mn zy kʿn ḥd ʾlp* Cowl 30[3]: thousand times more than now - **6)** in the combination *mn bʾtr d*, *mn bʾtr dmn šṭr ʿdwʾ hw kryzt* MPAT 64 i 2f.: after this document of *ʿdwʾ* (v. *ʿdw*) was made public (?, v. krz_1) - i) preceded by prep. $ʿd_7$, *ʿd zy ʾgwrʾ zk ytbnʾ* Cowl 30[27]: until this temple will be rebuilt (cf. however the par. clause in Cowl 31[26]: *zy ʿd ʾgwrʾ zk yt[bnʾ]* (v. also $ʿd_7$)); *ʾmrt qṭlth ʿd zy lʿd[n ʾ]ḥrn ... qrbtk qdm snḥʾryb* Aḥiq 49f.: I said: "I have killed him", until in aftertime ... I brought you before S.; cf. also Aḥiq 64 (dam. context) - j) preceded by prep. $ʿl_7$, *ʿl zy psmš[k] ʾmr* Driv 4[2*f.]: concerning P.'s having said (cf. also Cowl 42[4], heavily dam. context); *šgyʾ snḥʾryb mlkʾ rḥmny ʿl zy hḥytk* Aḥiq 51: king S. was well pleased with that I had kept you alive - k) preceded by prep. $ʿm_4$, *ʿm zy rm mnk* Aḥiq 142: with one that is higher than you - l) preceded by prep. *lqbl*, *lqbl zy bnh hwh qdmyn* Cowl 30[25]: as it was built before; *lqbl zy lqdmyn hwh mtʿbd* Cowl 32[10f.]: as it formerly was done; *lqbl zy ʾnh ʿbdt lk kn ... ʿbd ly* Aḥiq 52: as I did to you, so do to me; *ʾnh ... yhbth ... lqbl zy sbltny* Krael 9[16f.]: I ... give it ... because she did maintain me (cf. Cowl 38[9], Aḥiq 68, Driv 8[6], 9[2], CIS ii 164[3]); cf. also the combination *kl qbl zy*, *kl qbl zy mn ʿlʾ kt[yb]* MPAT 49 i 6: according to what is written above - m) preceded by prep. qdm_3, *qdm dtrʿh* MPAT-A 48[2] (= Frey 979 = SM 15): before the gate - **F)** introducing the second of two par. principal clauses, *trtyn mln špyrh wzy tltʾ rḥymh lšmš* Aḥiq 92: two things are agreeable, yea three (things) are a pleasure to Sh. (on this text, cf. Lindenberger APA 66; cf. also the expression *ʾp zy*, v. $ʾp_2$) - R.A.Bowman Pers a.l.: l. *zy* in Pers 62[3], cf. however Naveh & Shaked Or xlii 456f.: probably l. *l* (= l_5).

zyb v. kdb_3.

v. $ʾz_2$, *ʾzy*, $ʾḥd_4$, $ʾlp_3$, $ʾrw_2$, zbn_1, kdd_2, $pḥz_2$, *rḥym*, $šm_1$.

zyw cf. Frah xii 4 (*zyw, zʿyw*): splendour, cf. Nyberg FP 46, 81 :: Ebeling Frah a.l.: l. *zyn, zywn* = form of *zywn* (= high, eminent).

zywk **OffAr** Sing. abs. *zywk* Cowl 37^3 - ¶ subst. m. of uncert. meaning, cf. Cowl p. 134: < Iran. = poss. pay-day × Eilers Beamtennamen 27f., Grelot DAE p. 388 (n. e), Porten & Greenfield JEAS p. 81, Porten & Yardeni sub TADAE A 4.2: = n.p. (< Iran.).
zywn v. *zyw*.
zyyr **JAr** Sing. emph. *zyyrh* SM 49^7, 70^7 - ¶ subst. press.
zykrwn v. *zkrn*.
zyl$_1$ v. *zkr$_3$*.
zyl$_2$ v. *zy*.
zymw **Hebr** Milik DJD ii p. 164: the *zymw[* (uncert. reading) in DJD ii 45^7 = fine (< Greek ζημία).
zyn$_1$ v. *zwn$_1$*.
zyn$_2$ **OffAr** Sing. emph. *zyn›* RES 1300^9; Plur. + suff. 3 p.pl.m. *znyhwm* Cowl 31^8 - ¶ subst. weapon: Cowl 31^8 (par. text Cowl 30^8: *tlyhm*); exact meaning uncert., cf. Puech CISFP i 566: = axe? :: Lidzbarski Eph iii 24: = armour?? - Altheim & Stiehl FuF xxxv 173, 176: l. *zyn›* = Sing. emph. also in FuF xxxv 173^{7,12,14} in the comb. *zyn zyn› ›rwst* (highly uncert. context).
zyn$_3$ v. *dn$_1$*.
zyn$_4$ v. *zyw*.
zyny (< Iran., cf. Telegdi JA ccxxvi 242, Driv p. 83, Eilers AfO xvii 334, Hinz AISN 279) - **OffAr** Sing. abs. *zyny* Driv 12^8 - ¶ subst. damage, loss.
zyq cf. Frah i 18: wind (*zyq›*, *zyg›*). Kaufman AIA 114: < Akkad.? (cf. also Zimmern Fremdw 45: < Akkad.) - the same word (Plur. abs.) poss. also in AMB 11^8 (*]zyqyn*) = blast-demon.
zyr > Akkad. = railing?, cf. v.Soden Or xxxvii 269, xlvi 197, cf. however CAD s.v. *ziru* (: = prob. designation of a part of a boat's superstructure).
zyr‹wn **Hebr** Plur. abs. *zyr‹wnyn* SM 49^3 - ¶ subst. Plur. herbs, vegetables.
zyt **Ph** Sing. + suff. 1 p.s.?? (or = n.p.??) *zty* RES 1526 - **Hebr** Plur. abs. *zytym* DJD ii 30^{18} - **OffAr** Sing. abs. *zyt* Krael 7^{20}, Herm 2^{11} - ¶ subst. - **1)** olive; *mšḥ zyt* Krael 7^{20}, Herm 2^{11}: olive oil - **2)** olive-tree: DJD ii 30^{18} - Aimé-Giron BIFAO xxxviii 6: l. *zyt* (= Plur. cstr.) in Ph. text BIFAO xxxviii 3^6 (uncert. reading and interpret.) - for this word, cf. also Borowski AIAI 117ff.
v. *bzy$_1$*,*nzy*.
zk$_1$ v. *zky$_2$*.
zk$_2$ **OffAr** Sing. m. *zk* Cowl 5^{12,14}, 8^{25}, Krael 3^7, ATNS 1^5, KAI 273^7 (?, dam. context; on this word, cf. Humbach MStSW xxvi 39), Samar 1^{10} (= EI xviii 8*), etc., etc., *dk*Krael 9^{10}, *zky* Driv 3^7, 4^2, *znk* Cowl 8^8, 9^6; f. *zk* Cowl 5^{4,5,6}, ATNS 1^6, etc., etc., *dk*FX 136^{19}, *zky* Cowl 1^{4,6},

Driv 3^8, *dky* Cowl 14^9, *dk›* Cowl 14^6; Plur. abs. *›lk* Cowl 14^6 (for this reading, cf. e.g. Porten & Greenfield JEAS p. 18, Porten & Yardeni sub TADAE B 2.8 :: e.g. Cowl a.l.: l. prob. *›lky*), 16^4 (or l. *›lky*?, cf. Porten & Yardeni sub TADAE A 5.2), 20^8, 27^8, Krael 11^4, Driv 6^6, Beh 20, ATNS 1^6, Samar 5^4, etc., etc., *›lky* Cowl 13^6 (cf. however Porten & Greenfield JEAS p. 14, Porten & Yardeni sub TADAE B 2.7: l. *›lk*), 14^8, 54^{12} (for this reading, cf. Porten & Yardeni sub TADAE A 3.1 verso 3), Herm 7^3; cf. Frah xxiv 12 (*zk*), Paik 339-343 (*zk*), 349 (*znk*), Sogd ii 238, B 279, R 56, Chw Ir 57, GH iv 78ff., GIPP 68, SaSt 26, etc., etc., cf. Lemosín AO ii 266, 268 - **JAr** Sing. m. *zk* MPAT 48^{2,3}, *dk* MPAT 42^{14}, 47 i-ii recto 8 (?, heavily dam. context), 50C 1, 51^{7,8,11,13}, 52^{3,5,9,12}; Sing. f. *dk* MPAT 51^5 - ¶ dem. pronoun, this, that, Plur. these, those - **A)** used attributively - **1)** after noun with emphatic ending or pron. suff., *byt› znk* Cowl 8^8: this house; *spr› zk* Cowl 8^{27}: this document; *kmry› zy ḥnwb ›lk* Cowl 27^8: these priests of Chn.; *gbr› zk* ATNS 1^7: that man; *mš›lt› zk* ATNS 1^6: this interrogation; *ynqy› ›lky* Herm 7^3: these children; *ḥqlt› ›lk* ATNS 3^4: those fields; *‹bdy ›lk* ATNS 4^1: those slaves of mine; *›tr› dk* MPAT 52^3: this site; etc., etc. - **2)** after n.p., *ydnyh zk* Krael 8^{7,8}: the afore mentioned Y.; *yhwḥnn zk* Samar 1^{10} (= EI xviii 8*): the said Y.; *yhwdh zk* MPAT 48^3: that Y.; etc., etc. - **B)** preceding noun with emphatic ending or pron. suffix in apposition, *zk spr›* Cowl 8^{16}: this document; *›lk nksy›* Cowl 20^8: these goods; *zk ptp›* Driv 9^1: this portion; *zk zmn›* ATNS 18^6: that time; *zk b[y]t[›]* LA ix 331^4: this building/construction (uncert. example, dam. context); *›lk ›nšn* KAI 279^5: these men - **C)** used independently - **1)** *›lk ṣryḥy›* RES 1432^1: these are the chambers - **2)** resuming someone/something mentioned just before (cf. also Kaufman BiOr xxxiv 96), *zk ›bd* Driv 8^2: that (man) perished; *wk‹t ḥnzny šmh ... zk ptp› hb* Driv 9^1: and now, as to the one named Ch. ... give that (man) a provision; *bg› lm zy mn mr›y yhyb ly bmṣryn zk mnd‹m mn tmh l› mhytyn ‹ly* Driv 10$^{1f.}$: in regard to the fief which my lord has given to me in Egypt, as to that, they are not bringing me anything thence; *zk hyty* Driv 13^3: that (man) has brought; *›tr› dk ... dk zbnt* MPAT 52$^{5ff.}$: this site ... that I have sold - **3)** preceded by preposition, *bzk* Cowl 38^9: on this account; *b›lk* Cowl 71^{15}: in these (?, dam. context); *mn zky* Cowl 30^{21}: since then (:: Cowl p. 117, Leand 14: lapsus; cf. par. text Cowl 31^{20}: *[m]n zk ‹[dn]›*); *‹l zk* KAI 264^7: therefore.

v. *zkm*, *znh*, *prq*$_1$.

zk› v. *zky*$_2$, *mr›*.

zky$_1$ **OffAr** Qal Pf. 1 p.s., cf. Warka 10: *za-ki-it* - ¶ verb Qal to be pure (for this translation, cf. Driver AfO iii 50, Dupont-Sommer RA xxxix 45) - Altheim & Stiehl FuF xxxv 176: the *hzky* in FuF xxxv 173^9 = Haph Pf. 3 p.s.m. (= to lead to victory), diff. context, highly uncert.

interpret. - on this root, cf. also Blau PC 49 n. 9 - a form of this root also in RSF xvii 42[1] (QAL Impf. 2 p.s.m. *tzk*), cf. Garbini RSF xvii 42f.

zky$_2$ **Pun** Sing. f. abs. *zkʾ*CIS i 3889[3] (:: Dothan IOS vi 60 (div. otherwise): l. *z* (= *z*$_1$)+ *kʾ*$_2$ (= here)??) - **OffAr** Sing. abs. *zky* Aḥiq 46, cf. Warka 10: *za-ka-a-a* (cf. Driver AfO iii 50, Dupont-Sommer RA xxxix 45); Plur. m. abs. *dkyn*Cowl 21[6], 27[12] (heavily dam. context, highly uncert. reading, cf. Cowl a.l., Grelot DAE p. 403, cf. however Porten & Yardeni sub TADAE A 4.5: l. *rbyn* = QAL Pf. 1 p.pl. of *rby*$_1$ (= to grow, increase), uncert. interpret.); cf. Frah xxvi 4 (*dkyʾ*)- **Palm** Plur. m. abs. *dkn*CIS ii 4174[6] (cf. Cantineau Gramm 129, AfO xi 379, Ingholt Ber ii 98 n. 251 :: Rosenthal Sprache 50: = dem. pron. Sing. (cf. also Chabot CIS ii a.l.)), Ber ii 97[2], 99 i 2, 100 i 2 - **Hatra** Sing. m. emph. *zkyʾ* 79[1], 194[2], 203[3], 229[2] (*[z]kyʾ*) - ¶ adj. - **1)** pure: CIS i 3889[3] (said of reed, v. *qnh*$_1$) - **2)** ritually pure: Cowl 21[6]; cf. Ber ii 97[2], 99 i 2, 100 i 2, said of undefiled niches in a tomb - **3)** innocent: Aḥiq 46 (for the translation of the context, cf. Joüon MUSJ xviii 84) - **4)** victorious: Hatra 79[1], 194[2], 203[3], 229[2] (epithet of Hatrean king Sanatruq; cf. also Tubach ISS 247 (n. 48)) - Garbini with Amadasi sub ICO-Malta Np 17: l. poss. Sing. m. abs. *zk*in l. 1 (uncert. interpret., dam. context; cf. also Amadasi Guzzo Sem xxxviii 23) - Humbach IPAA 12: the *zkʾ*in IPAA 12[10] = Sing. m. emph., the pure one (highly uncert. interpret.; poss. *škn zkʾ* = inhabitant of Z.?) - for the (possibility of) differentiation between roots *zky/dky*in Aramaic, cf. Kaufman AIA 112. v. *mrʾ*.

zky$_3$ v. *zk*$_2$.

zkm **OffAr** *zkm* Cowl 9[2], 20[4], 43[2] (for this prob. reading, cf. Porten JNES xlviii 176, Porten & Yardeni sub TADAE B 5.5 :: Cowl a.l.: l. poss. *mm[r]* = QAL Inf. of *ʾmr*$_1$;heavily dam. context), 65 iii 2, *dkm*Krael 7[2]; cf. Nisa 258[4], 459[7,10], etc. (*zkm*), GIPP 38, 68 - ¶ dem. pronoun, the same; preceding noun with emphatic ending in apposition, *zkm dglʾ* Cowl 9[2]: the same company, cf. Cowl 20[4], 65 iii 2, Krael 7[2].

v. *zkm*, *znh*.

zkr$_1$ **OldCan** QAL Impf. 3 p.s.m. *ia-az-ku-ur-mi* EA 228[19] (cf. Rainey EI xiv 9*, Sivan GAG 148) - **Ph** QAL Impf. 3 p.s.m. + suff. 1 p.s. *yskrn* KAI 43[15] (for the *s*, cf. Garbini ISNO 44, FR 46a) - **Hebr** QAL Pf. 3 p.s.m. *zkr* KAI 192[4]; Part. pass. s.m. abs. *zkwr* SM 75[1], 105[2], 107[8,11]; pl. abs. *zkwryn* SM 76[1] - **Samal** QAL Impf. 3 p.s.m. *yzkr* KAI 214[17] (cf. e.g. Cooke NSI p. 168, Driver AnOr xii 47, Altheim & Stiehl AAW i 225, Gibson SSI ii p. 73 :: e.g. Donner KAI a.l., Greenfield RB lxxx 46 (n. 4), Dion p. 121f., Stefanovic COAI 176: = HAPH); HAPH Impf. 3 p.s.m. *yzkr* KAI 214[16] (cf. e.g. Cooke NSI p. 168, Koopmans 36, Donner KAI a.l., Greenfield RB lxxx 46f., Dion p. 121f., Gibson SSI ii p. 73 (prob.), Garr DGSP 55 :: e.g. Lidzbarski Handb 267, Driver AnOr xii 47, Altheim & Stiehl AAW i 225: = QAL) - **OffAr** QAL Pf. 3 p.pl.m. *dkrw*Cowl 34[6] (cf. e.g. Porten & Yardeni sub TADAE A 4.4 :: Ungnad ArPap 26, Grelot DAE p. 397 (n. g): l. *dbrw* = QAL Pf. 3 p.pl.m. of *dbr*$_2$);Impf. 3 p.s.m. + suff. 1 p.s. *yzkrny* Aḥiq 53; Part. pass. s.m. abs. *zkyr* BSOAS xxvii 284 (bis), *dkyr* Sumer xx 19 ii 1, 20 i 1; pl.m. abs. *dkyryn* Sumer xx 15[1], 18 ii 3 - **Nab** QAL Pf. 3 p.s.f. *dkrt*J 212[1] (= ARNA-Nab 42), 213, RB xlii 412 i, 417 i 1, ii 1, 418[1], etc. (for the interpret. as verbal form with optative meaning instead of Sing. cstr. of *dkrh*(= memory), cf. Cantineau Nab i 76, Savignac RB xlii 413, Milik ADAJ xxi 145 n. 5, id. sub ARNA-Nab 42); Pf. pass. 3 p.s.f. *dkyrt* ARNA-Nab 121 (= CIS ii 262; ?, or deviating form of Part. pass.?); Part. pass. s.m. abs. *zkyr* J 295, *dkyr* CIS ii 376[1], 385[1], 393bis 1, 400[1], IEJ xxxvi 56[1], etc., etc. (the reading *dkyr* CIS ii 316[1] false, l. *dkrwn*, cf. J 180[1]), *dkr*J 237, RB xli 593[1], IEJ xxvii 225 iii 1 (= CIS ii 2677); cstr. *dkyr* CIS ii 788[1], 1841, 2075; s.f. abs. *dkyrh* CIS ii 448[1], 786[1], RES 1411[1], 1412[1], 1413; pl.m. abs. *dkyryn* CIS ii 235A 1, 380[2], J 290, RES 1427, BSOAS xvi 225 lxxvii 1, 226 lxxix 1, ARNA-Nab 73, *dkyrn* CIS ii 812[1], 1115[1]; Part. pass. (Arabic formation) s.m. abs. (cf. Cantineau Nab i 80) *mdkwr* CIS ii 1331[1], 2768[1], Qedem vi 56 no. 219, *mdkr*CIS ii 1280 (cf. 1312?); m. pl. abs. *mdkryn* CIS ii 2662[1] (= IEJ xxvii 222 i) - **Palm** QAL Pf. 3 p.s.m. *zkr* ISC p. 541; 1 p.s. *zkrt* (??, cf. Cantineau Gramm 74, cf. however Rosenthal Sprache 24) CIS ii 4093[2]; Part. pass. s.m. abs. *dkyr* CIS ii 3973[7,9], 4207, PNO 2ter 1, 9, Inv ix 4 (Greek par. (μνησθη), etc., etc.; pl.m. abs. *dkyryn* CIS ii 3973[10], Inscr P 31[2], Inv D 25[1] (= Frey 825), PNO 52ter a 1, 4, 76c 2, SBS 61b 1, Syr xl 33[1], xlvii 413[1], Inv ix 5[1] (for the reading, cf. Fiema BASOR cclxiii 82; Greek par. (in Lat. letters) *mnest*), *dkyrn* PNO 56[1,3], 76b (?), 78[1], Inv D 25[5], *dkrn*(or Sing. cstr. of *dkrn*?) PNO 52[1], 56a 1 - **Hatra** QAL Impf. 3 p.s.m. *ldk[r]* 13[2] (cf. Aggoula Ber xviii 88, Degen ZDMG cxxi 124, cf. also Milik Syr xliv 298: l. *ldk[wr]* :: Safar Sumer vii 178, Caquot Syr xxix 96: l. *lrk* (cf. also Donner sub KAI 240)); + suff. 3 p.s.m. *ldkrhy*23[5] (cf. Milik RN vi/iv 55, Caquot Syr xl 15f., Degen NESE ii 100 :: Safar Sumer vii 182, Caquot Syr xxix 102: l. *ldkrh* (= *l*$_5$ + *dkrh* (= Sing. + suff. 3 p.s.m. of *dkr*$_2$) + *w* (cf. also Donner sub KAI 244)); Part. pass. s.m. abs. *dkr*8 (for the reading, cf. Altheim & Stiehl AAW ii 195f., cf. also Safar Sumer vii 176 :: Caquot Syr xxix 94: l. *dkyr* :: Altheim & Stiehl AAW ii 195f.: = QAL Imper. s.m. or Sing. cstr. of *dkr*$_2$), 9[1,2] (for the reading of both lines, cf. Safar Sumer vii 176, Altheim & Stiehl AAW ii 195f., Aggoula Ber xviii 88 :: Aggoula Ber xviii 88: = QAL Imper. s.m., cf. also Altheim & Stiehl AAW ii 195f.: = QAL Imper. s.m. or Sing. cstr. of *dkr*$_2$ :: Caquot Syr xxix 94: l. *dkyr*), *dkyr* 2, 4[8], 6[2], 80[7], 81[1], 134 (:: Caquot Syr xli 258, Vattioni IH a.l.: l. *dykyr*), etc.,

etc. (cf. also Assur 25g 1: *dkr*, Assur 6b 2, 12[1], 14[2], etc.: *dkyr*); pl.m. abs. *dkryn*24[2], 230[1], *dkyrn* 79[14], 207[3] (for the reading, cf. Aggoula Sem xxii 53 :: idem Syr lii 195: l. *dkyryn*), *dkyryn* 147, 154 (cf. also Assur 28a 2, 29b 1) - **JAr** Qal Part. pass. s.m. abs. *dkyr* MPAT-A 1[1] (= SM 21), 2[1] (= SM 58 = Frey 1197), 6[1], 8[1], 12[1] (= Frey 1195 = SM 71), 27[1] (with f. subject), etc., etc., *dkr*MPAT-A 28[1] (= SM 34 :: Fitzmyer & Harrington MPAT a.l.: restore *dk<y>r*), *dykr* MPAT-A 36[1](= SM 30 = Frey 987 (reading incorrectly *dkyr*); lapsus, cf. also Lidzbarski Eph i 314), *dyr* (with superscribed correction *dky*) MPAT-A 7[2] (for this explanation, cf. Naveh sub SM 65, Beyer ATTM 393 :: Fitzmyer & Harrington MPAT a.l.: l. l. 1: *dky[...*, l. 2: *d<k>yr...*; = Frey 1204), *ydkr*MPAT-A 43[1] (lapsus; for this uncert. reading, cf. Goldhar with Klein ZDPV li 137, Naveh sub SM 5, cf. however Klein ibid., Frey sub 971, Fitzmyer & Harrington MPAT a.l.: l. *dkyr*); s.f. abs. *dkyrh* MPAT-A 2[4] (= SM 59 = Frey 1198), 3[1] (= SM 60 = Frey 1199), 28[2]; pl.m. abs. *dkyrn* MPAT-A 34[1] (= SM 69), 55 (*[d]kyrn*; cf. Naveh sub SM 77: l. *dkyrn*; or = pl.f. abs.?, cf. also Fitzmyer & Harrington MPAT p. 303), *dkryn*MPAT-A 40[1] (*[d]kryn*; for this reading, cf. Naveh sub SM 57 :: Fitzmyer & Harrington MPAT a.l.: l. *[d]kyryn*), SM 37[3] (*dkry[n]*; for the reading, cf. Naveh EI xx 307), 81, *dkyryn* MPAT-A 5[1] (*[d]kyryn*; = SM 64 = Frey 1203), 13[1] (= SM 46), 22[1,9] (= SM 70[9,17]), 28[4] (= SM 34 = Frey 858), 35[1] (= SM 16), 48[1] (= SM 15 = Frey 979) - Aph Part. pl.m. abs. *mdkryn* AMB 15[20] - ¶ verb Qal to remember, passim - **1)** + obj., *yzkr nbš pnmw* KAI 214[17]: let him remember the soul of P.; *zkr ʾl bṭb* ISC p. 541: may El remember (her) for good; *dkrt ʾltw ḥlypw* RB xlii 412[1f.]: may Allāt remember Ch. (v. supra); *wkwl dldk[r] hnw dkyr lṭb* Hatra 13[3f.]: and everyone who remembers (i.e. mentions aloud) them may be remembered for good (v. supra); *mn dy lqryhy wlʾ ldkrhy lnšrʿqb lṭb* Hatra 23[4f.]: whoever will read this and will not mention him (sc. his name), i.e. *nšrʿqb* for good ... (v. supra); passim - **2)** Part. pass. remembered; *wlʾ lmr dkyr* Hatra 101[2]: and he will not say: may he be remembered; cf. the use in the following types of formulae (v. also *brk*₁; cf. also Negev IEJ xvii 253ff. for the meanings of these formulae) - **A)** formulae with single Part. and without exclamations - **Aa)** consisting of 2 elements: indication of person(s) and Part. - **1)** Part. + indication of person(s), *dkyr NP* CIS ii 376[1]: May NP be remembered; *dkyr NP wbnyhy* Hatra 206: may NP and his sons be remembered; *dkyr NP wNP* Hatra 221[1f.]: may NP and NP be remembered (cf. Qedem vi 54 no. 209, 55 no. 218); *dkyryn NP wNP* Sumer xx 15[1ff.]; *mdkryn NP wNP* IEJ xxvii 222 i 1ff. (= CIS ii 2662); cf. CIS ii 385[1], 393bis 1, 1280, 1331, Inv xii 52[2f.], SBS 60[7f.], Hatra 162, Assur 22[2ff], SM 103 (= Frey 826c), etc., etc.; cf. also *dkyr* + n.d. in *dkyr mrn* Hatra 279[2] (or = may (he) be remembered, our lord!, v. also sub Cb; cf. also *lṭb dkyr mmrn* Hatra

329) - **2)** indication of person(s) + Part., *NP dkyr* CIS ii 1373; cf. ARNA-Nab 18[1f.] - **3)** with deletion of person indication, *dkt' dy NP dkyr* Hatra 7: place of NP (v. *dkh₁*), may he be remembered - **Ab)** consisting of three elements, Part., indication of person(s) and *bṭb/lṭb* - **1)** Part. + indication of person(s) + *bṭb*, *dkyr NP ... bṭb* CIS ii 408: may NP be remembered for good; cf. CIS ii 493, 494, 499, 1233, 3973[10f.], IEJ xxvii 227 ii 1ff., EI x 182 vii, Inv xii 40, Assur 20[1f], etc., etc.; cf. *mdkwr NP bṭb* Qedem vi 56 no. 219, *mdkwr NP wNP bṭb* CIS ii 2768, cf. also *dkyr NP bṭb wNP wNP* IEJ xxvii 224 iv 1ff. (= CIS ii 2674; cf. Assur 27b 1f.) and *lmdk[wr] NP bṭb* CIS ii 2244 - **2)** Part. + *bṭb* + indication of person(s), *dkyr bṭb NP* CIS ii 1174; cf. CIS ii 1232, 1303, 2616, 2677 (cf. IEJ xxvii 225), 3229 (cf. also *dkyr bṭb'* (without NP) AAW v/1 85[2], cf. also Teixidor Syr xlviii 481) - **3)** indication of person(s) + Part. + *bṭb*, *NP ... dkyr bṭ[b]* BSOAS xvi 215 lv; cf. CIS ii 239 (= J 73, for the reading, cf. Milik sub ARNA-Nab 96), 1594 - **4)** Part. + indication of person(s) + *lṭb*, *dkyr NP lṭb* Hatra 54[1]; cf. Hatra 9[2], 43[2], 92, 96, Assur 23a, 28f. 1f., etc., etc. - **5)** Part. + *lṭb* + indication of person(s), *dkyr lṭb NP* Hatra 69[1ff.] (cf. Hatra 11, 305, 332); *[d]kryn lṭb kl qhlh ...* MPAT-A 40[1]: may the whole community be remembered for good; *dkyr lṭb NP* MPAT-A 2[1f.,4f.]; cf. MPAT-A 4[1f.], 5[1f.], 6, 8[1], 12[1], 14, 22[1], etc.; cf. also *dkyrn lṭb yhwy dkrnhwn* (v. *zkrn*) *lṭb kl qhlh qd[y]šh ...* MPAT-A 34[1f.]: may be remembered for good -may their memory be for good- the whole holy community ... - **6)** indication of person(s) + Part. + *lṭb*, *NP NP dkyryn lṭb* MPAT-A 22[9] (= SM 70[17]), cf. Hatra 207 (cf. Aggoula Sem xxii 53) - **7)** *lṭb* + Part. + indication of person(s), *lṭb dkyr NP* Hatra 148; cf. Hatra 24[2] (for the reading, cf. Degen ZDMG cxxi 125), 166, 170 - 8) with deletion of person indication, *ktb yhwdh zkwr lṭwb* SM 105[2]: Y. has written (this text), may he be remembered for good; *dkryn lṭb* Hatra 24[2] (for the reading of the context, cf. Degen ZDMG cxxi 125), cf. Hatra 6[2], 20[5], 22; cf. also SM 75[1], 76[1] - **Ac)** consisting of three elements: Part., indication of person(s) and *ṭb*, *dkyr ṭb NP* CIS ii 2075 - **Ad)** consisting of three elements: Part., indication of person(s) and *bkl ṭb* - **1)** Part. + *bkl ṭb* + indication of person(s), *dkyr bkl ṭb NP* CIS ii 1241, 3096[1] - **2)** Part. + indication of person(s) + *bkl ṭb* CIS ii 1570 (cf. also CIS ii 1488, 1577, cf. also *dkyr NP bkl ṭb bṭb* CIS ii 1026) - **3)** indication of person(s) + *bkl ṭb* + Part., *NP ... bkl ṭb dkyr* CIS ii 551[2f.] - **Ae)** consisting of three elements: Part., indication of person(s) and *bšlm* - 1) Part. + indication of person(s) + *bšlm*, *dkyr NP bšlm* CIS ii 750: may NP be remembered in peace - **2)** indication of person(s) + Part. + *bšlm*, *NP dkr bšlm* J 237 - **Af)** consisting of three elements: Part., indication of person(s) and *'d 'lm'*, *dkyr NP 'd 'lm'* Syr xl 42[1ff.]: may NP be remembered for ever - **Ag)** consisting of three elements: Part., indication of person(s) and *qdm*-phrase - **1)** Part.

+ indication of person(s) + *qdm*-phrase, *dkyr NP ... qdm yrḥbwl* PNO 2ter 1f., 5: may NP be remembered before Y.; cf. ADAJ xx 118 ii 1f. (= J 142), Sumer xx 19 ii 1ff., CIS ii 3973$^{7f.}$, Hatra 44, 88, 151, 153^{1}, 213, 268, 299, 320, Assur 25c, d, 29c, 34e (cf. also Assur 28b: *dkyr NP ... qdm ... wNP*) - **2)** Part. + *qdm*-phrase + indication of person(s), *dkyr qdm ʾln ʾnš ʾnš* Sem xxvii 117$^{6f.}$: may every person be remembered before those (sc. gods); cf. Inv xii 45$^{9f.}$ - **3)** indication of person(s) + Part. + *qdm*-phrase, *NP dkyr qdm brmryn* Hatra 116$^{1f.}$ - **4)** *qdm*-phrase + Part. + indication of person(s), *qdm mrn dkyr NP* Hatra 159 - **Ah)** consisting of three elements: Part., indication of person(s) and *bṭb wšlm/wbšlm*, *dkyr NP ... bṭb wšlm* CIS ii 509 (cf. CIS ii 785, 1305, 1375, etc., etc.); *dkyryn NP [wNP] bṭb wbšlm* ARNA-Nab 73 (v. also *brk*$_1$) - **Ai)** consisting of three elements: Part., indication of person(s) and *bkl ṭb wšlm*, *dkyr NP ... bkl ṭb wšlm* CIS ii 1257 - **Aj)** consisting of three elements: Part., indication of person(s) and *lṭb lšnpyr* - **1)** Part. + *NP* + *lṭb wlšnpyr*, *dkyr NP lṭb lšnpyr* Hatra 182 - **2)** NP + Part. + *lṭb wlšnpyr*, *NP dkyr lṭb wlšnpyr* Assur 34b - **Ak)** consisting of four elements: Part., indication of person(s), *bṭb wšlm* and *bṭb*, *dkyr bṭb wšlm NP ... bṭb* CIS ii 613 (cf. CIS ii 619, Qedem vi 57 no. 222) - **Al)** consisting of four elements: Part., indication of person(s), *bṭb* and *(l)ʿlm* - **1)** Part. + indication of person(s) + *bṭb* + *lʿlm*, *dkyr NP ... bṭb lʿlm* J 281 (cf. CIS ii 3200, Qedem vi 71 no. 261) - **2)** Part. + *ʿlm* + *bṭb* + indication of person(s), *dkyr ʿlm bṭb NP* CIS ii 788$^{1f.}$ - **Am)** consisting of four elements: Part. + indication of person(s) + *bṭb wšlm* + *ʿd ʿlm*, *dkyr bṭb wšlm NP ... ʿd ʿlm* CIS ii 2072 - **An)** consisting of four elements: Part., indication of person(s), *bṭb/lṭb* and *(mn) qdm*-phrase - **1)** Part. + indication of person(s) + *bṭb* + *(mn) qdm*-phrase, *dkyrn bny qrytʾ ... bṭb qdm gnyʾ* PNO 78: may the inhabitants of the village ... be remembered for good before G. (v. *gny*$_4$); *dkyr NP ... bṭb mn qdm dwšrʾ* CIS ii 443 - 2) Part. + indication of person(s) + *(mn) qdm*-phrase + *bṭb*, *dkyr NP qdm ʾbgl ... bṭb* PNO 17; *dkyr NP ... mn q[d]m ʾltw bṭb* RB xlii 415$^{5f.}$ - **3)** Part. + indication of person(s) + *lṭb* + *qdm*-phrase, *dkyr NP lṭb qdm mrn nšrʾ* Hatra 155 (cf. Hatra 167, 171, 175, 248, 279a, 295, Assur 6b 2f., 32d; cf. also Assur 29k: *dkyr NP lṭb w NP lṭb qdm*) - **4)** Part. + indication of person(s) + *qdm*-phrase + *lṭb*, *dkyr NP qdm mrn ... lṭb* Hatra 89 (cf. Hatra 24^{1}, 101, 322, Assur 25e 2, 27f) - **5)** Part. + *bṭb* + indication of person(s) + *qdm*-phrase: IEJ xxxvi 56^{1} - **6)** *lṭb* + Part. + indication of person(s) + *qdm*-phrase, *lṭb dkyr NP qdm ʾlhʾ* Hatra 169 - **Ao)** consisting of four elements: Part., indication of person(s), *bkl ṭb* and *bṭb*: CIS ii 1026 - **Ap)** consisting of four elements: Part., indication of person(s), *bkl ṭb* and Part.: CIS ii 551 - **Aq)** consisting of four elements: Part., indication of person(s), *lṭb wlšnpyr* and *qdm*-phrase - **1)** Part. + indication of person(s) +

lṭb wlšnpyr + *qdm*-phrase, *dkyr NP ... [l]ṭb wlšnpyr qdm mrn* Hatra 52[1f.] (cf. Hatra 74[3f.], 301) - **2)** Part. + indication of person(s) + *qdm*-phrase + *lṭb wlšnp(y)r*, *dkyr NP ... qdm mrn lṭb wlšnpyr* Hatra 26 (cf. Hatra 58, 90, 327, Assur 23c 2ff., 24, 26[2ff], 32h) -**Ar)** consisting of four elements: Part., indication of person(s), *bṭb wšlm* and *mn qdm*-phrase, *dkyr NP ... bṭb wšlm mn qdm dwšrʾ* CIS ii 401 - **As)** consisting of four elements: Part., indication of person(s), *qdm*-phrase and *ʿd ʿlm/lʿlm(ʾ)* - **1)** Part. + indication of person(s) + *qdm*-phrase + *ʿd ʿlm*, *dkr NP ... qdm ʾltw ... ʿd ʿlm* RB xli 593[1ff.] - **2)** Part. + indication of person(s) + *qdm*-phrase + *lʿlm*, *dkyr ʿqybsr ... qdm m[rtn] lʿlm* Assur 28h 3ff. (cf. Assur 31j 1ff.; cf. also Assur 27k (*lʿlmʾ*)) - **3)** *lʿlm* (?) + Part. + indication of person(s) + *qdm*-phrase, *[lʿ]lm dkyr NP qdm ʾlhʾ* Hatra 173 - **At)** consisting of five elements: Part., indication of person(s), *lṭb* (twice) and *qdm*-phrase - **1)** *lṭb* + Part. + *qdm*-phrase + indication of person(s) + *lṭb*, *lṭb dkyr qdmyk NP lṭ[b]* Hatra 150 (for reading of NP (*rmw*), cf. Safar Sumer xviii 45 (n. 41), Caquot Syr xli 261 :: Milik Syr xliv 292: l. *dkyr*) - **2)** *lṭb* + Part. + indication of person(s) + *qdm*-phrase + *lṭb* (*wNP*), *lṭb dkyr NP qdm mrn lṭb (wNP)* Hatra 174 - **Au)** consisting of five elements: Part., *ṭb*, *lʿlm ʿlmn*, indication of person(s) and *bṭb wšlm*, *dkyr ṭb lʿlm ʿlmn NP ... bṭb wšlm* CIS ii 1841 - **Av)** consisting of five elements, Part., *bṭb*, *lʿlm*, indication of person(s), and *bṭb*, *dkyr bṭb lʿlm NP bṭb* CIS ii 820 - **Aw)** consisting of five elements: indication of person(s), Part., *bṭb wšlm*, *lʿlm* and *mn qdm*-phrase, *NP dkyr bṭb wšlm lʿlm mn qdm dwšrʾ wmntw* J 184 (= prob. CIS ii 320F) - **Ax)** consisting of five elements, *lṭb*, Part., indication of person(s), *qdm*-phrase and *lʿlm*, *lṭb dkyr NP ... qdm mrn wgdʾ dy ʾbwlʾ lʿlm* Hatra 297 - bf Ay) consisting of five elements, Part., NP, *qdm*-phrase, *bṭb* and *lʿlm*, *dkyr ddlt ... qdm sry/w ... bṭb lʿlm* Assur 34 - **Az)** consisting of five elements, Part., NP, *qdm*-phrase, *lṭb wlšnpyr* and *lʿlm* (or related formula), *dkyr mlbyl ... qdm sry/w ... lṭb wlšnpyr lʿlm* Assur 25g (cf. also Assur 17 i 2ff. (*lymt [ʿ]lmyn*), 32j (*lymt [ʿ]lm[y]n*)) - **B)** formulae with two Part. and without exclamations - **Ba)** with repeated Part. *dkyr* - 1) comparable to the formula mentioned sub Ag 1, *dkyr dkyr NP qdm šmš* Hatra 2 - **2)** comparable to the formula mentioned sub An 3, *dkyr dkyr NP ... lṭb qdm ...* Hatra 48 - **Bb)** Part. pass. of *dkr₁* combined with Part. pass. of *brk₁* (:: Toll ZAW xciv 117: *dkyr* here to be related to *zkr₃*, *bryk* expressing strength?) - **1)** *dkyr wbryk* in formula comparable to the one mentioned sub Aa 1, *dkyr wbryk NP* CIS ii 3186 (cf. Sumer xx 18 ii 3ff., CIS ii 2839[1], 3119, Syr vii 129[6], Inv ix 28[2]) - **2)** *dkyr wbryk* in formula comparable to the one mentioned sub Ab 1, *dkyr wbryk NP bṭb* CIS ii 534, 899 - **3)** *dkyr wbryk* in formula comparable to the one mentioned sub Ag 2, *dkyryn wbrykyn qdm ʾlhy tdmr ʾnʾ NP* (etc.) Syr xlvii 413[1ff.] (poss. comparable to Ag 1: *dkyryn wbrykyn NP* *mn qdm[* SBS 61b) - **4)** *dkyr wbryk* in formula comparable to the one mentioned in Ag 1, but with indication of person between the two Part., *dkyr NP wbryk qdm šḥyrw* Hatra 146 (bis) - **5)** *dkyr wbryk* in formula comparable to the one mentioned sub An 4, *dkyr wbryk NP qdw/ym ʾsr wsry/w lṭb* Assur 27i 2f. - 6) *dkyr wbryk* in formula comparable to the one mentioned sub Aq 1, *dkyr wbryk NP ... lṭb wlšnpyr qdm mrn wmrtn wnrgwl* Hatra 81[1ff.] - **7)** *dkyr wbryk* in formula comparable to the one mentioned sub Aq 2, *[d]kyr wbryk NP qdm [m]rn lṭb wlšnpyr* Hatra 77 (cf. also Assur 27d) - **8)** *dkyr wbryk* in formula consisting of the same elements as those mentioned sub Aq but in the order *dkyr wbryk* + *qdm*-phrase + indication of person(s) + *lṭb (w)lšnpyr*, *dkyr wbryk qdm bʿšmyn ... NP ... lṭb wlšnpyr* Hatra 23[1f.] (cf. Hatra 25[1f.] with as last part of formula *lṭb lšnpyr*); cf. also *bryk wdkyr* in formula consisting of the same elements as those mentioned sub Aq, but in the order *bryk wdkyr*, *lṭb*, *wlš[pr]*, *NP*, *qdm*-phrase, *bryk wdkyr lṭb Wlš[pr] NP qdm ʾs[r]* Assur 14[2f] - **9)** with same elements as sub 8, but with both Part. separated by other elements, *bryk NP qdm gndʾ dkyr lṭb wlšnpyr* Hatra 296 - **10)** *dkyr wbryk* in formula comparable to the one mentioned sub Ay, *dkyryn [w]brykyn NP wNP qdm ʾlhʾ klhwn lṭ[b] wlšnpyr l[ʿ]lm* .... Assur 28a 2ff. - **C)** formulae combined with exclamation(s) - **Ca)** introduced by interjections *bl* (v. *bl$_5$*), *blʾ* (v. *blʾ$_2$*), *bly* (v. *bly$_3$*) - **1)** in formula comparable to the one mentioned sub Aa 1, *bl dkyr NP* Hatra 24[1] (cf. CIS ii 4207, Hatra 24[3,4], 48[1], 51, etc., etc.); *bly dkyr NP* CIS ii 243 (cf. CIS ii 273, 293, J 157[1], 255, 281, ARNA-Nab 17[3ff.], 65[1f.] (dam. text)) - **2)** in formula comparable to the one mentioned sub Aa 2, *bl NP dkyr* Hatra 136 - **3)** in formula comparable to the one mentioned sub Ab 4, *bl dkyr NP lṭb* Hatra 99 (cf. Hatra 24[3] (for the context, cf. Degen ZDMG cxxi 125), 103 (?), 128, 129, 302, 303, 310, 317, 318); *blʾ dkyr [NP] lṭb* CIS ii 246 - **4)** in formula comparable to the one mentioned sub Ab 6, *bl NP dkyr lṭb* Hatra 136 - **5)** in formula comparable to the one mentioned sub Aj, *bl dkyr NP lṭb wlšpr* Hatra 309 - 6) in formula comparable to the one mentioned sub Ab 7, *lṭb bl dkyr NP* Hatra 321 - **7)** in formula comparable to the one mentioned sub Ag 1, *bl dkyr NP qdm brmryn* Hatra 127 (cf. Hatra 161[1]) - **8)** in formula comparable to the one mentioned sub An 3, *bl dkyr NP lṭb qdm brmryn ...* Hatra 125[1f.] (cf. Hatra 298, 325) - **9)** in formula comparable to the one mentioned sub An 4, *bl dkyr NP qdm mrn ... lṭb* Hatra 160 - **10)** in formula comparable to the one mentioned sub Aa 1 but with repeated Part., *bl dkyr dkyr NP* Hatra 315[1f.] - **Cb)** introduced by *mrn* used as interjection (v. *mrʾ*) - **1)** in formula comparable to the one mentioned sub Aa 1, *mrn dkyr NP* Hatra 119 (cf. Hatra 181, 258[2f.] (?)) - **2)** in formula comparable to the one mentioned sub Ab 4, *mrn dkyr NP lṭb* Hatra 117 (cf. Hatra 121, 220) - **3)** in formula comparable to the one mentioned sub Ab 6, *mrn NP dkyr lṭb* Hatra 253 - **4)** in formula comparable to the one mentioned sub Ab 7, *mrn lṭb dkyr NP* Hatra 331 - **5)** in formula comparable to the one mentioned sub Ag 1, *mrn dkyr NP ... qdm mrn* Hatra 152 - **6)** in formula comparable to the one mentioned sub Ag 2, *[m]rn dkyryn qdmyk NP wNP* Hatra 147 - **7)** in formula comparable to the one mentioned sub Aj, *mrn dkyr NP lṭb wlšnpyr* Hatra 118 - **8)** in formula comparable to the one mentioned sub An 4, *[m]rn dkyr NP wNP wNP qdm mrn lṭb* Hatra 324+328 - **9)** introducing formula consisting of four elements: Part., indication of person(s), *bmrn* and *lṭb*, *mrn dkyr NP bmrn lṭb* Hatra 179: Our lord! may NP be remembered with our lord for good - **10)** introducing formula consisting of five elements: Part. + *qdm*-phrase + indication of person(s) + *ldkrn› ṭb›* + *l‹lm*, *mrn dkryn qdmyk NP NP ldkrn› ṭb› l‹lm* Hatra 230 - **11)** introducing formula consisting of six elements: Part. + indication of person(s), *lṭb*, *l‹lm*, *qdm*-phrase and *lṭb wlšnpyr*, *mrn dkyr NP lṭb l‹lm qdm ›lh[›] klhwn lṭb wlšnpyr* Hatra 184 - **Cc)** formulae extended with *šlm* used as exclamation (v. *šlm₂*) - **1)** in formula comparable to the one mentioned sub Aa 1, *dkyr NP wNP šlm* CIS ii 376 (cf. CIS ii 409, PNO 67) - **2)** in formula comparable to the one mentioned sub Ab 1, *dkyr NP bṭb šlm* IEJ xxvii 224 iii 1ff. (= CIS ii 2673), cf. CIS ii 2098, Inv xi 75 - **3)** in formula consisting of the same elements as the one sub Af in the order Part., *‹d ‹lm›* and indication of person(s), *dkyr ‹d ‹lm› [N]P šlm* SBS 61e (cf. also SBS 60[8ff.]) - **4)** in formula comparable to the one mentioned sub An 2, *dkyr NP qdm bl w›rṣw šlm bṭb* MUSJ xlii 177[1f.] - **5)** in formula comparable to the one mentioned sub Bb 1, *dkyr bryk NP NP wNP šlm* Sumer xx 20 i; *dkyr wbryk NP šlm* — CIS ii 3186, cf. also *dkyryn wbrykyn ḥṣdy› ›ln ... šlm NP NP*, etc. Syr xl 33[1-9]: may these harvesters ... be remembered and blessed, peace!, NP, NP, etc. - **D)** formulae in which *šlm* is used parallel to *dkyr* - **1)** formula comparable to those mentioned sub Ab 1, 3, *šlm NP wdkyr bṭb* CIS ii 3010; cf. also *dkyr bṭb NP wšlm* EI x 184 ii - **2)** formula comparable to the one mentioned sub Al 1, *šlm wdkyr NP bṭb l‹lm* ARNA-Nab 67 - **3)** formula consisting of the same elements as those mentioned sub Al in the order: indication of person(s) + *šlm wPart* + *bṭb* + *l‹lm*, *NP šlm wdkyr bṭb l‹lm* BSOAS xvi 226, 78 - **E)** in formula consisting of the same elements as those mentioned sub Al in the order: Part., *l‹lm›*, indication of person(s) and *bṭb*, preceded by form of *hwy₁*, *yhwh dkyr l‹lm› hw wbnwhy bṭb* SBS 60[6f.]: may he and his sons be remembered forever for good - **F)** with geographical indication in *dkyrn l‹lm bḥṭr› w‹rbw›w* Hatra 79[14]: may they be remembered forever in H. and A. - HAPH/APH to pronounce, to mention; *yzkr ›šm hdd* KAI 214[16]: he will pronounce the name (of) Hadad (i.e. he will invoke Hadad; v. also supra); *mdkryn ... šmh d ...* AMB 15[20]: who mention the name of ... - Starcky RB lxxiii 616: pro *]dkyr* in Inv xi 76[1] l. *ydkyr* (= APH Impf. 3 p.s.m.?), highly uncert. reading - Naveh sub SM 102: l. *dkyr* in l. 2 (highly uncert. reading, cf. du Mesnil du Buisson RB xlv 76: l. *dkr* = n.p., cf. Torrey Syn D p. 275 sub 21: l. *dkh* = n.p.) - the diff. *dkrʾ* in SM 104[6] = QAL Part. pass. s.m. emph.?? × du Mesnil du Buisson Bibl xviii 171 (n. 1), Frey sub 845 (reading incorrectly *dkrh*), Naveh sub SM 104: = Sing. emph. of *dkr*$_2$ :: Milik DFD 410f.: l. *dqrʾ* = *d*$_2$ + QAL Pf. 3 p.s.m. of *qrʾ*$_1$ - the *dkry* in PNO 77[1] poss. = lapsus for *dkyr* (cf. however Ingholt & Starcky PNO a.l.: = n.p.) - Segal ATNS a.l.: l. poss. a form of this root in ATNS 68 ii 1 (diff. reading, heavily dam. context) - a form *mdkyr* in CIS ii 1044 of uncert. reading, CIS ii a.l.: l. prob. (div. otherwise) *dkyr* (Greek par. μνησθῇ).

v. *bkr*$_1$, *dr*$_1$,*zkr*$_2$, *zkrn*, *rḥym*.

zkr$_2$ **Ph** Sing. abs. *skr* KAI 18[6], 53[1], DD 10[1] (or preferably cstr.?, v. *šm*$_1$), 16[1]; cstr. *skr* DD 5[1] (= RES 250, KI 15), 11[1] (for the forms with *s*, v. *zkr*$_1$)- **Pun** Sing. abs. *skr* CIS i 6000bis 4 (= TPC 84); cstr. *skr* KAI 123[4], 161[5] (cf. Février RA xlv 143), NP 130[1] (:: Krahmalkov JSS xxiv 27: = QAL Imper. s. (or pl.) m. of *zkr*$_1$),Punica xvi 2[3] (for reading of context, v. *dr*$_1$), *skʿr* KAI 165[7] (on this orthography, cf. FR 96c); + suff. 3 p.pl.m. *škʿrnm* KAI 160[1] (cf. Levi Della Vida RCL '55, 556 n. 2) - **Hebr** Sing. cstr. *zkr* IEJ vii 244[2], Frey 625 (dam. context) - **Samal** Sing. abs. *zkr* KAI 215[22] - **JAr** Sing. abs. *dkr*RES 1890 - ¶ subst. m. memory, memorial; context of KAI 215[22] obscure; cf. the following combinations - a) *mṣbt skr* KAI 53[1], DD 5[1], 10[1], 11[1]: memorial stele - b) *skr drʾ* KAI 165[7f.] (*skʿr d[ʿ]rʾ*, v. *dr*$_1$): memorial (stone) from his family, cf. NP 130[1], Punica xvi 2[3f.] - c) *skr kbd ʿl* ... KAI 123[4]: glorious memorial for ..., cf. KAI 161[5] - in KAI 43[3] l. prob. *skr* (Sing. abs. or cstr., dam. context), for this reading, cf. e.g. Honeyman JEA xxvi 57, v.d.Branden OA iii 252, cf. also Lipiński RTAT 250.

v. *zkr*$_{1,3}$, *nṣb*$_5$, *škn*$_1$.

zkr$_3$ **Hebr** Sing. m. abs. *zkr* AMB 4[15] - **Samal** Sing. m. abs. *zkr* KAI 214[30]; Plur. m. abs. (nom.) *zkrw* KAI 214[31]; m. abs. (casus obliquus) *zkry* KAI 214[28] (for the interpret. of these texts, cf. Poeb 44, Dion p. 33f., 130, cf. also for l. 31 Cooke NSI p. 171 :: - a) for l. 30, Lidzbarski Handb 268 (with reserve), Cooke NSI p. 163, 171 (with reserve), Donner KAI a.l.: = Sing. abs. of *zkr*$_2$- b) for l. 28, Lidzbarski Handb 268, Cooke NSI p. 162, 170, Friedr 35*, Donner KAI a.l., Altheim & Stiehl AAW i 225, Sader EAS 164: = Sing. + suff. 1 p.s. of *zkr*$_2$- c) for l. 31, Friedr 33*b, Donner KAI a.l., Friedrich FS Landsberger 427, Altheim & Stiehl AAW i 225, Segert ArchOr xxvi 568: = Sing. abs. of *zkrw* (= memory; cf. also Lidzbarski, Handb 268) - **OffAr** Sing. m. abs. *zkr* Krael 3[21], 7[28], *dkr* Cowl 15[17,20]; Plur. m. abs. *zkrn* Sam 7[7]; cf. Frah xi 6 (*zkl*),

xxvi 2 (*zkl*; cf. Nyberg FP 56, 105 :: Ebeling Frah a.l.: l. *zyl*$_1$ (= of small value)) - **Nab** Sing. m. emph. *dkr›*J 12[6] (= CIS ii 205); Plur. m. abs. *dkryn*CIS ii 209[2,5] - **Palm** Plur. m. abs. *dkryn* CIS ii 4214, Inv viii 58[2] (Greek par. ἄ[ρσε]σι); m. emph. *dkry›*CIS ii 4159[6], 4172[3], 4196, Syr xiv 184[2], Ber ii 109[3] (Greek par. ἄρσεσι), xix 71[7], *dkr›*Ber ii 60[2] - **JAr** Sing. m. abs. *dkr*AMB 7a 7, 7b 3 - ¶ adj. male, of the male sex.
v. *›rṣ*$_1$, *zkr*$_1$.

zkrw v. *zkr*$_3$,*zkrwt*$_1$.

zkrwn v. *zkrn*.

zkrwt$_1$ **OffAr** a Sing. emph. of this word (*zkrwt›*) has been supposed in KAI 273[1] (= memory, memorial), cf. Altheim & Stiehl ASA 269, AAW i 228 (cf. also idem Suppl 11f.: = mention, listing (cf. idem GMA 341)), Donner KAI a.l., In der Smitten BiOr xxviii 309, Kutscher, Naveh & Shaked Lesh xxxiv 126 (cf. also Andreas NGWG '32, 9). Reading however uncertain, cf. Degen Lesh xxxiv 315, ZDMG cxxi 125, 138, Humbach AIT 7ff., cf. also Cowley JRAS '15, 343: l. *ṣdwq* (Sing. abs.) = memorial.

zkrwt$_2$ v. *zngrwt*.

zkrn **Ph** Sing. abs. *zkrn* DD 14[2] (:: Krahmalkov OA xi 214: = Qal Pf. 3 p.s.m. + suff. 1 p.s. of *zkr*$_1$),*skrn* Mus li 286[3] - **Hebr** Sing. abs. *zykrwn* Frey 630b 1; + suff. 3 p.s.m. *zykrwnw*Frey 892[2] (for the reading, cf. Klein MGWJ lxxv 370); + suff. 3 p.s.f. *zkrwnh*Frey 630[3] - **OldAr** Sing. abs. *zkrn* KAI 222C 2f. - **OffAr** Sing. abs. *zkrn* Cowl 32[1,2] (for the transl. of these ll., cf. Wag 22), 61[10], 62 i 4 (or cstr.?), 63[10,12,14] (or cstr.?), 68 xi obv. 2 (or cstr.?), AJSL lviii 303B 4 - **Nab** Sing. abs. *dkrn*CIS ii 236[1] (for the context, cf. also Milik DFD 409f.), *dkrwn*CIS ii 163[1], 169[1] (?), 407, 3072, IEJ xi 130 iii 1, ADAJ xxi 139[1] (= CIS ii 476), etc.; cstr. *dkrwn*CIS ii 338[1] (for the forms with -*w*-, cf. Hopkins BSOAS xl 141) - **Palm** Sing. abs. *dkrn*CIS ii 3987[1], 3993[1], 4000[1], 4001[1], 4062[1], 4540[6], Inv xi 4[1], 6[5], xii 51[1], etc.; cstr. *dkrn*CIS ii 4180, PNO 52[1], 74[1]; emph. *dkrn›*CIS ii 4123[1]; + suff. 3 p.s.f. *dkrnh* DFD 163[6] - **Hatra** Sing. abs. *dkrn*149 (for the reading, cf. Vattioni IH a.l. :: Safar Sumer xviii 45, Caquot Syr xli 261: l. *dkyr* = Qal Part. pass. s.m. abs. of *zkr*$_1$); emph. *dkrn›*230[4], app. 3[1] (= KAI 257[1]; for the reading, cf. du Mesnil du Buisson Syr xix 147, Degen WO v 233, ZDMG cxxi 125, 136 :: Caquot Syr xxx 245, Donner KAI a.l.: l. Sing. abs. *dkrn*);+ suff. 3 p.s.m. *dkrnh*83[3]; Plur. abs. *dkrnyn*16[1,2] (for the reading, cf. Milik RN vi/iv 53 (n. 2), DFD 393, Teixidor Syr xliv 189, Degen WO v 234, Vattioni IH a.l. :: Safar Sumer vii 179, Caquot Syr xxix 98, Donner sub KAI 241 (div. otherwise): l. *dkrn*(Sing. abs.) *wn*- :: Altheim & Stiehl AAW ii 196 (div. otherwise): l. *dkrn* (Sing. abs.) *yn*- - **JAr** Sing. + suff. 3 p.pl.m. *dkrnhwn*MPAT-A 34[1] (for the reading, cf. Naveh sub SM 69 :: Fitzmyer & Harrington MPAT a.l.: l. *dkrwnhwn*)- ¶ subst.

m. - **A)** memory, memorial: Mus li 286[3], DD 14[2], CIS ii 4180[1], 4540[6], PNO 6a, 52[1], 74, Hatra 83[3]; said of tomb: CIS ii 4123[1] (cf. Greek par. μνημεῖον αἰώνιον γέρας for *dkrn› ... dy hw yqr bt ‹lm›*); cf. *yhwy dkrnhwn lṭb* MPAT-A 34[1]: may their memory be for good; *ldkrnh dy ‹lm›* DFD 163[6]: that she may be remembered forever (cf. Greek par. μνήμης χάριν), cf. also Hatra 230[4]; cf. *ph ynwḥ bzykrwn ṭb šmw›l* Frey 630b 1f.: here may rest in good memory Sh. ...; *zkrwnh thy lbrkh* Frey 661[3f.]: her memory be to blessing - **1)** *dkrwn (ṭb)* + l_5 - a) (good) memory for (someone, i.e. that people may remember him): CIS ii 163[1], 236[1] (v. supra), 426E, 478, Qedem vi 70 no. 254, PNO 41; *dkrnyn ṭbyn l‹qyb›* Hatra 16[1]: good memories for A., cf. Hatra 16[2], KAI 257[1]; *dkrn ṭb lNP qdm bl* Inv xii 51: good memory for NP before Bel, cf. ADAJ xx 127; *mrn dkrn lṭbyn lNP* Hatra 149: my lord, a memory for good for ... (for the reading, v. supra, v. *ṭb*$_2$); *dkrwn ṭb wšlm lNP* J 180[1f.]: good memory and well-being for NP, cf. IEJ xi 130 iii 1, CIS ii 459, ADAJ xxi 139[1] (cf. also CIS ii 3072); *dkrwn NP mn qdm dwšr› lNP br[h]* CIS ii 338: memorial of NP (i.e. erected by him) before D. on behalf of his son NP; *dkrn ṭb lNP mn qdm šmy›* CIS ii 236[1f.]: good memory for NP before the Heavens (for this reading, cf. Milik DFD 410; cf. also Hatra app. 3[1f.]) - b) memorial for (someone, i.e. that he may remember): KAI 222C 2f., Inv D 20, Inv xi 4[1f.], 6[5]; *dkrn ṭb lmr› ‹lm›* RIP 126[1], cf. CIS ii 3987[1], 4000[1], 4001[1], 4062[1], Inv xi 24[1f.], 74[1], xii 56[1], RIP 125[1] - **2)** + *qdm*$_3$, *ldkrn qdm bryk šmh* Inv xi 28[1f.]: as a memorial before the one whose name is blessed; cf. *dkrn ṭb qdm br[yk] šmh l‹lm›* Ber iii 84[1f.] - **B)** memorandum: Cowl 32[1,2] (on this text, cf. Greenfield CAL 290), 61[10] (prob. also in the other Cowl-instances); for the interpret. of the context, cf. e.g. Grelot DAE p. 415, Porten & Yardeni sub TADAE A 4.9; + *‹l*$_7$, memorandum concerning: Cowl 63[10], AJSL lviii 303B 4.
v. *zkr*$_1$.

zl **DA** Levine JAOS ci 200: l. *zl* = Sing. cstr. of *zl* (= shadow) in DA ii 15 (uncert. reading and interpret.; for the reading problems, cf. v.d.Kooij DA p. 131).

zlb v. *gnb*$_2$.

zlh **Samal** Sing. cstr. (v. infra) *zlt* KAI 215[10] - ¶ subst. prob. meaning cheapness (cf. e.g. Cooke NSI p. 174, 177, Dion p. 76, 404 n. 32, 415 n. 1, Delsman TUAT i 629; cf. also Dupont-Sommer AH i/2, 3: = adj. (cheap), Sing. f. cstr. or Plur. f. abs.).

zlw‹ **OffAr** Sing. abs. *zlw‹* Cowl 15[13], 36[4], Krael 7[15]; Plur. abs. *zlw‹n* Krael 7[18] - ¶ subst. m. exact meaning unknown, prob. bottle, jug (cf. also Fitzmyer FS Albright ii 155, WA 258; cf. Grelot RB lxviii 532, DAE p. 194: = decanter; Cowl a.l. & Krael a.l. = bowl).

zlyq **OffAr** Altheim & Stiehl FuF xxxv 173, ASA 269: the *zlyq* in FuF xxxv 173[12] = Sing. abs. of *zlyq* (= lustre, splendour).

zlm **DA** a form of this root poss. in ii 15 (uncert. reading, dam. context; cf. Hoftijzer DA p. 243).
zmbr v. zbr_2.
zmh v. *ywm*.
zmm v. *ʿny*$_1$.
zmn$_1$ **DA** Puech BAT 356, 360f.: l. *yzmn* = PAʿEL Impf. 3 p.s.m. of *zmn*$_1$ in i 3 + viiid 1 (= to convoke, to invite), diff. reading, cf. also idem FS Grelot 17, 19, 27, Lemaire BAT 318: l. *ymn* = Plur. abs. of *ywm*; for the reading, cf. also v.d.Kooij DA p. 155 - **OffAr** a verb *zmn* in RES 1785A 4? Uncert. reading, cf. Lidzbarski Eph i 325f. = to be intended.
zmn$_2$ (poss. < Akkad., cf. Kaufman AIA 91f., 143, cf. however Hinz AISN 143, Lipiński LDA 108f.: < Iran.; cf. also Zimmern Fremdw 63) - **Hebr** Sing. abs. *zmn* EI xx 256^8 - **OffAr** Sing. emph. *zmnʾ* ATNS 2^4, 18^6, 80^4 (?; *zmn[ʾ]*), cf. Paik 24 (*zmn*, *zmʾn*), 344 (*zmn*), 345 (*zmʾn*) - **Nab** Sing. abs. (or cstr.?) *zmn* CIS ii 158^5; cstr. *zmn* CIS ii 204^3; Plur. abs. *zmnyn* CIS ii 196^6 - **JAr** Sing. abs. *zmn* MPAT 40^{23}, 42^{19} (*[z]mn*), 46^5, IEJ xxxvi 206^7, DBKP 17^{41}; emph. *zm[nʾ]* MPAT 39^5 - ¶ subst. m. time, moment in time; *bzk zmnʾ* ATNS 18^6: at that time (dam. context); *mn zmn šṭr mwhbtʾ* CIS ii $204^{3f.}$: from the moment the deed of gift was issued; *zmnyn tryn* CIS ii 196^6: two times; *bkl zmn* EI xx 256^8: at any moment (cf. DBKP 17^{41}) - Grelot DAE 73 (n. h): l. poss. *[z]mnʾ* (= Sing. emph.) in MAI xiv/2, 66^8 (poss. restoration :: Dupont-Sommer MAI xiv/2, 66f., 76: l. *[ʾ]mnʾ* = QAL Impf. 1 p.s. of *mny*); v. also zbn_3.
zmr$_1$ **Hebr** PIʿEL Imper. pl.m. *zmrw* AMB 4^{11} - **OffAr**, cf. Frah xix 16 (*zml-lwn*) - ¶ verb PIʿEL to sing; *zmrw ldwyd ldwr wdr* (reading of *dwr* diff.) AMB 4^{11}: sing for D. forever.
zmr$_2$ **Hatra** m. Sing. emph. *zmrʾ* 219^2; f. Sing. emph. *zmrtʾ* Hatra 342^4 - ¶ subst. singer (prob. temple function): Hatra 291^2, 342^4 (cf. also Aggoula Syr lxiv 97) - Milik Bibl xlviii 556 n. 1, DFD 55ff.: the *zmrʾ* in Syr xxvi 45^6 (= Inv x 145) = Plur. emph., cf. however Starcky Syr xxvi 49ff.: = n.p. (cf. however idem CRAI '46, 393), cf. also Gawlikowski TP 35, 40 - the word (Sing. emph. *zmrʾ*) poss. also in short Nab. inscription, cf. RB xliii 578 (sub 22), or = n.p.? - Milik DFD 56: l. *zmrʾ* (= Sing. emph.) in CIS ii 457, 458 pro *nmrʾ* = n.p. (cf. CIS ii a.l., Cantineau Nab ii 121), less prob. interpret.
zmr$_3$ **Hebr** Sing. abs. *zmr* KAI 182^6 - ¶ subst. vintage (cf. e.g. Lemaire VT xxv 17ff. (also for older litt.), Lipiński OLP viii 84, cf. also Borowski AIAI 36, 38) × e.g. Dir p. 8, Février Sem i 36f., Albright BASOR xcii 23 n. 38, ANET 320, Gibson SSI i p. 2, 4, Smelik HDAI 28: = pruning.
zmr$_4$ v. *zpr*.
zmrt **Nab** Milik DFD 56: l. *zmrtʾ* (form?) = special type of singer in

CIS ii 454 (uncert. reading, highly uncert. interpret.).

zn_1 (< Iran., cf. e.g. Nöldeke Gramm § 146, Telegdi JA ccxxvi 242f., Ellenbogen 71f., HAL s.v., Hinz AISN 276, Brown Bibl lxx 204, cf. also Watson Bibl liii 194) - **OffAr** Sing. abs. *zn* Cowl 17[3] - ¶ subst. type, kind; in the expression *zn zn*, every type/kind, cf. Joüon MUSJ xviii 17f. - Altheim & Stiehl AAW v/1, 82, 84: the *zn*ʾ in Hatra app. 4[5] = Sing. emph. of zn_1 used adverbially (in the way of), improb. interpret.; prob. = (part of) n.p.

v. $tbnh_2$.

zn_2 v. $tbnh_2$.

zn_3 v. $tbnh_2$.

zn_4 v. zyn_2.

zn_5 v. z_1,*znh*.

znʾ v. *znh*.

zngrwyr v. *zngrwt*.

zngrwt cf. Frah ix 11: virility (< $zkrwt_2$,cf. Ebeling Frah a.l.; cf. however Nyberg FP 44, 74: l. *znglwyr*ʾ = *zngrwyr*ʾ (= ginger) < Sanskrit).

znh **Ph** Sing. m. *zn*KAI 1[2], 2[3], 9A 1, 3, 5, 10[4,5,12], 11, 29[1] (*[z]n*, for this reading cf. e.g. Burrows JRAS '27, 791, Röllig KAI a.l., Garbini ISN 63, Amadasi Guzzo Or lix 59f., cf. however Ginsberg FS Gaster 141, Gibson SSI iii p. 72, Garr DGSP 148f. n. 23, O'Connor AO vi 48 n. 3: l. *[š]n* = Sing. abs. of $šn_1$ (= ivory)), MUSJ xlv 262[1] (cf. FR 113b, Healy CISFP i 664, Del Olmo Lete FPI 41) - **DA** Plur. ʾ*l* i 3 (for this interpret., cf. e.g. Hoftijzer DA a.l., Caquot & Lemaire Syr liv 194 × e.g. Garbini Hen i 173, H. & M. Weippert ZDPV xcviii 84, 102, Levine BAT 333, Puech BAT 360, Wesselius BiOr xliv 593f.: = n.d.) - **Samal** Sing. m. *zn* KAI 214[1,14,16] (?, dam. context), 215[1,20] (on this form, cf. also Cook Maarav v/vi 64f.), *znh* KAI 215[22]; f. *z*ʾKAI 214[18,19] (dam. context); Plur. ʾ*l* KAI 214[29] - **OldAr** Sing. m. *znh* KAI 202A 17, B 14, 18, 19, 216[20], 222A 6f. (*[z]nh*), 36, 40, B 8f. (*zn[h]*), 28, 33, C 17, 224[14,17,23] (*zn[h]*); f. *z*ʾKAI 222A 35, 37, 224[9]; Plur. ʾ*l*KAI 202A 9, 16, B 8, ʾ*ln* (on this form, cf. Cook Maarav v/vi 64) KAI 222A 7, 38, B 7, 11f. (ʾ*l[n]*), 24, 38, 223C 2, 9, 224[7,9,19,20f.,27] - **OffAr** Sing. m. *znh* KAI 225[3,7], 226[2], 228A 4 (*zn[h]*, cf. Segal BSOAS xl 375, Degen GGA '79, 27, 49 n. 85 :: e.g. Cooke NSI p. 195, Donner KAI a.l., Gibson SSI ii sub 30, Segert AAG p. 176, Cook Maarav v/vi 64: l. *zn*), 260[6] (with f. noun, cf. also Lipiński Stud 159), 266[8] (for the reading, cf. Rosenthal with Ginsberg BASOR cxi 25 n. 4c, Fitzmyer Bibl xlvi 54, Gibson SSI ii sub 21, Porten BiAr xliv 36 :: e.g. Dupont-Sommer Sem i 44, 52, Donner KAI a.l., Shea BASOR ccxxiii 61: l. *zkm*), Cowl 2[10,11], 34[2] (with pl.f. noun), Krael 1[5,9], Driv 4[4], 6[5], Herm 1[13], 2[17], ATNS 2[2,4,6], Pers 1[3], CIS ii 38[1] (= Del 21; with pl. noun *š*ʿ*rn*), etc., etc., *zn*ʾKrael 9[16], Or lvii 16[3] (?, heavily dam. context), *dnh* Cowl 16[9], 54[8] (for the reading, cf. Porten

& Yardeni sub TADAE A 3.1 recto 7: l. *kdnh* (= k_1 + *dnh*) :: Cowl a.l.: l. prob. *bnwh[y]* = Plur. + suff. 3 p.s.m. of br_1),Krael 5[3], 10[3], Pers 43[3] (for the reading, cf. Naveh & Shaked Or xlii 455 n. 68 :: R.A.Bowman Pers a.l.: l. *znh*), 44[3], LA ix 331[3], *dn*ʾJAOS liv 31[1,5]; f. *z*ʾKAI 233[8], Cowl 21[3], 30[17], 42[7], ATNS 2[1], etc., *dh*Herm 5[7]; Plur. ʾ*lh* Cowl 2[13], 7[10], 13[13], Krael 3[7], 6[14], 7[41], Driv 8[3], BSOAS xxvii 272 iv 2, ATNS 4[3] (for the reading, cf. Porten & Yardeni, sub TADAE 8.7 :: Segal ATNS a.l.: l. ʾ*lk*), 4[6] (dam. context; cf. Porten & Yardeni, sub TADAE B 8.7 :: Segal ATNS a.l.: preferably = ʾlh_4 (= ʾ$lʾ_3$(= except))), 13[1], Samar 1[7] (= EI xviii 8*), etc., ʾ*ln* CIS ii 111[5]; for the presumed ʾ*lw* in KAI 271A 2, 5, v. ʾlp_3; cf. Frah xxiv 9 (*znh*), 11 (*znh*), Frah-S_2 19 (*ḥdnh*), Paik 348 (*znh*), 524 (*kdnh*), 576 (*lznh*), Nisa 14[1], 16[1], 17[1], 18[1], 19[2], etc. (*znh*), Sogd ii 238, B. 257, R. 56, Gi 60f., Ve 113, 123, ML 587, Syn 300[5], 301[5], 304[3,4], 305[4], 311[3], AJSL liii 139, ZDMG xcii 441[3], 442A 14, B 4, IrAnt vii 150 (cf. however Bogoljubov PaSb lxxxvi 102f.: l. *qʿr*ʾ = Sing. emph. of *qʿr* (= vessel, bowl)), BSOAS xxxiii 148[7], 152[11,12], GH iv 78ff., FS Nyberg 276 xiv, GIPP 27, 38f., 68, SaSt 14 (ʿ*lḥ* pro ʾ*lh*), 22, 27, cf. Lemosín AO ii 266 - **Nab** Sing. m. *znh* Chal 1, *dnh* CIS ii 164[1], 170[3], 182[1], IEJ xi 133[1], ARNA-Nab 16[1], MPAT 64 i 7, etc., etc., *dn*ʾIEJ xiii 113[2], xxi 50[1] (*[d]n*ʾ); f. *d*ʾ CIS ii 158[1], 160[1], 191[1], ARNA-Nab 79[5] (= CIS ii 200 = J 30), RB lxxii 95[1], MPAT 61[25] (= DBKP 15), etc., etc., *dh*RES 2052[1] (*[d]h*), 2064 (*[d]h*); Plur. ʾ*lh*CIS ii 207[3], 350[3], RES 1088[1], J 2[1], 12[6], IEJ xxix 112[5] (cf. Naveh IEJ xxix 113, 117; interpret. of context however highly uncert.), ʾ*ln* RES 1432[1] (for the reading, cf. Starcky SOLDV ii 523 n. 3, Couroyer RB lxix 154 :: Savignac RB xxii 441, RES sub 1432: l. ʾ*lk*), ʾ*nw* CIS ii 350[4,5], MPAT 64 iii 6 (on the Nab. Plur. forms, cf. also Levinson NAI 31ff.) - **Palm** Sing. m. *dnh*CIS ii 3908[1], 3909[1], 3916[1], SBS 32[1], 37[1], RIP 24[3] (Greek par. τοῦτο)[,4], Inv xii 2[1], etc., etc. (with f. noun ʿ*lt*ʾ *dnh*, cf. Inv xi 20[3], 32[3], xii 34[3]), *dn*ʾCIS ii 3911[3], Syr xxvi 45 ii 1, SBS 87 (?, heavily dam. context); f. *zh* DM ii 40 iv 2 (poss. reading); *dh*CIS ii 3903[1], 3969[1], 3975[3], SBS 23[1], 45[10] (Greek par. αὐτῇ), RIP 24[6], Inv xi 9[2], xii 1[1], etc., etc., *rh* (lapsus) CIS ii 4195[4], *d*ʾInv xi 79[3] (?, diff. context; followed by m. noun?, cf. also Silverman JAOS lxxxix 633); Plur. ʾ*ln* CIS ii 3913 i 6, 7, 3914[4], SBS 10[3], RIP 21[1,4], Inv xi 77[2], xii 39, etc., etc., *hln*RB xxxix 548[4], Syr xvii 280[4] (?, highly uncert. reading, cf. Milik DFD 310f.) - **Hatra** Sing. m. *hdyn*53[2] (for the reading, cf. Aggoula Ber xviii 95, Degen NESE ii 100, Vattioni IH a.l.), app. 3 (= KAI 257; for the reading, cf. also du Mesnil du Buisson Syr xix 148f.), ʿ*dyn* 101[2] (for the reading, cf. also Degen NESE ii 101 n. 9 (cf. also Caquot Syr xl 11, Vattioni IH a.l.) :: Safar Sumer xvii 34: = n.p.); f. *hd*ʾ282 (cf. also Assur 28a 4); Plur. m. *hlyn*281[10], ʾ*n*ʾ 50[3] (?; cf. Aggoula Ber xviii 95 :: Caquot Syr xxxii 54f.: l. ʾ*k*ʾ = there (for this reading, cf. also Safar

Sumer vii 245 (n. 32)) :: Vattioni IH a.l.: l. *ʾlʾ* (= Sing. emph. of *ʾ*l_1)? :: Teixidor Syr xli 281 n. 4: l. *ʾl[h]ʾ* = Plur. emph. of *ʾ*lh_1 :: Milik DFD 358f.: l. *ʾl[h]ʾ* = Sing. emph. of *ʾ*lh_1) - **JAr** Sing. m. *znh* MPAT 49 i 3, 5, 6, DJD ii 62 (uncert. reading, heavily dam. context), *dnh*MPAT 39^{6}, 40^{2,13}, 50c 1, 51^{3,11,14}, 52^{4,10}, 67^{1} (= Frey 1300), etc. *dnʾ*MPAT 40^{17}, Frey 1077, *dn* MPAT 40^{9,22}, MPAT-A 35^{1} (= Frey 980 = SM 16), AMB 3^{14}, *hdn*MPAT-A 5^{3,7} (= Frey 1203 = SM 64), 7^{4} (= Frey 1204 = SM 65), 15^{2} (= Frey 982 = SM 18), 16^{2} (= Frey 981 = SM 17), 29^{4} (= Frey 859 = SM 35), 30^{1} (= SM 26), 40^{2} (= SM 57 :: Hüttenmeister ASI 304: l. *ddn* = lapsus for *hdn*), 42^{4} (= SM 20), SM 23, 110, *hʾdn* MPAT-A 25^{2} (= Frey 976 = SM 12; cf. Naveh sub SM 12 :: Frey a.l., Fitzmyer & Harrington MPAT a.l.: = h_1 (= article) + Sing. abs. of *ʾ*dn_3 :: Renan MP 779: = h_1 + Sing. abs. of *ʾ*rn_1),*hdyn*MPAT-A 1^{4} (*[h]dyn*; = SM 21), 3^{2} (= Frey 1199 = SM 60), 12^{5} (= Frey 1195 = SM 71), 46^{1}, SM 40^{1}, Frey 826a, 990^{1}, Syn D A 1 (= SM 88), 6 (uncert. reading, cf. Torrey Syn D a.l., cf. however Naveh sub SM 88: l. hdy_3= Sing. f.), C_1 1 (= SM 89a), C_2 1 (= SM 89b), 20^{1} (= SM 101); f. *dh*MPAT 39^{7}, 40^{5}, 69^{1}, 141^{1} (= Frey 1222; J.Ar. text in Palm. script), MPAT-A 48^{1} (= Frey 979, cf. SM 15; with m. noun: *byt dh*), *dʾ*Mas 556^{4}, *hdh*MPAT-A 36^{3} (= Frey 987a = SM 30), 37^{2} (= Frey 987b = SM 31), 39^{1} (= SM 42), 45^{2} (for the reading, cf. Avigad BethSh iii 171, Fitzmyer & Harrington MPAT a.l. :: Avigad IEJ iv 95: l. *hdʾ*), 51^{1}, ZDPV xcvi 59^{1}, *ḥdh* (lapsus) MPAT-A 14^{1} (= SM 47; cf. also Hestrin IR p. 186, Naveh SM a.l.), *hdʾ* Frey 892^{1}; Plur. *ʾln* Mas 556^{4}, *hlyn*Syn D B 6 (= SM 88^{21}; dam. and diff. context; for the reading, cf. Naveh SM a.l.) - **Waw** Plur. m. *hlyn*AMB 6^{3} (for this reading, cf. Naveh & Shaked AMB a.l. :: Gordon Or xviii 340: l. *hnyn*= pron. pers. 3 p.pl.f. :: Dupont-Sommer Waw p. 14: = Plur. abs. of hn_2(= hwn_2 (= power, force)); cf. also Dupont-Sommer AIPHOS xi 120) - ¶ dem. pron., this, that/ these, those - **A)** as element in a phrase - **1)** as attribute in a noun phrase, *ʾrn zn* KAI 1^{2}: this sarcophagus; *nṣb hdd zn* KAI 214^{14}: this statue of Hadad; *ʿglʾ znh* KAI 222A 40: this calf; *mlkyʾ ʾl* KAI 202A 9: these kings; *šntʾ zʾ* Cowl 21^{3}: this year; *šnytʾ zʾ* ATNS 2^{1}: this mark (v. $šnt_2$); *ʾbšwnʾ znh* Pers 15^{4} (cf. Pers 19^{3}, 43^{3}, etc.; cf. however *ʾbšwn znh* Pers 3^{4} (cf. Pers 5^{2}, 20^{3}, etc.), *hwn rb znh* Pers 14^{2}: this large mortar (cf. Pers 31^{3}, etc.) and *sḥr znh rb* Pers 18^{2}: this large plate (cf. Pers 39$^{3f.}$)); *gṭʾ znh* Samar 3^{12}: this deed; *kprʾ dnh* CIS ii 197^{6}: this tomb; *ṣbwtʾ ʾln* CIS ii 3913 i 6: these things; *byt dh dʾwrḥwtyh* Frey 979^{1} (= MPAT-A 48^{1}; for the reading, v. *ʾ*$rḥ_2$): this hostel of his (v. also byt_2); etc., etc. - as attribute to a n.p., *mnky znh* ATNS 3^{7}: the said M.; *mnʾt dnh* CIS ii 200^{3}: the said M.; *hgrw dʾ* ARNA-Nab 79$^{4f.,5}$: the said H.; *gdrṣw dnh* Syr xlvii 314^{4}: the said G.; *šlmlt br mlkw dnh* RIP 24^{4}: the said Sh. the son of M.; *yhwḥnn znh* MPAT 49 i 3: the said Y. - **2)** as core element in a pronominal phrase, *znh sprʾ* Cowl 13^{2}: this document; *zʾ bʾyštʾ* Cowl 30^{17}: this evil; *zʾ šntʾ* ATNS 3^{3}: this year; *znh ṭʿmʾ* ATNS 2^{6}: this matter; *ʾlh mlyʾ* ATNS 13^{1}: these words; *znh ʾsrʾ* Samar 1^{11} (= EI xviii 8*): this covenant; *znh ʿbd zylh* Samar 1^{2} (= EI xviii 8*): this slave of his; *dʾ ʿmwd[ʾ]* Inv xi 79^{3}: this column; *ʿdyn ktbʾ* Hatra 101^{2}: this document; *hdyn byth* Syn D A 1 (= SM 88): this building; *bhdn ʾtrh qdyšh* MPAT-A 5^{7}: in this holy place; *hdh qbwrth* ZDPV xcvi 59^{1f}: this tomb; etc.; cf. *dʾ ʿly mnh* J 17^{9}: which is above it - **B)** used independently - **1)** not preceded by preposition, *ky zʾ zʾ ʾmr ly ...* KAI 233^{8}: for this, yes this, he said to me; *wkʿt zʾ* HDS 9^{1}: and now this (i.e. the following, cf. also Caquot HDS p. 12); *ʾlh tḥwmy bytʾ* Cowl 13^{13}: these are the boundaries of the house ...; *znh šmht* Cowl 34^{2}: these are the names; *wmhy dh zy* Herm 5^{7}: and what is this that ... (i.e. what does this mean that ...); *dnh ṣlmʾ* CIS ii 164^{1}: this is the statue; *dnh ṣlmʾ ḥrtt* RB lxxiii 237^{1}: this is the statue Ch. (i.e. of Ch.); *dʾ npš ptrys* RB lxxii 95^{1}: this is the funerary monument of P.; *wdʾ bywm ḥd* RES 676^{4}: and this was (i.e. happened) on the first day (cf. J 11^{9}); *zbdbwl br zbdʿth dnh* SBS 62: this is Z. the son of Z.; *brykyn ʾln klhwn* Inv xi $77^{1f.}$: may all these be blessed; *hdʾ qbwrtʾ* Frey 892^{1}: this is the tomb; *wšnt šmṭh dh w...* MPAT 39^{7}: and (if) this is the year of Release, and ...; *ʿbd hʾdn* MPAT-A 25^{2} (v. supra): he made this; etc.; cf. also *ʾnʾ dmšknʾ* Hatra 50^{3} (v. supra): those who belong to the sanctuary; *nsḥt dnh* CIS ii 209^{9} (= J 36): the copy of this; for the interpret. of the diff. *znh* in KAI $279^{3,4}$, cf. e.g. Dupont-Sommer JA ccxlvi 27, 33, Nober VD xxxvii 374, Altheim & Stiehl EW x 245, GH i 400f., ii 173, GMA 349f., ASA 26f., Garbini Kand 10f., 13 n. 2, Kutscher, Naveh & Shaked Lesh xxxiv 130, Rosenthal EI xiv 97* - **2)** preceded by prep. - a) preceded by b_2 - α) *bznh* Driv 3^{2}, 5^{1} (cf. Fales JAOS cvii 459), 10^{1}, 12^{7}, *bdnh* Syr xlvii 131^{1}, *bhdyn* MPAT-A 46^{1}: here - β) *bzʾ* KAI 224^{9}: in this respect - b) preceded by k_1, *kdnh* Krael 5^{3}: thus, as follows; *kdn yhy qym* MPAT 40^{9}: so let it be determined (cf. prob. also Cowl 54^{8} (v. supra; heavily dam. context), MPAT $40^{22f.}$) - c) preceded by *mn ʾḥry*, *mn ʾḥry znh* Samar 6^{5}: hereafter - d) preceded by *mn qdm(t)*, *mn qdm dh* MPAT 40^{5}: up to this (sc. time); *mn qdmt dnʾ* MPAT 40^{17}: up to this (sc. time), cf. MPAT 52^{4} - e) preceded by $ʿl_7$, *ʿ[l] dnh* Cowl 16^{9}: concerning this (cf. also Cowl 26^{6}, 30^{28}, SSI ii 28 obv. 4 (heavily dam. context)) - f) preceded by qdm_3, *wdkyr qdm ʾln ʾnš ʾnš* Sem xxvii $117^{6f.}$: and may everyone be remembered before these (i.e. the gods mentioned above) - g) preceded by *tḥwt*, *tḥwt hln*RB xxxix 548^{4}: in exchange for these - Kaplan EI xix 285: l. *dyʾn* in Frey 896^{1} = variant form of *hdyn* (highly uncert. interpret.) - Altheim & Stiehl FuF xxxv 175: *zn* in *hlzn* FuF xxxv 173^{3} = zn_5 (= *znh*), diff. context - Caquot & Lemaire Syr liv 203: both instances of *ʾl* in DA ii 6

= *’l*$_5$ (improb. interpret., cf. Hoftijzer DA a.l., Rofé SB 68, H.P.Müller ZDPV xciv 63 (n. 42): = n.d.) - e.g. Röllig KAI a.l., Gibson SSI ii p. 5: the *]zt* in KAI 232 prob. = s.f. demonstrative pronoun (heavily dam. context, uncert. interpret., cf. also Puech RB lxxxviii 545f., 556, 561 (div. otherwise): l. *[’ḥ]zt* = Sing. cstr. of *’ḥzh* (= annexation)).
v. *’ḥd*$_4$, *br*$_1$, *dnt*, *hykylyn*, *z*$_1$,*kdn*, *kwt*, *l’*$_2$, *lkdn’*, *mrzḥ*, *nwh*.

znzr v. *zrzr*.

znyh **Palm** Sing. emph. *znyt’* CIS ii 3913 ii 47 - ¶ subst. f. prostitute.

znk v. *zk*$_2$.

z‘wr v. *z‘r*$_2$, *‘bd*$_2$.

z‘yd v. *z‘yr*$_2$.

z‘yp v. *‘yp*.

z‘yr$_1$ v. *z‘r*$_2$.

z‘yr$_2$ **OffAr** Sing. m. abs. *z‘yr* Aḥiq 101 - ¶ adj. (?) of uncert. meaning and reading (reading *z‘yd* also poss.). Stummer OLZ ’14, 252f.: = frightening (cf. Rosenthal AH i/2, 10; cf. also Kottsieper SAS 20, 200: = vehement) :: Seidel ZAW xxxii 295, Cowl p. 233, 237, Lindenberger APA 82, 239 n. 211: = *z‘r*$_2$ (= swift, sharp) :: Grelot RB lxviii 183 (cf. also idem DAE p. 437): l. *z‘yd*= Sing. m. abs. (= prompt, quick, swift); *z‘yr kṣph mn brq* Aḥiq 101: his anger is more frightening (?) than lightning.
v. *z‘r*$_2$.

z‘p v. *‘yp*.

z‘q **OldCan** Niph Pf. 3 p.pl.m. *na-az-a-qú* EA 366[24] (par. to Akkad. *in4-né-ri-ru* :: Dhorme Rec Dhorme 502: < *nšq*$_2$ = par. to *narkabâti* in l. 25 (= chariots)) - **OffAr** Qal Pf. 3 p.s.m. *z‘q* Cowl 71[17] - ¶ verb Qal to cry: Cowl 71[17] - Niph to be called, to be mustered (cf. Finkelstein EI ix 3*).

z‘qh v. *ṣ‘qh*.

z‘r$_1$ **OffAr** the *tz‘ry* in Or lvii 25[3] = Qal/Pa‘el Imf 2 p.s.f. of *z‘r*$_1$ (resp. = to be small/to diminish) :: Degen NESE ii 73f.: l. *tzr‘y* = Qal Impf. 2 p.s.f. of *zr‘*$_1$.
v. *z‘r*$_2$.

z‘r$_2$ **OffAr** Sing. m. abs. *z‘yr*Aḥiq 114, 145, Beh 24 (Akkad. par. *mi-i-ṣi*), Sach 76 ii A 5 (dam. context), KAI 279[2] (cf. Altheim & Stiehl EW ix 193, cf. also Rosenthal EI xiv 97* (:: Levi Della Vida Editto 21, 33: to be combined with preceding *mn ’dyn*) × Kutscher, Naveh & Shaked Lesh xxxiv 130, 132: = Qal Part. act. s.m. abs. of *z‘r*$_1$(= to be little; cf. also Garbini Kand 8f., 18: prob. = Qal Pf. pass. 3 p.s.m. (to be diminished)) × Dupont-Sommer JA ccxlvi 24: = Qal Pf. 3 p.s.m. of *z‘r*$_1$ (or = Pa‘el of *z‘r*$_1$(= to diminish)?, cf. Altheim & Stiehl EW x 244, GH i 307, ii 171, ASA 269, GMA 347)),[3] (:: Altheim & Stiehl EW ix 194, GH i 401, 407: l. *wṣyd* = *w* + Sing. abs. of *ṣyd*$_1$ (= hunting booty), cf. however idem EW x 244, ASA 26, 269, GMA 348), Pers 31[3], 38[3], 48[5] (for the reading, cf. Naveh & Shaked Or xlii 456, Degen BiOr xxxi 127 :: R.A.Bowman Pers a.l.: l. *ḥzyd*, word of unknown meaning), 52[3] (for the reading, cf. Naveh & Shaked Or xlii 455, Degen BiOr xxxi 127 :: R.A.Bowman Pers a.l.: l. *[r]‘yn* = Sing. abs. of *r‘yn* (= desire, wish)), 87[4], 108[4], 112[5] (for the reading, cf. Naveh & Shaked Or xlii 456, Degen BiOr xxxi 126, Gershevitch Mem de Menasce 70 :: R.A.Bowman Pers a.l.: l. *[b]‘yd* = b_2 + *‘yd* (= Sing. abs. of *‘yd* (= festival)) :: Segal BSOAS xxxv 354: l. *b‘yr* = b_2 + *‘yr* (= nomen mensis)), 118[4], 123[3], 147[2] (*[z]‘yr*); Sing. m. cstr. *z‘yr*RES '41-45, 67[2], Sem xiv 72 conv. 1; emph. *z‘yr’*RES 1296[3], BIFAO xxxviii 58[11] (:: Segal Maarav iv 73f.: l. *gd/w’* (= n.p.? or n.g.?), *z‘r’* Cowl 81[41]; Sing. f. emph. *z‘yrt’*Sem xxi 85 conc. 3; Plur. m. abs. *z‘yrn*Cowl 37[7]; + suff. 3 p.pl.m. *z‘ryhm* Aḥiq 106 (on this form, cf. Kottsieper SAS 77f., 200) - **Nab** Sing. m. emph. *z‘yr’*CIS ii 350[1] - **Palm** Sing. m. abs. *z‘yr*CIS ii 3949[5]; f. abs. *z‘r’* CIS ii 3915[4]; Plur. f. abs. *z‘wrn*Inv x 114[4] - **JAr** Sing. emph. *z‘r’* Mas 420[4]; Plur. emph. *z‘wryh*MPAT-A 34[2] (= SM 69) - ¶ adj. small: CIS ii 350[1], 3915[4], RES 1296[3], Pers 31[3], 38[3] (on the use of *z‘yr* in Pers, cf. also R.A.Bowman Pers p. 48); small in number: Beh 24, Cowl 37[7], Inv x 114[4]; unimportant, less important, *’yš z‘yr* Aḥiq 114, 145: an unimportant (/less important) man (cf. also Lindenberger APA 101: or = young man?); used as *cognomen*, *ḥšwb z‘yr’* BIFAO xxxviii 58[11]: little Ch., cf. also Cowl 81[41]?, cf. also Mas 420[4]?? (v. also *zwmlyt*) - used substantively: a little; *z‘yr mlḥ* RES '41-45, 67[2]: a little bit of salt (:: Lindenberger APA 82, 239 n. 210: *z‘yr* poss. = $z‘yr_2$(= quickly)), cf. also Sem xiv 72 conv. 1; *z‘ryhm* Aḥiq 106: their small number (sc. of children); *z‘yr qṭln* KAI 279[3f.]: people kill (only) a small number (sc. of animals; cf. also Levine JAOS lxxxvii 186: ... to a small degree); *bz‘yr* CIS ii 3949[5] (prob. meaning): moderately, little (dam. context) - used substantively: an unimportant man; *kl qhlh q[dy]šh rbyh wz‘wryh* MPAT-A 34[1f.]: the complete holy community, the great ones and the unimportant ones - a form of this word poss. also in Cowl 72[5] (*z‘r?*), obscure context.

v. *zz*, $z‘yr_2$, $‘bd_2$.

z‘rrh **OffAr** Sing. emph. *z‘rrt’* Aḥiq 105 - ¶ subst. f., certain type of fruit, prob. of bitter taste (*z‘rrt’ mrrt’*), exact meaning unknown. Cowl a.l.: = fruit of sloe-tree; Ginsberg ANET 429, Grelot DAE p. 438, Lindenberger APA 89, 242f. n. 250, Kottsieper SAS 20, 200: = medlar (prob. related to Arab. *zu‘rūr-* with diff. meanings according to time and place).

zp_1 v. gp_1.

zph **OffAr** Sing. cstr. *zpt* Cowl 10[3] (cf. Leand 43i × Joüon MUSJ xviii 40f.: = Sing. abs. (acc.), cf. also Wesselius AION xxx 265ff. for this

poss. explanation); emph. *zpt'* Aḥiq 130, 131 (*[z]pt'*; for the reading of the context, cf. Puech RB xcv 590f.); cf. Frah xv 3 (cf. Nyberg FP 85 :: Ebeling Frah a.l.: = *zb*(= book), cf. Akkad *zīpu* = mould), xvii 1 (*zwp(m)h*) - ¶ subst. f. loan; *yhbt ly zpt ksp* ... Cowl 10^3: you have given to me as a loan silver ...; *tzp zpt'* Aḥiq 130: you will borrow (a loan).
v. *ntn*.

zp' v. *zr'*$_2$.

zpr Nyberg FP 43, 71: l. *zpl'* in Frah vii 13 = form of *zpr* (= stinking, indication of a kind of buck) :: Ebeling Frah a.l.: l. *zzr'*poss. to be read however *zmr'*(= Sing. emph. of *zmr*$_4$(= ibex))

zprn v.Soden Or xlvi 197: > Akkad. *zuprinnu* = brush (uncert. interpret.).

zpt = pitch > Akkad., cf. v.Soden Or xxxvii 269, xlvi 197, AHW s.v. *ziptu* (cf. also CAD s.v. *zibtu* B).

zq **OffAr**, cf. Frah vii 22 (*zky'*) - **Palm** Plur. abs. *zqyn* CIS ii 3913 ii 18 (*zqy[n]*), 22 (*zqy[n]*), 26, 29, 31 (Greek par. ἀ[σ]κοῖς), 98 (Greek par. ἀσκο[ῖς]), Syr vii 129^5 - ¶ subst. f. goat-skin (used to transport oil, wine, etc.); > Akkad., cf. v.Soden Or xxxvii 269, xlvi 197, AHW s.v. *b(/p)urussu(m)*, *ziqqu* IV, cf. also CAD s.v. *ziqqu* B - Segal, ATNS a.l.: l. *zq* (Sing. abs.) in ATNS 26^4 (reading and interpret. however highly uncert., cf. Shaked Or lvi 409) - on this word, cf. also Collini SEL iv 14.

zqyq₁ **Hatra** Sing. emph. *zqyq'* $410^{1,2}$; Plur. (?) emph. *zqyq'* 13^3 (cf. however Vattioni Or xxxiv 338f., Aggoula Syr lxvii 413:= Sing. emph., cf. also Safar Sumer vii 178 n. 26 :: Caquot Syr xxix 115: *zqyq'* = form of *zqyq*$_2$ (= the pure one; epithet of *mrtn*)) - ¶ subst. ghost, deified ancestor; *'prṭn zqyq'* Hatra 401^1: A. the ghost; for this indication of a divine being, cf. Milik Syr xliv 297ff., DFD 166, Vattioni Or xxxiv 338f., Aggoula Syr lxvii 413, cf. also Teixidor Syr xlvii 376f.

zqyq₂ v. *zqyq*$_1$.

zqn₁ **OldAr** Qal Impf. 3 p.s.m. *yzqn* KAI 223B 8 (cf. e.g. Dupont-Sommer Sf p. 105, 111, Donner KAI a.l., Fitzmyer AIS 80, 88, Degen AAG p. 18, 68 × Lemaire & Durand 117, 127, 142 (div. otherwise): l. *zqn* (= Qal Pf. 3 p.s.m.) :: Ben-Chayyim Lesh xxxv 246: = Aph Impf. 3 p.s.m. + suff. 1 p.s. of *nzq*$_1$) - ¶ verb Qal to grow old.

zqn₂ **Ph** Sing. + suff. 1 p.s. (nom./acc.) *zqn* KAI 24^7 - **OffAr**, cf. Frah x 28 (*dyk[n]'*)- ¶ subst. beard.

zqp v. *gbh*$_1$.

zr₁ **Pun** Sing. abs. *zr* KAI $69^{7,9,11}$, 74^7 - ¶ subst. small coin, exact value unknown.

zr₂ v. *zr*$_4$.

zr₃ v. *sr*$_2$.

zr$_4$ **Ph** Sing. m. abs. KAI 26A iii 16 (:: Gevirtz VT xi 143 n. 3: = *zr*$_2$(= corona?)), C iv 18, MUSJ xlv 262[6] (?; heavily dam. context), EpAn ix 5[2] - **Samal** Sing. m. abs. *zr* KAI 214[30,34] - ¶ adj. strange, other; *šʿr zr* KAI 26A iii 16: another gate (i.e. a gate which has nothing to do with the gate the context speaks of, the gate of Azitawaddu), cf. KAI 26C iv 18; *krm zr* EpAn ix 5[2]: another vineyard (cf. Mosca & Russell EpAn ix 10, cf. however id., ibid.: or = another vineyard (less probable interpret.)); *ʾš zr* KAI 214[34]: stranger (for the context, cf. Tawil JNES xxxii 480ff.) - substantivated adj.: stranger; *ʾm šmt ʾmrt ʾl bpm zr* KAI 214[29f.]: if I have put these words in the mouth of a stranger - poss. a form of this word in KAI 222B 40 (heavily dam. context).

zrb$_1$ **OffAr** Sach p. 235: l. *hzrb* (= HAPH Imper. s.m. of *zrb* (= to spur on, to prompt)) in Sach 76 ii A 4 (uncert. interpret., dam. and difficult context).

zrb$_2$ v. *rby*$_1$.

zrd **Hatra** Aggoula Syr lii 193: l. *zrd* (Sing. abs.) in 291[2] (= ring or coat of mail); highly uncert. reading and interpret.; Safar & As-Saliḥi Sumer xxvii 13: l. poss. *ʿbd* (= QAL Pf. 3 p.s.m. of *ʿbd*$_1$) or (ibid. n. 35): l. *bsr* = PAʿEL Pf. 3 p.s.m. of *bsr*$_1$(= to form); for the reading problems, cf. also Degen NESE iii 89.

zrw v. *ṣry*$_2$.

zrz **OffAr** word of uncert. meaning in RES 1785G (Sing. abs.). For the reading, cf. Lidzbarski Eph i 72; (Bogoljubov with) Hinz AISN 279: = belief.

zrzr (or *znzr*)= star > Akkad., cf. v.Soden Or xxxvii 269, xlvi 197, AHW s.v. *zanzīru*, CAD ibid.

zrḥ v. *mzrḥ*$_1$.

zry$_1$ **Nab** ITP Impf. 3 p.s.m. *yztry* in J 38[6]? Cantineau Nab i 73, ii 92: = to despise, to scorn, to disregard :: Lidzbarski Eph iii 270: l. *yštry*? (= form of ITP of *šry*$_1$).

zry$_2$ v. *zrʿ*$_1$.

zrk v. *zwk*.

zrm **DA** a form of this root poss. in ii 20 (*tzrm*), reading uncert., dam. context; for interpret., cf. Hoftijzer DA a.l. and p. 274 n. 10.
v. *ʾzr*$_2$, *mlk*$_5$.

zrnyk (< Iran., cf. Schaed 267, Hinz AISN 278) - **OffAr** Sing. abs. *zrnyk* Cowl 26[17]; emph. *zrnykʾ* Cowl 26[21] - ¶ subst. arsenic. The reading *zrnyk* (Sing. abs.) in Cowl 26[5] highly uncert., cf. Grelot Sem xx 27f., DAE p. 287 (n. j): pro *zrnyk zy* l. *ʿl* (= *ʿl*$_7$) *mn* (= *mn*$_4$) *zy*? (cf. also Porten & Yardeni sub TADAE A 6.2)

zrʿ$_1$ **OldAr** QAL Impf. 3 p.s.m. *yzrʿ* KAI 222A 36; *lzrʿ* Tell F 18f., 19 (:: Andersen & Freedman, FS Fensham 34: or = *l*$_1$ + QAL Pf. 3 p.s.m.) - **OffAr** QAL Impf. 2 p.s.m. + suff. 3 p.s.f. *tzrʿnh* MAI xiv/2, 66[4]; Inf.

+ suff. 3 p.s.m. *mzrʿh* MAI xiv/2, 66[3] (for this prob. reading, cf. Porten & Yardeni sub TADAE B 1.1 :: Dupont-Sommer MAI xiv/2, 66, 72: l. *mzrʿ* = Inf.); cf. Frah xviii 15 (*zrytwn*): to sow (cf. however Nyberg FP 49, 89: l. *zlytwn* = form of *zry*$_2$(= to scatter, to distribute), cf. also Toll ZDMG-Suppl viii 37) - **JAr** QAL Imper. s.m. + suff. 3 p.s.m. *zrʿnh* Syr xlv 101[14] (dam. context),[16] (*zrʿ[n]h*) - ¶ verb QAL to sow; for Tell F 18f., cf. Dion FS Delcor 146 - **1)** + obj., *wʾlp šʿryn lzrʿ* Tell F 19: and may he sow a thousand measures (for the context, cf. Greenfield & Shaffer RB xcii 53f.) - **2)** + double object, *zrʿnh sʿry* Syr xlv 101[16]: sow it with barley, cf. Syr xlv 101[14] - **3)** + obj. + *b*$_2$ - a) + obj. + *b*$_2$ (mat.), *tzrʿnh bzrʿ* MAI xiv/2, 66[4]: you must sow it with seed - b) + *b*$_2$ (loc.) + obj., *wyzrh bhn hdd mlḥ* KAI 222A 36: may Hadad sow in them salt (:: Ben-Chayyim Lesh xxxv 253: l. *bhm*?; for this text, cf. also Cardascia FS Seidl 27ff.) - a derivative of this root poss. in Syr xlv 101[11] (*zr[ʿ]*), heavily dam. text - on this root, cf. also Blau PC 48f. n. 9.

v. *zʿr*$_1$,*zrʿ*$_2$, *yld*$_1$.

zrʿ$_2$ **Ph** Sing. abs. *zrʿ* KAI 13[7], 14[8]; cstr. *zrʿ* KAI 14[11]; + suff. 3 p.s.m. *zrʿw* KAI 10[15]; + suff. 1 p.s. *zrʿy* KAI 43[11,15]; + suff. 3 p.pl.m. *zrʿm* KAI 14[22]; cf. Diosc ii 103: ζερα, Plin xxiv 71: *zura* (cf. FR 194a) - **Hebr** Sing. abs. *zrʿ* KAI 182[1f.] (:: Segal JSS vii 219: = QAL Imper. s.m. of *zrʿ*$_1$?),DJD ii 30[2] - **Samal** Sing. cstr. *zrʿ* KAI 214[20] (v. *ḥb*$_1$) - **OldAr** Sing. + suff. 3 p.s.m. *zrʿh* Tell F 8 - **OffAr** Sing. abs. *zrʿ* Cowl 13[8], Driv 8[2,4], ATNS 19[7], 20[4] (also in RES 493[6]?, uncert. reading, cf. Cowley PSBA xxxvii 221, RES sub 1801, cf. however Lidzbarski Eph ii 402: l. prob. *ydʿ*); cstr. *zrʿ* RES 493[2] (for this reading, cf. Cowley PSBA xxxvii 221, RES sub 1801, Dupont-Sommer ASAE xlviii 128, cf. however e.g. Lidzbarski Eph ii 401: prob. l. *ydʿ*), CIS ii 111[3], Sem xxxiii 94[6] (= TADAE A 5.1. :: Sznycer HDS 168, 175f.: l. *zpʿ*= word of unknown meaning); emph. *zrʿʾ* RES 956[5]; + suff. 3 p.s.m. *zrʿh* Aḥiq 85, CIS ii 113[12,14], Atlal vii 109[9]; + suff. 2 p.s.m. *zrʿk* KAI 225[11]; + suff. 1 p.pl.? *zrʿn* Cowl 68 v 2 (for the context, cf. Porten & Greenfield BIDG 56), AG 4bis 2 (for the reading, cf. Segal Maarav iv 71 :: Aimé-Giron AG a.l.: l. *ydʿn* = QAL Part. act. pl.m. abs. of *ydʿ*$_1$) - **Palm** Sing. abs. *zrʿ* CIS ii 4218[5] - **Hatra** Sing. + suff. 3 p.s.m. *zrʿh* 79[11] - **JAr** Sing. abs. *zrʿ* MPAT 52[2]; emph. *zrʿh* Syr xlv 101[14] (or + suff. 3 p.s.m.?); + suff. 3 p.s.m. *zrʿyh* MPAT-A 22[7], Syr xlv 101[15] (or Plur.?) - ¶ subst. m. - **1)** (act of) sowing: KAI 182[1f.] (on this text, cf. Borowski AIAI 34 (cf. also ibid. 53ff.)) - **2)** seed, grain: RES 493[2] (v. supra), Driv 8[2,4], ATNS 19[7], 20[4], MPAT 52[2], DJD ii 30[2] (for *byt zrʿ*, v. *byt*$_2$), Syr xlv 101[15] - **3)** seed, issue, posterity (:: v.d.Branden OA iii 257: *zrʿ* = male and female issue as opposed to *bn*$_1$= male issue): KAI 10[15], 14[11], 43[11,15], 214[20] (v. *ḥb*$_1$), Tell F 8, Aḥiq 85, Sem xxxiii 94[6] (prob.

interpret., context however dam.), Atlal vii 109[9], CIS ii 4218[5], MPAT-A 22[7], etc.; cf. *bn wzrʿ* KAI 14[8]: son and offspring; cf. also *ʾnh wbny wzrʿ zyly* Cowl 13[8]: I or my sons or my offspring; and cf. *S. mlkʾ wzrʿh wbnyhy klhwn dlʿlm* Hatra 79[11f.]: the king S., his offspring and all his descendants forever (Caquot Syr xl 5: *zrʿh* ... = his successor and all his (i.e. the successor's) descendants) - this word (Sing. abs. *zrʿ*) prob. also in KAI 195[10] (cf. Torczyner Lach i p. 96f., Michaud Syr xxxiv 47, Gibson SSI i p. 43ff. (or = *zrʿ*$_3$?), Reviv CSI 85f. (: = *zrʿ*$_3$), Lemaire IH i p. 117f., Briend TPOA 144, Pardee HAHL 96f., Conrad TUAT i 623 :: e.g. Albright BASOR lxx 15, Ginsberg BASOR lxxi 26, Hempel ZAW lvi 134f., de Vaux RB xlviii 196, Elliger ZDPV lxii 75, Röllig KAI a.l.: l. *yrʿ* = HIPH Impf. 3 p.s.m. of *rʿʿ* (for this reading, cf. also Diringer Lach iii p. 334; on this text, cf. also Heltzer Shn iii 279).
v. *mzrʿ*.

zrʿ$_3$ **OldCan** Sing. cstr. *zu-ru-uḫ̯* EA 287[27], 288[34] (cf. Sivan GAG 22, 216; for the form, cf. FR 88, Grave UF xii 223f., Steiner JAOS c 515) - **Hebr** Sing. abs. *zrʿ* TA-H 88[2] - **OffAr** Sing. + suff. 3 p.s.f. *drʿh*RES 492B 4, 5 - ¶ subst. - **1)** arm: RES 492B 4, 5 (cf. Driver AnOr xii 57) - **2)** hand: EA 287[27], 288[34] (Akkad. par. *qāt*) - 3) > strength: *ʾmṣ zrʿ* TA-H 88[2]: strengthen the arm > take strength (cf. e.g. Aharoni TA a.l. :: Conrad TeAv iii 112f.) - > Akkad. (arm, foreleg), cf. v Soden Or xxxv 7, xlvi 185, CAD s.v. *duraʾu* - Beyer & Livingstone ZDMG cxl a.l.: the *drʿʾ*in ZDMG cxl 2[2]: = Sing. emph. indicating the protecting arm of the deity.
v. *zrʿ*$_2$.

zrph cf. Ebeling Frah a.l.: l. *zrpn* (= Plur. abs. of *zrph*) in Frah xxvii 13 = heavy rains > winter (less prob. interpret., cf. Nyberg FP 107: l. Iran. word).

zrq$_1$ **OffAr** QAL Part. pass. s.m. abs. *zrq* CRAI '70, 163[1] (for the reading, cf. Humbach IPAA 12 :: Dupont-Sommer CRAI '70, a.l.: l. / + *rq* (= Sing. m. abs. of *rq*$_1$ (vanity))), IPAA 11[3] (:: Sundermann with IPAA 12: = QAL Pf. 3 p.s.m.) - ¶ verb QAL to sprinkle; Part. pass. the sprinkled one > the anointed one.

zrq$_2$ **Hatra** Sing. emph. *zrqʾ* 5[4], 232b 1 - ¶ adj. blue, prob. used as nickname: the blue one > the blue-eyed one?, cf. Degen JEOL xxiii 404, cf. also Donner sub KAI 238, 239, Altheim & Stiehl AAW ii 192.

zrr **Samal** Plur. abs. (gen./acc.) *zrry* KAI 214[10] - ¶ subst. of unknown meaning. For the context, v. *nṣb*$_5$.

zrt **OffAr** Sing. abs. *zrt* Cowl 36[3] - ¶ subst. measure: span. For poss. Egypt. origin, cf. Lambdin JAOS lxxiii 149f. (cf. also Trinquet SDB v 1213ff.).

zt$_1$ v. *zyt*.

zt$_2$ v. *z*$_1$, *znh*,*kwt*, *mḥzt*, *mlk*$_5$.

zt$_3$ **Ph** the diff. *sz zt* in KAI 27[22] (for this reading, cf. du Mesnil du Buisson FS Dussaud 424f., 433 (: = n.d.), Gaster Or xi 44, 67(: = onomatopaeic representation of hissing and spitting; cf. also Rosenthal ANET 658)) highly uncert. reading. Cross & Saley BASOR cxcvii 46 (nn. 28, 29): l. poss. *ssm* (= n.d.) ʾ- (cf. Röllig NESE ii 19, 25, Avishur PIB 248, de Moor JEOL xxvii 108, 110); Albright BASOR lxxvi 9 (n. 35): l. *szyt* (= n.p. f.), cf. also Röllig KAI a.l.; Caquot FS Gaster 50f., Garbini OA xx 286: l. *mṣʾ* = Sing. abs. of *mṣʾ*$_2$ (= *mwṣʾ* (= sunrise)); Gibson SSI iii p. 82f., 88: l. *mṣʾ* = QAL Pf. 3 p.s.m. of *mṣʾ*$_1$ (= to arrive); v.d.Branden BiOr xxxiii 13: l. *tn* (= QAL Imper. s.f. of *ytn*$_1$) *ʿzt* (= f. Sing. abs. of *ʿz*$_3$); cf. also Lipiński RTAT 266.
v. *mzzh*.

Ḥ

ḥ$_1$ v. *h*$_1$.
ḥ$_2$ v. *ḥbl*$_4$.
ḥ$_3$ (abbrev. of *ḥbr*$_2$), v. *khn*$_1$, *šlḥ*$_3$.
ḥ$_4$ v. *ḥṭh*.
ḥ$_5$ v. *ḥlr*.
ḥ$_6$ v. *ḥmr*$_5$, *mzḥ*.
ḥ$_7$ v. *ḥmr*$_6$.
ḥ$_8$ v. *ḥpn*.
ḥb$_1$ **Samal** Sing. emph. *ḥbʾ* KAI 214[20] (?; cf. Garb 260, Gibson SSI ii p. 74, cf. however also Koopmans 37, Donner KAI a.l., Segert AAG p. 189, Dion p. 60, 88, 137: = Sing. abs. of *ḥbʾ*$_2$, v. infra) - ¶ subst. of unknown meaning in the combination *zrʿ ḥbʾ*. Garb 260: = seed of the bosom, cf. also Donner KAI a.l.: = issue of the bosom (cf. Segert AAG p. 189: *ḥbʾ* = breast); Caquot Syr liv 135: = pleasant offspring (*ḥbʾ* < *ḥbb*$_1$); Gibson SSI ii p. 67, 74: seed to cherish (*ḥbʾ* < *ḥbb*$_1$); Dion p. 31, 88, 382 n. 12: *ḥbʾ* = marriage act, *zrʿ ḥbʾ* = fertile union.
ḥb$_2$ v. *ṣby*$_1$.
ḥb$_3$ v. *ḥbr*$_3$.
ḥbʾ$_1$ **OldCan** HIPH Pf. 3 p.s.m. *ḫi-iḫ-bi-e* EA 256[7] (cf. Siwan GAG 174f., 228) - ¶ verb HIPH to conceal (cf. Albright BASOR lxxxix 11 n. 19).
v. *ḥpr*$_1$, *yhb*.
ḥbʾ$_2$ v. *ḥb*$_1$.
ḥbb$_1$ **Pun** YIPH Part. s.m. cstr. *mḥb* KAI 121[1], 126[4,4f.,6]; YOPH Part. s.f. + suff. 3 p.s.m. *mḥbtʾ* KAI 162[3] (diff. context) - **Palm**, cf. Cantineau Gramm 87, 88: APH Pf. 3 p.s.m. *ʾḥb* (unpubl. text); Impf. 3 p.pl.m. *yḥb[w]n* (unpubl. text) - ¶ verb YIPH/APH to love; *mḥb ʾrṣ* KAI 126[4]:

patriotic (Lat. par.: *amator patriae*); *mḥb bn› ‹m* KAI 126[4f.]: loving the compatriots (Lat. par.: *amator civium*); *mḥb d‹t htmt* KAI 121[1], 126[6]: loving the perfect knowledge (Lat. par.: *amator concordiae*), three honorary titles - YOPH to be loved: KAI 162[3] (v. however supra).
v. *ḥb₁*,*ḥdy₁*, *mḥzy₂*.

ḥbb₂ **OffAr** Milik Bibl xlviii 553, 583: the *ḥbb* in Herm 4[9] = Sing. abs. of *ḥbb₂* (< Egypt.) = river (improb. interpret.; *ḥbb*= n.p., cf. also Kornfeld OAA 49; for the context, v. *zhr*; :: Swiggers Aeg lxi 67f.: = Sing. abs. of *ḥbb₃* (= love)).

ḥbb₃ v. *ḥbb₂*.

ḥbh v. *ḥwt*.

ḥbwrh **JAr** Sing. emph. *ḥbwrth* MPAT-A 13[1] (= SM 46) - ¶ subst. f. community, or: religious confraternity; *kl bny ḥbwrth qdyšth* MPAT-A 13[1]: all the members of the holy community (or: confraternity).
v. *ḥbrh*.

ḥbz₁ **OldAr** PA‹EL (cf. Rosenthal BASOR clviii 30 n. 14, Fitzmyer JAOS lxxxi 213, AIS 88, Degen AGG p. 70 (n. 57), Gibson SSI ii p. 56 :: Fitzmyer CBQ xx 463: = QAL, cf. also Donner KAI a.l.: = PA‹EL (or QAL)) Pf. 3 p.pl.m. *ḥbzw* KAI 224[24]; Inf. + suff. 3 p.pl.m. *ḥbzthm* KAI 223B 7 - ¶ verb PA‹EL to strike, to smite + obj. (for the etymology, cf. the litt. mentioned above and Greenfield ActOr xxix 5 n. 12, Hartman CBQ xxx 259), cf. however Tawil CBQ xlii 30ff.: = to commit a razzia against, to make an incursion into someone's territory (*ḥbz* being semantically equivalent to Akkadian *ḫabātu*).

ḥbz₂ v.Soden Or xlvi 186: Ar. *ḥbz(h)* = pot > Akkad.?, cf. idem AHW s.v. *ḫabazz(at)u*, cf. CAD s.v. *ḫabaṣu*.

ḥbzh v. *ḥbz₂*.

ḥbṭ v. *ḥzr₃*.

ḥby v. *yhb*.

ḥbl₁ **OffAr** PA‹EL Pf. 3 p.s.m. *ḥbl* Cowl 30[14]; + suff. 2 p.s.m. *ḥblk* Aḥiq 44; Impf. 3 p.s.m. *yḥbl* Aḥiq 36, KAI 228A 13, 260B 6; Part. pass. s.m. abs. *mḥbl* Cowl 27[2] (cf. Leand 32d), SSI ii 28 obv. 7 (cf. e.g. Gibson SSI ii a.l. :: (Glanzman with) Fitzmyer JNES xxi 16, 20, WA 225: = PA‹EL Part. act. of *ḥbl₂* (= to take as a pledge); or in both instances = noun Sing. abs.?) - **JAr** PA‹EL Part. act. s.m. emph. *mḥblh* AMB 7a 13, 7b 2 - ¶ verb PA‹EL, to damage, to ruin - **1)** + object - a) a monument or other object, *w›yš mnd‹m b›gwr› zk l› ḥbl* Cowl 30[14]: and no one damaged anything in that temple (:: Joüon MUSJ xviii 5: and no one damaged that temple in any way), cf. KAI 228A 13, 260B 6 - b) a person: Aḥiq 44 - **2)** + obj. + ‹*l₇*, *lmh hw yḥbl mt› ‹lyn* Aḥiq 36: why should he corrupt the land against us? - **3)** Part. act., indication of a demon, destroyer: AMB 7a 13, 7b 2 - **4)** Part. pass., what is damaged, corrupted; *wmḥbl l› ›yty* SSI ii 28 obv. 7: there will be no harm done; *wmndʿm mḥbl [lʾ] ʾštkḥ ln* Cowl 27²: nothing corrupted (i.e. nothing bad/damaging) was found in us (cf. Dion RB lxxxvi 569 n. 115, lxxxix 567f.) - a derivative of this root prob. (*ḥbl*) in AE '23, 42 no. 5 (dam. context).

ḥbl₂ v. *ḥbl₁*.

ḥbl₃ **Pun** Sing. abs. *ḥbl* (the reading of the *ḥ* uncert.) CIS i 3189³ - ¶ subst. m. sailor.

ḥbl₄ **Amm** Plur. abs. *ḥblm* AUSS xiv 145⁴ (heavily dam. context) - **OffAr** Plur. abs. *ḥbln* Cowl 37¹⁰ - ¶ subst. rope (for Cowl 37¹⁰, cf. e.g. Cowl p. 134, Driver JRAS '32, 81, Grelot Sem xiv 67, Porten & Yardeni sub TADAE A 4.2; for AUSS xiv 145⁴, cf. Cross AUSS xiv 147, Aufrecht sub CAI 94).

ḥbl₄ **OffAr**, cf. GIPP 52 - **Palm** CIS ii 4219¹, 4220⁴, 4221, Inv xi 50¹, xii 12⁷, RIP 3⁴, etc., etc. - **JAr** Frey 1077³, 1112, 1147b, 1148², 1151, 1156 (diff. reading), MPAT 37 i 2 (heavily dam. context), 141⁴ (= Frey 1222; in Palm. script) - ¶ (subst., misfortune >) exclamation: alas, used in funerary inscriptions (cf. Joüon Syr xix 186ff., Rosenthal Sprache 83, cf. also Díez Merino LA xxi 104f.) - also in Hebr. text?: Frey 1002³ - cf. also the diff. *ḥbl ḥblyk* in KAI 276⁷, for the diff. interpretations, cf. Nyberg Eranos xliv 239 (: = indigenous name of the Georgians; improb. interpret.); Tsereteli with Metzger JNES xv 24 (: *ḥblyk* with Pahlavi ending *-ik* or Aramaic pron. suff. 2 p.s.), cf. also Degen ZDMG cxxi 138: *ḥblyk* = Plur. + suff. 2 p.s.m., *ḥbl ḥblyk* = cstr. phrase (cf. Altheim & Stiehl ASA 269f.: *ḥblyk* = Plur. + suff. 2 p.s.m., *ḥbl ḥblyk* = woe, woe for you; cf. also Levi Della Vida with Altheim GH ii 295f.; cf. also Metzger JNES xv 20: = woe, woe [for her] (improb. interpret.)) :: Altheim & Stiehl WZKMU '55/56, 284, Suppl 80f., GH i 248, 251, Grelot Sem viii 17: *ḥblyk* = lapsus for Plur. abs. *ḥblyn*, cf. also Donner KAI a.l. (*ḥbl ḥblyk* = cstr. phrase); for the reading, cf. also Frye BiOr xi 134 - abbrev. *ḥ* in PNO 52bis? - cf. the *ḥblnʾ* in Frah S₂ 21 - Segal ATNS a.l.: l. poss. *ḥbl* (= Sing. abs.) *ʿl* (= *ʿl₇*) *ḥblʾ* (= Sing. emph.) *zy ln*: woe for our woe in ATNS 69b 2 (cf. also Ullendorff JRAS '85, 70: destruction upon destruction suffered by us), uncert. reading and dam. context - Segal ATNS a.l.: l. poss. *ḥblʾ* (= Sing. emph.) in ATNS 69b 7, uncert. reading, heavily dam. context.

ḥbṣ₁ v. *ḥbṣ₃*.

ḥbṣ₂ v. *ḥbz₂*.

ḥbṣ₃ **DA** Plur. abs. *ḥbṣn* Vd 3 (uncert. reading, cf. v.d.Kooij DA p. 150; dam. context) - ¶ subst. prob. meaning crowd, cf. Hoftijzer DA a.l. :: Puech FS Grelot 24f., 28: = QAL Part. act. pl.m. abs. of *ḥbṣ₁* (= to be confused, to be desoriented).

ḥbr₁ **Palm** PAʿEL (or lapsus for APH?; cf. Ingholt Ber v 107) Pf. 3 p.pl.m. *ḥbr* Ber v 106²; APH Pf. 3 p.s.m. *ʾḥbr* CIS ii 4194², 4195²,

4211^{1} (*'ḥ[br]*), Ber ii 76^{1}, 77^{1}, 78^{1}, 95, RB xxxix 532^{2} (Greek par. ἐξεχώρησεν); 1 p.s. + suff. 3 p.s.m. *'ḥbrth* CIS ii 4195^{6}; 3 p.pl.m. *'ḥbr* Ber ii 91^{1}, v 95^{4}; Inf. *'ḥbwr'* CIS ii 4214 (for this form, cf. Cantineau Gramm 89, Rosenthal Sprache 60, 72) - ¶ verb PA ‘EL (?, v. supra) to make a partner (partner functioning as object); + obj., *lšmš ... w'mdy ... ḥbr wrdn ... wyhb lh sṭr' grbyy'* Ber v 106$^{1ff.}$: L. ... and A. ... made W. ... a partner and sold him the northern wall - APH - **1)** to make a partner (partner functioning as object); *l'ḥbwr' bh 'yš* CIS ii 4214: to make someone a partner in it (i.e. in the tomb), cf. also Greek par. ἐπὶ τῷ κατὰ μηδένα τρόπον κοινωνόν αὐτοῦ προσλαβεῖν); *'lksdrys ... 'ḥbr bgy* (:: Cantineau sub Inv iv 7b: = lapsus for *lbgy*, cf. also Gawlikowski MFP p. 211: l. *[l]bgy*) *... bsṭr' ... dy 'ksdr' ... ṭksys dy gwmḥy' ḥmš' ...* RB xxxix 532$^{1ff.}$ (= Inv iv 7b): A. has made B. a partner in the wall of the exedra for a row of five niches (cf. Greek par. ἐξεχώρησεν Βαγγαίωι ... ἀρκτικοῦ πλευροῦ τῆς ... ἐξέδρας τάξεις νεκροθή[κ]ων πέντε; :: Gawlikowski MFP 174: ἐξεχώρησεν = exact translation of *'ḥbr*); *ywlys ... 'ḥ[br] b‘ly[t'] ... l[gys] ...* CIS 4211$^{1f.}$: Y. made G. a partner in the upper floor (cf. Greek par. [Ιούλιος ...] ... κοινωνὸν [προσελάβε]το ἐν τῷ ἀναγαί[ῳ]) - **2)** to make a partner > to cede to (with double object); *'ḥbrth mn 'ksdr' gwmḥyn tmny'* CIS ii 4195$^{6ff.}$: I have made him a partner, from the exedra eight niches (i.e. I have ceded him eight niches from the exedra) - **3)** to cede to (+ *l*$_5$ (= to)); *'ksdr' ... klh yhb w'ḥbr ml' ... ltybwl* Ber ii 76^{1}: M. has given and ceded to T. the complete exedra (cf. Ber ii 77^{1}, 78$^{1f.}$, 95); *nwrbl w'qmt ... 'ḥbr lnḥšṭb ... b'ksdr'* Ber ii 91^{1f}: N. and A. have ceded to N. ... part of the exedra; *'ḥbr lšmš ... mn m‘rt' dh lbwn'* CIS ii 4195$^{2ff.}$: L. has ceded to B. part of this hypogee; *'ḥbr lšmš ... mn m‘rt' dh lsry ... 'ksdr' dnh* CIS ii 4194^{2ff}: L. has ceded to S. from this hypogee this exedra; *mqymw ... w'qmt ... 'ḥbr lšlmn ... wltymw ... w'rḥq lhwn mn pnyn trtn* Ber v 95$^{2ff.}$: M. and A. have ceded to S. and T. and have transferred to them two stretches (?; v. *pny*, *rḥq*$_1$).
v. *ytn*$_1$.

ḥbr$_2$ **Pun** m. Plur. + 3 p.pl. *ḥbrnm* KAI 69^{19}, 159^{4}, RCL '66, 201^{3} - **OffAr** m. Plur. + suff. 3 p.s.m. *'ḥbrwhy* NESE iii 48 conv. 2 (:: Degen NESE iii 51f.: = lapsus for *ḥbrwhy*), *ḥbrwh'* RCL '62, 259 iii 2; f. Plur. abs., cf. Warka 16: *ḫa-ba-ra-an* - **Nab** m. Sing. + suff. 1 p.s. *ḥbry* MPAT 61^{25} (= DBKP 15); m. Plur. + suff. 3 p.s.m. *ḥbrwhy* RES 1423^{2}, J 246, IEJ xi 135^{2}, 137^{1}, *'ḥbrwh* J 18A 1f. (for the reading, cf. Milik sub ARNA-Nab 89); + suff. 3 p.pl. *ḥbryhm* RES 1160^{1} (for the reading, cf. Lidzbarski Eph iii 87 :: J 57: l. *ḥyryhm* = Plur. + suff. 3 p.pl.m. of *ḥyr*$_2$(= person of note, noble) :: CIS ii sub 235: l. *bnyhm* = Plur. + suff. 3 p.pl.m. of *br*$_1$,cf. also Levinson NAI 115f.) - **Palm** m. Sing. + suff. 3 p.s.m. *ḥbrh* MUSJ xxviii 46^{6} - **Hatra** m. Sing. + suff.

3 p.s.m. *ḥbrh* 212[4] (cf. Aggoula Ber xviii 10, Vattioni IH a.l. :: Teixidor Sumer xx 80: or = lapsus for *ḥbryhy*?, cf. also Milik DFD 392); Plur. + suff. 3 p.s.m. *ḥbryhy* 207[2], 209[3], 210, 213[2], 283[2], 284[2], *ḥbryh* 409 iii 3f. (:: As-Salihi Sumer xlv 103 (div. otherwise): l. *-ḥ* (= part of NP) *bryh* (= Sing. + suff. 3 p.s.m. of br_1)) - **JAr** m. Sing. + suff. 3 p.s.m. *ḥbryh* MPAT-A 22[2,3,4] (= SM 70[10,11,12]); Plur. abs. *ḥbryn* MPAT-A 34[6] (= SM 69) - ¶ subst. colleague, companion (in RES 1423 designation of the members of the same religious confraternity; cf. also Negev IEJ xiii 114, Teixidor Sumer xx 77, Syr xliv 188f., Milik DFD 391ff., Naveh IEJ xvii 188, Aggoula Sem xxii 54f., O'Connor JANES xviii 72ff., 80) - a form of this word poss. in KAI 222B 33 (*ḥb[*), cf. Dupont-Sommer Sf p. 82, Lipiński Stud 39 (cf. also Silverman JAOS xciv 270: or = derivative of root *ḥyb*? (= $ḥwb_1$)), for the reading difficulties, cf. also Fitzmyer AIS 70 (or l. *hn* = hn_3?)- for prop. form of this word in ICO-Spa 16, v. ytn_1.
v. $ḥbr_3$, khn_1, $šlḥ_3$.

ḥbr₃ **Hebr** Sing. cstr. *ḥbr* on coins from the Hasmonean period, cf. JC 12, 14, 17, 18, 18a, 19, 20, 20a, 21, 23, 24 (*ḥb[r]*), 25, 28, 29, 30, PEQ '67, 106 no. 2, 3, 5, '80, 11 no. 1-3 (cf. also Meshorer Mas coin 96, 101, 103; cf. also abbrev. *ḥb* JC 13, 22; v. also infra) - ¶ subst. community (kind of collegium or senate, cf. Meyshan PEQ '64, 49 (also for older litt.), cf. also Sperber PEQ '65, 85ff.); on coins from the Hasmonean period, *ḥbr yhdym* JC 14: the community of the Jews (cf. PEQ '80, 11 no. 1-3; cf. JC 18, 20, 20a, 21, 28: *ḥbr hyh(w)dym* (cf. also JC 19, 30), cf. JC 25: *hḥbr hyhwdym* (cf. also JC 24); cf. also shortened forms of this formula: JC 18a (*ḥbr hydy*), JC 17 (*ḥbr hyh*), JC 29 (*ḥbr hyhd*), JC 23 (*hḥbr hydy*), PEQ '67, 106 no. 5 (*ḥbr y*), JC 22 (*ḥb hyhw*), JC 13 (*ḥb yh*), PEQ '67, 106 no. 2 (*ḥbr*)); on these coin inscriptions, cf. O'Connor JANES xviii 74 (n. 42) - a word *ḥbr* prob. to be restored in KAI 222A 4, cf. e.g. Dupont-Sommer Sf p. 26f., Fitzmyer AIS 29, Gibson SSI ii p. 28f., 35, Na'aman WO ix 225, 227, Lemaire & Durand IAS 120, 131, O'Connor JANES xviii 73f. (n. 37): = $ḥbr_3$ × Lipiński Stud 24f.: = $ḥbr_2$(cf. however Sacchi RCL '61, 188f.: = name of people) - for such a word in Ph., cf. Katzenstein CISFP i 599ff.
v. *ʾrʾl,ḥbrh*, krk_1, *ṣbw*.

ḥbr₄ v. ytn_1.

ḥbrh **Pun** diff. word *ḥbʿrt* in KAI 145[9] (:: Cooke NSI p. 151: l. *ḥpʿrt*, unexplained, cf. also RES 2221), meaning unknown. Février Sem vi 25f.: = Sing. or Plur., covering (sc. golden covering of statues; improb. interpret.); v.d.Branden RSF i 166, 170: = Sing. abs. (= association, community; v. *ḥbwrh*); Krahmalkov RSF iii 196: = Plur. abs. of $ḥbr_3$(= tribe; improb. interpret.).

ḥbry v. ytn_1.

ḥbryt v. *ytn$_1$*.

ḥbš OldCan Sing. abs. *ḫa-ab-ši* EA 147^{12} - ¶ subst. of uncert. meaning: power?, cf. Böhl 37i; CAD s.v. *ḫapši*: = arm, force (cf. also Christian OLZ '25, 419f.: < root *ḥpš*) :: Ebeling with Knudt p. 1246: < Egypt. (= arm, force; cf. Ranke ibid. n. 1) :: Albright JPOS iv 169f.: related to Hebr. *ḥop̄šī* = free (v. *ḥpš$_2$*).

ḥbt v. *ḥwt*.

ḥg Nab Cantineau Nab ii 93: l. *ḥg* + suff. 3 p.s.m. (*ḥgh*) in CIS ii 2158 meaning pilgrimage (improb. interpret.).
v. *rbmg*.

ḥgb Palm Sing. emph. *ḥgbʾ* Sem xxvii 117^2 - ¶ subst., exact meaning unknown, prob. indicating either idol or building with cultic function (used in the context besides *mṣb*), cf. Aggoula Sem xxvii 118, 120ff.

ḥgg v. *ḥgy*, *mḥgh*.

ḥgh Nab Sing. emph. *ḥgtʾ* CIS ii 483^1 (= RES 1470) - ¶ subst. of unknown meaning. Garbini RSO xl 136: = protection, refuge, cf. also Donner sub KAI 278^5.

ḥgy OffAr the diff. *yḥgh* in KAI 278^5 poss. of this root, cf. Garbini RSO xl 135f.: = Impf. 3 p.s.m. of *ḥgy* (= to seek refuge); cf. however Dupont-Sommer CRAI '61, 21f., DCH 14: = Impf. 3 p.s.m. + suff. 3 p.s.m. of *ḥgg*/*ḥwg* (= to go around (in a religious/ritual sense)), cf. Levi Della Vida RSO xl 203f.: = to surround, to encircle; Ryckmans Mus lxxviii 468f.: < *ḥwg*/*ḥgg* = to cross a boundary (as a pilgrim); Gibson SSI ii p. 157: < *ḥgy* = *ḥgʿ* (= to efface; cf. already Kutscher with Naveh AION xvi 33 n. 47; improb. interpret.).

ḥgyr OffAr Sing. f. emph., cf. Warka 16, 41: *øha-gi-ir-ta-ʾ* - ¶ adj. limping, lame; used as subst. f. (Warka 16, 41): the limping woman.

ḥgʿ v. *ḥgy*.

ḥgr$_1$ v. *ḥgr$_2$*.

ḥgr$_2$ Pun Sing. cstr. *ḥgr* KAI 81^4 - **Nab** Sing. emph. *ḥgrʾ* J 329 (or = Sing. emph. of *ḥgr$_3$*?) - ¶ subst. m. wall, enclosure; *ḥgr hšmrt* KAI 81^4 : the protecting wall (v. *šmrh*) :: Clermont-Ganneau RAO iii 11f.: *ḥgr* = Qal Pf. 3 p.s.m. of *ḥgr$_1$*(= to surround with a fence).
v. *ḥgr$_3$*.

ḥgr$_3$ Nab Sing. emph. *ḥgrʾ* Atlal vii 105^1 - ¶ subst. poss. meaning: object dedicated to a god (designation of a basin dedicated to a god); cf. Aggoula Syr lxii 65, Beyer & Livingstone ZDMG cxxxvii 291 :: Livingstone Atlal a.l.: = *ḥgr$_2$*
v. *ḥgr$_2$*.

ḥgr$_4$ v. *qṣr$_4$*.

ḥd$_1$ v. *ʾḥd$_4$*, *ḥwd$_1$*, *kḥd*.

ḥd$_2$ (the number), v. *ʾḥd$_4$*.

ḥd$_3$ v. *ʾḥd$_4$*.

ḥdh **OffAr**, cf. Nisa-c $210^{5,6}$ (*ḥdh*; prob. reading :: Diakonov & Livshitz PaSb ii 145: l. in l. 5 *ḥw>/h* and in l. 6 *ḥwh*?): joy (in l. 6 in the comb. *šlm ḥdh wšrrt*; for a comparable construction, v. *šryr*).
v. *ḥdy₃*.

ḥdy₁ **OffAr** QAL Pf. 1 p.s. *ḥdyt* Cowl 41^2, Driv 13^4; Impf. 3 p.s.m. *yḥdh* Aḥiq 106; Part. act. s.m. abs. *ḥdh* Cowl 30^3, 31^3, 70^2, RES 1785B 5; s.f. emph. *ḥdyt>* Sem xxxiii 94^4 (for this poss. reading and interpret., cf. Porten Sem xxxiii 94, 98, Porten & Yardeni sub TADAE A 5.1 :: Sznycer HDS 168, 172f.: l. *ḥryth* = PA <EL Pf. 1 p.s. + suff. 3 p.s.m. of *ḥry₁* (= to kindle)); PA <EL Impf. 2 p.s.m. *tḥd[y]* Driv 13^2; HAPH Impf. 2 p.pl.m. *thḥdwn* Driv 11^4 (reading uncert.); cf. Frah xix 17 (*yḥdḥ-wn*; cf. Nyberg FP 50, 92 :: Ebeling Frah a.l.: l. *yḥbybwn* = PA <EL form of *ḥbb₁*(= to laugh); cf. also Toll ZDMG-Suppl viii 33f., 37) - **Hatra** QAL Pf. 3 p.s.m. *ḥdy* 30^9; Part. act. pl.m. abs. *ḥdyn* 79^4 (cf. e.g. Caquot Syr xl 3 :: Altheim & Stiehl AAW iv 245, 249 (div. otherwise): l. *yḥdyn* = Plur. abs. of *yḥd₂* (= excellent, eminent) :: Safar Sumer xvii 13 (n. 5; div. otherwise): for *ḥdyn bh* l. *ḥd/ryn bh* = tribal name) - ¶ verb QAL - **1)** to rejoice - a) + *b₂*, *bšgy> bnn lbbk >l yḥdh* Aḥiq 106: let not your heart rejoice in a multitude of children (cf. Greenfield FS Fitzmyer 50; cf. Hatra 79^4) - b) + *l₅*, *w>nh l[k] ḥdyt* Driv 13^4: and I am pleased with you - **2)** to jeer; *mn qṭlh wḥdy lh* Hatra $30^{8f.}$: whoever has killed him and has amused himself at his expense - PA <EL, HAPH (?, v. supra) to gladden; + *l₅*, *l>lhy> wl>ršm tḥd[y]* Driv 13^2: you will please his majesty and A. (cf. Driv 11^4; cf. Porten BiAr xlii 95) - a form of this verb also in RES 1689 (Palm.): *ḥdy*?? (= PA <EL Pf. 3 p.s.m. or Imper. s.m.??).
v. *>ḥd₄*.

ḥdy₂ v. *>ḥd₄*.

ḥdy₃ **Hatra** Sing. emph. *ḥdy>* 107^5 - ¶ subst. joy; *byt ḥdy> <ly>* Hatra 107^5: the high house of the joy (cf. Safar Sumer xviii 30, Altheim & Stiehl AAW iv 256, Milik DFD 379, Aggoula MUSJ xlvii 39, Syr lxv 207, Vattioni IH a.l., Drijvers SV 408 :: Caquot Syr xli 252: = the house of highest joy :: Tubach ISS 260 (n. 35; combining otherwise): *<ly> dsgyl* = the upper (room) of the *sgyl* :: Aggoula Ber xviii 98: *ḥdy>* = Sing. emph. of *ḥdy₄* (= breast, front)) - same word as *ḥdh*?
v. *>ḥd₄*, *>ḥr₅*.

ḥdy₄ cf. Frah x 32 (*ḥdyy>*): breast, cf. also Toll ZDMG-Suppl viii 32.

ḥdy₅ (= presence, directness), cf. Frah x 26 (*lḥdy>* = straight on, directly), cf. Nyberg FP 45, 76 :: Ebeling Frah a.l.: l. *zdq>* = form of *ṣdq₃*.

ḥdlh v. *dlt₂*.

ḥdn v. *>dn₁*.

ḥds v. *ḥdš₃*.

ḥdq v.Soden Or xlvi 186: = to press (together) > Akkad. (uncert.

interpret.).

ḥdr **Ph** Sing. cstr. *ḥdr* KAI 27^{19} (cf. e.g. Röllig KAI a.l., Cross & Saley BASOR cxcvii 46 × Baldacci BiOr xl 129: = Plur. cstr. (cf. also Gibson SSI iii p. 87 :: Garbini OA xx 285f.: = Sing. abs.) - **Pun** Sing. abs. *ḥdr* 161^3 (for the context, cf. Roschinski Num 112, 114); cstr. *ḥdr* CIS i 124^1, *ʿdr* BAr '38,/***pagina* (cf. Levi Della Vida OA iv 70, FR 35b) - **Hebr** Sing. abs. *ḥdr* IEJ v 165, HUCA xl/xli 151^3, IEJ xxxvi 206b 1 - ¶ subst. m. chamber, inner chamber; in IEJ v 165, HUCA xl/xli 151^3: burial-chamber; cf. *ḥdr bt ʿlm* CIS i 124^1: the burial-chamber, i.e. the house of eternity.

ḥdrh **Pun** Sing. abs. *ḥdrt* KAI 83; Sing. (cf. e.g. Cooke NSI p. 125f.) or Plur. (cf. e.g. Röllig KAI a.l.; v. also infra) abs. *ḥdrt* KAI 76B 3, 8 - ¶ subst. chamber (:: Stocks Ber iii 35: = tent); in KAI 76B prob. = chamber(s) in a sanctuary, cf. Cooke NSI p. 126 (cf. Lidzbarski sub KI 67: = *adyton* (cf. also idem Handb 271; Février Sem v 59: = sanctuary)) :: Lipiński VT xxiii 445: = sepulchral chamber (cf. also Röllig KAI a.l.: or = reference to the netherworld?); in KAI 83 the title *bʿlt hḥdrt* = indication of a goddess, exact meaning unknown, Garbini JSS xii 112: the lady of the netherworld (cf. also Lidzbarski sub KI 72 (cf. however idem Handb 271), Röllig KAI a.l.), Lipiński VT xxiii 444f.: the lady of the sepulchral chamber, Cooke NSI p. 131: the lady of the inner shrine? :: Stocks Ber iii 32: the lady of the nuptial tent (cf. also Hvidberg-Hansen TNT i 21, ii 18 n. 137).

ḥdš$_1$ **Ph** PIʿEL Pf. 3 p.s.m. *[ḥ]dš* CIS i 88^2 (on this text, cf. v.d.Branden FS Rinaldi 62f.) - **Pun** PIʿEL Pf. 3 p.s.m. *ḥdš* KAI 62^1, 72B 1 (cf. e.g. Röllig KAI a.l., Amadasi sub ICO-Spa 10 :: Littmann FuF '32, 179: l. *ḥrš* = QAL Pf. 3 p.s.m. of *ḥrš$_1$* (= to engrave), cf. also FR 131 (cf. however 143), JA xi/xvii 190^1, *ḥydš* KAI 138^6; 3 p.pl. *ḥdš* KAI 80^1 - **Nab** PAʿEL Pf. 3 p.s.m. *ḥdt* RB lxiv 215^3; + suff. 3 p.s.m. *ḥdth* CIS ii 349^3; 3 p.pl.m. *ḥdtw* CIS ii 235A 2 (= J 57) - **Palm** PAʿEL Pf. 3 p.s.m. *ḥdt* CIS ii 3957^2, 4288^4; 3 p.pl.m. *ḥdt* CIS ii 4198^2, DFD 217^1 - **Hatra** PAʿEL Pf. 3 p.s.m. *ḥdt*, cf. Assur 4^5 - ¶ verb PIʿEL/PAʿEL - **1)** to restore, to renew - a) + obj.: KAI 62^1, 80^1, CIS ii 349^3, 4198^2, RB lxiv 215^3, DFD 217^1 - b) + *l$_5$* (comm.): CIS ii 3957^2 - c) + obj. + *l$_5$* (comm.): KAI 72B 1ff. - **2)** to consecrate, to dedicate; + obj. + *l$_5$* (comm.): CIS ii 235A 2 (for this interpret., cf. Jaussen & Savignac J p. 214f.); cf. prob. also Assur 4^5 (cf. also Aggoula Assur a.l.) - v.Soden Or xlvi 186: derivative of this root > Akkad.

v. *ḥrš$_1$*, *pʿl*.

ḥdš$_2$ **Ph** Sing. abs. *ḥdš* KAI 37A 3, B 3; cstr. *ḥdš* KAI 37A 2 (for the reading, cf. Amadasi sub Kition C 1), B 2, 43^4 - **Pun** Sing. cstr. *ḥdš* CIS i 5510^8 - **Hebr** Sing. abs. *ḥdš* TA-H 5^{13}, 7$^{3f.,5,7}$, 8^{3,4}, 17^8, 32, AMB 4^{31}; Plur. abs. *ḥwdšym* IEJ vii 239^8 - ¶ subst. m. - **1)** new moon: KAI

37A 3, B 3, 43^{4}, CIS i 5510^{8}; *bḥdš yrḥ ʾtnm* KAI 37A 2: with the new moon of the month of E., cf. KAI 37B 2 - **2)** month: TA-H 5^{13} (on this text, cf. Pardee UF x 304, HAHL 38), IEJ vii 239^{8}; *mḥdš lḥdš* AMB 4^{31}: from month to month; *hššh lḥdš* TA-H 7$^{4f.}$: the sixth of the month (cf. TA-H 7$^{3f.,7}$, 8^{3,4}, 17^{8}, 32) - Owen Sar p. 103: the *ḥdṯ* in Sar 6^{2} = Sing. abs. of *ḥdš$_2$* (less prob. interpret., cf. Greenstein JANES viii 54, 56: the *ḥdṯ* (= Ph.) = n.d. or part of n.d.).

ḥdš$_3$ **Pun** Sing. m. abs. *ḥdš* RCL '66, 201^{1}; Plur. m. abs. *ḥdšm* KAI 81^{1} - **OldAr** Sing. m. abs. *ḥds*Tell F 11 (cf. Abou-Assaf, Bordreuil & Millard Tell F p. 43f.) - **OffAr** Sing. m. abs. *ḥdt* Cowl 8^{16}, 13^{12}, 36^{2} (cf. Porten & Yardeni sub TADAE B 6.2, Porten AN xxvii 90, 93: l. *ḥdt zy* :: Porten & Greenfield JEAS 118: l. *ḥdt l* :: Cowl a.l.: l. *ḥdth* (= Sing. f. abs.)), Krael 4^{8}, 7^{7}, etc., etc.; f. abs. *ḥdth* Cowl 36^{3}; f. emph. *ḥtʾ* (lapsus ??) RES 1300^{9} (cf. Chabot RES a.l., Grelot DAE p. 144); Plur. m. abs. *ḥdtn* Cowl 26^{10,14}; cf. Nisa 12, 13, 36^{2}, 41^{2}, 43^{2}, 282^{2}, 285^{2}, 294^{3}, 295^{2}, etc. (*ḥdt*), cf. GIPP 52 - **Palm** Sing. m. abs. *ḥdt* RTP 702 (:: Milik DFD 191: l. *ṣdt* related to *ṣyd$_1$*); m. emph. *ḥdtʾ* CIS ii 3913 i 8 - **Hatra** Sing. m. emph. *ḥdtʾ*, cf. Assur 27g - ¶ adj. new; said of - a) garment: Cowl 15^{7,9}, Krael 7^{6,7,8} (cf. also RES 1300^{9})^{,11} - b) object: Cowl 15^{16}, Krael 7^{17} (box?), cf. also Cowl 26^{10,14} (beams) - c) building: KAI 81^{1}, Krael 4^{8}, Assur 27g (cf. RCL '66, 201^{1}, said of gate) - d) wine, cf. *ḥdt* only for new wine: RTP 702 (cf. also Nisa-b 100^{3}, 1949^{2}, 2076^{2}, Nisa-c 223^{5}) - e) document; *šṭr ʾgryʾ ḥdtʾ* CIS ii 3913 i 8: the new document of lease (cf. Greek par. τῇ ἔνγιστα μισθώσει); *spr ḥdt wʿtyq* Cowl 8^{16}: a new document or an old one (cf. Cowl 13$^{11f.}$, Krael 9^{22}, 10^{15}, 12^{29} - used adv., anew: Tell F 11 (*ybl lknnh ḥds*: he shall bring (it) to erect it anew; cf. Akkad. par. *an-ḫu-su lu-diš*; :: Abou-Assaf MDOG cxiii 14: *ḥds* = something new, as object to *ybl*).

v. *z$_1$*,*mtnt*.

ḥdt$_1$ v. *ḥdš$_1$*.

ḥdt$_2$ v. *ḥdš$_3$*.

ḥw v. *hʾ$_1$*.

ḥwʾ$_1$ v. *ḥwy$_2$*.

ḥwʾ$_2$ v. *ḥdh*.

ḥwb$_1$ **OffAr** Qal Impf. 3 p.s.m. *yḥwb* Krael 10^{13}, ATNS 52 b 13; 1 p.s. *ʾḥwb* Krael 4^{14}, 10^{10}, 11^{6}; 1 p.pl. *nḥwb* Cowl 2^{15}, Krael 5^{14}; Part. act. (cf. Leand 39b, Segert AAG p. 124; or rather = adj.?, cf. Kutscher JAOS lxxiv 237, Jansma BiOr xi 215, Lipiński BiOr xxxiv 93, Lindenberger APA 267 n. 498, Freedman & Andersen FS Fitzmyer 24) s.m. abs. *ḥyb* Krael 7^{42}, Samar 1^{9} (= EI xviii 8*), 6^{9} (dam. context); act. s.f. abs. *ḥybh* Cowl 18^{3}; Paʿel Pf. 3 p.pl.m. + suff. 1 p.s. *ḥybwny* ATNS 9^{9} (for this prob. reading, cf. Porten & Yardeni sub TADAE B 8.6 :: Segal ATNS a.l.: l. *ngbr/dg* (word of unknown meaning)) - **Palm**

QAL Impf. 3 p.s.m. *yḥwb* RIP 199[12], Syr xiv 184[2], xvii 353[11]; Part. act. (or adj.?, cf. Cantineau Gramm 108f.) s.m. abs. *ḥyb* CIS ii 3913 ii 77, 102, 106, 113, 119; pl.m. abs. *ḥybyn* CIS ii 3913 ii 108; s.f. abs. *ḥyb'* CIS ii 3913 ii 146, 147 (*ḥyb[']*); pl.f. abs. *ḥybn* CIS ii 3913 i 4 - ¶ verb QAL - **1)** to be liable: Samar 1[9] (= EI xviii 8*; sc. liable to a penalty; cf. also Samar 6[9]) - a) + obj., *yḥwb sl'n .[...* Syr xvii 353[11]: he will be liable in the sum of ... *s.* (cf. prob. also RIP 199[12] (dam. context)); *'bydn šgyn ḥybn mks'* CIS ii 3913 i 4f.: many goods liable to taxation (cf. CIS ii 3913 ii 106, 108, 113, 119f., 146, 147) - b) + l_5: ATNS 52b 13 (dam. context) - c) + l_5 (comm.) + obj., *'nḥnh nḥwb lk ksp ...* Cowl 2[15]: we shall be liable to you in the sum of ... (cf. Krael 5[14], Syr xiv 184[2]); cf. also *'nh 'ḥwb w'ntn lky ksp ...* Krael 4[14f.]: I shall be liable and shall give to you the sum of ... (cf. Krael 10[10,13f.], 11[6]) - **2)** to be powerless, to be of no effect; *hn t'mr kwt ḥybh hy l' yštm' lh* Cowl 18[3]: if she speaks thus, she will be powerless, no heed shall be paid to her (cf. Krael 7[42]) - **3)** to be compulsory; + l_5 + Inf., *mks' ... ḥyb lmtḥšbw* CIS ii 3913 ii 102f.: the tax ... must be reckoned (cf. CIS ii 3913 ii 76f.?) - PA'EL to obligate + obj.: ATNS 9[9] (v. supra).
v. *hwy*$_1$, *ḥbr*$_2$, *yṣb*$_1$, *mḥzy*$_2$.

ḥwb$_2$ **OffAr** Sing. abs. *ḥwb* MAI xiv/ii 66[15] (for this prob. reading, cf. Porten & Yardeni sub TADAE B 1.1 (cf. also Bauer & Meissner SbPAW '36, 415, 421f. :: Torrey JAOS lviii 395: l. *ṣwb* = Sing. abs. of *ṣwb* (= misfortune), cf. also Dupont-Sommer MAI xiv/ii 67, 84f.: same reading, = interest??); on this text cf. also Grelot DAE p. 74 n. o); + suff. 1 p.s. *ḥwby* ATNS 35[5] (or l. *ḥwb'* = Sing. emph.?, cf. Porten & Yardeni sub TADAE B 4.7); Plur. abs. *ḥwbn* Samar 1[10] (= EI xviii 8*) - ¶ subst. obligation, debt: ATNS 35[5], MAI xiv/ii 66[15]; *l' dynn wl' ḥwbn* Samar 1[10] (= EI xviii 8*): without litigations or obligations - Porten & Yardeni sub TADAE B 1.1: l. poss. *ḥwb* (= Sing. cstr.) in MAI xiv/ii 66[19].

ḥwbh **JAr** Sing. cstr. *ḥwbt* DBKP 18[70] - ¶ subst. debt; *ḥwbt ksp* DBKP 18[70]: a debt of silver.

ḥwbs$_1$ v. *ḥwbš*.

ḥwbs$_2$ v. *ḥwbš*.

ḥwbš **OffAr** cf. Frah xvii 3 (*ḥwbš'* = prison), cf. Nyberg FP 48, 87 :: Ebeling Frah a.l.: l. *ḥwbsy'* (two words coinciding: *ḥwbs*$_1$(= prison) and *ḥwbs*$_2$(= bond, dead pledge)).

ḥwg v. *ḥgy*, *mḥgh*.

ḥwd$_1$ **Nab** Sing. abs. *ḥwd* CIS ii 215[6], *ḥd*CIS ii 209[7]; + suff. 3 p.s.m. *ḥwdwhy* CIS ii 212[6] - **JAr** Sing. abs. *ḥwd* MPAT 52[8] (for the reading, cf. Yaron BASOR cl 26, Beyer ATTM 322, 572 :: Milik Bibl xxxviii 263, J.J.Rabinowitz Bibl xxxix 487, Koffmahn DWJ 174, Fitzmyer & Harrington MPAT a.l.: pro *lḥwd* l. *lḥyn* = Plur. m. abs. of *lḥy*$_2$) - ¶

subst. solitude - **1)** preceded by prep. b_2 + l_5 (*blḥ(w)d*), only, exclusively: CIS ii 209[7], 215[6] (diff. context) - **2)** preceded by prep. l_5 - a) without pron. suff., *zbnt lkn bksp zwzyn šbʿyn wtmnyh ... lḥwd* MPAT 52[7f.]: I have sold to you for a price of seventy-eight *zūz* ... only (i.e. nothing more than the price mentioned; cf. also Beyer ATTM 323; :: Yaron BASOR cl 26: *wtql ḥd lḥwd* = and one shekel separately (i.e. extra); v. also supra) - b) + pron. suff., *yqbrwn yth ... lḥwdwhy* CIS ii 212[6]: they will bury him ... him only.
v. *ʾḥd*$_4$.

ḥwd$_2$ **OffAr** Sing. abs. *ḥwd* FuF xxxv 173[8] - ¶ subst. of uncert. meaning, Altheim & Stiehl FuF xxxv 176, ASA 254, 270 = mountain-top (diff. context).

ḥwdš v. *ḥdš*$_2$.

ḥwh$_1$ **OldAr** Sing. abs. *ḥwh* KAI 222A 31 - **OffAr** Sing. emph. *ḥwyh* (cf. Kutscher IOS i 117, Gibson SSI ii p. 140) - ¶ subst. m. serpent; for KAI 222A 31, cf. Hillers TC 55.

ḥwh$_2$ **Pun** Plur. abs. *ḥwt* KAI 161[9] (cf. Roschinski Num 112, 115 :: Février RA xlv 147: = Plur. cstr.) - ¶ subst. prob. meaning town, borough, settlement; cf. Février RA xlv 147, Röllig KAI a.l., Roschinski Num 112, 115 :: Berger RA ii 37, 43: = Sing. cstr. of *ḥwh*$_3$ (= life; cf. also Cooke NSI p. 150, Tomback CSL 103; on the subject, cf. also Amadasi Guzzo StudMagr xi 30).

ḥwh$_3$ v. *ḥwh*$_2$.

ḥwh$_4$ v. *ḥdh*.

ḥwṭ$_1$ **OffAr** QAL Pf. 3 p.s.m. *ḥṭ* Sem ii 31 conc. 6 (v. infra) - ¶ verb QAL to pay (cf. Levine JAOS lxxxiv 20 :: Rosenthal AH i/2, 10 s.v. *ḥṭ*: = Sing. abs. of *ḥṭ*$_2$ (= cash; cf. also Grelot DAE p. 370 n. i) :: Dupont-Sommer Sem ii 32: = QAL Pf. 3 p.s.m. of *ḥwṭ*$_2$); for the context, v. *qṭ*.

ḥwṭ$_2$ **OffAr** Impf. 3 p.s.m. + suff. 3 p.s.m. *yḥṭnh* RHR cxxx 20 conv. 1 (reading uncert.); cf. Frah xviii 10 (*ḥṭṭwn*), cf. Nyberg FP 89 :: Ebeling Frah a.l.: < root *ḥṭṭ*$_1$ - ¶ verb QAL to sew + obj.
v. *ḥwṭ*$_1$.

ḥwṭ$_3$ **OffAr** Sing. abs. *ḥwṭ* Cowl 15[25,28], Krael 2[9,10] - ¶ subst. string; only in the expression *mn ḥm ʿd ḥwṭ* (= totally), v. *ḥm*$_3$ - this word (Sing. abs. *ḥwṭ*) poss. also in Sach 76 ii B 5 (heavily dam. context).

ḥwy$_1$ **DA** PAʿEL Impf. 1 p.s. + suff. 2 p.pl.m. *ʾḥwkm* i 7 - **OffAr** PAʿEL Pf. 3 p.s.m. *ḥwy* ATNS 118 (?, *ḥwy[* ; heavily dam. context); + suff. 1 p.pl. *ḥwynʾ* Cowl 31[15]; Impf. 3 p.s.m. *yḥwh* ATNS 5[5] (or = APH?; uncert. reading; Porten & Yardeni sub TADAE B 8.3: l. *hḥwh* = HAPH Pf. 3 p.s.m.); + suff. 2 p.s.m. *yḥwk* Irâq xxxi 173[5] (dam. context; for the reading, cf. Segal Irâq xxxi 174); + suff. 1 p.s. *yḥwny* Herm 4[2], 6[2] (for this form, cf. Kutscher IOS i 116f.); 2 p.s.m. *tḥwh* Aḥiq 96 (dam.

context :: e.g. Lindenberger APA 71, 234 n. 48, Kottsieper SAS 12, 20, 201 : l. *tḥzh* = QAL Impf. 2 p.s.m. of *ḥzy*$_1$); 1 p.s. *ʾḥwh* Irâq xxxi 173^{1} (heavily dam. context); 3 p.pl.m. *[y]ḥww* Cowl 26^{5} (or APH?, for the heavily dam. context, cf. also Grelot Sem xx 27, DAE p. 287 n. h × Cowl a.l., Porten & Yardeni sub TADAE A 6.2: = QAL (= to see)); + suff. 1 p.pl.? *yḥwwnn[ʾ]* Cowl 34^{7} (or APH??, cf. Cowl a.l., Grelot DAE p. 397 n. i × Porten & Greenfield JEAS p. 84, Porten & Yardeni sub TADAE A 4.4: l. *yḥwwnn[y]* = Impf. 3 p.pl.m. + suff. 1 p.s.); 1 p.pl. *nḥwy* Cowl 26^{7} (or APH??, cf. Cowl a.l.; cf. however Porten & Yardeni sub TADAE A 6.2: = QAL Impf. 1 p.pl. (= to see), this form to be combined with prec. clause); Inf. *mḥwh* RES 1792B 8 (for this form, cf. Leand 31g, cf. however Grelot DAE p. 375 n. m: l. *mḥwy*); HAPH Pf. 3 p.s.m. + suff. 1 p.pl. *hḥwyn* Cowl 26^{7}, 30^{16}; 1 p.pl. *hḥwyn* Cowl 26^{8}, ATNS 6^{5}; Impf. 3 p.s.m. *yhḥwh* Aḥiq 93; 2 p.s.m. *[th]ḥwy* Aḥiq 208; Imper. pl.m. + suff. 3 p.s.m. *hḥwwhy* Driv 8^{5}; cf. Paik 356 (*ḥwh*), 357 (*ḥwyth*; cf. however de Menasce BiOr xi 162), GIPP 24, 28, SaSt 18f. - **Hatra** PA ʿEL Pf. 3 p.s.m. *ḥwy* 281^{11} - ¶ verb PA ʿEL (v. however supra) to show, to make known, to report - **1)** + obj., *nḥwy zy byd psmsnyt* ... Cowl 26^{7}: we report that by the hand of P. ... (v. however supra; cf. Hatra 281^{11}, for this text, cf. also Tubach ISS 274f. (n. 113)) - **2)** + double object, *yḥwny ʾpyk bšlm* Herm 4^{2}: may he show me your face in peace (cf. Herm 6^{2}), cf. also DA i 7 - **3)** + obj. + *l*$_5$, *lmḥwh ṭʿmʾ lhwšʿ* RES 1792B 8f.: to notify H. of the order (cf. Dupont-Sommer REJ cvii 43f.) - **4)** + obj. + *b*$_2$, *ḥwynʾ bwydrng* Cowl 31^{15}: he let us behold (our desire) on W. (i.e. he has revenged us on W.) - HAPH to show, to make known, to report - **1)** + *l*$_5$, *ʾnḥnh hḥwyn lšmšlk* Cowl 26^{8}: we have notified Sh. - **2)** + double object, *hḥwyn spyntʾ* Cowl 26^{7}: he has shown us the boat; cf. *hḥwwhy yhḥsn* Driv 8^{5}: do you notify him (that) he take possession - **3)** +*l*$_5$ (obj.): ATNS 6^{5} - **4)** + obj. + *b*$_2$, *hḥwyn bwydrng* Cowl 30^{16}: he let us behold (our desire) on W. (i.e. he has revenged us on W.) - for this verb, cf. Joüon Or ii 117ff., Rosenthal Sprache 65 n. 4 - Dion p. 27: the *ḥwyw* of KAI 214^{4} (diff. and dam. context) poss. = PA ʿEL Pf. 3 p.pl.m. of this root (cf. however Dion p. 381 n. 4: or = PA ʿEL Pf. 3 p.pl.m. of *ḥwy*$_2$?, cf. also Tawil Or xliii 48ff. (v. *šnm*$_1$) - a form of this root prob. in Aḥiq 208 (*[th]ḥwy* = HAPH Impf. 2 p.s.m.) - a form of this root poss. in Cowl 69A 1: *]ḥwhh*. v. *ʾḥ*$_1$, *ḥzy*$_1$, *ydʿ*$_1$, *yḥʾ*, *twḥyt*.

ḥwy$_2$ **Ph** PI ʿEL Pf. 3 p.s.m. *ḥwy* KAI 4^{2}; Impf. 3 p.s.m. (or rather 3 p.pl., cf. Lidzbarski OLZ '27, 458, cf. also Röllig KAI ii p. 16) + suff. 3 p.s.m*yḥww* KAI 12^{4} (or YIPH?); 3 p.s.f. + suff. 3 p.s.m. *tḥww* KAI 10^{9} (or YIPH?); Imper. s.m. in Αὐδονίς = *ḥw ʾdny* AnthGraeca vii 419,8 (the way a Phoenician is greeted); YIPH Pf. 3 p.s.m. *yḥw* KAI 26A i 3 (cf. FR 174, 267b also for litt.; interpret. as Inf. (abs.), cf. also Amadasi

Guzzo VO iii 89f., less prob.) - **Pun** QAL Pf. 3 p.s.m. *ḥw*ʾKAI 128[3], NP 66[3], Punica ix 6[2], x 2[3], *ʿwh* KAI 142[2], 158[2], NP 59[2] (= Punica xii 27), RES 173[2], Punica xx 4[2] (l. *rgʿṭ ʿwh* pro *rgʿṭʿ w<ʿw>h*), Sem xxxvi 33[2], *ʿwʾ* KAI 144[2], 165[7], NP 13[2] (= Punica xii 18bis), 25[3] (= Punica xi 4), 53[2] (= Punica xii 20), 61[2] (= Punica xii 29), Karth x 133[2] (cf. also Fantar Sem xxv 72 :: Garbini AION xxv 263: l. *ʿwʿʾ*), etc., etc., *ʿwʿ* KAI 157[2] (?, dam. context), NP 23[3] (= Punica xi 2), Punica ix 3[4], xi 16[2] (uncert. context), RES 168[3], cf. KAI 180a, b, c, d, IRT 879[3], 894[4]: *avo* (cf. Levi Della Vida OA ii 85 n. 43; cf. prob. also Aug xvi 541 no. 21: *a[v]o*; cf. poss. also Aug xvi 540 no. 8), cf. KAI 180e, PBSR xxii 115f.[2,4] (or rather = 3 p.s.f.?): *av* (in KAI 180e, Röllig KAI a.l.: l. *av?[o]*); 3 p.s.f. *ḥw*ʾKAI 140[7], 171[3], Punica ix 1[3], xiv 1[2], *ḥwʿ* NP 60[3] (= Punica xii 28), *hwʿ* NP 68[3] (= Punica ivA 8), *ʿwʾ* NP 22[3] (= Punica xi 1), 55[2] (= Punica xii 23), 56[2] (= Punica xii 24), *ʿwʿ* KAI 135[3], 142[3,6], 149[4], 169[2f.], NP 12[5], 54[3] (= Punica xii 22), 64[3] (= Punica xii 32; :: FR 174: = 3 p.s.m.), Sem xxxvi 35[3], etc., *ʿʿwʿ* KAI 143[3f.] (for this form, cf. Chabot sub Punica ix 2: lapsus for *ʿwʿ* :: Röllig KAI a.l.: *ʿʿwʿ* pro *ḥʿwʿ*; cf. also Sznycer Sem xxxiii 56), *ʿwḥ* NP 65[2] (= Punica xii 33; cf. Chabot Punica ibid., FR 174 :: Schroed 271: = 3 p.s.m.), cf. Aug xvi 540 no. 9 (cf. also Krahmalkov JSS xxiv 28): *ava* (uncert. interpret.; cf. poss. also Aug xvi 540 no. 11); Impf. 3 p.pl. (or s.m.?; uncert. context; cf. Février JA ccxxxvii 88) *yḥwʾ* KAI 153[4]; Imper. s.m. *[ḥ]wʾ* RES 1224 (cf. 1929; cf. e.g. Lidzbarski Eph i 162, Sznycer APCI 213 (n. 14)), cf. Poen 994, 1001: *avo* (Poen 998: *avo* with var. *vo*; cf. also *hav*, *havon* in Poen 1141, 1142, cf. also Sznycer PPP 144f.; a form of this root also in Poen 946??, cf. Schroed 291f., 312, L.H.Gray AJSL xxxix 77f.: l. *auo* = QAL Pf. 3 p.s.m.) - **Hebr** QAL Pf. 3 p.s.m. *ḥyh* Frey 630b 3; 3 p.pl.m. *ḥyw* DJD ii 30[19] - **OffAr** QAL Impf. 3 p.s.m. *yḥyh* Cowl 49[3]; 3 p.pl.m. *yḥywn* HDS 9[8]; HAPH Pf. 1 p.s. + suff. 2 p.s.m. *hḥytk* Aḥiq 51; Impf. 3 p.s.m. + suff. 1 p.s. *yhḥyny* Aḥiq 54; cf. Syr xxxv 321[53], 323[55], GIPP 37, SaSt 25 - **Nab** APH Pf. 3 p.s.m. *ʾḥyy* CIS ii 183[4], RES 83[12], 86[4] (= 471), 1434[6], Syr xxxv 227[4], RB xlii 408[5], IEJ xi 135[4], xiii 113[4], *ʾḥy* RES 468[5] - **Palm** QAL Pf. 3 p.s.m. *ḥyʾ* CIS ii 4358B 5, 4359[5], 4562[6], 4616[7], AAS iii 24 i 5, ii 5; 3 p.s.f. *ḥyt* RIP 39A 4 - ¶ verb QAL to live, passim; *ʿwʾ šnt ʿsr wʿmš* NP 13[2]: he lived fifteen years; *ḥyh ʾrbʿym wštym šnh* Frey 630b 3f.: he lived forty-two years (et passim); *kl mdʿm zy yḥyh bh ʾyš* Cowl 49[3]: everything whereby a man may live; *kl šbw wšḥyw ʿlyw* DJD ii 30[19]: everything which is on it, and which lives on it; cf. the peculiar clause *wʿwʾ bn šʿnt šbʿm* NP 52[2f.] (= Punica xii 19, for the reading of *ʿwʾ*, cf. Bourgade TO pl. 17 tun): he lived a son of seventy years (i.e. he lived to the age of seventy) - PIʿEL - **1)** to restore; + obj., *ḥwy kl mplt hbtm* KAI 4[2]: he restored all the ruins of the temples - **2)**

to keep alive; + obj., *wtḥww wtʾrk ymw wšntw* ... KAI 10[9]: may she give him life and prolong his days and years ... (cf. KAI 12[4]; v. supra; cf. Amadasi Guzzo WO xv 116f.) - YIPH/HAPH/APH to give life to, to vivify, to keep alive; + object, *yḥw ʾnk ʾyt dnnym* KAI 26A i 3: I vivified the D. (on this text, cf. Amadasi Guzzo WO xv 113ff.); *hḥytk wlʾ qṭltk* Aḥiq 51: I kept you alive and did not kill you (cf. Aḥiq 54); cf. also the stereotype designation of the Nab. king Rab'el II, *rbʾl mlkʾ mlk nbṭw dy ʾḥyy wšyzb ʿmh* RES 83[9ff.]: king R., king of the N., who vivifies and saves his people (passim in Nab. texts, cf. also Meshorer NC p. 75f.) - a form of this root poss. in Aḥiq 86: *]ḥyh*, cf. Grelot RB lxviii 181, DAE p. 435, Kottsieper SAS 11, 19, 101, 202: = Sing. abs. of *ḥyh$_2$*, Cowl a.l.: l. *[y]ḥyh* = QAL Impf. 3 p.s.m., cf. however Ginsberg ANET 428: l. *[l]ḥyh* = Sing. f. abs. of *lḥy$_2$* (cf. also Lindenberger APA 57f., Puech RB xcv 589) - a form of this root poss. also in KAI 179[3] (= IRT 889): *aun*, cf. Février JA ccxli 467: = Sing.(??) + suff. 1 p.pl. of *ḥy$_1$*, Levi Della Vida OA ii 87, Polselli OAC xiii 238: = QAL Imper. pl.m. + *n* energ. (cf. Vattioni Aug xvi 551), cf. however Vattioni AION xvi 45: = part of n.p., Krahmalkov JAOS xciii 61, 64: = Sing. + suff. 1 p.pl. of *ʾḥ$_1$* - Vattioni Aug xvi 543: the *ayo* in IRT 877[8] poss. = *avo* (v. supra) - Garbini AION xvii 69ff.: l. *aion* (= form of *ḥwy$_2$*) in ILA i 468[1f.,4] (= RIL 665; uncert. interpret.).
v. *ʾḥ$_1$*, *ḥwy$_1$*,*ḥy$_1$*, *kwn$_1$*, *ʿrṣ$_1$*, *šgʾ$_3$*.

ḥwy$_3$ v. *ḥwh$_1$*.

ḥwy$_4$ **Nab** Sing. emph. *ḥwyʾ* CIS ii 278[3] (= J 63[2] = ARNA-Nab 94[2] :: CIS ii a.l.: l. *twyʾ* = poss. ethnicum) - ¶ subst. of unknown meaning, prob. indication of function or profession or indication of origin.

ḥwyw v. *ḥwy$_1$*.

ḥwyn v. *ʾḥšyn*.

ḥwl$_1$ v. *ḥll$_1$*.

ḥwl$_2$ **Palm** Plur. + suff. 3 p.s.m. *ḥwlwh* MUSJ xxxviii 106[10] - ¶ subst. (or substantivated adj.?) unconsecrated place (i.e. loculus not yet used for burial).

ḥwlq v. *ḥlq$_3$*.

ḥwmh v. *ḥmh$_1$*.

ḥws Milik DFD 37: l. *ʾḥ[y]s* (= APH Pf. 3 p.s.m., to spare oneself, *npšh*) in DFD 37[3] (uncert. reading and interpret.).

ḥwpn v. *ḥpn*.

ḥwṣ$_1$ v. *ḥṣ$_2$*.

ḥwṣ$_2$ v. *ḥṣ$_4$*.

ḥwṣn v. *ḥṣ$_4$*.

ḥwr **Palm** Sing. emph. *ḥwrʾ* MUSJ xxxviii 106[11] - ¶ subst. (or substantivated adj.) in combination *ktl dy ḥwrʾ* prob. = wall with white material (i.e. plaster), cf. also Ingholt MUSJ xxxviii 117.

v. *ḥywr.*

ḥwry **OffAr** Sing. m. abs. *ḥwry* Driv 6[3] - ¶ adj. white; *qmḥ ḥwry* Driv 6[3]: white flour (or *ḥwry* = subst.? (= white flour), cf. Segert ArchOr xxiv 386f.).

ḥwš v. *dḥšpt,ḥšš.*

ḥwt **OffAr**, cf. Nisa 14[1], 16[1], 25[1], 26[1], 27[1], 45[3], 46[1], 48[1], etc. (*ḥwt*ʾ), Nisa 18[1], 19[2], 29[1], 30[1], 62[2], 67[3], 71[2], 72[2], 91[1], etc. (*ḥwth*), Nisa 21[1] (*ḥwtyn*), Nisa 562[1] (*ḥwṭ*ʾ), Nisa 356[2], 852[1] (*ḥt*ʾ; lapsus?), Nisa 449[1], 450[1], 485[1] (*ḥtw*ʾ, lapsus?); cf. Vinnikov VDI xlviii ('54), 116ff., Diakonov & Livshitz VDI lvi ('56), 109, Altheim & Stiehl WZKMU '55/56, 218f., Suppl 56f., EW x 248, ASA 35f., 269, AAW i 650f., ii 220f.: < *ḥbt*ʾ= *ḥ*ᵃ*bītā* (= jar; :: Diakonov & Livshitz Nisa-b p. 39: < Akkad. *øhuttu* = jar (less prob.) :: Henning Ir 27: *ḥwt*ʾ < *ḥbt*ʾ = Sing. emph. of *ḥbh*(= debt)); cf. also GIPP 53f.

ḥwtm v. *ḥtm₂*.

ḥzʾn v. *ḥzn.*

ḥzg **OffAr** Degen NESE i 56, Lipiński Stud 140f.: l. *ḥzg* in TH 5 rev. 7 (= AECT 57; highly uncert. reading, cf. also Friedrich TH p. 78: l. poss. *dzg*, dam. context). Lipiński ibid.: *ḥzg* (= Sing. m. abs.) = adj. *ḥzg*, var. of *ḥzq₂* (= mighty; uncert. interpret.).

ḥzh **Pun** Sing. abs. *ḥzt* KAI 69[11] - ¶ subst. of unknown meaning, prob. certain type of sacrifice; related to root *ḥzy₁*??: sacrifice connected with auspices/divination??, cf. e.g. Cooke NSI p. 120, Lagrange ERS 474, Röllig KAI a.l., v d Branden RSO xl 120, Amadasi sub ICO app. 3, SSMA 113, Kaiser TUAT i 265, cf. also Février REJ cxxiii 13: type of divination connected with a sacrifice; on this word, cf. also Urie PEQ '49, 70, Capuzzi StudMagr ii 74, Fuhs HZH 50.

ḥzw **OffAr** the *ḥzw* mostly read in KAI 270A 5 (cf. e.g. CIS ii sub 137, Cooke NSI p. 202f., Sach p. 239f., Donner KAI a.l., Grelot DAE p. 138, Levine JAOS lxxxiv 19, Fuhs HZH 46f.: = Sing. abs. (= vision, apparition)) prob. to be read *yḥ* (= part of n.p.), cf. Dupont-Sommer ASAE xlviii 120, 124f.

v. *mḥzt.*

ḥzwr cf. Frah vii 15 (*ḥzwl*ʾ): pig, swine (cf. also Lemosín AO ii 266).

ḥzy₁ **Ph** Qal Pf. *ḥz* KAI 24[11,12]; 1 p.s. *ḥzt* KI 38 (for the problems of the context, cf. also Puech Sem xxxii 53) - **DA** Qal Pf. 3 p.pl.m. *ḥzw* i 16 (:: Hackett BTDA 54 (n. 47): or = Qal Pf. 3 p.s.m.??); Impf. 3 p.s.m. *yḥz* DA v e 2 (on this prob. interpret., cf. (Hamilton with) Hackett BTDA 33, 98, Wesselius BiOr xliv 593f.; on the context, cf. however Knauf ZDPV ci 189, Puech BAT 360); 3 p.pl.m. *yḥzw* ii 13 (for the reading problems, cf. v d Kooij DA p. 127f.; on the form, cf. Halpern FS Lambdin 129 n. 50); Part. act. s.m. abs./cstr. *ḥzh* i 1 (cf. e.g. Hoftijzer DA a.l., Hackett BTDA 31, 98 :: Garbini Hen i

173: rather = QAL Pf. 3 p.s.m.) - **OldAr** QAL Part. act. pl.m. abs. *ḥzyn* KAI 202A 12; PA ʿEL Inf. *ḥzyh* KAI 222A 13 (cf. Fitzmyer JAOS lxxxi 194, AIS 40, Degen AAG p. 77, 78 (n. 82), Gibson SSI ii p. 38 × Dupont-Sommer Sf p. 36, Koopmans 48, Donner KAI a.l., Segert AAG p. 301, 304, Fuhs HZH 43 n. 202: = QAL Inf., cf. also Garbini RSO xxxiv 49 (n. 1), 51, Ben-Chayyim Lesh xxxv 250 (cf. also Muraoka AN xxii 100, 115 n. 120: = QAL Inf. cstr. or QAL Inf. cstr. + proleptic suff. (last interpret. less prob.)) :: Lipiński Stud 27f. (div. otherwise): l. *ḥzy* (= QAL Inf.) + h_2(less prob., cf. also Fales OA xvi 64, Degen WO ix 168); on this form, cf. also Garr DGSP 140, 163 n. 407; ITP Impf. 3 p.s.m. *ytḥzh* KAI 222A 28 (cf. e.g. Garbini RSO xxxvi 9ff., Fitzmyer JAOS lxxxi 196f., AIS 47, Donner KAI a.l., Degen WO iv 58, AAG p. 67, 78, Gibson SSI ii p. 31, 39, Rössler TUAT i 181 :: Dupont-Sommer Sf p. 45, 143, Koopmans 51 (div. otherwise; cf. Segert ArchOr xxxii 126, Stiehl AAW i 222): l. *lyt* + *ḥzh* (= QAL Part. act. s.m. abs.) - **OffAr** QAL Pf. 3 p.s.m. *ḥzh* RES 1785B 3, Aḥiq 94 (?, or = QAL Part. act. s.m. abs.?; dam. context; cf. also e.g. Sach p. 160, 162, Halévy RS xx 50, Baneth OLZ '14, 297 (div. otherwise): l. *mtḥzh* (= ITP Part. s.m. abs.), less prob. reading, cf. Lindenberger APA 67, 232 n. 126; on the reading, cf. also Kottsieper SAS 101), ATNS 45b 1, 59^3, 102a 3, 147^2 (?, *]ḥzh[*); 1 p.s. *ḥzyt* KAI 270A 2, Herm 4^5, ATNS 5^4 (or = QAL Pf. 2 p.s.m.?, cf. Porten & Yardeni sub TADAE B 8.3); 3 p.pl.m. + suff. 3 p.s.m. *ḥzwhy* HDS 9^7 (for this diff. reading, cf. Kaufman with Lipiński Stud 77 (cf. also Fales AION xxviii) 282, Lipiński WGAV 375) :: Caquot HDS a.l.: l. *ḥṣwhy* = QAL Pf. 3 p.pl.m. + suff. 3 p.s.m. of *ḥṣy*$_1$ (= to divide), cf. also Vattioni Or xlviii 138); + suff. 1 p.s., cf. Warka 7: *ḫa-za-ú-ni-ʾ*; 1 p.pl. *ḥzyn* Cowl 30^{17}, 31^{16}; Impf. 3 p.s.m. *[yḥ]zh* Aḥiq 163; 2 p.s.m. *tḥzh* KAI 233^{20}, Cowl 68 iii 3 (or = 3 p.s.f.?); 2 p.s.f. *tḥzy* KAI 270A 5 (for this reading, cf. Dupont-Sommer ASAE xlviii 120, 124, Grelot DAE p. 138 (n. d), Segert AAG p. 299 :: Fuhs HZH 46f.: l. poss. *ʾḥzy* = QAL Impf. 1 p.s. :: e.g. CIS ii sub 137, Cooke NSI p. 202f., Donner KAI a.l. (cf. also Levine JAOS lxxxiv 19, Degen GGA '79, 36): = lapsus for *ʾtḥzy* (= ITP Pf. 3 p.s.m.)), *tḥzyn* Sem ii 31 conv. 4; 1 p.s. *ʾḥzh* Aḥiq 205, Sem ii 31 conv. 5, *ʾḥzʾ* KAI 233^{14} (for the diff. reading, cf. Dupont-Sommer Syr xxiv 44 :: R.A.Bowman UMS xx 278, 281: = same form of *ḥzy*$_2$ (= to seize)); 2 p.pl.m. *tḥzw* KAI 233^{17}; Imper. s.m. *ḥzy* Cowl 30^{23} (:: Birkeland ActOr xii 87ff.: l. *ḥwy* = QAL Imper. s.m. of *ḥwy*$_1$(= to look)), 41^6, Aḥiq 101, Sem xxi conv. 1, Aeg xxxix 4 recto 4, CRAI '70, 163^1 (for the reading, cf. however Teixidor Syr xlviii 479), Beh 54 (for the context, cf. Greenfield & Porten BIDG 49), etc., etc.; pl.m. *ḥzw* Cowl 38^5, ASAE xxvi 27^1, NESE i 11^2 (for the reading, cf. Degen NESE i 11, Naveh & Shaked JAOS xci 380, Grelot DAE p. 504 (n. e), Porten Or lvii 78, Porten & Yardeni sub TADAE

A 3.10 :: Shunnar in GMA 114, 116 (cf. however idem CRM ii 278, 286f.): l. *ḥww* = PA‘EL Imper. pl.m. of *ḥwy*₁,cf. also Macuch JAOS xciii 59: l. prob. *ḥww* = PA‘EL Imper. pl.m. of *ḥwy*₁);Inf. *mḥzh* Aḥiq 37, 63, 108, KAI 279⁴, BSOAS xiii 82⁵ (dam. context); Part. act. s.m. abs. *ḥzh* Aḥiq 125 (cf. Cowl p. 287, Gressmann ATAT 460, Ginsberg ANET 429 :: Grelot RB lxviii 186, Lindenberger APA 114: or = Part. pass. s.m. abs., cf. also Grelot DAE p. 440, Puech Sem xxi 14 (n. 2)); f. s. abs. *ḥzyt* Herm 1¹¹, 7³ (for the form, cf. Wesselius AION xl 266); PA‘EL Impf. 3 p.s.m. + suff. 1 p.s. *yḥzny* Herm 1², 2², 3², 5² (cf. e.g. Bresciani & Kamil Herm al × Kutscher IOS i 112: = APH/HAPH); Part. act. s.m. abs. *mḥzh* KAI 226⁵ (cf. Fitzmyer AIS 40, Gibson SSI ii p. 98 :: e.g. Cooke NSI p. 190, Donner KAI a.l., Kutscher Lesh xxxi 34, Rosenthal ANET 661, Dupont-Sommer AH i/2, 4 (s.v. *mḥzh*), Fuhs HZH 44 n. 207, Garr DGSP 163 n. 407, Dion p. 159 (div. otherwise): l. *m*₁₁ + *ḥzh* (= QAL Part. act. s.m. abs.; cf. also Stefanovic COAI 197ff.); ITP Pf. 3 p.s.m. *ʾtḥzy* ATNS 67b 5 (heavily dam. context); Part. m. s. abs. *mtḥzh* Aḥiq 106; cf. Frah xx 14 (*ḥzytwn*), Paik 376 (*ḥzy*), 378 (*ḥzyt*), 379-381 (*ḥzytn*), 377 (*ḥz[*), Sogd R 56, ZDMG xcii 442A 14, GIPP 24, 54, SaSt 18 (cf. Lemosín AO ii 108ff., Toll ZDMG-Suppl viii 28, 37) - **Palm** QAL Pf. 3 p.pl.m. *ḥzw* RIP 199⁴ (dam. context); ITP Pf. 3 p.s.m. *ʾtḥzy* CIS ii 3913 i 7 (Greek par. δεδόχθαι), ii 114, 123, 129 - **Hatra** QAL Part. act. s.m. emph. *ḥzyʾ* app. 4⁶ (cf. Safar Sumer xvii 39f., Altheim & Stiehl AAW v/1, 81f., 84 (cf. also Vattioni IH a.l.) :: Caquot Syr xl 13, Teixidor Syr xli 273 (n. 3): = QAL Part. act. pl.m. emph. :: Milik DFD 395: = QAL Part. pass. s.m. emph. :: Tubach ISS 401f. (n. 698): = QAL Part. pass. s.f. abs.? :: Aggoula MUSJ xlvii 46, Sem xxvii 138: l. *ḥzyh* = QAL Pf. 3 p.s.m. + suff. 3 p.s.m.) - **JAr** QAL Imper. s.m. *ḥzy* Syr xlv 101²² (poss. also in l. 20: *ḥz[y]*, heavily dam. context); Part. act. pl.m. abs. *ḥzyn* AMB 15¹⁵ (dam. and diff. context); pass. s.m. abs. *ḥzh* IEJ xxxvi 206⁵,⁷; ITP Impf. 3 p.s.m. *ytḥzh* AMB 3¹⁴ - ¶ verb QAL to see, passim - **1)** + obj.: DA i 16 (for the context, v. *qq*₁), KAI 24¹², 233¹⁴, Aḥiq 63, HDS 9⁷, Herm 4⁵, ATNS 45b 1, etc.; *ḥzyt ‘bdʾ zk mhlk tn[h]* ATNS 5⁴: I saw this slave walking here; *ḥzy b‘ly ṭbtk* Cowl 30²³ᶠ·: look after your well-wishers (v. *ṭbh*₁), cf. Cowl 31²³, KAI 233¹⁷; *ḥzy ʾgrt ʾršm* Driv 12⁴: look at Arsham's letter (i.e. obey what is written in it); *bl ḥz pn š* KAI 24¹¹: he had never seen a sheep (i.e. prob. he never had a sheep in his possession, cf. Landsberger Samʾal 52, cf. also Fuhs HZH 49); *lmḥzh ʾyk ...* Aḥiq 37: to see how ... (object clause); *ḥzy hkyn ‘bdt* Syr xlv 101²²: look how I have acted; for the context of KAI 279⁴, v. *znh* - **2)** + *b*₂, *ḥzyʾ* (v. supra) *bḥlmʾ* Hatra app. 4⁶: seeing in dreams (v. *ḥlm*₃; :: Teixidor Syr xli 273 (n. 3): l. *ḥzyʾ wḥlmʾ*, Caquot Syr xl 13: l. *ḥzyʾ ḥlmʾ*); *ḥzh bʾrqʾ* RES 1785B 3: he looked to the earth (for the context, cf. Pardee

UF ix 211); in specialized meaning, *ḥzyn bhwn* Cowl 30[17]: we saw (our desire) upon them (i.e. we were revenged upon them), cf. Cowl 31[16] - **3)** + l_5 + Inf., *ḥzw ḥlqʾ zyly ... lmṭʿn bh* NESE i 11[2f.]: take care to load my share on it ... (for this interpret., cf. Degen NESE i 15) - **4)** + $ʿl_7$, *ḥzy ʿl ynqyʾ* PSBA '15, 222[2f.] (= RES 1793[8f.]): look after the children (cf. Cowl 41[6], Herm 1[11f.], 7[2f.]; cf. also Dion RB lxxxix 557) - **5)** + $ʿl_7$ + obj., *ḥzw ʿlyhm mh ṣbw* Cowl 38[5f.]: look after them in what they want (cf. also Joüon MUSJ xviii 5; v. *ṣby*1; cf. Dion RB lxxxix 567) - **6)** Imper. s.m. often used as interjection "behold": Aḥiq 101, RES 492A 4, 1298B 2, Sem xxi 85 conv. 1, etc.; cf. *kʿn ḥzy* Aeg xxxix 4 recto 4: now, behold (cf. also *kʿnt ḥzy* RES 492B 1, Sem xxi 85 conc. 2); *ʾn ḥzy* RES 492B 3 (cf. RES 1800): behold; Imper. pl.m. used as interjection "behold": ASAE xxvi 27[1] (cf. Dupont-Sommer JA ccxxxv 80), prob. also in CRAI '70, 163[1] (cf. Dupont-Sommer a.l.) - **7)** Part. act. (substantivated): seer, prophet: KAI 202A 12 (cf. also Ross HThR lxiii 4, 14ff.); cf. *ḥzh ʾlhn* DA i 1: seer of the gods (cf. also Weinfeld Shn v/vi 142) - **8)** Part. pass. in the expression *kdy ḥzh* IEJ xxxvi 206[5,7]: as is proper (cf. Broshi & Qimron ibid. 210) - PAʿEL - **1)** to make to see, to show; *yḥzny ʾpyk bšlm* Herm 1[2]: may he show me your face in peace (i.e. may he let me see you again in good health), cf. Herm 2[2], 3[2], 5[2] (or APH?, v. supra); cf. also Porten & Greenfield ZAW lxxx 227, Fales JAOS cvii 460 - **2)** to behold, to gaze (v. supra); + obj., *wbʿyny mḥzh ʾnh bny rbʿ* KAI 226[5]: and with my eyes I was beholding children of the fourth generation (for the context, cf. Tawil Or xliii 63ff.), cf. also KAI 222A 13 (on this text, cf. also Fuhs HZH 43; v. also supra) - ITP - **1)** to be seen, to show oneself, *wlytḥzh* (v. supra) *yrq* KAI 222A 28: and let not anything green be seen; *kmwtʾ zy [l]ʾ mtḥzh* Aḥiq 106: like death which does not show itself (cf. also Lindenberger APA 91: = which is unforeseen, unexpected?); *bkl ʾtr dytḥzh yt qmyʿh dn* AMB 3[13f.]: in every place where this amulet will be seen (for the construction, cf. Naveh & Shaked AMB p. 34) - **2)** + l_5 + *dy* ..., *ʾtḥzy lbwlʾ dy ʾrkwnyʾ ʾln ... dy* CIS ii 3913 i 7f.: it seemed good to the council of these archonts ... that (for the context, cf. Teixidor AO i 238; cf. CIS ii 3913 ii 131) - **3)** + *dy*, *ʾtḥzy dy yhwn yhbyn* CIS ii 3913 ii 123f.: it seemed good (i.e. it was decreted) that they should pay ... (cf. also Teixidor Sem xxxiv 62f.), cf. CIS ii 3913 ii 114, 129 - Dupont-Sommer JKF i 203, 210: l. *ḥzy* (= QAL Imper. s.m.) in AMB 7[22] (cf. also Scholem JGM 87; cf. Levine with Neusner HJB v 361: = QAL Part. act. s.m. abs.); uncert. reading, cf. Naveh & Shaked AMB a.l.: l. *gyzw* = peculiar form of QAL of *gwz* (= to pass., to vanish) :: Beyer ATTM 372f.: l. *ʿnn* (= QAL Part. act. pl.f. abs. of *ʿny*1) - the *ḥzʿnm* in KAI 34[4f.] (for the reading, cf. Cooke NSI p. 71 , Amadasi Guzzo Kition p. 99) poss. = *ḥz* (= QAL Part. act. pl.m. cstr.

of *ḥzy*$_1$) + *ʿnm* (= Plur. abs. of *ʿyn*$_2$), *ḥz ʿnm* = inspectors of the wells (cf. Halévy RS iii 183f., Sznycer AEPHE '70/'71, 160, Amadasi Guzzo Kition p. 99, Teixidor Syr li 322) :: Nöldeke ZA ix 403: = soothsayers :: Cooke NSI p. 71f.: = Plur. abs. of *ḥzʿn* (= prefect).
v. *bzy*$_1$,*z*$_1$,*ḥwy*$_1$,*ḥzh*, *mḥz*$_2$, *mḥzy*$_{1,2}$, *pḥz*$_2$.

ḥzy$_2$ v. *ḥzy*$_1$.

ḥzyd v. *zʿr*$_2$.

ḥzn$_1$ (< Akkad., cf. Zimmern Fremdw 6f., Kaufman AIA 55 (n. 115)) - **OffAr** Sing. cstr. *ḥzn* HDS 9^6, KAI 236 vs. 2 (= AECT 49; for the reading, cf. also Lipiński with Kaufman AIA 55 (n. 115), Lipiński Stud 95, 97, WGAV 381) - **JAr** Sing. emph. *ḥznh* MPAT-A 42^1 (= SM 20), *ḥzʾnh*MPAT-A 23 (= SM 28) - ¶ subst. - **1)** magistrate, mayor: HDS 9^6, KAI 236 vs. 2 (for the function, cf. Kinnier Wilson, The Nimrud Wine Lists (publ. by the Brit School of Arch in Irâq, 1972) p. 7f.); *ḥzn qrytʾ* HDS 9^6: the mayor of the city (cf. Caquot HDS 14, Lipiński ActAntHung xxii 376, Stud 79, 82, 99, also for Akkad. par.); for *ḥzn ʾglh* (magistrate of *ʾglh*), v. *ʾglh* - **2)** sexton, overseer of synagogue: MPAT-A 23, 42^1 - Torrey AASOR ii/iii 107 (cf. also Vattioni Or xlviii 139): l. *ḥznh* (= Sing. emph.) in RES 1265 (= overseer (of synagogue)); uncert. reading; Clermont-Ganneau sub RES 1265: l. *hlwy* (cf. ibid. for other interpret.) - Greek transcription ἀζζανα HUCA xxiii/ii 546, 6^1, ἀζανα BIES xxii 64^5 = Sing. emph. (cf. also Milik Bibl xlviii 559, 615, Vattioni Aug ix 463f.) - Lifshitz Frey Prol 33: perhaps l. *ḥzn* (= Sing. abs.) in Frey 294 (:: Frey a.l.: l. *ʾdn* = Sing. abs. of *ʾdn*$_1$).
v. *pḥz*$_2$.

ḥzn$_2$ v. *pḥz*$_2$.

ḥzʿn v. *ḥzy*$_1$.

ḥzq$_1$ **Hebr** QAL Imper. pl.m. *ḥzqw* Frey 1399^3 (reading of *w* uncert.); PIʿEL Imper. s.m. *ḥzq* DJD ii 44^7; HIPH Pf. 3 p.pl. *hḥzyqw* SM 76^2; HITP Imper. s.m. *hthzq* (sic) DJD ii 44^7 - **JAr** QAL Imper. s.m. *ḥzq* Frey 1397^2 - ITP Pf. 3 p.s.m. *ʾtḥzq* MPAT-A 1^3 (= SM 21), SM 84; 3 p.s.f. *ʾtḥzqt* MPAT-A 3^2 (= Frey 1199 = SM 60); 3 p.pl.m. *ʾtḥzqwn* MPAT-A 34^3 (= SM 69); Part. s.m. abs. *mtḥzq* MPAT-A 5^2 (= Frey 1203 = SM 64); pl.m. abs. *mtḥzqyn* MPAT-A 7^3 (= Frey 1204 = SM 65), 13^2 (= SM 46), SM 83 (*mtḥzq[yn]*) - ¶ verb QAL to be firm, courageous: Frey 1397^2, 1399^3 - PIʿEL to encourage; + obj.: DJD ii 44^7 (or: to strengthen?, cf. Pardee HAHL 132) - HIPH/ITP to donate, to contribute; in the expressions, *šhḥzyqw wʿšw* SM 76^2: who have contributed and made; *ʾtḥzqwn wʿbdwn psypsh* MPAT-A 34$^{3f.}$: they have contributed and made the mosaic; *mtḥzq wyhb* MPAT-A 5^2: contributing and giving; + *b*$_2$, *mtḥzqyn btqwnh dʾtrh [qdy]šh* MPAT-A 13$^{2f.}$: contributing to the repair of the synagogue (cf. MPAT-A 3^2, 7^3) - HITP to be courageous: DJD ii 44^7.

v. *yhb*.

ḥzq₂ v. *ḥzg*.

ḥzqy **OffAr** word of unknown meaning (prob. subst. Sing. abs.) in PF 173 (indication of title or function?).

ḥzr₁ **OffAr** Qal Pf. 3 p.pl.m. *ḥzrw* JRAS '29, 108[11] (reading uncert., cf. Cowley JRAS '29, 110f.: or l. *ḥzrwny*?? = Qal Pf. 3 p.pl.m. + suff. 1 p.s.) - ¶ verb Qal to turn round, to alter one's mind, cf. also Grelot DAE p. 142 - Fales sub AECT 52: the *ḥzrn* in AECT 52 side 1 poss. = Qal Part. pl.m. abs. of this root, cf. however Freydank AOF ii 135: = n.p.

ḥzr₂ **Pun** Yiph Inf. cstr. *ʾyḥzr* (= to take heed) in NP 130[4]??, cf. Février RHR cxli 21 (improb. interpret.), cf. also e.g. Cooke NSI p. 147f.: pro *bʾyḥzr d* l. *bʾyḥšbr*: in the island (*ʾy₁*) of Chashbar?

ḥzr₃ Ebeling Frah a.l.: l. in Frah xix 7 *ḥzyrtwn* < root *ḥzr₃* = to sift, to sieve, cf. however Nyberg FP 50, 91: l. *ḥḥbṭwn* = Haph of *ḥbṭ*= to throw.

ḥzr₄ for this subst. (= cup), cf. poss. Hesychius s.v. ἀσοῦρ.

ḥzr₅ **OffAr** word of unknown meaning, prob. noun, in ATNS 43b i 2, ii 4, 86b 1, 2 (context dam. and diff.; Segal ATNS a.l.: = lettuce or round fruit/apple/head of poppy??).

ḥḥ v.Soden Or xxxv 9, xlvi 187: (= thornbush, hook) > Akkad. *ḫaḫḫu* (= iron implement: hook?), cf. also id. AHW s.v. *ḫaḫøhu* III, CAD s.v. *ḫaḫḫu* C (uncert. interpret.).

ḥḥwr v. *ʾḥrn*.

ḥṭ₁ v. *ḥṣ₁*.

ḥṭ₂ v. *ḥwṭ₁*.

ḥṭ₃ v. *ḥṭh*.

ḥṭ₄ **Ph** Puech RSF iii 13f., 16: l. *ḥṭ* in Kition D 21 [4] (= Sing. abs. (= lock of hair)), against this reading however Dupont-Sommer MAIBL xliv 281, Amadasi Kition D 21 a.l., Coote BASOR ccxx 47.

ḥṭʾ₁ **Hebr** Qal Pf. 3 p.s.m. *ḥṭʾ* Frey 661[3] - **OffAr** cf. Frah app. 2 (*ḥṭywn*), cf. Toll ZDMG-Suppl viii 37 - **Palm** Qal Part. act. s.m. abs. *ḥṭʾ* Ber v 133[10] - ¶ verb Qal to sin; *lʾ ḥṭʾ mʿwlm* Frey 661[3]: he has never sinned; *mnw ... dy yzbn ... ʿl npšh ḥṭʾ* Ber v 133[1-3,8-10]: whoever sells ... is sinning against his soul.

v. *ḥṭp₂*.

ḥṭʾ₂ **OffAr** Plur. + suff. 2 p.s.m. *ḥṭʾyk* Aḥiq 50 - ¶ subst. offence, transgression.

v. *ḥṣ₁*.

ḥṭʾh **JAr** this subst. = sin (Sing. + suff. 3 p.s.m.?) poss. in SCO xxix 128 ii 3 (*ḥṭth*)?; cf. however Marrassini SCO xxix 129: preferably = Sing. emph. of *ḥṭh*.

ḥṭʾt v. *ḥṭh*.

ḥṭb **OffAr** Sing. m. (for Krael 7[7], cf. Driver PEQ '55, 93) abs. *ḥṭb* Cowl 15[7], *ḥṭyb* Krael 7[7] - ¶ adj. (or Part. pass.?, cf. Joüon MUSJ xviii 9) of uncert. meaning, poss. = striped (or: embroidered), for the interpret., cf. e.g. Cowl p. 47, Krael p. 210, Grelot RB lxxiv 435, DAE p. 193 n. f, Fitzmyer FS Albright ii 153.
v. *mšgb*.

ḥṭbt **OffAr** Sing. abs. *ḥṭbt* Herm 3[10] (cf. Wesselius AION xxx 266) - ¶ subst. indicating special type of garment, poss. striped, embroidered or coloured garment, cf. Bresciani & Kamil Herm a.l., Grelot RB lxxiv 435, DAE p. 158 n. f (cf. also litt. sub *ḥṭb*).

ḥṭh **Hebr** Plur. abs. *ḥṭm* TA-H 3[7], 31[1], 33[1,2,3,4,6] (*[ḥ]ṭm*),[7] (*ḥ[ṭ]m*),[8] (*[ḥ]ṭm*), BS i p. 73 no. 3 (*ḥṭ[m]*; cf. Aharoni a.l.), *ḥṭym* DJD ii 30[2,14], *ḥṭyn* DJD ii 44[9], *ḥnṭyn* DJD ii 24A 12 (*ḥ[n]ṭyn*), B 16, C 15, D 15 (uncert. reading), E 11, *ḥyṭyn* SM 49[22] - **Samal** Sing. abs. *ḥṭh* KAI 215[6,9]; Plur. abs. (cas obl.) *ḥṭy* KAI 214[6] - **OffAr** Sing. abs. *ḥnṭ*ʾ Cowl 81[28]; emph. *ḥnṭt*ʾ Aḥiq 129; Plur. abs. *ḥṭn* Cowl 49[2], *ḥnṭn* Cowl 81[2,3,4], NESE iii 39[3], Del 79bis 1 (for the reading, cf. Cardascia AM 66 :: Del a.l.: l. poss. *ḥnṭt[ʾ]* = Sing. emph.), etc. - **Palm** Plur. emph. *ḥṭ*ʾ (cf. Rosenthal Sprache 76 :: Cantineau Gramm 98: = Sing. emph.) CIS ii 3913 ii 59 - **JAr** Plur. abs. *ḥnṭyn* MPAT 52[2], Mas 555[4]; emph. *ḥnṭy*ʾ MPAT 53[1] (for the reading, cf. Beyer ATTM 351), *ḥṭyh* IEJ xxxvi 206[4], *ḥṭyyh* MPAT-A 11[3] (= Frey 1165 = SM 43; for the reading and interpret. of the context, cf. Naveh sub SM 43 :: Beyer ATTM 377, 577: = Qal Part. act. pl.m. emph. of *ḥṭṭ*₁ (= stone-cutter, engraver)) - ¶ subst. Sing./Plur., wheat - cf. the abbrev. *ḥ*ʾʾ in Frah iv 1 (cf. also Nyberg FP 65); the abbrev. *ḥ* in TA-Ar 13[2], BS i p. 79ff. no. 3[2], 5[3], 6[4], 10, 13 (prob. *ḥsp* = *ḥnṭyn sʾh plgh*, cf. Naveh Shn i 194 :: Naveh ibid.: or = Sing. abs. of *ḥsp*₂ (= clay)). Highly uncert. whether *ḥ* in TA-H 49[15,16] is abbrev. of

ḥṭh (cf. Aharoni TA a.l.: or = *ḥṭʾt*= sin-offering?) - for this word, cf. also Kislev Lesh xxxvii 83ff., 243ff., xlii 64ff., Borowski AIAI 88ff.
v. *ḥṭʾh*,*ḥṭṭ*₂.

ḥṭṭ₁ **Nab** Qal Pf. 3 p.s.m. *ḥṭ* Syr xxxv 243[3] - ¶ verb Qal to engrave (sc. inscription): Syr xxxv 243[3] - Lemaire & Durand IAS 122, 134: l. poss. *tḥṭ* in KAI 222A 32 = pass. form Impf. 3 p.s.f. of *ḥṭṭ* (= to be pulled out), poss. reading and interpret. :: Dupont-Sommer Sf p. 47, Segert ArchOr xxxii 120f., Fitzmyer JAOS lxxxi 198, AIS 50, Donner KAI a.l., Degen AAG p. 67, Gibson SSI ii p. 40 (div. otherwise): l. *[yš]tḥṭ* = Itp Impf. 3 p.s.m. of *šḥṭ*₂ (= *šḥṭ*₁; = to be destroyed; against this reading, cf. also Greenfield JBL lxxxvii 241); for this text, cf. also Weinfeld DSS 126 n. 2.
v. *ḥwṭ*₂,*ḥṭh*,*ḥṭṭ*₂.

ḥṭṭ₂ **Hatra** Safar Sumer xvii 40, Caquot Syr xl 13: the *ḥṭṭ* in app. 4[4] =

Sing. abs. of *ḥṭṭ* (= well), Vattioni IH a.l.: = plain (both interpret. less prob.); prob. = n.g., cf. Teixidor Syr xli 275, cf. also Altheim & Stiehl AAW v/1, 84f., Milik DFD 398f. (related to *ḥṭh*:= region suited for wheat and grain culture), Aggoula Sem xxvii 140f. (related to *ḥṭṭ*$_1$:= cultivated area), Tubach ISS 399, 400 n. 693 (preferably n.g. related to *ḥṭṭ*$_2$ (= well)).

ḥṭṭwt Ebeling Frah a.l.: l. poss. *ḥṭ(ṭ)wt* in Frah xiv 7: = sharpness, edge (highly uncert. reading and interpret., cf. also Nyberg FP 47, 84: l. Iran. word).

ḥṭy v. *ḥṭʾ*$_1$.

ḥṭyʾh **Nab** Sing. abs. *ḥṭʾyh* CIS ii 224^{11} - **Palm** Sing. + suff. 3 p.s.m. *ḥṭyʾth* RIP 199^{6,7,9} - ¶ subst. f. fine (in RIP 199 in a prob. religious context) - Cantineau Nab ii 172, O'Connor JNES xlv 216f., 219: prob. < Arab.

ḥṭyb v. *ḥṭb*.

ḥṭl **JAr** the diff. word *ḥṭlʾ* in RB lxi 208, IEJ xxxviii 164B vi 3 poss. = Sing. emph. of noun *ḥṭl* (= indication of function), or related to Hebr. n.p. *ḥṭyl*? (cf. Eshel & Mishgav IEJ xxxviii 171) :: Yadin Mess 62: l. *hṭlʾ* (= h_1 + Sing. abs. of *ṭlʾ*$_1$ (= *ṭlh*$_1$; = youth, young man; cf. also Eshel & Mishgav IEJ xxxviii 171f. n. 41)).

ḥṭm **Hatra** Sing. (or Plur.) emph. *ḥṭmʾ* 281^4 - ¶ subst. poss. meaning sledge-hammer (cf. Aggoula Syr lii 182, lxv 208, Vattioni IH a.l.) :: Safar Sumer xxvii 4 n. 2: = sunshade, cf. also Degen NESE iii 68 (cf. however ibid. 69) :: v.d.Branden BiOr xxxvi 341: = stone hewn to make it fit to be used in constructing vaults.

ḥṭp$_1$ **OffAr** the *ʾḥṭp* in RES 1793^{10} (= Egypt. n.p., cf. RES a.l.: = Aph Imper. s.m. of *ḥṭp* (= to hurry, to make haste)) prob. false reading, cf. Cowley PSBA '15, 222 (l 4), Grelot DAE p. 376 n. d: l. *ʾḥṭb* = np.

ḥṭp$_2$ **Palm** Qal Impf. 3 p.s.m. *yḥṭ[p]* Syr xvii 353^2 (cf. Cantineau Syr a.l., Milik DFD 300f. :: Gawlikowski TP 57: l. *yḥṭ[y]* = Qal Impf. 3 p.s.m. of *ḥṭʾ*$_1$)- ¶ verb Qal to plunder (used together with form of *gnb*$_1$).

v. *hnkt*.

ḥṭr$_1$ **Ph** Sing. cstr. *ḥṭr* KAI 1^2 - **Samal** Sing. abs. *ḥṭr* KAI 214^{20,25}; cstr. *ḥṭr* KAI 214^{3,9} - **DA** Sing. abs. *ḥṭr* i 11 - **OffAr** Sing. abs. *ḥṭr* Aḥiq 81; Plur. abs. (?, dam. context) *ḥṭrn* Cowl 69^5 (cf. also Porten & Yardeni sub TADAE B 8.5: or = Sing. + suff. 1 p.pl.?) - ¶ subst. m. (for KAI 1^2, cf. Vincent RB xxxiv 186, v.Dijk VT xix 441 n. 6, 444f., Dahood Or xlviii 97, Puech RB xcii 292, Schoors FS Fensham 194, Baldacci BiOr xl 125 :: Friedrich AfO x 82, FR 303, Röllig KAI a.l., Gibson SSI iii p. 16: in KAI 1^2: = f.) - **1)** rod: Aḥiq 81 (to punish a son); in DA i 11 poss. > punishment, cf. Hoftijzer a.l., Levine JAOS ci 199 (cf. also H.P.Müller ZAW xciv 218, 226, 239: = twig, shoot, indication of a human mediator bringing about disaster), cf. however Caquot & Lemaire Syr liv 199: = shepherd's crook (cf. also Rofé SB 66, Garbini Hen i 179, 185, Delcor SVT xxxii 57 (n. 19), Sasson UF xvii 300) - **2)** sceptre: KAI 214^{3,9,20,25} (cf. ibid. l. 15; v. also *ḥlbbh*); *ḥṭr mšpṭh* KAI 1^{2}: the sceptre of his rule (for this text, cf. Hillers TC 61, Avishur PIB 17ff., 64f., cf. also Tawil Or xliii 47 n. 48, Niehr HR 63f., Olivier JNSL vii 45ff.).

ḥṭr$_2$ v. *ḥṣr$_4$*.

ḥy$_1$ **Ph** Plur. abs. *ḥym* KAI 26A iii 3, C iii 17f., 42^{1}, 48^{4}, 52^{1}, BMQ xxvii 85, RSF xviii 35^{1}; cstr. *ḥy* KAI 43^{7,8,11}; + suff. 3 p.s.m. *ḥyy* KAI 40^{5}; + suff. 1 p.s. *ḥyy* KAI 35^{2} (= Kition B 1), 43^{11} - **Pun** Plur. abs. *ḥym* KAI 152^{3}, CIS i 135^{1}, 5510^{5}, NP 130^{3} (?, cf. Février RHR cxli 20; or rather = Plur. m. abs. of *ḥy$_2$*?), Punica x 2^{3} (*[ḥ]ym*), xii 23^{3} (= NP 55), *ʿym* KAI 134^{3}, 160^{1} (?, diff. context :: Février Sem iv 21: = Sing. cstr. of *ʿym* = violence > surplus?, cf. Röllig KAI a.l., cf. however Levi Della Vida RCL '55, 556 n. 2); cstr. cf. IRT 893^{3}: *baiae* (= *b$_2$* + Plur. cstr., cf. Vattioni Aug xvi 552); + suff. 3 p.s.m., cf. IRT 828^{3}: *baiaem* (= *b$_2$* + Plur. + suff. 3 p.s.m., cf. Levi Della Vida OA ii 78, Vattioni Aug xvi 538, cf. however Vattioni AION xvi 49: or = + suff. 3 p.pl.m.?), 893$^{2f.}$: *biaem* (= *b$_2$* + Plur. + suff. 3 p.s.m., cf. Vattioni Aug xvi 552); + suff. 1 p.s. *ḥyy* CIS i 6000bis 5 (= TPC 84; or = + suff. 3 p.s.m.?, cf. Février BAr '51/52, 56, CIS i a.l., Ferron StudMagr i 78) - **Hebr** Plur. abs. *ḥyy[m]* Frey 1399^{4}; cstr. *ḥyy* Frey 569^{5} (*ḥy[y]*), 661^{4}, 1536^{3} (= RES 863), *ḥyh* Frey 1398^{3}, *ḥy* Frey 571 - **Samal** Plur. abs. (cas obl.) *ḥy* KAI 25^{7} (:: Gibson SSI iii p. 41: poss. *ḥy* pro *ḥym* owing to lack of space, cf. also e.g. Röllig KAI a.l.) - **OldAr** Plur. cstr. *ḥyy* Tell F 7 (Akkad. par. *bulluṭ*; :: Kaufman Maarav iii 148, 165: or = PAʿEL Inf. of *ḥyy* (var. of *ḥwy$_2$*),cf. also Andersen & Freedman FS Fensham 20; cf. also Muraoka AN xxii 99f.); + suff. 3 p.s.m. *ḥywh* Tell F 14 (cf. in Akkad. par. text: *pa-lu-šú*) - **OffAr** Sing. abs. *ḥy* Sem ii 31 conc. 3, 7; Plur. abs. *ḥyn* Cowl 30^{3}, Aḥiq 11, RHR cxxx 20^{2}, Herm 3^{5}, 7^{1} (*[ḥ]yn*; Milik Bibl xlviii 556: l. *[ḥ]yyn* (less prob.)); cstr. *ḥyy* KAI 229^{4}, ATNS 35^{5} (or preferably: + suff. 1 p.s.?; for the reading, cf. Porten & Yardeni sub TADAE B 4.7 :: Segal ATNS a.l. (div. otherwise): l. *lḥyʾ* = Plur. emph. of *lḥy$_2$*), Atlal vii 109^{8}, Sem xxiii 95 verso 5 (for the context, cf. Fales AION xxvi 546, AECT p. 89f. and sub AECT 58, Kaufman Conn xix 120, 125, cf. also Lipiński ActAntHung xxii 379), IrAnt iv 122^{3}, ZDMG cxl 2^{2}; + suff. 3 p.s.m. *ḥywhy* IrAnt iv 122^{3}; + suff. 2 p.s.m. *ḥyyk* Krael 5^{12,13}; + suff. 1 p.s. *ḥyy* Cowl 8^{3,8}, Krael 5^{4}, 9^{2}, 10^{11,13}; cf. Frah x 34 (*ḥyʾ*) - **Nab** Plur. abs. *ḥyyn*?? (cf. Cantineau Nab ii 95) RES 2023^{4} (= CIS ii 163; :: Littmann PAES p. 77: = Plur. m. abs. of *ḥy$_2$*; for the context, v. *ʿd$_7$*); cstr. *ḥyy* CIS ii 158^{3}, 354^{2}, 442^{4}, RES 1434^{7}, RB lxxiii 244^{2}, PEQ '81, 22^{2}, etc.; + suff. 3 p.s.m. *ḥywhy* CIS ii 197^{4}, RES

468^{2}, ADAJ xxi 144^{3}, *ḥyyh* Syr xxxv 246^{4} - **Palm** Plur. cstr. *ḥyy* CIS ii 3973^{5}, 3978^{8}, 3983^{2}, 3986^{4}, Inv xi 2^{3}, xii 22^{5}, SBS 1a 2, RIP 140^{3}, etc., etc., *ḥyʾ* CIS ii 3902^{2}, 3974^{3}, 3981^{5}, 3990^{4}, Inv xi 8^{5}, RIP 134^{5}, etc., etc., *ṣyʾ* (lapsus) CIS ii 4018^{5}, *ḥy* CIS ii 4011^{6}, 4019^{5}, 4075^{5} (for this diff. reading, cf. Teixidor sub Inv xi 29), Inscr P 27^{1}, Rob 373^{1}, Inv D 47^{2} (?, for this reading, cf. Ingholt YClSt xiv 138f.; du Mesnil du Buisson sub Inv D 47 (div. otherwise): l. *ptybr[t]* < Iran. (= Sing. abs.) = recompensation (or id. ibid.: = title < Iran.)); + suff. 3 p.s.m. *ḥywhy* CIS ii 3902^{2}, 3973^{5}, 3974^{3}, 3983^{2}, Inv xi 4^{3}, xii 22^{5}, SBS 1a 2, RIP 135^{4}, etc., etc., *ḥywh* CIS ii 3991^{5}, 4000^{5}, 4011^{6}, 4024^{4}, Inv xi 8^{5}, etc., etc., *ḥywhw* CIS ii 4033^{6}, *ḥyw* CIS ii 4009^{5}, Inv xi 19^{4}, *ḥyh[y]* RIP 134^{4} (?, cf. Gawlikowski RIP a.l.: or l. *ḥyh*?), *ḥwh* (lapsus for *ḥywh*?, cf. Cantineau Gramm 97, CIS ii sub 4063, Rosenthal Sprache 47 n. 3) CIS ii 4063^{6}; + suff. 3 p.s.f. *ḥyyh* CIS ii 3988^{3} (= RIP 128), Inv xi 24^{3}, SBS 11^{6}, *ḥyh* CIS ii 3971^{5}, 4010^{4} (= Inv xi 23), 4014^{5}, 4027^{3}, 4087^{4}, RIP 228^{3} (??, heavily dam., highly uncert. context); + suff. 3 p.pl.m. *ḥyyhwn* CIS ii 3978^{8}, 3981^{4}, 4018^{7}, PNO 57, Inv xii 34^{4}, 46^{3}, 48^{3}, SBS 19^{6}, 25^{2}, RIP 113^{1} (*ḥyyh[wn]*), 116^{5}, Syr xii 130^{6}, xvii 274^{2}, DM ii 39 ii 6, *ḥyyhn* CIS ii 3911^{9}, 3996^{6}; + suff. 3 p.pl.f. *ḥyyhn* SBS 10^{5} - **Hatra** Plur. cstr. *ḥyy* 37^{6} (??; cf. Maricq Syr xxxii 282, Degen Or xxxvi 77 (n. 4), Milik DFD 372, cf. however Safar Sumer viii 193, Caquot Syr xxx 242: pro *wʿl ḥyy* l. *mlh nm(ʾ)* (?)), 107^{8}, 241^{1} (:: Degen JEOL xxiii 409, Vattioni IH a.l.: l. *ḥyʾ*), *ḥyʾ* 4^{5} (:: Altheim & Stiehl AAW ii 193: = Plur. emph.), 34^{7}, 62^{3}, 67, 68^{3}, 80^{6}, 139^{3}, 144^{5}, 191^{2}, 192^{3}, 195^{3}, 214^{2}, 223^{6,7}, 238^{2}, 243^{2}, 245^{3}, 272^{2,3}, 287^{3,6}, 288c 4, 290^{5,6,7}, app. 4^{9}, Mašr xv 512^{3,4} (cf. also Assur 4^{6}), *ḥy* 288c 6 (for this form, cf. Degen NESE iii 83), etc.; + suff. 3 p.s.m. *ḥyyhy* 20^{3} (for this reading, cf. Milik RN vi/iv 54, Altheim & Stiehl AAW ii 198f., Caquot GLECS ix 89, Degen Or xxxvi 77 (n. 1), Vattioni IH a.l. :: Safar Sumer vii 180, Caquot Syr xxix 99 (div. otherwise): l. *ḥyy* = Plur. cstr.), 140^{5}, 243^{2}, 245^{3}, 287^{6}, app. 3^{4} (cf. Degen ZDMG cxxi 125, 136 :: du Mesnil du Buisson Syr xix a.l., Caquot Syr xxx 245, Donner sub KAI 257, Vattioni IH a.l.: l. *ḥywhy*; Aggoula Syr lii 188f., Vattioni IH a.l.: l. *ḥyyhy* in 288b 9, less prob. reading, cf. Safar Sumer xxvii 10, Degen NESE iii 80 (sub b 10), 82: l. *ʿlyhy* = *ʿl*$_{7}$ + suff. 3 p.s.m.), cf. also Assur 4^{6}, *ḥyyh* 139^{4} (*ḥy[y]h*), *ḥyhy* 192^{3} (cf. Safar Sumer xviii 55, Degen Or xxxvi 78 :: Caquot Syr xli 268: l. *ḥyyh*), *ḥyy* 107^{8} (cf. also Degen Or xxxvi 77 (n. 5), Vattioni IH a.l. :: Altheim & Stiehl AAW iv 256: l. *ḥyw* = Plur. + suff. 3 p.s.m.; cf. however Milik DFD 378, 388: = Plur. + suff. 1 p.s.); + suff. 3 p.s.f. *ḥyyh* 35^{5}, *ḥyh* 31^{2}, 32^{4}; + suff. 3 p.pl.m. *ḥyyhwn* 34^{6}, *ḥyhn* 62^{2} (for this reading, cf. Safar Sumer xi 7, Caquot Syr xxxii 264, Donner sub KAI 253 :: Degen ZDMG cxxi 125, Vattioni IH a.l.: l. *ḥyyhn*) - **JAr** Plur. emph. *ḥyyh* MPAT-A 34^{5} (for the reading, cf. Naveh Lesh xxxviii

295f., sub SM 69, Fitzmyer & Harrington MPAT p. 295 :: Baramki & Avi-Yonah QDAP vi 76: l. *ḥyym* (= Hebr. Plur. abs.), cf. also Kutscher AH i/1, p. 69 (n. 57)) - ¶ subst. life (cf. Bravmann Mus lxxxiii 551ff., esp 556f.) - a) Sing. in the expression *ḥy lyhh* Sem ii 31 conc. 3, 7: by the life of Y. (cf. Dupont-Sommer Sem ii 34f.) - b) Plur. passim; cf. the following expressions and combinations - **1)** *ʿl ḥywhy wḥyʾ bnwhy* CIS ii 3902^{2}: for the benefit of his life (i.e. for his well-being) and the life of his sons (cf. HDS 151^{3}, PEQ '81, 22^{2,3,4}, CIS ii 3911$^{9f.}$, 3973^{5}, Hatra 4$^{5f.}$, 20^{3}, Assur 4$^{6f.}$, etc., etc.), cf. also *lḥyh wlḥyʾ brth* CIS ii 4014$^{5f.}$ (cf. also CIS ii 4046^{6}, 4061$^{5f.}$, PNO 15^{4}) and *lḥyy nbšh* IrAnt iv 115: for his own life (cf. IrAnt iv 122^{3}, Tell F 7 (Akkad. par. *ana bulluṭ*^{uṭ} *napšāti-šú*; cf. also Dion FS Delcor 144)) Atlal vii 105^{2}, 109^{8}, ZDMG cxl 2^{2} - **2)** *ḥyy ʿwlm* Frey 1536^{3}: eternal life (cf. Frey 569$^{5f.}$, 571), cf. also *ḥyy hʿwlm hbʾ* Frey 661^{4}: life in the coming world - **3)** *bḥywhy* Inv viii 57^{2}: during his life (cf. Lat. par. *[vi]vos* and Greek par. ζῶν); cf. also *bḥyy wbmwty* Cowl 8^{3,8}, Krael 10^{11,13}: for my lifetime and after my death (i.e. forever; cf. Yaron Law 80f., Porten Arch 230 (n. 87), Muffs 25f., 36 (n. 1), 39 n. 2, Boyarin JANES iii 59, Porten & Szubin JAOS cvii 236f.) - **4)** *ḥrpkrṭ ytn ḥym lʿms* BMQ xxvii 85: Ch. may give life to A. (cf. also Röllig WO v 119, Ferron RSF ii 84f.; cf. KAI 52^{1}); cf. also *ḥyn ʾrykn yntn lk* Cowl 30^{3}: may he grant you a long life - **5)** *spr ḥyyh* MPAT-A 34^{5}: the book of life - **6)** *šlm wḥyn šlḥt lk* Herm 3^{5}: I send you (wishes of) prosperity and life (cf. also RHR cxxx 20^{2} - **7)** *bn ššm št wšlš tm bḥym* KAI 152^{3}: sixty three years old, honest during (his) life (cf. Lat. par. *vixit annis lxiii honeste*); cf. also KAI 134^{3}, Punica xii 23^{3} (cf. for this text also Polselli CISFP i 775) - **8)** *[ḥ]ym ḥwʾ šbʿm wḥmš* Punica x 2^{3}: he has lived a life for seventy-five years(??) - Ebeling Frah a.l.: l. *ḥy* in Frah xi 2 = form of *ḥy*$_1$ (improb. interpret., cf. Nyberg FP 78: l. Iran. word here) - for *lmbḥyy* v. *l*$_5$ - for *mʿz ḥym*, v. *mʿz* - for *ʿd ḥyyn*, v. *ʿd*$_7$ - Naveh AION xvi 21f. n. 9: l. *ḥyy* (= Plur. cstr.) in IrAnt iv 115 (improb. reading, cf. Dupont-Sommer IrAnt iv 115ff.: l. *ḥzy* (= n.p.) - a form of this subst. poss. in Or lix 325^{1} (Sing. abs. *ḥy*), cf. Zauzich & Röllig Or lix 326 (uncert. reading and interpret.) - Livingstone Atlal vii 109f.: the *lḥyn* in Atlal vii 109^{3} = *l*$_5$ + Plur. abs. of *ḥy*$_1$ (less prob. interpret., cf. also Aggoula Syr lxii 66f., Beyer & Livingstone ZDMG cxxxvii 286f.: *lḥyn* = n.g.) - a form of *ḥy*$_1$ (*ḥym* Plur. abs.) in RES 1320 (= KAI 49,3)?; Kornfeld sub Abydos 3 (div. otherwise): l. *lḥy* (= Sing. abs. of *lḥh* (= youthful strength)), highly uncert. interpret. - cf. also *mḥy*$_4$.
v. *zy*,*ḥwy*$_2$,*ḥy*$_2$, *mrḥ*$_2$.

ḥy$_2$ **OldCan** Sing. m. abs. *ḫa-ia-ma* EA 245^{6} (cf. Siwan GAG 131, 223, Kossmann JEOL xxx 57) - **Ph** Plur. m. abs. *ḥym* KAI 13^{7}, 14^{12}, 53^{1}, CIS i 58^{1} (= Kition B 3), 59^{1} (= Kition B 4), Mus li 286^{3} - **Pun**

Sing. m. abs. *ḥy* OA iv 55; cstr. *ḥy* KAI 161[1] (v. infra); Plur. m. abs. *ḥym* KAI 161[1] (v. infra), CIS i 5510[5] (poss. interpret. :: Février BAr '41/42, 393, CIS i a.l.: = form of *ḥy*$_1$(*'vita eorum*›)), NP 130[3] (diff. context; cf. e.g. Cooke NSI p. 147 :: Février RHR cxli 20: = Plur. abs. of *ḥy*$_1$)- **Hebr** Sing. m. abs. *ḥy* KAI 196[12] (also with intended haplography *ḥyhwh* in KAI 193[9], and poss. in TA-H 21[5] (*ḥyh[wh]*; cf. Lehman JNES xxvi 93ff.)), AMB 1[23], 4[5]; Plur. m. abs. *ḥym* DJD ii 22[6], *ḥyym* Frey 661[5] (v. infra) - **Samal** Sing. m. abs. *ḥy* KAI 215[12] (for the context, v. *w*$_2$, *p*$_1$ :: Sader EAS 168 (div. otherwise): l. *›ḥy* = verbal form of *ḥyy*, he did live :: e.g. Cooke NSI p. 178, Donner KAI a.l.: = Plur. cstr. of *›ḥ*$_1$) - **OffAr** Sing. m. abs. *ḥy* Herm 5[9], 8[4] (?, dam. context); m. emph. *ḥy›* Cowl 70[2] (poss. also in RES 1785F 4, 6); Plur. m. abs. *ḥyn* KAI 225[10] (cf. e.g. Donner KAI a.l. :: e.g. Cooke NSI p. 186, 189, Gibson SSI ii p. 95: = Plur. abs. of *ḥy*$_1$),Beh 1, 6, 11 (Akkad. par. *bal-ṭu-tú*), Cowl p. 266 i 3 (cf. Greenfield & Porten BIDG 34f. (Akkad. par. *bal-ṭu-tú*)), ii 5 (cf. Greenfield & Porten BIDG 44f.), Cowl p. 268, 56[17] (cf. Greenfield & Porten BIDG 38f. (Akkad. par. *bal-ṭu-tú*)) - **Nab** Sing. m. abs. *ḥy* RES 527 (??) - **JAr** Sing. emph. *ḥy›* MPAT 40[11], 42[20] (cf. however Beyer ATTM 311: l. *ḥyh*), 52[6], *ḥyh* AMB 9[5] - ¶ adj. living, passim; *ḥy* AMB 1[23]: the living One (epithet of God; cf. Gordon JAOS cvii 133 :: Naveh & Shaked AMB p. 270: = form of *ḥy*$_1$);*mn dḥyh* AMB 9[5]: the One who lives (i.e. God) - cf. the following expressions and combinations - a) *ḥy YHWH* KAI 196[12]: (as truly as) the Lord lives (oath formula, cf. also KAI 193[9], TA-H 21[5] (v. supra)), cf. also *ḥy b‹l ›dr* OA iv 55, *ḥy ‹bdt* RES 527(??) - b) *›ḥlp lky šṭrh kdy ḥy›* MPAT 40[10f.]: I shall replace for you the document, as (long as) I am alive, cf. MPAT 42[19f.] (:: Yaron BASOR cl 28: *kdy ḥy›* = in a year's time) - c) *›l ḥy* AMB 4[5]: the living God - d) *kl dy bh wdy ḥy› ‹lh* MPAT 52[6]: all that is on it or which lives on it (cf. Milik Bibl xxxviii 259, Beyer ATTM 322 :: Fitzmyer & Harrington MPAT a.l.: and everything that is on it. (As for) whatever animal is on it ...) - e) Plur. the living (ones) - α) *ḥy ḥym* KAI 161[1] (epithet of a king): the living among the living ones (i.e. the most living one?, cf. Röllig KAI a.l. (cf. also Roschinski Num 114: indication of the king who after his death still works for his people), or = the life (Plur. cstr. of *ḥy*$_1$) of the living ones, cf. Berger RA ii 37, Février RA xlv 141 :: Cooke NSI p. 148f.: the life (= Plur. cstr. of *ḥy*$_1$)of life (= Plur. abs. of *ḥy*$_1$))- β) *bḥym* among the living, cf. *zr‹ bḥym* KAI 13[7]: posterity among the living; *mṣbt bḥym* CIS i 58[1]: a stele(/tombstone) among the living (cf. also *mṣbt skr bḥym* KAI 53[1]: a stele (as) a memory among the living); *skrn bḥym* Mus li 286[3]: a memorial among the living; *t›r bḥym tḥt šmš* KAI 14[12]: renown among the living under the sun; cf. also DJD ii 22[6] - γ) *ysḥw šmk w›šrk mn ḥyn* KAI 225[9f.]: they may snatch away

your name and your place from among the living - δ) *ṣrwr hḥyym* Frey 661^{5}: the bundle of the living (or: of life?) - the *ḥy*ʾ in MPAT 52^{7} poss. = Sing. m. emph., interpret. of context however diff., Milik Bibl xxxviii 259: *mʿlʾ wmpqʾ bh ḥyʾ* MPAT 52$^{6f.}$: = the right to enter and to leave for the living beings (uncert. interpret.), J.J.Rabinowitz Bibl xxxix 486: *ḥyʾ* = dittography, prob. mistake for *ʾtrʾ*, cf. also Fitzmyer & Harrington MPAT a.l.
v. *hykylyn,ḥy$_1$*.
ḥyb v. *ḥbr$_2$,ḥwb$_1$*.
ḥybw **Nab** unexplained word in CIS ii 978 (or l. *ḥyrw*?), v. also *ḥyr$_2$*.
ḥyd v. *ʾḥd$_4$*.
ḥydrn v. *ḥyrwn*.
ḥyh$_1$ **Pun** Sing. cstr. *ḥyt* Trip 38^{6}; + suff. 3 p.s.m. *ḥytnm* Trip 38^{6} (the *m* written above the *n*, poss. indication that *ḥytn* is a lapsus for *ḥytm*, cf. also Levi Della Vida LibAnt i 159, and cf. Amadasi Guzzo StudMagr xi 30: l. *ḥyt<n>m*), *ḥytm* KAI 126^{9} (for the reading, cf. Amadasi Guzzo StudMagr xi 30, IPT 66, 69 :: Levi Della Vida RCL '49, 405f., Röllig KAI a.l.: l. *hʿt* = *h$_1$* (= article) + Sing. abs. of *ʿt$_1$* (= time)) - ¶ subst. life.
ḥyh$_2$ **Ph** Plur. (cf. FR 65, 230a; or Sing.??) abs. *ḥyt* KAI 43^{9,10} - ¶ subst. f. animal (or collective??, v. supra).
v. *ḥwy$_2$, pṭm$_1$, tbʾh*.
ḥywh v. *pṭm$_1$*.
ḥywr **Hebr** Sing. f. emph. *ḥywrth* SM 49^{6} - ¶ adj. white; *ḥqlh ḥywrth* SM 49^{6}: the white field.
v. *ḥwr*.
ḥyṭ **Palm** Plur. emph. *ḥyṭʾ* (prob. reading) CIS ii 3913 ii 139 - ¶ subst. m. tailor.
ḥyṭh v. *ḥṭh*.
ḥyy v. *ḥwy$_2$,ḥy$_2$, šgʾ$_3$*.
ḥyl$_1$ v. *ḥlp$_1$*.
ḥyl$_2$ **Hebr** Sing. abs./cstr. *ḥyl* TA-H 24^{4} (?, heavily dam. context) - **OldAr** Sing. + suff. 2 p.s.m. *ḥylk* KAI 222B 31; + suff. 2 p.pl.m. *ḥylkm* KAI 222B 32 - **OffAr** Sing. abs. *ḥyl* Aḥiq 137 (for the reading, cf. Lindenberger APA 259 n. 416), KAI 266^{7}, FuF xxxv 173^{8}, ATNS 3^{6} (for this poss. reading, cf. Porten & Yardeni sub TADAE B 8.10; cf. however Segal ATNS a.l.: l. *zyl*); cstr. *ḥyl* Aḥiq 55, 61, JAOS liv 31^{4}; emph. *ḥylʾ* Cowl 20^{5}, Beh 5, 13, 20* (in the Beh instances Akkad. par. *ú-qu*), Krael 8^{2}, Driv 4^{1}, ATNS 24^{11}, etc., etc.; + suff. 2 p.s.m. *ḥylk* Cowl 71^{13} - **Palm** Sing. emph. *ḥylʾ* CIS ii 3946^{3}, 3947^{2,3} - ¶ subst. m. - **1)** force; *ḥrb ḥylk* Cowl 71^{13}: the sword of your strength (i.e. your mighty sword; cf. CIS ii sub 145, Joüon MUSJ xviii 41 :: Cowl p. 181: the sword of thy troops) - **2)** armed force, army (for Elephantine, cf.

Porten Arch 29ff.): KAI 222B 31, 32, Beh 5, 24, 40, Driv $4^{1,2}$, 5^{6}, JAOS liv 31^{4}, ATNS 24^{11}; *ḥyl ʾtwr* Aḥiq 55 (cf. ibid. 61): the army of Assyria (cf. Cowl a.l., Ginsberg ANET 428, Grelot DAE p. 450 × Altheim & Stiehl EW xii 11, ASA 93, 185: the aristocracy of Assur, cf. also Klíma ArchOr xxvi 614f.); *ḥylʾ zʿy[rʾ] rkby swsyn* Beh 30: a small force of cavalry (:: Klíma ArchOr xxvi 615: = aristocracy); *ḥylʾ zy swn* Cowl $25^{2f.}$: the garrison of S. (cf. Cowl 25^{4}, Krael $8^{2,3}$); for *rb ḥylʾ*, v. *rb₂* - **3)** collective: soldiers (cf. Joüon MUSJ xviii 41f.); *šmht ḥylʾ yhwdyʾ zy yhb ksp* Cowl 22^{1}: the names of the Judean soldiers who gave silver; *npyn dbr mṣryʾ ʿm ḥylʾ ʾḥrnn* Cowl 30^{8}: N. led out the Egyptians with the other soldiers (v. also *ʾḥrn*), cf. also Cowl 24^{33} (dam. context) - **4)** riches: Aḥiq 137 (?, dam. context; cf. also Lindenberger APA 134) - the *ḥl* in CIS i 5510^{7} poss. = Sing. abs. (= riches), cf. Février BAr '46/49, 172, CIS i a.l. :: Chabot BAr '41/42, 391, 393: prob. = QAL Pf. 3 p.pl.m. of *ḥll₄* (= to begin) - v.Soden Or xxxv 11, xlvi 187: > Akkad. (*ḫijālu, ḫiʾalu, ḫajālu*), cf. also idem AHW s.v. *ḫiʾālu* (cf. also Zadok WO xii 199, cf. however CAD s.v. *øhijālu*: l. *ṭijālu/ṭajālu*).
v. *ʾl₆,ḥlq₃, rbmg*.

ḥylp v. *ḥlq₃*.

ḥyṣwny **Hebr** Sing. f. abs. *ḥyṣwnyt* IEJ vii 241^{1} - ¶ adj. external, outer (said of sarcophagus).

ḥyr₁ v. *ḥbr₂*.

ḥyr₂ **Nab** Sing. abs. *ḥyr* CIS ii 1499^{2}, 1631^{5} - ¶ subst.? - **1)** in the expression *bḥyr* CIS ii 1499^{2}: for good - **2)** used adverbially, *ḥyr bṭb* CIS ii 1631^{5}: for the very best (*optime in bono*) - cf. also the enigmatic *ḥyr/bw*in CIS ii 978??

ḥyrh **Palm** Sing. emph. *ḥyrtʾ* CIS ii 3973^{3} - ¶ subst. f. citadel (cf. also Lipiński Or xlv 73 (n. 164); or n.g.?, cf. CIS ii a.l., cf. however Dussaud Syr xiv 77f.).

ḥyrw v. *ḥybw, ḥyr₂*.

ḥyrwn **Palm** Sing. abs. *ḥyrwn* RTP 113 (v. however infra) - ¶ subst. prob. meaning: rejoicing (for the etymology, cf. Caquot RTP p. 144; for the context, cf. Milik DFD 150; cf. however du Mesnil du Buisson TMP 444: l. *ḥydrnʾ* = Plur. emph. of *ḥydrn*(= small circle)).

ḥk **Pun** Sznycer PPP 141f.: the diff. *bocca* (var. *bua*) in Poen 1002 poss. = *b₂* + Sing. + suff. 2 p.s.m. of *ḥk₁* (= palate > mouth) or = *b₂* + suff. 2 p.s.m. (for this interpret., cf. also Schroed 294, 316, L.H.Gray AJSL xxxix 80); highly uncert. interpretations. J.J.Glück & Maurach Semitics ii 119: or = QAL Inf. cstr. of *bwʾ*+ suff. 2 p.s.m. (improb. interpret.).

ḥky **Pun** Sznycer PPP 128: the diff. *aocca* in Poen 949 = PIʿEL Impf. 1 p.s. of *ḥky* (= to await; cf. e.g. L.H.Gray AJSL xxxix 78), uncert. interpret. L.H.Gray AJSL xxxix 80: the variant *aode/aoda* poss. = QAL

Impf. 1 p.s. of *ʿdy*$_1$ (= to advance; highly uncert. interpret.; Schroed 315: prob. = NIPH Impf. 1 p.s. of *ydʿ*$_1$).

ḥkym v. *ḥkm*$_2$.

ḥkyr **Hebr** Sing. abs. *ḥkyr* DJD ii 24B 8, C 8 (*ḥk[yr]*), E 10, F 7 - ¶ subst. rent.

ḥkm$_1$ **OffAr** PAʿEL Pf. 3 p.s.m. *ḥkm* Aḥiq 1; + suff. 3 p.s.m. *ḥkmh* Aḥiq 10; 1 p.s. + suff. 3 p.s.m. *ḥkmth* Aḥiq 9 - ¶ verb PAʿEL to instruct, to inform; + obj., *wḥkmth* Aḥiq 9: and I instructed/taught him, cf. Aḥiq 10 (for the context, cf. also Grelot DAE p. 433 (n. d)); + *l*$_5$, *ḥkm lbrh* Aḥiq 1: he instructed/taught his son.
v. *ḥkm*$_2$.

ḥkm$_2$ **DA** Plur. m. (or f.??, cf. Hoftijzer DA p. 212 n. 78, 214, cf. also Rofé SB 67) abs. *ḥkmn* i 13 - **OffAr** Sing. m. abs. *ḥkym*Aḥiq 1, 28, 35, 178, cf. Warka 26: *ḫa-ki-mi* (cf. however Garbini HDS 30, 33: = QAL Part. act. s.m. abs. of *ḥkm*$_1$); m. emph. *ḥkymʾ*Aḥiq 12, 42, RES 1785A 1, KAI 264^5 (for the reading, cf. Lipiński Stud 180f. n. 3 :: e.g. Donner KAI a.l.: l. *ḥkym*= Sing. m. abs.; used as.f., cf. *ʾmr* in l. 3 × = Sing. f. abs., cf. e.g. Donner KAI a.l. for the following *špyrʾ*) - ¶ adj. wise, skilful: Aḥiq 1, 12, 28, etc.; substantivated adj.: a wise one, sage: Aḥiq 178; in DA i 13 poss. religious/cultic function, cf. Hoftijzer DA p. 212 n. 78, cf. also Levine JAOS ci 197, 199: skilled diviners.

ḥkmh **Ph** Sing. + suff. 1 p.s. *ḥkmty* KAI 26A i 13 - **Samal** Sing. + suff. 3 p.s.m. *ḥkmth* KAI 215^{11} - **OffAr** Sing. abs. *ḥkmh* Aḥiq 92, 169; emph. *ḥkmtʾ* Aḥiq 146; + suff. 3 p.s.m. *ḥkmth* Aḥiq 94; + suff. 1 p.s. *ḥkmty* Aḥiq 19 - ¶ subst. f. wisdom.

ḥkn$_1$ **OffAr** the *ḥknʾ* in KAI 267B poss. = n.p. (cf. e.g. Lepsius ZÄS xv 131, CIS ii sub 122, Lidzbarski Handb 274, Cooke NSI p. 201, Donner KAI a.l., Gibson SSI ii p. 120), cf. however Lipiński OLP viii 110: or = Sing. emph. of *ḥkn* (< Egypt.; = a sacred oil) :: Euting with Lepsius ZÄS xv 130: poss. = Sing. emph. of *ḥkn*$_2$ (= serpent, snake).

ḥkn$_2$ v. *ḥkn*$_1$.

ḥkr$_1$ **Hebr** QAL Pf. 1 p.s. *ḥkrty* DJD ii 24B 13, D 13 (*ḥk[r]ty*), E 8, F 10, *ḥkrt* DJD ii 24C 6, 8, 11, E 5 (*[ḥ]krt*), 7 - ¶ verb QAL to rent; *ḥkrt mšmʿwn* DJD ii 24C 8: I rented from Sh. (cf. DJD ii 24E 7); *ḥkrty hmk mn hywm* DJD ii 24B 13: from this day on I have rented from you (cf. DJD ii 24C 6, 11, E 5, 8).

ḥkr$_2$ **OffAr** Sing. abs. *ḥkr* ATNS 52a 3; emph. *ḥkrʾ* ATNS 18^4 - ¶ subst. rent (cf. Segal sub ATNS 18); *ḥkr zy šnh 2* ATNS 52a 3: rent of the second year.

ḥkrh **Hebr** this word (= act of renting) poss. in DJD ii 24K i 1: *ḥkr[t]* (heavily dam. context); pro *ḥrty* (lapsus) in DJD ii 24E 6 l. prob. *ḥkrty* (= Sing. + suff. 1 p.s.).

ḥl$_1$ v. *ḥlr*.

ḥl$_2$ **OldAr** Sing. abs. *ḥl* KAI 222A 25 (v. infra) - **OffAr** Sing. emph. *ḥl*ʾ Cowl 26^{7}, Aḥiq 111 - ¶ subst. sand: Aḥiq 111; in Cowl 26^{7} (dam. context) prob. = sandy beach/river-bank, cf. e.g. Cowl a.l., Grelot DAE p. 288, Porten & Yardeni sub TADAE A 6.2; *mlkt ḥl* KAI 222A 25: a kingdom of sand; for the diff. context, cf. however - **1)** Dupont-Sommer Sf p. 41f. (div. otherwise): pro *mlkt ḥl mlkt ḥlm* prob. l. *mlkt ḥlm lkt ḥlm* = dittography for *mlkt ḥlm* (= a dream-kingdom, a fancy-kingdom; cf. idem AH i/1, 4 n. 4, Koopmans 50 - **2)** Bauer AfO viii 6ff. (div. otherwise): pro *mlkt ḥl mlkt ḥlm zy* l. *mlkt ḥl mlkt ḥl* (= dittography) *mzy* (cf. Fitzmyer AIS 14f., 45), possible dittography, *mzy* = *m*$_{12}$ (= *mn*$_5$) + *zy* = as long as (cf. however Grelot RB lxxv 282); for the reading *mlkt ḥl mlkt ḥlm* (= a kingdom of sand, a kingdom of dream(s), cf. Donner KAI a.l., Rosenthal ANET 659, Lipiński Stud 49, Gibson SSI ii p. 31, 39, Lemaire & Durand IAS 133; for the context, cf. also Epstein Kedem i 39f., Degen AAG p. 10f. n. 49.
v. *ḥl*$_6$, *nyḥ*.

ḥl$_3$ **Palm** Sing. + suff. 3 p.s.m. *ḥlh* CIS ii 4052^{6}, 4206^{2,4} (cf. Cantineau sub Inv iv 1) Ber v 104^{2} - ¶ subst. maternal uncle; cf. *ḥlh*$_1$.

ḥl$_4$ v. *ḥyl*$_2$.

ḥl$_5$ = ball of dung > Akkad. *ḫallā*, cf. v.Soden Or xxxv 9, xlvi 187, cf. idem AHW s.v., cf. also CAD s.v. *ḫalla*.

ḥl$_6$ = vinegar > Akkad., cf. v.Soden Or xxxv 9, xlvi 187, cf. also idem AHW s.v. *ḫallu* IV, CAD s.v. *ḫallā* - Kottsieper SAS 18, 110, 202: this word (Sing. emph. *ḥl*ʾ) poss. in Aḥiq 190 (or = form of *ḥl*$_2$?,heavily dam. context, uncert. interpret.).
v. *ḥlh*$_2$.

ḥl$_7$ **OffAr** Sing. emph. *ḥl*ʾ Cowl 26^{12,15,20} - ¶ subst. of uncert. meaning; Grelot DAE p. 290 (n. c): < Egypt. = gun-wale?, cf. also Porten & Yardeni sub TADAE A 6.2.

ḥlʾ v. *ḥlh*$_5$.

ḥlb$_1$ = to milk > Akkad. *ḫalābu*, cf. v Soden Or xxxv 11, xlvi 188.

ḥlb$_2$ v. *ḥlbh*, *ḥšb*$_1$.

ḥlb$_3$ **Pun** Sing. abs. *ḥlb* KAI 69^{14}, 74^{10} (or = *ḥlb*$_4$?), 75^{1} (or = *ḥlb*$_4$?) - ¶ subst. fat; *wʿl ḥlb wʿl ḥlb* KAI 69^{14}: and upon fat and upon milk (or vice versa, cf. also Delcor Sem xxxviii 93) :: Dussaud Orig 321 n. 4: = dittography of *wʿl ḥlb* (= *ḥlb*$_4$).
v. *ḥlb*$_4$.

ḥlb$_4$ **Pun** Sing. abs. *ḥlb* KAI 69^{14} (v. sub *ḥlb*$_3$),CIS i 6024 (or = *ḥlb*$_3$??)- **OffAr** Sing. abs. *ḥlb* ATNS 23a 4, 52a 8, b 9; cf. Frah v 8 (cf. Nyberg FP 44, 68 :: Ebeling Frah a.l.: l. *ḥly*ʾ = Sing. emph. of *ḥly*$_2$ (= something sweet, delicacy, sweet drink)), vii 18 (on this ideogram, cf. also Lemosín AO ii 270) - ¶ subst. milk; > Akkad. *ḫilpu*, cf. v.Soden Or xxxv 11, xlvi 188.

v. *ḥlb$_3$*, *lqḥ*.

ḥlb$_5$ Palm word of uncert. meaning (*ḥl/nb/k*ʾ) and unknown meaning in Syr xlvii 413[5]: prob. = nominal form Plur. m. emph.

ḥlbbh Samal Sing. abs. *ḥlbbh* KAI 214[3,9] (*ḥl[bbh]*)[,10] (uncert. reading, cf. Gibson SSI ii p. 66, 70: l. *ḥlbt[y]* (v. *ḥlbh*); cf. also *ḥlbbh* in Koopmans no. 6[2], cf. Dion p. 88); + suff. 3 p.s.m. *ḥlbbth* KAI 214[19] (uncert. reading, cf. Gibson SSI ii p. 66, 70: pro *ḥlbbth* l. *lbbth* (= lapsus); × Poeb 46: l. *ḥlbbty* = Sing. + suff. 1 p.s.); + suff. 1 p.s. *ḥlbbty* KAI 214[13] (uncert. reading) - ¶ subst. of unknown meaning; poss. = reign, rule (cf. Poeb 46, Koopmans 32, Tawil Or xliii 46f., Dion p. 88 (cf. also Halévy RS i 145: = majesty, kingship)) :: Lidzbarski Handb 274, Eph iii 201: = blessing, prosperity (cf. also Friedrich ZS i 7, Friedr 38*, Donner KAI a.l., Sader EAS 163 (n. 30)). For this word, cf. also Gibson SSI ii p. 70, Rosenthal JBL xcv 154, Fales VO v 76f., Greenfield FS Cross 69.
v. *ḥlbh*.

ḥlbh Samal Sing. + suff. 1 p.s. *ḥlbt[y]* KAI 214[12] (uncert. reading, cf. e.g. Lipiński BiOr xxxiii 232, OLP viii 101, Gibson SSI ii p. 66, 70, cf. however Cooke NSI p. 159: l. *ḥlbt[*, Donner KAI a.l.: l. *ḥlbb/t[*; cf. also Poeb 46, Dion p. 28: = lapsus for *ḥlbbt[y]*)- ¶ subst.? of unknown meaning, the same word as (or lapsus for) *ḥlbbh*?,cf. however Lipiński BiOr xxxiii 232, OLP viii 101: prob. = PA ʿEL Inf. of *ḥlb$_2$* (= *ḥlp$_1$* (= to succeed)); uncert. interpret.; Gibson SSI ii p. 66, 70: Sing. + suff. 1 p.s. *ḥlbt[y]* also in KAI 214[10] (v. *ḥlbbh*).

ḥld$_1$ v. *ḥlp$_1$*.

ḥld$_2$ v. *rd$_3$*.

ḥlh$_1$ Nab Sing. + suff. 3 p.s.m. *ḥlth* J 13[2] (:: CIS ii 226 (div. otherwise): l. *brth* (= Sing. + suff. 3 p.s.m. of *brh$_3$*)) - ¶ subst. f. maternal aunt (= f. of *ḥl$_3$*)- Cantineau Nab ii 172: < Arab., cf. however O'Connor JNES xlv 218.

ḥlh$_2$ OffAr, cf. Nisa 190[4], 357[2], 470[8], 493b 2, 537[11], 722[4], etc.: vinegar; cf. GIPP 52 (:: Altheim & Stiehl ASA 270: = Sing. emph. of *ḥl$_6$*;poss. = Sing. + suff. 3 p.s.m. of *ḥl$_6$*, cf. Altheim & Stiehl ibid.).

ḥlh$_3$ Ph Sing. abs. *ḥlt* KAI 14[3,11]; cstr. *ḥlt* KAI 14[5,7,21] - **JAr** Sing. cstr. *ḥlt* MPAT 88[1]; emph. *ḥlth* MPAT 69[1] - ¶ subst. f.; in Ph. texts: sarcophagus; in J.Ar. texts: ossuary (cf. also Marcus JANES vii 89f.).
v. *mškb$_1$*.

ḥlh$_4$ Hebr Sing. abs. *ḥlh* SM 49[5,23] - ¶ subst. certain type of loaf, in the combination *pt ḥlh* - this word poss. also in SCO xxix 128 ii 2 (*ḥlth* = Sing. emph. or + suff. 3 p.s.m./f., heavily damn. context).

ḥlh$_5$ Ph Peckham Or xxxvii 305f., 315: the *ḥlt* in KAI 37A 10 = Plur. abs. of *ḥlh$_5$* (= cake), cf. e.g. also Masson & Sznycer RPC 48, Delcor UF xi 155f., Gibson SSI iii p. 125, 128 (prob. interpret.) - Harmatta ActAntHung vii 362, 385: the *ḥl*ʾin Cowl 81[49] prob. = Sing. abs. of

ḥlh$_5$ (cf. also Grelot DAE p. 112).
ḥlh$_6$ = cane basket > Akkad., cf. v.Soden Or xxxv 9, xlvi 187, cf. also idem AHW 312.
v. *slh*$_1$.
ḥlh$_7$ v. *slh*$_1$.
ḥlwp v. *nyḥ*.
ḥlwr Ebeling Frah a.l.: l. in Frah iv 4 *ḥlwr*, prob. = chick pea (highly uncert. reading, cf. Nyberg FP 42, 65).
ḥlṭ$_1$ v. *ḥlp*$_1$.
ḥlṭ$_2$ **OffAr** Plur. abs., cf. Warka 21, 25: *øḫa-la-ṭi-in-ni*, 33: *ḫa-la-ṭi-i-ni* (for ending *-i*, cf. Garbini HDS 32) - ¶ subst. prob. meaning: mixtures (cf. Dupont-Sommer RA xxxix 50 :: Driver AfO iii 52: = mixed herbs :: Gordon AfO xii 117: l. resp. *ḫa-la-ki-in-ni*, *ḫa-la-ki-i-ni* = *ʿlqyn* (= Plur. abs. of *ʿlq* (= leech)) - v.Soden Or xxxv 11, xlvi 188: Akkad. *ḫulūṭu* (prob. = certain kind of drink) poss. derived from the Ar. root *ḫlṭ* = to mix (mixed drink?).
ḥly$_1$ **OffAr** Qal Impf. 2 p.s.m. *tḥly* Aḥiq 148 (for the reading, cf. Lindenberger APA 149, 263 n. 457); Haph Impf. 3 p.s.m. *yhḥlh* Aḥiq 188 - ¶ verb Qal to be sweet, to be friendly: Aḥiq 148 - Haph to make sweet; *kpn yhḥlh mrrwtʾ* Aḥiq 188: hunger sweetens that which is bitter.
v. *ḥly*$_2$.
ḥly$_2$ **OffAr** Sing. f. abs. *ḥlyh* Aḥiq 131 - ¶ adj. (or Qal Part. act. of *ḥly*$_1$?)sweet, pleasant - Lipiński Stud 144f.: l. *ḥlyh* (= Sing. f. abs.) in NESE i 48[2f.] preceded by *nm* (= Qal Part. m. s. abs. of *nwm*); highly improb. interpret., cf. e.g. Degen NESE i a.l. (div. otherwise): l. *bn* (= Sing. cstr. of *bn*$_1$) *mḥlyh* (= n.p.).
v. *ḥlb*$_4$, *ḥly*$_3$.
ḥly$_3$ v. *ḥlʿ*.
ḥlym v. *ḥlyt*.
ḥlymw v. *mqlw*.
ḥlyph **OffAr** Sing. + suff. 3 p.pl.m. *ḥlypthm* Cowl 26[13] - ¶ subst. poss. meaning, equivalent, cf. Cowl p. 95 (also for other interpret.; cf. also Grelot DAE p. 291 (n. j) and Porten & Yardeni sub TADAE A 6.2: = replacement) :: Driver JRAS '32, 79f.: = Plur. + suff. 3 p.pl.m. (= relay, shift, sc. of sailors or workmen) :: Galling Studien 84: = patchwork.
ḥlyqh (< Arab., cf. Cooke NSI p. 220) - **Nab** Sing. cstr. *ḥlyqt* CIS ii 197[9], 199[3], 206[2] - ¶ subst. in the expression *kḥlyqt* = according to the nature of, like; *qbrʾ dnh ḥrm kḥlyqt ḥrmʾ dy mḥrm ldwšrʾ* CIS ii 206[2f.]: this tomb is an inviolable object like the inviolable object which is inviolably dedicated to D. (cf. however Milik Bibl xlviii 577).
ḥlyt **Palm** word of unknown meaning and uncert. reading in the ex-

pression *byt ḥlyt[ʾ]* in RTP 525 (the house of ...); cf. however du Mesnil du Buisson TMP 545: pro *ḥlyt[ʾ]* l. *ḥlym*(prob. reading) = n.p. (uncert. interpret.). Related to root *ḥlm$_1$* = to dream??

ḥlk v. *ḥlb$_5$*.

ḥll$_1$ **OffAr** ITP Impf. 3 p.s.f. *ttḥll* Aḥiq 168 - ¶ verb ITP prob. meaning: to be destroyed (cf. Cowl a.l., cf. also Grelot RB lxviii 191, DAE p. 445 (n. f), Kottsieper SAS 157f., 203), cf. however Lindenberger APA 171, 270 n. 524, 525: = to be swept away (< root *ḥwl$_1$* or root *ḥll* (variant of *ḥwl$_1$*)= to turn); for the restoration of the context, cf. already Driver JRAS '32, 88 - Gibson SSI ii p. 78, 82: l. *ḥll* (= PA ʿEL Pf. 3 p.s.m. = to pierce, to execute) in KAI 215[3] (uncert. reading, heavily dam. context).

ḥll$_2$ cf. Frah xix 5 (*yḥllwn*, *ḥllwn*): to wash.

ḥll$_3$ v. *ḥll$_5$*.

ḥll$_4$ v. *ḥyl$_2$*.

ḥll$_5$ v.Soden Or xxxv 9, xlvi 187: Akkad. *ḫālilu* (= a digging tool (made of iron)) prob. = QAL Part. act. of *ḥll$_3$*(= to hollow, to dig out (< Ar.)), cf. also CAD s.v. *ḫālilu*-A: prob. < Ar. (uncert. interpret.).

ḥlm$_1$ cf. Frah xix 19: to sleep - a form of this root poss. to be restored in ATNS 68 ii 3 (*[yḥ]lmwn* = QAL Impf. 3 p.pl.m.?), cf. Segal ATNS a.l.

v. *ḥlyt*,*ḥlm$_3$*, *kly$_1$*.

ḥlm$_2$ v. *ḥlm$_3$*.

ḥlm$_3$ **Ph** Sing. abs. *ḥlm* Syr xlviii 403[4] (cf. Röllig NESE ii 29, 33; uncert. interpret., diff. context × Caquot Syr xlviii 405f., Gaster BASOR ccix 19, 25, Lipiński RSF ii 52ff., Cross CBQ xxxvi 488f., Gibson SSI iii p. 90, de Moor JEOL xxvii 111: = QAL Part. act. s.m. abs. of *ḥlm$_1$*(= dreamer), cf. also the following interpret.: - **1)** Garbini OA xx 291f.: = Sing. m. abs. of *ḥlm$_6$* (= powerful, mighty) - **2)** Avishur PIB 267, 271, UF x 32, 35f.: = joint, hinge (place where the door is joined to close it; less prob. interpret.) - **3)** v d Branden BiOr xxxiii 13, xxxvi 202: = QAL Pf. 3 p.s.f. of *ḥlm$_2$*(= to become sound (improb. interpret.))) - **OldAr** Sing. abs. *ḥlm* KAI 222A 25 - **OffAr** Sing. abs. *ḥlm* KAI 270A 1 (cf. e.g. CIS ii sub 137, Cooke NSI p. 203, Donner KAI a.l., Porten Arch 275, Levine JAOS lxxxiv 19, 21 (for the context, cf. also Fuhs HZH 45f.) :: Dupont-Sommer ASAE xlviii 121f.: = Sing. abs. of *ḥlm$_5$* (= certain type of vegetable, borage)); + suff. 3 p.s.m./f. *ḥlmh* ATNS 68 i 6 (dam. context) - **Hatra** Sing. emph. *ḥlmʾ* 106B 4 (or Plur.??), 281[11]; Plur. emph. *ḥlmʾ* app. 4[6] (cf. Safar Sumer xvii 39 n. 95, 40, Segal Irâq xxix 9 n. 28, Milik DFD 395 :: Teixidor Syr xli 273 (n. 3): = Plur. emph. of *ḥlm$_4$* (= dream-interpreter) :: Aggoula MUSJ xlvii 46, Sem xxvii 138, 142: l. *ḥlmh* = Sing. emph. or + suff. 3 p.s.m. of *ḥlm$_3$*; the *ḥlm* with Vattioni IH a.l. prob. misprint) - ¶ subst.

dream; for KAI 222A 25, v. *ḥl$_2$*; *ḥlm ... ḥzyt* KAI 270A 1f.: I have seen a dream (i.e. I dreamed), cf. also Hatra 281^{11} (for the context, cf. also Degen NESE iii 68, 71); *ḥzy› bḥlm›* app. 4^6: seeing in dreams (for the reading, cf. Safar Sumer xvii 39, Segal Irâq xxix 9 n. 28, Milik DFD 395, cf. also Aggoula MUSJ xlvii 46, Sem xxvii 138, 142; v. *ḥzy$_1$* and also supra); *›lh› bḥlm› ›lp hnw* Hatra 106B 4f.: the god has instructed them in a dream (or dreams??).

ḥlm$_4$ v. *ḥlm$_3$*.

ḥlm$_5$ v. *ḥlm$_3$*.

ḥlm$_6$ v. *ḥlm$_3$*.

ḥl‹ **DA** derivative of this root poss. in v d 4 (reading uncert., cf. v.d.Kooij DA p. 150), meaning unknown (heavily dam. context) - Puech FS Grelot 17, 25, 28: l. *ḥly* = Sing. abs. of *ḥly$_3$*(= illness).

ḥlp$_1$ **Ph** QAL Imper. s.m. *ḥlp* KAI 27^{27} (cf. Cross & Saley BASOR cxcvii 47 (n. 34), Röllig NESE ii 19, Gibson SSI iii p. 83, de Moor JEOL xxvii 108 (cf. Avishur PIB 248, 255f.: or = Imper. s.f.) :: Caquot FS Gaster 51: = QAL Pf. 3 p.pl. (cf. Lipiński RTAT 266) :: Garbini OA xx 286: = QAL Pf. 3 p.s.m. :: du Mesnil du Buisson FS Dussaud 424f., 433, Albright BASOR lxxvi 10, Gaster Or xi 44, Röllig KAI a.l.: l. *ḥl* = QAL Imper. s.f. of *ḥyl$_1$*(= to be in travail) :: Torczyner JNES vi 26f., 29: l. *ḥld* = QAL Pf. 3 p.s.m. of *ḥld$_1$*(= to shine) :: v.d.Branden BiOr xxxiii 13: l. *ḥlṭ* = QAL Imper. s.f. of *ḥlṭ$_1$*(= to have sexual intercourse) - **Mo** QAL (or PI‹EL?) Impf. 3 p.s.m. + suff. 3 p.s.m. *yḥlph* KAI 181^6 - **OldAr** QAL Part. act. s.m. + suff. 3 p.s.m. *ḥlph* KAI 224^{22} (for the div. *whwy* (v. *hwy$_1$*) *ḥlph*, cf. Milik with Fitzmyer CBQ xx 462, AIS 118 and already Rosenthal BASOR clviii 30 n. 12; for the interpret., cf. e.g. Fitzmyer AIS 100f., 118, JSS xiv 198ff., Teixidor Syr xlviii 177, Degen ZDMG cxx 201, Greenfield IEJ xix 201, cf. also Gibson SSI ii p. 51, 55, Sader EAS 136 (n. 61) × the interpret. as Sing. + suff. 3 p.s.m. of *ḥlp$_2$* (noun) = successor, cf. e.g. Gibson SSI ii p. 51, 55 (cf. also Nober VD xxxvii 171f., Lipiński Stud 48) :: Rosenthal BASOR clviii 30 n. 12, Koopmans 68, Degen AAG p. 62 (cf. also p. 22 n. 88, ZDMG cxix 173, OLZ '71, 271, GGA '79, 30): *ḥlph* = Sing. + suff. 3 p.s.m. of *ḥlp$_4$* (= in his place); cf. also Nober VD xxxvii 171f.: *ḥlph* = Sing. + suff. 3 p.s.m. of *ḥlp$_4$* (still used as subst. = substitution), *whwy* = *waw* conversivum + QAL Pf. 3 p.s.m. of *hwy$_1$*: that there may be his substitution :: Dupont-Sommer Sf p. 131, 142f., AH i/1, 6, i/2, 3, Segert ArchOr xxxii 124 (div. otherwise): l. *whw* (= *hw$_1$*) *yḥlph*(= PA‹EL/APH Impf. 3 p.s.m. + suff. 3 p.s.m. of *ḥlp$_1$*) :: (Milik with) Fitzmyer CBQ xx 462: div. *whwy ḥlph* (= Sing. abs. of *ḥlph$_1$* = change)) - **OffAr** QAL (or PA‹EL?) Impf. 3 p.s.m. *yḥlp* Cowl 71^{14} (uncert. reading, dam. context), Aḥiq 18; HAPH Pf. 3 p.s.m. *hḥlp* ATNS 3^7; 2 p.s.m. *hḥlpt* ATNS 50^7 (dam. context); Impf. 1 p.s. *›hḥlp* ATNS 2^2 (reading however highly uncert.,

cf. Porten & Yardeni sub TADAE B 8.9); Imper. s.f. *hḥlpy* Sem ii 31 conc. 5; Inf. *hḥl[p]* ATNS 119^{1} (??, heavily dam. context) - **JAr** PA ʿEL Impf. 1 p.s. *ʾḥlp* MPAT 40^{12,24} (*[ʾ]ḥlp*), 42^{19} (*[ʾḥ]lp*), 46^{5}, IEJ xxxvi 206^{7}; 1 p.pl. *nḥlp* MPAT 45^{7} - ¶ verb QAL to go away, to disappear, to vanish: KAI 27^{27} - QAL or PI ʿEL/PA ʿEL to succeed - a) + obj., *wyḥlph bnh* KAI 181^{6}: and his son succeeded him, cf. KAI 224^{22} - b) + *l*$_5$ comm. + nom. specification (cf. Joüon MUSJ xviii 5), *whw yḥlp ly spr* Aḥiq 18: and he may succeed me as scribe - PA ʿEL to replace; + *l*$_5$ + obj., *ʾḥlp lky šṭrh* MPAT 40$^{10f.}$: I shall replace for you the document (cf. MPAT 40^{24}, 42^{19}, 45^{7}, 46^{5}, IEJ xxxvi 206^{7} (cf. also Milik DJD ii p. 109, Koffmahn DJW 71f.) - HAPH to exchange; + *l*$_5$ + obj., *hḥlpy ly šʿrn* Sem ii 31 conc. 5: send me barley in return; + *ʿm*$_4$ (with): ATNS 3^{7} (dam. context) - a form of this root poss. in ATNS 52b 4 (*ḥlpth*)??, cf. Segal ATNS a.l.
v. *ḥlbh*.

ḥlp$_2$ = substitute > Akkad., cf. v.Soden Or xxxv 9, xlvi 187, AHW s.v. *ḫalpu* III, cf. also CAD s.v. *ḫalpu* B - this subst. (Sing. emph. *ḥlpʾ*) also in Samar 7^{14}? (diff. reading), Groppe a.l.: = amount.
v. *ḥlp*$_{1,4}$.

ḥlp$_3$ **Nab** Sing. cstr. *ḥlp* CIS ii 212^{6} - ¶ subst. m. fate; *wyhwʾ bh ḥlp mwt* CIS ii 212^{6}: and the fate of death (i.e. death) will befall him (:: Cantineau Nab ii 96: i.e. a mortal accident).

ḥlp$_4$ **OffAr** Cowl 1^{3}, 9^{10,11}, 13^{4}, 44^{8,9}, Aḥiq 62, 69; + suff. 3 p.s.m. *ḥlpwhy* Driv 2^{3}; + suff. 2 p.s.m. *ḥlpyk* Aḥiq 21; + suff. 1 p.pl. *ḥlpn* (?, prob. reading) Cowl 83^{4} (v. however infra); cf. Nisa-b 22^{2,3,4}, 139^{2}, 149^{1}, 292^{3,5}, Nisa-c 240^{3}, etc. (*ḥlp*), cf. GIPP 52 - ¶ (subst., v. sub *ḥlp*$_2$ >)prep. - **1)** instead of, in the place of; *ytqṭl ... ḥlp ʾḥyqr znh* Aḥiq 62: let him be killed ... instead of this Aḥiqar (cf. Aḥiq 21, 69, Driv 2^{3}) - **2)** in return for; *bnyk ... šlyṭn bh ḥlp ʿbydtʾ zy ʾnt ʿbdt* Cowl 9$^{9f.}$: your children ... have power over it in return for the work which you have done; *yhbth lmpṭḥyh brty ḥlp nksyʾ zy yhbt ly* Cowl 13^{4}: I give it to my daughter M. in return for the goods which she gave me (cf. Cowl 1^{3}, 9^{1}, 44^{8,9}) - **3)** by way of: Nisa-b 22^{2,3,4}, 139^{2}, 796^{1f}, etc., etc. - the meaning of *ḥlpn* in Cowl 83^{4} obscure, cf. Cowl a.l.: on our account (?; is it really *ḥlp*$_4$?) - on this word, cf. Ribera AO viii 136ff.
v. *ḥlp*$_1$.

ḥlph$_1$ **Ph** Sing. abs. *ḥlpt* KAI 60^{7} - ¶ subst. equivalent, return; *ydʿ hgw lšlm ḥlpt ʾyt ʾdmm ...* KAI 60^{7}: the community knows how to requite the men ...
v. *ḥlp*$_1$,*ḥlph*$_2$, *mḥlph*.

ḥlph$_2$ **Palm** Sing. + suff. 3 p.s.m. *ḥlpth* Syr xiv 179^{1} - ¶ subst. of uncert. meaning. Cantineau Syr xiv a.l.: = substitute, lieutenant?? Same word as *ḥlph*$_1$?

ḥlṣ1 **Pun** QAL Part. pass. s.m. abs. *ḥlṣ* KAI 73[4] (= CIS i 6057, cf. e.g. Chabot sub RES 5, cf. also Février sub CIS i a.l., Krahmalkov JSS xxvi 186, cf. however Garbini RSO xlii 7f., Ferron Mus lxxxi 258, v.d.Branden BO xi 201, Gibson SSI iii p. 69f.: = PI ‘EL Pf. 3 p.s.f. and Ferron CB viii 53: = part of n.p. (cf. also Röllig KAI a.l.)); PI ‘EL Pf. 3 p.s.m. *ḥlṣ* KAI 73[5] (cf. e.g. Chabot sub RES 5, Ferron CB viii 53, Mus lxxxi 258, Gibson SSI iii p. 69f. :: Garbini RSO xlii 7f., v.d.Branden BO xi 201: = PI ‘EL Pf. 3 p.s.f. :: Krahmalkov JSS xxvi 186: = QAL Pf. 3 p.s.m.) - ¶ verb QAL Part. pass.: the saved one (diff. context: *ḥlṣ ʾš ḥlṣ pgmlyn* KAI 73[4ff.]: the saved one whom P. saved?) :: Krahmalkov JSS xxvi 186: = (the equipped one >) soldier; v. however supra - PI ‘EL to save (v. supra).
v. *ḥlq*1, *ḥṣl*1.

ḥlṣ2 **OffAr** Sing. emph. *ḥlṣh* Herm 3[6] (for the division of words, cf. Milik Bibl xlviii 552, 582, Grelot DAE p. 158 (n. e), Lipiński OLP viii 116, Swiggers AION xlii 137 :: Bresciani & Kamil Herm a.l. (div. otherwise): l. *srḥlṣh* = n.p., cf. also Gibson SSI ii p. 136) - ¶ subst. prob. meaning, something squeezed out (i.e. a certain type of oil), cf. Grelot DAE p. 158 (n. e), Lipiński OLP viii 116, Swiggers AION xlii 137 :: Milik Bibl xlviii 552, 582: = Sing. emph. of *ḥlṣ*3 (= hide of skinned animal, skin for wine, oil, etc.).
v. *srblwn*.

ḥlṣ3 v. *ḥlṣ*2.

ḥlq1 **OffAr** QAL Pf. 3 p.s.m. *ḥlq* WO vi 44A 4, B 3 (*ḥl[q]*), C 3 (for the reading, cf. Diakonov & Starkova VDI lii 168f., v however infra :: Dupont-Sommer Syr xxv 59, 61, Donner KAI sub 274, 275: l. *ḥlṣ* = QAL (or PA ‘EL?) Pf. 3 p.s.m. of *ḥlṣ*1(= to pull up, to land (sc. fishes)), REA-NS viii 170 A, B 4; cf. Frah xxi 8 (*ḥlkwn*), GIPP 23, SaSt 17 - **Nab** ITP Impf. 3 p.pl.m. *ytḥlqwn* BASOR cclxiii 78[2] - ¶ verb QAL - **1)** to divide; *ʾrtḥšsy ... ḥlq ʾrq byn qry* WO vi 44C: A. ... divided the land between the villages, cf. WO vi 44A, B, REA-NS viii 170A, B (for the interpret., cf. Henning Ir 37, Naveh WO vi 44f. :: Diakonov & Starkova VDI lii 168f.: or *ḥlq* = Sing. cstr. of *ḥlq*3) - **2)** to distribute: Frah xxi 8 - ITP exact meaning unknown, poss. = to allot or to divide among themselves: BASOR cclxiii 78[2] (dam. context) - Porten & Yardeni sub TADAE B 4.3: l. poss. *ḥlqn* (= QAL Pf. 1 p.pl.) in Cowl 2[15] :: Cowl a.l.: l. poss. *zyln* = *zy* + *l*5 + suff. 1 p.pl..
v. *ḥlq*4.

ḥlq2 v. *ḥlq*4.

ḥlq3 **OffAr** Sing. abs. *ḥlq* Cowl 28[3,5,7,9,10,12], 82[12]; cstr. *ḥlq* Krael 4[11]; emph. *ḥlqʾ* Cowl 28[3,5], Krael 4[9], NESE i 11[2] (for the reading, cf. Naveh & Shaked JAOS xci 380, Degen NESE i 11, 15, Golomb BASOR ccxvii 51f., Grelot DAE p. 504, Porten Or lvii 78, Porten & Yardeni sub

TADAE A 3.10 :: Macuch JAOS xciii 59: pro *ḥlqʾ zyly* l *ḥylyʾ* (= Plur. emph. of *ḥyl*$_2$(= the guardsmen)) *ʾlp* (= Sing. abs. of *ʾlp*$_3$) :: Shunnar with Altheim & Stiehl GMA 114, 116: pro *ḥlqʾ zyly* l. *ḥyl[p]ʾ ʾlp* (poss. = boatswain) :: Shunnar CRM ii 278ff., 286f.: l. poss. *ḥylnʾ* (= Sing. + suff. 1 p.pl. of *ḥyl*$_2$) *ʾln* (= these goods of ours, these workmen of ours)); + suff. 3 p.s.m. *ḥlqh* Cowl 28^{14}; + suff. 1 p.s. *ḥlqy* Krael 4^{19}, NESE i 11^3; Plur. abs. *ḥlqn* Cowl 82^7; cf. Frah x 27 (*ḥlkʾ*), cf. Nyberg FP 77 :: Ebeling Frah a.l.: = form of *ḥlq*$_5$ (= hairless, clean-shaven) - **Nab** Sing. abs. *ḥlq* J 4^7; cstr. *ḥlq* J $14^{2,3}$; + suff. 3 p.s.m. *ḥlqh* CIS ii 200^4 (= J 30 = ARNA-Nab 79)^{,5}, 213^6, 223^4; + suff. 3 p.s.f. *ḥlqh* CIS ii 213^5 - **Palm** Sing. + suff. 3 p.s.m. *ḥlqh*(?) Inv x 54^3 - **JAr** Sing. abs. *ḥwlq*MPAT-A 16^4 (= Frey 981 = SM 17); + suff. 1 p.s. *ḥ[l]qy* IEJ xxxvi 206^3 (diff. reading, dam. context, uncert. restoration, cf. Broshi & Qimron IEJ xxxvi 208); + suff. 3 p.pl.m. *ḥwlqhwn*MPAT-A 8^3, 48^2 (= Frey 979), *ḥwqhwn* MPAT-A 5^6 (= Frey 1203 = SM 64; lapsus) - ¶ subst. m. part, portion, share, passim; *znh ḥlq bytʾ zy ...* Krael $4^{11f.}$: this is the part of the house which ...; *whʾ znh ḥlqʾ zy mṭʾk bḥlq* Cowl 28^3: this is the share which comes to you as a share; *ḥlqy bʾgr ʾlpʾ* NESE i 11^3: my part in the rent of the ship; *wḥlqh mn gwḥyʾ mdnḥʾ* CIS ii 213^5: and her portion of the niches is the east side; *yhy lh ḥwlq ʿm ṣdyqyh* MPAT-A $16^{3f.}$ (v. *ṣdq*$_3$): let his share be with the righteous. v. *ḥlq*$_{1,4}$.

ḥlq$_4$ **DA** Sing. abs. (?) *ḥlq* ii 11 (dam. context; cf. Caquot & Lemaire Syr liv 205, cf. also Hoftijzer DA a.l.: or = *ḥlq*$_3$?,Garbini Hen i 183, 186 (cf. H.P.Müller ZAW xciv 219, 235): = Qal Inf. of *ḥlq*$_1$:: Levine JAOS ci 200: = Qal Inf. of *ḥlq*$_2$(= to pass. away; cf. also Hackett BTDA 30, 67f., 96, 129 = to perish) :: Dahood Bibl lxii 126 = Qal Part. act. s.m. abs. of *ḥlq*$_2$(= mortal one) ?) - ¶ subst. perdition (or = lost one, someone abandoned to perdition?, cf. Hoftijzer DA a.l.).

ḥlq$_5$ v. *ḥlq*$_3$.

ḥlqw **OffAr** Plur. emph. *ḥlqwtʾ* KAI 279^7 (v. infra) - ¶ subst. disposition of fate (cf. Kutscher, Naveh & Shaked Lesh xxxiv 130, 135 :: the interpret. of *ḥlqwtʾ* as Sing. emph., cf. Dupont-Sommer JA ccxlvi 31, Levi Della Vida Editto 27, Koopmans 177, Garbini Kand 16, 18, Teixidor Syr xlvi 349, Rosenthal EI xiv 97*f.: = fate, destiny (cf. also Altheim & Stiehl EW ix 97f. (cf. Altheim GH i 405, 407): = favourable lot, good luck > joy, idem EW x 245f.: = good allocation > luck (cf. also idem ASA 28f., 270, GMA 351, GH ii 174) :: Levine JAOS lxxxvii 186: = division, dispute). For the context, v. *ʾsr*$_1$.

ḥlr **OffAr** Plur. abs. *ḥlrn* Cowl 10^5, 11^2, Krael $2^{5,7}$, ATNS 19^3, etc., etc., *ḥlryn* Cowl 81^{20} - ¶ subst. certain weight, $\frac{1}{40}$ shekel (cf. e.g. Cowl p. xxxf., Porten Arch 67, Fitzmyer FS Albright ii 156 :: Krael p. 39: = 1/10 shekel) - abbrev. *ḥ* Krael $7^{14,15,27}$, ATNS $38^{7,8,9}$, 43a 4, 52a

6,8, 66b 2 - the *ḥl* in Cowl 81^{41} also abbrev. for *ḥlr*?? - Segal ATNS a.l.: the *ḥ* in ATNS 41^{2,3}, 42a 5, b 6, 44^{1}, 51^{1}, 95b 1,2 = abbrev. of *ḥlr* (context however dam. and diff.); idem ATNS a.l.: the *ḥ* in ATNS 44 ii 1 = abbrev. of *ḥlr* (improb. interpret., cf. Porten & Yardeni sub TADAE B 8.2 = part of n.p.).
v. *ḥmr$_6$*, *ḥpn*.

ḥm$_1$ **Palm** Sing. + suff. 3 p.s.m. *ḥmwhy* Ber xix 69^{3} - ¶ subst. father-in-law.

ḥm$_2$ **Hebr** Sing. cstr. *ḥm* KAI 200^{10} - ¶ subst. heat (for the context of KAI 200^{10}, cf. Pardee Maarav i 49ff. and litt. quoted there) - Yeivin BiOr xix 3ff.: l. *bḥ[m]* (= *b$_2$* + Sing. cstr. of *ḥm$_2$*) *[hy]wm* (= article + Sing. abs. of *ywm)* in KAI 200$^{3f.}$ (cf. also Röllig KAI a.l.), improb. reading, cf. Naveh IEJ x 131f.: l. *bḥṣrʾsm* (= *b$_2$* + n.l.), cf. also Naveh Lesh xxx 69, Cross BASOR clxv 42, 44, Amusin & Heltzer IEJ xiv 149ff., Talmon BASOR clxxvi 29f., Delekat Bibl li 456f., Gibson SSI i p. 28f., Lemaire Sem xxi 63 n. 4, Pardee Maarav i 35f., 41, Conrad TUAT i 250 - this word or word of the same root poss. in DA iv a 3 (cf. also Hoftijzer DA p. 277) - Driver JRAS '32, 83: this word (Sing. cstr.) poss. in Cowl 57^{2} (highly uncert. interpret.).
v. *lḥm$_4$*, *rḥm$_3$*.

ḥm$_3$ (< Akkad., cf. Kaufman AIA 53) - **OffAr** Sing. abs. *ḥm* Cowl 15^{25,28}, Krael 2^{8,10} - ¶ subst. straw (cf. Muffs 59 n. 1, 182, Fitzmyer FS Albright ii 163, WA 264f., Kaufman AIA 53, Grelot DAE p. 195 n. t, Porten & Greenfield JEAS p. 23, Porten & Yardeni sub TADAE B 2.6 (a.e.), cf. also Speiser JAOS liv 200ff. :: Driver JRAS '32, 78: = broom :: Cowl p. 46, 49: = shred); only in the expression *mn ḥm ʿd ḥwṭ* = from straw to string (i.e. totally; cf. also Yaron RB lxxvii 414).

ḥm$_4$ **Pun** Schroed p. 291f., 308, L.H.Gray AJSL xxxix 77f., 79: the second *am* in Poen 941 = *ḥm* used adverbially, ardently, hotly (highly uncert. interpret.).

ḥmʾ v. *ḥmh$_2$*.

ḥmd$_1$ **Ph** QAL Impf. 3 p.s.m. *yḥmd* KAI 26A iii 14, C iv 16 - ¶ verb QAL to covet, to try to secure a coveted object, cf. Marcus & Gelb JNES viii 120, Alt WO i 283f., cf. also v.d.Branden Meltô i 75, Bron RIPK 116, Swiggers BiOr xxxvii 341, Gibson SSI iii p. 63, Moran CBQ xxix 544, Greenfield Sem xxxviii 155 :: Dupont-Sommer RA xlii 167, 175: to love (cf. Rosenthal ANET 654: to have good intentions toward) -
v. *ḥmd$_2$*, *ḥmr$_7$*.

ḥmd$_2$ **OldCan** Sing. abs. *ḫa-mu-du* EA 138^{26} (× Böhl 37f.: = QAL Part. pass. of *ḥmd$_1$*,cf. also Siwan GAG 171, 223) - **OffAr** Plur. + suff. 3 p.s.f. *ḥmdyh* Krael 7^{19} (v. infra) - ¶ subst. something valuable, precious object; for Krael 7^{19}, cf. Krael a.l., Grelot RB lxxviii 532,

DAE p. 235, Porten & Greenfield JEAS p. 55 :: Porten & Yardeni sub TADAE B 3.8: l. *ḥmryh* = Plur. + suff. 3 p.s.f. of *ḥmr*$_{12}$ (= jewel).

ḥmd$_3$ v. *ḥmr*$_3$.

ḥmdh **Ph** Sing. abs. *ḥmdt* KAI 26A iii 17 - ¶ subst. good intention(s), cf. Dupont-Sommer RA xlii 175, Rosenthal ANET 654 × Greenfield Sem xxxviii 155: strong possessive desire (cf. Gibson SSI iii p. 53: = covetousness) × jealousy, envy.
v. *ḥmr*$_5$.

ḥmh$_1$ **OldCan** Sing. abs. *ḫu-mi-tu* EA 141^{44} (for this form, cf. also Greenfield PICS 95 n. 13, Garr DGSP 30, Siwan GAG 29, 223) - **Ph** Plur. abs. *ḥmyt* KAI 26A i 13, 17 (for a variant *ḥnyt*, cf. Dupont-Sommer RA xlii 163 n. 1; for the form, cf. Bron RIPK 64 :: FR 204a: = *ḥm* + *nisbe*-ending (cf. also Gibson SSI iii p. 58)) - **Mo** Sing. cstr. *ḥmt* KAI 181^{21} - **Hebr** Sing. abs. *ḥwmh*SM 79 (??, heavily dam. context, cf. also Naveh SM a.l.); cstr. *ḥwmt* SM 49^{13} - ¶ subst. f. - **1)** wall: EA 141^{44}, KAI 181^{21}, SM 49^{13} - **2)** fortress: KAI 26A i 13, 17 - for this word, cf. Marrassini FLEM 54ff.

ḥmh$_2$ **Samal** Sing. abs. *ḥm*ʾKAI 214^{33} (for the form, cf. Dion p. 60f., cf. however Ginsberg JAOS lxii 235 n. 31 × Lipiński BiOr xxxiii 233: l. *ḥr*ʾ = Sing. abs. of *ḥr*ʾ$_2$) - **OffAr** Sing. emph. *ḥmt[ʾ]* Aḥiq 140 (cf. e.g. Cowl a.l., Ginsberg ANET 429, Grelot DAE p. 442, cf. however Kottsieper SAS 16, 207: l. *ḥmt[y]* = Sing. + suff. 1 p.s. :: Lindenberger APA 138: l. prob. *ḥmt[y]* = Sing. + suff. 1 p.s. (= poison > poisoner)) - ¶ subst. f. wrath.

ḥmh$_3$ v.Soden Or xxxv 9, xlvi 186 (cf. also idem AfO xix 149): = summer > Akkad., cf. idem AHW s.v. *gummātu* (cf. however CAD s.v. *gumatu* = foreign word).

ḥmh$_4$ **Hebr** Sing. abs. *ḥmh* AMB 4^{20} - ¶ subst. sun.

ḥmh$_5$ v. *m*ʾ*š*$_1$.

ḥmy **Palm** Itp Part. pl.m. abs. *mtḥmn* (unpubl. text, cf. Cantineau Gramm 91) - **JAr** Qal Part. act. m. s. abs. (or cstr.??) *ḥmy* MPAT-A 22^6 (= SM 70^{14}); Itp Impf. 2 p.s.f. *[t]tḥmyn* AMB 12^{33} - ¶ verb Qal to see; *ḥmy styrth* MPAT-A 22^6: He who sees hidden things (i.e. God) - Itp to be seen: AMB 12^{33} - > Akkad., cf. v.Soden Or xlvi 187.
v. *ḥ*ʾ$_1$.

ḥmydh v. *ḥmr*$_5$.

ḥmyr$_1$ v. *ḥmr*$_2$.

ḥmyr$_2$ v. *ḥmr*$_2$.

ḥmyš v. *ḥmš*$_2$.

ḥmyšy v. *ḥmšy*.

ḥml v. *mlky*.

ḥmlh v. *ḥmr*$_5$.

ḥmm$_1$ **Palm** Aph Part. s.m. abs. (or cstr.??) *mḥm* RIP 162^2 - ¶ verb

APH to heat; *mḥm my*ʾ RIP 162[2]: bath-heater (litt. heater of water; for this function, cf. Gawlikowski Syr xlvii 321f., RIP a.l.) - derivatives of this root also in ATNS 95a 2 (*]ḥmy ḥmn*) and 96[2] (*ḥmy ḥm[*)??, Segal sub ATNS 95: *ḥmy ḥmn* poss. = very hot water (??).
v. *ḥmm*$_2$.

ḥmm$_2$ **OffAr** Sing. m. abs. *ḥmm* KAI 270A 4 - ¶ adj. (or = QAL Part. act. of *ḥmm*$_1$= to be hot?) hot, feverish (for the context, cf. litt. mentioned sub *ḥlm*$_3$).

ḥmn **Nab** Sing. emph. *ḥmn*ʾ RES 2053[1] - **Palm** Sing. emph. *ḥmn*ʾ CIS ii 3917[3], 3978[2], Syr xxvi 45 ii 1, FS Collart 198[2], JSS xxxiii 171[1]; Plur. emph. *[ḥ]mny*ʾ Inv xii 24 - ¶ subst. m. prob. meaning incense altar or chapel with such an altar, this last meaning in CIS ii 3917[3], JSS xxxiii 171[1] and prob. FS Colart 198[2], in the other texts the context does not allow decision; for the litt., cf. Ingholt FS Dussaud 795ff., Dupont-Sommer AIPHOS xiii 149ff., Starcky Syr xxvi 52, 55ff., SOLDV ii 517 n. 2, Elliger ZAW lvii 256ff., ZDPV lxvi 129ff., du Mesnil du Buisson TMP 200f., Milik DFD 306f., 341, Gawlikowski TP 84f., DM i 65f., FS Collart 198ff., Galling FS Elliger 65ff., Weippert ZDPV xci 93f., Fritz BN xv 9ff., Dietrich & Loretz UF xiii 99f., Tubach ISS 178 (n. 141), Nielsen SVT xxxviii 45ff., Teixidor PP 67f., Garbini FSR 180, Drijvers JSS xxxiii 165ff. - Naveh IEJ xxix 113, 116: this subst. (Sing. emph. *ḥmn*ʾ) in IEJ xxix 112[3] (interpret. of context however uncert.).

ḥms **Samal** Sing. abs. *ḥms* KAI 214[26] (dam. context) - **OffAr** Sing. abs. *ḥms* Aḥiq 140 - ¶ subst. violence; in the expression *šhd ḥms* Aḥiq 140: a false witness, cf. Lindenberger APA 138, 261 n. 434.

ḥmṣ$_1$ **OffAr** QAL (?) Pf. 2 p.s.m. *ḥmṣt* Cowl 45[3]; 1 p.s. *ḥmṣ[t]* Cowl 45[4] (for the reading and interpret., cf. Porten RB xc 566, Porten & Yardeni sub TADAE B 7.1 (cf. also Grelot DAE p. 97) :: Cowl a.l.: l. *ḥm[ṣt]* = QAL Pf. 2 p.s.m.) - ¶ verb QAL (?) to steal, to rob; + *mn*$_5$ (from (someone)), cf. also Driver JRAS '32, 82, Krael p. 58 n. 22, Porten RB xc 565 :: Cowl a.l.: = to defraud.

ḥmṣ$_2$ **Hebr** Sing. abs. *ḥmṣ* TA-H 2[7] - ¶ subst. vinegar; for the context of TA-H 2[7], cf. Aharoni TA a.l., Levine Shn iii 289, Pardee UF x 299.

ḥmṣ$_3$ **OffAr** Plur. abs. *ḥmṣyn* EI xv 67*[1] (on the reading, cf. Cross EI a.l.) - ¶ subst. m. kind of small pea.

ḥmr$_1$ **OffAr** QAL Pf. 3 p.s.m. *ḥmr* Aḥiq 47 - ¶ verb QAL to be angry + *ʿl*$_7$ (with).

ḥmr$_2$ **Edom** m. Sing. abs. *ḥmr* TeAv xii 97[6] - **OffAr** Sing. m. abs. *ḥmyr*Cowl 21[7] - ¶ adj. (or QAL Part. pass. of *ḥmr* = to leaven?) leavened (× in Cowl 21[7] = subst. *ḥmyr*$_2$(= leaven), cf. Grelot VT xvii 203, 206); interpret. of TeAv 97[6] uncert., cf. Israel RivBib xxxv 342.
v. *bṣyr*$_1$.

ḥmr$_3$ **DA** Sing. abs. *ḥmr* i 12 (cf. Hoftijzer DA a.l., TUAT ii 143,

H.P.Müller ZAW xciv 218, 227 × e.g. Caquot & Lemaire Syr liv 200, McCarter BASOR ccxxxix 51, H. & M. Weippert ZDPV xcviii 97, 103, Weinfeld Shn v/vi 144ff., Puech FS Grelot 23, 28: = *ḥmr*$_5$; cf. also Rofé SB 67 (n. 32) :: Garbini Hen i 180, 185, Delcor SVT xxxii 58: = Sing. abs. of *ḥmr*$_8$ (= mud)? (cf. also Dahood Bibl lxii 126) :: Levine JAOS ci 197, 199: = Sing. abs. of *ḥmr*$_4$ used collectively) - **OffAr** Sing. cstr. *ḥmr* Aḥiq 104 (cf. Cowl a.l., Grelot DAE p. 438 :: Lindenberger APA 84, 86, 241 nn. 236, 237: l. *ḥmd* (= Sing. cstr. of *ḥmd*$_3$(= delight)), cf. Kottsieper SAS 12, 20, 76f., 203 :: Epstein OLZ '16, 207, Ginsberg ANET 429: = *ḥmr*$_9$ (= veil)) - ¶ subst. wrath; for the context of DA i 12, v. *šty*$_1$.
v. *ḥmr*$_5$.

ḥmr$_4$ **Hebr** m. Plur. abs. *ḥmrm* TA-H 3^{5} - **OffAr** m. Sing. abs. *ḥmr* Cowl 44^{8}, Aḥiq 90, MAI xiv/2, 66^{14}, TA-Ar 1^{2}, 2^{1}, 12^{1} (× Aharoni TA a.l.: or = Sing. abs. of *ḥmr*$_{10}$ (= donkey-driver)?)^{,3}, 21^{1} (dam. context), 23^{1}, 24^{1}, 25^{1} (diff. reading), 31^{1}, 37^{2}; cstr. *ḥmr* MAI xiv/2, 66^{13}; emph. *ḥmr*ʾ Aḥiq 91, 110; Plur. abs. *ḥmrn* Cowl 54^{5,11}, *ḥmryn* Cowl 81^{29}; f. Plur. abs. *ḥmrʾn* Cowl 81^{16} (cf. also Leand 45d); cf. Frah vii 5 (*ḥmrʾ*, *ḥmlʾ*), Paik 400 (*ḥmrʾ*), GIPP 52 - **Palm** m. Sing. abs. *ḥmr* CIS ii 3913 ii 21, 28, 33; emph. *ḥmrʾ* CIS ii 3913 ii 10, 37 - **JAr** m. Plur. abs. *ḥmryn* MPAT 60^{1} - ¶ subst. m. donkey, ass, f. she-ass.
v. *ḥmr*$_{3,5}$.

ḥmr$_5$ **Ph** Sing. cstr. *ḥmr* IEJ xviii 227A 2 (*[ḥ]mr*), B 2 - **Edom** (?) Sing. abs. *ḥmr* BASOR lxxx 8^{1,2} - **OffAr** Sing. abs. *ḥmr* Cowl 30^{21}, 31^{20}, 81^{119} (for the context, cf. Harmatta ActAntHung vii 374), Sem ii 31 conv. 2 (for the reading, cf. Rosenthal AH i/1, 13, Grelot DAE p. 370 :: Dupont-Sommer Sem ii 31, 38: l. *ḥm*ʾ = n.p.), Aḥiq 79 (cf. e.g. Perles OLZ '11, 500f., Cowl a.l., Gressmann ATAT 457, Grelot DAE p. 435, Kottsieper SAS 18, 203 × Nöldeke AGWG xiv/4, 10, Baneth OLZ '14, 296, Ginsberg ANET 428, Lindenberger APA 43f.: = *ḥmr*$_4$ :: Torczyner OLZ '12, 402: = Sing. cstr. of *ḥmr*$_3$;cf. also Grelot RB lxviii 180), Driv 6^{3}, Atlal vii 108 ii (for the diff. and dam. context, cf. also Beyer & Livingstone ZDMG cxxxvii 292), etc., etc.; cstr. *ḥmr* Cowl 72^{2,4,10,17}; emph. *ḥmrʾ* Cowl 81^{39}, Aḥiq 92, 93, 209, Driv 12^{5,6}, Sach 81 i 2 (dif. and dam. context); cf. Frah v 5 (*ḥmlʾ*), Nisa 12, 13, 17^{2}, 19^{2}, 21^{2}, 41^{1}, 43^{1}, 44^{4}, 45^{3}, etc. (*ḥmr*), Nisa 17^{3}, 18^{3}, 20^{3}, 21^{3}, 22^{3}, 25^{2}, 26^{2}, 27^{2}, etc. (*ḥ*, abbrev.), GIPP 23, 52, SaSt 17 - **Palm** Sing. abs. *ḥmr* CIS ii 3973^{5}, RIP 199^{12}, Syr vii 129^{5}, RTP 39, 526, 541, 694, etc., etc.; emph. *ḥmrʾ* CIS ii 3913 ii 59, Syr vii 129^{4}, RTP 706 - ¶ subst. m. wine; *lšyʿʾlqwm ʾlhʾ ṭbʾ ... dy lʾ štʾ ḥmr* CIS ii 3973$^{4f.}$: to Sh. the good god ... who does not drink wine (cf. e.g. Hoftijzer RelAr 41, Milik DFD 211ff.); *ḥmrʾ ʿtyqʾ* Syr vii 129^{4}: matured wine; *ḥmr ṣydn* Cowl 72^{2}: wine from Sidon (cf. Cowl 72^{10,17}); *ḥmr mṣryn* Cowl 72^{4}: Egyptian

wine; *[ḥ]mr gt krml* IEJ xviii 227A 2: wine from G.-K. (cf. also *ḥmr yn gt kr[ml]* IEJ xviii 227B 2; v. also *yyn*) - abbrev. *ḥ*, v. supra sub Nisa; the same abbreviation poss. in Kition D 14[1], cf. Puech Sem xxix 36 - Sing. emph. (*ḥmrh*) poss. in J.Ar. text SM 88[19] (= Syn D B 4 = Frey 828b), heavily dam. context, cf. Naveh SM a.l. :: Obermann Ber vii 113, 116: l. *ḥmlh* (Sing. abs.) = mercifulness :: Torrey Syn 263f.: l. *ḥmydt* = Sing. cstr. of *ḥmydh*(= eager desire) - Garbini AION xxv 434f.: l. *ḥmr* (Sing. abs.) in BMB xxvi 46 (uncert. reading) :: v.d.Branden with Kaoukabani BMB xxvi 46 (div. otherwise): l. *ḥṣ* = Sing. cstr. of $ḥṣ_6$ (= basin) - on this word, cf. Delcor APCI 230f.
v. $ḥmr_{3,6}$.

ḥmr₆ **Hebr** Sing. abs. *ḥmr* TA-H 2[5] (cf. Aharoni TA a.l., Pardee UF x 297f. :: Lemaire IH i p. 162, Or lii 446, Delavault & Lemaire RSF vii 15, Pardee UF x 298 n. 48, Hospers SV 103f.: = $ḥmr_5$(on this interpret., cf. Cathcart VT xxix 247) :: Dahood Or xlvi 330: = $ḥmr_{11}$ (= wine-vat); cf. also Pardee UF x 298: or = $ḥmr_{11}$?, *ḥmr yyn* = *ḥomer*-wine, different from *bat*-wine, a different grade of wine kept in a different sized container) - **OffAr** Sing. abs. *ḥmr* ATNS 24[6] (dam. context, uncert. reading, cf. Shaked Or lvi 409L l. poss. *lp* + numerical sign), MAI xiv/2, 66[5] - ¶ subst. certain measure of capacity, *ḥomer* - **1)** a dry measure: MAI xiv/2, 66[5] (grain) - **2)** a wet measure: TA-H 2[5] (for wine; cf. Aharoni TA a.l.) - Segal ATNS a.l.: the *ḥ*in ATNS 69a prob. = abbrev. of $ḥmr_6$ (as a wet measure); the *ḥ* in ATNS 51[1] also abbrev. of $ḥmr_6$?? (Segal ATNS a.l.: = abbrev. of *ḥlr*)- the same abbrev. poss. in IEJ xxxv 19[3] (dam. context) - cf. also Barrois ii 247ff., Trinquet SDB v 1222ff., EM iv 852ff., Scott BiAr xxii 31f. - Naveh BASOR cxxxix 76: l. this noun (Sing. abs. *ḥmr*) in CIS ii 102[2] (poss. reading :: Herr sub SANSS-Ar 7 (div. otherwise): l. *ḥmdṣry* (= n.p.)).
v. $qšr_1$.

ḥmr₇ **Hatra** Sing. emph. *ḥmr*ʾ 35[2] (for the reading and interpret., cf. Aggoula Ber xviii 92 (cf. also Vattioni IH a.l.) :: Safar Sumer viii 190 (n. 30): l. a) *ḥmr*ʾ = Sing. emph. of $ḥmr_{10}$ (= donkey-driver, owner of donkeys, letter of donkeys) or b) *ḥmd*ʾ = Qal Part. pass. s.m. emph. of $ḥmd_1$(= the desired one (surname); cf. Donner sub KAI 249) :: Caquot Syr xxx 240f.: l. *ḥmd*ʾ = n.p.) - ¶ subst. wine-merchant.

ḥmr₈ **Palm** Plur. abs. *ḥmryn* MUSJ xxxviii 106[11] - ¶ subst. indicating certain type of building material, Plur. clay (?, cf. Ingholt MUSJ xxxviii 117).
v. $ḥmr_3$.

ḥmr₉ v. $ḥmr_3$.

ḥmr₁₀ **JAr** Plur. emph. *ḥmry*ʾ Mas 556[5] (diff. and dam. context) - ¶ subst. donkey-driver.
v. $ḥmr_{4,7}$.

ḥmr$_{11}$ v. *ḥmr*$_6$.

ḥmr$_{12}$ **OffAr** Bordreuil & Pardee Syr lxii 174: l. *ḥmr* (= Sing. abs. of *ḥmr*$_{12}$ (= seal)) in CIS ii 102 (poss. interpret.).
v. *ḥmd*$_2$.

ḥmš$_1$ v. *ḥmšm*.

ḥmš$_2$ **Ph** m. abs. *ḥmš* Mus li 286[8], RES 1504 (or = *ḥmš*$_3$?, cf. Chabot RES a.l., cf. also Bron & Lemaire CISFP i 766: or l. *ḥmš[t]*?); f. abs. *ḥmšt* Mus li 286[4] - **Pun** m. abs. *ḥmš* KAI 120[1], NP 66[3], 67[4] (= Punica ivA 7), Hofra 57[3], 64[1f.], Trip 51[5] (or cstr.?, diff. context), etc., *ʿmš* KAI 112[3f.], 135[4], 157[3], 169[4], NP 13[2] (= Punica xii 18b), 22[4] (= Punica xi 1), 23[5] (= Punica xi 2), 55[2f.] (= Punica xii 23), Karth x 133[3], Sem xxxvi 33[3], etc., etc.; f. abs. *ḥmšt* KAI 69[5], 76B 10 (dam. context) - **Hebr** m. abs. *ḥmš* Qadm v 46 (on jars; diff. interpret., cf. also Yeivin a.l.), Dir pes. 21 (or = *ḥmš*$_3$?; cf. Dir p. 282, Trinquet SDB v 1248, Scott BiAr xxii 38, BASOR clxxiii 54 (n. 3), I.T.Kaufman BASOR clxxxviii 39, Bron & Lemaire CISFP i 768; cf. for litt. Delavault & Lemaire RSF vii 31), SM 51[1] (dam. context), DJD ii 24E 10; cstr. (or abs.?) *ḥmš* DJD ii 24D 10, 30[14]; f. cstr. *ḥmšt* DJD ii 44[2] - **OffAr** m. abs. *ḥmš* IEJ xxv 118[3] (for script and language, cf. Naveh ibid. 120ff.); f. abs. *ḥmšh* Cowl 26[11,12,14,15,16], 65 vii 2, Krael 4[15]; cstr. *ḥmšt* CIS ii 1b, 2b (for the reading, cf. Degen NESE iii 11ff., GGA '79, 27 n. 54, 30 :: e.g. CIS ii a.l. and litt. mentioned with Degen NESE iii 11f.: l. *ḥmšʾ* = f. abs. :: Vattioni Aug xi 175: l. *ḥmšh* = f. abs.), Cowl 81[83] (*ḥmšt[*, on the context, cf. also Harmatta ActAntHung xxii 367f.: poss. = f. form of *ḥmšy* (= pentagonal)); cf. Frah xxix 5 (*ḥwmš(y)ʾ*, cf. Nyberg FP 57, 108 :: Ebeling Frah a.l.: l. *ḥʿmšyʾ*) - **Nab** m. abs. *ḥmš* CIS ii 183[2], 200[9], 206[9], 209[8], 1325[2], ARNA-Nab 16[2], DBKP 22[33], etc., on coins: cf. Meshorer NC no. 22 - **Palm** m. abs. *ḥmš* CIS ii 4053[4], 4173[1], 4174[8], 4199[14], Inscr P 32[4], MUSJ xxxviii 106[1], Sem xxxvi 89[5,7]; cstr. *ḥmš* MUSJ xxxviii 106[1], Sem xxxvi 89[4]; f. abs. *ḥmšʾ* CIS ii 3983[1] (= SBS 13), RB xxxix 532[3], Ber ii 107[1], SBS 18[1]; emph. *ḥmštʾ* Ber v 95[1] - **JAr** m. abs. *ḥmš* Mas 571[3]; cstr. *ḥmš* MPAT-A 52[7] (or abs.?), Syn D A 2 (= SM 88), C_1 1 (= SM 89A), C_2 1 (= SM 89B), DBKP 21 back; f. abs. *ḥmšh* MPAT 36[2], Mas 554[2], *ḥmyšh*MPAT-A 26[8] (= Frey 856 = SM 32) - ¶ cardinal number, five, passim; cf. the following constructions: *byrḥ ʾyr ywm ḥmštʾ* Ber v 95[1]: the fifth day in the month I.; *bḥmš lyrḥ* Hofra 64[1f.]: on the fifth of the month (cf. Hofra 57[3], 63[3f.] (= KAI 112)); *šnt ḥmš mʾh wʿšryn wḥmš* MUSJ xxxviii 106[1]: (in) the year five hundred and twenty five; *šnt tltyn wḥmš lḥrtt* CIS ii 206[9], ARNA-Nab 16[2]: the thirty-fifth year of Ch. (cf. CIS ii 1325[2], 4053[4f.], 4173[1], ADAJ xx 121[2f.], MPAT 149[2f.], SM 88[2] (= Syn D A), 89A 1f. (= Syn D C_1), B 1f. (= Syn D C_2), etc.); *bḥmš lmlky* RES 337[3]: in the fifth (year) of his reign; *šnt ʾrbʿ mʾh wtltyn wḥmš šnyn lḥrbn byt mqdšh* MPAT-A 52[5ff.]: the

year four hundred and thirty five of the years after the destruction of the Temple; *[tḥ]t mšlt ˓sr hmšlm p˓m˒t ˓sr wḥmš* KAI 120[1]: tribune of the people for the fifteenth time (cf. Lat. par. *trib(unic ia) pot(estate) xv*) - Beyer ATTM 372: l. poss. *ḥmš* (= m. abs.) in AMB 7[8f.] (improb. reading and interpret., cf. also Naveh & Shaked AMB a.l.) - Milik DFD 147: l. *ḥmš˒* (f.) in Inv x 13[7] (uncert. reading, cf. Starcky Inv x a.l.: l. *[ḥm]š*) - Segal ATNS a.l.: l. *ḥmšt* in ATNS 64b 7 = form of *ḥmš₂* (uncert. interpret.; = Sing. abs. of *ḥmšt* (= group of five??)).
v. *ḥmšm*.

ḥmš₃ **OffAr** Sing. abs. *ḥmš* CIS ii 12 - **JAr** Sing. abs. *ḥmš* MPAT 39[6] - ¶ subst. fifth part; for MPAT 39[6], cf. Koffmahn DJW 85f.
v. *ḥmš₂*.

ḥmšy **Pun** Sing. m. abs. *ḥmšy* KAI 76B 7 - **Hebr** Sing. m. abs. *ḥmyšy*SM 106[2] - **JAr** Sing. f. emph. *ḥmyšyt˒*IEJ xl 135[2] (on the context, cf. Yardeni IEJ xl 137) - ¶ ordinal number, fifth.
v. *ḥmš₂*.

ḥmšyn v. *ḥmšm*.

ḥmšm **Ph** *ḥmšm* KAI 19[8], Mus li 286[4,7] - **Pun** *ḥmšm* KAI 69[6], 101[4], 112[4], 130[3], NP 130[4], etc., *˓mšm* KAI 140[7], 165[7], RES 173[2], *˓mš* Karth x 133[3] (*˓mš w˓mš* lapsus for *˓mšm w˓mš*?, cf. Février Karth x a.l., Fantar Sem xxv 73 :: Garbini AION xxv 263f.: *˓mš w˓mš* = five and five) - **Mo** *ḥmšn* KAI 181[28] (cf. e.g. Cooke NSI p. 3, Röllig KAI a.l., Segert ArchOr xxix 223, 260, Andersen Or xxxv 91, Gibson SSI i p. 77 :: de Moor UF xx 155 (n. 18): = indication of units of fifty men :: Lipiński Or xl 339: = in battle array (= Qal Part. pass.m. pl. abs. of *ḥmš₁*(= to array for battle)), cf. also Smelik HDAI 35) - **OffAr** *ḥmšn* Cowl 26[14,15] - **Nab** *ḥmšyn* BAGN ii 88[6] - **Palm** *ḥmšyn* Inscr P 32[4], Sem xxxvi 89[4] - **JAr** *ḥmšyn*Syn D A 2, 9 (= SM 88), C_1 2 (= SM 89A), C_2 2 (= SM 89B; diff. reading, cf. also Naveh SM a.l.), Mas 571[2] - ¶ cardinal number, fifty, passim; cf. the following constructions: *bššt ḥmšm št lmlknm* KAI 112[4f.]: in the fifty-sixth year of their reign; *byrḥ ˒b šnt m˒tyn wḥmšyn w˒ḥdy* BAGN 88[5ff.]: in the month Ab (in) the year two hundred and fifty one; *bšnt ḥmš m˒h ḥmšyn wšyt* Syn D A 2f. (= SM 88): in the year five hundred and fifty six; cf. KAI 19[8], Inscr P 32[4] (= Inv ix 29) - Levi Della Vida FS Friedrich 309 n. 15: l. *ḥmšm* in the Pun. text KAI 127[4] (= BASOR lxxxvii 31 = IRT 294).

ḥmšn v. *ḥmšm*.

ḥmšt v. *ḥmš₂*.

ḥmt v.Soden AfO xix 149, Or xxxv 9, xlvi 186: *ḥmt* = to be angry > Akkad. *gummutu*, cf. also idem AHW s.v. (uncert. interpret.).

ḥn₁ **Ph** Sing. abs. *ḥn* KAI 10[10], 48[4]; + suff. 1 p.s. *ḥny* KAI 43[13] - **OldAr** Sing. + suff. 1 p.s. *ḥny* KAI 217[8] - **OffAr** Sing. cstr. *ḥn* Aḥiq 132 -

subst. - **1)** favour; *ḥn lʿn ʾlnm* KAI 10[10]: favour in the sight of the gods (cf. KAI 48[4]) - **2)** (quality) which procures favour; *ḥn gbr hymnwth* Aḥiq 132: the quality of a man which procures him favour is his trustworthiness; cf. also *mnḥt ḥny* KAI 43[13]: the gift which procures favour for me (for other interpret. of this diff. text, cf. Honeyman JEA xxvi 64, cf. also Gibson SSI iii p. 141) - for this word, cf. also Willi-Plein VT xxiii 95f. - a form of this word poss. also in KAI 145[10] (Sing. abs.; diff. context), cf. Février Sem vi 25f., cf. however v.d.Branden RSF i 166, 171 (div. otherwise): l. *ʾḥn* = Dual + suff. 1 p.pl. of *ʾḥ*₁; Krahmalkov RSF iii 188f., 197 (div. otherwise): l. *mḥnytn* (v. *ytn*₁; improb. interpret.) :: Halévy RS ix 282f., 285 (div. otherwise): l. *lʾnḥn* = n.p. - Bordreuil Syr lxv a.l.: the *ḥnt* on a seal (Syr lxv 443) = Plur. cstr. of *ḥn*₁ (highly uncert. interpret.).
v. *ʿn*₃.

ḥn₂ **OffAr** Plur. abs. *ḥnn* Cowl 26[11,14]; emph. *ḥnnyʾ* Cowl 26[19] (for the form, cf. Leand 52b) - ¶ subst. m. of uncert. meaning, prob. indicating some kind of beam, cf. Grelot DAE p. 290 n. y :: Kaufman AIA 56: = ship's cabin (for other litt., cf. Cowl p. 95; v. also *ḥnh* sub *ʾḥd*₄); on the subject, cf. also Sprengling AJT xxi 431 n. 1.

ḥn₃ Ebeling Frah a.l.: l. *ḥn* in Frah x 37: vagina (improb. interpret., cf. Nyberg FP 45, 77f.: l. Iran. word).

ḥn₄ cf. Paik 401: until, till, Syr xxxv 317[42]: as far as (cf. GIPP 52).

ḥnʾ₁ **Samal** QAL Pf. 1 p.s. *ḥnʾt* KAI 214[19]; PA ʿEL (cf. Friedr 26*, Dion p. 211) Pf. 3 p.s.m. + suff. 3 p.s.m. *ḥnʾh* KAI 215[12] (for both forms, cf. Dion p. 212f., Gibson SSI ii p. 73) - **Palm** QAL Impf. 3 p.s.m. *yḥnʾ* RTP 154 (cf. Caquot RTP p. 144) - ¶ verb QAL - **1)** to repose, to find rest: KAI 214[19] (cf. e.g. Cooke NSI p. 162, 168, Dion p. 31, Gibson SSI ii p. 67, 73 :: Poeb 46 n. 6, 47: = *ḥnʾ*₂ (= to cohabitate) :: Koopmans 37: or = *ḥnʾ*₃ (= to treat kindly)) - **2)** to reside; *ʿglbwl yḥnʾ* RTP 154: may A. reside(?) - PA ʿEL to place, to position; *wḥnʾh mrʾh mlk ʾšwr ʿl mlky* KAI 215[12]: and his lord the king of Assur positioned him over kings.
v. *mḥnh*

ḥnʾ₂ v. *ḥnʾ*₁.

ḥnʾ₃ v. *ḥnʾ*₁.

ḥnb v. *ḥlb*₅.

ḥngr = dagger > Akkad., cf. v.Soden Or xlvi 187 (cf. however CAD s.v. *ḫangaruakku*), cf. also Zadok WO xii 199.

ḥndw **OffAr**, cf. Nisa-b 257[2] (*ḥndwtʾ*; cf. GIPP 52): certain type of jar/vessel (cf. also Diakonov & Livshitz Nisa-b p. 39f.).

ḥndsyrm v. *knzsrm*.

ḥnh₁ **Pun** Sing. abs. *ḥnt* CIS i 151[5] (:: Février JA ccxlvi 445, Amadasi sub ICO-Sard-NPu 2 (div. otherwise): l. *tḥnt* (= Sing. abs. of *tḥnh* (=

favour)) :: Pili BO xxii 214, 217 (div. otherwise): l. *mtn* (= Sing. abs. of *mtn*$_2$) :: CIS i a.l.: l. *tḥkt* (without interpret.)) - ¶ subst. favour; *ʿbdʾ ... lm t ḥnt* CIS i 151[5]: they have done him a favour.

ḥnh$_2$ v. *ʾḥd*$_4$.

ḥnwṭ **Ph** Plur. abs. *ḥnwṭm* KAI 12[1] - **Pun** Plur. abs. *ḥnwṭm* KAI 64[1] - ¶ subst. m. of uncert. meaning; Renan sub CIS i 139: < Greek χωνευτά = molten images (cf. also Slouschz TPI p. 133f.); Dussaud Syr vi 273: = incense altar (for both interpret., cf. however Lidzbarski OLZ '27, 457f.; cf. CIS i sub 139 for other interpret., cf. also Amadasi sub ICO-Sard-Pu 23).

ḥnwkh v. *ḥnkh*.

ḥnwt **Nab** Plur. emph. *ḥnwtʾ* MPAT 64 i 12, iii 5 - **Palm** Sing. emph. *ḥnwtʾ* CIS ii 3913 ii 55 (Greek par. ἐργαστηρίων) - ¶ subst. f. shop -> Akkad. *ḫanūtu*, cf. v.Soden Or xxxv 9, xlvi 187 (cf. idem AHW s.v. *kibānu*) - Beyer ATTM 329, 582: l. *ḥnw* (= Sing. abs.) in MPAT 89[4] (highly uncert. reading and interpret.; cf. Avigad IEJ xvii 105: l. poss. *ḥny* = n.p., cf. also Fitzmyer & Harrington MPAT a.l.).

ḥnṭh v. *ḥṭh*.

ḥny **Hatra** Segal Irâq xxix 9 n. 28: l. *bdr* (v. *bdr*$_2$)*ḥny* (= form of this root: he attends) in app. 4[5] (improb. interpret.; cf. Safar Sumer xvii 38 (n. 93), 40, Caquot Syr xl 12f., Teixidor Syr xli 273, Milik DFD 394f., Aggoula Sem xxvii 138, Vattioni IH a.l.: l. *br* (= Sing. cstr. of *br*$_1$) + n.p. (*d/rḥny*).

v. *ḥnn*$_1$.

ḥnyʾh **Nab** CIS ii 1578, 2556[2], unexplained: = n.p.?

ḥnynh **Hebr** Sing. abs. *ḥnynh* Frey 634[6] - ¶ subst. grace; *tmṣʾ pny ʾl ḥnynh* Frey 634[5f.]: may she find grace with God.

ḥnyṣ **DA** Sing. abs. *ḥnyṣ* i 17 - ¶ subst. young pig.

ḥnk$_1$ **Pun** QAL Pf. 3 p.s.m. *ʾnk* BAr-NS i/ii 228[2] (?, cf. Garbini AION xxv 260f. :: Février BAr a.l. = *ʾnk*)- **Palm** QAL Pf. 3 p.s.m. *ḥnk* Syr xiv 171[4] - ¶ verb QAL to dedicate, to consecrate; + obj.: BAr-NS i/ii 228[2f.], Syr xiv 171[4] (*ḥnk hyklʾ dy bl*, he consecrated the temple of Bel).

v. *šnh*$_2$.

ḥnk$_2$ **OffAr** Sing. + suff. 3 p.s.m. *ḥnkh* Aḥiq 115 - ¶ subst. palate; *yšymwn ṭb bḥnkh lmʾmr* Aḥiq 115: they will put something good in his palate to speak (for the "palate" as an indication of the organ of speech, cf. also Lindenberger APA 103).

ḥnk$_3$ v. *ḥlb*$_5$.

ḥnkh **Hebr** Sing. abs. *ḥnwkh* SM 49[3]- **Palm** Sing. emph. *ḥnktʾ* RTP 93 - ¶ subst. - **1)** dedication, consecration: RTP 93 - **2)** *Chanukka*-festival: SM 49[3].

ḥnkt v. *hnkt*.

ḥnm **Pun** *ḥnm* CIS i 5522[4] (cf. Février Sem iv 15, CIS i a.l. ::

v.d.Branden BiOr xxiii 144: = QAL Pf. 3 p.s.m. + suff. 3 p.pl.m. of *ḥnn*$_1$ (= to favour, to bestow a favour on), cf. also idem GP § 243) - ¶ adv. gratuitously, without payment.
v. *ywm*.

ḥnmy› **OffAr** Cowl 75^{2}; word(s) of unknown meaning; Cowl a.l.: *wḥnmy›* = n.p.?; CIS ii sub 150: l. *ḥn my›* = *propitatio aquarum* (poss. referring to the offering of water to the deceased by Osiris).

ḥnn$_1$ **Ph** NIPH Part. s.m. abs. *nḥn* KAI 14^{12} (cf. e.g. Cooke NSI p. 36, Röllig KAI a.l., FR 164, Avishur PIB 195, Gibson SSI iii p. 111, Butterweck TUAT ii 592 :: Dahood UHP 66, Bibl lx 431: = QAL Part. act. s.m. abs. of *nḥn*$_1$ (= to groan) :: Rosenthal ANET 662 n. 2: = *nḥn*$_2$ (= *›nḥn*$_1$)?,placed here wrongly, the text being out of order?) - **Pun** QAL Impf. 3 p.s.f. + suff. 3 p.s.m. *tḥn›* CIS i 196^{5} - ¶ verb QAL + obj., to be benevolent, merciful towards someone: CIS i 196^{5} - NIPH to be pitied; Part. pitiable :: Poeb 20 n. 1: = favoured one, favorite - Grelot RB lxviii 182, DAE 436 n. i: l. *[ḥ]nynw* (= QAL pass. Pf. 3 p.pl.m.) = to be favoured, in Aḥiq 94 (cf. Lindenberger APA 68, Kottsieper SAS 19, 203; cf. also Cowl a.l.: l. *...]ynw* - Lemaire & Durand IAS 117, 126: l. a form of this root (*ḥnnt* = QAL Pf. 2 p.s.m.) in KAI 223A 13 (less prob. reading) - a form of this root in the diff. text PF 2043^{3} (*ytḥnwn*)?, or to be derived from root *ḥny,tḥn*?? - the *ḥnn* in KA 9B 1 prob. = n.p. (cf. Scagliarini RSO lxiii 208f. :: e.g. Hadley VT xxxvii 188: *ḥnn* = form of *ḥnn*$_1$).
v. *ḥnm,ḥnn*$_3$.

ḥnn$_2$ **Hatra** Aggoula MUSJ xlvii 20: *ḥnn›* in 258^{1} = Sing. emph. of *ḥnn*$_2$ (= pity, compassion), diff. context (cf. Degen JEOL xxiii 415, Vattioni IH a.l.: *ḥnn›* = n.p.).

ḥnn$_3$ **Palm** Sing. m. emph. *ḥnn›* CIS ii 4084^{2} (cf. Cantineau Gramm 108) - ¶ adj. clement, merciful - Cross FS Glueck 302, 306 n. 15, Lemaire RB lxxxiii 560, 566, Miller SVT xxxii 328ff. (n. 38), cf. also Conrad TUAT ii 560: l. *ḥnn*$_3$ (Sing. abs.) in SSI i 58B (uncert. reading; cf. Naveh IEJ xiii 85f.: l. *ḥnnt* = POL Pf. 2 p.s.m. of *ḥnn*$_1$(= to favour), cf. also Gibson SSI i a.l.

ḥnpw **Palm** Milik DFD 301f.: l. prob. *ḥn[pwt›]* (= Sing. emph. (= impiety)) in Syr xvii 353^{7} (poss. reading; cf. however Gawlikowski TP 57f.: l. *ḥr[...*?).

ḥnq **Ph** QAL Part. act. s.f. abs. *ḥnqt* KAI 27^{4} (cf. Dupont-Sommer RHR cxx 134, 137 × du Mesnil du Buisson FS Dussaud 424, 426, Albright BASOR lxxvi 8, Gaster Or xi 44, 51, Röllig KAI a.l., Zevit IEJ xxvii 111, 114, de Moor JEOL xxvii 108, Gibson SSI iii p. 83ff.: = QAL Part. act. s.f. cstr. × Torczyner JNES vi 21, 28, Rosenthal ANET 658, Lipiński RTAT 265, Garbini OA xx 283, Sperling HUCA liii 3, 5f.: = QAL Part. act. pl.f. abs. (cf. also Caquot FS Gaster 47: or = s.f.?) ×

Cross & Saley BASOR cxcvii 45, Avishur PIB 248, 251: = QAL Part. act. pl.f. cstr. (cf. also Röllig NESE ii 21: or = s.f.?) - ¶ verb QAL to strangle; *lḥnqt ʾmr* KAI 27[4f.]: oh strangler(s) of lamb(s) (v. supra and v. *ʾmr*$_3$; cf. also Butterweck TUAT ii 436) × say to the strangler(s) (v. supra and v. *ʾmr*$_3$). For the first solution, cf. Gaster Or xi 51f.

ḥnt$_1$ **OffAr** Sing. abs. *ḥnt* Aḥiq 83 (cf. e.g. Cowl a.l., Lindenberger APA 53 :: Krael p. 144: *lḥnt* = haplography for *llḥnt* = *l*$_5$ + Sing. f. abs. of *lḥn*$_2$ (cf. also e.g. Couroyer VT v 87f., Torrey JNES xiii 151)); emph. *ḥntʾ* RES 492B 1 (cf. Driver AnOr xii 57, cf. however Grelot DAE p. 140 n. n: = Sing. emph. of *ḥnt*$_3$ (= leather bag)); this word also in CIS ii 139A 2?? - ¶ subst. f. servant-girl, female slave (:: Lidzbarski Eph ii 238: *ḥntʾ* in RES 492B 1 indicates a transportable object) - for this word, cf. also Muraoka JSS xxxii 187 and on the etymology Lindenberger APA 227 n. 59.

ḥnt$_2$ v. *pḥnt*.

ḥnt$_3$ v. *ḥnt*$_1$.

ḥs$_1$ v. *ḥsyn*$_1$.

ḥs$_2$ **OffAr** Gignoux GIPP 23: l. ideogram *ḥs* (= wine) in Frah v 4, cf. however Nyberg FP 43, 68: = Iran. word.

ḥsg v. *šḥsgm*.

ḥsd **JAr** Sing. abs. *ḥsd* MPAT-A 13[4] - ¶ subst. piety.
v. *dm*$_1$.

ḥsy$_1$ **Palm** PAʿEL Pf. 3 p.s.m. *ḥsy* Syr xiv 177[3] - ¶ verb PAʿEL to consecrate; *ḥsy mn kysh* Syr xiv 177[3]: he has consecrated from his purse (i.e. at his own cost).

ḥsy$_2$ **OffAr** Plur. m. abs. *ḥsyn* KAI 279[7] - ¶ adj. pious, religious (cf. Dupont-Sommer JA ccxlvi 31f., Altheim GH ii 175, Garbini Kand 17, Donner KAI a.l., Kutscher, Naveh & Shaked Lesh xxxiv 136 :: Altheim & Stiehl EW ix 197, GH i 406, Levi Della Vida Editto 28, 34, Rosenthal EI xiv 98*: *ḥsyn* = *ḥsn*$_6$ (= strong; cf. however Altheim & Stiehl EW x 246, ASA 29f., 270).
v. *ḥsyh*.

ḥsy$_3$ v. *ḥsyh*.

ḥsyd **Pun** Sing. m. abs. *ḥsyd* KAI 145[7] - ¶ adj. prob. meaning, pious, kind.

ḥsyh (< Egypt.) - **OffAr** Plur. *ḥsyh* KAI 269[4] (cf. e.g. Cooke NSI p. 206, Lévy JA ccxi 282, 289f., Donner KAI a.l., Grelot Sem xx 21f., Lipiński OLP viii 109f., 114f. :: Grelot Sem xvii 73f., DAE p. 342: l. *ḥsyh[y]* = *ḥsy*$_3$(= *ḥsyh*) + suff. 3 p.s.m., cf. also Gibson SSI ii p. 121f. :: Rosenthal AH i/2, 10: = Plur. emph. of *ḥsy*$_2$, cf. Koopmans 169: = form of *ḥsy*$_2$,cf. also Degen ZDMG cxxi 137: = form of *ḥsy*$_2$,but *ḥsy*$_2$= *ḥsy*$_3$< Egypt.) - ¶ subst. Plur. the favoured ones, the beatified; for the context, cf. Couroyer Sem xx 18).

ḥsyn$_1$ **OffAr** Sing. m. abs. *ḥsyn* Cowl 26[13], Aḥiq 79, 105 (cf. Cowl a.l., Grelot RB lxviii 184, DAE p. 438, Kottsieper SAS 74, 204 × Perles OLZ '12, 56, Rosenthal AH i/2, 10: *ḥsyn* = Plur. abs. of *ḥs*$_1$(= bitter lettuce) :: Ginsberg ANET 429 (n. 12): = *ḥsyn*$_2$ (= endives); cf. also Lindenberger APA 89f., 281, Watson AO ii 255 (n. 20)); f. abs. *ḥsynh* Aḥiq 159 (for the dam. context, cf. Lindenberger APA 159f., 266 nn. 481-487) - **JAr** Sing. m. emph. *ḥsynh* AMB 7[15] - **Waw** Sing. emph. *ḥsyn*ʾ AMB 6[2] - ¶ adj. strong, mighty; *ʾlh rbh ḥsynh wdḥylh* AMB 7[15]: mighty, strong and terrifying God (cf. AMB 6[1f.]); *ʿqy ʾrz ... ḥsyn* Cowl 26[13]: planks of strong cedar-wood; *m[h] ḥsyn hw mn ḥmr* Aḥiq 79: what is stronger than wine (v. however *ḥmr*$_5$, for the context, cf. also Lindenberger APA 44f., 221f. nn. 8-14); said of certain kind of fruit (v. *zʿrrh*) with bitter taste Aḥiq 105: strong (said of taste), v. however supra.

ḥsyn$_2$ v. *ḥsyn*$_1$.

ḥsyn$_3$ v. *ḥsn*$_6$.

ḥsyr v. *ḥsr*$_2$.

ḥsyrh v. *ḥsr*$_2$.

ḥsk **Palm** Qal Pf. 3 p.s.m. *ḥsk* CIS ii 3932[5]; + suff. 3 p.pl.m. *ḥsknwn* CIS ii 3948[3] - ¶ verb Qal to save (sc. expenses); *wḥsk rzʾyn šgyʾyn* CIS ii 3932[5]: he spared (others) from many expenses (i.e. he spent money in a most generous way, cf. Greek par. οὐκ ὀλίγων ἀφειδήσαντα χρημάτων, spending lavishly no small sums); *ḥsknwn ... dnryn dy dhb ...* CIS ii 3948[3]: he saved them ... *denarii* of gold ... - cf. *ḥšk*$_1$.

ḥsl$_1$ **OldCan** (:: Böhl 37o: not a Canaanite gloss) Qal stat./pass. 3 p.pl. *ḫa-sí-lu* (cf. Rainey EA p. 72) EA 263[13] - ¶ verb Qal (pass.; v. supra) to be brought to an end, to be extinguished (cf. Held FS Landsberger 399ff.).

v. *ʾṣl*$_2$,*ḥsn*$_2$.

ḥsl$_2$ = weaned > Akkad., cf. v.Soden Or xxxv 11, xlvi 187 (cf. also idem AHW s.v. *ḫeslu*, CAD s.v. *ḫislu*).

ḥsn$_1$ **OffAr** Haph Pf. 3 p.s.m. *hḥsn* Cowl 20[7], ATNS 1[9], Samar 3[4]; Impf. 3 p.s.m. *yhḥsn* Driv 8[5]; 2 p.s.f. *thḥsn* Samar 2[9] (lapsus for *thḥsnn*?, dam. context); 1 p.s. *ʾhḥsn* Driv 8[3]; 1 p.pl. *nhḥsn* Cowl 28[14]; Imper. s.f. + suff. 3 p.s.m. *hḥsnhy* Cowl 8[26]; Inf. + suff. 3 p.s.m. *hḥsnwth* Cowl 44[7] (*[h]ḥsnwth*), 65 iii 3 (*hḥsnw[th]*, for the reading and context, cf. Porten & Yardeni sub TADAE B 5.2); Part. s.m. abs. *mhḥsn* Cowl 7[2], 8[2], 16[2], Krael 12[5], Driv 8[2], KAI 278[3] (with f. subject), ATNS 4[5] (for this reading, cf. Naveh IEJ xxxv 211, Shaked Or lvi 408 :: Segal ATNS a.l.: l. *mhṣdn* = Haph Part. s.m. abs. of *ṣdn* (= to manumit)), 10a 2 (*mhḥsn[]*), 75a 1, 151[2] (heavily dam. context), 169 (id.), OMRO lxviii 45[4], Samar 7[9] (heavily dam. context); pl.m. abs. *mhḥsnn* Cowl 26[3], 80[5] (for the reading cf. Porten & Yardeni sub TADAE A 5.5), ATNS

3[5]; cf. Frah xxi 3 (*yḥsnn*), Paik 383 (*hḥsn, hḥsnw, yḥsn, yḥsnwn*), 477 (*yḥsnwn*), Syr xxxv 327[61], Syn 313[3], GIPP 37, 52, SaSt 25 (cf. also Lemosíin AO ii 267, 269f.) - ¶ verb HAPH - **1)** to take possession of: Driv 8[3,5] (said of a fief for which one has to pay land-tax), ATNS 1[9] (said of villages); for ATNS 3[5], v. *hmkrygrb*; + obj., *wgbr ḥlqh nhḥsn* Cowl 28[14]: and we will each take possession of his share (sc. of his inheritance); *spr› zk ›nh yhbth lky ›nty hḥsnhy* Cowl 8[25f.]: I give this document to you, take it in your possession; + *qdm*₅ (in the presence of): Samar 3[4] - **2)** to have in possession, to be in possession of, to keep in possession: Driv 8[2] (said of a fief, for which one has to pay land-tax); *kršy qryt› zy mhḥsn kbbh* KAI 278[1ff.]: K. the town (v. *qryh*) which Kubaba possesses (sc. as overlord); *whw hḥsn wl› htyb lh* Cowl 20[7]: and he kept possession and did not return (them) to him; *spynt› zy mhḥsnn ›[nḥ]nh* Cowl 26[3]: the boat of which we have charge (on this text, cf. Sprengling AJT xxi 418 n. 2); + *l*₅ (obj.), *[znh ḥ]ql› [dg]ln mhḥsn lh* Cowl 16[2]: our detachment had this field in his possession (had it to its disposal; for the reading of the context, cf. also Porten & Yardeni sub TADAE A 5.2); Porten & Szubin BiOr xlii 284ff.: in Driv 8 and Cowl 16 the HAPH of *ḥsn* = to hold as hereditary lease (less prob. interpret.); cf. also Frah xxi 3, Paik 383, 477: to take, to hold - **3)** to give in possession, to transfer to; + double obj., *ṣdyq ›[nh lh]ḥsnwth psmy* Cowl 44[6f.]: I have the right to transfer it to Psami (cf. Porten Arch 318, Porten & Greenfield JEAS p. 122, Grelot DAE p. 95 (n. g, Porten & Yardeni sub TADAE B 7.3) :: Cowl a.l.: l. *›[p ›mr lh]ḥsnwth psmy* (= but P. claimed to own it) - **4)** Part. in the expression *mhḥsn byb byrt›* Cowl 8[2] (cf. Cowl 7[2], Krael 12[5], cf. also Cowl 33[6]), prob. interpret. of *mhḥsn* = κληροῦχος (= holder of land by military tenure), cf. Wag 177f., J.J.Rabinowitz Law 101f., Grelot Sem xx 31f., RB xcv 298: κληροῦχος in the fortress of Yeb :: Szubin & Porten JRAS '82, 3ff.: = hereditary property-holder, cf. Cowl sub 7[2]: = holding property in Yeb the fortress (cf. also Porten Arch 33 n. 25, Porten & Greenfield JEAS p. 9, 69, 125, Porten & Yardeni sub TADAE B 2.3 a.e.) - Dupont-Sommer CRAI '74, 137, FX p. 136, 152, Teixidor Syr lii 289: the diff. *mhṣsn* in FX 136[19] = lapsus for *mhḥsn* (HAPH Part. s.m. abs.; cf. also Teixidor JNES xxxvii 183f., Contini OA xx 233, Frei BiOr xxxviii 367), diff. context, uncert. interpret., for the context, v. *ktb*₁.
v. *ḥsn*₂.

ḥsn₂ (related to *ḥsl*₁? or = *ḥsn*₁??)- **OffAr** ITTAPH Pf. 3 p.pl.m. *›thḥsynn* KAI 279[4,5] (for the form, cf. Dupont-Sommer JA ccxlvi 28, Altheim & Stiehl EW ix 194, 196, x 245, GH i 401, ii 172 (n. 21), 176f., ASA 270, GMA 353, Nober VD xxxvii 373f., Garbini Kand 11, 20f., Donner KAI a.l., Kutscher, Naveh & Shaked Lesh xxxiv 134, Degen Or xliv 122 (cf. also Coxon JNES xxxvi 297)) - ¶ verb ITTAPH to cease, to give up: KAI 279^4; + *mn*$_5$ (to give up, to cease): KAI 279^5 (in both instances Greek par. πέπαυνται).

ḥsn$_3$ **OldAr** Plur. emph. *ḥsny*ʾ KAI 202B 8 - **OffAr** Plur. emph. *ḥsny*ʾ Cowl 27^{11} (poss. reading, cf. also Grelot DAE p. 403, cf. however Porten & Greenfield JEAS p. 88f.: l. *ḥpny*ʾ word of unknown meaning, Porten & Yardeni sub TADAE A 4.5 (div. otherwise): pro *bḥpny*ʾ l. *d/rḥpny*ʾ, word of unknown meaning) - ¶ subst. - **1)** fortification, stronghold: KAI 202B 8 - **2)** store: Cowl 27^{11} (cf. Cowl a.l., cf. however Lidzbarski Eph ii 217, Grelot DAE p. 403: = fortification).

ḥsn$_4$ **OffAr** Sing. abs. *ḥsn* Cowl 7^{5,8,9} (for the reading, cf. Porten Or lvi 92, Porten & Yardeni sub TADAE B 7.2), Driv 12^{10} (uncert. reading, cf. also Porten & Yardeni sub TADAE A 6.15: pro *kḥsn* l. *nks[n]* = Plur. abs. of *nks*$_3$), ATNS 30a 4 (for the reading, cf. Porten & Yardeni sub TADAE B 8.4 :: Segal ATNS a.l.: pro *kḥsn* l. *kʾyn* = QAL Part. pass. pl.m. abs. of *kʾy* (= to rebuke)) - ¶ subst. prob. meaning, force, violence, in the expression *kḥsn* = by force, forcibly (cf. Cowl a.l., Driv a.l., J.J.Rabinowitz Bibl xli 72ff., Porten & Greenfield JEAS p. 124f., Porten & Yardeni sub TADAE B 7.2 a.e., cf. also Porten & Szubin JNES xli 130 :: Grelot DAE p. 93, 325: *kḥsn* = as a burglar, *ḥsn* = *ḥsn*$_5$ (= burglar)?).
v. *ḥsn*$_6$.

ḥsn$_5$ v. *ḥsn*$_4$.

ḥsn$_6$ **OffAr** *ḥsn* Driv 4^3, *ḥsyn* Driv 7^{2,4,6,9}, ATNS 26^7 - ¶ adv. strictly, exactly; *ḥsyn nṭr* Driv 7^2: he took strict care of (cf. Driv 7^{4,6}); *ḥsyn ynṭrw* ATNS 26^7: let them guard strictly (said of people posted in the gates); *ḥsyn tštʾlwn* Driv 7^9: you will be strictly called to account (cf. Driv 4^3; cf. Driv a.l., Grelot DAE p. 307, 313f. :: J.J.Rabinowitz Bibl xli 73f.: *ḥsn/ḥsyn* = *ḥsn*$_4$).

ḥsp$_1$ **Ph** IPHT Impf. 3 p.s.m. (v. *ḥṭr*$_1$) *tḥtsp* KAI 1^2 (cf. FR 150) - ¶ verb IPHT prob. meaning to be broken (said of a sceptre; cf. e.g. Vincent RB xxxiv 184, 186f., Rosenthal ANET 661, Mazza RSF iii 21 (n. 12), Avishur PIB 17, 159, SSWP 544 (n. 3); cf. however Gevirtz VT xi 147 (n. 2): = to be stripped away (cf. Caquot with Elayi RCP 106f. n. 266; cf. also Hillers TC 39, 61 (n. 51), Dahood Or xlvi 466, xlviii 97, Bibl lx 432, Gibson SSI iii p. 14, 16 (: to be torn away); cf. however Blau PC 124 n. 49) :: Röllig KAI a.l., Galling TGI 49 (n. 3), Butterweck TUAT ii 583: = to be defoliated, cf. also Niehr HR 63f. (n. 213) :: Margalit Shn v 60*f. n. 19: = be wrung (dry), i.e. become brittle and fragile (and thus easily broken)).

ḥsp$_2$ **JAr** Sing. abs. *ḥsp* Mas 556^3 - ¶ subst. clay; *mn ḥsp* Mas 556^3: a clay vessel.
v. *ḥth*.

ḥsr$_{1}$ **OffAr** QAL Pf. 1 p.s. *ḥsrt* Driv 13^{4}; Part. act. (or adj., v. *ḥsr$_{2}$*) s.f. abs. *ḥsrh* Cowl 27^{7} - **Palm** QAL (or PA ʿEL?) Pf. 3 p.s.m. *ḥsr* Inv x 115^{2}, SBS 47B 3 (heavily dam. context) - ¶ verb QAL to lack, to be in want of: Driv 13^{4}; *myn lʾ ḥsrh* Cowl 27^{7}: it (i.e. the well) does not lack water (cf. Cowl a.l., Joüon MUSJ xviii 5, Degen GGA '79, 43) - QAL (or PA ʿEL?), *wḥsr lhwn mn kysh* Inv x 115^{2}: he spent for them much money from his purse - a form of this root in ATNS 184^{4} (*]ḥsr*, reading uncert., dam. context)?
v. *ḥsrn*, *mḥsr*

ḥsr$_{2}$ **Hebr** Sing. abs. *ḥsr* DJD ii 22^{11} - **OffAr** Sing. f. emph., cf. Warka 15: *ḫa-as-si-ir-ta-a*, 40: *ḫa-as-si-ir-t[a-a]* - **Palm** Sing. m. abs. *ḥsyr*CIS ii 3913 ii 127 - ¶ adj. defective, imperfect; substantivated - a) *ḫa-as-si-ir-ta-a* Warka 15 (cf. 40): the imperfect one, deficient one (cf. Gordon AfO xii 116 (cf. also Dupont-Sommer RA xxxix 48: the mutilated one) :: Landsberger AfO xii 256: = object with (some) deficiency :: Driver AfO iii 48, 51: = Sing. emph. of *ḥsyrh*(= deficiency)) - b) *ḥsyr* CIS ii 3913 ii 127: what is less; *hn ḥsyr thwh šqlʾ* = if she takes less - c) *[ʾm ytyr] ʾw ḥsr* DJD ii $22^{10f.}$ (for the restoration, cf. DJD ii $30^{3,14}$): more or less.
v. *ḥsr$_{1}$*.

ḥsr$_{3}$ **Hebr** word of unknown meaning in TA-H 98, cf. Aharoni TA a.l.

ḥsrn **OffAr** Sing. abs. *ḥsrn* Cowl $38^{9,10}$ (for this interpret. and the reading of the context, cf. Porten & Yardeni sub TADAE A 4.3, cf. also Grelot DAE p. 393 (n. 1) :: Cowl a.l.: = QAL Part. pl.m. abs. of *ḥsr$_{1}$*).
v. *ḥryb*.

ḥstmḥ **OffAr** word of unknown meaning in KAI 267^{1} (diff. context); CIS ii sub 122 (cf. also Cooke NSI p. 201, Gibson SSI ii p. 119f.): < Egypt., compounded of *ḥst* and *mḥ* = favoured by the god and faithful (uncert. interpret.); Donner KAI a.l., REHR 41: = compound (< Egypt.) of *ḥst* and *mḥ* (= the favoured one and revered one (said of the blessed dead)), probably misunderstood as *nomen abstractum* (veneration, i.e. the blessed state of the dead; uncert. interpret.); Quaegebeur with Lipiński OLP viii 109f.: pro *zy* (??) *ḥstmḥ* l *[p]ḥstmḥ* (< Egypt.), *pḥs* = the beatified one (m.), *tmḥ* = the revered one (f.), highly uncert. reading and interpret.

ḥpwš **OffAr** word of unknown meaning in Cowl $26^{18,19,20}$. Cowl a.l.: = adv. clear, fully??; Grelot DAE p. 292 n. s: noun of prob. non-Sem. origin (< Egypt.??) = extremity (said of beam), cf. also Porten & Yardeni sub TADAE A 6.2: = overcut? In both instances uncert. interpret.; cf. also Sprengling AJT xxi 433 n. 2.

ḥpy$_{1}$ **OffAr** HAPH Part. pl.m. abs. of this root (*mhḥpyn* (reading uncert.)) poss. in RES 1785A 2: = covering?? - cf. also Collini SEL vi

23, 38 n. 3.

ḥpy$_2$ v. *ḥpyw$_2$*.

ḥpyh (< Arab., cf. Milik BIA x 57, O'Connor JNES xlv 228f.) - **Nab** Sing. cstr. (v. infra) *ḥpyt* BIA x 55[5] (Greek par. προτρο[πῆς]), 58[3] (or in both instances = Sing. cstr. of *ḥpyw$_1$*?) - ¶ subst. care, effort (:: Graf & O'Connor BySt iv 56 (n. 16) = Plur. cstr. (= salutations)) - cf. *ḥpyw$_1$*.

ḥpyw$_1$ **Palm** Sing. emph. *ḥpywtʾ* Inv x 127[2] - ¶ subst. effort, par. with Greek σπουδῆς, cf. Milik DFD 26, 33, BIA x 57 :: Starcky sub Inv x 127: or = protection?? - cf. *ḥpyh*.

ḥpyw$_2$ **Hatra** word of diff. reading and uncert. meaning in 232b 4 (for the reading, cf. Degen JEOL xxiii 404). Safar Sumer xxiv 9: l. *ḥpyy* (?) = Plur. cstr. of *ḥpy$_2$*(= bare-footed; improb. interpret.); Degen JEOL xxiii 404: = n.l.??; Aggoula MUSJ xlvii 8: l. *ḥpyw* or *ḥpyz*, perhaps pro *dḥpyw/z* l. *rḥpʾ*?; perhaps *ʾlhʾ dḥpyw* (Sing. abs.) = the god of protection (i.e. the protecting god).

ḥpyz v. *ḥpyw$_2$*.

ḥpn **OffAr** Sing. abs. *ḥpn* Krael 2[5] (*scriptio anterior*, cf. e.g. Porten & Yardeni sub TADAE B 3.3), 7[20], Driv 6[4,5], ATNS 41[2], 68[6]; emph. *ḥpnʾ* Krael 2[6] (also as *scriptio anterior* in Krael 2[5] (cf. Yaron JSS xiii 207, Porten BiAr xlii 82)); Plur. abs. *ḥpnn* Cowl 15[16] (for this reading, cf. Lidzbarski Eph iii 131, Krael p. 147, Grelot Sem xiv 63, Fitzmyer FS Albright ii 157f., WA 260, Porten & Greenfield JEAS p. 20, Porten & Yardeni sub TADAE B 2.6 :: Cowl a.l.: pro *ḥpnn /// //* l. *ḥ*(= abbrev. of *ḥpnn*) */// /// //*), Krael 2[6], 7[20,21], Driv 6[3], Herm 2[13], 3[12], ATNS 77a 2, 126[4] (dam. context) - ¶ subst. f. certain measure of capacity, exact amount unknown, cf. Driv p. 60, Cazelles Syr xxxii 78 n. 4, Fitzmyer WA 260; Porten Arch 71: *ḥpn* = 1/10 *gryw*(= *sʾh*; cf. also Grelot Sem xiv 70 n. 2, RB lxxviii 533, DAE p. 155 n. f); used as dry measure and for liquids - for *ḥwpn*and *ḥ* used as ideograms, cf. Maricq Syr xxxv 319 n. 7, Altheim & Stiehl GMA 471 (for the relevant texts, cf. AJSL lvii 387, 390, 391, 416), cf. perhaps also the abbrev. *ḥ* in Nisa-b 2167[2,3,4,6,7,8]? - the abbrev. *ḥ* in Cowl 24[38,41], cf. Maricq Syr xxxv 319 n. 7, Porten Arch 70 n. 48, Grelot DAE p. 274 (. p) :: :: Epstein ZAW xxxiii 148: = abbrev. for *ḥlq$_2$* (= measure of capacity) :: Cowl a.l.: poss. = abbrev. for *ḥlrn* (= Plur. abs. of *ḥlr*); Segal ATNS a.l.: the *ḥ* in ATNS 42b 1 prob. = abbrev. of *ḥpn* (prob. interpret.); the same abbrev. also in Cowl 2[4] (for the reading, cf. Porten & Yardeni sub TADAE B 4.4 :: e.g. Cowl a.l.: l. poss. some numerical signs).

ḥpnyʾ v. *ḥsn$_3$*.

ḥpp$_1$ = to wash, to clean > Akkad., cf. v.Soden Or xxxv 10, xlvi 187, cf. also idem AHW s.v. *ḫapāpu* II, CAD s.v. *ḫapāpu*.

ḥpp$_2$ v. *ʾpy*.

ḥpṣ$_1$ **Nab** QAL (or PA‘EL?) Impf. 3 p.s.m. *yḥpṣ* J 33[4] (for the reading, cf. J a.l. :: Milik RB lxvi 560: l. prob. *ytpṣ* = ITP Impf. 3 p.s.m. of *pṣṣ* (= to belong to) :: CIS ii sub 215: l. *ytpq*? = form of *npq*$_1$ (for this reading, cf. Lidzbarski Eph iii 270); for the reading, cf. also RES sub 1150) - ¶ verb QAL (or PA‘EL?) of uncert. meaning: to keep for one's own?? (cf. J a.l.) + obj.

ḥpṣ$_2$ **Hebr** QAL Impf. 2 p.s.m. *tḥpṣ* DJD ii 30[23]; 3 p.pl.m. *yḥpṣw* DJD ii 44[6] - ¶ verb QAL to desire, to like; *yḥpṣw lbw* DJD ii 44[6]: they desire to come; *l‘śwt bw kl tḥpṣ* DJD ii 30[23]: to do there everything you like.
v. *‘pṣ*, *š*$_{10}$.

ḥpṣ$_3$ **OldAr** Sing. + suff. 1 p.s. *ḥpṣy* KAI 224[8] - ¶ subst. affair; *w’šlḥ ml’ky ’[l]wh lšlm wlkl ḥpṣy* KAI 224[8]: I will send my envoy to him to ask after his welfare (v. *šlm*$_2$) or on any matter of business that I have - L.H.Gray AJSL xxxix 83: the *epsi* in Poen 1142 = Sing. + suff. 1 p.s. (= my joy)??, cf. however Sznycer PPP 144 (without interpret.) :: J.J.Glück & Maurach Semitics ii 124f. (div. otherwise) *mepsi* = Sing. + suff. 1 p.s. of *npš* (my soul) :: Schroed 298f., 320f.: pro *ipsi* l. *ipsa* = QAL Impf. 1 p.s.. of *pṣy* (= to look).

ḥpqws (< Greek ἱππικός, cf. Teixidor MUSJ xlii 177; v. infra) - **Palm** Sing. abs. *ḥpqws* MUSJ xlii 177[1] - ¶ subst. prob. interpret., someone with equestrian rank, knight, important person, cf. however Milik DFD 26: = n.p. of semitic origin.
v. *hpq*, *hpqws*, *pyq’*.

ḥpr$_1$ **Hebr** Torczyner Lach i p. 159: l. QAL Impf. 3 p.s.m. + suff. 3 p.s.m. *yḥprhw* in KAI 198[2] (improb. reading, repeated with reserves by e.g. Gibson SSI i p. 48; cf. also Röllig KAI a.l. :: Albright BASOR lxx 16 (div. otherwise): l. prob. *hḥb’h* = HIPH Pf. 3 p.s.m. + suff. 3 p.s.m. of *ḥb’*$_1$)- **OffAr**, cf. Frah xviii 12 (*ḥplwn*) - **Palm** QAL Pf. 3 p.s.m. *ḥpr* CIS ii 4199[9], Inscr P 40[4]; 3 p.pl.m. *ḥpr* CIS ii 4159[1], 4171[1], 4172[1], 4173[3]; Impf. 3 p.s.m. *yḥpr* RB xxxix 539[2,4]; Part. act. pl.m. abs. *ḥpryn* Ber v 95[9] - **JAr** QAL Inf. *mḥpr* IEJ xxxvi 206[5] (for the context, cf. Broshi & Qimron IEJ xxxvi 211) - ¶ verb QAL to dig; *yhwn ḥpryn wbnn mqbrn* Ber v 95[9]: they will dig and build burial places; *ḥpr wṣbt m‘rt’ dh* CIS ii 4173[3]: they have dug and adorned this hypogeum; *wyḥpr wytqn lh mqbrt’* RB xxxix 539[4]: he will dig and prepare the burial place for himself - **1)** + obj., *ḥpr m‘rt’ dh* CIS ii 4172[1]: they dug this burial place; *ḥpr m‘rt’ dh wbnw* CIS ii 4171[1]: they dug this burial place and built (it); *m‘rt’ dnh ... ḥpr wbn’ wṣbt* ... Inv P 40[4] (= Inv iv 13): this burial place ... he has dug, built and adorned - **2)** + *l*$_5$ (comm.): RB xxxix 539[2] - **3)** + obj. + *l*$_5$ (comm.), *m‘rt’ dnh ḥpr ... lhwn* CIS ii 4159[1ff.]: this burial place they dug ... for themselves; *’ksdr’ dnh ... ḥpr wṣbt ... lh* CIS ii 4199[8ff.]: this exedra ... he dug and adorned for himself - cf. also Gawlikowski Ber xxi 13 n. 61.

ḥpr₂ **Hebr** a word *ḥpr* poss. to be read in Dir sig. 75 (= Vatt sig. eb. 75 = SANSS app. a 88; cf. Dir Tab xxi 12), for the reading, cf. Pilcher PEQ '19, 178ff., meaning unknown; Pilcher PEQ '19, p. 179ff., Dir p. 236: = n.p.?, Aharoni TeAv i 158 n. 3 (div. otherwise): pro *-h ḥpr* l. *hḥpr* (= h_1 + *ḥpr* (= nisbe-adjective, the Hepherite) :: Lemaire Syr liv 131 (div. otherwise): pro *-h ḥpr* l. ***hspr*** (= h_1 + spr_2 (cf. also Bordreuil Syr lii 118) :: Raffaeli with Pilcher PEQ '19, 178ff.: l. *wgr* (= *w* + gr_1(a sojourner), cf. also Heltzer AION xxi 191 (: the settler, dweller) :: Herr sub SANSS app. a 88 (div. otherwise): l. *ʾdnyhwpr* = np.

ḥpš₁ **DA** a form of this root poss. in i 12: *ḥpš[...*; cf. Hoftijzer DA a.l.: l. poss. QAL Part. pl.m. abs./cstr.: *ḥpš[n]/ḥpš[y]*: those who seek for ... (cf. also Garbini Hen i 179f., 185: = QAL Pf. 3 p.s.m.; Puech FS Grelot 17, 23, 28: l. *ḥpšw* = QAL Imper. pl.m.?), cf. however Caquot & Lemaire Syr liv 199f.: or is related to *ḥpš₂* (cf. also McCarter BASOR ccxxxix 51, 55) or to *ḥpš₃* (= military man) :: Levine JAOS ci 197, 199: l. *ḥpš[y]* = Sing. m. abs. of *ḥpšy* used adverbially: freely :: H.P.Müller ZAW xciv 218, 227 (nn. 82, 83) = Sing. abs. of *ḥpš₄* (= depth, downfall); on this word, cf. also Ringgren Mem Seeligmann 96, Hackett BTDA 50.
v. HbS.

ḥpš₂ **Ph** Sing. abs. *ḥpš* JEA x 16 - ¶ subst. m. freedman.
v. *ḥbš,ḥpš₁*.

ḥpš₃ v. *ḥbš,ḥpš₁*.

ḥpš₄ v. *ḥpš₁*.

ḥpšy v. *ḥpš₁*.

ḥṣ₁ **Ph** Sing. cstr. *ḥṣ* MUSJ xi 330[1] (= KAI 20), BASOR cxxxiv 6, cxliii 3, ccxxxviii 5, BMB xvi 106, 107, Syr lxvii 315, SEL vi 53[1], Mem Saidah 180[1], etc., (on the orthography in the Ph. instances, cf. Naveh Lesh xxx 66, Claassen AION xxi 289) - **OldAr** Plur. emph. *ḥṣyʾ* KAI 222A 38, B 29 (heavily dam. context, cf. e.g. Fitzmyer AIS 19, 67f., Degen AAG p. 14 n. 63, Lipiński Stud 36) - **OffAr** Sing. emph. *ḥṭʾ*Aḥiq 128 (cf. Grimme OLZ '11, 537, Ginsberg ANET 429, Grelot RB lxviii 187, DAE p. 441 :: Cowl a.l., Kottsieper SAS 15, 202: = Sing. abs. of *ḥṭʾ₂*(= sin)); + suff. 2 p.s.m. *ḥṭk*Aḥiq 126, 128; cf. Frah xiv 2 (*ḥṭyʾ*), Paik 384 (*ḥṭyʾ*), 385 (*ḥṭyʾ*), GIPP 23, 53, SaSt 17 - ¶ subst. m. arrow (for the background of KAI 222A 38, cf. Hillers TC 21, 27, 60) - for the arrow-heads with inscr *ḥṣ* + NP (MUSJ xi 330[1], BASOR cxxxiv 6, cxliii 3, ccxxxviii 5, BMB xvi 106, 107, SEL vi 53[1], etc.), cf. Milik & Cross BASOR cxxxiv 6f., Milik BASOR cxliii 4ff., Mazar VT xiii 312, Iwry JAOS lxxxi 27ff., Starcky Mem Saidah 179ff., Mitchell FS Tufnell 136ff., Puech RB xcii 164, 167, Sass UF xxi 356 - *ḥṣ* also found in the n.d. *ršp ḥṣ* KAI 32[3,4] (Reshep of the arrow; cf. e.g. CIS i sub 10, Albright FS Haupt 147, Virolleaud PRU ii p. 3, Matthiae OA ii 37, Vattioni AION xv 46, Liverani AION xvii 332ff., Driver FS Bakoš

97, Dahood Bibl xlix 356, liv 354f., v.d.Branden PO ii 411ff., Caquot & Masson Syr xlv 301f. (arrow > lightning, cf. also Röllig KAI a.l., Teixidor Syr xlvii 369), Conrad ZAW lxxxiii 172f., Dahood & Pettinato Or xlvi 232, Xella WO xix 52 :: Clermont-Ganneau RAO i 180: *ḥṣ* = *ḥṣ*$_2$ (= street), cf. Cooke NSI p. 57 :: Iwry JAOS lxxxi 31: *ḥṣ* = *ḥṣ*$_5$ (= luck, good fortune) - Milik BMB xvi 105: l. *ḥṣ* (without n.p.) on arrow-head (BMB xvi 105), highly uncert. reading.

ḥṣ$_2$ **Pun** Sing. abs. *ḥṣ* RCL '66, 201^{1} (:: Mahjoubi & Fantar RCL '66, 202f., 209: = *ḥṣ*$_6$ (= basin, v. also infra)) - **Hebr** Sing. cstr. *ḥwṣ* SM $49^{9,22}$ - ¶ subst. - **1)** street: RCL '66, 201^{1} (cf. Dupont-Sommer CRAI '68, 117, 119ff., Garbini RSO xliii 12, Ferron Mus xcviii 49, 60 :: Sznycer GLECS xii/xiii 6: = wall; v. also supra) - **2)** in the combination *lḥwṣ* = except, apart from: SM $49^{9,22}$.
v. *ḥṣ*$_1$,*pḥṣ*.

ḥṣ$_3$ v. *ḥṣy*$_2$.

ḥṣ$_4$ **OffAr** Plur. abs. *ḥṣn* Cowl 15^{16}, *ḥwṣn*Cowl 20^{6}, Krael 7^{17} - ¶ subst. prob. meaning palm leave (cf. Nöldeke ZA xx 148, Wag 61 n. 5, Leand 43o, Krael p. 212f., Grelot RB lxxviii 526ff., cf. also Porten Arch 91, Porten & Greenfield JEAS p. 20, Porten & Yardeni sub TADAE B 2.6/9, Fitzmyer FS Albright ii 157, Delsman TUAT i 261 :: Cowl p. 49: *ḥṣn*/*ḥwṣn*= Sing. abs. of *ḥṣn*$_1$ (= ivory), cf. also Reider JQR xliv 340 for Krael 7^{17}).

ḥṣ$_5$ v. *ḥṣ*$_1$,*ḥṣy*$_2$.

ḥṣ$_6$ v. *ḥmr*$_5$,*ḥṣ*$_2$.

ḥṣʾ v. *ḥṣy*$_1$.

ḥṣb **Hebr** Qal Part. act. pl.m. abs. *ḥṣbm* KAI $189^{4,6}$ - ¶ verb Qal Part. act. (or subst.?) miner, stone mason - for a poss. reading *ḥṣ[bm]* in KAI 189^{1}, cf. Puech RB lxxxi 200; this word also in the Ph. text RES 1513C??

ḥṣd **OldAr** Qal Impf. 3 p.s.m. *yḥṣd* Tell F 19 - **OffAr** Qal Impf. 2 p.s.m. *tḥṣd* MAI xiv/2, 66^{7}; Part. act. s.m. abs. *ḥṣd* KAI 234 Rs 1 (= AECT 47), 236 vs. 6 (= AECT 49), TH 3r 1 (??, highly uncert. reading, cf. e.g. Lipiński Stud 133: l. *ḥ*xx; heavily dam. context); pl.m. abs. *ḥṣdn* CIS ii 38^{5} (= Del 21 = AECT 3), 39^{5} (= Del 23 = AECT 9); cf. Frah xviii 17 (*ḥṣdlwn*, cf. Nyberg FP 89) - **Palm** Qal Part. act. pl.m. emph. *ḥṣdyʾ* Syr xl 33^{2} (for this reading, cf. Teixidor Syr xl 33ff. :: Teixidor Sumer xviii 63f. (english section): l. *ḥṣryʾ* = Plur. emph. of *ḥṣr*$_5$ (= settler) :: Teixidor Sem xxxiv 25: l. *ḥṣryʾ* = Plur. emph. of *ḥṣr*$_6$ (= storekeeper)) - ¶ verb Qal to reap, to harvest; *wlzrʿ wʾl yḥṣd* Tell F 18f.: may he sow but not harvest (for the context, cf. Greenfield & Shaffer RB xcii 53f.); + obj. (prob.): MAI xiv/2, 66^{7}; Part. act. (or subst.?, cf. e.g. Lipiński Stud 91): reaper, harvester.

ḥṣy$_1$ **Pun** Qal Part. s.m. abs. *[ḥ]ṣʾ*KAI 160^{3} (or cstr.?; cf. Février

Sem iv 22, Röllig KAI a.l.; dam. context, uncert. interpret.) - ¶ verb QAL to distribute, to divide + obj.
v. *ḥzy*₁.

ḥṣy₂ **Ph** Sing. cstr. *ḥṣy* RES 1204[5,6] (in l. 6 diff. construction, v. infra) - **Pun** Sing. abs. *ḥṣy* CIS i 169[11] (dam. context) - **Mo** Sing. cstr. *ḥṣy* KAI 181[8] - **Hebr** Sing. abs. *ḥṣy* TA-H 101 (cf. Aharoni a.l. :: Albright with Aharoni a.l.: *ḥṣy* poss. = *ḥṣ*₅(= luck)), TeAv ii 162, on coins of the first revolt: JC no. 161 (cf. Meshorer Mas coin 3492); cstr. Dir pes. 23, on coins of the first revolt: JC no. 149, 152, 155, 159 (cf. Meshorer Mas coin 1313, 1343, 2989) - **OffAr** Sing. abs. *ḥṣy* NESE iii 43[3], BIFAO xxxviii 58[10] (:: Segal Maarav iv 73f.: l. *hny* = these) - **Nab** Sing. cstr. *ḥṣ* on coins: NC no. 80, 84 - ¶ subst. half; *ḥṣy hsp* RES 1204[5]: half of the basin (cf. l. 6: *hḥṣy hsp*); *hn 1 wḥṣy hlg wrb‹t hlg* Dir pes. 23: one *hin* and three quarters of a *log*; *m 1 ḥṣy* NESE iii 43[3]: one *m.* and a half (cf. BIFAO xxxviii 58[10]: *k 1 ḥṣy 1*, prob. = one *k.* and a half; cf. however Aimé-Giron BIFAO xxxviii 60: *ḥṣy* = half-obol, cf. also Degen NESE iii 57); *ḥṣy hšql* coins of the first revolt (JC no. 149, 152, 155, 159): half a shekel (cf. JC no. 161: *ḥṣy* = half a shekel; cf. also *ḥṣ ksp* NC no. 80, 84: half a silver coin (half-obol); for the Hebr. and Nab. coins, cf. also Meshorer Proc v CJS i 82f. (Hebr.)); *ḥṣy lmlk* TeAv ii 160: half(-measure) of the king (poss. = capacity measure of one half of tenth part of a *bat*, cf. Aharoni TeAv ii a.l., TA p. 14 n. 17; cf. also inscription *ḥṣy* on sherd: TA-H 101, cf. Aharoni TA a.l.: poss. part of expression *ḥṣy lmlk*, v. also supra); *ḥṣy ymy bnh* KAI 181[8]: half of the days of his son, (for *his son*, v. *bn*₁,for *half*, cf. e.g. Lidzbarski Eph i 144, Bonder JANES iii 87f., Lipiński Or xl 330ff., H.P.Müller TUAT i 647 :: CF 38 (cf. also 39f. n. 13), Wallis ZDPV lxxxi 180ff.: = part, portion (cf. also Galling TGI 52 (n. 4), Reviv CSI p. 18) :: Liver PEQ '67, 19: = most (of the days of his son), cf. also Gibson SSI i p. 76: = much (of his son's days) :: Winckler AltOrForsch ii 403ff.: *ḥṣy* = amount, total amount?; for the context, v. also *›rb‹m*).

ḥṣyp v. *›ṣyl*.

ḥṣl₁ **OldAr** PA‹EL (cf. e.g. Donner KAI a.l., Gibson SSI ii p. 16 :: Degen AAG p. 69: = QAL) Impf. 1 p.s. + suff. 2 p.s.m. *›ḥṣlk* KAI 202A 14 - **OffAr** PA‹EL Inf. + suff. 1 p.s. *ḥṣltn[y]* KAI 266[7] (prob. reading, cf. Porten BiAr xliv 36 (cf. Porten & Yardeni sub TADAE A 1.1) :: Fitzmyer Bibl xlvi 52, WA 239, Gibson SSI ii p. 113, 115: l. *ḥṣlty* = PA‹EL Inf. + suff. 1 p.s. :: Koopmans 90: l. *ḥṣlty* = QAL Inf. + suff. 1 p.s. :: e.g. Dupont-Sommer Sem i 44, 51, Ginsberg BASOR cxi 25, Donner KAI a.l.: *hṣlty* = HAPH Inf. + suff. 1 p.s. of *nṣl* (cf. also Kaufman AIA 157 n. 81; cf. however Dupont-Sommer Sem i 51 n. 1, Ginsberg BASOR cxi 25 n. 4a, Donner KAI a.l.: or l. *ḥṣlty*?) - ¶ verb PA‹EL to save, to rescue; + obj.: KAI 266[7]; + obj. + *mn*₅ (from): KAI

202A 14 (cf. also Greenfield Proc v CJS i 179f.); *ḥṣl* prob. metathesis for *ḥlṣ*$_1$,cf. e.g. Nöldeke ZA xxi 382, Koopmans 27f., Donner KAI sub 202, Uffenheimer Lesh xxx 165f., Greenfield Proc v CJS i 175, Fitzmyer Bibl xlvi 52, Claassen AION xxi 295, Gibson SSI ii p. 15f., Miller SVT xxxii 314 n. 8.

ḥṣl$_2$ v. *ʾṣl*$_2$.

ḥṣn$_1$ v. *ḥṣ*$_4$.

ḥṣn$_2$ **Hatra** Sing. (cf. Vattioni IH a.l.; or Plur.?, cf. Degen NESE iii 68) emph. *ḥṣnʾ* 281^7 - ¶ subst. axe - Zimmern Fremdw 12: < Akkad. (less prob. interpret., cf. Kaufman AIA 54).

ḥṣp **OffAr** Sing. m. abs. *ḥṣp* ASAE xlviii 112 conc. 3 - ¶ adj. coarse (said of salt)?, cf. Dupont-Sommer ASAE xlviii 113.

ḥṣṣ inscription on tags from Massada, meaning unknown, cf. Yadin IEJ xv 112, Yadin & Naveh Mas p. 12.

ḥṣr$_1$ **Pun** *mḥṣrt* in KAI 161^{10} of diff. and uncert. interpret.; Février RA xlv 147: = Pɪ ʿᴇʟ (or Pᴜ ʿᴀʟ) Part. pl.f. abs. of *ḥṣr*$_1$ (= to bring forth grass), cf. however Roschinski Num 112, 116: = Pᴜ ʿᴀʟ Part. pl.f. abs. of *ḥṣr*$_2$ (= covered with settlements); Röllig KAI a.l.: *mḥṣrt* = subst. Sing. abs. (= green?) :: Berger RA ii 36f., 43: pro *mḥṣrt* l. *mḥqt* = form of root *ḥqq*$_1$ (*[ʾ]rṣʾt mḥqt* = the lands of the heritage) :: Cooke NSI p. 150: l. *mḥqt* = Plur. abs. of *mḥqh* (= inscription).

ḥṣr$_2$ v. *ḥṣr*$_1$.

ḥṣr$_3$ **Ph**, cf. Diosc ii 126, 130, 167, 178, 186, iii 105, 137, iv 36, 70, 85 (ατιρ, ασιρ, αστιρ; cf. Steiner ASSL 61, 67); cf. also Apul 66 (ann. sub 9): *Azir(guzol)* and Apul 9: *Atzic urur* (cf. however Steiner ASSL 60f.) - **OldAr** Sing. abs. *ḥṣr* KAI 222A 28 - ¶ subst. grass, herb; for certain etym. problems of *ḥṣr* in KAI 222A 28, cf. Kutscher SVT 171f., Blau PC 61, 133, Degen AAG p. 37 (n. 28), Ben-Chayyim Lesh xxxv 249, Gibson SSI ii p. 39, Halpern FS Lambdin 122 (n. 17); cf. also *ʾḥw* - for this word, cf. also Borowski AIAI 138.

ḥṣr$_4$ **Ph** Sing. cstr. *ḥṣr* KAI 27^7 (cf. FR 292, Röllig KAI a.l.), 60^{2,3} - **Palm** Sing. emph. *ḥṭrʾ* SBS 19^2 - ¶ subst. courtyard, enclosed court: KAI 27^7, 60^{2,3}; in SBS 19^2 prob. same meaning, cf. Garbini OA xiv 177: enclosed court × Dunant SBS a.l.: = enclosure-wall (in the context = basis-wall), for an interpret. as "wall", cf. also Degen WO viii 129f., Gawlikowski Syr li 96 - the same word (Sing. emph. *ḥṭrʾ*) also on Hatrean coins (Hatra app. 7): *ḥṭrʾ dšmš* (= n.l. = Hatra; cf. Caquot Syr xxix 114, cf. also Walker NumChron vi/xviii 167f. (type A), Vattioni Aug xi 79 no. 100, Milik DFD 362) and in KAI 200$^{3f.}$ (*ḥṣr ʾsm*, v. *ḥm*$_2$); cf. also n.l. Hazor - the reading *ḥ[ṣ]r* in KAI 10^4 (cf. e.g. CIS i sub 1, Cooke NSI p. 23, Lidzbarski sub KI 5) less prob., cf. Dupont-Sommer Sem iii 39, Gibson SSI iii p. 94, 97: l. *ḥ[ṣr]n*, Sing. abs. with the same meaning as *ḥṣr*$_4$ (cf. also Röllig KAI a.l.: l. *ḥ[..]n*) - for the etymology

of *ḥṣr$_4$*, cf. Malamat JAOS lxxxii 147.
v. *ḥṣrh*, *pḥṣ*, *qṣr$_6$*.

ḥṣr$_5$ v. *ḥṣd*.

ḥṣr$_6$ v. *ḥṣd*.

ḥṣrh **Pun** Sing. (or Plur.?) abs. (or cstr.?) *ḥṣrt* KAI 145[1] (for Sing., cf. e.g. Berger MAIBL xxxvi/2 144, 149, Février Sem vi 17, 20, Röllig KAI a.l. × e.g. Cooke NSI p. 152f., RES sub 2221, v.d.Branden RSF i 166f.: = Plur. abs. of *ḥṣr$_4$*,cf. also Krahmalkov RSF iii 188, 201; v. also *pḥnt*); cstr. *[ḥ]ṣrt* KAI 122[2] - ¶ subst. court (of a temple).

ḥṣrm v. *ʿšrm*.

ḥṣrn v. *ḥṣr$_4$*.

ḥṣt v. *pḥṣ*.

ḥql **OffAr** Sing. cstr. *ḥql* ATNS 78[1] (dam. context), 106[1,2,3]; emph. *ḥqlʾ* CIS ii 24 (= Del 17 = AECT 32), 27[1] (*ḥql[ʾ*, cf. Fales sub AECT 10; = Del 18), KAI 228A 18, MAI xiv/2, 66[7]; + suff. 3 p.s.m. *ḥqlh* CIS ii 53[1] (cf. however CIS ii a.l.: = Sing. emph.); + suff. 1 p.s. *ḥqly* MAI xiv/2, 66[3,8,12,14]; Plur. cstr. *ḥqly* CIS ii 31[1] (= Del 30 = AECT 16 (for the reading of the context, cf. also Kaufman JAOS cix 99)); emph. *ḥqlyʾ* Irâq xxxiv 133,5 (= AECT 37; dam. context) - **JAr** Sing. emph. *ḥqlh* SM 49[6] - ¶ subst. plot of land, field (Aggoula Syr lxii 62, 65: in KAI 228A 18 = oasis (uncert. interpret.); for the context, v. *šymh*).
v. *ḥqlh*.

ḥqlh **OffAr** Plur. cstr. *ḥqlt* ATNS 31[1]; emph. *ḥqltʾ* ATNS 3[4], 31[4], 48a ii 5, 56[5], 75a 2 (or = Sing.?), 78[2,3] (for these forms, cf. Wesselius BiOr xli 705: *ḥqlt* = Plur. of *ḥql*)- ¶ subst. plot of land, field.

ḥqq$_1$ **Ph** Qal Pf. 3 p.s.m. *ḥq* BMB xxvii 85 (for the reading, cf. Röllig WO v 120, cf. also Ferron RSF ii 80); Yiph Part. s.m. abs. *mḥq* CIS i 51[2] (for a discussion, cf. Amadasi sub Kition B 42) - **Samal** Qal Impf. 2 p.s.m. *tḥq* KAI 214[34] (cf. e.g. Friedr 24*, Dion p. 214 :: Garb 263: or < *nḥq*?; v. infra) - **Nab** Qal Part. pass. (?) s.m. abs. *ḥqq* MPAT 64 i 10 - ¶ verb Qal - **1)** to engrave: BMQ xxvii 85 (v. supra) - 2) to prescribe, to order; + *ʿl$_7$* (concerning), *tḥq ʿlyh* KAI 214[34]: you will give instructions concerning him (cf. Dion p. 35, 214 (cf. also Gibson SSI ii p. 69) × Rosenthal JBL xcv 154: < *ḥqq$_2$* (= to incite) :: e.g. Donner KAI a.l.: you will write concerning him?) cf. also Cooke NSI p. 171, Tawil JNES xxxii 478ff. (n. 22) - for MPAT 64 i 10, v. *pgʿwn* - Yiph Part. stone-cutter (uncert. interpret., cf. also Bonnet SEL vii 119).
v. *ʾtḥr*,*ḥṣr$_1$*.

ḥqq$_2$ v. *ḥqq$_1$*.

ḥqr v. *yqr$_1$*.

ḥr$_1$ **OffAr** Sing. emph. *ḥrʾ* Beh 34 (:: Sokoloff JAOS cix 686: = Plur. emph.); Plur. abs. *ḥrn* Aḥiq 217; cstr. *ḥry* Cowl 30[19], 31[18] - **Nab** Plur.

cstr. *ḥry* CIS ii 161 i 2, 990^{2}, 1296^{3}, 1705^{2} - **Palm** Plur. cstr. *ḥry* CIS ii 3901, 3913 ii 62, 4000^{4}, 4015^{4}, Inv xi 5^{3}, xii 56^{3}, MUSJ xxxviii 106^{4}, etc., *ḥr›* CIS ii 4482^{2}, MUSJ xxviii 46^{3}; + suff. 3 p.pl.m. *ḥryh[wn]* RIP 104^{5} (?) - ¶ subst. m. - **1)** person of note, noble: Cowl 30^{19}, 31^{18}; prob. used collectively: Beh 34 (cf. Akkad. par. *mār banūtu*) - **2)** in the combination *br ḥrn* - a) person of note, noble: Aḥiq 217 (dam. context) - b) freedman (*br ḥry NP*): CIS ii 161 i 2, 990^{2}, 4000^{3f}, 4173^{1}, 4174^{1}, etc.; f. *bt ḥry NP*: CIS ii 3901, 4340$^{2f.}$, Ber ii 91^{2}, *brt ḥry NP*: Ber v 124^{4}, Inscr P 40^{6}, Inv xi 5$^{2f.}$
v. *›ḥd$_4$*, *›ḥrn*.

ḥr$_2$ **OffAr** Segal ATNS a.l.: l. *ḥrn* (= Plur. abs. of *ḥr$_2$* (= free)) in ATNS 48^{5}?? (dam. context, highly uncert. reading and interpret.).

ḥr$_3$ v. *ḥrwt$_1$*.

ḥr$_4$ v. *ḥrm$_4$*.

ḥr›$_1$ **DA** Pa‹el Impf. 1 p.s. + coh. ending *›ḥr›h* (diff. and dam. context, cf. Hoftijzer **DA** p. 186f., 298 × Rofé SB 65: = Pa‹el Impf. 1 p.s. + suff. 3 p.s.f. :: Caquot & Lemaire Syr liv 195: = Sing. + suff. 3 p.s.m. of *›ḥr›*(= posterity (cf. also H.P.Müller ZAW xciv 220f., Puech BAT 356, 360, FS Grelot 18, 27)) :: Garbini Hen i 174f.: = Sing. abs. of *›ḥr›h*(= wrath), cf. also Koenig Sem xxxiii 80, 83, 88 :: McCarter BASOR ccxxxix 51f.: = Sing. emph. of *›ḥr$_3$* + adverbial. *-h* (= hereafter), cf. also Levine JAOS ci 196, 198, Hackett BTDA 35, 99, Sasson UF xvii 287, 293 :: Lemaire BAT 317f., CRAI '85, 279f.: *›ḥr›h* = form of adj. (= last; cf. also id. GLECS xxiv-xxviii 324f.: = Sing. m. emph. of *›ḥr›* (= last)) :: Wesselius BiOr xliv 593, 595: poss. = *›ḥ* (= Sing. abs. of *›ḥ$_2$*) + *r›h* (= Qal Pf. 3 p.s.m. of *r›y*)) - ¶ verb Pa‹el to kindle.

ḥr›$_2$ **Samal** Sing. abs. *ḥr›* KAI 214^{23} (for this form, cf. Rosenthal JBL xcv 154) - ¶ subst. wrath.
v. *ḥmh$_2$*.

ḥr›b v. *ḥrb$_7$*.

ḥrb$_1$ **Nab** Aph Pf. 3 p.pl.m. *›ḥrbw* CIS ii 964^{3} (for this reading, cf. Jaussen & Savignac RB xi 467, cf. also Lidzbarski Eph ii 77 :: CIS ii sub 964: l. *›ḥrpw* = Aph Pf. 3 p.pl.m. of *ḥrp$_2$* (= to collect fruits??); for this last reading, cf. also Clermont-Ganneau with Berger Revue Critique xxvi 492f., RAO iv 187ff.: *›ḥrpw* = Aph Pf. 3 p.pl.m. or Aph pass. Pf. 3 p.pl.m. of *ḥrp$_2$* (= resp. to give permission to pluck/pick or to be given permission to pluck/pick)) - **JAr** Aph Part. s.m. abs. *mḥrb* AMB 8^{8} (reading of *m* uncertain) - ¶ verb Aph to destroy, to devastate: AMB 8^{8}; + obj.: CIS ii 964^{3} (cf. also Negev IEJ xiii 123f.) - a form of this root also in JAOS liv 31^{2}: *tḥrb*. Torrey JAOS liv a.l.: = Inf. v from Arab.; or = Qal Impf. 3 p.s.f.? (= she was devastated?) - cf. Cantineau Nab ii 172: the *›ḥrbw* in CIS ii 964^{3} < Arab., however

O'Connor JNES xlv 218: not < Arab.
v. *ḥrb$_2$*, *ḥrb$_6$*, *ḥryb*.

ḥrb$_2$ **Hebr** Sing. abs. *ḥrb* DJD ii 45[7] - **Samal** Sing. abs. *ḥrb* KAI 214[9,25], 215[5] - **OldAr** Sing. abs. *ḥrb* KAI 224[13,14] - **OffAr** Sing. abs. *ḥrb* Cowl 71[13], Aḥiq 113 (:: Halévy RS xx 57: = Sing. abs. of *ḥrb$_5$* (= bustard, heron)); + suff. 3 p.s.m. *ḥrbh* Cowl 80[4] (dam. context; cf. however Porten & Yardeni sub TADAE A 5.5: or = form of *ḥrb$_1$*?);+ suff. 1 p.s. *ḥrby* Aḥiq 174 - ¶ subst. f. sword; as a symbol of devastation, *hwyt ḥrb b›rq y›dy* KAI 215[5]: I have been a sword (i.e. a devastator) in the land of Y. (v. also *hwy$_1$*; cf. also Landsberger Sam›al 63 n. 160: = a revenger?).
v. *ḥšb$_1$*.

ḥrb$_3$ v.Soden Or xxxv 11, xlvi 188: *ḥrb$_3$* = waste land, desert > Akkad. (cf. also idem AHW s.v. *ḫurbu*; cf. however CAD s.v. *ḫurbû*).

ḥrb$_4$ **Hebr** Plur. abs. *ḥrby[m]* DJD ii 22[3], *ḥrwbym* DJD ii 22[12] - ¶ subst. carob-tree.

ḥrb$_5$ v. *ḥrb$_2$*.

ḥrb$_6$ **Samal** Plur. f. abs. *ḥrbt* KAI 215[4] - ¶ adj. (or QAL Part. act. of *ḥrb$_1$*?,cf. e.g. Dion p. 128) devastated (said of town).

ḥrb$_7$ **Pun** Levi Della Vida Or xxxiii 7f., 13f., Amadasi IPT 132: the diff. *ḥr›b* in Trip 51[1] = adj. Sing. m. abs. (substantivated): dry, what is dry (diff. and uncert. context).

ḥrbwṣyn cf. Frah iv 23 (*ḥlbwṣyn›*): water-melon, cf. Nyberg FP 67.

ḥrbn **Hebr** Sing. cstr. *ḥrbn* SM 13[1] (= Frey 977) - **JAr** Sing. cstr. *ḥrbn* MPAT-A 50[7] (= Frey 1208), 51[7], 52[7] - ¶ subst. destruction; *lmspr ›rb‹ m›wt wtyš‹ym w›rb‹ šnh lḥrbn hbyt* SM 13: in the 494th year of the destruction of the Temple (:: Avigad BRF iii 52: ... the destruction (of the Temple). The house...; case of haplography), cf. also MPAT-A 50[7], 51[7], 52[7].

ḥrg **Nab** QAL Part. pass. s.m. abs. *ḥryg* J 30[4,6] (= CIS ii 200; for the reading in both instances, cf. Milik sub ARNA-Nab 79) - ¶ verb QAL Part. pass. forbidden; *ḥlqh ḥryg l›ḥr hgrw* J 30[4]: his part will be forbidden for the posterity of H. (sc. it will be forbidden to the posterity of H. to buy his part, etc.), cf. also J 30[5f.] - on this root, cf. also O'Connor JNES xlv 217 n. 20.

ḥrdh **Pun** Sing. abs. *ḥrdt* KAI 145[5] (or = Plur. abs.?, cf. Dahood Bibl lx 432) - ¶ subst. terror, awe; *b‹l ḥrdt* KAI 145[5]: the lord of terror (i.e. the one who inspires awe), epithet of a deity.

ḥrdl **Hebr** Sing. abs. *ḥrdl* SM 49[3] - ¶ subst. mustard-seed.

ḥrwb v. *ḥrb$_4$*.

ḥrwt$_1$ **Hebr** Sing. cstr. *ḥrwt* on coins of the first revolt, cf. JC 153b, 156, on coins of the second revolt, cf. JC 194, 199, 202, 203, 204, 205, 206, etc. (cf. Meshorer Mas coin 2048, 3000), *ḥrt* on coins of the first revolt, cf. JC 153 (cf. Meshorer Mas coin 1358, 3476) - **JAr** Sing. cstr. *ḥrwt* MPAT 43³ (*ḥr[wt]*), 44 i 1, IEJ xxxvi 206¹, *ḥrt* MPAT 51¹ - ¶ subst. freEdom., liberation; used in dating - a) on coins of the first revolt *ḥr(w)t ṣywn* (cf. JC 153, 153b, 156): the liberation of Sion - b) on coins of the second revolt - α) in the combination *[šn]t tlt lḥrwt yrw{w}šlm* MPAT 44 i 1: the third year of the liberation of Jerusalem (cf. IEJ xxxvi 206¹; cf. also on coins JC 194, 199, 202, etc.: *lḥrwt yrwšlm*) - β) in the combination *šnt tlt lḥrt yšrʾl* MPAT 51¹: the third year of the liberation of Israel (cf. on coins *š b lḥr yšrʾl* JC no. 176, 177 (*š [b l]ḥr yšrʾl*), 178, etc.: the second year of the liberation of Israel; *ḥr* (*ḥr*$_3$) here abbrev. of *ḥrwt*) - for the coins of the second revolt, cf. also Kanael IEJ xxi 39ff., Philonenko CRAI '74, 183ff., Schäfer BKA 62f., 85ff.

ḥrwt$_2$ = branch of date palm > Akkad., cf. v Soden Or xxxv 10, xlvi 187 (cf. also idem AHW s.v. *ḫaruttu* and CAD s.v. *ḫarūtu*).

ḥrz$_1$ **Pun** Sing. abs. *ḥrz* KAI 81⁴ - ¶ subst. of unknown meaning; Halévy RS ix 81: prob. = the upper part of the enclosure wall of the sanctuaries (cf. Cooke NSI p. 128); cf. also Röllig KAI a.l.: part of a building, upper part of the sanctuaries or the terrace on which they were erected; Slouschz TPI p. 158: = parapet; v.d.Branden BiOr xxxvi 202, PO i 209: = bastion.

ḥrz$_2$ **OffAr** word of uncert. reading and unknown meaning in TA-Ar 41 obv. 8. Aharoni TA a.l.: = bead?

ḥrṭyt **Pun** Plur. abs. *ḥrṭyt* KAI 81² - ¶ subst. of unknown meaning, connected with root *ḥrṭ* (to engrave)??, cf. e.g. Lidzbarski Eph i 21 (sculpture, engraving, sculptured object, cf. idem sub KI 69, cf. also Cooke NSI p. 128, Slouschz TPI p. 157, Röllig KAI a.l., v.d.Branden PO i 207f., Bonnet SEL vii 116f.), cf. however Marrassini FLEM p. 33 (n. 1): derivation of root *ḥrṭ* (= to engrave) less prob.

ḥry$_1$ v. *ʾtḥr*, *ḥdy*$_1$.

ḥry$_2$ prob. = same root as *ḥry*$_1$, v. *ʾḥd*$_4$.

ḥry$_3$ cf. Frah ii 1: = plowed land (*ḥrytʾ*, cf. Nyberg FP 62).

ḥryb **JAr** Plur. m. abs. *ḥrybyn* MPAT 40⁸,²² (*ḥr[yby]n*; cf. however Beyer ATTM 308, 584: l. in both instances *ḥsrnyn* = Plur. abs. of *ḥsrn*(= loss, depreciation)) - ¶ adj. ruined (said of goods; or = Qal Part. pass. of *ḥrb*$_1$?).

ḥrm$_1$ **Mo** Hiph 1 p.s. + suff. 3 p.s.f. *hḥrmth* KAI 181¹⁷ - **OffAr** a form of this verb poss. also in ASAE xxvi 27⁴ (*[y]ḥrmh*), cf. Dupont-Sommer JA ccxxxv 82f., cf. also Grelot DAE p. 368 n. e: = Aph Impf. 3 p.s.m. + suff. 3 p.s.m. :: Aimé-Giron ASAE xxvi 27, 29: poss. l. *yrmh* = Qal Impf. 3 p.s.m. + suff. 3 p.s.m. of *rmʾ* (= *rmy*$_1$? (= to return (something) to) ??) - **Nab** Paʿel/Aph Part. pass. s.m. abs. *mḥrm* (cf. Cantineau Nab i 80, ii 99, cf. however also Cantineau Nab i 80: or =

QAL Part. pass.?) CIS ii 206[3] - **Hatra** APH Pf. 3 p.s.m. *ʾḥrym* 245[2] - ¶ verb HIPH/APH to consecrate, to devote; *ʾs 8 ... dy ʾḥrym lʿbdʾ dy sgyl* Hatra 245[2]: 8 *as* ... which he devoted to construction of the *sgyl* (v. s.v.); *wʾhrg kl[h] ... ky lʿštr kmš hḥrmth* KAI 181[16f.]: and I killed her totality ... because I had consecrated her to A.-K. (for the background, cf. e.g. Brekelmans Herem 32, Mattingly SMIM 233ff.) - PAʿEL Part. pass. devoted, consecrated to (l_5).
v. *ʾḥz*.

ḥrm₂ v. *ḥrm₄*.

ḥrm₃ **Nab** Sing. abs. *ḥrm* CIS ii 197[8], 199[3], 206[2]; abs./cstr. *ḥrm* CIS ii 350[3]; cstr. *ḥrm* CIS ii 197[9], 199[3]; emph. *ḥrmʾ* CIS ii 199[7], 206[2]; Plur. abs. *ḥrmyn* CIS ii 350[4]; emph. *ḥrmyʾ* CIS ii 350[4,5] - ¶ subst. m. - **1)** consecrated object, inviolable object; *kprʾ wktbh dnh ḥrm kḥlyqt ḥrm nbṭw* CIS ii 197[8f.]: this tomb and this its inscription are consecrated objects after the manner of what is held consecrated by the N., cf. CIS ii 199[3f.], 206[2f.] (cf. however Milik Bibl xlviii 577; v *ḥlyqh*); *qbrʾ dnh ... ḥrm wḥrg dwšrʾ* CIS ii 350[1ff.]: this tomb ... is a consecrated and forbidden (i.e. inviolable) object (dedicated to) Dushara - **2)** consecration formula (by which a certain object is placed under the protection of a deity; *pʾyty ʿmh ldwšrʾ ʾlhʾ bḥrmʾ dy ʿlʾ* CIS ii 199[7]: and he shall be charged to (i.e. shall pay to) the god D. on account of the consecration formula mentioned above (sc. the formulae in ll. 4ff.; :: Brekelmans Herem 25: = inviolability); *šṭry ḥrmyn* CIS ii 350[4,5]: the deeds containing the consecration formula :: Parrot Malédictions 44, 81 (cf. also Cooke NSI p. 241, Brekelmans Herem 24): deeds relating to consecrated things - :: Cantineau Nab ii 99 interpreting meanings 1) and 2) of $ḥrm_2$ as two different words - a form of this word poss. also in the Palm. text CIS ii 3927[3], cf. Chabot sub CIS ii a.l.: *ḥr[my]ʾ* (Plur. emph.; *pia munera*), cf. also Milik DFD 3 (cf. Gawlikowski TP 51, Ber xxiv 37): l. *ḥrmʾ* (= Sing. emph., sacred distribution (of food)), cf. Greek par. ἐπίδοσιν (αἰωνίαν), cf. also Cantineau Gramm 100 - Milik DFD 3f.: l. *ḥr[mʾ]* (= Sing. emph.) or rather *ḥr[mtʾ]* (= Sing. emph. of *ḥrmh* (= sacred enclosure)) in Inv xi 80[5], highly uncert. interpret. - v.d.Toorn ZAW xcviii 283ff.: the *ḥrm* in Cowl 7[7] = Sing. cstr. of $ḥrm_3$ (improb. interpret., *ḥrm* = part of n.d., cf. e.g. Cowl a.l., Porten Arch 156ff.).

ḥrm₄ **Pun** Sing. abs. *ḥrm* CIS i 324[3] - ¶ subst. of unknown meaning denoting a profession, manufacturer of fishing-nets?, Tomback CSL s.v.: = fisherman (?), cf. also Dahood: poss. = Plur. cstr. of *ḥrm* (= fisherman) or = QAL Part. act. pl.m. cstr. of $ḥrm_2$(= to fish; less prob. interpret.). The same word also in KAI 51 Rs 2?, in the expression *rb ḥrm lym* (Tomback s.v.: = chief fisherman of the sea; v. ym_1 :: Aimé-Giron BIFAO xxxviii 13f.: *ḥrm* = Plur. abs. of $ḥr_4$(= Syrian,

Phoenician); Röllig KAI a.l.: *ym* in this title poss. = *ywm* (Sing. abs.)).
ḥrmh v. *ḥrm*$_3$.
ḥrn **OldAr** Sing. abs. *ḥrn* KAI 223B 12 - ¶ subst. wrath; *ywm ḥrn* KAI 223B 12: the day of wrath.
ḥrsh$_1$ **Pun** Sing. (or Plur.?) *ḥrst* KAI 145^{8} - ¶ subst. of unknown meaning; poss. certain type of building or part of it, cf. Cooke NSI p. 155, Février Sem vi 21ff., Bonnet SEL vii 116 :: v.d.Branden RSF i 169: = Plur. abs. of *ḥrsh*$_2$ (= bas-relief) (cf. Berger MAIBL xxxvi/2, 161: = sculptures, Chabot sub RES 2221: = sculpture) :: Halévy RS ix 280, 285: = objects of clay, pottery > masonry :: Krahmalkov RSF iii 194 (div. otherwise): l. *ʾḥrst*= abnormal spelling of *ʾrṣt* (= Sing. abs. of *ʾrṣh*(= district)) - on this word, cf. also Clermont-Ganneau RAO iii 338.
ḥrsh$_2$ v. *ḥrsh*$_1$.
ḥrp$_1$ **DA** QAL (or PA ʿEL) Pf. 3 p.s.f. *ḥrpt* i 9f. (cf. Hoftijzer DA p. 200, Garbini Hen i 177, 185, Delcor SVT xxxii 55f., McCarter BASOR ccxxxix 51, 54, H.P.Müller ZAW xciv 218, 225f., Hackett BTDA 29, 47, 96, 129, Puech BAT 359 :: Sasson UF xvii 288, 299: prob. = QAL Part. act. s.f. cstr. (cf. Puech FS Grelot 22) :: Levine JAOS ci 199 = QAL Part. act. pl.f. abs. of *ḥrp*$_1$ (cf. also H. & M. Weippert ZDPV xcviii 94) :: Wesselius BiOr xliv 594, 597: = Pf. 2 p.s.m. :: Caquot & Lemaire Syr liv 199: = Sing. cstr. of *ḥrph* (= contumely, defamation) :: Lemaire BAT 318, CRAI '85, 280: poss. = Sing. abs. of *ḥrpt* (= bat) ?) - ¶ verb QAL (or PA ʿEL) to offend, to revile, to defame; + obj. (for the context, v. *ss*$_3$) - Lemaire RB lxxxiii 562f., 567: l. in small Hebr. text (no. 7$^{1f.}$) *ḥrpk* = QAL Part. act. s.m. + suff. 2 p.s.m. (poss. reading and interpret.; for the *ḥ*, cf. also Naveh IEJ xiii 80f. (n. 11), Miller SVT xxxii 323ff.).
ḥrp$_2$ v. *ḥrb*$_1$.
ḥrph v. *ḥrp*$_1$.
ḥrpt v. *ḥrp*$_1$.
ḥrṣ$_1$ v. *ḥrṣ*$_5$, *ʿrṣ*$_1$.
ḥrṣ$_2$ v. *ḥrṣ*$_4$.
ḥrṣ$_3$ **Pun** Sing. abs./cstr. (uncert. context) *ḥrṣ* Punica xiv 3^{5} - **OldAr** Sing. abs. *ḥrṣ* KAI 202A 10 - **OffAr**, cf. Frah iii 6 (*ḥlkyʾ*) - ¶ subst. - **1)** moat: KAI 202A 10 - **2)** canal: Frah iii 6 (cf. Ebeling Frah a.l.: < root *ḥrq* (= to cut, to incise, to carve), cf. however Nyberg FP 64: *ḥlkyʾ* = form of *hlk*$_5$(= watercourse)) - **3)** exact meaning unknown, poss. pit; *nʿspʾ ʿṣmyʿ bḥrṣ* ... Punica xiv 3^{5}: her bones are gathered in the pit (?) ... - for this word, cf. also Kaufman AIA 53f. - on this word, cf. Masson RPAE 73f.
ḥrṣ$_4$ **Ph** Sing. abs. *ḥrṣ* KAI 10^{5} (first instance; cf. e.g. CIS i sub 1, Cooke NSI p. 22f., Röllig KAI a.l., Gibson SSI iii p. 95ff., Garbini

AION xxvii 407 :: Harr 104: = *ḥrṣ*$_5$), 11, 13^{5}, 24^{12}, 38^{1}, 60^{3}, Mus li 286^{5} (prob. reading) - **Pun** Sing. abs. *ḥrṣ* CIS i 327^{5}, 328^{4}, 329^{4}, KAI 81^{2} (:: v.d.Branden PO i 208: = *ḥrṣ*$_5$), 145^{10} (:: Krahmalkov RSF iii 196: = QAL Pf. 3 p.pl. of *ḥrṣ*$_2$= to attack (militarily)), CRAI '68, 117^{6} - cf. also Lipiński BiOr xxxi 119 - ¶ subst. gold; > Greek χρυσός, cf. Masson RPAE 37f.
v. *ḥrṣ*$_5$.

ḥrṣ$_5$ **Ph** Sing. abs. *ḥrṣ* KAI 10^{4,5} (second instance; cf. Harr 104, Garbini AION xxvii 406f., Bonnet SEL vii 116 :: e.g. CIS i sub 1, Cooke NSI p. 22f., Dupont-Sommer Sem iii 39, Röllig KAI a.l., Rosenthal ANET 656, Gibson SSI iii p. 95ff.: = *ḥrṣ*$_4$),60^{5} (cf. e.g. Lidzbarski Handb 281, KI p. 42, Chabot sub RES 1215, Harr 104, Röllig KAI a.l., Gibson SSI iii p. 149, 151, Bonnet SEL vii 115 :: e.g. Cooke NSI p. 94, 98: = *ḥrṣ*$_4$),DD 13^{1} (cf. Milik DFD 426, Gibson SSI iii p. 121f. :: Durand & Duru DD a.l., Caquot Sem xv 31: = *ḥrṣ*$_4$),Antas 5^{1} (:: Garbini AION xix 322: = QAL Part. pass. s.m. abs. of *ḥrṣ*$_1$(= to sculpture), cf. also Fantar sub Antas 5: = adj. of this root :: Fantar ibid.: or = Sing. abs. of *ḥrṣ*$_4$)- ¶ subst. carving, chiselling, carved work; *mš ʾbn ḥrṣ* Antas 5^{1}: statue of carved stone; *mṣbt ḥrṣ* KAI 60^{5}: a chiselled stele (cf. DD 13^{1}); *hptḥ ḥrṣ zn* KAI 10^{4}: this carved door (cf. KAI 10^{5}).
v. *ḥrṣ*$_4$.

ḥrq v. *ḥrṣ*$_3$.

ḥrr **Hebr** Sing. abs. *ḥrr* DJD ii 30^{25} - **JAr** Sing. abs. *ḥrr* MPAT 45^{5}, IEJ xxxvi 206^{7} - ¶ subst. litigation; *kl ḥrr [w]tgr* MPAT 45^{5}: every litigation and claim, cf. DJD ii 30^{25}, IEJ xxxvi 206^{7} (cf. also Koffmahn DWJ 168).

ḥrrt v.Soden Or xxxv 10, xlvi 187: = throat > Akkad. (less prob. interpret., cf. Kaufman AIA 54, 144f., cf. also CAD and v.Soden AHW s.v. *ḫarurtu*.

ḥrš$_1$ **OldCan** QAL Impf. 1 p.s. *aḫ-ri-šu* EA 226^{11} (*aḫ-ri-[šu]*, cf. Rainey EI xiv 10* (n. 37), EA p. 72, Sivan GAG 155, 225), 365^{11} - **OffAr** QAL (?) Impf. 1 p.pl. *nḥrt* MAI xiv/2, 66^{8} (reading however uncert., cf. Porten & Yardeni sub TADAE B 1.1: or l. *nḥdt/nḥwt* (without interpret., v. also infra)) - **Palm** QAL Part. act. s.m. emph. *ḥrtʾ* Inv D 17 - ¶ verb QAL - **1)** to plough: EA 226^{11}, 365^{11}; this meaning poss. also in MAI xiv/2, 66^{8} (cf. Dupont-Sommer MAI xiv/2, 76 (diff. context) :: Grelot DAE p. 73 (n. g): = to divide :: Bauer & Meissner SbPAW '36, 419: = to dig or l. *nḥdt* = PAʿEL Impf. 1 p.pl. of *ḥdt*$_1$ (= *ḥdš*$_1$);v. however supra) - **2)** to engrave; Part. act. (or subst.?) = engraver: Inv D 17 (?, cf. Cantineau Syr xix 164) - Vattioni AION xvi 54f.: *aross* in IRTS 24^{5}: = QAL Pf. 3 p.s.m. (to engrave; uncert. reading and interpret., cf. also Levi Della Vida OA ii 75f.: poss. = part of n.p.).

v. ḥdš₁,ḥrš₄,₆, ḥrt₃.

ḥrš₂ **Pun** a form of this root poss. in Poen 1027: *ierasan*; cf. Schroed 297, 318f.: = YIPH Impf. 1 p.s. + suff. 3 p.s.m. (= to silence, to put to silence); L.H.Gray AJSL xxxix 82: = QAL Impf. 3 p.s.m. (coh.) (= to be deaf) :: du Mesnil du Buisson BiOr xviii 111: *ierasan* = that he may be favorable (QAL Impf. 3 p.s.m. of *rṣy*?); cf. also Garbini StudMagr xii 90f.

v. ḥrš₉.

ḥrš₃ **Nab** the form *ḥryš*ʾ CIS ii 350³ = QAL Part. pass. s.m. emph. of *ḥrš₃* with meaning "protected" (i.e. sacred)??, cf. Hoffmann with Lidzbarski Handb 281 × Milik RB lxvi 560: = name of the throne of Dushara :: Clermont-Ganneau RAO ii 130, Hommel FS de Vogüé 298, Cantineau Nab i 91, ii 99: = name of a goddess, consort of Dushara.

ḥrš₄ **Ph** Sing. abs. *ḥrš* CIS i 64³ (= Kition B 9), 81³f· (*ḥ[r]š*; for the reading, cf. also Amadasi sub Kition B 26), EI xviii 117¹ (= IEJ xxxv 83); cstr. *ḥrš* RES 1207² (= Kition B 46); Plur. abs. *ḥršm* KAI 37A 14 (= Kition C 1 A) - **Pun** Sing. abs. *ḥrš* CIS i 274², 325⁵, 4875³, 51794; cstr. *ḥrš* CIS i 326³, 3333; Plur. abs. *ḥršm* KAI 100⁶ (cf. however Röllig KAI iii p. 9: = QAL Part. act. of *ḥrš₁*)- **Hebr** Sing. abs. *ḥrš* DF 12 - ¶ subst. m. handicraftsman, artisan, *faber*; *rb ḥrš* CIS i 64³: chief artisan; *ḥrš* ʾrnt CIS i 3333: box-maker (cf. also CIS i 326³); *ḥrš* ʿglt RES 1207²: wheelwright; *ḥršm šyr* KAI 100⁶: wood-craftsmen - cf. also *bn ḥrš* EI xviii 117¹: handicraftsmen, artisans (cf. Dothan EI a.l., IEJ xxxv 84).

v. ḥrš₅.

ḥrš₅ **Pun** Sing. abs. *ḥrš* KAI 72B 4, 81⁹, CIS i 5510¹¹, Monte Sirai ii 80³, cf. IRT 889²: *ars* - ¶ subst. craftmanship; in the combination *b ʿl ḥrš* KAI 72B 4, 81⁹, CIS i 5510¹¹, Monte Sirai ii 80³ (cf. IRT 889²: *bal ars*): chief craftsman, architect (or = *ḥrš₄*?),on this interpret., cf. also Bonnet SEL vii 115.

ḥrš₆ **Ph** Sing. abs. *ḥrš* KAI 26A iii 1 (*[ḥ]rš*), C iv 5 (cf. however Röllig KAI iii p. 9: = QAL Inf. cstr. of *ḥrš₁*)- ¶ subst. ploughing; *b ʿt ḥrš* KAI 26C iv 4f.: at ploughing time (cf. Gibson SSI iii p. 61) :: Lipiński RTAT 259: at pruning time.

ḥrš₇ **Pun** Sing. cstr., cf. Poen 937: *chirs* (cf. e.g. Sznycer PPP 95 :: J.J.Glück & Maurach Semitics ii 111 (div. otherwise): l. *hychir* (= HIPH Pf. 3 p.s.m. of *nkr₂* (= to know)) + *sa* (= *š₁₀*)), Poen 947: *ers* (on these transcriptions, cf. Quittner ZDMG-Suppl iv 298)- ¶ subst. sherd; *chirs aelichot* Poen 937 (cf. Poen 947 *ers ahelicot*): the sherd of hospitality.

ḥrš₈ **OffAr** Sing. emph. *ḥrš*ʾ Cowl 81³⁷,³⁸ - ¶ word of unknown meaning, denoting object of bronze (cf. Cowl p. 199; *ḥrš*ʾ *zy nḥš* Cowl 81³⁷); Harmatta ActAntHung vii 352 (cf. also Grelot DAE p. 110 (n. c)): =

plough (improb. interpret.) - Segal ATNS a.l.: this word also in ATNS 50[9] (*ḥrš*, Sing. abs.), uncert. reading and interpret.

ḥrš₉ **DA** Plur. m. abs. *ḥršn* i 15 (:: Levine JAOS ci 197, 199: = Plur. abs. of *ḥrš₁₀* (= incantation)) - **OffAr** Sing. m. abs., cf. Warka 18, 43: *ḫa-ri-iš*; cstr. *ḥrš* Aḥiq 216 (?, v. infra) - ¶ adj. (substantivated; or = QAL Part. act. of *ḥrš₂*?),deaf, deaf and dumb; *šmʿw ḥršn mn rḥq* DA i 15: the deaf ones heard from afar (cf. also Weinfeld Shn v/vi 145); *ḥrš ʾdnyn* Aḥiq 216: someone deaf of ears (:: Cowl a.l.: a deaf man, ears; dam. context); *a-ma-ár ša-ṭi-e qu-um ḫa-ri-iš* Warka 18, 43: speak, stupid one, rise dumb one.

ḥrš₁₀ v. *ḥrš₉*.

ḥrt₁ v. *ḥrš₁*,*ḥrt₃*.

ḥrt₂ v. *ḥrwt₁*.

ḥrt₃ **Pun** Sing./Plur. abs. *ḥrt* CIS i 6002[2]; Sing./Plur. cstr. *ḥrt* OA v 199 - ¶ subst. word of unknown meaning; Ferron OA v 198f.: = ashes, burned remains (cf. also Bonnet SEL vii 117); cf. however for CIS i 6002 RES sub 10: = Sing. of subst. denoting profession (someone using ink to adorn vases/urns), or = QAL Pf. 3 p.s.m. (or 1 p.s.) of *ḥrt₁*(= *ḥrš₁*;= to write??), cf. Lidzbarski Eph i 170, Harr 104, cf. also Février sub CIS i 6002: or = QAL Imper. s.m. of *ḥrt₁*:: Garbini Monte Sirai ii p. 86 n. 1 = QAL Pf. 1 p.s. of *ḥrš₁*(= to write, to engrave).

ḥrts (< Greek χόρτος, cf. Cross EI xv 68*) - **OffAr** Sing. abs. *ḥrts* EI v 67*[3] - ¶ subst. fodder, food for cattle.

ḥš₁ **Palm** Sing. emph. *ḥšʾ* Inv x 127[2] - ¶ subst. m. solicitude, care; *ḥšʾ ṭb[ʾ]* Inv x 127[2]: goodwill, favour, benevolence (cf. Greek par. εὔνοια; cf. also Starcky sub Inv x 127).
v. *ḥšš*.

ḥš₂ **Pun** Levi Della Vida LibAnt i 59, Amadasi IPT 119: the diff. *ḥš* in Trip 38[5] poss. = Sing. abs. of noun *ḥš* (= sorrow, grief), poss. interpret.

ḥšʾ **OffAr** PAʿEL Part. s.m. abs., cf. Warka 28: *mi-ḫa-áš-še-e* - ¶ verb PAʿEL to silence, to put to silence, cf. Landsberger AfO xii 250f., Dupont-Sommer RA xxxix 51 :: Gordon (and Ginsberg) AfO xii 117: = verbal form or subst. derived from the root *ḥšš* (= to pain).

ḥšb₁ **Pun** QAL Part. act. s.m. abs. (or cstr.?) *ḥšb* KAI 161[2]; PIʿEL Part. pl.m. abs. *mḥšbm* CRAI '68, 117[7], on coins Müll 2,76, CHC 586 no. 14 (× Mahjoubi & Fantar RCL '66, 209: = Plur. abs. of *mḥšb₂* with same meaning) - **DA** QAL Imper. s.m., or Inf. abs. in i 14, v. infra - **Nab** PAʿEL Pf. 3 p.s.m. *ḥšb* MPAT 64 ii 5 (?, *ḥšb[*, dam. context); 2 p.s.m. *ḥšbt* MPAT 64 i 11; Impf. 2 p.s.m. *tḥšb* MPAT 64 i 10; 1 p.pl. *nḥšb* MPAT 64 i 13 - **Palm** ITP Inf. *mtḥšbw* CIS ii 3913 ii 103 (for this form, cf. Cantineau Gramm 91, Rosenthal Sprache 60f.) - **Hatra** PAʿEL Pf. 1 p.s. *[ḥ]šbyt* 49[3] (cf. Milik RN vi/iv 56 n. 2, Syr xliv 297, Vattioni IH p. 41 (uncert. interpret.) :: Safar Sumer ix 245 (n. 26): l.

šbyt = PA ʿEL Pf. 3 p.s.m. of *šbt₁* (= to repose > to die) :: Caquot Syr xxxii 54: l. *šbyt* = Sing. abs. of *šbt₃* (= rest) :: Altheim & Stiehl AAW iv 265: l. *šbyt* = verbal form Pf. 1 p.s. (I have collected/demanded payment)) - ¶ verb QAL to weigh, to consider; + obj. in the epithet of a king, *ḥšb nʿm* KAI 161[2]: who devises good, the well-disposed; *ḥšb ḥšb wḥšb ḥ[šb]* DA i 14f.: prob. meaning, consider carefully and consider carefully (each pair with different subject; one *ḥšb* in each pair is either QAL Imper. s.m. (cf. Hoftijzer DA p. 216f.) or QAL Inf. abs. (cf. H.P.Müller ZDPV xciv 62 n. 36, ZAW xciv 218, 229, H. & M. Weippert ZDPV xcviii 99 :: H.P.Müller ZDPV xciv a.l. the first *ḥšb* of each pair = verbal form), the other *ḥšb* is Sing. abs. of *ḥšb₃* (= consideration; other possibility: each pair consists of two Imper., cf. Hoftijzer DA p. 216f.) :: McCarter BASOR ccxxxix 51, 56: in each pair one *ḥšb* = Sing. abs. of *ḥšb₂* (= esteemer), the other one = QAL Part. act. s.m. abs. (cf. also Hackett BTDA 29, 53, 96: the first *ḥšb* = QAL Part. pass. s.m. abs., the second one = QAL Pf. 3 p.s.m., the third one = QAL Part. act. s.m. abs., the fourth one = QAL Pf. pass. 3 p.s.m.) :: Rofé SB 67: at least one *ḥšb* = Sing. abs. of *ḥšb₄* (= band), cf. also Garbini Hen i 180f., 185, H.Weippert LJPM 90 n. 35 :: Garbini Hen i 181, 185: the last *ḥšb* = QAL Pf. 3 p.s.m. :: Sasson UF xvii 288, 303 (n. 45), 308: the first three instances of *ḥšb* = QAL Inf. abs., in the fourth instance l. *ḥ[rb]* = Sing. abs. of *ḥrb₂*:: Levine JAOS ci 197, 199: in all instances *ḥšb* = QAL Part. act. s.m. abs. (= augurer)? :: Puech FS Grelot 24, 28: in all instances *ḥšb* prob. = QAL Pf. 3 p.s.m.? (on the problem, cf. also Naveh IEJ xxix 135, Weinfeld Shn v/vi 144, 146)) - PI ʿEL/PA ʿEL to calculate, to evaluate; + obj.: MPAT 64 i 11; + obj. + *b₂*: MPAT 64 i 10 (for context, v. *pgʿwn*); + obj. + *byn*, *klʾ nḥšb byny lbynyk* MPAT 64 i 13: we shall evaluate all between you and me (sc. together) :: J.J.Rabinowitz BASOR cxxxix 13: *nḥšb* = hebraism (NIPH Part. s.m. abs.; it is considered as nothing between me and between you); Part.: accountant, person charged with or responsible for accounts, comptroller: RCL '66, 201[7], on coins (cf. Müll 2,76; prob. = *quaestores*; cf. also Huss 465 (n. 73), 493, Polselli StudMagr xii 83ff.) - ITP to be calculated: CIS ii 3913 ii 103 - Halévy RS i 219, 230: l *nḥ[š]b* in KAI 215[10] (= NIPH Part. s.m. abs., esteemed), cf. Dupont-Sommer AH i/1, 7, i/2, 3: *l[n]ḥ[š]b* (cf. also Dion p. 39, 208f.; for the reading of the *ḥ*, cf. D.H.Müller WZKM vii 38bis, Cooke NSI p. 172, 177, Koopmans ii 16, Gibson SSI ii p. 78, 84 (Gibson: l. *[h]ḥ[l]b*? = HAPH Pf. 3 p.s.m. of *ḥlb₂*(= to cause to succeed, to give authority); poss. explanation)) :: Lidzbarski Handb 443 : l. *hwšb*? (cf. Halévy RS vii 342: = HOPH Pf. 3 p.s.m. of *yšb₁*; Donner KAI a.l.: = HAPH Pf. 3 p.s.m. of *yšb₁*); cf. also Degen ZDMG cxix 175 - v.Soden Or xlvi 187: > Akkad.: to calculate.

v. *ḥšb$_2$*, *mḥšb$_1$*.

ḥšb$_2$ **Ph** Sing. abs. *ḥšb* CIS i 74[4] (= Kition B 19; dam. context) - ¶ subst. m. (or = Qal Part. act. of *ḥšb$_1$*?): comptroller?, quaestor?
v. *ḥšb$_1$*.

ḥšb$_3$ v. *ḥšb$_1$*.

ḥšb$_4$ v. *ḥšb$_1$*.

ḥšbn$_1$ **OffAr** Sing. cstr. *ḥšbn* Cowl 81[1] - **Palm** Sing. cstr. *ḥšbn* CIS ii 3913 ii 75, 115, Inv x 127[2] - **JAr** Sing. cstr. *ḥšbn* DBKP 17[41] - ¶ subst. account; *ḥšbn ʿnbyʾ zy ktbt* Cowl 81[1]: the account (cf. however Harmatta ActAntHung vii 339: = calculation) of the produce which I wrote; *kl dy ʿll. lḥšbn tgrʾ* CIS ii 3913 ii 115: everything that enters into the reckoning of the merchants (i.e. everything that comes into the market; cf. Greek par. ὅσα εἰς ἐμπορείαν φέρεται); *lḥšbn* Inv x 127[2]: because of, on account of; *lḥšbn pqdwn* DBKP 17[41]: on account of deposit (cf. Greek par.: εἰς λόγον παραθήκης) - Sing. + suff. 3 p.s.m. (*ḥš[bn]h*) prob. to be restored in CIS ii 3913 ii 133 (cf. Reckendorf ZDMG xlii 334, 338, Cooke NSI p. 331; cf. however CIS ii sub 3913: l. *ḥš[ḥt]h* = Sing. + suff. 3 p.s.m. of *ḥšḥh* (= use), cf. also Teixidor AO i 245).
v. *ḥšbn$_2$*.

ḥšbn$_2$ **Hatra** Sing. emph. *ḥšbnʾ* 49[3] (:: Altheim & Stiehl AAW iv 265: = Sing. emph. of *ḥšbn$_1$*)- ¶ subst. comptroller, treasurer; *ḥšbnʾ dbyt bʿšmn* Hatra 49[3]: the comptroller/treasurer of the temple of B.

ḥšhrsrt (< Iran., cf. Périkhanian REA-NS viii 172) - **OffAr** Sing. abs. *ḥšhrsrt* REA-NS viii 170A 3, B 3 - ¶ subst. the one who allied to Xhathra.

ḥšwk v. *ḥšk$_2$*.

ḥšḥh v. *ḥšbn$_1$*.

ḥšy (< Arab., cf. Brockelmann Semitistik 148, Cantineau Nab ii 172, Altheim & Stiehl AAW i 191, Garbini HDS 36, cf. also O'Connor JNES xlv 225ff.) - **Nab** J 17[8] - ¶ prep. with the exception of, except (for the context, v. *yld$_2$*).

ḥšk$_1$ **OffAr** Haph Impf. 2 p.s.m. *thḥšk* Aḥiq 81 - ¶ verb Haph to withhold; + obj. + *mn$_5$*, *ʾl thḥšk brk mn ḥṭr* Aḥiq 81: do not withhold your son from the rod (i.e. do not leave your son unpunished), for this text, cf. also Lindenberger APA 49f., 224f. nn. 35-37 - cf. *ḥsk*.

ḥšk$_2$ **Ph** Sing. abs. *ḥšk* KAI 27[19] - **DA** Sing. abs. *ḥšk* i 8, 9 (dam. context) - **OffAr** Sing. emph. *ḥšwkʾ*Aḥiq 125 (for this form, cf. Leand 43r[00], Kottsieper SAS 114, 205; cf. also Degen GGA '79, 25) - **Palm** Sing. emph. *ḥšd/rkʾ* Ber iii 99[3] (lapsus for *ḥšwkʾ*,cf. Milik DFD 182f. :: Ingholt Ber iii 99, 103: l. *ḥškkʾ* = Sing. emph. of *ḥškk* (= darkness)) - ¶ subst. darkness; *ḥdr ḥšk* KAI 27[19]: dark room (diff. context; cf. e.g. Gaster Or xi 48f. (*bḥdr ḥšk* = epithet of *ʿptʾ*, cf. also Torczyner JNES vi 26, Albright BASOR lxxvi 9, Röllig KAI a.l., Avishur PIB 255), Cross & Saley BASOR cxcvii 46 (combining *bḥdr ḥšk* with *ʿbr*, cf. also Röllig NESE ii 19 (cf. also p. 24f.), Gibson SSI iii p. 83) :: Garbini OA xx 285f.: *ḥdr* = Sing. abs., *ḥšk* = subject of following *ʿbr*); *qrth bḥšwkʾ* (v. supra) Ber iii 99[3]: she invoked him in darkness (i.e. in a difficult situation).

ḥškk v. *ḥšk*$_2$.

ḥšl$_1$ **OffAr** QAL Impf. 3 p.s.m. *yḥšl* Driv 8[6]; Part. act. s.m. abs. *ḥšl* Driv 8[6] - ¶ verb QAL of uncert. meaning: to give, to pay? (meaning derived from context, cf. Grelot DAE p. 317 n. 1); Driv p. 70f.: < Akkad. (improb. interpret., cf. Kaufman AIA 54f.); *hlkʾ lqbl zy qdmn pmwn ʾbwhy hwh ḥšl yḥšl ʿl bytʾ zyly* Driv 8[5f.]: a tax to (the rate) which P. his father used to pay formerly, he must pay to my estate.

ḥšl$_2$ v. *bqrlḥš,gll*.

ḥšq v. *msʿ*.

ḥšš **Hebr** QAL Part. act. pl.m. abs. *ḥwššyn* SM 49[26] - **JAr** APH Impf. 2 p.s.f. *tyḥšyn* AMB 3[5] (for this form, cf. Sokoloff DJPA s.v. :: Naveh & Shaked AMB a.l.: or = < root *ḥwš*, preferably = PAʿEL Impf. 2 p.s.f.) - ¶ verb QAL to take into consideration, to consider; + *l*$_5$: SM 49[26] - APH to cause pain to, to make suffer; + *l*$_5$ (obj.): AMB 3[5] - du Mesnil du Buisson TMP 569: the diff. *ḥš* in TMP 569[3] = QAL Pf. 3 p.s.m. of *ḥšš* (= to suffer), improb. interpret. (cf. Gawlikowski Sem xxiii 121ff.: *ḥš* = lapsus for *ḥšʾ* = Sing. emph. of *ḥš*$_1$ (= affection)?) - Meehan ZDPV xcvi 64f.: the diff. *ḥšyšth* in ZDPV xcvi 59[2] poss. = a composite < *ḥšyš* (= PAʿEL Imper. s.m. of *ḥšš* (= to have respect)) + *(y)th* = *yt* + suff. 3 p.s.f. (highly uncert. interpret.).

v. *dḥšpṭ*, *ḥšʾ*.

ḥštrʾ **OffAr** Dupont-Sommer JKF i 46f.: l. this word in JKF i 46[4] (= kingdom, royalty; < Iran.) or l. *ḥštrp[nʾ]* = Sing. emph. of *ḥštrpn*.

ḥštrpn (< Iran., cf. Chaumont JA cclvi 19f., 28 n. 44, 30 n. 88, cf. also Diakonov & Livshitz Nisa-b p. 23, PaSb ii 142f., Benveniste Titres 103, Dupont-Sommer CRAI '76, 648ff., Mayrhofer FX p. 181f.) - **OffAr** Sing. emph. *ḥštrpnʾ* FX 136[4] (Greek par. ξαδράπης) - ¶ subst. satrap, governor of a province (cf. also Henning JRAS '53, 134, Frye BAG 89f.); *ḥštrpnʾ zy bkrk wtrmyl* FX 136[4f.]: the satrap (governing) in K. and T. - this word Sing. emph.(?) poss. to be restored in RES 954[5] (*ḥšt[rpnʾ]*, cf. Lidzbarski Eph iii 66 (Greek par. l. 3: σαδράπησιν) - cf. also the n.d. *ḥštrpty* (= Lord of power) in FX 137[25] (cf. Dupont-Sommer CRAI '76, 648ff., Mayrhofer FX 184f.).

v. *ḥštrʾ*.

ḥt **DA** Sing. abs. (?, dam. context) *ḥt* i 9 (cf. e.g. Hoftijzer DA a.l., TUAT ii 142, Lemaire CRAI '85, 280, Sasson UF xvii 288, 298 :: McCarter BASOR ccxxxix 51, 54, Hackett BTDA 25, 29, 45, 129: l. *ḥt[m]*

(= Sing. abs. of *ḥtm*$_2$) :: Puech BAT 356: l. *ḥtt* (= Sing. abs. of *ḥtt*$_2$ (= terror)) :: Wesselius BiOr xliv 594, 597: l. *ḥt[mh]* = QAL Part. pass. s.f. abs. of *ḥtm*$_1$) - ¶ subst. fear.

ḥtyl OffAr Plur. abs. *ḥtyln* Cowl 37^{10} - ¶ subst. prob. meaning: string, cf. Cowl p. 134, Driver JRAS '32, 81, cf. however Grelot Sem xiv 67, Porten & Greenfield JEAS p. 80, Porten & Yardeni sub TADAE A 4.2: = mat. (cf. also Driver JRAS '32, 81 (: or = basket?), Grelot DAE p. 389).

ḥtm$_1$ Pun QAL Pf. 3 p.s.m. *ḥtm* KAI 124^{4}, CIS i 5522^{5} (?, cf. Février Sem xi 6, CIS i a.l., v.d.Branden BiOr xxiii 143 :: Février Sem iv 14: = QAL Part. pass. s.m. abs.) - **Hebr** QAL Imper. s.m. *ḥtm* TA-H 4^{2}, 17^{6}; Part. act. pl.m. abs. *ḥwtmym* DJD ii 29^{9}, 30^{9}; pass. s.m. abs. *[ḥ]tm* TA-H 10^{4} (?, uncert. reading, heavily dam. context, cf. also Pardee UF x 308, HAHL 44) - **OffAr** QAL Impf. 3 p.pl.m. *yḥtmwn* Samar 1^{12} (= EI xviii 8*); Imper. pl.m. *ḥtmw* Cowl 21^{9} (for the reading, cf. Cowl a.l., (Ginsberg with) Porten Arch 313f., Porten & Greenfield JEAS p. 78, Porten & Yardeni sub TADAE A 4.1 :: Vincent Rel 247: = PA ʿEL Imper. pl.m. (= to lock up carefully) :: Joüon MUSJ xviii 66, Grelot VT xvii 206f.: l. *stmw* = QAL/PA ʿEL Imper. pl.m. of *stm* (= to keep apart, to conceal); cf. also Grelot VT iv 382f.); cf. Frah xxiii 2 (*ḥtymwn*), Paik 444-446 (*ḥtymwn*), GIPP 24, SaSt 17 (cf. Toll ZDMG-Suppl viii 35) - **JAr** QAL Pf. 3 p.pl.m. *ḥtmw* MPAT 51^{14} (for this reading, cf. Milik RB lxi 183, Bibl xxxviii 265, Puech RQ ix 214, 220 × Birnbaum PEQ '57, 116, 130: l. *ḥtm* = QAL Part. pass. s.m. abs., cf. also Beyer ATTM 320) - ¶ verb QAL - **1)** to seal (up) - a) a document: MPAT 51^{14} (v. supra), cf. also Samar 1^{12}; Part. act. = sealer > witness: DJD ii 29^{9}, 30^{9} (cf. Koffmahn DWJ 178f.) - b) a jar (cf. Aharoni sub TA-H 17^{6}, Pardee UF x 302, HAHL 36f., Conrad TUAT i 252): TA-H 4^{2}; + obj. + *b*$_2$, *ḥtm ʾth bḥtmk* TA-H 17$^{6f.}$: seal it (sc. the jar) with your seal - c) a chamber: Cowl 21^{9} (v. supra; cf. also Malamat EI xviii 325ff.) - d) diff. text CIS i 5522^{5}; Février CIS a.l.: = to seal :: v.d.Branden BiOr xxiii 143, 145: > to fix (sc. a certain object to a wall) - **2)** to complete: KAI 124^{4} (?, uncert. interpret., cf. Levi Della Vida RCL '49, 403, Röllig KAI a.l., v.d.Branden PO i 438; cf. however Jongeling SV 413: = to seal?) - a form of this root (*ḥtm*) in Sem xxxix 32 conv. 1 (on the poss. interpret., cf. Lozachmeur Sem xxxix 34), dam. context - the diff. *ḥtmʾ* in Nisa-b 483^{1}, 526^{1}, 661^{1}, 676^{1}, Nisa-c 27^{1}, 31^{2}, 36^{2} (in 31 and 36 uncert. reading) poss. = QAL Part. pass. s.m. emph.: sealed (said of a jar) - a form of this root (*mḥtm*) in EI xx 256^{13} (= PU ʿAL Part. s.m. abs.??).
v. *ḥt*.

ḥtm$_2$ Ph Sing. abs. *ḥtm* KAI 51^{9} (*ḥ[t]m*; uncert. reading, heavily dam. context), JKF i 44 (or cstr.?), Sem xxvii 32 i 3, 33 i 3 (cf. however

Teixidor Syr lvi 370f.: both instances in Sem xxvii forgery?); cstr. *ḥtm* Syr xxxii 42 (Ph.?, cf. also Herr sub SANSS-Ar 78, Bordreuil sub CSOI-Ar 85); Plur. abs. *ḥtmm* KAI 51[9f.] - **Amm** Sing. cstr. *ḥtm* SANSS-Amm 9 (= Vatt sig. eb. 225 = Jackson ALIA 74 no. 36 = CAI 55 = CSOI-Amm 76; or = Ar.?, cf. Naveh BASOR ccxxxix 76), 45 (= Vatt sig. eb. 229 = CAI 57; for the reading, cf. Teixidor Syr xlv 362), 46 (45 and 46 prob. forgeries, cf. Naveh & Tadmor AION xviii 448ff., Herr SANSS a.l., cf. however Garbini AION xviii 453f., xx 252 (= LS 101), cf. also Bordreuil Syr l 183) - **Hebr** Sing. abs. *ḥtm* Dir sig. 97 (= Vatt sig. eb. 97 = SVM 185); + suff. 2 p.s.m. *ḥtmk* TA-H 13[3], 17[6f.] - **OffAr** Sing. abs. *ḥtm* Syr xlv 362, lxvii 505 (in both instances *ḥtm zy NP*); cstr. *ḥtm* CIS ii 66 (= CSOI-Ar 125), 100 (= Gall 163 = SANSS-Ar 72), 101 (= Gall 169 = SANSS-Ar 71 = CSOI-Ar 128), 105 (= Gall 48), Driv p. 4 n. 1, Gall 40, 47, 160 (:: Driver RSO xxxii 48 (div. otherwise): l. *ḥwmdt*ʾ = n.p.), PF 281 (*[ḥ]tm*), PTT p. 53 n. 52, Schmidt Persepolis ii p. 26 (taf. 7; on this text, cf. also R.A.Bowman Pers p. 6f., Hinz FS Nyberg 381), Syr lxiii 425, JRAS '86, 24, KAI 236 vs. 1 (= AECT 49); emph. *ḥtm*ʾ ATNS 26[4] (?, dam. context); cf. GIPP 53 - **JAr** Sing. cstr. *ḥtm* Eph i 141 (for the reading, cf. Lipiński Stud 191 (n. 9)) - ¶ subst. m. seal - this word poss. also in PF 2043 (Plur. emph. *ḥtmy*ʾ), context of uncert. reading and interpret. - Cowl a.l.: the *ḥwtm*in Cowl 76[1] = Sing. abs. of *ḥtm₂* (improb. interpret., cf. Porten & Yardeni sub TADAE A 5.4: = part of n.p.).
v. *ḥt*.

ḥtm₃ **Ph** Sing. abs. *ḥtm* KAI 58 - ¶ subst. of uncert. meaning denoting a function/profession: signet-officer?, sealer? or maker of seals? (cf. e.g. CIS i sub 118, Cooke NSI p. 100, Röllig KAI a.l.).

ḥtn₁ **OffAr** Sing. emph. *ḥtn*ʾ ATNS 148[2] (or = *ḥtn₂*??, dam. context); + suff. 3 p.s.m. *ḥtnh* Herm 6[3] - **Nab** Sing. abs. *ḥtn* CIS ii 209[7] - **JAr** Sing. + suff. 3 p.s.m. *ḥtnh* MPAT-A 26[4,5] (= Frey 856 = SM 32), Frey 290[1] (uncert. interpret.; or = Sing. emph.?) - ¶ subst. m. son-in-law, brother-in-law (or more generally: relation by marriage?, cf. Mitchell VT xix 110f.).
v. *ḥtn₂*.

ḥtn₂ **DA** Sing. abs. *ḥtn* ii 7 - ¶ subst. bridegroom; for the context, cf. Hoftijzer DA p. 226 (:: Garbini Hen i 185: = near relative (= *ḥtn₁*)).
v. *ḥtn₁*.

ḥtn₃ **OffAr** Sing. cstr. *ḥtn* RES 1785G (uncert. reading) - ¶ subst. of unknown meaning; Clermont-Ganneau RAO iii 69 (div. otherwise): l. *bhtḥtn* = *b₂* + *htḥtn* (= marriage).

ḥtp v. *prr₁*.

ḥtpy (< Egypt. *ḥtp.ṯ*, cf. e.g. CIS i sub 123, Cooke NSI p. 202, Donner KAI a.l., REHR 39) - **OffAr** Sing. abs. *ḥtpy* KAI 268[1] - ¶ subst. prob.

meaning: offering, cf. e.g. CIS i sub 123, Cooke NSI p. 202, Donner KAI a.l., REHR 39 :: (Quaegebeur with) Lipiński OLP viii 11 (n. 142): = libation altar).

ḥtr OffAr QAL (?) Pf. 3 p.s.m. *ḥtr* FX 173³ (v. however infra) - ¶ verb QAL (?) uncert. meaning (heavily dam. context); Dupont-Sommer FX a.l.: = to cross, *ḥtr bym* FX 173³: he has crossed the sea (uncert. interpret.).

ḥtt₁ v. *mḥth, tḥt.*

ḥtt₂ v. *ḥt.*

Ṭ

ṭ₁ for this mark/symbol on seals, in stamps and on jars (for a survey, cf. Colella RB lxxx 549ff. and Syr xlvii 364 no. 41, DJD iii Pl vii 2, cf. also IEJ xviii 227A 3), cf. Yadin SH viii 9ff., Cross EI ix 20ff., IEJ xviii 231f., Avigad IEJ xxiv 52ff., Stern BiAr xxxviii 52, Goldwasser & Naveh IEJ xxvi 15ff. (cf. also Lapp. BASOR clxxii 27f.) :: Colella RB lxxx 549ff. (cf. also Teixidor Syr lii 275): = abbrev. of *ṭpʾ* (= QAL Part. pass. of *ṭpʾ* (= to close, to seal)) :: Delavault & Lemaire Sem xxv 31ff. (cf. also Lemaire RB lxxxiii 57f., Lemaire & Vernus Sem xxviii 55 n. 2): = abbrev. of *ṭb₂* (cf. however Teixidor Syr liii 323).

ṭ₂ v. *šṭ₁.*

ṭʾb OffAr QAL Part. act. s.m. abs. *ṭʾyb* FX 173⁴ (:: Dupont-Sommer FX 174: = QAL pass. Pf. 3 p.s.m.) - ¶ verb QAL to please, to be pleasant to + *l₅*; cf. also *ṭyb.*

ṭʾṭ OffAr Vattioni Or xlviii 145 (ad no. 155): in the Aramaic endorsement of TC xii 58 l. *ṭʾṭ* < Akkad. *uṭṭatu* = barley (highly uncert. reading and interpret.).

ṭʾr v. *ṭhr.*

ṭb₁ Hebr Sing. abs. *ṭb* KAI 194², 195² (uncert. reading), Lach viii obv. 2 - OffAr Sing. + suff. 2 p.s.m. *ṭwbk* Beh 55 (for the interpret. of the context, cf. Greenfield & Porten BIDG 49) - ¶ subst. goodness, well-being; *yšmʿ YHWH ... šmʿt ṭb* KAI 194¹ᶠ·: the Lord give to hear ... good tidings (cf. also the other Hebr. texts); *[wʾl b]ṭwbk ʾymnš thwh* Beh 55: nor in your well-being be insecure (?) - a form of this subst. (Sing. abs. *ṭb*) poss. in Or lix 325¹ (cf. Zauzich & Röllig Or lix 326; uncert. reading and interpret.).
v. *ṭby₃.*

ṭb₂ Hebr Sing. m. abs. *ṭwb* Frey 630b 1, 1070; Plur. m. abs. *ṭwbyn* DJD ii 22,1-9² (on the context cf. Koffmahn DWJ 160f.) - OldAr Sing. m. abs. *ṭb* KAI 216¹⁶, 222B 6, 224³,²² (for the context, v. *mk*); Sing. f. abs. *ṭbh* Tell F 5 (Akkad. par. *ṭābu*) - OffAr Sing. m. abs. *ṭb* KAI

226^{3}, 276^{9} (for the context, v. *hwy*$_1$, *prnwš* :: Grelot Sem viii 13: = orthographic variant of Sing. f. abs. *ṭbh*), Cowl 27^{19,21}, Aḥiq 109, Driv 3^{5}, 5^{8}, WO vi 44D 5, etc.; cstr. *ṭb* Aḥiq 165; emph. *ṭbʾ* MAI xiv/2, 66^{5}, RES 1785F 4, 6; Plur. m. abs. *ṭbn* Aḥiq 14, 113, 157, *ṭbyn* RES 1785F 3 (diff. context); Sing. f. abs. *ṭbh* Aḥiq 57; emph. *ṭbtʾ* Aḥiq 42; cf. Frah xiii 12 (cf. Nyberg FP 47, 83), cf. also GIPP 35, 65, 67, Paik 447, LuG ii 47f., SaSt 24 - **Nab** Sing. m. abs. *ṭb* CIS ii 163A, 228, 243, etc., etc.; emph. *ṭbʾ* CIS ii 184^{3} (cf. Milik Syr xxxv 227, 231), AAW v/1, 85^{2} (cf. also Teixidor Syr xlviii 481) - **Palm** Sing. m. abs. *ṭb* CIS ii 3913 ii 69, 3973^{11}, 4001^{1}, PNO 2ter 11, etc., etc.; emph. *ṭbʾ* CIS ii 3973^{4,9}, 3981^{4}, 3983^{1}, 4014^{12}, 4028^{2}, PNO 6b, c, Inv xi 11^{6} (or rather = Plur. m. emph., cf. Aggoula Sem xxix 110), etc., etc.; Plur. m. emph. *ṭbyʾ* CIS ii 3955^{7}, Syr xii 130^{5}, PNO 7a, Inv xii 55^{2}, SBS 14^{2}, etc., *ṭbʾ* FS Collart 327^{4}; Sing. f. emph. *ṭbtʾ* Syr xii 134^{3}, xvii 349^{4} (cf. also Milik DFD 280f.), AAS xv/1, 90^{2} - **Hatra** Sing. m. abs. *ṭb* 6^{2}, 9^{2}, 13^{2,3}, 23^{2,5}, 25^{2,3}, 200^{1} (cf. Teixidor Sumer xxi 89, Milik DFD 405, Vattioni IH a.l. :: Safar Sumer xviii 60 (n. 25), Caquot Syr xli 269f.: = part of n.p.), etc., etc. (cf. also Assur 6b 3, 12^{4}, 17 i 5, etc., etc.); emph. *ṭbʾ* 230^{4}, app. 3^{1} (= KAI 257; for the reading, cf. du Mesnil du Buisson Syr xix 147, Degen WO v 233, ZDMG cxxi 125, 136 :: Caquot Syr xxx 245, Donner KAI a.l.: l. Sing. abs. *ṭb*; the reading *ṭbnʾ* in Vattioni IH a.l. prob. misprint); Plur. m. abs. *ṭbyn* 16^{1,2}, 17 (for the reading in these instances, cf. Milik RN vi/iv 53 (n. 2), 54, DFD 393, 400, Teixidor Syr xliv 189, Degen WO v 234, Vattioni IH a.l. :: Safar Sumer vii 179, Caquot Syr xxix 98, Donner sub KAI 241 (div. otherwise): l. *nṭbwn* = Sing. abs. of *nṭbwn* (= commemoration) :: Altheim & Stiehl AAW ii 196f. (div. otherwise): l. *ynṭbwn* = Aᴘʜ Impf. 3 p.pl.m. of *ṭbb* (= to proclaim (gloriously))), 149 (in the combination *lṭbyn*, diff. context; :: Safar Sumer xviii 45: pro *lṭbyn* l. *ṭbyn* = benefactions :: Caquot Syr xli 261 : pro *lṭbyn* l. *ṭbyn* used adverbially (favorably) :: Vattioni IH a.l.: pro *dkrn lṭbyn* l. *dkrn ṭbyn* = good memories; v. also *zkrn*) - **JAr** Sing. m. abs. *ṭb* MPAT 41^{5}, MPAT-A 1^{1} (= SM 21), 2^{1} (= Frey 1197 = SM 58), 2^{5} (= Frey 1198^{2} = SM 59), 3^{1} (= Frey 1199 = SM 60), SM 81, 83, 104^{3,6} (= Frey 845), etc., etc. - ¶ adj. - **1)** good, firm, in good condition; *by ṭb* KAI 216^{16}: a suitable palace; *šm ṭb* KAI 226^{3}: a good name; *mʾn ṭb* Aḥiq 109: a good vessel; *ʿṭh ṭbh* Aḥiq 57: a good counsel (cf. Aḥiq 42); *ʾlh rḥmn zy tṣlwth ṭbh* Tell F 5: the merciful god, to whom it is good to pray; *dkrn ṭb* PNO 6a: a good memorial (for other examples, v. *zkrn*); *mh ṭb bʿyny* KAI 224^{3}: whatever is good in my eyes (i.e. whatever seems fitting to me); *hn ʿl mrʾn ṭb* Cowl 30^{23}: if it is good to our lord (i.e. if it seems good to your lordship), cf. Cowl 27^{19,21}, 31^{22}, Driv 3^{5} (cf. Dion RB lxxxix 550f.), cf. also Aḥiq 86 (dam. context); *hn ʿlyk kwt ṭb* Driv 5^{8}: if it thus be good to thee (cf. Driv 10^{2};

cf. Benveniste JA ccxlii 305, Driv p. 55: = calque < Iran., cf. however Whitehead JNES xxxvii 134 (n. 106)); *kzy ḥ[z]yt 'npy 'srḥ'dn ... ṭbn* Aḥiq 14: when I saw the face of A. ... good (i.e. favourable); *gbr ṭb* Aḥiq 163, 164: a good man (i.e. a man of good character); *[']rtḥš[sy] mlk ... ṭb* WO vi 44D 4f.: king A. ... the good (cf. Périkhanian REA-NS iii 19, viii 172); *'lh' ṭb'* PNO 27: the good god (cf. PNO 33[2], SBS 10[4], etc.); *gny' ṭb'* PNO 6b, c, etc.: the good *genius*; *'štr[t'] 'štr' ṭbt'* Syr xii 134[2f.]: A. the good goddess; *l'zyz ṭb'* RIP 151[3]: for A. the good one; *qmy' ṭb* AMB 4[1]: a proper amulet; *qmy' ṭb l'str* AMB 13[2]: an amulet proper for E.; *qmy' ṭb m'syh y'yth* AMB 2[1]: an amulet proper to heal Y. (cf. AMB 2[11]); cf. also the combinations (used as divine epithets): *ṭb' wrḥmn'* CIS ii 3974[2f.]: the good and merciful one (for other examples, v. *rḥmn*); *rḥmn' ṭb'* CIS ii 4022[3]: the merciful (and) good one (for other examples, v. *rḥmn*), *ṭb' wrḥmn' wtyr'* CIS ii 4046[1ff.]: the good, merciful and compassionate one (for other examples, v. *rḥmn*, also for comparable epithets); *ṭb' wškr'* PNO 20: the good and renumerating one (for other examples and comparable expressions, v. *rḥmn*, *škr$_3$*); cf. also *ṭb'* CIS ii 4053[7]: the good one (referring to an unmentioned god; epithet of the anonymous god: CIS ii 4081[1]) - **2)** substantivated: something good, what is good; *yšymwn ṭb bḥnkh lm'mr* Aḥiq 115: they put something good in his palate to say; *ṭb' wlḥy' nplg* MAI xiv/2, 66[5f.]: we will divide what is good and bad (sc. of the yield); *mh ṭb šg[y'] kby[k]* Aḥiq 165: what is the good of your many thorns (v. *mh$_2$*); *lqdm bryk šmh l'lm' 'bd ml' 'l ḥywhy bṭb* DM ii 38 iii: for the one whose name is blessed for ever M. made (this) for his life for good; for the memento-formulae with *bṭb*, *lṭb*, *bkl ṭb*, etc., v. *brk$_1$*, *zkr$_1$*, *šlm$_2$*, cf. also *NP lṭb* Hatra 177: (may) NP (be remembered) for good (complete text?); cf. also the expression *l'lm' ṭb'* CIS ii 4081[5]: for a good eternity (or = lapsus?) - for the unexplained *ṭb* in Cowl 22[135], cf. Cowl a.l., Silverman JAOS lxxxix 695 n. 22, cf. also Grelot DAE p. 364 n. e: l. *ṭby* - Cohen KB a.l.: l. *ṭb* (= Sing. m. abs.) in KB xix (cf. however Lipiński ZAH i 64: l. *ṭby* (= n.p.)).
v. *ṭ$_1$*, *ṭbh$_1$*, *ṭby$_3$*, *ṭm*, *mk*, *mlk$_3$*, *šb*.

ṭb'rš' v. *myṭb*.

ṭbb v. *ṭb$_2$*.

ṭbh$_1$ **Hebr** Sing. abs. *ṭwbh* SM 75[1], 76[1] - **OldAr** Sing. cstr. *ṭbt* KAI 216[15]; emph. *ṭbt'* KAI 222C 4f. (*ṭbt[']*), 223B 2 (:: Dupont-Sommer Sf p. 143, Segert ArchOr xxxii 122: = Plur. f. emph. of *ṭb$_2$*in all Sf instances); Plur. emph. *ṭbt'* KAI 222C 19 (× e.g. Segert ArchOr xxxii 122, Fitzmyer AIS 155, Gibson SSI ii p. 43: = Plur. f. emph. of *ṭb$_2$*)- **OffAr** Sing. abs. *ṭbh* Aḥiq 123; emph. *ṭbt'* Aḥiq 9, 24; + suff. 3 p.s.m. *ṭbth* KAI 266[8] (cf. e.g. Meyer FS Zucker 257, Gibson SSI ii p. 115, cf. also Bea Bibl xxx 514, Ginsberg BASOR cxi 26, McHardy DOTT

254 :: Fitzmyer Bibl xlvi 54: prob. = Plur. + suff. 3 p.s.m., cf. also Donner KAI a.l. :: Dupont-Sommer Sem i 51, Koopmans 90: = Plur. f. + suff. 3 p.s.m. of *ṭb*$_2$);+ suff. 2 p.s.m. *ṭbtk* Cowl 30^{24}, 31^{23}; + suff. 2 p.pl.m. *ṭbtkm* JRAS '29, 108 conc. 4; Plur. (or Sing.??) + suff. 1 p.s., cf. Warka 34: *ṭa-ba-ti-ia* - **Hatra** Sing. (or Plur.?) emph. *ṭbtʾ* 107^{5}, 229a 2, 343^{6}, 363^{2} - ¶ subst. f. - **1)** goodness, benevolence: Aḥiq 9, 24; cf. also *hn npqh ṭbh mn pm ʾ[nšʾ]* Aḥiq 123: if there goes forth good (i.e. benevolent words) from the mouth of a man (or: of men), cf. Warka 34; *ʾhpk ṭbtʾ wʾšm [l]lḥyt* KAI 222C 19f.: I will overturn the good and make it into evil (cf. Dupont-Sommer Sf p. 88, 93, Donner KAI a.l., Greenfield ActOr xxix 11 n. 35, HDS 51, cf. also Gibson SSI ii p. 35 :: Moran JNES xxii 173ff., Lipiński Stud 53: = friendship, good relations, alliance, cf. Fitzmyer AIS 21, 76, cf. also McCarthy BASOR ccxlv 63f.); *ʾlhʾ rbʾ ʿbd ṭbtʾ* Hatra 107$^{4f.}$: the great god who does good (or: good things); *snṭrwq m[lkʾ z]kyʾ wʿbyd ṭbtʾ* Hatra 229a 1f.: S. the victorious and benevolent king (cf. Hatra 189$^{3f.}$, cf. Milik DFD 361; cf. also Hatra 346^{4}, 363^{2}) - cf. the expression *bʿly ṭbtk* Cowl 30$^{23f.}$, 31^{23}: your friends (cf. also JRAS '29, 108 conc. 3f.), in the meaning: those who are entitled to your goodness (for the interpret., cf. e.g. Cowl a.l., Cowley JRAS '29, 109, Wag 21, Joüon MUSJ xviii 77, Koopmans 131, Galling TGI 87, Fishbane JBL lxxxix 316, Weinfeld Lesh xxxviii 236f., Grelot DAE p. 142 n. d, p. 411 n. b, cf. also Porten & Yardeni sub TADAE A 4.7/8: your obligees; for *zkwr lṭwbh* SM 75^{1} (cf. SM 76^{1}), v. comparable expressions sub *zkr*$_1$ - **2)** prosperity, abundance: KAI 216^{15} - 3) good relations > alliance (v. also sub 1: *bʿly ṭbtk*); *ʿdyʾ wṭbtʾ z[y] ʿbdw ʾlhn* KAI 223B 2: the covenant and the alliance that the gods have made (cf. e.g. Moran JNES xxii 173ff., Greenfield ActOr xxix 10 (n. 28), Fitzmyer AIS 81 (cf. also ibid. 74), Lipiński Stud 53, cf. also Hillers BASOR clxxvi 46f., Weinfeld Lesh xxxviii 231ff., Fox BASOR ccix 41f. :: Donner KAI ii p. 257: *ṭbtʾ* = the good, what is good (cf. also Dupont-Sommer Sf p. 106f.)); *wṭbth ʿbdk nṣr* KAI 266^{8}: your servant has guarded his alliance (i.e. your servant has remained faithful; cf. Croatto AION xviii 388f., cf. also Fitzmyer Bibl xlvi 53f., WA 239f., Vattioni AION xvii 210 :: Ginsberg BASOR cxi 26, Bright BiAr xii 46, Bea Bibl xxx 515, Meyer FS Zucker 258, Horn AUSS vi 31, Shea BASOR ccxxiii 61, Gibson SSI ii p. 114: his servant remembers his kindness :: Dupont-Sommer Sem i 45: and your servant has safeguarded his goods (sc. of the Pharao; cf. also McHardy DOTT 251, 254)) - Fitzmyer AIS 73f. (cf. also ibid. 19), Lipiński Stud 53: prob. transl. the *ṭbt[ʾ]* in KAI 222C 4f. with good relations/alliance (uncert. interpret., cf. Grelot RB lxxv 284 and Gibson SSI ii p. 33, 43 (: welfare)).

ṭbh₂ v. *ṭbḥ*.

ṭbwt **OffAr** Sing. abs. *ṭbwt* KAI 276[11]; emph. *ṭbwt*ʾ JA ccliv 440[2] (for the reading, cf. (Naveh with) Shaked JRAS '69, 119f., cf. also Kutscher, Naveh & Shaked Lesh xxxiv 128 :: Dupont-Sommer JA ccliv a.l., 455, 462a: l. *ṭlnt*ʾ = Sing. emph. of *ṭlnyt* (= shadow) or l. *ṭnnt*ʾ? = Sing. emph. of *ṭnnt* (= zeal, envy)) - ¶ subst. goodness, beauty; *zy br* ʾ*ynš l*ʾ *dm*ʿ *yhwh mn ṭbwt* KAI 276[10f.]: to whom no one could be compared in beauty (cf. e.g. Donner KAI a.l. :: Metzger JNES xv 20, Altheim & Stiehl ASA 270: = goodness; cf. Greek par. ἥτις τὸ κάλλος. ἀμείμητον εἶχε) - As-Salihi Sumer xliv 105: l. ʾ*l ṭbw* in Hatra 412 ii 6 (ʾl_1 or ʾl_8 + *ṭbw*?), cf. however Aggoula a.l.: l. ʾ*lt*ʾ = Aramaic form of the name of the goddess AlLat. (uncert. interpret.).

ṭbḥ **Pun** Sing. abs. *ṭbḥ* CIS i 237[5], 238[2], 239[6], 376[3], 3345[4,5], 4876[3], 4879[5], *ṭbh*CIS i 4877[5], Hofra 85[3] (for the reading, cf. Février BAr '55/56, 157 :: Berthier & Charlier Hofra a.l.: l. *pṭbḥ* = lapsus for *pṭrḥ* denoting the same function as *pytr*ʿ (v. *ptr*$_2$)) - **OldAr** Plur. emph. *ṭb[ḥ]y*ʾ PEQ '68, 42 - **OffAr** Plur. emph. *ṭbḥy*ʾ TA-Ar 37[3] (dam. context) - **Palm** Sing. emph. *ṭbḥ*ʾ CIS ii 4069[2] - ¶ subst. m. butcher, cook (:: Widengren HDS 224: < Akkad.).

ṭby$_1$ **OffAr** Sing. emph. *ṭby*ʾ Aḥiq 120; cf. Frah vii 16 (*ṭyb*ʾ) - ¶ subst. gazelle: Aḥiq 120 (for the problems of the context, cf. Cowl p. 240, Ginsberg ANET 429 n. 19, Lindenberger APA 109, 249 nn. 316-318 :: Grelot RB lxviii 186: > young lady?)

ṭby$_2$ **OffAr** Sing. m. abs. *ṭby* REA-NS viii 170A 2, B 2 - ¶ adj. good; in REA-NS 170A 2, B 2 used as epithet of a king, cf. Périkhanian REA-NS viii 172.

ṭby$_3$ **OldAr** *ṭby* KAI 222B 6 (v. infra) - ¶ poss. exclamation (happy be ...) < Plur. cstr. of *ṭb*$_1$,cf. Fitzmyer AIS 16f., 60, Lipiński Stud 33, Sader EAS 130, cf. also Rössler TUAT i 182: *ṭby mlk[* = happy be the king/kingship (v. *mlk*$_3$) :: e.g. Dupont-Sommer Sf p. 61f., 70, 143, Degen AAG p. 13, 44, 61, 68 (div. otherwise): l. *ṭb* (= Sing. abs. of *ṭb*$_2$used adverbially) *ymlk* (= Qal Impf. 3 p.s.m. of *mlk*$_1$, may he reign well, cf. also Donner KAI a.l.); Lemaire & Durand IAS 136f.: or l. ʿ*dy* (= Plur. cstr. of ʿ*d*$_1$), highly uncert. reading.

ṭbyʿ **JAr** Sing. abs. *ṭby*ʿ MPAT 41[5] - ¶ subst. coinage (?; cf. Milik DJD ii p. 112, Fitzmyer & Harrington MPAT a.l. × e.g. Birnbaum JAOS lxxviii 15, MarDeed 20, Koopmans 199: = Qal Part. pass. s.m. abs. of *ṭb*ʿ$_1$(?): coined, cf. also Beyer ATTM 309, 588; on the context of MPAT 41[5], cf. also Koffmahn DJW 117).

ṭbyt **Palm** the diff. *ṭbyt* in Inscr P 31[9] poss. = adverb: well, cf. Cantineau Inscr P a.l., sub Inv ix 28, Aggoula Sem xxxii 111, 116, cf. also du Mesnil du Buisson RES '45, 77, 81, Gawlikowski Syr xlviii 415 (for the context, v. *šm*ʿ$_1$).

ṭblh (< Lat. *tabula*) - **JAr** Sing. abs. *ṭblh* MPAT-A 36[3] (= Frey 987a

= SM 30), 37^{2} (*ṭb[lh]*; = Frey 987b = SM 31), IEJ xxxii 8^{2} (heavily dam. context) - ¶ subst. f. prob. *tabula ansata*, cf. e.g. Fitzmyer & Harrington MPAT-A 36 a.l. (for *tabula ansata* executed as mosaic, cf. e.g. also SM 33 and EI viii 183f.; cf. also L.I.Levine IEJ xxxii 8f.).

ṭb‘$_1$ **Pun** PI‘EL Pf. 3 p.s.m. *ṭ’b’‘* Trip 43 (cf. Levi Della Vida RCL '63, 470f., Amadasi Guzzo IPT 22, Röllig BiOr xxvii 379; however reading of *b* uncert. (l. *p*?)) - ¶ verb PI‘EL to fulfill; + obj. (a vow): Trip 43, v. however supra.
v. *ṭby‘*,*šṭ*$_1$.

ṭb‘$_2$ **Ph** Plur. abs. *ṭb‘m* Mus li 286^{5} (prob. reading); cstr. *ṭb‘* RES 1204^{2} (?, :: RES sub 1204, Cooke NSI p. 44, Teixidor Sem xxix 10f.: = Sing. cstr.) - ¶ subst. certain type of weight/coin; *mšqly 10 ṭb‘m* Mus li 286^{5}: his weight is 10 *ṭ*. (cf. Honeyman Mus li a.l.); *ksp 1070 ṭb‘ ṣr* RES 1204^{2}: a sum of 1070 Tyrian *ṭ*. (:: RES sub 1204: = a sum of 1070 (shekels), coinage of Tyre, cf. Cooke NSI p. 44, cf. also Bordreuil Syr lvii 489: in this context = standard (of measure); for another (less prob.) reading of the context, Teixidor Sem xxix 10f., v. also *ksp*$_2$) - on this word, cf. also Healy CISFP i 666.
v. *rb‘*$_5$.

ṭb‘h **Ph** Plur. abs. *ṭb‘t* KAI 51^{10} - ¶ subst. imprint, mark (cf. Aimé-Giron BIFAO xxxviii 9 :: Röllig KAI a.l.: = Sing. abs. (= signet-ring)).

ṭhwr v. *ṭhr*.

ṭḥnh **OffAr** Segal ATNS a.l.: l. *ṭḥnt* (= Plur. cstr. of *ṭḥnh* (= mill)) in ATNS 20^{5} (highly uncert. reading).

ṭhr **Pun** Sing. m. abs. *ṭr* Punica ix 9^{2}, *ṭ’r*Punica ix 9b 3 (= Punica xi 35) - **Hebr** Sing. m. abs. *ṭhwr*Mas 456 - ¶ adj. pure; *blb ṭr* Punica ix 9^{2}: with a pure heart (cf. Punica ix 9b 2f.; cf. Dussaud CRAI '46, 379f., Février JA cclv 61ff. :: Chabot sub Punica ix 9: l. = *blbṭ(’)r* = n.p.); *ṭhwr lqdš* Mas 456: clean for hallowed things - Yadin & Naveh Mas a.l.: the *ṭwhr* in Mas 457 = variant form of *ṭhwr*.

ṭhrh **Pun** Sing. abs. *ṭhrt* NP 130^{4} - **Hebr** Sing. cstr. *ṭhrt* Mas 449^{2} (*ṭh[rt]*), 450^{2} (*ṭh[rt]*), 452^{3} - ¶ subst. f. purity: NP 130^{4} (diff. context, cf. e.g. Cooke NSI p. 147f., Février RHR cxli 21); *ṭhrt hqdš* Mas 452^{3}: the purity of hallowed things (cf. Mas 449$^{2f.}$).

ṭwb$_1$ v. *ṭb*$_1$.

ṭwb$_2$ v. *ṭb*$_2$.

ṭwbh v. *ṭbh*$_1$.

ṭwhr v. *ṭhr*.

ṭwḥ **Hebr** QAL Pf. 3 p.s.m. *ṭḥ* SM 75^{3} - ¶ verb QAL to plaster, to coat; + obj. (wall) + *b*$_2$ (with): SM 75^{3f}; cf. *ṭḥy*$_2$.

ṭwr$_1$ v. *ṣr*$_1$.

ṭwr$_2$ **Nab** Plur. emph. *ṭwry’* CIS ii 350^{2} - ¶ subst. wall (for this interpret., cf. Cantineau Nab ii 101, Milik RB lxvi 556, 559, Levinson

NAI 164; for other interpret., cf. CIS ii a.l.) - cf. also Marrassini FLEM 104f. (n. 1).

ṭwš **DA** a form of this root (Qal Part. pass. s.m. abs.: *ṭš*; = to cover) poss. in DA ii 15 (cf. Hoftijzer DA p. 243; uncert. reading and interpret., cf. also Caquot & Lemaire Syr liv 207) - Dupont-Sommer JKF i 203: the *ṭwš* in AMB 7^9 = Qal Imper. s.m. of *ṭwš* (improb. interpret., cf. Scholem JGM 186, Naveh & Shaked AMB a.l.: = part of a magical name).

ṭwt v. *mṭwtw*.

ṭḥy₁ Ebeling Frah a.l.: the *ṭḥṭwn* in Frah app. 11 = form of *ṭḥy₁* (= to reach), improb. interpret., cf. Nyberg FP 99: = transcription of Iranian word.

ṭḥy₂ = to coat, to cover > Akkad., cf. v.Soden Or xlvi 196, AHW s.v. *ṭeḫû* II; cf. *ṭwḥ*.

ṭḥn **OffAr** Qal Pf. 3 p.s.m. *ṭḥnw* KAI 233^8 (cf. e.g. Dupont-Sommer Syr xxiv 39, Donner KAI a.l., Gibson SSI ii p. 107 :: e.g. Lidzbarski ZA xxxi 199: *lṭḥnw* = Qal Impf. (jussive) 3 p.pl.m.); cf. Frah xix 6 (*ṭḥnn*) - ¶ verb Qal to grind (+ *l₅* comm. (for)) = to be the slave of ? (cf. Dupont-Sommer Syr xxiv 39, Gibson SSI ii p. 107).

ṭḥnh **OffAr** Segal ATNS a.l.: l. *ṭḥnt* (= Plur. cstr. of *ṭḥnh* (= mill)) in ATNS 20^5 (highly uncert. reading).

ṭyb **OffAr** Qal Pf. 3 p.s.m. *ṭyb* Cowl 2^9, 14^5, 20^9, 43^7, Krael 3^6, SSI ii 28 obv. 2 (for the reading of the context, cf. Porten FS Bresciani 431f., Porten & Yardeni sub TADAE A 3.3., v. also *lbb₂*), etc., *ṭb* Cowl 15^5; 3 p.s.f. *ṭybt* Aḥiq 67 - ¶ verb Qal to be content, to be satisfied; *wṭyb lbbn bgw* Cowl 2^9: and our heart is content therewith, cf. Cowl $15^{5f.}$, 20^9, Krael $12^{6,26}$ (for this expression, cf. Muffs 27-194, cf. also Yaron Bibl xli 254, 380f., Law 105f., RB lxxvii 408ff., Boyarin JANES iii 60f., Levine FS Morton Smith 38ff., Szubin & Porten BASOR cclii 35, Malul ZA lxxv 72); cf. also *wṭyb lbby bmwm'h dk'* Cowl $14^{5f.}$: and my heart was content with that oath, cf. Krael $3^{6f.}$, $12^{14f.}$; cf. also the expression *lbby l' ṭyb 'p 'mk* SSI ii 28 obv. 2: my heart is not glad (and) likewise your mother (for the context, v. supra) - **2)** to be pleasant, to please; + *ʿl₇*, *...]ṭybt ʿl knwth* Aḥiq 67: (it) seemed good to (pleased) his companions - cf. also *ṭ'b*.

ṭymy (< Greek τιμή) - **JAr** Sing. cstr. *ṭymy* MPAT-A 2^2 (= Frey 1197 = SM 58) - ¶ subst. cost, price.

ṭyn **OffAr** Sing. abs. *ṭyn* KAI 260^8; cf. Frah ii 4 - ¶ subst. clay, loam, ground, earth; *qnynh ṭyn wmyn wmndʿmth* KAI 260^8: his acquest, ground and water and everything that is his (= his whole acquest).

ṭyq **OffAr** word of unknown meaning in the combination *lḥm ṭyq* in ATNS 20^3 (subst. or adj. Sing. (m.) abs.?); Segal ATNS a.l.: poss. to be connected with *tyq* = chest? (less prob. interpret.).

ṭyr v. *gly*.

ṭyš v. *dhmpṭypṭyš*.

ṭyšm v. *tš‘m*.

ṭksys v. *ṭkss*.

ṭkss (< Greek τάξις) - **Palm** Sing. abs. *ṭkss* FS Miles 50 ii 6, *ṭksys*CIS ii 4171^{3}, 4173^{2}, RB xxxix 532^{3} (Greek par. τάξεις), Ber ii 101^{4} - ¶ subst. row (in all texts said of funerary niches) - on this word, cf. also Brown Bibl lxx 208f.

ṭl$_1$ **DA** Sing. abs. *ṭl* ii 36 (dam. context) - ¶ subst. dew - L.H.Gray AJSL xxxix 83: the *tal* in Poen 1142 = Sing. abs. of *ṭl$_1$* (highly uncert. interpret., cf. also Schroed 298f., 321, Sznycer PPP 144f.).

ṭl$_2$ **OffAr** Sing. emph. *ṭl’* Krael 5^{9} (v. infra); + suff. 3 p.s.m. *ṭlh* Beh 5 (Akkad. par. *ṣilli*), 13 (*ṭ[l]h*; Akkad. par. *ṣilli*), 28 (Akkad. par. *ṣilli*), Cowl p. 269 vii 3 (= BIDG 1 10; Akkad. par. *ṣilli*) - ¶ subst. - **1)** shadow; *mn ṭl’ lsmš’* Krael 5^{9}: from the shadow to the sun (i.e. from slavery to liberty), cf. Falk JJS v 116, Ginsberg JAOS lxxiv 158, J.J.Rabinowitz Law 31f., Koopmans 115, Yaron Law 39, Verger RCL ’64, 303 (cf. also idem RGP 171f.), Porten Arch 220, Grelot DAE p. 226 (n. g), Porten & Greenfield JEAS p. 46, Porten & Yardeni sub TADAE B 3.6 (cf. also Hillers JBL xcvii 178, 180) :: Cazelles Syr xxxii 80 (n. 4): by virtue of the protection of Sh. :: Driv p. 86: *ṭl’* = *ṭl’$_2$*, *mn ṭl’* = absolutely :: Rosenthal (with Krael p. 185): *mn ṭl’* = adverb (therefore, consequently), cf. also Black JSS i 66 :: Krael p. 185f.: *mn ṭl’ l* = before or *mn ṭl’* = thereupon (cf. also Volterra RSO xxxii 692f.) :: Milik RB lxi 595: = *rite*, as it should be - **2)** protection; *bṭlh zy ’hw[rmzd]* Beh 5: under the protection of A. (cf. Beh 28, Cowl p. 269 vii 3 (cf. Akkad. par. *ina ṣilli ša U.*, cf. also Kaufman AIA 58)); cf. *ṭll$_2$*.
v. *ṭl’$_2$*.

ṭl’$_1$ v. *ḥṭl*, *ṭlh$_1$*.

ṭl’$_2$ **OffAr** Sing. abs. (or Sing. emph. of *ṭl$_2$*?, v. infra) *ṭl’* Driv 13^{3} (v. however infra) - ¶ subst. (?) of uncert. meaning in the expression *lṭl’*; Driv p. 86: all right, in order, Milik RB lxi 595: *accurate*, precisely, Grelot DAE p. 327 (n. c): punctually :: Cazelles Syr xxxii 80: *ṭl’* = Sing. emph. of *ṭl$_2$*,all combining *lṭl’* with preceding clause, connection with following clause not to be excluded however; for the etymology, cf. Driv p. 86: cf. J.Ar. *ṭl’y* = patch, Hebr. *ṭlw’* = flecked, speckled, spotted, therefore *lṭl’* = *ad punctum* (highly uncert. interpret., moreover reading highly uncert., cf. Porten & Yardeni sub TADAE A 6.16: l. *lhn* (= *lhn$_1$*) *l’*).
v. *ṭl$_2$*.

ṭlh$_1$ **Hebr** Sing. abs. *ṭlh* Frey 1206^{1} (= SM 67), SM 27^{1}, 70^{3}, *ṭl’* Frey 1162^{1} (= SM 45) - ¶ subst. Aries (sign of the Zodiac) - L.H.Gray AJSL xxxix 79: *tloti* in Poen 941 = Plur. + suff. 1 p.s. (= my lambs), highly

uncert. interpret., cf. also Schroed 307, Sznycer PPP 120ff.
v. *ḥṭl*.

ṭlh₂ **Ph** Garbini AION xxv 435f.: l. *ṭlh* (= Sing. abs.) in the combination *ḥmr ṭlh* (= boiled wine) in BMB xxvi 46, uncert. interpret. :: v.d.Branden with Kaoukabani BMB xxvi 46 (div. otherwise): l. *nṣḥ* = Sing. abs. of *nṣḥ₃* (= sprinkling).

ṭly₁ **OffAr** Plur. abs. *ṭlyn* CIS ii 111[2] - **Palm** Sing. emph. *ṭly᾿* CIS ii 4139[1], PNO 14[2], Inv xi 13[4]; Plur. emph. *ṭly᾿* Inv ix 28[8] (= Inscr P 31; for the form, cf. Rosenthal Syr xix 170 :: du Mesnil du Buisson RES '45, 80f.: = Sing. emph. of *ṭly₂* (= roof)) - ¶ subst. m. - **1)** young man, boy; as epithet in CIS ii 4139[1]: *m῾ny ṭly᾿* (M. the younger one, junior, cf. also Ingholt FS Michałowski 474 n. 75) - **2)** servant: CIS ii 111[2], PNO 14[2] (:: Ingholt Ber iii 90 n. 66: = (temple-)boy), Inv xi 13[4] (cf. Silverman JAOS lxxxix 632, Aggoula Sem xxix 111 :: Teixidor sub Inv xi 13: = junior); in Inv ix 28[8] prob. = temple-boy, oblate, cf. Ingholt Ber iii 90f. n. 66, FS Michałowksi 474 n. 75 (cf. also idem with Cantineau sub Inscr P 31), Milik DFD 275, cf. also Gawlikowski Syr xlviii 414 (n. 4), 415, Aggoula Sem xxxii 111, 115.

ṭly₂ v. *ṭly₁*.

ṭlyw **Palm** Sing. abs. *ṭlyw* Ber iii 99[6] - ¶ subst. youth; *mn ṭlyw ῾d sybw* Ber iii 99[6]: from youth to old age.

ṭll₁ **Palm** Pa῾el Pf. 3 p.s.m. *ṭll* CIS ii 3917[4] - ¶ verb Pa῾el to cover; + obj. (a large room?): CIS ii 3917[4] - Segal ATNS a.l.: l. *tṭl* = Qal Impf. 2 p.s.m. (= to protect) in ATNS 55a i 4 (uncert. interpret., diff. and dam. context).

ṭll₂ **OldAr** Sing. abs. *ṭll* KAI 222B 42 (in relation to the orthography, cf. Lipiński Stud 44, cf. however Dupont-Sommer Sf p. 85, Segert ArchOr xxxii 119) - **OffAr** Sing. cstr. *ṭll* Cowl 38[5]; + suff. 3 p.s.m. *ṭllh* Cowl p. 265[4] (cf. Greenfield & Porten BIDG 54), BIDG 56 xxi 1 (*ṭll[h]*; Akkad. par. *ṣilli*); + suff. 2 p.s.m. *ṭllk* Cowl 71[15] - ¶ subst. - **1)** protection; *bṭllh z[y] ᾿hw[rmzd]* Cowl p. 265[4]: under the protection of A. (cf. Akkad. par. *ina ṣilli ša U.*, cf. also Kaufman AIA 58); *᾿štdrw ῾m wydrng ... bṭll ᾿lh šmy᾿ ῾d šzbwny* Cowl 38[4f.]: they interceded with W. under the protection of (i.e. with the help of) the God of Heaven until they rescued me (cf. Dion RB lxxxix 566 (n. 217)) - **2)** in the diff. text KAI 222B 42 poss. = shadow?? (v. however supra, cf. also Donner KAI a.l., Fitzmyer AIS 19, 72; Lipiński Stud 44: = protection) - the interpret. of Cowl 71[15] (dam. context) remains unclear :: Cowl a.l.: = shadow > spirit, soul - cf. *ṭl₂*.

ṭlm > Akkad., cf. v.Soden Or xxxvii 268, xlvi 196, cf. also idem AHW s.v. *ṭullummā᾿u* (= evildoer; cf. also idem AHW s.v. *ṭullumum*).

ṭlmh **JAr** Sing. abs. *ṭlm᾿* IEJ xl 135[5] - ¶ subst. a loaf of bread.

ṭlnyt **Hebr** Sing. abs. *ṭlnyt* AMB 4[15] - **JAr** Sing. abs. *ṭlny* AMB 13[8];

emph. *ṭlnyth* AMB 7a 6, 13, 7b 3; Plur. abs. *ṭlnyn* AMB 11^{8} - ¶ subst. phantom, spectre, ghost (cf. also PS 1470) :: Dupont-Sommer JKF i 206: the gloomy one, epithet of Lilith; *šydh ṭlnyth ʾn dkr wʾn nq[bh]* AMB 7b 13: a demon (or) a phantom be it male or female; cf. *hṭlnyt wrwḥ zkr wnqbh* AMB 4^{15}: the phantom and the male and female spirit. v. *ṭbwt*.

ṭlpḥ **OffAr** Plur. abs. *ṭlpḥn* Cowl $2^{4,5}$, $3^{5,6}$ (*[ṭ]lpḥn*)^{,8}, ASAE lv 277 rect. 1, AG 87a 14 - ¶ subst. lentil (cf. e.g. Löw AP p. 182f., Perles OLZ '11, 500, Lidzbarski Eph iii 258, Porten Arch 84 n. 103 :: Cowl p. 5: = bean, cf. also Bresciani ASAE lv 278 - cf. poss. also *ṭrp[.]ʾ[.]* in MPAT 38^{3}, restored by Milik DJD ii p. 89 as *ṭrpwʾḥ* variant form of *ṭlpḥ*.

ṭlpḥt **OffAr** Naveh IEJ xxxv 211: l. this word (Sing. abs.) = lentils poss. in ATNS iii :: Naveh ibid. (div. otherwise): or l. *pḥt* (= Sing. cstr. of *pḥh*) :: Segal ATNS a.l.: l. *]ṭ l* (= *l*$_5$) *ght* (= n.p.).

ṭm **Palm** Plur. cstr. *ṭmʾ* CIS ii 3907^{1} (:: Díez Merino LA xix 78: l. *ṭbʾ* (interpret.?)) - **Hatra** Sing. (or Plur.?, cf. Degen NESE iii 94, cf. also Vattioni IH a.l.) + suff. 3 p.pl.m. *ṭmhwn* 293^{4} (:: Aggoula MUSJ xlix 472: = Paʿel Pf. 3 p.s.m. + suff. 3 p.pl.m. of *ṭmʾ*$_1$ or l. *lṭmhwn* = Paʿel Impf. 3 p.s.m. + suff. 3 p.pl.m. of *ṭmʾ*$_1$) - **JAr** Plur. cstr. *ṭmy* MPAT 70^{2} (against the authenticity of this text, cf. Garbini OA xxiv 67ff.) - ¶ subst. Sing. (v. however supra) bones: Hatra 293^{4} - Plur. bones: CIS ii 3907^{1}, MPAT 70^{2}; for the word, cf. Degen NESE iii 94, Kaufman AIA 50 n. 91.

ṭmʾ$_1$ **OffAr** a form of this root prob. in Sem xiv 72 ii 1: *ṭmʾw*; Dupont-Sommer Sem xiv a.l.: = Qal Pf. 3 p.pl.m. (= to be impure) or = Paʿel Pf. 3 p.pl.m. (= to render impure); heavily dam. context.
v. *ṭm*.

ṭmʾ$_2$ **OffAr** Plur. m./f. abs. *ṭmʾn* Sem xxxix 32 conv. 2 (dam. context) - **JAr** Sing. f. abs. *ṭm[ʾh]* AMB 13^{11} - ¶ adj. impure; *rwḥ ṭm[ʾh]* AMB 13^{11}: an impure spirit.

ṭmʾ$_3$ **Pun** the diff. *ṭmʾ* in Trip 51^{1} explained by Levi Della Vida Or xxxiii 7 as poss. < Greek τόμος (resp. Lat. *tomus*) = department, section (highly uncert. interpret., cf. also Amadasi IPT 132).

ṭmn v. *mmn*.

ṭmš **Palm** the diff. *ṭmš* in Inv D 52 explained by du Mesnil du Buisson a.l. as Qal pass. Pf. 3 p.pl.m. (= to be inundated), highly uncert. reading and context.

ṭnʾ$_1$ **Ph** Piʿel Pf. 3 p.s.m. *ṭnʾ* DD 9^{2}, BMB xiii 52^{2} (:: v.d.Branden Mašr liv 736 n. 10: l. *ynʾ* = lapsus for *yṭnʾ* (= Yiph Pf. 3 p.s.m.)); Yiph Pf. 3 p.s.m. *yṭnʾ* CIS i 13^{2} (= Kition A 27), 14^{6} (= Kition A 3^{5}), 58^{2} (= Kition B 3), 88^{2} (= Kition F 1), 89^{2} (= KAI 39), Kition A 30^{2}, KAI 26A i 9 (cf. FR 174, 267b, cf. also for litt.; interpret. as Inf.

(abs.) less prob.), etc.; 3 p.s.f. *yṭnʾ* CIS i 11^{2} (= Kition A 1 = KAI 33), 93^{3} (= KAI 40); 1 p.s. *yṭnʾt* CIS i 46^{2} (= Kition B 1 = KAI 35), 57 (= Kition B 2), 115^{2} (= KAI 54), KAI 43^{3}; 3 p.pl. *yṭnʾ* CIS i 60$^{1f.}$ (= Kition B 5); Impf. 3 p.pl. + suff. 3 p.s.f. *yṭnʾy* KAI 60^{5} (cf. e.g. Cooke NSI p. 98, Gibson SSI iii p. 151, Krahmalkov RSO lxi 77ff. :: FR 170: = YIPH Inf. cstr. + suff. 3 p.s.f.) - **Pun** QAL Part. pass. s.f. abs. *ṭnʾt* KAI 153^{1}, *ṭnt* CIS i 5510^{7}; pl.m. abs. *ṭnʾm* CIS i 3920^{4}, KAI 65^{4}, 101^{5}, 173^{6} (also in KAI 96^{5}?? = CIS i 5523, cf. Levi Della Vida RSO xxxix 305, or div. otherwise l.: *mṭnʾm* = PUʿAL Part. pl.m. abs.??, cf. Röllig KAI a.l., cf. however Février sub CIS i 5523, Sznycer ACSCS i 214), RCL '66, 201^{3}; PIʿEL Pf. 3 p.s.m. *ṭnʾ* KAI 102^{2}, 112^{1}, 141^{1}, 153^{2} (:: FR 64c, 187: = Pf. 3 p.s.m. + suff. 3 p.s.m.), 161^{3}, RES 779^{3}, 936^{2}, 1544, Hofra 250$^{3f.}$, Punica xii 30^{2}, NP 130^{1}, *ṭynʾ* KAI 119^{2}, 123^{2}, 127, 143^{2}, RES 785^{2}, Punica ix 3^{4}, *ṭʿnʾ* KAI 172^{4} (or = QAL?, cf. Friedrich AfO x 82 n. 13; for the reading, cf. e.g. idem ibid., Röllig KAI a.l. :: e.g. CIS i sub 149, Lidzbarski Handb 434, sub KI 100, Cooke NSI p. 158, Amadasi sub ICO-Sard-NPu 5, Sznycer ACSCS i 215: l. *ṭynʾ*), *ṭmʿ* BAr '55/56, 30 no. 1^{2} (lapsus; for this diff. reading, cf. Février sub IAM 1); 3 p.s.f. *ṭnʿ* KAI 168$^{2f.}$; 1 p.s. *ṭnʾt* CIS i 6000bis 4 (= TPC 84); 3 p.pl. *ṭnʾ* KAI 74^{1} (cf. KAI 69^{1}), 3917^{1}, *ṭnʿ* KAI 166$^{2f.}$ (??, cf. Schroed 270, Lidzbarski Handb 437f., FR 170, context however diff., cf. also Chabot sub Punica xi 7); + suff. 3 p.s.f. *ṭnyʾ* CIS i 152^{5} (cf. e.g. FR 187 :: CIS i a.l.: = PIʿEL Pf. 3 p.pl.), Punica xvi 2^{1}; PUʿAL Pf. 3 p.s.f. (cf. e.g. Février GLECS ix 26, FR 170 :: Friedr 170: = QAL Part. pass.) *ṭnʾ* KAI 134^{1}, 144^{1}, 151^{1}, 171^{1}, Punica iv 4^{1}, xi A 1^{1}, 8^{1}, RES 779^{1}, etc., *ṭnʿ* KAI 150^{1}, *ṭnḥ* Punica xii 27^{1}, 32^{1}, *ṭn* RES 169^{1}, *ṭʿnʾ* KAI 133^{1}, 154^{1}, 158^{1}, 166^{1}, Punica xi A 7^{1}, xii 22^{1}, 30^{1}, etc., *ṭʿnʿ* KAI 143^{1}, 169^{1}, NP 12^{1}, 13^{1} (sub Punica xii 18), Punica xi A 4^{1}, 6^{1}, etc., *ṭʿnh* KAI 157^{1} (?, or l. (div. otherwise) *ṭʿn hʿbn*?), RES 178^{1} (?, or l. (div. otherwise) *ṭʿn ʿ[bn]*?), Sem xxxvi 33^{1}, *ṭʿʾn* KAI 135^{1} (:: Lidzbarski Handb 436, Chabot sub Punica xii 18, Röllig KAI a.l.: = *ṭʿ<nʾ> ʾ<b>n*), *ṭʿʾ* Punica xii 17^{1} (lapsus); 3 p.pl. *ṭnʾ* KAI 139^{2} (cf. e.g. Sznycer Sem xxvii 50f. :: Röllig KAI a.l.: = PIʿEL Pf. 3 p.s.m./pl.); YIPH Pf. 3 p.s.m. *yṭnʾ* RES 906^{2} - ¶ verb QAL to erect; Part. pass. - **1)** erected; said of a stone: KAI 153^{1}; said of a gift (prob. certain monument): CIS i 5510^{7} - 2) said of people, appointed; *ṭnʾm ʿl mlkt z* KAI 101^{5}: those appointed over this work, cf. KAI 65^{4}, 96^{5} (v. supra), 173^{6}, CIS i 3920^{4}, RCL '66, 201^{3} - PIʿEL to erect - **1)** without object: KAI 119^{2} (memorial stone), RES 1544 (votive stele), cf. also KAI 74^{1} (tariff of temple) - **2)** + obj., *ṭʿnʾ t hmʾš st bnʾ* KAI 172^{4} (v. supra): his son has erected this statue - **3)** + l_5, *ṭʿnʾ ʾbn z llqy ... ṭnʾ lʾ ʿym* Punica xii 30: this stone was erected for L. ..., his brother erected (it) for him; cf. Punica xii 31, cf. also KAI 123^{2}, RES 779^{3f}, etc. - **4)** + *l₅* + obj. (or vice versa), *ṭnʾ* ʾ*bn z lmtnbʿl* RES 936²ᶠᶠ·: he has erected this stone for M.; cf. CIS i 152⁵ (uncert. object), KAI 127 (obj.: statue), 161³ (obj.: stele), 168²ᶠ· (obj.: stone), NP 130¹ (obj.: memorial stone) - Pu ʿAL to be erected (said of stones); + *l₅* KAI 133¹, 134¹, 135¹, 143¹, Punica iv 4¹, etc., etc. - YIPH to erect - **1)** + obj.: KAI 26A i 9f. - **2)** + obj. + *b₂*: KAI 60⁵ - **3)** + *l₅*: CIS i 13²ᶠ· (a stone?), 146ᶠᶠ· (a stone), 57¹ᶠ· (= Kition B 2; a stone), 58²ᶠ· (= Kition B 3; a memorial stone), 60¹ᶠᶠ· (a memorial stone), CIS i 88² (= Kition F 1; a statue), KAI 41¹ᶠᶠ· (a statue; cf. KAI 39²ᶠ·), 59¹ (a memorial stone), DD 9²ᶠ· (a stone) - **4)** + *l₅* + *b₂*: KAI 43³ (a statue) - **5)** + *l₅* + *ʿl₇*, *mṣbt ʾz ʾš yṭnʾ ʾrš* ... *lʾby* ... *wlʾmy* ... *ʿl mškb nḥtnm* KAI 34: this pillar is it which A. erected to his father ... and to his mother ... over their resting-place; cf. also KAI 35¹ᶠᶠ·. - **6)** + *mn₅*, *[s]mlt ʾz ʾš yṭn wyṭnʾ mnḥšt yʾš* ... KAI 33² (= Kition A 1): this statue is it which Y. has given and erected of bronze (for the context, v. *nḥšt*) - **7)** + *ʿl₇*, *hsmlm hʾl ʾš yṭnʾ btšlm* ... *ʿl bn bny* KAI 40³ᶠ·: these statues are (those) which B. has erected ... for her grandsons - **8)** + *ʿl₇* + *l₅*, *sml ʾz ʾš ndr wyṭnʾ ʿbdʾ* ... *ʿl bny* ... *lʾdny* Kition A 30: this statue is it which A. has vowed and erected for his son ... to his lord.

ṭn ʾ₂ **Ph** Peckham Or xxxvii 305f., 314: l. poss. *ṭnʾ* (= Sing. cstr. of *ṭn ʾ₂* (= basket)) in KAI 37A 10 (cf. also Gibson SSI iii p. 124f., 128), diff. reading (cf. Masson & Sznycer RPC 48f. :: Healy BASOR ccxvi 53, 55: poss. l. *spʾ* = Sing. abs. of *sp ʾ₁* (= food)) :: Cooke NSI p. 65ff., Röllig KAI a.l.: l. *n ʿr*, without interpret.

ṭnnt v. *ṭbwt*.

ṭs **OffAr** Plur. abs. *ṭsn* Cowl 26¹⁶ - ¶ subst. m. plate; *ṭsn zy nḥš* Cowl 26¹⁶: plates of bronze (in a list of building materials for a boat); cf. also Grelot DAE p. 292 n. n.

ṭ ʿ ʾ v. *ṭ ʿy*.

ṭ ʿwn₁ **Palm** Sing. abs. *ṭ ʿwn* CIS ii 3913 ii 99 - ¶ subst. error, mistake; *ṭ ʿwn dy ktb* CIS ii 3913 ii 99f.: a mistake (/mistakes) in the document.

ṭ ʿwn₂ v. *ṭ ʿn₂*.

ṭ ʿy **Palm** QAL Pf. 3 p.s.m. *ṭ ʿʾ* CIS ii 3913 ii 100 - ¶ verb QAL to commit a mistake.

ṭ ʿyn v. *ṭ ʿn₁*.

ṭ ʿm₁ **OffAr** QAL Pf. 1 p.s. *ṭ ʿmt* Aḥiq 105; Impf. 3 p.s.m. *yṭ ʿm* KAI 233⁸ (× Gibson SSI ii p. 107: = QAL pass.; v. also infra; or poss. = HAPH Impf. 3 p.s.m.?); + suff. 3 p.s.m. *yṭ ʿmnhy* Aḥiq 209; HAPH Pf. 3 p.s.m. *hṭ ʿm* Sem xxiii 95 recto 5 (cf. Bordreuil Sem xxiii 100, 102, Fales AION xxvi 547, sub AECT 58, Lipiński WGAV 377, Teixidor Syr lvi 392 :: (Naveh with) Kaufman Conn xix 120, 122 (n. 30): = *h₅*(= variant of *h ʾ₂*)+ QAL Imper. s.m. *ṭ ʿm* (= to taste, to eat) :: Wesselius AION xlv 508 (div. otherwise): l. *ṭ ʿm* =

PAʿEL Pf. 3 p.s.m. (= to feed)) - ¶ verb QAL to taste; + obj.: Aḥiq 105, 209; in KAI 233[8] of uncert. interpret. (dam. context): > to consider (something) palatable/acceptable, to decide?, cf. Dupont-Sommer Syr xxiv 40, Donner KAI a.l. × Gibson SSI ii p. 107 (v. supra): = QAL pass. (= to be tasted > to be palatable/acceptable; cf. also Kaufman Conn xix 122 (n. 31)) :: Bowman UMS xx 277: = to taste - HAPH (v. however supra) uncert. meaning, to make acceptable, to impose an agreement concerning?; (+ obj.): Sem xxiii 95 recto 5 (cf. Bordreuil Sem xxiii 100, 102; cf. also Lipiński ActAntHung xxii 378f., Fales AION xxvi 544f., 547, sub AECT 58); cf. Teixidor Syr lvi 392: = to order, to arrange.

ṭʿm₂ **OffAr** Sing. abs. *ṭʿm* Cowl 17[2] (for the prob. reading, cf. Porten RB xc 406, 410, Porten & Yardeni sub TADAE A 6.1, Lipiński Or lvii 435), 26[22,23,25], 34[7], Driv 3[6,7,8], 5[8], Herm 1[12], AJSL lviii 303A 7, ATNS 14[5] (*ṭʿm[]*), 15[3]; cstr. *ṭʿm* Samar 4[7]; emph. *ṭʿmʾ* Driv 4[4], 6[6], 7[10], 8[6], 10[5], 12[1*], ATNS 2[2] (*ṭʿm[ʾ]*)[,6], 14[4] (heavily dam. context, diff. reading, cf. also Garbini RSO lxi 212), RES 1792B 9, Sem xiv 72 conv. 4 (*ṭʿm[ʾ]*); + suff. 2 p.s.m. *ṭʿmk* Cowl 41[7] (dam. context, cf. e.g. Porten & Greenfield ZAW lxxx 229, Dion RB lxxix 558, Porten & Yardeni sub TADAE A 3.5); + suff. 1 p.s. *ṭʿmy* Irâq xxxi 173[4] (dam. context) - **Nab** Sing. emph. *ṭʿmʾ* CIS ii 161 ii 2, J 255, RES 624 (= CIS ii 466; *ṭʿm[ʾ]*) - ¶ subst. m. - **1)** order (for this special meaning, cf. Zimmern Fremdw 10, Kaufman AIA 109 (n. 390), Lipiński ZAH i 66): Cowl 26[22,23,25], Driv 3[6,7,8], ATNS 15[3], Sem xiv 72 conv. 4, etc.; for context, v. also *ydʿ₁*, *šym₁*; *bʿl ṭʿm* Cowl 26[23]: the one who drafts the order, chancellor (< Akkad. *bēl ṭēmi*; for the reading, cf. Porten & Yardeni sub TADAE A 6.2) - **2)** decision, resolution, in the expression *mn ʿl ṭʿmʾ* CIS ii 161 ii 2, J 255, RES 624: because of a decision, on account of a decision; *ʾdrmw ... wnqydw mn ʿl ṭʿmʾ bny ʿbdmlkw* CIS ii 161 ii 1f.: A. ... and N. on account of a decision sons (i.e. adoptive sons) of A. :: Clermont-Ganneau RAO i 61, Cooke NSI p. 250: = Sing. emph. of *ṭʿm₃* (= graff, graft, sapling) - **3)** poss. > authority (cf. Cowl a.l., Grelot DAE p. 397 n. h): Cowl 34[7]; *ʿwd ṭʿm lʾ ʿd yhwy lhn* Cowl 34[7]: moreover, they will have no further authority (for the context, v. also *ʿwd₅*; cf. also Verger RCL '64, 77 n. 11; cf. however Porten & Yardeni sub TADAE A 4.4: may another decree no more be (delivered) to them) - **4)** > matter, affair: Herm 1[12] (cf. Bresciani & Kamil Herm a.l., Porten & Greenfield ZAW lxxx 226, 229, Kutscher IOS i 114); cf. *[ʿ]l ṭʿm nḥm[yh]* Samar 4[7]: concerning N.; this meaning prob. also in ATNS 2[2,6]; the same meaning poss. in Cowl 41[7], cf. Porten & Greenfield ZAW lxxx 229, Porten Arch 274, cf. however also Cowl a.l.: = desire, wishes, Porten & Yardeni sub TADAE A 3.5: instruction.

ṭʿm₃ v. *ṭʿm₂*.

ṭʿmh **Palm** Plur. emph. *ṭʿmtʾ* CIS ii 3913 ii 109 (cf. Greek par. τῶν βρωτῶν) - ¶ subst. Plur. victuals.

ṭʿn₁ **OffAr** QAL Pf. 1 p.s. *ṭʿnt* Aḥiq 111; 3 p.pl.m. + suff. 2 p.s.m. *ṭʿnwk* Cowl 6[6]; Pf. pass. 1 p.s. *ṭʿynt* Cowl 8[24]; Impf. 3 p.s.m. + suff. 3 p.s.m. *yṭʿnnhy* Aḥiq 91 (:: Lindenberger APA 63: or form of QAL pass.); Inf. *mṭʿn* NESE i 11[3] - **Palm** QAL Part. pass. pl.m. abs. *ṭʿynyn* CIS ii 3913 ii 118 (Greek par. ἔνγομοι) - ¶ verb QAL - **1)** to carry: Aḥiq 111 (+ obj.) - **2)** to load; + obj. + *b₂*: NESE i 11[2f.] (on a ship); cf. also *wṭʿwn gmlʾ yṭʿnnhy* Aḥiq 91: he will load upon him a camel's load × Leand 33a: he will carry it (a camel's load); cf. also Part. pass., laden: CIS ii 3913 ii 118 (cf. e.g. Cooke NSI p. 330, 338 :: Klíma FS Bakoš: = Plur. abs. of *ṭʿyn*(= being with young; cf. however Teixidor Syr xlviii 483) - **3)** to impose (something upon someone); + obj. + *l₅* + obj., *ṭʿnwk ly mwmʾh* Cowl 6[6]: they imposed upon you an oath to me (cf. also Muffs 32 n. 1) - QAL pass., *wmwmʾ ṭʿynt lh* Cowl 8[24]: an oath to him was imposed upon me (cf. Porten & Greenfield JEAS p. 10, Grelot DAE p. 179, Porten & Yardeni sub TADAE B 2.3 × I took an oath to him, cf. Cowl a.l.).

ṭʿn₂ **OffAr** Sing. cstr. *ṭʿwn*Aḥiq 91 - **Palm** Sing. abs. *ṭʿwn*CIS ii 3913 ii 23, 26, 66, 130; cstr. *ṭʿwn*CIS ii 3913 i 13, ii 7, 8, 17, 21, 24, 29, etc.; emph. *ṭʿwnʾ*CIS ii 3913 ii 16, 34, 36, 59, 109, 144?; Plur. abs. *ṭʿwnyn*CIS ii 3913 i 13 (the Greek par. text of CIS ii 3913 uses γόμος), *ṭʿnyn* RTP 117 (diff. reading, cf. Seyrig & Caquot RTP p. 17 (cf. also Caquot ibid. p. 145): l. *kʿnyn* = word of unknown meaning (= Plur. abs. of *kʿn₁*), cf. however Starcky ibid. p. 17: l. *ṭʿnyn*, cf. also Caquot RTP p. 145, Gawlikowski TP 72 (n. 34)) - ¶ subst. load, passim - as *nomen regens* in a construct-phrase - 1) the *nomen rectum* indicating the one who is carrying; *ṭʿwn gmlʾ* Aḥiq 91: the camel-load (for the context, cf. Epstein ZAW xxxiii 228), cf. CIS ii 3913 ii 7, 8, 17, 30, 31 (cf. in Greek par. γόμου καμηλικοῦ); *ṭʿwn ḥmrʾ* CIS ii 3913 ii 37: the donkey-load, cf. CIS ii 3913 ii 10 (Greek par. γόμου ὀνικ[οῦ]); *ṭʿwn qrs* CIS ii 3913 i 13: a waggon-load (cf. Greek par. γόμος καρρικὸς); cf. also the corresponding *dy*-construction *ṭʿwnyn dy gmlyn* CIS ii 3913 i 13: camel-loads; *ṭʿwnʾ dy gmlʾ* CIS ii 3913 ii 36: the camel-load - 2) the *nomen rectum* indicating what is carried; *ṭʿwn dhnʾ* CIS ii 3913 ii 29, 31: a load of fat; *ṭʿwn n[wny]ʾ mlyḥyʾ* CIS ii 3913 ii 34: a load of salted fishes; cf. *ṭʿwnʾ dy ḥṭʾ wḥmrʾ wtbnʾ* CIS ii 3913 ii 59: a load of wheat and wine and straw (cf. Greek par. γόμου πυρικοῦ οἰνικοῦ); cf. also *ṭʿwn gmlʾ dy [m]šḥʾ* CIS ii 3913 ii 17: a camel-load of oil (cf. CIS ii 3913 ii 7); *ṭʿwn ḥmr [d]y mšḥʾ* CIS ii 3913 ii 21: a donkey-load of oil (cf. in the Greek par. resp. γόμου ἐλεηροῦ, γόμου ἐλαιηροῦ = a load of oil).

ṭp₁ **OffAr** Sing. abs. *ṭp* Cowl 26[10,18] - ¶ subst. of unknown meaning: plank, beam?? (cf. Ungnad ArPap 16, Holma Öfversigt af Finksa

Vetenskaps-Societetens Förhandlingar '15B no. 5, 4f., Cowl a.l., Degen NESE iii 87, cf. also Grelot DAE p. 289 n. t: < Egypt.?; and cf. Perles OLZ '11, 499 with improb. etymology).
v. *ṭp*$_2$.

ṭp$_2$ **Hatra** Sing./Plur. emph. *ṭpʾ* 290^{4} (cf. Degen NESE iii 87 :: Teixidor Sem xxx 66f.: = Plur. emph. of *ṭp*$_1$(= beam) :: Aggoula Syr lii 191f.: = Qal Pf. 3 p.s.m. of *ṭpʾ* (= to join, to adjoin) :: Safar Sumer xxvii 12: l. *ṭwʾ* (misprint for *ṭpʾ*) = Qal Pf. 3 p.s.m. (= to close)). ¶ subst. of unknown meaning, poss. denoting building material or part of a building: Aggoula Syr lxv 205: = platform; cf. Degen NESE iii 87: compare *ṭp*$_1$(highly uncert. comparison); Vattioni IH a.l.: = Plur. emph. (= the annexes (outbuildings)).

ṭpʾ v. *ṭ*$_1$,*ṭp*$_2$,*ṭpyʾ*.

ṭpḥ **Hebr** Plur. abs. *ṭpḥym* Mas $585^{2,4}$ - ¶ subst. a hand's breadth.

ṭpyʾ **Edom** (?) Plur. abs. *ṭpyʾn* BASOR lxxx $8^{1,2}$ (v. infra) - ¶ subst. of uncert. meaning, poss. = jar (cf. (Youtie with) Glueck BASOR lxxx 8 (n. 11), Delavault & Lemaire Sem xxv 32f. :: Albright BASOR lxxx 8 (n. 11): = Qal Part. pass.f. pl. abs. of *ṭpʾ* (= to close, to seal); cf. also Colella RB lxxx 548).

ṭpyh **Palm** Sing. emph. *ṭpytʾ* SBS 20^{3}; Plur. emph. *ṭpytʾ* SBS 19^{1} (v. infra) - ¶ subst. exact meaning unknown, architectural term, prob. indicating special type of base of a column, cf. Garbini OA xiv 176f., cf. also Degen WO viii 130 :: Caquot GLECS vii 78, Dunant SBS a.l.: = capital of a column, crowning (Dunant: in both instances = Sing. emph.).

ṭpsr v. *dpsr*, *ṭpsrs*.

ṭpsrs **OffAr** the diff. *ṭpsrsn* in ATNS 37^{6} poss. = Plur. emph. of *ṭpsrs*, subst. of unknown meaning, poss. related to *ṭpsr* = scribe (v. *dpsr*),context however heavily dam.

ṭpp v. *ʿwp*$_1$.

ṭpr = hoof > Akkad., cf. v.Soden Or xxxvii 268, xlvi 196, cf. also idem AHW s.v. *ṭupru*.

ṭpš v. *npš*.

ṭr v. *ṭhr*.

ṭrʾ$_1$ v. *nṣr*$_1$.

ṭrʾ$_2$ Dietrich ASS 181: > Akkad. *ṭerû* (= to beat); uncert. interpret.
v. *ymʾ*, *nṣr*$_1$.

ṭrd **JAr** Qal Pf. 3 p.s.f. *ṭrdt* AMB 15^{6} - ¶ verb Qal to lock, to bolt: AMB 15^{6} (context however heavily dam.).

ṭrymysyn (< Greek τριμήσιον) - **JAr** Sing. abs. *ṭrymysyn* MPAT-A 27^{1} (= SM 33 = Frey 857), 29^{2} (= SM 39 = Frey 859), $56^{2f.}$ (*ṭr[ym]ysyn*, for the reading, cf. Naveh sub SM 74 :: Fitzmyer & Harrington MPAT a.l., Hüttenmeister ASI 121: l. on l. 2 *ṭr[ymysyn]*), *ṭrysyn* MPAT-A 28^{4}

(= SM 34 = Frey 858; the original mosaic shows a blank space with room for two letters: *ym* after *ṭr*) - ¶ subst. a coin worth the third part of the *aureus*.

ṭrysyn v. *ṭrymysyn*.

ṭrm **Hebr** *ṭrm* TA-H 5[12] - ¶ particle; in TA-H 5[12] used in the combination *bṭrm* = before; *bṭrm y'br hḥdš* TA-H 5[12f.]: before the month passes.

ṭrn **Hatra** (m.) Sing. emph. *ṭrn'* 324 (for the reading, cf. e.g. As-Saliḥi Sumer xxxi 183 :: Degen NESE iii 106: l. *ṭkn'* (or l. *ṭknb*??) = n.p.) - ¶ subst. (or adj.) of uncert. meaning; Aggoula Sem xxvii 132: poss. = epithet, the hard one (cf. also Vattioni IH sub 324), or = epithet, silex. v. *'ṭrn*.

$ṭrp_1$ **OffAr** *ṭrpy[k]* Aḥiq 97, uncert. form (poss. subst. Plur. + suff. 2 p.s.m.) of the root *ṭrp*, cf. Cowl a.l. (: = destruction?; cf. also Koopmans 142), cf. also Grelot DAE p. 437 (: > prejudice, or = form of $ṭrp_2$ (= wink of an eye; cf. idem RB lxviii 182), Lindenberger APA 74: = grief, trouble :: Kotsieper SAS 20, 169f., 205f.: = good quality, excellence.

$ṭrp_2$ v. $ṭrp_1$.

ṭrpw'ḥ v. *ṭlpḥ*.

ṭrps v. prq_1.

ṭrq v. *trq*.

Y

y_1 **Pun** *y'* KAI 165[1] (for this interpret., cf. Levi Della Vida OA iv 65, 67, v.d.Branden RSF ii 146 :: Chabot sub Punica xvi 1 (div. otherwise): l. *sbqy'*, meaning unknown :: Février BAr '51/52, 40f., 43, Röllig KAI a.l. (div. otherwise): l. *tbqy ''lk* (for the first word, v. *sbq*, the first ' of the second word being the article, cf. also Röllig BiOr xxvii 379)) - **Hebr** *yh* SSI i 58B (bis; cf. Cross FS Glueck 302, 306 n. 17 :: Naveh IEJ xiii 86, Gibson SSI i a.l., Lemaire RB lxxxiii 560: the second *yh* = n.d. :: Naveh ibid., Gibson ibid.: the first *yh* = part of n.g. :: Lemaire RB lxxxiii a.l.: = part of n.d.) - **DA** *y* ii 10 (cf. Hoftijzer DA p. 232, 285, Rofé SB 68 :: Caquot & Lemaire, v. $'nš_3$) - **OffAr** *yh* Aḥiq 127, 129 - ¶ exclamation, oh; *y' 'lk* KAI 165[1]; oh passer-by; *y'nš* DA ii 10: oh mankind (v. $'nš_3$); *yh bry* Aḥiq 127, 129: oh my son - Kornfeld sub Abydos 15: l. ' (= y_1) twice in RES 1349[2] (improb. reading and interpret.) - cf. *'yh*.

y_2 v. *ywm*.

y_3 v. ymn_2.

y_4 unexplained abbreviation (?) in the combination *y* + *A* attested several times on tags from Massada, cf. Yadin IEJ xv 113, Yadin & Naveh Mas 17f.

y'₁ **Pun** Sing. m. abs. *y'* KAI 76A 5, B 2, 5 - ¶ adj. beautiful, good (said of fruits); *pr y'* KAI 76 B 2: good fruit, cf. KAI 76 A 2, B 5.

y'₂ v. *y₁*.

y'b **OffAr** QAL Impf. 3 p.s.m. *yy'b* RES 1790[5] (highly uncert. context) - ¶ verb QAL to desire (v. supra); related to *'by*?
v. *n'b*.

y'yrt **Nab** word of unknown meaning in MPAT 64 recto ii 8 (Starcky RB lxi 166: = QAL Pf. 1 p.s. of *yrt₁* (= *yrš*); improb. interpret.).

y'ny v. *hy₂*.

y'nq v. *ynq₂*.

y'ṣ v. *y'ṣ*.

y'r **OffAr** Sznycer HDS 168f.: l. *by'r* in Sem xxxiii 94[2] = *b₂* + Sing. abs. of *y'r* (= river or = n.g.), improb. reading and interpret., cf. Porten Sem xxxiii 94, 96: l. *bzy hw* (cf. also Porten & Yardeni sub TADAE A 5.1; prob. reading).

ybb **Pun** Rocco AION xxiv 478: l. *bb* in GR ii 36 no. 20[3] = QAL Imper. s.m. of *ybb* (= to act impetuously; highly uncert. reading and interpret., cf. Polselli GR a.l.).

ybyš **Palm** Sing. m. abs. *ybyš* CIS ii 3913 ii 116 (Greek par. τὸ ξηρόφορτον = load of dry goods); Plur. m. abs. *yby[šyn]* CIS ii 3913 ii 7 - **JAr** Plur. m. abs. *ybyšyn* SM 49[4] - ¶ adj. dry: SM 49[4]; Sing. and Plur. (substantivated) dry goods: CIS ii 3913 ii 7, 116.

ybl₁ **DA** PA'EL (cf. H. & M. Weippert ZDPV xcviii 96) or HAPH? (cf. Garbini Hen i 179, Puech FS Grelot 23) :: McCarter BASOR ccxxxix 55, Hackett BTDA 29, 49, 96: = PU'AL (cf. also Weinfeld Shn v/vi 146) :: Levine JAOS ci 199, Sasson UF xvii 300: = YIPH) Impf. 3 p.s.m. *yybl* i 11 - **Samal** PA'EL (cf. e.g. Cooke NSI p. 176, Friedr 23*, Dion p. 216, Donner KAI iii p. 34; or QAL?, cf. Kutscher IOS i 114) Pf. 3 p.s.m. *ybl* KAI 215[6,14,21] (second instance; ?, cf. e.g. Cooke NSI p. 180, Donner KAI a.l. × Dion p. 42: = Sing. abs. of *ybl₂*) - **OldAr** QAL Impf. 3 p.s.m. *ybl* Tell F 11 (cf. Abou-Assaf, Bordreuil & Millard Tell F p. 24, 32, Wesselius BiOr xl 182, Muraoka AN xxii 111 n. 22, Sader EAS 19 (n. 39) :: Kaufman Maarav iii 166f., Gropp & Lewis BASOR cclix 5, Huehnergard BASOR cclxi 93, Sasson ZAW xcvii 90, 96: = QAL Impf. 3 p.s.m. of *nbl₁* (= to grow old, to wear out, to become worn) :: Greenfield & Shaffer Irâq xlv 113f., Fales Syr lx 246: = QAL Impf. 3 p.s.m. of *nbl₂* (= variant of *npl₁* (= to fall); cf. also Puech RB xc 596, Pardee JNES xliii 254 n. 6) :: Stefanovic COAI 71f.: = QAL Impf. 3 p.s.m. of *bly₁* (cf. Wesselius SV 56, 58); on this form cf. also Sasson ZAW xcvii 96f. (n. 9), Andersen & Freedman FS Fensham 23) - **OffAr** QAL Pf. 3 p.s.m. *ybl* PF 1587[1] (cf. Hallock PF a.l., or = QAL pass.?, cf. Elam. par. text); + suff. 2 p.s.m. *yblk* ASAE xxvi 25B 3; 1 p.s. + suff. 2 p.s.m. *ybltk* Aḥiq 48; 3 p.pl.m. + suff. 1 p.s. *yblwny* ATNS 29 ii 8; 2 p.pl.m. *ybltwn* NESE i 11[5]; Impf. 1 p.pl. *nbl* Cowl 2[9]; Imper. s.m. + suff. 1 p.s. *blny* Aḥiq 52; Inf. *mwbl* Cowl 2[13] (cf. Leand 38d :: Sach p. 101f., Wag 38: = Sing. abs. of *mwbl* (= load)), NESE i 11[4]; QAL pass. Pf. 3 p.s.m. *ybyl* ATNS 2[4]; Part. pl.m./f. abs. *ybyln* ATNS 65b 5 (?; or = Pf. 1 p.pl., dam. context); HOPH (cf. Grelot RB lxxiv 434, Segert AAG p. 278, Kaufman BiOr xxxiv 95 × Kutscher IOS i 114 (cf. also Bresciani & Kamil Herm p. 382, Lindenberger APA 258 n. 413): = QAL pass. :: Bresciani & Kamil ibid.: or *ybl* = QAL and *ywbl* = APH) Impf. 3 p.s.m. *ybl* Herm 1[14], 2[18], 3[14], 5[10], 6[11], *ywbl* Herm 7[5]; cf. Frah xx 21 (*yblwn*, cf. Ebeling Frah a.l. :: Nyberg FP 51, 94: or l. *ydlwn* = form of *dry*(= to carry)), 22 (*yblwn*, cf. Nyberg FP 51, 94 :: Ebeling Frah a.l.: l. *dbrwn* = form of *dbr*$_2$),SaSt 24, Paik 460-462 (*yblwn*), GIPP 37, cf. also Lemosín AO ii 108, Toll ZDMG-Suppl viii 38 - **Nab** QAL Pf. 2 p.pl.f. *ybltyn* IEJ xxix 112[9] (cf. Naveh IEJ xxix 113, 119; uncert. interpret., diff. context) - **Palm** APH Impf. 3 p.s.m. + suff. 3 p.s.f. *[y]wblnh* CIS ii 4058[7] (dam. context; cf. Milik DFD 181, cf. also Chabot CIS ii a.l.) - **JAr** APH Pf. 1 p.s. *ʾblt* IEJ xl 135[2,6,9], 142[2,4] (for the reading problems, cf. Yardeni IEJ xl 137f.) - ¶ verb QAL to bear, to convey, to transport (:: Wesselius BiOr xl 182: in Tell F 11 = to go?) - **1)** + obj., *ʾnḥnh nbl ʿbwrʾ[* Cowl 2[9]: we will convey the corn; cf. IEJ xl 142[2] - **2)** + obj. + *b*$_2$, *yblwny bmt nbyh* ATNS 29 ii 8: they brought me in the region of N. (dam. context) - **3)** + obj. + *b*$_2$ (temp.) + *lwt*: IEJ xl 135[2ff] - **4)** + obj. + *l*$_5$ (temp.) + *lwt*: IEJ xl 135[5ff.] - **5)** + obj. + *l*$_5$, *ybltk lbytʾ zyly* Aḥiq 48: I took you to my house; cf. Aḥiq 52 - **6)** + n.g. + obj., *ybl prs ptp* PF 1587[1f.] (v. however supra): he has brought the rations to P. - **7)** + acc. comm.: *yblk* ASAE xxvi 25: he will bring to you (cf. Bogaert Bibl xlv 227) - **8)** + *l*$_5$, *lmwbl lgbryʾ ʾlh* Cowl 2[13]: to bring (it) to those men; *lmwbl lbyty* NESE i 11[4]: to bring (it) to my house - **9)** + *mn*$_5$ + obj.: IEJ xl 135[9] - **10)** + *ʿl*$_7$, *ybltwn ʿl btyn* NESE i 11[5f.]: you have brought (it) to our houses - QAL pass. to be transported, to be brought; *ybyl lhm lmwmʾ ʿl znh* ATNS 2[3]: he was transported to them to swear about this - PAʿEL to bear, to convey, to transport - **1)** + obj. + noun without prep., *bnt mwqʾ šmš ybl mʿrb* KAI 215[14]: the daughters of the east he brought to the west - **2)** + *b*$_2$ + obj., *bʾšr rḥln yybl ḥṭr ʾrnbn* DA i 11: in the place fit for breeding ewes the staff will bring hares (cf. Hoftijzer DA p. 205f., TUAT ii 143 :: Caquot & Lemaire Syr liv 199: in the place where the staff (i.e. the shepherd's crook) brought the ewes (i.e. let them graze), the hares ... (cf. also Rofé SB 66, Smelik HDAI 79) - APH to bring; + obj. + *lwt*: CIS ii 4058[7] (dam. context) - HOPH (v. supra) to be conveyed, to be brought; + name without prep., *ʾpy ywbl* Herm 7[11]: it must be

brought to O. (cf. Herm 1^{14}, 2^{18}, 3^{14}, 5^{10}, 6^{11}) - the diff. *ᵓbl* in Herm 8^4 = QAL Impf. AION xvi 51: l. in IRT 906^5 *v[y]byl* = derivative of *ᵓbl*$_1$(= to mourn??; heavily dam. context) - Vattioni AION xvi 51: l. in IRT 906^5 *v[y]byl* = derivative of *ybl*$_1$?, or of *bwl* (with same meaning)?, cf. however idem Aug xvi 550: l. *v[.]byl* ... = *w* + *b*$_2$ + *l*$_5$ (or l. (div. otherwise): *v[y]by l* ... (derivative of *bwᵓ*+ *l*$_5$??)); for this text, cf. also Levi Della Vida OA ii 71ff. - a comparable instance also in IRT 901^5??: *[y]bil* (cf. Vattioni AION xvi 50, Aug xvi 552 (div. otherwise): l. *[y]bi* = YIPH Pf. 3 p.s.m. of *bwᵓ* + *l*$_5$, cf. also Milik with Vattioni AION xvi 50: *ybili* = form of root *y/wb* (misprint for *y/wbl*?), Krahmalkov JSS xxiv 26 (div. otherwise): *bili* = *bl*$_3$ (improb. interpret.); or *bili* = *b*$_2$ + *l*$_5$??) :: Polselli StudMagr xi 40 (div. otherwise): l. *abi* = Sing. + suff. 3p.s.m. of *ᵓb*$_1$.
v. *ᵓbl*$_5$, *ybl*$_3$.

ybl$_2$ **Pun** Sing. abs. *ybl* KAI 69^7, CIS i 3915^2 - ¶ subst. ram :: Renan sub CIS i 165: = he-goat; the difference in Pun. texts between *ᵓyl*$_2$and *ybl*$_2$ uncert.; Dussaud Orig 139f.: *ybl*$_2$ = castrated ram, *ᵓyl*$_2$= non-castrated ram; cf. Capuzzi StudMagr ii 50f., v. however *ᵓyl*$_2$(cf. also Lagrange ERS 474: *ybl*$_2$ = ram or used to indicate sheep in general) - Zadok WO xii 200: *ybl*$_2$ > Akkad. *jabilu* (cf. also v.Soden AHW s.v.).
v. *ybl*$_{1,3}$.

ybl$_3$ **Samal** the meaning of the difficult *ybl* (first instance) in KAI 215^{21} uncert.; prob. = subst. Sing. abs./cstr. (v. also *ᵓmn*$_3$), cf. e.g. Cooke NSI p. 180, Lagrange ERS 497, Koopmans 76, Gibson SSI ii p. 85: = produce? × Dion p. 42: = *ybl*$_2$ :: Donner KAI a.l.: poss. = PAᶜEL Pf. 3 p.s.m. of *ybl*$_1$ :: Halévy RS i 238, 241: = river, brook; difficult context.

ybl$_4$ **Ph** Diosc iv 29: ιεβαλ = ἄγρωστις (= dog's tooth grass), cf. Löw AP 407.

ybᶜ v. *nbᶜ*.

ybš **Palm** Sing. emph. *ybšᵓ* CIS ii 4047^4 - ¶ subst. the dry ground, the land; *bymᵓ wbybšᵓ* CIS ii 4047^4: on sea and land (i.e. everywhere); Milik DFD 294: read same expression in Inv xi 35^3 (uncert. reading, cf. also Teixidor Inv xi a.l.).

ygn **Pun** this word prob. in ICO-Malta-NPu 11 (uncert. interpret., cf. Amadasi ICO a.l.): = work; the same word poss. in KAI 119^6: *yᶜgn*?: = effort, work?, cf. Février RA l 187, Röllig KAI a.l., Amadasi IPT 80f. (diff. context, cf. also Levi Della Vida RCL '55, 560: other word divisions poss., v. *nšᵓ*$_1$).

yd **OldCan** Sing. (prec. by *b*$_2$) + suff. 3 p.s.m. *ba-di-ú* EA 245^{35} (cf. Siwan GAG 133, 209) - **Ph** Sing. abs. *yd* KAI 24^{13} (:: Degen ZDMG cxxi 127: or = Sing. + suff. 1 p.s.?); cstr. *yd* KAI 24^6 (second instance); + suff. 3 p.s.m. *yd* KAI 24^6 (first instance; cf. Cross & Freedman JNES x 228, CF 17, FR 112, 240.13 (cf. also Koopmans 12 (with wrong derivation), Gibson SSI iii p. 36)); or = Sing. abs.?, cf. e.g. Röllig KAI a.l.); + suff. 1 p.s. *yd* KAI 24[7] (cf. FR 240.13); Dual cstr. *yd* KAI 30[4] (cf. Dupont-Sommer RA xli 205f., Masson & Sznycer RPC 15 × Honeyman Irâq vi 107, Albright BASOR lxxxiii 16, Röllig KAI a.l., FR 240.13: = Sing. cstr.); in combination with b_2 with loss of *y* (cf. e.g. FR 63a, 80a, 252c, Garbini ISNO 64, Blau & Loewenstamm UF ii 30, Garr DGSP 52 :: Gordon Or xxi 121, Rabin JJS vi 111ff.: *bd*= b_2 + *d* (= hand); cf. also Garbini RSO xlvi 136): *bd* KAI 60[1], CIS i 87[1,3] (= Kition C_2; dam. context), EpAn ix 5[6] - **Pun** Dual + suff. 3 p.s.m., cf. KAI 178[1]: *iadem* (or = Dual abs.?, cf. e.g. Levi Della Vida LibSamal. iii 109, FR 76a, 86a, 226a, 240.13, 241, Röllig KAI a.l.); in combination with b_2 with loss of *y* (v. supra) *bd*: CIS i 269[3], 270[2], 272[3], 274[4], 2998[2], 4901[3], 4902[4]; + suff. 3 p.s.m. *bdy* KAI 277[6] (v. *ʾrš*$_1$) - **Edom** Sing. cstr. (in combination with b_2 with loss of *y*, v. supra) *bd* RB lxxiii 399[3] (dam. context) - **Hebr** Sing. cstr. *yd* KAI 197[7], TA-H 17[9], 24[15], DJD ii 24B 2, D 2, E 2, I i 2, 49 i 2; Dual cstr. *ydy* KAI 196[7], EI xx 256[2]; + suff. 2 p.s.m. *ydyk* KAI 196[6] (cf. e.g. Diringer Lach iii p. 334, Albright BASOR lxx 15, Hempel ZAW lvi 135f. (n. 9), Röllig KAI a.l., Gibson SSI i p. 45 (cf. Pardee HAHL 100f.) :: Albright BASOR lxxxii 22 (n. 18): l. *ydyk[m]* = Dual + suff. 2 p.pl.m. :: e.g. de Vaux RB xlviii 197f.: l. *ydy* = Dual cstr. :: Albright BASOR lxxiii 20 (n. 26): l. *ydym* = Dual abs. :: Albright ANET 322: l. *ydynw* = Dual + suff. 1 p.pl.; for the reading, cf. also Birnbaum PEQ '39, 104: l. *ydyb* (unexplained)) - **DA** Sing. + suff. 3 p.s.m./f. *ydh* xd 2 - **Samal** Sing. + suff. 1 p.s. *ydy* KAI 214[2,8] (for both instances, cf. Dion p. 151 :: Friedr 37*, Donner KAI a.l., Gibson SSI ii p. 70); + suff. 3 p.s.m. *ydh* KAI 214[25]; Dual + suff. 3 p.s.m. *ydyh* KAI 214[29]; + suff. 1 p.s. *ydy* KAI 214[12] (cf. Donner KAI a.l. × Dion p. 151, Gibson SSI ii p. 67: = Sing. + suff. 1 p.s.) - **OldAr** Sing. abs. *yd* KAI 222B 25, 34; cstr. *yd* KAI 202A 12, 223B 14, 224[11]; + suff. 3 p.s.m. *ydh* KAI 222B 27, 224[2], Tell F 18; + suff. 1 p.s. *ydy* KAI 224[2,5,10,13] (× Degen AAG p. 58 (n. 32): or = Dual + suff. 1 p.s.; cf. also Fitzmyer AIS 155); Dual + suff. 1 p.s. *ydy* KAI 202A 11, B 15 (dam. context) - **OffAr** Sing. abs. *yd* Irâq xxxiv 133a (uncert. interpret., cf. Fales sub AECT 45 (div. otherwise): l. *ydyʾ* = Dual emph. :: Kaufman JAOS cix 100: l. *ʿwz* = Sing. abs. of *ʿwz* (= *ʿz*$_1$)), ATNS 28b 4; cstr. *yd* KAI 267[4], Cowl 22[120], 24[36], 26[7], Krael 13[4], Driv 13[2], Herm 3[6], 5[5], RES 1300[4], NESE i 11[6], BS 47[1], Pers 1[1], ATNS 9[1], etc., etc.; + suff. 3 p.s.m. *ydh* Cowl 28[4,6], 81[32,33,34], Aḥiq 171, Driv 4[1], JRAS '29, 111[7], Herm 6[7], NESE i 11[3]; + suff. 2 p.s.m. *ydk* Cowl 10[12,14,19,20], 42[13], Aḥiq 193, Driv 4[2], NESE i 11[7] (reading of *d* highly uncert., cf. also Macuch JAOS xciii 60; for reading *ydk*, cf. Naveh & Shaked JAOS xci 381, Degen NESE i

11, 19, Golomb BASOR ccxvii 49, 52, cf. also Grelot DAE 504, Porten Or lvii 80, Porten & Yardeni sub TADAE A 3.10: l. *ydk[m]* = Sing. + suff. 2 p.pl.m. :: (Shunnar with) Macuch JAOS xciii 60: l. *ywm[ʾ]* = Sing. emph. of *ywm* :: Shunnar with Altheim & Stiehl GMA 115: pro *bydk* l. *byswn* (= in Syene)); + suff. 2 p.s.f. *ydky* Cowl $8^{18,22}$, 43^{7}, Herm 6^{6}; + suff. 1 p.s. *ydy* Herm 2^{5}, 3^{4}, FuF xxxv 173^{6} (prob. interpret., v. infra); + suff. 3 p.pl.m. *ydhm* ATNS 77a 3; + suff. 2 p.pl.m. *ydkm* Cowl 38^{9}, NESE i 11^{2}; + suff. 1 p.pl. *ydn* Cowl $2^{3,13}$, 3^{4}; Dual abs. *ydyn* Cowl $15^{8,26}$, Krael 7^{8}; cstr. *ydy* Aḥiq 122, Krael 9^{17}; + suff. 2 p.s.m. *ydyk* Aḥiq 123; + suff. 1 p.s. *ydy* Aḥiq 155; + suff. 3 p.pl.m. *ydyhm* KAI 233^{9}; Plur. + suff. 3 p.pl.m. *ydhyhm* KAI 233^{5} (*ydh[yh]m*, for the reading, cf. Dupont-Sommer Syr xxiv 36 :: Lidzbarski AUA p. 10, 12: l. *ydh[w]m* = Sing. + suff. 3 p.pl.m. (on this reading, cf. Bowman UMS xx 279) :: Silverman JAOS xciv 271: l. *bydh[y]m*? = metathesis for *bydyhm*)^{,9} (*ydhy[hm]*, for the reading, cf. Dupont-Sommer Syr xxiv 41 :: Lidzbarski AUA p. 12: l. *ydhm* or *ydhwm* = Sing. + suff. 3 p.pl.m. ?)^{,12} (for the reading, cf. Dupont-Sommer Syr xxiv 43 :: Lidzbarski AUA p. 8, 12: l. *ydhwm* = Sing. + suff. 3 p.pl.m.); cf. Frah x 30 (*ydh*), Paik 464 (*ydʾ*), 465 (*ydh*), Nisa 49^{2}, 54^{3}, 55^{3}, 56^{2}, 58^{2}, 69^{1}, 74^{2}, 75^{3}, 76^{4}, etc. (*yd*), Nisa-b 2167^{3} (*ydyh*; ?, diff. context), GIPP 37, 56, 67, SaSt 25, cf. Toll ZDMG-Suppl viii 29 - **Nab** Sing. cstr. *yd* CIS ii 197^{3}, 198^{9}, 221^{5}, J 5^{3}; + suff. 3 p.s.m. *ydh* CIS ii 197^{2}, 198^{9}, 206^{5}, $207^{3,6}$, 215^{2}, 221^{5}, 222^{3}, 224^{2}, J 5^{3}, RB xli 591,1, Mas 515, ADAJ xxiv 43 ii, IEJ xxxvi 56^{6}; + suff. 3 p.s.f. *ydh* CIS ii 204^{4}; + suff. 3 p.pl.m. *ydhm* BIA x 55^{4} - **Palm** Sing. + suff. 1 p.s. *ydy* MUSJ xxxviii 106^{3}; Dual + suff. 3 p.s.m. *ydwh* CIS ii 3976^{4} - **JAr** Sing. cstr. *yd* MPAT 61^{26} (= DBKP 15); + suff. 3 p.s.m. *ydh* MPAT 55^{4}; + suff. 2 p.pl.m. *dkwn* Mas 554^{3} (in *bdkwn* = *bydkwn*, cf. Yadin & Naveh Mas a.l.); Dual cstr. *ydy* SM 40^{2} - ¶ subst. f. - **A)** hand, passim; *kp yd* ATNS 28b 4: the palm of the hand; *ydyhm ktbt* KAI 233^{9}: their own hands have written; cf. *ʾšʾlt ktb ydy lywlys* MUSJ xxxviii 106^{3}: I have lent the writing of my hand to J. (i.e. I have written for J.); *ydh tṣmqn* DA xd 2: his/her hand will wither; v. *mṭʾ*, *šlḥ*$_1$ - **1)** prec. by prep. *b*$_2$ - a) followed by pron. suff. referring to the subject of the clause, with one's own hand, personally; *mlkʾltw ... ktbydh* (haplography for *ktb bydh*) RB xli 591.1: M. has written with his own hand (cf. Mas 515, ADAJ xxiv 43 ii, IEJ xxxvi 56^{6}); *hnḥt ly ktwn 1 bydk* Cowl 42^{13}: bring me a coat personally; *hnʿlt ly tmt bydh lbš 1* Krael 2^{4}: T. from her side has brought in to me one garment (cf. Krael $2^{8,10,16}$, Cowl $15^{6,7,24f.,27f.}$); *mn dy ynpq bydh ktp tqp* CIS ii $197^{2f.}$: whoever will bring forward with his own hand a legitimate document (cf. CIS ii 198^{9}, 206^{5}, 207^{3}, 215^{2}, etc.) - b) in the hands of, at someone's service, in the possession of; *wntn bydy hdd*

... *ḥṭr ḥlbbh* KAI 214[2f]: and Hadad ... gave the sceptre of ruling (?, v. *ḥlbbh*) in my hand (i.e. put it at my disposal; cf. KAI 214[8f.]; cf. also Tawil Or xliii 46f.); *wspr› znh bydk* Cowl 10[12]: while this deed is in your possession (cf. Cowl 8[18,22], 10[14,19,20], 38[4], 43[7], 44[4], 81[14,28], CIS ii 204[4], 207[6], etc.; *wntn bydy hdd* KAI 214[2]: Hadad has given to me (cf. KAI 214[8]); *›yty ly ›lp ḥ[d]h bydkm* NESE i 11[2]: I have a ship that you have (at the moment) at your disposal (cf. also NESE i 11[6f.]); *mst ksph zy hwh bydy nttn* (prob. lapsus for *ntnt*) Herm 2[4f.]: the quantity of silver which was in my possession, I have given ... (cf. Herm 6[6f.]); *ntn nḥm šmn byd hkty* TA-H 17[8f.]: N. gave the oil to the Kitti; *hn y›ḥdn ršy‹› bknpy lbšk šbq bydh* Aḥiq 171: if the wicked take hold of the skirts of your garment, leave (it) in his hand (cf. Aḥiq 193); *tql› dy ›yty ly bdkwn* Mas 554[3]: the shekel that you owe me; cf. also *lbl gzly ›dm bd špḥ klš* EpAn ix 5[6]: so that no one might seize it (i.e. landed property) from the possession of the family of K. - c) by the hand of, through; *zy hwšrt ‹ly byd ›n›* Driv 13[2]: which you have sent me by the hand of A. (cf. Cowl 24[36], 26[7], RES 1300[4], Herm 3[6], 5[5], RSO xxxii 404[2,3]; *[b]yd ḥzyn wbyd ‹ddn* KAI 202A 12: through seeers and messengers (v. *‹dd*$_2$); *byd tgr* BS 47[1]: through/by a merchant (cf. BS 48[2], cf. also RB lxxiii 399[3] (*bd*)); *yhwḥnn br ›lks byd yhwsp brh* MPAT 61[26] (= DBKP 15): Y. son of A. by the hand of his son Y. (signature of witness to a Greek document); *tm bd* (v. supra) *ṣdnym* KAI 60[1]: it was resolved by the Sidonians; *›š ṣdn bd ›dnm bd NP* CIS i 4901[3]: a freedman by the hand of his lord (by the hand of) NP (cf. CIS i 269[3], 270[2], 272[3], 275[4], 2998[2], 4902[4], etc. (v. *ṣdn*, cf. also Heltzer OA xxiv 80, UF xix 435); for KAI 277[6], v. *›rš*$_1$;with poss. meaning: with the help of, cf. FuF xxxv 173[6] (diff. context) - d) in the power of; *kt byd mlkm* KAI 24[6]: I was in the power of kings; *ḥd ‹m› zy bydy* KAI 224[5]: any of the people who are under my control (cf. KAI 224[10,13]); *thskrm bydy* KAI 224[2]: you must surrender them into my hands; *ky l› bydy ›nš[›] m[nš]› rglhm* Aḥiq 122: it is not in the power of men to lift up their foot (cf. Aḥiq 123) - **2)** prec. by prep. *bn*$_5$, v. *byn*$_2$ - **3)** prec. by prep. *l*$_5$ - a) with *yd* in the status abs., *w›nk tmkt mškbm lyd* KAI 24[13]: I grasped the M. by the hand (cf. e.g. Torrey JAOS xxxv 365, 368, Rosenthal ANET 501, Röllig KAI a.l., Avishur PIB 209, 213, Gibson SSI iii p. 35, 38, cf. also FR 282.4, Sperling UF xx 335 :: v.d.Branden BiOr xxxvi 203: I took the M. in my hand :: Lidzbarski Eph iii 238: *lyd* = being at (their) side (cf. also Degen ZDMG cxxi 127)) - b) with *yd* in the status cstr. or + pron. suff. - α) at the disposal of; *krbr ‹bd ›bšwn lyd dtmtr gnzbr›* Pers 12[2f.]: K. has made a pestle at the disposal of (intended for) the treasurer D. (cf. Pers 1[2ff.], 7[3ff.], 8[2ff.], 9[2ff.], 10[3ff.], etc., etc. (:: Degen BiOr xxxi 125f.: during the term of office of ... D.)); *rmn 1 ‹bd hwn znh rb lyd bgpt gnzbr› qdm mzddt ›pgnzbr[›]* Pers 39[3ff.]: R. made this large mortar at the disposal of the treasurer B. before (i.e. under supervision of) M. the sub-treasurer (cf. Pers $32^{2ff.}$, $36^{1f.}$, $47^{2ff.}$, $53^{3ff.}$, etc.); *phrbrn ʿbd hwn ... qdm ʾrywhš ʾp[g]n[zb]rʾ lyd b[gpt gnzbrʾ]* Pers $116^{2ff.}$: P. made a mortar ... before (i.e. under the supervision of) A. the sub-treasurer at the disposal of the treasurer B. (for the interpret. of *lyd* in these Pers texts, cf. Naveh & Shaked Or xlii 451f., Gignoux RHR clxxxi 87, Bernard StIr i 169, 171; cf. however Levine JAOS xcii 72, Segal BSOAS xxxv 354, Degen BiOr xxxi 125f.: = under the authority of (cf. Oelsner OLZ '75, 476: = under the responsibility of; on the interpret., cf. also Hinz FS Nyberg 377 :: Bowman Pers p. 39f., 68: = beside); *kspʾ hbw lyd ʾr[mty]dt* NESE i 11^{6}: give the silver to A.; *lyd* with the same meaning also in the Nisa-texts (for the interpret. of Nisa-texts, cf. Henning Ir 27 (n. 2), Bernard StIr i 71 :: Diakonov & Livshitz Nisa-b p. 44, PeSb ii 143: = under the command/management of (cf. also Sznycer Sem xii 117, 118, 119, Chaumont JA cclvi 14, 32, Naveh & Shaked Or xlii 451)) - β) under the authority of, under the command of; *ḥylʾ zy lydh* Driv 4^{1}: the troop which is under his command (cf. ATNS 9^{1} (for the reading *zy lyd ʾwstn*, cf. Porten & Yardeni sub TADAE B 8.6); *bsrk byrtʾ lyd mtrk sgnʾ* Pers 18^{1}: in the fortress of S. (which is) under the authority of the governor M. (cf. Pers 1^{1}, $4^{1f.}$, 5^{1}, $6^{1f.}$, 8^{1}, 9^{1}, etc., etc.; for the interpret., cf. Segal BSOAS xxxv 354, Levine JAOS xcii 76f., Gignoux RHR clxxxi 87, Naveh & Shaked Or xlii 451f., Degen BiOr xxxi 125f., Teixidor Syr l. 431 (cf. Oelsner OLZ '75, 476: under the responsibility of; cf. also Delaunay CC 210f. (nn. 55, 56), 216) :: Bernard StIr i 170: at the disposal of (cf. also Gershevitch Mem de Menasce 59f., Hinz FS Nyberg 377) :: Bowman Pers p. 39, 68 (with wrong interpret. of context): beside (v. *hst*, *srk*$_2$, *prk*$_6$ (v. *bz*$_1$), *prkn*$_2$) - **4)** prec. by prep. *mn*$_5$ - a) from, from the side of; *yqḥw mn ydy* KAI 214^{12}: they accept from my hands (i.e. from me), cf. KAI 224^{2}, Tell F 17f.; *ktb tqp mn yd ʿydw* CIS ii 197^{3}: a valid document from the hand of A., cf. CIS ii $198^{9f.}$, 221^{5}, J 5^{3} (cf. also CIS ii 206^{5}, 207^{3} containing the same expression with *mn* instead of *mn yd*) and also CIS ii 224^{2f} (*mn yd hynt dʾ ktb ʾw tqp*) - b) cf. the expression *tqm dmy mn yd šnʾy* KAI 224^{11}: you will avenge my blood from the hand of my enemies (i.e. you will avenge my death on my enemies), cf. also KAI 223B 14 and *lmhwʾ [š]wh mn ydhm* BIA x 55^{4}: that it may be established by their hands (poss. interpret., cf. O'Connor DRBE 606, 619 n. 19; cf. also Milik BIA x 56; restoration of the text however uncert.) - **5)** prec. by prep. *ʿl*$_7$ - a) at the disposal of; *whbqydm ʿl yd ʾlyšʿ* TA-H $24^{14f.}$: and place them at the disposal of E. (cf. also Pardee UF x 319; Lemaire Sem xxiii 15f.: place them at the disposal of/under the responsibility of E.; second proposal less prob.; cf. also idem IH i 194: under the command of); *yhbt ʿl ydn šʿ[rn]* Cowl 2^{3}: you have delivered to us barley (cf. Cowl

2^{13}, 26^{21}, ATNS 77a 3, NESE i 11^{3}); *ʾšlmt ʿl ydwh* CIS ii 3976^{4}: she has been entrusted to his hands (i.e. to him); cf. also RES $1791^{1ff.}$?, cf. however Lidzbarski Eph iii 120: = through, by; cf. prob. also BSh 3^{3}, 28^{3} - b) through, by means of: SM 40^{2} (?, dam. context: *ywdn ... ʿbd hdyn ʿmwdh ʿl ydy[* , Y. ... made this column by means of (?) ...), v. also sub 5a - c) on the authority of: DJD ii 24B 2, D 2, E 2 (in the opening section of contracts, cf. also Milik DJD ii p. 126), cf. also *ʿl ydy* in EI xx 256^{2} - **B)** time; *lbš 1 zy ʿmr ... ṣbʿ ydyn* Cowl $15^{7f.}$: one woollen garment ... dyed two times (cf. Driver PEQ '55, 93, Grelot DAE p. 193 (n. g), cf. however Porten & Greenfield JEAS p. 21: = dyed double well, or two-toned? (cf. also Porten & Yardeni sub TADAE B 2.6 a.e.) :: Fitzmyer FS Albright ii 153f., WA 256f.: on two/both edges? :: Cowl p. 48, Krael p. 205, 210: = on both sides), cf. Krael 7^{8}, 14a - **C)** side; *byn yd zʾ wlbbʾ* Irâq xxxiv 133a: between this side and the centre (cf. Akkad. par. *bir-ti idi lìb-bi*), reading and interpret. of Ar. text however uncert., v. supra and cf. Fales sub AECT 45 - the interpret. of *lqbl zy ydkm* in Cowl 38^{9} uncert. (diff. context), Cowl a.l.: according to your ability (cf. Grelot DAE p. 393, Porten & Greenfield JEAS p. 82, Porten & Yardeni sub TADAE A 4.3) - Schroed 313, Sznycer PPP 101: the *id* in Poen 938: = *yd* (Sing. abs.; :: L.H.Gray AJSL xxxix 80: = *ʿ*d_2 (= witness > testimony) cf. also J.J.Glück & Maurach Semitics ii 112: = I see or better (div. otherwise) l. *yid* = HIPH Impf. 1 p.s. of *ʿ*wd_1 (= to observe)) - a poss. *yd* (Sing. abs.) in PF 2043^{3} (highly uncert. context) - a form of *yd* also in the diff. text HUCA xl/xli 159^{3} (Hebr.), prob. l. *ydh* = Sing. + suff. 3 p.s.m. (*scriptio anterior yh* (lapsus) *l* (= l_5)), cf. however Dever HUCA xl/xli 159, 161: l. *yd* (Sing. abs.; *scriptio anterior yhh* = lapsus for *yhyh* (= QAL Impf. 3 p.s.m. of *hyy*)) :: Garbini AION xxviii 192f.: l. *yd* (= Sing. abs.) *kl* (= Sing. abs. (or cstr.?) of kl_1) :: Teixidor Syr xlix 428: l. *yh* :: Mittmann ZDPV xcvii 144, 146f. (div. otherwise): l. *ydh* = HIPH Impf. 3 p.s.m. of ydy_1 (= to praise) :: Lemaire RB lxxxiv 599: l. *-yh* (cf. also Zevit BASOR cclv 44) :: Naveh BASOR ccxxxv 28 (div. otherwise): l. *-y w-* :: Spronk BAAI 308 (nn. 4, 5): l. *dyh* (= Sing. + suff. 3 p.s.m. of dy_1)+ *hlʾ* (= over there); for the context, v. *ʾ*rr_1 - Février & Fantar Karth xii a.l.: the *ydʾ* in Karth xii 53^{1} = Dual cstr. (cf. also v.d.Branden RSF v 56f., 61), poss. interpret. :: Krahmalkov RSF iii 178, 184, 201: = PIʿEL Pf. 3 p.pl.m. of ydy_2(= to cast down) - the βιδ in Inv D 51^{1} poss. = part of n.p., cf. Milik Syr xliv 290ff., cf. however Levi Della Vida FDE '22-23, 367f., du Mesnil du Buisson sub Inv D 51: = b_2 + Sing. cstr. of *yd* - Owen Sar p. 102, 104: l. *yd[y]* in Sar 2^{1} (= Dual + suff. 1 p.s.), less prob. interpret., cf. Greenstein JANES viii 54ff.: l. *yd* = part of Ph. n.p. - Broshi & Qimron IEJ xxxvi 207: the *ymy* in IEJ xxxvi 206^{1} prob. = lapsus for *ydy* (= Dual cstr.), diff. and dam. context - Naveh & Shaked

AMB a.l.: the diff. *lyd›* in AMB 15[7] poss. = *l*$_5$ + Sing. emph. of *yd* (= near there?? or at that time??), highly uncert. interpret. - Segal ATNS a.l.: l. *yd* (= Sing. cstr.) in ATNS 8[13] (highly uncert. reading, cf. also Porten & Yardeni sub TADAE B 5.6) - v.d.Branden BO xii 215, 218: l. *bdk* in KAI 50[5] (= *bd* (v. supra) + suff. 2 p.s.m.).
v. *›ḥd*$_4$, *z*$_1$, *zy,plk*$_1$.

ydw‘ **OffAr** the *ydw‘* in TA-Ar 1[3], 2[2], 3[2], 5[2], etc. prob. = n.p. (cf. Naveh TA-Ar p. 153f., 175).

ydy$_1$ **OffAr** HAPH Pf. 1 p.s. *hwdt* Samar 2[11], *hdt* Samar 3[10] (dam. and diff. context) - **Palm** APH Pf. 3 p.pl.m. *›wdw* Inv x 114[4]; Part. s.m. abs. *mwd›* CIS ii 3989[2], 3998B 2, 4007[2], 4009[3], 4012[2], 4066[3] (*mw[d›]*, Greek par. εὐχαρίστ[ως]), Inv xi 1[2], 15[2], 16[2], xii 34[2], RIP 148, Ber iii 92[3] (*mzd›* printer's error), etc., etc.; s.f. abs. *mwdy›* CIS ii 4006[2], 4010[2], 4020A 2, B 2, 4080[4], 4083[2], Inv xi 21[1], 23[2], RIP 147 (*[m]wdy›*), 149, RB xxxix 548[3], Ber iii 99[2]; pl.m. abs. *mwdn* CIS ii 3949[2], 3981[1], PNO 37[5f.], DM ii 44[2], *mwdyn* PNO 38[4], *mdyn* PNO 72[8] - **JAr** APH Part. s.m. abs. *mwdy* DBKP 17[40] (written in combination with following *›nh*), *mdy* DBKP 18[70], *md›* DBKP 20[41]; ITTAPH (cf. Rosenthal JBL xci 552) Pf. 3 p.s.m. *›ytwdy* MPAT 39[2], EI xx 256[3] (Aramaic form in Hebr. context, cf. Broshi & Qimron EI xx 258) - ¶ verb APH - **1)** to acknowledge, to attest - a) + obj., *hwdt dyn›* Samar 2[11]: I acknowledge the claim (dam. context), cf. Samar 3[10] - b) + *b*$_2$, *mdy ›nh bḥwbt ksp* DBKP 18[70]: I acknowledge the debt of silver - c) + *l*$_5$ + *dy*, *mwd› hw lywlys ... dy ...* MUSJ xxxviii 106[5f.]: he acknowledges to Y. ... that ... (cf. Inv x 114[4], RB xxxix 548[3], DBKP 17[40]); *md› ›nh lk dy ‘l dy ›‘bd ...* DBKP 20[41f.]: I acknowledge to you what is (written) above (i.e.) that I will act ... - **2)** to return thanks - a) used absolutely, *‘bd wmwd› yrḥbl› ... dy ...* Inv xi 1[2f.]: Y. has made, returning thanks (sc. to the deity) ... because ... (cf. Inv xi 15[2], 16[2], 23[2], xii 34[2], RIP 137[2], 148, DM ii 38 ii 2f., etc.), cf. also *‘bd wmwd› l‘lm› whblt ...* RIP 135[2f.]: W. has made, returning thanks, forever ... - b) + *l*$_5$, *mwd› ‘nnw lrḥmn›* Inv xi 37[1f.]: A. is returning thanks to the merciful one (cf. CIS ii 3981[1,3], 3989[1f.], 4006[1f.], PNO 38[4f.], Inv xi 21[1], RIP 149, MUSJ xxxviii 125[1ff.], etc.) - c) followed by a noun/name not prec. by prep., *mwd› ‘b› b‘šmn* Sem xxvii 106: A. is returning thanks to B. (cf. also Drijvers Sem xxvii 110), cf. CIS ii 4020A 1f., B 1f., 4083[1f.], etc. - ITTAPH to declare, to acknowledge: MPAT 39[2] (cf. Yaron JJS xi 158, Koffmahn 83f.; diff. and dam. context), EI xx 256[3f.].
v. *yd*.

ydy$_2$ v. *yd*.

ydyn v. *dn*$_1$.

yd‘$_1$ **Ph** QAL Impf. 3 p.pl.m. *yd‘* KAI 60[7]; Inf. cstr. *d‘t*KAI 2[1]; Part. act. s.m. abs. *yd‘* KAI 60[7] (cf. Harr 106 × FR 158, Gibson SSI iii p. 151:

= QAL Pf. 3 p.s.m.; cf. also v.d.Branden GP p. 89) - **Pun** QAL Inf. cstr. (v. infra) *dʿt*KAI 121^{1}, 126^{6} - **Hebr** QAL Pf. 2 p.s.m. *ydʿth* KAI 192^{6} (cf. e.g. de Vaux RB xlviii 188f., Gibson SSI i p. 38 × + suff. 3 p.s.m., cf. e.g. CF 53, Diringer Lach iii p. 332, H.P.Müller WO viii 65 n. 2, Cross FS Iwry 45, 46 n. 4 (on the problem, cf. also Pardee HAHL 80) :: H.P.Müller UF ii 237: + suff. 3 p.s.f. :: Torczyner Lach i p. 43: = QAL Pf. 1 p.s. + suff. 3 p.s.m.; cf. also Cassuto RSO xvi 167ff., Lemaire IH i p. 99), 193^{8} (cf. e.g. Ginsberg BASOR lxxi 26, Elliger PJB '38, 47 n. 1, Cassuto RSO xvi 172, 393, Pardee HAHL 86 :: e.g. Albright BASOR lxx 13, lxxiii 18, Dussaud Syr xix 264 n. 3, CF 53, Diringer Lach iii p. 332, Röllig KAI a.l.: + suff. 3 p.s.m. :: H.P.Müller UF ii 238 n. 86, WO viii 65 n. 2: + suff. 3 p.s.f. :: Torczyner Lach i p. 56: = QAL Pf. 1 p.s. + suff. 3 p.s.m.; cf. also Yeivin BiOr xix 7 n. 52), TA-H 40^{9} (cf. Aharoni TA p. 71f., Pardee UF x 293, 325 (cf. also Zevit MLAHE 19, Scagliarini Hen xii 135) :: v.Dyke Parunak BASOR ccxxx 26, 28: + suff. 3 p.s.m.); Impf. 3 p.s.m. *ydʿ* KAI 194^{10} (or Pf.?, cf. Pardee HAHL 93, 243), TA-H 40^{13} (cf. Aharoni TA-H a.l., Pardee UF x 323; or = QAL Part. act. s.m. abs.?, cf. also Dion RB lxxxix 553); Inf. cstr. *dʿt*DJD ii 44^{4}; Part. pass. s.m. abs. *ydʿ* DJD ii 42^{2} - **DA** QAL Inf. cstr. *dʿt*ii 17 (v. *pr*$_{3}$; :: Lemaire CRAI '85, 277: pro *ldʿt* l. poss. *ydʿt* = QAL Pf. 2 p.s.m.) - **OldAr** QAL Part. act. s.m. abs. *ydʿ* KAI 223C 8 (cf. Veenhof BiOr xx 144, Fitzmyer AIS 185, Degen AAG p. 74, GGA '79, 45 (cf. Segert AAG p. 362) :: Dupont-Sommer Sf p. 143: = QAL Pf. 3 p.s.m. :: Gibson SSI ii p. 45: = QAL Impf. 3 p.s.m.) - **OffAr** QAL Pf. 3 p.s.m. *ydʿ* Cowl 30^{30}, 31^{29}, ATNS 19^{8} (*ydʿ[* ; uncert. reading); 3 p.pl.m. *ydʿw* RES 1805B 3 (dam. context); Impf. 3 p.s.f. *tdʿ* Aḥiq 187 (for this reading and interpret., cf. Lindenberger APA 185); 2 p.pl.f. *tdʿn* Herm 5^{2}; Imper. s.m. *dʿ* NESE iii 48 conv. 9; Part. act. s.m. abs. *ydʿ* Aḥiq 116 (or = Pf. 3 p.s.m.??, cf. also Lindenberger APA 104 :: Kottsieper SAS 206: = QAL Impf. 3 p.s.m.)), 177 (:: Kottsieper SAS 206: = QAL Impf. 3 p.s.m.), Driv 4^{4}, 6^{6}, KAI 266^{6} (or Pf.?; on this text, cf. Dion RB lxxxix 553), etc.; Part. pass. s.m. abs. *ydyʿ* Cowl 38^{7} (for this prob. reading, cf. Grelot DAE p. 393 n. h, Porten & Greenfield JEAS p. 82, Porten & Yardeni sub TADAE A 4.3), Driv 4^{3} (dam. context), 7^{8}, *ydʿ* Aḥiq 217 (?, or = Part. act.?, cf. Leand 38d); HAPH Pf. 1 p.pl. *hwdʿn* Cowl 30^{29}; 3 p.pl.m. *hwdʿw* BSOAS xiii 82^{8} (dam. context; for the reading, cf. Henning ibid. 88 :: Rosenthal Forschung 34 n. 1, Henning BSOAS xiii 82, 84: l. *hwdʿn* (= Pf. 1 p.pl.) :: Birkeland ActOr xvi 232: l. *hwnʿn*?); Imper. s.m. *hwdʿ* Beh 52; pl.m. *[hw]dʿw* NESE i 11^{7} (for the reading, cf. also Porten Or lvii 78, Porten & Yardeni sub TADAE A 3.10); ITP Impf. 3 p.s.m. *yty[dʿ]* Cowl 27^{10}; cf. Frah xxiii 8 (*ydʿytwn*, cf. Nyberg FP 53, 98, Toll ZDMG-Suppl viii 37f., 40 :: Ebeling Frah a.l.: l. *ḥwytwn* = form of *ḥwy*$_{1}$),Paik 466, 467 (*ydʿh*), 468-470 (*ydʿtn*), 497 (*yndʿy*), GIPP 37, 53,

67, SaSt 24 - **Palm** QAL Part. act. s.m. abs. *yd'* MUSJ xxxviii 106[4] (or = Pf. 3 p.s.m.?) - **JAr** QAL Part. act. s.m. abs. *yd'* MPAT 49 i 4, MPAT-A 34[4] (= SM 69; or = Pf. 3 p.s.m.?); Part. pass. s.m. abs. *ydy'* MPAT 59[3] - ¶ verb QAL - **1)** to know, to be informed - a) + obj., *]kl' zy 'byd ln 'ršm l' yd'* Cowl 31[29]: all that was done to us, A. knew nothing (of it); *td'n zy md'm lh mpqn ln* ... Herm 5[2f.]: you must know that one has not brought us anything ...; *yd' hṣdnym kyd' hgw* ... KAI 60[7]: the Sidonians shall know, that the community is able ...; cf. KAI 194[10], 266[6], Aḥiq 116, 187, AG 4bis 2f., NESE iii 48 conv. 9, MPAT 49 i 4, MPAT-A 34[4]; cf. the formula *bgsrw yd' ṭ'm' znh* Driv 6[6]: B. is cognizant of this order (cf. Driv 4[4], 7[10], 8[6], 9[3], 10[5], cf. also Eilers AfO xvii 327 n. 17) - b) + *b*$_2$, *bznh zy 'byd ln kl'* (added later) *'ršm l' yd'* Cowl 30[30]: of all which was done to us, A. knew nothing - c) Part. act., *zy lyd'* KAI 223C 8: the witless one (cf. Veenhof BiOr xx 142ff., Tawil JNES xxxii 480, Lemaire & Durand IAS 143) - d) Part. pass. + *l*$_5$, *kn ydy' yhwy lk* Driv 7[8]: thus let it be known to you (cf. Cowl 38[7] (for the reading of the context, cf. Porten & Yardeni sub TADAE A 4.3, v. also supra), Driv 4[3], MPAT 59[3], cf. also Benveniste JA ccxlii 305, Kutscher PICS 135ff., Porten IrJu 13*) - e) Inf., *ld't* KAI 2[1]: beware! (litt. to know), v. also infra sub 3 - 2) to be able - a) + Inf., *l' yd'th qr' spr* KAI 193[8f.]: you are unable to read a letter (for the context, v. supra and *qr'*$_1$), cf. MUSJ xxxviii 106[4] - b) + *l*$_5$ + Inf., *yd' hgw lšlm ḥlpt 'yt 'dmm 'š* ... KAI 60[7]: the community knows how to recompense the men who ... - **3)** Inf. > subst., knowledge; *'ṣlk bd't* DJD ii 44[4]: may it be with you in knowledge (i.e. may it be known to you; cf. Milik DJD ii a.l. :: Pardee HAHL 132: (who) are known to you); cf. also the honorary title *mḥb d't htmt* KAI 121[1], 126[6]: loving the perfect knowledge (Lat. par. *amator concordiae* (for this title, cf. also Amadasi IPT 60) :: Dahood UHP 61: *d't* = friendship); for DA ii 17, v. *pr*$_2$ - HAPH to make known, to give instructions: Cowl 30[29] (cf. Dion RB lxxxix 552f.) - a) + obj., *hwd' 'yk zy* ... Beh 52: make known how ... - b) + *l*$_5$ + *'l*$_7$, *[hw]d'w l'rmtydt 'lwhy[* NESE i 11[7]: inform A. about it - ITP to be made known; *yty[d'] lmr'n* Cowl 27[10]: it will be made known to our lord - a form of this root poss. also in KAI 188[2] (*hd'm* = HIPH Imper. s.m. + suff. 3 p.pl.m.?), cf. Michaud PA 62 (n. 4), Milik DJD ii 97 n. 2, Gibson SSI i p. 14f., Teixidor Syr l. 418 :: Sukenik PEQ '33, 153, Lipiński OLP viii 86, BiOr xxxv 287: l. *hr'm* = *h*$_1$ + *r'm* (= QAL Part. act. pl.m. abs. of *r'y*$_1$; for this reading, cf. also Greenfield JAOS xciv 510 and cf. Dir p. 71f.: l. *hr'm* or *hrdm*?) or l. *hd'm*? :: Albright PEQ '36, 212f., Mosc p. 38: l. *hp'm* = *h*$_1$ + Sing. abs. of *p'm*$_2$ = now (cf. however Albright ANET 321), cf. also Röllig KAI a.l. with same reading: = at last? :: Birnbaum Sam p. 11f., Galling ZDPV lxxvii 180f.: l. *hw'm* = *hw*$_1$+ *'m*$_4$ :: Lemaire RB lxxix

569 (cf. idem IH i 246ff.) div. otherwise: l. *hr‘mh* = HIPH Imper. s.m. + suff. 3 p.pl.m. (+ paragogical ending) of *r‘y*$_1$: = to make (someone) pasture > to give (someone) food - a form of this root prob. in IEJ xxix 112^2 (highly uncert. interpret., Naveh IEJ xxix 116: = PA‘EL Imper. s.m.).

v. *’rṣ*$_1$,*d‘k*,*zr‘*$_2$,*ḥky*, *mnd‘*$_1$, *r’y*, *r‘h*$_2$.

yd‘$_2$ v. *yr‘*.

yh v. *y*$_1$.

yhb **DA** QAL Impf. 2 p.s.f. *thby* i 9 (on the form, cf. Hackett BTDA 45f.; :: Wesselius BiOr xliv 594, 596f. (n. 7): l. prob. *tḥby* = QAL (?/NIPH/HOPH) Impf. 2 p.s.f. of *ḥb’*$_1$/*ḥby*(= to conceal)) - **Samal** a form of this root poss. in KAI 214^{12}: *yhb* (reading of *y* uncert.), cf. Donner KAI a.l.: = QAL Pf. 3 p.s.m., Dion p. 216: = QAL pass. Impf. 3 p.s.m., cf. however Poeb 44 n. 4, Gibson SSI ii p. 66, 67, 71, Lipiński BiOr xxxiii 232, OLP viii 101: l. *’hb* = QAL Impf. 1 p.s.; on this form, cf. also Faber ZDMG cxxxvii 282 - **OldAr** QAL Pf. 3 p.s.m. *yhb* Tell F 10 (Akkad. par. *iqēš*); Impf. 2 p.s.m. *thb* KAI 222B 38 (cf. Degen AAG p. 74 n. 73, Grelot RB lxxix 615) - **OffAr** QAL Pf. 3 p.s.m. *yhb* Cowl 8^{25}, 13^3, 22^1, Driv 12^3, Herm 1^8 (cf. Bresciani & Kamil Herm p. 373, 379, Hoftijzer SV 109 × Porten Arch 270, Porten & Greenfield ZAW lxxx 226, 228, JEAS p. 152, Kutscher IOS i 113, Grelot DAE p. 152, Gibson SSI ii p. 130f., Porten & Yardeni sub TADAE A 2.3: = QAL Pf. pass. 3 p.s.m. :: Bresciani & Kamil Herm p. 424, Hayes & Hoftijzer VT xx 99f.: = QAL Impf. 3 p.s.m. :: Milik Bibl xlviii 550: = QAL Part. pass. s.m. abs.), 2^{16} (with fem subject; cf. Kutscher IOS i 116, cf. however Bresciani & Kamil Herm p. 424: = QAL Impf. 3 p.s.m.; Swiggers AION xli 146: lapsus for *yhbt* (= QAL Pf. 3 p.s.f.?)), $6^{3,7}$, KAI 233^7, 236 Rs 7 (:: Lipiński Stud 96, 103 n. 3, Fales sub AECT 49: = QAL Impf. 3 p.s.m. (cf. also Lipiński WGAV 381)), Del 77^1, ATNS 3^4, etc., etc.; + suff. 3 p.s.f. *yhbh* Krael 12^{24}; 3 p.s.f. *yhbt* Cowl 13^4; 2 p.s.m. *yhbt* Cowl 2^3, 13^4, 5^3, 10^3, Krael $1^{3,7}$, $3^{5,7}$, 8^4, 11^3, $12^{5,13,15,25}$, Aḥiq 170 (*[y]hbt*, or = Pf. 1 p.s.? :: Kottsieper SAS 41, 197 (div. otherwise): l. *hbt* (= QAL Pf. 1 p.s. of *hbt* (= to strike down, to destroy)), ATNS 130^2 (or = 3 p.s.f.?, dam. context), Samar 1^8 (= EI xviii 8*; *yhb[t]*), 4^{10}; + suff. 3 p.s.m. *yhbthy* Cowl 43^7; + suff. 3 p.s.f. *yhbth* Krael 7^3; 2 p.s.f. *yhbt* Samar 6^8; 1 p.s. *yhbt* Cowl $8^{3,13,20}$, 47^3 (for the reading of the context, cf. Porten & Yardeni sub TADAE B 5.4 l. 6), Aḥiq 169, Krael 4^2, 6^{14}, Driv 8^5, NESE i 11^4, ATNS 2^5, etc., etc.; + suff. 3 p.s.m. *yhbth* Cowl $8^{8,25}$, $13^{4,7,16}$, Krael $4^{4,12}$, $9^{3,12,16}$, 10^7; 3 p.pl.m. *yhbw* Cowl 1^3, 27^4, 31^5, $81^{39,111}$ (cf. Cowl a.l., Harmatta ActAntHung vii 371, Grelot DAE p. 116; or = QAL pass. Pf. 3 p.pl.m.?), FX 136^{11} (Greek par. ἔδωκαν); 1 p.pl. *yhbn* Cowl $1^{2,6}$, 37^4, Krael $3^{3,10,13}$, 12^3, ATNS 6^{6b} (dam. context), etc.; + suff. 3 p.s.f. *yhbnh* Cowl 1^5; Pf. pass. 3 p.s.m. *yhyb* Cowl 17^3 (cf. Grelot

DAE p. 282, cf. also Porten RB xc 412, Porten & Yardeni sub TADAE A 6.1), 69^{13} (for the reading, cf. Porten & Yardeni sub TADAE B 8.5), ATNS 9^{2} (for the reading, cf. Porten & Yardeni sub TADAE B 8.6 :: Segal ATNS a.l.: l. *yhb* = QAL Pf. 3 p.s.m.)^{,10}, 28b 7 (for the reading, cf. Porten & Yardeni sub TADAE B 8.4 :: Segal ATNS a.l.: l. *yhb* (= QAL. Pf. 3 p.s.m.)), $38^{15,16,18}$ (or = Part. pass. s.m. abs.?), 39^{3}, 42b 3, 108^{1} (?, dam. context), *yhb* Herm $2^{8,9,10}$ (cf. Grelot RB lxxiv 434, Porten & Greenfield JEAS p. 155, Gibson SSI ii p. 134, Hoftijzer SV 111, Porten & Yardeni sub TADAE A 2.2 :: Bresciani & Kamil Herm p. 387, Grelot DAE p. 154: = QAL Pf. 3 p.s.m. (cf. also Milik Bibl xlviii 582, Kutscher IOS i 116) :: Bresciani & Kamil Herm p. 424: = QAL Impf. 3 p.s.m.); 3 p.s.f. *yhybt* ATNS 10a i 7 (for the reading, cf. Porten & Yardeni sub TADAE B 8.2 :: Segal ATNS a.l.: l. *yhyb* (= QAL Part. pass. s.m. abs.; dam. context)), *yhbt* Driv 12^{1}; 3 p.pl.m. *yhybw* ATNS 67b 6, *yhbw* Driv 12^{5} (or = QAL Pf. 3 p.pl.m.?, cf. Porten & Yardeni sub TADAE A 6.15); Imper. s.m. *hb* Cowl $42^{5,11}$ (for this prob. reading, cf. Porten & Yardeni sub TADAE A 3.8), Driv 9^{1}, $12^{4,7,10}$, TA-Ar 5^{1}, BS 50^{1}, ATNS 43b i 1; + suff. 3 p.s.m. *hbh* Cowl 39^{4} (prob. reading, cf. also Porten & Yardeni sub TADAE A 3.7), 42^{6}; s.f. *hby* Cowl 8^{19}, RSO xxxv 22^{4}; + suff. 3 p.s.m. *hbhy* Cowl 13^{16}, Sem xxi 85 conv. 2; + suff. 3 p.s.f. *hbyh* RES 492B 2 (?; cf. Degen GGA '79, 40), *hbh* RSO xxxv 22^{3} (for the reading of the context, cf. Porten FS Bresciani 434f., Porten & Yardeni sub TADAE A 3.4); pl.m. *hbw* Cowl 38^{9}, Driv $6^{2,4,5}$, NESE i 11^{3} (cf. Grelot DAE p. 505 :: Shunnar CRM ii 281, 287: l. *hbh* (= QAL Imper. s.m.))^{,6}; + suff. 3 p.s.m. *[h]bwhy* NESE i 11^{7} (cf. Degen ibid. 19f., Naveh & Shaked JAOS xci 379, 381, Porten Or lvii 78, 80, Porten & Yardeni sub TADAE A 3.10 :: Shunnar CRM ii 285ff. (div. otherwise): l. *bwhyl[h]* = n.p.); Part. act. s.m. abs. *yhb* Herm 3^{9} (:: Bresciani & Kamil Herm p. 424: = QAL Imper. s.m.); s.f. abs. *yhbt* Herm 2^{14} (cf. Wesselius AION xxx 266); pl.m. abs.? *yhbn* RES 492A 3 (cf. RES 1800); Part. pass. s.m. abs. *yhyb* Cowl $24^{18a,35}$, 69^{10} (or = QAL pass. Pf. 3 p.s.m.?; for the reading of the context, cf. also Porten & Yardeni sub TADAE B 8.5), 74^{8}, Driv 8^{5}, 10^{1}, *yhb* Cowl 24^{39} (cf. Leand 38d), Driv 2^{1}, Del 98^{1}, *hyb* (lapsus) Cowl 72^{4}; s.f. abs. *yhbh* Cowl 17^{2} (for this prob. reading and interpret., cf. Porten RB xc 406, 411, Porten & Yardeni sub TADAE A 6.1. :: Cowl a.l., Grelot DAE p. 281 (n. f): l. *yhbnh* (= QAL Pf. 1 p.pl. + suff. 3 p.s.f.); pl. m. abs. *yhybn* FX 136^{13}; ITP Impf. 3 p.s.m. *ytyhb* Cowl $26^{18,21,24}$ (for this prob. reading, cf. Porten & Yardeni sub TADAE A 6.2; dam. context), SSI ii 28 obv. 5; Part. s.m. abs. *mtyhb* Cowl 72^{1} (uncert. reading; :: CIS ii sub 146: l. *mtk[t]b* = ITP Part. s.m. abs. of ktb_1); cf. Frah xxi 10 (*yḥbwn*), Paik 503-506 (*yḥbwn*), ZDMG xcii 442A 15, GIPP 37, SaSt 25 (cf. also Lemosín AO ii 267) - **Nab** QAL Pf. 3 p.s.m. *yhb* CIS ii 204^{2}; 3 p.pl.m.

yhbw CIS ii 158⁶; Impf. 3 p.s.m. *yhb* CIS ii 199⁶; Part. pass. s.m. abs. *yhyb* CIS ii 209⁹ - **Palm** QAL Pf. 3 p.s.m. *yhb* CIS ii 3959³ (= SBS 44B; Greek par. παρασχό[ν]τα), RB xxxix 547², Syr xii 122⁵, xix 159 i 2, Ber ii 76¹, 77¹, PNO 2ter 6; 3 p.s.f. *yhbt* RB xxxix 548⁴; 3 p.pl.m. *yhb* Ber v 106³; Part. act. s.m. abs. *yhb* CIS ii 3913 ii 133; pl.m. abs. *yhbyn* CIS ii 3913 ii 124 - **Hatra** QAL Pf. 3 p.s.m. *yhb* 191¹ (for the reading, cf. Safar Sumer xviii 54, cf. however Caquot Syr xli 267 :: Vattioni IH a.l. (div. otherwise): l. *qdm* (= qdm_3)), 192¹, 200² (cf. Safar Sumer xviii 60f., Caquot Syr xli 269, cf. however Teixidor Sumer xxi 89, Milik DFD 405f., Vattioni IH a.l.: *yhb* = part of n.p.), 225¹, 246¹; 3 p.pl.m. *yhb* 242¹ - **JAr** QAL Pf. 3 p.s.m. *yhb* MPAT-A 2¹ (= Frey 1197 = SM 58), 27³ (= Frey 857 = SM 33), 29² (= Frey 859 = SM 35), 29³ (cf. Naveh sub SM 35 :: Fitzmyer & Harrington MPAT a.l.: = QAL Pf. 3 p.pl.m.; cf. also Frey sub 859), 32² (= Frey 855 = SM 39), 41⁴ (for the reading, cf. Naveh sub SM 29, Beyer ATTM 394 :: Fitzmyer & Harrington MPAT a.l. (div. otherwise): l. *hdh*), 44¹ (dam. context; = Frey 1196 = SM 87), 54³ (dam. context; = SM 78), 56² (= SM 74), *hb* (in *dhb*) MPAT-A 27¹ (= Frey 857 = SM 33); 2 p.s.m. *[y]hbt* Syr xlv 101²¹ (?, dam. context); 1 p.s. *yhbt* IEJ xl 132²,⁴,⁶,⁹, DBKP 19²⁸; 3 p.pl.m. *yhbw* MPAT-A 40⁴ (= SM 57), *yhbwn* MPAT-A 27²,⁴ (= Frey 857 = SM 33), *hbwn* (in *dhbwn*) MPAT-A 26⁸ (= Frey 856 = SM 32), 28⁴ (= Frey 858 = SM 34); Imper. s.m. *hb* Mas 558¹, 561, 562¹, 564², 565², 572¹ (heavily dam. context), 573², 574², 575², 582¹; Part. act. s.m. abs. *yhb* MPAT 48² (or = QAL Pf. 3 p.s.m.?, cf. Beyer ATTM 316), MPAT-A 5² (cf. e.g. Fitzmyer & Harrington MPAT a.l., Naveh sub SM 64 :: Vincent & Carrière RB xxx 589, Kutscher (mentioned by Naveh sub SM 64), Sokoloff Maarav i 81: = QAL Pf. 3 p.s.m.; = Frey 1203), 5³ (?, cf. also Sokoloff Maarav i 81 (with other interpret. of context) × Fitzmyer & Harrington MPAT a.l.: = QAL Pf. 3 p.s.m. :: Naveh sub SM 64: = QAL Impf. 3 p.s.m. :: Vincent & Carrière RB xxx 589f.: l. *[yy]hb* = QAL Impf. 3 p.s.m., cf. also Frey sub 1203), *yhyb* MPAT-A 22² (= SM 70¹⁰); cf. PEQ '38, 238²: ιαεβ (for reading and interpret., cf. Peters OLZ '40, 218, 220, Beyer ATTM 353, cf. also Milik LA x 154f.); + encl of 1 p.s. *yhbn'* MPAT 40⁸, *yhbnh* MPAT 40²¹; pl.m. abs. *yhbyn* MPAT 46⁴; ITP Impf. 3 p.pl.m. *ytyhbw* Syr xlv 101¹⁹; Part. s.m. abs. *mtyhb* MPAT-A 43¹ (for this diff. reading, cf. Naveh sub SM 5, cf. however Klein ZDPV l. 136f., Fitzmyer & Harrington MPAT a.l.: pro *dmtyhb* l. *r* (= abbrev. of *rby* = Sing. m. + suff. 1 p.s. of rb_2) *mtyh* (= n.p.) *b[r]* (cf. also Frey sub 971); Beyer ATTM 387: l. *mtḥzq* = ITP Part. s.m. abs. of $ḥzq_1$)- ¶ verb QAL - **1)** - A) active, to give (specific meanings dependent on context), passim - a) + obj., *šmšdlh yhb š'ry'* KAI 236 Rs 7f.: Sh. has given the barley; *dhbwn ... ḥmyšh dynryn* MPAT-A 26⁸: who have given ... 5 *denarii* (cf. KAI 222B 38 (cf. also

Lipiński Stud 42), Cowl 38^{9}, Hatra 242$^{1ff.}$, MPAT-A 27^{1,2,3}, 28^{4}, etc.); cf. *hb ʿrbn* Cowl 42^{5}: give security; *yhwn yhbyn mk[sʾ]* CIS ii 3913 ii 123f.: they should pay the tax; *ʾksdrʾ ... klh yhb wʾḥbr mlʾ* Ber ii 76^{1}: the exedra ... the whole of it, bestowed and gave in partnership M. ... (cf. Ber ii 77^{1}; for the use of the terminology, cf. Ingholt Ber ii 76) - b) + obj. + *bšm*, *yhb š[mʿ]wn(?)... wʾntth ksp r 3 bšm ksp mlḥʾ* OLZ '27, 1043$^{1ff.}$: S. ... and his wife have paid a sum of 3 *r.* as salt-tax (uncert. interpret.) - c) + obj. + l_5, *zk bytʾ yhbth lk* Cowl 13$^{15f.}$: this house, I have given it to you (cf. KAI 233^{7}, Cowl 1^{5}, 8^{8}, Driv 6^{4,5}, Herm 2^{14}, RSO xxxv 22^{3}, CIS ii 204^{2}, 3959$^{3f.}$ (= SBS 44B), Hatra 246$^{1ff.}$, MPAT 48$^{2f.}$ (dam. context; poss. = to pay), DBKP 19^{28}, Mas 564^{2}, 573$^{2f.}$), etc.; cf. also *mndʿ[m] ʾḥrn zy lqḥt klʾ htb hb lmspt* Driv 12$^{6f.}$: anything else that you have taken, all of it, restore (it) to M.; *bgh zy pmwn zk yhbt lpṭswry* Driv 8^{5}: the domain of P. I give to P. (sc. on lease); *wyhbth ly* Krael 7$^{3f.}$: and you gave her to me (sc. for marriage; cf. *wyhbh ly lʾntw* Krael 12$^{24f.}$: he gave her to me in marriage) - d) + obj. + *lyd*, *kspʾ hbw lyd ʾr[mty]dt* NESE i 11^{6}: give the silver to A. - e) + obj. + mn_5, *dyhb ṭymy psypsh mn dydh* MPAT-A 2$^{1ff.}$: who gave the cost of the mosaic from his resources (for the context, v. also *zy*) - f) + obj. + *ʿl yd*, *ḥlqy ... hbw ʿl ydh* NESE i 11^{3}: my part ... give (it) to him - g) + b_2, *whwy lqḥ šʿrn mn tšy wyhb bgšrn* Herm 3^{9}: take barley from T. and exchange (it) for beams (:: e.g. Bresciani & Kamil Herm a.l., Gibson SSI ii p. 136l and give the price in beams (i.e. pay in beams)) - h) + b_2 + l_5, *bʾgr yhbt lh* Cowl 69A 12: I did give to him as payment (for the reading of the context, cf. Porten & Yardeni sub TADAE B 8.5) - i) + l_5, *yhb lh* Tell F 10: he has offered (it) to him (sc. Hadad); *ʾrqʾ zk zy yhbt lky* Cowl 8$^{12f.}$: this land which I give to you (cf. Cowl 1^{6}, 8^{20} (cf. Muffs 23 n.), 38^{9} (for the reading, cf. Porten & Yardeni sub TADAE A 4.3), Krael 9^{6,8,18}, FX 136$^{11f.}$, ATNS 6^{6} (for the dam. and diff. context, cf. also Porten & Yardeni sub TADAE B 8.12), 28b 6 (dam. context), Samar 4^{10}, 6^{8}), etc., etc.; cf. *whn kspʾ znh ... [... lʾ ʾš]lmt yhbt lk* Cowl 29^{6}: and if I do not pay (and) give to you this silver ... (cf. Cowl 45^{7}); *bytʾ zy zbn wyhbn lk* Krael 12$^{6f.}$: the house which we sold and gave over to you (cf. Krael 3$^{10f.,13}$, 12^{15,17,25,29}, cf. also Driv 12^{10}); ου ιαεβ λαχ PEQ '38, 238^{2} (v. supra): He (sc. God) is giving to you - j) + l_5 + obj., *ʾnh yhbt lky ... by 1* Cowl 8^{3} (for the reading, cf. e.g. Porten & Greenfield JEAS p. 8, Porten & Yardeni sub TADAE B 2.3): I give to you ... one house (cf. Cowl 8^{25}, Krael 3$^{3f.}$ (for the context, cf. Porten & Szubin JNES xli 123ff.), 4$^{2f.}$, 9$^{2f.}$, Herm 2^{16}, TA-Ar 5^{1}, etc.); cf. also *dy yhb lʾbgl šlṭnʾ* PNO 2ter 6f.: who gave the power to A.; *whn lʾ šlmt wyhbt lk kntyʾ ʾlk* Krael 11^{5}: and I do not pay back and give to you that spelt; *yhbt lky kspʾ znh* Cowl 35^{7}: I have paid to you this silver (cf. Krael 11^{8}); *yhb lhn prs tnh* Herm 1$^{8f.}$: he has given them (i.e.

prob. offered them, cf. Hoftijzer SV 109) a salary (cf. also Milik Bibl xlviii 581: *yhb* meaning here to grant; for the form *yhb* and the litt., v. supra); *zbn wyhbn lk bytn* Krael 12^{3}: we have sold and given over to you our house (cf. Krael $3^{3f.}$, 12^{12}, Ber v 106^{3}); *yhb krs› ... lbnyn› dy [sgy]l ›s 8* Hatra $192^{1f.}$: K. has given 8 *as* for the (re)construction of the S. (v. also *bnyn*; for the reading of the context, cf. Aggoula MUSJ xlvii 42); *yhb ›b› ... lsgyl ›s 60* Hatra 225^{1}: A. has given 60 *as* for the S. (i.e. for the (re)construction of the S.; for the reading of the context, cf. Aggoula MUSJ xlvii 45, Vattioni IH a.l., cf. also Degen JEOL xxiii 412 n. 35 reading *ln[r]gwl* pro *lsgyl* (cf. Safar Sumer xxi 39, Degen WO v 229), less prob. reading; v. also *›s_1*); *hb lyrḥmyh lḥm* Mas 574^{2}: give Y. bread (cf. Mas $561^{1f.}$); cf. also IEJ xl $132^{2,4,6,9}$ - k) + l_5 + l_5 + Inf., *yhbt l[...] lmntn* NESE i 11^{4}: I have given (it) to ... to give ... - l) + l_5 + obj. + l_5 + Inf., *yhbt ly tr‹ byt› zylk lmbnh ...* Cowl 5^{3}: you have given to me the gateway of your house to build ... (cf. Cowl 9^{14}) - m) + l_5 + noun without prep., *yhbt lk ps šrt* Krael 12^{9} : I gave (it) to you as additional portion (cf. Krael 10^{9}) - n) + l_5 + noun without prep. + obj. (or + double obj.?), *yhbt l[y] dmwhy ksp šqln [5]* Krael 1^{7}: you gave me as its price (5) *sh.* of silver; *yhbt ly zpt ksp šqln 4* Cowl $10^{3f.}$: you have given to me as a loan 4 *sh.* of silver (cf. Cowl $15^{4f.}$, Krael $3^{5f.}$, $7^{4f.}$, $12^{5,13f.,25f.,32}$) - o) + noun without prep. + obj., *hb byt ḥpr ›ry› 5* BS $50^{1f.}$: give to the house of Ch. 5 beams (?, v. *›r_2*; diff. context, cf. Naveh TeAv vi 192) - p) + noun without prep. + obj. + l_5, *yhb mnt› mnth dy m‹rt› ... lyrḥy* RB xxxix $547^{2f.}$: he has given to Y. as part his part of the hypogee (cf. Krael 9^{3}) - q) + obj. + l_5 + noun without prep., *yhbth lk ps šrt* Krael 10^{7}: I gave it to you as additional portion - r) + l_5 + obj. + b_2, *yhbt ly ksp šqln 5 bdmy hyr›* Krael 1^{3}: you paid the sum of 5 *sh.* silver as price of the *hyr* (v. *hyr*) - s) + obj. + l_5 + b_2, *hbh lh bksp› zy ...* Cowl 42^{6}: sell to him for the silver that ... - t) + l_5 + obj. + *ḥlp*$_4$, *yhbn lky plg mn[t]› zy ... ḥlp plg mnt› zy ...* Cowl $1^{2f.}$: we have given to you half the share which ... in exchange for half the share which ... (cf. Cowl 44^{8}) - u) + obj. + l_5 + *ḥlp*$_4$, *wyhbth lmpṭḥyh brty ḥlp nksy› zy ...* Cowl 13^{4}: I have given it to my daughter M. in exchange for the goods that ... - v) + l_5 + b_2, *yhb ly mšlm ... bdmwh[y]* Cowl 13^{3}: M. sold (it) to me for its price (cf. Del 77) - w) + l_5 + l_5 (obj.), *›nh yhbt lky lbyt›* Cowl 13^{2}: I have given you the house - x) + l_5 + l_5 (obj.) + *ḥlp*$_4$, *yhbt lky lbyt› znh ḥlp nksyky* Cowl $13^{5f.}$: I have given you this house in return for your goods - y) + l_5 + *lqbl*, *yhbt lky ... lqbl sbwl[* Cowl $43^{3f.}$: I have given (it) to you ... in consideration of the support - z) + l_5 + *mn*$_5$, *wyhbyn lk mn dlnh* MPAT 46^{4}: and giving to you from what is ours (dam. context) - aa) + *mn*$_5$, *yhb mn kysh* Syr xii 122^{5}: he has given from his purse - bb) + *‹l*$_7$, *whn ›yty ksp hby ‹lwhy* RSO xxxv 22^{4}: and if there is silver, give it to him (prob. interpret., dam.

context, for the reading, cf. *ʿl*$_7$) - cc) + *ʿl yd*, *zy yhbt ʿl yd[n]* Cowl 3[14]: which you delivered to us (heavily dam. context) - dd) + *ʿl yd* + obj., *yhbt ʿl ydn šʿ[rn]* Cowl 2[3]: you have delivered to us barley (dam. context) - ee) + *tḥwt* + *l*$_5$, *tḥwt hln yhbt lh* RB xxxix 548[4]: in exchange of which she has given (it) to him - B) passive, to be given (specific meanings dependent on context) - a) + *b*$_2$, *zy yhyb bmkl* Cowl 24[35]: which was delivered as food; *zy yhbw bbbʾl gbrn 5* Driv 12[5]: who were delivered at B., 5 men (v. however supra); *wyhyb bḥd[* ANS 42b 3: and it was given for one ... (?, dam. context); for ATNS 38[18], v. *yd* - b) + *l*$_5$, *yhyb ltbʾ* Cowl 73[8]: given to T. (cf. Cowl 17[3], 69A 10, 13 (for the reading of the context, cf. Porten & Yardeni sub TADAE B 8.5), Del 98, ATNS 28b 7 (v. supra)); *hn yhb lky nqyh* Herm 2[8]: if a lamb is given to you (cf. Herm 2[9,10]); *kspʾ yhyb lh* ATNS 39[3]: silver was given to him (cf. ATNS 9[10]) - c) + *l*$_5$ + *mn*$_5$, *lʿlym ʾḥrn zyly mny lʾ yhyb* Driv 8[5]: it was not given by me to any other of my servants - d) + *mn*$_5$ + *l*$_5$, *mn mrʾy yhyb ly* Driv 10[1]: it has been given to me by my lord (cf. Driv 2[1]; on this formula, cf. Kutscher PICS 149) - e) + *mn*$_5$ + noun without prep., *mn mtʾ yhybn ksp <m>nh ḥd wplg* FX 136[13]: by the town there was given in silver one and a half *m.* (cf. Greek par. καὶ δίδοται τρία ἡμιμναῖα παρὰ τῆς πόλεως) - f) + *ʿl*$_7$ (to?): ATNS 38[15] (dam. context) - g) + *ʿl*$_7$ + *l*$_5$ + Inf., *bbl lm ʾgrt mn ʾršm yhbt ʿl ps[mš]k* (?)... *lmntn* ... Driv 12[1f.]: a letter from A. was delivered in B. to P. ... to assign ... - **2)** active, to place, to put - a) + obj.: DA i 9 (for the context, v. *smr*$_3$) - b) + obj. + *bn*$_5$ + *l*$_5$, *kl mn dyhyb plgw bn gbr lḥbryh* MPAT-A 22[2]: everyone who will set discord between a man and his fellow - c) + *b*$_2$, *yhbw bgw mḥrmtʾ dʾ* CIS ii 158[6]: they have placed in this sanctuary (cf. CIS ii 209[9]) - d) + *ʿl*$_7$, *nḥšyʾ zy yhbw ʿl tmryʾ zy pḥy* Cowl 81[111]: the bronze bands which they put (or: which were put) on the date-palms of P. (?, highly uncert. interpret.; for the context, v. also *nḥš*$_6$) - Itp to be given, to be supplied; *ʿqyʾ zy ytyhb* Cowl 26[18]: the pieces of wood which are supplied (cf. also Syr xlv 101[19], diff. context; Cowl 72[1], dam. context) - a) + *b*$_2$, ... *zrnykʾ kbrytʾ bmtqlt prs ytyhb* Cowl 26[21]: ... arsenic (and) sulphur are to be supplied by Persian weight - b) + *l*$_5$, *wytyhb lkn* SSI ii 28 obv. 5: it (sc. the salary) will be given (i.e. paid) to you - c) + *ʿl yd* + *l*$_5$, *ytyhb ʿl yd šmw* ... *lʿynyn* ... Cowl 26[21f.]: let it be delivered to S. ... for the purpose of ... - v.Soden Or xxxvii 269, xlvi 197: Qal Imper. s.m. *hb* > Akkad. *(i)b* in *(i)binna* (= give me), improb. interpret. (cf. CAD s.v. *bī*, cf. also v.Soden AHW s.v. *bīn*) - Lemaire & Durand IAS 117, 127: l. poss. *thb* (= Qal Impf. 2 p.s.m.) in KAI 223B 17 (highly uncert. reading) - Gawlikowski TP 57: l. poss. *yhbw* (= Qal Pf. 3 p.pl.m.) in Syr xvii 351[10] (highly uncert. reading; Milik DFD 304 (div. otherwise): l. *[lhn]*; cf. also Cantineau Syr xvii a.l.) - a form of this root prob. also in BS i p. 81 no. 16[2]: *]hbwh* = Qal

Imper. pl.m. + suff. 3 p.s.m./f.? (cf. Naveh BS i a.l. (n. 22), Shn i 94) - a form of this root (*yhb[*) in Or lvii 50 iii - Aggoula Assur a.l.: the diff. *whb* in Assur 27e 2: = *w* + *hb* (= QAL Pf. 3 p.s.m. of variant of *yhb*), uncert. interpret., diff. context.
v. *ʾb$_1$*, *hwy$_1$*, *hyr*, *zhb*.

ywd$_1$ **OffAr** Sing. abs. *ywd* Cowl 28[4,5] - ¶ subst. m. poss. meaning mark (cf. Ginsberg with Porten Arch 204 n. 15, Porten & Greenfield JEAS p. 28), cf. however Cowl a.l., Grelot DAE p. 205: = the sign *yod* (used as a mark); for the context, v. *šnt$_1$*; cf. also Segal sub ATNS 5 n. 19.

ywd$_2$ **OffAr** Sing. abs. *ywd* Or lvii 35[6,7] (or l. *ywr* ?) - ¶ subst. of unknown meaning (on this word, cf. Porten Or lvii 37) - the same word prob. also in FS Volterra vi 530 A1, D1 (:: Bresciani ibid. 531: = n.g.).

ywdn (<Iran., cf. Shaked with Porten EI xiv 172) - **OffAr** Sing. emph. *ywdnʾ* Cowl 27[5] (for the reading, cf. Porten EI xiv 172, Porten & Greenfield JEAS p. 86, Porten & Yardeni sub TADAE A 4.5 (cf. already Ungnad ArPap p. 9 :: Cowl a.l., Grelot DAE p. 402 n. g: l. *gwrnʾ* = Sing. emph. of *gwrn*= store-house, granary) - ¶ subst. barley-house (for litt., v. supra).

ywz (< Iran., cf. Driv p. 68, Eilers AfO xvii 334, Grelot DAE p. 316 n. e, Hinz AISN 275) - **OffAr** Sing. emph. *ywzʾ* Driv 8[2,4] - ¶ subst. m. revolt, insurrection.

ywm **Ph** Sing. abs. *ym* KAI 37A 7, 15, 17 (= Kition C 1[6,14,16]), 43[11], 60[1], Mus li 286[2], ATNS xii (*ym[* ; highly uncert. reading, cf. Naveh IEJ xxxv 211: pro *9 ym* l. *900*), xv (??); Plur. abs. *ymm* KAI 14[3,13], 26A iii 1, 5, C iii 20, 32[1] (= Kition A 2), 33[1] (= Kition A 1), 37B 4, 40[1], CIS i 13[1] (= Kition A 27; *[y]mm*), 21[1] (cf. RES 1531), 88[1] (= Kition F 1), RES 1213[1]; Plur. cstr. *ymt* KAI 4[5], 7[5], EpAn ix 5[2,7], 5C 2; + suff. 3 p.s.m. *ymw* KAI 10[9] (cf. FR 235); + suff. 3 p.s.f. *ymy* KAI 29[2] (cf. however Amadasi Guzzo Or lix 60: or = Plur. + suff. 3 p.s.m.?, cf. already Burrows JRAS '27, 791); + suff. 1 p.s. *ymy* KAI 24[12], *ymty* KAI 26A i 5, ii 1, 5, 7, 15, 17; + suff. 3 p.pl.m. *ymm* KAI 11[1] (heavily dam. context; **Hebr**?) - **Pun** Sing. abs. *ym* KAI 76B 1, 7, 113B 1, 2, Hofra 98[4], RES 304[1], 331[3f.], Punica xix 1, MAIBL xvi 397[1], 401[1], etc. - **Mo** Plur. abs. *ymn* KAI 181[5]; cstr. *ymy* KAI 181[8]; + suff. 3 p.s.m. *ymh* KAI 181[8] (on this form, cf. Halpern FS Lambdin 130 (n. 54)); + suff. 1 p.s. *ymy* KAI 181[6,9,33] - **Amm** Plur. abs. *ywmt* Ber xxii 120[7] (on this form, cf. Jackson ALIA 39, 42) - **Hebr** Sing. abs. *ywm* DJD ii 24B 13, C 6, 11, E 5, 8, AMB 4[29], *ym* KAI 192[3], 194[3], TA-H 1[4], 24[19], 40[11] (diff. and dam. context, cf. Aharoni TA a.l., Pardee UF x 325 :: Aharoni BASOR cxcvii 30, 32: = Sing. abs. of *ym$_1$*); cstr. *ym* KAI 189[3] (the *ywm* in KAI prob. printer's error; on the orthography, cf. Zevit MLAHE 21f., Sarfatti Maarav iii 63ff.); Plur. abs. *ymm* KAI

200^{5,7,9} (for KAI 200, v. infra), TA-H 2^{4} - **Samal** Plur. cstr. *ywmy* KAI 215^{10}, *ymy* KAI 214^{12} (diff. reading; cf. Dion p. 147, Gibson SSI ii p. 67, Lipiński OLP viii 101 :: e.g. Cooke NSI p. 162, Donner KAI a.l., Sader EAS 163: = Plur. + suff. 1 p.s.?); + suff. 3 p.s.m. *ywmyh* KAI 215^{9}; + suff. 1 p.s. *ywmy* KAI 215^{8} (cf. Cooke NSI p. 174, Donner KAI a.l., Dion p. 152, Gibson SSI ii p. 81 × or = Plur. cstr.?, cf. also Dion p. 147; dam. context), *ymy* KAI 214^{9,10} (on the Yaudic instances, cf. Garr DGSP 36) - **OldAr** Sing. abs. *ywm* KAI 222A 12, B 31 (or = cstr.?, cf. Lambdin FS Albright ii 318 n. 7), C 20 (× Beyer ZDMG cxx 202, Degen GGA '79, 43: = Sing. cstr.); cstr. *ywm* KAI 223B 12; Plur. + suff. 3 p.s.m. *ywmh* KAI 222C 15f. (cf. Dupont-Sommer Sf p. 91, Segert AAG p. 119 × Fitzmyer AIS 75, Degen AAG p. 56 (n. 27), GGA '79, 24: = Sing., cf. Beyer ZDMG cxx 202, Ben-Chayyim Lesh xxxv 246), *ywmwh* Tell F 7 (cf. Akkad. par. *ūmē-šú*); + suff. 3 p.pl.m. *ywmyhm* KAI 223C 17 - **OffAr** Sing. abs. *ywm* Cowl 1^{4}, 5^{1,6}, Krael 1^{1}, 2^{7,9}, Driv 6^{3,6}, ATNS 35^{4} (cf. Segal ATNS a.l.; highly uncert. reading, cf. Porten & Yardeni sub TADAE B 4.7: l. *yqwm* (= QAL Impf. 3 p.s.m. of *qwm*$_{1}$)), etc., etc., *ym* RES 799^{1}; cstr. *ywm* Cowl 30^{21}, Aḥiq 168, KAI 226^{4}, RSO xxxii 404^{1}, ATNS 41^{8}; emph. *ywm›* Cowl 8^{9}, 14^{7}, 15^{4}, Krael 2^{4}, 3^{11}, 4^{4}, Driv 6^{5}, Aḥiq 96 (for the reading, cf. e.g. Sach p. 163, Ungnad ArPap 71, Lindenberger APA 71 :: Cowl a.l.: l. *ytr›* (= Sing. m. emph. of *ytr*$_{3}$, overmuch, cf. also Leand 61l, Ginsberg ANET 428, Grelot DAE p. 436)), ATNS 41^{1}, KAI 228A 4, etc., etc., *ym›* RES 1792A 3, 4; Plur. abs. *ywmn* Cowl 45^{7} (*ywm[n]*, for the reading, cf. Porten RB xc 573f., Porten & Yardeni sub TADAE B 7.1), 71^{4}, Aḥiq 49, 52, Krael 3^{20}, 11^{7}, ATNS 4^{8}, *ymyn* Krael 9^{17}, *ymn* KAI 233^{16} (?; cf. also Stefanovic COAI 203); cstr. *ywmy* CIS ii 43^{5} (= Del 26; for the uncert. reading, cf. Fales sub AECT 13; interpret. of context diff., cf. Del a.l., Fales JAOS cix 98 (div. otherwise): l. *ywm* (= Sing. abs.)), Cowl 30^{13}, KAI 266^{3}, *ywm* (lapsus?) Cowl 31^{12}, *ywmt* ATNS 34^{3}; emph. *ywmy›* Driv 6^{6}; + suff. 3 p.s.m. *ywmwhy* ATNS 52b ii 4 (heavily dam. and uncert. context); + suff. 2 p.s.m. *ywmyk* Aḥiq 102, Beh 58 (Akkad. par. *ūmē-ka*); + suff. 1 p.s. *ywmy* KAI 226^{3}; cf. Frah xxvii 3, 8 (cf. Nyberg FP 56, 106; *ywm*), xxviii 1ff. (*ywm*), Paik 471 (*ywm*), Nisa-c 100+91^{1} (*ywm›*), Sogd R 56, Syn 300^{2}, 301^{2}, 304^{1}, 305^{2}, 306^{1}, 307^{1}, 308^{1,2}, 311^{1}, GIPP 38, 68, SaSt 26 - **Nab** Sing. abs. *ywm* CIS ii 211^{9}, 219^{7}, J 22^{3}, RES 676^{5}, RB xliv 266,3, MPAT 64 i 8 (*[y]wm*), BASOR cclxiii 78^{4}; emph. *ywm›* J 38^{4}; Plur. + suff. 3 p.s.m. *ywmwhy* CIS ii 224^{5} (uncert. reading, cf. J p. 197) - **Palm** Sing. abs. *ywm* CIS ii 3981^{1}, 3987^{3}, 3994a 7, 4010^{7}, 4210^{4}, Inv xi 37^{3}, RIP 135^{5}, 142^{3} (diff. reading of context, cf. Milik DFD 294: l. *ywm ‹šrt›*, cf. however Gawlikowski sub RIP 142: l. *ywm yšrḥ›* (unexplained, cf. also Michałowski FP v p. 114f.) or *ywmy* (= Plur. cstr.) *šrḥ›* (cf. Aggoula Syr liv 284: l. *ywmy* *šrḥ*ʾ = the days of rejoicing, v. also *šrḥ*)), etc., etc., *ym* Inscr P 28[3], Inv ix 35bis(?) - **Hatra** Sing. abs. *ywm* 49[1], 288b 4, 6 (cf. also Assur 6b 1, 14[1], 17 i 1, etc.); Plur. cstr. *ymt*, cf. Assur 17 i 5, 32j 5; + suff. 3 p.s.m. *ymth* 23[4] (for this reading, cf. Milik RN vi/iv 54, Degen ZDMG cxxi 125, NESE ii 100, Vattioni IH a.l. :: Caquot Syr xl 15f.: l. *zmth* (cf. also idem Syr xxix 102) = Sing. + suff. 3 p.s.m. of *zmh*(= hair), cf. also idem GLECS ix 89, Donner sub KAI 244 (without explanation), Ingholt AH i/1, 45, i/2, 45 (diff. reading, cf. Safar Sumer vii 182 (no transcription), Krückmann AfO xvi 47 n. 63: l. poss. *w/dmth*, without explanation) - **JAr** Sing. abs. *ywm* MPAT-A 52[3], IEJ xl 132[7]; cstr. *ywm* IEJ xl 132[3,5], 135[3,8], 144[5]; emph. *ywm*ʾ MPAT 40[2,13], 49 i 7, 8, 51[3], 52[10], *ywmh* Syr xlv 101[6] (??, dam. context), AMB 1[11] (*ywm*ʾ misprint), *ymh* MPAT 51[3,11]; Plur. abs. *ywmyn* MPAT-A 52[4], Syr xlv 101[10,15], *ymyn* MPAT 42[15] - ¶ subst. m. day, passim, cf. also *ktb šm hym* TA-H 1[4]: write the name of the day (i.e. write down the date, cf. Aharoni TA a.l., Pardee UF x 294); *ywm šbh* RSO xxxii 404[1]: the day of the Sabbath (cf. IEJ xl 132[3,5], 135[3,8]); *ywm yld*ʾ *zy* .. : ATNS 41[8]: the birthday of ... (cf. also Shaked Or lvi 410, v. also *plny*); *ywm rwḥ* Aḥiq 168: the day of tranquillity (i.e. a calm day; v. *rwḥ*$_3$); *mst ywm*ʾ ATNS 41[1]: the daily amount; cf. also *wʿdy*ʾ ʾ*ln zy gzr brg*ʾ*[yh] ... qdm ywm wlylh* KAI 222A 7, 12: this treaty which B. has concluded ... in the presence of day and night (cf. Moran Bibl xliii 319, Delcor VT xvi 18) - **1)** in dates, *ywm šbʿt*ʾ CIS ii 3987[3]: the 7th day; *ywm 1 btšrn* CIS ii 4363[6f.]: the first day of (the month) T. (cf. e.g. Syr xlvii 413[5]); *b 18 l*ʾ*lwl hw ywm 28 lpḥns* Cowl 5[1]: on the 18th of E., i.e. the 28th of P. (cf. e.g. Cowl 6[1], 8[1], Syr xli 285[1]); *bym* ʿ*šrt wšlšt lyrḥ* Mus li 286[2]: on the 13th day of the month; *bywm 6 lp*ʾ*py* Cowl 37[15]: on the 6th day of P. (cf. also FuB xiv 13[2f.?], dam. context); *bywm ḥd b*ʾ*b* CIS ii 219[7] (= J 4); on the first day of A.; *bywm 14 bt[šry]* Hatra 288b 4: on the 14th day of T. (cf. Hatra 49[1f.], 288b 6, Assur 17 i 1, 20[1], 22[1], 25e 1, etc.); *bywm tltt bḥd*ʿ*šr ywmyn byrḥ* ʾ*lwl bšnt ...* MPAT-A 52[3f.]: on the third day (sc. of the week) on the 11th day of the month E. in the year ...; *bymm 6 lyrḥ bl* KAI 32[1] (= Kition A 2): on the 6th day of the month B.; *byrḥ nysn ywm 20 šnt ...* RIP 135[5f.]: in the month N. on the 20th day (in the) year ...; *ywm ḥd bšbh* IEJ xl 132[7]: the first day of the week - **2)** *ywm*ʾ *znh*, *ym*ʾ *znh*, *ywm*ʾ *dnh*, *ymh dnh* e.g. RES 1792A 3, MPAT 40[2,13], etc.: now, at this moment; *znh ywm*ʾ Cowl 30[20], 31[29]: now, at this moment; cf. also ʾ*nh ... ywm*ʾ *dnh zbnt lk ymh dnh lbth dyly* MPAT 51[3]: today I have sold to you ... today my house; *mn zky w*ʿ*d ywm šnt 17 ldryhwš* Cowl 30[21]: from that moment until the (present) day in the 17th year of Darius (?, lapsus?, cf. Cowl a.l.); *mn ywm*ʾ *znh w*ʿ*d* ʿ*lm* Cowl 8[9]: from now on and forever (cf. Muffs 30f. n. 2; cf. Cowl 14[6f.], 15[4], 20[9,10], 28[7], 43[4], Krael 2[4], 4[4f.], 7[4], 14[4] (dam.

context); cf. also ... *‘d ‘lmn* Krael 3^{11}, 12^{23} and ... *ywm› znh znh* Krael 10^{8} (dittography?, cf. Krael a.l., Porten & Szubin JAOS cvii 231)); *mn ymh dnh wl‘lm* MPAT $51^{11,11f.}$, 52^{10}: from now on and forever; *hywm* DJD ii 24C 6, E 5: now, at this moment (cf. also TA-H 24^{19}); *mn hywm ‘d swp ‘rb hšmṭh* DJD ii 24E 8f.: from now until the end of the year preceding the sabbatical year (cf. DJD ii 24B 13f., C 11f.); *ywm› hw* Cowl 22^{120}: on that day (i.e. on the day the document was issued; :: Macuch JAOS xciii 60: *ywm›* and *hw* part of different constituents) - **3)** *kl ywm* CIS ii 3981^{11}, Inv xi 44^{4}, DM ii 38 ii 4: always (cf. Inv xi 37^{3}; cf. also Aggoula Sem xxix 113); *bkl ywm* DJD ii 47^{4}: always (?, dam. context); *kl ymyn* MPAT 42^{15}: all the days - **4)** *ym md ym* KAI 43^{11}: day by day; *ywm lywm* Driv 6^{3}: day by day; *mywm ly[wm]* AMB 4^{29}: from day to day - **5)** *lywm›* Driv $6^{3,5}$: daily; *lymt [‘]lmyn* Assur 17 i 5f.: for ever and ever (cf. Assur 32j 5) - **6)** *‘t kym* KAI 192^{3}, 194^{1}, Lach viii 2: at this very moment (*‘t* = *‘t*$_2$, cf. e.g. Joüon RES ’38, 85f., de Vaux RB xlviii 187, Gibson SSI i p. 37, Lemaire IH i 97f. :: Michaud Syr xxxiv 43: *‘t* = *‘t*$_1$ (cf. also Chapira RES ’45, 110f.) :: Torczyner Lach i p. 109ff.: *‘t* = *‘t*$_2$, *kym* = adverb (thus), cf. also Lipiński OLP viii 89 (n. 34), BiOr xxxv 286) - 7) *bym n‘m wbrk* Punica xix 1: on a favorable and blessed day (cf. MAIBL xvi 397^{1}, 401^{1}, 403^{1}, 407^{1}, etc. ; cf. *bym n‘m ›š* (?; reading uncert.) *bym brk* RES $331^{3f.}$: on a favorable day, i.e. (?) on a blessed day; cf. also *ym n‘m* Hofra 98^{4}: a favorable day; *ym n‘m hym z lmgn* KAI 113b: a favorable day is this day for M. (cf. *bym n‘m lmlk* Punica xviii/3 1^{2}: on a favorable day for M. (for this reading, cf. Berthier & Charlier sub Hofra 116, cf. also Chabot sub Punica xviii/iii :: e.g. Eissfeldt Molk 30, Dussaud CRAI ’46, 380: *mlk* = Sing. abs. of *mlk*$_5$)) - **8)** *bywm ḥd bkp ḥdh* Cowl 15^{28}: on one day, at one stroke (i.e. all together at one moment (cf. Krael $7^{24,28}$; v. also *kp*$_1$)), cf. also *bywm* ATNS 35^{4}: a day, daily - **9)** Plur. with spec transl. and/or meaning, *l‘d[n ›]ḥrn wlywmn ›ḥrnn šgy›n* Aḥiq 49f.: until in after time and many days after (i.e. after a long time); *‘[d] lywmn ›ḥrnn* Aḥiq 52: until other days (i.e. until a certain period of time has elapsed); *ymn rbn* KAI 181^{5}: during a long period; *wyšmḥ bywmt rbm wšnt rḥqt* Ber xxii $120^{6ff.}$: and may he be glad during many days and faraway years (v. *šmḥ* for the context; :: Krahmalkov BASOR ccxxiii 56 (n. 6): *b* = because of) - a) designating the duration of someone’s life, *h›rk ywmy* KAI 226^{3}: he has prolonged the duration of my life (cf. Beh 58, Tell F 7); *wbgn šḥrw ‘l ymth dy mn dy lqryhy* ... Hatra 23^{4}: and the invocation of Sh. against the lifetime of the one who will read it ...; *w›n› ymyn sb* Krael 9^{17}: and I was very old; *bl› bywmyk* Aḥiq 102: before your time (cf. also Lindenberger APA 83); *‘l ywmwhy* CIS ii 224^{5} (= J 34, uncert. reading): during his lifetime; cf. also the comparison *kywmy šmyn wmyn* KAI 266^{3}: (a life) like the days of the

Heavens and the Waters (for the context, v. also *mym*) - b) designating more specially the duration of someone's reign, *bymy* KAI 24^{12}: during my reign; *tʾrk bʿlt gbl ymt špṭbʿl wšntw ʿl gbl* KAI $7^{4f.}$: may the lady of G. prolong the days and years of Sh. (i.e. his reign) over G. (cf. KAI $4^{5f.}$, 10^{9}, 26A i 5, $181^{6,8}$ (:: Lipiński Or xl 330f.: = life), 214^{9}, 223C 17, Cowl 30^{13}, ATNS 34a 3, EpAn ix 5^{2} (on this text, cf. also Long & Pardee AO vii 213), etc.; cf. also *yṣrw ʾlhn mn ywmh wmn byth* KAI 222C 15f.: may the gods keep (him) all his days and his whole house) - c) in the expressions *kymm* and *zh ymm*: KAI $200^{5,7}$ and 200^{9} (for the reading, cf. Cross BASOR clxv 43 n. 29 :: Naveh IEJ x 134f.: pro *ymm* l. *ynm* = unknown measure of capacity (cf. however idem IEJ xiv 158; cf. also Elizur with Sarfatti Lesh xxxiv 154) :: Yeivin BiOr xix 4f.: *ynm* = QAL Impf. 3 p.s.m. of *nwm* (= to slumber) :: Vogt Bibl xli 183: *ynm* (l. 9) = QAL Part. act. s.m. + encl. *mem* of *yny* (= to oppress) :: Michaud VT x 454: pro *ymm* (l. 9) l. *ʿnn* (= n.p.)) - *kymm* in KAI $200^{5,7}$ prob. = within the fixed time (cf. Gibson SSI i p. 28f.: for the days agreed) :: Cross BASOR clxv 45 n. 44, clxviii 23: according to the regular (periodic) practice = as usual, regularly (cf. also Amusin & Heltzer VDI lxxxv 120f., IEJ xiv 150ff., Talmon BASOR clxxvi 32 (cf. also Mettinger SSO 97), Veenhof Phoenix xi 250, Naveh Lesh xxx 70, Vinnikov ArchOr xxxiii 547ff., Silverman JAOS xciv 269f., Weippert FS Rendtorff 460 (n. 28); cf. also Suzuki AJBI viii 5, 10f. = according to the regular quota) :: Röllig KAI a.l.: as daily :: Lemaire Sem xxi 61, 69f. (cf. also idem IH i 261, 263): = these days (cf. Briend TPOA 135, Conrad TUAT i 250, Smelik HDAI 90) :: Booij BiOr xliii 644f. (nn. 10,12-14): for days (indeed) :: Pardee Maarav i 36f., 43f., HAHL 20ff.: a few days ago :: Albright ANET 568 (n. 6): *ymm* in l. 5 = *ywm* + adv. ending, *kymm* = as usual (cf. also Teixidor Syr l. 417) :: Garbini AION xxii 98f., 102: *ymm* = adverb (*ymm*$_2$; cf. also Garbini BSOAS xxxv 625), *kymm* = according to the daily quota :: Delekat Bibl li 462f.: *ymm* = adverb, *kymm* = halfway through the day - *zh ymm* in KAI 200^{9} prob. = exactly within the fixed time :: Naveh Lesh xxx 70: regularly (*zh* adding a notion of precision; cf. Veenhof Phoenix xi 250, Talmon BASOR clxxvi 33f.) :: Cross BASOR clxv 43 (n. 34), 45: pro *ymm* l. *<k>ymm* = regularly (*zh* connected with preceding word; cf. also Röllig KAI a.l.; cf. however Naveh IEJ xiv 158 n. 3) :: Amusin & Heltzer VDI lxxxv 120, 122, IEJ xiv 150ff.: (in) these (postulated) days (cf. also Gibson SSI i p. 29f.: over the afore mentioned days) :: Pardee Maarav i 37, 48f., HAHL 21f.: at that time (= *zh*), a few days ago (= *ymm*; cf. Conrad TUAT i 250) :: Vinnikov ArchOr xxxiii 547, 549: it is several days now that ... (cf. Lemaire Sem xxi 72f., IH i 261, 265, Briend TPOA 135, Sasson BASOR ccxxxii 60, Smelik HDAI 90; cf. also Booij BiOr xliii 643f. (n. 6): now for (many) days; cf. Weippert

FS Rendtorff 461 (n. 31)) :: Garbini AION xxii 102: exactly the daily quota (*ymm* = adverb *ymm*$_2$), cf. also Suzuki AJBI viii 5, 11, 13ff.: = the exact quota :: Delekat Bibl li 463, 467: *ymm* = adverb (during the day; *zh* to be connected with prec. word) :: Albright with Cross BASOR clxv 45 n. 48, ANET 568: pro *ymm* l. *ḥnm*= for no reason - cf. also *kymn* KAI 233^{16} in heavily dam. context; cf. Dupont-Sommer Syr xxiv 34, 46: every year? (cf. also Koopmans 86, Donner KAI a.l., Gibson SSI i p. 29, ii p. 105, 109f.; cf. however Cross BASOR clxviii 23: regularly (:: Lidzbarski ZA xxxi 201f.: *kymn* = n.p.)) - Starcky RB lxxiii 615: l. *kl ywm* in Inv xi 6^{10} - Starcky ibid. 616: l. *ywm šbʿtʾ* (pro ...*] šbʿtʾ*) in Inv xi 70^{4} - Lipiński RTAT 251: l. poss. Sing. abs. *ym* in KAI 43^{14} - Sznycer PPP 75f.: the diff. *lymmoth* in Poen 934: = *l*$_5$ + Plur. abs. of *ywm* (:: Schroed 290, 310: = Sing. abs. of *ʿlmt* = former time :: L.H.Gray AJSL xxxix 78f.: = Plur. abs. of *lmh* (= assembly); for a discussion, cf. also Glück & Maurach Semitics ii 105ff.) - abbrev. *y* poss. in *by 7* RTP 721: on the seventh day? - cf. *ymm*$_1$.
v. *ʾḥrn*, *ʾmh*$_2$, *ʾrk*$_2$, *bn*$_1$, *bʿl*$_1$, *zbḥ*$_2$, *zmn*$_1$, *ḥm*$_2$, *ḥrm*$_4$, *yd*, *ym*$_1$, *ll*$_2$, *mym*, *rzn*, *šd*$_1$, *šmš*$_2$.

ywn$_1$ **DA** Sing. abs. *ywn* i 11 - ¶ subst. dove (cf. e.g. Caquot & Lemaire Syr liv 198f., Garbini Hen i 178, McCarter BASOR ccxxxix 51, 55, H. & M. Weippert ZDPV xcviii 96, 103, Hoftijzer TUAT ii 143 :: Hoftijzer DA a.l.: = *ywn*$_2$ (= marsh, swamp)).

ywn$_2$ v. *ywn*$_1$.

ywntʾ **OffAr** word of unknown meaning (Sing./Plur. emph.?) in FuF xxxv 173^{11}; Szemerényi with Altheim & Stiehl FuF xxxv 177: related to *ywn* = Greece; Altheim & Stiehl ibid.: < Iran. = hero, young man (taking *ywntʾ* as Plur.; improb. interpret.).

ywṣyt v. *twḥyt*.

ywr v. *ywd*$_2$

yzb v. *kdb*$_3$.

yzp **OffAr** QAL Pf. 1 p.s. *yzpt* Krael 11^{3}; Impf. 2 p.s.m. *tzp* Aḥiq 130; Imper. s.m. *zp* Aḥiq 129 - ¶ verb QAL to borrow - **1)** + obj.: Aḥiq 129; cf. *tzp zptʾ* Aḥiq 130: you will borrow - **2)** + *mn*$_5$ (= from): Krael 11^{3}, Aḥiq 130.
v. *ntn*.

yzq v. *nzq*$_1$.

yḥ v. *yrḥ*$_2$.

yḥʾ **OffAr** Nyberg FP 50, 91: l. *mḥwḥy* + *tʾ* in Frah xix 14 = HAPH Part. of *yḥʾ* (:: Ebeling Frah a.l.: l. *mʾwʿd-wyt* = form of *mwʿd*), cf. however Toll ZDMG Suppl viii 39: = PAʿEL form of *ḥwy*$_1$- **Palm** APH Part. s.m. abs. *mwḥʾ* CIS ii 3913 ii 125 (cf. Rosenthal Sprache 65 n. 4 :: Nöldeke with Reckendorf ZDMG xlii 415: prob. = lapsus for *mḥwʾ* (= APH Part. s.m. abs. of *ḥwy*$_1$):: Cantineau Gramm 86: l. *mḥwʾ* =

Pa‘el Part. s.m. abs. of *ḥwy*$_1$(cf. also Teixidor AO i 250)) - ¶ verb Aph poss. meaning: to prescribe, to decree; ***hyk dy nmwsʾ mwḥʾ*** CIS ii 3913 ii 125: as the law prescribes(?); cf. also Frah xix 14: Haph Part. = announcement, presentation (v. however supra) - cf. also *twḥyt*.

yḥbwr **Nab** Sing. emph. *yḥbwrʾ* IEJ xxix 112^1 (v. infra) - ¶ subst. of unknown meaning; Naveh IEJ xxix 114: poss. = smoke (uncert. interpret., diff. context).

yḥd$_1$ **DA** Itp Pf. 3 p.pl.m. *ʾtyḥdw* i 7 (on the reading, cf. also Hackett BTDA 119, Or liii 63 n. 28) - **OldAr** Haph Pf. 3 p.s.m. *hwḥd* KAI 202A 4 - ¶ verb Haph to gather; ***hwḥd ʿly brhdd ... ʿšr mlkn*** KAI 202A 4f.: B. gathered against me ... 10 kings - Itp to assemble: DA i 7 (:: Sasson UF xvii 295, AUSS xxiv 151f.: sc. to conspire) - Lipiński OLP viii 93f.: l. *yḥd* in SSI i p. 58A 1 (= form of this root (= to single out); prob. reading, uncert. interpret.) :: Naveh IEJ xiii 83f., Veenhof Phoenix xi 252f. (uncert. reading), Cross FS Glueck 301, Gibson SSI i a.l., Lemaire RB lxxxiii 558f.: l. *YHWH* (cf. also Weippert ZDPV lxxx 162).

yḥd$_2$ **Pun** Schroed 290, 308, Sznycer PPP 65ff.: *iad* in Poen 932: = *yḥd*$_2$ (= together with); Sznycer PPP 69: > at the same time :: J.J.Glück & Maurach Semitics ii 105 (div. otherwise): l. *i* (= suff. 1 p.s. connected with prec. word) + *ad* (= *ʿwd*$_5$); for the context, v. also *hn*$_3$.
v. *ḥdy*$_1$,*yḥdn*, *pḥd*$_2$.

yḥdn **OldCan** Sing. + suff. 1 p.s. *ya-ḫu-du-un-ni* EA 365^{24} (cf. Rainey EA 73 (cf. also Thureau-Dangin RA xix 97 n. 3, Held JAOS lxxxviii 94 n. 81, Tawil JBL xcv 410 n. 43, Sivan GAG 286) :: CAD s.v. *ya-ḫudunni*: = *yḥd*$_2$ + suff. 1 p.s.) - ¶ subst. aloneness; ***ya-ḫu-du-un-ni*** EA 365^{24}: I alone.

yḥl$_1$ **Hebr** a form of this root (= to expect, to wait) *tyḥl* (= Pi‘el/Niph Impf. 3 p.s.f.) poss. in AMB 4^{19} (diff. context).

yḥl$_2$ (< Iran.??, cf. Chabot sub CIS ii 3956, cf. however Rosenthal Sprache 97) - **Palm** Sing. emph. *yḥlʾ* CIS ii 3956^5 (for the reading, cf. Cantineau sub Inv v 7, Milik DFD 116, Gawlikowski TP 89) - ¶ subst. of uncert. meaning, prob. indicating material of which statues were made, a certain type of metal?, cf. Gawlikowski TP 89; the interpret. onyx (cf. e.g. CIS ii a.l., Cantineau sub Inv v 7) less prob. (cf. Gawlikowski ibid.).

yḥnwn **Nab** Sing. emph. *yḥnwnʾ* IEJ xxix 112^1 - ¶ subst. henna (cf. also Naveh IEJ xxix 114; interpret. of context however uncert.).

yṭʾ **JAr** Milik Syr xlv 101: l. *yṭʾ* (= he will bring, cf. ibid. 102) in Syr xlv 101^{15} (uncert. reading and interpret.).

yṭb **Ph** (**Hebr** ?) Yiph *yṭb* KA 11^2 (heavily dam. context) - **Samal** Haph Pf. 3 p.s.m. + suff. 3 p.s.m. *hyṭbh* KAI 215^9 - **OldAr** Qal

Impf. 3 p.s.f. *tyṭb* Tell F 15 (Akkad. par. *ṭu-ub-bi*; :: Pardee JNES xliii 255: or = OPH Impf. 3 p.s.m.? (cf. however Huehnergard BASOR cclxi 93)); HAPH Pf. 1 p.s. + suff. 3 p.s.m. *hyṭbth* KAI 216[12] - **OffAr** HAPH Pf. 2 p.s.m. *hwṭbt* Cowl 6[11], ATNS 8[2] (dam. context); 2 p.pl.m. *hwṭbtm* Cowl 20[8] - ¶ verb QAL to be agreeable; *ʾmrt pmh ʾl ʾlhn wʾl ʾnšn tyṭb* Tell F 14f.: the word of his mouth will be agreeable to gods and men (cf. Dion FS Delcor 145) - HAPH to make good - a) + obj. + b_2, *hwṭbtm lbbn bʾlk nksyʾ* Cowl 20[8]: you have satisfied our heart concerning these goods - b) + obj. + mn_5, *whyṭbh mn qdmth* KAI 215[9]: he made it better than it was before (for the context, v. also $qdmh_1$), cf. KAI 216[12f.] - c) + obj. + $ʿl_7$ (or + b_2), *whwṭbt lbby ʿl ʾrqʾ zk* Cowl 6[11f.]: you have satisfied my heart about this land (for litt. on this and comparable expressions, v. *ṭyb*) - (Gordon with) Ginsberg BASOR lxxi 26 n. 5, de Vaux RB xlviii 196 (cf. also Galling TGI 65 n. 1): l. *yʾṭb* in KAI 195[9f.] (= variant of *yyṭb* (= HIPH Impf. 3 p.s.m. of *yṭb*)) :: Elliger ZDPV lxii 75f. (cf. also Galling TGI 65 (n. 1)): l. *yʾṭm* = NIPH Impf. 3 p.s.m. of *ʾṭm*(= to permit (one's ears) to be stopped up (> to permit oneself to be lead astray into disobedience)) :: Michaud Syr xxxiv 47 (div. otherwise; cf. Lemaire IH i 117): l. *yʾ* (= lapsus for *ybʾ* (= HIPH Impf. 3 p.s.m. of *bwʾ*))*ṭbyhw* (= n.p.), v. infra (cf. also Reviv CSI p. 85f. l. *yʾ* = *y<b>ʾ* (= QAL Impf. 3 p.s.m. of *bwʾ*)):: Torczyner Lach i p. 96f. (div. otherwise): l. *yʾr* (= QAL Impf. 3 p.s.m. of $ʾrr_1$)*byhw* (= b_2 + *YHW* (= n.d.)) :: Albright BASOR lxx 15, lxxiii 17, lxxxii 21 (cf. also ANET 322, Hempel ZAW lvi 134f.): l. *yyṭb* = HIPH Impf. 3 p.s.m. of *yṭb*; the reading *yʾṭb* however also less prob., cf. Gibson SSI i p. 43ff. (div. otherwise): l. poss. *yʾ[..] ṭbyhw* = verbal form + n.p. (for the difficulties of the reading, cf. also Diringer Lach iii 334, Röllig KAI a.l.).

v. w_2.

yyn **OldCan** Sing. abs. *ye-nu* TeAv iii 137[2] (Akkad. par. *ka-ra-nu*) - **Ph** Sing. cstr. *yn* IEJ xviii 227B 2 (the reading *yn* in IEJ xviii 227A 2, cf. Delavault & Lemaire RSF vii 15, less prob.), xxxvii 27 no. 4[3] - **Amm** Sing. abs. *yn* AUSS xiii 2[7,8] - **Hebr** Sing. abs. *yyn* TA-H 1[3], 2[2,5], 3[2], 4[3], 8[5], 10[2], 11[3] (dam. context), TeAv v 83, SM 49[5,23], *yn* Dir ostr 5[3], 6[3] (= KAI 185), 10[3], 11[1], 12[3] (cf. 12[1]), 13[3], 14[3], 35[3] (uncert. reading), 36[3] (uncert. reading), 44[3] (?, dam. context), 53[1], 54[1] (= KAI 187; or = cstr. in 53/54?, cf. e.g. Avigad IEJ xxii 5), 57[1] (dam. context), 62; cstr. *yyn* TA-H 1[9], IEJ xxii 3 (v. however infra) - **OffAr** Sing. abs. *yyn* BASOR cclxiv 46[2] (reading however uncert., cf. Yassine & Teixidor BASOR cclxiv 47) - ¶ subst. m. wine; *yyn hʾgnt* TA-H 1[9f.]: wine of the craters (for the type of wine meant, cf. Aharoni TA a.l., Pardee UF x 296f., HAHL 31f., Hospers SV 103f., Conrad TUAT i 251 :: Aharoni IEJ xvi 3 n. 8: = wine preserved in special type of vessel); *yn yšn* Dir ostr 5^3, 6^3, 10^3, etc.: old wine; *yn ʿz* IEJ xxxvii 27 no. 4^3: wine from Gaza (:: Naveh IEJ xxxvii 29: or = strong wine?, *ʿz* = Sing. m. abs. of $ʿz_3$); *yyn kḥl* IEJ xxii 3: wine of K. (?, n.g.?, cf. Avigad IEJ xxii a.l. (cf. also Stern BiAr xxxviii 51, Zevit MLAHE 17) × Demsky IEJ xxii 233f.: = dark wine (*kḥl* being adj. = dark coloured; cf. also Paul IEJ xxv 42ff.); *yyn ʿšn* TeAv v 83: "smoked" wine (cf. Demsky TeAv vi 163, cf. also Ussishkin TeAv v 83f.; or *ʿšn* = n.l.??; v. also $ʿšn_1$); *ḥmr yn* IEJ xviii 227B 2: fermented wine (?, cf. Cross IEJ xviii 227 (n. 15), cf. also Lemaire IH i 162, Delavault & Lemaire Sem xxv 39, RSF vii 15f.; for TA-H 2^5, v. $ḥmr_6$) - on the etymology, cf. v.Selms JNSL iii 76ff., Delcor APCI 224ff., Beekes MStSW xlviii 21ff.

ykd v. *tkd.*

ykl **Hebr** QAL Part. act. pl.m. abs. *yklm* TA-H 40^{14} - **OffAr** QAL Impf. 3 p.s.m. *ykl* Cowl 1^5, 13^{11}; 2 p.s.m. *tkl* RES 1792A 4, B 2, *twkl* PSBA '15, $222^{4f.}$ (= RES $1793^{10f.}$; cf. Kutscher Kedem i 55, Grelot DAE p. 376 (n. e)); 1 p.s. *ʾkl* Cowl $10^{11,12}$, 13^8, $15^{31,35}$, $47^{7,8}$, Aḥiq 26, Krael 2^{13}, NESE iii 16^1 (:: Vattioni AION xxx 355: reading of *l* uncert.), Irâq xxxi 173^6, AE '23, 40 no. 2^8; 3 p.pl.m. *yklwn* Cowl 10^{18}, Krael 10^{15}; 3 p.pl.f. *tkln* Herm 1^4 (cf. Bresciani & Kamil Herm a.l., Porten & Greenfield ZAW lxxx 227, JEAS p. 153 × Grelot DAE p. 151, Gibson SSI ii p. 131: = 3 p.s.f., cf. also Kutscher IOS i 117), 5^5; 1 p.pl. *nkl* Cowl 1^4, Krael 3^{12} - **Nab** QAL Impf. 3 p.s.m. *ykl* CIS ii 220^2 - ¶ verb QAL -1) to be able, in jur. contexts also: to have the right to (cf. also Muffs p. 36f. n. 2; cf. *khl*) - a) followed by verbal form (same tense, same person), *tkln thytn ln tqm* Herm 5^5: you will be able to send us castor oil (cf. Herm 1^4, Irâq xxxi 173^6); *lʾ nkl ngrky* Cowl 1^4: we will not have the right to sue you; *lʾ ykl gbr ʾḥrn yhnpq ... spr ḥdt* Cowl $13^{11f.}$: no one else will have the right to produce ... a new document (cf. Cowl $1^{5f.}$, $10^{11,12}$, Krael 2^{13}, 3^{12}, NESE iii $16^{1f.}$ (= Cowl 49; cf. also Porten & Yardeni sub TADAE B 4.1), AE '23, 40 no. 2^8 - b) + l_5 + Inf., *[ʾy]nnw yklm lšlḥ* TA-H $40^{13f.}$: we are not able to send - c) + *zy* + hypotactic clause, *wlʾ ykl ʾnš zy yzbn* CIS ii 220^2: and no one will have the right to sell - **2)** to trust (someone with) + obj. + $ʿl_7$, *ʾl twkl hmw ʿl ʾḥrnn* RES $1793^{10f.}$: do not trust them to others (cf. e.g. Sukenik & Kutscher Kedem i 54f., Greenfield IEJ xix 203f. (n. 24), Grelot DAE p. 376 (n.e.) :: Dupont-Sommer REJ '46/47: *twkl* = APH Impf. 2 p.s.m. of $ʾkl_1$) - on the use of this verb, cf. Lipiński LDA 109f. - on the use of *ykl* in juridic documents, cf. J.J.Rabinowitz Law 104f., cf. also Greenfield Mem Yalon 72f.

v. *khl*, tk_1, $tklh_1$.

$\mathbf{yld_1}$ **Ph** QAL (or YIPH?) Impf. 3 p.s.m. *yld* KAI 26A iii 9 (for the reading, cf. e.g. Bron RIPK 110, Avishur PIB 224, Gibson SSI iii p. 50, 62 :: O'Callaghan Or xviii 178, 188: l. *ylʿ*?, cf. also Röllig KAI

a.l. (cf. however ibid. ii p. 339), Dahood Bibl xliii 225 (< root *lʿʿ* = to overflow), C iv 10 - **OffAr** QAL Pf. 2 p.s.f. *yldty* Krael 4[5,17,20], *ylty* Krael 5[5,8] (cf. Segert AAG p. 114, Degen GGA '79, 23), *lydty* (lapsus for *yldty*) Krael 5[6]; Impf. 3 p.s.f. *tld* Cowl 15[33], ATNS 50[3]; Part. act. s.m. abs. (or cstr.), cf. Warka 26: *ya-a-li-di* (?); cf. Frah xxii 1 (*ylydwn*, cf. Nyberg FP 52, 96 (cf. also Toll ZDMG-Suppl viii 35) :: Ebeling Frah a.l.: l. *zrʾwn* = form of *zrʿ*$_1$),cf. also GIPP 38 - **Nab** ITP Impf. 3 p.s.m. *ytyld* CIS ii 209[2] - **JAr** QAL Pf. 3 p.s.f. *ylydt* AMB 15[1]; Part. pass. s.m. abs. *ylyd* MPAT 68[4] (or preferably = QAL pass. Pf. 3 p.s.m.?, cf. Beyer ATTM 347, 597) - ¶ verb QAL to bear, to give birth to; + obj.: AMB 15[1]; + *l*$_5$, *bnn zy tld ly* Cowl 15[32f.]: the children she will bear to me (cf. Krael 4[5,17,20], 5[5,6,8]); + *mn*$_5$, *tld mnh* ATNS 50[3]: she will bear by him (?, dam. context); in KAI 26A iii 9, C iv 10 an interpret. as QAL as well. poss. as as YIPH (= to beget); Part. pass. born: MPAT 68[4] - ITP to be born; *mh dy ytyld lḥlpw dnh mn dkryn* CIS ii 209[2]: as many male children as shall be born to the said Ch. - a form of this root prob. in ATNS 52b 7 (diff. reading), cf. Segal ATNS a.l.: l. *yld* = Sing. cstr. of *yld*$_2$.
v. *yld*$_2$, *yrd*, *rd*$_3$.

yld₂ (forms with initial. *w* < Arab.?; cf. Cantineau Nab ii 171f., Diem ZDMG cxxiii 228 n. 11) - **Nab** Sing. abs. *yld* MPAT 64 i 8; cstr. *yld* CIS ii 207[2], 217[3], *wld*CIS ii 209[3] (highly uncert. reading, cf. RES 1290D); + suff. 3 p.s.m. *yldh* CIS ii 197[2], 199[2], 201[3], 206[1], 208[2], 210[2], 214[2], 219[2], 221[1], J 5[2], ARNA-Nab 16[2], *wldh*CIS ii 220[1]; + suff. 3 p.s.f. *yldh* CIS ii 224[2], *wldh*CIS ii 223[2], 225[2], J 17[8f.] ({*w*}*wldh*; O'Connor JNES xlv 216f.: < Arab. :: O'Connor JNES xlv 226: or = QAL Pf. 3 p.s.m. + suff. 3 p.s.m. of *wld*$_1$(= *yld*$_1$));+ suff. 3 p.pl.m. *yldhm* CIS ii 200[2], 202[3], 212[2,5], 213[7], 215[2], 216[2], 217[2], J 38[3]; + suff. 3 p.pl.f. *yldhm* CIS ii 199[3], *wldhm*J 3[2] (= CIS ii 210), 14[2] (= CIS ii 203; cf. also Ben Chayim EI i 137) - **Palm** Sing. emph. *wldʾ*RB xxxix 536[2] (cf. Rosenthal Sprache 40 n. 2, 95 n. 1 :: Cantineau Gramm 116: = *w* (copula) + *ldʾ*(= Sing. emph. of a subst. derived from the root *yld* with loss of initial. *y*- or lapsus); Plur. emph. *wldʾ*Syr xlviii 413[3] (?, dam. context; cf. Gawlikowski ibid. 417, 420, TP 77) - **JAr** Sing. + suff. 3 p.s.m. (or Sing. emph.) *wldh*AMB 12[4] (*wld[h]*; heavily dam. context)[,34] - ¶ subst. with collective meaning, children, issue: CIS ii 197[2], 200[2], 201[2], J 5[2], etc.; with wider meaning, posterity: CIS ii 202[3], 207[2], RB xxxix 536[2], etc. - Février RHR cxli 20: l. *yld* (Sing. abs.) in NP 130[3] (reading uncert. though poss., improb. interpret., word division unclear).
v. *yld*$_1$,*yld*$_3$, *yld*$_4$.

yld₃ **OffAr** Sing. emph. *yldʾ* ATNS 41[8] - **Hatra** Sing. + suff. 3 p.s.m. *yldh* (in *byldh*, v infra) 79[3] - ¶ subst. birth; *ywm yldʾ zy* ... ATNS 41[8]: the birthday of... (cf. also Shaked Or lvi 410, v. also *plny*); in the combination *byldh* (haplography of *by* (= Sing. cstr. of *byt$_2$*)+ *yldh*) = litt. house of his birth (house taken in the astrological sense of the word in Hatra 79^3, cf. (Starcky with) Teixidor Syr xli 280 n. 2, Milik DFD 379f.); *byldh dgnd*ʾ Hatra 79$^{3f.}$: = the day of the ascension of his Fortune (sc. of the king), equivalent with the birthday of the king, cf. also Aggoula Ber xviii 96, MUSJ xlvii 31 (v. also *byt$_2$*) :: Caquot Syr xl 36: *byldh dgnd*ʾ = his fortunate birthday :: Altheim & Stiehl AAW iv 245, 249: *yldh* = Plur. + suff. 3 p.s.m. of *yld$_2$*:: Safar Sumer xvii 13 n. 4, 16: *bbyldh* = *b$_2$* + noun of unknown meaning *byld/r* + suff. 3 p.s.m.

yld$_4$ **OffAr** Sing. abs. *yld* ATNS 8^4 - ¶ subst. someone born (in/from); *yld bzn by* ATNS 8^4 (for the reading, cf. Porten & Yardeni sub TADAE B 5.6): a slave born in this house (prob. interpret. :: Segal ATNS a.l.: l. *yld* (= Sing. cstr. of *yld$_2$*) *bzn br* = children of B. the son of ...).

yly **Palm** APH Part. (pass.?) s.f. emph. *mwly*ʾ Inv viii 6^4, 8^4, 37b 2; pl.m. abs. *mwln* CIS ii 4172^2 - ¶ verb APH - **1)** to be near to (prob. interpret.); *trn mwln twpr*ʾ CIS ii 4172^2: two (sc. *loculi*) near to the *twpr* (v. s.v.), cf. e.g. Chabot CIS ii a.l., Milik DFD 193 - **2)** in the expression *wh*ʾ *npš*ʾ *dh mwly*ʾ *bšmš* Inv viii 6^4, 8$^{3f.}$, 37b 2, of uncert. meaning; Milik DFD 193: this soul is near to Shamsh (i.e. has a close relation with Sh.); Gawlikowski Ber xxi 9 (n. 30): this soul is protected by Shamsh; Dussaud with Cumont CRAI '33, 261 n. 1: this stele is (the one of) the freedman (freed) by Shamsh; Cantineau sub Inv viii 6: *mwly*ʾ = subst. (*mwly$_1$*) Sing. emph. (= plenitude (achievement; cf. also du Mesnil du Buisson TMP 254), less prob. interpret.), or = Sing. emph. of *mwly$_2$* (= highest duties rendered to the dead?; improb. interpret.); cf. also Cantineau Gramm 90, Rosenthal Sprache 50 n. 2, Díez Merino LA xxi 132.

ylk v. *hlk$_1$*, *mlk$_5$*.

yll$_1$ **OffAr** HAPH Pf. 3 p.s.m. *hyll* Aḥiq 41 - ¶ verb HAPH to lament. v. *myll*.

yll$_2$ **Pun** Février BAr a.l.: l. *yll* in BAr '46/49, 253^4 (= Sing. cstr.) = moaning.

yllh **OldAr** Sing. abs. *yllh* KAI 222A 30 - ¶ subst. lamentation.

ylp v. *ʾlp$_5$*.

ym$_1$ **Ph** Sing. abs. *ym* KAI 14^{16,18}, 15, 51 Rs 2, MUSJ xlv 262^5 (cf. Starcky MUSJ xlv 262, 271, Röllig NESE ii 2, 11, Schiffmann RSF iv 172, 176 :: v.d.Branden BiOr xxxiii 12, xxxvi 202 (div. otherwise): l. *-h wnʿm* (v. *hwn$_3$*)) - **Pun** Plur. abs. *ymm* KAI 145^5 (uncert. interpret., cf. e.g. Cooke NSI p. 152, 154, Röllig KAI a.l.: or = Plur. abs. of *ywm*?,for this last interpret., cf. also Février Sem vi 20, v.d.Branden RSF i 166, 168, Krahmalkov RSF iii 192) - **OffAr** Sing. emph. *ym*ʾ Cowl 71^{20} (uncert. reading, cf. Cowl p. 182), Aḥiq 117, 208, RES 1785C, ATNS 26^{13}; cf. Frah iii 2 (*ymy*(*my*ʾ)), 3 (:: Ebeling Frah a.l.: or l. *gm*ʾ = *gmh*

(= ditch, trench)), Syr xxxv 317[42], GIPP 38, 67, SaSt 26 - **Palm** Sing. emph. *ym›* CIS ii 4047[4], Inv xi 35[3] (?, uncert. reading, cf. Milik DFD 294) - **JAr** Sing. emph. *ymh* AMB 9[7], 15[16], *y›m›* SM 91A 4 (= Frey 834), C 2 (= Frey 835); :: Torrey Syn 269f.: l. in both texts *l›m›* = *l*$_5$ + *›m›* (= *ym›*)), cf. also Ellis & Ingholt Syn 456 - ¶ subst. sea; in ATNS 26[13] prob. indicating the Nile (cf. Segal ATNS a.l., Shaked Or lvi 13; *bby ym›* ATNS 26[13]: the gates of the Nile (i.e. the side of the Nile)); for *›rṣ ym* in KAI 14[16,18], *ym šmm rmm* in KAI 15, v. *›rṣ*$_1$; for *hwn ym* in MUSJ xlv 262[5], v. *hwn*$_3$; for *rzn ymm* in KAI 145[5], v. supra and *rzn*; for *bym› wbybš›* CIS ii 4047[4], Inv xi 35[3] (?), v. *ybš*; for *rb ḥrm lym* KAI 51 Rs 2, v. *ḥrm*$_4$ - Rocco StudMagr vii 14: l. *ym* (= Sing. abs.) in StudMagr vii 12[5] (highly uncert. interpret., dam. context).
v. *ywm,ym›*, *mym*.

ym$_2$ v. *ywm,šd*$_1$.

ym› **OffAr** QAL Pf. 3 p.s.m. *ym›* Cowl 44[2] (cf. e.g. Cowl a.l., Grelot DAE p. 95 :: Porten & Yardeni sub TADAE B 7.3: or = QAL Impf. 3 p.s.m. (cf. also Porten & Greenfield JEAS p. 122)), ATNS 2[1] (dam. context; *ym›[* ; Segal ATNS al.: or = Sing. emph. of *ym*$_1$?),5[4] (*[y]m›*, uncert. context), 17[3], 54[9] (*[y]m›*, heavily dam. context); 2 p.s.m. *ym›t* Cowl 6[8,11]; 2 p.s.f. *ym›ty* Cowl 14[5,8]; 1 p.s. *ym›t* Cowl 8[24]; Impf. 2 p.s.m. *tm›* Cowl 45[6] (*tm›[* ; for this prob. interpret., cf. Yardeni with Porten RB xc 568, Porten & Yardeni sub TADAE B 7.1); Inf. *mwm›* Cowl 6[6], ATNS 2[4]; Part. act. pl.m. abs. *ymyn* ATNS 17[7] (heavily dam. context; or = QAL Pf. 1 p.pl.?); HAPH Pf. 3 p.s.m. *hwmy* ATNS 27[2]; 1 p.s. + suff. 2 p.s.m. *hwmytk* SSI ii 37[2] (cf. Cross BASOR clxxxiv 9 n. 19, Teixidor Syr xlv 376, Lipiński Stud 151, 153, Gibson SSI ii a.l. :: Benveniste with Dupont-Sommer CRAI '66, 47, 52: < Iran., = adj. Sing. m. cstr. (= having good mutual relations; cf. Dupont-Sommer CRAI '66, 52: = devout, devoted) :: (de Menasce with) Delcor Mus lxxx 307f., 312: < Iran. = subst. Sing. cstr. (= a good/happy abode; cf. also Altheim & Stiehl AAW v/1, 73f.: = what is well-built)); ITTAPH Part. s.m. abs. *mtwmy* FX 136[20] (cf. Dupont-Sommer CRAI '74, 137, FX p. 153f., Teixidor JNES xxxvii 184 (n. 23), Contini EVO ii 205 :: Dupont-Sommer FX p. 136f., 153 (div. otherwise): pro *mtwmy hnṣl* l. *mtwm* (adv. ever, always, = *mtm*$_2$) *yhnṣl* (= HAPH Impf. 3 p.s.m. of *nṣl*, cf. Contini OA xx 233), cf. also Rosenthal JNES xxxvii 86, Faber FUCUS 224, ZDMG cxxxvii 280) - **Palm** QAL Pf. 3 p.s.m. *ymh* Syr xvii 353[9] - **Waw** APH Part. s.m. abs. + affixed pron. 1 p.s. *mwmn›* AMB 6[7] (cf. Naveh & Shaked AMB a.l. :: Gordon Or xviii 339f.: l. *mwmyyn›* = lapsus for *mwmyn›* = APH Part. s.m. abs. + affixed pron. 1 p.s. :: Dupont-Sommer Waw p. 18: l. *mwm* (= Sing. cstr. of *mwm* (= dirt)) *my›* (= Plur. cstr. of *mym*); cf. also idem AIPHOS xi 121) - ¶ verb QAL to swear, to take an oath - **1)** + *b*$_2$ (by): Syr xvii 353[9],

AMB 6^7 - **2)** + b_2 (by) + *ʿl dbr* (concerning): Cowl 6^6 - **3)** + l_5 (to): Cowl 8^{24} - **4)** + l_5 (to) + b_2 (by): Cowl 6^{11}, $44^{2f.}$ (for the reading of the context, cf. Porten & Yardeni sub TADAE B 7.3) - **5)** + l_5 (to) + ʿl_7 (concerning): Cowl 14^8 - **6)** + l_5 (to) + ʿl_7 (concerning) + b_2 (by): Cowl 14^5 - **7)** + l_5 (to) + *ʿl dbr* (concerning): Cowl 6^8 - **8)** + ʿl_7 (concerning): ATNS 2^4 - HAPH to adjure; + obj.: ATNS 27^2 (context however heavily damaged, Segal ATNS a.l.: or = to swear in?); + obj. + divine names, *hwmytk bl wnbw* SSI ii $37^{2f.}$: I adjure you (by) Bel and Nabu (:: Cross BASOR clxxxiv 9 n. 19: or = I adjure thee, B. and N. ...) - ITTAPH Part., solemnly promised; *hn ʾyš mtwmy hnṣl mn kndwṣ ʾlhʾ* FX $136^{20f.}$: if someone takes away from the god K. what has been solemnly promised (compare Greek par.: καὶ ἐποιήσαντο ὅρκους ... τοῖς θεοῖς τούτοις ... καὶ μὴ μετακινήσειν μηδαμὰ ...) - Grelot DAE p. 444 n. c.: l. *yhw[m]ʾnhy* (= HAPH Impf. 3 p.s.m. + suff. 3 p.s.m.) in Aḥiq 161 (dam. context; for this reading, cf. also Lindenberger APA 163, 267 n. 498, UF xiv 111) :: Nöldeke AGWG xiv/4, 17: l. *yhṭrʾnhy* = HAPH Impf. 3 p.s.m. + suff. 3 p.s.m. of $ṭrʾ_2$ :: Cowl a.l.: l. poss. *yhw[h]* (= QAL Impf. 3 p.s.m. of hwy_1)+ *[d]ʾnhy* (= QAL Part. act. s.m. + suff. 3 p.s.m. of dyn_1)).
v. hwn_2,*mʾzl*, mlk_1.

ymyn v. ymn_2.

$\mathbf{ymm_1}$ **Nab** Sing. emph. *ymmʾ* J 2^4 - ¶ subst. day, for the context, v. $prš_1$; cf. *ywm*.

$\mathbf{ymm_2}$ v. *ywm*.

$\mathbf{ymn_1}$ v. *tymn*.

$\mathbf{ymn_2}$ **Hebr** Sing. abs. *ymn* KAI 189^3; + suff. 3 p.s.m. *ymynw* AMB 4^{32}; + suff. 2 p.s.m. *ymynk* AMB 1^1 - **OffAr** Sing. abs. *ymn* Krael 5^3; cstr. *ymn* Cowl $28^{4,6}$; + suff. 3 p.s.m./f. ATNS 90^3 - **Nab** Sing. emph. *ymynʾ* CIS ii 213^6, J 14^3 (:: CIS ii sub 203: l. *ytqbrwn* = ITP Impf. 3 p.pl.m. of qbr_1) - **Palm** Sing. cstr. *ymyn* Ber i 38^{12}; emph. *ymynʾ* CIS ii 4172^2, 4199^4, 4204^2, Ber ii 60^1, 91^3, 98^1, FS Miles $38^{1,2}$, etc., *ymnʾ* Ber ii 95; + suff. 2 p.s.m. *ymynk* CIS ii 4172^2, 4195^7, Ber ii 76^1, 78^2, 101^6, 110^1 (Greek par. δεξίοις), RIP 51^2 (= Inv xii 14), FS Collart 161^3, etc. - ¶ subst. right side, passim - **1)** *ymynʾ*, at the right side, to the right; *wnpl ḥlq hgrw ymynʾ ʾmyn ḥmš* J 14^3: and five cubits to the right fell to the share of H.; *gwḥyʾ md[n]ḥ ymynʾ* CIS ii 213^6: niches at the south (litt. right) east side - **2)** *bymn*, at the right side (of), to the right (of); *bymn šnytt mqrʾ ʾrmyt* Cowl 28^4: at the right of a tattoo in the Aramaic language (cf. Cowl 28^6); *šnyth ʿl ydh bymn* Krael 5^3: there is a tattoo on his hand at the right; cf. also ATNS 90^3 - **3)** *lymynʾ*, at the right side: CIS ii 4172^2 (v. *pny*) - **4)** *mn ymyn*, *mymn*, to the right (of), at the right side (of); *hyt zdh bṣr mymn* KAI 189^3: there was a fissure (?, v. *zdh*) in the rock at the right side (i.e. at

the south side; context however dam., transl. from the right/south side also poss., cf. e.g. Gibson SSI i p. 22, Puech RB lxxxi 199, 202); *ʾḥbrth ... gmḥyn tmnyʾ mn ymynk ʾrbʿʾ* CIS ii 4195[6f.]: I have made him a partner ... (for) eight niches, four at your right side (cf. Ber v 109 ii 8f.) - **5)** - a) *ʿl ym(y)nʾ*, at the right (side); *ḥdʾ ʿl ymynʾ kdy ʾnt ʿll.* CIS ii 4199[4f.]: one at the right side when you enter (cf. CIS ii 4204[2], Ber ii 60[1], 91[3], 95, RB xxxix 538[2], FS Miles 38[1,2], etc.) - b) *ʿl ymyn*, at the right (side) of; *ʾksdrʾ mʿlyk ʿl ymynk* Ber ii 76[1]: the exedra to your right, when you enter (cf. Ber i 38[12], ii 78[2], 101[6], RIP 51[2], etc.) - for AMB 4[32], v. *šbʿ₂* - Negev IEJ xv 93: the *y* in Nab. stone-dresser's marks from Avdat poss. = abbrev. of *ymyn* (uncert. interpret., cf. the combinations *ʾy*, *dy*, *yg* (Avdat, IEJ xv 189) and the combinations *ḥy*, *ky*, *ṭy*, *yy* and *ly* (temple of Ramm RB, xliv 250; Savignac and Horsfield RB a.l.: the second *y* here = abbrev. of unknown interpret., Negev IEJ xv 193: *y* poss. = number 5)).
v. *ymny*.

ymny **Palm** m. Sing. emph. *ymnyʾ* Ber ii 86[6], 88[6], 97[1], 104[2]; Plur. abs. *ymnyyn* Ber v 124[2]; emph. *ymyny[ʾ]* RIP 163[2] (prob. reading, cf. Gawlikowski a.l. :: Michałowski FP '59, 214: l. *ymynʾ* = Sing. emph. of *ymn₂*)- ¶ adj. - **1)** right, right-hand: Ber ii 97[1], v. 124[2] - **2)** southern: Ber ii 86[2], 88[6], 104[2], RIP 163[2].

ymnt v. *nḥt₄*.

ymtn v. *mwt₁*.

yn v. *yyn*.

ynṭs **Nab** CIS ii 373; word of unknown meaning, cf. Lidzbarski Eph ii 267, Cantineau Nab ii 104 (: = QAL Impf. form of root *nṭs* = to be able, to be wise??).

yny **OldAr** HAPH Impf. 3 p.s.m. *yhwnh* KAI 223B 16; + suff. 3 p.s.m. *yhwnnh* KAI 223B 16 - ¶ verb HAPH to oppress; + obj.: KAI 223B 16.
v. *ywm*.

ynm **Hebr** TA-H 19; word of unknown meaning; Aharoni TA a.l.: poss. = n.l., Elizur with Sarfatti Lesh xxxiv 154: = unknown measure of capacity.
v. *ywm*.

ynq₁ **OldAr** HAPH Impf. 3 p.pl.f. *yhynqn* KAI 222A 22, 23, 223A 2 (*[yhy]nqn*), *lhynqn* Tell F 20, 21 (:: Andersen & Freedman FS Fensham 36: = *l₁* + Pf. 3 p.pl.f.); Part. pl.f. abs. *[mhy]nqn* KAI 222A 21 - **OffAr** QAL Inf. *mwnq* Aḥiq 120; APH Impf. 3 p.s.m. + suff. 3 p.s.m. *ynyqnhy* Aḥiq 92 (diff. form, cf. Strack ZDMG lxv 833, Cowl p. 236: poss. < root *nwq*? (cf. also Kottsieper SAS 136, 218); Leand 38c: lapsus for *yynqnhy*?; Kaufman AIA 77 (n. 238): poss. < root *nqy*?, less prob. interpret.; on the form, cf. also Lindenberger APA 66f., 232 nn. 120-123) - ¶ verb QAL to suck; + obj., *lhn lmwnq dmh* Aḥiq 120: only to

suck its (sc. the kid's) blood - HAPH/APH - **1)** to suckle; + obj., *wšbʿ š'n yhynqn 'mr* KAI 222A 23: seven sheep shall suckle a lamb (cf. KAI 222A 22, 22f., 223A 2, Tell F 20, 20f., 21; cf. also Hillers TC 61f.); Part. substantivated, wet-nurse: KAI 222A 21 - **2)** to give to drink + obj.: Aḥiq 92 (v. however supra) - Rofé SB 63, 68: l. *'hnq* (= HAPH Impf. 1 p.s.) in DA ii 12 (less prob. interpret.; for the reading, cf. v.d.Kooij DA p. 125f.).
v. *mynwq*.

ynq_2 **OffAr** Plur. emph. *ynqy'* Cowl 40^3, SSI ii 28 rev. 5, Herm 7^3, KAI 270B 3 (for the reading, cf. Dupont-Sommer ASAE xlviii 120 :: CIS ii 137, Donner KAI a.l.: l. *y'nqy'*),RES 1793^9 (= PSBA xxxvii 222^3), *ynqyh* RSO xxxv 22^2 (dam. context) - ¶ subst. m. child, small child - the form *ynq'* in RES 1793^6 diff., prob. = Sing. emph., cf. Dupont-Sommer REJ cvii 49 (n. 37), Grelot DAE p. 376 (n. g), cf. however Dupont-Sommer REJ a.l.: = lapsus for *ynqy'*? (cf. also Kutscher Kedem i 56) - v.Soden Or xxxvii 270, xlvi 188: > Akkad. (young lamb?; uncert. interpret., cf. also CAD s.v. *janūqu* (: = foreign word? of unknown meaning), v.Soden AHW s.v.: *janūqu* = certain type of meat (in cultic context)).

ysb v. *yšb₁*.

ysd_1 **JAr** QAL Pf. 3 p.pl.m. *ysdw* SM 88^9 (:: Torrey Syn D p. 263 (A 9): l. *šdrw* = PAʿEL Pf. 3 p.pl.m. of *šdr₁*) - ¶ verb QAL to found, to establish: SM 88^9 (dam. context).
v. *swr₃*.

ysd_2 **Ph** Sing. + suff. 3 p.s.f. *ysdh* KAI 10^{14} (for this diff. reading, cf. Dupont-Sommer Sem iii 43, cf. also Röllig KAI a.l., Gibson SSI iii p. 94 :: Dunand BMB v 83, 85: pro *ysdh* l. *hsr* (= he will take away) *h* (also discussion of previous readings) - ¶ subst. base.

ysk **Pun** NIPH Impf. 3 p.s.f. *tysk* KAI 89^6 (:: Février sub CIS i 6068: = PUʿAL?) - ¶ verb NIPH to be poured out (said of lead): KAI 89^6 - a form (PUʿAL Pf. 3 p.s.f.) *ysk* prob. in KAI 89^1, cf. however Röllig KAI a.l.: = YOPH Pf. 3 p.s.f. of *nsk₁*; cf. Février sub CIS i 6068, cf. also Lidzbarski sub KI 85.

ysp **Ph** QAL (or YIPH) Pf. 1 p.pl. + suff. 3 p.pl.m. *yspnnm* KAI 14^{19}; Impf. 3 p.s.m. *ysp* KAI 10^{11}; a form of this root in MUSJ xlv 262^4, Starcky MUSJ xlv 262, 270f., Röllig NESE ii 2, 10: l. prob. *ysp[t]* = QAL or YIPH Pf. 1 p.s., cf. however Schiffmann RSF iv 172) - **Pun** QAL (or YIPH) Pf. (or Impf.?) 3 p.s.m. *ysp* CIS i 5510^6 (v. infra) - **Mo** QAL Pf. 1 p.s. *yspty* KAI 181^{29}; Inf. cstr. *spt* KAI 181^{21} (cf. also Solá-Solé IS 121f.) - **OldAr** HAPH Pf. 1 p.s. *hwsp[t]* KAI 202B 4f. - **OffAr** HAPH Pf. 3 p.s.m. *'wsp* KAI 279^8 (cf. e.g. Altheim & Stiehl EW x 246, ASA p. 30, 271, GMA 353, GH ii 176, Levi Della Vida Editto 30, Garbini Kand 17, Donner KAI a.l., Kutscher, Naveh & Shaked Lesh xxxiv 136,

Segert AAG p. 518 :: Dupont-Sommer JA ccxlvi 32: *›wsp* = adv., still :: Altheim & Stiehl EW ix 197, GH i 398, 406f.: pro *w›wsp* l. *wy›wsp* (= *w* + APH Impf. 3 p.s.m. :: Koopmans p. 178: or l. *ywsp*? = APH Impf. 3 p.s.m.); Impf. 3 p.pl.m. *yhwspwn* Cowl 26[18]; 2 p.pl.m. *thwspwn* Driv 7[9]; Inf. *hwsph* Cowl 26[17] (for this interpret., cf. Driver JRAS '32, 80, cf. also Grelot DAE p. 292 :: Cowl p. 96, Leand 38j: = APH Imper. s.m. + coh. ending, cf. also Porten & Yardeni sub TADAE A 6.2: = overcut?) - ITP Pf. 3 p.s.m. *›twsp* ATNS 19[4]; Impf. 3 p.pl.m. *ytwspw* ATNS 19[6] - **Nab** APH Pf. 3 p.s.m. *›wsp* RB lxiv 215[3] - **Hatra** APH Impf. 3 p.s.m. *lwsyp* (cf. Degen NESE ii 101 (n. 11); for the reading, cf. also Safar Sumer xviii 46 :: Caquot Syr xli 261f.: l. *lysyp* = PA‘EL Impf. 3 p.s.m. of *swp$_1$* (= to destroy) :: Vattioni IH p. 65: l. *lysp* (poss. to be connected with root *ysp* or *›sp$_1$*)) - ¶ verb QAL (or YIPH), HAPH, APH to add - **1)** + obj.: KAI 202B 4f.; cf. *hwsph kbry kršn ‘šrh* Cowl 26[17]: the adding of (i.e. plus) 10 k. sulphur - **2)** + obj. + *‘lt*, *wyspnnm ‘lt gbl ›rṣ* KAI 14[19f.]: we added them to the territory of the land - **3)** + *b$_2$*, *wḥdt yth w›wsp bh* RB lxiv 215[3f.]: and he restored it and added to it (sc. to the temple) - **4)** + *l$_5$* + Inf. + *‘lt*, *kl ›dm ›š ysp lp‘l ml›kt ‘lt mzbḥ zn* KAI 10[11f.]: everyone who will do further work on this altar - **5)** + *‘l$_7$*, *lspt ‘l dybn* KAI 181[21]: to add it to (the territory of) Diban (cf. KAI 181[29]); *wl› thwspwn ‘l byt› zyly* Driv 7[9]: and do not add (them; i.e. members of the domestic staff) to my estate; cf. also Cowl 26[18] - **6)** + *‘lt* + l$_5$: CIS i 5510[6] (for the diff. context, cf. Chabot BAr '41/42, 393, Février BAr '46/49, 161, 171 CIS i a.l.) - **7)** in diff. formula, *hwtyr lklhm ›nšn w›wsp yhwtr* KAI 279[8]: it has benefitted all men and will continue(?) to benefit (sc. them), for this interpret., cf. Garbini Kand 17f., Donner KAI a.l., Kutscher, Naveh & Shaked Lesh xxxiv 130, 136 (for other transl., cf. Altheim & Stiehl EW x 247, ASA 32, Rosenthal EI xiv 97*f.) - Teixidor Syr lvi 382: the *lspt* in RES 930[1] poss. = *l$_5$* + QAL Inf. cstr. of *ysp* or *l$_5$* + Sing. abs. of *›sph*(= assembly); highly uncert. interpretations - ITP to be added; *ksp› zy ›twsp ‘l mks pṭ›sy* ATNS 19[4]: the (amount of) silver that was added to the tax of P.

v. *›sp$_1$*.

ysr$_1$ **DA** Lemaire BAT 317f., CRAI '85, 279f.: l. poss. *htysrh* = HITP Inf. cstr. of *ysr* (= to be corrected, to be punished) in DA ii 2 (restored by adding parts of DA iii), highly uncert. reading and interpret.

v. *›sr$_1$*.

ysr$_2$ **OffAr** Segal ATNS a.l.: the *hwsrt* in ATNS 46[4] = HAPH Pf. 2 p.s.m. of *ysr$_2$* (= to remove), diff. and dam. context, uncert. interpret., reading *hwsdt* also possible.

ysr$_3$ v. *›br$_1$*.

y‘gn v. *ygn,nš›$_1$*.

y‘ṭ v. *y‘ṣ*.
y‘l$_1$ v. *‘ll$_1$*.
y‘l$_2$ v. *‘ll$_1$*.
y‘nh v. *‘ny$_1$*.
y‘p v. *‘wp$_1$*.
y‘ṣ **Pun** QAL Part. act. s.m. abs. *y’ṣ*RES 906[1] (prob. interpret.) - **OffAr** QAL Part. act. s.m. cstr. *y‘ṭ* Aḥiq 12 - ¶ verb QAL to advise; Part. act.: counsellor - a derivative of this root in Palm. Inv D 40[4]?? (highly uncert.).
v. *‘wṣ*, *pṣy*.
y‘r **Pun** Sing. abs. *yr* KAI 100[6]; cf. also Augustine Enarr in Ps 123:8 (on Ps 124:5): *jar* - **Mo** Plur. abs. *y‘rn* KAI 181[21] - ¶ subst. - **1)** wood; *hḥršm šyr* KAI 100[6]: wood-craftsmen - **2)** forest, parkland: KAI 181[21] (cf. also de Geus SV 26, 28 n.p.: indication of special type of sanctuary).
yp’ **Pun** Février RA l 188, Röllig KAI a.l.: l. *yp’* (= adj. Sing. m. abs.) in KAI 119[7] (*km yp’*, as (it is) fitting (highly uncert. interpret.; cf. also Amadasi IPT 82)) :: Levi Della Vida RCL ’55, 560 (div. otherwise): pro *km yp’* l. *bmyp’* = *b$_2$* + Sing. abs. of *myp’* (= embellishment; cf. IPT 81); or l. *kmyp’* = *k$_1$* + *myp’* (as embellishment)?
ypd v. *hn$_3$*,*pwd*.
yph **Hebr** Sing. f. abs. *yph* Mas 516 (cf. also Mas 520); Plur. abs. *ypwt* DJD ii 24B 16, C 15, D 16 - ¶ adj. beautiful, good; in combination *ḥnṭyn ypwt* DJD ii 24B 16, C 15, D 15f.: wheat of good quality; *dblh ktwšh yph* Mas 516: a well pressed fig-cake.
v. *ptt$_1$*.
yp‘$_1$ **DA** Lemaire BAT 317f., CRAI ’85, 279f.: l. poss. *yp‘t* (= QAL Pf. 3 p.s.f. of *yp‘$_1$* (= to appear)) in DA ii 2 (highly uncert. reading and interpret.); cf. also Puech BAT 356, 360: l. *šm‘t* = QAL Pf. 2 p.s.m. of *šm‘$_1$*.
v. *yp‘$_2$*.
yp‘$_2$ **DA** Hoftijzer DA p. 187f.: l. *yp‘* in i 2 = subst. Sing. abs. (= blaze, blazing fire, cf. Wesselius BiOr xliv 593, 595: = shining), diff. context, uncert. interpret.; Rofé SB 65: = verbal form of *yp‘$_1$* (= to come, = HIPH Impf. 3 p.s.m.?; cf. also Lemaire BAT 317f., CRAI ’85, 279f.: = QAL Pf. 3 p.s.m. of *yp‘$_1$*); cf. however e.g. Caquot & Lemaire Syr liv 195, Garbini Hen i 174, McCarter BASOR ccxxxix 51f., Levine JAOS ci 196, H.P.Müller ZAW xciv 216, 220, 240 (div. otherwise): l. *yp‘l* = QAL Impf. 3 p.s.m. of *p‘l$_1$* (cf. also H. & M. Weippert ZDPV xcviii 86, 103: or *yp‘l* = NIPH(/QAL pass.) Impf. 3 p.s.m. (cf. also Koenig Sem xxxiii 80, 83, 88, Puech BAT 356, 360)).
ypq$_1$ **OldCan** QAL Pf. 1 p.s. *ia-pa-aq-ti* EA 64[23] (cf. Rainey EA p. 61 s.v. *abāku*, Loretz & Mayer UF vi 493f. :: Krahmalkov JNES xxx

141f.: < root *ypq$_2$* = to remove :: Knudtzon EA a.l.: l. *ia-pa-ak-ti*, cf. ibid. p. 1358 s.v. *abāku*, cf. also CAD s.v. *abāku* A 3b: related to West Sem *hpk*)- ¶ verb QAL to find, to acquire.
v. *pwq$_1$*.

ypq$_2$ v. *ypq$_1$*,*pwq$_1$*.

yṣ' **OldCan** QAL Impf. 3 p.s.m. *ji-ṣa* EA 151^{70} (gloss to *li-sà-ḫír*, cf. Ebeling with Knudtzon EA p. 1546, Rainey EA p. 88 s.v. *sa-ḫāru*); HIPH Impf. 3 p.s.m. + suff. 1 p.s. *ia-ṣí-ni* EA 282^{14} (gloss to *yi-ki-im-ni*, cf. Ebeling with Knudtzon EA p. 1546, Rainey EA p. 69 s.v. *ekēmu*; for both instances, cf. also Böhl 37q) - **Ph** QAL Pf. 3 p.s.m. *yṣ'* KAI 27^{26} (cf. e.g. Avishur PIB 248, UF x 34, Garbini OA xx 292, Gibson SSI iii p. 83, de Moor JEOL xxvii 111; or = Impf. 3 p.s.m.? (cf. e.g. Röllig KAI a.l.) or = Part. act. m. s. abs.? :: Caquot FS Gaster 51, Garbini OA xx 286: = YIPH Pf. 3 p.s.m.), Syr xlviii 396^{3} (cf. Caquot Syr xlviii 403, Röllig NESE ii 29, Liverani RSF ii 35, 37, Gaster BASOR ccix 19 (n. 3), Avishur PIB 267 :: Lipiński RSF ii 51f., RTAT 267, vd Branden BiOr xxxiii 13, Gibson SSI iii p. 89f.: = YIPH Pf. 3 p.s.m. :: v.d.Branden BO iii 43, 47: = YIPH Imper. s.m. (= to sprout) :: Cross CBQ xxxvi 488 (n. 21): = QAL Inf. abs.); Part. act. pl.m. abs. *yṣ'm* CIS i 91^{2} - **Pun** QAL Part. act. pl.m. abs., cf. Poen 939: *lusim* (lapsus for *iusim*, cf. e.g. Sznycer PPP 108, cf. also id. APCI 211; cf. poss. also *lus* in Poen 949, lapsus for *ius<im>*?, cf. Sznycer PPP 129) - **Hebr** QAL Inf. cstr. + suff. 1 p.s. *ṣ'ty* TA-H 16^{3} (on the reading of the context, cf. Pardee UF x 311, HAHL 49); a form of this root poss. also in Lach xxi 4 (or 3f.), cf. Diringer PEQ '43, 98, Lach iii p. 339 (n. 2), Ginsberg BASOR lxxx 13 - ¶ verb QAL to go out, to leave: EA 151^{70}, Syr xlviii 396^{3}, CIS i 91^{2} (uncert. context), Poen 939; *yṣ' šmš* KAI 27^{26}: the sun has risen (v. however supra); + *mn$_5$*, *kṣ'ty mbytk* TA-H 16$^{3f.}$: as I left your house - HIPH to take away, to save; + obj.: EA 282^{14} (cf. Rainey EA p. 69 s.v. *ekēmu*) - a form of this root also in RES 1204^{1} ?, cf. Catastini RSF xiii 6.
v. *š'l$_1$*, *šnṣy*.

yṣb$_1$ **OffAr** PA 'EL Part. pass. s.m. abs. *myṣb* Krael 9^{22} (cf. Kutscher JAOS lxxiv 237, Yaron Bibl xli 274, Grelot DAE p. 246 n. r, Porten & Greenfield JEAS p. 60, Porten & Yardeni sub TADAE B 3.10 :: Krael a.l.: l. *myḥb* = lapsus for *mḥyb* (= PA 'EL Part. pass. s.m. abs. of *ḥwb$_1$*) :: J.J.Rabinowitz Law 114: l. *myḥb* < Egypt. (= legitimate) - ¶ verb PA 'EL Part. pass. valid (said of document).

yṣb$_2$ **OffAr** Sing. m. abs. *yṣb* Krael 10^{17} - ¶ adj. valid (said of a document; cf. also Weinfeld UF viii 410).

yṣd v. *ṣd'$_1$*.

yṣlh **Pun** Sing. (or Plur.) abs. *yṣlt* KAI 69^{4,6,8,10,13} - ¶ subst. of unknown meaning indicating part of victim; poss. = joint/shoulder joint, cf. e.g. Cooke NSI p. 118, Prätorius ZDMG lx 165, Lidzbarski sub KI 63, Lagrange ERS 470, 473, Röllig KAI a.l., Amadasi ICO p. 177, Rosenthal ANET 656f., cf. however Dussaud Orig 148f.: = thigh, cf. also vd Branden RSO xl 117, Capuzzi StudMagr ii 65f. (for other interpret., cf. also CIS i sub 165) - on this word, cf. also Amadasi Guzzo SSMA 116.

yṣʿ v. *ṣʿy*.

yṣp **OffAr** QAL Impf. 2 p.s.m. *tṣp* Herm 3^{3}; 2 p.s.f. *tṣpy* Herm 1^{4}, 4^{8}, 8^{14}; 2 p.pl.m. *tṣpw* Herm 2^{3}, 3^{12}, 8^{8}; Part. act. m. s. abs. *yṣp* Herm 3^{12}, 8^{10} (dam. context); pl.m. abs. *yṣpn* Herm 4^{8} - ¶ verb QAL to be concerned, to worry; + l_5, *ʾl tṣpw lh* Herm 1^{4}: do not be concerned about him (cf. Herm 2^{3}, $3^{3,12,12f.}$, 4^{8}, $8^{8f.,14f.}$) - for the use of this verb in formulae in the Herm. papyri, cf. Dion RB lxxxvi 571ff.

yṣq **Ph** the *yṣq* in RES 828A 1 = subst. Sing. abs. meaning "cast statue"?, cf. Lidzbarski Eph ii 161.

yṣr **Pun** Sing. abs. *yṣr* CIS i 137^{2}, Mozia vi 96B 3 (= SMI 16) - ¶ subst. m. potter.

yṣt **Hebr** Milik DJD ii p. 167: read *yṣtw* (= HIPH Impf. 3 p.pl.m. of *yṣt* (= to burn)) in DJD ii 47^{5}? (uncert. reading and interpret.; dam. context).

v. *ṣtt*.

yqb **Ph** Kornfeld sub Abydos 15: l. *ʾqb* in RES 1349^{2} (= QAL Impf. 1 p.s. of *yqb* (= to enter)?); highly uncert. interpret. :: the emendation (div. otherwise) *ʾqrʾ* (= QAL Impf. 1 p.s. of $qrʾ_1$), cf. RES a.l.

yqd **OldAr** Impf. 3 p.s.m. *yqd* KAI 222A 37; 3 p.s.f. *tqd* KAI 222A 35, 37 - **OffAr** QAL Part. act. f. s. abs. *yqdh* Aḥiq 103 - **JAr** QAL Impf. 3 p.s.m. *yqwd* AMB 10^{5} - ¶ verb to burn (intrans.); *ʾšh yqdh hy* Aḥiq 103: it is a burning fire (for the context, cf. Lindenberger APA 84); + b_2, *ʾyk zy tqd šʿwtʾ zʾ bʾš* KAI 222A 35: just as this wax is burned by fire, cf. KAI 222A 37 (for the contexts, cf. Fitzmyer AIS 52f., Weinfeld Lesh xxxviii 234 (n. 13)); cf. also AMB $10^{4f.}$ (heavily dam. context).

yqy v. *rkn*.

yqyr **OffAr** Sing. m. abs. *yqyr* Aḥiq 93, 108, 111; Plur. abs. *yqyrn* JA ccliv 440^{5} (for the reading, cf. Shaked JRAS '69, 119, Kutscher, Naveh & Shaked Lesh xxxiv 128f. :: Dupont-Sommer JA ccliv 440, 460, 462bis, 463: l. *gmyrn* = QAL Part. pass.m. pl. abs. of gmr_1(= instructed ones, scholars) or l. *gmyln* (= variant of *gmyrn*), cf. also Teixidor Syr xlvi 350); Sing. f. abs. *yqyrh* Aḥiq 95; emph. *yqyrtʾ* Aḥiq 130; cf. Frah xxvi 8 (*ykl*) - ¶ adj. - **1)** heavy: Aḥiq 111; *[z]ptʾ yqyrtʾ* Aḥiq 130: a heavy loan - **2)** precious: Aḥiq 93, 108 (// *špyr*); *ʾp lʾlhn yqyrh hy* Aḥiq 95: even to the gods it is precious - **3)** the *yqyrn* in JA ccliv 440^{5} indication of the elders, cf. Shaked JRAS '69, 121, Kutscher, Naveh & Shaked Lesh xxxiv 129.

yqp₁ **OldAr** Fitzmyer AIS 18f., 68, 158: the lettergroup *tqpyqpy* in KAI 222B 29 (left unexplained by e.g. Dupont-Sommer Sf p. 64, 80, Donner KAI a.l., Degen AAG p. 14 n. 63) = *tqp* (= QAL Impf. 2 p.s.m.) + *yqpy* (= QAL Part. act. pl.m. + suff. 1 p.s.) both forms of the root *yqp* (= to go around, to surround), you must surround those who surround me (poss. interpret.); cf. also Sader EAS 131 (n. 51): *tqp* (= QAL Impf. 2 p.s.m. of *yqp₁* (= to take position)) *yqpy* (= Sing. + suff. 1 p.s. of *yqp₂* (= position)), cf. however Lipiński Stud 36f.: *tqp* = QAL Impf. 2 p.s.m. of *nqp* (= to smite :: Lipiński ibid.: or = PA ʿEL (= to smite)) :: Lipiński Stud 37: *yqpy* = PA ʿEL Impf. 3 p.s.m. + suff. 1 p.s. of root *qp* (= to encom pass.); cf. also Lemaire & Durand IAS 124, 138.

yqp₂ v. *yqp₁*.

yqr₁ **OffAr** HAPH Pf. 2 p.s.m. *hwqrt* Aḥiq 176 (cf. however Kottsieper SAS 18, 207: or = Pf. 1 p.s.? :: Ungnad ArPap p. 78: l. *hḥqrt* = HAPH Pf. 2 p.s.m. of *ḥqr*(= to pride oneself or = to spy out?)); Imper. s.m. *hwqr* Aḥiq 98 - **Palm** APH Pf. 3 p.s.f. *ʾwqrt* CIS ii 4518A 3 - ¶ verb HAPH/APH - **1)** to make heavy; + obj., *[ʿl] zy š[mʿt] hwqr lbb* Aḥiq 98: over what you hear harden your heart (i.e. be reserved; on this text cf. Lindenberger APA 75, 236 n. 167, Greenfield FS Fitzmyer 50) - **2)** to honour: Aḥiq 176; + obj., *ʾwqrt ... ʾḥwh wbnwhy* CIS ii 4518A 3f.: she has honoured her brother and his sons - L.H.Gray AJSL xxxix 77f.: *chor* in Poen 942 = QAL Impf. 3 p.s.m. of *yqr₁* (improb. interpret.; cf. also Sznycer PPP 122ff. on this line).

v. *qrʾ₁*, *qry₁*.

yqr₂ **Palm** Sing. abs. *yqr* Inscr P 11⁴; cstr. *yqr* CIS ii 3940⁴, 3943⁵, 3948⁴, 3949⁴, 3950³, 4160³ (Greek par. τειμὴν), Inv xi 81³, Ber xix 69³, etc., *qr* (in *lqr* pro *lyqr*) CIS ii 4192; emph. *yqrʾ* SBS 48⁷; + suff. 3 p.s.m. *yqrh* CIS ii 3915⁵, 3917⁶, 3920³, 3921², 3922³, Inv xi 71³, SBS 37⁴, 48⁸ (Greek par. τειμῆς), etc., etc.; + suff. 3 p.s.f. *yqrh* CIS ii 3954³, 4518A 3, 4542², AAS xxxvi/xxxvii 168 no. 9⁵; + suff. 3 p.pl.m. *yqrhwn* CIS ii 3930⁵, 3931⁴, 4121², 4124³, 4163⁴, Inv xi 85², RIP 24⁶, etc., etc., *yqrhyn* Inv x 119b 3, *yqrhn* CIS ii 4122³, 4123bis 4, 4130², Ber ii 88⁸, etc.; Plur. abs. *yqryn* SBS 45⁶, DFD 13¹⁰ - **Hatra** Sing. cstr. *qr* (in *lqr* pro *lyqr*) 65⁵ (cf. Aggoula MUSJ xlvii 29f., Vattioni IH p. 45f. :: Safar Sumer xi 8f. (n. 25 (div. otherwise)): l. *lqrt* = l_5 + *qrt* (= QAL Inf. of *qrr₁* (= to make cold > to appease)) :: Caquot Syr xxxii 266 (div. otherwise): l. *qrtgryʾ* = Plur. emph. of *qrtgr* (< Iran., meaning unknown)) - **JAr** Sing. + suff. 3 p.s.f. (or Sing. emph.) *yqrh* MPAT-A 12⁶ (= Frey 1195 = SM 71), 28¹ (*[y]qrh*)ʾ³ (= Frey 855 = SM 34) - ¶ subst. - **1)** honour; frequently in the expression *lyqr ...*: in honour of; cf. e.g. *lqrh* Ber xix 66¹⁰: in his honour (Greek par. αὐτοῦ τειμῆς χάριν); *lyqrhwn dy ʿlm* RIP 24⁶: to their everlasting honour (cf. however Aggoula Syr liv 282: transl. rather, to their honour upon earth), etc.,

etc. (cf. also Díez Merino LA xxi 106 (n. 60)); *lyqrhn ʿd ʿlmʾ* CIS ii 4123bis 4: to their everlasting honour; *lyqrhwn lʿlmʾ* FS Miles 50 ii 9: to their everlasting honour; *lqr tgryʾ* Hatra 65^5: in honour of the merchants; *lyqrh dknyštʾ* MPAT-A 12^6: in honour of the congregation; *lyqr* followed by name of deity poss. in RIP $125^{2f.}$ (cf. Starcky AAS vii 101, Gawlikowski RIP a.l., TP 64f., cf. however Milik DFD 251); cf. also the expressions *yqr bt ʿlmʾ* CIS ii 4192: the magnificent tomb (× Joüon Syr xix 100: tomb serving as a honorary monument, cf. also Gawlikowski Ber xxi 14 (n. 70); cf. Greek par. in Inv iv 22: αἰώνιος τειμή and Inv 6b: μνημεῖον αἰώνιον γέρας (cf. also Milik DFD 222)); *yqrhwn dy bt ʿlmʾ* CIS ii 4121^2: their magnificent tomb (v. however supra), cf. Syr lxii 271^5 - cf. also the diff. expression *ʿm yqrʾ dy bwlʾ wdms* in SBS 48^7, Cantineau Syr xvii 280f. (relating it with following words): = at the expense of Senate and People (cf. also Dunant SBS a.l.: = with contribution of Senate and People, relating it to preceding words); Milik DFD 312 (relating it to following words): = with the consent (litt. honour) of Senate and People (cf. also Gawlikowski TP 27: in consequence of a honorary decree of Senate and People, relating it to following words) - **2)** honour, preferment; *yqryn šgyʾyn* SBS 45^6: many honours/preferments; *bdgmyn wyqryn wṣ[l]myn* DFD 13^{10}: by decrees, honours and statues (cf. Greek par. ψηφίσμασι καὶ ἀνδριᾶσι τειμηθέντα).

yrʾh **Ph** v.d.Branden BO 12, 215: l. *y[r]ʾt* (= Sing. cstr. of *yrʾh* (= respect, regard)) in KAI 50^5 (uncert. reading and interpret.).

yrd **Ph** QAL Impf. 3 p.s.m. *yrd* KAI $27^{24f.}$ (for this reading, cf. Cross & Saley BASOR cxcvii 46f., Röllig NESE ii 19, de Moor JEOL xxvii 108, 110 :: Albright BASOR lxxvi 10, Röllig KAI a.l., FR 158: l. *tld* = QAL Impf. 3 p.s.f. of yld_1 (cf. also Gaster Or xi 44) :: du Mesnil du Buisson FS Dussaud 424, 433: l. *twd* (Sing. abs.) = favour? :: v.d.Branden BO iii 43, 47: l. twr_3 (= turtle- dove > innocent child) :: v.d.Branden BiOr xxxiii 13: l. *nkd* (Sing. abs.) = offspring :: Gibson SSI iii p. 88: l. *ʾwr* = PIʿEL Pf. 3 p.s.m. of $ʾwr_1$ (= to make light; cf. Lipiński RTAT 266) :: Caquot FS Gaster 51, Garbini OA xx 286: l. *ʾwr* = Sing. abs. of $ʾwr_2$ (= light; cf. Avishur PIB 248, cf. also Torczyner JNES vi 27)); YIPH Pf. 3 p.s.m. + suff. 3 p.pl.m. *yrdm* KAI 26A i 20 (cf. FR 158, 267b also for litt., interpret. as Inf. abs. (cf. also Loewenstamm JANES ii 53, Chiera Hen x 134f.) less prob. :: Dupont-Sommer RA xlii 171: poss. < root *rdy* = to dominate, cf. also idem ArchOr xviii^3 45, cf. however idem JKF ii 192) - **Pun** QAL Part. act. s.m. abs. *yrd* KAI 145^8 (cf. Février Sem vi 21, v.d.Branden RSF i 166, 169; diff. context, for other interpret., cf. Krahmalkov RSF iii 188f., 193, 201: = QAL Pf. 3 p.s.m., Cooke NSI p. 155: poss. = form of YIPH Pf. (cf. also Röllig KAI a.l., BiOr xxvii 379)) - **Mo** QAL Impf. 1 p.s. *ʾrd* KAI 181^{32}; Imper. s.m.

rd KAI 181[32] - **Hebr** QAL Pf. 3 p.s.m. *yrd* KAI 193[14] (cf. however Hoftijzer FS Hospers 87, 91 n. 18); Impf. 3 p.s.m. TA-H 40[10f.] (*[y]rd*, v. however infra); HOPH Pf. 3 p.s.m. *hwrd* DJD ii 24B 12 (dam. context, uncert. interpret., cf. Milik ibid. p. 128) - ¶ verb QAL to descend: KAI 181[32] (cf. however Segert ArchOr xxix 241); *yrd šr ḥṣb*ᵓ *... lb*ᵓ *mṣrymh* KAI 193[14ff.]: the commander of the army has descended on his way (litt. to go) to Egypt; *[bṭrm y]rd ym* TA-H 40[10f.]: before sunset (cf. Aharoni TA a.l., cf. however Pardee UF x 325, HAHL 65) - **1)** + *b*$_2$, *yrd b*ᶜ*mq* KAI 145[8]: descending in the valley (v. however supra) - **2)** + *l*$_5$, *w*ᵓ*[l] yrd lmzzt* KAI 27[24f.]: let him not descend to my doorposts (diff. context; v. *mzzh*) - YIPH to bring down, to deport (cf. also Puech RB xxxviii 97); + obj.: KAI 26A i 20 - HOPH to be sent away: DJD ii 24B 12 (v. however supra).
v. *rd*$_3$.

yrḥ$_1$ **Ph** Sing. abs. *yrḥ* KAI 26A iv 3, C v 7 - ¶ subst. moon - the same noun (Sing. abs. *yrḥ*) prob. also in off Ar RES 1785F 3.

yrḥ$_2$ **Ph** Sing. abs. *yrḥ* KAI 14[1], 32[1] (= Kition A 2), 33[1] (= Kition A 1), 37A 1, 2, B 2 (= Kition C 1), 38[2], 43[6,7,12], Mus li 286[2], etc.; cstr. *yrḥ* CIS i 13[1] (= Kition A 27; or abs.?, v. also *zbḥ*$_2$); Plur. abs. *yrḥm* BIFAO xxxviii 3[9] (dam. context) - **Pun** Sing. abs. *yrḥ* KAI 81[5], 110[3], 111[3], 112[4], 119[3], 137[5], 159[5], CIS i 124[2], 179[5], Hofra 57[3], 61[3], 64[3], Trip 51[5]; cstr. *yrḥ* KAI 277[4] (or abs.?; v. also *zbḥ*$_2$) - **Hebr** Sing. cstr. *yrḥ* KAI 182[3,4,5,7] (v. infra); Dual cstr. *yrḥw* KAI 182[1,2,6] (cf. Lemaire VT xxv 15ff., Lipiński OLP viii 82f., Conrad TUAT i 247 (for a comparable though historically incorrect interpret., cf. Ginsberg ArchOr viii 146, cf. also Halpern FS Lambdin 132f.) :: Garbini AION vi 124ff., ISNO 114, Gibson SSI i p. 3: = Plur. cstr. (nom.) :: Albright BASOR xcii 22ff.: = Dual + suff. 3 p.s.m., interpreting the Sing. form *yrḥ* in ll. 3, 4, 5, 7 as Sing. + suff. 3 p.s.m. (cf. also (Skehan with) CF 46f. (n. 11), Cross FS Glück p. 305 n. 3, Rainey JBL cii 630, Knauf ZAH iii 14) :: Segal JSS vii 212ff.: l. *yrḥ 2* = two months; for proposed interpret. of this form, cf. Cassuto SMSR xii 108f., Dir p. 5f., Mosc p. 8ff., Lemaire VT xxv 15ff., Lipiński OLP viii 82ff., Zevit MLAHE 6) - **OffAr** Sing. abs. *yrḥ* Cowl 2[1], 10[1,5], Krael 2[1], 3[1], 4[1], RES 438[3], FX 136[1], Beh 32 (Akkad. par. *ar-ḫi*), ATNS 6[2] (highly uncert. reading, cf. Porten & Yardeni sub TADAE B 8.12), etc., etc.; emph. *yrḥ*ᵓ Cowl 11[3,4] Lidzb Ass 5[5] (= AECT 50), 6[4] (= AECT 51; cf. also Lipiński Stud 108, 110), ATNS 29[4], FX 136[15]; Plur. abs. *yrḥyn* Cowl 81[21], *yrḥn* Cowl 45[8]; cf. Frah xxvii 2 (*byrḥ*), xxviii 31 (*byrḥ*), Paik 510 (*yrḥ*ᵓ), 511 (*byrḥ*), Nisa-b 2167[1], Nisa-c 164[2] (*yrḥ*), Sogd R 56, ZDMG xcii 441[1], 442B 1, Syn 300[1], 301[1], 304[1], 305[1], 306[1], 307[1], 308[1,2], 310[1], 311[1], BSOAS xxxiii 147[1], GIPP 21, 68, SaSt 16 - **Nab** Sing. abs. *yrḥ* CIS ii 158[4], 161[6], 170[1], 182[3], 184[3], IEJ xi 137[2] (for the reading, cf. Naveh IEJ xvii 188), etc., etc., *yḥ* (lapsus) CIS ii 213[8] - **Palm** Sing. abs. *yrḥ* CIS ii 3902[2], 3911[2], 3913 i 1, 3914[5], 3915[5], Inv xi 1[7], 2[4], xii 1[3], 22[1], SBS 7[2], 10[1], 48[9] (Greek par. μηνὸς), Syr lxii 257 (Greek par. μηνεὶ), Sem xxxvi 89[1], etc., etc., *yḥ*(lapsus) CIS ii 4028[7] - **Hatra** Sing. abs. *yrḥ* 34[1], 36[1], 62[1], 65[1], 108[1], 235[3], 288a 1, 293[1], 294[1], app. 4[1], 6[1], 11[1], cf. also Syr xl 125 - **JAr** Sing. abs. *yrḥ* MPAT-A 50[3] (= Frey 1208), 51[4] (cf. Frey 1208), 52[4]; Plur. abs. *[y]rḥyn* MPAT 62[13] (diff. reading, cf. Greenfield sub DBKP 27) - ¶ subst. m. month, passim; *yrḥw ʾsp* KAI 182[1]: two months of ingathering (v. *ʾsp*$_2$; cf. KAI 182[1f.,2,3], etc.); cf. also the following expressions: *yrḥ byrḥ* Cowl 11[5], 17[3] (cf. however (Yardeni with) Porten RB xc 412: l. prob. *yrḥ kyrḥ*, cf. also Porten & Yardeni sub TADAE A 6.1), ATNS 25[3] (cf. Dion RB lxxxix 548f.), *yrḥ lyrḥ* Cowl 11[9], *yrḥ md yrḥ* KAI 43[12]: month by month, monthly (cf. also *yrḥ yrḥ* Cowl 67 viii 1? (heavily dam. context)); *kl yrḥn wšnn* Cowl 45[8]: every month and year (cf. Yaron JNES xx 128); *yrbh ʿly ksp ḥlrn 2 ltql 1 lyrḥ 1 hwh ksp ḥlrn 8 lyrḥ ḥd* Cowl 10[4ff.]: (interest) from me shall accrue (at the rate of) 2 *ḥ*. silver per shekel per month, being 8 *ḥ*. silver per month (cf. Cowl 11[4] and *lyrḥʾ* Cowl 11[3]); *lmbyrḥ ḥyr* KAI 81[5]: since the month Ch.; *hn lʾ šlmt lk kl kspk ... ʿd yrḥ tḥwt ...* Cowl 11[7f.]: if I do not pay you all your silver ... by the month of T. ...; *byn yrḥ[ʾ zn]h* Cowl 29[6]: within this month (??, heavily dam. text, cf. Cowl a.l.; for the context, cf. also Porten & Yardeni sub TADAE B 4.5); *lrš yrḥʾ* FX 136[15]: at the beginning of the month (i.e. of every month) - in dates: - a) *yrḥ tḥwt* Krael 11[1]: in the month T. (cf. KAI 236 Vs. 6f., Lidzb Ass 5[5f.], MAI xiv/2, 66[1]) - b) *byrḥ bl* KAI 14[1]: in the month of B. (cf. KAI 38[2], 43[6], 110[3], 119[3], Cowl 20[1], Krael 7[1], CIS ii 158[4], 161[6], 3911[2], Inv xi 1[7f.], xii 1[3], SBS 7[2], RIP 24[6] (*byrḥ nysn*, Greek par. μηνὶ ξανδικῷ), Hatra 34[1], 36[1], 62[1], MPAT-A 51[4], etc., etc.); *byrḥ nysn ywm 18* CIS ii 3913 i 1: in the month of N. on the 18th day (cf. RIP 135[5], 141[2f.]; cf. also RIP 142[2f.]); *byrḥ ʾb bywm 15* PNO 55D 4: in the month of A. on the 15th day; *bywm tltt bḥdʿšr ywmyn byrḥ ʾlwl* MPAT-A 52[3f.]: on the third day (sc. of the week) on the 11th day in the month of E.; *bryš yrḥ mrḥšwn* MPAT-A 50[3f.]: at the beginning of the month of M.; *bḥdš yrḥ pʿlt* KAI 37B 2: with the new moon of the month of P. (cf. KAI 37A 2); for a survey of Palm. material, cf. also Díez Merino LA xxi 79ff. - c) *ywm 4 lyrḥ tḥwt* Cowl 10[1]: on the fourth day of the month T. (cf. Cowl 13[1], Krael 3[1], 4[1], etc.); *bymm 6 lyrḥ bl* KAI 32[1]: on the sixth day of the month of B. (cf. KAI 33[1], 40[1], CIS i 13[1]); *bʿsr wšmn lyrḥ mrpʾm* KAI 111[2f.]: on the 18th (day) of the month of M. (cf. KAI 112[3f.], 137[5], Hofra 57[3], Cowl 2[1], etc.) - Aharoni TA p. 40f.: l. *yrḥ* (= Sing. abs.) *ṣḥ* (name of month) in TA-H 20[2] (cf. e.g. Gibson SSI i p. 51; cf. also Heltzer Shn iii 279f.; highly uncert. reading, cf. Weippert ZDPV lxxx 183, Naveh Lesh xxx 72, Teixidor Syr xliv 170,

cf. also Lemaire VT xxiii 243ff., IH i p. 184 (cf. idem Or lii 446, Lipiński OLP viii 91): l. poss. *gr' bn 'zyhw*, prob. reading) - Milik Syr xliv 297: l. *[y]rḥh* (= Sing. emph.) in Hatra 49^3 (improb. reading; cf. for other reading proposals, Caquot Syr xxxii 54: l. *?ḥṣ*, Milik RN vi/iv 56 n. 2: l. *r/dḥṣ*, Vattioni IH a.l.: l. *dḥṣ* (all without interpret.).
v. *rwḥ₁*.

yry₁ OldCan QAL pass. Impf. 3 p.s.f. *tu-ra* EA 245^8 (cf. Rainey EA p. 65) - ¶ verb QAL pass. to be shot (said of a mare hit by an arrow).

yry₂ v. *hwr'h*.

yrkh Hebr Dual cstr. *yrkty* IEJ xxxii 195^3 (or div. otherwise, l. *yrktyw* (= Dual + suff. 3 p.s.m.??); heavily dam. context) - ¶ subst. recess.

yr' OffAr Cowl p. 213, 231: l. poss. *yr'k* in Aḥiq 43 (= QAL or PA'EL Pf. 3 p.s.m. + suff. 2 p.s.m. of *yr'* = to injure (cf. also Driver AnOr xii 55)), less prob. reading, cf. Grelot DAE p. 449 n. c: l. *brk* (= Sing. + suff. 2 p.s.m. of *br₁*;cf. also Fitzmyer Bibl lvi 256) :: Rosenthal AH i/1, 15, i/2, 11: l. *yd'k* (= QAL Pf. 3 p.s.m. + suff. 2 p.s.m. of *yd'₂*(= to abandon); for this text, cf. also Degen ZDMG cxix 174) :: Ginsberg ANET 428 (n. 1): l. *yd'k* = QAL Impf. 3 p.s.m. of *d'k*?:: Epstein ZAW xxxii 132: l. *yb'k* = Impf. pass. of *b'k*(= to be trampled upon)??, cf. Nöldeke AGWG xiv/4, 9; cf. also Sach p. 153: l. *y[..]k*.

yrq OldAr Sing. abs. *yrq* KAI 222A 28 - **OffAr**, cf. Frah vi 1 (*ylk'*) - ¶ subst. 1) verdure: KAI 222A 28 (for the context, cf. Greenfield ActOr xxix 15 (n. 44); cf. also Fronzaroli RCL '60, 129 and cf. *'ḥw*) - **2)** vegetables: Frah vi 1.

yrqn = yellowness > Akkad. *jarqānu* = a certain type of garden-herb, cf. v.Soden Or xxxv 12, xlvi 188, cf. also idem AHW s.v. *jarqānu*.

yrš Mo QAL Impf. 3 p.s.m. *yrš* KAI 181^7 - **Hebr** QAL Part. act. pl.m. cstr. *yršy* DJD ii 22,1-9^3, *ywršy* DJD ii 22,1-9^{11}; + suff. 3 p.s.m. *yršw* DJD ii 30^{23} - **OldAr** QAL Impf. 3 p.s.m. *yrt* KAI 222C 24 (for the form, cf. Blau IOS ii 73; for other interpret., cf. Dupont-Sommer Sf p. 94, Segert Arch Or xxxii 119, Fitzmyer AIS 150, Degen WO iv 50 n. 10, AAG p. 43, Röllig WO vi 130, Ben-Chayyim Lesh xxxv 248f., Gibson SSI ii p. 43, Lipiński OLP viii 98, Coxon ZDMG cxxix 15, 21 :: Rosenthal ANET 660 (n. 10), Kaufman Maarav iii 173, Garr DGSP 119 (div. otherwise): l. *yrtš[y/h]* = IPHT Impf. 3 p.s.m. of *ršy₁*) - **OffAr** QAL Impf. 3 p.s.m. + suff. 3 p.s.f. *yrtnh* Cowl 15^{21}, Krael 7^{35} - **Palm** QAL Pf. 3 p.s.m. *wrš* (cf. Cantineau Gramm 73, 150, Blau PC 46 n. 2: < Arab. (cf. also Diem ZDMG cxxiv 251)) - ¶ verb QAL - **1)** to take possession of; + obj. (territory): KAI 181^7 (through conquest) - **2)** to inherit - a) + obj., *'l yrt šr[š]h 'šm* KAI 222C 24f.: may his stock inherit no name - b) + obj. + *b₂*, *'sḥwr hw yrtnh bnksyh* Cowl 15^{21}: A., he shall inherit from her her goods (cf. Krael 7^{35}, dam. context, cf. also Porten & Greenfield JEAS p. 56), for the context, cf. Freund

WZKM xxi 177, Yaron Gifts 14f., Law 69f., Hoftijzer BiOr xxi 221f., Porten Arch 211, 225, Fitzmyer FS Albright ii 160, Gottlieb JSS xxvi 196f. - QAL Part. act. heir: DJD ii 22,1-9[3,11], 30[22].
v. *wrš*h, *y*ʾ*yrt*,*yrt*$_2$, *trš*$_2$.

yršh_1 v. *wršh*.

yršh_2 **Pun** Sing. abs. (?, dam. context), cf. IRT 828[2] *yrysoth* (cf. Levi Della Vida OA ii 78, Vattioni AION xvi 49; prob. interpret.) - ¶ subst. meaning originally heritage; exact meaning in context unknown; Levi Della Vida OA ii 78f.: = possession, substance; Vattioni AION xvi 49, Aug xvi 538: = testament.

yrt_1 v. *y*ʾ*yrt*,*yrš*,*ytr*$_1$.

yrt_2 **Nab** Sing. abs. *yrt* CIS ii 206[3]; cstr. *yrt* MPAT 64 recto i 7 - **JAr** Sing. + suff. 2 p.pl.m. *yrtkn* MPAT 45[5], 52[12]; + suff. 3 p.pl.m. *yrthn* MPAT 52[9,10]; Plur. + suff. 3 p.s.m. *yrtwhy* DJD ii 23[6] (for this poss. reading, cf. Beyer ATTM 312); + suff. 2 p.s.m. *yrtyk* MPAT 41[13], 44 xxiii 2 (*yrty[k]*; heavily dam. context) - ¶ subst. m. (or QAL Part. act. m. of *yrš*$_1$ (= *yrš*?)) heir: CIS ii 206[3], MPAT 41[13], 44 xxiii 2 (v. supra), 64 recto i 7; used collectively, heirs: MPAT 45[5], 52[9,10,12]. For meaning, cf. also ʾ*ṣdq*- > Akkad. *jāritu*, cf. v.Soden Or xxxv 12, xlvi 188, idem AHW s.v., cf. also CAD s.v., cf. already Meissner AfO xi 154 - the diff. *yrth* in KAI 260[8] poss. = *yrt*$_2$ (= Sing. + suff. 3 p.s.m.), cf. Littmann Sardis 29, Lidzbarski ZA xxxi 130 (cf. also Donner KAI a.l.) :: Lipiński Stud 155, 160f.: l. *yrth* = Sing. + suff. 3 p.s.m. of *yrt*$_3$ (= inheritance), cf. also Millard JSS xxi 177 (cf. however Degen WO ix 170) :: Kahle & Sommer KlF i 77, Driver AnOr xii 54: l. *ypth* = QAL Impf. 3 p.s.m. + suff. 3 p.s.m. of *ptt*$_1$ (= to destroy) :: Cowley CRAI '21, 13: l. *ypth* = QAL Impf. 3 p.s.m. of *pty*$_1$ (= to be stretched, to be knocked down) :: Driver AnOr xii 54: or *ypth* = lapsus for *yptnh/yptwnh* (= QAL Impf. 3 p.pl.m. + suff. 3 p.s.m. of *ptt*$_1$) :: Donner KAI a.l.: or l. *ypth* = PA ʿEL Impf. 3 p.s.m. + suff. 3 p.s.m. of *pty*$_1$ (= to break down); cf. also Torrey AJSL xxxiv 198.

yrt_3 v. *yrt*$_2$.

yrtw = inheritance > Akkad. *jāritūtu*, cf. v.Soden Or xxxv 12, xlvi 188, cf. also CAD s.v., cf. already Meissner AfO xi 154.

yš **Hebr** *yš* SM 49[20,24,26], (combined with *š*$_{10}$) DJD ii 24C 7 (*š*ʾ*yš*), 30[23] (*šyš*), ʾ*š*EI xx 256[12] (*š*ʾ*š*) - ¶ subst. (prob. related etymologically to ʾ*yty*, ʾ*t*$_3$), orig. meaning: presence, existence, to be translated: there is; *kl šyš ly* DJD ii 30[23]: everything that is mine; *qṣt* ʿ*pr š*ʾ*yš b*ʿ*yr* ... DJD ii 24 C 7f.: a plot which is in I. ...; *w*ʾ*m yš mqwm š* ... SM 49[26]: if there is a place where ...; *yš* ʾ*wmryn* SM 49[20]: there are people who say ... (cf. SM 49[24]); *kwl š*ʾ*š* ʿ*l hšṭr hz*ʾ EI xx 256[12]: everything which stands in this document (sc. what is written in it) - poss. the same word in Karth xii 54[1] (ʾ*š*),cf. Krahmalkov RSF iii 178f., 186, 200, v.d.Branden

RSF v 62.
v. ʾš$_1$,*lyš*$_1$, š$_{10}$.

yšb$_1$ **Ph** QAL Pf. 3 p.s.m. *yšb* KAI 26A i 11 (cf. FR 158, 267b also for litt.; interpret. as Inf. (abs.) (cf. also Gai Or li 254ff.) less prob.; or interpret. as YIPH Pf. 3 p.s.m. + suff. 3 p.s.m. preferable?, cf. v.d.Branden Meltô i 41, 76, Lipiński RTAT 258, Puech RB lxxxviii 100, Amadasi Guzzo VO iii 94, Gibson SSI iii p. 47, 57f., Swiggers BiOr xxxvii 338); 1 p.s. *yšbt* KAI 24[9]; Impf. 3 p.s.m. *yšb* KAI 24[14]; Inf. cstr. *šbt* KAI 26A ii 7, 13 (cf. e.g. FR 158, O'Callaghan Or xviii 187, Röllig KAI a.l. , Avishur PIB 224, 231 × Dupont-Sommer RA xli 166: = Sing. abs. of *šbt*$_3$ (= rest (< root *šbt* = to rest) :: Loewenstamm CSBA 34f.: = Sing. abs. of *šbh*$_2$ (= withdrawal)); + suff. 3 p.pl.m. *šbtnm* KAI 26A i 17; Part. act. s.m. abs. *yšb* KAI 26A iii 8 (:: Amadasi Guzzo VO iii 102: or = form of YIPH?), C iv 8 (for both A ii 8 and C iv 8 :: Bron RIPK 109 (cf. also Pardee JNES xlii 67) : = QAL Impf. 3 p.s.m.), CIS i 102a 1 (??, cf. RES 1305, FR 158) - YIPH Pf. 3 p.s.m. *yšb* KAI 26A ii 18 (cf. FR 158, 267b also for litt. (cf. also Chiera Hen x 134f.); interpret. as Inf. (abs.) less prob.), EpAn ix 5[5] (cf. also Long & Pardee AO vii 263, Elayi SCA 64; or perhaps = QAL Pf. 3 p.s.m.?; cf. also Mosca & Russell EpAn ix 14f.); + suff. 3 p.pl.m. *yšbm* KAI 26A i 20 (cf. also FR 158, 267b); 1 p.s. *yšbt* KAI 26A ii 1; 1 p.pl. *yšrn* (prob. lapsus for *yšbn*) KAI 14[16]; + suff. 3 p.s.m. *yšbny* KAI 14[17] - **Pun** QAL Inf. cstr. + suff. 3 p.s.m., cf. Poen 938: *sibitthim* (cf. e.g. Sznycer PPP 103f. :: FR 158: = QAL Inf. cstr. + suff. 3 p.pl.m., cf. also J.J.Glück & Maurach Semitics ii 112f.); Part. act. s.m. cstr. (or pl. cstr.?, cf. v.d.Branden RSF i 168) *yšb* KAI 145[3] - **Mo** QAL Pf. 3 p.s.m. *yšb* KAI 181[10,31]; Impf. 3 p.s.m. *yšb* KAI 181[8,19]; HIPH Impf. 1 p.s. ʾ*šb* KAI 181[13] - **Hebr** QAL Part. act. s.m. abs. *yšb* TA-H 18[10] (cf. Aharoni TA a.l., Freedman IEJ xix 56, Pardee UF x 315, 317ff., HAHL 55, 241 (cf. also Weinberg ZAW lxxxvii 363ff., Eissfeldt FS Altheim i 79f., Smelik HDAI 105) × Albright ANET 569: = QAL Impf. 3 p.s.m. (interpret. of context less prob.) × Fritz WO vii 138ff.: = QAL Impf. 3 p.s.m. of *šwb* (interpret. of context less prob.) :: Levine IEJ xix 49ff.: = HIPH Impf. 3 p.s.m. of *šwb* (cf. already Aharoni IEJ xvi 6 n. 14)), *ywšb* DJD ii 24B 4, C 4 (*[yw]šb*), D 4, E 3, 42[4] (for the reading, cf. e.g. de Vaux RB lx 270, Ginsberg BASOR cxxxi 26, Birnbaum PEQ '55, 23, Bardtke ThLZ lxxix 301, Milik DJD ii a.l. (also for further litt.) :: I.Rabinowitz BASOR cxxxi 21f.: pro *šywšb* ʾ*byt* l. *šyyšr*ʾ (= orthographic variant of *šy*ʾ*šrh* = š$_{10}$ + PIʿEL Impf. 3 p.s.m. + suff. 3 p.s.f. of ʾ*šr*$_1$ (= to certify)) *byt*) - **DA** QAL Imper. pl.m. *šbw* i 7 (for the reading problems, cf. v.d.Kooij DA p. 105, cf. also McCarter BASOR ccxxxix 51, 53) - **Samal** QAL Pf. 1 p.s. *yšbt* KAI 214[8]; 3 p.pl.m. *yš[bw]* KAI 214[8] (or = Impf. 3 p.pl.m.?, cf. Dion 486 n. 9); Impf. 3 p.s.m. *yšb* KAI 214[15,20,25]; Part. pass. pl.f.

abs. *yšbt* KAI 215^4; HAPH Pf. 3 p.s.m. + suff. 1 p.s. *hwšbny* KAI 215^{19}; 1 p.s. *hwšbt* KAI 214^{19} - **OldAr** QAL Impf. 3 p.s.m. *yšb* KAI 224^{17} (:: Garbini RSO xxxiv 49: = Part. act. m. s. abs.); 3 p.pl.m. *y[šb]n* KAI 224^6 (cf. e.g. Dupont-Sommer Sf p. 144, Fitzmyer AIS 110, Degen AAG p. 74, Donner KAI a.l.); Imper. pl.m. *šbw* KAI 224^7; Part. act. s.m. cstr. *ysb* Tell F 5, 16; HAPH Pf. 3 p.s.m. + suff. 1 p.s. *hwšbny* KAI 216^5 - **OffAr** QAL Pf. 3 p.s.m. *ytb* Cowl 6^2, Krael 13^3 (cf. e.g. Grelot DAE p. 421; or = Part. act. m. s. abs.? or Impf. 3 p.s.m.? (cf. Krael a.l.)); Impf. 3 p.s.f. *ttb* Cowl 15^{23}, Krael 7^{26} (prob. interpret., cf. Nöldeke ZA xx 148, Krael p. 215, Ginsberg ANET 223, Fitzmyer FS Albright ii 162, WA 264 :: Jampel MGWJ li 622 n.: to be taken transitively (she will put), cf. also Yaron JSS iii 13 :: Cowl p. 49: = QAL Impf. 3 p.s.f. of *twb*$_1$ (cf. also Grelot DAE p. 195 (cf. however n. s), 236) :: Driver AnOr xii 55, J.J.Rabinowitz VT vi 104: = APH Impf. 3 p.s.f. of *twb*$_1$ (= to pay, to return) :: Porten & Greenfield JEAS p. 22, 54, Porten & Yardeni sub TADAE B 2.6 a.e.: = APH Impf. 3 p.s.f. of *ytb* (= to place, to put) :: Segal sub ATNS 21: = QAL Impf. 3 p.s.f. of *ytb*$_2$ (= to give, to pay); cf. also Yaron Law 59); Imper. s.m. *tb* Cowl 9^6; Part. act. s.m. abs. *ytb* Beh 22 (cf. e.g. Greenfield & Porten BIDG p. 36 :: Leand 38d: = Pf. 3 p.s.m.; Akkad. par. *a-ši-ib*), AG 99^2 (:: Segal sub ATNS 21: = QAL Impf. 3 p.s.m. of *ytb*$_2$ (= to give, to pay)), ATNS 30a 6 (for this uncert. reading, cf. Porten & Yardeni sub TADAE B 8.4 :: Segal ATNS a.l.: l. *ktb* = QAL Pf. 3 p.s.m. of *ktb*$_1$); Plur. m. + suff. 3 p.s.m., cf. Warka 13: *ia-a-ti-ib-a-a-ʾi-i*, cf. Warka 38 (*ia-a-ti-ib-a-a-[ʾi]-i*; for the suffix, cf. Kienast MStSW x 72ff., Degen GGA '79, 24, on this form, cf. also Kaufman JAOS civ 89); cf. Frah xx 1 (*ytybwn*), Paik 479 (*yṭybw* replacing *ytybw*?), 512 (*ytybwn*), GIPP 38, SaSt 26, cf. Toll ZDMG-Suppl viii 35 - **Palm** QAL Pf. 3 p.s.m. *ytb* Syr vii 129^3; Part. act. pl.m. abs. *ytbyn* RIP 143^4 - **JAr** QAL Part. act. s.m. abs. *ytb* MPAT 39^4, 40^3; pl.m. abs. *ytbn* MPAT 42^{11}; s.f. abs. *ytbʾ* MPAT 40^{4,15}, 50G (??, heavily dam. context) - ¶ verb QAL - **1)** to sit down, to be seated: DA i 7; cf. *ta-ra-ḫa ú-ma-ʾ ia-a-ti-ib-a-a-ʾi-i* Warka 13: the gate and those who are seated there (cf. Warka 38) - a) + *b*$_2$, *ʾrtḥššš mlkʾ ytb bkrsʾh* Cowl 6^2: king A. sat on his throne - b) + *ʿl*$_7$, *wʾnk klmw ... yšbt ʿl ksʾ ʾby* KAI 24^9: and I K. sat upon my father's throne (cf. KAI 26A i 11, 214^{8,15,20,25}, 224^{17}) - c) + *tḥt*, *ʾš yšb tḥtn* KAI 24^{14}: who shall sit (sc. on the throne) in my place - **2)** to preside over (*ʿl*$_7$): Syr vii 129$^{3f.}$ (for the context, v. *qsm*$_1$) - **3)** to live, to reside; *gubulim lasibitthim* Poen 938: the territory of his residing (i.e. where he lives; cf. *habitare* in Lat. par.); *lšbtnm dnnym bnḥt lbnm* KAI 26A i 17f.: so that they (sc.) the D. might dwell with their hearts at peace (or: so that the D. might dwell in them ..., cf. Gibson SSI iii p. 59, Pardee JNES xlvi 140, cf. e.g. already O'Callaghan Or xviii 186; on the context, cf. Greenfield

EI xiv 74f.) - a) + noun, *[y]hwn ytbn byty* MPAT 42^{11}: they will live at my house (v. also infra); *ʿmʾ yšb ʾdmt* KAI 145^{3}: his people living in the country (v. however *ʿm*$_1$); *hdd ysb skn* Tell F 15f.: Hadad residing in S. (cf. Tell F 5; in both instances Akkad. par. *a-šib*; cf. Tsumura VT xxxviii 236 n. 3: translate 'the one who is enthroned'); for AG 99^{2}, v. *tqm*$_2$ - b) + *b*$_2$, *ʿm z ʾš yšb bn* KAI 26A iii 7f.: this people who dwell in it (sc. the town), cf. KAI 181^{8,10,19,31}, 224^{6}, Beh 22, MPAT 39^{4}, 40$^{3,4f.,15f.}$, DJD ii 24B 4, C 4, E 3 (cf. *ywšb ʾbyt mškw* DJD ii 42^{4}: living in B.M., cf. Milik DJD ii p. 158 for *ʾbyt*); *tb bgw* Cowl 9^{6}: dwell on it (sc. on the plot in question; for the context, cf. Muffs p. 24f. (n. 2)) - c) + *l*$_5$, *šbw lthtkm* KAI 224^{7}: stay where you are (cf. Fitzmyer AIS 110, Greenfield ZAW lxxiii 226ff., ActOr xxix 4) - d) + *lwt*, *ytbyn lwth* RIP 143^{4}: living with her - e) Part. pass., inhabitated (said of a town): KAI 215^{4}; Inf. cstr. (v. supra), living; *šbt nʿmt* KAI 26A ii 7, 13: gracious living - Yiph, Hiph, Haph - **1)** to make to sit: KAI 215^{19} - a) + obj. + *ʿl*$_7$, *hwšbny mrʾy ... ʿl krsʾ ʾby* KAI 216$^{5ff.}$: my lord ... seated me upon my father's throne - **2)** to make to reside, to settle, to establish - a) + obj., *dnnym yšbt šm* KAI 26A i 21f.: I settled the D. there; *wyšb ʾnk hʾlm z* KAI 26C iii 15f. (for the text, cf. also Gibson SSI iii p. 52): and I made this god ... dwell (sc. in it, cf. par. text KAI 26A ii 18f. with *bn* = in it), cf. also KAI 14^{17} (for the context, v. also *ʾdr*$_1$) - b) + obj. + *b*$_2$, *wʾšb bh ʾt ʾš šrn* KAI 181^{13}: and I settled in it the men of Sh. (cf. KAI 26A i 20f.); *whwšbt bh ʾlhy* KAI 214^{19}: and I made my god to dwell in it (sc. the temple; cf. KAI 26A ii 18f., EpAn ix 5^{5}) - Schroed 291f., 314: l. *susibiti* (= *š*$_{10}$ + Qal Inf. cstr. + suff. 3 p.s.m. in Poen 948 (cf. also L.H.Gray AJSL xxxix 77f.: l. *susibiti(m)* = *š*$_{10}$ + Qal Inf. cstr. + suff. 3 p.pl.m. and Krahmalkov Or lvii 57, 60: l. *sussibti* = *š*$_{10}$ + Qal Inf. cstr. + suff. 3 p.s.m.); emendation of this text highly uncert., cf. also Sznycer PPP 128 - Aufrecht sub CAI 80: the *ytb* in AUSS xiii 2^{9} = Qal Pf. 3 p.s.m. (less prob. interpret., cf. e.g. Cross AUSS xiii a.l., Jackson ALIA 52, 56: = n.p.) - the *šbt* in BASOR cclxiv 47^{3} (= CAI 144) = Qal Inf. cstr.? (poss. reading, interpret. of context however uncert.) - Naveh sub SM 5: l. *mtytb* (= Itp Part.) in MPAT-A 43^{1} (uncert. reading), cf. Klein ZDPV li 137, Frey sub 971, Fitzmyer & Harrington MPAT a.l. (div. otherwise): l. *mtyh* (= n.p.) - Aufrecht sub CAI 144: the *yšb* in BASOR cclxiv 47^{5} = form of this root (poss. interpret., dif. and dam. context) - Bron RIPK 128: the *ʾšb* in KAI 26C iv 20 prob. = Yiph Impf. 1 p.s. of *yšb*$_1$ (highly uncert. context, cf. also Alt WO i 279, Dupont-Sommer RA xlii 178, Röllig KAI a.l. (div. otherwise): = *ʾš*$_4$ + *b*$_2$).

v. *ḥšb*$_1$, *šbr*$_1$, *šbt*$_1$, *šwb*, *šyt*$_1$.

yšb$_2$ **Pun** Plur. abs. *yšbm* KAI 130^{1,5} - ¶ subst. m. seat.

yšbr **OffAr** Sing. abs. *yšbr* Del 45 (uncert. reading, cf. also Stevenson

Contracts p. 147f. :: Pinches OAG p. 46, 62: l. *šb*ʾ) - ¶ subst. (?) of uncert. meaning (v. also supra); Stevenson Contracts p. 148: < Akkad. *išparu* = weaver?

yšṭ v. *šwṭ$_1$*.

yšmn **OldAr** Sing. abs. *yšmn* KAI 222A 32 (cf. e.g. Dupont-Sommer Sf p. 47, Fitzmyer AIS 50, Rössler TUAT i 181 × Gibson SSI ii p. 31, 40f.: = QAL Impf. 3 p.s.m. of *šmn$_1$* = to ripen) - ¶ subst. desert; *lyšmn* KAI 222A 32: into desolation (v. however supra).

yšn **Hebr** Sing. m. abs. *yšn* KAI 183[3], 185[4], Dir ostr 5[3], 9[3], etc. - ¶ adj. old (said of wine), cf. also Paul IEJ xxv 44.

yšʿ$_1$ **Mo** HIPH Pf. 3 p.s.m. + suff. 1 p.s. *hšʿny* KAI 181[4] - **Hebr** HIPH Imper. s.m. *hwšʿ* IEJ xiii 86 ii - ¶ verb HIPH to save, to deliver: IEJ xiii 86 ii; + obj. + *mn$_5$* (from): KAI 181[4] - a form of this root is poss. contained in the enigmatic letter group *thhwšʿlh* HUCA xl/xli 159[3], cf. Dever HUCA xl/xli 159: div. *thhwš ʿlh* poss. = he defaces it, cf. however idem ibid. 162: div. poss. *hwšʿ* (= HIPH Inf. cstr.) *lh*?, *th* unexplainable (cf. also Lemaire RB lxxxiv 599, 601, Miller SVT xxxii 317f., Mittmann ZDPV xcvii 144, 147, Hadley VT xxxvii 51, 59, Spronk BAAI 308 (n. 6), Margalit VT xxxix 373, Conrad TUAT ii 557: *hwšʿ* = HIPH Pf. 3 p.s.m. (Lemaire ibid., Angerstorfer BN xvii 9, Hadley VT xxxvii 59: or Imper. s.m., cf. also Naveh BASOR ccxxxv 29f. n. 10; cf. also Zevit MLAHE 18, BASOR cclv 43, 45, O'Connor VT xxxvii 228f., Tigay FS Cross 174f., Smelik HDAI 139)); :: Garbini AION xxviii 193 (div. otherwise): *hhwšʿ* = *h$_1$* (article) + *hwšʿ* (= HIPH Inf. cstr.) :: Shea VT xl 110, 112f. (div. otherwise): l. *šʿlh* = Sing. + suff. 3 p.s.m. of *šʿl$_3$* (= hollow of the hand, handprint); v. also *ʾšr$_7$*.

v. *yšʿ$_2$*, *šyʿ$_1$*.

yšʿ$_2$ **Mo** Sing. abs. *[y]šʿ* KAI 181[3f.] (uncert. restoration, accepted by most authors; cf. however e.g. Segert ArchOr xxix 207: poss. l. *[m]šʿ*, cf. also Smend & Socin IKM 12f., 17, Halévy RS viii 236, 238, Auffret UF xii 110 (n.6); cf. particularly Lipiński Or xl 327f. on sentence division; his restoration *[n]šʿ* = NIPH Part. s.m. abs. of *yšʿ$_1$*used as adverb (= victorious) less prob. - ¶ subst. deliverance, salvation (v. however supra).

yšʿ$_3$ v. *tšʿ$_1$*.

yšr$_1$ (Pun. and Ar. forms poss. not from same root, cf. Kaufman AIA 110f. (n. 399), Degen ZDMG cxxi 135) - **Pun** PIʿEL Part. s.m. abs. *myšr* KAI 161[2] (:: Roschinski Num 114: = Sing. cstr. of *myšr* (= justice)); YIPH Part. s.f. abs. *mʿšrt* KAI 123[5] (or pl.f. abs.?), *mhšʿrt* Punica xii 23[3] (= NP 55; for both forms, cf. Levi Della Vida AfrIt vi 29, FR 158, 161, cf. also Röllig KAI 123 a.l., Sznycer PPP 74f., Amadasi IPT 59 × Lidzbarski Handb 306: *mhšʿrt* = form of root *ʾšr$_1$*(= to be happy, honest); for the last mentioned text, cf. Polselli CISFP i 775)

- **OffAr** HAPH/APH Pf. 3 p.s.m. *hwšr* Herm 5^{4}; 2 p.s.m. *hwšrt* Krael 13^{4}, Driv $13^{2,3}$; 2 p.s.f. *hwšrty* Cowl 39^{3}, *ʾwšrty* Herm 4^{4}; 1 p.s. *hwšrt* KAI 233^{6} (*[h]wšrt*, cf. Bowman UMS xx 279; dam. context), Cowl 42^{1} (for the reading, cf. Bresciani RSO xxxv 20, Porten & Yardeni sub TADAE A 3.8), Driv 2^{1} (= Driv F ix 6; for this prob. reading, cf. Yardeni with Szubin & Porten JNES xlvi 39ff., Porten & Yardeni sub TADAE A 6.4), 3^{1}, 5^{1}, 13^{1}, Sem ii 31 conv. 2, RES 492A 6 (cf. RES 1800; for the interpret. of the context, cf. Grelot DAE p. 139f.); + suff. 3 p.s.m. *hwšrth* Sem ii 31 conv. 3; 2 p.pl.f. *hwšrtn* Herm 5^{7}; Impf. 3 p.s.f. *twšr* Herm 2^{7}; 2 p.s.f. *tšry* Herm 1^{10}; 1 p.s. *ʾwšr* Sem ii 31 conc. 1f.; 2 p.pl.m. *thwšrw* Sem xxxix 32 conc. 4; Imper. s.m. *hwšr* KAI 233^{14}, Herm 3^{7}, RSO xxxii 403^{4}, Sem xiv 72 conc. 2, 3, conv. 3 (*hwš[r]*; dam. context), RES 1296^{1} (= AG 3a), 1299B 3 (*[hw]šr*; dam. context; or = Pf. 3 p.s.m.?); s.f. *hwšry* RES '41-45, 67^{1}, Herm 2^{13}, RES 496^{5} (dam. context); pl.m. *hwšrw* Driv 9^{3}, ASAE xlviii 112A 1, RES 492A 8 (cf. RES 1800; for the reading, cf. Grelot DAE p. 140 n. 1), 1299B 4 (heavily dam. context, or = Pf. 3 p.pl.m.?), FS Driver 55^{3}; + suff. 3 p.s.m. *hwšrwhy* RES 492A 5; Inf. + suff. 3 p.pl.m. *mwšrthm* Herm 2^{13}; *hwšr* RES 1792B 9 obscure form; cf. Nisa-b 54^{2} (*[h]wšrt*), Nisa-c 210^{5}, 287^{2} (*hwšrt*), DEP 153^{1}, cf. also GIPP 53, 54 - ¶ verb PIʿEL to conduct: KAI 161^{2}, *myšr ʾrṣt* KAI 161^{2}: the regent of the countries (cf. also Février RA xlv 142, Niehr UF xvii 234; uncert. interpret.) - HAPH/APH to send - a) + obj.: Sem ii 31 conc. 1f., conv. 3 - b) + obj. + l_5: Herm 2^{13}, $5^{7f.}$; *šlm wšrrt šgyʾ hwšrt lk* Driv 3^{1}: I send you much greetings of peace and prosperity (cf. Driv 5^{1}, 13^{1}, Cowl 42^{1} (for the reading, v. supra; on this formula, cf. Fitzmyer JBL xciii 215, Dion RB lxxxix 537, Greenfield IrJu 6), Nisa-c $210^{4f.}$, $287^{1f.}$, cf. also SSI ii 28 obv. 1, Nisa-b 54^{2} - c) + l_5: KAI 233^{6} (dam. context), Herm 1^{10}, 4^{4}, FS Driver 55^{3} (dam. context), RSO xxxii 403^{4}, Sem xxxix 32 conc. 4 - d) + l_5 + obj.: KAI 233^{14}, Herm 2^{7}, 3^{7}, 5^{4}, RES 492A 5, 5f., 8f. (v. supra), 1296^{1} (= AG 3 a), RES '41-45, $67^{1f.}$, Sem xiv 72 i conc. 3, ASAE xlviii 112A 1f. - e) + l_5 + *byd* (= by the hand of, through): Krael 13^{4} (dam. context) - f) + $ʿl_7$ + *byd* + obj., *hwšrt ʿly byd ʾnʾ ... ktn* Driv $13^{3f.}$: you sent me through A. ... a garment (cf. however Porten & Yardeni sub TADAE A 6.16: l. *hwšrt [hyty] ʿly ...*) - YIPH Part. honest, beneficient: KAI 123^{5} (*pʿlt mʿšrt* = (a) beneficient act(s)), Punica xii 23^{3} (v. however supra; for the last mentioned text, cf. Polselli CISFP i 775); perhaps a form of the same root in NP 130^{5} (*mʿšrt* = YIPH Part. f. s./pl. abs. or noun Sing./Plur. abs.), cf. also Février RHR cxli 21f.: either noun = justice (< *yšr*; cf. also Sznycer PPP 74f.) or = felicity (< *ʾšr*$_1$), highly uncert. context, word division unclear - a form of this root prob. in KAI 214^{33}, cf. e.g. Cooke NSI p. 161, 171, Donner KAI a.l.: l. *yšrh* (cf. also Dion 35, 132: = justice, correctness), cf. however

Gibson SSI ii p. 69, 76 (div. otherwise): l. *yšr* (= Sing. m. abs. of *yšr*₂) - a form of this root also in Cowl 82[12]? (*yšr*), Cowl a.l.: = form of *yšr*₂ - a form of this root also in Cowl 54[12]? (*h/yšd/rt*; for this reading, cf. Porten & Yardeni sub TADAE A 3.1 verso 3).

yšr₂ **Ph** Sing. m. abs. *yšr* KAI 4[7] - **Pun** Sing. m. abs. *yšr* CIS i 6000bis 3 (= TPC 84; cf. e.g. Lidzbarski Eph i 165 (for the reading), Février BAr '51/52, 75, CIS i a.l., Ferron StudMagr i 72, 78, v.d.Branden BO xxiii 156 :: Slouschz TPI p. 179: l. *yzr* (< root *ʾzr*) = n.d.) - ¶ adj. right, rightful; *mlk yšr lpn ʾl gbl* KAI 4[6f.]: a rightful king in the sight of the gods of G. (for the context, v. also *ṣdq*₃).

v. *yšr*₁.

yšrh v. *yšr*₁.

yt v. *ʾyt*₃,*ḥšš*, *ʿtd*₁.

ytb₁ v. *yšb*₁.

ytb₂ v. *yšb*₁,*šwb*.

ytyr v. *ytr*₃.

ytm **Ph** Sing. abs. *ytm* KAI 14[3,13], 24[13] - ¶ subst. orphan (a fatherless one); *ytm bn ʾlmt* KAI 14[3,13]: an orphan, the son of a widow - l. poss. *ytm* (= Sing. abs.) in Syr xlviii 403[5f.] (cf. Caquot Syr xlviii 405f., Gibson SSI iii p. 89, 92 (cf. also Avishur PIB 267, 271, UF x 32, 36)), cf. however Röllig NESE ii 29, 34 (div. otherwise): l. *tm* (= Sing. m. abs. of *tm*₃; de Moor JEOL xxvii 111: = Sing. cstr. of *tm*₁; Garbini OA xx 292: = QAL Pf. 3 p.s.m. of *tmm*₁); Gaster BASOR ccix 19, 26: l. *ytm* = QAL Impf. 3 p.s.m. of *tmm*₁ (for other readings and interpret. of the context, cf. also Lipiński RSF ii 53, v.d.Branden BiOr xxxiii 13).

ytmʾl v. *ʾtml*.

ytn₁ (for this root, cf. FR 159) - **Ph** QAL Pf. 3 p.s.m. *ytn* KAI 9A 4 (cf. FR 267b also for litt.; interpret. as Inf. abs. less prob. :: Février Sem ii 23: = QAL Part. act. s.m. abs.), 14[18], 31[1], 32[2] (= Kition A 2), 38[1], 39[2], 41[1], DD 13[1], EpAn ix 5C 1, 5[1,2,3,4,6], etc.; 3 p.s.f. *ytn* KAI 33[2] (= Kition A 1); 1 p.s. *ytt* KAI 43[9], 50[5] (?, dam. context), Mus li 286[4] (*[y]tt*)[,5]; 3 p.pl.m. *ytn* KAI 24[8] (cf. Collins WO vi 185f. × e.g. Halévy RS xx 24, 28 (also for older litt.), Bauer ZDMG lxvii 686f., Lidzbarski Eph iii 231, Rosenthal ANET 654 (n. 2), Gibson SSI iii p. 35, 37, de Moor UF xx 167, Sperling UF xx 324, 333, Fales WO x 19, H.P.Müller TUAT i 639: = QAL Pf. 3 p.s.m. (diff. interpretations of context; cf. also Swiggers RSO xlv 4 n. 13: = Pf. 3 p.s.m. or 3 p.pl.m.) × Landsberger Samʾal 53 (cf. also Torrey JAOS xxxv 365): = pass. form of root *ytn* :: Lidzbarski Eph iii 231 n. 2: or = QAL Pf. 1 p.pl.? :: Dahood Bibl lx 571 (n. 3), Baldacci BiOr xl 126: = QAL pass. Pf. 3 p.s.f.), RES 367 i 2 (cf. Delavault & Lemaire RB lxxxiii 569ff., cf. however Lidzbarski Eph i 285ff.; :: Teixidor Syr lvi 383: *ytn* with s.f. subject), EI xviii 117[1] (= IEJ xxxv 83); 3 p.pl.m. *ytnw* KA 12[1] (heavily dam. context; or =

Hebr ? (Impf. 3 p.pl.m.)); Impf. 3 p.s.m. *ytn* KAI 52^{1} (:: e.g. Slouschz TPI p. 65, Röllig KAI a.l.: or = QAL Pf. 3 p.s.m.?), BMQ xxvii 85 (cf. Egypt. par.: *dy*); 3 p.s.f. *ttn* KAI 10^{9}; 2 p.s.f. *tntn* KAI 50$^{3f.}$ (cf. e.g. Dupont-Sommer PEQ '49, 56, Röllig KAI a.l., FR 158 (cf. v.Soden Mem Brockelmann 179) × Aimé-Giron ASAE xl 439f.: = NIPH Impf. 3 p.s.f. (cf. also v.d.Branden GP § 235, BO xii 215, 217); Inf. + suff. 3 p.s.m. *tty* KAI 26A iii 4, C iii 19 - **Pun** QAL Pf. 3 p.s.m. *ytn* KAI 277^{2}, CIS i 3775^{1}, 4945^{2}, RES 79^{1}, Punica xviii/ii 92^{4}, Mozia vi 105^{2} (= SMI 24), ix 156^{1} (= SMI 37), StudMagr iv 3^{2}, RSF v 131^{3} (dam. context), 133^{2} (*yt[n]*; heavily dam. context), 135^{3} (dam. context), Trip 51^{8} (??, diff. reading, dam. context), MC 57^{2}; 1 p.s. *ytnty* KAI 145^{6} (?, reading of last 2 consonants uncert.; cf. FR 155, 158, v.d.Branden RSF i 166, 169, Krahmalkov RSF iii 189, 193, 201 :: Halévy RS ix 277: l. *ytn* (or *ytnty*?) = n.p., cf. also Cooke NSI p. 151f., 154, RES 2221 :: Février Sem vi 20: l. *ytnty* = QAL Pf. 2 p.s.m. + suff. 3 p.s.m. :: Berger MAIBL xxxvi/2, 158: l. *ytns*? = n.p.; on this form, cf. also Sznycer APCI 212 (n. 7), 217f.); 3 p.pl.m. *ytn* ICO-Spa 16^{4} (for the context, v. infra), *ytn*ʾ KAI 126^{9}, 160^{1} (cf. Levi Della Vida RCL '55, 556 n. 2 (with diff. interpret. of context) :: Février Sem iv 20: = QAL Pf. 3 p.s.f., cf. also Röllig KAI a.l.), *yʿtn*ʾ Karth xii 53^{2} (:: Krahmalkov RSF iii 178 (div. otherwise): l. *yʿtn* (= QAL Pf. 3 p.s.m.) + ʾ*t*$_{5}$), 54^{2}; Impf. 3 p.s.m. *ytn* KAI 69^{21}, CIS i 169^{10} (?); Inf. cstr. *tt* KAI 163^{1} (highly uncert. context), CIS i 3917^{2,3}; NIPH Pf. 3 p.s.f. *ntn* KAI 69^{18}, 74^{11} (?, *nt[n]*); 3 p.pl.m. *nntn* KAI 137^{6} (cf. FR 154) - ¶ verb QAL to give - **1)** + obj.: KAI 10$^{9f.}$, RES 827, 1204^{6}, Karth xii 53^{2}, 54^{2} (for both contexts, v. *šbʿh*$_{1}$) - **2)** + obj. + *b*$_{2}$, *ʿlmt ytn bš wgbr bswt* KAI 24^{8}: they gave a maid for the price of a sheep and a man for the price of a garment (v. however supra; cf. Swiggers RSO lv 3f.: = description of barter) - **3)** + obj. + *l*$_{5}$ (or + *l*$_{5}$ + obj.): KAI 14$^{8f.}$, 26A iii 4f., C iii 19f., 31^{1}, 41$^{1ff.}$, 50$^{3f.}$, CIS i 3775^{1}, 3917^{2}, Mus li 286^{4,5}, EI viii 117^{1f}, EpAn ix 5^{1,4}, 5C 1; cf. *kšmʿ qlʾ brkʾ ʿzrʾ ytn lʾ nʿm* Punica xviii/ii 92$^{3f.}$: because he has heard his voice, blessed him, helped him and gave him goodness (i.e. was good to him); *ḥrpkrt ytn ḥym lʿbdy* KAI 52$^{1f.}$: may H. grant life to his servant ... (cf. BMQ xxvii 85) - **4)** + obj. + *l*$_{5}$ + *b*$_{2}$; *krm zr ytn l bʾdrwz* EpAn ix 5^{2}: another vineyard (v. *zr*$_{4}$) he gave him in A. - **5)** + *l*$_{5}$: KAI 32$^{3f.}$, CIS i 3917^{9}, RES 930, 1213$^{3f.}$, Mozia ix 156^{1}, EpAn ix 5^{6} - **6)** + *l*$_{5}$ + Inf., *ytn*ʾ *lʿbd b...* KAI 126^{9}: they gave (the right) to use ... (cf. Lat. par. *uti conce[ssit]*) - **7)** + *l*$_{5}$ + *b*$_{2}$: EpAn ix 5^{3} (diff. context, cf. Mosca & Russell EpAn ix 12) - NIPH to be given; *wntn lpy hktbt* KAI 69^{18}: and it shall be given according to the document - a) + ʾ*t*$_{6}$, *wnntn* ʾ*t hkhnm* KAI 137$^{6f.}$: they were handed over to the priests - cf. the following combinations - a) *ytn* + YIPH of *ṭn*ʾ$_{1}$: KAI 33^{2} (= Kition A 1), 39^{2}, 41$^{1f.}$, CIS i 88^{2} (= Kition

F 1), Kition 29^{2} - b) *ytn* + YIPH of *qdš*$_1$: KAI 43^{9} - c) *p‘l* + *ytn*, *’šr qdš ’z ’š p‘l w’š ytn tbry’* KAI 277$^{1ff.}$: this holy place which made and which gave T. ... - Garbini RSO xlii 4ff.: l. the context of ICO-Spa 16^{4} (v. also supra): *‘štrt ḥrr ytn k* = A. of Chrr. They have given, because ... (prob. reading, division and interpret.; for the reading *hrr*, cf. also Fuentes Estañol sub CIFE 14.01) :: Gibson SSI iii p. 65f.: l. *‘štrt ḥr rbtn k* = A. of Chr our mistress (= Sing. + suff. 1 p.pl. of *rb*$_2$), because ... :: Krahmalkov OA xi 208, 212f.: l. *‘štrt ḥbr ytn k* = A. of Iberia. She (QAL Pf. 3 p.s.f.) granted (it) because ... :: Solá-Solé RSO xli 98, 103f. (cf. also Amadasi sub ICO-Spa 16): l. *‘štrt ḥbry tnt k* = A. the companion (Sing. m. cstr. of *ḥbry*,or Sing. f. cstr. of *ḥbry*(with elision of *t*) or lapsus (/haplography) *ḥbry tnt* for *ḥbryttnt*) of Tinnit, because ... :: Heltzer OA vi 265, 267f.: l. *‘štrt ḥbry tnt k* = A. her companion (= Sing. + suff. 3 p.s.f. of *ḥbr*$_2$) is T. (i.e. the companion of T.), because ... :: Vattioni Or xxxvi 178ff.: l. *‘štrt ḥbry tnt k* = A., the magicians of (= QAL Part. act. pl.m. cstr. of *ḥbr*$_1$ (orig. = to bind)) T., because ... (cf. Dahood Ps ii 60) :: v.d.Branden RSO xliv 104, 106f.: l. *‘štrt ḥbr ytnt k* = A. the joy of (= Sing. cstr. of *ḥbr*$_4$)the hierodules (= Plur. abs. of *ytnh*), because ... - Garbini Malta ’64, 84: the diff. *lyytn* (ICO-Malta 27) poss. = *l*$_5$ + suff. 1 p.s. + *ytn* (= QAL Pf. 3 p.s.m. or Impf. 3 p.s.m. (Amadasi ICO-Malta a.l.: or = n.p.?)) - a form of this root (*ytn*) in RES 1320^{1}? (cf. however Kornfeld sub Abydos 3: = part of n.p.) - a form of this root (*ytn*) prob. also in KAI 145^{10} (:: Février Sem vi 25f.: l. prob. *kwn* = PI‘EL Pf. 3 p.s.m. of *kwn*$_2$ (= to establish)), diff. context, cf. v.d.Branden RSF i 166, 171: = QAL Pf. 3 p.pl., Halévy RS ix 282, 285: = QAL Pf. 3 p.s.m., Krahmalkov RSF iii 188f., 197 (div. otherwise): l. *mḥnytn* = Plur. + suff. 3 p.pl.m. of *mḥnt* (= camp; improb. interpret.), Février Sem vi 26: if reading *ytn* poss. = QAL Impf. 3 p.s.m. - Ferron MC 59: the *ytn* in CIS i 3789^{2} = QAL Pf. 3 p.s.m. (uncert. interpret., heavily dam. context, cf. also CIS i a.l.: = part of n.p.) - Puech Sem xxix 20f.: l. *ytn* (= QAL Impf. 3 p.pl.) in KAI 30^{6} (heavily dam. context, uncert. interpret.) - v.d.Branden BO xiv 196, 200: the *tt* in KAI 162^{5} = QAL Inf. cstr. - cf. also *ntn*.
v. *zt*$_3$,*ytn*$_2$.

ytn$_2$ Pun Sing. cstr. *ytn* KAI 145^{11} (v. infra), *y‘tn* Karth xii 50^{2}, 51^{1} (:: v.d.Branden RSF v 60: = QAL Inf. cstr. of *ytn*$_1$;v. also infra) - ¶ subst.?, the giving, presentation (for the context, v. *šb‘h*); for the reading of KAI 145^{11}, cf. e.g. Cooke NSI p. 151, 155f. (without interpret.), RES sub 2221, Février & Fantar Karth xii 50f., Sznycer Sem xxii 42f. :: reading *bytt* pro *bytn*, cf. Röllig KAI a.l. (: *ytt* = form of root *ytn*), Krahmalkov RSF iii 188f., 197, 200 (: *bytt* = Plur. f. of *byt*$_2$ (= verses)) :: reading *kytn* pro *bytn*, cf. vd Branden RSF i 166, 171 (= *k*$_2$ + QAL Pf. 1 p.pl. of *ytn*$_1$):: reading *kytt* pro *bytn*, cf. Février Sem vi 20, 26

(= k_2 + QAL Pf. 2 p.s.m. of *ytn*$_1$).For Karth xii 50[2], 51[1], cf. Février & Fantar Karth xii a.l.: transl. *by‘tn* by "by giving" :: Krahmalkov RSF iii 177f., 181, 200: *by‘tn* = Sing. + suff. 1 p.pl. of *by‘t*(= terror).

ytnh v. *ytn*$_1$.

ytr$_1$ **Hebr** HIPH Pf. 3 p.s.m. *hytyr* SM 49[10] - **OldAr** HAPH Pf. 3 p.s.m. *hwtr* Tell F 15 - **OffAr** HAPH/APH Pf. 3 p.s.m. *hwtyr* KAI 279[8]; 3 p.pl.m. *hwtyrn* JA ccliv 440[4]; 2 p.pl.f. *›trtn* Herm 4[5] (cf. Bresciani & Kamil Herm a.l., cf. also Hayes & Hoftijzer VT xx 105 :: Grelot DAE p. 160f. (n. b): = ITP Impf. 1 p.s. + energ. ending of *yrt*$_1$,*rwt* or *rtt*$_1$ (= to procure for oneself)? :: Swiggers AION xlii 138f.: = APH Pf. 2 p.pl.f. of *twr*$_1$ (= to answer) :: Milik Bibl xlviii 553, 583: = PA‘EL Pf. 2 p.s.m. + suff. 3 p.s.m. of *’tr*$_1$ (= to replace)); Impf. 3 p.s.m. *yhwtr* KAI 279[8]; 3 p.pl.m. *yhwtrwn* JA ccliv 440[4] (for the reading, cf. Naveh with Shaked JRAS ’69, 119, cf. also Kutscher, Naveh & Shaked Lesh xxxiv 128f. :: Dupont-Sommer JA ccliv 440, 457f.: l. *yhwtlwn* = variant form of *yhwtrwn*) - ¶ verb HAPH/APH - **1)** to add - a) + obj.: SM 49[10] - b) + *›l*$_6$, *›l zy qdm hwtr* Tell F 15: he has added to what was before (Akkad. par. *eli ma-ḫ-re-e ú-šá-tir*; cf. Greenfield FS Rundgren 150, Kaufman Maarav iii 168, Sader EAS 20 n. 41) - **2)** to have left, to have still (left): Herm 4[5] (diff. context, v. supra; :: Porten & Yardeni sub TADAE A 2.1: = to have in abundance) - **3)** to benefit, to be profitable; + *l*$_5$: KAI 279[8] (for the context, v. *ysp*) - **4)** to grow; + *b*$_2$, *›p hwtyrn wyhwtrwn bptystykn›* (for *b*$_2$ pro *l*$_5$, cf. Naveh with Shaked JRAS ’69, 119) JA ccliv 440[4]: also they have grown and will grow in obedience (for the background, cf. also Benveniste JA ccliv 449) - a HAPH Pf. form prob. to be restored in KAI 273[8] (*hwt[yr...]*), cf. e.g. Humbach AIT p. 8, 11, Degen Lesh xxxiv 315ff., ZDMG cxxi 125. v. *›šr*$_4$,*ytr*$_2$, *mšb*$_1$, *n‘tr*, *ntn*.

ytr$_2$ **Hebr** Sing. cstr. (?, dam. context) *ytr* TA-H 5[14] - **Samal** Sing. + suff. 3 p.s.m. *ytrh* KAI 215[4] (diff. context; cf. e.g. Cooke NSI p. 173, 176, Donner KAI a.l., Gibson SSI ii p. 79, 82, Dion p. 152 :: Lipiński BiOr xxxiii 232, OLP viii 102: = QAL Part. act. s.f. abs. of *ytr*$_1$(= to abound)) - **OffAr** Sing. emph. *ytr›* ATNS 23b 4 (for the reading, cf. Segal ATNS a.l.) - ¶ subst. rest.

ytr$_3$ **Hebr** Sing. m. abs. *ytyr*DJD ii 30[3,14] - **OffAr** Sing. m. abs. *ytyr*Cowl 30[3], 70[2] (for this reading, cf. Porten FS Bresciani 438, Porten & Yardeni sub TADAE A 5.3.), Driv 6[6]; cstr. *ytyr*Driv 6[6]; f. emph., cf. Warka 17, 42: *ia-ti-ir-ta-›* - **Palm** Sing. m. abs. *ytyr*CIS ii 3913 i 11, ii 127; cstr. *ytyr*CIS ii 3913 ii 48 - **JAr** Sing. m. abs. *ytyr* MPAT 52[3], IEJ xl 144[12] (*[y]tyr*) - ¶ 1) adj. exceeding, superabundant: Warka 17, 42 (cf. Dupont-Sommer RA xxxix 48); *md‘m ytyr* CIS ii 3913 i 11: anything further - **2)** substantivated adj., *ytyr dnr›* CIS ii 3913 ii 48: more than a dinar (cf. Driv 6[6]); *dnr› ›w ytyr* CIS ii 3913 ii 126f.: a

dinar or more - **3)** adv., *ytyr mn ywm ḥd* Driv 6^{6}: more than a day; *ytyr mn zy kʿn ḥd ʾlp* Cowl 30^{3}: a thousand times more than now; *ʾm ytyr ʾw ḥ[sr]* DJD ii 30^{14}: more or less (cf. DJD ii 30^{3}, cf. also MPAT 52$^{2f.}$); *ytyr mn dnh* IEJ xl 144^{12}: in addition to this.
v. *ywm.*

ytry **OffAr** CRAI '70, 163^{3bis} - ¶ prep. (?) prob. meaning: more than, cf. Dupont-Sommer CRAI '70, 163, 169, Humbach IPAA p. 15.

ytrn **OffAr** Sing. cstr. *ytrn* ATNS 19^{2}, 149^{2} (?, *ytrn[* ; :: Lemaire Syr lxi 341: pro *wytrn* poss. l. *ḥtnn*) - ¶ subst. prob. meaning: what is left over, in the context of ATNS 19^{2}: what still has to be paid?? (Segal sub ATNS 19^{2}: = balance or surplus?).

K

k$_1$ prep. (cf. also Pennacchietti AION xxiv 181ff.) - **1)** comparative: as; *kqdm* KAI 43^{12}: as aforetime; *thwy mlkth kmlkt ḥl* KAI 222A 25: let his kingdom become as a kingdom of sand (for the context, v. however *ḥl$_2$*); *ptpʾ hb lh ... kʾḥrnn* Driv 9$^{1f.}$: give to him ... the same provision as to others; *nsbl bzkwr brk kbr zy ...* Krael 5^{12}: we will provide for Z. your son, like a son who ... (or to be classified as normative?) - **2)** comparative (with a feature of normativity): as, in accordance with; *kmdt št bktb[t]* KAI 69^{17}: according as is set down in the document; *kkl ʾšr šlḥ ʾdny kn ʿšh ʿbdk* KAI 194$^{2f.}$: in accordance with all (instructions) that my lord has sent, so has your servant acted ... (cf. KAI 194$^{3f.,10ff.}$); *hn kn hw kmlyʾ ʾlh zy ptsry šlḥ ʿ[ly]* Driv 8^{3}: if it is as (described in) this account which P. has sent to me; *knsḥt dnh* CIS ii 209^{9} (= J 36): according to the copy hereof; *kktbw tgryʾ tdmryʾ* Inv x 114^{3}: as the Tadmorean merchants have written; *ktb plṭyh ... sprʾ znh kpm kwnyh* Cowl 5^{15}: P. ... wrote this document at the dictation of K. (cf. Cowl 6^{17}, 8^{28}, 9^{16}, Krael 3^{22b}, 4^{22}, ATNS 3^{6}, etc.); for *kḥd(h)*, v. *ʾḥd$_4$*; *thwʾ ly lʾnth kdyn m[šh]* MPAT 41^{3}: you shall be my wife according to the law of Moses; *knmsʾ* MPAT 42^{11}: legitimately (cf. also MPAT 61^{24}, 64 i 4); for *kzy/kdy*, v. *zy*; for *kdn(h)*, v. *znh* - **3)** temp. on, in, during; *ʿt kym ʿt kym* KAI 192^{2}: at this very moment (cf. also KAI 194^{1}); *kymm* KAI 200^{5,7}: within the fixed time (prob. meaning; v. also *ywm*); *kymn* KAI 233^{16}: every year (?, v. also *ywm*); *kṣʾty mbytk* TA-H 16$^{3f.}$: when I left your house; for *kʾšr*, v. *ʾšr$_7$*; for *kzy/kd(y)*, v. *zy* - **4)** instrumental?? (cf. Leand 62g), *kḥsn* Cowl 7^{5,8}, Driv 12^{10}: by force, forcibly (v. also *ḥsn$_4$*) - **5)** as so-called *kaph veritatis*, *šmʿt kʿmlʾ zy ʿmlt* Cowl 40^{2}: I have heard of the trouble which you took; *kʿšq ʿbyd ly* Cowl 16^{8}: a wrong was done to me (cf. Cowl 16^{5,9}); *kzy kznh ʿbyd* Cowl 30^{15}: when this was done (cf. Cowl 37^{8}?; for Aḥiq 107, v. *rḥmn*) - cf. poss. also

KAI 4[6]: *yʾrk ... ymt yḥmlk ... ʿl gbl kmlk šdq* ... : may they ... prolong the days of Y. ... over G., as a righteous king ... (for this interpret., cf. e.g. Albright JAOS lxvii 156f., Degen ZDMG cxxi 126, Silverman JAOS xciv 268 :: e.g. Röllig KAI a.l., Rosenthal ANET 653, Gibson SSI iii p. 18f.: *k* = *k*$_3$ (= *ky*) and restore *h*ʾ at the end of l. 7: because he is a righteous king).
v. *znh,kwt, ky, km*$_2$.

k$_2$ v. *k*ʾ$_1$.

k$_3$ v. *k*$_1$, *ky, kl*$_1$, *krt*$_1$, *qdm*$_2$.

k$_4$ v. *knt*$_2$.

k$_5$ v. *ksp*$_2$, *mḥṣ*$_2$.

k$_6$ v. *kp*$_1$.

k$_7$ v. *kr*$_1$.

k$_8$ v. *krš*$_1$.

k$_9$ v. *ktš*.

k$_{10}$ v. *p*$_4$.

k$_{11}$ v. *qrbn*.

k$_{12}$ **OffAr** the obscure abbrev. *k* in Cowl 81[61] prob. = part of n.p., cf. however Harmatta ActAntHung vii 366: pro *k 10* l. *kp* (= n.p.), cf. also Grelot DAE p. 112 (n. a).

kʾ$_1$ **OffAr** Sing. abs. Cowl 81[61,64,81,85,131]; Plur. abs. *k*ʾ*n* Cowl 81[106] - ¶ subst. certain measure of capacity: Cowl 81[61,64,81,85,106,131] (for liquids); 1 *k*ʾ poss. = 12 *lg* (cf. Driver JRAS '32, 84f.), the same measure also in ATNS 45a 1, 2, 3, 4, 5, b 7, AG 87a 4, 9, 10, 11, 12, 13, 18, 19, 20, 21, 22, 23, 24, b 8, 13 (*k*ʾ)??, cf. however Porten Arch 82 n. 91: *k*ʾ = *k*$_4$ (abbrev. of *knth*, v. *knt*$_2$) + ʾ$_7$ (= abbrev. of ʾ*rdb*)prob. interpret., cf. also the *kntn* ʾ in ATNS 45b 2, 4, 6, 8 - Harmatta ActAntHung vii 365f.: prob. < Egypt.

kʾ$_2$ **Pun** *k*ʾ Or xxxiii 4[1] (poss. interpret., cf. Levi Della Vida Or xxxiii 8f., 13, FR 248a), KAI 146[1] (?; *[k]*ʾ), 159[8] (?; *[k]*ʾ), cf. Poen 939, 1006: *cho*, Poen 949: *co* - **Nab** *k*ʾ RES 529[1] (highly uncert. interpret.), IEJ xxix 112[2] (interpret. of context highly uncert.) - **Palm** *k*ʾ CIS ii 3932[4] - **JAr** *kh* MPAT 70[1] (cf. however Garbini OA xxiv 67ff., who doubts the authenticity of this text) - ¶ adv. here: Poen 1006 - **1)** prec. by *l*$_5$, ʾ*ty lk*ʾ *yt lgyny*ʾ CIS ii 3932[4]: he has brought the legions hither (cf. MPAT 70[1]) - **2)** prob. prec. by prep. *mn*$_5$: Poen 939, 949 (cf. Sznycer PPP 107, 129) - for Hatra 8 (*k*ʾ), v. *hn*ʾ - Sznycer PPP 125f.: the *cona* in Poen 942 = *k*ʾ$_2$ + *n*ʾ (= interjection indicating deprecation), uncert. interpret., Schroed 291, 308, Gray AJSL xxxix 77f. (div. otherwise): l. *econa* = Qal Impf. 3 p.s.m. of *kwn*$_1$ + *n*ʾ - Altheim & Stiehl FuF xxxv 176: the *lkh* in FuF xxxv 173[7,12(bis)] = *l*$_5$ + *kh*$_2$ (= *k*ʾ$_2$) = here (uncert. interpret., diff. context; cf. also Altheim & Stiehl ASA 254, 272).
v. *hlk*$_2$,*hn*$_3$,*hnkt, z*$_1$,*zky*$_2$, *šyt*$_1$.

k'$_3$ v. *kh$_1$*.
k'$_4$ v. *ky*.
k'y v. *ḥsn$_4$*.
k'yt **Ph** word of unknown meaning in CIS i 111a 1, b 1: for interpret. proposals, cf. CIS i a.l.
k'l v. *q'l$_1$*.
k'n v. *mn$_5$*.
k'nyš v. *hy$_2$*.
kb **OffAr** Sing. emph. *kb'* Sach 76A i 5 (for the reading, cf. Lidzbarski Eph iii 256, Greenfield Or xxix 99f., cf. also Grelot DAE p. 377 :: Sachau p. 234: l. *rb'* = Sing. emph. of *rb$_2$* (cf. also Ungnad ArPap 103) or = n.l.? (cf. also Koopmans 150)); Plur. abs. *kbn* Aḥiq 166; + suff. 2 p.s.m. (?) *kby[k]* Aḥiq 165 - ¶ subst. thorn: Aḥiq 165, 166 (cf. also Lindenberger APA 168); with coll. meaning: Sach 76A i 5.
kbd$_1$ **OldCan** PI'EL Impf. 3 p.s.m. *yu-ka-bi-id* EA 245[39] (cf. Sivan GAG 177, 237, cf. also Steiner JAOS c 515) - **Ph** PI'EL Impf. 3 p.pl.m. *ykbd* KAI 24[14,15] - **Hebr** PU'AL Part. s.m. abs. *mkwbd* SM 75[2] - ¶ verb PI'EL to honour: EA 245[39]; + *l$_5$*, *mškbm 'l ykbd lb'rrm* KAI 24[14]: may the M. not honour the B., cf. KAI 24[14f.] - PU'AL to be honoured, Part. the honoured one: SM 75[2] - Naveh EI xv 301f.: l. *mkbdm* in Hazor ii p. 72 (= SSI i p. 18 A) = PI'EL Part. pl.m. abs. of *kbd$_1$* (= the food-servers), poss. reading and interpret., cf. however Yadin Hazor ii a.l., Gibson SSI p. 18: l. *mkbrm* = n.p. - a derivative of this root prob. in TK 302 (no. 5; *]kbd*), or = part of n.p.?
kbd$_2$ **Pun** Sing. abs. *kbd* KAI 123[4], 161[5] - ¶ subst. glory, honour; for both KAI 123 and 161, v. *zkr$_2$*.
v. *kbdh*, *'bd$_1$*.
kbd$_3$ **Ph** Sing. m. abs. *kbd* IEJ xviii 117[1f.] (= IEJ xxxv 83) - ¶ adj. valuable, magnificent; *'gn kbd* IEJ xviii 117[1f.]: a valuable basin (for this interpret., cf. Dothan IEJ xviii a.l.).
kbdh **Pun** Sing. cstr. *kbdt* CIS i 6000bis 7 (cf. Février BAr '51/52, 78, sub CIS i a.l., Ferron StudMagr i 77f. :: Lidzbarski Eph i 168f. (div. otherwise): l. *bkbd* (= *b$_2$* + Sing. cstr. of *kbd$_2$*)*t'ṣmty* (= Sing./Plur. + suff. 1 p.s./3 p.s.m. of *t'ṣmh* (= strength, might)) - ¶ subst. glory, honour; *bkbdt 'ṣmty* CIS i 6000bis 7: in honour of his bones.
kbdw v. *kbrw*.
kbh **Amm** word (?) or part of word (?) in BASOR cxciii 8[5] (for the reading, cf. Puech & Rofé RB lxxx 532, 534, Fulco BASOR ccxxx 41f., Sasson PEQ '79, 118, 123, Shea PEQ '81, 105, 107f.); Puech RB lxxx 534: = *kbh[lh]* = *k$_3$* + Sing. abs. of *bhlh*(= fright, consternation), Rofé ibid.: *kbh* = *k$_4$* + *b$_2$* + suff. 3 p.s.f.., Sasson PEQ '79, 118, 123: = PI'EL Pf. 3 p.s.m. of *kby* (= to be quenched), Shea PEQ '81, 105, 107f., Aufrecht sub CAI 59: = PI'EL Inf. abs. of *kby*, uncert. interpretations;

Fulco BASOR ccxxx 42f.: meaning unknown (for the reading *kbh* and its interpret., cf. also Aufrecht BASOR cclxvi 88) :: Horn BASOR cxciii 8, 12, v.Selms BiOr xxxii 5, 8, Shea PEQ '79, 18f.: l. *krh* = QAL Pf. 3 p.s.m. of *kry*$_1$ (cf. however Horn BASOR cxciii 12: reading *kbh* equally poss.) :: Cross BASOR cxciii 17, 19 ((n. 15): l. *krh* = Sing. + suff. 3 p.s.f. of *kr*$_3$ (= laver) :: Albright BASOR cxcviii 38, 40: l. *krh* = a) Sing. abs. of *krh* (= feast, banquet; cf. also Dion RB lxxxii 32f. (n. 56)), or b) QAL Inf. abs. of *kry*$_3$ (= to invite to a feast (related to *qry*$_1$)); for the reading *krh* and its interpret., cf. also Garbini AION xx 253, Sivan UF xiv 223, 228).

kby **OffAr** PA ʿEL Impf. 2 p.s.m. *tkbh* Aḥiq 100 (for the reading, cf. Lindenberger APA 79, 237 n. 191) - ¶ verb PA ʿEL to extinguish; + obj., *ʾl tkbh mlt mlk* Aḥiq 100: do not extinguish (i.e. do not suppress, cf. Cowl a.l.) the word of a king (cf. Ginsberg ANET 428: treat not lightly..., cf. also Rosenthal AH i/2, 11).
v. *kbh*.

kbyr **OffAr** Sing. m. abs. *kbyr* Aḥiq 136, 147 (:: Kottsieper SAS 16, 192: = *k*$_1$ + Sing. abs. of *byr*$_2$(= nitwit, blockhead)); cstr. *kbyr* KAI 276[4]; cf. Frah xxv 27 (*kbyr* :: Ebeling Frah a.l.: l. *kby* = lapsus for *kbyr*), Paik 523 (*kbyr*), GIPP 25, 55, SaSt 18 - ¶ adj. great, mighty; for KAI 276[4] and context, v. *nṣyḥ* - subst. adj. something big, grand: Aḥiq 136, 147 (for this text, v. *skl*$_1$).

kbl$_1$ **OffAr** Dupont-Sommer CRAI '47, 181f.: the *kblky* in CRAI '47, 181 conc. 2 = QAL (PA ʿEL) Pf. 3 p.s.m. + suff. 2 p.s.f. of *kbl* (= to bind > to render barren, said of a woman; uncert. interpret., cf. also Verger OA iii 56f., RGP 114f.).

kbl$_2$ v. *ky*.

kbl$_3$ **Hebr** Plur. abs. *kblym* DJD ii 43[5] - **OffAr** Sing. emph. *kblʾ* Cowl 30[16] (v. infra); Plur. cstr. *kbly* TADAE A 4.6[16] (heavily dam. context; *kbly[]*) + suff. 3 p.s.m. *kblwhy* Cowl 31[15] - ¶ subst. chain, fetter; *ʾny ntn t kblym brglkm* DJD ii 43[5f.]: I will put fetters on your feet - in Cowl 30[16], 31[15], poss. > anklet (as a sign of honour or distinction, cf. e.g. J.W.Epstein ZAW xxxii 128, Cowl a.l., Grelot DAE p. 410 (n. t), Porten & Greenfield JEAS p. 93, 97, Porten & Yardeni sub TADAE A 4.7 × Lipiński BiOr xxxi 120: = *kbl*$_5$ (cf. Akkad. *kaballu*; = leg of a shoe, legging) :: Ginsberg ANET 492 (n. 14): = fetter (cf. Galling TGI 86 (n. 14): = stocks?)); for these texts, cf. also Porten Arch 288 n. 19, Grelot RB xcv 297f. and v. *klby*.

kbl$_4$ **Pun** Sing. + suff. 3 p.s.m. *kblm* CIS i 5600[6] - ¶ subst. of uncert. meaning; Février JA ccxliii 56, sub CIS i a.l.: = offering - Février AIPHOS xiii 166f.: l. *kbl* (= Sing. abs.) in KAI 163[3] (cf. also Röllig KAI a.l.), highly uncert. interpret. - Février JA ccxliii 56: l. *kbl* (= Sing. abs.) in Hofra 25[2] (less prob. interpret., cf. also Berthier & Charlier Hofra a.l.: *kbl* = k_1 + *bl* (= n.d), cf. also Elayi SCA 59; uncert. interpret.) - Février with Berthier & Charlier sub Hofra 103, JA ccxliii 56 (cf. also Elayi SCA 58f.): l. *ʾt*$_5$ + *kblm* (= Sing. + suff. 3 p.s.m.) in Hofra 103[3] (improb. reading, cf. Berthier & Charlier Hofra a.l.: l. *ʾš* (= Sing. cstr. of *ʾš*$_1$) *kbnm* (= n.l.?), poss. interpret.) :: Krahmalkov RSF iii 182: l. *klbnm* (= Plur. + suff. 3 p.pl.m. of *klb*$_3$ (= their cages)) - Février with Berthier & Charlier sub Hofra 105, JA ccxliii 156: l. *bkblʾ* in Hofra 105[3] (= b_2 + Sing. + suff. 3 p.s.m.), less prob. reading, cf. Berthier & Charlier Hofra a.l.: prob. l. *bkrlʾ* (poss. = b_2 + n.l., division however unclear (cf. also Elayi SCA 59)).

kbl$_5$ v. *kbl*$_3$.

kblh v. *byt*$_2$.

kbn v.Soden Or xxxv 12, xlvi 188: subst. = wrapping, band, ring > Akkad. (cf. also id. AHW s.v. *kabnu*), uncert. interpret., cf. also CAD s.v. *kabnu* (= certain type of tree?), *kušāru*.
v. *lbnh*$_1$.

kbs$_1$ v. *kbs*$_2$.

kbs$_2$ **Pun** Sing. abs. *kbs* TPC 63[1] - ¶ subst. (or QAL Part. act. of *kbs*$_1$(= to wash)?) fuller (for the reading and interpret., cf. e.g. Lidzbarski Handb 293, Sznycer Sem xxvi 86ff.) - Israel UF xxi 234 (n. 14): the *kbs* in Irâq xix 140 ii 4 = Sing. abs. of this subst. (poss. interpret., cf. however e.g. Segal Irâq xix 143, Albright BASOR cxlix 34 n. 14: = n.p., Garbini AION xvii 94f.: = gentilicium?).

kbʿ v. *prʿ*$_2$.

kbr$_1$ **Samal** QAL Pf. 3 p.s.f. *kbrt* KAI 215[9]; HAPH Pf. 3 p.s.m. *hkbr* KAI 215[4] - **OffAr** QAL Impf. 3 p.pl.m. *ykbrw* ATNS 54[4] (heavily dam. context, reading *ykbdw* also poss.); HAPH Pf. 3 p.s.m. *hkbr* ATNS 52b ii 2 (*hkbr[*; heavily dam. context) - ¶ verb QAL to be plentiful; *wkbrt ḥṭh wšʿrh* KAI 215[9]: and wheat and barley were plentiful - HAPH to make numerous; + obj., *whkbr qyrt ḥrbt mn qyrt yšbt* KAI 215[4]: and desolate towns he made more numerous than inhabited ones.
v. *kbr*$_2$.

kbr$_2$ **Samal** Sing. abs. *kbr* KAI 215[12] (for the reading, cf. e.g. Lidzbarski Handb 293, 443 (:: id. ibid.: = n.l.?), Halévy RS i 219, 232, Cooke NSI p. 177f. (:: id. ibid.: or = n.l. ?), Donner KAI a.l. :: Gibson SSI ii p. 80: l. *kbr[y]* = Plur. m. abs. (casus obliquus) of *kbr*$_3$ (= powerful) :: Dion p. 40: l. *kbr* = k_1 + Sing. abs. of *br*$_1$(cf. however Garbini AION xxvi 125)) - **OldAr** Sing. cstr. *kbr* Tell F 8 (cf. Abou-Assaf, Bordreuil & Millard Tell F p. 46, 52; or preferably = PAʿEL Inf. of *kbr*$_1$?,cf. Andersen & Freedman FS Fensham 21, Kaufman Maarav iii 165, Muraoka AN xxii 99f., Gropp & Lewis BASOR cclix 49) - ¶ subst. - **1)** might (prob. interpret.); *mlky kbr* KAI 215[12]: powerful kings - the same expression *mlky kbr* has been read by e.g. Cooke NSI p. 172, Donner KAI a.l. in

KAI 215[10] (cf. also Lidzbarski Handb 443, cf. however Dion p. 39: l. *m[lky ...]*, Gibson SSI ii p. 78, 84: unreadable (cf. also Halévy RS i 219, 230: l. *mn p[..*, cf. however idem RS vii 342)) - **2)** abundance; *kbr šnwh* Tell F 8: the multiplication of his years (cf. Akkad. par. *šúm-ud šanāti-šu*).

kbr₃ v. *kbr₂*,*qbr₁*.

kbr₄ JAr this word (*[k]br*) = already, poss. in DJD ii 8 i 5 (cf. Milik DJD ii a.l.).

kbrh Ph Sing. cstr. *kbrt* KAI 19[1] (= DD 4) - ¶ subst. region, side (exact meaning unknown, cf. e.g. Röllig KAI a.l., v.d.Branden BO vii 71); *ʿrpt kbrt mṣʾ šmš* KAI 19[1]: the portico of the west quarter/side.

kbrw Samal Sing. abs. *kbrw* KAI 214[11] (for this reading, cf. e.g. Lidzbarski Handb 293, 441, Halévy RS i 141, 149 (n. 2), vii 334, 338, Cooke NSI p. 159, 167, Donner KAI a.l., Gibson SSI ii p. 66 × D.H.Müller WZKM vii 52, 58, 132, Dion p. 28: l. *kbdw*(Sing. abs.) = honour, prestige) - ¶ subst. f. greatness.

kbry OffAr Sing. abs. *kbry* Cowl 26[17]; emph. *kbrytʾ* Cowl 26[21] - ¶ subst. sulphur.

kbš OffAr QAL Impf. 3 p.s.m. + suff. 3 p.s.m. *ykbšnhy* Krael 8[5]; Part. act. s.m. abs./cstr. *kbš* Aḥiq 92 (v. infra), 152 (?, dam. context; for the context, cf. Lindenberger APA 152) - **JAr** QAL Part. pass. s.m. abs. *kbyš* AMB 11[6] - ¶ Verb QAL - **1)** to bind; *kbyš bšwšln* AMB 11[6]: bound by chains - **2)** to subdue; + obj., + noun, *ykbšnhy ʿbd* Krael 8[5]: he will subdue him as a slave (i.e. he will treat him as a slave) - exact meaning of root in Aḥiq 92 uncert. (*kbš ḥkmh*), Cowl a.l.: one who restrains wisdom? (cf. comm. p. 236, cf. also Nöldeke AGWG xiv/4, 11); Grelot RB lxviii 182, DAE p. 436: (when) one has wisdom in one's possession (*kbš* = QAL Pf. 3 p.s.m.??); Ginsberg ANET 428: who guards wisdom; Driver AnOr xii 56: one who acquires wisdom (cf. comm.), Kottsieper SAS 19, 208f.: one who collects wisdom, Lindenberger APA 65, 67, 232 n. 125: one who masters wisdom :: Perles OLZ '12, 55: one who hides wisdom - a form of this root probably in Cowl 64 xxiii 1 (*kbš[*), cf. also Lindenberger APA 220.

kgh v. *kkh*.

kd₁ Ph Sing. cstr. *kd* ClRh iii 67 no. 18 (dam. context; for the reading, cf. e.g. Amadasi Guzzo Sem xxxviii 18f.) - **Pun** Sing. cstr. *kd* ICO-Spa 2 (?; for this interpret., cf. Solá-Solé Sef xv 48; reading less. cert.; word div. uncert., cf. also Amadasi ICO-Spa a.l.) - **Hebr** Plur. abs. *kdyn* Mas 454[1] - **OffAr** Sing. emph. *kdʾ* Cowl 37[13] (for the reading, cf. e.g. Cowl a.l., Grelot DAE p. 390, Porten & Greenfield JEAS p. 80, Porten & Yardeni sub TADAE A 4.2, cf. however Sach p. 51, 53: poss. l. *krʾ* = Sing. emph. of *kr₁* (cf. also Ungnad ArPap 19, Wag 28)); Plur. abs. *kddn* RES 1300[7] - ¶ subst. f. (cf. Mas 454[1f.]) pitcher, jar - *knd* (< *kd₁*)

> Akkad., cf. v.Soden Or xxxv 12, xlvi 188 (cf. also Zimmern Fremdw 33, v.Soden AHW s.v. *kandu*, CAD s.v. *kandu*) - > Greek κάδος, cf. Masson RPAE 42ff. (for the relation of *kd₁* and κάδος and Lat. *cadus*, cf. Brown VT xix 155ff.) - for this word, cf. also Welten Stempel 54f., Amadasi Guzzo Sem xxxviii 17ff., Heltzer UF xxi 203, 206f. - the same word also in Lev ix 19 no. 9, cf. Puech Lev ix 20 (??, highly uncert. interpret.).

v. *tkd*.

kd₂ v. *zy*.

kdb₁ OffAr PA ʿEL Part. s.m. abs. *mndb* ATNS 4³ (lapsus for *mkdb*, cf. Porten with Shaked Or lvi 408, Porten & Yardeni sub TADAE B 8.7 :: Segal ATNS a.l.: = PA ʿEL Part. s.m. abs. of *ndb₁* (= to donate)) - ¶ verb PA ʿEL to deceive; *mnky mndb bʾlk mlyʾ* ATNS 4³: M. deceives with these words (v. supra).

v. *kdb₃, kzb*.

kdb₂ OffAr Plur. abs. *kdbn* Beh 51 (cf. Greenfield & Porten BIDG p. 46f. (cf. Akkad. par. *pir-ṣa-a-tú*) :: Cowl a.l.: = Plur. m. abs. of *kdb₃* (= liar)); cf. Frah x 27, GIPP 25, SaSt 18 - ¶ subst. lie.

kdb₃ OffAr Sing. m. abs. *kdb* Cowl 8¹⁷, Krael 10¹⁶; m. emph. *kdbʾ* Aḥiq 133; cf. Frah ix 8 (*kzbʾ*, cf. Nyberg FP 74; :: Ebeling Frah a.l.: l. *yzbʾ* or *zybʾ*?) - ¶ adj. (or QAL Part. act. of *kdb₁*?)deceitful, false; in Cowl 8¹⁷, Krael 10¹⁶ said of a document: forged; subst. adj., liar: Aḥiq 133.

v. *kdb₂, šʿl₁*.

kdbh OffAr Sing. cstr. *kdbt* Aḥiq 132; + suff. 3 p.s.m. *kdbth* Aḥiq 133 (or = Plur.?, cf. Ben Chayim EI i 136, Ginsberg ANET 429) - ¶ subst. untruthfulness, mendacity; Sach p. 196f., Cowl a.l.: l. *kdbtʾ* (= Sing. emph.) in Beh 56 (dam. context; highly uncert. reading, cf. Greenfield & Porten BIDG p. 48f.: l. poss. *swd/rtʾ*, word of unknown meaning; for the reading, cf. also Lemaire Or lv 349).

kdd₁ v. *tkd*.

kdd₂ OffAr Plur. emph., cf. Warka 11: *[k]i-da-di-e* (for this reading, cf. Gordon Or ix 32, cf. already Landsberger AfO xii 256f. n. 48 and also Dahood Bibl xlvi 327 :: Dupont-Sommer RA xxxix 36, 46: l. *qú-da-di-e* = Plur. m. emph. of *qdd₂* (= small), for this interpret., cf. also Landsberger AfO xii 256f. n. 48 :: Driver AfO iii 48, 51: l. *ki-ṭa-ṭi-e* = Plur. m. emph. of *qṭṭ* (= small) :: Gordon AfO xii 116: l. *[d]i-da-di-e* = *dy₂* + Plur. emph. of *dd₂*(= breast), i.e. they of the breasts (= sucklings) :: Kaufman AIA 86 (n. 279), Margalit UF xvi 161f.: l. *[d]i-da-qé-e/[d]a-da-qé-e* = Plur. emph. of *ddq*(= child)) - ¶ subst. child.

kdd₃ Hebr/JAr Plur. abs. *kddyn* Mas 551 - ¶ subst. of uncert. interpret.; Yadin & Naveh Mas a.l.: = *qddyn* = Plur. of *qydh* (= a seasoning plant?); uncert. interpret.

kdh **OffAr** Harmatta ActAntHung vii 362: l. *kd[h]* or *qd[h]* in Cowl 81^{49} = cinnamon.
kdwn v. *kwdn*.
kdy$_1$ v. *tkd*.
kdy$_2$ v. *zy*.
kdm (< Akkad. < Sum., cf. Kaufman AIA 66) - **OffAr** Sing. abs. *kdm* Irâq iv 18^2 (reading uncert.) - ¶ subst. gold-, silversmith, in the comb. *br kdm* = gold-, silversmith or son of the jeweller (?, cf. Driver Irâq iv a.l., Meissner AfO xiv 202 n. 1, cf. however Vattioni Aug x 519: = n.p.).
kdn **JAr** Fitzmyer & Harrington MPAT a.l.: *kdnyn* in MPAT 89^3 = QAL Part. pass. pl.m. abs. of *kdn* (= to join; highly uncert. interpret.) :: Beyer ATTM 329, 603: = QAL Part. act. pl.m. abs. of *kdn* (= to build) :: Avigad IEJ xvii 104: = *k*$_1$ + *dnyn*(= combination of *dnn* and *dyn*) = such, cf. also Puech RB xc 487, 489: l. *kdnwn* (= *k*$_1$ + *dnwn* (= those)) = thus.
kdš v. *qdš*$_2$.
kh$_1$ **DA** *kh* i 2 (for the context, cf. Hoftijzer **DA** p. 186) - **OldAr** *kh* KAI 222C 1 (:: Vriezen JEOL xvii 209 (div. otherwise): l. *k*$_3$ + *hʾmrn* = HAPH Pf. 1 p.pl. of *ʾmr*$_1$) - **OffAr** *kʾ*KAI 233^8 (dam. context) - in text in unknown West-semitic dialect *kh*: Sem xxxviii 52^1 (or = fraud?, cf. however Bordreuil & Pardee Sem xxxviii 65ff.) - ¶ adv. thus - Lipiński Stud 41: l. *kh* pro *kd* (uncert. reading and interpret.) in KAI 222B 36 (less prob. reading) - Gibson SSI ii p.66f., 73: l. poss. *kʾ* in KAI $214^{16,17}$ (in both instances uncert. reading; for other reading, cf. de Moor NYC ii 31).
kh$_2$ v. *hnkt*,*kʾ*$_2$.
khy **OffAr** diff. word in KAI 268^3 poss. = adv., thus (for older interpret., cf. CIS ii sub 123 :: Lipiński OLP viii 111: = *k*$_1$ + *hy*$_1$).
khl **OldAr** QAL Impf. 3 p.s.m. *ykhl* KAI 222B 25; 1 p.s. *ʾkhl* KAI 222B 33, 223B 6 - **OffAr** QAL Pf. 1 p.pl. *khln* Krael 3^{22a}; Impf. 3 p.s.m. *ykhl* Cowl 5^8, 43^5 (for the reading, cf. Porten & Yardeni sub TADAE B 5.5), Krael 3^{17}, 4^{13}, 7^{41}, 9^{18}, 10^{12} (for the *scriptio anterior ykl* (= QAL Impf. 3 p.s.m. of *ykl*),cf. Porten & Szubin JAOS cvii 231), 12^{27}; 3 p.s.f. *tkhl* Krael 7^{39}; 2 p.s.m. *tkhl* Aḥiq 81; 1 p.s. *ʾkhl* Cowl $5^{6,11}$, 6^{12}, 14^7, Krael 1^4, 4^{12}, 6^{14} (for the reading and *scriptio anterior*, cf. Szubin & Porten BASOR cclxix 33), etc.; 3 p.pl.m. *ykhlwn* Cowl 8^{15}, 20^{11}, ATNS 26^6, *ykhylwn* Krael 9^{21} (:: Krael p. 243: = HAPH Impf. 3 p.pl.m.; cf. Milik RB lxi 251, Kutscher JAOS lxxiv 237, Lindenberger APA 297 n. 1; cf. however Porten & Yardeni sub TADAE B 3.10: the second *y* erased); 1 p.pl. *nkhl* Cowl 20^{10}, 25^{10}, Krael 3^{13}, $12^{25,26}$; Part. act. s.m. abs. *khl* Krael 9^{17} - ¶ verb QAL to be able, to have the right to, to be allowed - **1)** followed by a verbal form of the same conjugation & person, *wlykhl*

bry [l]yšlḥ yd bbr[k] KAI 222B 25: nor will my son be able to raise (his) hand against your son; *l' 'khl 'mr lmḥsh* Cowl $5^{11f.}$: I shall not be able to say to M.; *l' tkhl thnṣln[hy* .. Aḥiq 81: you will not be able to save (him ...); *l' ykhl br wbrh ln ygrnk zyn wzbb* Krael $3^{16f.}$: and son or daughter of ours shall not be able to institute suit or process against you; etc., etc. (cf. also Muffs 36f. n. 2, 197f.); cf. the following examples, *l['] nkhl 'nḥnh wbnyn wbntn w'ḥyn w'yš zyln qryb wb'l qryh l' ykhlwn yršw[nk]m* Cowl $20^{10f.}$: we shall not be able, we, our sons or daughters, our brothers, or any person who is related to us, one near or a civilian (they) shall not be able to institute suit or process against you; *l' 'khl 'nh ... wbr wbrh ly 'ḥ w'ḥh ly w'yš ly ykbšnhy* Krael $8^{4f.}$: I shall not be able, I, ... a son or daughter of mine or brother or sister of mine or any person who is related to me, to subdue him; *wl' 'khl 'nh wbr wbrh ly 'ḥ w'ḥh ly w'yš ly nqwm* Krael 8^6: I shall not be able, I or son or daughter of mine or brother or sister of mine or any person related to me, to rise up ...; cf. also *[l]' tkhl yhwyšm' wl' t'bd ...* Krael $7^{39f.}$: Y. shall not be able to abstain from making ... - **2)** + l_5 + Inf., *l' 'khl ... lmršh 'lyk* Cowl $28^{7f.}$: I will not be able ... to institute a suit against you (cf. Greenfield Mem Yalon 72f.); *ykhlwn lmqrq* ATNS 26^6: they will be able to flee; *l' 'khl lmplḥ ...* Aḥiq 17: I will not be able to work ... - **3)** + b_2, *l' khl hwyt bydy* Krael 9^{17}: I had no command (anymore) over my hands (:: Greenfield IEJ xix 205 n. 26: *bydy* = lapsus for *lmplḥ bydy*) - Dupont-Sommer Sf p. 62, 84, Fitzmyer AIS 18, 72, Lipiński Stud 43: l. *[tk]hl* in KAI 222B 39 (poss. emendation) - for the use of this verb, cf. also Lipiński LDA 109f.

khn$_1$ **Ph** m. Sing. abs. *khn* KAI 43^5; cstr. *khn* KAI 11, $13^{1,2}$, 32^3 (= Kition A 2), RES 307^2 (= DD 6); Plur. abs. *khnm* KAI 59^2 (cf. e.g. Renan sub CIS i 119, Cooke NSI p. 101, Garbini AION xvii 96 :: Röllig KAI a.l.: = grammatical mistake :: Driver FS Bakoš 102, Dahood Or xxxiv 172, Bibl xlvii 412, xlix 90, Teixidor Syr xlviii 456: = Plur. cstr. + enclitic *mem*); f. Sing. cstr. *khnt* KAI 14^{15} - **Pun** m. Sing. abs. *khn* KAI 65^{11} (cf. e.g. Lidzbarski Eph iii 283, Röllig KAI a.l., v.d.Branden BiOr xxxvi 158 (n. 23); reading however highly incert., cf. Chabot JA xi/10, 9, cf. also Guzzo Amadasi ICO p. 117, 120: l. *wḥ* = *w* + *ḥ* (= abbrev. for *ḥbrm* = Plur. + suff. 3 p.s.m. of *ḥbr$_2$*??)), 69^{20}, 72B 3, $74^{2,6,8}$, 75^3, 159^7, CIS i 244^4, 246^4, 3917^2, 6000bis 5 (= TPC 84), Hofra 29^3, 69^3, 70^3, Punica xii 11^2 (cf. Jongeling NINPI 51 :: Chabot Punica a.l.: = Sing. cstr.), ICO-Malta-npu 19 (reading uncert.), *kḥn* RES 1552^3, *k'n* Hofra 65^3 (uncert. context), 66^2, 71^2, *kn* Hofra 235^1 (in the comb. *h'kn* = *h'* (variant of *h$_1$*) + *kn* (or = *h* (= *h$_1$*) + *'kn* (= lapsus for *k'n*)?)), *phn* CIS i 5268^2 (prob. lapsus for *khn*, cf. Février CIS i a.l.); cstr. *khn* CIS i 243^4, 245^3, 379^1, 4861^6, $4862^{5f.}$, 5955^1 (= TPC 17), Hofra 68^3; Plur. abs. *khnm* KAI 65^{10}, $69^{3,5,7,9}$, $74^{2,3,4}$, $81^{8,9}$,

93$^{3,3f.}$ (= TPC 12), 95^{1} (= TPC 50), 96^{8} (= CIS i 5523), 137^{7}, CIS i 4857^{6}, 4858^{5}, etc., etc., *khnym* KAI 161^{6} (diff. context; cf. Cooke NSI p. 150, FR 222b, Roschinski Num 112, 115 :: Février RA xlv 144f., Röllig KAI a.l.: = Plur. abs. of *khn$_2$* (= *kn$_2$*) = base (of a column) :: v.d.Branden RSF ii 144: = Plur. abs. of *khny* (= something belonging to a priest > priestly chamber)); f. Sing. abs. *khnt* KAI 70^{1}, 93^{1} (= TPC 12), 145^{45}, RES 7^{1} (= CIS i 5942 = TPC 4), 501^{1} (= CIS i 5961 = TPC 23), 502 (= CIS i 5941 = TPC 3), 509 (= CIS i 5947 = TPC 9), 796^{1} (= RES 2001 = CIS i 5987 = TPC 49), *kʿnt* Hofra 72^{2}, *knt* KAI 140^{2} (cf. Lat. par. *sacerdos magna*), *kḥnt* CIS i 5994^{1} (= TPC 56); Plur. abs. *khnt* RES 540^{1} (= CIS i 5949 = TPC 11), Hofra 67^{3} - **Hebr** m. Sing. abs. *khn* IEJ xxxvi 39^{3}, Frey 903, 1317a, DF 22^{3}, SM 75^{2,5}, Vatt sig. eb. 348 (diff. reading), Sem xxxvi 44, Mas 441, on coins of the first and second revolt: JC no. 12, 14, 15, 17, 17a, 18, 18a, 197, etc. (cf. also Meshorer Mas coin 96, 101, 103), *kh* (lapsus?) JC no. 13 (for the coins of the second revolt, cf. Schäfer BKA 99), *kwhn* Frey 1411, Qadm xvii 60 (on coin, cf. e.g. Barag BiAr xlviii 166ff., Cross SVT xl 21); cstr. *khn* Vatt sig. eb. 323 (= SANSS-Hebr 57), SM 106^{9}; Plur. abs. *khnm* RB lxxxviii 236, *khnym* Frey 1394^{3} (cf. Kutscher SY 353), *kwhnym* Frey 1001 (Greek par. ἱερέων), 1002 - **DA** f. Sing. abs. *khnh* i 13 (dam. context) - **OffAr** m. Sing. emph. *khnʾ* Cowl 30^{18}, 81$^{8, 39?}$; Plur. emph. *khnyʾ* Cowl 30^{1,18}, 38^{1,12} - **Nab** m. Sing. cstr. *khn* CIS ii 506, 526^{2}, 611, 766^{2}, 1236^{2}, 1748^{2}, 1885^{2}, 2491$^{2f.}$, RB xli 591 ii 2, *kh* (lapsus) CIS ii 1750^{3}; emph. *khnʾ* CIS 2665^{2} (cf. Negev IEJ xxvii 222), xliii 578 xxiii, ARNA-Nab 17^{5} - **JAr** m. Sing. emph. *khnʾ* MPAT-A 56^{1} (= SM 74), Frey 824^{1}, Mas 461, *khnh* MPAT 68^{1}, 139^{1} (= Frey 1221; for the context, cf. also Puech RB xc 499f.), MPAT-A 2^{1} (= Frey 1197 = SM 58), Syn D A 5 (= SM 88), C$_1$ 5 (= SM 89a), C$_2$ 4 (*[k]hnh*; = SM 89b) - ¶ subst. m. priest, f. priestess: passim; *khn dʾr* Vatt sig. eb. 323: the priest of D. (cf. SM 106^{9}); *khn bʿlt* KAI 11: the priest of B.; *khnt ʿštrt* KAI 14^{15}: the priestess of A. (cf. KAI 13^{1,2}, 32^{3}, RES 307^{2} (= DD 6), CIS i 243^{4}, 245$^{2f.}$, 4861$^{6f.}$, 4862$^{5f.}$, 5955^{1}, ii 506, 526$^{2f.}$, 611, 766^{2}, 1236^{2}, 1748^{2}, 1885^{2}, 2491$^{2f.}$, Hofra 68^{3}; the *khn tʾ* in CIS ii 506, 766, 1748, 1750 (v. supra), 1885, 2491 = priest of T. :: Milik DFD 56: *khntʾ* (form?) = special type of priest, cf. also Starcky RB lxxxiii 445), *khn šbʿlšmm* CIS i 379: priest of B.; *hkhnt šrbtn* RES 7$^{1f.}$: the priestess of our lady (cf. also RES 2001^{1}, cf. Février Rob 368f.; cf. also Punica xii 11^{2}?, cf. Jongeling NINPI 51); *hkhn lrbbtn* KAI 72B 3: the priest of our lady (cf. KAI 159^{7}); *khnyʾ zy YHW ʾlhʾ* Cowl 38^{1}: the priests of the god Y.; *hkhn hgdl* IEJ xxxvi 39^{3}, JC no. 12 (cf. JC no. 13, 14, 17, 18, etc.): the high-priest; *khnʾ rbʾ* Cowl 30^{18}: the high-priest (cf. Mas 461; cf. also the unpublished *khnʾ rbʾ* in IEJ xv 84); *rb (h)khnm* KAI 65^{10}, 81^{8,9}, 93$^{3,5f.}$ (= TPC 12), 95^{1} (= TPC 50), 96^{8}, CIS i 4857^{6},

4858[5], 4859[5,6f.], 5955[2f.], etc.: the high-priest (title used for a woman in KAI 95[1] (= TPC 50)); *[r]b khn* CIS i 244[3f.]: the high-priest (cf. also *rb ḥk'n* Hofra 65[3] (uncert. reading), *hrb hk'n* Hofra 66[2]); *rb (h)khnt* CIS i 5949[1], Hofra 67[3]: high-priestess - for *khn* in Nab. inscriptions, cf. also Catastini JSS xxxii 274ff. - Puech RB xc 495f.: l. poss. *kwhnt'* (= f. Sing. emph.) in IEJ xvii 110 iii l. 1 (highly uncert. reading) - Pili BO xxii 216: l. *knm* = m Plur. abs. in CIS i 151[4] (highly uncert. interpret., cf. e.g. Amadasi sub ICO Sard Npu 2 (dividing otherwise) l.: *bn* (= Sing. cstr. of bn_1) *m-*.
v. *hnkt*, *'ybydh*, *qrbn*.

khn₂ v. khn_1.

khnh v. *hnkt*, khn_1.

khny v. khn_1.

khnt v. khn_1.

khs' v. *krs'*.

kw v. *kwh*.

kw' v. ks'_1.

kwd v. *tkd*.

kwdn **OffAr** Plur. abs. *kwdnn* AG 90 (*kdwnn*prob. misprint); cf. Frah vii 6 (*kwdnt'*; for the reading, cf. Nyberg FP 43, 70 :: Ebeling Frah a.l.: l. *kwtyn'*) - **Palm** Sing. emph.? *kwdn[']* CIS ii 3913 ii 39 - ¶ subst. mule.

kwh **OffAr** Plur. abs. *kwn* Krael 4[8], 9[13], 12[13], *kwyn* Cowl 25[6], Krael 3[5] (cf. Leand 43t, Segert ArchOr xxxiii 122; or = Plur. of *kw*with same meaning?) - **Nab** Plur. emph. *kwy'* RES 2025[2] (:: Chabot sub RES 90: l. *kry'* prob. = Plur. emph. of kry_4 (= cistern), cf. also Levinson NAI 175) - ¶ subst. window - this word (Sing. emph. *kwt'*) in Aḥiq 211?, or (div. otherwise): l. *bkwt'* = Sing. emph. of *bkw*(= weeping)?, cf. Kottsieper SAS 23, 209.
v. bwt_4.

kwhn v. khn_1.

kwhnh v. $kḥn_1$,

kwz **Nab** Littmann BSOAS xv 15f. (sub 44d): l. poss. *kwzh* (= Sing. + suff. 3 p.s.m. of *kwz* (= jug)) or l. *kwz'* (= Sing. emph. of *kwz* or = n.p.); uncert. interpret.
v. *'rkw*.

kwzbrh cf. Frah vi 5 (*kwzblt'*): coriander.

kwy v. ks'_1, ksy_1, $qdḥ_1$.

kwk₁ **JAr** Sing. emph. *kwkh* MPAT 67[1] (= Frey 1300) - ¶ subst. m. sepulchral chamber (for this word, cf. Kutscher EI viii 270ff. and v. also qwq_2).

kwk₂ v. krk_1.

kwkb/kwkp v. *kkb*.

kwl$_1$ **OffAr**, cf. Frah xix 1 (*kylwn*), cf. Toll ZDMG-Suppl viii 36 - **Palm** APH Impf. 3 p.s.m. + suff. 3 p.s.f. *ykylnh* CIS ii 3913 ii 73 (cf. Greek par. παραμετρησάτω) - ¶ verb APH to measure; + obj.: in CIS ii 3913 ii 73 (object = salt) - Segal ATNS a.l.: l. *kl* (= QAL Pf. 3 p.s.m.) in ATNS 52a 11 (diff. context; highly uncert. interpret.).
v. *ʾnḥ$_2$*,*kl$_2$*, *kly$_1$*, *qʾl$_1$*.

kwl$_2$ v. *kl$_1$*.

kwl$_3$ v. *kl$_1$*.

kwlb$_1$ **Pun** Plur. abs. *kwlbm* Karth xii 51 ii 1 - ¶ subst. of unknown meaning, prob. architectural term in the comb. *kwlbm mšʾm* = elevated (?, v. *nšʾ$_1$*) ...; cf. Février & Fantar Karth xii 51f.: poss. = capital (of a column) :: idem ibid.: or < Lat. *columna*? :: v.d.Branden RSF v 57, 60, BiOr xxxvi 202: = *kwlb$_2$* (= hatchet), in Plur. = arms :: Krahmalkov RSF iii 178, 182, 201: = *kwlb$_3$* (= cage, basket > prison, imprisonment).

kwlb$_2$ v. *kwlb$_1$*.

kwlb$_3$ v. *kwlb$_1$*.

kwlyh **JAr** Sing./Plur. + suff. 3 p.s.m./f. *kwlyth* AMB 10[7] - ¶ subst. kidney.

kwmr v. *kmr$_2$*.

kwmtr cf. Frah iv 20 (*kwmtlʾ*): pear.

kwn$_1$ **OldCan** QAL Imper. s.m. *ku-na* EA 147[36] (cf. Böhl 32m; cf. however CAD s.v. *kânu* B) - **Ph** QAL Pf. 3 p.s.m. *kn* KAI 24[3] (cf. e.g. Lidzbarski Eph iii 226, Röllig KAI a.l., Gibson SSI iii p. 35 :: Torrey JAOS xxxv 365: = *kn$_4$*),[5], KAI 26 i 5, 9, 16, ii 7, 15, 16 (:: v.d.Branden Meltô i 50: = QAL Pf. 3 p.pl.m.; v. also *ll$_2$*), 40[5]; 3 p.s.f. *kn* KAI 26A iii 7, C iv 6; 1 p.s. *kt* KAI 24[6,10,11]; 3 p.pl.m. *kn* KAI 11, 26A i 14, 19 ii 1, 3, C iv 8; Impf. 3 p.s.m. *ykn* KAI 14[8,11], 26A iii 8, iv 2, C v 6; 3 p.pl.m. *ykn* KAI 43[15]; Inf. cstr. *kn* KAI 19[10]; + suff. 3 p.s.m. *kny* KAI 18[6]; + suff. 3 p.s.f. *kny* KAI 26A ii 14 (:: Gibson SSI iii p. 60: + suff. 3 p.s.m.); + suff. 3 p.pl.m. *knnm* KAI 14[20] - **Pun** QAL Pf. 3 p.s.m. *kn* KAI 69[11], 76A 5 (?, or = QAL Part. act. s.m. abs.?, cf. FR 166), 134[2] (for the reading, cf. Chabot sub Punica ix 2bis, Röllig KAI ii p. 340 (or l. *bn*? = Sing. cstr. of *bn$_1$*,cf. Chabot Punica a.l.) :: Röllig KAI a.l. (div. otherwise): l. poss. *ʾwḥ* = QAL Pf. 3 p.s.m. of *ḥwy$_2$*), 165[3] (for this interpret., cf. Levi Della Vida OA iv 65, 67 :: Février BAr '51/52, 41, 43 (div. otherwise): l. *mkn* (= Sing. abs. of *mkn$_1$*) :: v.d.Branden RSF ii 145f. (div. otherwise): l. *mkn* = Sing. cstr. of *mkn$_1$*, cf. also Röllig KAI a.l.), RCL '66, 201[1], Or xxxiii 4[6] (diff. context, cf. Levi Della Vida ibid. p. 7),[8] (diff. and dam. context), cf. Poen 934, 935: *chon*, Poen 944: *con*; 3 p.s.f. *knʿ* KAI 136[4]; 3 p.pl.m. *kn* KAI 69[4,6,8,10], 74[4,5,8] (or = 3 p.s.f. in KAI 69 & 74 (except in 74[8])?), 80[1], *knʾ* KAI 130[3], 137[2]; Impf. 3 p.s.m. *ykn* KAI 69[3,7] (*yk[n]*),[15], 74[6], 76B

4; 3 p.pl.m. *ykn* KAI 69[13]; Inf. *kn* KAI 162[6], Trip 51[1] (diff. context, cf. Levi Della Vida ibid. p. 7, Amadasi IPT 131f.), CIS i 151[4] (cf. also Février JA ccxlvi 444, Guzzo Amadasi sub ICO-Sard-Np 2), NP 2[4] (= Trip 2) - ¶ verb QAL - **1)** to be, to exist, to happen; *bmqmm b'š kn 'šm r'm* KAI 26A i 14f.: in places where there were wicked men (cf. KAI 26A i 9); *kl hmlkm 'š kn lpny* KAI 26A i 19: all the kings who were before me (cf. KAI 11; cf. also Sperling UF xx 326); *šm 'ztwd ykn l'lm* KAI 26A iv 2: may the name of A. last forever (cf. KAI 26C v 5f., cf. also Dietrich & Loretz UF ii 356); *kt byd mlkm* KAI 24[6]: I was in the hands (i.e. in the power) of kings; *'š kn' bhšt hy* KAI 130[3]: who were in function in that year (cf. KAI 80[1]); *kn bnh* (for this reading instead of *bmh*, cf. Lipiński RSF ii 49) KAI 24[3]: there was B. (i.e. B. reigned); etc. - a) + l_5: to belong to; *'l ykn lm šrš* KAI 14[11]: may they have no root (cf. KAI 14[8]); *lknnm lṣdnm l'lm* KAI 14[20]: that they belong to the Sidonians for ever; *wkn bymty kl n'm ldnnym* KAI 26A i 5f.: and in my days the D. had everything (that was) pleasant (cf. KAI 26A ii 15f., 43[15]); *wkn h'rt ... lb'l hzbḥ* KAI 69[4]: and the hide ... will belong to the person offering the sacrifice (cf. KAI 69[6,8,13,14], 74[4,5], etc.); etc. - b) + l_5 + l_5, *lkny ly lskr ... tḥt p'm 'dny* KAI 18[6]: that it may be to me (for) a memorial ... under the foot of my lord - c) + *'l_7*, *kn' 'l mlkt ...* KAI 137[2]: (they) were in charge of the work ... - **2)** to be + predicate, *bmqmm 'š kn lpnm nšt'm* KAI 26A ii 3f.: in the places which were formerly dreaded; *wkn hqrt z b'lt šb'* KAI 26A iii 7: may this town be owner of plenty (cf. KAI 26A iii 7f., C iv 6f., 7f.); *bl 'š 'bd kn lbt mpš* KAI 26A i 15f.: no one had been servant of the house of M. (for the construction, v. *'bd_2*); *hndr 'š kn ndr 'bnm ... bḥyy* KAI 40[5]: the vow which their father ... had vowed during his lifetime (for the construction, v. *ndr_1*); *wkn' š'nt 'sr wšmn r'š'* KAI 136[4f.]: during 18 years she was ... (v. *r'š'*); cf. Poen 934, 935 - a) + predicate + l_5, *lkny mšmr l'mq 'dn* KAI 26A ii 14: that it might be a protection for the plain of A.; *lmy kt 'b wlmy kt 'm* KAI 24[10]: to some I was a father and to some I was a mother (on this text, cf. Guzzo Amadasi VO iii 96, Sperling UF xx 334 (n. 110)).

v. *k'_2*, *kn_4*, *kny*, *ndr_1*, *ktb_2*, *qry_1*, *tk_1*.

kwn$_2$ **Hebr** HOPH Part. s.f. abs. *mwknt* Frey 634a 3 - **OldAr** PAL (cf. also Gropp & Lewis BASOR cclix 51) Pf. 3 p.s.m. *knn* Tell F 10; Impf. 3 p.s.m. + suff. 3 p.s.f. *lknnh* Tell F 11 (cf. Kaufman Maarav iii 150 (n. 31), JAOS civ 572, Pardee JNES xliii 254, Muraoka AN xxii 83, 95 :: Abou-Assaf, Bordreuil & Millard Tell F p. 32, 50, 63 (div. otherwise): *knnh* = Inf. :: Puech RB xc 596: = PAL Inf. + suff. 3 p.s.m. :: Andersen & Freedman FS Fensham 23f.: poss. = l_1 + PA'EL Pf. 3 p.s.m. + suff. 3 p.s.f.) - **OffAr**, cf. Nisa 229[6] (*ytkyn*), 563[14] (*ytkynw*), GIPP 68 - **Hatra** APH Pf. 3 p.s.m. *'kyn* 6[1] (cf. Caquot Syr xxix 93, Altheim &

Stiehl AAW ii 195, Teixidor Sumer xxi 89*, Aggoula Ber xviii 87, Milik DFD 405, Vattioni IH a.l. :: Safar Sumer vii 175 (n. 22), Krückmann AfO xvi 142: *ʾkyn*= adverb: thus), 200^5, 410^2 (:: As-Salihi Sumer xliv p. 103: l. *hkyn* = HAPH) - ¶ verb PAL to erect: Tell F 10, 11 (a statue, cf. Kaufman Maarav iii 166 :: Greenfield & Shaffer Irâq xlv 113f.: = to dedicate) - APH to erect: Hatra 6^1 (a statue :: Caquot Syr xxix 93: = to execute); + obj. + *b*$_2$ (loci): Hatra 200$^{5f.}$ - HOPH Part. designated, ready; *mwknt bkl mṣwwt* Frey 634a 3f.: ready in all prescriptions - a form of this root poss. also in DA ii 14 (reading and context diff.), Hoftijzer DA p. 241f., 293: = NIPH Impf. 3 p.s.m. (= to be quiet, to be firm), cf. also Caquot & Lemaire Syr liv 206 (with different context interpret.), cf. however H.P.Müller ZAW xciv 219, 236: = APH Impf. 3 p.s.m.: (= to consolidate) - v.Soden Or xxxv 12, xlvi 188: second D-stem of *kânu* in Akkad. < Ar. influence (cf. idem AHW s.v. *kânu(m)*, cf. however CAD s.v. *kânu* A 8 (= K p. 171)).
v. *hlk*$_1$, *ytn*$_1$.

kwn$_3$ **OffAr** Sing. + suff. 3 p.s.m. *kwnh* Krael 12^{21} - ¶ subst. m. window - Lipiński ZAH i 66: < Neo-Babyl.

kwn$_4$ v. *krk*$_1$.

kws **Hebr** word of unknown meaning in TA-H 38^1; Aharoni TA a.l.: *hkws* = *h*$_1$ + Sing. abs. of *kws* (= small night bird) used as n.p.

kwsh v. *kysh*.

kwr$_1$ v. *ksʾ*$_1$.

kwr$_2$ (< Akkad. < Sum., cf. Kaufman AIA 62 (n. 148)) - **OffAr** Plur. emph. *kwry* CRAI '70, 163^{2bis}, IPAA 11^4; cf. Frah iii 7 (*kwʾlʾ*) - ¶ subst. fish (for the context of CRAI '70, 163^{2bis}, IPAA 11^4, cf. Humbach IPAA p. 12f.).

kwr$_3$ v. *kr*$_1$.

kwrkwr **JAr** Plur. emph. *kwrkwryʾ* AMB 11^{5,10} - ¶ subst. of uncert. meaning; bones?, for eventual etymologies, cf. Naveh & Shaked AMB a.l.

kwrsʾ v. *krsʾ*.

kwt **OffAr** *kwt* Cowl 18^3 (for the reading, cf. Kutscher with Muffs 43 n. 1, Porten & Greenfield JEAS p. 116, Porten & Yardeni sub TADAE B 6.4, Porten AN xxvii 101 :: Cowl a.l.: l. *kzt* = *k*$_1$+ *zt*$_2$(= f. Sing. of *znh*)= like this > so), Krael 7^{33,39,42} (for this reading, cf. Porten & Yardeni sub TADAE B 3.8), Driv 5^8, 10^2, Herm 1^7, *kwtʾ* Aḥiq 20 - **Nab** *kwt* CIS ii 199^8, 200^5 (= J 30; for the reading, cf. Milik sub ARNA-Nab 79)^{,8}, 205^{10}, 206^8, 209^9, 224^{13}, J 38^8 - **Palm** *kwt* CIS ii 3913 i 6, ii 96, 3917^6, 3932^6, Inscr P 6^4, Syr xii 122^6 - ¶ adverb - **1)** thus, so; *hn tʿbd kwt* Krael 7^{33}: if she does so (cf. Cowl 18^3 (v. supra)); *hn ʿlyk kwt ṭb* Driv 5^8: if it thus be good to you (cf. Aḥiq 20, Krael 7^{39}, Driv 10^2) - a) in the expression *bdyl kwt* CIS ii 3917$^{5f.}$, Inscr. P

6[4], Syr xii 122[6]: for that reason, it is for that reason that ... - b) in the expression *btr kwt* CIS ii 3913 ii 95f., prob. meaning: after that, afterwards, cf. Lidzbarski Handb 230 and the expressions *bdyl kwt*, *mṭl kwt* :: Reckendorf ZDMG xlii 387, Cooke NSI p. 328, 338, CIS ii sub 3913: *btr* = adverb (afterwards), based on reconstructed Greek par. - c) in the expression *mṭl kwt* CIS ii 3913 i 6 (Greek par. περὶ τούτου), 3932[6]: for that reason, it is for that reason that ... - d) in the comb. *kzy ... kwt ...* , *kzy ʿbd ʾnh lḥrwṣ kwt tʿbd bnt ʿly* Herm 1[7]: as I am doing for Ch., thus may B. do for me - **2)** likewise; *pʾyty ʿmh ldwšrʾ ʾlhʾ ... slʿyn ʾlp ... wlmrʾnʾ ḥrtt mlkʾ kwt* CIS ii 199[7f.]: he shall be charged to the god D. ... a thousand *selac*'s ... and to our lord the king Ch. likewise (i.e. the same amount; cf. CIS ii 205[10], 206[8], 209[9], 224[13], J 38[8]) - Porten & Yardeni sub TADAE A 6.2: l. *kwth* in Cowl 26[24] = *kwt* (used as prep.) + suff. 3 p.s.m./f. (according to it), heavily dam. and uncert. context.
v. *ʾyt*$_3$, *bwt*$_4$.

kwtʾ v. *kwt.*

kwtyn v. *kwdn*

kwtl v. *ktl.*

kzb$_1$ **OffAr** PAʿEL Impf. 3 p.s.m. *ykdb* Beh 50 (Akkad. par. *ú-par-ra-ṣu*), 51; Part. act. s.m. abs. *mkdb* Aḥiq 134 - ¶ verb PAʿEL to lie: Beh 50, 51; Part. subst., liar: Aḥiq 134 - the *ʾkzb* in Lach viii rev. 1 (heavily dam. context) may be explained as PIʿEL Impf. 1 p.s. (cf. Torczyner Lach i 129, Albright BASOR lxxxii 23), cf. however Elliger PJB '38, 58, ZDPV lxii 81, Lemaire IH i 124ff.: l. *ʾkzb* = n.l.; cf. also Diringer Lach iii p. 335.
v. *kdb*$_1$.

kzb$_2$ v. *kdb*$_3$.

kzy v. *zy.*

kḥ **Hebr** Sing. constr. *kḥ* AMB 4[32] (dam. context) - ¶ subst. strength.

kḥd **Amm** two forms of this root prob. in BASOR cxciii 8[3]: *]kḥd ʾkḥd*, poss. = Inf. abs. + Impf. 1 p.s., cf. Palmaitis VDI cxviii 120, 122f., 125, Dion RB lxxxii 29f., 32, Fulco BASOR ccxxx 41f.; *ʾkḥd* = HIPH form? (cf. Jackson ALIA 17, 26, cf. also Aufrecht sub CAI 59), cf. however Fulco BASOR ccxxx a.l.: both forms PIʿEL (cf. also Sivan UF xiv 231); exact meaning unknown, Palmaitis VDI cxviii 122f., 125, Dion RB lxxxii a.l., Fulco BASOR ccxxx a.l., Jackson ALIA 10, 17, Aufrecht sub CAI 59: = to obliterate, to extirpate, to annihilate, to destroy :: R.Kutscher Qadm v 27f.: l. *kḥd ʾkḥdw* = Inf. abs. + Impf. 1 p.s. + suff. 3 p.s.m. :: Puech & Rofé RB lxxx 532f., 536: l. *kḥd ʾkḥdm* = Inf. abs. + Impf. 1 p.s. + suff. 3 p.pl.m. (with same meaning; cf. also Dion RB lxxxii 33f.: this reading poss., Shea PEQ '79, 17f., '81, 105 (l. *ʾkḥd[m]*) :: Cross BASOR cxciii 17f. (div. otherwise): l. *kḥd ʾkḥd[h]w* = Inf. abs.

+ Impf. 1 p.s. + suff. 3 p.s.m. (with same meaning), cf. also Sasson PEQ '79, 118, 120 :: Horn BASOR cxciii 8, 10 (n. 19): l. *]kḥd* (poss. = rest of Niph-form (= to be destroyed)) *ʾkḥd/b/r* (without interpret.) :: v. Selms BiOr xxxii 7f. (n. 22): l. poss. *[ʾ]kḥd ʾkḥd* (*ʾkḥd* in both instances = *ʾ*k_2(= prep. as) + *ḥ*d_1 (= one) = the one like the other) :: Albright BASOR cxcviii 38f.: l. *kḥd ʾkḥd* (*kḥd* = k_1 + *ʾḥ*d_4 (with loss of *ʾ*), or + *ḥ*d_1; *ʾkḥd* = *ʾ*k_2 + *ḥ*d_1) = as one man, all together; cf. also Garbini AION xx 253, 256: l. *kḥd ʾkhr* (*ʾkhr* = broken Plur.?)).

kḥl v. *yyn*.

kṭl v. *qṭ*l_1.

ky **Ph** *k* KAI 10[9], 13[4,6], 14[5,6,13], 26A ii 10, 15, 30[2] (dam. context; cf, H.P.Müller ZA lxv 109), 38[2], etc. - **Pun** (on the situation in Punic, cf. Jongeling FS Hospers 101ff.) *k* KAI 61A 5, 63[3], 68[5], 88[5], 98[4], 102[4], 104[3], 105[4], etc., etc., *kʾ*KAI 89[3] (= CIS i 6068), 106[3], 111[5], 113A 3, 159[7], CIS i 2595[6], 3390[3], Hofra 29[3], 36[3], etc., etc., *kʿ* Punica iv A 1[1], B 1, Hofra 101[3], 104[2], NP 8[1], etc., *kh* Punica xvii 3[4], *kḥ* Punica xii 3[5], 11[3], xvii 11[4], xviii/ii 105[2], Hofra 251[3], *ky* Karth xii 53[2], cf. Poen 931: *chy*, 938: *chi* (diff. context, for other proposals, cf. Sznycer PPP 102f., J.J.Glück & Maurach Semitics ii 112f.), 941: *co*, IRT 865: *c* (cf. Vattioni AION xvi 42, Aug xvi 541; uncert. interpret.), IRTS 24[5]: *ch* (cf. Vattioni AION xvi 54f., Aug xvi 549, cf. also Krahmalkov RSF vii 175, 178: l. *ch[y]*; uncert. interpret., cf. also Levi Della Vida OA ii 76: *ch* = part of n.p.) - **Mo** *ky* KAI 181[4,5,17,27,28], BASOR clxxii 7[2] (cf. also Schiffmann ZAW lxxvii 325) - **Hebr** *ky* KAI 189[3], 192[4], 193[6,8] (for the context, v. *ʾmr*$_1$), 194[4,9,10,12], 196[3] - **DA** *ky* i 9 - **OldAr** *ky* KAI 202A 13, 224[22] - **OffAr** *ky* KAI 233[8], 266[6], Aḥiq 95, 98, 99 (and passim in Aḥiq) - **Palm** *ky* SBS 47[2] (uncert. interpret., dam. context) - ¶ particle - **1)** used as introduction of principal clause, verily, surely; *kʾnk ʾšmnʿzr mlk ṣdnm ... wʾmy ... ʾm* (lapsus for *ʾš*) *bnn* KAI 14[13ff.]: surely I E. king of the Sidonians and my mother ... are those who have built (cf. KAI 14[12]); *ky lʾ bydy ʾn[š]ʾ m[nš]ʾ rglhm* Aḥiq 122: verily, it is not in the power of men to lift up their foot (cf. Aḥiq 123) - **2)** used as introduction of clause element; *byrḥ ... kbn bdʿštrt* CIS i 4[1ff.]: in the month of ... B. has built (cf. however Elayi SCA 58f.: pro *kbn* l. poss. *kbl* = QAL Pf. 3 p.s.m. of *kbl*$_2$(= to offer)) - **3)** used as introduction of casus pendens (cf. also H.P.Müller WO viii 66), inasmuch, with regard to; *wkyʾmr ʾdny lʾ ydʿth qrʾ spr ḥYHWH ʾm nsh ʾyš* KAI 193[8ff.]: for inasmuch as my lord said: can't you read a letter?, as the Lord lives, no man has dared ...; *wky šlḥ ʾdny ʿl dbr byt hrpd ʾyn šm ʾdm* KAI 194[4ff.]: and with regard to the orders my lord sent in the matter of B.H., there is no one there ...; cf. KAI 14[6ff.] - **4)** used as introduction of a subordinate clause - a) introduction of object clause, *ydʿ hṣdnym kydʿ hgw* KAI 60[7]: The Sidonians may know that the community knows

...; *wyd' ky 'l mš't lkš nḥnw šmrm* KAI 194[10f.]: he may know that we are watching for the beacons of L. (cf. Poen 931, 941, KAI 266[6]); cf. poss. also DA i 9 (cf. Hoftijzer DA p. 199f., 202) - b) because, for; *w'l ybqš bn mnm k'y šm bn mnm* KAI 14[4f.]: let no one seek anything in it, for they did not lay anything in it (cf. KAI 13[4,6]); *wbn 'nk hqrt z ... k b'l wršp ... šlḥn lnbt* KAI 26A ii 9ff.: and I rebuilt this city ... for B. and R. .. had sent me to build (it); *wt'rk ymw wšntw 'l gbl kmlk ṣdq h'* KAI 10[9]: and may she prolong his days and years over G., for he is a legitimate king; *'mry mlk yšr'l wy'nw 't m'b ymm rbm ky y'n.p. kmš b'rṣh* KAI 181[4f.]: Omri king of Israel had oppressed Moab for a long time, because K. was angry with his land; *w['l] zy š[m't] hwqr lbb ky ṣnpr hy mlh* Aḥiq 98: and concerning what you hear be reserved for a word is (like) a bird; cf. KAI 60[3], 89[3f.], 181[4,17,27,28], 189[3], 194[12], 202A 13, 224[22], 233[8] (?), Aḥiq 95, 98, etc.; cf. also the stereotyped formula on Phoen. and Pun. votive stelas *kšm' ql* KAI 38[2], *kšm' ql'* KAI 102[4]: because he/they listened to his voice, and comparable formulae, cf. KAI 39[3], 41[6], 47[3], 61A 5, 63[3], 68[5], 88[5], 98[4], 104[3], DD 7[4], 8[4], 14[2], Antas 78[3], Mozia vi 104[3], RSF iii 51 vii 3f., ICO-Spa 16[4f.], etc., etc. - c) (so) that, in the combination *my ... ky*; *my 'bdk klb ky zkr 'dny ['|bdk* KAI 192[3ff.]: what is your servant (but) a dog, that my lord remembers his servant? (cf. KAI 196[2f.]) - **5)** in the combination *ky 'm*: KAI 194[9], prob. meaning: but, however (for this interpret., cf. Albright BASOR xcvii 26, Cross BASOR cxliv 24f., Albright with Cross BASOR cxliv 26, Röllig KAI a.l., Lipiński OLP viii 90, cf. also Lemaire IH i p. 110, 112, cf. however Gibson SSI i p. 42f.: = except, unless (cf. Dahood Or xlvi 330) :: Torczyner Lach i p. 79, 82: = because; the context of the *ky 'm* in SBS 47[2] too much dam. for interpret. (cf. Dunant SBS p. 61 (n. 2)) - **6)** prec. by the prep. *'l*$_7$, Karth xii 53[2]: because; also in Driv F xi 20 (??, heavily dam. context, uncert. reading), Driver a.l.: = because?? - Baldacci BiOr xl 130: the *k* in Syr xlviii 483[7] poss. = *k*$_3$(= *ky*), improb. interpret.; prob. = *k*$_1$(cf. e.g. Gibson SSI iii p. 90).
v. *k*$_1$,*kh*$_1$, *kl*$_1$, *km*$_2$, *kn*$_4$, *smr*$_3$, *'b*$_1$, *p*$_1$, *p'l*$_1$, *qdm*$_2$, *šyt*$_1$.

kyb **OffAr** Plur. cstr. *kyby* Cowl 71[2] (context however heavily dam.) - ¶ subst. suffering.

kyḥz 'yl **DA** diff. comb. in ii 23 (cf. also *kyḥz'.* in xiib 2), interpretation unknown, cf. Hoftijzer **DA** p. 266f.

kyl$_1$ v. *kly*$_1$, *q'l*$_1$.

kyl$_2$ **Nab** Sing. emph. *kyl'* J 325 - ¶ subst. m. land measurer, land surveyor (cf. also Negev RB lxxxiii 227).

kyl$_3$ v. *kl*$_3$.

kym **OldAr** KAI 224[1]. ¶ word, exact meaning unknown (dam. context); Dupont-Sommer BMB xiii 30, Sf p. 129, Garbini RSO xxxiv 52, Degen AAG p. 61, Segert AAG p. 236 (cf. also Rössler TUAT i 186) =

adv. likewise (comparable to Akkad. *kīam*; cf. also Kaufman AIA 154); Fitzmyer CBQ xx 452f., AIS 153f.: = conjunction, just as (comparable to Akkad. *kīma*), cf. however Fitzmyer AIS 97, 176, 186: = adverb, indeed; Gibson SSI ii p. 51f.: = prep., like, in the manner of (comparable to Akkad. *kīma*); cf. also Koopmans p. 62, Donner KAI a.l.
v. *ywm*.

kyn v. kn_4.

kys **Palm** Sing. cstr. *kys* CIS ii 3985[1] (= Inv vi 1, RIP 152), Inv xii 43[3]; + suff. 3 p.s.m. *kysh* CIS ii 3902[1], 3936[4], 3959[6] (= SBS 44), 3970[2], Inv x 44[5], 115[2], Inscr P 40[5], SBS 40[7], RIP 25[8,12], 127[9], Syr xii 122[5], xiv 177[3], lxii 274 i 4, Ber ii 60[1]; + suff. 3 p.pl.m. *kyshwn* CIS ii 3914[5], 3955[6], 4159[1], 4201[2], Inv xii 48[1], 49[8] - **Hatra** Sing. + suff. 3 p.pl.m. *kyshwn* 214[2] - ¶ subst. purse; *mn kysh* CIS ii 3902[1]: on his costs (the comb. with mn_5 in all Palm. texts and in Hatra) - Segal ATNS a.l.: l. *kys[* (= Sing. abs. or cstr.?) in ATNS 2[5] (less prob. reading, cf. Porten & Yardeni sub TADAE B 8.9 (div. otherwise): l. *lḥšy[* without interpret.).

kysh **JAr** the *kysh* in Mas 546 poss. = Sing. abs. of *kysh* (= fodder) or l. *kwsh* = Sing. abs. of *kwsh*(= kind of liquid measure), cf. Yadin & Naveh Mas a.l.

kyst v. *myst*.

kyp v. kp_2.

kypḥ **Pun** Sing. abs. *kypḥ* CIS i 362[2] - ¶ subst. of unknown meaning, prob. indication of function or title (prec. by $ʾ_9$ = article; cf. Harr 110); Slouschz sub TPI 553: *ʾkypḥ* = n.p.

kyṣ v. $qṣ_1$.

kytwn v. ktn_2.

kk **OffAr**, cf. Frah x 21: tooth, molar; cf. also Kaufman AIA 61 (n. 143).

kkb **Pun** Plur. abs. *kkbm* KAI 277[10] (cf. e.g. Dupont-Sommer JA cclii 292, Février CRAI '65, 11, OA iv 175, Garbini OA iv 45f., FSR 220, RSF xvii 185ff., Levi Della Vida OA iv 46f., v.d.Branden Meltô iv 108f., Fischer & Rix GGA '68, 68, 70, Lambdin FS Albright ii 329 n. 24, Amadasi sub ICO-app. 2, Röllig KAI a.l., WO v 116 (n. 38), Heurgon BAr-NS iv 250, Altheim & Stiehl AAW iv 225, Teixidor Syr xlviii 456f. :: Dahood Or xxxiv 170ff., Bibl xlvi 326, Ps i 176, RPIM 146 n. 45, Nober VD xliii 204f.: = Plur. cstr. + enclit. *mem*; cf. also Fitzmyer JAOS lxxxvi 287, 295f., Naveh Lesh xxx 236 (n. 6), Parker UF ii 248: both solutions poss.; v. also infra) - **OffAr** Plur. cstr. *[k]wkb[y]* Aḥiq 116 (for this reading, cf. already Perles OLZ '11, 502); cf. Frah i 15 (*kwkbʾ*, *kwkpʾ*) - ¶ subst. star; *šnt km hkkbm ʾl* KAI 277[10f.]: years like (i.e. as numerous as) these stars (for the interpret., v. litt. mentioned supra, especially Heurgon BAr-NS iv 250) :: Dahood Or xxxiv 170ff., Bibl xlvi 326, Ps i 176, Nober VD xliii 204f., Penar NSPBS 46, Herrmann UF xiv 95 n. 13: like the stars of El :: v.d.Branden Meltô iv 108f.: like the divine stars (*ʾl* = *$ʾl_1$* used as an adjective); on this text, cf. also Carratelli PP xx 303ff., Gibson SSI iii p. 154, 158f.

kkh **Hebr** *kkh* DJD ii 24C 19, D 19, $30^{6,25}$, 42^{6} - **OffAr**, cf. Sogd ii 221 (*kgh*)?- ¶ adv. thus; *lʿmt kkh* DJD ii 24C 18f.: conform what is written above (cf. DJD ii 24D 19, $30^{6,\ 24f.}$); *ʿl kkh* DJD ii 42^{6}: concerning this, on this point.

kkr **Pun** Sing. abs.? *kkr* CIS i 171^{2}; Plur. abs. *kkrm* CIS i 171^{4}; cstr. *kkrʾ* Or xxxiii 4^{2} (or l. *kkrm* = Plur. abs.?, cf. Levi Della Vida Or xxxiii 4f., 8, 14; cf. also FR 225b, 312b: l. *kkrʾ*) - **OffAr** Sing. abs. *knkr* Cowl 26^{17}; Plur. abs. *kkrn* Cowl 50^{9} (reading uncert.), 83^{29}, Sach 81 ii 3, *knkrn* Cowl 31^{27}, *knkryn* Cowl 30^{28} - **Nab** Plur. abs. *kkryn* DBKP 22^{33} (prob. reading, cf. also Greek par. τάλαντα) - **Palm** Plur. abs. *kkryn* Sem xxxvi 89^{5} (for the reading, cf. Gawlikowski Sem xxxvi 92, v. also infra) - **JAr** Plur. abs. *kkryn* DBKP 21^{31} back (Greek par. τάλαντα) - ¶ subst. m. talent (weight; 1 talent = 60 *minae* (cf. also Ben-David PEQ '78, 28: Phoen. talent = 21.9 kg)); for the problems of the *kkryn* in Sem xxxvi 89^{5}, cf. Gawlikowski Sem xxxvi 93: *kkr* here indication of small coin "grain" (related to Greek κοκκάριον; uncert. interpret.) - cf. also Barrois ii 253ff., Wambacq VD xxix 342f., Trinquet SDB 1241ff., Scott BiAr xxii 32ff.

v. *$krš_1$*.

kl_1 **Ph** Sing. abs. *kl* KAI 24^{6}, 60^{3} (or cstr.?), EpAn ix 5^{6}; cstr. (or abs.?) *kl* KAI 4^{2}, 9B 5 (dam. context), 6 (dam. context), $10^{11,16}$, $13^{3,5}$, $14^{4,6,7,20}$, 19^{9}, 26A i 5, 9, 12, ii 19 (cf. e.g. Dupont-Sommer RA xlii 166, Röllig KAI a.l., Bron RIPK 96f., Gibson SSI iii p. 51 :: Honeyman PEQ '49, 27, 34: = Qal Inf. of *kwl_2*(= to sustain, to nourish)), C iii 18, iv 1, 3, $27^{11,12}$, $50^{3,4}$, MUSJ xlv 262^{2} (?, dam. context), etc.; + suff. 3 p.s.m. *klʾ* KAI 51 vs. 8 (??, heavily dam. context; cf. also Aimé-Giron BIFAO xxviii 8) - **Pun** Sing. abs. *kl* KAI 81^{1} (or cstr.?), 96^{1} (or cstr.?), cf. Poen 935: *chil* (var. *chyl*; or cstr.?); cstr. (or abs.?) *kl* KAI $69^{13,14,15,16,20}$, $75^{2,3,4}$, $81^{2,3}$, 126^{9}, CIS i 3915^{4}, etc.; + suff. 3 p.s.m. *klʾ* KAI 161^{6} (for this poss. interpret., cf. Février RA xlv 143f., Röllig KAI a.l., Roschinski Num 112, 115; cf. however Lidzbarski Handb 295, Cooke NSI p. 150: *klʾ* = *k_3*(= *ky*) + *l_5* + suff. 3 p.s.m.?) - **Mo** Sing. cstr. (or abs.?) *kl* KAI $181^{4,5,11,20,24,28}$; + suff. 3 p.s.f. *kl[h]* KAI 181^{16} - **Amm** Sing. abs. *kl* BASOR cxciii 8^{2} (cf. Horn BASOR cxciii 9, Cross ibid. 18, Albright BASOR cxcviii 38f., Dion RB lxxxii 32 (n. 50), Shea PEQ '79, 18, Sasson PEQ '79, 118, 120 × R. Kutscher Qadm v 27f., Puech & Rofé RB lxxx 534ff., v.Selms BiOr xxxii 7f., Fulco BASOR ccxxx 41f., Jackson ALIA 25: = Sing. cstr.; cf. also Garbini AION xx 254); cstr. *kl* BASOR cxciii 8^{3} (cf. however Cross BASOR cxciii 18 n.

9: or = Sing. abs.?)^{,4} - **Hebr** Sing. abs. *kl* 194^{2} (or cstr.?)^{,3} (or cstr.?), TA-H 21^{7} (??, dam. context), 60^{1} (diff. context :: Lemaire IH i p. 216f.: pro *kkl 4* (?) l. *kprh* = prob. n.p.), SM 49^{12}, *kwl*DJD ii 24B 13, D 12, 30^{4} (or cstr.?)^{,19} (idem)^{,23} (idem); cstr. (or abs.?) *kl* KAI 193^{11}, 194^{11}, 200^{10}, DJD ii 17A 2 (*k[l]*), 30^{25}, 42^{7}, 43^{5}, 46^{7,8}, 47^{4}, 51 ii (dam. context), TA-H 88^{1} (*k[l]*, dam. context), SSI i p. 58A 1 (cf. Naveh IEJ xiii 84, Weippert ZDPV lxxx 162, Gibson SSI i a.l., Lemaire RB lxxxiii 558, 566 :: Lipiński OLP viii 94: pro *kl h᾿rṣ h* ... l. *klh* (= Sing. abs. of *klh*$_1$ (= totality)) *᾿rṣh* :: Cross FS Glueck 301: pro *᾿lhy kl h᾿rṣ h* ... l. *᾿lhykh ᾿rṣh*; for the context, v. *᾿lh*$_1$, *᾿rṣ*$_1$), Frey 634^{3}, 973 (= SM 3), 974^{1} (= SM 1), AMB 1^{7}, EI xx 256^{8}, *kwl*DJD ii 24C 18, EI xx 256^{12}; + suff. 3 p.pl.m. *klm* DJD ii 22, 1-9^{2}, *kln* Mas 450^{2} (dam. context), 452^{2} (dam. context) - **DA** Sing. abs. *kl* i 16 (:: Hackett BTDA 29, 54, 132: l. *skl* = Sing. abs. of *skl*$_6$ (= fool; for the reading, cf. also v.d.Kooij DA p. 117)), ii 5 (diff. context, cf. Hoftijzer DA p. 222f.) - **Samal** Sing. cstr. (or abs.?) *kl* KAI 215^{22}; + suff. 3 p.s.m. *klh* KAI 215^{19}; + suff. 3 p.s.f. *klh* KAI 215^{17} - **OldAr** Sing. abs. *kl* KAI 216^{8,15}, 222A 26, B 2, 34, C 22, 224^{8,16,28,29}; cstr. (or abs.?) *kl* KAI 202A 9, 16, B 5, 8, 222A 6, 10, 12, B 22, 23, C 6, 223A 7, B 9, C 13, 15, 224$^{1,4,7,14,16f.,23}$; + suff. 3 p.s.m. *klh* KAI 222A 5; + suff. 3 p.pl.m. *klm* Tell F 4; + suff. 3 p.pl.f. *kln* Tell F 3, 5 (:: Blau FS Andersen 5f.: *klm/kln* prob. = adverb 'in its entirety') - **OffAr** Sing. abs. *kl* KAI 267A 1, 270B 2 (cf. CIS ii sub 137, Cooke NSI p. 203, Koopmans 170, Levine JAOS lxxxiv 19f., Grelot DAE p. 138 (n. f) :: Dupont-Sommer ASAE xlviii 120: l. *᾿l*$_3$), Cowl 15^{19}, 30^{14}, Krael 2^{10}, Driv 3^{5}, Herm 3^{7}, ATNS 8^{5}, 9^{8}, etc.; cstr. (or abs.?) *kl* KAI 228A 19, 279^{3}, Cowl 6^{16}, 10^{9,10}, Krael 2^{11,12}, Herm 1^{12}, NESE i 11^{1}, iii 48^{4}, ATNS 8^{10}, etc., etc., cf. Warka 14: *kul* (cf. Dupont-Sommer RA xxxix 47), 39: *kul* (?, heavily dam. context); emph. (cf. Joüon MUSJ xviii 49f., Fitzmyer Bibl xxxviii 178ff. (cf. also Degen GGA '79, 22: -᾿ = adv. ending) :: Montgomery JAOS xliii 391ff., Driver JRAS '32, 88, Segert AAG p. 103: -᾿ = adv. ending prob. < old accusative case ending, cf. also BL 25h, Leand 47b) Cowl 26^{13,17}, 30^{11}, Krael 13^{1}, Driv 8^{2}, SSI ii 28 rev. 5, ATNS 46^{1}, etc.; + suff. 3 p.s.m. *klh* Krael 4^{20} (or = Sing. emph.?, cf. Fitzmyer Bibl xxxviii 183f.), SSI ii 28 obv. 6 (cf. also Fitzmyer JNES xxi 20, WA 224); + suff. 3 p.s.f. *klh* Cowl 15^{20} (or = Sing. emph.?, cf. Fitzmyer FS Albright ii 160f.), Aḥiq 12, 55 (or = Sing. emph.?, cf. Fitzmyer Bibl xxxviii 183f.), Herm 4^{4,12} (or = Sing. emph.? in both instances); + suff. 2 p.s.m. *kl[k]* Aḥiq 166 (for this prob. restoration, cf. Lindenberger APA 169); + suff. 3 p.pl.m. *klhm* KAI 279^{2,4,7,8}; + suff. 3 p.pl.m. or f.? *klhn* Driv F 2b i 2; cf. Frah xxv 26 (*kr᾿*), xxviii 31 (id.), xxx 3 (id.), Paik 535 (*kl᾿*), 536, 537 (*kl*), Nisa-b 2167^{9} (*kl᾿*), GIPP 25, 55, SaSt 18 - **Nab** Sing. abs. *kl* CIS ii 197^{6}, 199^{4}, 204^{4}, 206^{6,8}, etc., etc.; cstr. (or abs.?) *kl* CIS ii 206^{3,6},

212^4, 551^2, etc., etc.; emph. *kl*ʾ CIS ii 757^2 (or l. *bl*ʾ? v. *bl*ʾ$_3$), MPAT 64 i 13 (cf. Starcky RB lxi 165, Fitzmyer & Harrington MPAT a.l. :: J.J.Rabinowitz BASOR cxxxix 13: *kl*ʾ = *k*$_1$ + *l*ʾ$_1$); + suff. 3 p.s.m. *klh* CIS ii 197^7, 206^5, 209^{5,6}, etc., etc.; + suff. 3 p.s.m. (or f.?) *klh* BASOR cclxiii 77^1; + suff. 3 p.s.f. *klh* J 12^{2,3} (or + suff. 3 p.s.m.?, v. infra); + suff. 3 p.pl.m. *klhm* CIS ii 211^{6,8}, 350^{3,4}, RES 1401^3 - **Palm** Sing. abs. *kl* CIS ii 3913 i 13, 3998B 1 (v. however infra), PNO 56^4, RIP 145^3, MUSJ xxxviii 106^7; cstr. (or abs.?) *kl* CIS ii 3915^4, 3916^4, 3930^4, 3949^4, Inv xi 37^3, xii 35^4, RIP 143^5, etc., etc., *kwl* CIS ii 4011^5; + suff. 3 p.s.m. *klh* CIS ii 3917^4, 3946^2, 3971^3, 3981^6, 4009^6, Inv xi 8^6, RIP 143^5, etc., *llh* (lapsus) CIS ii 3949^{4,6}; + suff. 3 p.s.f. *klh* CIS ii 3915^4, 3916^4, 3930^4, 3952^4, 3985 (= Inv vi 1 = RIP 152), SBS 1a 1, 2a 1, Inv xii 19^1, 35^4, etc.; + suff. 3 p.pl.m. *klhn* CIS ii 3923^3, 3972^4, 4036A 4, 4051^3, Inscr P 34^6, SBS 34^{1,4}, RIP 143^4, *klhwn* CIS ii 3913 ii 68, 3953^3, 3955^3, 3973^{11}, RIP 108^5, 119^6, 134^5, Inv xi 6^8, 17^5, 20^6, 25^3, 77^2, *kwlhwn* CIS ii 4048^5 - **Hatra** Sing. abs. *kwl* 13^3 (for the reading, cf. e.g. Caquot Syr xxix 96f., Milik Syr xliv 298, Aggoula Ber xviii 88, Degen ZDMG cxxi 104, Vattioni IH a.l. :: Safar Sumer vii 178: pro *w* l. *y*, cf. also Krückmann AfO xvi 146, Donner KAI sub 240 (cf. however id. ibid. ii p. 296)), 34^3 (for the uncert. reading, cf. Milik DFD 373, Vattioni IH a.l. :: e.g. Safar Sumer viii 189f., ix 18, Caquot Syr xxx 239: pro *bnyt kwl* l. *bt* (?) *tk*(?)*dm* (= n.p.)), 74^6 (or cstr.?), 343^4; cstr. (or abs.?) *kwl* 173^2; + suff. 3 p.s.m. *klh* 20^4 (for the reading, cf. Milik RN vi/iv 54, Teixidor Syr xliv 189, Degen Or xxxvi 77 n. 1, ZDMG cxxi 125, Aggoula Ber xviii 89, Vattioni IH a.l. :: Safar Sumer vii 120, Caquot Syr xxix 99, Krückmann AfO xvi 147 (n. 52), Donner KAI a.l. (div. otherwise): pro *lh klh* l. *lhklh* = *l*$_5$ + Sing. + suff. 3 p.s.m. of *hkl* (= *hykl*)), 290^7, *kwlh* 35^8, 74^7 (for this reading, cf. e.g. Caquot Syr xxxii 270 :: Vattioni IH a.l.: l. *kwl*ʾ), *kwlyh* 173^2; + suff. 3 p.s.f. *klh* 35^7 (for this reading, cf. Aggoula Ber xviii 92, Degen ZDMG cxxi 125, Milik DFD 353, 366 :: Safar Sumer viii 191, Caquot Syr xxx 240, Donner sub KAI 249: = part of n.p. :: Vattioni IH a.l.: l. *kl*ʾ (misprint?)); + suff. 3 p.pl.m. *klhn* 403^3; *klhwn* 23^1 (for this reading, cf. Krückmann AfO xvi 147 n. 59, Milik RN vi/iv 54, Caquot Syr xl 15, Degen ZDMG cxxi 125, Vattioni IH a.l. :: Safar Sumer vii 182, Caquot Syr xxix 102, Donner sub KAI 244: l. *klhyn*), 52^5 (for this reading, cf. e.g. Safar Sumer ix 246, Degen ZDMG cxxi 125, Vattioni IH a.l. :: Caquot Syr xxxii 55f.: or l. *klhyn*? :: Altheim & Stiehl AAW ii 203: l. *klhyn* (cf. also Donner sub KAI 251)), 79^{11}, 151^2 (*kl[hwn]*), 184^2, 213^3, 284^2 (*klh[wn]*; cf. Degen NESE iii 75 :: Safar Sumer xxvii 7, Aggoula Syr lii 184: l. *klh* (+ suff. 3 p.s.m.) :: Vattioni IH a.l.: l. *kl*ʾ (misprint?)), 287^7 (*klh[wn]*, cf. Degen NESE iii 77, 79 :: Aggoula Syr lii 186f., Vattioni IH a.l.: l. *klh* (+ suff. 3 p.s.m.); cf. also Safar Sumer xxvii 8: l. *kl*...; heavily dam. context), 325^3, 343^4 (cf. also

Assur 28a 4), *kwlhwn* 74^{6}, 75^{2}; cf. also Jensen MDOG lx 19 no. 28 - **JAr** Sing. abs. *kl* MPAT-A 5^{1} (= Frey 1203 = SM 64), 22^{2} (= SM 70^{10}), 30^{1} (= SM 26), 45^{1}, 47^{1}, 49 i 6, Syn D B 5 (= SM 88^{20}); abs. (or cstr.?) *kl* MPAT $52^{6,10,11}$, 55^{2}, 61^{24} (= DBKP 15), 69^{1}, MPAT-A 46^{3}, DBKP 20^{42}, *kwl* MPAT 51^{7}, IEJ xxxvi 206^{6}, xl 135^{9}; cstr. (or abs.?) *kl* MPAT 40^{22} (cf. however Beyer ATTM 308: l. *kwl*), 42^{15}, 45^{5}, 53^{3}, MPAT-A 5^{5} (= Frey 1203 = SM 64), $11^{4,6}$ (= Frey 1165 = SM 43), 13^{1} (= SM 46), 22^{5} (= SM 70^{13})^{,8} (= SM 70^{16}), 26^{7} (= Frey 856 = SM 32), 33^{1} (= SM 50), $34^{1,6}$ (= SM 69), 40^{1} (= SM 57), SM 53^{2} (= Frey 963), Syn D A 13 (= SM 88), B 8 (= SM 88^{23}), Syr xlv 101^{10}, DBKP 17^{41}, *kwl*MPAT $40^{6,8,19}$, 59^{2}, IEJ xxxvi 206^{7}, EI xx 161*, DBKP 17^{42}, Mas 556^{2}, etc.; emph. *kl*ʾ IEJ xl 132^{12}, 144^{11}; + suff. 3 p.pl.m. *klhwn* Syn D A 14 (= SM 88), B 3 (= SM 88^{18}); + suff. 3 p.pl.f. *klhyn* Syn D B 2 (for this reading, cf. Naveh sub SM 88^{17} :: Torrey Syn D a.l.: l. *klhwn*; for the context, v. also ʾ$š_1$ sub Plur. f.); + suff. 1 p.pl. *kln* MPAT 46^{3} (:: Beyer ATTM 314: l. *ʿln*) - ¶ subst. totality, completeness - **A)** in the absolute state, not being an element in an appositional construction - **1)** all, everyone (referring to animate objects); *kl šlḥ yd* KAI 24^{6}: everyone put forth his hand; *wkl ḥzw* ... DA i 16: and all saw ...; cf. KAI 216^{8} - **2)** all, everything (referring to inanimate objects); *ʾt hkwl* DJD ii 24B 12f.: everything; *dkl ʾḥyd wʿl kl prys* RIP 145^{3}: who is all-powerful and is extending himself over everything; cf. poss. *mrʾ kl* CIS ii 3998B 1 (= Inv vi 5): the lord of everything (cf. also Aggoula Syr liv 283, cf. however Gawlikowski sub RIP 130, TP 94: l. *mrʾ kl [ʿlmʾ]* = the lord of the whole universe) - **3)** to be translated adverbially; *ʾnt ʾnttk wbrk kl 3* Cowl $6^{4f.}$: you, your wife and your son, altogether 3 (persons), cf. KAI 267^{1}; (following five names) *kl gbrn 5* Cowl 33^{5}: all together five men; (at the end of a list of expenses) *kl rʿy 814* Cowl 73^{17}: total 814 *r.*; (at the end of a list of garments) *kl lbšn ... 8* Krael 7^{13}: in all 8 garments ...; cf. also ATNS 8^{5} (for the context, cf. Porten & Yardeni sub TADAE B 5.6), 9^{8} (for the context, cf. Porten & Yardeni sub TADAE B 8.6), 28b 5 (for the context, cf. Porten & Yardeni sub TADAE B 8.4), IEJ xl 135^{9}, 144^{11}, cf. also IEJ xxxviii 164B ii 7 (and prob. also ibid. A 13: *[k]l*); cf. the comp. use of *bkl* (at the end of a list of expenses) *bkl rʿy 10* Cowl 73^{6}: in total 10 *r.* (the reading *bkl* in Krael 7^{19} improb., cf. Porten & Yardeni sub TADAE B 3.8: pro *bkl* l. *1 kl*) - **B)** *kl* as *nomen regens* in a construct group, or as first element in an appositional construction - **1)** combined with indefinite pronoun - a) in the comb. *kl mn*, whoever; *kl mn ynpq bydh* CIS ii 215^{2}: whoever will bring forward in his own hand ...; *kl mn yzbn* CIS ii 197^{6}: whoever will sell; *kl mn dhw* PNO 56^{4}: whosoever ...; *kl mn dyhyb plgw* ... MPAT-A 22^{2}: everyone who will set discord ... (cf. MPAT-A 5^{1}, 30^{1}, 45^{1}, 47^{1}), etc. - b) in the comb. *kl mh/ʾ*: whatever (:: CF 28: *klmh* in

KAI 222A 26 = Sing. abs. of *klmh₂* (= reproach, humiliation)); *kl mh šqnw yšrʾl* SM 49[12]: whatsoever the Israelites buy; *ʿqr klmh mlk* KAI 222B 2: the descendance of whatever king; *bkl mh zy ymwt br ʾnš* KAI 224[16]: in every case that a man dies (cf. e.g. Dupont-Sommer Sf p. 131, Donner KAI a.l., Degen AAG p. 129, 131f., Gibson SSI ii p. 49, 54 (cf. also Ben-Chayyim Lesh xxxv 252, Beyer ZDMG cxx 203), cf. however e.g. Fitzmyer AIS 99, Lipiński Stud 56: in whatever way (less prob. interpret.)); *kl mh ṭbt byty* KAI 216[15]: all the abundance of my house (cf. KAI 222A 16, 224[28,29]); cf. also *dy klmʾ gns klh* CIS ii 3913 i 13: of any kind whatsoever (cf. Greek par. παντὸς γένους); *ʿl kwl mʾ ʾnš kwlh* Hatra 74[6f.]: against whatever person whosoever (for the reading, cf. Milik DFD 401, 403, Vattioni IH a.l. :: e.g. Safar Sumer xi 13, Caquot Syr xxxii 270, Donner sub KAI 256, Ingholt AH i/1, 44: pro *mʾ* l. *mn*; :: Milik DFD 401, 403, Vattioni IH a.l: transl. concerning everything (what) anyone ...) - c) in the comb. *kl mnm*, whatsoever, cf. KAI 13[5], 81[2,3] - d) in the comb. *kl mndʿm/mdʿm/mdʿn*: everything whatsoever, cf. Cowl 21[7], 49[3] (cf. Degen NESE iii 18,23 :: Cowl a.l., Leand 37d: anything), CIS ii 3959[5] (= SBS 44; Greek par. ἐν πᾶσιν); cf. also *kl dy bhm mndʿm* CIS ii 350[5]: anything whatsoever of all that is in them; cf. poss. also *kl ḥd wḥd* SM 53[2]: everyone (cf. Naveh SM a.l.) - **2)** *k(w)l* followed by a relative clause, *kl ʾš ytn l mtš* EpAn ix 5[6f]: all that M. has given to him; *wpʿl ʾyt kl ʾš ʿlty* KAI 60[3f.]: and he did all that he was required to do; *km kl ʾš pʿl* KAI 96[1]: according to everything he did; *kkl ʾšr šlḥ ʾdny* KAI 194[2]: according to everything my lord sent (to me); *kl šbw* DJD ii 30[19]: everything therein; *kl šyš ly* DJD ii 30[23]: everything I have; *kwl šʾš ʿl hštr hzʾ* EI xx 256[12]: everything that is in this document (i.e. is written in it); *kl zy tṣbh* Herm 3[7]: everything you want; *ʿbd kʿyr kl dy ʿlʾ ktyb* BASOR cclxiii 78[3]: he did other than all of that which is written above; *wkwl dldk[r]* (v. *zkr₁*) Hatra 13[2]: everyone who mentions aloud; *kwl dy bh* MPAT 51[7]: everything that is in it; *kl dypth ʿlwy* MPAT-A 46[3f.]: anyone who will open (it, sc. the tomb) on him; cf. KAI 81[1], 194[3f.], 222B 34, C 22, 224[8], Poen 935, DJD ii 30[4,23], Cowl 15[19], ATNS 46[3,4], CIS ii 204[4], Hatra 343[4], MPAT 52[6,10,11], 55[2f.], 64 i 12, ii 1, 2, 69[1], etc. - **3)** *kl* followed by a noun in the Sing. - a) the noun expressing a collectivity, or a totality determined in itself, or through additional grammatical means, *kl hrʿ* KAI 26A i 9: all the evil (:: Gibson SSI iii p. 47: every evildoer); *bkl gbl ʿmq ʾdn* KAI 26A ii 1f.: in the whole territory of the plain of A. (× e.g. Röllig KAI a.l., Gibson SSI iii p. 49: on all the borders of the plain of A; v. *gbl₁*); *kl hʿm* KAI 181[11]: the whole people, all the people; *kl byt yšrʾl* DJD ii 42[7]: the whole house of Israel; *kl kspk* Cowl 11[7f.]: all your silver (cf. *kl ksp krš 1 š 8* NESE i 11[5]: all the silver (involved), i.e. 1 k. 8 sh.); *kl qhlh qd[y]šh* MPAT-A 34[1f.]: the whole holy assembly; cf. KAI 50[4], 181[24], 202B 5,

8f. (v. *gbl*$_1$), 222A 6, 279[3], SSI i p. 58A 1 (v. supra), MPAT-A 22[5,8], 40[1], 64 i 4; cf. *kl* followed by a name, *kl dybn* KAI 181[28]: the whole of D.; *kl yšrʾl* MPAT-A 34[6]: all Israel (cf. MPAT-A 33[1f.]) - b) the noun not expressing a collectivity or a totality, *kl mmlkt wkl ʾdm* KAI 10[11]: every king and every person; *kl zbḥ* KAI 69[14]: every offering; *kl khn* KAI 69[20]: every priest; *kl spr* KAI 193[11]: every letter; *kwl šnh wšnh* DJD ii 24C 18: every year; *kl zmn* EI xx 256[8]: every moment; *kl gbr zy* KAI 224[1f.]: every man who ...; *bkl ʾtr* Aḥiq 97: everywhere; *kl ʾnwš dy* J 38[7]: everyone who ...; *kl mšk* CIS ii 3913 ii 67: each skin; *kl ywm* Inv xi 37[3]: every day; *kwl gbr yhwdy dy tṣbyn* MPAT 40[6f.]: any Jewish man that you please; *kwl ʾnšʾ* Mas 556[2]: every person; *kwl mn ḥsp* Mas 556[3]: every clay vessel; cf. KAI 13[3], 14[4,6f.,20], 26A i 5, 12, C iii 18, iv 1, 69[13,15,16], 75[2,3,4,5], CIS i 5632[4], DJD ii 17A 2, 24B 16, 30[25], 43[5], 46[8], 47[4], Herm 1[12], 2[15], 3[10], Cowl 30[2], NESE i 11[1], CRAI '47, 181 conc. 4f., Inv xi 6[10] (for the reading, cf. Starcky RB lxxiii 615), 44[4], MPAT 40[19], 45[5], 53[3], 59[2], MPAT-A 5[5], 26[7], Syn D B 8, etc. - **4)** *kl* followed by a noun in the Plur., *kl ʾln g[bl]* KAI 10[16]: all the gods of G.; *kl hmlkm* KAI 26A i 19: all the kings; *wkl bn ʾlm* KAI 27[11]: and all the gods (:: Gaster Or xi 58f.: *wkl* = Sing. cstr. of *wkl*(= chieftain, governor); cf. also Avishur PIB 252); *kl šnʾy* KAI 181[4]: all my enemies; *kl ʾḥy* KAI 200[10]: all my colleagues; *bkl mqwmwt yšrʾl* SM 1: on all the places of Israel (i.e. everywhere where Jews are living); *kl mlkyʾ* KAI 222B 22: all the kings; *kl dqln* KAI 228A 19: all palm-trees; *kl yrḥn* Cowl 45[8]: every month; *kl nwnyk* Cowl 45[6]: all your fishes; *kl ʾsryʾ* ATNS 8[10]: all the bonds (v. *ʾsr*$_3$); *kl dmy lbšʾ* ATNS 50[10]: all the costs of clothing; *kl ʿbdn* ATNS 50[12]: all slaves; *kl bny zydʾlhy* RES 1427C: all the sons of Z.; *kl ymyn* MPAT 42[15]: all days; *kl bny ḥbwrth qdyšth* MPAT-A 13[1]: all the members of the holy community; cf. KAI 27[12], 50[3], 69[16], 194[11], 202A 9, 16, 215[22], 222A 10, B 23, 223C 13, 15, 15f., 224[4,7,14,16f.,23], MPAT 40[8,22], MPAT-A 11[4,6f.], SM 3, Syr xlv 101[10] - **C)** *kl* in absolute state as last element of an appositional group, *ʾlhyʾ kl* Cowl 39[1]: all the gods; *yhwdyʾ kl zy tnh* Cowl 30[26f.]: all the Judeans who are here; *ʾgwry ʾlhy mṣryn kl* Cowl 30[14]: all the temples of the gods of Egypt (cf. poss. DA ii 5); etc.; cf. also this construction combined with the one mentioned sub B 4, *kl gbryn zy ... kl* Cowl 30[16f.]: all the men who ... alltogether - **D)** *kl* in the emphatic state - **1)** used independently, to be translated adverbially, ATNS 46[1], IEJ xl 132[12] (in all) - **2)** as first element in an appositional group - a) followed by relative clause, *klʾ zy ʿbyd ln* Cowl 31[29]: all that was done to us (dam. context) - b) followed by a noun in the Plur., *klʾ mlyʾ* Cowl 30[29]: the whole matter (cf. Hoftijzer VT ix 317f. :: Fitzmyer Bibl xxxviii 181, WA 212: = contamination of *kl mlyʾ* and *mlyʾ klʾ*) - **3)** as last element in an appositional group after a Plur. or a Sing. indicating a collectivity or a determined totality or a name, *ʾlhyʾ klʾ* Cowl 41[1]: all the gods; *yhwdyʾ klʾ zy tnh* Cowl 31[26]: all the Judeans who are here; *ʾtwr klʾ* Aḥiq 43: the whole of Assyria; *ʿbwr ʿrqtʾ klʾ* Driv 12[6]: the whole crop from the land; *nšy bytn klʾ* Driv 8[2]: all the women of our house; *bznh zy ʿbyd ln klʾ* Cowl 30[30]: concerning all this which was done to us; *ynqyʾ klʾ* SSI ii 28 rev. 5: all the children; etc.; cf. also *wmṭll ʿqhn zy ʾrz klʾ zy ʿm šyryt ʾšrnʾ wʾḥrn zy tmh hwh klʾ bʾšh šrpw* Cowl 30[11f.]: and the whole roof of cedar wood with the rest of the timber and other things which were there all (of it) they burnt with fire; cf. alo *ʿqy ʾrz ... knkr ḥd mnn ʿšrh klʾ* Cowl 26[17]: planks of cedar wood ... 1 talent 10 minae in all (cf. prob. also Cowl 26[13] :: Cowl a.l., Grelot DAE p. 291: connect *klʾ* with following clause) - **E)** *kl* with pronominal suff. - **1)** used independently, *kln* MPAT 46[9]: all of us - **2)** with non-proleptic suffix as first element in an appositional group, *wʾhrg kl[h] šbʿt ʾlpn g[b]rn* KAI 181[16]: and I killed all of it (i.e. the town), 7000 men - **3)** *kl* with proleptic suffix as first element in an appositional group, *klhm ʾnšn* KAI 279[2]: all men (cf. KAI 279[2,4,7,8]) - **4)** *kl* with pronominal suff. as second element in an appositional group - a) the first element being either a Plur. or a Sing. indicating a collectivity or a totality determined in itself or through additional grammatical means, *ʾkhnym ʾš ʿl mrm klʾ* KAI 161[6]: the priests who (are appointed) over the whole high place (uncert. interpret., v. *khn₁*, *mrm* and supra); *byth klh* KAI 215[19]: the whole of his house; *prskn zy kly klh* SSI ii 28 obv. 6: the whole of your salary which has been withheld; *ʾlhyʾ klhm* CIS ii 211[6]: all the gods (cf. Tell F 4); *gnsyʾ klhwn* CIS ii 3913 ii 68: all kinds; *mṭltʾ dh klh* SBS 1a 1: this whole portico; *ʾtrʾ klh* PNO 2ter 7f.: the whole region; *bny byth klhwn* Inv xi 20[6]: all the members of his household; *ʾln klhwn* Inv xi 77[2]: all these; *ʾlhʾ klhwn* Hatra 23[1]: all the gods; *ḥbryhy klhwn* Hatra 213[2f.]: all his colleagues; *mrʾlhʾ klhwn* Hatra 325[3]: the lord of all the gods; *nšyh klhyn* Syn D B 2 (v. supra): all the women; cf. KAI 215[17], SBS 1b 1, 2a 1, 3[1], 4a 1, 34[1,4], 40[6], Inv xi 6[8], 8[6], 17[5], 25[3], xii 19[1], 48[2,2f.], 49[5f.,7], RIP 119[5f.], Hatra 35[7], 79[11], 151[2], Assur 28a 3f., Syn D A 14, etc., etc., cf. poss. also KAI 51 vs. 8; cf. *kl* + pron. suff. preceded by name, *ʾrm klh* KAI 222A 5: the whole of Aram; cf. *mt kln* Tell F 3, 5: all countries (the pron. suff. not corresponding grammatically as to number with the prec. noun (cf. Akkad. par. *kal ālāni*); cf. also *nhr klm* Tell F4 (cf. also Kaufman Maarav iii 148, Muraoka AN xxii 93f.)); cf. also with repeated *kl* + pron. suff., *dnh kprʾ dy ʿbdw wšwḥ ... w ... bnth ... lhm klh klh* (*wl ... ʾḥwthm wlgryhm klh*) J 12[1ff.]: this is the tomb which W. built ... and ... his daughters ... for themselves the whole of it (and for ... their sisters and their clients the whole of it (sc. the tomb)) :: Jaussen & Savignac J a.l.: ... *bnth ... lhm klh klh* = his daughters ... for every one of them, *wlgryhm klh* = for all their clients - b) the first element being introduced by *kl*, *bkl ṣbw klh* CIS ii 3930[4]: in every case; *bkl ʾtr klh* RIP 143[5]: everywhere (v. *ʾšr*$_4$); *bkl gns klh* RIP 156[15] (= CIS ii 3966): of every kind; *kwl ʾlh kwlyh* Hatra 173[2]: every god whosoever; etc. - c) the first element being a Sing. not indicating a collectivity or a totality, *ktb klh* CIS ii 197[7]: any document whatsoever; *grhm klh* J 12[5]: whosoever of their clients (:: Jaussen & Savignac J a.l: the whole body of their clients); *wlʾ ršy ʾnwš klh* CIS ii 209[4f.]: and nobody whosoever has the right; *zwn klh* BASOR cclxiii 77[1]: any kind of provision (:: Hammond, Johnson & Jones BASOR cclxiii 78: *klh* = apposition of preceding string: altogether); *mn dy rḥym lhwn kwlh* Hatra 35[7f.]: everyone who is dear to them (cf. Hatra 20[4], 74[7]) - **F**) poss. as first element in a compound conjunction - 1) *kl lmṭl dy* MUSJ xxxviii 106[7]: (completely) in such a way that :: Ingholt MUSJ xxxviii 113: the preceding *mdʿn* also part of this compound conjunction - **2**) *kl qbl zy* MPAT 49 i 6: = according to what ... - on the use of *kl* in Ar. texts from Egypt, cf. Fitzmyer Bibl xxxviii 170ff., WA 205ff. - L.H.Gray AJSL xxxix 77f.: the *cil* in Poen 945 = Sing. abs. (cf. also Schroed 291f., 311, Krahmalkov Or lvii 59), cf. however Sznycer PPP 127 - Levi Della Vida OA ii 74: the *chulam* in IRT 906[5] poss. = Sing. + suff. 3 p.pl.m., cf. however Reynolds PBR xxiii 142 (with reserve), Vattioni Aug xvi 550: = n.p. (cf. also Vattioni AION xvi 50: = part of n.p.) - Milik DFD 300, Gawlikowski TP 57: l. *klh* (Sing. + suff. 3 p.s.m.?) in Syr xvii 353[2] (prob. reading, dam. context) :: Cantineau Syr xvii a.l.: l. *]mh* - Naveh & Shaked Or xlii 453 n. 54: the *kl* in Pers 94[3], 95[3] = Sing. abs. (uncert. interpret.; cf. R.A.Bowman sub Pers 94: = n.p., sub 95: = n.p. or pro *kl 2* l. *kly* (= n.p.) *1* or *kl* = Sing. abs. (cf. also Segal BSOAS xxxv 354)) - Segal ATNS a.l.: l. *kln* (= Sing. + suff. 1 p.pl.) in ATNS 10a ii 5 (*scriptio anterior*), highly uncert. reading, cf. also Porten & Yardeni sub TADAE B 8.2.

v. *yd*,*kl*$_2$, *kly*$_{1,3}$, *kll*$_2$, *klmh*$_1$, *lylh*, *mʾkl*, *mskh*$_1$, *meškn*$_2$, *nd*, *plk*$_1$, *pnh*$_1$.

kl$_2$ **Hebr** Sing. abs. *kl* KAI 182[5] (:: Ginsberg BJPES ii 49: = PIʿEL Inf. abs. of *kly*$_1$ :: Lemaire Sem xxi 64ff.: = derivative of *kly*$_1$ (= end) :: Lidzbarski PEQ '09, 29, Dir p. 8: = Sing. abs. of *kl*$_1$,cf. already Macalister Gezer ii 25, RES sub 1201 :: Driver PEQ '45, 6: = Sing. cstr. of *kl*$_1$:: Cassuto SMSR xii 111f.: l. poss. *klh* = PIʿEL Inf. abs. of *kly*$_1$; v. infra) - ¶ subst. (cf. e.g. Torczyner BJPES xiii 4f., Gibson SSI i p. 2ff., cf. however Février Sem i 35f., McDaniel Bibl xlix 214: (or) = QAL Inf. (cstr.) of *kwl*$_1$:: Segal JSS vii 219: = QAL Imper. s.m. of *kwl*$_1$) measuring, act of measuring (?, exact meaning unknown (cf. also e.g. Ronzevalle PEQ '09, 109, Michaud PA 23, 25f., Naveh IEJ x 132 n. 5, Cross BASOR clxv 44 n. 42, Röllig KAI a.l., Amusin & Heltzer IEJ xiv 151, Brock JSS xvi 112, Dahood JNSL ii 21f., CISFP i 597f., Conrad TUAT i 248, Borowski AIAI 36, 68, Smelik HDAI 28, Weippert

FS Rendtorff 460 n. 27; cf. also Delekat Bibl li 460f.) :: Brown LP i 3: = threshing? :: Garbini AION vi 123f.: = the getting in (of the crops), the ingathering; for other readings, cf. Mosc p. 13ff.).

kl$_3$ **Palm** Plur. abs. *klyn* RTP 280, *kln* RTP 867 (uncert. interpret., or = Dual?, cf. du Mesnil du Buisson TMP 476) - ¶ subst. meaning uncert.; poss. = some kind of measure (cf. du Mesnil du Buisson TMP 476, 583 n. 2, cf. also Caquot RTP a.l., p. 451: or = vase?) - du Mesnil du Buisson TMP 476, 585: the same word (Plur. abs. *kyln*)in Inv D 18^{1,3,4,6} (poss. interpret., diff. context) - Segal ATNS a.l.: l. poss. *kyln* (= Plur. abs. of *kl$_3$*) in ATNS 52a 11 (uncert. reading, diff. context). v. *kly$_3$*.

kl›$_1$ **OffAr** QAL Pf. 1 p.s. + suff. 2 p.s.m. *klytk* Cowl 5^{7,13}; 3 p.pl.m. *klw* Cowl 37^{15}; + suff. 3 p.s.m. *klwhy* Cowl 37^{13}; Impf. 3 p.s.m. *ykl›* Cowl 5^{9,10}; 1 p.s. + suff. 2 p.s.m. *›kl›nk* Cowl 5^{6}; 3 p.pl.m. *[y]kl›w* FS Driver 54 conc. 3 (dam. context; or l. *]kl›w* = QAL Imper. pl.m.?, cf. Naveh AION xvi 25), *[y]klw* Driv 1^{2} (dam. context; cf. also Segal JSS iv 70); Part. act. pl.m. abs. *klyn* Cowl 37^{14} (cf. Grelot DAE p. 390, Porten & Greenfield JEAS p. 80, Porten & Yardeni sub TADAE A 4.2 :: Cowl a.l., Leand 40f., Driver JRAS '32, 81, Segert AAG p. 295: = QAL Pf. 1 p.pl.); pass. s.m. abs. *kly* SSI ii 28 obv. 6 - **JAr** ITP Impf. 3 p.s.m. *ytkl* AMB 7b 2 (lapsus for *ytkly*?, cf. Dupont-Sommer JKF i 212, cf. also Beyer ATTM 373: = lapsus for *ytklwn* (= ITP Impf. 3 p.pl.m.)); 3 p.pl.m. *ytklwn* AMB 7a 5, 12 - ¶ verb QAL to withhold, to detain, to prevent; *ḥwry zy klw* Cowl 37^{15}: Ch. whom they had detained (cf. Grelot DAE p. 390, Porten & Greenfield JEAS p. 80, Porten & Yardeni sub TADAE A 4.2 :: Cowl a.l.: ... Ḥori, what they had withheld) - **1)** + obj., *hn klytk ›ntn lk ksp›* .. Cowl 5^{13}: if I restrain you (sc. from building) I will have to pay you silver .. (cf. Cowl 5^{7}); cf. also *ykl› mnhm* Cowl 5^{10}: he will restrain one of them - **2)** + obj. + *l$_5$* + Inf., *›kl›nk lmbnh* Cowl 5^{6}: I will restrain you from building - **3)** + obj. + *‹l$_7$*, *klwhy ‹l kd›* Cowl 37^{13}: they detained him because of the pitcher (cf. Grelot DAE p. 390, Porten & Greenfield JEAS p. 80, Porten & Yardeni sub TADAE A 4.2 :: Cowl a.l.: they had withheld it on account of the pitcher) - **4)** + *l$_5$* obj., *wklyn lhn* Cowl 37^{14}: they were detaining them (v. supra) - **5)** + *l$_5$* obj. + *l$_5$* + Inf., *ykl› lmḥsh ... lmbnh* Cowl 5^{9}: he will restrain M. ... from building - **6)** + *mn$_5$* + obj., *[y]kl›w mnh lḥm wmyn* FS Driver 54 conc. 3: one must withhold from him bread and water - **7)** Part. pass. withheld; *[p]rskn zy kly* SSI ii 28 obv. 6: your salary which has been withheld - ITP to be withheld, to be restrained, to be warded off; *dytklwn rwḥ byšth wšydh ...* AMB 7a 12: that the evil spirit and the demon may be restrained - **1)** + *mn$_5$*, *dytklwn rwḥh byšth wṭlnyth ... mn šlw zh* AMB 7a 5f., 7: that the evil spirit and the phantom (v. *ṭlnyt*) ... be withheld from the one who owns this.

v. *kl'$_2$*, *kly$_1$*, *klt*, *tkl$_1$*.

kl'$_2$ **Mo** Plur. (or Dual?, v. infra) cstr. *kl'y* KAI 181[23] - ¶ subst. of uncert. meaning used in the description of a water system (in the comb. *kl'y h'šw[ḥ]*, v. also *'šwḥ*), poss. to be derived from the root *kl'$_1$*,cf. Michaud PA 39 (n. 6), Syr xxxix 126: = support, supporting wall, cf. also Segert ArchOr xxix 242, 265: prob. = inclosing wall (cf. also Dussaud MPJ 8 (n. 3), v.Zijl 191), Gibson SSI i p. 76, 81: = bank (for reservoir) (cf. also de Moor UF xx 154), Jackson & Dearman SMIM 98, 118: = retaining wall, Cooke NSI p. 3, 13: = sluices? (v. however infra), Lidzbarski KI p. 8: = reservoir in cellar-vault (cf. Vriezen & Hospers PI p. 20: = basin, cistern (?, v. however infra)) × related to *kl'* (= double), in Dual, cf. Yadin IEJ xix 18 (n. 18), BiAr xxxii 70 n. 18: *kl'y h'šw[ḥ]* = the twofold underground water system (twofold prob. denoting the two elements typical of *'šwḥ*-systems: the shaft and the tunnel), cf. de Geus SV 26, 28 n. q, cf. Briend TPOA 91; cf. also Lipiński Or xl 335f., UF ii 80: = the twofold shaft of access to the *'šwḥ*, Galling BiOr xxii 244 (n. 5), TGI 53 (n. 15) = the two levels of the system (for the interpret. as Dual, cf. also Cooke NSI p. 13, Vriezen & Hospers PI p. 20, Reviv SCI p. 27); cf. also Röllig KAI a.l.

kl'h **Hebr** Milik DJD ii a.l.: the diff. *kl't* in DJD ii 30[3,15] (= Sing. cstr.) poss. = enclosure (uncert. interpret.).

klb$_1$ **Ph** Plur. abs. *klbm* KAI 24[10], 37B 10 - **Hebr** Sing. abs. *klb* KAI 192[4], 195[4], 196[3] (:: Torczyner Lach i p. 39f.: *klb ky* poss. = haplography for *klbk* (= Sing. + suff. 2 p.s.m.) *ky* :: Jepsen MiOr xv 4f.: *klb* = n.p. (improb. interpret., cf. H.P.Müller UF ii 235 n. 63, Teixidor Syr xlviii 461f.)) - **OffAr** Plur. emph. *klby'* KAI 233[7] (:: Fales JAOS cvii 468f.: = Plur. emph. of *klb$_5$* (< Akkad.; = auxiliary)), AG 87b 9; cf. Frah ix 1 (*klb'*) - **Hatra** Plur. abs. *klbn* 72 (cf. Caquot Syr xxxii 269, Milik DFD 166, Vattioni IH a.l. :: Safar Sumer xi 12 (n. 41), Aggoula Ber xviii 96 (div. otherwise): l. *klbn'* = Plur. emph. of *klb$_1$*) - ¶ subst. m. dog; KAI 24[10], Hatra 72 - **1)** used in a formula expressing subservience (cf. Margalith VT xxxiii 492ff.), *my ʿbdk klb ky ...* KAI 192[3f.]: what is your servant but a dog that ... (cf. KAI 195[3f.], 196[3]; on this formula, cf. Coats JBL lxxxix 14ff.) - **2)** prob. used as indication of hierodule, sacred prostitute: KAI 37B 10 (cf. e.g. CIS i sub 86, Thomas VT x 425f., Amadasi sub Kition C 1 (p. 117), Astour JBL lxxxv 186, Masson & Sznycer RPC 65f., Delcor UF xi 161ff., Gibson SSI iii p. 130 :: v.d.Branden BO viii 258: persons participating in the cult while wearing dogs' masks (cf. Peckham Or xxxvii 317, cf. also Healy BASOR ccxvi 56)), not meant as euphemism (:: v.d.Branden BMB xiii 92); cf. also e.g. Cooke NSI p. 67f., Röllig KAI a.l. - this subst. (Sing. abs./cstr.) poss. in Lach xii 1 (cf. e.g. Lemaire IH i p. 130, Pardee HAHL 107f.), or = *k$_1$* + Sing. cstr. of *lb*??

v. *klb$_2$*, *klby*, *mkn$_1$*, *plb*.

klb$_2$ **Hatra** Sing. emph. *klb›* 70, 71 (v. infra) - ¶ subst. master of the dogs (used as epithet of Nergal), cf. Safar Sumer xi 11 (n. 38), cf. also Segal Irâq xxxv 68 × Caquot Syr xxxii 268f., Vattioni AION xv 50 (n. 77), IH a.l., Milik DFD 165ff., Aggoula Syr liv 284, Drijvers EM 171f., ActIr xvii 171, 179: *klb›* = Sing. emph. of *klb$_1$*(the Dog, epithet of Nergal) × Donner sub KAI 255: = Sing. emph. of *klb$_1$*, *nrgl klb›* = Nergal of the dog (or *klb›* in this case = Plur. emph. of *klb$_1$*??,Nergal of the dogs); on the subject, cf. also As-Saliḥi Irâq xxxiii 114, Greenfield FS Asmussen 137f.

klb$_3$ **OldCan** Sing. abs. *ki-lu-bi* EA 74[46], 79[36], 81[35], 105[9], 116[18] (*ki-lu[-bi]*) - ¶ subst. bird-trap.
v. *kbl$_4$*.

klb$_4$ v. *klby*.

klb$_5$ v. *klb$_1$*, *klby*.

klby **OffAr** Sing. emph. *klby›* Cowl 30[16], 31[15] (cf. Wag 21, Krael p. 105 n. 15, Rowley DOTT 263f., Galling TGI 86, Grelot DAE p. 410 (n. s), Briend TPOA 158 × e.g. Cowl a.l., Ginsberg ANET 492, Lipiński BiOr xxxi 120, Porten & Yardeni sub TADAE A 4.7: = Plur. emph. of *klb$_1$*:: Porten & Greenfield JEAS p. 93, 97: = Plur. emph. of *klb$_4$*(= ax)? :: Fales JAOS cvii 468f.: = Plur. emph. of *klb$_5$*(< Akkad.; = auxiliary); on the subject, cf. Porten Arch 288 n. 19, Grelot RB xcv 297f.) - ¶ adj. doglike; substantivated: the doglike one, the cur (v. however supra).

kldy **Palm** Sing. emph. *kldy›* Ber i 38[7] - ¶ subst. m. chaldean, astrologer (cf. Ingholt Ber i 39); *›kldy*in CIS ii 4357[5], 4358B 3, 4359[3], AAS iii 24A 3, 24B 3 = surname or indication of function (cf. also Lidzbarski Eph i 197; on the form, cf. Stark PNPI 67, cf. however Degen BiOr xxix 212); :: Lidzbarski Eph i 198: l. *›kldy* pro *›knby* in CIS ii 3986[3].

klh$_1$ **Pun** Sing. + suff. 3 p.s.m. *klty* CIS i 124[2] (:: Praetorius ZDMG lx 167, Harr 111: + suff. 1 p.s.) - ¶ subst. poss. meaning completeness (cf. CIS i a.l., Amadasi sub ICO-Malta 2) × Harr 111: = expenses (= subst. or PI‘EL Inf. cstr. of *kly$_1$*; cf. also Praetorius ZDMG lx 167: *klh* = fortune, wealth).
v. *kl$_1$*,*klt*.

klh$_2$ **Palm** Sing. + suff. 3 p.s.m. *klth* MUSJ xlvi 189[2] - ¶ subst. f. daughter-in-law.

kly$_1$ **Ph** PI‘EL Inf. cstr. *klt* Syr xlviii 403[5] (for the reading, cf. Röllig NESE ii 29, 34 :: Caquot Syr xlviii 403, 405f., Gaster BASOR ccix 19, Lipiński RSF ii 52f., v.d.Branden BiOr xxxiii 13, Avishur PIB 267, 271, UF x 32, 36, Gibson SSI iii p. 89, 91f., de Moor JEOL xxvii 111 (div. otherwise): pro *-h lklt* l. *hlmt* = QAL Pf. 1 p.s. of *hlm$_1$*(= to strike) :: Garbini OA xx 291f. (div. otherwise): l. *hlk* (= QAL Pf. 3 p.s.m. of *hlk*$_1$):: Cross CBQ xxxvi 487ff. (div. otherwise): l. *ky ḥlm* (= QAL Pf. 3 p.s.m. of *ḥlm*$_1$(= to dream)) :: Teixidor AO i 108: l. *ḥlmt* (without interpret.)) - **Pun** PI῾EL Pf. 1 p.pl. *kyln* KAI 145^{11} (for this prob. interpret., cf. e.g. Cooke NSI p. 155, RES sub 2221, Röllig KAI a.l., v.d.Branden RSF i 166, 171 :: Février Sem vi 26: = QAL Pf. 1 p.pl. of *kll*$_1$ (= to complete) :: Krahmalkov RSF iii 188, 197: = *kl*$_1$+ suff. 1 p.pl.) - **Hebr** PI῾EL Pf. 3 p.s.m. *kl* KAI 200^6 (for the reading, cf. Cross BASOR clxv 43 n. 30; for the interpret., cf. Naveh IEJ x 132 n. 5, 133f., Lesh xxx 70, 80, Yeivin BiOr xix 5, Amusin & Heltzer IEJ xiv 151f., Röllig KAI a.l., Albright ANET 568, Lemaire Sem xxi 61, 64ff., IH i 261f., Briend TPOA 135, Pardee Maarav i 36f., 41f., HAHL 21, 237, Smelik HDAI 90 :: Cross BASOR clxv 45, Talmon BASOR clxxvi 34, Delekat Bibl li 460f., 463, Gibson SSI i p. 29, Garbini AION xxii 101f., Teixidor Syr lii 279, Dahood Or xlvi 331, Booij BiOr xliii 643, Suzuki AJBI viii 5, 11ff., Rainey JBL cii 632, Conrad TUAT i 250: = QAL Pf. 3 p.s.m. of *kwl*$_1$/*kyl*$_1$(= to measure (cf. also Borowski AIAI 68, Weippert FS Rendtorff 460 n. 27) :: Vinnikov ArchOr xxxiii 547f.: = Sing. cstr. (or abs.?) of *kl*$_1$);1 p.s. *klt* KAI 200^8 (for the reading, cf. Naveh IEJ xiv 158, Delekat Bibl li 457, Lemaire Sem xxi 71f., Briend TPOA 135, Gibson SSI i p. 29f., Scagliarini Hen xii 137 :: Cross BASOR clxv 43 n. 33: l. *klt[y]*; for the interpret., cf. Naveh IEJ x 133, 135, Lesh xxx 70, Vinnikov ArchOr xxxiii 547, Vogt Bibl xli 183, Yeivin BiOr xix 5f., Amusin & Heltzer IEJ xiv 151f., Röllig KAI a.l., Albright ANET 568, Lemaire Sem xxi 61, 65f., IH i 261f., Pardee Maarav i 36f., 41f., 48, 63, HAHL 21, 237, Smelik HDAI 90 :: Cross BASOR clxv 45, Talmon BASOR clxxvi 34, Delekat Bibl li 457, 460f., 463, Gibson SSI i p. 89f., Garbini AION xxii 101f., Booij BiOr xliii 643f., Suzuki AJBJ viii 5, 11ff., Teixidor Syr lii 279, Conrad TUAT i 250: = QAL Pf. 1 p.s. of *kwl*$_1$/*kyl*$_1$(= to measure; cf. also Borowski AIAI 68, Weippert FS Rendtorff 460 n. 27) :: Michaud VT x 454 = QAL Inf. cstr. of *kly*$_1$); Impf. 3 p.s.m. *ykl* KAI 200^5 (cf. Naveh IEJ x 131, 134, Lesh xxx 70, Yeivin BiOr xix 4f., Amusin & Heltzer IEJ xiv 151f., Vinnikov ArchOr xxxiii 547, Lemaire Sem xxi 61, 64f., IH i 261f., Briend TPOA 135, Pardee Maarav i 36, 41f., HAHL 21, 237, Smelik HDAI 90 :: Cross BASOR clxv 44 (n. 42), Talmon BASOR clxxvi 31, Röllig KAI a.l., Brock & Diringer FS Thomas 41f., McDaniel Bibl xlix 214, Gibson SSI i p. 28f., Garbini AION xxii 101f., Teixidor Syr lii 279, Dahood Or xlvi 331, JNSL ii 22, CISFP i 597 n. 21, Booij BiOr xliii 643, Suzuki AJBJ viii 5, 9f., Conrad TUAT i 250: = QAL Impf. 3 p.s.m. of *kwl*$_1$/*kyl*$_1$(= to measure; cf. also Borowski AIAI 68, Weippert FS Rendtorff 460 n. 27) :: Albright ANET 568 (div. otherwise): l. *yklw* = PI῾EL Impf. 3 p.pl.m. of *kly*$_1$) - ¶ verb PI῾EL - **1)** to complete, to finish: KAI 145^{11} (diff. context), 200^5 - a) + obj. (harvest), KAI 200$^{6,8f.}$ - **2)** to destroy, to

destruct; + obj. (an eye): Syr xlviii 403⁵ (v. supra) - Röllig NESE ii 29, 34: pro *ky h-* in Syr xlviii 403[4f.]: l. *klh* = PI ʿEL Imper. s.m. of kly_1 (uncert. reading and highly uncert. interpret.) - Levi Della Vida OA ii 74: *]chyly* in IRT 906[5] = PI ʿEL Pf. 3 p.s.m. of kly_1 (= to add; highly uncert. interpret.); cf. Vattioni AION xvi 50f.: l. *[y]chyl(y)* = YIPH Pf. 3 p.s.m. of kwl_1(= to pay), cf. however idem Aug xvi 550: l. *[y]chyl v.*, *[y]chyl* = YIPH Pf. 3 p.s.m. of kly_1 (= to pay (or = YIPH Impf. 1 p.s.?)) - Tomback JNSL viii 105f.: a form of this root (*kl* = PI ʿEL Pf. 3 p.s.m.) = to complete in RES 16[2] (uncert. interpret., cf. also Lidzbarski Eph i 295f. (div. otherwise): l. *klt* (= QAL Pf. 1 p.s. of $kl{}^{\flat}_1$(= to forbid)), on the context, cf. also Slouschz TPI p. 206).
v. *ʾklh*, kl_2,klh_1.

kly₂ v. $klʾ_1$.

kly₃ **Pun** Sing. abs. *kl* CIS i 1948[3] (v. infra) - **Mo** Plur. cstr. *[k]ly* KAI 181[17f.] (thus reconstructed by most authors, cf. e.g. Cooke NSI p. 12, v.Zijl 191 (n. 6), Röllig KAI a.l., Gibson SSI i p. 75 (cf. also Auffret UF xii 117 (n. 17)), cf. however Blau Maarav ii 154ff. (n. 56), cf. de Geus SV 26, 28 n. o, Mattingly SMIM 237; cf. also Lipiński Or xl 335: l. *[ʾ]ly* = Plur. cstr. of $ʾyl_2$(poss. interpret.) :: Lemaire Syr lxiv 208f.: l. *ʾ[rʾ]ly* = Plur. cstr. of *ʾrʾl*,cf. also Lidzbarski Handb 225, 415, Beeston JRAS '85, 146ff.) - **JAr** Plur. abs. *klyn* AMB 1[14] (?, uncert. interpret., diff. context) - ¶ subst. vessel; *pʿl kl* CIS i 1948[3]: the maker of vessels (cf. also CIS i sub 1948) :: Slouschz TPI p. 315: *kl* = Sing. abs. of kl_1,*pʿl kl* = someone who does everything, i.e. unskilled labourer - for KAI 181[17f.], v. supra - the same word (Plur. abs. *kln*) in ATNS 99[2]? (*kln bblyn* = Babylonian vases?), or to be connected with kl_3??

klyṭ v. *lyṭʾ*.

klyl **JAr** Sing. emph. *klylh* MPAT-A 35[1] (dam. context; = Frey 1980 = SM 16) - ¶ subst. m. circle (text written on circular bronze chandelier).
v. *klyly*.

klyly **Hatra** Sing. emph. *klylyʾ* 253[2] - ¶ nisbe-adj.? the man of K.? (cf. Degen JEOL xxiii 414, Aggoula MUSJ xlvii 19, Vattioni IH a.l.) or connected with *klyl*(cf. Safar Sumer xxiv 20 (n. 38): the one of the crown, Degen JEOL xxiii 414: the one of the crown/garland/turban; cf. Vattioni IH a.l.; cf. Aggoula MUSJ xlvii 19: the one of the arch (i.e. its sculptor)).

klyrk (< Greek χιλίαρχος) - **Nab** Sing. emph. *klyrkʾ* CIS ii 201[2], ADAJ xxvi 203 (cf. also Jobling & Tanner SEL vi 135) - ¶ subst. m. captain over a thousand, for the context of CIS ii 201[3], v. *hpstywn*; cf. also Negev RB lxxxiii 225 (and cf. Benveniste Titres 67ff.).

klklyh **OffAr** Cowl p. 139: the *klklyh* in Cowl 39[3] = everybody (cf. Leand 18 o); improb. interpret., prob. = n.p., cf. Driver JRAS '32, 82, Grelot DAE p. 128 (n. d).

kll$_1$ OffAr a form of this root (*] kllh*) prob. in AE '23, 42 no. 13; Giron AE '23 a.l.: = PA ‘EL Pf. 3 p.s.m./f. (= to complete, to finish).
v. *kly$_1$*.

kll$_2$ Pun Sing. abs. *kll* KAI 69[3,5,7,9,11] (*kl[l]*); Plur. abs. *kllm* 74[5], CIS i 3915[2] - ¶ subst. indicating a certain type of offering, the exact nature of which is diff. to ascertain; *kll* in KAI 69[3,5,7,9] prob. = expiatory sacrifice (cf. Lagrange ERS 470, 472, Dussaud Orig 142ff., Février JA ccxliii 50) :: CIS i sub 165: = holocaust (cf. also Lidzbarski Handb 296, Cooke NSI p. 113f., 117, Ginsberg AJSL xlvii 53, Röllig KAI a.l., Rosenthal ANET 656: = whole offering, cf. also Urie PEQ '49, 69ff.) :: v.d.Branden RSO xl 115f.: = general rule (in the first instance in l. 3 and in ll. 5, 7, 9; cf. also Baker ZAW xcix 191 (n.13)) - the comb. *šlm kll* in KAI 69[3,5,7,9] prob. = holocaust (cf. Lagrange ERS 470, 472, Dussaud Orig 142ff., Février JA ccxliii 50, cf. also v.d.Branden RSO xl 117f.) :: Cooke NSI p. 113f., 118: whole thank-offering (cf. also CIS i sub 165) :: Rosenthal ANET 656: complete whole-offering (cf. Röllig KAI a.l.: or = substitute offering) :: Dietrich, Loretz & San Martín UF vii 561f.: the *kll* in *šlm kll* to be connected with following word, *kll lkhnm* = completely for the priests, *kll* = *kll$_4$* (= adverb); on the *šlm kll*, cf. also Urie PEQ '49 69ff.) - the Plur. in KAI 74[5], CIS i 3915[2] prob. indicating the *kll* and the *šlm kll*, cf. e.g. Dussaud Orig 145, 150, Röllig KAI a.l. - for these offerings, cf. also Amadasi sub ICO app. 3, SSMA 111ff., Capuzzi StudMagr ii 45ff., Janowski UF xii 254f. - v.d.Branden FS Rinaldi 57, 63: l. *kll* (Sing. abs.) in CIS i 88[2] (used adv. = according to the rule), uncert. reading and interpret. (cf. CIS a.l., Cooke NSI p. 73: l. *kl[h]* = entirely).

kll$_3$ Hatra word of unknown meaning (Sing. emph.? or n.p.??) *kll›* in 202[10]?

kll$_4$ v. *kll$_2$*, *lkdn›*.

klm v. *kl$_1$*.

klmh$_1$ OldAr Sing. abs. *klmh* KAI 222A 30 (cf. Tawil BASOR ccxxv 60f. :: e.g. Dupont-Sommer Sf p. 20, 46, Donner KAI a.l., Fitzmyer AIS 15, 48, Gibson SSI ii p. 31, 41, Lemaire & Durand IAS 114, 122: = *kl$_1$*+ *mh$_2$*) - ¶ subst. parasite, louse (for the context, cf. Tawil BASOR ccxxv 60f.; the etym. relation with J.Ar. *qlmh*, Syr *qlm* (cf. Tawil a.l.) improb.).

klmh$_2$ v. *kl$_1$*.

kln v. *kl$_1$*.

klš Ph *klš* RES 1527, word of unknown meaning, cf. *klšy 100* RES 1523, also of unknown meaning.

klšy v. *klš*.

klt Pun word of uncert. meaning in CIS i 6001[2], poss. = Sing. cstr. of *klt* (= vase); Février CIS a.l.: = Sing. abs. of *klt* (= vase) :: Lidzbarski

Eph i 295f.: = Qal Pf. 1 p.s. of (prob.) *kl*ʾ$_1$(= to forbid)? :: Berger sub RES 16: = Sing. abs. of *klh*$_1$(= death); cf. also Slouschz TPI p. 205f.

km$_1$ **Nab** Plur. cstr. *kmy* RB lxxiii 244^1 - ¶ subst. m. indicating unknown object; for a discussion, cf. Starcky & Strugnell RB lxxiii 246.

km$_2$ **Ph** *km* KAI 10^7, 11, 19^9, 24^{6,10,13}, 26A iv 2, C v 6, 43^{12} (for the reading, cf. Honeyman JEA xxvi 57), EpAn ix 5^7 - **Pun** *km* KAI 81^{1,4}, 89^6, 96^1, 119^7, 138^4 (for this interpret., cf. Février Sem ii 25f., Sznycer Sem xxx 36, 40 :: e.g. Lidzbarski Eph iii 287, Röllig KAI a.l.: pro *km b* l. in l. 4f. *km*ʿ = orthographical variant of *km*$_2$), 161^5 (v. infra), 277^{10}, CIS i 6000bis 5 (= TPC 84), NP 130^6 (v. infra) - **Hebr** *kmw* DJD ii 22^6 (reading uncert.), *kmh* DJD ii 43^6 - ¶ prep. as, like - **1)** used comparatively; *šm* ʾ*ztwd ykn l*ʿ*lm km šm šmš wyrḥ* KAI 26A iv 2f.: may the name of A. last forever like the name of the sun and the moon (cf. KAI 26C v 6f.); *šnt km hkkbm* ʾ*l* KAI 277$^{10f.}$: years as many as these stars (v. also *z*$_1$); cf. also KAI 24^{10,13}, CIS i 6000bis 5 (diff. context) - with the meaning "as well as", cf. KAI 81^1, 96^1 (in both instances prob. interpret.); Février RA xlv 144, Röllig KAI a.l.: l. *km* with this meaning in KAI 161^5 (uncert. interpret.; cf. Roschinski Num 112, 115: or (div. otherwise): l. *km*ʾ = as, like); Février RHR cxli 22: l. *km* with this meaning in NP 130^6 (highly uncert. interpret.) - **2)** used normatively; *km bkt*ʿ*b* KAI 138$^{4f.}$ (v. also supra): conform to the document (cf. also KAI 43^{12}); Février RA l 188, Röllig KAI a.l.: l. *km* with normative meaning also in KAI 119^7 (highly uncert. interpret.; for the context, v. also *yp*ʾ) - **3)** used as conjunction; *km tysk* ʾʿ*prt* KAI 89^6: as the lead is poured out - **4)** followed by ʾ*š*$_4$/*š*$_{10}$ - a) used comparatively; *b*ʾ*rn zn ... škbt bswt wmr*ʾ*š* ʿ*ly ... km* ʾ*š lmlkyt* ʾ*š kn lpny* KAI 11: in this coffin ... I lie ... in a robe and with a head-dress on me ... as was the custom with the royal ladies who were before me; *wkt byd mlkm km* ʾ*š* ʾ*klt zqn* KAI 24$^{6f.}$: and I was in the hands of the kings, as if I had eaten my beard (diff. context, cf. also ʾ*kl*$_1$, *š*$_{10}$) - with the meaning "just as"; ʿ*rpt ...* ʾ*š bn ... l*ʿ*štrt ... km* ʾ*š bn* ʾ*yt kl* ʾ*ḥry* KAI 19$^{1ff.}$: the portico ... which they built ... for A. ... just as they built all the rest ... (cf. KAI 81^4, dam. context; cf. also DJD ii 43$^{6f.}$) - b) used temporarily; *km* ʾ*š qr*ʾ*t* ʾ*t rbty* KAI 10^7: when (or: as often as?) I called upon my lady (cf. e.g. Cooke NSI p. 19, Gibson SSI iii p. 95, 98 (cf. also Rosenthal ANET 656) × Dupont-Sommer Sem iii 37: = because; cf. also CIS i sub 1); *km* ʾ*š ygl* ʾ*yt msnzmš* EpAn ix 5^7: when M. drove him into exile; *kmw šbḥym* DJD ii 22^6: as long as (I am) alive - Février JA ccxlvi 445f.: l. *km* (as well as) in CIS i 151^6 (uncert. interpret.; cf. Amadasi sub ICO Sard-Npu 2; cf. also Pili BO xxii 218: l. *k*ʾ).

v. *m*ʾ*š*$_1$, *mglh*, *mplh*, *tm*$_3$.

km› v.Soden Or xxxv 13, xlvi 189: = how much > Akkad. *kima›* - Segal ATNS a.l.: l. *km›* (= as) in ATNS 55a 4 (heavily dam. context, uncert. reading and interpret.).
v. *km*$_2$.
kmh v. *km*$_2$.
kmw$_1$ v. *km*$_2$.
kmw$_2$ v. *kmr*$_2$.
kmn **Ph** Sing. abs. *kmn* KAI 51 verso 7 - **Hebr** Sing. abs. *kmn* SM 49[3,23] - ¶ subst. cummin; > Greek κύμινον, cf. Masson RPAE 51f. - on this word, cf. also Ellenbogen 85, Lipiński ZAH i 67, Borowski AIAI 97f.
kms v. *›škmst*.
km‹ v. *km*$_2$.
kmr$_1$ **JAr** Dupont-Sommer JKF i 207: l. derivative of this root (*mkmrh/t*) in AMB 7[9] (noun or part.?), meaning unknown; improb. reading and interpret., cf. Naveh & Shaked AMB a.l.: l. *mkmry* = part of magical name.
kmr$_2$ **Ph** m. Sing. cstr. *kmr* RES 1519B (= Kition F 2B) - **Pun** m. Plur. cstr. *kmr* KAI 159[7] (reading however uncert., cf. e.g. Cooke NSI p. 146) - **OffAr** m. Sing. abs. *kmr* Cowl 13[15], 76[1] (for the reading, cf. Porten & Yardeni sub TADAE A 5.4 :: Cowl a.l.: l. *kmw* (without interpret.));cstr. *kmr* KAI 225[1], 226[1], RN vi/xiii 17[2], ATNS 56[1], *kwmr* CSOI 140 (diff. reading); emph. *kmr›* KAI 228B 2, AG 99[1], 104b, c, 110bis 2 (for the reading of the context, cf. Dupont-Sommer Syr xxxiii 81: pro *kmr› ›s*l. *kmr› zy*), ASAE lv 277 verso 3 (v. infra), 281, Syr lxvii 332[2] (Greek par. ὁ ἱερεὺς), FX 136[9] (Greek par. ἱερέα),[14,22] (Greek par. ἱερεῖ); Plur. abs. *kmrn* Cowl p. 318[11], AE '23, 42 no. 11[1]; emph. *kmry›* Cowl 27[3,8], 30[5], KAI 228A 23 (for this reading, cf. e.g. Gibson SSI ii p. 149, 151, cf. however Aggoula Syr lxii 62, 65: l. *kmry* = Plur. cstr.) - **Nab** m. Sing. cstr. *kmr* CIS ii 170[4]; Plur. emph. *kmry›* BASOR cclxiii 78[2] - **Palm** m. Plur. cstr. *kmry* CIS ii 3919[4], 3968, RTP 15, 17, Syr xii 133[3] (for the reading, cf. Starcky with Teixidor sub Inv xi 87 and (idem with) Milik DFD 219), etc., etc.; emph. *kmry›* Inv xi 68[1] (*kmr[y›]*; for the reading and interpret. of the context, cf. Milik DFD 103, cf. however Gawlikowski TP 37: l. *kmr[yh]* = Plur. + suff. 3 p.s.m.), 100[2], SBS 38[4], 47[4] (*[k]mry›*, heavily dam. context), Syr xiv 177[4], RTP 10, 11, etc., etc., *kmr›* CIS ii 3929[3] (for this interpret., cf. also Milik DFD 85f., cf. however Gawlikowski Ber xix 81 n. 53, TP 37 (n. 45): l. *kmrh* = Plur. + suff. 3 p.s.m.), SBS 48[3] (= Syr xvii 280[4]; diff. and uncert. reading, cf. Gawlikowski Ber xix 146) - **Hatra** m. Sing. cstr. *kmr* 384; emph. *kmr›* 5[3], 25[1], 27[6], 34[5], 39, 51 (the second instance highly uncert. reading, cf. Safar Sumer ix 246, cf. also Caquot Syr xxxii 55; Milik DFD 400: l. *dmr[l]h[›]* (equally uncert. reading, cf. also Aggoula Sem

xxvii 141)), 145^{2}, 279a, 286^{2}, 388 (v. infra), 405^{2,6}, 407; f. Sing. cstr. *kmrt* (cf. Safar Sumer viii 189, Caquot Syr xxx 239, Ingholt AH i/1, 46; cf. however Milik DFD 366: l. *kmrt[ʾ]* (= f. Sing. emph.; cf. also Vattioni IH a.l.; less prob. reading)) - ¶ subst. m. priest, f. priestess; cf. e.g. *kmr šhr* KAI 225$^{1f.}$: the priest of Sh. (cf. KAI 226^{1}); *kmr ʾsyt[ʿʾ]* ATNS 56^{1}: the priest of Isis-the-great; *kmr ʾlt* CIS ii 170^{4}: the priest of A.; *kmry bl* RTP 15: the priests of B. (cf. e.g. RTP 17); *kmryʾ zy ḥnwb* Cowl 27^{3}: the priests of Ch. (cf. e.g. Cowl 27^{8}, 30^{5}, ASAE lv 281 (for the reading, cf. Milik Bibl xlviii 566 n. 3)); *kmryʾ dy bl* RTP 11: the priests of B. (cf. e.g. RTP 10, 12, Inv xi 100$^{2f.}$); *kmrʾ dʾtrʿtʾ* Hatra 5^{3}: the priest of A.; etc., etc.; *kmr mnbg* RN vi/xiii 17^{2}: priest of M. (= n.l., cf. Seyrig RN vi/xiii 11 (n. 2)); *kmrn bbty ʾlhyʾ* Cowl p. 318^{11}: the priests in the temples of the gods; *kmrʾ rbʾ* (for the reading of the context, v. *rb*$_2$) Hatra 25^{1}: the high-priest (:: Altheim & Stiehl AAW ii 201: poss. = the priest of the great (god)) - the *br kmrʾ* in Hatra 388 poss. = son of the priest, cf. however Aggoula Syr lxvii 398: *kmrʾ*, priest, used as gentilicium (= or *kmrʾ* = name) - for the tribe/clan of the *bny kmrʾ* in Palmyre, as indication of a class of priests, cf. Ingholt Ber iii 11, Syr xiii 289 n. 1, du Mesnil du Buisson TMP 463, Milik Bibl xlviii 577 n. 4, DFD 36ff., Gawlikowski TP 28, 36f., Syr li 94 (cf. also Greek par. Χωνειτῶν φυλή), cf. however Garbini AION xviii 76f. - cf. poss. also ASAE lv 277 verso 3f. (*bbny kmrʾ ʾšmn* = among (i.e. belonging to) the *bny kmrʾ* of E., a class of priests? (cf. also Milik Bibl xlviii 577, 617 (*kmrʾ* = Plur. cstr.)) :: Bresciani ASAE lv 281 n. 1: *bbny* poss. = variant of *bbly* (= Babylonian)?; cf. also Garbini AION xvii 95f.) - *kmrh* > Akkad. *kumirtu*, cf. v.Soden Or xxxv 13, xlvi 189 (cf. also idem AHW s.v. *kumirtu*, CAD s.v.).
v. *dyr*,*pḥr*$_1$, *rḥym*.

kmrh v. *kmr*$_2$.

kn$_1$ v. *khn*$_1$.

kn$_2$ v. *khn*$_1$.

kn$_3$ v. *kn*$_4$, *ptystyknʾ*.

kn$_4$ **Ph** *kn* KAI 9A 2, 51 recto 4 (dam. and diff. context; or = Qal Inf. cstr. of *kwn*$_1$?,cf. also Aimé-Giron BIFAO xxxviii 15), 60^{7}, MUSJ xlv 262^{1} (cf. e.g. Starcky MUSJ xlv 262f., Röllig NESE ii 2f. × Cross IEJ xxix 41: = *kn*$_5$; v. also *hn*$_3$) - **Pun** *kʿn* Punica xii 8^{2}, xvii 2^{4}, *pʿn* Punica xii 8^{2} (prob. lapsus for *kʿn*; or l. *kʿn*?, cf. Jongeling NINPI 5), *kḥn* Punica xii 6^{3}, 9^{3} (for the reading, cf. Jongeling NINPI 5 :: Chabot Punica a.l.: l. *kḥt*), cf. poss. Poen 935: *chem* = lapsus pro *chen* (variant reading *them*; cf. Sznycer PPP 84f. :: J.J.Glück & Maurach Semitics ii 108f.: = *ky* + *ʾm*$_3$) - **Hebr** *kn* KAI 194^{3}, DJD ii 7 iii 2 (heavily dam. context), AMB 4^{14} - **OldAr** *kn* KAI 222A 35, 37, 38, 39, 40, 41, 42, B 43, C 21, Tell F 10 (cf. Abou-Assaf, Bordreuil & Millard Tell

F p. 24, 32, Zadok TeAv ix 125, Wesselius SV 56, Muraoka AN xxii 83, 111 n. 23, Gropp & Lewis BASOR cclix 46, 51, Vattioni AION xlvi 360, Delsman TUAT i 636 :: Kaufman Maarav iii 162, 166: = *kn*$_6$ (= conditional particle), if, when, cf. also Greenfield & Shaffer Irâq xlv 113; for the context, cf. Pardee JNES xliii 254 n. 5) - **OffAr** *kn* Cowl 20^{7}, 21^{4}, 26^{2}, Driv 3^{2}, $4^{1,2}$, 8^{3} (cf. however Porten & Yardeni sub TADAE A 6.11: l. prob. *knm*), Beh 37 (Akkad. par. *ki-a-am*), Aḥiq 145 (:: Kottsieper SAS 16, 209: or = Sing. m. abs. of *kn*$_3$(= honest?)), ATNS 1^{10}, 2^{5}, 4^{10} (for the reading, cf. Shaked Or lvi 409, Porten & Yardeni sub TADAE B 8.7 :: Segal ATNS a.l.: l. *kz* (= when)), KAI $264^{3,4}$, 267A 3, SSI ii 28 obv. 4, rev. 6, JA ccliv 440^{4} (for the reading, cf. Dupont-Sommer a.l., cf. however Kutscher, Naveh & Shaked Lesh xxxiv 128: l. *[k]n*; dam. context), etc., etc.; cf. Frah xxv 33 (cf. Nyberg FP 104), Paik 538, GIPP 25, 55, SaSt 18 - **JAr** *kn* MPAT 39^{7}, 49 i 5, 53^{2} - ¶ adv. thus, passim; *kn ydyʿ yhwy lk hn mn grdʾ ... mndʿm ksntw yhwh ...* Driv 7^{8}: thus let it be known to you, (that) if the domestic staff ... will suffer some kind of loss ... (cf. Driv 4^{3}); *kn yhwy* ATNS 12^{2}: thus let it be (cf. ATNS 1^{10}; for the context of this text, cf. Porten & Yardeni sub TADAE B 8.8); *kn šmyʿ ln lʾmr ...* SSI ii 28 rev. 6: thus we have heard: ...; *whn kn lʾ ʾʿbd* MPAT 39^{7}: if I do not do so (cf. MPAT 53^{2}); cf. also in introduction of direct speech, *ʿbdyk ... kn ʾmryn hn ʿl mrʾn ṭb ...* Cowl $30^{22f.}$: your servants ... say as follows: if it seems good to our lord ... (cf. Cowl $26^{3,9}$, 33^{7}, Driv 3^{2}, 4^{1}, 10^{1}, Beh 37, SSI ii 28 obv. 4, KAI $264^{3,4}$; cf. Dion RB lxxxix 549f.); *kn ʾmrt kpm ...* ATNS 3^{6}: she spoke as follows: according the instruction of ... (for the reading, cf. Porten & Yardeni sub TADAE B 8.10); *kn ktyb* ATNS $27^{3,5}$: thus it was written; *kn ʾmr zy šmʿ hwyt ...* MPAT 49 i 5: he spoke thus: I have heard ...; cf. also the introductory formulae *kʿnt hlw kn* RES 1792A 1: well then, it is thus (v. also *hlw*) and *hlw kn*, *hlw kn šlḥ lʾmr ...* RES 492B 5: well it is thus: he has sent saying ... - **1)** corresponding with a preceding expression - a) with *ʾyk zy*, *ʾyk zy tqd šʿwtʾ zʾ bʾš kn tqd ʾrpd* KAI 222A 35: just as this piece of wax burns with fire thus will A. be burned (cf. KAI 222A 37, 38, etc.) - b) with *k*$_1$, *kkl ʾšr šlḥ ʾdny kn ʿšh ʿbdk* KAI $194^{2f.}$: in accordance with all (the instructions) that my lord has sent, so has your servant acted; Lipiński Stud 45: this construction also in KAI 222B 43 (poss. interpret.; dam. and diff. context) - c) with *lqbl*, *lqbl zy ʾnh ʿbdt lk kn ... ʿbd ly* Aḥiq 52: according as I did for you, so ... do to me - **2)** for *kn* in the comb. *hʾ kn* introducing the second part of a comparison, v. *hʾ*$_2$ - **3)** corresponding with a following *kzy* - a) with final meaning, *kn ʿbd kzy ... lʾršm tḥd[y]* Driv 13^{2}: act thus so that ... you will please A. (cf. ATNS 26^{11}); *htb hb lhm kn kzy [ms]pt qbylt twbʾ lʾ yšlḥ* Driv 12^{10}: restore (it) to them in this way that M. may not again send a complaint; *ʾntm* *qmw qblhm kn kzy mlh bʾyšh lʾ yhškḥwn lkm* Cowl 38[6f.]: you stand by them so they shall not find a fault with you; etc. - b) with comparative meaning, *ʿbdw ʿl bytʾ zyly kn kzy pqydyʾ [qd]myʾ hww ʿbdn* Driv 7[7f.]: attach (them) to my estate, just as the former officers used to do - c) with explicative meaning, *tnh kn šmyʿ ly kzy pqydyʾ ...* Driv 7[3]: here I hear thus that the officers ... - **4)** preceded by prep. - a) preceded by *ʾḥr_5*, *ʾḥry*, v. *ʾḥr_5* - b) preceded by l_5 - α) with final meaning, in order that: KAI 60[7] - β) in the combination *qdmn lkn* (?, diff. and dam. context), *hn lw glyn ʾnpyn ʿl ʾršm qdmn lkn lʾ kznh ...* Cowl 37[8]: if we had shown ourselves in the presence of A. formerly, this would not ... (v. *gly*; cf. for interpret. of context also Porten & Greenfield JEAS p. 81, Porten & Yardeni sub TADAE A 4.2 :: Grelot DAE p. 389: *lkn* = consequently :: Cowl a.l., Leand 63c: *lkn* poss. = 'but') - c) preceded by mn_5: Cowl 20[7] = consequently, therefore (cf. also Cowl 41[4], dam. context) - d) preceded by $ʿl_7$: KAI 9A 2, Aḥiq 117, 187 = consequently, therefore; cf. also *kn* preceded by *ʿl dbr* (v. dbr_3) - **5)** *kn* repeated in the formula *kʿn kʿn*, *kʿn kʿn brkʾ šmʾ ql* Punica xvii 2[4f.]: just because he has blessed her (and) heard (her) voice, cf. Punica xii 6[3], 8[2], 9[3] (for the reading, v. supra) - the reading *kn* in MPAT-A 40[3] highly uncert., cf. also Naveh sub SM 57 (Beyer ATTM 366: l. poss. *ʿwd* = $ʿwd_5$) - Altheim & Stiehl ASA 271: the *kyn*in FuF xxxv 173[2,4,5] (*ky[n]*)[,7,8,11] = kn_4 (diff. context) - Beyer ATTM 372: l. *lkn* (= l_5 + kn_4) in AMB 7[8] (uncert. reading and interpret., diff. context).

v. kwn_1, $krš_1$, mn_5, *npš*, $rbʿ_3$.

kn_5 **Hebr** IEJ vii 239[1], DJD ii 46[4] - ¶ adv. here.

v. kn_4, mn_5, *rwndkn*.

kn_6 v. kn_4.

knʾ v. *ptystyknʾ*.

knb v. mkn_1.

knbwn **Hebr** Sing. abs. *knbwn* Mas 430 - ¶ subst. round cake, in Mas 430 used as nickname (cf. Yadin & Naveh Mas a.l.).

knd v. kd_1.

kndws v. *kndwṣ*.

kndwṣ (< Lyc., cf. Dupont-Sommer CRAI '74, 142, FX 145, cf. also Laroche CRAI '74, 121f., Teixidor JNES xxxvii 183) - **OffAr** Sing. abs. *kndwṣ* FX 136[7,12,16,21], *kndws*FX 136[22] - ¶ subst. honorific title for a god (lord; cf. Greek par. βασιλεῖ, βασιλέως), prob. used here as n.d. (cf. Frei BiOr xxxviii 367); for the meaning, cf. also litt. mentioned supra.

kndsyrm v. *knzsrm*.

kndr (< Lat. *quadrans*?, v. infra) - **Pun** Plur. abs. *kndrm* KAI 130[2] (= Trip 12) - ¶ subst. indicating certain coin; Levi Della Vida IRT p. 12: prob. = *quadrans* = 1/4 *as*, cf. also Amadasi IPT 44; uncert. interpret., reading *ktdrm* equally poss.

knwn (< Akkad., cf. Littmann Syr xix 171, Rosenthal Sprache 90, Kaufman AIA 62, 146, 148 n. 41 :: Gawlikowski TP 85 n. 110) - **Palm** Sing. emph. *knwn›* CIS ii 3952[4], 3977[4] (= RIP 132), RIP 143[1], Syr xii 138[4] (*k[n]wn›*; for this poss. reading, cf. Milik DFD 317, cf. also Gawlikowski TP 78: l. *[kn]wn›*); Plur. abs. *knwnyn* Inv xi 7[3] - ¶ subst. m. brazier; *knwn› dy nḥš›* CIS ii 3952[4]: a brazier of bronze; in CIS ii 3977[4], RIP 143[1], Inv xi 7[3] prob. indication of a small stone altar on which incense was burned, cf. Chabot Choix 47, Teixidor Sumer xxi 86, Gawlikowski TP 85, Aggoula Syr liv 284.
knwt v. *zbnwt*.
knzsrm **OffAr** the diff. *knzsrm* in Driv 8[1*] (*k[nz]srm*)[,1], 9[1*,1], 10[1*,1] (cf. also *kndsyrm*Driv 11[1] and *ḥn[d]syrm*Driv 11[1*]) = n.p., cf. Kitchen RHA lxxvi (xxiii) 25ff., cf. also Eilers AfO xvi 326 (n. 14), Garbini ISNO 50, Grelot DAE p. 316 (n. b), 476, Degen GGA '79, 21, Porten & Yardeni sub TADAE A 6.11/12/13 :: Kamil with Driv[1] p. 26: < Iran. = chief of the treasury (cf. Segert AAG p. 95, Coxon ZDMG cxxix 13; cf. however de Menasce BiOr xi 162, Henning with Driv p. 67 and Greenfield Mem Henning 181 (n.7)).
kny **Ph** PI‹EL Inf. cstr. *knt* KAI 60[5] - ¶ verb PI‹EL to appoint; *lknt gw ‹rb* KAI 60[5f.]: to appoint the community as guarantor (v. *‹rb*$_5$) - Février & Fantar Karth xii 54: the *kn›* in Karth xii 54[1] = PI‹EL Pf. 3 p.pl. (highly uncert. interpret., cf. also v.d.Branden RSF v 57, 62, BiOr xxxvi 202: = QAL Pf. 3 p.s.f. or 3 p.pl. of *kwn*$_1$:: Krahmalkov RSF iii 179, 186: = QAL Pf. 1 p.pl. of *kwn*$_1$).
knyšh **JAr** Sing. *knyšt›* MPAT-A 12[6] (= Frey 1195 = SM 71), *knyšth* MPAT-A 28[1,3] (= Frey 858 = SM 34) - ¶ subst. f. synagogue, congregation; *d[yhb]t* (for the reading, cf. Naveh sub SM 34) *ḥd dynr lyqrh dknyšth* MPAT-A 28[3]: who gave one dinar for the honour of the congregation (cf. MPAT-A 12[5f.], 28[1]).
v. *knšh*.
knkr v. *kkr*.
knm **OffAr** *knm* KAI 279[5], ATNS 2[3], 21[5] - ¶ adv. thus, similarly; *knm ›mrn* ATNS 2[3]: thus we said (for KAI 279[5], cf. e.g. Dupont-Sommer JA ccxlvi 29, Altheim & Stiehl EW ix 198, x 245, ASA 271, GH 400 :: Kutscher, Naveh & Shaked Lesh xxxiv 134: = too, also).
v. *›pm*, *kn*$_4$.
knn$_1$ **Palm** Sing. cstr. *knn* Inv D 15[5] - ¶ subst. fixation (reading and interpret. highly uncert., cf. Cantineau Syr xix 164).
knn$_2$ v. *hlk*$_1$.
knn$_3$ v. *lkdn›*.
knp **Samal** Sing. cstr. *knp* KAI 215[11] - **OffAr** Dual cstr. *knpy* Aḥiq 171 - ¶ subst. skirt (of a garment).
v. *›ḥz*.

knprs (< Greek κανηφόρος) - **Ph** Sing. cstr. *knprs* KAI 40[2] - ¶ subst. basket bearer (cultic function); cf. also Röllig KAI a.l.

knṣwl‘t (< Lat. *consulatus*) - **Pun** Sing. abs. *knṣwl‘t* Karth xii 50[1] (cf. Février & Fantar Karth xii a.l., Krahmalkov RSF iii 178f., 204 :: v.d.Branden RSF v 56, 59 (div. otherwise): l. *nṣwl‘t* = Sing. abs. (= ruin)), 52[3] - ¶ subst. consulate, consulship.

knr **OldAr** Sing. abs. *knr* KAI 222A 29 - ¶ subst. lyre (for KAI 222A 29, cf. Greenfield ActOr xxix 15); > Greek κινύρα, cf. also Boisacq 457, Brown JSS x 206f., Or l. 386ff. - on the etymology, cf. Ellenbogen 116f.
v. *mkn$_1$*.

knš$_1$ **OffAr** QAL Part. pass. pl.m. + suff. 3 p.s.m., cf. Warka 12: *ka-niš-a-a-[’i-i]*; ITP Pf. 3 p.pl.m. *’tknšw* Beh 1 (*’tknš[w]*; Akkad. par. *ip-ḫu-ru-nim-ma*), 4 (*[’]tknšw*, Akkad. par. idem), 8 (Akkad. par. idem), 10 (Akkad. par. idem), Cowl 269 iv 2 (*[’]tknšw*; cf. Greenfield & Porten BIDG 24 l. 8); Impf. 3 p.pl.m. *ytknšwn* Cowl 71[8] - **Palm** QAL Part. pass. s.f. abs. *knyš’* CIS ii 3913 i 3 (Greek par. ἀγομένης); ITP Part. pl.m. abs. *mtknšyn* CIS ii 3913 ii 132 - ¶ verb QAL; Part. pass. assembled; *kd hwt bwl’ knyš’ mn nmws’* CIS ii 3913 i 3: when the council was assembled by law; *ka-niš-a-a-[’i- i]* Warka 12: those who are assembled there - ITP to be assembled, to assemble, to rally; *wytknšwn ’lhy mṣryn* Cowl 71[8]: and the gods of Egypt will be assembled; *b’tr dy mtknšyn* CIS ii 3913 ii 132: in the place where they assemble (cf. l. 131: *b’tr dy dms*); *[mr]dy’ ’tknšw ’[z]lw l‘rqh zy whmws* Beh 10: the rebels rallied (and) went against W. - > Akkad. *kanāšu* (= to gather, said of harvest), cf. v.Soden Or xxxv 12, xlvi 188, AHW s.v. *kanāšu* II; cf. also Deller Or xxxiii 260 (n. 2), Zadok WO xii 199 - the *knš’* in KAI 160[3] poss. = QAL Part. act. pl.m. cstr., cf. Février Sem iv 22, Röllig KAI a.l. (cf. also the diff. *knš* in KAI 159[1]?, Février Sem iv 22: related to *knš’* in KAI 160[3] :: Clermont-Ganneau RAO iii 31 n. 5: < *censor*?; rather to be explained as n.p.).

knš$_2$ v. *npš*.

knš$_3$ cf. Frah xii 9 (*knš(y)’*; cf. Nyberg FP 81) - v.Soden Or xxxv 12, xlvi 188, AHW s.v. *kanšu* II: > Akkad. *kanšu* = ‘Arbeitskommando’, cf. however also CAD s.v. *kanšu* (s.) = donkey caravan (< West-Sem.).

knšh > Akkad. *kiništu* (*/kinaštu/kinaltu/kinartu*) = a class of priests of low status, cf. v.Soden Or xxxv 13, xlvi 189, AHW s.v. *kiništu*, cf. also CAD s.v. *kiništu*.
v. *knyšh*.

knt$_1$ (< Akkad., cf. Zimmern Fremdw 46, Kaufman AIA 64, 145, 157f., cf. also Lipiński ZAH i 67) - **OffAr** Sing. + suff. 3 p.s.m. *knth* Aḥiq 90, 163; + suff. 3 p.pl.m. *knthm* Cowl 17[7]; Plur. + suff. 3 p.s.m. *knwth* ATNS 9[3a] (for the reading, cf. Porten & Yardeni sub TADAE B 8.6),[10], 30a 2, Cowl 6[6], 17[1,5,6] (for the reading, cf. Porten RB xc 406, Porten

& Yardeni sub TADAE A 6.1), Krael 7^{38}, Driv 3^7, 5^7, FX $136^{8,23}$ (cf. Dupont-Sommer FX a.l., Contini OA xx 233 :: Garbini SMEA xviii 271f., Teixidor JNES xxxvii 184 (div. otherwise): l. *›wrn* (= n.g.) *wth* (= *wt* (var. of *›yt*$_3$) + suff. 3 p.s.m.)), etc., etc.; + suff. 1 p.pl. *knwtn* Samar 5^7 - ¶ subst. m. companion, colleague (for the exact meaning, cf. Porten Arch 48 n. 77, cf. also Grelot VT iv 351); the Plur. in FX $136^{8,23}$ used instead of Sing.? (cf. Dupont-Sommer FX 145f.), cf. for *kndwṣ ›lh› kbydšy wknwth* FX 136^7 and *kndws ›lh› wknwth* FX $136^{22f.}$ the Greek par. βασιλεῖ Καυνίῳ καὶ >Αρκεσιμαι (l. 7f.), βασιλέως Καυνίου καὶ Αρκεσιμα (ll. 15f., 22f.), cf. also Lycian par. l. 8f., 17f., 24f., 28f.
v. *knt*$_2$.

knt$_2$ OffAr Plur. abs. *kntn* Cowl 10^{10}, Krael 11^3, ATNS 45a 6, 45b 2, 4, 6, 8, 181^2 (?, heavily dam. context; or = Sing. + suff. 1 p.pl. of *knt*$_1$??);emph. *knty›* Krael 11^5, *kntny›* Krael 11^4 (prob. lapsus) - ¶ subst. emmer, cf. Fronzaroli RCL '69, 297, Kislev Lesh xxxvii 87, 92 - abbrev. *k* prob. in Krael 11^4, *kp 2 s›n 3* = emmer 2 *peras* and 3 *seah* (cf. prec. line *kntn prsn 2 s›n 3*; cf. Alrik BASOR cxxxvi 24 n. 2, Porten & Greenfield JAOS lxxxix 156 n. 22, JEAS p. 67 :: Yaron JSS xiii 211: *kp 2* = in two instalments (*kp* = *kp*$_1$), cf. also Alrik BASOR a.l. :: Krael a.l.: *kp 2* = two times (i.e. a double amount; *kp* = *kp*$_1$, cf. also Grelot DAE p. 253)).

knt$_3$ Pun the unexplained *kntm* in KAI 163^1 poss. = Sing. of *knt* (without interpret.) + suff. 3 p.s.m.?, Février AIPHOS xiii 166, 170: = Sing. + suff. 3 p.s.m. of *knt* (= solemn declaration?).

ks$_1$ Ph Sing. cstr. *ks* Kadm xviii 91 (= BASOR ccxxxviii 15 :: Sznycer Kadm xviii 93: or = poss. Sing. abs.?; for the reading and interpret. of the context, cf. also Puech RB xc 375ff., xciii 168), Kadm xviii 92 n. 1 - **OffAr** Sing. abs. *ks* Cowl 36^4 (cf. Porten & Greenfield JEAS p. 118, Porten & Yardeni sub TADAE B 6.2, Porten AN xxvii 90, 93 × Cowl a.l.: or l. *kp* = Sing. abs. of *kp*$_1$ (= bowl, ladle)), Krael 7^{14}; cstr. *ks* Cowl $61^{4,14}$; emph. *ks›* RES 1296^3 (v. infra), 1299A 2?, IrAnt iv 115; Plur. abs. *ksn* Cowl 15^{12}, ATNS 9^5, *ksyn* Cowl $61^{1,3,13}$ - **Hatra** Plur. emph. *ks›* (for this reading, cf. Degen NESE iii 91; reading of › however uncert., cf. e.g. Safar Sumer xxvii 14 (n. 39) :: Aggoula Syr lii 194f.: reading *ks* (= Sing. cstr.) preferable, cf. also Vattioni IH a.l.) - ¶ subst. m. cup; in RES 1296^3 *ks›* rather = Sing. emph. of *ks*$_2$ (= sack)?, cf. RES sub 1296, AG sub 3a (cf. however Lidzbarski Eph iii 122, Grelot DAE p. 137: = cup) - on this word, cf. Amadasi Guzzo Sem xxxviii 16f.
v. *kp*$_1$.

ks$_2$ v. *ks*$_1$.

ks›$_1$ OffAr Qal (or Pa‘el?) Impf. 3 p.pl.m. *yks›n* KAI 233^{16} (for the reading, cf. e.g. R.A.Bowman UMS xx 278, 281, Dupont-Sommer Syr xxiv 31, 46, Donner KAI a.l., Gibson SSI ii p. 104, 109 :: Lidzbarski ZA xxxi 195, 201, AUA p. 8, 13: l. *ykwʾn* = PA ʿEL Impf. 3 p.pl.m. of *kwʾ* (= to burn; variant of *kwy*)),[18] (for the reading, cf. Dupont-Sommer Syr xxiv 31, 47, Donner KAI a.l., Gibson SSI ii p. 104 :: Lidzbarski ZA xxxi 195, 202, AUA p. 8, 13: l. *ykwrn* = PA ʿEL Impf. 3 p.pl.m. of kwr_1(= to slay), cf. R.A. Bowman UMS xx 278, 281: l. *ykwrn* = pass. form, to be overthrown); cf. however Gibson SSI p. 110: l. *yksʾn* = QAL pass., poss. interpret.) - ¶ verb QAL (or PA ʿEL?) poss. meaning to pursue (cf. e.g. Gibson SSI ii p. 105, 109 :: Donner KAI a.l. (cf. also Dupont-Sommer Syr xxiv 46): = to bind, to catch :: R.A.Bowman UMS xx 278, 281: = to hide?)

ks ʾ₂ **Pun** PI ʿEL (or YIPH) Part. pl.m. abs. *mksʾm* RCL '66, 201^5 - ¶ verb PI ʿEL (or YIPH); Part. meaning unknown; Garbini RSO xliii 13: (denominative verb of *ksʾ₃*) = those of the seat (indication of certain category of magistrats), poss. explanation :: Fantar RCL '66, 207: (denominative verb of *ksʾ₃*) = makers (and merchants) of seats :: Dupont-Sommer CRAI '68, 127: (= PI ʿEL Part. of *ksy₁*) = packers :: Ferron Mus xcviii 56f.: < *ksʾ₃* = those who live along the same street (i.e. in the context the merchants living in the same street).

ks ʾ₃ v.Soden AHW s.v. *kussû*: < Akkad. < Sum. (cf. also Salonen Möbel 58f., Lipiński ZAH i 67; cf. however Kaufman AIA 28f.) - **Ph** Sing. cstr. *ksʾ* KAI 1^2, 24^9, 26A 1,11 - ¶ subst. m. (for KAI 1^2, cf. Vincent RB xxxiv 186, v.Dijk VT xix 441 n. 6, 444f., Dahood Or xlviii 97, Baldacci BiOr xl 125 :: Friedrich AfO x 81f., FR 303, Röllig KAI a.l., Gibson SSI iii p. 16: in KAI 1^2 = f. (cf. also Schoors FS Fensham 194)) throne; for the context of KAI 1^2, cf. Gibson SSI iii p. 16; on this word, cf. also Ishida BZAW cxlii 105f.
v. *ksʾ₂*,*ksʾh*, *krsʾ*, *mṭnʾ*, *myst*.

ks ʾ₄ **Ph** Plur. abs. *ksʾm* KAI 43^{12} - ¶ subst. full-moon; cf. also Akkad. *kusīu* (= piece of head gear, turban) in lex. text, poss. < West-Sem. (Aramaic?), cf. Kaufman AIA 65, CAD s.v. :: Zimmern Fremdw 63: Akkad. poss. > West-Sem.

ks ʾh (for etym., cf. *ksʾ₃*) - **Pun** Sing. abs. *ksʾt* KAI $122^{1,2}$ - ¶ subst. throne; *ksʾt šhnskt lʾlm ʿwgsṭs* KAI 122^1: the throne for the molten image of the divine Augustus; v. *krsʾ*.

ksh **OffAr** Sing. + suff. 2 p.s.m. *kstk* Aḥiq 205 - ¶ subst. fodder (cf. Ungnad ArPap 80, Ginsberg ANET 430, Lindenberger APA 203f., Kottsieper SAS 23, 210 × = Sing. + suff. 2 p.s.m. of *kst₁* (= covering) :: Cowl p. 226, 247 (cf. also Grelot RB lxviii 193, DAE p. 447): = *kst₁* (= cushion > saddle)).

kswt **JAr** Sing. abs. *kswt* MPAT 62^{12} (= DBKP 27; diff. reading, cf. Greek par. ἀμφιαζμοῦ) - ¶ subst. clothing (for the context of MPAT 62^{12}, v. *mzwn*).

ksy$_1$ **Ph** PI ʿEL Pf. 3 p.s.m. + suff. 3 p.s.m. *ksy* KAI 24^{12} (cf. Lidzbarski Eph iii 237f., Friedrich ZS i 5f., CF p. 18 (cf. Gibson SSI iii p. 38: or = Pf. 3 p.pl. + suff. 3 p.s.m.; cf. also Avishur PIB 213) :: Harr 112: = PU ʿAL Pf. 3 p.s.m. (cf. also FR 174, 176b, Röllig KAI a.l., Segert ArchOr xxix 227 (n. 158), GPP p. 190, Dahood Bibl lx 431, de Moor UF xx 168, Swiggers BiOr xxxvii 341); on the form, cf. also Garr DGSP 142) - **DA** PA ʿEL Impf. 2 p.s.m. *tksn* ii 10 (for the word division and interpret., cf. Hoftijzer DA p. 231, 297f. (cf. also Lemaire CRAI '85, 277) × Knauf ZDPV ci 190: = QAL Impf. 2 p.pl.m. × e.g. Caquot & Lemaire Syr liv 204, Garbini Hen i 172, 186, Levine JAOS ci 200 (div. otherwise): l. *mtksn* = ITP Part. pl.m. abs., those who are covered :: Hackett BTDA 26, 65, 94, 99: l. *tksn* = PA ʿEL Impf. 2 p.s.m. + suff. 3 p.s.m. (cf. also Rofé SB 62, 68 (+ suff. 3 p.s.f.), Garr DGSP 111)) - **OffAr** PA ʿEL Impf. 2 p.s.m. *tksh* Aḥiq 103 (cf. e.g. Cowl a.l., Grelot RB lxviii 183, DAE p. 437, Kottsieper SAS 176, 210 :: Baneth OLZ '14, 298, Lindenberger APA 85, 241 n. 234, 279: lapsus for *tkwh* = QAL or PA ʿEL Impf. 3 p.s.f. of *kwy*(= to burn; cf. also Ginsberg ANET 428)); 1 p.s. + suff. 2 p.s.f. *ʾksnky* Aḥiq 118; ITP Impf. 3 p.pl.m. *ytkswn* Cowl 38^{11} - **JAr** ITP Part. s.f. abs. *mksyʾ* MPAT 41^{10} (cf. e.g. Birnbaum MarrDeed 19, Milik sub DJD ii 20 (or: = PU ʿAL Part.), Fitzmyer & Harrington MPAT a.l. :: Birnbaum JAOS lxxviii 17f.: l. *mbsyʾ* = PA ʿEL Part. of *bsy*(= to be negligent)) - ¶ verb PI ʿEL/PA ʿEL to cover - **1)** + obj.: Aḥiq 103; *wbymy ksy bṣ* KAI $24^{12f.}$: and in my days byssus covered him (cf. e.g. Röllig KAI a.l. × Gibson SSI iii p. 35, 38: and in my days they covered him with byssus; v. also supra) - **2)** + double object, *ʾksnky mšky* Aḥiq 118: I will cover you with my hide; cf. poss. also DA ii 10, v. however supra - ITP - **1)** to be hidden; + *mn*$_5$, *lʾ ytkswn mn ʿnny* Cowl 38^{11}: they will not be hidden from A. - **2)** to be clothed: MPAT 41^{10} - a form of this root (*ks[h/y]*) prob. in Aḥiq 109 (= QAL Pf. 3 p.s.m. (*ksh*), PA ʿEL Pf. 3 p.s.m. (*ksy*) or QAL Part. act. s.m. abs.), cf. also Lindenberger APA 95, 245 n. 271.
v. *ksʾ*$_2$,*kst*$_1$, *kšt*.

ksy$_2$ **Hatra** Sing. emph. *ksyʾ*, cf. Assur 7^2 - ¶ subst. cover, lid.
v. *nsyk*.

ksyd **Hatra** Sing. (or Plur.) emph. *ksydʾ* 281^5 (for this reading, cf. Degen NESE iii 70, Vattioni IH a.l. :: Safar Sumer xxvii 4f. (n. 5): l. *ksyrʾ* = Sing. emph. of *ksyr* (= axe, pickaxe); cf. also Aggoula Syr lii 182, lxv 209) - ¶ subst. indicating certain tool, stone-mason's axe, hatchet? (cf. Aggoula Syr lii 182f., cf. also Vattioni IH a.l., Safar Sumer xxvii 4 n. 5) or: paring chisel? (cf. Degen NESE iii 70).

ksyr v. *ksyd*.

ksl > Akkad. *kaslu* (= land drained by ditches), cf. v.Soden Or xxxv 12, xlvi 188 (cf. also idem AHW s.v. *kaslu* II), cf. also CAD s.v.

ksntw (< Iran.?, cf. Benveniste JA ccxlii 300, de Menasce BiOr xi 162, Driv p. 64, Eilers AfO xvii 333, Grelot DAE p. 313 n. a, Hinz AISN 150) - **OffAr** Sing. abs. *ksntw* Driv 7[2]* (reading highly uncert., cf. Porten & Yardeni sub TADAE A 6.10)[,2,6,8] - ¶ subst. m. damage, loss.

kss v. *nqy*$_1$.

ksṭrwn **Hatra** Safar Sumer xxiv 26 n. 60 (cf. also Tubach ISS 263 n. 47): l. *ks[sṭrwn]* (= balcony, colonnade; < Greek?) in 272[2] (highly improb. restoration, cf. also Aggoula MUSJ xlvii 24).

ksp$_1$ v.Soden Or xxxv 13, xlvi 189: > Akkad. ***kuspu*** = shame (cf. also AHW s.v.; poss. interpret., cf. however CAD s.v.: ***kusup libbi*** = heartbreak).

ksp$_2$ **Ph** Sing. abs. *ksp* KAI 3[2] (for this diff. reading, cf. e.g. Dunand BMB ii 101, Torczyner Lesh xiv 159f., Dupont-Sommer ArchOr xvii[1] 161f., Martin Or xxx 62 (cf. also Röllig KAI a.l., Gibson SSI iii p. 11) :: Albright BASOR lxxiii 12 (n. 13): l. *sg* or *sr* (= QAL Imper. s.m. of *swg* (= to withdraw) or *swr*$_1$ (for the reading *sg*, cf. also idem JAOS lxvii 158)) :: Iwry JAOS lxxxi 32f.: l. *sg* = Sing. abs. of *sg*$_2$ (= strife) :: McCarter & Coote BASOR ccxii 18 (n. 12): l. *sg* = QAL Part. act. s.m. abs. of *swg* (= to backslide, to prove faithless; for a derivation of the root *swg*, cf. also Dahood Bibl lx 433) :: Obermann JBL lviii 234, 242: l. *sg* = Sing. m. abs. of *šgʾ*$_3$ :: v.d.Branden RSF ii 138f.: l. *[w]sp* = *w* + Sing. abs. of *sp*$_2$ (= destruction)), 13[4], 24[12], 43[14] (*k[s]p*), 50[3,5], 51 rs. 4 (?, heavily dam. context), RES 1204[2] (diff. reading, cf. Cooke NSI p. 43, Chabot RES a.l. :: Teixidor Sem xxix 10f.: l. *lg* (= Sing. abs. of *lg*) *p* (= abbrev. of *pʿmym* = Plur. abs. of *pʿm*$_2$)), Mus li 286[4,7]; cstr. *ksp* KAI 60[6] - **Pun** Sing. abs. *ksp* KAI 69[3,5,7], 74[7], CIS i 3915[5], 5522[4], RCL '66, 201[7] - **Amm** Sing. abs. *ksp* AUSS xiii 2[6] (= CAI 80) - **Hebr** Sing. abs. *ksp* KAI 191B 1 (for the reading, cf. Avigad IEJ iii 142), TA-H 16[5] (*[k]sp*; diff. reading)[,8] (dam. context; ?, cf. also Pardee UF x 312, HAHL 49), 29[6] (dam. context), IEJ xii 30[2], DJD ii 22[4], 30[20], EI xx 256[6] - **Samal** Sing. abs. *ksp* KAI 215[11] - **OldAr** Sing. abs. *ksp* KAI 216[10f.] - **OffAr** Sing. abs. *ksp* KAI 226[7], 227 vs. 2, CIS ii 43[3] (= Del 26 = AECT 13), Cowl 1[7], 2[15], Krael 1[3,7], 2[6] (for the dittography of *ksp*, cf. Yaron JSS xiii 207 (n. 1)), Herm 2[6], TA-Ar 41 obv. 6, RSO xxxv 22[4], MAI xiv/2, 66[12], FX 136[13], ATNS 4[1], 9[4], Samar 1[10] (= EI xviii 8*), etc., etc.; cstr. *ksp* Cowl 15[23], Krael 7[22,25], Del 79[1], RES 1295[2], 1298A 5, ATNS 38[5,14]; emph. *kspʾ* KAI 263, Cowl 5[10,13], 48[2] (for the reading of the context, cf. Porten & Yardeni sub TADAE B 2.5, cf. also Porten GCAV 256), Krael 2[6], CIS ii 30[1] (= Del 19 = AECT 21), NESE i 11[6], ATNS 19[2,4], Samar 1[3,8] (= EI xviii 8*), 2[7], 4[9], etc., etc., ***ksph*** Herm 2[4], 6[6]; + suff. 3 p.s.m. *ksph* Cowl 71[30]; + suff. 2 p.s.m. *kspk* Cowl 10[7,11,12,18], 11[4,8], Krael 3[22a], 11[9,11]; + suff. 2 p.s.f. *kspky* Cowl 35[9]; cf.

Frah xvi 2 (*ksp*), 5 (*ksp›*), GIPP 26, 55, Sogd R 49 - **Nab** Sing. abs. *ksp* CIS ii 200[7,8] (for the reading, cf. also Milik sub ARNA-Nab 79), 206[7], 212[8], 224[12], BASOR cclxiii 77[1], on coins, cf. Meshorer NC no. 79, 80, 83, 84; emph. *ksp›* BASOR cclxiii 77[1] - **Palm** Sing. cstr. *ksp* CIS ii 3994a, b, c 2, MUSJ xxviii 56; emph. *ksp›* CIS ii 3902[1], 3945[4], 3951[5] - **JAr** Sing. abs. *ksp* MPAT 39[4], 41[5], 43[5], 48[3,4], 50e 4 (?, dam. context), 51[5], 52[7], MPAT-A 5[5] (*[k]sp*; = Frey 1203 = SM 64), DBKP 17[41], 18[70]; cstr. *ksp* MPAT 42[13]; emph. *ksp›* MPAT 44 i 5, 48[2], 52[8], *ksph* IEJ xxxvi 206[5]; + suff. 3 p.s. or pl. *ksph[* Syn D B 3 (= SM 88[18]) - ¶ subst. m. silver, (silver coins >) money, passim (these two meanings diff. to distinguish in many texts); *mlkn rbrbn b‹ly ksp wb‹ly zhb* KAI 216[10f.]: powerful kings, possessors of silver and possessors of gold (cf. KAI 24[12], 215[11]); *›yn [ph] ksp wzhb* KAI 191B 1: there is no silver nor gold here; *mh dy y›t› lh mn ksp wdhb* BASOR cclxiii 77[1]: whatever comes to him of silver and gold; *bn dhb bn [k]sp bn kl mqmh [d]hy›* MPAT-A 5[4ff.]: either gold or silver or any object whatsoever; cf. also *mn ksp ‹nwšt›* CIS ii 3994a, b, c 2f.: at the expense of the Treasury (cf. MUSJ xxviii 56); *‹lt mṣbt z yš›n bksp ›lm b‹l ṣdn drkmnm 20* KAI 60[6]: for this stele let the citizens of Sidon draw 20 d. from the temple treasury (:: Dahood Bibl lx 430: *ksp ›lm* = the finest silver); *ksp hlk›* Del 79[1]: the money for (paying) the tax; *ksp šn›h* Cowl 15[23], Krael 7[25]: divorce money (v. *šn›h*); *ksp mlḥ›* OLZ '27, 1043[2f.]: salt-tax (?, cf. Lidzbarski a.l.); *ksp nqpt›* ATNS 38[13f.]: the silver used for expenditure; *ksp ktbtyk* MPAT 42[13]: the sum of your contract; cf. also the following formulae, *ksp ‹šrt* KAI 69[3]: the sum of 10 silver (coins); *ksp 40* AUSS xiii 2[6] (= CAI 80): 40 (pieces) of silver; *ksp šql 1* KAI 69[7]: the sum of one shekel; *ksp š 47* CIS ii 64[2]: the sum of 47 shekels; *ksp kršn 5* Cowl 1[7]: the sum of 5 *k.* silver (cf. however also *ksp ṣryp kršn ‹šrh* Cowl 28[10f.]: the sum of 10 *k.* refined silver (v. *ṣrp*$_1$)); *ksp sl‹yn ›lp ḥd* CIS ii 224[12]: the sum of one thousand *s.*; *ksp zwzyn šb‹yn wtmnyh* MPAT 52[7]: the sum of 78 *z.*; *šṭr ksp mn[* FuB xiv 13[1], 23[1]: document about the silver *m.*[...; *ksp› znh krš ḥd* Cowl 29[6]: this sum of one *k.* silver; *ksp› zk zw[z]yn m›tyn* MPAT 48[2]: that sum of two hundred *z.*; etc., etc.; *kršn 10 lksp* ATNS 40[4]: 10 *k.* in silver; *›rb‹ ksp* IEJ xii 30[2]: four (shekels) of silver (v. *›rb‹*; followed by two signs meaning *4 royal shekels*, cf. Naveh IEJ xiii a.l.); *8 šql ksp* LidzbAss 5[1f.]: the sum of 8 shekels silver; *ksp š[mw]nym wšmwnh zwz sl‹yn ‹šrym wštym* DJD ii 30[20f.]: the sum of 88 *z.* (i.e.) 22 *s.*; *ḥṣ ksp* NC no. 80, 84: a half silver obol (v. also *mḥṣ*$_2$); *m‹h ksp* NC no. 79, 83: a silver obol; for *ksp r 2 l‹štrt›*, *ksp š 1 l10*, *ksp r 2 lkrš 1*, *ksp zwz*, v. resp. *rb‹*$_3$, *šql*$_3$, *zz* - Milik DJD ii p. 151: this word (*ksp*) poss. also in DJD ii 33[4] (highly uncert. interpret.) - abbrev. *k*:Cowl 22[21,22,24,27,28], etc., etc. (cf. also Grelot DAE p. 358), v. also *mḥṣ*$_2$ - Fales sub AECT 28: l. poss. *ksp›* (= Sing. emph.) in CIS ii 20 (= Del

7), uncert. reading :: e.g. Delaporte sub Del 7: l. *hykl*ʾ (= Sing. emph. of *hykl*);for the context, v. also *qdm*$_3$.
v. *br*$_4$,*ksp*$_3$, *kst*$_1$, *qdm*$_3$.

ksp$_3$ **Pun** Sing. abs. *ksp* KAI 89^{6} (= CIS i 6068); + suff. 3 p.s.f. *ksp*ʾ KAI 89^{4} (cf. Février sub CIS i 6068 :: e.g. Cooke NSI p. 135, Röllig KAI a.l, NESE ii 32 (div. otherwise): l. *ksp* = Sing. abs. (v. infra), cf. also Berger CRAI '99, 180, 184 n. 1) - ¶ subst. incantation (for this interpret., cf. Février sub CIS i 6068 (cf. also Lidzbarski Eph i 33, 175f., Chabot sub RES 1590) :: e.g. Halévy RS ix 264, Cooke NSI p. 135, Clermont-Ganneau RAO iii 314, 317, 319, iv 93f., Levi Della Vida RSO xiv 313, Ferron ZDMG cxvii 222, Röllig NESE ii 32: = *ksp*$_2$).

kspy **OffAr** the *kspy* and derived forms (in Cowl $13^{18,19}$, Krael $3^{2,23b,24}$, $4^{4,11}$, $12^{4,12}$, AG 5^{6}) = Caspian, cf. Lagrange RB xvi 263, AG p. 16, 18, Driver JRAS '32, 77f., AnOr xii 58f., Kutscher JAOS lxxiv 234, Grelot Sem xxi 101ff., Lipiński BiOr xxxi 119 :: Cowl a.l., Krael a.l.: prob. = silverman :: Eilers AfO xvii 334: = priest.

kst$_1$ **Pun** Sing. abs. *kst* CIS i 6051^{1} (cf. Lidzbarski Eph iii 55f., Clermont-Ganneau RAO viii 95f. :: Février CIS i a.l.: prob. = QAL Part. pass. s.f. abs. of *ksy*$_1$) - **OffAr** Sing. abs. *kst* Herm 1^{10} (cf. Milik Bibl xlviii 550, 581, 617, Porten & Greenfield ZAW lxxx 228, JEAS p. 152, Porten Arch 268, Grelot RB lxxviii 527 (n. 32), DAE p. 152 (n. l), Gibson SSI ii p. 130, 132, Hoftijzer SV 109, Porten & Yardeni sub TADAE A 2.3 :: Grelot RB lxxiv 434, Kutscher IOS i 110 (cf. also Bresciani & Kamil Herm a.l.): poss. = Sing. abs. of *kst*$_2$ (= money)) - ¶ subst. - **1)** covering (?, dam. context): CIS i 6051^{1} (v. supra) :: Clermont-Ganneau RAO viii 96: = cushion - **2)** garment, clothing: Herm 1^{10} (v. supra; for the context, v. *b*$_2$ sub 5) - this word also in Del 94^{2}, or = lapsus for *ksp*$_2$??- on nominal derivatives of the same root > Greek, cf. Masson RPAE 22ff.
v. *ksh*.

kst$_2$ v. *kst*$_1$.

k‘yr v. *‘yr*$_3$.

k‘n$_1$ v. *ṭ‘n*$_2$.

k‘n$_2$ v. *khn*$_1$.

k‘n$_3$ v. *kn*$_4$.

k‘n$_4$ **(k‘nt/k‘t)** - (for the poss. construction of these words, cf. BL 68u; cf. also Levine Shn iii 287) - **OldAr** *k‘t* KAI 224^{24} - **OffAr** *k‘n* Cowl 9^{5}, 18^{2}, 27^{6}, Krael 7^{41}, Driv 2^{2}, 3^{5}, Herm 7^{2}, NESE iii 48^{13}, ATNS 14^{3} (or l. *k‘nt*?), 26^{7}, 59^{4}, etc., etc., *k‘nt* Cowl 4^{6}, 37^{2}, RES 492A 1, B 1, 493^{1}, 494B 2, 1792A 1, B 3, JRAS '29, 108^{2}, Sem ii 31 conc. 1, 6, xxi 85 conc. 2, *k‘t* Cowl $17^{2,3}$, 21^{3}, Driv 3^{6}, 4^{1}, Herm $1^{3,5,6}$, SSI ii 28 obv. 2, 3, etc., etc.; cf. Frah xxv 23 (*k‘n*), Paik 541 (*k‘n*), 591 (in comb. *lk‘n*), Nisa-c 287^{9} (*k‘n*), Sogd R 49, DEP 154 recto 1 (*k‘t*), verso

23 (*k‘n(m)*), BSOAS xxxiii 147^{4}, 152^{8}, GIPP 25, 27, 55, SaSt 18 - ¶ adv. now; *wk‘t hšbw ’lhn šybt* ... KAI 224^{24}: but now the gods have restored the fortunes of ...; *’ḥḥpy zy k‘n pqyd ‘bd ḥlpwhy* Driv 2$^{2f.}$: A. who now has been made (i.e. is) an officer in his place (cf. Cowl 30^{3}); *mn zy ḥnnyh bmṣryn ‘d k‘n* Cowl 38^{6}: from the time that Ch. was in Egypt till now; cf. prob. also NESE iii 48^{5} (cf. Degen ibid. 52) - used as interjection to underline the following words (cf. also Alexander JSS xxiii 164) - **1)** introducing a new subject (or aspect of a subject already mentioned) in letters, *k‘n*: Cowl 9^{5}, 27^{6} (for the context, cf. e.g. Grelot DAE p. 402f. (n. h)), 30^{4}, 42^{10}, Driv 3^{5}, 5^{8}, *k‘nt*: Sem ii 31 conc. 6, RES 1792B 3, *k‘t*: Cowl 17^{2}, Herm 1^{9,10,11}, 2^{8,11}, SSI ii 28 obv. 2, 3, etc., etc. - cf. also introducing the first subject of a letter after the address and/or the greeting formula(e) (cf. e.g. Dion RB lxxxix 532, 536, 546), *k‘n, ’l ’my... šlm ’ḥty ... wk‘n ‘lyky mtkl ’nh* Herm 7$^{1f.}$: to my mother ... greetings to my sister ... and now I am relying on you; *k‘nt, ’l mr’y ... k‘nt bkl ywm zy [...* Cowl 37$^{1f.}$: to my lords ... now on every day that [...; *k‘t, mn ’ršm ’l ’rmpy wk‘t psmšk pqyd’ zyly šlḥ* Driv 4^{1}: from A. to A. and now P. my officer has sent (cf. Cowl 26^{1}, Driv 7^{1}, 8^{1}, 9^{1}, 10^{1}, 11^{1}, 12^{1}); *šlm byt nbw ... brktky lptḥ ... šlm bntsrl ... wk‘t šlm {l}lḥrwṣ* Herm 1$^{1ff.}$: greetings to the temple of N. ... I bless you by Ptah ... greetings to B. ... and now, it is well with Ch. (cf. Herm 4$^{1ff.}$, 5$^{1f.}$, NESE i 11^{1}) - cf. *k‘t* introducing the apodosis, *kdy mt’h ydy wk‘t ‘bd ’nh lh* Herm 3^{4}: as far as I am able, look, I am taking care of him (cf. e.g. Degen NESE iii 37, Hoftijzer SV 113) - **2)** introducing direct discourse: RES 1295^{5} - **3)** in the following comb. - a) *k‘t ’rh* (= *’rh$_2$*) Herm 1^{5}: now, look (introducing a new subject in a letter) - b) *k‘n h’* (= *h’$_2$*) Cowl 37^{7}: now, look (introducing a new subject in a letter), cf. Cowl 38^{5}; *k‘nt h’* Sem ii 31 conc. 1: now, look (introducing the first subject matter following the greeting formula) - c) *k‘n hlw* KAI 270A 1: now, look (introducing a letter); *k‘nt hlw* RES 1792A 1: now, look (introducing a letter; cf. JRAS '29, 108 conc. 1f., introducing the first subject matter of a letter following the greeting formula; RES 1792A 3, introducing a new aspect of the subject matter of a letter); *k‘t hlw* Herm 1^{8}, 2^{4}: now, look (introducing a new subject in a letter); cf. also *k‘t zy mlty lbty l’mr lh š’l ‘l ḥrwṣ k‘t hlw kzy ‘bd ’nh lḥrwṣ ...*, Herm 1$^{6f.}$: now, because you are filled with anger against me saying: "He is not caring for Ch.", now, behold, as I am doing for Ch. ...; v. also *hlw* - d) *k‘n ḥzy* Aeg xxxix 4 recto 4: now, look (introducing a new aspect of the subject matter of a letter); *k‘nt ḥzy* Sem xxi 85 conc. 2: now, look (introducing a new aspect of the subject matter of a letter), cf. also RES 492B 1; v. also *ḥzy$_1$* - e) *k‘n lw* FS Driv 54 conc. 1, prob. with same meaning, v. *lw* - **4)** *k‘t* introducing a juridical text, *k‘t z’* HDS 9^{1}: and now this - Bresciani & Kamil Herm. a.l.: l. *[k]‘n* in Herm 6^{6},

less prob. restoration, cf. e.g. Milik Bibl xlviii 548, Porten & Greenfield IOS iv 21, JEAS p. 162, Gibson SSI ii p. 141, Porten & Yardeni sub TADAE A 2.6: l. *[s]wn* = n.l. - Segal ATNS a.l.: l. prob. *k‘n* in ATNS 16^{2} (less prob. reading, cf. Porten & Yardeni sub TADAE B 8.10: l. prob. *mn* (= *mn$_5$*)).
v. *lwk‘y*.

k‘nt v. *k‘n$_4$*.

k‘s$_1$ **Pun** QAL (??) Pf. 3 p.s.m. *k‘s* KAI 124^{4} - ¶ verb QAL (??) of uncert. meaning and etymology; *k‘s lp‘l* KAI 124^{4}, prob. corresponding to Lat. par. *f(aciendum) c(uravit)*, cf. Levi Della Vida RCL ’49, 402, RSO xxxix 307f., idem with Volterra RCL ’52, 176, Röllig KAI a.l., v.d.Branden PO i 437 (cf. also Dahood Bibl xlvi 330).

k‘s$_2$ **OffAr** QAL Part. act. s.m. abs. *k‘s* Aḥiq 189 - ¶ verb QAL to be vexed, to be angry - on this root, cf. Blau PC 123 (n. 46).

k‘t v. *k‘n$_4$*.

kp$_1$ **DA** Dual + suff. 3 p.s.m. *kpwh* ixa 3 (?, cf. Hoftijzer DA p. 263, 286 (n. 9); heavily dam. context) - **OffAr** Sing. abs. *kp* Cowl 15^{28}, Krael 7^{24,28}, 11^{4}; cstr. *kp* ATNS 28b 4; Dual cstr. *kpy* Cowl 3^{21} (context however dam.), 13^{17} (for this prob. reading, cf. Porten & Yardeni sub TADAE B 2.7 :: Cowl a.l., Yaron Law 17, Volterra FS Tisserant i 443f., Porten & Greenfield JEAS p. 16: l. *bky* (of diff. interpret.) :: SC p. 41: l. *bry* (cf. also (Bowman with) Porten Arch 245 (n. 20), Grelot DAE p. 188 n. j)); + suff. 2 p.s.m. *kpyk* Aḥiq 103; + suff. 2 p.pl.m./f. *kpykn* Cowl 44 (*scriptio anterior* l. 1; for the reading, cf. Porten & Yardeni sub TADAE B 7.3); Plur. abs. *kpn* Cowl 15^{16}, Krael 7^{19} - ¶ subst. f. - **1)** hand: Aḥiq 103 (:: Grelot DAE p. 438: *kpyk* = your face; cf. also Fitzmyer Bibl lvi 256); *b‘bdt kpykn* Cowl 44 (*scriptio anterior* l. 1; v. supra): by the work of your hands; cf. *ktb h[wš‘] bkpy n[pšh]* Cowl 3^{21}: H. wrote with his own hands (for this reading, cf. Porten & Yardeni sub TADAE B 4.3) - **2)** palm (of the hand); *kp yd* ATNS 28b 4: the palm of the hand - **3)** sole (of the foot); *kp rgl* ATNS 28b 4: the sole of the foot - **4)** in the expression *bywm ḥd bkp ḥdh* Cowl 15^{28}: at one day, at one stroke (cf. also Krael 7^{24,28}; cf. Peiser OLZ ’07, 627, Fitzmyer FS Albright ii 164) - **5)** a certain object, poss. = laddle: Cowl 15^{16}, 36^{4}, Krael 7^{19} (for a discussion on the meaning, cf. Grelot RB lxxviii 530ff.; cf. also Cowl a.l.: or = bowl?) - the *k*in Krael 4^{7}, 12^{7,8,16} poss. = abbrev. of linear measure *kp* (= handbreadth), cf. Krael p. 173, cf. however Grelot DAE p. 222 n. d: or = abbrev. of Egyptian *kyḏ* with same meaning; for a discussion of the exact length, cf. Grelot ibid.; cf. also Cowl 63^{11}? - Porten & Yardeni sub TADAE B 8.6: l. poss. *kp* (= Sing. cstr.) *yd* (= Sing. abs. of *yd*) = the palm of the hand in ATNS 9^{7} (:: Segal ATNS a.l.: l. *ksn* = Plur. abs. of *ks$_1$*)and ibid. l. prob. *kp* (= Sing. cstr.) *rgl* (= Sing. abs. of *rgl$_2$*) = the

sole of the foot (:: Segal ATNS a.l.: l. *krbyl* (= Sing. abs.) = cap(s)) - Porten & Yardeni sub TADAE A 3.11: l. *kpn* (= Sing. + suff. 1 p.pl.) in Aeg xxxix 4 verso 1 (poss. reading (cf. also Porten FS Bresciani 439f.), uncert. interpret.; cf. Bresciani Aeg xxxix 7: l. *kwn* (= n.l.), Milik Aeg xl 79f. (div. otherwise): l. *mnkwn* (= n.p.), cf. also Hoftijzer VT xii 342: or *mnkwn* = *mn*$_5$ + suff. 2 p.pl.m.??).
v. *br*$_4$,*knt*$_2$,*ks*$_1$.

kp$_2$ **OffAr**, cf. Frah xvi 3 (*kyph*;:: Ebeling Frah a.l.: l. *ksph* = lapsus for *kyph*),10 (*kyp*ʾ) - **Hatra** Sing. (or Plur. ?) emph. *kp*ʾ Ibr 9^{2}; Plur. emph. *kp*ʾ 344^{9} - ¶ subst. stone; in Hatra Ibr 9^{2} (*]šwr*ʾ *dy kp*ʾ*[*: the stone wall) and Hatra 344^{9} (cf. Hatra 344^{4}) building material, cf. also Aggoula Syr lxv 210; in Frah xvi 3 = gem, jewel - Degen WO v 225: l. Sing. cstr. *kp* in Hatra 216, 217 (less prob. interpret.), cf. Safar Sumer xxi 35 (n. 8; div. otherwise): l. *kp*ʿ*nny* = n.p. :: Aggoula MUSJ xlvii 43 (div. otherwise): l. *rp*ʿ*nny* in Hatra 217 = n.p. (cf. also Vattioni IH a.l.: l. *rp*ʿ*nny* in Hatra 216, 217 = n.p.) - Rocco AION xix a.l.: l. *kp* (= Sing. abs. (= rock or sea coast)) in GR i 61 no. 31B 1 (= GR ii 88 no. 70^{1}), highly uncert. reading and interpret., cf. Guzzo Amadasi GR a.l.
v. *kph*.

kpʾ **OffAr** Itp Pf. 3 p.s.m., cf. Warka 8: *it-ka-pi-*ʾ - ¶ verb Itp to be tipped up, cf. Driver AfO iii 50, Dupont-Sommer RA xxxix 45.

kph **Hatra** Sing. emph. *kpt*ʾ 408^{1,3,7,8} (:: As-Salihi Sumer xlv 102: = Plur.) - **Palm** Sing. emph. *kpt*ʾ CIS ii 3912, 4172^{2}, 4187, 4194^{7}, Ber v 95^{8}, Syr xix 159 i 2; Plur. emph. *kpy*ʾ Ber ii 104^{4} (cf. Ingholt Ber ii 105f.); + suff. 3 p.pl.m. *kpyhn* Inv xi 81^{1} - **JAr** Sing. emph. *kpth* MPAT-A 17^{2} (= SM 7; cf. Beyer ATTM 396, 609 :: Naveh SM a.l.: or = Sing. + suff. 3 p.s.m. or = Plur. emph. (or + suff. 3 p.s.m.) :: Urman IEJ xxii 18, Fitzmyer & Harrington MPAT a.l.: = Plur. emph.) - ¶ subst. f. arch, vaulted room/niche, vault, cf. Ingholt Ber v 97f., Milik DFD 177ff., Aggoula Syr lxvii 408; cf. Greek par.: τὴν καμάραν (CIS ii 3912), τῇ ψαλίδι (CIS ii 4187) - exact meaning in MPAT-A 17^{2} (= SM 7) unknown (heavily dam. context; v. supra) - Milik DFD 178: l. prob. *kpy*ʾ (= Plur. emph.) in Inscr P 57^{1} (poss. though uncert. reading; cf. however Cantineau Inscr P a.l.: l. *kpry*ʾ = Plur. emph. of *kpr*$_4$ (= tomb)) - Milik DFD 179, 363: the diff. *kpy*ʾ in Hatra 140^{1} = Plur. emph., *mr*ʾ *kpy*ʾ = the lord of the niches (highly uncert. interpret.; Safar Sumer xviii 41 (n. 32): = Sing. emph. of *kpy*$_3$ (= curved, bent; used to describe an older person), cf. also Caquot Syr xli 259; Vattioni IH a.l.: *kpy*ʾ = n.p. (with same meaning)) - Aggoula Assur a.l.: the *kp*ʾ in Assur 11 ii 1 poss. = Sing. abs. of *kph* (highly uncert. interpret.), cf. Jensen SbPAW '19, 1050: Sing./Plur. of *kp*$_2$.

kpwtk (< Iran., cf. Bowman Pers p. 45, 63, 67f., Bernard StIr i 173

n. 8) - **OffAr** Sing. m. abs. *kpwtk* Pers 122[2] - ¶ adj. (used to describe a stone) pigeon-coloured (blue?? (cf. Bowman Pers p. 63, 67f.: usual translation lapis-lazuli in this instance inappropriate), cf. also Bernard StIr i 173f. n. 8: stone in question = green) - Naveh & Shaked Or xlii 456: pro *bprk rb* (for *bprk* v. *bz₁*; *rb* = Sing. m. abs. of *rb₂*; for this reading, cf. Bowman Pers a.l, Levine JAOS xcii 76) l. in Pers 5[3] *bz* (= *bz₁*) *kpwtk* (highly uncert. reading; cf. also Degen BiOr xxxi 127, for a partial reading).

kpy₁ **JAr** Naveh & Shaked AMB a.l.: the diff. *tkyn* in AMB 12[10] poss. lapsus for *tkpyn* = Qal Impf. 2 p.s.f. of *kpy₁* (= to force); ?, uncert. interpret., diff. context.

kpy₂ **Nab** the diff. *kpy>* in RES 837C poss. = Sing. emph. of *kpy₂* (adj.; = of stone), cf. Cantineau Nab ii 107 (cf. also Savignac RB xv 594), cf. however Chabot sub RES 837.

kpy₃ v. *kph*.

kpyr **Samal** the diff. *kpyry* in KAI 214[10] (= Plur. abs. casus obl.?, cf. however Sader EAS 163: = Plur. + suff. 1 p.s.) = villages? (v. *kpr₃*), cf. e.g. Fitzmyer AIS 119, Greenfield Lesh xxxii 363 (n. 22), Delcor JSS xviii 49, Dion p. 28, 130, Gibson SSI ii p. 55, cf. also Halévy RS ii 56, vii 349, cf. however Donner KAI a.l.: = n.l.? (cf. also Cooke NSI p. 166f.: poss. = tribal name or n.l.); or = young lion > warrior?? (v. infra; cf. also Landsberger Sam>al 50 n. 127, 64 n. 165: > lion statues (at gate)) - the diff. *kpyry* in KAI 215[10] (= Plur. abs. casus obl.?) poss. = young lions > warriors, cf. also Dahood Or xlv 382 (cf. also Landsberger Sam>al 50 n. 127: *b<ly kpyry* = certain type of deity, the lords of the young lions, less prob. interpret.), cf. however Lagrange ERS 493, Donner KAI a.l., Fitzmyer AIS 119, Greenfield Lesh xxxii 363 (n. 22), Delcor JSS xviii 49, Lipiński OLP viii 102, Dion p. 39, 130, Gibson SSI ii p. 79, Sader EAS 167f. (n. 44): = villages (v. *kpr₃*).

kpl **Nab** Sing. cstr. *kpl* CIS ii 217[7] - ¶ subst. double; *kpl dmy* ... CIS ii 217[7]: double the price of ... (for CIS ii 217[7], cf. Greenfield Mem Yalon 70f.) - Garbini PP xxxiii 144: l. *kpln* as Ar. inscription on amphora (= Dual abs. of *kpl*), uncert. reading and interpret., cf. Teixidor Syr lvi 387.

kpn₁ **JAr** Qal Part. act. s.f. abs. *kpnh* AMB 7[17,20]; s.f. emph. *kpnth* AMB 7[19] - ¶ verb Qal to be hungry.

kpn₂ **OffAr** Sing. abs. *kpn* Aḥiq 188 - ¶ subst. m. hunger.

kps₁ **Ph** Sing. abs. *kps* RES 1356[2] - ¶ subst. indicating function: carpenter??

kps₂ v. *ps₁*.

kpp₁ **Pun** Qal Inf. cstr. *kp* CIS i 5510[3] (on this text, cf. Krahmalkov RSO lxi 75f.) - ¶ verb Qal meaning uncert.: to put away, to take away (??) :: Chabot BAr '41/42, 393, Février CIS i a.l., FR 164: = to break

(cf. also v.d.Branden BiOr xxxvi 202, Hvidberg-Hansen TNT ii 38 n. 347) :: Dahood Bibl lx 432: = to bend double.
v. *kpt*.

kpp$_2$ Hatra Plur. emph. *kppʾ* 290^{4} - ¶ subst. architectural term, exact meaning unknown, poss. = vaulted room (cf. Caquot Syr lii 192, cf. also Aggoula Syr lii 192, lxv 204f., Vattioni IH a.l.: vaulted rooms) or arch (cf. Safar Sumer xxvii 11f. (n. 32), Degen NESE iii 85f., Teixidor Sem xxx 66).

kpṣ Palm a form of this root in RIP 199^{12} (*mkpṣ*; for the reading, cf. Strelcyn with Michałowski FP '59, 215, Gawlikowski Sem xxiii 115f., RIP a.l. :: Milik DFD 184, 287: l. *mnpṣ* = PAʿEL Part. s.m. abs./cstr. of *npṣ* (= to vomit)); meaning unknown, poss. = PAʿEL/APH Part. s.m. abs./cstr. of *kpṣ* (cf. Gawlikowski Sem xxiii 116, RIP a.l.: // Akkad. *kapāṣu* = to take in, to swallow; highly uncert. interpret.) or = Sing. cstr. of noun *mkpṣ*? (meaning unknown).

kpr$_1$ OffAr QAL (or PAʿEL?) Pf. 3 p.s.m. *kpr* Cowl 37^{14} (for this interpret., cf. Cowl a.l. × Porten & Greenfield JEAS p. 80, Porten & Yardeni sub TADAE A 4.2: = Sing. cstr. of *kpr$_5$* (= compensation)); 1 p.s. *kprt* CRAI '47, 181 conc. 3, 4 - **Palm** QAL (or PAʿEL?) Pf. 3 p.pl.m. (or Imper. pl.m.??) *kprw* CIS ii 3913 ii 122 - ¶ verb QAL (or PAʿEL?); in Cowl 37^{14} poss. = to pardon or to give compensation (v. however supra), dam. and uncert. context; in CIS ii 3913 ii 121ff. also diff. context, *ktb ... ʿl gldyʾ dy gmly[ʾ] ʾp ʾln kprw dy mks lʾ gbn*: he wrote concerning the camel hides: also for those on which they do not levy tax, one has to give compensation, cf. however Ingholt PBP 105 (n. 14): *kprw* = they have paid their dues :: Teixidor AO i 242: = ... they (i.e. the archonts and the judges) also have denied that they (i.e. the publicans) do not levy tax (cf. Syriac *kpr*; cf. also Rosenthal Sprache 87 n. 4); v. also supra; in CRAI '47, 181 conc. 3, 4 poss. = to refuse (cf. Dupont-Sommer CRAI '47, 182).

kpr$_2$ v. *qpl$_1$*.

kpr$_3$ OldAr Plur. + suff. 3 p.s.f. *kpryh* KAI $224^{23,26}$ - **OffAr** Sing. cstr. *kpr* AECT F 1 - ¶ subst. village: AECT F1 (for this prob. interpret. in KAI $224^{23,26}$, cf. e.g. Fitzmyer AIS 119, Gibson SSI ii p. 51, 55f., Lipiński Stud 48, 57), cf. however Noth ZDPV lxxvii 155 (n. 104), Donner KAI a.l.: = storehouse-building - Fales sub AECT 18: l. poss. *kpr* (= Sing. cstr.) in Del 32 (uncert. reading, cf. also Kaufman JAOS cix 99).
v. *kpyr*.

kpr$_4$ (< Liḥy., cf. Cantineau Nab ii 108, cf. also Gawlikowski Ber xxi 12 (n. 50), O'Connor JNES xlv 217ff. - **Nab** Sing. emph. *kprʾ* CIS ii $197^{6,8}$, $198^{1,5,10}$, etc., etc. - ¶ subst. m. tomb - for the relationship with Greek κοπρών, κοπρία = dung (cf. Clermont-Ganneau RAO i 146f.), cf.

Wright PEQ '69, 113ff., Gawlikowski Ber xxiv 39f.
v. *wgr,kph*.

kpr$_5$ v.d.Branden BO xii 215, 218: l. *kpr* = *kpr$_5$* (= interest) in KAI 50[4], highly uncertain reading and interpret.
v. *kpr$_1$*.

kprh v.Soden Or xxxv 13, xlvi 189: Akkad. *kup(p)artu* = purification, prob. based on Ar. nominal form *quttāl* (uncert. interpret.).

kprt **Ph** Sing. cstr. *k[p]rt* DD 13[1] (for the reading, cf. Caquot Sem xv 30, Milik DFD 425f., Gibson SSI iii p. 121 :: Dunand & Duru DD a.l.: l. *k[š]rt* = Sing. cstr. of *kšrh* (= sculpture)) - ¶ subst. prob. meaning: lioness/sphinx (cf. Caquot Sem xv 30, Milik DFD 426) × Gibson SSI iii p. 121f.: = propitiatory offering :: Caquot Sem xxv 30f.: or = lid, cover.

kpt **Pun** the diff. *kpt* in CIS i 5510[4] poss. = QAL Part. act. s.f. abs. of *kpp* (cf. e.g. Garbini JSS xii 112, FR 164, Röllig BiOr xxvii 379, v.d.Branden BiOr xxxvi 202 (: or = Pf. 3 p.s.f.?), cf. however Chabot BAr '40/41, 390, 393, Février BAr '46/49, 171: = QAL Pf. 3 p.s.f. of *kpp$_1$* :: Dahood Bibl lx 432: = QAL Pf. pass. 2 p.s.m. of *kpp$_1$*); meaning uncert., v. *kpp$_1$*.

kṣ v. *qṣ$_1$*.

kṣd v. *kṣr$_1$*.

kṣyd v. *kṣyr$_1$*.

kṣyr$_1$ **OffAr** Sing. abs. *kṣyr* Aḥiq 127 (:: Ungnad ArPap 74: or l. *kṣyd* (= Sing. abs.) = aim) - ¶ subst. prob. meaning harvest, v. however *kṣr$_1$*.

kṣyr$_2$ v. *kṣr$_1$*.

kṣyr$_3$ v. *ʾṣyl*.

kṣp (< root *qṣp*, cf. e.g. Cowl a.l., Claassen AION xxi 297, Lindenberger APA 82f., Kottsieper SAS 42, 210f.) - **OffAr** Sing. + suff. 3 p.s.m. *kṣph* Aḥiq 101 (for the reading, cf. Cowl a.l., Lindenberger APA 82f., 239 n. 212 :: Perles OLZ '11, 501: l. *kṣ[r]h* related to *kṣr$_1$*) - ¶ subst. m. fury, wrath.

kṣr$_1$ (< root *qṣr$_1$*, cf. e.g. Cowl a.l., Claassen AION xxi 297, Kottsieper SAS 42, 211) - **OffAr** HAPH Imper. s.m. *hkṣr* Aḥiq 127 (:: Ungnad ArPap 74: or l. *hkṣd* = HAPH Imper. s.m. of *kṣd*(= to realize one's aims); v. also infra) - ¶ verb HAPH prob. meaning to harvest; in the expression *hkṣr kl kṣyr* Aḥiq 127: gather every harvest (cf. e.g. Cowl a.l., Grelot DAE p. 441, Lindenberger APA 121, Kottsieper SAS 15 :: Grimme OLZ '11, 536: = exert yourself in every way (*hkṣr* = HAPH Imper. s.m. of *kṣr$_2$* (= to exert oneself), *kṣyr* = Sing. abs. of *kṣyr$_2$* (= exertion)); cf. also Ginsberg ANET 429).
v. *kṣp*.

kṣr$_2$ v. *kṣr$_1$*.

kṣr$_3$ **OffAr** Segal Maarav iv 70: l. *kṣr*ʾ in AG 2[2] (= Sing. emph. of *kṣr$_3$* (= fuller)); *rb kṣr*ʾ = chief of the fullers (uncert. interpret.) :: Aimé-Giron AG a.l. (div. otherwise): l. *ṣd*ʾ, cf. *ṣydh* = game, fish, food. v. *kṣr$_7$*.

kṣr$_4$ **Hatra** Plur. emph. *kṣr*ʾ 344[5,10] (v. infra) - ¶ subst. cobble, for this interpret., cf. Aggoula Syr lxiv 94, cf. however Aggoula Syr lxv 210: or = Sing. emph. of *kṣr$_5$* (variant of *qṣr$_3$* = straw))?.

kṣr$_5$ v. *kṣr$_4$*.

kṣr$_6$ v. *kṣry*ʾ.

kṣr$_7$ (< *qṣr$_7$*) - **Hatra** Sing. m. emph. *kṣr*ʾ 13[3] (for the reading, cf. Aggoula Ber xviii 88f., Vattioni IH a.l. :: Caquot Syr xxix 96: l. *nṣr*ʾ = QAL Part. s.m. emph. of *nṣr$_1$*, cf. also Donner sub KAI 240 :: Krückmann AfO xvi 146: = Sing. m. emph. of *nṣr$_3$* (= victorious (cf. also Safar Sumer vii 178)) :: Milik Syr xliv 298, Degen ZDMG cxxi 124: l. *nṣr*ʾ = n.p.; v. also infra; prob. related form ʾ*kṣr*ʾ in 98, 104 (v. infra)) - ¶ adj. short, used as cognomen: the short one: 13[3] (:: Aggoula Ber xviii 88f., Vattioni IH a.l.: = Sing. emph. of *kṣr$_3$* (= fuller), v. also supra). The ʾ*kṣr*ʾ in 98, 104 prob. the same meaning, cf. Caquot Syr xl 10 :: Aggoula Ber xviii 97 (div. otherwise): l. *kṣr*ʾ = Sing. emph. of *kṣr$_3$* (= fuller; cf. also Vattioni IH a.l.: ʾ*kṣr*ʾ = fuller) :: Safar Sumer xvii 32 (n. 78): < Greek = exile, the exiled one.

kṣry v. *kṣry*ʾ.

kṣryʾ **Hatra** the *kṣry*ʾ in Hatra 58[3] poss. = n.p. (cf. Vattioni IH a.l.) :: Caquot Syr xxxii 263: two poss. interpret. - a) Plur. emph. of *kṣr$_6$* = camp (< Lat. *castra*, cf. also Safar Sumer xi 4 (n. 4)) - b) Plur. emph. of *kṣry*= nisbe adj. < *kṣr$_6$*(= the man of the camp, soldier) :: Ingholt AH i/2, 46: or = Plur. emph. of *ksr* < Lat. *Caesar*.

kṣt **OffAr** Segal ATNS a.l.: the diff. *kṣt* (Sing. abs.) in ATNS 18[5] prob. = equivalent of *qṣt$_2$* (= total; *bkṣt* = in total); dam. context, uncert. interpret. - Segal ATNS a.l.: the diff. *kṣt* (Sing. cstr.) in ATNS 19[5] = equivalent of *qṣt$_1$* or *qṣt$_2$* (= total); dam. context, uncert. interpret. - the same word also in ATNS 93[2] (*kṣ[*)??

kr$_1$ (< Akkad. < Sum., cf. Zimmern Fremdw 21, Kaufman AIA 65, cf. also Lipiński ZAH i 68) - **Hebr** Plur. abs. *kwryn*DJD ii 24B 17 (*[k]wryn*),D 16 (diff. reading), 44[3] - **OffAr** Sing. abs. *kr* Del 79bis 1 (= AM 66); Plur. abs. *krn* Del 46[2], 47[2], 72[2], 74[2], 75[3], 76[3], 104[1], Irâq iv 18[3], FuB xiv 16[3] (dam. context), 17[2], 18[2], 19[1,2] (for this poss. reading, cf. Vattioni Or xlviii 141 sub no. 175), 20[3] (or pro *krn* l. *kr 1*?), PF 2043[1] (?, uncert. context) - **Nab** Plur. abs. *kryn* DBKP 22[33] (prob. reading, cf. Greek par. κόρους) - **Hatra** Sing. abs. *kr*, cf. Assur 27e 2 (diff. context) - ¶ subst. a dry measure: *gur*, used for grain, dates and the like - abbrev. *k*(= *kr$_1$*) prob. in BSh-Ar 1[2], 2[2], 3[2], 4[2], 10, 30[3] and in DBKP 21 back (prob. reading, cf. Greek par. κόρους) - > Greek κόρος,

cf. also Barrois ii 248, Trinquet SDB v 1222, EM iv 852ff.
v. *kd*$_1$,*qr*$_3$.

kr$_2$ Ebeling Frah a.l.: l. in Frah vii 7 *kryʾ*, *kyrʾ* = sheep, cf. however Nyberg FP 43, 70: l. resp. *klbʾ* (= form of *qrb*$_7$ (= sheep)) and *kynʾ* (= form of *qn*$_1$ (= cattle)), cf. also idem MP 4.

kr$_3$ v. *kbh*.

kr$_4$ **Ph** Lipiński RAI xix 43: the *kr* in the indication of a deity *bʿl kr* (in EI ix 10*, EpAn ix 5[5]) = Sing. abs. of *kr*$_4$ (= furnace); poss. interpret., cf. also Mosca & Russell EpAn ix 14, Elayi SCA 64 :: Barnett EI ix 10f.: = Sing. abs. of *kr*$_5$ (= pasturage), cf. also Tomback CSL 149.

kr$_5$ v. *kr*$_4$.

kr$_6$ v. *lkd*$_1$.

kr$_7$ v. *krš*$_1$.

krʾ v. *kry*$_1$.

krb$_1$ **Ph** Grelot Or xxvi 273ff.: l. *krb* (= Qal or Piʿel Pf. 3 p.s.m.) = to offer in KAI 22 (highly improb. interpret., cf. e.g. Yeivin RB lxv 586f., Milik ibid. 589, BMB xvi 105f., Röllig KAI a.l., Cross BASOR ccxxxviii 7, Gibson SSI iii p. 6, 8, Naveh EHA 40 for a discussion of the context (: *kr*/*krb* = part of n.p.)).

krb$_2$ **Pun** the *krbm* in KAI 96[2] (= CIS i 5523) poss. = Plur. abs. of *krb*$_2$ indicating certain object?, cf. also Février CB vii 123, CIS i sub 5523: = cherub.

krbyl v. *kp*$_1$.

krblh (word of unknown origin, cf. CAD s.v. *karballatu*, v.Soden AHW s.v., cf. also Kaufman AIA 63, cf. however Fraenkel HUCA xxxi 83f.: < Indo-European? :: Zimmern Fremdw 36: prob. < Akkad.) - **OffAr** Sing. abs. *krblh* Cowl 55[11]; Plur. abs. *[k]rbln* Cowl 57[3] - ¶ subst. headgear, hat.

krh v. *kbh*.

krwz$_1$ **Nab** Sing. cstr. *krwz* MPAT 64 i 3; emph. *krwzʾ* MPAT 64 i 3, 4, 5; Plur. abs. *krwzyn* MPAT 64 ii 4 - ¶ subst. of unknown meaning; Starcky RB lxi 169: = sale by auction :: J.J.Rabinowitz BASOR cxxxix 12: = proclamation (made by the court, that the unpaid creditor has the right to seize goods from a defaulting debtor), cf. also Shaffer Or xxxiv 32ff., Fitzmyer & Harrington MPAT a.l. - related to *krwz*$_2$? - cf. *ʾkryz* (sub *krz*$_1$).

krwz$_2$ v. *krwz*$_1$,*krz*$_2$.

krwṭ v. *prwṭ*.

krz$_1$ **Nab** Qal Pf. 3 p.s.m. *krz* MPAT 64 i 4; Pf. pass. 3 p.s.f. *kryzt* MPAT 64 i 3; Part. pass. s.m. abs. *kryz* BASOR cclxiii 78[2] (for this reading, cf. Jones BASOR cclxxv 43 :: Hammond, Johnson and Jones BASOR cclxiii a.l. (div. otherwise): l. *ʾkryz*= Sing. cstr. of *ʾkryz*(= proclamation)) - ¶ verb Qal meaning uncert.; Jones BASOR cclxxv

43: = to assign, to decree, to allot :: Starcky RB lxi 165, 169: in MPAT 64 = to buy at an auction (+ obj.) :: Shaffer Or xxxiv 32ff., Fitzmyer & Harrington MPAT a.l.: = to proclaim (v. *krwz*$_1$;cf. also J.J.Rabinowitz BASOR cxxxix 12).

krz$_2$ (not < Greek κήρυξ, but < Iran., cf. Schaed 254, Eilers Beamtennamen 19f., cf. also Brown Bibl lxx 211) - **OffAr** Sing. emph. *krz›* Sumer xx 13[5] - **Palm** Sing. emph. *krwz›* Syr xl 34[8] - ¶ subst. herald (cf. Teixidor Sem xxxiv 26ff. :: Teixidor Syr xl 36, xliv 187f., Safar Sumer xx 14: or = cognomen).
v. *krwz*$_1$.

krḥ **Hatra** Sing. emph. *krḥ›* 278[1] - ¶ subst. prob. meaning enclosure wall (cf. Degen JEOL xxiii 419f.); transl. *cella* less prob., cf. Safar Sumer xxiv 29 (n. 63), Aggoula MUSJ xlvii 26, Vattioni IH a.l. - for this word, cf. also Marrassini FLEM 63.

kry$_1$ **Pun** QAL Pf. 3 p.s.m. *kr›*Trip 18[2] - ¶ verb QAL to cut out, to hew; + obj.: Trip 18[2].
v. *kbh,krt*$_1$, *mkrth*.

kry$_2$ **Pun** QAL (?) Impf. 3 p.s.m. *ykry* Or xxxiii 4[3] - ¶ verb QAL poss. meaning to buy (for this highly uncert. interpret., cf. Levi Della Vida Or xxxiii a.l.).

kry$_3$ v. *kbh*.

kry$_4$ **OffAr** Altheim & Stiehl FuF xxxv 176, ASA 252: this word (= well) in FuF xxxv 173[4] (*kry my*) :: idem ASA 271: = Plur. cstr.); uncert. interpret.
v. *kwh*.

krk$_1$ **Hebr** Sing. abs. *krk* DJD ii 43[2] (for the reading, cf. Ginsberg BASOR cxxxi 25, Sonne PAAJR xxiii 95f., Birnbaum PEQ '54, 24f., Bardtke ThLZ lxxix 296, Yeivin At i 105, Lipiński BiOr xli 157f., Schäfer BKA 125 (cf. also Yadin BK 137) × Milik DJD ii a.l.: l. *(h)brk* = n.l. :: Milik RB lx 277, 283, Cross RB lxiii 47 n. 4 (div. otherwise): l. *ḥbrk* = Sing. + suff. 2 p.s.m. of *ḥbr*$_3$;on the reading problems, cf. Pardee HAHL 130) - **OffAr**, cf. Frah i 12 (*krk›*; cf. Nyberg FP 61 :: Ebeling Frah a.l.: l. *kwk›*< Akkad. < Sum. = darkness) - **Nab** Sing. emph. *krk›* CIS ii 350[2], J 1[1] (:: CIS ii sub 199: l. *kwn›* = Sing. emph. of *kwn*$_4$(= foundation); cf. also Levinson NAI 172) - **Palm** Sing. emph. *krk›* RTP 8 - ¶ subst. - **1)** fortification, fortified town: Cowl 26[3,8] (for both instances, v. however supra), RTP 8 (cf. Caquot RTP p. 146; cf. also Gawlikowski TP 14f.; *krk* as (part of) n.l., cf. CIS ii 3928[3], 3948, cf. also Rosenthal Sprache 37, 98) - **2)** enclosure before a tomb: CIS ii 350[2], J 1[1] (for the situation presupposed in this text, cf. J p. 141f. and the photography J p. 358; cf. also Milik RB lxvi 558, Levinson NAI 99, 175) - for the word, cf. Marrassini FLEM 98ff. - e.g. Cowl sub 26, Grelot DAE p. 288 (n. o): the *krky›* in Cowl 26[3,8] = Plur. emph. of *krk$_1$* (improb. interpret., cf. Herzfeld PE 280f., Segal PEQ '74, 163, sub ATNS 26, Teixidor JAOS cv 732f., Porten & Yardeni sub TADAE A 6.2: = Plur. emph. of *krky* (= Carian)).

krk$_2$ = roll > Akkad., cf. v.Soden Or xxxv 13, xlvi 188, AHW s.v. *kerku* B; cf. also CAD s.v. *kirku* II.

krkm > Akkad. *kur-ru-ku-um-mu* STU ii 50[5] (cf. v. Weiher a.l.): suffron crocus, cf. also Löw AP 219.

krm$_1$ **Pun** YIPH Pf. 3 p.pl.m. *›ykrm›* KAI 145[13] (:: Krahmalkov RSF iii 183: = YIPH Pf. 3 p.s.m. + suff. 3 p.s.m. (= to honour)); HIPH Pf. 3 p.s.m. *hykrm* Karth xii 52[2] (cf. Krahmalkov RSF iii 178, 183, 202, v.d.Branden RSF v 56f. :: Février & Fantar Karth xii a.l.: lapsus for *hykrt* = HIPH Pf. 3 p.s.m. of *krt$_1$*) - ¶ verb YIPH in KAI 145[13] poss. meaning to give freely, to pay the costs of (+ obj.; cf. Berger MAIBL xxxvi/ii 142f., 163, Halévy RS ix 284f., Cooke NSI p. 155, Lidzbarski Eph i 50, Chabot sub RES 2221, Février Sem vi 28, Röllig KAI a.l., Février & Fantar Karth xii 52; v. also supra); the same meaning prob. in Karth xii 52[2] :: v.d.Branden RSF v 57: = to occupy oneself with :: Krahmalkov RSF iii 178, 183, 202: = to honour.
v. *krt$_1$*.

krm$_2$ **Ph** Sing. abs. *krm* EpAn ix 5[2,2f.,6]; Plur. abs. *krmm* EpAn ix 5[4] - **Amm** Sing. abs. *krm* Ber xxii 120[4] - **Hebr** Sing. cstr. *krm* Dir ostr 20[2], 53[2], 54[1f.] (= KAI 187), 55[1f.], 58[2], 60[1], 61[1] - **Samal** Sing. abs. *krm* KAI 214[7] - **OffAr** Sing. cstr. *krm* Del 27[1] (= AECT 29), At ix-x 201[1]; emph. *krm›* ATNS 30a 6; Plur. emph. *krmy›* Aḥiq 40; cf. Frah v 1 (*klm›*), Paik 544 (*krm›*), Nisa 14[1], 15[1], 16[1], 18[1], 21[1], 22[1], 24[1], 26[2], 27[1], etc. (*krm›*), Nisa-c 385[2] (*krmn*; dam. context), GIPP 25, 55 - ¶ subst. m. vineyard; in KAI 214[7] prob. with coll. meaning (cf. also Baldacci VT xxxi 365: in Ber xxii 120[4] with coll. meaning) - on this word, cf. Delcor APCI 231ff., Borowski AIAI 103f.

krml v. *pry$_2$*.

krn v. *qrn*.

krs$_1$ cf. Frah x 36 (*klsh*, *kršh*): belly.
v. *krsy*.

krs$_2$ **Pun** Sing. abs. *krs* Or xxxiii 4[3] - ¶ subst. of unknown meaning; Levi Della Vida Or xxxiii 10, 14: < Greek χρῆσις = profit, gain; Vattioni AION xvi 38f.: = vase, amphora poss. related to Greek κρωσσός (v. *krsy*).

krs› **OldAr** Sing. cstr. *krs›* KAI 216[7]; + suff. 3 p.s.m. *krs›h* Tell F 13 (Akkad. par. *[iṣ]kussî-šú*); + suff. 1 p.s. *khs›y* KAI 224[17] (lapsus for *krs›y*?, cf. Dupont-Sommer BMB xiii 34, Fitzmyer AIS 98, 115, Greenfield ActOr xxix 6 n. 13, Degen AAG p. 21 n. 86 (cf. also Lemaire & Durand IAS 146) × Segert ArchOr xxxii 121, Donner KAI a.l., Gibson SSI ii p. 48f., 55: variant form for *krs›y*; cf. however Garbini RSO xxxiv

44) - **OffAr** Sing. abs. *krs*ʾ NESE ii 40 ii (or = Sing. emph.?, cf. Röllig
a.l.), *kwrs*ʾAM-NS ii 171 i 4; emph. *krs*ʾʾ Aḥiq 133, Atlal vii 109⁵;
*kwrsy*ʾ AM-NS ii 169, 171 ii 5, 174⁴ (*y* superscribed); + suff. 3 p.s.m.
*krs*ʾh Cowl 6² - **JAr** Sing. + suff. 3 p.s.m. (or emph.) *krsyh* AMB 7a 5,
15, 7b 1 - ¶ subst. throne (for the context of Tell F 13, v. *mwddw*; for
AM-NS ii 169, 171 i 4, ii 5, 174⁴, v. *nsb*) - for the etymology, v. *ks*ʾ₃, cf.
also Degen GGA '79, 19, Kaufman AIA 29 (n. 83), Lindenberger APA
299 n. 12, H.P.Müller VT xxxvi 427 (n. 23).
v. *ks*ʾ₃, *ks*ʾh,*krsy*, *nsb*.

krsy **Ph** Plur. abs. *krsym* CIS i 22 (= Kition A 9), 44² (= Kition B 40),
88³,⁵,⁶ (= Kition F 1), Krug 33a - ¶ subst. of uncert. meaning, only in
the comb. *mlṣ krsym*; Harr 112: Plur. = title of a group? or *krsy* =
throne? (for this last mentioned interpret., cf. also CIS i sub 22, Cooke
NSI p. 60f., 73, Lidzbarski sub KI 21 :: v.d.Branden BMB xiii 91, FS
Rinaldi 58, 63: = Plur. of *krs₁*> intestines (cf. Capuzzi StudMagr ii
73f.) :: Vattioni AION xviii 72f.: = vase (v. *krs₂*)).

krʿ v.Soden Or xlvi 188: = to bow > Akkad. *karāʾu* (?); cf. also
v.Weiher ad STU ii 24⁸.

krp **OffAr** Sing. emph. *krp*ʾ FX 136⁷ (reading uncert.: *d/r/k d/r/k p*
ʾ, cf. Dupont-Sommer FX 145, Mayrhofer FX 183) - ¶ subst. of uncert.
meaning (v. supra); Dupont-Sommer FX 145: < Iran. = sanctuary,
cult (cf. however Mayrhofer FX 183f., cf. also Dupont- Sommer CRAI
'74, 137, 149, Teixidor Syr liii 335, JNES xxxvii 183, PP 105; on the
subject, cf. also Frei BiOr xxxviii 370), cf. Greek par. βωμόν; cf. also
Garbini SMEA xviii 270: = cult.

krph **Hatra** Sing. emph. *krpt*ʾ, cf. Assur 27g (uncert. interpret., diff.
context; cf. Aggoula Assur a.l.: = Plur.) - ¶ subst. furniture (v. however
supra).

krpty (< Iran., cf. Humbach IPAA p. 15, Hinz AISN 148) - **OffAr**
Sing. abs. *krpty* IPAA 11⁷ - ¶ subst. caravan-route.

krṣ (< root *qrṣ₁*, cf. e.g. Cooke NSI p. 206, Claassen AION xxi 297; cf.
however Kaufman AIA 63: < Akkad. *karṣu*) - **OffAr** Plur. cstr. *krṣy*
KAI 269² - ¶ subst. calumny, slander (cf. e.g. Held JCS xv 12 :: Degen
ZDMG cxxi 137, Or xliv 124); *wkrṣy* ʾyš lʾ ʾmrt KAI 269²: and she
has not slandered anyone (cf. Greenfield IEJ xix 203 n. 19).

krš₁ (< Iran., cf. Driv¹ p. 38, Eilers AfO xvii 333) - **OffAr** Sing. abs.
Cowl 15⁶, 20¹⁵, Krael 2¹⁶, 3⁶, NESE i 11⁴ (cf. Degen NESE i 11, 17,
Grelot DAE p. 504 :: Shunnar GMA 114f. (div. otherwise): l. *kršn* (=
Plur. abs.; cf. however idem CRM ii 281, 287)), ATNS 20²,³, etc., etc.;
Plur. abs. *kršn* Cowl 1⁷, 2¹⁵, 5⁷, Krael 1⁸, 3¹⁵, Driv F 2A 17¹, JNES
xlix 291¹, ATNS 4¹, etc., etc. - ¶ subst. m. certain type of weight, coin,
karaš = 10 *shekel* = 83 1/3 gr. (cf. Cowl p. xxxf., Wag 214, Driv¹ p. 38,
Porten Arch 66, Cameron PTT p. 37, Hinz ZDMG cx 237, Fitzmyer

FS Albright ii 143, 152, WA 255f.; for the context, v. *rb*ʿ$_2$) - abbrev. *k*in Cowl 36b 1 (cf. also Porten & Greenfield JEAS p. 119); ATNS $38^{11,17}$, $41^{6,7,9}$, 43a 4 (heavily dam. context), 66a 3, 66b 5, 6 (heavily dam. context), cf. Segal ATNS a.l.; cf. poss. also the abbrev. *k*in BIFAO xxxviii 58^9 (:: Segal Maarav iv 73: pro *k 1* l. *kn* (= *kn*$_4$))and in DJD ii 9^{1-6} - the diff. *kr* in KAI 43^{14} poss. = abbrev. of *krš*?? (cf. Lidzbarski sub KI 36, Honeyman JEA xxvi 64 n. 13, Röllig KAI a.l., Lipiński RTAT 251 n. 35, Gibson SSI iii p. 141, cf. also v.d.Branden OA iii 259 :: Cooke NSI p. 88: = abbrev. of *kkr*?:: Bordreuil Syr lxv 438: l. *krš* (= Sing. abs. of *krš*$_1$) - Segal Maarav iv 72: l. *k*(= abbrev. of *krš*) *2* in BIFAO xxxviii 58^1, less prob. reading, cf. Aimé-Giron BIFAO a.l.: l. *ntn* = n.p.
v. *br*$_4$,*m*ʿ*h*$_1$, *spr*$_2$, *rb*ʿ$_3$.

krš$_2$ v. *byk*.

kršn **Hebr** Plur. abs. *kršnyn* Mas 543 - ¶ subst. indicating a kind of vetch.

krt$_1$ **Ph** QAL Pf. 3 p.s.m. *krt* KAI $27^{8f.}$ (for the reading, cf. Dupont-Sommer RHR cxx 134, Caquot JANES v 48, cf. also Albright BASOR lxxvi 8 n. 14, Gibson SSI iii p. 85, Garbini OA xx 282ff. × Cross & Saley BASOR cxcvii 44 (n. 7), Röllig NESE ii 18, 21: l. *krrt* = lapsus for *krt* × Gaster Or xi 44, Röllig KAI a.l., v.d.Branden BiOr xxxiii 12, Avishur PIB 248, de Moor JEOL xxvii 108: l. *kkrt* = *k*$_3$ + *krt* (cf. also Baldacci BiOr xl 128; v. infra) :: Teixidor AO i 106: l. *kyrt* (without interpret.) :: du Mesnil du Buisson FS Dussaud 424, 427: l. *k[n]rt* = *k*$_3$ + Sing. abs. of *nrh* (= torch, light); for the interpret., cf. Cross & Saley BASOR cxcvii 45, Caquot JANES v 48 (: or = pass. Pf. 3 p.s.f.), Röllig NESE ii 18, Lipiński RTAT 265, Garbini OA xx 283f., Gibson SSI iii p. 82 × Gaster Or xi 44, Röllig KAI a.l.: = Pf. pass. 3 p.s.f. (QAL or PUʿAL?) × Avishur PIB 248, 252, de Moor JEOL xxvii 108, Sperling HUCA liii 3, 6: = QAL Pf. 3 p.pl. :: Albright BASOR lxxvi 8: = QAL Pf. 3 p.s.f. (cf. also FR 131, v.d.Branden BO iii 43f., Baldacci BiOr xl 128, Cross HThR lv 237) :: Dupont-Sommer RHR cxx 135, 138: = QAL Imper. s.f. :: Torczyner JNES vi 22: = QAL Pf. 2 p.s.m.),[10] (cf. Gaster Or xi 44, Caquot JANES v 48, Röllig NESE ii 18, 21f., Lipiński RTAT 265, Avishur PIB 248, 252, Gibson SSI iii p. 82, Garbini OA xx 283f., Sperling HUCA liii 3, 7, de Moor JEOL xxvii 108 :: du Mesnil du Buisson FS Dussaud 424, Albright BASOR lxxvi 8, Cross & Saley BASOR cxcvii 45: = QAL Pf. 3 p.s.f. (cf. also FR 131, Baldacci BiOr xl 128) :: Torczyner JNES vi 22: = QAL Pf. 2 p.s.m. :: Dupont-Sommer RHR cxx 135, 138: = QAL Imper. s.f.) - **Pun** HIPH Pf. 3 p.s.m. *hykrt* Karth xii 50^2 (v. infra) - **Mo** QAL Pf. 1 p.s. *krty* KAI 181^{25} (cf. e.g. Lidzbarksi Handb 299, sub KI 1, Michaud PA 40 (n. 1), Segert ArchOr xxix 211, 226 (cf. however id., ibid. 242), Lipiński Or xl 336ff., de Geus

SV 26 × e.g. Röllig KAI a.l., Gibson SSI i p. 77, 82 (cf. also Cooke NSI p. 13): = QAL Pf. 1 p.s. of *kry*$_1$;cf. also Reviv CSI p. 28) - ¶ verb QAL to cut (for KAI 181[25], v. supra and v. *mkrth*); with special meaning: to conclude a treaty; *krt ln ʾlt ʾlm ʾšr krt ln wkl bn ʾlm* KAI 27[8ff.]: he has made an eternal pact with us, Ashur, and all the gods, has made (a pact) with us (cf. McCarthy TaC 92ff.; for the problems involved, v. also supra) - prob. a form of this root in KAI 214[11]: *(.)krt*, cf. Halévy RS i 149f., Lagrange ERS 493f.: = QAL Pf. 3 p.s.m. (cf. also D.H.Müller WZKM vii 52, Cooke NSI p. 159, 167, Dion p. 28, 381) × Gibson SSI ii p. 67f., 71: = QAL Part. pass. s.m. abs. (cf. also Driver AnOr xii 47, reading however *krt[h]*) × Koopmans 35: l. *[n]krt* = NIPH Pf. 3 p.s.m.; for the context, v. also *ʾmn*$_3$ - HIPH Février & Fantar Karth xii 50: the *hykrt* in Karth xii 50[2] = HIPH Pf. 3 p.s.m. (= to construct by cutting, i.e. to construct of hewn stone; cf. however Krahmalkov RSF iii 178, 180, 202: = to cut off, to extirpate) :: v.d.Branden RSF v 56, 59: l. *hykrm* = HIPH Pf. 3 p.s.m. of *krm*$_1$.
v. *krm*$_1$,*krt*$_2$, *mkrth*.

krt$_2$ **Pun** Sing. abs. *krt* (reading uncert.) Hofra 94[2] (or = QAL Part. act. s.m. abs. of *krt*$_1$?) - ¶ subst. (v. however supra) indication of function: stone-cutter, quarryman? (highly uncert. interpret.).

krtys v. *qrṭys*.

krtk **OffAr** Zadok WO xvi 174: the *krtk* in ATNS 5[1] poss. = subst. Sing. abs. (= traveller, wanderer, migrant), less prob. interpret., cf. Segal ATNS a.l., Porten & Yardeni sub TADAE B 8.3: = Cretan.

kšd **DA** a form of this root (*kšd*) poss. in v q 2 (reading uncert., heavily dam. context)??, cf. also Hoftijzer DA p. 259.

kšy v. *qdḥ*$_2$.

kšyṭ (< root *qšṭ*, cf. Cowl p. 244, Greenfield Lesh xxxii 364, Kutscher IOS i 108, Kottsieper SAS 42, 211) - **OffAr** Sing. emph. *kšyṭʾ* Aḥiq 158 - ¶ subst. (or substantivated adj.): truth.

kšyr **Hebr** Plur. m. abs. *kšyry[n]* Mas 449[2], 452[3] - **OffAr** Plur. m. abs. *kšyrn* ATNS 26[7,14] - **Palm** Sing. m. emph. *kšyrʾ* CIS ii 3913 ii 121 - ¶ adj. capable, competent - **1)** excellent; *gbrn kšyrn mny byn bbyʾ* ATNS 26[7]: appoint (i.e. post) capable men in the gates (cf. ATNS 26[14]); *qrblwn kšyrʾ* CIS ii 3913 ii 121: the excellent Corbulo (cf. Greek par. Κουρβούλων ὁ κράτιστος); :: Dahood Bibl xliv 532: < Can. - 2) suited: Mas 449[2]; *kšyry[n] lṭhrt hqdš* Mas 452[3f.]: suited for the purity of hallowed things.

kšyš v. *qšyš*.

kšmy v. *qysm*.

kšr **Hebr** QAL Part. act. s.f. abs. (v. infra) *kšrh* Frey 1536[1] (= RES 863A) - **OffAr** QAL Impf. 3 p.s.m. *ykšr* ATNS 48[2]; 3 p.pl.m. *ykšrwn* ATNS 48[1,7]; Part. act. s.m. abs. (v. infra) *kšr* Driv 11[5] (for this reading, cf. Porten & Yardeni sub TADAE A 6.14; dam. context) - **Palm** QAL Part. act. s.m. abs. (v. infra) *kšr* CIS ii 3913 ii 105, Syr xvii 351^{10} - ¶ verb QAL to be suitable; + l_5: ATNS $48^{1,2,7}$ (in all instances, dam. context); Part. act. (or adj.?) pious, just, suitable; *kšr dy [yh]n mksy᾽* ... CIS ii 3913 ii 105: it is right that the taxes will be ... (cf. Greek par. δεῖ ... τὰ τέλη λογεύεσθαι); *mh dy kšr* Syr xvii 351^{10}: what is right (for the context, cf. Milik DFD 304, Gawlikowski TP 57).

kšrh v. *kprt*.

kšryn v. *bšrwn*.

kšt **Pun** Garbini with Bisi AION xix 557: l. *kšt* in AION xix 556^1 = QAL Part. pass. pl.f. abs. of ksy_1(highly uncert. reading and interpret., cf. also Bisi a.l. (div. otherwise): l. *nš᾽t* = Sing. abs. (= offering (equally uncert.)) or (ibid. n. 8): l. *š᾽t* = Sing. abs. of $šnh_2$).

kt᾽ **Pun** word of uncert. meaning in Hofra 82^3: nom. gent.??; Février (sub Hofra 82): l. *bt᾽* = bt_2 + suff. 3 p.s.m. (improb. interpret.).

ktb₁ **Ph** QAL Pf. 1 p.s. *[k]tbt* KAI 43^{13} (cf. e.g. Clermont-Ganneau Et ii 175, Cooke NSI p. 87, RES sub 1211, Honeyman JEA xxvi 58, Röllig KAI a.l., Gibson SSI iii p. 136); Inf. cstr. *ktb* KAI 60^4 - **Pun** QAL Pf. 3 p.s.m. *ktb* CIS i 6022^1 (dam. context), Punica xviii/i 15^4 (cf. FR 131 × Février CB viii 30f.: = Pf. 3 p.s.f.); 1 p.s. *ktbt* RES 1543^4 (:: Février BAr '51/52, 263, HDS 192f., Bonnet SEL vii 112: = Pf. 2 p.s.m.), *k῾tbty* KAI 145^6 (cf. Berger MAIBL xxxvi/2, 158, Lidzbarski Eph i 49, Cooke NSI p. 154, FR 131, v.d.Branden RSF i 166, 169, Krahmalkov RSF iii 188f., 193 :: Février Sem vi 19f.: l. *k῾trty* = k_4 + PI῾EL Pf. 3 p.s.m. + suff. 3 p.s.m. of $῾tr_1$ (= to grant); on this form, cf. also Sznycer APCI 212 n. 6, 217); Part. pass. s.m. abs. *ktb* CIS i 6000bis 8 (= TPC 84; cf. Février CIS i a.l. × Ferron StudMagr i 78, Bonnet SEL vii 112: = QAL Part. act. s.m. abs. :: Harr 113: = QAL Pf. 3 p.s.m./pl.m. :: Chabot sub RES 13 (div. otherwise): or l. *yktb* = QAL Impf. 3 p.s.m.); PI῾EL Pf. 3 p.s.m. *kytb* KAI 160^2 (?; for this interpret., cf. Février Sem iv 21, Röllig KAI a.l., FR 143); NIPH Part. s.f. abs. *nktbt* NP 130^4 (cf. e.g. Cooke NSI p. 148, Février RHR cxli 21; diff. context) - **Hebr** QAL Pf. 3 p.s.m. *ktb* SM 105^1, DJD ii 24D 20; + suff. 3 p.s.f. *ktbh* DJD ii $42^{8,9}$ (cf. Birnbaum PEQ '55, 32 n. 14 :: de Vaux RB lx 272, Milik DJD ii p. 292: + suff. 3 p.s.m. (cf. also Pardee JBL xcvii 341f., HAHL 245 :: Lehmann & Stern VT iii 392, Sonne PAAJR xxiii 93: = Part. act. s.m. emph., scribe; cf. also Ginsberg BASOR cxxxi 27, Yeivin At i 101), 48^7 (?, heavily dam. context, cf. also Milik DJD ii p. 292: + suff. 3 p.s.m.); 2 p.s.m. *ktbth* TA-H 7^6 (cf. e.g. Aharoni TA a.l., Pardee UF x 293, Zevit MLAHE 28, Scagliarini Hen xii 135 :: v.Dyke Parunak BASOR ccxxx 26, 28: = QAL Pf. 2 p.s.m. + suff. 3 p.s.m.; or rather = QAL Pf. 1 p.s. + suff. 3 p.s.m./f.?; on the form, cf. also Rainey JBL cii 633); 1 p.s. *ktbty* KAI 194^3; Impf. 2 p.s.m. *tktb* KAI $196^{8f.}$; Imper. s.m. *ktb* TA-H

1^{4} (or Inf. abs.?, cf. Pardee UF x 294), DJD ii 50 i 2 (?, heavily dam. context) - **OldAr** Qal Pf. 1 p.s. *ktbt* KAI 222C 2; 1 p.pl. *[k]tbn* KAI 222C 1 (for this reading and restoration, cf. e.g. Fitzmyer AIS 18f., 73, Donner KAI a.l., Degen AAG p. 16 (n. 69), Gibson SSI ii p. 32f., 43 :: Vriezen JEOL xvii 209f.: l. *[n]qbn* = Qal Pf. 1 p.pl. of *nqb$_1$*) - **OffAr** Qal Pf. 3 p.s.m. *ktb* Cowl 2^{18,22}, 3^{21}, Krael 1^{10}, 2^{14}, MAI xiv/2, 66^{17}, IrAnt iv 115, FX 136^{19} (cf. Dupont-Sommer FX 137, 152f. × Teixidor Syr lii 289: = Sing. abs. of *ktb$_2$* (v. also infra) :: Teixidor JNES xxxvii 184: = Qal Part. pass. s.m. abs.), ATNS 6^{7}, 8^{10}, etc., etc.; 3 p.s.f. *ktbt* Cowl 10^{23}, 68 iv rev., KAI 233^{9} (uncert. interpret., cf. Lidzbarski AUA p. 11, R.A.Bowman UMS xx 280, Dupont-Sommer Syr xxiv 40, Donner KAI a.l., Gibson SSI ii p. 107 :: Lidzbarski ZA xxxi 199: = Qal Pf. 1 p.s. (cf. also Baneth OLZ '19, 56)); 2 p.s.m. *ktbt* Krael 8^{4}; 1 p.s. *ktbt* Cowl 9^{4,14}, 13^{9,12}, 81^{1} (cf. Driver JRAS '32, 83, Harmatta ActAntHung vii 339f., Grelot DAE p. 106 (n. d) :: Cowl a.l.: = Qal Pf. 3 p.s.f.), Krael 6^{16} (for the reading and the *scriptio anterior ktyb*, cf. Szubin & Porten BASOR cclxix 33, Porten & Yardeni sub TADAE B 3.7), 10^{16}, Herm 6^{5}, SSI ii 28 rev. 6; + suff. 3 p.s.m. *ktbth* Cowl 8^{17}; 1 p.pl. *ktbn* ATNS 3^{1} (dam. context); Impf. 2 p.s.m. *tktb* Cowl 11^{6}; 1 p.s. *ʾktb* FS Driver 55^{4} (?, heavily dam. context); 3 p.pl.m. *yktbwn* NESE iii 34 conv. 4, Irâq xxxi 174^{2} (*[y]ktbwn*; heavily dam. context), ATNS 81^{5} (*[yk]tbwn*?, heavily dam. context); + suff. 3 p.s.f. *yktbwh* RES 492B 4; 1 p.pl. *nktb* Cowl 28^{14}; Inf. *mktb* BSOAS xiii 82^{7}; Qal pass. Pf. 3 p.s.m. *ktyb* Cowl 17^{3} (for this interpret., cf. Grelot DAE p. 282, Porten RB xc 412 :: Cowl a.l.: = Qal Part. pass. s.m. abs.), ATNS 27^{3,5}, Samar 3^{12}, 8^{13} (*kty[b]*); Part. pass. s.m. abs. *ktyb* Cowl 5^{10,13}, 10^{8}, 35^{8}, 48^{2}, Krael 11^{5} (for the reading, cf. Porten & Yardeni sub TADAE B 3.13 :: e.g. Krael a.l., Porten & Greenfield JEAS p. 66: l. *ktyb[n]* = Qal Part. pass. pl.m. abs.)^{8,9,10,12}, 12^{22}, 13^{8}, ATNS 8^{11} (*kt[yb]*, cf. Porten & Yardeni sub TADAE B 5.6 :: Segal ATNS a.l.: l. *kt[b]* = Qal Pf. 3 p.s.m.), *ktb* Cowl 3^{20}, Krael 10^{7,16} (as predicate with pl. subject; Porten & Szubin JAOS cvii 232: = lapsus for *kt(y)bn* (= Qal Part. pass. pl.m. abs.)), 12^{29}, KAI 233^{12} (:: R.A.Bowman UMS xx 277: = Qal Pf. 3 p.s.m.); pl.m. abs. *ktybn* Cowl 2^{11,13}, 18^{2}, 25^{8}, Krael 4^{12}, 6^{9}, 7^{23,28}, 9^{16}, 10^{7}, *ktbn* Krael 3^{17}, 9^{12}, 10^{11,15}; pl.f. abs. *ktybn* Krael 9^{16}; cf. Frah xv 5 (*ktyb*, cf. Nyberg FP 47, 85 :: Ebeling Frah a.l.: l. *qṭʾ* (= form of *qṭ*)), xxiii 1 (*yktybwn*), Paik 481 (*ykwymwn*), 482 (*yktybwn*), GIPP 38, 55, SaSt 25f. (cf. also Toll ZDMG-Suppl viii 28, 33, 35) - **Nab** Qal Pf. 3 p.s.m. *ktb* CIS ii 224^{5} (cf. Jaussen & Savignac sub J 34 :: CIS ii a.l.: = Sing. abs. of *ktb$_2$*), J 188, 190, 334^{2}, RB xli 591,1 (*ktbydh* haplography for *ktb bydh*), RES 528^{1} (??), Mas 515 (*ktbydh* haplography for *ktb bydh*), ADAJ xxiv 43 ii (*ktbydh* haplography for *ktb bydh*), IEJ xxxvi 56^{6} (*ktbydh* haplography for *ktb* *bydh*); + suff. 3 p.s.m. *ktbh* MPAT 61[25] (= DBKP 15), Mas 514[1], *ktbyh* Mas 514[2]; 1 p.s. *ktbt* DBKP 22[34]; Impf. 3 p.s.m. *yktb* CIS ii 206[4,6], 209[6], 219[4], 223[3], J 5[7]; 1 p.s. *›ktb* MPAT 64 i 5 (cf. Starcky RB lxi 171 (: or = APH pass. Pf. 3 p.s.m.; less prob. interpret.) :: e.g. Fitzmyer & Harrington MPAT p. 165, 324: = APH Pf. 3 p.s.m.); 3 p.pl.m. *yktbwn* CIS ii 212[4]; Inf. *mktb* CIS ii 210[4]; Part. act. s.m. cstr. *ktb* RES 1479[2] (uncert. interpret.), J 18[4]; emph. *ktb›* CIS ii 416, 825[2], 2667[4f.], J 190; QAL pass. Pf. 3 p.s.m. *ktyb* MPAT 64 i 4, 8, iii 3; 3 p.s.f. *ktybt* MPAT 61[25] (for the reading, cf. (Naveh with) Greenfield sub DBKP 15 :: e.g. Fitzmyer & Harrington MPAT a.l.: l. *ktbnn* = QAL Pf. 1 p.pl.); Part. pass. s.m. abs. *ktyb* CIS ii 197[8], 198[7], 199[5,7], RB xliv 266,3, MPAT 61[25] (= DBKP 15), etc.; pl.m. abs. *ktybyn* MPAT 64 i 2; pl.f. abs. *ktbn* DBKP 22[34] (diff. and dam. context; Yadin & Greenfield DBKP a.l.: or = QAL Pf. 1 p.pl.??); ITP Impf. 3 p.s.m. *ytktb* J 38[7] (reading uncert.); 2 p.s.m. *ttrtb* J 5[5] (prob. lapsus for *ttktb*, cf. Jaussen & Savignac J p. 153 and RES sub 1286) - **Palm** QAL Pf. 3 p.s.m. *ktb* CIS ii 3913 ii 104, 121, Syr xiv 183[3] (heavily dam. context; cf. also Gawlikowski TP 43: = Sing. cstr. of *ktb_2*, Milik DFD 227: = QAL Part. pass. s.m. of *ktb_1*); 1 p.s. *ktbt* CIS ii 4214; 3 p.pl.m. *ktbw* Inv x 114[3]; Part. act. s.m. emph. *ktb›* PNO 47a 5 (or = Sing. emph. of *ktb_3* (= *ktwb*?)); QAL pass. Impf. 3 p.s.m. *yktb* CIS ii 3913 i 8 (cf. Rosenthal Sprache 56, 62, cf. however Cantineau Gramm 82ff.: = QAL Impf. 3 p.s.m.? :: Duval REJ viii 61: = ITP Impf. 3 p.s.m., cf. also CIS ii sub 3913), *wktb* CIS ii 3913 i 9 (lapsus for *yktb*? or for *wyktb*?, cf. CIS ii sub 3913, Rosenthal Sprache 13; cf. also Cantineau Gramm 83; :: Cooke NSI p. 334 (div. otherwise): = QAL Pf. 3 p.s.m. or 3 p.pl.m.); Part. pass. s.m. abs. *ktyb* CIS ii 3913 i 4, ii 68, 87, 89, Syr xvii 353[3], RIP 25[11]; ITP Part. s.m. abs. *mtktb* CIS ii 3913 i 5 - **Hatra** QAL Pf. 1 p.s. *ktbt*, cf. Assur 11 i 4, 21 ii 4, *ktbyt* 24[1,3] (cf. also Assur 27h); Impf. 3 p.s.m. *lktwb* 74[7]; QAL pass. Pf. 3 p.s.m. *ktyb* 235[3] (cf. Aggoula MUSJ xlvii 12, Degen JEOL xxiii 406 :: Safar Sumer xxiv 11, Vattioni IH a.l.: = QAL Part. act. s.m. abs.) - **JAr** QAL Pf. 3 p.s.m. *ktb* MPAT 42[23] (with f. subject, cf. Milik Bibl xxxviii 257, DJD ii p. 117), 51[16] (with f. subject, cf. Milik Bibl xxxviii 257), 52[15] (*[k]tb*, dam. context)[,18], SM 101[3] (= Frey 826a), DBPK 21 back; + suff. 3 p.s.m. *ktbh* MPAT 56[7], 61[24] (= DBKP 15), DBKP 17[42], 18[69,72], 19[29] (*ktb[h]*), 20[42], *ktbyh* MPAT 62[13] (= DBKP 27); 1 p.s. *ktbt* MPAT 54[1], AMB 1[12]; 3 p.pl.m. *ktbw* DBKP 18[71] (reading of *w* uncert.); Impf. 3 p.s.m. *yktwb* MPAT-A 34[5] (= SM 69); Part. pass. s.m. abs. *ktyb* Syr xlv 101[9] (heavily dam. context; or = QAL pass. Pf. 3 p.s.m.?), *ktb* MPAT 61[24] (cf. Yadin & Greenfield sub DBKP 15 :: Fitzmyer & Harrington MPAT a.l.: = Sing. abs. of *ktb_2*), DBKP 17[42], 18[69], 20[42] - ¶ verb QAL to write, passim; *›dnmrdk ktb* ATNS 26[17]: I. has written (it) (end of official document; letter?); *ktb pqṭnwty* ATNS 11[3]: P. has written (it) (written by a witness under an official document; cf. ATNS 11[4-6]); *ʾnʾ ʾzʾ ktbt* Assur 21 ii 3f.: I, A., have written (it; at the end of inscription, cf. Assur 11 i 4, cf. also Assur 27h, Hatra 24[1,3]) - **1)** + obj. - a) what is written = the contents of the writing; *ktb šm hym* TA-H 1[4]: write (/note) the name of the day - b) what is written = the result of the writing; *ktb ktbʾ* AE '23 42 no. 16: he has written the inscription; *wspr mrḥq ktb* Cowl 8[25]: he wrote a deed of renunciation (cf. Krael 2[14]); *ktbt ʾgrtʾ zʾ* SSI ii 28 rev. 6: I have written this letter (cf. MPAT 52[18] (for the context, v. *spr₃*), 64 i 5, ASAE xxxix 353[3], 357[1f.,9] (heavily dam. context), etc.); *dth dk ktb zy ...* FX 136[19]: this decree he has written, who ... (cf. Dupont-Sommer FX 137, 152f. × Teixidor Syr lii 289: this decree is a document that ...; v. also supra), cf. J 334[2] - c) what is written upon; *ktb ʾbʾṣr ksʾ znh* IrAnt iv 115: A. has written (on) this cup (for the context, cf. also Teixidor Syr xliv 185; v. also *ḥy₁*) - d) + obj. + *b₂*, *yktbwn ythwn bspr ḥyyh* MPAT-A 34[5]: He will write them (sc. their names) in the book of life - e) + obj. + *byn₂*, *wspr plgnn nktb bynyn* Cowl 28[14]: and we will write between us our deed of partition - f) + obj. + *kpm*, *ktb plṭyh br ʾḥyw sprʾ znh kpm qwnyh* Cowl 5[15]: P. the son of A. wrote this document conform the instructions of Q. (for the context, v. *pm₁*), cf. Cowl 6[16f.], Krael 5[15f.], 7[42f.], etc., etc. - g) + obj. + *l₅* + *ʾḥr₅*, *wspr ktbt lh ʾḥrwhy* Cowl 9[4]: and I have written for her a deed concerning it - h) + obj. + *l₅* + *ʿlʾ*, *wspr ktb ly ʿlʾ* Cowl 13[3]: and he wrote a document for me about it (cf. Cowl 13[9f.], Krael 8[4]) - i) + obj. + *lwt* (= *l₅* + *wt*), *ʾktb krwzʾ hw lwtk* MPAT 64 i 5: I will write this *krwz* for you (v. *krwz₁*, v. also supra) - j) + obj. + *ʿl₇*, *yktbwh ʿl drʿh* RES 492B 4: they shall write it upon her arm (= RES 1800; for the context, cf. Driver AnOr xii 57) - k) + obj. + *ʿl pm*, *wktb sprʾ gmryh br ʾḥyw ʿl pm šhdyʾ ...* Cowl 11[16]: G. the son of A. wrote the deed basing himself on the evidence of the witnesses ... (for the context, v. *pm₁*); *ktb mkbnt br nrgy [sp]rʾ znh ʿl pm pty* MAI xiv/2, 66[17f.]: M. the son of N. wrote this deed conform the instructions of P. (for the context, v. also *pm₁*) - l) + obj. + *ʿlt*, *ʾyt rʿt z lktb hʾdmm ʾš ... ʿlt mṣbt* KAI 60[4f.]: that the men who ... should write this decision on a stele - **2)** + *ʾl₆*, *hlʾ tktb ʾl[...* KAI 196[8f.]: will you not write to [them] (for the reading, cf. e.g. Gibson SSI i p. 45) - **3)** + *b₂*: BSOAS xiii 82[7] (on) - a) + *b₂* + obj., *wlʾ yktb bqbrʾ dnh ktb klh* CIS ii 206[4f.]: and he will not write about the tomb any document whatever (cf. CIS ii 206[6], 210[4], 212[4], 219[4f.], cf. also CIS ii 223[3]) - b) + *bydh*, *mlkʾltw ... ktbydh* (v. supra) RB xli 591,1: M. ... has written with his own hand (cf. Mas 515, ADAJ xxiv 43 ii, IEJ xxxvi 56[6]) - c) + *bpky*, *ktb h[wšʿ] bkpy n[pšh]* Cowl 3[21]: H. wrote with his own hands (for the reading, cf. Porten & Yardeni sub TADAE B 4.3); cf. also Cowl 13[17f.] (for the reading, cf. Porten & Yardeni sub TADAE B 2.7) - **4)**

+ *kpm*, *ktb mʿwzyh br ntn kpm ydnyh* Cowl 25^{17}: M. son of N. wrote (this) conform the instructions of Y. (v. pm_1), cf. Krael 1^{10}, 3^{22b}, 4^{22}, 8^{9} - **5)** + l_5 - a) l_5 = to, *ktb lsṯṯyls* CIS ii 3913 ii 104: he wrote to S. (cf. CIS ii 3913 ii 121) - b) l_5 = for, *spr ... zy ktb qwnyh lmḥsh* Cowl 5^{20}: deed ... which Q. wrote for M. (cf. Cowl 2^{22}, Krael 4^{25}, 5^{18}, etc., etc.) - c) + l_5 + obj., *lʾ ktbt lk sprʾ znh* Cowl 9^{14}: I did not write this deed for you (cf. Krael 12^{31}, CIS ii $209^{6f.}$) - d) + l_5 + obj. + $ʿl_7$, *wktb lhm spr ʿlyhm* Cowl 42^{4}: and write for them a deed concerning them; *wtktb ly nbz ʿl kl ksp* Cowl $11^{6f.}$: and you shall write me a receipt for all the silver - e) + l_5 + $ʿl_7$ (concerning): Cowl 8^{23} (cf. Herm 6^{5}, Milik Bibl xlviii 548: in this context *ktb* = to sign (less prob. interpret., cf. also Porten & Greenfield IOS iv 20)) - f) + *lʿl* (= l_5 + $ʿl_7$) + obj., *wlktwb lʿlwhy* (v. $ʿl_7$) *mdʿn dbš* Hatra $74^{7f.}$: and he will write upon it something bad (for the context reading, cf. Milik DFD 401, 403f., Vattioni IH a.l. :: e.g. Caquot Syr xxxii 270: pro *lʿlwhy ...* l. *ʿlyh m?? d/rbš*; v. also $bʾš_2$) - g) + *lpny*: TA-H 7^{6}, v. pnh_1 - **6)** + mn_5, *]mn npšh ktb* MPAT 42^{13}: she (v. supra) wrote for herself (i.e. as interested party, v. also *npš*, and below sub 7b) - **7)** + $ʿl_7$ - a) *ʿl* = concerning, *ktb ydnyh br hwšʿ ʿl byt yznyh* Cowl 25^{20}: Y. the son of H. wrote (it) concerning the house of Y. - b) + *ʿl npš*, *šlm b[r]t šmʿwn ʿl npšh ktb* (v. supra) MPAT 51^{16}: Sh. daughter of Sh. wrote for herself (i.e. as interested party (v. *npš*), cf. prob. also MPAT 52^{15}; v. also supra sub 6) - c) + *ʿl hdlt*, *ktbty ʿl hdlt* KAI 194^{3}, diff. expression, poss. = I wrote on the door (as place for public announcements), cf. Albright BASOR lxi 14, lxx 14, Gordon BASOR lxvii 31 n. 7, Burrows JAOS lvi 491ff., de Vaux RB xlviii 194f., Diringer Lach iii 333, Gibson SSI i p. 42, cf. also Michaud PA 79 (n. 1) :: Chapira RES '41/'45, 121: I have written on the door-leaf (of the building, prob. the date of the completion of the building) :: Février SDB vi 953: I have written on a tablet (cf. Röllig KAI a.l., Albright BASOR cxcviii 39 (> Greek δέλτος), Dahood Or xli 318, cf. also Galling FS Albright ii 210f., TGI 76 (n. 1), Hicks VT xxxiii 51ff., 55: writing board; cf. also Reider JQR xxix 236: I have written in a notebook) :: Torczyner Lach i p. 80, JQR xxxix 376: I have written on a sheet of papyrus (cf. Ginsberg BJPES iii 77ff.) :: Dussaud Syr xix 260: I have written on a papyrus scroll :: Lemaire IH p. 110f.: I have written on the column of the scroll (cf. also Brock & Diringer FS Thomas 42f., Millard BAT 307, Weinfeld BAT 367, Conrad TUAT i 622) :: Hempel ZAW lvi 133 (cf. also Hammershaimb with Michaud JA ccxxxix 80): I have written concerning the poor (*dlt* = Plur. abs. of *dlh*(= the poor), cf. also Thomas JSS x 12); cf. Eissfeldt BAGN i 80: = proverbial expression, meaning something like 'hinter den Spiegel stecken'; cf. also Cassuto RSO xvi 174, Greenfield JAOS xciv 511, Reviv CSI p. 81f., Pardee HAHL 91f. - d) + *ʿl pm*, *ktb hwšʿ ʿl pm ʾḥyʾb* Cowl

2^{18}: Ch. has written conform the instructions of A.; *ktbt ‘l pm bbt’* DBKP 22^{34}: I have written by order of B. (v. also *pm*) - QAL pass. to be written: ATNS $27^{3,5}$, Samar 8^{12f}, CIS ii 3913 i 8f., MPAT 61^{25} (v. supra), 64 i 4 (dam. context), 8, iii 3 (dam. context) - **1)** + b_2, *bšmr[yn] gṭ’ znh ktyb* Samar 3^{12}: this document is written in Sh.; *wyktb bšṭr ’gry’ ḥdt’* CIS ii 3913 i 8 : it should be written down in the new contract of lease; *wktb ‘m nmws’ qdmy’ bgll’* CIS ii 3913 i 9 : they will be written down (v. supra) together with the former law on the stele (v. *gll*) - QAL Part. pass., written, described, mentioned; *wš’rt nksyh zy ktybn* Krael $7^{27f.}$: and the rest of her goods, which are described (sc. above), cf. Krael 7^{23}, MPAT 61^{24} (= DBKP 15), DBKP 17^{42}, 18^{69}, 20^{42} - a) + b_2, *spry ktb bps [...* CIS i 6000 bis 8: his document written on [this] tablet (v. however supra); *byt’ zy tḥwmwhy ktybn bspr’ znh* Krael 10^{7}: the house, the boundaries of which are described in this document; *byt’ zy tḥwmwhy wmšḥth ktybn wmlwhy ktybn bspr’ znh* Krael 9^{16}: the house the boundaries and measurements of which are described - and the details of which are described - in this document (for the context, cf. also Grelot DAE p. 245 (n. n)); cf. Cowl 10^{8}, 18^{2}, Krael 12^{22}, CIS ii 3913 ii 87, MPAT 64 i 2, etc. - b) + l_5 + b_2, *mn dy ktyb lh tn’ mqbr bšṭry ḥrmy’* CIS ii 350^{5}: he for whom a contract to bury is written down in the deeds containing the consecration formulae (v. also *ḥrm₃*) - c) + mn_5 - **1)** + *mn l‘l* (= l_5 + ‘l_1), *hyk dy ktyb mn l‘l* CIS ii 3913 ii 68: as it is written above (cf. RIP 25^{11} :: Bounni AAS xi/xii 150f.: connect *ktyb* with following *lbt*) - **2)** + *mn ltḥt* (= l_5 + *tḥt*), *zy ktyb mn ltḥt* CIS ii 3913 i 4: what is written below - **3)** + *mn ‘l(’)*, *ksp’ zy ktyb mn ‘l’* Cowl 5^{10}: the silver mentioned above; *zk byt’ zy tḥwmwhy ktybn mn ‘l* Cowl 25^{8}: this house, the boundaries of which are described above; cf. Cowl 5^{13}, $35^{7f.}$, Krael $11^{8,9}$, etc. - **4)** + *mn ‘l* + b_2, *byt’ znh zy tḥwmwhy mn ‘l ktb bspr’ znh* Krael $10^{15f.}$: this house, the boundaries of which are described above in this document (v. supra) - d) + ‘l_7, *šmy ktb ‘l ydhyhm* KAI 233^{12}: my name is written on their hands; *zy l’ ktb ‘l spr ’nttky* Krael 10^{7}: which is not mentioned in your marriage contract - e) + *‘l’*, *mh dy ‘l’ ktyb* CIS ii $199^{6f.}$: what is written above (cf. CIS ii 198^{7}, 212^{7}, 217^{7}); *lhn lmn dy ‘l’ ktyb* CIS ii 197^{8}: except the people mentioned above (cf. CIS ii 199^{5}); *‘bd‘bdt ’bwh ‘l’ ktyb* (reading uncert.) CIS ii 224^{4}: his father A., mentioned above - QAL Part. act. (or = *ktb₃* (= *ktwb*)?), scribe: CIS ii 416, 825^{2}, $2667^{4f.}$, J 18^{4}, 190, RES 1479^{2} (v. however supra), PNO 47a 5 - PI‘EL to inscribe: KAI 160^{2} (v. however supra) - NIPH Part. prescribed: NP 130^{4} (v. supra) - ITP - **1)** to be written; + b_2, *mtktb b’gwry’* CIS ii 3913 i 5: written in the contract of lease (v. also *’gr₃*) - **2)** to inscribe for oneself; + l_5 + b_2 + obj., *ytktb lh bh mwhbh* J 38^{7}: he will inscribe for himself on it a title-deed of donation (?, uncert. interpret.; or: for

whom there will be written on it a ..., cf. Brockelmann OLZ '34, 690) - Cowl a.l.: the *ktb* in Cowl 42[14] poss. = QAL Pf. 3 p.s.m. (dam. context; Porten & Yardeni sub TADAE A 3.8: = QAL Part. pass. s.m. abs.) - for the *ktb* (mistakenly explained as QAL Pf. 3 p.s.m.) in BSOAS xvi 227 no. 81[2], cf. Strugnell BASOR clvi 31 (div. otherwise): l. *ʾlktbʾ* = n.d. - for the *ktbʾ* (mistakenly explained as QAL Part. act. s.m. emph.) in J 142[1], cf. Strugnell BASOR clvi 31 (div. otherwise): l. *tym lktbʾ* = n.p. - *mktbh* in RES 492A 2, B 7 poss. = QAL Inf. + suff. 3 p.s.m./f., cf. e.g. Lidzbarski Eph ii 241, 401, for A 2, cf. also Grelot DAE p. 139 × Grelot DAE p. 141: in B 7 = PUʿAL Part. s.f. abs. :: Halévy RS xii 57, 64f., Chabot RES a.l.: = Sing. + suff. 3 p.s.m. of *mktb* (= letter) - for this root and its derivatives in Punic, cf. Bonnet SEL vii 111ff.
v. *yhb*,*yšb*$_1$,*ktb*$_2$, *ktwm*, *mktb*, *šwb*, *tʾrh*.

ktb$_2$ **Pun** Sing. cstr. (?, diff. context; Février Sem ii 26: = Sing. abs.) *ktʿb* KAI 138[5] (for this reading, cf. Dussaud BAr '17, 166, Février Sem ii 26, Sznycer Sem xxx 36, 40 :: Röllig KAI a.l. (div. otherwise): l. *knʿ* = QAL Pf. 3 p.pl. of *kwn*$_1$:: Lidzbarski Eph iii 290 (div. otherwise): l. poss. *kn* (= QAL Pf. 3 p.s.m. of *kwn*$_1$):: Dussaud BAr '14, 619f. (div. otherwise): l. *ʿknʿk* (= first part of n.p.)) - **Hebr** Sing. + suff. 3 p.s.m. *ktbh* HUCA xl/xli 159[1] (cf. Dever ibid. 159, Avigad with Dever ibid. 160 n. 39, Garbini AION xxviii 192f., Catastini Hen vi 133, O'Connor VT xxxvii 224, Zevit BASOR cclv 43f. × Mittmann ZDPV xcvii 141f., Hadley VT xxxvii 51, 53 = QAL Pf. 3 p.s.m. + suff. 3 p.s.f. of *ktb*$_1$,cf. also Cross with Dever HUCA xl/xli 160 n. 39, Naveh BASOR ccxxxv 28, Zevit MLAHE 17, Spronk BAAI 308, Margalit VT xxxix 373, Shea VT xl 110, Smelik HDAI 139 :: Lemaire RB lxxxiv 599ff., Angerstorfer BN xvii 9: = PIʿEL Pf. 3 p.s.m. + suff. 3 p.s.f. (?) of *ktb*$_1$,cf. Zevit BASOR cclv 44: or = PIʿEL 3 p.s.m. + suff. 3 p.s.f. (?) of *ktb*$_1$) - **OffAr** Sing. abs. *ktb* FX 136[19] (cf. Teixidor Syr lii 289 :: Dupont-Sommer FX 137, 152f. = QAL Pf. 3 p.s.m. of *ktb*$_1$;v. infra); emph. *ktbʾ* AE '23, 42 no. 16 - **Nab** Sing. abs. *ktb* CIS ii 197[3,7], 198[9], 206[5,6], 209[7], 212[4], 215[3], 219[5], 222[4], 224[3,10]; cstr. *ktb* MPAT 64 i 3, 4; emph. *ktbʾ* CIS ii 198[10], 207[6], J 18[4], RES 529[3] (?; cf. Levinson NAI 177); + suff. 3 p.s.m. *ktbh* CIS ii 197[8], DBKP 22[32,33]; Plur. abs. *ktbyn* MPAT 64 ii 4 - **Palm** Sing. abs. *ktb* CIS ii 3913 ii 100; emph. *ktbʾ* CIS ii 3998B 6 (= RIP 130[15]); Plur. emph. *ktbyʾ* Syr xvii 353[4,8] - **Hatra** Sing. emph. *ktbʾ* 101[2], 235[2] - **JAr** Sing. emph. *ktbh* MPAT 51[14] (*k[t]bh*), SM 101[2] (= Frey 826a) - ¶ subst. m. something written - **1)** document: MPAT 51[14], 64 i 3, 4, ii 4, CIS ii 197[3,7], 198[9], 3913 ii 100 (for the context, v. *ṭʿwn*$_1$), Syr xvii 353[4,8] (for the context, cf. also Milik DFD 301ff.), etc. - **2)** inscription: AE '23, 42 no. 16, CIS ii 197[8], 206[6], 212[4], 219[5], 224[10], RIP 130[15], J 18[4], SM 101[2] - *dth dk ktb zy mhṣsn* (prob. lapsus for *mhḥsn* (v. *ḥsn*$_1$)) FX 136[19]: this law is a document giving title of possession (?,

uncert. interpret.; cf. Teixidor Syr lii 289, cf. however Dupont-Sommer FX 137, 151f.: = this law, he has written (it), (he) who is master (of the decision), less prob. interpret., v. also supra) - a Dual abs. (*[k]tbyn*) in DJD ii 29 verso 3?? (cf. Milik DJD ii a.l.) - on this word in Nab. texts, cf. Greenfield Mem Yalon 73f.
v. *ktb_1*.

ktb_3 v. *ktb_1*.

ktb_4 **Palm** Sing. cstr. *ktb* MUSJ xxxviii 106^3 - ¶ subst. in the comb. *ktb ydy* = the writing of my hand (i.e. my writing-skill).

$ktbh_1$ **Pun** Sing. abs. (or cstr.) *ktbt* KAI 69^{18} (cf. l. 17: *ktb[t]*); cstr. *ktbt* KAI 124^3 - **OffAr** Sing. emph. *ktbt›* RES 492B 4, ASAE xxxix 353^3 (reading *ktybt›* erroneous), *ktybt›* ASAE xxxix $357^{2,9}$ (*ktyb[t›]*, diff. reading) - **JAr** Sing. cstr. *ktbt* MPAT 63^1; + suff. 2 p.s.f. *ktbtyk* MPAT 42^{10} (*[k]tbtyk*)^{,13,16} (*[kt]btyk*), v. infra - ¶ subst. f. what is written - **1)** document, text (for KAI 124^3, v. *dbr_3* and for the context, v. also *b_2* sub 3a); in RES 492B 4 indicating a mark of ownership on the arm of a slave, cf. Driver AnOr xii 57 - **2)** specialized meaning, marriage deed: MPAT $42^{10,13,16}$, 63^1 (or = *$ktbh_2$*?).

$ktbh_2$ v. *$ktbh_1$*.

ktdr v. *kndr*.

ktwb **Palm** Sing. emph. *ktwb›* Syr vii 129^7 - ¶ subst. scribe, secretary (cf. Milik DFD 151, Aggoula Syr lii 206, cf. already Ingholt Syr vii 138).
v. *ktb_1*.

ktwm **JAr** the diff. *ktwm* in AMB 4^1 poss. = lapsus for *ktwb* (= QAL Imper. s.m. of *ktb_1*),cf. Naveh & Shaked AMB a.l.

ktwn v. *ktn_2*.

ktybh v. *$ktbh_1$*.

ktl **Hebr** Plur. + suff. 3 p.s.m. *kwtlyw* SM 75^3 - **Palm** Sing. abs. *ktl* MUSJ xxviii 106^{11}; emph. *ktl›* RIP $127^{3,4}$; + suff. 3 p.s.f. *ktlh* SBS 9 - ¶ subst. wall: SBS 9, SM 75^3; *wktl› dy qd[m] bt gb› wktl› dy br› w ... ktl› dy [l]bn›* RIP $127^{3ff.}$: the wall which is before the water-reservoir, the outside wall and ... the mudbrick wall; for *ktl dy ḥwr›*, v. *ḥwr* - prob. not < Akkad., cf. Kaufman AIA 65 (cf. also Garbini AION xxiii 275) :: e.g. Zimmern Fremdw 32, 45, Marrassini FLEM 21f. : < Akkad.

ktm **Pun** Février BAr '51/52, 42f.: l. *ktmm* (= Plur. abs. of *ktm* (= stone with inscription)) in KAI 165^4 (cf. v.d.Branden RSF ii 145f.: = plaquette), less prob. interpret., cf. Levi Della Vida OA iv 63, 65 (div. otherwise; for this division of words, cf. also Chabot sub Punica xvi 1): l. *ktm* (= *nomen gentis*) *m-* (v. *$mṣ›_1$*).

ktn_1 **Ph** Sing. abs. *ktn* KAI 24^{12} (or = *ktn_2*?) - **OffAr** Sing. abs. *ktn* Cowl 20^5, 26^{14}, 55^{10} (heavily dam. context, for the reading, cf. Porten & Yardeni sub TADAE A 3.2 recto 5 :: Cowl a.l. l. *ntn* (= form of

ntn)), Krael 7[11,12] (dam. context)[,13], SSI ii 28 rev. 4, NESE iii 16[2] (= addition to Cowl 49), ATNS 10a ii 1, 20[4], 64a 11; emph. *ktn*ʾ Cowl 26[20] - ¶ subst. - **1)** flax: ATNS 10a ii 1, 20[4] - **2)** linen: KAI 24[12], Cowl 29[5], 26[14], etc. (cf. Driver JRAS '32, 78f. :: Cowl a.l.: = cotton) - for the etymology, cf. e.g. Zimmern Fremdw 37 (prob. < Akkad.), Kaufman AIA 28.
v. *ktn*$_2$, *qṭy*$_2$, *qtn*.

ktn$_2$ **OffAr** Sing. abs. *ktn* Cowl 42[10], Driv 13[3] (or = *ktn*$_1$?, cf. however Grelot DAE p. 327 n. b), Herm 2[11], SSI ii 28 rev. 4 (for this prob. reading, cf. Porten FS Bresciani 432, cf. also Porten & Yardeni sub TADAE A 3.3), *ktwn* Cowl 42[8,9,13], SSI ii 28 rev. 2, ASAE xlviii 112B 2; emph. *ktnh* Herm 4[4,6]; + suff. 3 p.s.m. *ktwnh* Aḥiq 41, *kytwnh* ATNS 51[2] (or + suff. 3 p.s.f.?, dam. context); + suff. 2 p.s.m. *ktwnk* SSI ii 28 rev. 2; + suff. 1 p.s. *ktwny* ASAE xxvi 27[1], Sach 76 ii B 2, 6 (for the reading, cf. Lidzbarski Eph iii 256 :: Sach a.l.: l. *rtwny* (= n.p.?)) - ¶ subst. m. (cf. Cowl 42[10]; cf. however Herm 4[4,6]: f.) tunic, garment - for the etymology, cf. e.g. Kaufman AIA 28; for the relationship with Greek κιτών, χιτών, etc., cf. e.g. Fensham VT xii 196ff., Kutscher JSS x 25f., Brown JSS x 219, xxv 7ff., Masson RPAE 27ff.
v. *ktn*$_1$.

ktp$_1$ **Hebr** Sing. cstr. *ktp* IEJ v 165 - ¶ subst. side; for the context, v. *ṣr*$_1$ - for *ktp*$_1$, cf. also Kallai IEJ xv 177.

ktp$_2$ **JAr** Plur. emph. *ktpty*ʾ Mas 556[5] (diff. and dam. context) - ¶ subst. porter.

ktr$_1$ **Pun** QAL Inf. cstr., cf. Poen 949: *ctor* (cf. Sznycer PPP 129 :: L.H.Gray AJSL xxxix 80: = Sing. abs. of *ktr*$_2$ (= mansion) :: Schroed 287, 291f.: = lapsus for *sor* (= Sing. abs. of *š*ʿ*r*$_1$)) - **OffAr** PAʿEL Part. s.m. abs. *mktr* Beh 6 (*mkt[r]*, Akkad. par. *i-dag-ga-lu-*ʾ), 11 (*[m]ktr*; Akkad. par. *i-dag-ga-lu*); cf. Frah xx 11 (*ktlwn*), cf. Toll ZDMG-Suppl viii 38 - ¶ verb QAL to wait for: Poen 949 (diff. context, uncert. interpret.; v. supra) - PAʿEL - **1)** to remain, to stay: Frah xx 11 - **2)** to wait for + *l*$_5$: Beh 11 (cf. prob. also Beh 6) - a form of this root in DA v c 2?? (cf. Hoftijzer a.l.) - v.Soden Or xxxv 12f., xlvi 188, AHW s.v. *katāru* II: > Akkad. *katāru* = to wait, cf. however CAD s.v. *katāru* B: = to think, to hesitate?
v. *ntyrh*.

ktr$_2$ v. *ktr*$_1$.

ktrt **Pun** Sing. abs. *ktrt* KAI 160[1] (or Plur.?; for this prob. interpret., cf. Levi Della Vida RCL '55, 556 n. 2 :: Février Sem iv 21, Röllig KAI a.l. (cf. also Teixidor Syr xlv 357): = *qṭrt*), *kt*ʿ*rt* KAI 119[2] - ¶ subst. capital (architectural term; cf. also Amadasi IPT 76).

ktš **Hebr** QAL Part. pass. s.f. abs. *ktwšh* Mas 516 - **Samal** QAL (or PAʿEL?) Impf. 3 p.pl.m. + suff. 3 p.s.m. *lktšh* KAI 214[31] (cf. e.g. Gibson ii p. 69, 76, Dion p. 34 :: e.g. Cooke NSI p. 163, 171, Friedr 17*, Donner KAI a.l., Sader EAS 164: = Impf. 3 p.s.m. + suff. 3 p.s.m.); 3 p.pl.f. + suff. 3 p.s.f. *lktšnh* KAI 214[31] (for the forms, cf. Dion p. 166ff., 463 :: Dahood Or xlv 383: = l_1 + QAL Pf.) - **OffAr** QAL (or PA ‘EL?) Pf. 3 p.s.m. *ktš* Driv 12[9]; 2 p.s.m. *ktšt* Cowl 7[5]; 1 p.s. *ktšt* Cowl 7[9]; 3 p.pl.m. + suff. 1 p.s. *ktšwny* ATNS 30a 5 (cf. also Porten & Yardeni sub TADAE B 8.4); Impf. 3 p.s.m. *yktš* (?) AG 58[2]; 3 p.pl.m. *yktšwn* AG 70; cf. GIPP 55 - ¶ verb QAL to press; Part. pass.: pressed; *dblh ktwšh* Mas 516: a pressed fig-cake (cf. also Yadin & Naveh Mas a.l.) - QAL (or PA ‘EL) to beat, to crush - 1) + obj., *grd› ... ktš* Driv 12[8f.]: he has beaten up the domestic staff ... (cf. ATNS 30a 5) - 2) + b_2, *plktšh b›bny* KAI 214[31]: let them pound him with stones (i.e. let them stone him to death; for the context, cf. also Poeb 44) - **3)** + l_5, *wktšt l›ntty* Cowl 7[5]: you struck my wife (cf. Cowl 7[9]) - the *k* in Mas 517 poss. abbrev. for *ktwš* (= QAL Part. pass.; cf. Yadin & Naveh Mas a.l.).

ktt v. *nt‘*.

L

l1 particle with precative function - **1)** + Pf., cf. *li pho caneth yth bynuthi* Poen 932: that I may find my daughters here; *lš‘m[›] ›t q›l[›]* Punica xi 18[3f.]: may he hear his voice (for this interpret., cf. Sznycer PPP 61f. :: Chabot Punica a.l.: *l* is part of prec. n.p.); *lšm› ql›* Hofra 216[3]: may he hear his voice (cf. Sznycer PPP 61f.); cf. also FR 257e, 317c - **2)** + Impf., *lyšm‘ ql›* Hofra 32[3]: may he hear his voice (cf. Sznycer PPP 61f., FR 257e, 317b, Röllig CISFP i 384 × Février with Berthier & Charlier Hofra p. 34 (div. otherwise): l. *ly* (= orthogr. variant of l_1) + *šm‘* (= QAL Pf. 3 p.s.m. of *šm‘*$_1$)) - for KAI 27[22], v. ›l_3 - cf. also the Impf. instances with modal function where *ly* > *l*: KAI 214[23] (v. *btk*),[24] (*lmn‘* :: Garb 262: = l_5 + QAL Inf. of *mn‘*, v. also *mn‘*),[30,31] (*lktšh, lktšnh* :: Dahood Or xlv 383, v. also *ktš*), Tell F 11, 12, 18f., 19, 20, 21, 22 (cf. Friedr 17*, 41*, Dion p. 166f., Abou-Assaf, Bordreuil & Millard Tell F p. 58f., Kaufman Maarav iii 150, Muraoka AN xxii 96ff., cf. however also Huehnergard JAOS ciii 576ff., 589f.) - Rocco AION xxiv 475f.: l_1 + Imper. in ibid. ll. 1, 3, 4 (= GR ii no. 20; highly uncert. interpret., diff. context, cf. also Polselli GR ii a.l.) - on l_1, cf. also Garr DGSP 118f.
v. *ll*$_3$, *lqṭ*, *mr›*, *ptḥ*$_1$.

l2 v. *l›*$_1$.

l3 v. l_5, *nss*$_1$, *pḥṣ*.

l4 v. *l›*$_2$.

l5 for transcriptions - **1)** from Ph./Pun., cf. a) *l*: IRT 828[1] (for the context, v. *ʾb*$_1$), IRTS 24^2 (for the context, v. *ʾb*$_1$), OA ii 83^2 (for the context, v. *ʾb*$_1$), λ: KAI 175^1 - b) *li*: Poen 9352, IRT 873^4 (cf. Levi Della Vida OA ii 79, 93, Vattioni AION xvi 45, Aug xvi 542, Polselli OAC xiii 236f.), cf. poss. also LibAnt i 45^1 (for this interpret., cf. Février BAr-NS i 226, cf. also Vattioni Aug xvi 553f.) - c) *ly*: IRT 827^1 (cf. Levi Della Vida OA ii 85, 93, Vattioni AION xvi 47f., Aug xvi 538f., Krahmalkov JSS xvii 72), 906^3 (cf. Vattioni AION xvi 50, Aug xvi 550 :: Levi Della Vida OA ii 73, 93: = *l*$_5$ + suff. 3 p.s.m.), λυ: KAI 175^2 - d) *la*: Poen 938 (cf. Sznycer PPP 104), λα: KAI 174^8 (poss. interpret., cf. Sznycer Sem viii 9 :: Röllig KAI a.l. (div. otherwise): l. λ (= *l*$_5$) :: Milik MUSJ xxxi 10: l. [α]λα = *ʿlt*) - e) *lo* (+ suff. 3 p.s.m.): Dréd 5^{19} (= IRT 886e; highly uncert. interpret., cf. Levi Della Vida OA ii 82, 93, Vattioni Aug xvi 546) - f) *lu*: IRT 901^5 (prob. interpret.; for the context, v. *bn*$_1$ sub Sing. f.; :: Polselli StudMagr xi 40: l. *ly*) - g) Levi Della Vida OA ii 78f., 93: the diff. *lil* in IRT 828^2 = lapsus for *l*$_5$ (diff. context, uncert. interpret., v. also *ʾš*$_1$) - **2)** from Aramaic, cf. λα in the transcribed text PEQ '38, 238^1 (cf. e.g. Peters OLZ '40, 218f., Beyer ATTM 353; cf. also Milik LA x 154f.) - > Akkad. *la* (< Ar.), cf. v. Soden Or xxxv 13, xlvi 189 (cf. idem AHW s.v. *la*), cf. also CAD s.v. *la* (prep.): < NWSem.; cf. also Frah xxiv 1-5, 9 (in the combinations *ly*, *lk*, *lnh*, *lkwm*, *lznh*), xxv 1 (in the comb. *lʾlʾ*, v. also *ʿl*$_1$), Paik 579, 580 (*lḥw*), 586 (*ly*), 587 (*lk*), 588 (*lkm*), 589 (*lkwm*), 590 (in the comb. *lkʿn*), 591 (*ln*), 592, 593 (*lnh*), 594 (in the comb. *lʿyny*), 596, 597 (in the comb. *lṣd*), Sogd B 275, Syr xxxv 325^{59}, BSOAS xxxiii 152^{11}, GIPP 26, 27, 56, SaSt 22 (cf. Toll ZDMG-Suppl viii 39f.) - ¶ prep. (on this prep., cf. also Pennachietti AION xxiv 181ff.) - **1)** indicating direction, local-terminative: to, towards; *hksp ʾš šlḥt ly* KAI 50^3: the silver which you have sent to me; *hḥṣ z lmqm šʿr hḥdš* RCL '66, 201^1: this street (leading) to the square of the new gate (for the context, cf. Dupont-Sommer CRAI '68, 121f., v. also *ḥṣ*$_2$, *mqm*$_1$); *šlḥ lzp mhrh* TA-H 17^5: send (it) quickly to Z.; *whʿbr ʾby mn dmšq lʾšr* KAI 215^{18}: and he brought my father (i.e. his mortal remains) across from D. to A.; *ʾtw lbyrt yb* Cowl 30^8: they came to the fortress of Yeb; *blny lbytk* Aḥiq 52: take me to your house; *ʾl thrkb ḥtk lṣdyq* Aḥiq 126: do not shoot your arrow at a righteous man; *mn mwʿh lmʿrb šmš* Krael 12^7: from east to west; *lʾ ... ybyl lhm* ATNS 2^4: he was not brought to them; *lmnpq lṣd pnh* ATNS 26a 3: to go out in the direction of P. (v. *pnh*$_1$); *ʾtyh ltpmt* Herm 1^{10}: send it to T.; *lmwšrthm lkn* Herm 2^{13}: to send them to you; *šlḥt lnbwntn* Cowl $54^{2f.}$: I have sent (a message) to N.; *ʿwtʾl ... dy nḥt lšrʾ* J $109^{1f.}$: A. ... who has descended to S.; *ʿlymyʾ dy mtʾʿlyn ltdmr* CIS ii 3913 ii 2: the slaves who are imported into T.; *mʿlyk lgw* FS Miles 38^2: when you proceed (further) the inside; *šlḥt lk try ḥmryn* MPAT 60^1: I have sent to you two asses; *glʾ lbbl* MPAT 68^5: he went into exile to B.; *lkh htyt* MPAT 70[1]: I have brought hither (v. *ʾty*$_1$); etc., etc. - a) with *verba dicendi*, *ʾmr lʾḥty* KAI 50[2]: speak to my sister; *wyʾmr ly kmš* KAI 181[14]: and K. said to me; *wyʾmr lzy lydʿ* KAI 223C 7f.: and he will say to the witless one; *ʾmr ʿnnyh ... lmšlm* Krael 2[1f.]: A. has said to M.; *qr lh wʿny* CIS ii 4038[4]: he has called to him and he (i.e. the god) has answered; *ʾlyšʿ ʾmr lk* MPAT 55[2f.]: E. says to you; *qbln lpḥwtʾ* SSI ii 28 obv. 4: we have complained to the officials; etc. - b) at the beginning of a message/letter, *snyʾ lrmnʾ* Aḥiq 165: bramble to pomegranate; *šmʿwn ... lyhwntn* MPAT 53[1]: Sh. ... to Y.; *mšmʿwn ... lyšʿ* DJD ii 43[1]: from Sh. ... to Y.; etc.; cf. also *lḥšt lʿtʾ* KAI 27[1]: incantation against A. (for this interpret., cf. e.g. du Mesnil du Buisson FS Dussaud 424f., Dupont-Sommer RHR cxx 134f., Torczyner JNES vi 19, 28, Rosenthal ANET 658, Röllig KAI a.l., Avishur PIB 248f., Garbini OA xx 280, 283, 287, 292, Sperling HUCA liii 3, Gibson SSI iii p. 83f., (cf. however Caquot Syr xlviii 379 n. 1, JANES v 46f.) :: e.g. Albright BASOR lxxvi 7 (n. 7), Gaster Or xi 44, Cross & Saley BASOR cxcvii 45, Röllig NESE ii 18ff.: = *l*$_3$ (= exclamation: ôh); cf. also Cross CBQ xxxvi 488 (n. 16); v. also *lḥšh*); cf. also KAI 27[4] (:: Teixidor AO i 106: reading *dl* preferable to *wl* and interpret. of *l* as *l*$_5$ highly uncert.),[19], Syr xlviii 396[1] - c) with verbal form of *ktb*$_1$, *bʾgrtʾ dy ktb lsṭṭyls* CIS ii 3913 ii 104: in a letter he wrote to S. (cf. CIS ii 3913 ii 121) - d) with verbal form of *ptḥ*$_1$, *wtrʿʾ .. ptyḥ lšwq mlkʾ* Krael 12[21]: and the gate ... opens towards the royal street; *zbnt lk ... lbth dyly dy ptyḥ ṣpn lgh drty dy tptḥnh lgh btk* MPAT 51[3f.]: I have sold to you ... my house which opens at the north side into my courtyard so that you may open it into your house (v. *ptḥ*$_1$) - e) with verbal forms of *verba movendi* used figuratively, *hn mṭt mrbytʾ lršʾ* Cowl 10[6]: if the interest is added to the capital; *kl dy ʿll. lḥšbn tgrʾ* CIS ii 3913 ii 115: everything that comes into the market (v. *ḥšbn*$_1$) - **2)** indicating the presence on a certain place, locative: on, at; *wmḥsm ḥrṣ lpy* KAI 11: there is a golden bridle on my mouth (v. *mḥsm*); *ʾl ykn lm šrš lmṭ wpr lmʿl* KAI 14[11f.]: may they have no root below nor branches above (for the context, v. *pry*$_2$); *lʿlyh lh byt štbr ltḥtyh lh tmy zy ḥnwm ʾlhʾ* Krael 3[7f.]: to the north of it is the house of Sh., to the south of it the *tmy* of the god Ch. (v. *ʿlyh*, *tmy*$_2$); *byty ʾnh drgmn lmwʿ šmš mn[h]* Cowl 6[8]: my house (of me, D.) is to the east of it; *ʾwṣrʾ zy mlkʾ dbq lh* Krael 3[9]: the king's treasury adjoins it; *mndʿm mḥbl [lʾ] ʾštkḥ ln* Cowl 27[2]: nothing bad was found in us (v. *ḥbl*$_1$); *kl ʿrbn zy tškḥ ly* Cowl 10[9]: any security that you may find with me; *wšbq kl gšr zy tškḥ lmmh* Herm 3[10]: and leave every beam you will find with M. (for this interpret., cf. e.g. Porten & Greenfield ZAW lxxx 225, Porten Arch 101, Hayes & Hoftijzer VT xx 103, Grelot DAE p. 158 :: Bresciani & Kamil Herm a.l., Gibson SSI ii p. 136: *lmmh* is beginning of a new clause: for M.);

l'l mnh CIS ii 3911[3f.]: on him; *lgw mn ṣlmy ʾln* RIP 21[3f.]: behind these images; *nk[s]yhwn dlbr wlgw* Hatra 79[8f.]: their possessions which are outside and inside (i.e. all their possessions); etc. - a) with a verbal form of the root *dbq* used figuratively, *wlbby lh dbq lh* Herm 4[5]: and my heart is not attached to it (i.e. I do not like it) - b) combined with form of *ʿyn*$_2$, *lʿn ʾlnm wlʿn ʿm ʾrṣ z* KAI 10[10]: before the gods and the people of this land; *lʿynwhy* Cowl 41[7]: in his presence (dam. context); etc. - c) combined with form of *pnh*$_1$, *lpny ʾdrʾ ʾlpqy wʿm ʾlpq[y]* KAI 126[7]: before the notables of L. and the people of L. (for the context, v. *ʿm*$_1$); *wʾsḥb hm lpny kmš* KAI 181[18]: and I dragged them before K.; etc. - d) for *lyd*, v. *yd* sub A 3 - **3)** with temporal meaning: in, during; *lʾḥrh* KAI 226[8]: in the future; *lqdmyn* Cowl 32[10]: formerly (cf. Nisa-b 526[1], etc., cf. also *l[qd]mt* Nisa-b 1318 + 1406[6]); *lʿlm* RIP 105[5]: for ever; *lmḥr ywm ʾḥrn* Cowl 1[4]: tomorrow or another day (v. *ʾḥrn*); *lywmn ʾḥrnn šgyʾn* Aḥiq 49f.: many days after; *lmmṭh mrd[y]ʾ ʾtknšw* Beh 8: upon arrival the rebels rallied; *lrš yrḥʾ* FX 136[15]: at the beginning of the month; *lšnt 23 lyrḥ tšrʾ* PF 1820: in the 23rd year, in the month T. (in this combination normally: *byrḥ*, cf. e.g. PF 1816, 1819); v. also *pnh*$_1$ - **4)** with temporal meaning: to; *mšbt lšbt* AMB 4[30]: from week to week (cf. AMB 2[29,30f.,31]) - **5)** with possessive meaning: belonging to, of; *lʿzm ʿbd ʿzrbʿl* Gall 14 (= SANSS-App A 71; the reading *ʿzbʿl* mistaken): (seal) belonging to A., the servant of A.; *lṣr/lṣdnym/lṣdn* on Ph. coins (coin) of Tyre/of the Sidonians/of Sidon (cf. Hill cvi, cxxxiii, Meshorer Mas 3676); cf. also *lnrgl trz* on coin (BMQ xxxvi 98; for the reading, cf. Teixidor Syr li 316); *lnḥm ʿbdy* Dir bol 7 (= SANSS-Hebr 13): (seal) of N. (the son of) A.; *ldmlyhw bn nryhw* Dir sig. 19 (= Vatt sig. eb. 19 = SANSS-Hebr 151, cf. also for the reading Dir a.l.): seal of D. the son of N.; *lṣdq* TA-H 93: (jar) belonging to Ṣ.; *lbnḥdš* ... KAI 55[1]: of B. ...; *lšʾyl kmrʾ zy nbw* AG 99[1]: (sarcophagus) of Sh. the Priest of N.; *bymn šnytt mqrʾ ʾrmyt kznh lmbṭḥyh* Cowl 28[4f.]: at the right of the tattoo in the Aramaic language (reading) thus: belonging to M.; *mšlm br zkwr ʾrmy zy swn ldgl wryzt* Krael 2[2f.]: M. the son of Z., Aramean from S., belonging to the detachment of W. (v. *dgl*$_1$; for *mn dgl* with the same meaning, v. *mn*$_5$); *lḥyn br kwzʾ* CIS ii 227: (tomb) of Ch. the son of K.; *lrmʾl br ḥyw* J 45: (graffito) of R. the son of Ch. (cf. J 46); *lbny ḥšš* RTP 457: (Tessere) of the Bene Ch.; etc., etc.; for *lmlk* (belonging to the king) on weights, measures and jars, v. *mlk*$_3$; cf. the following usages: - a) as so-called *l-genitivi*, *ksʾt lṭbry* KAI 122[2]: the throne of T.; *lḥn lyhw ʾlhʾ* Krael 3[3]: *lḥn* (v. *lḥn*$_2$) of the god Y.; *lʾ hwt ʾrq ldrgmn zyly* Cowl 6[7]: it was not the plot of D. (i.e.) mine; *pyʾ br pḥy ʾrdykl lswn* Cowl 14[1f.]: P. the son of A. architect of S.; *br lk* Krael 3[14]: a son of yours; *lṣlmyn lmqymw br mqymw ʿrymʾ wb[n]why qrbw mqymw br mqymw ʿrymʾ wyrḥybwlʾ* ... InscrP 36: M. the son of M., A. and

Y. ... have offered statues of M. the son of M. A. and his children; cf. also *lṭnnw br ḥnʾl npšʾ* RES 1093[1]: the tomb of Ṭ. (cf. *lmlkw ḥyrn lṣlm* Inv xi 95, *lbwrpʾ ... lṣlm* Inv xi 98a, *lṣlm rpbwl...* Inv xi 98b 1); etc. - b) used in indications of dates - α) preceding an indication of a person, *bšnt 37 lmlk pmyytn* KAI 33[1]: in the 37th year of king P.; *b 35 lmlk* IEJ xxxvii 28D: in the 35th (year) of the king (cf. IEJ xxxvii 28E); *bšnn 7 lmlkʾ drwš* MAI xiv/2, 66[7]: in the 7th year of king D. *byrḥ tšry šnt šbʿ lqldys qysr* CIS ii 170[1f.]: in the month T. of the 7th year of the emperor C.; *[šn]t trtyn lnrwn qsr* MPAT 39[1]: the second year of the emperor N.; etc. - β) preceding the indication of a period, *bšnt ʿsr wʾrbʿ lmlky mlk ʾšmnʿzr* KAI 14[1]: in the 14th year of the reign of king E.; *bymm 6 lyrḥ bl* KAI 32[1]: on the sixth day of the month B.; *b 1 lḥdš* TA-H 7[3f.]: on the first of the month; *ywm ḥd lṭbt* FuB xiv 13[2f.]: the first day of the month Ṭ.; *b 18 lʾlwl* Cowl 5[1]: on the 18th (day) of (the month) E.; *[b ... lḥtḥwr* ATNS 30a 5: on the ...th (day) of (the month) Ch. (for the context, cf. Porten & Yardeni sub TADAE B 8.4); *b 3 llšbṭ* Samar 3[11]: on the third (day) of (the month) Sh. (cf. Samar 6[1]); *[byw]m 10 ltšry* Assur 29j 1: on the 10th day of (the month) T.; *šnt tlt lḥrt yšrʾl* MPAT 51[1]: the 3rd year of the liberation of Israel; *b 5 lʾyr* Mas 564[1]: on the fifth of (the month) I.; etc., etc. - c) in combination with a *nota relationis*, *ʾdn ʾš ly* KAI 43[9,10]: my lord; *qbʿm šl ksp* Mus li 286[4]: goblets of silver; *hʾš šlʾ* NP 130[3]: her husband; *hkhn šlʾ* Punica xii 11[2]: his priest (for the reading, cf. Jongeling NINPI 51; cf. also KAI 100[5]); *bymarob syllohom* Poen 933: under their protection; *hprnsyn šl byt mškw* DJD ii 42[1]: the administrators of B.M.; *ʿbdn hmw zly* KAI 233[13]: they are my servants; *bytʾ zyly* Cowl 5[4]: my house; *ʿlym zyly* Driv 8[1]: a servant of mine; *dgl[ʾ] zy ln* ATNS 3[6]: our detachment (for the reading, cf. Porten & Yardeni sub TADAE B 8.10); *kprʾ dy lhgrw* CIS ii 203[1]: the tomb of H.; *bgrmṭyʾ dy lh* InscrP 6[3]: during his secretaryship; *drth dyly* MPAT 51[10]: my courtyard; etc., etc.; for *nota relationis* + l_5 without antecedent, cf. *hn hšb zyly* KAI 224[20]: if he has returned mine (i.e. my fugitive); *ynṣr zylk* KAI 225[13f.]: may what is yours be guarded (v. *nṣr*$_1$); *zyly hy* Cowl 8[25]: it belongs to me; *mn dy lh* CIS ii 158[3]: from what is his (i.e. at his expense); etc., etc. - d) in the description of measures, *gmydh 1 zy qmr ḥdt lʾmn 6 b 4* Krael 7[7]: a new woollen garment of six cubits by four (v. *gmydh*); *pʿrʿr ḥd lʾmn tryn* Cowl 26[12]: a prow of two cubits (cf. Krael 7[6], etc.) - e) cf. also *lšr lhš[b]* KAI 200[12f.]: it is to the official (it is his duty) to return; for *ʾyty l*, v. *ʾyty*; for *hwy* + *l*, v. *hwy*$_1$ sub 1a); for *kwn* + *l*, v. *kwn*$_1$ sub 1a) - f) as so-called *lamed auctoris*: HUCA xl/xli 159[4] (*lʾnyhw*), cf. Dever HUCA xl/xli 159, 162, Lemaire RB lxxxiv 599, 602 (uncert. interpret.) - **5)** used as so-called *l-commodi/l-incommodi*: for, to; *qr z bny špṭbʿl ... lbʿlt gbl* KAI 7[1,3f.]: the wall which Sh. built for the mistress of G.;

ʾrn [z]n mgn ʾmtbʿ ... mtt lʿštrt ... KAI 29: this casket A. ... gave as a gift to A. (for the context, v. *znh*); *wpʿl ʾnk lrbty bʿlt gbl hmzbḥ nḥšt zn* KAI $10^{3f.}$: and I made this altar of bronze for my lady the mistress of G.; *mʾš z ṭynʾ lʾdn šdrpʾ bdmlqrt* KAI 127: B. has erected this statue for the lord Sh.; *hndr ʾš kn ndr ʾbnm ... lʾdnnm lršp* KAI 40^{5}: the vow which their father has vowed to their lord R.; *lzbḥm 2 qr 1* KAI 37A 9 (= Kition C 1): for the two sacrificers 1 *qr*; *wʾʿš hbmt zʾt lkmš* KAI 181^{3}: and I made this high place for K.; (in a list of deliveries) *lytb dšʾ* ... AUSS xiii 2^{9} (= CAI 80): for Y. hay ... (cf. ll. 3, 4, 5, 6); *wʿt ntn lktym yyn ...* TA-H $1^{1ff.}$: and now, give wine to the *Kittiyim*; *lšmryw mbʾrym nbl [yn] yšn* KAI $183^{1ff.}$: from Sh. from B. a jar of old wine; *hqmt nṣb zn lhdd* KAI 214^{1}: I have erected this stele for H.; *kʿšq ʿbyd ly* Cowl 16^{5}: a wrong was done to me; *bʿw bʾyš lʾgwrʾ zk* Cowl 30^{17}: they sought to do evil to that temple; *mḥʾh lʿlym* Aḥiq 83: a blow for a slave; *dšnyʾ lywm yldʾ zy plnyh* ATNS 41^{8}: presents for the birthday of P. (v. *plny*); *bnyky zy yldty ly* Krael 4^{7}: your children that you have borne me; *ḥlkyʾ zy mlkw ly* Driv 12^{4}: the Cilicians they promised me; *zbnt mšḥ zyt lyqh* Herm 2^{11}: I have bought olive oil for Y.; *šlm llḥrwṣ tnh* Herm $1^{3f.}$: it is well with Ch. here; *hb lpʾl š s 1* TA-Ar 5^{1}: give to P. barley, 1 *seah*; *npšh sy ḥmrt dy bnh lh ʾdymt bʿlh* CIS ii 162: the funerary monument of Ch., which O. her husband has constructed for her; *ḥdtw ʾtrʾ dnh lmrʾ bytʾ* CIS ii 235A 2: they have restaured this sanctuary (v. *ʾšr$_4$*) for the Lord of the House; *ʿltʾ dh lmlkbl wʾlhy tdmr qrb ṭbrys* CIS ii $3903^{1f.}$: this altar Ṭ. has offered to M. and the gods of T.; *ʿltʾ dnh ʿbdt mky ... lḥyh wlḥyʾ brth* CIS ii $4014^{2f.,5f.}$: this altar M. has made for her life and for the life of her daughter; (cf. also *ʿl ḥywhy ... wlḥyy bny ...* Inv xi $6^{6f.}$; v. also *ḥy$_1$*); *ʾḥbr lšmš mn mʿrtʾ dh lbwnʾ* CIS ii $4195^{2ff.}$: L. has ceded to B. part of this hypogee; *ʾqym ywlys ʾwrlys ... lyqr rḥmh* CIS ii $3940^{2ff.}$: J.A. had erected (it) ... in honour of his friend; *mwdʾ zbydʾ ... lbryk šmh* RIP $112^{1f.}$: Z. is returning thanks ... to the one whose name is blessed (for *ydy$_1$* + *l_5* and related constr., v. s.v.); *bwlʾ wdmws lywlys ʾwrlys ʿgʾ* CIS ii $3934^{1f.}$: (token of gratitude) of the Senate and the People for J.A.; *ṣlmtʾ dy ʾbw ... dy ʾqymlh ʾšʾ* Hatra $30^{1ff.}$: statue of A. ... which A. has erected for her; *dkrn ṭb lNP qdm bl* Inv xii 51: good memory for NP before Bel; *dkrn ṭb lmrʾ ʿlmʾ* RIP 126^{1}: a memorial for the lord of the universe (i.e. that he may remember; for both *dkrn*-instances, v. *zkrn* sub A 1); *lbryk šmh lʿlmʾ ... ʿbd ...* RIP $134^{1f.}$: to the one whose name is blessed forever ... he made ... (cf. the construction *bryk šmh lʿlmʾ ... ʿbd* RIP $135^{1f.}$, with same meaning, v. also *ʿbd$_1$*; cf. also *bryk šmh ... mwdʾ lh* RIP $121^{1f.}$; or rather *(l)bryk šmh* in these texts to be explained as superscription?); *yhb krsʾ ... lbnynʾ dy [sgy]l ʾs 8* Hatra $192^{1f.}$: K. has given ... 8 *as* for the building of the S. (for the context, v. *ʾs$_1$*, *bnyn*); *ʾḥlp lky šṭrʾ*

MPAT 40[10f.]: I shall replace for you the document; *kwkh dnh ‘byd lgrmy ’bhtnh* MPAT 67[1f.] (= Frey 1300): this sepulchral chamber was made for the bones of our fathers; cf. also the introductory formula of Ph./Pun. votive inscriptions, *l’dnn lmlqrt ... ’š ndr ‘bdk* KAI 47[1f.]: to our lord M., which your servant has vowed ...; *lrbt ltnt pn b‘l wl’dn lb‘l ḥmn ’š ndr knmy* KAI 79[1ff.]: to the lady, to T., the face of Ba‘al and the lord Ba‘al Ch., which K. vowed; etc., etc. - a) used with the function of the so-called *dativus ethicus* (cf. also Degen GGA ’79, 45); *thk lh ’n zy ṣbyt* Cowl 15[28f.]: she shall go away whither she wants; *’zlt ly byty* Aḥiq 22: I ‘for myself’ went away to my house; *’štmr lk* Aḥiq 97: beware yourself - b) cf. also *yyn l’rb‘t hymm* TA-H 2[2f.]: wine for four days; *npqth byrḥ p’py b 1 lp’py lšrt’ ḥmr ṣydn* Cowl 72 ii 1f.: expenses in the month P.: on the first of P. for dinner wine from Sidon (cf. Cowl 72 ii 3, 13, etc.); *lmnyn* MPAT 38[1]: for the counting (introducing a list of deliveries) - c) in the combination *šlḥ lšlm ...*, *’ḥk ḥnnyhw šlḥ lšlm ’lyšb wlšlm bytk* TA-H 16[1f.]: your brother Ch. greets E. and your house (cf. TA-H 21[1f.]); *lšlmky šlḥt sprh znh* Herm 1[12f.]: this letter is to send you my best wishes; cf. Herm 2[17], RHR cxxx 20 conv. 2, etc. - d) for *hwy* + l_5 comm., v. hwy_1 sub 2 - e) with a verbal form of the root *šm‘*, *l’ yštm‘ lh* Cowl 18[3]: no heed shall be paid to her (cf. Krael 7[42], Driv 4[1,3,3f.]) - **6)** used as the so-called *l objecti*, *w’nš l’ yhn[pq] ṣlmšzb ... mn byt’ znh wl[zr]‘h* KAI 228A 20ff.: no one shall eject Ṣ. ... from this temple nor his seed; *kštt l’ntty* Cowl 7[5]: you struck my wife; *’nh yhbt lky lbyt’* Cowl 13[2]: I have given you my house; *hškḥt l’ḥyq[r]* Aḥiq 76: I found A.; *qṭlw lmrdy’* Beh 3: they have killed the rebels; *tpmt w’ḥtsn msbln lh* Herm 1[5]: T. and A. are supporting him; *l’ šbw lntn* FS Driver 54 conv. 1: they have not taken N. captive; *bl ybrk lbny bwdl’* RTP 92: may Bel bless the sons of B.; *lṣlmyn lmqymw ... wb[n]why qrbw mqymw ... wyrḥbwl’* InscrP 36: M. ... and Y. have offered statues of M. ... and his children (cf. also Inv xi 92 with deletion of verbal form?, cf. also Inv xi 95, 98a, b); *mn dy lqrhy l‘dyn ktb’* Hatra 101[2]: whoever will read this inscription; *zbnt lk ymh dnh lbth dyly* MPAT 51[3]: I have sold to you this day the house which belongs to me; etc., etc.; - **7)** indicating a relation (as to) or with normative function; *wkl ’ḥy y‘nw ly* KAI 200[10]: all my companions will testify for me (cf. KAI 200[11]; v. also $‘ny_1$); *l‘ṣh bk lyt‘ṣ* DA ii 9: as to counsel, one will not ask you for it (cf. Hoftijzer DA a.l. :: Caquot & Lemaire Syr liv 204: = *l obje‘ti*); *lṭ‘mt’ hy bnm[w]s’* CIS ii 3913 ii 109: as to the victuals, it is (written) in the law; *shd lh yrḥbwl ’lh’* CIS ii 3932[6]: the god Y. testified concerning him; etc.; cf. also *lksp šqln 6* ATNS 35[2]: in silver 6 *šh.* (cf. ATNS 20[2]) - a) in the combination *l’npy*, *’qhy ’šh l’npy kršn 10* ATNS 40[4]: pieces of fire wood at the cost of 10 *k.* - b) in the combination *lmdt*, *ytn ln ’dn mlkm ’yt d’r ... lmdt ‘ṣmt ’š p‘lt* KAI 14[18f.]: the lord of kings gave us

D. ... in conformity with (i.e. as a reward for) the striking deeds which I performed - c) in the combination *lpy*, *wntn lpy hktbt* KAI 69[18]: it will be given according to the text (cf. KAI 119[5]); *lpy m*ʾ*s*ʾ ʾ*bty* KAI 126[8]: because of the deeds of his fathers (cf. Latin par. *ob merita maiorum eius*) - d) cf. also the diff. text KAI 71: *l*ʾ*dn l*ʿ*zz mlk*ʿ*štrt wl*ʿ*bdm l*ʿ*m* ʾ*gdr* (= belonging to the lord, to the mighty one M., and to his servant, in accordance with (the law/custom of) the people of G. (?; cf. Sznycer Sem xxv 55f. :: Solá-Solé Sef xxi 251ff.: ... his servants belonging to the people of G. :: Röllig KAI a.l., Amadasi sub ICO-Spa 12: to the lord, to the mighty one M., and his servants the people of G.) - e) cf. also expressions like, *mn dy rḥym lh* Hatra 116[3]: whoever he cares for; *mn dy špr lhwn* SBS 38[5]: because he has made himself agreeable to them - f) used with verbal form of the root *dm*ʾ, *mdy dm*ʾ *lhwn* CIS ii 3913 ii 114: whatever is comparable to them - g) used with a verbal form of the root *š*ʾl_1, *YHWH yš*ʾ*l lšlmk* TA-H 18[2f.]: may the Lord seek your welfare - h) used with a verbal form of the root *yṣp*, ʾ*l tṣpw lh* Herm 1[4]: do not be concerned about him (etc., v. *yṣp*) - i) used with a verbal form of the root *brk*$_1$, *brktk lb*ʿ*l ṣpn* KAI 50[2f.]: I mention you in blessing formulae in (the name of) B.-S.; etc., v. also *brk*$_1$ sub 4, 6a - **8)** indicating the result of an action, *p*ʿ*ln b*ʿ*l ldnnym l*ʾ*b wl*ʾ*m* KAI 26A i 3: B. made me a father and a mother to the D.; *lkny ly lskr* KAI 18[6]: that it may be to me (for) a memorial; *mh ktbt ... lzkrn* KAI 222C 1ff.: what I have written as a reminder (cf. also Inv x 28[1], and poss. Inv xi 3[2]); cf. poss. also KAI 222A 32 (v. however *yšmn*) - a) for *dkyr lṭb* (may he be remembered for good) and related instances, v. *zkr*$_1$, *šlm*$_2$ - **9)** with distributive function, *lḥd lywm*ʾ Driv 6[3]: for each one daily; *lgbr lgbr* Cowl 2[7]: to each man (cf. Cowl 22[1]); *yrbh* ʿ*ly ksp ḥlrn 2 ltkl 1 lyrḥ 1* Cowl 10[4f.]: it shall be due from me, silver (at the rate of) 2 *ḥ.* per shekel per month; *yrḥ lyrḥ* Cowl 11[9]: month by month (cf. Driv 6[3]); *[mn kl] mšk ... lmšk*ʾ ʾ*sryn 2* CIS ii 3913 ii 56: from every skin ... (one has to pay as tax) per skin two *as*; *l*ʾ*rḥ ḥd*ʾ *d 1* CIS ii 3913 ii 60: per journey (i.e. for every journey) 1 *denarius* - **10)** passive participle + l_5 used instead of finite verbal form, *šmy*ʿ *ly* Driv 7[3]: I have heard; *kn šmy*ʿ *ln* SSI ii 28 rev. 6: thus we have heard; *ydy*ʿ *yhwy lk* Driv 7[8]: you may know (cf. MPAT 59[3]); etc.; cf. also Hatra 141?; for this construction, cf. Friedrich AfO xviii 124f., Kutscher JBL lxxvi 337 - **11)** l_5 + Inf. (for Ph. and Pun., cf. also FR 268) - a) as a complement of a verbal form with final function, *kl šlḥ yd llḥm* KAI 24[6]: and each put forward his hand to eat (it; v. *lḥm*$_2$); *wbn* ʾ*nk ḥmyt ... lšbtnm dnnym bnḥt lbnm* KAI 26A i 17f.: and I built fortresses ... so that the D. might dwell in them with their minds at peace; *šlḥn lbnt* KAI 26A ii 11: they commissioned me to build (it); *wyspnnm* ʿ*lt gbl* ʾ*rṣ lknnm lṣdnm l*ʿ*lm* KAI 14[19f.]: and we added them to the territory of the country that they might belong to the S. forever; *ys chon ... liful* Poen 935: which he was ... to do (i.e. which he had to do; cf. Lat. par. *quod faciendum fuit*); *wʾḥzh lspt ʿl dybn* KAI 181[20f.]: and I have taken it to add it to D.; *ʿbdk hwšʿyhw šlḥ lhg[d] l[ʾd]ny* KAI 193[1f.]: your servant H. has sent (a message) to report to my lord; *ʾnšw šlḥ lqḥt* KAI 193[18]: his men he has sent to get; *hnh šlḥty lhʿyd bkm hym* TA-H 24[18f.]: behold, I have sent to warn you today; *[ʾy]nnw yklm lšlḥ* TA-H 40[13f.]: we are not able to send; *qrny lbnʾ* KAI 214[13]: he called me to build; *[wmn y]ʾmr lhldt* KAI 223C 1f.: who will purpose to efface (v. *ʾmr*$_1$ sub 8); *w[zy] yqwm ʿl mptḥyh ltrkwth mn byth* Cowl 15[29f.]: and who will rise up against M. to drive her out his house; *[ʾ]tyt bytk lmntn ly [l]brtk* Cowl 15[3]: I came to your house that you might give me your daughter; *ʾgrh mnk yštlḥ ... ʿl ʾgwrʾ ... lmbnyh* Cowl 30[24f.]: let a letter be sent from you ... concerning the temple ... to rebuild it; *yhbt ly trʿ bytʾ zylk lmbnh ʾgr 1* Cowl 5[3f.]: you have given to me the gateway of your house to build one wall (v. *ʾgr*$_3$); *lʾ ... ybyl lhm lmwmʾ ʿl znh ...* ATNS 2[4]: he was not brought to them to swear about this ...; *zbnt ... mšḥ bšm lmtyh lkn* Herm 3[10f.]: I have bought ... perfumed oil to be brought to you; *ḥzw ḥlqʾ zyly ... lmṭʿn bh* NESE i 11[2f.]: take care to load my share upon it (v. *ḥzy*$_1$ Qal sub 3); etc. - b) giving a further determination of a preceding verbal form or noun, *bmqmm .. ʾš yštʿ ʾdm llkt drk* KAI 26A ii 4: in places ... where a man was afraid to walk on a road; *dbr mlk ʾšmnʿzr ... lʾmr ngzlt* KAI 14[2f.]: king E. said as follows: I was snatched away; *wbrk bʿl ... ʾyt ʾztwd ḥym ... ltty .. lʾztwd ʾrk ymm* KAI 26A iii 2ff.: Baʿal may bless ... A. with life ... by giving to A. length of days (:: Barré Bibl lxiv 411ff.: *ltty* = l_5 + Inf. used independently as a precative construction); *gubulim lasibitthim* Poen 938: regions where he lives (Lat. par.: *in ... habitare ... regionibus*); *bʿwd šlš ʾmt lhnq[b]* KAI 189[2]: while there were still three cubits to be cut through; *lʾ ʾkhl ʾklʾnk lmbnh* Cowl 5[6]: I shall not be able to restrain you from building; *wlʾ hškḥt ksp wnksn lšlmh lky* Cowl 13[5]: I did not find money and goods to pay you; *ʾnt mšlm šlyṭ lmlqḥ lk* Cowl 10[16f.]: you M. have the right to take for yourself ...; *wmyn lʾ ḥsrh lhšqyʾ ḥylʾ* Cowl 27[7]: it never lacks water to supply the garrison; *yšymwn ṭb bḥnkh lmʾmr* Aḥiq 115: they would put something good in his palate to speak; *kpn lmnšʾ mšḥ* Krael 7[19]: ladles to carry oil; *bbʾ zylk lmnpq* Krael 10[4]: your gate (through which) to go forth; *lʾ šnṣyw lmnʿl bbyrtʾ* Driv 5[7]: they did not succeed in entering the fortress; *ʾškḥ ʾš lmwšrthm* Herm 2[12f.]: I will find a man to deliver them; *lʾ ršy ʾnwš lmktb* CIS ii 210[3f.]: no one has the right to write; *ktb lmqbr* CIS ii 209[7]: a deed of burial; *mksʾ dy qṣbʾ ʾpy dnr ḥyb lmtḥšbw* CIS ii 3913 ii 102f.: the tax to be paid by the butchers must be reckoned by the *dinar* (v. *qṣb*$_2$); *lʾ yhwn [šl]ṭyn ʾw lmbʿd ʾw lʾḥbwrʾ bh ʾyš* CIS ii 4214: they will not have the

right either to renounce nor to make someone a partner in it (i.e. in the tomb; v. *b'd*$_1$, *ḥbr*$_1$); *'t ršy' bnpšky lmhk wlmhy ...* MPAT 40[5f.]: you are free on your part to go and to be ...; etc. - c) negation + *l*$_5$ + Inf. (used absolutely), *'bl lptḥ* KAI 70[4]: not to be opened (on tomb); cf. *wl' lmptḥ* MPAT 67[4] (= Frey 1300), 70[4] (cf. however Garbini OA xxiv 67ff.: text is fraud), 95b (= Frey 1359b), also on tombs (cf. also EI xx 161*) - d) used as so-called predicate in a nominal clause, *kl zbḥ 'š 'dm lzbḥ* KAI 69[14]: each sacrifice which one may offer; *wkl 'š lsr t 'bn z* KAI 79[6ff.]: and everyone who will remove this stone; *kl 'š lgnb t 'bn z* CIS i 3784[1f.]: everyone who will steal this stone (cf. poss. also CIS i 5510[3] (v. also *kpp*$_1$)) :: FR 268.2: pro 'who will' translate 'who is about to' - **12)** *l*$_5$ in combination with other prep. (for *l*$_5$ + *wt*, v. *'yt*$_3$) - a) *l*$_5$ + *b*$_2$, *lkhnm ksp '[grt] 10 lb'ḥd* KAI 69[12]: the priests will have 10 silver *a.* apiece (for KAI 153[4], v. *šd*$_1$) - b) *l*$_5$ + *mn*$_5$ (cf. also Zevit JANES vii 106ff.), *lmn'ry* KAI 24[12]: from his youth; *lmmṣ' šmš w'd mb'y* KAI 26A i 4f., ii 2: from the rising of the sun to its setting; for KAI 145[14], v. *m'l*$_2$ - c) *l*$_5$ + *mn*$_5$ + *b*$_2$ (cf. also Zevit JANES vii 106ff.), *lmbḥyy* KAI 35[2]: during my life-time (cf. also *lmbmḥy'* in Trip 8[3], v. *mḥy*$_3$); *lmbyrḥ ḥyr* KAI 81[5]: since the month Ch.; *lmb'bn ...* KAI 141[4]: from the stone ... (for the context, v. *'t*$_6$); *'gl 'š qrny lmbmḥsr* KAI 69[5]: a calf whose horns are still wanting; *lmbmlktm* KAI 124[2], 126[11]: (poss. meaning) according to the work necessary for them (v. *ml'kh*$_1$); *lmb'nšm* KAI 130[2]: (poss. meaning) according to the contributions (v. however *'nš*$_2$); *lmbšm g'y* KAI 124[1]: in the name of Gaius (cf. Lat. par. *nomine [C.]*); the same comb. prob. also in Trip 51[4], cf. Levi Della Vida ibid. 11, Amadasi IPT 134 n. 1 - d) *l*$_5$ + *'l*$_7$, for MUSJ xxxviii 106[9,11] and Hatra 74[8], v. *'l*$_7$; for KAI 224[2], v. *mll*$_1$ - e) *'ḥr*$_5$ + *l*$_5$, *'ḥr ly[w]mn 'ḥrnn tlth* Aḥiq 39: after three more days - f) *mn*$_5$ + *l*$_5$, *dy mn l'l ktyb* RIP 25[11]: which is written above - g) *'d*$_7$ + *l*$_5$, *'[d] lywmn 'ḥrnn* Aḥiq 52: until other days - **13)** for *l*$_5$ combined with conjunction *mṭl*, v. *kl*$_1$ - for a discussion of the diff. *l* in the Samaria ostraca, cf. Gibson SSI i 6f. (also for older litt.), cf. also Rainey PEQ '70, 45ff., BASOR cclxxii 71ff., Mettinger SSO 90ff., Cross AUSS xiii 8ff., Shea IEJ xxvii 16ff., ZDPV ci 16ff., Lemaire IH i 75f., Sarfatti Maarav iii 75f. - for *l* as poss. abbrev. of *lmlk*, v. *mlk*$_3$.
v. *'l*$_6$, *l'*$_1$, *lk*, *mlk*$_3$.

l'$_1$ cf. Frah xxv 40 (*l'*), Paik 573 (*l'*), 595 (in the comb. *l'yty*), Nisa-b 477[1], 621[2], 2067[3] (*l'*), Sogd ii 222, B 257, Ka 17, 19, 21, R 48, Ta 476, 480, Ve 113, BSOAS xxxiii 152[15], GIPP 26, 56, SaSt 21 - not attested in Ph./Pun. (cf. FR vii, 249 n. 1, 318,1; for MUSJ xlv 262[5], v. *'gd*$_1$), in Moab. and Sam'al. (cf. Friedr 41*, Dion 166, 303) - variant spellings: - **1)** *l* KAI 222A 28, B 21, 25, 31, C 17, 223B 3, 6, C 8, 224[5,9,21], etc. (the spelling *l'* not attested for OldAr., cf. also Degen AAG p. 64),

$226^{4,6,8}$, 233^8 (cf. Dupont-Sommer Syr xxiv 39; cf. also Abou-Assaf, Bordreuil & Millard Tell F p. 59 n. 1), DA ii 7, 9, 17 (spelling *l'* not attested in DA; cf. also Hoftijzer DA p. 285), cf. also *l* in the comb. *l'd*: Cowl 28^{13}, 34^7, Krael 11^8, Herm 2^{12}, v. *'wd*$_5$); this spelling poss. also in Sem xiv 72 ii 1 (cf. Dupont-Sommer a.l.); on the orthography, cf. also Andersen & Freedman FS Fitzmyer 9, Kottsieper SAS 81 - **2)** *lh*: TH i vs. 4 (for this interpret., cf. Lipiński Stud 118, 120, Kaufman BiOr xxxiv 94 :: Friedrich TH a.l., Degen NESE i 51: = *l*$_5$ + suff. 3 p.s.m. :: Fales sub AECT 53: poss. = *lh*$_2$ (= variant of *lw*)), Herm 1^5 (cf. e.g. Bresciani & Kamil Herm a.l., Gibson SSI ii p. 130 :: Kutscher IOS i 112: = *l*$_5$ + suff. 3 p.s.m.),^{6}, $2^{3,10}$ (v. *hn*$_3$), $3^{4,11}$, 4^5, $5^{3,4,7,8}$ (only in Herm 1^8 the spelling *l'* (cf. e.g. Bresciani & Kamil Herm a.l., Porten & Greenfield ZAW lxxx 220, Gibson SSI ii p. 127, 130, Porten & Yardeni sub TADAE A 2.3 :: Milik Bibl xlviii 549: = *l'*$_2$, cf. also Huehnergard JAOS ciii 572 n. 23)) - **3)** *lw'* DJD ii 45^2, 47^5; the *lw'* in Syr xiv 184^2 (Palm.) contraction of *l'*$_1$ + *hw'*$_2$? (cf. Cantineau Gramm 135 :: Rosenthal Sprache 83: prob. contamination of *l'* and *lw* :: Aartun UF v 3ff.: = *l*$_2$ + *w*) - **4)** *lw* in the comb. *blw* DJD ii 50 i 2 (heavily dam. context; cf. *bl'* in DJD ii 22^5) - ¶ adverb of negation - **A)** used in non-modal context - **1)** preceding a verbal form - a) preceding a Pf. form, *lšmw 'my ...* KAI 226^6: they did not lay with me ...; *l' hwt 'rq ldrgmn* Cowl 6^7: it was not (i.e. no longer) the land of D.; *l' š'ylt* ATNS 12^1: she was not interrogated; *spr lh šlḥty* Herm 1^5: you did not send a letter (v. supra); *l' 'th 'sts* NESE iii 48^5: A. did not come (for the reading, cf. Degen ibid. 53); *wl' šbq bny ddy* MPAT 64 i 7: my uncle B. did not leave; etc., etc. - b) preceding an Impf. form, *l' nr'h 't 'zqh* KAI $194^{12f.}$: we do not see A. (for the context, v. *'yt*$_3$); *lyqtl* KAI 224^{18}: he will not be killed; *byt ly'l hlk* DA ii 7: a traveller will not enter a house (for the context, v. *'ll*$_1$, cf. DA ii 9, v. *mlk*$_2$); *l' nkl ngrky* Cowl 1^4: we shall not be able to sue you; *l' ykhl 'nnyh wl' y'bd dyn [ḥdh] wtrtyn ... lyhwyšm'* Krael $7^{37f.}$: A. will not be able to refuse the sexual connexion ... with Y. (for the context, v. *dn*$_1$; cf. also Kaufman BiOr xxxiv 96); *l' y'bd* CIS ii 198^7: he will not do; *wl' yh' šlyṭh* MUSJ xxxviii $106^{8f.}$: he will not be allowed ...; *wl' ldkrhy* Hatra $23^{4f.}$: and he will not read (for the reading, v. *zkr*$_1$); *whn kn l' ''bd* MPAT 39^7: and if I will not act thus ...; etc., etc. - **2)** not preceding a verbal form - a) functioning in a nominal clause on clause level, *ky lṭb h'* KAI 224^{22}: for he is not good (for the context, v. *mn*$_5$); *byt' znk l' šlyṭ 'nt lzbnh* Cowl 9^6: you have not the right to sell this house; *lh šbq 'nh lh* Herm 3^4: I shall not leave him; *l' 'ḥy hw ḥrwṣ* Herm 1^8: is not Ch. my brother? (v. also supra); *l' ršy 'nwš lmktb* CIS ii $210^{3f.}$: no one has the right to write; *l' 'yty lh yld* MPAT 64 i 8: he has no offspring; *pgryn ... mks l' ḥybyn* CIS ii 3913 ii 108: dead bodies ... are not liable to taxation; *l' 'ytyny* *yd‘* MPAT 49 i 4: I did not know ...; *ršh l' 'yty lk* MPAT 51[5]: there is no authorisation for you (for *l' 'yty*, v. also *'yty*); cf. also, *mnd‘m ... l' mhytyn ‘ly* Driv 10[2]: they are not bringing me anything ...; *l' šbqn ln lmbnyh* Cowl 30[23]: they do not allow us to build it; *zy l' ktb ‘l spr 'nttky* Krael 10[7]: it is not written on your marriage document; *md‘m lh mpqn ln mn swn* Herm 5[2f.]: they do not send us anything from S.; *'lh' dy l' št' ḥmr* CIS ii 3973[4f.]: the god who does not drink wine - b) not functioning on clause level, *ld‘t* DA ii 17: foolishness (for the context, v. *pr₃*); *l' 'nḥn yhbnh lky* Cowl 1[5]: *we* did not give it to you; *l' 'nh ktbth* Cowl 8[17]: *I* shall not have written it; *l' dyn wl' dbb* Cowl 8[14]: without (the possibility to contest the preceding stipulation(s) in) a lawsuit or process; *l' ‘d zmn' ybyl lhm* ATNS 2[4]: *not until (i.e. by) the appointed time,* was he brought to them (cf. also Porten & Yardeni sub TADAE B 8.9); *[zb]nyn wl' z‘wrn* Inv x 114[4]: several times; *ḥdh kpnh wl' 'klh* AMB 7[17]: one who is hungry but does not eat; *wl' lmptḥ* MPAT 67[4]: not to be opened (against the authenticity of this text, cf. however Garbini OA xxiv 67ff.); *wl' m‘l* MPAT 51[10]: no entrance; cf. also in an expression poss. preceded by *b₂*, *[b]l' bywmyk* Aḥiq 102: before your time - **B)** used in a modal context, *hn yqrq mny ... ḥd pqdy 'w ḥd 'ḥy ... lt'mr lhm* KAI 224[4f.]: if any of my officers ... or any of my brothers flees from me, ... you may not say to them ...; *l' tnpq bšwq' zy bynyn* Cowl 5[12f.]: you shall not go out into the street which is between us; *hn y'mr kwt l' yštm‘ lh* Krael 7[42]: if he should speak thus, he shall not be heard; *l' yḥywn* HDS 9[8]: they may not live; *wl' ytptḥ* CIS ii 226[2]: it should not be opened; *‘l kl 'nwš ... dy l' yzbn qbr' dnh* CIS ii 206[3f.]: it is incumbent on everyone ... that he do not sell this tomb; *wdy l' ytqbr bkpr' dnh lhn ...* CIS ii 208[3]: that no one is to be buried in this tomb except ...; *w'nš l' yptḥ* CIS ii 4218[3]: and no one should open ...; *wl' ldbrhn* Hatra 79[12]: let they not lead them (for the context, v. *qṭyr₁*); etc.; cf. also *l' dy yrhn yth* CIS ii 217[5]: he should not give it as a security - for the comb. *‘d l'*, v. *‘d₇* - the diff. *l'w* in DJD ii 32[5] remains unexplained, cf. Milik DJD ii a.l. - Puech RB xci 91ff.: the *wl'* in At xiv 56[2] to be translated: except (poss. interpret.).

v. *'pl₂*, *bl₃*, *bl'₁*, *bql*, *hn₃*, *kl₁*, *lhn₁*, *lwl'*, *lyš₂*, *ml'₁*, *‘l'*, *ṣ'n*, *ṣnl*.

l'₂ **Nab** CIS ii 235A, B, 298[1], 647[1], 1427[1], J 122, ARNA-Nab 16[3] - **Hatra** 13[1] (for the reading, cf. Krückmann AfO xvi 146 (n. 34), Milik Syr xliv 298, Degen ZDMG cxxi 124, Vattioni IH a.l. :: Safar Sumer vii 178 n. 24: l. *lh* :: Caquot Syr xxix 96f., Donner sub KAI 240: leave l. 1 out); cf. also Assur 14[1] - ¶ exclamatory particle, yea, oh, certainly; for this interpret., cf. Jaussen & Savignac sub J 122, Cantineau Nab i 105 (cf. also Huehnergard JAOS ciii 590) :: Joüon MUSJ xviii 98ff.: = optative particle; for other interpretations, cf. Chabot sub RES 1160, 1291 - the same particle prob. also (spelled *l*) in CIS ii 2244[1], cf. Joüon

MUSJ xviii 99 - this particle also (spelled *l*) in KAI 204 (*ll'bdb'lt* = l_4 (= l'_2) + l_5 + n.p.)?, cf. Garb 256 (or: *ll'bdb'lt* = dittography for *l'bdb'lt* ??), Donner KAI a.l. :: Gibson SSI ii p. 18: *ll'bdb'lt* = l_5 + n.p. (consisting of *l* = *lw* + status-constructus group) - Teixidor Syr xlviii 481: l. *l'* (= l'_2) in AAW v/1, 85[1] :: Altheim & Stiehl AAW a.l.: l. *dnh*$_3$ (= *znh*).
v. *bl'*$_3$, *l'*$_1$.

l'w v. *l'*$_1$.

l'y **JAr** QAL Pf. 3 p.pl.m. *l'yw* SM 88[13] (= Syn D A) - ¶ verb QAL to toil; *'mlw wl'yw* SM 88[13]: they laboured and toiled - this root prob. also in *l'ty* CIS i 6000bis 5 (= TPC 84), Ferron StudMagr i 74f.: = QAL Inf. cstr. + suff. 3 p.s.m. of *l'y* (= to wear oneself out), cf. also Février CIS i a.l.: < root *l'y* (= to be able), cf. also Février BAr '51/52, 76, v.d.Branden BO xxiii 156, 158: = nominal form of this root (*l'h* Sing. + suff. 3 p.s.m. (= force, power)) :: Lidzbarski Eph i 166f. (div. otherwise): l. *'ty* = Sing. + suff. 1 p.s. of *'t*$_1$.

l'yt v. *lyš*$_2$, *skl*$_3$.

l'yty v. *lyš*$_2$.

l'm$_1$ (< Akkad., cf. Kaufman AIA 67 (n. 180), 144, 156, cf. also Beyer Or lvii 82f.) - **OffAr** Sing. cstr. *l'm* CIS ii 38[6] (= Del 21 = AECT 3), KAI 236 Rs 1 (= AECT 49), Sem xxiii 95 recto 4 (= AECT 58), *lm* CIS ii 39[6] (= Del 23 = AECT 9) - ¶ subst. eponym-year.
v. *'m*$_2$.

l'm$_2$ **OffAr** word of unknown meaning in Cowl 46[7]; Cowl p. 152: poss. = but? related to *lm*$_2$? (cf. also Porten & Yardeni sub TADAE B 6.3) :: Sach p. 117: = *l'm*$_3$ (= people, nation)??

l'm$_3$ v. *l'm*$_2$, *lḥm*$_2$.

l'm$_4$ v. *sgyl*.

lb **Ph** Sing. abs. *lb* KAI 26A ii 8, 14; + suff. 1 p.s. *lby* KAI 26A i 13; + suff. 3 p.pl.m. *lbnm* KAI 26A i 18 - **Pun** Sing. abs. *lb* KAI 145[11], Punica ix 9[2], 9b 2 - **Hebr** Sing. abs. *lb* AMB 4[18] (or = cstr.?); cstr. *lb* KAI 193[6]; + suff. 3 p.s.m. *[l]bh* TA-H 40[4] - **OffAr** Sing. + suff. 3 p.s.m. *lbh* Cowl 71[6] (highly uncert. reading; cf. Cowl a.l.: *b* is more like *d*) - **JAr** Sing. + suff. 3 p.s.m./f. *lbh* AMB 10[5] (dam. context) - ¶ subst. m. heart - **1)** as centre of feelings and emotions of someone, *b'šr lb* KAI 145[11]: with joy of heart (v. also *'šr*$_3$); *bnḥt lbnm* KAI 26A i 18: with their heart at peace (cf. KAI 26A ii 8, 13f.); *lb ['[bd[k] dwh* KAI 193[6f.]: the heart of your servant is sick (for the context, v. *dwh*); *ḥzw 'm yḥpṣw lbw* DJD ii 44[6]: see that they are satisfied (each) in his heart - **2)** indicating the inclination and disposition of someone, *bn'm lby* KAI 26A i 13: because of the goodness of my heart; *blb ṭr* Punica ix 9[2]: with a pure heart (cf. Punica ix 9b 2f.; for this interpret., v. *ṭhr*); cf. also TA-H 40[4f.] (v. *nṭy*) and poss. AMB 4[18] - poss. two forms (*lby*, *lb*) in

DA ii 32, cf. Hoftijzer DA a.l. - for a poss. form in KAI 222B 35, v. *lqḥ* - pro *᾽ntt lby* (= Sing. + suff. 1 p.s.) in KAI 264[8f.] (cf. Donner KAI a.l.: = the woman of my heart; cf. also Chabot sub RES 1785E: or l. *᾽ntt byl* = the wife of B.? (cf. Lidzbarski Eph i 69)) l. prob. *᾽ntt by* (= the woman of the house, cf. Lipiński Stud 180f. (n. 3)) - Rocco StudMagr vii a.l.: l. *lb* (= Sing. abs.) in StudMagr vii 12[1] (uncert. reading and interpret.) - cf. lbb_2.

v. *bw᾽*, bl_1, klb_1, ll_2, *lqḥ*, *mglb*.

lb᾽ **OffAr** Sing. abs. *lb᾽* Aḥiq 117 - ¶ subst. occurring in diff. clause, *᾽ryh [l᾽ ᾽y]ty bym᾽ ‘l kn yqr᾽wn lqp᾽ lb᾽* Aḥiq 117: there is no lion in the sea, therefore they call the mass of waters (?, v. qp_1) *lb᾽* (indicating the existence of a *lb᾽* = lion and a *lb᾽* of unknown meaning, but used in maritime context), cf. Epstein ZAW xxxii 135f., Cowl a.l., Ginsberg ANET 429 (n. 18), Grelot RB lxviii 185, DAE p. 439 (n.e.), Kottsieper SAS 21, 212 (cf. also Lindenberger APA 105ff., 247 n. 299, 248 n. 305, 249 n. 311: *lb᾽* indicating both the lion (cf. Akkad. *labbu*) and a sea-dragon (cf. Akkad. *Labbû*; cf. also Watson OA ii 256 (n. 30); uncert. interpret.); related to Greek λέων, cf. Koehler ZDPV lxii 122, Fronzaroli RCL '68, 281 (n. 53) - cf. also Frah xxx 14 (*lb‘᾽*).

lbb **Hebr** Sing. + suff. 3 p.s.m. *lbbh* KA 9 B 2 - **DA** Sing. abs. *lbb* ii 12 (v. infra; :: Hackett BTDA 26, 68, 84 (div. otherwise): l. *lbbm* = Sing. + suff. 3 p.pl.m.); cstr. *lbb* ii 14; + suff. 3 p.s.m. *lbbh* ii 12 - **OldAr** Sing. cstr. *lbb* KAI 224[15,16] (*[l]bb*); + suff. 2 p.s.m. *lbbk* KAI 223B 5 (*lbb[k]*), 224[14] - **OffAr** Sing. abs. *lbb* Aḥiq 98; cstr. *lbb* Aḥiq 65, 163; emph. *lbb᾽* Aḥiq 104, 137, Irâq xxxiv 133a (= AECT 45); + suff. 3 p.s.m. *lbbh* Aḥiq 109, 159; + suff. 2 p.s.m. *lbbk* Cowl 15[5], Aḥiq 82, 106, Krael 2[14]; + suff. 1 p.s. *lbby* Cowl 6[12], 14[5], 15[15], 40[3], 43[7], 67 v 1 (*lbb[y]*; for reading and context, cf. Porten & Yardeni sub TADAE B 5.2), Aḥiq 169, Krael 1[4], Herm 4[5], SSI ii 28 obv. 1 (*lbb[y]*; for this poss. reading, cf. Porten FS Bresciani 431f., Porten & Yardeni sub TADAE A 3.3, Lipiński Or lvii 435 :: e.g. Bresciani RSO xxxv 18, 20: l. *br[y]* = Sing. + suff. 1 p.s. of br_1 (cf. also e.g. Grelot DAE p. 125, Gibson SSI ii p. 144f.)); + suff. 3 p.pl.m. *lbbhm* Aḥiq 162; + suff. 1 p.pl. *lbbn* Cowl 2[9], 20[8,9], Krael 3[6], 12[6,14,26]; cf. Frah x 35 (*lbb(m)h*; cf. Toll ZDMG-Suppl viii 29) - ¶ subst. m. - **A)** heart - **1)** as centre of feelings and emotions of someone, *bḥmr lbb᾽* Aḥiq 104: with wrath of heart; *wšgy᾽ bnn lbbk ᾽l yḥdh* Aḥiq 106: let not your heart rejoice in a multitude of children; *wṭb lbbk bgw* Cowl 15[5f.]: and your heart is content therewith (cf. Cowl 2[9], 6[11f.], 14[5], etc.); cf. also *blbb mn n᾽nḥ nqr blbbh n᾽nḥ* DA ii 12: in the (i.e. his) heart who is sighing?, is a blinded one (v. nqr_1) sighing in his heart? (cf. also Hoftijzer DA a.l.) :: Caquot & Lemaire Syr liv 205: in the heart (= Sing. cstr.) of whom sighs the offshoot; it is in his heart that he sighs (cf. also Garbini Hen i 183, 186, H.P.Müller

ZAW xciv 219, 235) - **2)** indicating the inclination and disposition of someone, *lbby zy yhbt lk* Aḥiq 169: my heart which I gave you (cf. also Greenfield FS Fitzmyer 50); *ʾšbqn ʿl lbbk* Aḥiq 82: I leave (you) to your own heart; *ʾl thšgʾ lbbʾ* Aḥiq 137: lead not your heart astray (v. *šgʾ$_1$*); *ʾyš [šp]yr mddh wlbbh ṭb* Aḥiq 159: a man of becoming conduct and whose heart is good; *lbby lh dbq lh* Herm 4^5: my heart is not attached to it (i.e. I do not like it); cf. also *klbbh* KA 9 B 2: according to his wish - **3)** as centre of reflection and thought, *[lʾ ydʿ] ʾyš mh blbb knth* Aḥiq 163: a man does not know what is in the heart of his fellow; *hn ysq ʿl lbbk* KAI 224^{14}: if the idea comes to your mind (cf. KAI 224^{16}); *[ʿl] zy š[mʿt] hwqr lbb* Aḥiq 98: over what you hear, harden your heart (i.e. be reserved), cf. KAI 223B 5 (for the context, cf. Greenfield ActOr xxix 6) - **4)** indicating the authority that one can have over someone or something, *lʾ ʾkl ʾnṣl lpltу mn tḥt lbbk* Krael $2^{13f.}$: I will not be able to take away P. from under your heart - **B)** the centre, inside of an object; *mʾn ṭb ks[h] mlh blbbh* Aḥiq 109: a good vessel hides a thing within itself; *byn yd zʾ wlbbʾ* Irâq xxxiv 133a: between this side and the centre (cf. Akkad. par. *bir-ti idi lìb-bi*; reading and interpret. of Ar. text however uncertain, cf. Fales sub AECT 45, v. also *yd*) - cf. *lb*.

lbbh **Amm** Sing. abs./cstr. *lbbt[* AUSS xiii 2^7 (or = Plur.?, cf. Sivan UF xiv 227, Aufrecht sub CAI 80; v. also infra) - ¶ subst. prob. meaning: fine flour, cf. Cross AUSS xiii 6f., cf. however Jackson ALIA 52, 57: = Plur. abs./cstr. of *lbbh* (= cake).

lbh (< Akkad., cf. Kaufman AIA 66, 145, cf. also v.Soden AHW s.v. *libbātu*, Gibson SSI ii p. 110; or = *lbt*?, cf. also Wesselius AION xxx 267) - **OffAr** Sing. abs. *lbt* SSI ii 28 rev. 3 (for the reading, cf. e.g. Bresciani RSO xxxv 18, Porten FS Bresciani 432, Porten & Yardeni sub TADAE A 3.3 :: Gibson SSI ii a.l.: l. *lbt[y]* = Sing. + suff. 1 p.s.); cstr. *lbt* KAI 233^{19}; + suff. 2 p.s.m. *lbtk* Cowl 41^4; + suff. 1 p.s. *lbty* KAI $233^{19,20}$, Herm 1^6 (cf. Porten & Greenfield ZAW lxxx 222, 228, Porten Arch 269f. n. 12, Kutscher IOS i 112f., Gibson SSI ii p. 130f., Degen Or xliv 123, Hoftijzer SV 108, Porten & Yardeni sub TADAE A 2.3 :: Bresciani & Kamil Herm a.l., Milik Bibl xlviii 581, Hayes & Hoftijzer VT xx 99: = l_5 + *bty* (= n.p.)); + suff. 2 p.pl.m. *lbtkm* Cowl 37^{11} - ¶ subst. wrath, anger; in all instances combined with form of *mlʾ$_1$* (comb. < Akkad., cf. Kaufman AIA 66, Degen Or xliv 123; on the formula, cf. also Fitzmyer CBQ xxiii 461, Dion RB lxxxix 556 (n. 155)); the suffix combined with *lbt-* indicates the person against whom the wrath is kindled (for the instances, v. *mlʾ$_1$*).

lbwnh v. *lbnh$_2$*.

lbwš$_1$ v. *lbš$_2$*.

lbwš$_2$ **Hatra** Milik DFD 373: the *lbwšʾ* in 34^5 = Sing. emph. of *lbwš$_2$* (= dresser; cf. also Abbadi PIH 33 (n. 1)), cf. however Aggoula Ber xviii 92: = part of n.p. *gbrlbwš›* :: Vattioni IH a.l.: = part of n.p. *‹bdbwš›* (for related interpret. and reading, cf. Ingholt AH i/2, 43 (s.v. *bwš›*): l. *bwš›* (= n.p.) or rather *lbwš›* = n.p., Caquot Syr xxx 239 (div. otherwise): l. *bwš›* = n.p.; cf. also Safar Sumer viii 190).

lbyn **Hatra** Safar Sumer xxiv 19 (n. 35): the diff. *lbyn›* in 247[2] = Plur. emph. (= gold plates; cf. also Vattioni IH a.l.), cf. however Degen JEOL xxiii 413 (n. 38): less prob. interpret. (or = *l*$_5$ + *byn›*?), cf. also idem NESE ii 101 :: Aggoula MUSJ xlvii 17: l. prob. *lbyr›* = *l*$_5$ + Sing. abs. of *byrh*?.

lbn$_1$ Ebeling AfO xvi 215, v.Soden Or xxxvii 263, xlvi 192: = white poplar > Akkad. in comb. *puru-ḫ libnu* (an aromatic essence; cf. also v.Soden AHW s.v.) - for this word, cf. Knauf MUGP 28 (n. 144).

lbn$_2$ v. *lbnh$_1$*.

lbn$_3$ **Pun** Sing. m. abs. *lbn* KAI 76B 5 - **Hebr** Plur. m. abs. *lbnyn* SM 49[24] - ¶ adj. white; said of figs: KAI 76B 5; said of bulbous root: SM 49[24]; cf. Diosc iii 102, 122, iv 190: λαβον (in the comb. αβιβλαβον); cf. also Löw AP p. 402, FR 76a, 78a, 196a, Garr DGSP 33 - Greek λίβανος < derivation of the same root, cf. Masson RPAE 53f.

lbnh$_1$ **OffAr** Plur. abs. *lbnn* CIS ii 69, Cowl 3[18], 10[9], Krael 11[11] - ¶ subst. brick - in Cowl 3[18], 10[9], Krael 11[11] in the combination *by zy lbnn* = house of bricks (cf. e.g. Sach p. 107, Wag 41, Hoftijzer VT ix 315, Ginsberg JNES xviii 149 (n. 19), Porten Arch 101, Grelot DAE p. 82f. n. d, Degen GGA '79, 26 :: Cowl p. 9: = some sort of bank or counting house (*lbnn* prob. = Plur. of *lbn$_2$* (= table), cf. Brown JSS x 203 n. 4) :: Krael p. 264: = the house of the children (*lbnn* = *l*$_5$ + Plur. abs. of *br$_1$* (cf. also Segert AAG p. 173)); cf. also Kutscher JAOS lxxiv 237, Yaron JNES xx 188, JSS xvi 241f., for the context of Krael 11[10f.], v. also *lqḥ*) - this subst. Plur. emph. *[l]bn›* poss. also in RIP 127[5], cf. Al-Hassani & Starcky AAS vii 111f., 114 (: or l. *[t]bn›* = Sing. emph. of *tbn$_1$*), Gawlikowski RIP a.l., TP 116 (cf. also Degen JEOL xxiii 413 n. 38), cf. however Milik DFD 257: l. *[k]bn›* = Sing. emph. of *kbn* (= enclosure; reading *[l]bn›*, *[t]bn›* or *[›]bn›* (= Plur. emph. of *›bn$_2$*) less prob.) - for the etymology, cf. Kaufman AIA 66, and litt. quoted there - prob. > Greek λιβανωτός, cf. Masson RPAE 54.

lbnh$_2$ **Pun** Sing. abs. *lbnt* KAI 76B 6 - **OffAr** Sing. abs. *lbwnh* Cowl 30[21] (*lbw[n]h*), 31[21], 33[11]; emph. *lbwnt›* Cowl 30[25], 32[9] - ¶ subst. f. frankincense - this word poss. also in KAI 161[8], *lbn[t]*, cf. already Février RA xlv 146, 148 - on this word, cf. Brown JSS xxv 16ff., Nielsen SVT xxxviii 60f., Knauf MUGP 28 (n. 144), on its use in Elephantine, cf. also Nielsen SVT xxxviii 81f.

v. *lbnh$_3$*.

lbnh$_3$ **Edom** (?) Sing. cstr. *lbnt* NESE i 48[1] (for this interpret., cf. Milik LA ix 334, Dahood CBQ xxii 407, Cross BASOR cxciii 23, Degen

NESE i a.l., Ullendorff JSS xviii 267f. (cf. also Teixidor Syr l. 430), Lemaire RB lxxxi 65ff. :: Israel RivBib xxvii 179, 183 : = Sing. abs. :: Dupont-Sommer Lach iii 358f., AIPHOS xiii 143ff., Albright BASOR cxxxii 46f., Aharoni IEJ xviii 163, Lesh xxxv 4, Lipiński Stud 144f. (dividing otherwise): l. *lbnt*› = Sing. emph. of *lbnh*$_2$ :: Albright FS Myers 26ff. (div. otherwise): l. *lbnt*› = *l*$_5$ + f. Plur. emph. of *br*$_1$) - ¶ subst. incense altar (cf. Dahood CBQ xxii 407, Degen NESE i 47f., Ullendorff JSS xviii 268, Lemaire RB lxxxi 67; poss. the same word as *lbnh*$_2$) :: Milik LA ix 334, Cross BASOR cxciii 23 = *lbnh*$_2$ (= incense used pregnantly for incense altar (v. also supra)) :: Nielsen SVT xxxviii 47f.: = *lbnh*$_2$ (= frankincense; cf. also idem ibid. 82).

lbnh$_4$ Hebr Sing. abs. *lbnh* AMB 4^{20} - ¶ subst. moon.

lbr v. *br*$_3$.

lbš$_1$ OffAr QAL Part. pass. s.m. abs./cstr., cf. Warka 20: *la-bi-iš*, Warka 24: *la-bi-šú* (for the forms, cf. also Garbini HDS 31, 33); pl.m. abs. *lbšn* Cowl $30^{15,20}$, 31^{14}; APH Pf. 1 p.s. + suff. 3 p.s.m., cf. Warka 31: *al-bi-iš-te-e*; Part. act. s.m. abs. *mlbš* Herm 4^{6} (cf. Gibson SSI ii p. 138, Coxon JAOS xcviii 418 :: Bresciani & Kamil Herm a.l.: or = PA‘EL?, cf. also Kutscher IOS i 117 = PA‘EL) - ¶ verb QAL Part. pass. clothed; ›*nḥn*› ... *šqqn lbšn hwyn* Cowl 30^{15}: we were clothed in sackcloth (cf. also Cowl 30^{20}, 31^{14}); *la-bi-šú šá-am-Lat. ru-ga-zi-e* Warka 24: clothed in a garment of wrath (cf. Warka 20; for the context, cf. Dupont-Sommer RA xxxix 49f.) - APH (v. supra) - 1) to clothe oneself, to wear; *ktnh zy htty ly swn hy mlbš* ›*nh* Herm $4^{6f.}$: the garment you brought to me to S. that one I am wearing (cf. Kutscher IOS i 104, 106, Kaufman BiOr xxxiv 95: *hy* used here as object; or *ktnh* ... *hy* = casus pendens?) - **2)** to clothe (someone else); + double object, *al-bi-iš-te-e ša-am-lat* ... Warka 31: I clothe him with the garment of ... - the *lbš* in Dir sig. 76 (= Vatt sig. eb. 76 = SANSS-Ph 9) prob. = (part of) n.p. (for a discussion, also of older litt., cf. Lemaire Sem xxvii 29ff.).

lbš$_2$ DA Sing. abs. *lbš* ii 10 - **OffAr** Sing. abs. *lbš* Cowl $15^{7,10}$, Krael 2^{4}, $7^{6,8}$, SSI ii 28 rev. 2,5, *lbwš* Cowl 14^{4}, Krael 11^{11}, ATNS $146^{2,4}$ (??, both in heavily dam. context); cstr. *lbš* Herm 3^{8}; emph. *lbš*› RHR cxxx 20^{4}, ATNS 50^{10}; + suff. 2 p.s.m. *lbšk* Cowl 68 iii obv. 4, Aḥiq 171, SSI ii 28 rev. 2; + suff. 1 p.s. *lbšy* KAI 226^{7} (cf. e.g. Cooke NSI p. 190, Donner KAI a.l., or = Plur. + suff. 1 p.s.?, cf. e.g. Gibson SSI ii p. 97f.), ATNS 44 i 7 (for the reading, cf. Porten & Yardeni sub TADAE B 8.2 :: Segal ATNS a.l.: l. *lbš*› = Sing. emph.); Plur. abs. *lbšn* Krael 7^{13}; cstr. *lbšy* Cowl 20^{5}; + suff. 3 p.s.f. *lbšyh* Krael $7^{17,23}$; cf. Frah viii 1 (*lbwš(y)*› (:: Ebeling Frah a.l.: l. *ṣrbwṣy*› = eagle)) - ¶ subst. m. garment, piece of clothing; used with coll. meaning: Cowl 14^{4}, Krael 11^{11}, ATNS 50^{10}.
v. *bšr*$_2$, *šy*$_1$.

lbt v. *lbh*.

lg **Hebr** Sing. abs. *lg* Dir pes. 23, 24, Bibl xl 986 (cf. DJD iii p. 37) - **OffAr** Sing. abs. *lg* Cowl 81^{70,79}; Plur. abs. *lgn* Cowl 81^{62,63,65,66}, RES 1301^{2,3,4}, etc., etc., *lgyn* RCL '62, 259 i 1,2 (*lg[yn]*), ii 2, 3, 4, 5, 6, iii 1, etc. - **JAr** Sing. abs. *lg* Mas 593, 594, 595^2 - ¶ subst. liquid measure, +/- 1/2 l., cf. Dir p. 287, Driver JRAS '32, 84f. (for Cowl 81), Barrois ii 248ff., Trinquet SDB v 1226, de Vaux IAT i 305f., EM iv 853ff., Milik DJD iii p. 48ff., Ben-David PEQ '71, 122, Schmitt BRL 205; for this word, cf. also Grelot Sem xxiii 104, DAE p. 119f. - Segal ATNS a.l.: the *lght* in ATNS iii poss. = Plur. abs. of *lg* (improb. interpret., cf. also Segal a.l.: preferably = l_5 + n.p.).
v. *ksp*$_2$.

lgywn v. *lgyn*.

lgyn ((< Greek λεγεών/λεγιών) < Lat. *legio*, cf. Cantineau Gramm 157, Rosenthal Sprache 91f.) - **Palm** Sing. emph. *lgywn›* CIS ii 3944^5, 3962^2, Inv x 81^2, xii 33^1; Plur. emph. *lgyny›* CIS ii 3932^4 - ¶ subst. legion; v. also *›rb‹*.

lgm **Ph** Plur. abs. *lgmm* EI xviii 117^5 (= IEJ xxxv 83) - ¶ subst. of uncert. meaning indicating a certain kind of object; Dothan EI xviii 118, IEJ xxxv 88: = decanter (< Greek λάγυνος), cf. Hebr./Ar. *lg(y)n*, *lgmm* < *lgnm* or lapsus for *lgnm* (uncert. interpret.).

lgr v. *rgl*$_2$.

ld› v. *yld*$_2$.

ldd v. *lwd*.

ldp **Pun** word of unknown meaning in CIS i 3056^2, *ḥn› bn bd‹štrt hldp šhrqḥ*: Ch. the son of B. the *ldp* who is a perfumer (??).

lh$_1$ v. *hn*$_3$, *l›*$_1$.

lh$_2$ v. *l›*$_{1,2}$.

lhbh **Pun** Février RA xlv 145: l. *lhb‹t* (= Sing. abs. or cstr. of *lhbh* (= flame)) in KAI 161^7 (cf. also Röllig KAI a.l., Roschinski Num 112, 115); highly uncert. context, cf. also e.g. Cooke NSI p. 148, 150: l. *lhr‹t* = l_5 + h_1 (article) + *r‹t* (= Sing. abs. of *r‹w* (= good pleasure)).

lhh v. *m›š*$_1$.

lhy v. *m›š*$_1$.

lhn$_1$ (< *l›*$_1$ + *hn*$_3$, cf. BL 70q, 111e) - **OffAr** Cowl 8^{11}, 9^{6,7}, 37^5, Aḥiq 107, Krael 4^{16,20}, FS Driver 54 conc. 4, ATNS 4^5, etc., etc. - **Nab** CIS ii 197^8, 208^3, 210^6, etc. - ¶ **1)** conjunction - a) but, however (with strictly adversative meaning); *wtb bgw ... lhn byt› znk l› šlyṭ ›nt lzbnh* Cowl 9^6: live thereon, but you have no power to sell this house; *w›nš l› šlyṭ ... lm‹bdh ‹bd lhn bry yhwh* Krael 8$^{8f.}$: no man shall have power ... to enslave him as a slave, but my son he shall be (cf. Cowl 9^{7,9}, 33^{11}); *wl› ršyn w›lt wbnyh dy yzbnwn ... kpr› dnh ... lhn dy yhwh kpr› hw lw›lt wlbnyh ... l‹lm* CIS ii 212$^{3ff.}$: W. and her sons shall not be

allowed to sell ... this tomb ... but the said tomb shall belong to W. and her sons ... for ever - b) with less pregnant adversative meaning, introducing another side of a mentioned subject: Krael 4[16f.], 7[33] (cf. poss. also Cowl 34[6]), cf. Yaron JSS iii 26f. - c) in the combination *l*ʾ ... *lhn*, *l*ʾ *ytqbr bqbr*ʾ *dnh* ʾ*nwš klh lhn mn dy ktyb lh tn*ʾ *mqbr* CIS ii 350[5]: no one shall be buried in this tomb except him who has in writing a document allowing to bury; *wl*ʾ *lmqbr bh* ʾ*nwš rḥq lhn* ʾ*ṣdq* CIS ii 210[5f.] (for the reading, cf. J 3): no one not belonging to the family is to be buried here but only the legitimate heirs; *w*ʾ*yš* ʾ*ḥrn l*ʾ *yšlṭ bbyth klh lhn bny zy yldty ly* Krael 4[19f.]: no other person shall have power over this whole house, except my children you bear me (cf. Cowl 8[11], 13[12], Aḥiq 107, 154, Krael 9[22], CIS ii 208[3], J 5[6]), cf. also *l*ʾ *[yš*ʾ*]l šlm ṭby*ʾ *lhn lmwnq dmh* Aḥiq 119f.: he does not greet the gazelle except to suck its blood (for the context, v. *ṭby₁*) - **2)** cf. also the foll. diff. elliptic constructions, ʾ*yty ly* ʾ*nth* ʾ*ḥrh lhn mpṭḥyh wbnn* ʾ*ḥrnn lhn bnn zy tld ly* Cowl 15[32f.]: I have another wife besides M. and other children than the children whom she shall bear to me (cf. Cowl 15[33]); *l*ʿ*nw dwšr*ʾ *wmnwtw ... mn dy ... yqbr bh* ʾ*nwš lhn lmn dy* ʿ*l*ʾ *ktyb* CIS ii 197[5ff.]: may D. and M. ... curse everyone who bury anyone in it, except those who are mentioned above - Wesselius BiOr xli 589ff.: l. *[l]hn* in KAI 224[18] (prob. restoration) :: e.g. Dupont-Sommer BMB xiii 29, Donner KAI a.l., Fitzmyer AIS 98, Degen AAG p. 22, Gibson SSI ii p. 48, Lemaire & Durand 119: l. *[w]hn* = *w* + *hn₃*.
v. *ṭl*ʾ*₂*, *lwh*.

lhn₂ **OffAr** KAI 228A 8 (heavily dam. context), 10 - ¶ conjunction, for that reason, consequently (:: Grelot RB lxix 283: < Canaan. :: BL 68x: < Hebr.).

lw **Samal** KAI 214[13,31], 215[11] - **OffAr** Cowl 37[8], Aḥiq 35, 81, FS Driver 54 conc. 1 - ¶ deictic particle - occurring in the comb. - **1)** *hn/hnw lw* - a) + Pf., *hn lw glyn* Cowl 37[8]: if we had revealed ... (for the context, v. *gly*; cf. also Joüon MUSJ xviii 22) - b) + Impf., ʾ*l thḥšk brk mn ḥṭr hn lw l*ʾ *tkhl thnṣln[hy]* Aḥiq 81: do not leave your son unpunished (v. *ḥšk₁*), or else you will not be able to save him (cf. Grelot RB lxviii 180, DAE p. 435, Ginsberg ANET 428 (cf. however Lindenberger APA 49f.: take *hn lw l*ʾ together (= otherwise followed by question: otherwise can you save him?)) :: Cowl a.l.: ... if thou canst not keep him ... :: Kottsieper SAS 19, 213: ... if you could not ... :: Joüon MUSJ xviii 22: ... even if you cannot keep him ...; cf. also Segert AAG 434, Lindenberger APA 50) - c) + nom. clause, *hn lw [*ʾ*ḥ]yq[r] zk šb*ʾ *spr ḥkym ... lmh hw yḥbl mt*ʾ Aḥiq 35f.: even if this old man A. is a skilful scribe why should he ruin the land (:: Ginsberg ANET 427: otherwise this old man A. is a wise scribe ... and is liable to corrupt the land ...; cf. also Joüon MUSJ xviii 22); *whnw lw šḥt* KAI

214[31f.]: if you have destroyed indeed (for the context, v. *šḥt*$_1$, *›šr*$_4$; for the interpret. of *lw*, cf. Montgomery JAOS liv 421, 424, Dion p. 175, 298f. :: Lidzbarski Handb s.v. *lw*, Cooke NSI p. 163, Friedr 41*, Garb 264, Koopmans 35, Donner KAI a.l., Segert AAG 434: = conjunction, if :: e.g. Clermont-Ganneau Et ii 202, Halévy RS vii 337, Lagrange ERS 498, Poeb 48 n. 4, Solá-Solé IS 125: = negation); for *hn lw*, cf. also Huehnergard JAOS ciii 571 (n. 22) - 2) *k‹n lw* FS Driver 54 conc. 1 (cf. Dupont-Sommer a.l., Naveh AION xvi 25 (:: Naveh ibid.: or = lapsus for *k‹n hlw*? (cf. also Huehnergard JAOS ciii 571 n. 23)), Dion p. 300) - 3) *lw* ... *lw* KAI 215[11] repetition of asseverative particle, surely (cf. Montgomery JAOS liv 424, Dion p. 39) > as well ... as (cf. also Dion p. 299) :: e.g. Lidzbarski Handb s.v. *lw*, Cooke NSI p. 174, 177, Lagrange ERS 497, Koopmans 35, Donner KAI a.l.: = *sive* ... *sive*, whether ... or :: Gibson SSI ii p. 81, 84, Huehnergard JAOS ciii 571 (n. 21): though ... though ... :: Segert AAG 434: = if (irrealis?) :: Halévy RS vii 349: = neither ... nor (repetition of negation) - the same particle with asseverative meaning prob. also in KAI 214[13], cf. Montgomery JAOS liv 421, Dion p. 175, 298f. :: Lidzbarski Handb s.v. *lw*, Cooke NSI p. 162, 167, Garb 264, Donner KAI a.l., Gibson SSI ii p. 67: = conjunction, if :: e.g. Halévy RS vii 336, Poeb 48 n. 4: = negation.

v. *l›*$_{1,2}$, *lwl›*, *ptḥ*$_1$.

lw› v. *l›*$_1$.

lwbr **OffAr** diff. word in Cowl 26[13,17], either subst. Sing. abs. or undeclinable adj. (cf. Grelot DAE p. 291 n. g); meaning: 'what is old' or 'old' (cf. Perles OLZ '11, 499, Cowl a.l., Grelot DAE p. 291f.). Perhaps with the special meaning: seasoned (cf. Cowl a.l., Couroyer RB xxx 468), cf. however Grelot DAE p. 291f.: = used; occurring in the expressions: *‹qy ›rz lwbr* Cowl 26[13,17] (occurring next to *‹qy ›rz ḥdṭn* (Cowl 26[14]), *lwbr wtbyrn* Cowl 26[13] (also said of planks)). For the relation with the Akkad. *labāru*, cf. Kaufman AIA 66 and litt. quoted there (cf. also Grelot DAE p. 291 n. g); cf. also Whitehead JNES xxxvii 133 n. 90: kind of wood.

lwd (cf. e.g. Fitzmyer JAOS lxxxi 207f., AIS 76, Koopmans 58, Degen AAG p. 75f., Gibson SSI ii p. 43, Greenfield & Shaffer Irâq xlv 114; or < *ldd*?, cf. Milik Bibl xlviii 571 n., Donner KAI ii p. 258, Kaufman Maarav iii 166; or < root *lyd*?, cf. Gropp & Lewis BASOR cclix 49f. :: Gevirtz VT xi 144 n. 2 (cf. Dupont-Sommer Sf p. 93, Fitzmyer AIS 76, Milik Bibl xlviii 571 n., Stefanovic COAI 152 (n. 2)): // Hebr. *lwz*) - **OldAr** QAL Impf. 3 p.s.m. *yld* Tell F 11 (Akkad. par. *ú-na-ka-ru*), 16 (Akkad. par. *i-pa-ši-ṭu-ni*); Imper. s.m. *ld* KAI 223C 9 (cf. e.g. Veenhof BiOr xx 144, Fitzmyer AIS 91, Degen AAG p. 19 (n. 77), Gibson SSI ii p. 44, 46 :: Dupont-Sommer Sf p. 117, 122: l. *ld[t]* = QAL Pf. 1 p.s., cf. also

Donner KAI a.l.); Inf. *ld* KAI 223C 6, *mld* Tell F 9 (Akkad. par. *nasa-ḫ*; :: Andersen & Freedman FS Fensham 21: = Pa‘el Inf. :: Vattioni AION xlvi 360: or = Sing. abs. of noun *mld* (= elimination)?); Haph Impf. 1 p.s. *ʾhld* KAI 222C 18; Inf. (cstr., cf. Kaufman BiOr xxxiv 95) *hldt* KAI 223C 2 - ¶ verb Qal to efface; + obj. + *mn*$_5$, *mn yld šmy mn mʾnyʾ* Tell F 16: whoever will efface my name from the movable objects ... (cf. Tell F 11, KAI 223C 6f., 9f.); > to remove, *wlmld mrq mnh* Tell F 9: to remove illness from him (sc. the king, cf. Akkad. par.: *ana nasa-ḫ murṣi šá zumri-šú*) - Haph to efface - **1)** + obj. + *mn*$_5$, *lhldt spry[ʾ ʾ]ln mn bty ʾlhyʾ* KAI 223C 2f.: to efface these inscriptions from the sacred stones - **2)** + *mn*$_5$, *ʾhld mn mlwh* KAI 222C 18f.: I shall efface some of its words.
v. *lḥm*$_2$.

lwh **OffAr** Kottsieper SAS 12, 20, 213: l. *lw[t]* (= Sing. cstr. of *lwh* (= proximity)) in Aḥiq 97; uncert. reading and interpret., cf. Grelot DAE p. 107 (n. b): l. *lwt* = *l*$_5$ + *wt* (= towards), cf. also e.g. Cowl a.l., Lindenberger APA 73: l. *lhn* (= *lhn*$_1$ (= but)).

lwḥ$_1$ v. *šlḥ*$_3$.

lwḥ$_2$ **OffAr** Sing. abs. *lwḥ* Cowl 79^{3,4}; emph. *lwḥʾ* NESE iii 34 conv. 2 - **Nab** Sing. emph. *lwḥʾ* ADAJ xxi 146 n. 11^2 (dam. context) - ¶ subst. f. - **1)** board (?): Cowl 79^{3,4} (diff. and dam. context, cf. also RES sub 1796) - **2)** tablet (?): NESE iii 34 conv. 2, ADAJ xxi 146 n. 11^2 (both in diff. and dam. context) - on this word, cf. Galling FS Albright ii 208ff. - cf. also *lḥ*$_1$.

lwḥšh v. *lḥšh*.

lwṭ **OffAr** Qal Impf. 2 p.s.m. *tlṭ* Aḥiq 96 (for reading of *l*, cf. Sach p. 163 :: Sach p. 163, Ungnad ArPap 71, Lindenberger APA 71, 234 n. 146, Puech RB xcv 589, Muraoka JSS xxxii 187f.: l. *tl[w]ṭ* (cf. also Kottsieper SAS 12, 156, 213) :: e.g. Cowl p. 236, Ginsberg ANET 428, Grelot RB lxviii 182, DAE p. 436: l. *tbṭ* = Qal Impf. 2 p.s.m. of *bṭṭ*$_1$ (= to chatter)); 3 p.pl.m. *ylwṭwn* Aḥiq 151 (cf. also Ben-Chayyim EI i 136) - **Waw** Qal Impf. 2 p.s.m. *tlṭ* AMB 6^{14} (cf. Dupont-Sommer Waw p. 11, 27, Gordon Or xviii 339; uncert. reading and interpret., cf. Del Medico AIPHOS ix 182, Naveh & Shaked AMB a.l.: = Sing. emph. of *tlṭ* (= sea; < Greek θάλαττα)) - ¶ verb Qal to curse; for the context of Aḥiq 96, v. *ywm*.
v. *mlʾ*$_1$.

lwy$_1$ **OffAr** Qal (or Pa‘el?) Impf. 3 p.s.m. *ylwh* Aḥiq 164 - ¶ verb Qal (or Pa‘el?) to accompany; + *‘m*$_4$: Aḥiq 164.

lwy$_2$ v. *lyn*$_1$.

lwy$_3$ **Hebr** Sing. abs. *lwy* Frey 974^2 (= SM 1), SM 80, MPAT-A 9^1 (= SM 3b; in Ar. context), 27^1 (= SM 33; in Ar. context) - **JAr** Sing. emph. *lywyʾ* SM 82 - ¶ subst. levite.

lwk‘y (< Prakrit *loke*, cf. Shaked JRAS ’69, 119f., Kutscher, Naveh & Shaked Lesh xxxiv 128) - **OffAr** Sing. abs. *lwk‘y* JA ccliv 440^{3} (for the reading, cf. Shaked JRAS ’69, 119, Kutscher, Naveh & Shaked Lesh xxxiv 128 :: Dupont-Sommer JA ccliv 440, 456: l. / *wk‘n* = word divider + *w* + *k‘n*$_4$) - ¶ subst. world, people (cf. also Benveniste JA ccliv 449; // with *’rq* in same line).

lwl’ **OffAr** diff. word (?, heavily dam. context) in Cowl 71^{20}; CIS ii sub 145: = *lw* + *l’*$_1$ (= unless), cf. however Cowl a.l. (also for other interpret.).

lwlyt = arrowhead > Akkad., cf. v.Soden Or xxxv 14, xlvi 189 (cf. also idem AHW s.v. *lūlī-tu*, cf. CAD s.v.).

lwn$_1$ v. *lyn*$_1$.

lwn$_2$ v. *lyn*$_1$.

lwn$_3$ v. *lyn*$_1$.

lwqbl v. *qbl*$_3$.

lwš **OffAr** Qal Imper. pl.m. *lšw* RES 1793^{2} (cf. Cowley PSBA xxxvii 222 (with reserve), Grelot DAE p. 376 :: Chabot RES a.l.: = Qal Pf. 3 p.pl.m.; for the context, v. *lḥm*$_4$); cf. Frah xix 8 (*lyšwn*, cf. Toll ZDMG-Suppl viii 36) - **JAr** Qal Impf. 2 p.s.m. *tlwš* MPAT 49 i 9 (uncert. context, cf. also Beyer ATTM 318: l. *tlyš* = Qal Part. pass. s.m. abs. of *tlš* (= to pull out)) - the diff. *lš’* in Antas 70^{6} = form of this root?? (cf. also Fantar Antas p. 73; highly uncert. interpret.) - ¶ verb Qal to knead + obj.: RES 1793^{2}, MPAT 49 i 9.
v. *lyš*$_1$.

lwt$_1$ **Palm** Pa‘el Pf. 3 p.s.m. *lwt* MUSJ xxxviii 106^{6} - ¶ verb Pa‘el to make a partner; + *l*$_5$ (obj.) + *b*$_2$: MUSJ xxviii 106^{6} (cf. Ingholt MUSJ xxviii 111f.).

lwt$_2$ v. *’yt*$_3$.

lwtn v.Soden Or xxxv 14, xlvi 189: Akkad. *lamūtānu* < Ar. (root *lwy*; = attendant, a type of slave), highly uncert. interpret., cf. v.Soden AHW s.v. (: ?), cf. however Albright RA xvi 184, CAD s.v. *lamutānu*.

lḥ$_1$ **Pun** Sing. abs. *lḥ* KAI 145^{8} (v. infra; :: Silverman JAOS xciv 269: = Sing. m. abs. of *lḥ*$_2$ (= moist) :: Krahmalkov RSF iii 188f., 194, 203 (div. otherwise): l. *hlḥ* = Qal Pf. 3 p.s.m. of *‘ly*$_1$) - ¶ subst. tablet (prob. interpret., cf. Halévy RS ix 280, Cooke NSI p. 155, Février Sem vi 21, 26 (: = tariff), Röllig KAI a.l. (: = tariff or memorial tablet), v.d.Branden RSF i 169 (: = memorial tablet), cf. also Berger MAIBL xxxvi/2, 160) - cf., also *lwḥ*$_2$.
v. *’ḥd*$_4$.

lḥ$_2$ v. *lḥ*$_1$.

lḥ$_3$ v. *lḥy*$_2$.

lḥh v. *ḥy*$_1$, *lḥy*$_2$.

lḥy$_1$ **OffAr** Qal Impf. 3 p.pl.m. *ylḥwn* Aḥiq 124 (cf. however Lindenberger APA 113, Kottsieper SAS 176, 213: = PA‘EL, Muraoka JSS xxxii 188: APH poss.) - ¶ verb QAL to do evil; + *l*$_5$, *ʾlhn ylḥwn lhm* Aḥiq 124: the gods will do evil unto them (cf. Ginsberg ANET 429, cf. also Grelot DAE p. 440, Lindenberger APA 113, Kottsieper SAS 22 :: Cowl a.l.: = to curse, cf. also Grelot RB lxviii 186).

lḥy$_2$ **OldAr** Sing. f. abs. *lḥyh* KAI 222A 26 (cf. Pardee JNES xxxvii 197), C 6f. (*lḥ[yh]*); Plur. f. abs. *lḥyt* KAI 222C 20 (cf. Segert ArchOr xxxii 122, Fitzmyer AIS 77, 155, Degen AAG p. 52, Gibson SSI ii p. 43, Wesselius AION xxx 265ff. :: Dupont-Sommer Sf p. 93: = Sing. f. abs.), 224^{2} - **OffAr** Sing. m. abs. *lḥh* KAI 225^{10}, Aḥiq 130, 138 (:: Grelot RB lxviii 188: or = cursed?), 200; m. emph. *lḥyʾ* Cowl 30^{7}, 31^{6}, 32^{6}, Driv 5^{7}, MAI xiv/2, 66^{6}; f. abs. *lḥyh* Aḥiq 124; f. emph. *lḥytʾ* Aḥiq 134, 198 (*lḥy[tʾ]*; dam. context); + suff. 1 p.s. *lḥyty* Aḥiq 139; Plur. m. emph. *lḥyʾ* ATNS 26^{17} - ¶ adj. - **1)** bad - a) said of a person, wicked, reprobate; *wydrng zk lḥyʾ* Cowl 30$^{6f.}$, 31^{6}: that wicked W.; *wydrng lḥyʾ zk*, Cowl 32^{6}: idem; cf. Driv 5^{7}, Aḥiq 130, ATNS 26^{17}, etc. - b) said of someone's death, miserable, evil: KAI 225^{10} - c) said of words, *wymll mln lḥyt* KAI 224^{2}: he will speak evil words, i.e. he will instigate rebellion (cf. Greenfield ActOr xxix 8f., Weinfeld UF viii 387 (n. 78, 80), cf. also Tawil JNES xxxii 478 n. 20) - **2)** substantivated adj. - a) m. form, *ṭbʾ wlḥyʾ nplg kḥdh* MAI xiv/2, 66$^{5f.}$: the good and the bad we will share alike (cf. e.g. Dupont-Sommer MAI a.l.), sc. of the produce of the land - b) f. form, what is bad, evil; *kl mh lḥyh bʾrq wbšmyn* KAI 222A 26: all manner of evil on earth and in heaven (cf. also KAI 222C 6f., 20); said of words, *whn lḥyh tnpq [mn] pmhm* Aḥiq 124: if an evil thing comes forth from their mouth (cf. Ginsberg ANET 429, cf. also Grelot DAE p. 440, Kottsieper SAS 22, 213 :: Cowl a.l., Grelot RB lxviii 186: = curse); said of an action, *y‘bd lḥytʾ* Aḥiq 134: he does something bad (i.e. he causes misfortune; cf. Ginsberg ANET 429, cf. also Grelot DAE p. 442, Lindenberger APA 131, 258 nn. 407-408, Kottsieper SAS 15, 213 :: e.g. Cowl a.l., Grelot RB lxviii 188: = curse), cf. Aḥiq 198 (v. supra); said of something happening to someone, *[mny] npqt lḥyty* Aḥiq 139: my misfortune has proceeded from myself (cf. Ginsberg ANET 429, Grelot DAE p. 442, Lindenberger APA 137 (cf. also Kottsieper SAS 9, 16: pro *[mn]* l. *[mn bny]* = from my children) :: e.g. Cowl a.l. (cf. also Grelot RB lxviii 188): = curse) - Garbini with Hölbi AGPPS i 134f.: the *lḥ* in ibid. 134 = Sing. m. abs. of *lḥy*$_2$ (uncert. interpret.).

v. *ḥwd*$_1$, *ḥwy*$_2$, *ḥy*$_1$.

lḥm$_1$ **Mo** HIPHT Impf. 1 p.s. *ʾltḥm* KAI 181^{11,15}; Inf. cstr. + suff. 3 p.s.m. *hltḥmh* KAI 181^{19}; Imper. s.m. *hltḥm* KAI 181^{32} - ¶ verb HIPHT to make war, to fight; + *b*$_2$ (against), *wʾltḥm bqr* KAI 181^{11}: and I fought against the town (i.e. I besieged the town), cf. KAI 181^{15,32};

bhltḥmh by KAI 181[19]: while he was warring against me.
v. *lḥm$_2$*, *nd.*

lḥm$_2$ **Ph** QAL Inf. cstr. *lḥm* KAI 24[6] (for the reading, cf. Herrmann OLZ '53, 297 (n. 1) :: v.Arendonk with Bauer ZDMG lxviii 227: l. *l'm* = Sing. + suff. 1 p.s. of *l'm$_3$* (= people) :: Sperling UF xx 329: pro *lḥm* l. *ldm* = QAL Inf. + suff. 3 p.pl.m. of *lwd* (= to extirpate)) - ¶ verb QAL to eat, to devour: KAI 24[6] (cf. Lidzbarski Eph iii 228, Friedr 137, Landsberger Sam'al 51, Koopmans 12, de Moor UF xx 167 (cf. Gibson SSI iii p. 34, 36: or + suff. 3 p.s.m.?, cf. Rosenthal ANET 654 (less prob. interpret.)) :: Bauer ZDMG lxvii 686, Collins WO vi 184 (n. 8), v.d.Branden RSF ii 141: = Sing. abs. of *lḥm$_4$* :: Koopmans 12: or *llḥm* = *l$_5$* + *hlḥm* (= NIPH Inf. cstr. of *lḥm$_1$*) :: Harr 114: = QAL (or PI'EL?) Inf. cstr. of *lḥm$_1$* (cf. also Tawil CBQ xlii 36 (n. 31), Sader EAS 157) :: Herrmann OLZ '53, 297, Röllig KAI a.l.: l. *hlḥm* (supposing that *h* in *lpnyhm* from preceding line belongs here) = NIPH Inf. cstr. of *lḥm$_1$* (against this interpret., cf. Fales WO x 10 n. 15); cf. also Avishur PIB 208, 211).

lḥm$_3$ v.Soden Or xxxv 13, xlvi 189: D-stem of Akkad. *la-ḫāmu* = to distillate, to make beer < Ar. *lḥm* = to be right, apt (cf. also id. AHW s.v. *la-ḫāmu* I; improb. interpret., cf. CAD s.v. *la-ḫāmu* B).

lḥm$_4$ **Pun** Sing. abs. *lḥm* KAI 76B 3 (dam. context; or cstr.?), 4 - **Hebr** Sing. abs. *lḥm* KAI 197[3] (for this poss. reading, cf. e.g. Michaud Syr xxxiv 52, 54, Lemaire IH i 127, Pardee HAHL 105), TA-H 1[8f.], 2[4], 3[7f.], 5[6] (dam. context), 6[4] (*lḥ[m]*, dam. context), 12[6] - **OldAr** Sing. abs. *lḥm* KAI 222A 24 (diff. context; cf. however Garbini AION xvii 91f.: = Sing. abs. of *lḥm$_5$* (= war, struggle, combat) :: Epstein Kedem i 39: = *lḥm$_6$* (= thread); for the context, v. also *šwṭ$_1$*), B 38, 39, 224[5,7], Tell F 22; + suff. 3 p.s.m. *lḥmh* Tell F 17 (Akkad. par. *akal-šú*), 18 (Akkad. par. idem); + suff. 1 p.s. *lḥmy* KAI 222B 38 (the same form also in KAI 222B 37?, cf. Lipiński Stud 42, cf. also Donner KAI a.l., Fitzmyer AIS 71) - **OffAr** Sing. abs. *lḥm* Cowl 71[8], Aḥiq 86, 189, NESE iii 34 conc. 5, JRAS '29, 108[13], FS Driver 54 conc. 3, ATNS 20[3] (or = Sing. cstr.?); cstr. *lḥm* Aḥiq 33; emph. *lḥm'* Sach 76 i B 5, Sem xxxix 32 conv. 3, ATNS 52a 9; + suff. 3 p.pl.m. *lḥmhn* RES 1793[1] (for this interpret., cf. Cowley PSBA xxxvii 222, Grelot DAE p. 376 :: Chabot sub RES 1793 (div. otherwise): l. *lḥm* (= Sing. abs.)); cf. Frah iv 10 (*lḥm'*), GIPP 27, 56, SaSt 22 - **Palm** Sing. abs. *lḥm* CIS ii 4218[7], Syr xvii 353[1] - **JAr** Sing. abs. *lḥm* MPAT 49 i 11, IEJ xl 144[14], Mas 554[3] (*[l]ḥm*; ?), 557[2], 560[2], 561[2], 565[3], 567[2], 569[1], 571[1], 572[2], 574[2], 577[2], 579[2] (*[l]ḥm*), 582[1], 583[3]; emph. *lḥm'* Syr xlv 101[21] (dam. context) - ¶ subst. m. bread, food, passim; for the context of KAI 222B 38, 224[5,7], v. *nsk$_1$*; for the context of ATNS 20[3], v. *ṭyq*; *lḥmh wmwh* Tell F 17: his bread and water (i.e. the food for the deity; cf. also Tell F 18; cf. Greenfield & Shaffer

RB xcii 52f., Greenfield FS Cross 70f.); *lḥm wmyn* FS Driver 54 conc. 3: bread and water (as the normal fare of a prisoner, cf. also Greenfield JAOS lxxxv 257); *[b]šr wlḥm wm[...* Syr xvii 353[1]: meat and bread and ..[... (dam. context); *wntn lktym b ⁰ 2 yyn ... w 300 lḥm* TA-H 2[1ff.] (for the problems of additional sign before 300, cf. Aharoni TA a.l., Pardee UF x 298): give the K. two baths of wine ... and 300 (loaves of) bread (cf. NESE iii 34 conc. 5: *lḥm 10* in dam. context); *[ḥ]d mn rby ʾby zy lḥm ʾby [ʾkl]* Aḥiq 33f.: one of my father's officers who ate the bread of my father (i.e. who dwelt at the court of my father); *hn grsw lḥmhn lšw* ... RES 1793[1f.]: if they have consumed (?, v. *grs*) their bread, knead ... - the *lḥm* in Cowl 57[2] of highly uncert. reading (cf. Cowl a.l.: *m* looks like *zn*; heavily dam. context) and interpret. (cf. also Driver JRAS '32, 83: = l_5 + $ḥm_2$??).
v. $lḥm_2$, $šlh_1$, *tḥm*.
lḥm₅ v. $lḥm_4$, *tḥm*.
lḥm₆ v. $lḥm_4$.
lḥn₁ v. *nd*.
lḥn₂ (< Akkad., cf. e.g. Porten Arch 200, Kaufman AIA 66 (n. 176)) - **OffAr** m. Sing. abs. *lḥn* Krael 2[2], 3[3,25], 4[2], 6[2], 9[2], 10[1], 12[1,10]; emph. *lḥnʾ* Cowl 63[9,12], Krael 4[23], 9[23,27], 10[9,17], 12[33], AG 102; s.f. abs. *lḥnh* Krael 12[2] - ¶ subst. m. certain type of temple servant, f. wife of the preceding, cf. Eilers AfO xvii 323 (cf. also Segert ArchOr xxiv 388f., 401, Gordon JNES xiv 57), Landsberger SVT xvi 204, Porten Arch 200f., Grelot RB lxxix 616, Kaufman AIA 66 (n. 176), cf. Couroyer BiOr xxvii 250 n. 9, Porten & Greenfield JEAS p. 37, Demsky IEJ xxxi 100ff., Porten & Yardeni sub TADAE B 3.2 and elsewhere, cf. also Krael p. 144f., Milik RB lxi 248, Teixidor Sumer xxi 88, Greenfield SVT xxxii 119f., Degen BLKA i 30f. :: Torrey JNES xiii 150f., Reider JQR xliv 339, Couroyer VT v 83ff., Kutscher JAOS lxxiv 234: = cantor, singer :: Driver AnOr xii 59: = maker of (wooden) bowls/dishes; cf. also Cazelles Syr xxxii 77 n. 4.
v. $ḥnt_1$, *nd*.
lḥnh v. $lḥn_2$.
lḥṣ₁ v. *pḥṣ*.
lḥṣ₂ **OldAr** Sing. cstr. *lḥṣ* KAI 223C 10 - ¶ subst. affliction, torment; *blḥṣ ʿlb* KAI 223C 10: by crushing torment.
lḥš **OffAr** QAL (or PAʿEL?) Pf. 3 p.s.m. *lḥš* Cowl 71[23] (dam. context) - ¶ verb QAL (or PAʿEL?) to whisper: Cowl 71[23].
lḥšh **Ph** Sing. abs. *lḥšt* KAI 27[1] (v. infra), Syr xlviii 396[1] (:: Cross CBQ xxxvi 488: = Plur. abs.) - **JAr** Sing. abs. *lwḥšh* AMB 1[16] - ¶ subst. incantation, spell (:: Teixidor OA i 106: pro *lḥšt lʿtʾ* l. *lḥšt* (= Sing. cstr.) *ʿtʾ* in KAI 27[1]; for the context of KAI 27[1], Syr xlviii 396[1], v. l_5) :: Dahood CBQ xxii 407f. n. 30: or = amulet?

v. *ʾš*$_1$.

lṭr (< Greek λίτρα, cf. e.g. CIS i sub 143, Honeyman Mus li 295, Röllig KAI a.l.) - **Ph** Plur. abs. *lṭrm* Mus li 286[5] (prob. reading) - **Pun** Plur. abs. *lṭrm* KAI 66[1] - ¶ subst. certain weight, +/- 330 gr.

ly$_1$ v. *l*$_1$.

ly$_2$ v. *tḥt*.

lyd v. *lwd*.

lyh **Pun** Février Sem iv 20f.: l. *lyt* (Sing. cstr.) in KAI 160[1] = community, association (cf. also Röllig KAI a.l.), improb. interpret., cf. Levi Della Vida RCL '55, 556 n. 2 (div. otherwise): l. *ly* (= *l*$_5$ + suff. 3 p.s.m.) + *t* (= *ʾyt*$_3$).

lywy v. *lwy*$_3$.

lyṭʾ **Pun** word (?) of unknown meaning in KAI 145[9] (diff. reading); v.d.Branden RSF i 170: = *l*$_5$ + YIPH Inf. cstr. of *nṭʿ*$_1$ (= to plant, to place); Février Sem vi 20, 23: l. *klyṭm* = Plur. abs. of *klyṭ* < Greek κάλαθος (= (corinthian) capital of a column); Krahmalkov RSF iii 188f., 195, 203: l. *plyṭm* = PIʿEL Pf. 3 p.s.m. + suff. 3 p.s.m. of *plṭ*; Berger MAIBL xxxvi/2, 161: prob. = n.p.

lyl v. *lylh*, *ll*$_2$.

lylh **Mo** Sing. abs. *llh* KAI 181[15] (for this form, cf. e.g. Cooke NSI p. 12, v.Zijl 174f., Segert ArchOr xxix 219, 222, 243, Röllig KAI a.l., Gibson SSI i p. 80, Blau Maarav ii 144 n. 5, Jackson & Dearman SMIM 114) - **DA** Sing. abs. *lylh* i 1 (for this form, cf. Hoftijzer DA p. 288f. (n. 14), Hackett BTDA 32 (n. 8)) - **Samal** Sing. abs. *lylʾ* KAI 214[24] (for the diff. interpret. of this form, cf. Ronzevalle FS de Vogüé 522, Montgomery JAOS liv 422, Ginsberg JAOS lxii 236 n. 38, Donner KAI a.l., Friedrich FS Landsberger 426, Gibson SSI ii p. 74, Dion p. 110, Lipiński BiOr xxxiii 233, Degen GGA '79, 28; cf. however Garb 260: = Sing. emph. of *lyl* (= night); cf. also Segert AAG p. 193, Hoftijzer DA p. 186f. n. 9) - **OldAr** Sing. abs. *lylh* KAI 222A 12 (for the diff. interpret. of this form, cf. e.g. Bauer AfO viii 5, CF 27, Dupont-Sommer Sf p. 35, Koopmans p. 48, Segert ArchOr xxxii 123, AAG p. 193, Fitzmyer JAOS lxxxi 193, AIS 38f., 143, 153, Degen AAG p. 10 n. 46, 26, GGA '79, 28, Kutscher IOS i 104 n. 4, Gibson SSI ii p. 37, Hoftijzer DA p. 288f. n. 14, Andersen & Freedman FS Fitzmyer 8 :: Garb 266: = Sing. emph. of *lyl*) - ¶ subst. night; *bllh* KAI 181[15]: throughout the night (cf. Dahood FS Horn 434) - Epstein ZAW xxxiii 228, Lindenberger APA 71f., 234 n. 149, 281f.: l. prob. *[ly]lh* (= Sing. abs.) in Aḥiq 96 (prob. restoration :: e.g. Cowl a.l., Grelot DAE 436: l. *[kl* (= Sing. cstr. of *kl*$_1$) *m]lh* (= Sing. abs. of *mlh*)); for the reading problems, cf. however Puech RB xcv 589f.: l. poss. *sph* (= Sing. + suff. 3 p.s.m. of *sp*$_2$) - cf. also *lyly*, *ll*$_2$.

lyly **OffAr**, cf. Frah xxvii 4 (*lylyʾ*) - **Nab** Sing. emph. *lylyʾ* J 2[4] - **JAr**

Sing. emph. *lyly*ʾ AMB 12[14] - ¶ subst. night - cf. also *lylh*, *ll*$_2$.

lyn$_1$ **Ph** YITP Pf. 3 p.pl.m. *ytlnn* KAI 24[10] (cf. FR 166 (cf. also 149), Naveh JAOS xciii 588f., IEJ xxviii 206, Swiggers ZDMG cxxxi 226ff. (v. however infra; cf. also Poeb 36 n. 5) × Segert GPP p. 141, 194: = HITPOL Impf. 3 p.pl.m. (cf. also Herrmann OLZ '53, 296, v. however infra); or = YITP Impf.? (cf. Gibson SSI iii p. 37; v. however infra); for the problems involved, cf. also Coxon JAOS xcviii 419 n. 22 :: Halévy RS xx 28, Landsberger Kultische Kalender 108 n. 2: l. *ytlwn* = HITP Impf. 3 p.pl. of *lyn*$_1$ (cf. also Friedrich ZS i 6 (n. 2), Poeb 36 n. 5) :: v. Arendonk with Bauer ZDMG lxviii 227, Albright JPOS vi 84f., Gressmann AIAT 442, Harr 114 , Koopmans 13, Friedr 135a, 174, CF 18: l. *ytlwn* = HITP Impf. 3 p.pl. of *lwy*$_2$ (= to curb oneself, to bend; cf. also Silverman JAOS xciv 268: = to wind, to accompany) :: v.d.Branden GP p. 81, 99: l. *ytlwn* = YITP pf 3 p.pl.m. of *lwn*$_2$ (= to growl, to grumble) :: Lidzbarski Eph iii 233, Torrey JAOS xxxv 367: l. *ytlkn* = HITP Impf. 3 p.pl. of *hlk*$_1$) - ¶ verb YITP (HITP?, v. supra) to spend the night (cf. Poeb 36 (n. 5), cf. also Halévy RS xx 28, Landsberger Kultische Kalender 108 n. 2, Samʾal 52 (v. however supra) :: Herrmann OLZ '53, 295ff., Röllig BiOr xix 24, KAI a.l., Collins WO vi 187, FR 149, 166, Segert GPP p. 141, 194, 292, Avishur PIB 208, 212, Gibson SSI iii p. 35, 37, de Moor UF xx 167, Garr DGSP 126, 133, H.P.Müller TUAT i 639: < *lwn*$_2$ = to growl, to grumble, to murmur, to complain :: Sader EAS 158, 159 n. 20: < *lwn*$_3$ = to be maltreated) - a form of this root (QAL Part. act. s.m. abs. or Pf. 3 p.s.m.: *ln*) poss. in TA-H 40[11] (cf. Aharoni TA a.l., Pardee UF x 323).
v. *hykylyn*, *nd*, *nṣḥ*$_2$.

lyn$_2$ **Pun** Tomback JNES viii 106: the *lyn* in CIS i 5090[3] poss. = Sing. abs. of *lyn*$_2$ (= lodger), uncert. interpret., cf. also CIS i a.l.: poss. = Sing. m. abs. of *lyn*$_3$ (= 'blandus').

lyn$_3$ v. *lyn*$_2$.

lyṣ **Ph** YIPH Part. s.m. abs. *mlṣ* RES 1357[2]; cstr. *mlṣ* CIS i 22 (*ml[ṣ]*; = Kition A 9), 44[2] (= Kition B 40), 88[3,5,6] (= Kition F 1); pl.m. abs. *mlṣm* KAI 26A i 8 (v. infra) - **Pun** YIPH Part. s.m. abs. *mlṣ* CIS i 350[4], Hofra 163[3] (for this reading, cf. Berthier & Charlier Hofra p. 240, cf. also Février BAr '55/56, 157; reading *mls* Hofra a.l. less prob.) - ¶ verb YIPH Part. - **1)** indication of function, prob. interpreter: RES 1357[2], CIS i 350[4], Hofra 163[3], also occurring in the diff. expression *mlṣ (h)krsym* (v. *krsy*) - **2)** (humbug >) bad one, wicked person: KAI 26A i 8, cf. Dupont-Sommer RA xlii 170: arrogant one (cf. however idem Oriens ii 121f.: or = proud one > noble?), Honeyman PEQ '49, 26, 31: traitor, Leveen & Moss JJS i 192f.: scorner, Levi Della Vida RCL '49, 277: reckless, presumptuous one, Marcus & Gelb JNES viii 119: rebel (cf. also Röllig KAI a.l., Bron RIPK 51ff., Gibson SSI iii p.

47, 57), Pedersen ActOr xxi 39, 50: audacious one, Rosenthal ANET 653: wicked one, Lipiński RTAT 258: violent one, Avishur PIB 223, 228: mocker (cf. also Swiggers BiOr xxxvii 338) :: Richardson VT v 434ff.: = fluent speaker > (court) advisor :: v.d.Branden Meltô i 36, 77: = intermediary (god) :: Albright with O'Callaghan Or xviii 185: = demigod (cf. Alt WO i 280f., cf. also Gordon Introduction 199: *mlṣm* = *lares* (cf. however Gordon JNES viii 109, 113: = dignitary)) :: Dunand BMB viii 30: *mlṣm* = Plur. abs. of *mlṣ* (= robber; < root *lṣṣ*) :: Lipiński SV 48, 50 n. c: *mlṣm* = Plur. abs. of *mlṣ*$_2$ (= hiding-place); cf. Zolli Sef x 166: *mlṣm* = Plur. abs. of *mlṣ*$_1$ (= rest) :: Gevirtz Maarav v/vi 145ff.: *mlṣm* = Plur. abs. of *mlṣ*$_3$ (= divine intermediary).

lyš$_1$ **DA** Sing. abs. *lyš* ii 13 (??, diff. and dam. context, cf. Hoftijzer DA a.l., cf. however Garbini Hen i 184, 186: prob. = *lyš*$_2$ (cf. also Levine JAOS ci 200, 202, H.P.Müller ZAW xciv 236 n. 147) :: Caquot & Lemaire Syr liv 206, Ringgren Mem Seeligmann 94: = QAL Part. pass. s.m. abs. of *lwš* :: Rofé SB 63, 68 (dividing otherwise): l. *kl yš* :: Hackett BTDA 26, 30, 69f., 94, 97, 134 (div. otherwise): l. poss. *yšbm* = APH Impf. 3 p.s.m. + suff. 3 p.pl.m. of *šwb*) - ¶ subst. lion.

lyš$_2$ **OldAr** + suff. 3 p.s.m. *lyšh* KAI 216^6 - **OffAr** *l›yt* RES '41/45, 67 conc. 3, *l›yty* Krael 7^{29}, RES '41/45, 67 conc. 6; cf. Frah xxv 43 (*l‹yt*), Paik 595 (*l‹yty*), Dep 154 verso 2, GIPP 26 - **Palm** *lyt* Syr xvii 353^{5,6} (dam. context; cf. Cantineau Syr a.l., Gawlikowski TP 57f. :: Milik DFD 301ff. (div. otherwise): l. *bdlyt* = *b*$_2$ + Sing. cstr. of *dlyt* (= in association with ...)) - **JAr** *l›yty* MPAT 51^{12} - ¶ comb. of adverb of negation *l›*$_1$ and noun *›yš/t(y)* (v. *›yty*, *›t*$_3$): there is not; *whn mlḥ l›yt bbyt›* RES '41/45, 67 conc. 3: if there is no salt in the house - *lyš/l›t(y)* + *l*$_5$, *hlw l›yty ly mlḥ* RES '41/45, 67 conc. 5ff.: see I have no salt; *wbr zkr wnqbh l›yty lh* Krael 7$^{28f.}$: he has no male or female child; *mlyn l›yty ly* MPAT 51$^{12f.}$: there are no claims for me (i.e. I have no claims); *by ṭb lyšh l›bhy* KAI 216^{16}: my ancestors did not have a good house. v. *ḥzy*$_1$, *lyš*$_1$, *sk*$_1$, *skl*$_3$.

lyškh **Pun** this subst. (Sing. abs. *lyškt*) = chamber in BAr '50, 111??, cf. Février ibid. 111f. (dam. context).

lyt v. *lyš*$_2$.

lk **Amm** The *lk* in BASOR cxciii 8^{1,2,8} prob. = *l*$_5$ + suff. 2 p.s.m. (cf. Horn BASOR cxciii 9f. (v. however infra), Cross BASOR cxciii 18f., Albright BASOR cxcviii 38, Palmaitis VDI cxviii 125, R.Kutscher Qadm v 27, Puech & Rofé RB lxxx 534, Dion RB lxxxii 29, 32f., Sasson PEQ '79, 118ff., 124, Garr DGSP 82f.; cf. also Fulco BASOR ccxxx 41, Shea PEQ '79, 17f. for ll. 1 & 8) :: Fulco BASOR ccxxx 41f., Shea PEQ '79, 17f.: in l. 2 pro word divider + *lk* l. *‹lk* = *‹l*$_7$ + suff. 2 p.s.m. (cf. also Horn BASOR cxciii 9f.) :: v. Selms BiOr xxxii 7: l. *lk* in ll. 1, 2, 8 = dem. pronoun, this (cf. also Garbini AION xx 255, LS 106: l. *lk* in ll. 1, 2, 8 = particle) :: Horn BASOR cxciii 9f.: or (div. otherwise) l. *bʿlk* = Sing. + suff. 2 p.s.m. of *bʿl$_2$*.

lkd$_1$ Ph a form of this root poss. in KAI 37B 8: *lkd*; CIS i sub 86: = PUʿAL Pf. 3 p.pl. (= they were chosen by lot (cf. also Healey BASOR ccxvi 55, 57)); Peckham Or xxxvii 306: = QAL Pf. 3 p.pl. (= they caught); Röllig KAI a.l.: = Sing. abs. of *lkd$_2$* (= trap); for a discussion, cf. also Harr p. 115, Amadasi sub Kition C 1, Masson & Sznycer RPC 63f., Puech Sem xxix 33f. :: v.d.Branden BO viii 248, 261 (div. otherwise): l. *kr* (= basin).

lkd$_2$ v. *lkd$_1$*.

lkdn› OffAr sign group (reading probable) in JA ccliv 440[3] (cf. Shaked JRAS '69, 119f., Kutscher, Naveh & Shaked Lesh xxxiv 128), prob. meaning: in this manner, conform = *l$_5$* + *k$_1$* + *dn›$_2$* (= *znh*)?, cf. Shaked JRAS '69, 120, Kutscher, Naveh & Shaked Lesh xxxiv 128 (*›rq lkdn›* = the world according to this manner // Prakrit: *loke anūppatiṭīpaṃne*, v. also *›nwpṭyptmnh*) :: Dupont-Sommer JA ccliv 440, 456: l. word divider + *knn›* = Sing. emph. of *knn$_3$* (= variant form of *kll$_4$* (= totality)).

lkḥ v. *lqḥ*.

lkn v. *kn$_4$*.

ll$_1$ v. *›ll*.

ll$_2$ OldCan Sing. abs. *l[e-e]l* EA 243[13] (for the reading, cf. Rainey EA p. 79; cf. also CAD s.v. *līla*) - **Ph** Sing. abs. *ll* KAI 26A ii 17 (v. infra) - ¶ subst. night; *wbl kn mtm ldnnym ll. bymty* KAI 26A ii 16f. (cf. the variant texts B, C: *wbl kn mtm ll. bymty ldnnym*): there was no night whatsoever (i.e. no adversity) for the D. in my days (cf. Gordon Or xxi 122, Röllig KAI a.l., Ginsberg FS Gaster 135f., Avishur PIB 224, 232, Dupont-Sommer FX 153, Gibson SSI iii p. 51, 60 (cf. also Rosenthal ANET 654, Greenfield IEJ xxxii 180) :: O'Callaghan Or xviii 179, 187 (dividing otherwise): l. *wbl kn* (= QAL Pf. 3 p.pl.m. of *kwn$_1$*) *mtm* (= Plur. abs. of *mwt$_2$* (= pestilence)) *llb* (= *l$_5$* + Sing. cstr. of *lb*) *ymty* = in the midst of my days (:: Dahood Meltô i 50f.: same division of words, but *mtm* = Plur. abs. of *mt$_5$*, dead people (because of violence)) :: reading *mtmll* (based on variant texts & presupposing corruption of text A), differently explained: - a) = HITP Part. s.m. abs. of *mll$_2$* (= to fade, to wither), cf. Friedrich FuF xxiv 79 (= languishing, distressed, cf. also H.P.Müller TUAT i 643), Dupont-Sommer RA xlii 166, 173, JKF ii 193ff., Bron RIPK 91ff., 151 (= unfortunate, hapless (cf. also Del Olmo Lete AO i 289)), Lipiński RSF ii 48f. (= wearied, restless), SV 49, 50 n. g (= obstreporous), RTAT 259 (n. 68) (= disgruntled), cf. also Pedersen ActOr xxi 40, 53 (= sufferer < *mll* (= to bow down)) - b) = HITP Part. s.m. abs. of *mll$_3$* (= to cut), cf. Dunand BMB viii 27, 31 (= massacred), Marcus & Gelb JNES vii 195, 197, viii 117, 119 (= injured person) - c) = HITP Part. s.m. abs. of *mll$_1$*, cf. Gordon JQR xxxix 47 n.

18 (= adversary; cf. also idem JNES viii 111, 115; cf. also Dahood Bibl xliv 71f.: = speaking derisively) - d) HITP Part. s.m. abs. of *mwl*$_1$ (= to attack), cf. Honeyman Mus lxi 53 (= provoking, attacking; cf. also idem PEQ '49, 27, 33; Alt WO '49, 275, 282 (= adversary); Swiggers BiOr xxxvii 340: poss. = sneering) - e) HITP Part. s.m. abs. of *mwl*$_2$ (= to cut), cf. Obermann JAOS Suppl ix 29, 37 (= seeking to cut off, cf. idem Conn xxxviii 26, 41) :: Barnett, Leveen & Moss Irâq x 65, 70 (div. otherwise): l. *mtml* (= *mn*$_5$ + *tml* (= heretofore)) *lbymty* (= *l*$_5$ + *b*$_2$ + Plur. + suff. 1 p.s. of *ywm* (= as in my days)); on the subject, cf. also Röllig ZDPV lxxiii 185) - cf. also *lylh*, *lyly*.

ll$_3$ **Pun** Sznycer PPP 122ff.: the *iule* in Poen 942 (lapsus for *lule*; var. *lula*) poss. = reduplicated form of *l*$_1$ (particle with precative function), cf. however Schaed 287, 291f., 308, L.H. Gray AJSL xxxix 77f. (div. otherwise): l. *lu* (= *l*$_1$) + *le* (= *l*$_5$).

ll$_4$ v. *ll*ʾ.

llʾ **OffAr**, cf. Frah x 11 = ear(ring), cf. Ebeling Frah a.l.: = variant form of Akkad. *lulmû*, cf. also CAD s.v. *lulmû*: related to *lulû* B, cf. however Nyberg FP 75: = form of *ll*$_4$ (= foolish).

llb **JAr** Plur. abs. *llbyn* MPAT 60^3 - ¶ subst. *lulav*.

llh v. *lylh*.

lm$_1$ v. *l*ʾ*m*$_1$.

lly Gibson SSI iii p. 87 (cf. already du Mesnil du Buisson FS Dussaud p. 424) l. *llyn* (= Plur. abs.) in KAI 27^{19} (= night creature), possible reading and interpret., cf. however e.g. Röllig KAI a.l.: l. *lly* (= name of a demon) :: v.d.Branden BO iii 43, 47: l. *llyt* (name of a female demon), cf. also Avishur PIB 255: l. *llyt* or *llyn*.

lm$_2$ (Huehnergard JAOS ciii 590 (n. 190): < *la* + *mā* or *-m*) - **DA** ii 5, 6, xii c 2 (or = *l*$_5$ + *m*$_1$ (= *mh*$_2$)?, cf. e.g. Kaufman BASOR ccxxxix 73, Levine JAOS ci 196, Hackett BTDA 29, 38, Cook Maarav v/vi 65; in all instances dam. context) - **OffAr** Cowl 10^{11,13}, 17^2, Aḥiq 2, 3, Beh 39 (Akkad. par. *um-ma*), Driv 10^{1,2}, ATNS 70^1 (heavily dam. context), etc., etc. (:: Kaufman Conn xix 121f., BiOr xxxiv 94, BASOR ccxxxix 73: *lm* < *l*ʾ*m* < *l*ʾ*mr* = *l*$_5$ + QAL Inf. of ʾ*mr*$_1$ (against this theory, cf. also Teixidor Syr lvi 391, Wesselius AION xlv 507 (n.4)) :: Segert AAG p. 233: the affirmative *lm* (v. infra sub 1) different from *lm* introducing direct discourse (v. infra sub 2), last mentioned *lm* < *l*ʾ*mr*; on *lm*, cf. also Leand 61d) - ¶ adv. - **1)** with affirmative meaning, *zkrn lm yhwy lk* Cowl 32^2: let it be indeed a memorandum for you (cf. Cowl a.l., Porten & Greenfield JEAS p. 99 × Grelot DAE p. 415, Porten & Yardeni sub TADAE A 4.9: memorandum, you must ...; for the background, cf. also Cowl p. 122); *dḥlt lm* ʾ*ḥyqr* Aḥiq 45: I, A., indeed was afraid; ʾ*mr ly* ʾ*l tdḥl lm [tḥ]yy* ʾ*ḥyqr* Aḥiq 54f.: he said to me: Fear not, surely you shall live, A.; *bbl lm* ʾ*grt mn* ʾ*ršm yhbt* Driv 12^1: a letter from A. was

delivered in B. indeed ...; etc. - **2)** introducing direct speech, *l› ›kl ›mr lk lm* (written above the line) *šlmtk bkspk* Cowl 10[11f.]: I will not be able to say to you: I paid you your silver; *l› ›kl ›qbl ‘lyk ... lm lqḥt mny ‘rbn* Cowl 10[12f.]: I shall not be able to complain against you ...: you have taken from me security; *yštlḥ lm ›šrn› znh ytyhb ‘l yd šmw* Cowl 26[21]: let word be sent: this *›šrn* (v. *›šrn*) is to be given to Sh.; *[sn]y› šdr lrmn[›] lm sny› lrmn›* Aḥiq 165: the bramble sent to the pomegranate: bramble to pomegranate ...; *kmry› ... hmwnyt ‘m wydrng ... lm ›gwr› zy yhw ›lh› ... yh‘dw mn tmh* Cowl 30[5]: the priests ... in agreement with W. ... (said): the temple of the God Y. ... let them remove from there; etc.
v. *›m$_2$*, *l›m$_3$*.

lmd$_1$ v. *mdh$_1$*.

lmd$_2$ v. *mr›*.

lmdy v. *›mr$_1$*.

lmh v. *ywm*.

lmn (< Greek λιμήν) - **Palm** Sing. emph. *lmn›* CIS ii 3913 ii 1 - ¶ subst. prob. meaning custom-house (cf. also Cooke NSI p. 335, Teixidor Sem xxxiv 59).

lnm **Hebr** S.Lévy & Edelstein RB lxxix 336: inscription on jar: *lnm* + numerical indication, cf. however Lemaire RB lxxx 559: l. *lnmš* = *l$_5$* + n.p. (prob. interpret.).

lsn Ebeling Frah a.l.: l. *lsn* in Frah xiv 8 = spear (cf. poss. Akkad. *lišānu* = blade of a sword or ass. *lisnu* = certain type of weapon?), improb. interpret., cf. Nyberg FP 47, 84: l. Iran. word.

l‘g **Pun** Rocco StudMagr a.l.: l. *l‘g* (= QAL Imper. pl.m. of *l‘g* (= to deride)) in StudMagr vii 12[2] (highly uncert. reading and interpret.).

l‘y **Samal** QAL Impf. 3 p.s.f. *tl‘y* KAI 214[32] - ¶ verb QAL to be weary (said of an eye); cf. also Dion p. 384, Gibson SSI ii p. 76.

l‘l›t **Pun** Levi Della Vida Or xxxiii 10: the *l‘l›t* in Trip 51[3] = Plur. abs. (= sale by auction) of a noun composed of *l$_5$* and *‘l$_7$*, diff. context, highly uncert. interpret., cf. also Amadasi IPT 133.

l‘n (< Arab., cf. Cantineau Nab ii 172, Altheim & Stiehl AAW i 191, Diem ZDMG cxxiii 228 (n. 11), O'Connor JNES xlv 218, 220; cf. however Hoftijzer DA p. 244) - **Nab** QAL Pf. 3 p.s.m. *l‘n* CIS ii 199[4], 211[6], J 17[6,9]; 3 p.pl.m. *l‘nw* CIS ii 197[5]; Impf. 3 p.s.m. *yl‘n* CIS ii 198[3], 206[8], J 2[4] - ¶ verb QAL to curse + obj.

l‘nh$_1$ (< Arab., cf. *l‘n*) - **Nab** Sing. cstr. *l‘nt* CIS ii 211[8], 217[8] - ¶ subst. curse; *l‘nt dwšr›* CIS ii 211[8]: curse uttered by D., cf. CIS ii 217[8].
v. *l‘nh$_2$*.

l‘nh$_2$ **DA** Sing. abs. *l‘nh* ii 17 (cf. Hoftijzer DA a.l. :: Caquot & Lemaire Syr liv 207: = *l$_5$* + QAL Inf. of *‘ny$_1$* (cf. Garbini Hen i 186) :: McCarter BASOR ccxxxix 59 n. 1: l. prob. *l‘mh* = *l$_5$* + Sing. + suff.

3 p.s.m. of *‘m*$_1$ (cf. also Levine JAOS ci 201, Hackett BTDA 26, 30, 73, 94, 133) :: Lemaire CRAI ’85, 277 (dividing otherwise): l. *l‘m* = l_5 + Sing. abs. of *‘m*$_1$) - ¶ subst. poss. meaning (poisonous herb, poison >) wretchedness, iniquity; *dbr l‘nh* DA ii 17: an iniquitous word (or = *l‘nh*$_1$?, cf. Hoftijzer DA a.l.).

l‘‘ v. *yld*$_1$.

l‘t v. *‘td*$_1$.

lp$_1$ **Ph** Plur. abs. *lpm* EI xviii 117[4] (= IEJ xxxv 83; reading of *p* uncertain, cf. also Dothan IEJ xxxv 91) - ¶ subst. of uncert. meaning, indicating a certain object; Dothan EI xviii 118, IEJ xxxv 87f.: < Greek λοπάς (= fLat. dish, plate) or λέβης (= kettle, cauldron), prob. indicating some kind of cooking vessel.

lp$_2$ v. *’lp*$_5$, *ḥmr*$_6$.

lpn Ebeling Frah a.l.: l. *lpn* in Frah xiv 8 (= shield; Ebeling Frah a.l.: cf. Akkad. *lapnu* of unknown meaning; improb. interpret., cf. CAD, v.Soden AHW s.v. *lap/bnu*), cf. also Nyberg FP 47, 84: l. Iran. word.

lpny (< *lpn* (= l_5 + Plur. cstr. of *pnh*) + ending *-y*, cf. e.g. FR 204a :: e.g. Friedrich ZS i 6 n. 1: = l_5 + Plur. cstr. of *pnh*$_1$, v. also infra) - **Ph** Plur. m. abs. *lpnym* KAI 24[10] (:: Lipiński RSF ii 50: = l_5 + Dual of *pnh*$_1$ (= before) :: Poeb 36 n. 4: prob. lapsus for *lpnyhm*, v. infra, cf. also CF 17); Plur. + suff. 3 p.pl.m. *lpnyhm* KAI 24[5] (cf. e.g. Gibson SSI iii p. 36 :: reading *lpnyhm* (v. *lḥm*$_2$) :: Poeb 34 n. 4, CF 16, Lipiński RSF ii 50: = l_5 + Plur. + suff. 1 p.s. of *pnh* + pers. pron. *hm* (= they were before me)) - **Pun** Sing. m. abs. *lpny* KAI 110[3], 137[5], Hofra 64[2] - ¶ adj. which precedes, which is earlier; *hmlkm hlpnym* KAI 24[9f.]: the former kings; *lyrḥ mp‘ lpny* Hofra 64[2]: the earlier (i.e. the first) month M. (cf. KAI 110[3], 137[5]; cf. also Chabot sub RES 1858); subst. adj., predecessor; *hlpnyhm* KAI 24[5]: their predecessors (v. also supra; on the problems of this construction, cf. also Montgomery JBL xlvii 196f.) - for this word, cf. also Sperling UF xx 327.

lpp v. *pp*$_2$.

lqwt Ebeling Frah a.l.: l. *lqwt’* in Frah xiii 7 (= disciple; to be related to Akkadian *liqûtu* = adopted child), cf. however Nyberg FP 47, 82: l. *lky’n’* = *raqyānā* (for *ra‘yānā*)? = thought > disciple, pupil (uncert. interpret.).

lqḥ **Ph** QAL Pf. 3 p.s.m. *lqḥ* KAI 37B 7 (for this interpret., cf. e.g. Peckham Or xxxvii 306 (cf. also 322 n. 4), Masson & Sznycer RPC 27, 62f., Amadasi sub Kition C 1, Healey BASOR ccxvi 53, Gibson SSI iii p. 127 (cf. also Puech Sem xxix 33) × passive form Pf. 3 p.s.m. (PU‘AL or pass. QAL), cf. Masson & Sznycer RPC 62f., Amadasi sub Kition C 1 :: Cooke NSI p. 69 (cf. also Lidzbarski sub KI 29): = QAL Pf. 3 p.pl. or PU‘AL Pf. 3 p.pl. (for this last interpret., cf. also CIS i sub 86) :: v.d.Branden BMB xiii 92, BO viii 248, 261 (div. otherwise): l. *lqḥm*

= QAL Part. act. pl.m. abs.; cf. also Röllig KAI a.l.) - **Pun** QAL Pf. 3 p.s.m. *lqḥ* Hofra 103[3] (for this interpret., cf. Février JA ccxliii 56 :: Berthier & Charlier Hofra a.l.: = l_5 + *qḥ* (= n.p.)??); Impf. 3 p.s.m. *yqḥ* KAI 69[20], 75[3]; Inf. cstr. *qḥt* KAI 76B 5; NIPH Pf. 3 p.pl. *nlqḥ*ʾ KAI 122[2] - **Mo** QAL Impf. 1 p.s. *ʾqḥ* KAI 181[17,20] - **Hebr** QAL Pf. 3 p.s.m. *lqḥ* KAI 200[9]; + suff. 3 p.s.m. *lqḥh* KAI 194[6]; 2 p.s.m. *lqḥt* TA-H 3[8], 17[3f.] (cf. e.g. Aharoni TA a.l., Gibson SSI i p. 53, Pardee UF x 312, Scagliarini Hen xii 137; or rather, cf. Lipiński OLP viii 92 (dividing otherwise): l. *lqḥ* (= QAL Inf. abs.) + gm_2, cf. also idem BiOr xli 157); Impf. 3 p.s.m. *yqḥ* KAI 200[8], DJD ii 42[3] (for the reading, cf. e.g. de Vaux RB lx 270f., I.Rabinowitz BASOR cxxxi 21f., Teicher JJS iv 132, Lehmann & Stern VT iii 391, Bardtke ThLZ lxxix 299, J.J.Rabinowitz Bibl xxxv 198 :: Birnbaum PEQ '55, 22, Yeivin At i 96f., Milik DJD ii a.l.: l. *lqḥ* = QAL Pf. 3 p.s.m. (cf. also Pardee HAHL 123; v. also infra)); Imper. s.m. *q[ḥ]* TA-H 12[1] (heavily dam. context; on the reading, cf. Pardee HAHL 46); Inf. cstr. *qḥt* KAI 193[18]; Part. act. s.m. abs. *lwqḥ* DJD ii 22[11], 30[3,15,22]; NIPH Impf. 3 p.s.m. *ylqḥ* TA-H 111[4] (dam. context) - **DA** QAL Impf. 3 p.s.m. *yqḥ* ii 13 (diff. context; for the reading, cf. v.d.Kooij DA p. 128; cf. also Hoftijzer DA a.l., Rofé SB 63, Levine JAOS ci 200, 202, H.P.Müller ZAW xciv 219, 236, Hackett BTDA 30, 70, 99 :: Caquot & Lemaire Syr liv 206 (div. otherwise): pro *bmyqḥ.mwt* l. *bmy rḥmwt* (= b_2 + *my* (= Plur. cstr. of *mym*) + *rḥmwt* (= Sing. abs. (= tenderness)), cf. also Garbini Hen i 186, Ringgren Mem Seeligmann 94 (cf. Delcor SVT xxxii 62: *my rḥmwt* referring to *semen virile*)) :: McCarter with Hackett BTDA 70f.: l. *my* (= Plur. cstr. of *mym*) *rḥ* (= Sing. abs. of $rḥ_2$ (= scent)) :: Lemaire CRAI '85, 277: l. poss. *bny* (= Plur. cstr. of br_1) *rḥmwt* (= entrails)); Imper. s.m. *qḥ* x d 2 (uncert. interpret., heavily dam. context :: Garbini Hen i 180, 185: = QAL Inf.?) - **Samal** QAL Pf. 3 p.s.m. *lqḥ* KAI 215[17]; Impf. 3 p.pl.m. *yqḥw* KAI 214[10] (*yqḥ[w]*; for this reading and the context, v. $ʾšr_4$),[12] - **OldAr** QAL Impf. 3 p.s.m. *yqḥ* KAI 222B 27, *ylqḥ* Tell F 17 (Akkad. par. (*i-ma-ḫar-šú*)), KAI 222B 35 (for this form, cf. Hoftijzer Mus lxxvi 199, Segert ArchOr xxxii 120, Donner KAI a.l., Fitzmyer AIS 70, 150, 159 :: v.Soden WZUH xvii 183 n. 2: poss. = *iqattal*-form (cf. also Meyer OLZ '74, 473) :: Degen AAG p. 41 n. 38 (div. otherwise): or l. *ylq* (= QAL Impf. 3 p.s.m. of *lqq* (= to lick)) + *ḥlb* (= Sing. abs. of $ḥlb_4$); cf. however Donner BiOr xxvii 248); 3 p.s.f. *tlqḥ* Tell F 18; 2 p.s.m. *tqḥ* KAI 224[2]; Inf. *mlqḥ* Tell F 10 (Akkad. par. *ma-ga-ri*); QAL pass. Impf. 3 p.pl.f. *yqḥn* KAI 222A 42 (diff. reading, cf. e.g. Dupont-Sommer Sf p. 60, Segert ArchOr xxxii 120, Fitzmyer AIS 16, Degen AAG p. 12, Gibson SSI ii p. 32 :: Lipiński Stud 31f. (div. otherwise): l. *yqḥ* (= QAL pass. Impf. 3 p.s.m.) + *w*) - **OffAr** QAL Pf. 3 p.s.m. *lqḥ* Cowl 20[6], Driv 12[6,9,10], PF 857 (diff. context), ATNS 43a ii 5 (?, heavily dam. context), KAI 236 vs. 4 (= AECT 49; cf. also Lipiński Stud 95, 100 (cf. id. WGAV 381), prob. interpret. :: e.g. Lidzbarski sub LidzbAss 4, Donner KAI a.l., Vattioni Aug x 521: = n.p.), *lkḥ* (*sic*) PF 2059; 2 p.s.m. *lqḥt* Cowl 7^{6}, 10^{13}, Driv $12^{7,8}$; 1 p.s. *lqḥt* Cowl 7^{9}, 16^{4}; 3 p.pl.m. *lqḥw* Cowl 27^{18}, 30^{12}, 34^{6}, Driv 3^{5}, ATNS 28b 3; Pf. pass. 3 p.s.f. *lqyḥt* Cowl p. 265^{1} (cf. also Greenfield & Porten BIDG p. 54); Impf. 3 p.s.m. *yqḥ* ATNS 7^{8}, *ylqḥ* Aḥiq 172 (*[y]lqḥ*); 2 p.s.m. *tlqḥ* Krael 11^{10}; *tlqḥn* Aḥiq 119 (on this form, cf. Kottsieper SAS 136); 1 p.s. *ʾlqḥ* Sem ii 31 conc. 4, MAI xiv/2, 66^{9}; 3 p.pl.m. *ylqḥw* ASAE xxvi 25B 5 (cf. Driver PEQ '45, 12); + suff. 3 p.s.f.? *yqḥwnh* Cowl 67 xviii (cf. Leand 3p); Imper. s.f. *qḥy* KAI 269^{3}; Inf. *mlqḥ* Cowl 9^{11}, $10^{9,17}$; + suff. 3 p.s.f. *mlqḥh* Cowl 9^{9}, 48^{3}; Part. act. s.m. abs. *lqḥ* Herm 3^{9}; Itp Impf. 3 p.s.m. *ytlqḥ* Cowl 8^{17}, Herm 1^{9} - **JAr** Haph Pf. 1 p.s. *hqḥt* DBKP 18^{68} - ¶ verb Qal to take (either with or without authorization); *[yhwh] lh lmlqḥ* Cowl 9^{11}: it will be hers to take; *wmndʿ[m] ʾḥrn zy lqḥt* Driv $12^{6f.}$: and anything else that you have taken; cf. Driv 12^{8}, ASAE xxvi 25B 5; cf. also Part. act. with meaning "buyer": DJD ii 22^{11}, $30^{3,15,22}$ - cf. also the foll. constructions: - **1)** + obj., *kl khn ʾš yqḥ mšʾt* KAI 69^{20}: every priest who shall exact a payment; *lqḥh šmʿyhw* KAI 194^{6}: Sh. has taken him (i.e. into custody; cf. also Pardee HAHL 92); *wyqḥ ʾt bgd ʿbdk* KAI 200^{8}: and he took your servant's garment away (i.e. against his will), cf. also KAI 200^{9} (for KAI $200^{8,9}$, cf. Delekat Bibl li 463f., Pardee Maarav i 47f., Lemaire IH i 264); *lʾ šlyṭh hy lmlqḥh* Cowl 9^{9}: she has no power to take it (i.e. in possession; for this text, cf. Greenfield Conn xix 91, cf. also Aḥiq 171f.); *nksy lqḥw* Driv 3^{5}: they took my property (i.e. they seized it); *wmndʿmtʾ zy hwh bʾgwrʾ zk ... lqḥw wlnpšhwm ʿbdw* Cowl $30^{12f.}$: and everything that was in that temple ... they took and made their own (cf. also Cowl 7^{6}, 27^{18}; v. also *ʿbd*$_{1}$); *wylqḥ lbkh ʾw[* KAI 222B 35: and he will take L. (n.l.; for this text, v. supra; for this interpret., cf. Dupont-Sommer Sf p. 64, 83, Fitzmyer AIS 19, 70, Degen AAG p. 15, cf. however Lipiński Stud 40 (div. otherwise): l. *wylqḥ lbk* (= Sing. + suff. 2 p.s.m. of *lb*) *hʾ* (= *hʾ*$_{1}$) = he will take your heart away (i.e. he will make you loose heart)), cf. KAI 76B 5, Hofra 103^{3}, Driv 12^{6}, PF 2059; cf. also *lmlqḥ ʾmrt pmh* Tell F 9f.: to accept the words of his mouth; *npšk[y] ʾlqḥ* Sem ii 31 conc. 3f.: I will take your life (i.e. I will kill you; for the reading, cf. Rosenthal AH i/1, 12, v. also *npš*) - 2) + obj. + *l*$_{5}$, *...] brtk lmlqḥh lʾntw* Cowl 48^{3}: ... your daughter, to take her in marriage - **3)** + obj. + *mn*$_{5}$, *nksn mn bytk ... lʾ lqḥt* Cowl 7^{9}: I did not take goods from your house; *nksn lqḥ mnh* Driv 12^{9}: he has taken property from it (i.e. the domestic staff); *mrʾy hdd lḥmh wmwh ʾl ylqḥ mn ydh* Tell F 17f.: may my lord H. not accept the bread and water (he offers) from his hand (cf. Tell F 18; on these texts, cf. Greenfield & Shaffer RB xcii 51ff., Shn v/vi

123f., Greenfield FS Cross 70f., Sasson ZAW xcvii 100); *whwy lqḥ š‘rn mn tšy* Herm 3^{9}: acquire barley from T. (cf. Hoftijzer SV 114 n. r; for the context, v. also *yhb*); *gldy ’l tlqḥn mny* Aḥiq 119: take not my skin from me (said by the goat to the leopard); cf. the expression *]tqḥ mly’ mn ydh* KAI 224^{2}: you shall [not] accept the words from him - **4)** + l_5: ATNS 7^{5} (dam. context) - **5)** + l_5 + obj., *’nt mšlm šlyṭ lmlqḥ lk kl ... ‘rbn* Cowl 10$^{16f.}$: you M. have a right to take for yourself any ... security (cf. Cowl 10^{9}) - **6)** + l_5 + *mn*$_5$, *wtlqḥ lk mn by zy lbnn ‘bd w’mh ... ‘d tšlm bkspk* Krael 11$^{10f.}$: you may take for yourself from the house of bricks the slaves and handmaiden ... until you are paid your silver (for the context, cf. Hoftijzer VT ix 315; v. also *mn*$_5$) - **7)** + *mn*$_5$, *lqḥt mzh* KAI 193^{18}: to take (provisions?) from here (on the text, cf. Hoftijzer FS Hospers 85ff., 90 n. 7, 91 n. 17; v. also z_1); *’sḥwr ’bwkm lqḥ mn šlwmm* Cowl 20^{6}: A. your father received (them) from Sh.; *mh zy lqḥt .. mn grd’* Driv 12$^{9f.}$: whatever you have taken ... from the domestic staff; cf. DJD ii 42^{3} (for the context, cf. Sonne PAAJR xxiii 88, Milik DJD ii a.l.; v. also supra), cf. also ATNS 28b 3 (dam. context) - **8)** + *mn yd*, *yqḥw mn ydy* KAI 214^{12}: they accepted from my hands (i.e. from me; cf. also Greenfield & Shaffer RB xcii 51f.) - **9)** + *mn*$_5$ + obj., *[w]’qḥ mm’b m’tn ’š* KAI 181$^{19f.}$: I took from M. 200 man (cf. KAI 181$^{17f.}$); *wlqḥt mšm 1 šmn* TA-H 17$^{3f.}$: and take from there one (jar of) oil (v. however supra), cf. also KAI 269^{3}: *mn qdm ’wsry myn qḥy* (= take water from Osiris (cf. e.g. Lévy JA ccxi 299ff., Donner KAI a.l., REHR 43f.)) - QAL pass. to be taken: KAI 222A 42 (dam. context, v. also supra), Cowl 265^{1} (dam. context, v. supra) - NIPH to be taken: TA-H 111^{4} (dam. context); the meaning of *nlqḥ’* in KAI 122^{2} diff. to ascertain (context highly uncert.), cf. Levi Della Vida AfrIt vi 27 n. 1: to be included in (*b*)?, Février JA ccxxxix 8: to be offered? (or: to be bought??), cf. also Röllig KAI a.l. - HAPH to give in marriage; + obj. + l_5: DBKP 18^{68} (cf. Greenfield IEJ xxxvii 248, 250, DBKP a.l.) - ITP to be taken, to be accepted - **1)** + b_2, *wl’ ytlqḥ bdyn* Cowl 8^{17}: it shall not be accepted in suit - **2)** + *qdmt* + b_2, *wytlqḥ qdmthn bswn* Herm 1^{9}: and it (i.e. the salary) will be taken (i.e. received) in their presence (i.e. by them personally) in S. (cf. Bresciani & Kamil Herm a.l., cf. also Kutscher IOS i 110, 113, Hoftijzer SV 109; cf. Porten & Greenfield ZAW lxxx 228: this interpret. poss., cf. Milik Bibl xlviii 550, 581: it may only be received in their presence in S. :: Porten & Greenfield ZAW lxxx 226, 228, JEAS p. 152, Porten Arch 270, Porten & Yardeni sub TADAE A 2.3: it will be taken before them (i.e. ahead of them) to S. (cf. also Gibson SSI ii p. 130f.) :: Hayes & Hoftijzer VT xx 100ff.: it must be acquired for them in S. :: Grelot DAE p. 152 (n. j): it (i.e. the amount of their salary) has to be deducted from their account at S.) - on the forms of this root, cf. also Garr DGSP 146f.

v. ʾšr$_4$, ṣʿqh, qḥk.

lqṭ **OldAr** QAL Impf. 3 p.pl.m. *llqṭw* Tell F 22 (:: Andersen & Freedman FS Fensham 39: prob. = l_1 + QAL Pf. 3 p.pl.m.; Akkad. par. *lil-qu-te*) - ¶ verb QAL to glean; *wmn qlqltʾ llqṭw ʾnšwh šʿrn* Tell F 22: may his men glean barley from the dunghill.

lqy v.Soden Or xlvi 189: = to be beaten, to suffer (a beating) > Akkad. *laqāʾu* II (uncert. interpret.).
v. *qbb*.

lqnh **Pun** Février AIPHOS xiii 169f.: the *lqnʾt* in KAI 162[5] poss. = Plur. abs. of *lqnh* (< Greek λεκάνη; = basin (highly uncert. interpret., diff. context)).

lqq v. *lqḥ*.

lqš **Hebr** Sing. abs. *lqš* KAI 182[2] - ¶ subst. prob. meaning late rain (> late rain vegetation, cf. e.g. Février Sem i 38, Michaud PA 23f., Talmon JAOS lxxxiii 183f., Gibson SSI i p. 2f., Greenfield JAOS xciv 510, Smelik HDAI 27 (cf. also Dalman i 411 (n. 1)), cf. however e.g. Dir p. 7, Mosc p. 12, 19, Ginsberg ArchOr viii 146, Driver PEQ '45, 6, Albright BASOR xcii 22 (nn. 31, 32), ANET 320, Röllig KAI a.l., Lipiński OLP viii 84, Conrad TUAT i 247, Borowski AIAI 34: late seed, late sowing/planting :: Dahood CISFP i 598: late harvest; the reference to a par. Akkad. month-name (*liqqaše*, cf. Tsevat HUCA xxix 117 n. 44) incorrect, cf. v.Soden AHW s.v. *niqali*, Gröndahl PTU 168.

lšʾ v. *lwš*.

lšn **Ph/Pun**, cf. Diosc iv 127: λασουν (Sing. cstr. in the comb. λασουναφ, name of a plant: βούγλωσσον; varr.: αλσουν- (cf. Schroed 90), αυσαν-, ανσαν-) and Apul xli note 13: *lasim* (Sing. cstr. in the comb. *lasimsaph*) - **DA** Sing. abs. *lšn* ii 17 - **Samal** Sing. abs. *lšn* KAI 214[9] - **OldAr** Sing. abs. *lšn* KAI 224[21]; + suff. 2 p.s.m. *lšnk* KAI 224[17f.] - **OffAr** Sing. abs., cf. Warka 5: *li-iš-šá-an*, 8: *li-iš-šá-ni*; cstr. *lšn* Aḥiq 105 (:: Kottsieper SAS 20, 214: = Sing. abs.); + suff. 3 p.s.m., cf. Warka 25: *liš-šá-ni-e* (cf. also Warka 21: *liš-šá-n[i-e]* (for the forms in Warka, cf. also Garbini HDS 31f.); + suff. 1 p.s., cf. Warka 3: *li-iš-šá-ni-ʾ*; cf. also Aḥiq 156: *lšn[* (for the context, v. *nsḥ*)); cf. Frah x 22 - **JAr** Sing. abs. *lšn* MPAT-A 22[3] (= SM 70[11]) - ¶ subst. m. - **1)** tongue (organ of speech): Aḥiq 156, Warka 3, 5, 8, 21, 25, DA ii 17 (cf. Hoftijzer a.l. :: Caquot & Lemaire Syr liv 207: = (bad) language; cf. also Levine JAOS ci 201) - **2)** word: Aḥiq 105; *lšn byš* MPAT-A 22[3]: an evil tongue (i.e. slander); with unfavourable meaning in the foll. contexts, *ltšlḥ lšnk bnyhm* KAI 224[17f.]: you shall not let loose your tongue among them (i.e. you will not stir up trouble among them; cf. also Greenfield ActOr xxix 6); *ltšlḥ lšn bbyty wbny bny* KAI 224[21]: you shall not let loose your tongue in my house nor among my sons (i.e. you shall not stir up trouble in my house nor among my sons); cf. also KAI 214[9], *ḥrb*

wlšn = sword and slander (cf. e.g. Cooke NSI p. 166, Gibson SSI ii p. 71).
v. $mšn_1$.

ltk **Hebr** Sing. abs. *ltk* DJD ii 24E 12 - ¶ subst. certain measure of capacity: = 1/2 *kor*, cf. e.g Barrois ii 248ff., Trinquet SDB v 1222.

HANDBUCH DER ORIENTALISTIK

Abt. I: DER NAHE UND MITTLERE OSTEN

ISSN 0169-9423

Band 1. Ägyptologie

1. *Ägyptische Schrift und Sprache.* Mit Beiträgen von H. Brunner, H. Kees, S. Morenz, E. Otto, S. Schott. Mit Zusätzen von H. Brunner. Nachdruck der Erstausgabe (1959). 1973.
   ISBN 90 04 03777 2
2. *Literatur.* Mit Beiträgen von H. Altenmüller, H. Brunner, G. Fecht, H. Grapow, H. Kees, S. Morenz, E. Otto, S. Schott, J. Spiegel, W. Westendorf. 2. verbesserte und erweiterte Auflage. 1970. ISBN 90 04 00849 7
3. HELCK, W. *Geschichte des alten Ägypten.* Nachdruck mit Berichtigungen und Ergänzungen. 1981. ISBN 90 04 06497 4

Band 2. Keilschriftforschung und alte Geschichte Vorderasiens

1-2/2. *Altkleinasiatische Sprachen [und Elamitisch].* Mit Beiträgen von J. Friedrich, E. Reiner, A. Kammenhuber, G. Neumann, A. Heubeck. 1969. ISBN 90 04 00852 7

3. SCHMÖKEL, H. *Geschichte des alten Vorderasien.* Reprint. 1979. ISBN 90 04 00853 5

4/2. *Orientalische Geschichte von Kyros bis Mohammed.* Mit Beiträgen von A. Dietrich, G. Widengren, F. M. Heichelheim. 1966. ISBN 90 04 00854 3

Band 3. Semitistik

Semitistik. Mit Beiträgen von A. Baumstark, C. Brockelmann, E. L. Dietrich, J. Fück, M. Höfner, E. Littmann, A. Rücker, B. Spuler. Nachdruck der Erstausgabe (1953-1954). 1964. ISBN 90 04 00855 1

Band 4. Iranistik

1. *Linguistik.* Mit Beiträgen von K. Hoffmann, W. B. Henning, H. W. Bailey, G. Morgenstierne, W. Lentz. Nachdruck der Erstausgabe (1958). 1967. ISBN 90 04 03017 4

2/1. *Literatur.* Mit Beiträgen von I. Gershevitch, M. Boyce, O. Hansen, B. Spuler, M. J. Dresden. 1968. ISBN 90 04 00857 8

2/2. *History of Persian Literature from the Beginning of the Islamic Period to the Present Day.* With Contributions by G. Morrison, J. Baldick and Sh. Kadkanī. 1981. ISBN 90 04 06481 8

3. KRAUSE, W. *Tocharisch.* Nachdruck der Erstausgabe (1955) mit Zusätzen und Berichtigungen. 1971. ISBN 90 04 03194 4

Band 5. Altaistik

1. *Turkologie.* Mit Beiträgen von A. von Gabain, O. Pritsak, J. Benzing, K. H. Menges, A. Temir, Z. V. Togan, F. Taeschner, O. Spies, A. Caferoglu, A. Battal-Tamays. Reprint with additions of the 1st (1963) ed. 1982. ISBN 90 04 06555 5
2. *Mongolistik.* Mit Beiträgen von N. Poppe, U. Posch, G. Doerfer, P. Aalto, D. Schröder, O. Pritsak, W. Heissig. 1964. ISBN 90 04 00859 4
3. *Tungusologie.* Mit Beiträgen von W. Fuchs, I. A. Lopatin, K. H. Menges, D. Sinor. 1968. ISBN 90 04 00860 8

Band 6. Geschichte der islamischen Länder

5/1. *Regierung und Verwaltung des Vorderen Orients in islamischer Zeit.* Mit Beiträgen von H. R. Idris und K. Röhrborn. 1979. ISBN 90 04 05915 6

5/2. *Regierung und Verwaltung des Vorderen Orients in islamischer Zeit.* 2. Mit Beiträgen von D. Sourdel und J. Bosch Vilá. 1988. ISBN 90 04 08550 5

6/1. *Wirtschaftsgeschichte des Vorderen Orients in islamischer Zeit.* Mit Beiträgen von B. Lewis, M. Rodinson, G. Baer, H. Müller, A. S. Ehrenkreutz, E. Ashtor, B. Spuler, A. K. S. Lambton, R. C. Cooper, B. Rosenberger, R. Arié, L. Bolens, T. Fahd. 1977.
ISBN 90 04 04802 2

Band 7.

Armenisch und Kaukasische Sprachen. Mit Beiträgen von G. Deeters, G. R. Solta, V. Inglisian. 1963. ISBN 90 04 00862 4

Band 8. Religion

1/1. *Religionsgeschichte des alten Orients.* Mit Beiträgen von E. Otto, O. Eissfeldt, H. Otten, J. Hempel. 1964. ISBN 90 04 00863 2

1/2/2/1. BOYCE, M. *A History of Zoroastrianism. The Early Period.* Rev. ed. 1989. ISBN 90 04 08847 4

1/2/2/2. BOYCE, M. *A History of Zoroastrianism. Under the Achaemenians.* 1982. ISBN 90 04 06506 7

1/2/2/3. BOYCE, M. and GRENET, F. *A History of Zoroastrianism. Zoroastrianism under Macedonian and Roman Rule.* With F. Grenet. Contribution by R. Beck. 1991. ISBN 90 04 09271 4

2. *Religionsgeschichte des Orients in der Zeit der Weltreligionen.* Mit Beiträgen von A. Adam, A. J. Arberry, E. L. Dietrich, J. W. Fück, A. von Gabain, J. Leipoldt, B. Spuler, R. Strothman, G. Widengren. 1961. ISBN 90 04 00864 0

Ergänzungsband 1

1. HINZ, W. *Islamische Maße und Gewichte umgerechnet ins metrische System.* Nachdruck der Erstausgabe (1955) mit Zusätzen und Berichtigungen. 1970. ISBN 90 04 00865 9

Ergänzungsband 2

1. GROHMANN, A. *Arabische Chronologie und Arabische Papyruskunde.* Mit Beiträgen von J. Mayr und W. C. Til. 1966. ISBN 90 04 00866 7
2. KHOURY, R. G. *Chrestomathie de papyrologie arabe.* Documents relatifs à la vie priveé, sociale et administrative dans les premiers siècles islamiques. 1992. ISBN 90 04 09551 9

Ergänzungsband 3

Orientalisches Recht. Mit Beiträgen von E. Seidl, V. Korošc, E. Pritsch, O. Spies, E. Tyan, J. Baz, Ch. Chehata, Ch. Samaran, J. Roussier, J. Lapanne-Joinville, S. Ş. Ansay. 1964. ISBN 90 04 00867 5

Ergänzungsband 5

1/1. BORGER, R. *Das zweite Jahrtausend vor Chr.* Mit Verbesserungen und Zusätzen. Nachdruck der Erstausgabe (1961). 1964. ISBN 90 04 00869 1

1/2. SCHRAMM, W. *[Einleitung in die assyrischen Königsinschriften, 2:] 934-722 v. Chr.* 1973. ISBN 90 04 03783 7

Ergänzungsband 6

1. ULLMANN, M. *Die Medizin im Islam.* 1970. ISBN 90 04 00870 5
2. ULLMANN, M. *Die Natur- und Geheimwissenschaften im Islam.* 1972. ISBN 90 04 03423 4

Ergänzungsband 7

GOMAA, I. *A Historical Chart of the Muslim World.* 1972. ISBN 90 04 03333 5

Ergänzungsband 8

KORNRUMPF, H.-J. *Osmanische Bibliographie mit besonderer Berücksichtigung der Türkei in Europa.* Unter Mitarbeit von J. Kornrumpf. 1973. ISBN 90 04 03549 4

Ergänzungsband 9

FIRRO, K. M. *A History of the Druzes.* 1992. ISBN 90 04 09437 7

Band 10

STRIJP, R. *Cultural Anthropology of the Middle East. A Bibliography.* Vol. 1: 1965-1987. 1992. ISBN 90 04 09604 3

Band 11

ENDRESS, G. & GUTAS, D. (eds.). *A Greek and Arabic Lexicon.* (*GALex*) Materials for a Dictionary of the Mediæval Translations from Greek into Arabic.

Fascicle 1. Introduction—Sources—ʾ – ʾ-kh-r. Compiled by G. Endress & D. Gutas, with the assistance of K. Alshut, R. Arnzen, Chr. Hein, St. Pohl, M. Schmeink. 1992. ISBN 90 04 09494 6

Fascicle 2. ʾ-kh-r – ʾ-ṣ-l. Compiled by G. Endress & D. Gutas, with the assistance of K. Alshut, R. Arnzen, Chr. Hein, St. Pohl, M. Schmeink. 1993. ISBN 90 04 09893 3

Band 12

JAYYUSI, S. K. (ed.). *The Legacy of Muslim Spain.* Chief consultant to the editor, M. Marín. 2nd ed. 1994. ISBN 90 04 09599 3

Band 13

HUNWICK, J. O. and O'FAHEY, R. S. (eds.). *Arabic Literature of Africa.*

Volume I. *The Writings of Eastern Sudanic Africa to c. 1900.* Compiled by R. S. O'Fahey, with the assistance of M. I. Abu Salim, A. Hofheinz, Y. M. Ibrahim, B. Radtke and K. S. Vikør. 1994. ISBN 90 04 09450 4

Band 14

DECKER, W. und HERB, M. *Bildatlas zum Sport im alten Ägypten. Corpus der bildlichen Quellen zu Leibesübungen, Spiel, Jagd, Tanz und verwandten Themen.* Bd.1: Text. Bd. 2: Abbildungen. 1994. ISBN 90 04 09974 3 (Set)

Band 15

HAAS, V. *Geschichte der hethitischen Religion.* 1994. ISBN 90 04 09799 6

Band 16

NEUSNER, J. (ed.). *Judaism in Late Antiquity.* Part One: The Literary and Archaeological Sources. 1994. ISBN 90 04 10129 2

Band 17

NEUSNER, J. (ed.). *Judaism in Late Antiquity.* Part Two: Historical Syntheses. 1994. ISBN 90 04 09799 6

Band 18

OREL, V. E. and STOLBOVA, O. V. (eds.). *Hamito-Semitic Etymological Dictionary.* Materials for a Reconstruction. 1994. ISBN 90 04 10051 2

Band 19

AL-ZWAINI, L. and PETERS, R. *A Bibliography of Islamic Law, 1980-1993.* 1994. ISBN 90 04 10009 1

Band 20

KRINGS, V. (éd.). *La civilisation phénicienne et punique.* Manuel de recherche. 1995 ISBN 90 04 10068 7

Band 21

HOFTIJZER, J. and JONGELING. K. *Dictionary of the North-West Semitic Inscriptions.* With appendices by R.C. Steiner, A. Mosak Moshavi and B. Porten. Part One: ʾ - L.
Part Two: M - T. 1995
ISBN 90 04 09817 8 (*Vol. 1*)
ISBN 90 04 09820 8 (*Vol. 2*)
ISBN 90 04 09821 6 (*Set*)